PrincetonReview.com

THE BEST 381 COLLEGES

2017 Edition

By Robert Franek, Kristen O'Toole, David Soto,
and The Staff of The Princeton Review

2017 Edition

Penguin
Random
House

The Princeton Review
24 Prime Parkway, Suite 201
Natick, MA 01760
E-mail: editorialsupport@review.com

ISBN 978-1-101-92006-0

Production: Best Content Solutions, LLC
Production Editor: Melissa Duclos

Printed in the United States of America on partially recycled paper.

Editorial
Robert Franek, SVP, Publisher
David Soto, Director of Content Development
Kristen O'Toole, Editorial Director
Pia Aliperti, Editor
Stephen Koch, Survey Manager

Random House Publishing Team
Tom Russell, VP, Publisher
Alison Stoltzfus, Publishing Manager
Jake Eldred, Managing Editor
Suzanne Lee, Design
Ellen L. Reed, Production Manager

ACKNOWLEDGMENTS

Each year we assemble an awesomely talented group of colleagues who work together to produce our updated college profiles, and our 25th edition this year is no exception. Everyone involved in this effort—authors, editors, data managers, production specialists, and designers—goes above and beyond to make *The Best 381 Colleges* an exceptional student resource guide. For twenty-five years, we have worked to collect and publish what prospective college students really want: The most honest, accessible, and pertinent information about the colleges they are considering attending.

My sincere thanks go to everybody who has contributed to this tremendous project over the past quarter century. A special thank you goes to our authors, Jen Adams, Alex Dryden, Jordan Foster, and Andrea Kornstein, for their dedication in poring through tens of thousands of surveys to produce the campus culture narratives of each school we profiled. Very special thanks goes to Kristen O'Toole and Pia Aliperti for their editorial commitment and vision, and our Student Survey Manager, Stephen Koch, who continues to work in partnership with school administrators and students. My continued thanks go to our data guru, David Soto, for his successful efforts in collecting and accurately representing the statistical data that appear with each college profile. The scope of this project and its deadline constraints could not have been realized without the calm presence of Scott Harris of Best Content Solutions and production editor Melissa Duclos—their dedication, focus, and attention to detail continue to impress and remind me of what a pleasure it is to work on this project each year. Special thanks also go to Jeanne Krier, my trusted colleague, media advisor, and friend, for the dedicated work she has done on this book and the overall series since its inception. I would also like to make special mention of Tom Russell and Alison Stoltzfus, our Penguin Random House publishing team, for their continuous investment and faith in our ideas. Last, I thank my Princeton Review Partner Team, Kate Walker, Michelle Bergland, Casey Cornelius, Vincent Jungels, Clark Rothrock, and Young Shin for their confidence in me and my content team and for their commitment to providing students the resources they need to succeed academically and find the colleges that fit them best.

Robert Franek
Senior VP—Publisher
Lead Author—*The Best 381 Colleges*

Contents

PART I: INTRODUCTION

25 Years of The Princeton Review's College Rankings

1992	Edition	2017
250	Colleges profiled	381
30,000	Student surveys	143,000
120	Average surveys per campus	375
67	Survey questions	84

"There was a void in the college guide market and we have filled it with this book."

Twenty-five years ago, The Princeton Review opened the first edition of *The Best Colleges* with this bold statement. In 1992, no other book provided in-depth descriptions of schools along side statistics covering admissions, financial aid, and student body demographics.

Then, as now, no other guide was based on the input of so many students. Then, as now, we at The Princeton Review believe that current students are the real experts about life at a particular college or university—only they can give you the most candid and informed feedback on what life is really like on campus. More than a million students have participated in our surveys over the past quarter century, and we are pleased to continue to publish what we believe is the most substantive resource you need to find the college that will fit you best.

We've added (and dropped) schools from the book; we've exponentially increased our student survey results; and we've changed or renamed many of the 60+ categories in which we've ranked top 20 colleges based on student feedback. Our guiding conviction, however, remains the same: That there is no single "best" college, only the best college for you. The profiles and ranking lists in this book can help you find the school that best fits your unique personality and goals.

What college is right for me?

We encourage students to consider their wants and needs across three categories: academics, campus culture, and financial aid.

Academics

Does the college you're considering offer classes and learning opportunities that interest you? You don't need to declare a college major until your junior year of college—but you're more likely to succeed if you're excited about and engaged by the options available to you. Consider your learning style: do you prefer informative lectures or lively discussions? Research and analysis, or hands-on experience and practice? Writing papers or working in small groups? Look for the academic experience you'll need to feel challenged and engaged, and what support you'll need for success—peer tutoring, accessible professors, mentorship, and career services are just some of the options you might find on campus. Check out course and program descriptions, reviews of professors, and sit in on some classes if you're able to visit campus.

Campus Culture

Do you want a big school or a small one? A hip urban campus or a verdant quad in the country? A college where everyone cheers on the basketball team, or one where every theater production gets a standing ovation? Every college has its own special vibe.

You can start narrowing down your list by making some decisions about the size of the student body and geographical location, and then move on to aspects you can identify by visiting campus, talking to current students and trusting your gut instincts: the personalities, politics, and interests of the student body. Take quality of life into account, too, and try to check out the dorms, food, and recreational facilities on campus.

Financial Aid

The cost of college is one of the biggest concerns for student, parents, counselors. We hear that from the students we work with and see it on our annual College Hopes & Worries Survey. It's important to be realistic about your family's finances and avoid taking on unreasonable debts in the name of your education—but it's also important not to cross a school off your list because of a scary sticker price.

Many colleges and universities offer incredible financial aid packages (sometimes as a combination of grants and scholarships, which means no debt at all!). Raising your grades and your SAT or ACT scores will help you become more eligible for merit-based financial aid. And more and more data on college outcomes—that is, career placement rates and average starting salaries—is becoming available, which can help you assess the value of investing your tuition dollars in a particular college.

Check out our list of 200 "best value" schools on page 56, and read more about getting the most bang for your tuition buck in Colleges That Pay You Back.

Getting Into Selective Colleges: An Overview for High School Students

College admission is all about compatibility. As an applicant, you are looking for an environment where you can thrive academically and personally, and it is the job of an admission officer to identify students who will make great additions to a unique campus community.

Your path to college begins your first year in high school. Grades and test scores are important factors in college admission, but admissions officers are also looking for curious and engaged candidates who will round out a diverse first-year class.

Grades

Most admissions officers report that your GPA and the rigor of your high school curriculum are the most important elements of your college application.

- Choose your high school classes carefully. Challenge yourself with honors, AP, and IB courses when they are available.

- Your grades count for all four years of high school. When colleges review your transcript, they often look at grade trends across subjects and course levels.

- Even if you had a rough first year of high school, there's still time to turn your grades around. Many schools will reward your upward trajectory.

Test Scores

SAT and/or ACT scores take the lead, but admissions officers consider your performance on other standardized tests as well.

- The PSAT is optional your sophomore year, but your junior year PSAT scores can qualify you for scholarship programs such as the National Merit® Scholarship, which can help cover the cost of tuition and get you into a great college. It's also good practice for the SAT.

- Many selective colleges require you to submit SAT Subject Test scores, and some colleges grant course credit for excellent performance. It's a good idea to sit for the Subject Tests right after you finish the related classes in high school.

- Strong performances on AP exams are can indicate your potential for academic achievement to college admission officers. More than 1,400 colleges and universities accept high scores on AP exams for course credits.

- Most schools view the ACT and SAT equally, so it's completely up to you which test you take (you can even take both!). The Essay section of the SAT and the Writing section of the ACT are both optional, but some colleges may require them.

- Test optional schools: Schools that are test optional do not require standardized test scores as part of a complete application. Since your test scores could qualify you for merit scholarships even at test optional schools, it's still a smart idea to take (and prep for!) at least one standardized test.

Extracurriculars

What you do with your time shows colleges who you are and what qualities you'll bring to campus.

- Commitment to a sport, hobby, religious organization, or job over four years of high school is key. Colleges would much rather see you excited about a few worthwhile endeavors than marginally involved with a ton of clubs.

- If an after-school job is cutting into your extracurricular time, don't worry! Work experience demonstrates maturity and responsibility on your college application.

- Summer counts, too! Some students enroll in university programs to start earning college credits. Others volunteer or find a summer job. Whatever you do, your experience can make your college application rise to the top of a competitive applicant pool.

What Should You Do This Summer?

Ahhh, summer. The possibilities seem endless. You can get a job, intern, travel, study, volunteer, or do nothing at all. Here are a few ideas to get you started:

- **Go to college:** No, not for real. However, you can participate in summer programs at colleges and universities at home and abroad. Programs can focus on anything from academics (stretch your brain by taking an intensive science or language course) to sports to admissions guidance. This is also a great opportunity to explore college life firsthand, especially if you get to stay in a dorm. Summer is also a time when families on vacations can squeeze in a college visit while they're in "the neighborhood." Even if classes aren't in session when you are able to tour a campus, the more colleges you can visit the better informed your final college choice will be.

- **Prep for the PSAT, SAT, or ACT:** So maybe it's not quite as adventurous as trekking around Patagonia for the summer (it's also not as expensive!) or as cool as learning to slam dunk at basketball camp, but hey, there's nothing adventurous or cool about being rejected from your top-choice college because of unimpressive test scores. Plus, you'll be ahead of the game if you can return to school with much of your PSAT, SAT, and ACT preparation behind you.

- **Research scholarships:** College is expensive. While you should never rule out a school based on cost, the more scholarship money you can secure beforehand, the more college options you will have. You'll find loads of info on financial aid and scholarships (including a scholarship search tool) on our site, PrincetonReview.com.

Applying for Financial Aid

The cost of college has been the biggest concern among respondents to our annual College Hopes & Worries survey for the past three years. Educate yourself on how financial aid works, so you can make the right choices for you and your family.

- Be aware that applying to college and applying for financial aid are two separate processes.

- Schools usually have their own net-price calculators so that families can get a sense of what their out-of-pocket costs would look like. Check out each prospective school's financial aid website as you research your college list.

- The Free Application for Federal Student Aid (FAFSA) is released on October 1 of every year. The form asks for information about your income and the size of your household to determine your expected family contribution (EFC) toward your college tuition.

- Schools may also use their own forms, or use the CSS/Financial Aid PROFILE Form for non-federal aid.

- Your financial aid package is intended to meet your need and will consist of

    o grants and scholarships

    o federal work-study

    o student loans

- Outside organizations offer scholarships tailored to academic interests, talents, extracurricular activities, career goals, geographic location, and many more factors. Keep an eye on deadlines which could fall as early as the summer before senior year.

Some of Our Other Helpful Books

The Princeton Review's *Paying for College Without Going Broke* is the only annually updated guide to financial aid that has detailed, line-by-line strategies for completing the highly complicated FAFSA for the upcoming school year (as well as the CSS/PROFILE form) to one's best advantage. It explains how the financial aid process works and reveals strategies—all legal—for maximizing your eligibility for aid. Authored by Kal Chany, one of the nation's most widely sourced experts on college funding, it also includes annually updated information on education tax breaks, college savings programs, and student and parent loans. Check out Kal Chany's "26 Tips for Getting Financial Aid . . ." on pages 7–8.

Colleges That Create Futures: 50 Schools That Launch Careers By Going Beyond the Classroom salutes an extraordinary group of institutions with compelling commitments to helping their students segue to successful careers and post-graduate accomplishments.

K & W Guide to College Programs & Services for Students with Learning Disabilities or Attention Deficit/ Hyperactivity Disorder profiles 350 schools highly recommended for such students. It includes strategies to help them successfully apply to the best programs for their needs, plus advice from specialists in the field of learning disabilities.

26 Tips for Getting Financial Aid, Scholarships, and Grants and for Paying Less for College

by Kalman A. Chany, author of *Paying for College Without Going Broke*

(Penguin Random House/Princeton Review Books)

Getting financial aid

1. Learn how financial aid works. The more and the sooner you know about how need-based aid eligibility is determined, the better you can take steps to maximize such eligibility.

2. Apply for financial aid no matter what your circumstances. Some merit-based aid can only be awarded if the applicant has submitted financial aid application forms.

3. Don't wait till the student is accepted to apply for financial aid. Do it when applying for admission.

4. Complete all the required aid applications. All students seeking aid must submit the FAFSA (Free Application for Federal Student Aid); other forms may also be required. Check with each college to see what's required and when.

5. Get the best scores you can on the SAT or ACT. They are used not only in decisions for admission but they can also impact financial aid. If your scores and other stats exceed the school's admission criteria, you are likely to get a better aid package than a marginal applicant.

6. Apply strategically to colleges. Your chances of getting aid will be better at schools that have generous financial aid budgets. (Check the "Colleges That Pay You Back" list and Financial Aid Ratings for schools in this book and on princetonreview.com.)

7. Don't rule out any school as too expensive. A generous aid award from a pricey private school can make it less costly than a public school with a lower sticker price.

8. Take advantage of education tax benefits. A dollar saved on taxes is worth the same as a dollar in scholarship aid. Look into Coverdells, 529 plans, education tax credits, and loan deductions.

Scholarships and grants

9. Get your best possible score on the PSAT: It is the National Merit Scholarship Qualifying Test and also used in the selection of students for other scholarships and recognition programs.

10. Check eligibility and deadlines for grants and scholarships from your state. Some (but not all) states will allow you to use such funds out of state.

11. Look for scholarships locally. Find out if your employer offers scholarships or tuition assistance plans for employees or family members. Also look into scholarships from your community groups and high school, as well as your church, temple, or mosque.

12. Look for outside scholarships realistically: they account for less than five percent of aid awarded. Research them at princetonreview.com or other free sites. Steer clear of scholarship search firms that charge fees and "promise" scholarships.

Paying for college

13. Start saving early when the student is an infant. Too late? Start now. The more you save, the less you'll have to borrow.

14. Invest wisely. Considering a 529 plan? Compare your own state's plan which may have tax benefits with other states' programs. Get info at savingforcollege.com.

15. If you have to borrow, first pursue federal education loans (Perkins, Stafford, PLUS). Avoid private loans at all costs.

16. Never put tuition on a credit card. The debt is more expensive than ever given recent changes to interest rates and other fees some card issuers are now charging.

17. Try not to take money from a retirement account or 401(k) to pay for college. In addition to likely early distribution penalties and additional income taxes, the higher income will reduce your aid eligibility.

Paying less for college

18. Attend a community college for two years and transfer to a pricier school to complete the degree. Plan ahead: Be sure the college you plan to transfer to will accept the community college credits.

19. Look into "cooperative education" programs. Over 900 colleges allow students to combine college education with a job. It can take longer to complete a degree this way. But graduates generally owe less in student loans and have a better chance of getting hired.

20. Take as many AP courses as possible and get high scores on AP exams. Many colleges award course credits for high AP scores. Some students have cut a year off their college tuition this way.

21. Earn college credit via "dual enrollment" programs available at some high schools. These allow students to take college level courses during their senior year.

22. Earn college credits by taking CLEP (College-Level Examination Program) exams. Depending on the college, a qualifying score on any of the thirty-three CLEP exams can earn students three to twelve college credits. (See Princeton Review's Cracking the CLEP-5th Edition.)

23. Stick to your college and your major. Changing colleges can result in lost credits. Aid may be limited/not available for transfer students at some schools. Changing majors can mean paying for extra courses to meet requirements.

24. Finish college in three years if possible. Take the maximum number of credits every semester, attend summer sessions, and earn credits via online courses. Some colleges offer three-year programs for high-achieving students.

25. Let Uncle Sam pay for your degree. ROTC (Reserve Officer Training Corps) programs available from U.S. Armed Forces branches (except the Coast Guard) offer merit-based scholarships up to full tuition via participating colleges in exchange for military service after you graduate.

26. Better yet: Attend a tuition-free college. Check out the nine institutions in this book on the "Tuition-Free Schools Honor Roll" list on p. 55.

Great Schools for 20 of the Most Popular Undergraduate Majors

Worried about having to declare a major on your college application? Relax. Most colleges won't require you to declare a major until the end of your sophomore year, giving you plenty of time to explore your options. However, problems may arise if you are thinking about majoring in a program that limits its enrollment—meaning that if you don't declare that major early on, you might not get into that program at a later date.

On the flip side, some students declare a major on their application because they believe it will boost their chances of gaining admission. This can be problematic, however, if you later decide to change your major. It involves switching from one school within the college to another (e.g., from the school of arts and sciences to the school of business, for example), it can be difficult.

Never choose a college solely on the prestige of a particular program. College will expose you to new and exciting learning experiences. (Choosing a school based on program availability is a different story.) You may also want to investigate opportunities to design your own major. A commitment to a major would limit you in many ways.

How Did We Compile These Lists?

Each year we collect data from more than 2,000 colleges on the subject of—among many other things—undergraduate academic offerings. We ask colleges not only to report which undergraduate majors they offer, but also which of their majors have the highest enrollment and the number of bachelor's degrees each school awarded in these areas. The list below identifies (in alphabetical order) twenty of the forty "most popular" majors that the schools responding to our survey reported to us. We also conduct our own research on college majors. We look at institutional data, and we consult with our in-house college admissions experts as well as our National College Counselor Advisory Board (whom we list on pages 839–840) for their input on schools offering great programs in these majors. We thank them and all of the guidance counselors, college admissions counselors, and education experts across the country whose recommendations we considered in developing these lists. Of the nearly 3,000 four-year colleges across the United States, those on these lists represent only a snapshot of the many offering great programs in these majors. Use our lists as a starting point for further research.

Great Schools for Accounting Majors

- Agnes Scott College
- Alfred University
- Assumption College
- Auburn University
- Babson College
- Baylor University
- Bentley University
- Birmingham-Southern College
- Boston College
- Boston University
- Brigham Young University (UT)
- Bryant University
- Bucknell University
- Calvin College
- City University of New York—Baruch College
- City University of New York—Brooklyn College
- City University of New York—Hunter College
- City University of New York—Queens College
- Claremont McKenna College
- Clemson University
- College of Charleston
- Cornell University
- DePaul University
- Drexel University
- Duquesne University
- Elon University
- Emory University
- Fairfield University
- Fordham University
- George Mason University
- Georgetown University
- Hofstra University
- Indiana University—Bloomington
- Iowa State University
- James Madison University
- Lehigh University
- Le Moyne College
- Marquette University
- Miami University
- New York University
- Northeastern University
- Pennsylvania State University—University Park
- Pepperdine University
- Rider University
- Rochester Institute of Technology
- St. Bonaventure
- Seton Hall University
- Southern Methodist University
- Stonehill College
- Suffolk University
- Temple University
- Texas A&M University—College Station
- Transylvania University
- The University of Alabama at Birmingham
- University of Houston
- University of Illinois at Urbana-Champaign
- University of Michigan—Ann Arbor
- University of Mississippi
- University of Pennsylvania
- University of Southern California
- The University of Texas at Austin
- The University of Texas at Dallas
- Washington and Jefferson College

Great Schools for Agriculture Majors

- Angelo State University
- Arizona State University
- Auburn University
- Berea College
- California State University Stanislaus
- The Catholic University of America
- Clemson University
- College of the Atlantic
- College of the Ozarks
- Colorado State University
- The Cooper Union for the Advancement of Science and Art
- Cornell University
- Gettysburg College
- Green Mountain College
- Illinois Institute of Technology
- Iowa State University
- Kansas State University
- Louisiana State University
- New Jersey Institute of Technology
- North Carolina State University
- Pennsylvania State University—University Park
- Prescott College
- Purdue University—West Lafayette
- Texas A&M University—College Station
- Texas Christian University
- Truman State University
- Tuskegee University
- University of Arizona
- University of Arkansas—Fayetteville
- University of California—Davis

- University of Florida
- University of Georgia
- University of Hawaii—Manoa
- University of Idaho
- University of Illinois at Urbana-Champaign
- University of Kentucky
- University of Maine
- University of Maryland—College Park
- University of Massachusetts Amherst
- University of Missouri—Columbia
- University of Nebraska—Lincoln
- The University of Tennessee at Knoxville
- University of Vermont
- University of Wisconsin—Madison
- University of Wyoming
- West Virginia University

Great Schools for Biology Majors

- Agnes Scott College
- Albion College
- Amherst College
- Austin College
- Allegheny College
- Baylor University
- Berea College
- Brandeis University
- Brown University
- Carleton College
- Case Western University
- Christopher Newport University
- Clark University
- Clemson University
- Colby College
- College of Charleston
- The College of Idaho
- The College of New Jersey
- College of Saint Benedict/ Saint John's University
- Colorado College
- Colorado State University
- Cornell University
- Creighton University
- Denison University
- Dickinson College
- Drexel University
- Duke University
- Earlham College
- Eckerd College
- Emory University
- Florida Southern College
- George Mason University
- Goucher College
- Guilford College
- Harvard College
- Haverford College
- Hillsdale College
- Hofstra University
- Howard University
- Illinois Wesleyan University
- Indiana University—Bloomington
- Johns Hopkins University
- Juniata College
- Le Moyne College
- Louisiana State University
- Loyola University—Chicago
- Massachusetts Institute of Technology
- Millsaps College
- Mount Holyoke College
- New College of Florida
- The Ohio State University—Columbus
- Ohio University—Athens
- Pomona College
- Randolph-Macon College
- Reed College
- Rice University
- St. Bonaventure University
- Saint Louis University
- St. Olaf University
- Salisbury University
- State University of New York—Stony Brook
- Swarthmore College
- Temple University
- Texas A&M University—College Station
- Transylvania University
- United States Coast Guard Academy
- The University of Alabama at Birmingham
- University of California—Davis
- University of California—Los Angeles
- University of California—San Diego
- University of California—Santa Barbara
- The University of Chicago
- University of Dallas
- University of Delaware
- University of Denver
- University of Georgia
- University of Hawaii at Manoa
- University of Houston
- University of Kansas
- University of New England
- University of New Mexico
- The University of North Carolina at Chapel Hill

- University of the Pacific
- University of Scranton
- The University of Texas at Dallas
- Wabash College
- Washington University in St. Louis

- Whitman College
- Willamette University
- Wofford College
- Xavier University of Louisiana

Great Schools for Business/Finance Majors

- Alfred University
- Arizona State University
- Babson College
- Bentley University
- Berea College
- Boston College
- Brigham Young University (UT)
- Bryant University
- California State University, Stanislaus
- Calvin College
- Carnegie Mellon University
- Champlain College
- Chapman University
- Christopher Newport University
- City University of New York—Baruch College
- City University of New York—Brooklyn College
- Cornell University
- DePaul University
- Emory University
- Florida State University
- Indiana University—Bloomington
- Iowa State University
- Lehigh University
- Massachusetts Institute of Technology
- Miami University (OH)

- New York University
- Northwestern University
- Ohio University—Athens
- Portland State University
- Rice University
- Roanoke College
- Seattle University
- San Diego State University
- Stetson University
- University of Arkansas—Fayetteville
- University of California—Berkeley
- University of California—Los Angeles
- The University of Chicago
- University of Florida
- University of Houston
- University of Illinois at Urbana-Champaign
- University of Michigan—Ann Arbor
- University of Notre Dame
- University of Pennsylvania
- University of Richmond
- University of Southern California
- The University of Texas at Austin
- The University of Texas at Dallas
- University of Virginia
- Villanova University
- Washington University in St. Louis

Great Schools for Communications Majors

- Baylor University
- Boston College
- Boston University
- Bradley University
- City University of New York—City College
- City University of New York—Hunter College
- Clemson University
- College of Charleston
- Cornell University
- Denison University
- DePaul University
- Duquesne University
- Eckerd College
- Elon University
- Emerson College
- Fairfield University
- Fordham University

- Gonzaga University
- Gustavus Adolphus College
- Hollins University
- Indiana University—Bloomington
- Iowa State University
- Ithaca College
- James Madison University
- Lake Forest College
- Loyola University—New Orleans
- Marist College
- Muhlenberg College
- New York University
- Northwestern University
- Pepperdine University
- Quinnipiac University
- Ripon College
- Salisbury University

- Seton Hall University
- St. John's University (NY)
- Stanford University
- Suffolk University
- Syracuse University
- University of California—San Diego
- University of California—Santa Barbara
- University of Iowa
- University of Maryland—College Park
- University of San Diego
- University of Southern California
- University of Tampa
- The University of Texas at Austin
- University of Utah

Great Schools for Computer Science/Computer Engineering Majors

- Auburn University
- Boston University
- Bradley University
- Brown University
- California Institute of Technology
- Carnegie Mellon University
- Champlain College
- Clemson University
- Drexel University
- Florida State University
- George Mason University
- Georgia Institute of Technology
- Gonzaga University
- Hampton University
- Harvey Mudd College
- Illinois Institute of Technology
- Iowa State University
- Johns Hopkins University
- Lehigh University
- Massachusetts Institute of Technology
- Missouri University of Science and Technology
- New Jersey Institute of Technology
- Northeastern University
- Northwestern University
- Pennsylvania State University—University Park
- Princeton University
- Rice University
- Rensselaer Polytechnic Institute
- Roanoke College
- Rochester Institute of Technology
- Seattle University
- Stanford University
- State University of New York at Binghamton
- Texas A&M University—College Station
- United States Air Force Academy
- University of Arizona
- University of California—Berkeley
- University of California—Los Angeles
- University of California—Riverside
- University of Illinois at Urbana-Champaign
- University of Maryland, Baltimore County
- University of Massachusetts Amherst
- University of Michigan—Ann Arbor
- University of Washington
- Worcester Polytechnic Institute

Great Schools for Criminology Majors

- American University
- Auburn University
- Florida State University
- Guilford College
- Indiana University of Pennsylvania
- North Carolina State University
- The Ohio State University—Columbus
- Ohio University—Athens
- Quinnipiac University
- Suffolk University
- University of Delaware
- University of Denver
- University of Maryland—College Park
- University of Miami
- University of New Hampshire
- University of South Carolina—Columbia
- University of South Florida
- University of Utah
- Valparaiso University
- Virginia Wesleyan College
- Whittier College

Great Schools for Education Majors

- Auburn University
- Barnard College
- Bucknell University
- City University of New York—Brooklyn College
- City University of New York—Hunter College
- Colgate University
- College of the Ozarks
- The College of William & Mary
- Columbia College (MO)
- Columbia University
- Cornell College
- Cornell University
- Duquesne University
- Elon University
- Gonzaga University
- Goucher College
- Hillsdale College
- Indiana University—Bloomington
- Knox College
- Loyola Marymount University
- Marquette University
- McGill University
- Miami University (OH)
- Monmouth University (NJ)
- Nazareth College
- New York University
- Northeastern University
- Northwestern University
- The Ohio State University—Columbus
- Prescott College
- Simmons College
- Skidmore College
- Smith College
- Trinity University (TX)
- University of Maine
- University of Mississippi
- The University of Montana—Missoula
- Vanderbilt University
- Villanova College
- Wagner College
- Wellesley College
- William Jewell College
- Xavier University (OH)

Great Schools for Engineering Majors

- California Institute of Technology
- Carnegie Mellon University
- Columbia University
- The Cooper Union for the Advancement of Science and Art
- Cornell University
- Drexel University
- Duke University
- Franklin W. Olin College of Engineering
- Georgia Institute of Technology
- Harvard College
- Harvey Mudd College
- Illinois Institute of Technology
- Johns Hopkins University
- Manhattan College
- Massachusetts Institute of Technology
- Michigan Technological University
- Missouri University of Science and Technology
- Montana Tech of the Univ. of Montana
- Pennsylvania State University—University Park
- Princeton University
- Purdue University—West Lafayette
- Rensselaer Polytechnic Institute
- Rose-Hulman Institute of Technology
- Stanford University
- Stevens Institute of Technology
- Texas A&M University—College Station
- United States Merchant Marine Academy
- University of California—Berkeley
- University of California—Los Angeles
- The University of Texas at Austin
- University of Wisconsin—Madison
- Virginia Tech
- Webb Institute
- Worcester Polytechnic Institute

Great Schools for English Literature and Language Majors

- Amherst College
- Auburn University
- Bard College (NY)
- Barnard College
- Bates College
- Bennington College
- Boston College
- Brown University
- Bryn Mawr College
- City University of New York—Hunter College
- Claremont McKenna College
- Clemson University
- Colby College
- Colgate University
- Columbia University
- Cornell University
- Dartmouth College
- Denison University
- Duke University
- Emory University
- Fordham University
- George Mason University
- Gettysburg College
- Gordon College
- Grinnell College
- Harvard College
- Johns Hopkins University
- Kalamazoo College
- Kenyon College
- Marlboro College
- Oberlin College
- Pitzer College
- Pomona College
- Princeton University
- Reed College
- Rice University
- Sewanee—The University of the South
- Smith College
- Stanford University
- St. Mary's College of Maryland
- State University of New York—University at Albany
- Syracuse University
- Tufts University
- University of California—Berkeley
- The University of Chicago
- University of Michigan—Ann Arbor
- The University of North Carolina at Asheville
- University of Notre Dame
- University of Utah
- Vassar College
- Washington University in St. Louis
- Wellesley College
- Williams College
- Yale University

Great Schools for Environmental Studies Majors

- Allegheny College
- Bates College
- Bowdoin College
- Catawba College
- Colby College
- College of the Atlantic
- Colorado College
- Dickinson College
- Eckerd College
- Emory University
- The Evergreen State College
- Green Mountain College
- Harvard College
- Hobart and William Smith Colleges
- Juniata College
- Middlebury College
- New College of Florida
- Northeastern University
- Occidental College
- Pitzer College
- Pomona College
- Portland State University
- Prescott College
- Sewanee—The University of the South
- Sonoma State University
- State University of New York at Binghamton
- State University of New York—College of Environmental Science and Forestry
- University of California—Berkeley
- University of California—Santa Cruz
- University of Colorado—Boulder
- University of Idaho
- The University of Montana—Missoula
- University of New Hampshire
- The University of North Carolina at Asheville
- The University of North Carolina at Chapel Hill
- University of Oregon
- University of Redlands
- University of the Pacific
- University of Vermont
- Warren Wilson College
- Washington College

Great Schools for History Majors

- Bates College
- Bowdoin College
- Brown University
- Centre College
- Colgate University
- College of the Holy Cross
- The College of Wooster
- Columbia University
- Davidson College
- Drew University
- Furman University
- Georgetown University
- Grinnell College
- Hampden-Sydney College
- Harvard College
- Haverford College
- Hillsdale College
- Kenyon College
- Marlboro College
- Oberlin College
- Princeton University
- Ripon College
- Trinity College (CT)
- Tulane University
- University of Virginia
- Wabash College
- Williams College
- Yale University

Great Schools for Health Services Majors

- Bellarmine University
- Boston University
- Clemson University
- The College of Idaho
- College of the Ozarks
- Creighton University
- Drexel University
- Duquesne University
- Fairfield University
- Gettysburg College
- Gustavus Adolphus College
- Hampton University
- Howard University
- Ithaca College
- Johns Hopkins University
- Kalamazoo College
- Loyola University—Chicago
- Monmouth University (NJ)
- Nazareth College
- Northeastern University
- Ohio University—Athens
- Purdue University—West Lafayette
- Quinnipiac University
- Sacred Heart University
- St. Anselm College
- Saint Louis University
- Seton Hall University
- Simmons College
- State University of New York—Stony Brook University
- Stephens College
- Suffolk University
- Texas A&M University—College Station
- Texas Christian University
- Tulane University
- The University of Alabama at Birmingham
- University of Central Florida
- University of Cincinnati
- University of Delaware
- University of Florida
- University of Houston
- University of Louisville
- University of Miami
- University of New England
- University of North Dakota
- University of Oklahoma
- University of Rhode Island
- University of Utah
- University of Wyoming
- Wagner College
- Washington University in St. Louis
- West Virginia University
- Westminster College (UT)
- Wheaton College (IL)
- William Jewell College
- Xavier University (OH)

Check out our free downloadable resource, The Princeton Review's *Guide to Green Colleges* at www.princetonreview.com/green-guide.

Great Schools for Journalism Majors

- American University
- Arizona State University
- Auburn University
- Ball State University
- Boston University
- Bowling Green State University
- Carleton College
- Duke University
- Emerson College
- The George Washington University
- Hampton University
- Howard University
- Indiana University—Bloomington
- Iowa State University
- Ithaca College
- Kansas State University
- Loyola University—New Orleans
- New York University
- Northwestern University
- Ohio University—Athens
- Pennsylvania State University—University Park
- St. Bonaventure University
- State University of New York—Stony Brook University
- Syracuse University
- Temple University
- The University of Alabama at Tuscaloosa
- University of Arizona
- University of Arkansas—Fayetteville
- University of Florida
- University of Georgia
- University of Kansas
- University of Kentucky
- University of Idaho
- University of Illinois at Urbana-Champaign
- University of Iowa
- University of Maryland—College Park
- University of Minnesota—Twin Cities
- University of Mississippi
- University of Missouri—Columbia
- The University of Montana—Missoula
- University of Nebraska—Lincoln
- The University of North Carolina at Chapel Hill
- University of Oklahoma
- University of Oregon
- University of Southern California
- The University of Texas at Austin
- University of Wisconsin—Madison
- Washington State University

Great Schools for Marketing and Sales Majors

- Babson College
- Baylor University
- Bentley College
- Duquesne University
- Fairfield University
- Hofstra University
- Indiana University—Bloomington
- Iowa State University
- James Madison University
- Loyola Marymount University
- Miami University (OH)
- Providence College
- Seattle University
- Siena College
- Syracuse University
- Texas A&M University—College Station
- The University of Alabama—Tuscaloosa
- University of Central Florida
- University of Cincinnati
- University of Dayton
- University of Michigan—Ann Arbor
- University of Mississippi
- University of Pennsylvania
- University of South Florida
- The University of Texas at Austin

Great Schools for Mathematics Majors

- Agnes Scott College
- Bowdoin College
- Bryant University
- Bryn Mawr College
- California Institute of Technology
- Carleton College
- College of the Holy Cross
- The College of Idaho
- Grinnell College
- Hamilton College
- Hampton University
- Harvard College
- Harvey Mudd College
- Haverford College
- Macalester College
- Massachusetts Institute of Technology
- Randolph College
- Reed College
- Rice University
- St. Lawrence University
- St. Olaf College
- State University of New York— University at Albany
- United States Coast Guard Academy
- The University of Chicago
- University of Rochester
- Wabash College

Great Schools for Mechanical Engineering Majors

- Auburn University
- Bradley University
- California Institute of Technology
- Clarkson University
- Colorado State University
- The Cooper Union for the Advancement of Science and Art
- Drexel University
- Franklin W. Olin College of Engineering
- Georgia Institute of Technology
- Grove City College
- Harvey Mudd College
- Illinois Institute of Technology
- Iowa State University
- Lehigh University
- Massachusetts Institute of Technology
- Michigan Technological University
- Missouri University of Science and Technology
- New Jersey Institute of Technology
- North Carolina State University
- Ohio Northern University
- Princeton University
- Purdue University—West Lafayette
- Rochester Institute of Technology
- Rose-Hulman Institute of Technology
- Stanford University
- Stevens Institute of Technology
- United States Military Academy
- University of California—Berkeley
- University of Illinois at Urbana-Champaign
- University of Maryland—Baltimore County
- University of Michigan—Ann Arbor
- Worcester Polytechnic Institute

Great Schools for Nursing Majors

- Angelo State University
- Baylor University
- Bellarmine University
- Creighton University
- Calvin College
- The Catholic University of America
- Drexel University
- Duquesne University
- Fairfield University
- Florida Southern College
- Indiana University of Pennsylvania
- Loyola University—Chicago
- Montana Tech of the University of Montana
- Ohio Northern University
- St. Anselm College
- Saint Louis University
- Texas Christian University
- The University of Alabama at Tuscaloosa
- University of Delaware
- University of Louisville
- University of North Dakota
- University of Pennsylvania
- University of Rhode Island
- University of Wyoming
- Valparaiso University
- Villanova University
- Washington State University
- Xavier University (OH)

Great Schools for Political Science/Government Majors

- American University
- Amherst College
- Bard College (NY)
- Bates College
- Bowdoin College
- Brigham Young University (UT)
- Bryn Mawr College
- Carleton College
- Claremont McKenna College
- Clark University
- College of the Holy Cross
- Columbia University
- Connecticut College
- Davidson College
- Dickinson College
- Drew University
- Franklin & Marshall College
- Furman University
- George Mason University
- The George Washington University
- Georgetown University
- Gettysburg College
- Gonzaga University
- Grinnell College
- Harvard College
- Kenyon College
- Macalester College
- McGill University
- Princeton University
- Scripps College
- Stanford University
- Swarthmore College
- Syracuse University
- University of Arizona
- University of California—Berkeley
- University of California—Los Angeles
- University of Washington
- University of Wisconsin—Madison
- Vassar College
- Wake Forest University
- Yale University

Great Schools for Psychology Majors

- Agnes Scott College
- Albion College
- Allegheny College
- Assumption College
- Barnard College
- Bates College
- Bucknell University
- Carleton College
- Carnegie Mellon University
- Christopher Newport University
- City University of New York—Hunter College
- Clark University
- Coe College
- College of the Holy Cross
- Colorado State University
- Columbia University
- Cornell University
- Dartmouth College
- DePaul University
- Duke University
- Earlham College
- Florida State University
- George Mason University
- Gettysburg College
- Guilford College
- Hampton University
- Hanover College
- Harvard College
- James Madison University
- Lewis & Clark College
- Loyola University New Orleans
- Loyola University—Chicago
- Mills College
- Moravian College
- Mount Holyoke College
- New York University
- The Ohio State University—Columbus
- Ohio Wesleyan University
- Pitzer College
- Portland State University
- Princeton University
- Quinnipiac University
- Randolph College
- Roanoke College
- Simmons College
- Smith College
- Spelman College
- Stanford University
- Stetson University
- Stonehill College

- Temple University
- Texas A&M University—College Station
- Union College (NY)
- University of Arizona
- University of California—Davis
- University of California—Los Angeles
- University of California—Riverside
- University of California—Santa Barbara
- University of California—Santa Cruz
- University of Connecticut
- University of Florida
- University of Houston
- University of Idaho
- University of Mary Washington
- University of Maryland-College Park
- University of Massachusetts-Amherst
- University of Michigan—Ann Arbor
- University of Minnesota—Twin Cities
- The University of Montana
- University of Nebraska—Lincoln
- University of Pittsburgh—Pittsburgh Campus
- University of Puget Sound
- University of San Francisco
- The University of South Dakota
- University of South Florida
- University of Southern California
- The University of Tennessee at Knoxville
- The University of Texas at Austin
- University of Utah
- Vassar College
- Washington & Jefferson College
- Washington College
- Washington University in St. Louis
- Wesleyan University
- Xavier University of Louisiana
- Yale University

How We Produce This Book

This Year's Edition

In the twenty-four years since the first edition of this book, our *Best Colleges* guide has grown considerably. We've added more than 130 colleges to the guide and deleted several along the way. How we choose the schools for the book, and how we produce it, however, has not changed significantly over the years (with the exception of how we conduct our student survey—more on this follows).

To determine which schools will be in each edition, we don't use mathematical calculations or formulas. Instead we rely on a wide range of input, both quantitative and qualitative. Every year we collect data from more than 2,000 colleges that we use for *The Complete Book of Colleges* and *Colleges That Pay You Back*, this book, and our online profiles of schools. We visit dozens of colleges and meet with their admissions officers, deans, presidents, and college students. We talk with hundreds of high school counselors, parents, and students. Colleges also submit information to us requesting consideration for inclusion in the book. As a result, we are able to maintain a constantly evolving list of colleges to consider adding to the book. Any college we add to the guide, however, must agree to support our efforts to survey its students via our anonymous student survey. (Sometimes a college's administrative protocols will not allow it to participate in our student survey; this has caused some academically outstanding schools to be absent from the guide.) Finally, we work to ensure that our roster of colleges in the book presents a wide representation of institutions by region, character, and type. Here you'll find profiles of public and private schools, Historically Black Colleges and Universities, men's and women's colleges, science- and technology-focused institutions, nontraditional colleges, highly selective schools, and some with virtually open-door admissions policies.

For this year's edition, we added three schools to the guide: Manhattan College, San Diego State University, and University of New Haven.

Our ranking lists in this edition are based on our surveys of 143,000 students attending the 381 colleges in the book. We surveyed about 375 students per campus on average, though that number varies depending on the size of the student population. We've surveyed anywhere from twenty-some students at Deep Springs College (100 percent of the all-male student body) to more than 1,000 collegians at such colleges as Drexel University, Clemson University, and the United States Military Academy.

All of the institutions in this guide are academically terrific in our opinion. The 381 schools featured—our picks of the cream of the crop colleges and universities—comprise only the top 14 percent of the approximately 2,800 four-year colleges in the nation. These are all very different schools with many different and wonderful things to offer. We hope you will use this book as a starting point (it will certainly give you a snapshot of what life is like at these schools), but not as the final word on any one school. Check out other resources. Visit as many colleges as you can. Talk to students at those colleges—ask what they love and what bothers them most about their schools. Finally, form your own opinions about the colleges you are considering. At the end of the day, it's what YOU think about the schools that matters most, and that will enable you to answer that all-important question: "Which college is best for me?"

> "We worked to create a guide that would help people who couldn't always get to the campus nonetheless get in-depth campus feedback to find the schools best for them."

About Our Student Survey for Our *Best Colleges* Books

Surveying tens of thousands of students on hundreds of campuses is a large undertaking. In 1992, when we published the first edition of this book, we had surveyed an average of 125 students on each of the 250 campuses we profiled. We conducted that survey in person on the college campuses, setting up tables in central locations at which students filled out the surveys. Sometimes in order for us to collect surveys from a wide range of students, first years to seniors, this process took place over several days and at a variety of campus locations.

As you might imagine, today all of our surveys are completed online. The process is more efficient, secure, and representative, and we are able to gather opinions from far more students per college than we had reached previously. The average number of student surveys (per college) upon which our ranking lists are annually tallied is now 375 students per campus (and at some schools we hear from more than 3,000 students).

Our student survey is also now a continuous process. Students submit surveys online from all schools in the book and they can submit their surveys at any time during the academic year at http://survey. review.com. (Our site will accept only one survey from a student per academic year per school. We also officially conduct surveys of students at each school in the book once every three years on average, working with administrators to reach out to their students. We conduct these "official" surveys more often than once every three years if the colleges request that we do so (and we can accommodate their request) or if we deem it necessary to capture dramatic changes on a campus. And of course, surveys we receive from students outside of their schools' normal survey cycles are always factored into the subsequent year's ranking calculations, so our pool of student survey data is continuously refreshed.

The survey has more than 80 questions in four main sections: "About Yourself," "Your School's Academics/Administration," "Students," and "Life at Your School." We ask about all sorts of things, from "How many out-of-class hours do you spend studying each day?" to "How do you rate your campus food?" Most questions offer an answer choice on a five-point scale: students fill in one of five boxes on a grid with headers varying by topic (e.g., a range from "Excellent" to "Awful"). Once the surveys have been completed and responses stored in our database, every college is given a score (similar to a GPA) for its students' answers to each question. This score enables us to compare student opinion from college to college and to tally the ranking lists. Most of the lists are based on students' answers to one survey question; some lists are based on answers to several survey questions. But all of our 62 ranking lists are based entirely on our student survey results.

Once we have the student survey information in hand, we write the college profiles. Student quotations in each profile come from our surveys (eight survey questions invite the students to tell us in their own words what they think about various aspects of their student body and campus experiences). We chose quotations that represent sentiments expressed by the majority of survey respondents from the college; or, that illustrate one side or another of a mixed bag of student opinion, in which case there will also appear a counterpoint within the text. We send draft profiles to administrative contacts at each school for comments and corrections. We take careful measures to review the school's suggestions against the student survey data we collected and make appropriate changes when warranted.

How This Book is Organized

Each of the colleges and universities in this book has its own two-page profile. To make it easier to find and compare information about the schools, we've used the same profile format for every school. Look at the sample pages below: Each profile has nine major components. First, at the very top of the profile you will see the school's address, telephone, and fax numbers for the admissions office, the telephone number for the financial aid office, and the school's website and/or e-mail address. Second, there are two sidebars (the narrow columns on the outside of each page, which consist mainly of statistics) divided into the categories of Campus Life, Academics, Selectivity, and Financial Facts. Third, there are four headings in the narrative text: Students Say, Admissions, Financial Aid, and From the Admissions Office. Here's what you'll find in each part:

The Sidebars

The sidebars contain various statistics culled from our surveys of students attending the school and from questionnaires that school administrators complete at our request in the fall of each year. Keep in mind that not every category will appear for every school—in some cases the information is not reported or not applicable. We compile the eight ratings—Quality of Life, Fire Safety, Green Rating, Academic, Profs Interesting, Profs Accessible, Admissions Selectivity, and Financial Aid—listed in the sidebars based on the results from our student surveys and/or institutional data we collect from school administrators.

These ratings are on a scale of 60–99. If a 60* (60 with an asterisk) appears as any rating for any school, it means that the school reported so few of the rating's underlying data points by our deadline that we were unable to calculate an accurate rating for it. (These measures are outlined in the ratings explanation below.) Be advised that because the Admissions Selectivity Rating is a factor in the computation that produces the Academic Rating, a school that has 60* (60 with an asterisk) as its Admissions Selectivity Rating will have an Academic Rating that is lower than it should be. Also bear in mind that each rating places each college on a continuum for purposes of comparing colleges within this edition only. Since our ratings computations may change from year to year, it is invalid to compare the ratings in this edition to those that appear in any prior or future edition.

Finally, these ratings are quite different from the ranking lists that appear in Part 2 of the book, "School Rankings and Lists." The ratings are numerical measures that show how a school "sizes up," if you will, on a fixed scale. Our sixty-two ranking lists report the top twenty (or in some cases bottom twenty) schools of the 381 in the book (not of all schools in the nation) in various categories. They are based on our surveys of students at the schools and/or institutional data. We don't rank the schools in the book 1 to 381 hierarchically. Here is what each heading in the sidebar tells you, in order of their appearance:

Quality of Life Rating

On a scale of 60–99, this rating is a measure of how happy students are with their campus experiences outside the classroom. To compile this rating, we weighed several factors, all based on students' answers to questions on our survey. They included the students' assessments of: their overall happiness; the beauty, safety, and location of the campus; comfort of dorms; quality of food; ease of getting around campus and dealing with administrators; friendliness of fellow students; and the interaction of different student types on campus and within the greater community.

> "Ratings are quite different from the ranking lists. The ratings are numerical measures that show how a school 'sizes up,' if you will, on a fixed scale. Our sixty-two ranking lists report the top twenty (or in some cases bottom twenty) schools of the 381 in the book (not of all schools in the nation) in various categories."

Fire Safety Rating

On a scale of 60–99, this rating measures how well prepared a school is to prevent or respond to campus fires, specifically in residence halls. We asked schools several questions about their efforts to ensure fire safety for campus residents. We developed the questions in consultation with the Center for Campus Fire Safety (www.campusfiresafety.org). Each school's responses to seven questions were considered when calculating its Fire Safety Rating. They cover:

1. The percentage of student housing sleeping rooms protected by an automatic fire sprinkler system with a fire sprinkler head located in the individual sleeping rooms.

2. The percentage of student housing sleeping rooms equipped with a smoke detector connected to a supervised fire alarm system.

3. The number of malicious fire alarms that occur in student housing per year.

4. The number of unwanted fire alarms that occur in student housing per year.

5. The banning of certain hazardous items and activities in residence halls, like candles, smoking, halogen lamps, etc.

6. The percentage of student housing fire alarm systems that, if activated, result in a signal being transmitted to a monitored location, where security investigates before notifying the fire department.

7. The percentage of student housing fire alarm systems that, if activated, result in a signal being transmitted immediately to a continuously monitored location.

Schools that did not report answers to a sufficient number of questions receive a Fire Safety Rating of 60* (60 with an asterisk). You can also find Fire Safety Ratings for our best 381 colleges (and several additional schools) in *The Complete Book of Colleges*, 2017 Edition. On page 55 of this book, you'll find a list of the schools with 99 (the highest score) Fire Safety Ratings.

Green Rating

We asked all the schools we collect data from annually to answer a number of questions that evaluate the comprehensive measure of their performance as an environmentally aware and responsible institution. The questions cover: 1) whether students have a campus quality of life that is both healthy and sustainable; 2) how well a school is preparing students not only for employment in the clean energy economy of the twenty-first century, but also for citizenship in a world now defined by environmental challenges; and 3) how environmentally responsible a school's policies are.

Additionally, The Princeton Review, the Association for the Advancement of Sustainability in Higher Education (AASHE), and *Sierra* magazine, have collaborated on an effort to streamline the reporting process for institutions that choose to participate in various higher education sustainability assessments. The intent of this initiative is to reduce and streamline the amount of time campus staff spend tracking sustainability data and completing related surveys.

To address this issue these groups worked to establish the Campus Sustainability Data Collector (CSDC). The CSDC was based off of the STARS Reporting Tool and was available for all schools (free of charge) who wanted to submit data to these groups in one single survey. For our most recent collection, the CSDC was replaced with the launch of STARS 2.0. The new version of STARS offers a basic level of access at no cost to institutions.

Please find more information here:

http://www.princetonreview.com/green-data-partnership/

Each school's responses to ten questions were considered when calculating The Princeton Review's Green Rating.

They include:

1. The percentage of food expenditures that go toward local, organic, or otherwise environmentally preferable food.

2. Whether the school offers programs including mass transit programs, bike sharing, facilities for bicyclists, bicycle and pedestrian plan, car sharing, carpool discount, carpool/vanpool matching, cash-out of parking, prohibiting idling, local housing, telecommuting, and condensed work week.

3. Whether the school has a formal committee that is devoted to advancing sustainability on campus.

4. Whether school buildings that were constructed or underwent major renovations in the past three years are LEED certified.

5. The schools overall waste-diversion rate.

6. Whether the school offers at least one sustainability-focused undergraduate major, degree program, or equivalent.

7. Whether the school's students graduate from programs that include sustainability as a required learning outcome or include multiple sustainability learning outcomes.

8. Whether the school has a formal plan to mitigate its greenhouse gas emissions.

9. What percentage of the school's energy consumption is derived from renewable resources.

10. Whether the school employs a dedicated full-time (or full-time equivalent) sustainability officer.

Colleges that did not supply answers to a sufficient number of the green campus questions for us to fairly compare them to other colleges receive a Green Rating of 60*. On page 55 of this book and on our website at www.princetonreview.com/green-honor-roll, you'll find a list of the schools with 99 (the highest score) Green Ratings.

Check out our free downloadable resource, The Princeton Review's *Guide to Green Colleges* at www.princetonreview.com/green-guide.

Type of school
Whether the school is public or private.

Affiliation
Any religious order with which the school is affiliated.

Environment
Whether the campus is located in an urban, suburban, or rural setting.

Total undergrad enrollment
The total number of undergraduates who attend the school.

"% male/female" through "# countries represented"

Demographic information about the full-time undergraduate student body, including male to female ratio, ethnicity, and the number of countries represented by the student body. Also included are the percentages of the student body who are from out of state, attended a public high school, first-year students living on campus, and belong to Greek organizations.

Survey Says . . .

A snapshot of key results of our student survey. This list names survey topics about which the body of students we surveyed at the school—as a group—showed a statistically higher consensus of opinion in their answers to our questions on those topics (as compared with their answers to questions on other topics). See the end of this section for a detailed explanation of items on the list.

Academic Rating

On a scale of 60–99, this rating is a measure of how hard students work at the school and how much they get back for their efforts. The rating is based on results from our surveys of students and data we collect from administrators. Factors weighed included how many hours students reported that they study each day outside of class, students' assessments of their professors' teaching abilities and of their accessibility outside the classroom and the quality of students the school attracts as measured by admissions statistics.

% of students returning for sophomore year

The percentage of degree-seeking first-year students returning for sophomore year.

4-year graduation rate

The percentage of degree-seeking undergraduate students graduating in four years or less.

6-year graduation rate

The percentage of degree-seeking undergraduate students graduating within six years.

Calendar

The school's schedule of academic terms. A "semester" schedule has two long terms, usually starting in September and January. A "trimester" schedule has three terms, one usually beginning before Christmas and two after. A "quarterly" schedule has four terms, which go by very quickly: the entire term, including exams, usually lasts only nine or ten weeks. A "4-1-4" schedule is like a semester schedule, but with a month-long term in between the fall and spring semesters. (Similarly, a "4-4-1" has a short term following two longer semesters.) It is always best to call the admissions office for details.

Student/faculty ratio

The ratio of full-time undergraduate instructional faculty members to all undergraduates.

Profs interesting rating

On a scale of 60–99, this rating is based on levels of surveyed students' agreement or disagreement with the statement: "Your instructors are good teachers."

Profs accessible rating

On a scale of 60–99, this rating is based on levels of surveyed students' agreement or disagreement with the statement: "Your instructors are accessible outside the classroom."

Most common regular class size; Most common lab size

The most commonly occurring class size for regular courses and for labs/discussion sections.

Most popular majors

The majors with the highest enrollments at the school.

Admissions Selectivity Rating

On a scale of 60–99, this rating is a measure of how competitive admission is at the school. This rating is determined by several factors, including the high school class rank of entering first year students, test scores, and percentage of applicants accepted.

% of applicants accepted

The percentage of applicants to whom the school offered admission.

% of acceptees attending

The percentage of accepted students who eventually enrolled at the school.

applicants offered a place on the wait list

Number of qualified applicants offered a place on waiting list

% accepting a place on wait list

The percentage of students who decided to take a place on the wait list when offered this option.

% admitted from wait list

The percentage of applicants who opted to take a place on the wait list and were subsequently offered admission. These figures will vary tremendously from college to college, and should be a consideration when deciding whether to accept a place on a college's wait list.

of early decision applicants

The number of students who applied under the college's early decision or early action plan.

% accepted early decision

The percentage of early decision or early action applicants who were admitted under this plan. By the nature of these plans, the vast majority who are admitted ultimately enroll.

Range SAT Critical Reading, Range SAT Math, Range SAT Writing, Range ACT Composite

The average and the middle fifty percent range of test scores for entering first-year students.

Nota Bene: The score ranges published in this edition are from the old SAT, administered prior to March 2016. For the most up-to-date information on SAT score concordance, college and university admission policies, and the new SAT, please visit PrincetonReview.com.

Don't be discouraged from applying to the school of your choice even if your combined SAT scores are 80 or even 120 points below the average, because you may still have a chance of getting in. Remember that many schools value other aspects of your application (e.g., your grades, how good a match you make with the school) more heavily than test scores.

Minimum TOEFL

The minimum test score necessary for entering first-year students who are required to take the TOEFL (Test of English as a Foreign Language). Most schools will require all international students or non-native English speakers to take the TOEFL in order to be considered for admission.

Average HS GPA

The average grade point average of entering first-year students. We report this on a scale of 1.0–4.0 (occasionally colleges report averages on a 100 scale, in which case we report those figures). This is one of the key factors in college admissions.

% graduated top 10%, top 25%, top 50% of class

Of those students for whom class rank was reported, the percentage of entering first-year students who ranked in the top tenth, quarter, and half of their high school classes.

Early decision/action deadlines

The deadline for submission of application materials under the early decision or early action plan.

Early decision, early action, priority, and regular admission deadlines

The dates by which all materials must be postmarked (we suggest "received in the office") in order to be considered for admission under each particular admissions option/cycle for matriculation in the fall term.

Early decision, early action, priority, and regular admission notification

The dates by which you can expect a decision on your application under each admissions option/cycle.

Nonfall registration

Some schools will allow incoming students to register and begin attending classes at times other than the fall term, which is the traditional beginning of the academic calendar year. Other schools will allow you to register for classes only if you can begin in the fall term. A simple "yes" or "no" in this category indicates the school's policy on nonfall registration.

Applicants also look at

These lists are based on information we receive directly from the colleges. Admissions officers are annually given the opportunity to review and suggest alterations to these lists for their schools, as most schools track as closely as they can other schools to which applicants they accepted applied, and whether the applicants chose their school over the other schools, or vice versa.

Financial Aid Rating

On a scale of 60–99, this rating is a measure of the financial aid the school awards and how satisfied students are with the aid they receive. It is based on school-reported data on financial aid and students' responses to the survey question, "If you receive financial aid, how satisfied are you with your financial aid package?" On page 55 of this book you'll find a list of the schools with 99 (the highest score) Financial Aid Ratings.

Annual in-state tuition

The tuition at the school, or for public colleges, the cost of tuition for a resident of the school's state. Usually much lower than out-of-state tuition for state-supported public schools.

Annual out-of-state tuition

For public colleges, the tuition for a non-resident of the school's state. This entry appears only for public colleges, since tuition at private colleges is generally the same regardless of state of residence.

Required fees

Any additional costs students must pay beyond tuition in order to attend the school. These often include fitness center fees and the like. A few state schools may not officially charge in-state students tuition, but those students are still responsible for hefty fees.

Tuition and fees

In cases when schools do not report separate figures for tuition and required fees, we offer this total of the two.

Comprehensive fee

A few schools report one overall fee that reflects the total cost of tuition, room and board, and required fees. If you'd like to see how this figure breaks down, we recommend contacting the school.

Room and board

Estimated annual room and board costs.

Books and supplies

Estimated annual cost of necessary textbooks and/or supplies.

Average freshman/undergraduate need-based scholarship

The average need-based scholarship and grant aid awarded to students with need.

% needy frosh receiving need-based scholarship or grant aid

The percentage of all degree-seeking first-year students who were determined to have need and received any need-based scholarship or grant.

% needy UG receiving need-based scholarship or grant aid

The percentage of all degree-seeking undergraduates who were determined to have need and received any need-based scholarship or grant.

% needy frosh receiving non-need-based scholarship or grant aid

The percentage of all degree-seeking first-year students, determined to have need, receiving any non-need based scholarship or grant aid.

% needy ugrads receiving non-need-based scholarship or grant aid

The percentage of all degree-seeking undergraduates, determined to have need, receiving any non-need based scholarship or grant aid.

% needy frosh receiving need-based self-help aid

The percentage of all degree-seeking first-year students, determined to have need, who received any need-based self-help aid.

% needy ugrads receiving need-based self-help aid

The percentage of all degree-seeking undergraduates, determined to have need, who received any need-based self-help aid.

% frosh receiving any financial aid

The percentage of all degree-seeking first-year students receiving any financial aid (need-based, merit-based, gift aid).

% UG receiving any financial aid

The percentage of all degree-seeking undergraduates receiving any financial aid (need-based, merit-based, gift aid).

% UG borrow to pay for school

The percentage who borrowed at any time through any loan programs (institutional, state, Federal Perkins, Federal Stafford Subsidized and Unsubsidized, private loans that were certified by your institution, etc., exclude parent loans). Includes both Federal Direct Student Loans and Federal Family Education Loans (prior to the FFEL program ending in June 2010).

% frosh and ugrad need fully met

The percentage of needy degree-seeking students whose needs was fully met (excludes PLUS loans, unsubsidized loans, and private alternative loans).

Average % of frosh and ugrad need met

On average, the percentage of need that was met of students who were awarded any need-based aid. Excludes any aid that was awarded in excess of need as well as any resources that were awarded to replace EFC (PLUS loans, unsubsidized loans, and private alternative loans).

Average Indebtedness

The average per-undergraduate borrower cumulative principal borrowed of those who borrowed at any time through any loan programs (Federal Perkins, Federal Stafford Subsidized and Unsubsidized, institutional, state, private loans that institution is aware of, etc. Includes both Federal Direct Student Loans and Federal Family Education Loans.).

Nota Bene: The statistical data reported in this book, unless otherwise noted, was collected from the profiled colleges from the fall of 2015 through the spring of 2016. In some cases, we were unable to publish the most recent data because schools did not report the necessary statistics to us in time, despite our repeated outreach efforts. Because the enrollment and financial statistics, as well as application and financial aid deadlines, fluctuate from one year to another, we recommend that you check with the schools to make sure you have the most current information before applying.

Students Say

This section shares the straight-from-the-campus feedback we get from the school's most important customers: The students attending them. It summarizes the opinions of first-year students through seniors we've surveyed and it includes direct quotes from scores of them. When appropriate, it also incorporates statistics provided by the schools. The Students Say section is divided into three subsections: Academics, Life, and Student Body. The Academics section describes how hard students work and how satisfied they are with the education they are getting. It also often tells you which programs or academic departments students rated most favorably and how professors interact with students. Student opinion regarding administrative departments also works its way into this section. The Life section describes life outside the classroom and addresses questions ranging from "How comfortable are the dorms?" to "How popular are fraternities and sororities?" In this section, students describe what they do for entertainment both on-campus and off, providing a clear picture of the social environment at their particular school. The Student Body section will give you the lowdown on the types of students the school attracts and how the students view the level of interaction among various groups, including those of different ethnic, socioeconomic, and religious backgrounds.

All quotations in these sections are from students' responses to open-ended questions on our survey. We select quotations based on the accuracy with which they reflect overall student opinion about the school as conveyed in the survey results.

Admissions

This section lets you know which aspects of your application are most important to the admissions officers at the school. It also lists the high school curricular prerequisites for applicants, which standardized tests (if any) are required, and special information about the school's admissions process (e.g., Do minority students and legacies, for example, receive special consideration? Are there any unusual application requirements for applicants to special programs?).

Financial Aid

Here you'll found out what you need to know about the financial aid process at the school, namely what forms you need and what types of merit-based aid and loans are available. Information about need-based aid is contained in the financial aid sidebar. This section includes specific deadline dates for submission of materials as reported by the colleges. We strongly encourage students seeking financial aid to file all forms—federal, state, and institutional—carefully, fully, and on time.

The Inside Word

This section gives you the inside scoop on what it takes to gain admission to the school. It reflects our own insights about each school's admissions process and acceptance trends. (We visit scores of colleges each year and talk with hundreds of admissions officers in order to glean this info.) It also incorporates information from institutional data we collect and our surveys over the years of students at the school.

From the Admissions Office

This section presents the key things the school's admissions office would like you to know about their institution. For schools that did not respond to our invitation to supply text for this space, we excerpted an appropriate passage from the school's catalog, web site, or other admissions literature. For this section, we also invited schools to submit a brief paragraph explaining their admissions policies regarding the SAT (especially the Writing portion of the exam) and the SAT Subject Tests. We are pleased that nearly every school took this opportunity to clarify its policies as we know there has been some student and parent confusion about how these scores are evaluated for admission.

Survey Says

Our Survey Says list, located in the Campus Life sidebar on each school's two-page spread, is based entirely on the results of our student survey. In other words, the items on this list are based on the opinions of the students we surveyed at those schools (not on any quantitative analysis of library size, endowment, etc.). These items reveal popular or unpopular trends on campus for the purpose of providing a snapshot of life on that campus only. The appearance of a Survey Says item in the sidebar does not reflect the popularity of that item relative to its popularity among the student bodies at other schools. To ascertain the relative popularity of certain items/trends on campus, see the appropriate ranking (e.g., for the Survey Says item "Career Services are Great," see the "Best Career Services" ranking). Some of the terms that appear on the Survey Says list are not entirely self-explanatory; these terms are defined below.

Different types of students interact: We asked students whether students from different class and ethnic backgrounds interacted frequently and easily. When students' collective response is "yes," the heading "Different types of students interact" appears on the list. When the collective student response indicates there are not many interactions between students from different class and ethnic backgrounds, the phrase "Students are cliquish" appears on the list. Note: This topic is not based on demographic data about the student body.

No one cheats: We asked students how prevalent cheating is at their school. If students reported cheating to be rare, the term "No one cheats" shows up on the list.

Students are happy: This category reflects student responses to the question "Overall, how happy are you?"

Students are very religious or Students aren't religious: We asked students how religious students are at their school. Their responses are reflected in this category.

Diverse student types on campus: We asked students whether their student body is made up of a variety of ethnic groups. This category reflects their answers to this question. This heading shows up as "Diversity lacking on campus" or "Diverse student types on campus." It does not reflect any institutional data on this subject.

Students get along with local community: This category reflects student responses to a question concerning how well the student body gets along with residents of the college town or community.

Career services are great: This category reflects student opinion on the quality of career/job placement services on campus.

AN IMPORTANT NOTE ABOUT SAT SCORES

The SAT underwent major changes in March 2016. The score ranges published in this book reflect the test prior to the change, i.e., the most recent available data at the time of printing. Fall 2016 is the first admission cycle that will use scores from the new SAT.

The College Board has released a great deal of information on score concordance, or relating scores from one version of the exam to another. They recommend converting your new SAT score to an old one to see if it falls within the score range at your target schools.

The concordance tables provided below are intended as a guide to help students and parents relate scores and score ranges between the new and old SAT exams, and are based on the latest available information as of May 2016. Please visit PrincetonReview.com for the most up-to-date information on SAT score concordance.

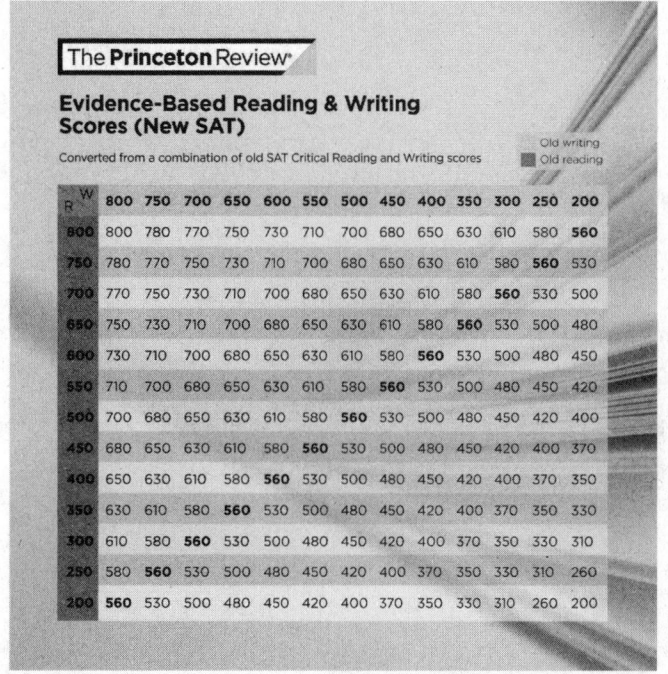

The Princeton Review®

Evidence-Based Reading & Writing Scores (New SAT)

Converted from a combination of old SAT Critical Reading and Writing scores

Old writing
Old reading

R\W	800	750	700	650	600	550	500	450	400	350	300	250	200
800	800	780	770	750	730	710	700	680	650	630	610	580	560
750	780	770	750	730	710	700	680	650	630	610	580	560	530
700	770	750	730	710	700	680	650	630	610	580	560	530	500
650	750	730	710	700	680	650	630	610	580	560	530	500	480
600	730	710	700	680	650	630	610	580	560	530	500	480	450
550	710	700	680	650	630	610	580	560	530	500	480	450	420
500	700	680	650	630	610	580	560	530	500	480	450	420	400
450	680	650	630	610	580	560	530	500	480	450	420	400	370
400	650	630	610	580	560	530	500	480	450	420	400	370	350
350	630	610	580	560	530	500	480	450	420	400	370	350	330
300	610	580	560	530	500	480	450	420	400	370	350	330	310
250	580	560	530	500	480	450	420	400	370	350	330	310	260
200	560	530	500	480	450	420	400	370	350	330	310	260	200

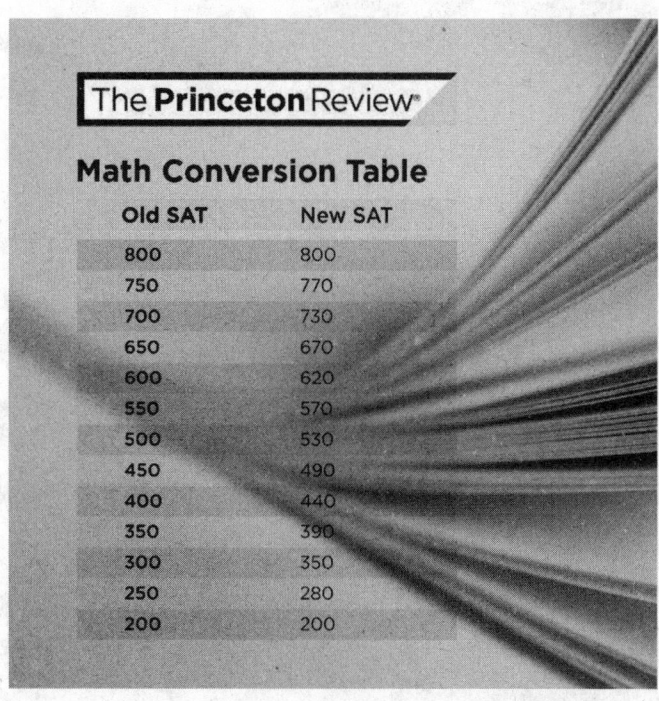

The Princeton Review®

Math Conversion Table

Old SAT	New SAT
800	800
750	770
700	730
650	670
600	620
550	570
500	530
450	490
400	440
350	390
300	350
250	280
200	200

About Our College Ranking Lists

Finding a college that has terrific academics is easy. There are hundreds of academically great colleges out there. Their campus cultures, student bodies, and school offerings, however, differ widely. Finding the academically great school that is right for you is the tough part. Hence, we compile not one ranking list but sixty-three unique lists, each one reporting the top twenty (or in some cases bottom twenty) schools from our *Best Colleges* book in a specific category.

None of our lists are based on what we think of the schools (though members of the media, the public, and school administrators mistakenly credit or blame us for the results, saying "According to The Princeton Review, X school is the best in the nation for…" or "The Princeton Review ranks Y school the tenth most…."). In fact, the only thing we say is that all of the 381 colleges in this book are outstanding (hence, the "Best" designation). It's what students think of their schools—how they rate various aspects of their colleges' offerings and what they report to us about their campus experiences—that results in a school's appearance on our ranking lists.

Here you won't find the colleges in the book ranked hierarchically, 1 to 381. We think such lists—particularly those driven by and perpetuating a "best academics" mania—are not useful for the people they are supposed to serve (college applicants). More and more college administrators—including several at schools ranked high on these lists—agree. In fact, the primary reason we developed this book was to give applicants and parents better and broader information that will help them winnow a list of colleges right for them.

About 80 percent of the schools in our book end up on one or more of the lists in each edition. To college officials happy about the lists their schools are on, we say don't thank us, we're just the messengers. To college officials unhappy about the lists their schools are on, we say don't blame us, we're just the messengers.

All of these ranking lists are based entirely on students' answers to questions on our surveys (e.g., our "Best Campus Food" list and inverse list, "Is it Food?" are each based on the single survey question, "How do you rate your campus food?") or students' answers to a combination of survey questions (e.g., our "Party Schools" list and our inverse list, "Stone-Cold Sober Schools" are each based on students' answers to survey questions concerning the use of alcohol and drugs on their campuses, the popularity of the frat/sorority scene on their campuses, and the number of hours they say they study each day outside of class time).

Each list covers one of many aspects of a college's character that can be helpful in deciding if it's the right or wrong school for an individual student. The lists report on a wide range of issues that may be important, either singly or, more likely, in combination. Our ranking lists cover: financial aid, campus facilities and amenities, extracurriculars, town-gown relations, the student body's political leanings, social life, race/class relations, LGBTQ-friendly (or not so friendly) atmosphere, career services, athletic facilities, and more.

> "It's what students think of their schools—how they rate various aspects of their colleges' offerings and what they report to us about their campus experiences—that results in a school's appearance on our ranking lists."

This year we added a new ranking list: "Most Active Student Government."

The ranking list categories that members of the media cover the most are our "Party Schools" and "Stone-cold Sober Schools" lists. Our "Party Schools" list has even been the subject of a "Doonesbury" cartoon (which appears on the frontispiece of this book). This list draws a wide range of reaction every year. Some students complain that their college didn't make the list. Others are irate because their college did.

Some people incorrectly assume that schools on our "Party Schools" list are not advisable to attend because they imagine that the social scene dominates over academic pursuits on those campuses. As we've noted, all the colleges and universities we profile in this book are academically excellent, and "work hard, play hard" is a favorite phrase of our survey respondents across many, many schools with a diverse array of social scenes.

Inversely, some people incorrectly assume that schools on our "Stone-cold Sober Schools" list are not advisable to attend because they imagine the social scene on those campuses is lacking. Skim each college's profile, however, and you'll find plenty of extracurricular activity: sports, games, clubs, and concerts.

We recommend all schools on these lists (and all 381 schools in this book) as outstanding institutions to earn one's college degree and have a fun time.

However, no one should assume that any one of these 381 outstanding colleges—regardless of which ranking list(s) it may (or may not) be on—is insulated from the influences of alcohol and drugs on its campus. An oft-quoted Harvard University School of Public Health 2002 study found that (then) 45 percent of undergraduates, in general, had engaged in binge drinking (consuming five or more alcoholic beverages in one sitting for men, four drinks or more for women).[1] These facts are alarming, as they should be. College administrators face tremendous challenges in creating and enforcing campus alcohol and drug use/abuse policies (and media have reported on how several institutions have toughed their policies subsequent to their appearances on our lists). Many colleges struggle with problems resulting from the prevalence of bars and liquor stores near their campuses; at some universities there are more than 100 such establishments within a few miles from the campus. "Dry campus" policies often exacerbate the problem, driving drinking off-campus, making it even more dangerous for students.

Over a decade ago, some administrators at colleges that had repeatedly made our "Party Schools" list claimed that our reporting this list promoted drinking on their campuses. (They were administrators at colleges receiving millions of dollars of funding through a program administrated within the American Medical Association to address their campuses' and communities' alcohol problems.) After these administrators (and their AMA program director) made news in 2002 with this claim, USA TODAY published an editorial that cited their unique affiliation and praised our reporting our ranking list as a "public service."

None of our lists promote behavior of any kind: They report what students on campuses told us about their opinions of their schools.

What our lists promote is information. What we say to college students is this: If you're going to drink, do it safely, responsibly, and (obviously) legally. If you're going off campus to drink, don't drive back—get a designated driver and never, ever drive drunk. Don't use alcohol or drugs as a badge of your coolness. Don't let any alcohol or drug-related situation put you in danger of getting hurt or hurting others—it's simply not worth it. Last, being responsible doesn't only apply to yourself—keep an eye on your friends, and never leave them passed out, alone, or at risk.

Finally, a grateful note to all the college officials, counselors, advisors, students, and parents who have made this annual guide possible by supporting us these past twenty-five years. Our ranking lists, rating scores, and profiles have factored in data from more than 2 million students and thousands of administrators. To all who have completed our past surveys and all who will do so this year: thanks. Your input is essential to our book. We know that it has helped students find "best fit" colleges ideal for them, and brought to the colleges in our book many outstanding applicants who otherwise may not have considered these "best" (in our opinion) colleges.

---

1 *Harvard University School of Public Health. "College Student Binge Drinking Rates Remain High Despite Efforts by School Administrations." www.hsph.harvard.edu/news/press-releases/2000-releases/press03142000.html.*

WE WANT TO HEAR FROM YOU

To all of our readers, we welcome your feedback on how we can continue to improve this guide. We hope you will share with us your comments, questions, and suggestions. Please contact us at editorialsupport@review.com. We welcome it.

To college applicants, we wish you all the best in your college search. And when you get to your campuses and settle in to your college life, come back to us online; participate in our survey for this book at http://survey.review.com. Let your honest comments about your schools guide prospective students who want your help answering the $64,000 question (goodness knows, the sticker price at some schools may be that high or even higher!): "Which is the best college for me?"

PART 2

School Rankings and Lists

We present our 62 "Top 20" ranking lists in eight categories.

Schools by Type

Under each list heading, we tell you the survey question or assessment that we used to tabulate the list. We tally student responses to several questions on our survey for our lists "Best Classroom Experience," "Best Quality of Life," and the five lists in our Schools by Type rankings (including our "Party Schools" and "Stone-Cold Sober Schools" lists). Be aware that all of our 62 ranking lists are based entirely on our student surveys. They do not reflect our opinions of the schools. They are entirely the result of what students attending these schools tell us about them: It's how students rate their own schools and what they report to us about their campus experiences at them that make our ranking lists so unusual. After all, what better way is there to judge a school than by what its customers—its students—say about it?

Honor Rolls

Colleges That Pay You Back

ACADEMICS/ADMINISTRATION

Best Classroom Experience

Based on a combination of survey questions concerning teachers, classroom/lab facilities, classes attended, and amount of in-class discussion

1. Sarah Lawrence College
2. Bennington College
3. Reed College
4. Franklin W. Olin College of Engineering
5. Mount Holyoke College
6. Bard College
7. Scripps College
8. Claremont McKenna College
9. University of Richmond
10. Thomas Aquinas College
11. Whitman College
12. United States Military Academy
13. Earlham College
14. Centre College
15. Haverford College
16. Carleton College
17. Colby College
18. Bowdoin College
19. St. Olaf College
20. Lawrence University

Students Study the Most

How many out-of-class hours do you spend studying each day?

1. United States Military Academy
2. Harvey Mudd College
3. Reed College
4. The University of Chicago
5. Carleton College
6. Grinnell College
7. Franklin W. Olin College of Engineering
8. The Cooper Union for the Advancement of Science and Art
9. Hamilton College
10. Carnegie Mellon University
11. California Institute of Technology
12. Webb Institute
13. Swarthmore College
14. Middlebury College
15. St. John's College (NM)
16. The College of Wooster
17. United States Coast Guard Academy
18. Brown University
19. Bowdoin College
20. Columbia University

Students Study the Least

How many out-of-class hours do you spend studying each day?

1. Trinity College Dublin
2. Kansas State University
3. Indiana University of Pennsylvania
4. St. John's University
5. National University of Ireland Maynooth
6. West Virginia University
7. University of Mississippi
8. Champlain College
9. City University of New York—Baruch College
10. Monmouth University (NJ)
11. Becker College
12. University of Central Florida
13. Emerson College
14. Warren Wilson College
15. Rider University
16. University of Rhode Island
17. University of South Carolina—Columbia
18. Stephens College
19. University of Miami
20. University of Louisville

Professors Get High Marks

Are your instructors good teachers?

1. Wellesley College
2. St. John's College (NM)
3. Bennington College
4. Franklin W. Olin College of Engineering
5. Swarthmore College
6. Hillsdale College
7. Reed College
8. Marlboro College
9. Sarah Lawrence College
10. Middlebury College
11. College of the Atlantic
12. Bard College
13. Claremont McKenna College
14. Mount Holyoke College
15. Carleton College
16. St. John's College (MD)
17. Harvey Mudd College
18. Wabash College
19. Wake Forest University
20. Hamilton College

Professors Get Low Marks

Are your instructors good teachers?

1. New Jersey Institute of Technology
2. United States Merchant Marine Academy
3. Stevens Institute of Technology
4. University of Hawaii at Manoa
5. State University of New York—Stony Brook University
6. University of California—San Diego
7. University of Connecticut
8. University of Louisville
9. McGill University
10. St. John's University
11. Michigan Technological University
12. City University of New York—Queens College
13. University of North Dakota
14. Howard University
15. Illinois Institute of Technology
16. California Institute of Technology
17. University of Pittsburgh—Pittsburgh Campus
18. Hampton University
19. Louisiana State University
20. Purdue University—West Lafayette

Most Accessible Professors

Are your instructors accessible outside the classroom?

1. United States Military Academy
2. Claremont McKenna College
3. United States Coast Guard Academy
4. Colby College
5. Rose-Hulman Institute of Technology
6. St. John's College (MD)
7. Centre College
8. Wake Forest University
9. Rhodes College
10. Wabash College
11. Whitman College
12. St. John's College (NM)
13. Swarthmore College
14. Bard College
15. College of the Holy Cross
16. Harvey Mudd College
17. United States Naval Academy
18. Carleton College
19. Villanova University
20. Wellesley College

Least Accessible Professors

Are your instructors accessible outside the classroom?

1. United States Merchant Marine Academy
2. University of New Mexico
3. The University of Alabama at Tuscaloosa
4. University of California—Santa Cruz
5. McGill University
6. St. John's University
7. University of Kentucky
8. Howard University
9. New Jersey Institute of Technology
10. State University of New York—University at Albany
11. University of North Dakota
12. Hampton University

13. University of Hawaii at Manoa
14. Portland State University
15. Trinity College Dublin
16. University of Massachusetts Amherst
17. Louisiana State University
18. University of California—Los Angeles
19. University of California—San Diego
20. City University of New York— Queens College

Best Science Lab Facilities
Based on students' assessment of science lab facilities

1. Harvey Mudd College
2. Trinity University
3. United States Naval Academy
4. University of Scranton
5. St. Olaf College
6. Johns Hopkins University
7. Rose-Hulman Institute of Technology
8. Lehigh University
9. California Institute of Technology
10. Union College
11. Middlebury College
12. Bowdoin College
13. Grinnell College
14. Stanford University
15. Christopher Newport University
16. Wheaton College (MA)
17. St. Lawrence University
18. Washington University in St. Louis
19. Emory University
20. Nazareth College

Most Popular Study Abroad Program
How popular is studying abroad at your school?

1. Worcester Polytechnic Institute
2. Centre College
3. Elon University
4. University of Dallas
5. Goucher College
6. Union College
7. Hobart and William Smith Colleges
8. University of Denver
9. Gettysburg College
10. St. Olaf College
11. Susquehanna University
12. Juniata College
13. University of Richmond
14. University of San Diego
15. St. Lawrence University
16. Dickinson College
17. Bates College
18. Carleton College
19. Syracuse University
20. University of Delaware

Best Health Services
Based on students' assessments of student health services/facilities on campus

1. University of Wisconsin—Madison
2. University of Arizona
3. United States Military Academy
4. Baylor University
5. Pennsylvania State University— University Park
6. Union College
7. University of California—Davis
8. University of Iowa
9. University of Utah
10. Calvin College
11. University of Central Florida
12. University of California—Los Angeles
13. United States Air Force Academy
14. Washington State University
15. The College of New Jersey
16. Wabash College
17. Stanford University
18. University of Minnesota— Twin Cities Campus
19. Auburn University
20. Rice University

Best Career Services
Based on students' rating of campus career/ job-placement services

1. Bentley University
2. Northeastern University
3. Wake Forest University
4. Southwestern University
5. Clemson University
6. Rose-Hulman Institute of Technology
7. Claremont McKenna College
8. Wabash College
9. Pennsylvania State University— University Park
10. University of Iowa
11. Washington University in St. Louis
12. The College of New Jersey
13. United States Naval Academy
14. Worcester Polytechnic Institute
15. Illinois Wesleyan University
16. Rhodes College
17. United States Military Academy
18. Bryant University
19. Elon University
20. University of Illinois at Urbana-Champaign

Best College Library
Based on students' assessment of library facilities

1. The University of Chicago
2. United States Military Academy
3. Columbia University
4. Stanford University
5. University of Iowa
6. Rhodes College
7. Vassar College
8. Yale University
9. Harvard College
10. Colgate University
11. Middlebury College
12. Mount Holyoke College
13. University of Wisconsin—Madison
14. Princeton University
15. Dartmouth College
16. Washington University in St. Louis
17. Wake Forest University
18. University of Denver
19. The College of William & Mary
20. University of Oklahoma

This Is a Library?
Based on students' assessment of library facilities

1. Bradley University
2. Clarkson University
3. Juniata College
4. University of Dallas
5. Salisbury University
6. University of Tampa
7. United States Merchant Marine Academy
8. United States Coast Guard Academy
9. New Jersey Institute of Technology
10. College of the Atlantic
11. Colorado College
12. Stevens Institute of Technology
13. Illinois Institute of Technology
14. University of North Dakota
15. Tuskegee University
16. Transylvania University
17. Prescott College
18. Bard College at Simon's Rock
19. Catawba College
20. Duquesne University

Great Financial Aid
Based on students' assessments of how satisfied they are with their financial aid package

1. Vassar College
2. Princeton University
3. Bowdoin College
4. Vanderbilt University
5. Pomona College
6. Claremont McKenna College
7. Colgate University
8. St. Olaf College
9. Pitzer College
10. Stanford University
11. Macalester College
12. Columbia University
13. Reed College
14. University of Wisconsin—Madison
15. Wellesley College
16. Yale University
17. Trinity College (CT)
18. Haverford College
19. The Cooper Union for the Advancement of Science and Art
20. Franklin W. Olin College of Engineering

Financial Aid Not So Great
Based on students' assessments of how satisfied they are with their financial aid package

1. State University of New York—Purchase College
2. Spelman College
3. Duquesne University
4. Suffolk University
5. New York University
6. Ohio University—Athens
7. The University of Texas at Austin
8. Hampton University
9. University of New Hampshire
10. The University of North Carolina at Greensboro
11. State University of New York at Binghamton
12. University of Hawaii at Manoa
13. Pennsylvania State University—University Park
14. Quinnipiac University
15. University of Kentucky
16. The Evergreen State College
17. University of Mary Washington
18. University of Missouri
19. Seton Hall University
20. State University of New York—University at Albany

Best-Run Colleges
Overall, how smoothly is your school run?

1. Elon University
2. Bowdoin College
3. Claremont McKenna College
4. Brigham Young University (UT)
5. Washington University in St. Louis
6. Rose-Hulman Institute of Technology
7. Webb Institute
8. Vanderbilt University
9. Stanford University
10. United States Coast Guard Academy

11. University of Richmond
12. Wheaton College (IL)
13. Emory University
14. United States Naval Academy
15. Kansas State University
16. Christopher Newport University
17. Tulane University
18. University of Oklahoma
19. Baylor University
20. Colby College

Administrators Get Low Marks
Overall, how smoothly is your school run?

1. Hanover College
2. University of Hawaii at Manoa
3. Illinois Institute of Technology
4. New Jersey Institute of Technology
5. Mills College
6. State University of New York—Purchase College
7. Warren Wilson College
8. Bard College
9. Whittier College
10. Marlboro College
11. City University of New York—Queens College
12. University of California—Berkeley
13. Beloit College
14. Earlham College
15. United States Merchant Marine Academy
16. Hampton University
17. New York University
18. Howard University
19. The Catholic University of America
20. Alfred University

Their Students Love These Colleges
Overall, how satisfied are you with your school?

1. Virginia Tech
2. Kansas State University
3. Clemson University
4. Claremont McKenna College
5. University of Dayton
6. The College of New Jersey
7. Colby College
8. The College of William & Mary
9. Whitman College
10. University of Vermont
11. University of Iowa
12. University of Wisconsin—Madison
13. Worcester Polytechnic Institute
14. Vanderbilt University
15. University of California—Santa Barbara
16. Yale University
17. Fairfield University
18. Auburn University
19. Bowdoin College
20. Stanford University

QUALITY OF LIFE

Happiest Students
Overall, how happy are you?

1. Rice University
2. Vanderbilt University
3. University of Dayton
4. Auburn University
5. University of Iowa
6. Kansas State University
7. Virginia Tech
8. University of California—Santa Barbara
9. Colby College
10. Claremont McKenna College
11. Clemson University
12. St. Mary's College of Maryland
13. The College of New Jersey
14. University of Vermont
15. University of Oklahoma
16. The College of William & Mary
17. Lake Forest College
18. Rhodes College
19. Worcester Polytechnic Institute
20. Saint Anselm College

Least Happy Students
Overall, how happy are you?

1. Montana Tech of the University of Montana
2. New Jersey Institute of Technology
3. United States Coast Guard Academy
4. United States Naval Academy
5. Clarkson University
6. University of Hawaii at Manoa
7. United States Merchant Marine Academy
8. McGill University
9. Simmons College
10. Illinois Institute of Technology
11. Marlboro College
12. University of California—Berkeley
13. University of Mary Washington
14. Wheaton College (MA)
15. University of Louisville
16. Transylvania University
17. St. John's University
18. University of New Orleans
19. California State University, Stanislaus
20. Portland State University

Most Beautiful Campus
Based on students' rating of campus beauty

1. Rhodes College
2. Bennington College
3. Elon University
4. Bucknell University
5. Florida Southern College

6. University of Vermont
7. The College of New Jersey
8. Pepperdine University
9. Colgate University
10. Rollins College
11. Vanderbilt University
12. Scripps College
13. University of San Diego
14. Southern Methodist University
15. Colby College
16. College of the Atlantic
17. University of Colorado Boulder
18. St. Mary's College of Maryland
19. University of Mississippi
20. The College of William & Mary

Least Beautiful Campus
Based on students' rating of campus beauty

1. University of Dallas
2. Harvey Mudd College
3. New Jersey Institute of Technology
4. State University of New York—
   Purchase College
5. Clarkson University
6. Illinois Institute of Technology
7. Montana Tech of the University of Montana
8. State University of New York
   at Binghamton
9. State University of New York—
   College of Environmental Science
   and Forestry
10. Rochester Institute of Technology
11. Xavier University of Louisiana
12. University of Louisville
13. City University of New York—
    Baruch College
14. University of New Orleans
15. United States Merchant Marine Academy
16. Drexel University
17. The University of Tennessee at Knoxville
18. The University of South Dakota
19. Case Western Reserve University
20. University of North Dakota

Best Campus Food
Based on students' rating of campus food

1. University of Massachusetts Amherst
2. Bowdoin College
3. Cornell University
4. Virginia Tech
5. St. Olaf College
6. College of the Atlantic
7. James Madison University
8. Saint Anselm College
9. Washington University in St. Louis
10. Bryn Mawr College
11. University of Scranton

12. Bates College
13. Scripps College
14. Gettysburg College
15. Vanderbilt University
16. Muhlenberg College
17. University of San Diego
18. College of Saint Benedict/
    Saint John's University
19. Seattle University
20. Goucher College

Is It Food?
Based on students' rating of campus food

1. Hampden-Sydney College
2. Ohio Northern University
3. Catawba College
4. University of New England
5. Stetson University
6. Bryant University
7. United States Merchant Marine Academy
8. Mercer University—Macon
9. St. John's College (NM)
10. Drew University
11. New College of Florida
12. Virginia Wesleyan College
13. Bentley University
14. The Catholic University of America
15. State University of New York—
    Purchase College
16. United States Military Academy
17. Siena College
18. Truman State University
19. Bard College at Simon's Rock
20. Alfred University

Best College Dorms
Based on students' rating of dorm comfort

1. Washington University in St. Louis
2. Christopher Newport University
3. Bowdoin College
4. Emory University
5. Scripps College
6. Bennington College
7. Skidmore College
8. Bryn Mawr College
9. State University of New York—
   College of Environmental Science
   and Forestry
10. Amherst College
11. Franklin W. Olin College of Engineering
12. Loyola University Maryland
13. Elon University
14. Smith College
15. Mount Holyoke College
16. University of Dayton
17. University of Scranton
18. Kansas State University

19. Whitman College
20. College of the Atlantic

Is That a Dorm?
Based on students' rating of dorm comfort

1. College of the Ozarks
2. United States Coast Guard Academy
3. Whittier College
4. Clarkson University
5. Transylvania University
6. University of Miami
7. Hampton University
8. United States Merchant Marine Academy
9. Xavier University of Louisiana
10. State University of New York—Purchase College
11. United States Naval Academy
12. Washington & Jefferson College
13. United States Military Academy
14. Prescott College
15. Illinois Institute of Technology
16. Virginia Wesleyan College
17. Wagner College
18. Hampden-Sydney College
19. Ohio Wesleyan University
20. Mercer University—Macon

Best Quality of Life
Based on The Princeton Review's Quality of Life Rating (page 23)

1. Virginia Tech
2. Claremont McKenna College
3. Kansas State University
4. Bowdoin College
5. Scripps College
6. Tulane University
7. Vanderbilt University
8. University of Dayton
9. Rice University
10. Rhodes College
11. Southern Methodist University
12. Whitman College
13. Villanova University
14. University of Richmond
15. Washington University in St. Louis
16. Middlebury College
17. Carleton College
18. Stanford University
19. Pomona College
20. Brown University

POLITICS

Most Conservative Students
Based on students' assessment of their personal political views

1. Brigham Young University (UT)
2. Baylor University
3. Thomas Aquinas College
4. University of Dallas
5. College of the Ozarks
6. Grove City College
7. Hillsdale College
8. Hampden-Sydney College
9. United States Naval Academy
10. United States Air Force Academy
11. United States Coast Guard Academy
12. Wheaton College (IL)
13. United States Military Academy
14. Texas A&M University—College Station
15. University of Louisiana at Lafayette
16. Angelo State University
17. Wofford College
18. Bryant University
19. University of Dayton
20. Kansas State University

Most Liberal Students
Based on students' assessment of their personal political views

1. Sarah Lawrence College
2. Bennington College
3. Marlboro College
4. Reed College
5. Ithaca College
6. Earlham College
7. Scripps College
8. Grinnell College
9. Bard College
10. Warren Wilson College
11. Oberlin College
12. Mills College
13. College of the Atlantic
14. Whitman College
15. Hamilton College
16. Carleton College
17. Clark University
18. Mount Holyoke College
19. Skidmore College
20. Brown University

Most Politically Active Students
How popular are political/activist groups?

1. The George Washington University
2. Macalester College
3. Vassar College
4. Reed College

5. United States Military Academy
6. United States Naval Academy
7. United States Air Force Academy
8. Bennington College
9. Bard College
10. Hampden-Sydney College
11. New College of Florida
12. Sarah Lawrence College
13. Gonzaga University
14. Hillsdale College
15. The Catholic University of America
16. Ithaca College
17. Columbia University
18. Bowdoin College
19. The College of Wooster
20. University of Richmond

Election? What Election?
How popular are political/activist groups?

1. Becker College
2. University of New England
3. The University of Montana
4. Monmouth University (NJ)
5. University of Tampa
6. Scripps College
7. Assumption College
8. Ohio Northern University
9. University of Massachusetts Amherst
10. Nazareth College
11. Villanova University
12. University of Rhode Island
13. Wheaton College (MA)
14. Simmons College
15. Earlham College
16. Auburn University
17. Skidmore College
18. University of New Haven
19. University of Minnesota—Twin Cities Campus
20. Alfred University

CAMPUS LIFE

Lots of Race/Class Interaction
Do different types of students (black/white, rich/poor) interact frequently and easily?

1. Rice University
2. Illinois Institute of Technology
3. Wesleyan University
4. University of Miami
5. City University of New York—Brooklyn College
6. Whitman College
7. Virginia Tech
8. Drew University

9. Claremont McKenna College
10. The College of William & Mary
11. Clark University
12. United States Military Academy
13. Loyola University New Orleans
14. University of Vermont
15. Swarthmore College
16. New York University
17. Suffolk University
18. Rhodes College
19. The College of New Jersey
20. United States Coast Guard Academy

Little Race/Class Interaction
Do different types of students (black/white, rich/poor) interact frequently and easily?

1. The Catholic University of America
2. Bucknell University
3. Roanoke College
4. Chapman University
5. Providence College
6. Miami University
7. Franklin and Marshall College
8. Colgate University
9. Rhodes College
10. University of Arkansas—Fayetteville
11. Trinity College (CT)
12. Furman University
13. Hobart and William Smith Colleges
14. Gettysburg College
15. Ithaca College
16. Amherst College
17. Wake Forest University
18. Auburn University
19. University of San Diego
20. Illinois Wesleyan University

LGBTQ-Friendly
Do students, faculty and administrators treat all persons equally, regardless of their sexual orientation and gender identity/expression?

1. Sarah Lawrence College
2. College of the Atlantic
3. Warren Wilson College
4. University of Wisconsin—Madison
5. Stanford University
6. Grinnell College
7. Emerson College
8. The College of William & Mary
9. Mount Holyoke College
10. Brown University
11. Harvey Mudd College
12. Smith College
13. Bennington College
14. Bard College
15. Bryn Mawr College

16. Bowdoin College
17. Oberlin College
18. Drew University
19. Mills College
20. Yale University

LGBTQ-Unfriendly
Do students, faculty and administrators treat all persons equally, regardless of their sexual orientation and gender identity/expression?

1. Wheaton College (IL)
2. Hampden-Sydney College
3. College of the Ozarks
4. Gordon College
5. Brigham Young University (UT)
6. Auburn University
7. Baylor University
8. Calvin College
9. Grove City College
10. The University of Tennessee at Knoxville
11. Hillsdale College
12. University of Dallas
13. University of Arkansas—Fayetteville
14. Wake Forest University
15. Montana Tech of the University of Montana
16. Lehigh University
17. The Catholic University of America
18. University of North Dakota
19. Indiana University of Pennsylvania
20. University of Utah

Most Religious Students
Are students very religious?

1. Thomas Aquinas College
2. Brigham Young University (UT)
3. Wheaton College (IL)
4. University of Dallas
5. Hillsdale College
6. College of the Ozarks
7. Gordon College
8. Calvin College
9. Baylor University
10. Kansas State University
11. Saint Anselm College
12. Grove City College
13. The Catholic University of America
14. Creighton University
15. Christopher Newport University
16. University of Oklahoma
17. Mercer University—Macon
18. University of Louisiana at Lafayette
19. Ohio Northern University
20. University of Dayton

Least Religious Students
Are students very religious?

1. Reed College
2. Sarah Lawrence College
3. Bennington College
4. Beloit College
5. Marlboro College
6. Whitman College
7. Bard College
8. Vassar College
9. Hamilton College
10. Lewis & Clark College
11. Emerson College
12. Bowdoin College
13. Wesleyan University
14. Oberlin College
15. Colorado College
16. Mills College
17. Grinnell College
18. State University of New York—Purchase College
19. Champlain College
20. Hobart and William Smith Colleges

TOWN LIFE

College City Gets High Marks
Based on students' assessment of the surrounding city or town

1. Vanderbilt University
2. Tulane University
3. Columbia University
4. New York University
5. University of San Francisco
6. University of Pittsburgh—Pittsburgh Campus
7. The George Washington University
8. Boston University
9. Stevens Institute of Technology
10. Suffolk University
11. San Diego State University
12. Fairfield University
13. College of Charleston
14. City University of New York—Baruch College
15. University of Vermont
16. Champlain College
17. University of Colorado Boulder
18. University of Denver
19. Illinois Institute of Technology
20. Emory University

College City Gets Low Marks
Based on students' assessment of the surrounding city or town

1. United States Coast Guard Academy
2. New Jersey Institute of Technology
3. United States Military Academy
4. Wheaton College (MA)
5. Hofstra University
6. Wabash College
7. Hampden-Sydney College
8. State University of New York at Binghamton
9. Earlham College
10. Tuskegee University
11. University of the Pacific
12. Bates College
13. St. Lawrence University
14. Hillsdale College
15. Albion College
16. University of Connecticut
17. Wittenberg University
18. Mercer University—Macon
19. University of Scranton
20. Clarkson University

Town-Gown Relations Are Great
Do students get along well with members of the local community?

1. Auburn University
2. College of the Ozarks
3. United States Naval Academy
4. Rhodes College
5. Kansas State University
6. Nazareth College
7. Virginia Tech
8. University of Mississippi
9. Clemson University
10. University of Iowa
11. Loyola University New Orleans
12. Stevens Institute of Technology
13. Texas A&M University—College Station
14. Wheaton College (IL)
15. Michigan Technological University
16. Gordon College
17. Stephens College
18. Saint Michael's College
19. United States Military Academy
20. University of Oklahoma

Town-Gown Relations Are Strained
Do students get along well with members of the local community?

1. Bennington College
2. Dickinson College
3. Trinity College (CT)
4. Colorado College
5. Lehigh University

6. New Jersey Institute of Technology
7. United States Merchant Marine Academy
8. Duke University
9. Bates College
10. Wheaton College (MA)
11. Earlham College
12. Vassar College
13. Beloit College
14. Indiana University of Pennsylvania
15. Illinois Institute of Technology
16. Washington & Jefferson College
17. Hofstra University
18. Temple University
19. Chapman University
20. Bucknell University

EXTRACURRICULARS

Best Athletic Facilities
Based on students' rating of campus athletic facilities

1. Pennsylvania State University—University Park
2. Purdue University—West Lafayette
3. Auburn University
4. Kansas State University
5. University of Illinois at Urbana-Champaign
6. West Virginia University
7. Grinnell College
8. Wabash College
9. Loyola University Maryland
10. Ohio University—Athens
11. Worcester Polytechnic Institute
12. University of Iowa
13. Rose-Hulman Institute of Technology
14. Calvin College
15. Colorado College
16. The College of Wooster
17. University of Colorado Boulder
18. Lake Forest College
19. University of Arizona
20. University of Utah

Students Pack the Stadiums
How popular are intercollegiate sports?

1. Syracuse University
2. West Virginia University
3. University of Southern California
4. Gonzaga University
5. Clemson University
6. Pennsylvania State University—University Park
7. Kansas State University
8. University of Oklahoma
9. Auburn University
10. Xavier University (OH)

11. University of Kansas
12. Marquette University
13. University of Iowa
14. United States Air Force Academy
15. Florida State University
16. University of Wisconsin—Madison
17. University of Arizona
18. University of Nebraska—Lincoln
19. University of Connecticut
20. University of Louisville

There's a Game?
How popular are intercollegiate sports?

1. College of the Atlantic
2. Thomas Aquinas College
3. Bennington College
4. Reed College
5. St. John's College (NM)
6. Marlboro College
7. Champlain College
8. State University of New York— Purchase College
9. Harvey Mudd College
10. Carnegie Mellon University
11. Sarah Lawrence College
12. The University of Chicago
13. Prescott College
14. Lawrence University
15. Clark University
16. Brown University
17. New College of Florida
18. Stephens College
19. Franklin W. Olin College of Engineering
20. Emerson College

Everyone Plays Intramural Sports
How popular are intramural sports?

1. University of Dayton
2. United States Military Academy
3. Wabash College
4. Colorado College
5. Mercer University—Macon
6. Providence College
7. Rose-Hulman Institute of Technology
8. Gonzaga University
9. Washington State University
10. Clemson University
11. Gettysburg College
12. Florida Southern College
13. United States Naval Academy
14. Kansas State University
15. University of Nebraska—Lincoln
16. Grove City College
17. University of Colorado Boulder
18. Bryant University
19. University of Vermont
20. Florida State University

Nobody Plays Intramural Sports
How popular are intramural sports?

1. Sarah Lawrence College
2. Marlboro College
3. Stephens College
4. Bard College
5. New College of Florida
6. Bennington College
7. Cornell College
8. Randolph College
9. Prescott College
10. The Cooper Union for the Advancement of Science and Art
11. College of the Atlantic
12. State University of New York— Purchase College
13. Mills College
14. Reed College
15. Simmons College
16. Warren Wilson College
17. Mount Holyoke College
18. State University of New York— College of Environmental Science and Forestry
19. Beloit College
20. City University of New York— Baruch College

Best College Radio Station
How popular is the radio station?

1. Ithaca College
2. Fordham University
3. Hofstra University
4. University of Puget Sound
5. Bates College
6. Syracuse University
7. Emerson College
8. DePauw University
9. St. Bonaventure University
10. Carleton College
11. Saint Michael's College
12. Chapman University
13. Reed College
14. Drew University
15. Washington State University
16. Franklin and Marshall College
17. Hobart and William Smith Colleges
18. Truman State University
19. Brown University
20. Earlham College

Best College Newspaper
How do you rate your campus newspaper?

1. Columbia University
2. University of Virginia
3. Brown University
4. Ithaca College

5. Syracuse University
6. Pennsylvania State University—University Park
7. Fordham University
8. Cornell University
9. Hillsdale College
10. University of Wisconsin—Madison
11. University of Iowa
12. Marlboro College
13. Yale University
14. College of Saint Benedict/Saint John's University
15. Wake Forest University
16. Hampden-Sydney College
17. Washington State University
18. University of Florida
19. West Virginia University
20. University of California—Santa Barbara

Best College Theater
How do you rate college's theater productions?

1. Muhlenberg College
2. Sarah Lawrence College
3. Wagner College
4. State University of New York—Purchase College
5. Bennington College
6. Stephens College
7. Drew University
8. Carnegie Mellon University
9. Catawba College
10. Emerson College
11. Bard College
12. Clark University
13. Wesleyan University
14. Ithaca College
15. Wabash College
16. Fordham University
17. Columbia University
18. The University of Chicago
19. Elon University
20. Brown University

Students Most Engaged in Community Service
Based on students' rating of their commitment to community service

1. Tulane University
2. Rhodes College
3. United States Coast Guard Academy
4. The College of William & Mary
5. Creighton University
6. Saint Anselm College
7. Brandeis University
8. Christopher Newport University
9. Boston College
10. Loyola University Maryland

11. Pitzer College
12. Loyola Marymount University
13. Warren Wilson College
14. University of Dayton
15. Hillsdale College
16. United States Naval Academy
17. Wake Forest University
18. State University of New York—College of Environmental Science and Forestry
19. Stevens Institute of Technology
20. University of Scranton

Most Active Student Government
Based on a combination of survey questions concerning student run political groups, and the active and effective presence of student government on campus.

1. Bucknell University
2. Reed College
3. United States Military Academy
4. The College of William & Mary
5. Moravian College
6. Stephens College
7. Dickinson College
8. Bentley University
9. Bowdoin College
10. City University of New York—Baruch College
11. Mercer University—Macon
12. St. Lawrence University
13. Elon University
14. Bellarmine University
15. College of Saint Benedict/Saint John's University
16. University of Richmond
17. University of Virginia
18. United States Air Force Academy
19. Juniata College
20. Purdue University—West Lafayette

SOCIAL SCENE

Lots of Greek Life
How popular are fraternities/sororities?

1. Bucknell University
2. Transylvania University
3. Southern Methodist University
4. Miami University
5. Gettysburg College
6. Rhodes College
7. Lehigh University
8. University of Illinois at Urbana-Champaign
9. University of Delaware
10. Worcester Polytechnic Institute
11. University of Mississippi
12. Vanderbilt University

13. Wofford College
14. University of Iowa
15. DePauw University
16. Syracuse University
17. University of Oklahoma
18. University of Arkansas—Fayetteville
19. Chapman University
20. Bradley University

Lots of Beer
How widely used is beer?

1. University of Wisconsin—Madison
2. University of Dayton
3. Bates College
4. Beloit College
5. Lehigh University
6. University of Florida
7. West Virginia University
8. Colgate University
9. Syracuse University
10. University of Illinois
    at Urbana-Champaign
11. Bucknell University
12. Florida State University
13. University of Mississippi
14. Tulane University
15. University of Delaware
16. Pennsylvania State University—
    University Park
17. College of Charleston
18. Wake Forest University
19. University of Iowa
20. Grinnell College

Got Milk?
How widely used is beer?

1. Brigham Young University (UT)
2. City University of New York—
   Brooklyn College
3. College of the Ozarks
4. Wheaton College (IL)
5. City University of New York—
   Baruch College
6. Gordon College
7. City University of New York—
   Queens College
8. Grove City College
9. Calvin College
10. Wesleyan College (GA)
11. United States Air Force Academy
12. Stephens College
13. Mills College
14. Thomas Aquinas College
15. Spelman College
16. St. John's University
17. Illinois Institute of Technology
18. Simmons College

19. University of California—Davis
20. Angelo State University

Lots of Hard Liquor
How widely used is hard liquor?

1. Tulane University
2. Connecticut College
3. Colgate University
4. University of Iowa
5. University of Wisconsin—Madison
6. University of California—Santa Barbara
7. University of Illinois at Urbana-Champaign
8. Marlboro College
9. Syracuse University
10. Bucknell University
11. Juniata College
12. Wake Forest University
13. Providence College
14. University of Georgia
15. College of Charleston
16. University of Maine
17. Grinnell College
18. Fairfield University
19. Santa Clara University
20. West Virginia University

Scotch and Soda, Hold the Scotch
How widely used is hard liquor?

1. Brigham Young University (UT)
2. College of the Ozarks
3. Wheaton College (IL)
4. City University of New York—
   Baruch College
5. United States Air Force Academy
6. Gordon College
7. Calvin College
8. City University of New York—
   Queens College
9. Thomas Aquinas College
10. Illinois Institute of Technology
11. City University of New York—
    Brooklyn College
12. United States Military Academy
13. Grove City College
14. Mills College
15. City University of New York—City College
16. University of California—Davis
17. St. John's University
18. Stephens College
19. United States Naval Academy
20. University of Central Florida

Reefer Madness
How widely used is marijuana?

1. Ithaca College
2. University of California—Santa Cruz

3. Skidmore College
4. The Evergreen State College
5. University of Vermont
6. Eckerd College
7. Green Mountain College
8. Marlboro College
9. University of Rhode Island
10. University of Colorado Boulder
11. Bard College
12. Reed College
13. Wesleyan University
14. State University of New York—
College of Environmental Science
and Forestry
15. University of Wisconsin—Madison
16. University of California—Santa Barbara
17. University of Maine
18. Warren Wilson College
19. Bennington College
20. St. Lawrence University

Don't Inhale
How widely used is marijuana?

1. United States Coast Guard Academy
2. United States Naval Academy
3. United States Military Academy
4. Brigham Young University (UT)
5. United States Air Force Academy
6. United States Merchant Marine Academy
7. College of the Ozarks
8. Thomas Aquinas College
9. Wheaton College (IL)
10. City University of New York—
Baruch College
11. Calvin College
12. Hillsdale College
13. Gordon College
14. Illinois Institute of Technology
15. Stephens College
16. University of Dallas
17. Simmons College
18. Rose-Hulman Institute of Technology
19. City University of New York—
Queens College
20. Baylor University

SCHOOLS BY TYPE

Party Schools
Based on a combination of survey questions concerning the use of alcohol and drugs, hours of study each day, and the popularity of the Greek system

1. University of Wisconsin—Madison
2. West Virginia University
3. University of Illinois
at Urbana-Champaign

4. Lehigh University
5. Bucknell University
6. University of Iowa
7. University of Mississippi
8. Syracuse University
9. Tulane University
10. Colgate University
11. University of California—Santa Barbara
12. University of Delaware
13. University of Rhode Island
14. Wake Forest University
15. College of Charleston
16. University of Maine
17. University of Vermont
18. University of Florida
19. University of Colorado Boulder
20. Florida State University

Stone-Cold Sober Schools
Based on a combination of survey questions concerning the use of alcohol and drugs, hours of study each day, and the popularity of the Greek system

1. Brigham Young University (UT)
2. College of the Ozarks
3. Wheaton College (IL)
4. United States Air Force Academy
5. Gordon College
6. Thomas Aquinas College
7. Calvin College
8. United States Military Academy
9. City University of New York—
Baruch College
10. United States Naval Academy
11. United States Coast Guard Academy
12. Mills College
13. City University of New York—
Queens College
14. Grove City College
15. Simmons College
16. Stephens College
17. Baylor University
18. Bellarmine University
19. Hillsdale College
20. Webb Institute

Future Rotarians and Daughters of the American Revolution
Based on a combination of survey questions concerning the political persuasion, the use of drugs, the popularity of student government, and the level of acceptance of the LGBTQ community on campus

1. Hillsdale College
2. College of the Ozarks
3. Wheaton College (IL)
4. University of Dallas

5. Brigham Young University (UT)
6. Thomas Aquinas College
7. Grove City College
8. Gordon College
9. United States Naval Academy
10. Baylor University
11. Calvin College
12. Kansas State University
13. Auburn University
14. United States Military Academy
15. United States Air Force Academy
16. Hampden-Sydney College
17. Saint Anselm College
18. Mercer University—Macon
19. University of Louisiana at Lafayette
20. Ohio Northern University

Birkenstock-Wearing, Tree-Hugging, Clove-Smoking Vegetarians

Based on a combination of survey questions concerning the political persuasion, the use of drugs, the popularity of student government, and the level of acceptance of the LGBTQ community on campus

1. Reed College
2. Bennington College
3. Marlboro College
4. Sarah Lawrence College
5. Ithaca College
6. Bard College
7. Wesleyan University
8. Oberlin College
9. Beloit College
10. Warren Wilson College
11. Skidmore College
12. State University of New York—Purchase College
13. Lewis & Clark College
14. Colorado College
15. Brown University
16. Champlain College
17. Carleton College
18. Goucher College
19. Clark University
20. McGill University

Deep Springs Honor Roll

Since Deep Springs is a two-year college (and the only one in *The Best 381 Colleges*), we remove it from our rankings tallies in order to avoid comparing "apples and oranges." Instead we present this list of some ranking categories in which Deep Springs ranks high (or low, as it were) among the best colleges in our book.

Active Student Government
Happiest Students
Professors Get High Marks
Most Accessible Professors
Best Run Colleges
Most Beautiful Campus
Best Campus Food
Most Liberal Students
Least Religious Students
Got Milk?
Scotch and Soda, Hold the Scotch
Don't Inhale
Stone-Cold Sober Schools
Great Financial Aid
Lots of Race/Class Interaction
Town-Gown Relations Are Great
Best Commitment to Community Service

We salute theses schools that received a 99 (the highest score) in the tallies for our "Financial Aid," "Fire Safety," and "Green" Ratings—three of eight ratings on some of the school profiles in this book and at www.PrincetonReview.com. Our school ratings are numerical scores (Note: They are not ranking lists) that show how a school "sizes up" on a fixed scale. They are comparable to grades and based primarily on institutional data we collect directly from the colleges.

Financial Aid Honor Roll

Schools are listed in alphabetical order. See page 28 for information on how our "Financial Aid Rating" is determined.

Bowdoin College
Colgate University
Haverford College
Middlebury College
Pomona College
Princeton University
Reed College
Thomas Aquinas College
Vanderbilt University
Vassar College

Fire Safety Honor Roll

Schools are listed in alphabetical order. See page 24 for information on how our "Fire Safety Rating" is determined.

Bay Path University*
Bentley University
Cazenovia College*
DePaul University
Dominican University of California*
Duquesne University
Five Towns College*
Framingham State University*
Husson University*
Lincoln University (MO)*
Millersville University of Pennsylvania*
Molloy College*
Mount Saint Mary's University*
Mount St. Joseph University*
New Jersey Institute of Technology
Plymouth State University*
Saint Mary-of-the-Woods College*
Southeastern University*
Texas Woman's University*
University of Maine—Fort Kent*
University of Minnesota, Crookston*
University of Saint Joseph*
University of South Florida St. Petersburg*
Worcester State University*

Green Honor Roll

Schools are listed in alphabetical order. See page 24 for information on how our "Green Rating" is determined.

American University
Ball State University*
California State University, Sacramento*
Carnegie Mellon University
Chatham University*
Colby College
College of the Atlantic
Colorado State University
Cornell University
Dickinson College
Green Mountain College
Lewis & Clark College
Santa Clara University
Smith College
Stanford University
State University of New York College of Environmental Science and Forestry
University of California—Irvine*
University of California—Santa Cruz
University of Maryland—College Park
University of New Hampshire
University of Washington

Tuition-Free Schools Honor Roll

The following schools have been excluded from our ranking and ratings dealing with financial aid:

Berea College
College of the Ozarks
Deep Springs College
United States Air Force Academy
United States Coast Guard Academy
United States Merchant Marine Academy
United States Military Academy
United States Naval Academy
Webb Institute

We commend these schools on their ability to do the seemingly impossible: not charge tuition. While some charge students for room and board and other fees, the overall cost of attendance at these schools is very low, and at some schools: free! (Note: We do not include these schools in our ranking lists dealing with financial aid, since they would have an unfair advantage over schools that charge even a moderate tuition.)

Schools marked with an asterisk do not appear in the *Best 381 Colleges.* You can find those school profiles in *The Complete Book of Colleges,* 2017 Edition.

The Princeton Review released its current list of Colleges That Pay You Back in February 2016. We selected the 200 schools based on forty weighted data points, including academics, cost, financial aid, and student debt to statistics on graduation rates, alumni salaries and job satisfaction. Alumni survey information was provided by PayScale.com. For detailed profiles of all these great schools, see our companion book, *Colleges That Pay You Back.*

Agnes Scott College
Allegheny College
Amherst College
Arizona State University
Babson College
Barnard College
Bates College
Bentley University
Berea College
Boston College
Boston University
Bowdoin College
Bradley University
Brandeis University
Brigham Young University (UT)
Brown University
Bryn Mawr College
Bucknell University
California Institute of Technology
California State University, Long Beach
Carleton College
Carnegie Mellon University
Case Western Reserve University
Centre College
City University of New York—Baruch College
City University of New York—Brooklyn College
City University of New York—City College
City University of New York—Hunter College
Claremont McKenna College
Clarkson University
Clark University
Clemson University
Coe College
Colby College
Colgate University
College of the Holy Cross
The College of New Jersey
College of the Ozarks
College of Saint Benedict/
    Saint John's University
The College of William & Mary
The College of Wooster
Colorado College
Columbia University
Connecticut College
The Cooper Union for the Advancement
    of Science and Art
Cornell University
Creighton University
Dartmouth College
Davidson College
Deep Springs College

Denison University
DePauw University
Dickinson College
Drake University
Duke University
Emory University
Florida State University
Franklin and Marshall College
Franklin W. Olin College of Engineering
Furman University
George Mason University
The George Washington University
Georgetown University
Georgia Institute of Technology
Gettysburg College
Gonzaga University
Grinnell College
Grove City College
Hamilton College
Hampden-Sydney College
Harvard College
Harvey Mudd College
Haverford College
Hobart and William Smith Colleges
Illinois Institute of Technology
Illinois Wesleyan University
Indiana University—Bloomington
Iowa State University
James Madison University
Johns Hopkins University
Kalamazoo College
Kenyon College
Lafayette College
Lake Forest College
Lawrence University
Lehigh University
Lewis & Clark College
Loyola University Maryland
Macalester College
Massachusetts Institute of Technology
Mercer University—Macon
Miami University
Michigan Technological University
Middlebury College
Missouri University of Science and Technology
Montana Tech of the University of Montana
Mount Holyoke College
Muhlenberg College
New College of Florida
North Carolina State University
Northeastern University
Northwestern University

Oberlin College
Occidental College
The Ohio State University—Columbus
Oklahoma State University
Penn State—University Park
Pepperdine University
Pomona College
Princeton University
Purdue University—West Lafayette
Reed College
Rensselaer Polytechnic Institute
Rhodes College
Rice University
Rochester Institute of Technology
Rose-Hulman Institute of Technology
Rutgers, The State University of New Jersey—
    New Brunswick
Santa Clara University
Scripps College
Skidmore College
Smith College
Southern Methodist University
Southwestern University
St. Lawrence University
St. Olaf College
Stanford University
State University of New York at Binghamton
    (Binghamton University)
State University of New York at Geneseo
State University of New York—College of
    Environmental Science and Forestry
State University of New York—
    Maritime College
State University of New York—
    Stony Brook University
State University of New York—
    University at Buffalo
Stevens Institute of Technology
Stonehill College
Swarthmore College
Texas A&M University—College Station
Trinity College (CT)
Trinity University
Truman State University
Tufts University
Tulane University
Union College (NY)
United States Air Force Academy
United States Coast Guard Academy
United States Merchant Marine Academy
United States Military Academy
United States Naval Academy
University of Arizona
University of California—Berkeley
University of California—Davis
University of California—Irvine
University of California—Los Angeles
University of California—Riverside

University of California—San Diego
University of California—Santa Barbara
University of California—Santa Cruz
The University of Chicago
University of Colorado Boulder
University of Dayton
University of Delaware
University of Denver
University of Florida
University of Georgia
University of Houston
University of Idaho
University of Illinois at Urbana-Champaign
University of Maryland—Baltimore County
University of Maryland—College Park
University of Massachusetts Amherst
University of Michigan—Ann Arbor
University of Minnesota—Twin Cities Campus
The University of North Carolina at Asheville
The University of North Carolina
    at Chapel Hill
University of Notre Dame
University of Oklahoma
University of Pennsylvania
University of Pittsburgh—Pittsburgh Campus
University of Richmond
University of Rochester
University of San Diego
University of Southern California
The University of Tennessee at Knoxville
The University of Texas at Austin
The University of Texas at Dallas
The University of Tulsa
University of Virginia
University of Washington
University of Wisconsin—Madison
Vanderbilt University
Vassar College
Villanova University
Virginia Tech
Wabash College
Wagner College
Wake Forest University
Washington University in St. Louis
Webb Institute
Wellesley College
Wesleyan University
Westminster College of Salt Lake City
Wheaton College (IL)
Whitman College
Willamette University
William Jewell College
Williams College
Wofford College
Worcester Polytechnic Institute
Yale University

Colleges That Pay You Back contains seven ranking lists, all of which focus on different aspects of financial aid and career preparation.

Top 50 Colleges That Pay You Back

The fifty schools that received the highest overall rating used to determine inclusion in *Colleges That Pay You Back* 2016 Edition.

1. California Institute of Technology
2. Princeton University
3. The Cooper Union for the Advancement of Science and Art
4. Harvey Mudd College
5. Massachusetts Institute of Technology
6. Stanford University
7. Yale University
8. University of California—Berkeley
9. Rice University
10. Harvard College
11. Brown University
12. Columbia University
13. Vanderbilt University
14. University of Virginia
15. Colgate University
16. Amherst College
17. University of Pennsylvania
18. Dartmouth College
19. Duke University
20. Cornell University
21. Pomona College
22. Brigham Young University (UT)
23. Swarthmore College
24. University of California—Los Angeles
25. Washington University in St. Louis
26. Williams College
27. Rose-Hulman Institute of Technology
28. Carleton College
29. Tufts University
30. The University of Chicago
31. Haverford College
32. Babson College
33. Worcester Polytechnic Institute
34. Claremont McKenna College
35. University of California—Santa Barbara
36. Johns Hopkins University
37. Missouri University of Science and Technology
38. Bowdoin College
39. University of California—San Diego
40. Hamilton College
41. Middlebury College
42. University of Florida
43. Lehigh University
44. Carnegie Mellon University
45. New College of Florida
46. Gettysburg College
47. Lafayette College
48. Wesleyan University
49. Emory University
50. Macalester College

Top 25 Colleges That Pay You Back for Students With No Demonstrated Need

To create this list, we used the same methodology for our overall rating, but removed need-based aid information. If you don't qualify for financial aid, these are your twenty-five best value schools.

1. California Institute of Technology
2. Brigham Young University (UT)
3. Harvey Mudd College
4. University of California—Berkeley
5. Massachusetts Institute of Technology
6. Stanford University
7. University of Virginia
8. Princeton University
9. Yale University
10. University of California—Los Angeles
11. Rice University
12. The College of William & Mary
13. Brown University
14. University of Florida
15. University of California—Santa Barbara
16. Rose-Hulman Institute of Technology
17. Colgate University
18. Virginia Tech
19. New College of Florida
20. University of Wisconsin—Madison
21. Missouri University of Science and Technology
22. University of Illinois at Urbana-Champaign
23. The University of Texas at Austin
24. Duke University
25. Georgia Institute of Technology

Best Alumni Network

These twenty-five schools have the strongest and most active alumni networks, based on students' ratings of alumni activity and visibility on campus, and PayScale.com's percentage of alumni who would recommend the school to prospective students.

1. Dartmouth College
2. Pennsylvania State University—University Park
3. Texas A&M University—College Station
4. Claremont McKenna College
5. Wabash College
6. St. Lawrence University
7. Clemson University
8. Hampden-Sydney College
9. Wellesley College
10. Virginia Tech
11. University of Virginia
12. Bucknell University
13. Southern Methodist University
14. Gettysburg College
15. Ohio State University—Columbus
16. Union College (NY)
17. University of Florida
18. Lehigh University
19. DePauw University
20. Florida State University
21. University of Georgia
22. Cornell University
23. New College of Florida
24. Stanford University
25. Colgate University

Best Schools for Internships

This top twenty-five list is based on students' ratings of accessibility of internships at their school.

1. The George Washington University
2. Claremont McKenna College
3. Rose-Hulman Institute of Technology
4. Northeastern University
5. Wabash College
6. Southern Methodist University
7. Franklin W. Olin College of Engineering
8. Dartmouth College
9. Rhodes College
10. Amherst College
11. Gettysburg College
12. Bentley University
13. Villanova University
14. California Institute of Technology
15. Harvey Mudd College
16. University of Dayton
17. Stanford University
18. DePauw University
19. Worcester Polytechnic Institute
20. Cornell University
21. State University of New York—Maritime College
22. George Mason University
23. Bradley University
24. University of Georgia
25. St. Lawrence University

Best Career Placement

This top twenty-five list is based on students' ratings of career services at their school, and on PayScale.com's median starting and mid-career salary information.

1. Harvey Mudd College
2. Massachusetts Institute of Technology
3. California Institute of Technology
4. Stanford University
5. Rose-Hulman Institute of Technology
6. Stevens Institute of Technology
7. State University of New York—Maritime College
8. Babson College
9. Carnegie Mellon University
10. Worcester Polytechnic Institute
11. Rensselaer Polytechnic Institute
12. Rice University
13. Princeton University
14. Clarkson University
15. The Cooper Union for the Advancement of Science and Art
16. Cornell University
17. Yale University
18. Colgate University
19. University of Pennsylvania
20. Georgia Institute of Technology
21. Santa Clara University
22. Duke University
23. Lehigh University
24. University of California—Berkeley
25. Tufts University

Best Financial Aid

The twenty-five schools in *Colleges That Pay You Back* 2016 Edition that received the highest financial aid rating. (see page 28)

1. Vassar College
2. Princeton University
3. Yale University
4. Trinity College (CT)
5. Pomona College
6. Amherst College
7. Vanderbilt University
8. Reed College
9. Haverford College
10. Colgate University
11. Middlebury College
12. Macalester College
13. Wellesley College
14. Grinnell College
15. Columbia University
16. Rice University
17. Swarthmore College
18. Bates College
19. Washington University in St. Louis
20. Bryn Mawr College
21. Claremont McKenna College
22. Dartmouth College
23. Stanford University
24. Bowdoin College
25. Franklin W. Olin College of Engineering

Best Schools for Making an Impact

These twenty-five schools were selected based on student ratings and responses to our survey questions covering community service opportunities at their school, student government, sustainability efforts, and on-campus student engagement. We also took into account PayScale.com's percentage of alumni from each school that reported that they had high job meaning.

1. The University of North Carolina at Asheville
2. Macalester College
3. Clark University
4. Oberlin College
5. Furman University
6. Colorado College
7. Brown University
8. Wesleyan University
9. Whitman College
10. St. Lawrence University
11. Mercer University—Macon
12. Pomona College
13. University of Colorado Boulder
14. Carleton College
15. Middlebury College
16. Wheaton College (IL)
17. University of Dayton
18. Mount Holyoke College
19. University of Denver
20. Emory University
21. Westminster College of Salt Lake City
22. Stanford University
23. Lawrence University
24. Tufts University
25. Lewis & Clark College

PART 3

THE BEST
381 COLLEGES

AGNES SCOTT COLLEGE

141 EAST COLLEGE AVENUE, DECATUR, GA 30030-3770 • ADMISSIONS: 404-471-6285 • FAX: 404-471-6414

STUDENTS SAY "..."

Academics

Agnes Scott College is a small women's liberal arts college that is "all about creating intelligent, confident, well rounded women." With just 900 or so students, there is a pervasively "caring and intellectual atmosphere" at a school that students claim is "dedicated to the enrichment of young women's lives." "Agnes Scott College is a school that focuses on education and experience for women who have any size plan, big or small, for their lives."

The "phenomenal" professors at Agnes Scott are "indescribably amazing." Their passion for the subjects they teach "shines through in everything that they do." If a student shows that they are trying, but still not grasping the material, then the professors will usually go out of their way to help. "Every professor that I have had has encouraged students to meet them if they have any questions," says a junior. "You can get to know your professors personally." Discussion is encouraged, and the classroom is "a place where you can speak your mind and actually be heard by your professors and peers." "Every day my thought process is challenged and I learn more about myself and how the world functions," says a history major. Most classes require papers rather than exams, which students find "challenging and more rewarding."

There are "rich opportunities as a consequence of small size" (such as extra tutoring on writing skills and "great opportunities for networking"), and "students get opportunities that most graduate students exclusively get at other universities." In addition, the financial aid is "exceptional" and the administration "actually listens to the students and tries to improve" when issues are raised, and "you can complain directly to the person in charge."

Life

This "fun, quirky little college" provides "a very safe space that is conducive for learning." "People study very hard here which encourages you to study hard as well," says a student. With the honor code in place (everyone must sign upon matriculation), "We don't have to worry about anyone taking our things when we're not looking or while we're asleep. We all look out for one another."

While academics and extracurriculars dominate the week, Scotties let their hair down on weekends. There is "a very modern artsy feel to this city [Decatur] and school," which is "close enough to Atlanta to enjoy the nightlife, and far enough to enjoy nature." "Many music groups come to Atlanta when they're on tour," and students also go to nearby shops, open mics, and museums, or to parties at other colleges or (occasionally) on campus ("where Emory, Morehouse, and Georgia Tech boys are invited"). "We have friends here of course, but we all go out off campus when wanting to hang out or do something fun," says a student.

Students universally agree that there needs to be "better dining hall food," and some say that the Wellness Center is "slightly unorganized" and "isn't as helpful as it should be." Luckily, "there are a lot of nice restaurants within the walk."

Student Body

The "smart, ambitious women" who attend Agnes Scott are a "hodgepodge," as the school "truly invests in diversity." "You would be hard pressed not to fit in somewhere," says a student. This "sisterhood of women...are willing to help" and are "very assertive" and "not afraid to speak their minds." Everyone here is "almost always active in something (not restricted to just sports)" and LGBT support and membership are big. While everyone is "friendly and open-minded," most everyone is "at least somewhat feministic" and "very liberal."

FINANCIAL AID: 404-471-6395 • E-MAIL: ADMISSION@AGNESSCOTT.EDU • WEBSITE: WWW.AGNESSCOTT.EDU

THE PRINCETON REVIEW SAYS

Admissions

Very important factors considered include: rigor of secondary school record, academic GPA, talent/ability, character/personal qualities. *Important factors considered include:* standardized test scores, application essay, recommendation(s), extracurricular activities, volunteer work. *Other factors considered include:* class rank, interview, first generation, alumni/ae relation, geographical residence, state residency, work experience, level of applicant's interest. SAT or ACT required for some. TOEFL required of all international applicants. High school diploma is required and GED is accepted. *Academic units recommended:* 4 English, 3 math, 2 science, 2 science labs, 2 foreign language, 2 social studies.

Financial Aid

Students should submit: FAFSA. Regular filing deadline is 5/1.The Princeton Review suggests that all financial aid forms be submitted as soon as possible after October 1. *Need-based scholarships/grants offered:* Federal Pell, FSEOG, State scholarships/grants, Private scholarships, College/university scholarship or grant aid from institutional funds. *Loan aid offered:* Direct Subsidized Stafford Loans, Direct Unsubsidized Stafford Loans, Direct PLUS Loans. Applicants will be notified of awards on a rolling basis beginning 3/1. Federal Work-Study Program available. Institutional employment available.

The Inside Word

Agnes Scott waives the application fee for those who apply online; all it will cost you is your time. Take the time to craft a solid application if you want to be considered seriously, as this is a very competitive school where admissions officers give each candidate a very careful look. A strong application that creates a compelling portrait may well overcome moderate shortcomings in high school grades or test scores, especially if bolstered by an enthusiastic interview during a campus visit.

THE SCHOOL SAYS "..."

From the Admissions Office

"During four years at Agnes Scott, you'll grow as a person, discovering your strengths and building confidence. Through SUMMIT, a unique global learning and leadership development initiative, you will choose a major, build your leadership skills and gain global perspectives, all while guided by a four-person board of advisors. Your SUMMIT advisor, peer advisor, faculty advisor and career mentor will help you adjust to college, choose classes and activities, and build connections to strengthen your academic experience and boost your professional readiness.

"You'll spend four years with brilliant women who won't suffer fools, stand for injustice or tolerate prejudice; with confident women who never settle, but question, confront and debate. Study with professors who will push you to the limits and then challenge you again.

"Explore your world, whether that's in your backyard or across an ocean. Become immersed in other cultures. Hone your leadership skills, whether you chart your own course, rally others around a cause or just set an example for your peers. Gain professional experience through research projects and internships with *Fortune* Global 500 companies or local, national or international nonprofits.

"After four years at Agnes Scott, you will never be the same. You will be a better you: more reflective, more intelligent, more cultured, more prepared to lead; you'll be ready for the world.

"If you've read this far, why not visit campus? We'd love to meet you, show you our world and help you plan your SUMMIT. Schedule your visit at agnesscott.edu/visit."

SELECTIVITY
Admissions Rating	87
# of applicants	1,461
% of applicants accepted	62
% of acceptees attending	30
# of early decision applicants	29
% accepted early decision	100

FRESHMAN PROFILE
Range SAT Critical Reading	550–690
Range SAT Math	510–640
Range SAT Writing	550–670
Range ACT Composite	24–29
Minimum internet-based TOEFL	80
Average HS GPA	3.7
% graduated top 10% of class	29
% graduated top 25% of class	62
% graduated top 50% of class	93

DEADLINES
Early decision	
Deadline	11/1
Notification	12/1
Early action	
Deadline	11/15
Notification	12/15
Regular	
Priority	1/15
Deadline	3/15
Notification	4/15
Nonfall registration?	No

APPLICANTS ALSO LOOK AT
AND OFTEN PREFER
University of Georgia

AND SOMETIMES PREFER
Georgia Institute of Technology

AND RARELY PREFER
Mercer University—Macon

FINANCIAL FACTS
Financial Aid Rating	85
Annual tuition	$38,232
Room and board	$11,520
Required fees	$240
Books and supplies	$1,000
Average frosh need-based scholarship	$27,535
Average UG need-based scholarship	$27,336
% needy frosh rec. need-based scholarship or grant aid	100
% needy UG rec. need-based scholarship or grant aid	100
% needy frosh rec. non-need-based scholarship or grant aid	26
% needy UG rec. non-need-based scholarship or grant aid	25
% needy frosh rec. need-based self-help aid	80
% needy UG rec. need-based self-help aid	83
% frosh rec. any financial aid	100
% UG rec. any financial aid	99
% UG borrow to pay for school	76
Average cumulative indebtedness	$33,050
% frosh need fully met	27
% ugrads need fully met	25
Average % of frosh need met	84
Average % of ugrad need met	85

ALBION COLLEGE

611 EAST PORTER, ALBION, MI 49224 • ADMISSIONS: 517-629-0321 • FAX: 517-629-0569

STUDENTS SAY "..."

Academics

Armed with a "great reputation" and a "small-town feeling," Albion College provides undergraduates with a "rigorous but rewarding" academic experience replete with "huge opportunities." Students here truly appreciate that Albion works diligently to foster an environment that "encourages questions [and] thinking" all the while aiming to "provide personal attention to each student." While the college certainly offers a "great liberal arts education," undergrads are especially quick to highlight the strong science, premed, and business programs. Indeed, students like to boast that Albion "has a very high rate of students being accepted into medical school." And business majors point to the Gerstacker Institute for Business and Management, which allows students to "gain real-world experience" and even the potential to walk away with "a job offer." Of course, regardless of discipline or department, Albion undergrads are full of praise for their teachers. As one thrilled student eagerly shares, "The professors care about their students' success and are always there to help." Importantly, they are "very knowledgeable in their material and try to make sure you learn as much as possible." Further, they are "easily approachable," "extremely passionate about their work," and always "available for discussions." As one content undergrad sums up, "I would say that the overall experience has been great, and I couldn't be more pleased with my decision to attend Albion College."

Life

While Albion students are often quite "studious" during the week, once the weekend rolls around they certainly know how to get "crazy [and] exciting." Fortunately, there "is almost always something going on on campus." Indeed, the "Union Board plans lots of free activities, concerts, comedians, etc." Moreover, those interested in the party scene will be delighted to discover that fraternities and sororities are very popular at Albion. As one thrilled undergrad notes, "Greek life is fantastic. It really is the cornerstone of our campus. Every weekend there is a party or something going on at the fraternities. Whether you are into drinking or not, the guys there know how to have a good time." While students bemoan the fact that "there's not much to do in the city of Albion," they do take solace in finding other off campus options. As another satisfied student reveals, "Bigger cities like Jackson and Battle Creek are only a fifteen- or twenty-minute drive away, so if you're looking for a day at a mall, that's always an option. Plus, the college sponsors sending buses and vans to take students to places like Ann Arbor or Lansing. Generally you can find something to do."

Student Body

At first glance, Albion College appears to be "a microcosm of upper-class metro-Detroit and Chicago." Therefore, it's not surprising that a "slightly right-leaning, white, and Greek-loving [student body seems to be] the norm." However, those seeking more diversity should fear not! One student assures us, "I have met anarchists and proud communists. There is a mix, but you have to dig for it." Beyond race and political affiliation, undergrads here find their peers to be "serious about school but also very fun and friendly." Moreover, they are "bright individuals that want to succeed" and certainly people who "value their education." They also seem to have "a million interests," which they vigorously pursue through a number of extracurricular activities and programs. As one socially satisfied undergrad sums up, "I think there is a club or niche here where everyone can find a group of people they fit in with. I truthfully would feel comfortable sitting down at a table with any one of my classmates in the cafeteria and having lunch with them."

FINANCIAL AID: 517-629-0440 • E-MAIL: ADMISSION@ALBION.EDU • WEBSITE: WWW.ALBION.EDU

THE PRINCETON REVIEW SAYS

Admissions

Very important factors considered include: rigor of secondary school record, academic GPA, standardized test scores. *Important factors considered include:* class rank. *Other factors considered include:* application essay, recommendation(s), interview, extracurricular activities, talent/ability, character/personal qualities, alumni/ae relation, geographical residence, state residency, racial/ethnic status, volunteer work, work experience. SAT or ACT required; SAT Subject Tests considered if submitted. ACT with or without writing accepted. SAT with or without Essay component accepted. TOEFL required of all international applicants. High school diploma is required and GED is accepted. *Academic units recommended:* 4 English, 4 math, 3 science, 2 science labs, 2 foreign language, 2 social studies.

Financial Aid

Students should submit: FAFSA. Priority filing deadline is 2/15.The Princeton Review suggests that all financial aid forms be submitted as soon as possible after October 1. *Need-based scholarships/grants offered:* Federal Pell, FSEOG, State scholarships/grants, Private scholarships, College/university scholarship or grant aid from institutional funds. *Loan aid offered:* Direct Subsidized Stafford Loans, Direct Unsubsidized Stafford Loans, Direct PLUS loans, Federal Perkins Loans. Applicants will be notified of awards on a rolling basis beginning 3/15. Federal Work-Study Program available. Institutional employment available.

The Inside Word

Albion's growing reputation means that earning a coveted acceptance letter is no easy feat. Academic success takes precedence, and applicants should have taken a challenging high school curriculum including a handful of honors and advanced placement courses. Of course, admissions officers are also concerned about maintaining a vibrant community, so careful attention will also be paid to essays and extracurricular activities.

THE SCHOOL SAYS "..."

From the Admissions Office

"As an Albion student, you'll be equipped to make an impact. You'll be prepared to go on to the nation's top graduate and professional schools and to assume leadership roles in the sciences and medicine, business, law, education, the arts, and social services. To do that, your education will take you beyond the classroom, beyond our campus, and beyond conventional thinking. It will help you discover what you're meant to do with your life. And it will prepare you to live it well.

"You'll identify your goals through a four-year individualized career plan and build a strong foundation in the liberal arts. You'll sharpen your career focus and develop skills through internships and other real-world, hands-on experiences like those in our prestigious institutes in business, public policy and service, sustainability and the environment, education, and pre-medicine and the sciences. Your creativity and curiosity may be satisfied through a multitude of research experiences available as early as your freshman year through our Foundation for Undergraduate Research, Scholarship and Creative Activity and the Prentiss M. Brown Honors Program.

"On our residential campus, you can choose from more than 100 campus organizations catering to a wide range of interests. Our athletic teams regularly head to NCAA Division III postseason play, and our equestrian team members compete regionally and nationally.

"Check us out online at www.albion.edu or visit us to learn if Albion will be right for you."

SELECTIVITY

Admissions Rating	75
# of applicants	2,803
% of applicants accepted	79
% of acceptees attending	20
# offered a place on the wait list	0

FRESHMAN PROFILE

Range SAT Critical Reading	500–590
Range SAT Math	420–570
Range ACT Composite	22–27
Minimum paper TOEFL	550
Minimum internet-based TOEFL	79
Average HS GPA	3.42

DEADLINES

Early action	
Deadline	12/1
Notification	1/15
Nonfall registration?	Yes

FINANCIAL FACTS

Financial Aid Rating	84
Annual tuition	$40,570
Room and board	$11,610
Required fees	$470
Books and supplies	$800
Average frosh need-based scholarship	$32,079
Average UG need-based scholarship	$27,732
% needy frosh rec. need-based scholarship or grant aid	100
% needy UG rec. need-based scholarship or grant aid	100
% needy frosh rec. non-need-based scholarship or grant aid	98
% needy UG rec. non-need-based scholarship or grant aid	96
% needy frosh rec. need-based self-help aid	83
% needy UG rec. need-based self-help aid	83
% frosh rec. any financial aid	100
% UG rec. any financial aid	99
% UG borrow to pay for school	68
Average cumulative indebtedness	$37,138
% frosh need fully met	24
% ugrads need fully met	21
Average % of frosh need met	91
Average % of ugrad need met	84

ALFRED UNIVERSITY

ALUMNI HALL, ONE SAXON DRIVE, ALFRED, NY 14802-1205 • ADMISSIONS: 607-871-2115 • FAX: 607-871-2198

CAMPUS LIFE

Quality of Life Rating	82
Fire Safety Rating	88
Green Rating	60*
Type of school	Private
Affiliation	No Affiliation
Environment	Rural

STUDENTS

Total undergrad enrollment	1,960
% male/female	49/51
% from out of state	24
% frosh live on campus	98
% ugrads live on campus	76
% African American	8
% Asian	2
% Caucasian	67
% Hispanic	7
% Native American	<1
% Pacific Islander	0
% Two or more races	3
% Race and/or ethnicity unknown	11
% international	3
# of countries represented	4

SURVEY SAYS...

Great library
Career services are great
Students are friendly

ACADEMICS

Academic Rating	75
% students returning for sophomore year	75
% students graduating within 4 years	44
% students graduating within 6 years	62
Calendar	Semester
Student/faculty ratio	12:1
Profs interesting rating	78
Profs accessible rating	72

Most classes have 10–19 students.
Most lab/discussion sessions have
10–19 students.

MOST POPULAR MAJORS

Business/Commerce; Ceramic Arts and
Ceramics; Psychology

STUDENTS SAY ". . ."

Academics

Alfred University is a small school with an impressive range of world-class majors. The school is known for its "excellent art program," particularly its ceramics and glass majors, as well as for its engineering and psychology programs. While some students at Alfred focus only on their majors, students happily report that there are a "variety of academic opportunities" and that it's "easy to take subjects outside your major." This is appreciated by many, including one art student who likes that Alfred offers "other majors versus a traditional art [school] setting. If I had decided to change majors, Alfred has almost every opportunity." Alfred's "outstanding, talented, dedicated" faculty is one of its biggest draws. An English writing student gushes that professors "bring a level of vibrancy and academic encouragement through enthusiasm to the classroom." "The professors are always pushing you to reach your full potential" and are "always willing to put time into student independent projects." Students also rave about the small classes sizes. "It is the closest to one-on-one teaching you can get," a clinical and counseling psychology major notes, and "the classroom size is perfect for a more personalized education."

Life

Alfred's "beautiful," "small" campus and its "somewhat rural location" are big draws for students looking for a quieter academic experience with a strong "sense of community." Of course, its location means the weather isn't exactly tropical. One student notes that it can feel like "it's basically winter here for about 80 percent of the school year, and it snows constantly." Luckily, "there is always something to do on weekends and week days," for distraction, such as "student club productions…and fundraisers and an excellent selection of movies shown on campus." On top of that, "there are so many clubs and options that you can find something to do," and "every sports team is supported, and superfans are at every event." "the facilities are amazing," particularly the "great" art buildings and the engineering facilities. Alfred's "strong equestrian program" and barn are also a big draw. Students find some of Alfred's dorms to be "pretty outdated," and there's a bit of grumbling about the "hit-or-miss" and "expensive" dining facilities.

Student Body

Alfred has a "warm" atmosphere, and "You can't go down the street without receiving a smile." Students are "friendly, outgoing, and involved," and many do community service work and are active in one of Alfred's many clubs or organizations. The prominent art school means that there's a large presence of creative types on campus, and the equally prominent engineering school ensures a good mix of personalities. One student notes, "A pretty significant gap between the prevalent, spunky art students and the more reclusive engineers," but another adds that this means students are "well-acquainted with people from a variety of studies and backgrounds and with a variety of interests." Most people believe that "everyone finds their own little niche," but they appreciate that it "definitely does not mean they stay there—you are allowed to float between everything." In fact, "more often than not, you'll see engineers rubbing elbows with philosophy majors and artists chilling with math and chemistry majors."

ALFRED UNIVERSITY

FINANCIAL AID: 607-871-2159 • E-MAIL: ADMISSIONS@ALFRED.EDU • WEBSITE: WWW.ALFRED.EDU

THE PRINCETON REVIEW SAYS

Admissions

Very important factors considered include: rigor of secondary school record, class rank, academic GPA, extracurricular activities, character/personal qualities. *Important factors considered include:* standardized test scores, application essay, recommendation(s), volunteer work, work experience. *Other factors considered include:* interview, talent/ability, first generation, racial/ethnic status, level of applicant's interest. SAT or ACT required; SAT Subject Tests considered if submitted. ACT with or without writing accepted. TOEFL required of all international applicants. High school diploma is required and GED is accepted. *Academic units required:* 4 English. *Academic units recommended:* 4 English, 4 math, 3 science, 3 science labs, 1 foreign language, 3 social studies.

Financial Aid

Students should submit: FAFSA, Institution's own financial aid form, State aid form, Noncustodial PROFILE, Business/Farm Supplement. Regular filing deadline is 3/15.The Princeton Review suggests that all financial aid forms be submitted as soon as possible after October 1. *Need-based scholarships/grants offered:* Federal Pell, FSEOG, State scholarships/grants, Private scholarships, College/university scholarship or grant aid from institutional funds. *Loan aid offered:* Direct Subsidized Stafford Loans, Direct Unsubsidized Stafford Loans, Direct PLUS loans, Federal Perkins Loans, College/university loans from institutional funds. Applicants will be notified of awards on a rolling basis beginning 2/15. Federal Work-Study Program available. Institutional employment available.

The Inside Word

Alfred is a fine university with a solid local reputation. The allure for arts students is obvious—Alfred's programs in the arts are especially well-regarded—and as a result, competition is fiercest among applicants for these programs. A killer portfolio, even more than great grades and standardized test scores, is your most likely ticket in. Competition for the engineering school is also tight. Applicants will need to have thrived in a rigorous high school program.

THE SCHOOL SAYS "..."

From the Admissions Office

"The admissions process at Alfred University is the foundation for the personal attention each student can expect during their time at AU. Each applicant is evaluated individually and receives genuine, individual care and consideration.

"The best way to discover all Alfred University has to offer is to come to campus. We truly have something for everyone with more than fourty courses of study, twenty-one NCAA Division III sports and two IHSA sports and over eighty student-run clubs and organizations. You can tour campus; meet current students, faculty, coaches and staff; attend a class; and eat in our dining hall—experience firsthand what life at AU is like.

"Alfred University is a place where students are free to pursue their interests—all of them—no matter how varied or different. Academics, athletics, co-ops, study abroad, internships, special interests—they're all part of what makes you who you are and who you are going to become."

SELECTIVITY

Admissions Rating	80
# of applicants	3,417
% of applicants accepted	70
% of acceptees attending	22
# offered a place on the wait list	91
% accepting a place on wait list	36
% admitted from wait list	33
# of early decision applicants	49
% accepted early decision	92

FRESHMAN PROFILE

Range SAT Critical Reading	490–590
Range SAT Math	510–610
Range SAT Writing	460–570
Range ACT Composite	22–27
Minimum paper TOEFL	550
Minimum internet-based TOEFL	80
Average HS GPA	3.2
% graduated top 10% of class	16
% graduated top 25% of class	43
% graduated top 50% of class	84

DEADLINES

Early decision	
Deadline	12/1
Notification	12/15
Regular	
Priority	2/1
Deadline	8/1
Nonfall registration?	Yes

APPLICANTS ALSO LOOK AT AND OFTEN PREFER

Rochester Institute of Technology; Clarkson University

AND SOMETIMES PREFER

State University of New York–University at Buffalo; Ithaca College

FINANCIAL FACTS

Financial Aid Rating	83
Annual tuition	$27,824
Room and board	$11,618
Required fees	$950
Books and supplies	$1,150
Average frosh need-based scholarship	$20,371
Average UG need-based scholarship	$18,189
% needy frosh rec. need-based scholarship or grant aid	100
% needy UG rec. need-based scholarship or grant aid	99
% needy frosh rec. non-need-based scholarship or grant aid	78
% needy UG rec. non-need-based scholarship or grant aid	62
% needy frosh rec. need-based self-help aid	90
% needy UG rec. need-based self-help aid	89
% frosh rec. any financial aid	96
% UG rec. any financial aid	92
% frosh need fully met	11
% ugrads need fully met	14
Average % of frosh need met	87
Average % of ugrad need met	83

ALLEGHENY COLLEGE

ALLEGHENY COLLEGE, MEADVILLE, PA 16335 • ADMISSIONS: 814-332-4351 • FAX: 814-337-0431

STUDENTS SAY "..."

Academics
Allegheny College in western Pennsylvania is a school "where people exude passion about what they are involved in," and the curriculum is "all about applying your knowledge to your experiences." The school allows students to combine completely unrelated majors and minors (in fact, it requires both), which means students "practically create [their] own education," and a student has "the freedom to dabble in my many areas of interest." "Allegheny students are known for their 'unusual combinations' of interests such as a major in biology and a minor in dance," explains a student. This "unique and valuable educational experience" provided by a school that "truly cares about the learning process" is a boon to students looking to forge any path in life (as well as those who are unsure), and the small population means that there are "many researching opportunities." "Faculty members reach out to students about internship and research opportunities often."

The "amazing," "very passionate" professors "go above and beyond to make sure their students understand the material." Professors are "great about teaching the material to you in a variety of ways until you understand." "I have never once felt dumb or like I couldn't handle something after getting help one on one," says a student. "I love my professors. I consider some of them to be friends, and most of them to be mentors," says another. Professors focus on student contribution "in and out of the classroom," so there are lectures, but students are the main focus. If you would rather have peers look at your work, then "there are plenty of consultants and tutors who are more than willing to help." The "workload is large," and the academics are demanding, but "the school is very understanding of how special and different each student is and tries to help each student excel in their own way."

Life
Attending Allegheny "is a lot of work," but "there is still time to be social and make the best friends of your life." "It can get wild on weekends," but for the most part people "are very studious during the week," and "students care for their grades." With so much leeway in academic studies, it's not surprising that the administration is concerned with "making sure that there is a place for everyone." Student activities are well-organized and plentiful, and the school works just as hard at "promoting [a] statement of community." The school organizes many late night activities: "We always have some type of performer, like comedians, musicians, or magicians." "There is a place for everyone with the different clubs and organizations on campus," says another. "If you get involved enough, you'll rarely have a boring moment," says a student. The "mutual respect [among] students, faculty, and the administration" feeds into the overall happy satisfaction with life, and "most students find their area either through work, class, sports, or clubs." Greek life is healthy here, but not overpowering. Some say that food services "are repetitive and not very good"; luckily, the green, scenic campus "has many open spaces," and the school's commitment toward sustainability has always been apparent.

Student Body
Allegheny's strong emphasis on community invites "very diverse" students who are "completely accepting and understanding of everyone's needs, interests, and feelings." Upperclassmen are "really welcoming to freshmen," and "the importance of being unique" is stressed from the get-go. Everyone is fun loving, but "always knows when to stop socializing and get to work." This "mixed bag" all get along well, but "we usually have at least a tiny nerdy side." Cliques aren't that common among this group of 2,100 "liberal, idealistic, and global thinkers," and though students normally find their niche within the first three semesters, they "are always eager to meet new people and do new things." Students say that there "is a lot of support to help minority students fit in."

FINANCIAL AID: 800-835-7780 • E-MAIL: ADMISSIONS@ALLEGHENY.EDU • WEBSITE: WWW.ALLEGHENY.EDU

THE PRINCETON REVIEW SAYS

Admissions

Very important factors considered include: rigor of secondary school record, class rank, academic GPA. *Important factors considered include:* recommendation(s), interview, extracurricular activities, character/personal qualities, level of applicant's interest. *Other factors considered include:* standardized test scores, application essay, talent/ability, first generation, alumni/ae relation, geographical residence, racial/ethnic status, volunteer work, work experience. SAT or ACT considered if submitted; SAT Subject Tests considered if submitted. ACT with Writing recommended. SAT with Essay component recommended. TOEFL required of all international applicants. High school diploma is required and GED is accepted. *Academic units required:* 4 English, 3 math, 3 science, 2 foreign language, 3 social studies, 1 academic elective.

Financial Aid

Students should submit: FAFSA. Priority filing deadline is 2/15.The Princeton Review suggests that all financial aid forms be submitted as soon as possible after October 1. *Need-based scholarships/grants offered:* Federal Pell, FSEOG, State scholarships/grants, Private scholarships, College/university scholarship or grant aid from institutional funds. *Loan aid offered:* Direct Subsidized Stafford Loans, Direct Unsubsidized Stafford Loans, Direct PLUS loans, Federal Perkins Loans. Applicants will be notified of awards on a rolling basis beginning 3/1. Federal Work-Study Program available. Institutional employment available.

The Inside Word

A whopping 70 percent of Allegheny's student body is in the top 25 percent of their class. The typical admit here has solid high school grades in a demanding curriculum and above-average standardized test scores. The school's stellar admissions officers are known to take the time to get to know applicants' full profiles and prove to be strong advocates for students during the admissions process.

THE SCHOOL SAYS " . . ."

From the Admissions Office

"Allegheny is the premier college in the country for students with 'Unusual Combinations' of interests and talents. Students develop combinations of majors and minors in areas that may, at first glance, seem unrelated: biology and economics; political science and music; history and psychology. There is an abiding passion for learning and life and shared inquiry that spans individuals as well as areas of study. Building on a combination of academic disciplines and passions, every student completes a comprehensive Senior Project. This significant piece of original scholarly work has a creative, analytical or experimental focus and the experience culminates with an oral defense in front of faculty experts and mentors. The project demonstrates the skills most prized by employers and graduate schools: the ability to complete a major assignment, to work independently, to analyze and synthesize information and to write and speak persuasively. Exploring academic disciplines from multiple perspectives leads students to extraordinary outcomes. Biochemistry majors highlight their skills learned in communication arts to start marketing careers at the Environmental Protection Agency. English majors collaborate with our pre-health advisors and enjoy acceptance rates to graduate and medical schools between 80 and 100 percent—twice the national average. Over and over again, we hear from leaders in business, government, medicine, education and community service that the future belongs to individuals who are innovators, inventors, and big picture thinkers, those who think both analytically and creatively. It is this preparation for the global marketplace that Allegheny is known for providing."

SELECTIVITY

Admissions Rating	86
# of applicants	4,324
% of applicants accepted	68
% of acceptees attending	17
# offered a place on the wait list	239
% accepting a place on wait list	100
% admitted from wait list	7
# of early decision applicants	188
% accepted early decision	60

FRESHMAN PROFILE

Range SAT Critical Reading	503–630
Range SAT Math	510–620
Range SAT Writing	480–618
Range ACT Composite	22–29
Minimum paper TOEFL	550
Minimum internet-based TOEFL	80
Average HS GPA	3.7
% graduated top 10% of class	35
% graduated top 25% of class	65
% graduated top 50% of class	91

DEADLINES

Early decision	
Deadline	11/15
Notification	12/15
Regular	
Deadline	2/15
Notification	4/1
Nonfall registration?	Yes

APPLICANTS ALSO LOOK AT AND OFTEN PREFER
Kenyon College; Oberlin College

AND SOMETIMES PREFER
University of Pittsburgh; Gettysburg College

AND RARELY PREFER
Washington & Jefferson College; Juniata College

FINANCIAL FACTS

Financial Aid Rating	87
Annual tuition	$43,750
Room and board	$11,170
Required fees	$500
Books and supplies	$1,000
Average frosh need-based scholarship	$32,544
Average UG need-based scholarship	$29,000
% needy frosh rec. need-based scholarship or grant aid	100
% needy UG rec. need-based scholarship or grant aid	100
% needy frosh rec. non-need-based scholarship or grant aid	21
% needy UG rec. non-need-based scholarship or grant aid	17
% needy frosh rec. need-based self-help aid	86
% needy UG rec. need-based self-help aid	87
% frosh rec. any financial aid	99
% UG rec. any financial aid	99
% frosh need fully met	42
% ugrads need fully met	36
Average % of frosh need met	92
Average % of ugrad need met	91

AMERICAN UNIVERSITY

4400 Massachusetts Avenue, Northwest, Washington, D.C. 20016-8001 • Admissions: 202-885-6000 • Fax: 202-885-1025

STUDENTS SAY "..."

Academics

American University exploits its Washington, D.C., location—that facilitates a strong faculty, prestigious guest lecturers, and "a wealth of internship opportunities"—to offer "incredibly strong programs" in political science and international relations. "The poli-sci kids are all going to be president one day, and the international studies ones are all going to save the world," a student insists. The school of communication also excels, and the school works hard to accommodate "interdisciplinary majors and the opportunities associated with studying them," which include "taking advantage of the resources of the city. The school values learning out of the classroom as much as learning in the classroom." As you might expect from a school with a strong international relations program, "AU's study abroad program is one of the best." Although AU "does not have the automatically recognizable prestige of nearby Georgetown," that's not necessarily a drawback; on the contrary, "the administration and professors go out of their way to ensure a great academic experience," in part because the school is trying to "climb in the rankings and gain recognition as one of the nation's top universities." However, some concede, "The university could improve programs in other fields, aside from its specialties in international studies, public affairs, business, and communication."

Life

"The greatest strength of AU is the activity level both politically and in the community," students tell us. "Whether it was signs in windows, talk in the class or in the hallways, t-shirts, or canvassing in Metro-accessible Virginia, students on both sides took [the 2014 midterm election] religiously." As one student explains, "Let's put it this way: A politician who comes to campus is likely to draw about 90 percent of the student population [and] an AU basketball game, about 9 [percent]." Students get involved in the community through "campus outreach by student-run organizations," which many see as "the school's greatest asset." The typical undergrad is "incredibly engaged and active...Students seek internships in every line of work, becoming actively involved in a field of interest before graduation." When it's time to relax, "Washington, D.C., offers limitless opportunities to explore." Many "enjoy partying and hanging out off-campus and on campus (even though AU is a 'dry campus')," but there are also "a lot of people who don't drink and have a very good time just using what D.C. has to offer: museums, restaurants, parks, cinemas, theaters, and shops." As one student sums it up: "The city is the school's greatest resource. You will never run out of things to do in Washington."

Student Body

AU attracts a crowd that "tends to be very ideologically driven." "Liberals run the show," most here agree, although they add that "Plenty of students don't fit this mold, and I've never seen anyone rejected for what they believe." The campus "is very friendly to those with alternative lifestyles (GLBT, vegetarian, green-living, etc.)," but students with more socially conservative inclinations note that "while AU boasts about the many religious groups on campus, there is still a general antipathy toward piety." The perception that some departments outshine others is reflected in the way students perceive each other; one says, "You have the political studies know-it-alls, the international studies student who thinks he is going to save the world, the artsy film/communication students, and the rest [who] are unhappy students who couldn't get into George Washington or Georgetown."

FINANCIAL AID: 202-885-6100 • E-MAIL: ADMISSIONS@AMERICAN.EDU • WEBSITE: WWW.AMERICAN.EDU

THE PRINCETON REVIEW SAYS

Admissions

Very important factors considered include: rigor of secondary school record, academic GPA, level of applicant's interest. *Important factors considered include:* application essay, recommendation(s), extracurricular activities, talent/ability, character/personal qualities, volunteer work. *Other factors considered include:* standardized test scores, first generation, alumni/ae relation, geographical residence, racial/ethnic status, work experience. SAT or ACT considered if submitted. High school diploma is required and GED is accepted. *Academic units required:* 4 English, 3 math, 3 science, 2 science labs, 2 foreign language, 2 social studies, 3 academic electives. *Academic units recommended:* 4 English, 4 math, 4 science, 3 foreign language, 4 social studies, 4 academic electives.

Financial Aid

Students should submit: FAFSA, CSS/Financial Aid PROFILE. Regular filing deadline is 1/10. The Princeton Review suggests that all financial aid forms be submitted as soon as possible after October 1. *Need-based scholarships/grants offered:* Federal Pell, FSEOG, Private scholarships, College/university scholarship or grant aid from institutional funds. *Loan aid offered:* Direct Subsidized Stafford Loans, Direct Unsubsidized Stafford Loans, Direct PLUS loans, Federal Perkins Loans, College/university loans from institutional funds. Applicants will be notified of awards on or about 4/1. Federal Work-Study Program available. Institutional employment available.

The Inside Word

Despite strong competition from other area powerhouses, American sees a strong application pool that allows it to be very selective. Admissions rates have declined significantly in recent years. In addition to asking students to indicate their intended field of study, the university is also interested in clear demonstrations of interest on the part of applicants.

THE SCHOOL SAYS "..."

From the Admissions Office

"A college-centered research university, AU's undergraduate experience is built on the pillars of Washington, D.C. as a laboratory for learning, distinguished faculty, engaged learners, and a culture of innovation. Its rigorous curriculum features high impact educational experiences that challenge you to combine serious theoretical study with meaningful real-world experiences. Whatever major you choose, you will acquire a solid foundation in liberal arts while pursuing in-depth study in your chosen field. You won't be confined to a single course of study or even be limited to traditional learning venues and methodologies. We encourage you to learn in every imaginable way—across disciplines, departments, and schools. Beyond that, we offer innovative programs that take you out of the classroom and into the realm of experience. Washington, D.C., is a laboratory for learning. Few locations can compare when it comes to internships of global importance. AU places special emphasis on balancing classroom time with active learning and application of knowledge. Eighty-seven percent of responding graduates held one or more internships. For all who participate, internships provide a firm foundation in both academic and practical achievement. Our post-graduation census of 2015 graduates (with a response rate of 80 percent) speaks to excellent post-graduation outcomes: Eighty-nine percent of 2015 AU grads were employed, enrolled in graduate school, or both, within six months of graduation. More than half (55 percent) of those working secured jobs before completing their degrees. Eighty-four percent of new AU grads who work hold a position related to their degree or career objective."

SELECTIVITY

Admissions Rating	92
# of applicants	16,735
% of applicants accepted	35
% of acceptees attending	30
# offered a place on the wait list	2,778
% accepting a place on wait list	10
% admitted from wait list	3
# of early decision applicants	805
% accepted early decision	87

FRESHMAN PROFILE

Range SAT Critical Reading	590–690
Range SAT Math	560–650
Range SAT Writing	570–670
Range ACT Composite	26–30
Minimum paper TOEFL	550
Minimum internet-based TOEFL	80
Average HS GPA	3.7

DEADLINES

Early decision	
Deadline	11/10
Notification	12/31
Other ED	
Deadline	1/10
Notification	2/15
Regular	
Deadline	1/10
Notification	4/1
Nonfall registration?	Yes

APPLICANTS ALSO LOOK AT AND OFTEN PREFER

The George Washington University; Georgetown University; Brown University; Tufts University; Boston College; College of William and Mary; Harvard College; Yale University

AND SOMETIMES PREFER

Boston University; New York University

AND RARELY PREFER

Northeastern University; Fordham University

FINANCIAL FACTS

Financial Aid Rating	82
Annual tuition	$44,046
Room and board	$14,526
Required fees	$547
Books and supplies	$800
% needy frosh rec. need-based scholarship or grant aid	93
% needy UG rec. need-based scholarship or grant aid	84
% needy frosh rec. non-need-based scholarship or grant aid	27
% needy UG rec. non-need-based scholarship or grant aid	30
% needy frosh rec. need-based self-help aid	94
% needy UG rec. need-based self-help aid	92
% frosh rec. any financial aid	82
% UG rec. any financial aid	73

AMHERST COLLEGE

CAMPUS BOX 2231, AMHERST, MA 01002 • ADMISSIONS: 413-542-2328 • FAX: 413-542-2040

CAMPUS LIFE

Quality of Life Rating	90
Fire Safety Rating	84
Green Rating	76
Type of school	Private
Affiliation	No Affiliation
Environment	Town

STUDENTS

Total undergrad enrollment	1,795
% male/female	50/50
% from out of state	86
% frosh from public high school	62
% frosh live on campus	100
% ugrads live on campus	98
% African American	12
% Asian	14
% Caucasian	42
% Hispanic	13
% Native American	<1
% Pacific Islander	<1
% Two or more races	5
% Race and/or ethnicity unknown	4
% international	10
# of countries represented	54

SURVEY SAYS...

Students politically aware
Students always studying
Students are happy
Internships are widely available
School is well run
Great financial aid
No one cheats
Students aren't religious
Students love Amherst, MA
Dorms are like palaces
Easy to get around campus
Recreation facilities are great
Alumni active on campus

ACADEMICS

Academic Rating	98
% students returning for sophomore year	98
% students graduating within 4 years	88
% students graduating within 6 years	95
Calendar	Semester
Student/faculty ratio	8:1
Profs interesting rating	94
Profs accessible rating	93

Most classes have 10–19 students.
Most lab/discussion sessions have
10–19 students.

MOST POPULAR MAJORS
Economics; Biology; History

STUDENTS SAY "..."

Academics

A crown jewel of the liberal arts college scene, Amherst College is an intimate and academically demanding school in western Massachusetts, where its 1,800 students from all across the country come to collaborate on "the highest of academic problems." There is an "openness that pervades every aspect of the school," from the open curriculum (which eliminates core requirements) to an administration that is "all about student feedback." Students say the school fosters "a vibrant life of the mind" through a "stellar academic and athletic combination" and "endless resources and funding for absolutely everything." Amherst professors are "unbelievably well-read," "insert unique insights into class discussions and maintain high levels of discourse on controversial topics." Relationships with professors "flourish due to how accessible they are and how much we, as students, interact with them"; they truly care about the students and "want to get to know them." "I've been invited to professors' houses for holiday parties, have met their children, and learned from their experiences," says one student. The ability to learn across disciplines and at other schools in the Five College Consortium gives students the freedom to take classes they are genuinely interested in, leading to "livelier discussions and allowing [them] to focus on what [they] want to." An emphasis on social consciousness both inside and outside of the classroom "raises the intellectual ability of . . . students" and "[challenges] students to embrace the 'uncomfortable.'" The workload is "often heavy" but "fulfilling," and the school "encourages hard work and breeds an atmosphere of perfection" that is roundly received by the student populace.

Life

While Amherst is "roughly in the middle of nowhere," the Five College Consortium brings thousands of students to this "beautiful area," making Amherst the second largest booking venue in New England. The town is "small but is extremely geared toward college students" and "social life is extremely fun and inviting." "It's honestly impossible to get bored here with five campuses of exciting academic and social events open to you," says a student. Fun "comes in many forms," such as sledding, going for hikes, and spectating at sports games. The nearby town of Northampton is a popular outing, and Amherst just renovated its old 1920s Powerhouse to serve as a party and event space (it has a "nightclub vibe that has been very popular"). There are "endless opportunities for campus involvement" and a "profound focus on diversity." Students "are encouraged to join essentially any group they would like" from the start of freshman year. Even with Amherst's emphasis on athletics, "you're going to see the football players in the library more than you will see them in the gym." There are always activities put on by student organizations, and students often have trouble choosing which ones to attend "since virtually all of them are compelling."

Student Body

Students tout their small campus's socioeconomic and racial diversity. "Everyone in this community is engaged in their own passions and supportive of others' passions," which "creates an energizing environment of curiosity, determination, and success." "Everyone has a story, a talent, an experience that I never would get to be in contact with if it wasn't for meeting them here," says a student. Smarts and talent are common traits, and students tend to be "preppy," "athletic," and "socially conscious." Though students tend to fall into loosely defined groups and friend sets, "those groups tend to be very flexible." "Every type of group that you would hope to be a part of exists here," and people are almost always involved in multiple activities but "do not carry out one or the other half-heartedly."

FINANCIAL AID: 413-542-2296 • E-MAIL: ADMISSION@AMHERST.EDU • WEBSITE: WWW.AMHERST.EDU

THE PRINCETON REVIEW SAYS

Admissions

Very important factors considered include: rigor of secondary school record, academic GPA, standardized test scores, application essay, recommendation(s), extracurricular activities, talent/ability, character/personal qualities, first generation. *Important factors considered include:* class rank, volunteer work. *Other factors considered include:* alumni/ae relation, geographical residence, racial/ethnic status, work experience. ACT with Writing recommended. SAT with Essay component recommended. TOEFL required of all international applicants. High school diploma or equivalent is not required. *Academic units recommended:* 4 English, 4 math, 3 science, 1 science lab, 2 social studies, 2 history.

Financial Aid

Students should submit: FAFSA, CSS/Financial Aid PROFILE, Noncustodial PROFILE, Business/Farm Supplement. Priority filing deadline is 2/15.The Princeton Review suggests that all financial aid forms be submitted as soon as possible after October 1. *Need-based scholarships/grants offered:* Federal Pell, FSEOG, State scholarships/grants, Private scholarships, College/university scholarship or grant aid from institutional funds. *Loan aid offered:* Direct Subsidized Stafford Loans, Direct Unsubsidized Stafford Loans, Direct PLUS loans, Federal Perkins Loans, College/university loans from institutional funds. Applicants will be notified of awards on or about 4/1. Federal Work-Study Program available. Institutional employment available.

The Inside Word

Membership certainly has its benefits at Amherst College. For the price of entry to this school, students also gain entrance to the prestigious Five College Consortium, which allows enrolled students to take courses for credit at no additional cost at any of the four other participating consortium members (Hampshire College, Mount Holyoke College, Smith College, and the University of Massachusetts Amherst). And this deal isn't just confined to the classroom: Students can use other schools' libraries, eat meals at the other cafeterias, and participate in extracurricular activities offered at the other schools. And don't worry about how you'll get there—your bus fare is covered, too.

THE SCHOOL SAYS " . . ."

From the Admissions Office

"Founded in 1821, Amherst College is considered to be among the premier liberal arts colleges in the nation, enrolling nearly 1,800 bright, talented and diverse students. A need-blind admission policy and generous, no-loan financial aid packages ensure that exceptional students from across the country and around the world can be admitted to Amherst based on their accomplishments and promise, regardless of family income. Located in Amherst, Massachusetts, a town of 35,000 people in an area of great natural beauty in the western part of the state, the College's 1,000-acre campus includes top-notch academic, athletic and residential facilities. Awarding the BA degree in thirty-eight different majors in the humanities, social sciences and natural sciences, Amherst offers an Open Curriculum, which allows students great independence and flexibility in the design of their educational programs, unconstrained by distribution or area requirements. Through the Five College Consortium, Amherst students can also take courses and participate in activities at Smith, Mount Holyoke and Hampshire Colleges and the University of Massachusetts Amherst, providing access to an unusually broad and diverse collection of curricular and extracurricular options. Amherst's small classes and low student-faculty ratio foster one-on-one interactions with professors and fellow students, and provide exceptional opportunities for undergraduate research with talented, accomplished faculty, all of which contribute to an uncommonly engaging intellectual and personal experience within a lively community."

SELECTIVITY

Admissions Rating	98
# of applicants	8,568
% of applicants accepted	14
% of acceptees attending	39
# offered a place on the wait list	1,398
% accepting a place on wait list	46
% admitted from wait list	5
# of early decision applicants	483
% accepted early decision	36

FRESHMAN PROFILE

Range SAT Critical Reading	680–780
Range SAT Math	680–780
Range SAT Writing	680–770
Range ACT Composite	31–34
Minimum internet-based TOEFL	100
% graduated top 10% of class	86
% graduated top 25% of class	96
% graduated top 50% of class	100

DEADLINES

Early decision	
Deadline	11/15
Notification	12/15
Regular	
Deadline	1/1
Notification	4/1
Nonfall registration?	No

APPLICANTS ALSO LOOK AT AND OFTEN PREFER

Princeton University; Yale University; Harvard College

AND SOMETIMES PREFER

Brown University; Williams College; Stanford University; Dartmouth College

AND RARELY PREFER

Tufts University; Vassar College; University of Virginia

FINANCIAL FACTS

Financial Aid Rating	96
Annual tuition	$49,730
Room and board	$13,210
Required fees	$832
Books and supplies	$1,000
Average frosh need-based scholarship	$49,514
Average UG need-based scholarship	$49,134
% needy frosh rec. need-based scholarship or grant aid	100
% needy UG rec. need-based scholarship or grant aid	99
% needy UG rec. non-need-based scholarship or grant aid	0
% needy frosh rec. need-based self-help aid	80
% needy UG rec. need-based self-help aid	88
% frosh rec. any financial aid	54
% UG rec. any financial aid	58
% UG borrow to pay for school	25
Average cumulative indebtedness	$15,756
% frosh need fully met	100
% ugrads need fully met	100
Average % of frosh need met	100
Average % of ugrad need met	100

ANGELO STATE UNIVERSITY

ASU STATION #11014, SAN ANGELO, TX 76909-1014 • ADMISSIONS: 325-942-2041 • FAX: 325-942-2078

STUDENTS SAY "..."

Academics

As a member of the Texas Tech University System, Angelo State in San Angelo is "committed to providing big time opportunities with a small school atmosphere." Students commend the "committed professors teaching small classes that prepare students for their careers," noting that their instructors are "willing to help solve a problem or talk about the material." As one student explains, "The student body is extremely friendly and make[s] me feel like I am a part of a really big family." Students praise the pre-med, accounting, nursing, and physical therapy programs. The school has its share of traditional and non-traditional students, but the two seem to mix easily. A non-traditional student comments, "I was a little nervous about how I would be perceived ... but I have been treated equally in relation to others on campus." As with any school, the quality of professors will run the gamut, but Angelo State students praise their "amazing" professors who "really care about their students' success." Students note, "You are an individual to them not just another number." One student goes so far as to credit a professor with a major personal academic change: "I have had the pleasure of being taught by some of the most amazing professors here. One was so influential I decided to change my major to biochemistry after taking the class for [non-majors]."

Life

Even though San Angelo is a small town, students say it "offers different things to do in your free time," including "a bowling alley, movie theatre and many outdoor adventure activities." The school owns "a lake facility [where] students may rent kayaks, bikes and [there are] picnic facilities." There's always something happening on campus, according to students, like "mixers, game nights, karaoke, poetry readings," or "some kind of exhibition or event going on in the University Center." Intramural sports are popular, as are intercollegiate ones. Angelo State is a Division II school and cheering on the Rams during various seasons and sports is a highlight. As one student notes, "You can always find things to [do], especially when there's a game." That's not to say that students aren't serious about their studies. "I go to class in the mornings and go to work in the evenings and then come straight home study and get ready for class the next day," says one public relations major. Others see Greek life as a way to be "involved on campus," and some even say "a bigger Greek life would make the school just that much better." There are so many different activities on campus, from clubs to volunteer organizations, that "you have to try really hard to not become involved at this school."

Student Body

At Angelo State, "Texas charm is prevalent on campus and ... you will rarely meet a stranger." The school "has students from all over the world," but even the non-native Texans have "all got the kind Texan heart." In the classroom, Angelo State is "an amazingly diverse mixture of traditional and non-traditional students," and around campus, "everyone knows everyone and you become a big family." Says one psychology major, "Angelo State is very friendly and welcoming yet highly conservative." Underscoring the tight-knit community feeling of the school, one business administration major says, "Everyone has a different story on why they are earning a degree. Some come from wealthy families while others are obtaining loans just to get through, but together we are RamFam." It's hard to be a stranger on the Angelo State campus, as one student gushes: "Everyone on campus is so friendly and will do anything they can to help someone who is lost or new to school. There are so many opportunities to meet people and make long lasting friendships and connections."

FINANCIAL AID: 325-942-2246 • E-MAIL: ADMISSIONS@ANGELO.EDU • WEBSITE: WWW.ANGELO.EDU

THE PRINCETON REVIEW SAYS

Admissions

Very important factors considered include: class rank, standardized test scores. *Important factors considered include:* rigor of secondary school record. *Other factors considered include:* academic GPA. SAT or ACT required. ACT with or without writing accepted. TOEFL required of all international applicants. High school diploma is required and GED is accepted. *Academic units recommended:* 4 English, 4 math, 4 science, 2 foreign language, 1 visual/performing arts, and 2 units from above areas or other academic areas.

Financial Aid

Students should submit: FAFSA. Priority filing deadline is 4/1.The Princeton Review suggests that all financial aid forms be submitted as soon as possible after October 1. *Need-based scholarships/grants offered:* Federal Pell, FSEOG, State scholarships/grants, Private scholarships, College/university scholarship or grant aid from institutional funds, Federal Nursing Scholarships. *Loan aid offered:* Direct Subsidized Stafford Loans, Direct Unsubsidized Stafford Loans, Direct PLUS loans, Federal Perkins Loans, Federal Nursing Loans, State Loans, College/university loans from institutional funds. Applicants will be notified of awards on a rolling basis beginning 4/1. Federal Work-Study Program available. Institutional employment available.

The Inside Word

The admissions criteria for Angelo State are fairly straightforward for first-year students and require applicants to submit a high school transcript, SAT or ACT scores, and an online application. Depending on the applicant's class rank, specific standardized test requirements must be met (for example, for applicants in the top 10 percent of their class, there is no minimum score, but for those in the next 40 percent, a minimum of a 17 on the ACT or an 820 on the SAT is required). Angelo State will still review applications for those prospective students who don't meet the minimum requirements, and they may be still be admitted.

THE SCHOOL SAYS "..."

From the Admissions Office

"Undergraduate students at Angelo State University engage in faculty-mentored projects and research experiences. Living Learning Communities include shared courses, study groups, social activities and educational activities, both in and outside the classroom. ASU also promotes community involvement through numerous organizations and outreach programs. ASU shines with superb records of graduates' acceptance into professional schools. Over 50 percent of pre-med students are accepted into medical school, well above the statewide average of 35 percent. More than 90 percent of students who complete the pre-veterinary program, maintain a high GPA and complete the entrance requirements are accepted into veterinary school. All graduates of ASU's Honors Program who have applied to graduate programs or professional schools, including medicine and law, have been accepted. Additionally, since 1998, ASU students have maintained a 100 percent passing rate on the Texas Examination of Educator Standards (TExES) teacher certification test for secondary mathematics.

"Because of strong academics and a substantial gift aid program, including the Carr Scholarship Program, which annually awards scholarships totaling approximately $4 million, ASU remains one of the top educational values in Texas. About 73 percent of ASU students receive gift aid, financial support that does not have to be repaid to the university. ASU also encourages healthy student lifestyles while fostering leadership development through 100-plus student organizations, a thriving intramurals program, and modern recreation and fitness facilities. ASU student-athletes just completed one of the most successful years in school history, competing in newly renovated, state-of-the-art facilities, including a new on-campus football stadium."

SELECTIVITY

Admissions Rating	72
# of applicants	3,291
% of applicants accepted	89
% of acceptees attending	45

FRESHMAN PROFILE

Range SAT Critical Reading	420–530
Range SAT Math	440–540
Range SAT Writing	400–500
Range ACT Composite	18–24
Minimum paper TOEFL	550
Minimum internet-based TOEFL	79
% graduated top 10% of class	11
% graduated top 25% of class	34
% graduated top 50% of class	67

DEADLINES

Regular	
Deadline	8/27
Nonfall registration?	Yes

FINANCIAL FACTS

Financial Aid Rating	83
Annual in-state tuition	$4,860
Annual out-of-state tuition	$16,560
Room and board	$7,702
Required fees	$3,004
Books and supplies	$1,200
Average frosh need-based scholarship	$3,819
Average UG need-based scholarship	$3,315
% needy frosh rec. need-based scholarship or grant aid	79
% needy UG rec. need-based scholarship or grant aid	85
% needy frosh rec. non-need-based scholarship or grant aid	67
% needy UG rec. non-need-based scholarship or grant aid	35
% needy frosh rec. need-based self-help aid	79
% needy UG rec. need-based self-help aid	76
% frosh rec. any financial aid	87
% UG rec. any financial aid	81
% frosh need fully met	20
% ugrads need fully met	14
Average % of frosh need met	91
Average % of ugrad need met	82

ARIZONA STATE UNIVERSITY

PO BOX 870112, TEMPE, AZ 85287-0112 • ADMISSIONS: 480-965-7788 • FAX: 480-965-3610

STUDENTS SAY ". . ."

Academics

Known as a research behemoth and one of the largest public universities in the United States, Arizona State University pairs world-renowned programs and "unlimited resources" with a high degree of expectation for student accomplishment. The school's six locations offer "many different campus experiences with the resources of a monster university," and its roughly 57,200 undergraduates from 112 countries in the metropolitan Phoenix campuses provide huge capital and a diverse environment. From among more than 300 academic programs to choose from (and students can also create their own interdisciplinary majors), the nursing school is "excellent," and the Walter Cronkite School of Journalism and Mass Communication is "the best of its kind." Barrett, The Honors College is a highly regarded, "small, close-knit community," and the size of the school actually leads to easier collaboration between disciplines because, as one student puts it, "we have more access." The professors are all "titans of their respective industries and have been brought here because of their enthusiasm and qualification." Most teachers are "available, helpful, and truly cared that I learned." They "use their work experiences to teach students" and do not strictly follow the book; the entire academic system is built around practical education, although many admit that the "advising services are not good" and could use some work. "Ask a peer for help before you ask [advisers], especially if you want to switch your major from their college to another one," says a student. Each of the six locations has a different vibe or concentration: Tempe is "more of a party scene," Downtown Phoenix is "very focused on public service," Polytechnic is "techy, nerdy, and quiet," and West is artsy. In general, ASU is "a vast and diverse school" that is "about creating well-rounded individuals."

Life

Make no mistake, "the school is extremely large, and can be intimidating at first." However, with so many different opportunities students say "you can very easily make the school seem small by integrating into club sports, academic pursuits, and various student groups." In addition to opportunities related to "education, sports, clubs, everything and anything you want to be involved in" there are "always huge university-sanctioned events going on all over campus." Swimming and sun bathing are also very popular (there is a pool at almost every campus housing complex and at the student rec center). However, parking can be a real problem here. The "party school" reputation that seems to follows ASU is mainly rebuked by students, who say that "if you look for the party, you can find it, but that is not the main focus for the majority of students." The smaller campuses, especially, tend to be quieter and mainly alcohol-free. People enjoy hanging out on campus or on Mill Avenue (where the bars are located); sports are also "a big deal," including playing intramurals, watching college and national games, and going to games at the stadiums. Students "also go up north to Sedona for hiking or Flagstaff for snowboarding."

Student Body

So many people attend ASU that "it is impossible for the student population to not be incredibly diverse." Most everyone "has a busy school schedule, a part-time job, and is involved in an organization." Students are prone to "hang out with students in their same major" or on the same campus, and most people tend to be "studious yet involved in many other extracurricular activities." "It seems that everyone finds their niche after a couple months or the first year," says a philosophy major. "Between [57,200] students, you can find whatever community you want."

FINANCIAL AID: 480-965-3355 • E-MAIL: ADMISSIONS@ASU.EDU • WEBSITE: WWW.ASU.EDU

THE PRINCETON REVIEW SAYS

Admissions

Very important factors considered include: class rank, academic GPA, standardized test scores. *Important factors considered include:* rigor of secondary school record. *Other factors considered include:* state residency. SAT or ACT recommend; SAT Subject Tests required for some. ACT with or without writing accepted. SAT with or without essay component accepted. TOEFL required of all international applicants. High school diploma is required and GED is accepted. *Academic units required:* 4 English, 4 math, 3 science, 3 science labs, 2 foreign language, 1 social studies, 1 history, and 1 unit fine art or career or technical education.

Financial Aid

Students should submit: FAFSA. Priority filing deadline is 1/1. The Princeton Review suggests that all financial aid forms be submitted as soon as possible after October 1. *Need-based scholarships/grants offered:* Federal Pell, FSEOG, State scholarships/grants, Private scholarships, College/university scholarship or grant aid from institutional funds, United Negro College Fund. *Loan aid offered:* Direct Subsidized Stafford Loans, Direct Unsubsidized Stafford Loans, Direct PLUS loans, Federal Perkins Loans, State Loans. Applicants will be notified of awards on a rolling basis beginning 3/1. Federal Work-Study Program available. Institutional employment available.

The Inside Word

With an acceptance rate of 82 percent, ASU is somewhat selective and clearly outlines all the requirements and academic standards for admission on its website. The applications of students who do not meet all the standards undergo an "individual review" and are carefully evaluated by the admissions team. Students interested in Barrett, The Honors College should apply for admission only after first submitting an application to ASU, though they may apply to Barrett before they are officially admitted to the university.

THE SCHOOL SAYS "..."

From the Admissions Office

"ASU is breaking down the walls of the traditional academic experience to increase the impact of education and research in local and global communities. As a New American University, ASU is committed to interdisciplinary connections, academic excellence, and societal impact. We are bold and forward-thinking, and we see challenges as opportunities. With 300-plus undergraduate majors, ASU is a learning environment where personal expression is valued as much as research and discovery. ASU champions intellectual and cultural diversity and welcomes students from all 50 states and more than 130 nations. Our distinguished faculty receives prestigious honors including the Nobel Prize and membership in the National Academies. Student achievements include Rhodes, Fulbright, Marshals, and Goldwater scholars, National Merit Scholars, and National Hispanic Scholars.

"ASU has five unique campuses in metropolitan Phoenix, and a site in Lake Havasu City. ASU's Downtown Phoenix campus features state-of-the-art living and learning facilities. The campus creates strong learning and career connections for over 10,000 students with media, health care, corporate, and government organizations. The Polytechnic campus, located in Mesa, Arizona, is home to 4,000 students who are exploring professional and technical programs. Thousands of square feet of new laboratory space make way for project-based learning.

"ASU welcomes more than 51,000 students studying at the historic Tempe campus. The Sun Devils athletic complex, performing arts facilities, and high-tech research space create a dynamic and engaging learning environment.

"At the West campus in northwest Phoenix, ASU offers business, education, and interdisciplinary arts and science programs to more than 3,600 students. The campus's award-winning architecture and lush landscaping are designed to create a close-knit learning community."

SELECTIVITY
Admissions Rating	80
# of applicants	33,575
% of applicants accepted	82
% of acceptees attending	38

FRESHMAN PROFILE
Range SAT Critical Reading	500–620
Range SAT Math	510–630
Range ACT Composite	22–28
Minimum paper TOEFL	500
Minimum internet-based TOEFL	61
Average HS GPA	3.5
% graduated top 25% of class	61
% graduated top 50% of class	90

DEADLINES
Regular	
Priority	2/1
Nonfall registration?	Yes

APPLICANTS ALSO LOOK A AND SOMETIMES PREFER
University of Arizona

FINANCIAL FACTS
Financial Aid Rating	82
Annual in-state tuition	$9,484
Annual out-of-state tuition	$24,784
Room and board	$11,232
Required fees	$674
Books and supplies	$1,081
Average frosh need-based scholarship	$12,181
Average UG need-based scholarship	$12,049
% needy frosh rec. need-based scholarship or grant aid	98
% needy UG rec. need-based scholarship or grant aid	92
% needy frosh rec. non-need-based scholarship or grant aid	14
% needy UG rec. non-need-based scholarship or grant aid	8
% needy frosh rec. need-based self-help aid	57
% needy UG rec. need-based self-help aid	71
% frosh rec. any financial aid	91
% UG rec. any financial aid	85
% UG borrow to pay for school	57
Average cumulative indebtedness	$23,210
% frosh need fully met	23
% ugrads need fully met	19
Average % of frosh need met	70
Average % of ugrad need met	60

ASSUMPTION COLLEGE

500 SALISBURY STREET, WORCESTER, MA 01609-1296 • ADMISSIONS: 508-767-7285 • FAX: 508-799-4412

STUDENTS SAY "..."

Academics

Located in the liberal arts college haven of Worcester, MA, Assumption College is "a tight knit, faith-based community where everyone is part of a family." The small school focuses on "educating aware and prospective young adults to become active and productive members of society while maintaining human core values" through "service, meaningful discussions, and liberal arts classes." Assumption is definitely all about education ("especially if you are a science major"), but there is also "a big push for sports" at this Division II school, and perhaps as a result the college's sense of community is "amazing." "We are one school, we are Assumption," says a student. The "beyond helpful" professors here are "engaging," "approachable," and "have a diversity of teaching styles," as well as being "willing to talk to you whenever you need it and [caring] about your well-being." They "bring their personal experiences into the classroom" to make studies "interesting and enjoyable," and the application of the liberal arts curriculum to small classes means that students "receive a greater impact" from their learning. "The professors here at Assumption all love what they do and it is obvious in the classroom," says a junior. However, some do admit that the school is "limited on the number of courses offered" which "can make getting into classes a little difficult." This "very welcoming and inclusive institution" focuses on giving its student every resource possible to help them succeed and be happy; tutoring is provided at the academic center, campus jobs are "abundant," and the Career and Internship Center admirably aids students in finding jobs after graduation. "Guidance counselors, teachers, [and] coaches are truly a blessing to have at this college," says a student. Overall, Assumption "helps foster well rounded, creative, intelligent and caring young adults to be successful and morally sound in their future endeavors."

Life

Life at Assumption is great. It's "easy to meet new people" and "there is a great sense of belonging." "Assumption does a great job of getting people involved one way or another," says a student. The "beautiful, diverse and secured campus" is "easily recognizable" from brochures, and those who get to take advantage of it "are very invested in academics, sports, extracurriculars, and social experiences." There is always an activity going on and "always something to do if you want to get off campus" in the college town of Worcester. Housing is guaranteed all four years and around 90 percent of students choose to take advantage of this, but "weekends can be dead sometimes" when students leave campus.

The school is "strict as far as drinking goes": Make no mistake, Assumption is "a VERY Catholic school" that "has a very conservative feel." This doesn't mean there's not fun to be had; though during the week "everyone is either in the library or involved in clubs/sports," once Thursday hits "upperclassmen flock to Leits off campus while underclassmen stick to their dorms." "Friday and Saturday are the go to nights for parties" for those that choose to so; however, a large majority go to the events the campus activities board puts on "like Bingo Nights, movie nights, trivia, [and] family feud." "They are really fun and have some amazing prizes like iPads, TV, etc." says a student.

Student Body

Though there's a lack of socioeconomic diversity—"generally middle-class Caucasians [who] are heterosexual"—students can be separated into "student-athletes and non-student-athletes." Most students "come from Catholic upbringings or have attended Catholic school but are not necessarily religious." New England preppy is a classic style; girls are usually seen in "leggings, Ugg boots, a North Face jacket." People here are "generally happy" and "very sociable and approachable" in all aspects of the college; everyone is "courteous and [will] hold doors open or lend you a calculator in class if your forgot yours." Overall, the student body "is like no other": People "genuinely care about each other and it makes for a wonderful experience."

FINANCIAL AID: 508-767-7158 • E-MAIL: ADMISS@ASSUMPTION.EDU • WEBSITE: WWW.ASSUMPTION.EDU

THE PRINCETON REVIEW SAYS

Admissions

Very important factors considered include: academic GPA, application essay. *Important factors considered include:* rigor of secondary school record, recommendation(s), interview, volunteer work, level of applicant's interest. *Other factors considered include:* class rank, standardized test scores, extracurricular activities, talent/ability, character/personal qualities, first generation, alumni/ae relation, racial/ethnic status. SAT or ACT considered if submitted. ACT with or without writing accepted. SAT with or without Essay component accepted. TOEFL required of all international applicants. High school diploma is required and GED is accepted. *Academic units required:* 4 English, 3 math, 2 science, 2 foreign language, 2 history, 5 academic electives. *Academic units recommended:*

Financial Aid

Students should submit: FAFSA. Regular filing deadline is 2/15. The Princeton Review suggests that all financial aid forms be submitted as soon as possible after October 1. *Need-based scholarships/grants offered:* Federal Pell, FSEOG, State scholarships/grants, Private scholarships, College/university scholarship or grant aid from institutional funds. *Loan aid offered:* Direct Subsidized Stafford Loans, Direct Unsubsidized Stafford Loans, Direct PLUS loans, Federal Perkins Loans, State Loans. Applicants will be notified of awards on a rolling basis beginning 2/16. Federal Work-Study Program available. Institutional employment available.

The Inside Word

Around three-quarters of those who apply to Assumption are admitted; keeping in mind that the applicant pool is somewhat self-selective, average students shouldn't have a hard time getting in. Assumption uses the Common Application and submitting standardized test scores is optional.

THE SCHOOL SAYS "..."

From the Admissions Office

"Students flourish at Assumption College. Established in 1904 by the Augustinians of the Assumption, the College is a Catholic coeducational institution known for its classic liberal arts curriculum and strong programs in business and professional studies. Approximately 2,000 undergraduates choose among forty-three majors and forty-eight minors, gaining the depth and breadth of knowledge that is the foundation of lifelong success. The educational experience is grounded in the Catholic intellectual tradition, which cultivates both the intellect and personal values and the academic atmosphere is marked by individual attention and the quest for excellence. Undergraduates and graduate students engage with a highly credentialed faculty and staff in a thriving community that fosters critical intelligence, thoughtful citizenship and compassionate service. With a student/faculty ratio of just 12:1, Assumption's professors challenge students to ask questions, find their answers and grow intellectually, socially and spiritually. Students gain important professional experience through intriguing internships and independent research projects. Ninety-eight percent of our Class of 2015 was employed or in graduate school within six months of graduation.

"Assumption's beautiful 185-acre campus is situated in a residential neighborhood minutes from downtown Worcester, Massachusetts, and 90 percent of the College's undergraduate population lives on campus, with housing guaranteed all four years. The campus is lively seven days a week with academic programming, activities sponsored by student clubs and organizations, community service opportunities, campus ministry programs; and intercollegiate, intramural and club sports. The College's campus in Rome, Italy utilizes the city as the classroom and enriches students' academic and cultural pursuits."

SELECTIVITY

Admissions Rating	77
# of applicants	4,769
% of applicants accepted	76
% of acceptees attending	16
# offered a place on the wait list	289
% accepting a place on wait list	38
% admitted from wait list	15

FRESHMAN PROFILE

Range SAT Critical Reading	510–600
Range SAT Math	510–600
Range ACT Composite	23–26
Minimum paper TOEFL	550
Minimum internet-based TOEFL	80
Average HS GPA	3.4
% graduated top 10% of class	12
% graduated top 25% of class	43
% graduated top 50% of class	81

DEADLINES

Early action	
Deadline	11/1
Notification	12/15
Regular	
Deadline	2/15
Nonfall registration?	Yes

FINANCIAL FACTS

Financial Aid Rating	84
Annual tuition	$35,510
Room and board	$11,264
Required fees	$650
Books and supplies	$1,000
Average frosh need-based scholarship	$20,067
Average UG need-based scholarship	$21,066
% needy frosh rec. need-based scholarship or grant aid	100
% needy UG rec. need-based scholarship or grant aid	100
% needy frosh rec. non-need-based scholarship or grant aid	22
% needy UG rec. non-need-based scholarship or grant aid	16
% needy frosh rec. need-based self-help aid	75
% needy UG rec. need-based self-help aid	81
% frosh rec. any financial aid	98
% UG rec. any financial aid	98
% frosh need fully met	26
% ugrads need fully met	23
Average % of frosh need met	72
Average % of ugrad need met	75

AUBURN UNIVERSITY

108 MARY MARTIN HALL, AUBURN, AL 36849-5149 • ADMISSIONS: 334-844-4080 • FAX: 334-844-6436

CAMPUS LIFE

Quality of Life Rating	94
Fire Safety Rating	89
Green Rating	87
Type of school	Public
Affiliation	No Affiliation
Environment	Town

STUDENTS

Total undergrad enrollment	21,786
% male/female	51/49
% from out of state	34
% frosh from public high school	86
% frosh live on campus	64
% ugrads live on campus	21
# of fraternities (% ugrad men join)	32 (20)
# of sororities (% ugrad women join)	19 (39)
% African American	7
% Asian	2
% Caucasian	84
% Hispanic	3
% Native American	1
% Pacific Islander	<1
% Two or more races	1
% Race and/or ethnicity unknown	1
% international	1
# of countries represented	58

SURVEY SAYS...

Students are happy
Lab facilities are great
Great library
Career services are great
School is well run
Great financial aid
Students are friendly
Students are very religious
Students get along with local community
Students love Auburn, AL
Recreation facilities are great
Lots of beer drinking
Everyone loves the Tigers
Alumni active on campus

ACADEMICS

Academic Rating	72
% students returning for sophomore year	90
% students graduating within 4 years	44
% students graduating within 6 years	73
Calendar	Semester
Student/faculty ratio	19:1
Profs interesting rating	75
Profs accessible rating	82

Most classes have 20–29 students.
Most lab/discussion sessions have
10–19 students.

MOST POPULAR MAJORS

Mechanical Engineering; Business
Administration and Management; Secondary
Education and Teaching

STUDENTS SAY "..."

Academics

Located in the heart of Alabama, Auburn University is called home by more than 20,000 undergraduates, making it one of the state's largest universities. Established before the Civil War, the school's environment is "challenging, captivating, unique and yet still timeless," and students say the university "provides you plenty of resources and opportunities to get a top-notch education." The school channels its efforts into developing young professionals through a "nurturing education, extracurricular involvement opportunities, and professional skill development." Classes may not be easy, "but the work pays off." Professors here are "approachable," "go out of their way to help you learn if you ask them," and "bring material to life." "My professors at Auburn University make it clear that they are there to teach me," says a student. While a few professors are difficult to follow or are more focused on research than on teaching, "graduate student assistants are helpful in assisting professors in understanding how to make material more exciting to learn." Along with "excellent diversity in courses/majors," students say that Auburn provides solid academic support and a faculty that is "always very intelligent on the subjects at hand." The science and the "very challenging engineering programs" benefit from updated facilities and classrooms (though some say that liberal arts programs "get less attention") with the added bonus of "many internship/co-op opportunities advertised and available." "I believe I have received a wonderful education from Auburn University," says a contented student.

Life

This "welcoming place" has "an Old South small town feeling," beautiful campus, and an "amazing new recreation center," where students can work out. There are more than 300 organizations for students to join, and "student involvement is high." Greek life is big here, but "it's definitely possible to fit in without being a part of Greek life." The city of Auburn "has a safe downtown area where students can go to bars" on weekends, and there is a nearby state park where people go for fun. There's also a "good food atmosphere in the community," and Birmingham and Atlanta are always doable options for travel and concerts. Sports (both watching and playing) "drive a ton of campus life and help unite the student body." "Football Saturdays at Auburn are second to none," says a student. "I was looking for a large school with an SEC football team but also a good academic program," says one student athlete within Auburn's famous athletic program. The student voice is also "very respected" among the administration and "can cause tangible change": the Student Government Association "is very strong at Auburn."

Student Body

Many here are "white," "Republican," and "tend to be conservative." The typical student is "friendly," an Alabama native, and "someone who would say 'hello' walking along the concourse to class" or "would lend a hand in a time of need." "There is so much school spirit" here (in no small part due to the football team) and most everyone "is highly obsessed with football," which "has almost a religious following of fans." "Alabama students love Alabama football, Auburn students love Auburn," says one student of the communal loyalty in which one can rest assured that "the Auburn Family has your back."

FINANCIAL AID: 334-844-4634 • E-MAIL: ADMISSIONS@AUBURN.EDU • WEBSITE: WWW.AUBURN.EDU

THE PRINCETON REVIEW SAYS

Admissions

Very important factors considered include: academic GPA, standardized test scores, application essay. *Important factors considered include:* rigor of secondary school record, extracurricular activities, talent/ability, character/personal qualities, first generation, alumni/ae relation, geographical residence, state residency, volunteer work, work experience, level of applicant's interest. *Other factors considered include:* recommendation(s). SAT or ACT required. ACT with Writing required. SAT with or without Essay component accepted. TOEFL required of all international applicants. High school diploma is required and GED is accepted. *Academic units required:* 4 English, 3 math, 2 science, 1 science lab, 3 social studies. *Academic units recommended:* 2 science labs, 1 foreign language, 4 social studies.

Financial Aid

Students should submit: FAFSA. Priority filing deadline is 3/1.The Princeton Review suggests that all financial aid forms be submitted as soon as possible after October 1. *Need-based scholarships/grants offered:* Federal Pell, FSEOG, State scholarships/grants, Private scholarships, College/university scholarship or grant aid from institutional funds. *Loan aid offered:* Direct Subsidized Stafford Loans, Direct Unsubsidized Stafford Loans, Direct PLUS loans, Federal Perkins Loans, Federal Nursing Loans, College/university loans from institutional funds. Applicants will be notified of awards on a rolling basis beginning 10/2. Federal Work-Study Program available. Institutional employment available.

The Inside Word

Auburn admissions officers have nearly 17,000 applications to sort through each year, and admission here is somewhat selective. Applicants are evaluated as individuals, and those who fall short of the average GPA, curricular, and standardized test score standards for incoming freshmen should know that the admissions committee is also looking for those with unique talents and abilities that will contribute substantially to campus life. Letters of recommendation, essays, and extracurricular activities are the make-or-break point for borderline candidates. Applicants' test scores must be submitted directly from the testing agencies.

THE SCHOOL SAYS "..."

From the Admissions Office

"Auburn University is a comprehensive land, sea, and space-grant university serving Alabama and the nation. The university is especially charged with the responsibility of enhancing the economic, social, and cultural development of the state through its instruction, research, and extension programs. In all of these programs, the university is committed to the pursuit of excellence. The university assumes an obligation to provide an environment of learning in which the individual and society are enriched by the discovery, preservation, transmission, and application of knowledge; in which students grow intellectually as they study and do research under the guidance of competent faculty; and in which the faculty develop professionally and contribute fully to the intellectual life of the institution, community, and state. This obligation unites Auburn University's continuing commitment to its land-grant traditions and the institution's role as a dynamic and complex, comprehensive university."

SELECTIVITY

Admissions Rating	85
# of applicants	19,414
% of applicants accepted	78
% of acceptees attending	33

FRESHMAN PROFILE

Range SAT Critical Reading	530–630
Range SAT Math	540–650
Range SAT Writing	520–620
Range ACT Composite	24–30
Minimum paper TOEFL	550
Minimum internet-based TOEFL	79
Average HS GPA	3.8
% graduated top 10% of class	31
% graduated top 25% of class	62
% graduated top 50% of class	89

DEADLINES

Early action	
Deadline	10/1
Notification	10/15
Regular	
Priority	2/1
Deadline	6/1
Notification	2/15
Nonfall registration?	Yes

APPLICANTS ALSO LOOK AT AND SOMETIMES PREFER

University of Florida; University of Georgia; The University of Alabama at Tuscaloosa; Clemson University; Georgia Institute of Technology; University of Mississippi; The University of Tennessee at Knoxville; Louisiana State University

FINANCIAL FACTS

Financial Aid Rating	81
Annual in-state tuition	$8,808
Annual out-of-state tuition	$26,424
Room and board	$12,584
Required fees	$1,616
Books and supplies	$1,200
Average frosh need-based scholarship	$8,635
Average UG need-based scholarship	$7,440
% needy frosh rec. need-based scholarship or grant aid	81
% needy UG rec. need-based scholarship or grant aid	72
% needy frosh rec. non-need-based scholarship or grant aid	15
% needy UG rec. non-need-based scholarship or grant aid	9
% needy frosh rec. need-based self-help aid	66
% needy UG rec. need-based self-help aid	77
% frosh rec. any financial aid	50
% UG rec. any financial aid	44
% UG borrow to pay for school	41
Average cumulative indebtedness	$27,782
% frosh need fully met	19
% ugrads need fully met	13
Average % of frosh need met	50
Average % of ugrad need met	44

AUSTIN COLLEGE

900 North Grand Ave, Suite 6N Sherman, TX 75090-4400 • Admissions: 903-813-3000 • Fax: 903-813-3198

STUDENTS SAY "..."

Academics

"Individual attention" is the name of the game at Austin College. Indeed, the small size of the school allows for a lot of "one-on-one interaction" and provides students with "many opportunities to get involved on campus." Additionally, students are grateful that Austin seems to maintain a healthy financial aid office. A psychology major concurs stating, "This college was very generous in helping fund my education." Undergrads are also excited about Austin's "excellent study abroad program." As one thrilled biology major brags, "I have already traveled to Trinidad for three weeks and I am planning to study in Cuba for three weeks as well as a semester abroad in Australia." Students also rave about the college's "GREAT pre-medicine program," "strong Japanese program" and excellent five year education program. Importantly, undergrads find their professors to be "very accessible." They are generally "willing to help and give us opportunities to advance ourselves outside the classroom as well as inside the classroom." Moreover, professors are "devoted to teaching their students how to think, not memorize." Finally, they "encourage their students to engage the material and ask meaningful questions."

Life

Despite its small size, Austin College is certainly a hotbed of activity. Truly, there are a myriad of clubs and events from which to choose. As one amazed senior shares, "I have played in a woodwind ensemble, done swing dancing and English country dancing, [attended] theater performances, art displays, choir, band and symphony concerts." She continues gushing, "There [have even been] mini carnivals with rock walls, live music, food, and inflatable race courses." And undergrads here are quick to tip their (metaphorical) hats to the Campus Activities Board (CAB) which "[throws] events almost every day." These might include "making wax hands...[and] pumpkin painting." Additionally, "CAB also hosts bigger events such as Kangapalooza where the college brings in three bands to play for the student body." While there are plenty of school events, a handful of students feel that "house parties sponsored by Greek groups are usually what encompass social life at Austin." Some students itching to get off campus are dismayed by hometown Sherman which doesn't seem to offer much beyond "Target and a few book stores." However, others insist there is more than meets the eye. As an optimistic international relations major sums up, "At first, Sherman seemed really small to a big city girl like me. But it really grows on you and now I love it! There are lots of great little hole-in-the-wall restaurants with awesome food. And if you need some city time, Dallas is about an hour away!"

Student Body

Undergrads here emphatically insist that "there is no typical student at AC." As one biology major explains, "Personalities range from frat-tastic jock to the gothic president of the English Country Dancing club." Fortunately, most everyone is "very welcoming." Indeed, "the environment here is so warm and friendly that the students easily fit in." Nevertheless, despite the reported uniqueness of the student body, there are some commonalities to be found. For starters, most undergrads here are "motivated in their studies" as well as "engaged in other extracurricular activities." Many students also describe their peers as "laid back," "pretty liberal" and "open minded." Of course, Austin does net "a lot of local Texas kids." However, there are definitely "some foreign students thrown in [there]" and students appreciate the diversity they bring to campus. And if you're still wary, this junior is moved to assuage your fears, "After coming to campus it doesn't take long to realize that even though most of us call Texas home, we are in no way defined by the Texas stereotype. Don't be deceived; the differences in socio-economic status, religion, political beliefs, and general perspective on life could not be more varied."

AUSTIN COLLEGE

FINANCIAL AID: 903-813-2900 • E-MAIL: ADMISSION@AUSTINCOLLEGE.EDU • WEBSITE: WWW.AUSTINCOLLEGE.EDU

THE PRINCETON REVIEW SAYS

Admissions

Very important factors considered include: rigor of secondary school record, academic GPA. *Important factors considered include:* standardized test scores, application essay, recommendation(s), character/personal qualities. *Other factors considered include:* class rank, interview, extracurricular activities, talent/ability, geographical residence, state residency, religious affiliation/commitment, volunteer work, work experience, level of applicant's interest. SAT or ACT required; SAT Subject Tests considered if submitted. ACT with Writing recommended. TOEFL required of all international applicants. High school diploma is required and GED is accepted. *Academic units required:* 4 English, 3 math, 3 science, 1 science lab, 2 foreign language, 2 social studies, 1 visual/performing arts. *Academic units recommended:* 4 English, 3 math, 4 science, 2 science labs, 2 visual/performing arts.

Financial Aid

Students should submit: FAFSA. Priority filing deadline is 2/1.The Princeton Review suggests that all financial aid forms be submitted as soon as possible after October 1. *Need-based scholarships/grants offered:* Federal Pell, FSEOG, State scholarships/grants, Private scholarships, College/university scholarship or grant aid from institutional funds. *Loan aid offered:* Direct Subsidized Stafford Loans, Direct Unsubsidized Stafford Loans, Direct PLUS loans, Federal Perkins Loans, State Loans. Applicants will be notified of awards on a rolling basis beginning 1/15. Federal Work-Study Program available. Institutional employment available.

The Inside Word

Austin College takes a holistic approach to the admissions game. Indeed, the school does its best to get a feel for who each applicant is beyond his or her GPA and test scores. Therefore, expect your recommendations, extracurricular activities, and essay to be heavily vetted. Additionally, the college is impressed with students who challenge themselves academically. Admissions officers are frequently more impressed with a B in an honors course than an A in a standard college prep class.

THE SCHOOL SAYS "..."

From the Admissions Office

"If you want to be anonymous, choose a different school. But if you dream of connecting with others, exploring the world, and discovering more about yourself, then Austin College is exactly where you belong.

"Learning happens in classroom discussions led by talented professors, dedicated to teaching and passionate about their work, who act as partners in education with students. Faculty and students often work together in research projects and learning opportunities in which sometimes the answers discovered aren't as important as the process of inquiry and discovery.

"Students come to Austin College for exceptional academic offerings in more than fifty-seven areas of study in the humanities, sciences, and social sciences. Over the past 5 years, 82 percent of graduates completed an internship as career preparation. More than 38 percent of first-year alumni attend graduate school with the highest numbers going to medical and law school. Graduates have an 80 percent acceptance rate into healthcare programs. In the last two years, 93 percent of graduates, seeking employment, have found a job after graduation. Many graduates receive prestigious honors like Fulbright grants or Teach for America positions.

"Few schools the size of Austin College offer a greater emphasis on all things global. Sixty percent of the 2015 Graduates had at least one international study experience, either during January Term or a semester abroad program. For the past decade, an average 70 percent of graduates have had an international experience."

SELECTIVITY	
Admissions Rating	87
# of applicants	3,357
% of applicants accepted	54
% of acceptees attending	20

FRESHMAN PROFILE	
Range SAT Critical Reading	530–670
Range SAT Math	540–650
Range SAT Writing	520–640
Range ACT Composite	22–27
Minimum paper TOEFL	550
Average HS GPA	3.6
% graduated top 10% of class	36
% graduated top 25% of class	71
% graduated top 50% of class	93

DEADLINES	
Early decision	
Deadline	11/1
Notification	12/4
Early Action I	
Deadline	12/1
Notification	1/5
Early Action II	
Deadline	1/15
Notification	3/1
Regular	
Deadline	3/1
Notification	4/1
Nonfall registration?	No

APPLICANTS ALSO LOOK AT AND SOMETIMES PREFER
Baylor University; Texas A&M University–College Station; Texas Christian University; Southwestern University

AND RARELY PREFER
University of Dallas

FINANCIAL FACTS	
Financial Aid Rating	85
Annual tuition	$37,130
Room and board	$12,082
Required fees	$185
Average frosh need-based scholarship	$28,997
Average UG need-based scholarship	$27,001
% needy frosh rec. need-based scholarship or grant aid	100
% needy UG rec. need-based scholarship or grant aid	99
% needy frosh rec. non-need-based scholarship or grant aid	55
% needy UG rec. non-need-based scholarship or grant aid	19
% needy frosh rec. need-based self-help aid	69
% needy UG rec. need-based self-help aid	72
% frosh rec. any financial aid	99
% UG rec. any financial aid	98
% frosh need fully met	66
% ugrads need fully met	65
Average % of frosh need met	95
Average % of ugrad need met	94

THE BEST 381 COLLEGES ■ 83

BABSON COLLEGE

231 FOREST STREET, BABSON PARK, MA 02457 • ADMISSION: 781-239-5522 • FAX: 781-239-4006

CAMPUS LIFE

Quality of Life Rating	93
Fire Safety Rating	95
Green Rating	93
Type of school	Private
Affiliation	No Affiliation
Environment	Village

STUDENTS

Total undergrad enrollment	2,141
% male/female	52/48
% from out of state	73
% frosh live on campus	100
% ugrads live on campus	78
# of fraternities (% ugrad men join)	3 (14)
# of sororities (% ugrad women join)	3 (27)
% African American	5
% Asian	12
% Caucasian	38
% Hispanic	10
% Native American	<1
% Pacific Islander	<1
% Two or more races	2
% Race and/or ethnicity unknown	6
% international	26
# of countries represented	77

SURVEY SAYS...

Students are happy
Career services are great
Internships are widely available
School is well run
Students love Babson Park, MA
Everyone loves the Beavers
Active minority support groups

ACADEMICS

Academic Rating	88
% students returning for sophomore year	96
% students graduating within 4 years	85
% students graduating within 6 years	89
Calendar	Semester
Student/faculty ratio	14:1
Profs interesting rating	92
Profs accessible rating	89
Most classes have 30-39 students.	

MOST POPULAR MAJORS

Business Administration and Management

STUDENTS SAY "..."

Academics

A private business school in Massachusetts, Babson College provides a "culture of entrepreneurship" and "fosters collaboration through group work and unconventional assignments." "We live and breathe business," says one business administration major, of the tight-knit, "diverse" group of undergraduate and graduate students on campus. Babson seeks to create an environment of "entrepreneurship among a community of goal-driven and disciplined students," and integral to this vision is the mandatory course Foundations of Management and Entrepreneurship. Through this course first-year Babson "students get to work in small teams to start and run an actual business of their choosing, [and there] is always a friendly competition between all of the companies to make the most profit and unit sales." Students say their "professors are passionate about the course material and bring their real-life experience into the classroom. The academics are rigorous, but worthwhile." With its focus on "experiential" and hands-on learning from day one, Babson employs professors who are "often industry experts with established careers." Students explain that their instructor's "experience leads to broader discussions of why material is important, and they open up their networks to students as we look for internships and jobs." As a "small college, attendance and participation are extremely important," and "professors want to make connections with their students . . . It is not uncommon to hear about professors recommending or referring students to internships and full-time positions with their extensive networks."

Life

Chronically busy Babson students take advantage of the school's policy of not offering classes on Friday and explore "Boston quite often" when they're not participating in the myriad on-campus organizations and clubs. With "so many student organizations, meetings, and events," it's difficult to be bored at Babson, and the business-minded students are often at "work on their own start-ups" or taking an Uber into nearby Wellesley "to blow off some steam." Greek life and sports—both intramural and intercollegiate—play key roles on campus. "The small class sizes make it very easy to make friends and establish new relationships," students explain, and "days without meetings for clubs and organizations are rare." Juggling multiple obligations isn't just a matter of clubs either: "Many students run their own businesses and manage that with school work and social lives."

Student Body

Babson students stress the diversity on campus. This varied population means that "a lot of diverse perspectives are brought about during discussions." At Babson, "wealth on campus is prevalent," and students describe each other as "business savvy, typically type-A over-achievers." But the atmosphere "is not overly competitive. It is collaborative and entrepreneurial" and "all of [the students] are aware that they have the power to shape the future." Even at a school where business is the name of the game, "everybody at Babson seems willing to help whenever they can whether it is emotional support or help with academics." Many "Babson students are already entrepreneurs and businesspeople, and are at school to learn and have access to the numerous resources provided." In short, "the average student at Babson is well read, wildly ambitious, and heavily involved in extracurricular organizations on campus."

FINANCIAL AID: 781-239-4015 • E-MAIL: UGRADADMISSION@BABSON.EDU • WEBSITE: WWW.BABSON.EDU

THE PRINCETON REVIEW SAYS

Admissions

Very important factors considered include: rigor of secondary school record, class rank, academic GPA, standardized test scores, application essay, recommendation(s), extracurricular activities, character/personal qualities. *Important factors considered include: Other factors considered include:* interview, talent/ability, first generation, alumni/ae relation, geographical residence, state residency, racial/ethnic status, volunteer work, work experience, level of applicant's interest. SAT or ACT required. ACT with or without writing accepted. SAT with or without Essay component accepted. TOEFL required of all international applicants. High school diploma is required and GED is accepted. *Academic units required:* 4 English, 4 math, 3 science, 4 foreign language, 4 social studies.

Financial Aid

Students should submit: FAFSA, CSS/Financial Aid PROFILE, Noncustodial PROFILE. Regular filing deadline is 2/15.The Princeton Review suggests that all financial aid forms be submitted as soon as possible after October 1. *Need-based scholarships/grants offered:* Federal Pell, FSEOG, State scholarships/grants, Private scholarships, College/university scholarship or grant aid from institutional funds. *Loan aid offered:* Direct Subsidized Stafford Loans, Direct Unsubsidized Stafford Loans, Direct PLUS loans, State Loans. Applicants will be notified of awards on or about 4/1. Federal Work-Study Program available. Institutional employment available.

The Inside Word

Babson's prominence as a noteworthy undergraduate business school continues to rise. Incoming students are evaluated on their academic performance (high school GPAs and standardized test scores) as well as non-academic factors including leadership, creativity, and enthusiasm. Writing ability is a valued commodity, and prospective students should be ready for the supplemental writing section of the application. Babson offers three fall application plans for first-years—Early Decision, Early Action, and Regular Decision—in addition to a new program, January G.A.P. Enrollment, which allows students to apply for the spring semester.

THE SCHOOL SAYS "..."

From the Admissions Office

"Nationally recognized as the number one school in entrepreneurship for eighteen years, Babson College defines entrepreneurship education for the world. Our learning concepts provide students with the ability to adapt to ever-changing business environments, the experience to hit the ground running upon graduation, and the know-how to discover opportunities that will create economic and social value everywhere. We believe, as do our graduates and their employers, in the value of an integrated approach combined with experiential education. As a business school where one-half of the classes are in liberal arts, Babson emphasizes creativity, innovation, and risk-taking as essential to learning the foundation of business.

"Babson's close-knit community provides students with the opportunity to form close relationships with faculty and staff. An average class size of twenty- nine and student/faculty ratio of ten to one allow faculty to serve as role models and mentors committed to helping our students grow. With about 85 percent holding a doctoral degree, these accomplished business executives, authors, entrepreneurs, scholars, researchers, and artists bring an intellectual diversity and real-world experience that adds depth to Babson's programs. Most importantly, faculty members teach 100 percent of the courses. At Babson, students receive a world-class education that is innovative and creative, yet practical. They study business, learn about leadership, and undertake a transformative life experience preparing them to create an authentic, powerful brand of success. Our students make friends, find mentors, and develop long-lasting relationships that will thrive long after graduation."

SELECTIVITY	
Admissions Rating	94
# of applicants	7,516
% of applicants accepted	26
% of acceptees attending	27
# offered a place on the wait list	1,384
% accepting a place on wait list	43
% admitted from wait list	0
# of early decision applicants	354
% accepted early decision	43

FRESHMAN PROFILE	
Range SAT Critical Reading	580–720
Range SAT Math	620–720
Range SAT Writing	590–660
Range ACT Composite	27–30
Minimum paper TOEFL	600
Minimum internet-based TOEFL	100

DEADLINES	
Early decision	
Deadline	11/1
Notification	12/15
Early action	
Deadline	11/1
Notification	1/1
Regular	
Priority	11/1
Deadline	1/1
Notification	4/1
Nonfall registration?	Yes

FINANCIAL FACTS	
Financial Aid Rating	90
Annual tuition	$48,288
Room and board	$15,376
Books and supplies	$1,050
Average frosh need-based scholarship	$38,761
Average UG need-based scholarship	$36,320
% needy frosh rec. need-based scholarship or grant aid	89
% needy UG rec. need-based scholarship or grant aid	96
% needy frosh rec. non-need-based scholarship or grant aid	11
% needy UG rec. non-need-based scholarship or grant aid	15
% needy frosh rec. need-based self-help aid	84
% needy UG rec. need-based self-help aid	82
% frosh rec. any financial aid	53
% UG rec. any financial aid	50
% UG borrow to pay for school	42
Average cumulative indebtedness	$32,982
% frosh need fully met	60
% ugrads need fully met	55
Average % of frosh need met	98
Average % of ugrad need met	97

BARD COLLEGE (NY)

OFFICE OF ADMISSIONS, ANNANDALE-ON-HUDSON, NY 12504 • ADMISSIONS: 845-758-7472 • FAX: 845-758-5208

STUDENTS SAY "..."

Academics

Bard College is "built on a very unique philosophy of the liberal arts," one that "truly values education for the sake of self-growth." To that end, every student's academic "experience is entirely customizable." Nevertheless, no matter their course load, all undergrads here are taught to think "critically, [to continually ask] questions...and [to follow through on] those questions." But these students wouldn't have it any other way! Certainly, prospective students should take note—the academics here are quite "rigorous." And virtually every major culminates in a massive "senior project" that requires "substantial independent work."

Inside the classroom, students are greeted by "incredible" professors who genuinely "care about teaching and mentoring." They are also "strong researchers as well" and make a concerted effort to "bring their research into [their classes] and into the community." They truly look to "involve students in almost everything they do." As one photography major boasts, "The classes are what make Bard an amazing school. I could not be happier academically."

Life

Though this is a small campus in a small town, there is no lack of engaging activity. For starters, the college itself sponsors "a multitude of cultural events, from having Edward Snowden speak [remotely]...to great bands playing at one of our venues." Bard also has a thriving performing arts scene. "There's probably a student production to see on average every other week or more. Students, [even] as non-majors, can easily produce their own shows. Plus, we have the Fisher Center, a Broadway-sized theatre that often hosts operas, dance troupes, and plays." Undergrads who tend to be more of the outdoorsy type will be thrilled to discover that "Bard is also surrounded by hiking trails, with easy access to our own private waterfall!" Of course, during those cold winter nights, "'Netflix and chill' is a reliable option." Even in inclement weather, "it's generally pretty easy to find people to go build snowmen with or go ice skating." Lastly, for those curious, Bard maintains a "very low-key party scene." A history major further explains, "Most of the larger parties happen at off-campus houses in Red Hook or Tivoli, the two surrounding towns where many students live. It can get repetitive, but I enjoy how you end up seeing/partying with similar people every weekend."

Student Body

When asked to describe their peers, undergrads here are quick to note that their fellow students are "unique, free-spirited, deviant, and epitomize critical thinking." Indeed, the average Bard student loves "intellectual conversations and enjoy[s] rehashing...topics [discussed in class]." An anthropology major further expounds, "We are always critiquing some aspect of the school, then relating this critique to one of the larger societal structures that we live in." Therefore, it's none too surprising when a sociology major tells us that "Bardians are [also] go-getters, self-motivated, driven, and thoughtful. We challenge authority and all social conventions." We've also been assured that "there isn't much competition between students when it comes to grades or classes. People are just supportive of the projects their peers are working on." Many undergrads here readily admit that they "felt in some way like outsiders in high school." Fortunately, once they arrive at Bard, "a lot of people seem to bond over their weirdness." Perhaps this supremely satisfied student puts it best, "I have been spoiled by my friendships here at Bard; I don't know where else I could find people this interesting and relationships this fulfilling."

FINANCIAL AID: 845-758-7526 • E-MAIL: ADMISSION@BARD.EDU • WEBSITE: WWW.BARD.EDU

THE PRINCETON REVIEW SAYS

Admissions

Very important factors considered include: rigor of secondary school record, academic GPA, application essay, recommendation(s), extracurricular activities, talent/ability, character/personal qualities. *Important factors considered include:* volunteer work, work experience. *Other factors considered include:* class rank, standardized test scores, interview, first generation, alumni/ae relation, geographical residence, state residency, religious affiliation/commitment, racial/ethnic status, level of applicant's interest. ACT with or without writing accepted. TOEFL required of all international applicants. High school diploma is required and GED is accepted. *Academic units recommended:* 4 English, 4 math, 4 science, 3 science labs, 4 foreign language, 4 social studies, 4 history.

Financial Aid

Students should submit: FAFSA, CSS/Financial Aid PROFILE, State aid form, Noncustodial PROFILE. Regular filing deadline is 2/15.The Princeton Review suggests that all financial aid forms be submitted as soon as possible after October 1. *Need-based scholarships/grants offered:* Federal Pell, FSEOG, State scholarships/grants, Private scholarships, College/university scholarship or grant aid from institutional funds. *Loan aid offered:* Direct Subsidized Stafford Loans, Direct Unsubsidized Stafford Loans, Direct PLUS loans, Federal Perkins Loans, College/university loans from institutional funds. Applicants will be notified of awards on or about 4/1. Federal Work-Study Program available. Institutional employment available.

The Inside Word

We won't mince words; gaining admission to Bard is definitely competitive. Successful applicants tend to have high school transcripts rife with honors and advanced placement courses. And a strong college prep curriculum is clearly a must. Beyond that, admissions officers want students who appear to be independent thinkers with a thirst for knowledge. After all, those are the type of individuals who will likely take advantage of all Bard has to offer. Lastly, submitting ACT or SAT scores is optional.

THE SCHOOL SAYS "..."

From the Admissions Office

"An alliance with Rockefeller University, the renowned graduate scientific research institution, gives Bardians access to Rockefeller's professors and laboratories and to places in Rockefeller's Summer Research Fellows Program. Almost all our math and science graduates pursue graduate or professional studies; 90 percent of our applicants to medical and health professional schools are accepted.

"The Globalization and International Affairs (BGIA) Program is a residential program in the heart of New York City that offers undergraduates a unique opportunity to undertake specialized study with leading practitioners and scholars in international affairs and to gain internship experience with international-affairs organizations. Topics in the curriculum include human rights, international economics, global environmental issues, international justice, managing international risk, and writing on international affairs, among others. Internships/tutorials are tailored to students' particular fields of study.

"Civic engagement has become a large and growing part of student life at Bard, with a high percentage of students participating in a wide variety of local, national, and international programs sponsored by the college or initiated by students.

"Beyond the central campus, Bard has created global programs and satellite campuses from Berlin to the West Bank, offering students unique opportunities for study abroad and making Bard's student body strongly international."

SELECTIVITY

Admissions Rating	92
# of applicants	7,044
% of applicants accepted	32
% of acceptees attending	20
# offered a place on the wait list	200
% accepting a place on wait list	84
% admitted from wait list	11

FRESHMAN PROFILE

Range SAT Critical Reading	590–690
Range SAT Math	570–680
Minimum paper TOEFL	600
Minimum internet-based TOEFL	100
% graduated top 10% of class	49
% graduated top 25% of class	76
% graduated top 50% of class	96

DEADLINES

Early decision	
Deadline	11/1
Early action	
Deadline	11/1
Notification	1/1
Regular	
Deadline	1/1
Nonfall registration?	No

APPLICANTS ALSO LOOK AT AND OFTEN PREFER
New York University

AND SOMETIMES PREFER
Oberlin College; Reed College; Vassar College

AND RARELY PREFER
Sarah Lawrence College; Skidmore College; Ithaca College; Hampshire College; Macalester College

FINANCIAL FACTS

Financial Aid Rating	84
Annual tuition	$49,226
Room and board	$14,118
Required fees	$680
Books and supplies	$950
Average frosh need-based scholarship	$38,766
Average UG need-based scholarship	$37,785
% needy frosh rec. need-based scholarship or grant aid	98
% needy UG rec. need-based scholarship or grant aid	97
% needy frosh rec. non-need-based scholarship or grant aid	0
% needy UG rec. non-need-based scholarship or grant aid	0
% needy frosh rec. need-based self-help aid	85
% needy UG rec. need-based self-help aid	82
% frosh rec. any financial aid	70
% UG rec. any financial aid	72
% UG borrow to pay for school	54
Average cumulative indebtedness	$28,261
% frosh need fully met	30
% ugrads need fully met	25
Average % of frosh need met	81
Average % of ugrad need met	78

BARD COLLEGE AT SIMON'S ROCK (MA)

84 ALFORD ROAD, GREAT BARRINGTON, MA 01230 • ADMISSIONS: 800-235-7186 • FAX: 413-541-0081

STUDENTS SAY "..."

Academics

There's no one else doing what Bard College at Simon's Rock is doing. The small, selective "early college" aims "to create a good experience for passionate younger students" through small class sizes, engaging class discussion, and "catering to each student as an individual." All 400 Simon's Rock students come to this "haven for young, bright minds" after tenth or eleventh grade, and while half of the students receive an associate's degree after two years and transfer to other institutions, others moderate into the Simon's Rock bachelor's degree program. The small size of the school "allows for almost unlimited rule-bending, as long as it is beneficial," and the "ability to create your own major" is one of the most lauded academic aspects. "No one has ever told me that a project wasn't my place because I'm an undergrad or that I couldn't do something because there wasn't enough oversight," says a student. "I have been constantly encouraged to pursue my interests by way of independent research, tutorials, internships, etc., and given support at every step of the way."

The school's "idyllic location" in the middle of the Berkshire Mountains provides the perfect setting for students who mean to get down to business with their studies, and "the professors here make the difficulty and volume of course work worth it." "They are what is amazing about this school." There will be a lot of writing for any class, but "pretty much all the professors are more than happy to help outside of the classroom." "My chemistry professor became upset when she realized that she wouldn't be able to teach a class for a week due to break," says one student. Classes are very oriented around discussion, typically are less than fifteen students, and "nothing's off the [table] for questioning and examination." Though all who attend here admit that it is "definitely not a walk in the park," they agree that "you will learn an incredible amount and be prepared for the future."

Life

Because it is an early college, the administration "is more strict about normal college pastimes (partying, etc.)," but most students spend time hanging out with friends on campus, or going into town (though "there is very little to do" there). "We're far from a party school, but we make our own fun," says a student of the dry campus. People's hobbies "tend toward the academic and/or geeky," and "fun is a *Doctor Who* viewing party or rehearsing for *Rocky Horror*." "It's not uncommon to go to the dining hall and discuss the anti-feminism of *Twilight* at one table, Occupy Wall Street at another table, and tell chemistry puns at another table." (Though, the food doesn't have many fans: "Each day I feel as if the dining hall food is progressively getting worse.") Many students here study away during their junior year, and student activities are initiated and run by students, "which means that if you want to start a club or activity group, you're given full support." Mainly, Rockers "spend a significant portion of our time studying. We think about work and talk about work."

Student Body

Students come from every end of the spectrum, but they are all here for the same reason: "We were ready to learn, and we weren't going to let a high school diploma stand in our way." The student body is "99 percent genius"; this is a "liberal, open-minded, bright, precocious" group full of "rigor and self-determination." Most of the incoming students are sixteen or seventeen years of age, but "They can still obtain a bachelor's degree in four years, just like at most other undergraduate schools." This is truly a "ragtag bunch of future political workers and the ragtag misfits from high school mixed in with some cool (albeit tough) professors." "I would say there is relatively little pressure to fit in at all, since a lot of us are high school misfits in the first place," says a student. Unsurprisingly, "you get to know your fellow students very well, as the size of the school is very small."

BARD COLLEGE AT SIMON'S ROCK (MA)

FINANCIAL AID: 413-528-7297 • E-MAIL: ADMIT@SIMONS-ROCK.EDU • WEBSITE: WWW.SIMONS-ROCK.EDU

THE PRINCETON REVIEW SAYS

Admissions

Very important factors considered include: rigor of secondary school record, academic GPA, application essay, interview, talent/ability. *Important factors considered include:* recommendation(s), character/personal qualities. *Other factors considered include:* class rank, standardized test scores, extracurricular activities, first generation, alumni/ae relation, volunteer work, work experience, level of applicant's interest. SAT or ACT considered if submitted. ACT with or without writing accepted. TOEFL required of all international applicants. High school diploma or equivalent is not required.

Financial Aid

Students should submit: FAFSA, CSS/Financial Aid PROFILE, State aid form, Noncustodial PROFILE. The Princeton Review suggests that all financial aid forms be submitted as soon as possible after October 1. *Need-based scholarships/grants offered:* Federal Pell, FSEOG, State scholarships/grants, Private scholarships, College/university scholarship or grant aid from institutional funds. *Loan aid offered:* Direct Subsidized Stafford Loans, Direct Unsubsidized Stafford Loans, Direct PLUS loans, Federal Perkins Loans. Applicants will be notified of awards on a rolling basis. Federal Work-Study Program available. Institutional employment available.

The Inside Word

Because Simon's Rock boasts healthy application numbers, it's in a position to concentrate on matchmaking. To that end, admissions officers seek students with independent and inquisitive spirits. Applicants who exhibit academic ambition while extending their intellectual curiosity beyond the realm of the classroom are particularly appealing. Successful candidates typically have several honors and advanced placement courses on their transcripts, as well as strong letters of recommendation and well-written personal statements. An interview is required for all applicants.

THE SCHOOL SAYS "..."

From the Admissions Office

"Bard College at Simon's Rock is the only four-year college of the liberal arts and sciences specifically designed to provide bright, highly motivated students with the opportunity to begin college in a residential environment immediately after the tenth or eleventh grade.

"Students also have the option of entering through two special programs:

"1) Bard Academy at Simon's Rock, the nation's first boarding and day high school program designed specifically to prepare students to enter college at Simon's Rock after two years. The curriculum is created and taught by the same college faculty already noted for engaging younger scholars and provides intellectual challenge. At the end of the 10th grade, students begin their undergraduate studies at the College.

"2) Pathway to Academic Choice and Excellence (PACE) offers a three-year path to the Associate of Arts for students who are ready for the challenge of college at a younger age but need further instruction to advance their English language skills. PACE students receive dedicated instruction leading to proficiency in reading, writing, and speaking American English. Students scoring between 65-99 on the TOEFL are eligible for consideration.

"Approximately half of our students transfer after the sophomore year and complete their junior and senior years of college elsewhere. The most common transfer destinations are Bard College, Brown University, Cornell University, New York University, Smith College, Stanford University, University of California—Berkeley, and The University of Chicago. For those who choose to complete the BA at Simon's Rock, the graduation rate exceeds 90 percent."

SELECTIVITY

Admissions Rating	87
# of applicants	199
% of applicants accepted	89
% of acceptees attending	66
# offered a place on the wait list	0

FRESHMAN PROFILE

Range SAT Critical Reading	640–750
Range SAT Math	610–650
Range SAT Writing	610–700
Range ACT Composite	28–30
Minimum paper TOEFL	600
Minimum internet-based TOEFL	100
Average HS GPA	3.5
% graduated top 10% of class	51
% graduated top 25% of class	20
% graduated top 50% of class	14

DEADLINES

Regular	
Round 1	12/1
Round 2	2/1
Round 3	4/1
Round 4	6/1
Nonfall registration?	Yes

APPLICANTS ALSO LOOK AT AND OFTEN PREFER

Bard College; Boston College; Boston University; Brown University; Columbia University; Cornell University; Eugene Lang College The New School for Liberal Arts; New York University; Northeastern University; University of California—Los Angeles; University of Wisconsin—Madison; Washington University in St. Louis

FINANCIAL FACTS

Financial Aid Rating	81
Annual tuition	$49,102
Room and board	$13,660
Required fees	$1,757
Books and supplies	$1,000
Average frosh need-based scholarship	$32,268
Average UG need-based scholarship	$31,957
% needy frosh rec. need-based scholarship or grant aid	97
% needy UG rec. need-based scholarship or grant aid	99
% needy frosh rec. non-need-based scholarship or grant aid	0
% needy UG rec. non-need-based scholarship or grant aid	0
% needy frosh rec. need-based self-help aid	69
% needy UG rec. need-based self-help aid	71
% frosh rec. any financial aid	90
% UG rec. any financial aid	86
% UG borrow to pay for school	61
Average cumulative indebtedness	$24,098
% frosh need fully met	17
% ugrads need fully met	13
Average % of frosh need met	68
Average % of ugrad need met	71

BARNARD COLLEGE

3009 BROADWAY, NEW YORK, NY 10027 • ADMISSIONS: 212-854-2014 • FAX: 212-854-6220

STUDENTS SAY "..."

Academics

Barnard is a small school, an urban school, a resource-rich school, a school that "offers so many opportunities." In some ways, Barnard College combines all the desirable traits one would want from an all-women's liberal arts college. Located in New York City, here "you get the best of both worlds," both a "small academic setting" as well as having "full access to the Ivy League institution (Columbia University) right across the street." The school's size means it "provides a small, close community" where students will "see familiar faces often." Among those familiar faces are the professors themselves, who are "really engaging and make the material approachable and interesting." Classes are a mix between lectures and discussions, and even in the larger classes professors "definitely make time for students to come talk to them." Students say educators here are adept at "creating an environment to learn from and be inspired by classmates through the discussions held." The "phenomenal" education experience at Barnard may be "challenging and very stressful" at times, but students are "so grateful" for those challenges. And while the school itself may be small, "you can cross Broadway and feel that large, Ivy League University feel." Graduates from Barnard should expect to experience a "transition from a young female college student to an adjusted global citizen."

Life

Finding things to do at Barnard? "It's easy—we live in New York." When you live in "one of the greatest cities on Earth," you are "open to a wide range of things to do such as shows, film festivals, amazing restaurants, etc." As one student puts it, while there is a thriving party scene on campus, "put down your vodka and go to the Met." Students even enjoy free admission to many such attractions. But while the opportunities for entertainment and cultural activities are limitless in a city like New York—the museums, sports venues, book stores, music venues, cultural centers and more are too numerous to list—"a lot of fun events take place on campus." There are a number of clubs on campus, busy students often spend time "just chilling" because "everyone is working or going to office hours, or pursuing an internship, a personal job, etc.," and neighboring Columbia offers a "phenomenal Greek life" for those interested in that scene. No matter their chosen form of distraction from school work and extracurriculars, students here "are intensely dedicated to pursuing their interests, whether that be artistic, academic, pre-professional, or athletic ones."

Student Body

Finding a single trait to define a school full of "cool, creative, confident, well-spoken, and determined" women who are "aware that [they are] in the cosmopolitan NYC" may seem difficult, but the repeated refrain of students makes it clear that there is something that unites Barnard students: They are ambitious. These are "driven, intelligent" women who are "extremely interested, dedicated, and passionate about something." What that something may be varies—"biology, dance, theatre, architecture, economics, or international relations" and more—but the "strong, powerful, intelligent personalities" make them who they are. These "motivated individuals" sometimes "have a tendency to overload," but "all Barnard women are very proactive and use all resources available...to achieve their goals." That said, while students here are "ambitious, driven, and hard workers," it is "not at the cost of physical or mental health: they know how to have fun, too." Barnard women tend to be well-dressed and embrace the cosmopolitan side of New York City. One student comments, "I know of very few students here who feel they don't fit in or haven't found their niche," and maybe that is because a Barnard student is one who is "smart, independent, and ready to take on the world."

FINANCIAL AID: 212-854-2154 • E-MAIL: ADMISSIONS@BARNARD.EDU • WEBSITE: WWW.BARNARD.EDU

THE PRINCETON REVIEW SAYS

Admissions

Very important factors considered include: rigor of secondary school record, academic GPA, application essay, recommendation(s), character/personal qualities. *Important factors considered include:* class rank, standardized test scores, extracurricular activities, talent/ability, volunteer work, work experience. *Other factors considered include:* interview, first generation, alumni/ae relation, geographical residence, racial/ethnic status, level of applicant's interest. ACT with or without writing accepted. SAT with or without Essay component accepted. TOEFL required of all international applicants. High school diploma or equivalent is not required. *Academic units recommended:* 4 English, 3 math, 3 science, 3 foreign language, 3 history.

Financial Aid

Students should submit: FAFSA, CSS/Financial Aid PROFILE, State aid form, Noncustodial PROFILE. Regular filing deadline is 2/15. The Princeton Review suggests that all financial aid forms be submitted as soon as possible after October 1. *Need-based scholarships/grants offered:* Federal Pell, FSEOG, State scholarships/grants, Private scholarships, College/university scholarship or grant aid from institutional funds. *Loan aid offered:* Direct Subsidized Stafford Loans, Direct Unsubsidized Stafford Loans, Direct PLUS loans, Federal Perkins Loans. Applicants will be notified of awards on or about 3/31. Federal Work-Study Program available. Institutional employment available.

The Inside Word

Barnard may have a highly competitive selection process—indeed, early decision applications have increased dramatically in recent years—but you wouldn't know it based on the admissions staff, who are surprisingly open and accessible. It comes as no surprise that the admission committee's expectations are high, given the school's long and impressive tradition of excellence, but those expectations reflect a genuine interest in who potential students are and what's on their minds.

THE SCHOOL SAYS "..."

From the Admissions Office

"Barnard College is a small, distinguished liberal arts college for women that is partnered with Columbia University and located in the heart of New York City. Barnard students are wide ranging in their interests and passions, but they also share in a distinctive experience that creates an enduring bond: they live and learn in an environment where women always come first, where they're surrounded by other smart and inspiring women, and where they have access to a wide array of opportunities, both on and off campus. The Barnard community thrives on high expectations. By setting rigorous academic standards and giving students the support they need to meet those standards, Barnard enables them to discover their own capabilities.

"The college enrolls women from all over the United States and around the world. More than forty countries, including Australia, Brazil, China, Denmark, France, India, Morocco, Russia, Turkey, and Zimbabwe are represented in the student body. Students pursue their academic studies in more than forty majors and are able to cross register at Columbia University. Students may participate in Division I Varsity Columbia University athletic teams, in more than thirty club sports, and in a wide variety of intramural sports, and have access to over 500 student clubs and organizations at Barnard and Columbia.

"Applicants for the entering class must submit scores from the SAT Reasoning test and two SAT Subject Tests of their choice, or the ACT with the writing component."

SELECTIVITY
Admissions Rating	98
# of applicants	6,655
% of applicants accepted	20
% of acceptees attending	49
# offered a place on the wait list	1,195
% accepting a place on wait list	11
% admitted from wait list	5
# of early decision applicants	748
% accepted early decision	43

FRESHMAN PROFILE
Range SAT Critical Reading	640–730
Range SAT Math	620–720
Range SAT Writing	650–740
Range ACT Composite	29–32
Minimum paper TOEFL	600
Minimum internet-based TOEFL	100
Average HS GPA	3.9
% graduated top 10% of class	81
% graduated top 25% of class	94
% graduated top 50% of class	99

DEADLINES
Early decision	
Deadline	11/1
Notification	12/15
Regular	
Deadline	1/1
Notification	4/1
Nonfall registration?	No

APPLICANTS ALSO LOOK AT AND OFTEN PREFER
Brown University; Columbia University; University of Pennsylvania; Yale University; Princeton University; Stanford University

AND SOMETIMES PREFER
Northwestern University; University of Chicago; Wellesley College

AND RARELY PREFER
Boston College; Bryn Mawr College

FINANCIAL FACTS
Financial Aid Rating	94
Average frosh need-based scholarship	$44,840
Average UG need-based scholarship	$40,661
% needy frosh rec. need-based scholarship or grant aid	98
% needy UG rec. need-based scholarship or grant aid	98
% needy frosh rec. non-need-based scholarship or grant aid	0
% needy UG rec. non-need-based scholarship or grant aid	0
% needy frosh rec. need-based self-help aid	100
% needy UG rec. need-based self-help aid	100
% frosh rec. any financial aid	53
% UG rec. any financial aid	48
% UG borrow to pay for school	44
Average cumulative indebtedness	$20,008
% frosh need fully met	98
% ugrads need fully met	98
Average % of frosh need met	100
Average % of ugrad need met	100

BATES COLLEGE

23 Campus Avenue, Lewiston, ME 04240 • Admissions: 207-786-6000 • Fax: 207-786-6025

STUDENTS SAY ". . ."

Academics

Located in Lewiston, Maine, Bates College is a small liberal arts college that invites intellectual exploration and tailors every education to the individual student. This "unbelievably tight-knit community" thrives on an "everyone is welcome" atmosphere and an open classroom environment in which everyone is "challenged to express their opinions, try something new and stand up for a cause." "I've honestly never felt competitive in a class at Bates," says a student. Between academic studies, extracurriculars, volunteering, and employment, students here are known for being "well-rounded, curious, and supportive of all aspects of Bates life." Classes are small here which means that students can really take advantage of their professors' time and attention. The "dynamic" teachers here "make you think and come up with your own opinion about issues." They are "incredibly passionate people who are not afraid to stand on a desk, play devil's advocate, and urge you to think critically about the material you are learning." "The most important thing I've learned so far is how to come up with an intelligent stance on an issue or idea," says a student. A Short Term at the end of the year allows students to explore one subject in depth, and the "flexible calendar" also encourages studying abroad (which the majority of students do). The extensive and "helpful" alumni network demonstrates "a fundamental love for the school," and students are given plenty of additional support through "advising and residential life staff, student leadership opportunities, [and] fun and engaging school-wide traditions." "I couldn't ask for more helpful professors, a more helpful administration, or a variety of classes that suit the needs and requirements of my major," sums up a student.

Life

Bates students are a busy group, but they also appreciate the weekends and having fun with friends. There are "dances, theater productions, and a multitude of other events to go to any day of the week"; students also "really enjoy eating out and going to on-campus events like Wind Down Wednesdays," hosted by various student groups," and "the Village Club Series on Thursdays" when musical groups and performers play for campus. Students say that the Bates security plus a "pretty strict no-hard-alcohol policy" is "quite effective" at restricting underage alcohol consumption as well as maintaining a safe campus environment. The food and dining are "absolutely amazing at Bates": Fare here is "all extremely healthy, organic, and naturally sourced," plus "there's food for every dietary restriction." Opportunities to serve the community surrounding campus are abundant, and students take advantage of the outdoor activities Maine has to offer. The student-run Outing Club, in particular, "hosts events every weekend, from skiing at our nearby mountains to sunrise paddles to backpacking trips" and "has a room full of gear that's free to check out." The nights start early and end early here, mostly because "students want to get up early the next day to ski, hike, or just do something with their day." With Portland and Boston being so close, "you can always switch up your scenery when you need city life."

Student Body

Bates students have a range of interests and passions—"no student does just one thing"—and "are not a judgmental group." Everyone finds their niche, and there "is a ton of crossover and interaction between different people." In order to "fit in" here, a student "just has to be friendly and willing to make new friends." A normal lunch conversation "will span from the divine cheese quesadillas in Commons to the implications of language-use and its impact on creating a culture of apathy and ableism." Many here are New Englanders, so there are a fair number of "really preppy" students, and everyone "enjoys the great outdoors."

FINANCIAL AID: 207-786-6096 • E-MAIL: ADMISSION@BATES.EDU • WEBSITE: WWW.BATES.EDU

THE PRINCETON REVIEW SAYS

Admissions

Very important factors considered include: rigor of secondary school record, class rank, academic GPA, application essay, recommendation(s), extracurricular activities, talent/ability, character/personal qualities, level of applicant's interest. *Important factors considered include:* interview, first generation, geographical residence. *Other factors considered include:* standardized test scores, alumni/ae relation, state residency, racial/ethnic status, volunteer work, work experience. SAT or ACT considered if submitted; SAT Subject Tests considered if submitted. ACT with or without writing accepted. TOEFL required of all international applicants. High school diploma is required and GED is not accepted. *Academic units required:* 4 English, 3 math, 3 science, 2 science labs, 2 foreign language, 3 social studies, 3 history. *Academic units recommended:* 4 English, 4 math, 4 science, 3 science labs, 4 foreign language, 4 social studies, 4 history.

Financial Aid

Students should submit: FAFSA, CSS/Financial Aid PROFILE, Noncustodial PROFILE. Regular filing deadline is 2/15. The Princeton Review suggests that all financial aid forms be submitted as soon as possible after October 1. *Need-based scholarships/grants offered:* Federal Pell, FSEOG, State scholarships/grants, Private scholarships, College/university scholarship or grant aid from institutional funds. *Loan aid offered:* Direct Subsidized Stafford Loans, Direct Unsubsidized Stafford Loans, Direct PLUS loans, Federal Perkins Loans. Applicants will be notified of awards on or about 4/1. Federal Work-Study Program available. Institutional employment available.

The Inside Word

Bates looks for students who challenge themselves in the classroom and beyond. A student's academic rigor, essays, and recommendations may be even more important than his or her GPA and test scores. The essay, in particular, is a chance to stand out—Bates is most interested in what has changed and inspired their applicants. Interviews are encouraged, and candidates who opt out of these face-to-face meetings may place themselves at a disadvantage.

THE SCHOOL SAYS ". . ."

From the Admissions Office

"Bates College is widely recognized as one of the finest liberal arts colleges in the nation. The curriculum and faculty challenge students to develop the essential skills of critical assessment, analysis, expression, aesthetic sensibility, and independent thought. Founded by abolitionists in 1855, Bates graduates have always included men and women from diverse ethnic and religious backgrounds. Bates highly values its study abroad programs, unique calendar (4-4-1), and the many opportunities available for one-on-one collaboration with faculty through seminars, research, service-learning, and the capstone experience of senior thesis. Co-curricular life at Bates is rich; most students participate in club or varsity sports; many participate in performing arts; and almost all students participate in one of more than 110 student-run clubs and organizations. More than two-thirds of alumni enroll in graduate study within ten years.

"The Bates College Admission Staff reads applications very carefully; the high school record and the quality of writing are of particular importance. Applicants are encouraged to have a personal interview, either on campus or with an alumni representative. Students who choose not to interview may place themselves at a disadvantage in the selection process. Bates offers tours, interviews, and information sessions throughout the summer and fall. Drop-ins are welcome for tours and information sessions. Please call ahead to schedule an interview. At Bates, the submission of standardized testing (the SAT, SAT Subject Tests, and the ACT) is not required for admission. After three decades of optional testing, our research shows no differences in academic performance and graduation rates between submitters and nonsubmitters."

SELECTIVITY

Admissions Rating	96
# of applicants	5,044
% of applicants accepted	25
% of acceptees attending	38
# offered a place on the wait list	1,595
% accepting a place on wait list	44
% admitted from wait list	4
# of early decision applicants	589
% accepted early decision	42

FRESHMAN PROFILE

Range SAT Critical Reading	640–720
Range SAT Math	640–710
Range SAT Writing	640–710
Range ACT Composite	29–32
% graduated top 10% of class	69
% graduated top 25% of class	95
% graduated top 50% of class	100

DEADLINES

Early decision	
Deadline	11/15
Notification	12/20
Other ED	
Deadline	11/15
Other ED	
Notification	12/20
Regular	
Deadline	1/1
Notification	4/1
Nonfall registration?	Yes

APPLICANTS ALSO LOOK AT AND OFTEN PREFER

Dartmouth College; Brown University; Williams College

AND SOMETIMES PREFER

Bowdoin College; Middlebury College; Wesleyan University

AND RARELY PREFER

Bucknell University; Connecticut College; Trinity College (CT)

FINANCIAL FACTS

Financial Aid Rating	97
comprehensive fee	$62,540
Books and supplies	$800
Average frosh need-based scholarship	$38,752
Average UG need-based scholarship	$38,921
% needy frosh rec. need-based scholarship or grant aid	100
% needy UG rec. need-based scholarship or grant aid	100
% needy frosh rec. non-need-based scholarship or grant aid	0
% needy UG rec. non-need-based scholarship or grant aid	0
% needy frosh rec. need-based self-help aid	99
% needy UG rec. need-based self-help aid	98
% frosh rec. any financial aid	42
% UG rec. any financial aid	42
% frosh need fully met	100
% ugrads need fully met	100
Average % of frosh need met	100
Average % of ugrad need met	100

BAYLOR UNIVERSITY

One Bear Place #97056, Waco, TX 76798-7056 • Admissions: 254-710-3435 • Fax: 254-710-3436

CAMPUS LIFE

Quality of Life Rating	90
Fire Safety Rating	95
Green Rating	83
Type of school	Private
Environment	City

STUDENTS

Total undergrad enrollment	14,189
% male/female	42/58
% from out of state	27
% frosh live on campus	99
% ugrads live on campus	3
# of fraternities (% ugrad men join)	17 (15)
# of sororities (% ugrad women join)	21 (28)
% African American	7
% Asian	6
% Caucasian	64
% Hispanic	14
% Native American	<1
% Pacific Islander	<1
% Two or more races	5
% Race and/or ethnicity unknown	<1
% international	3
# of countries represented	79

SURVEY SAYS...

Students are happy
Classroom facilities are great
Lab facilities are great
Great library
Career services are great
School is well run
Great financial aid
Students are very religious
Recreation facilities are great
Everyone loves the Bears

ACADEMICS

Academic Rating	81
% students returning for sophomore year	89
% students graduating within 4 years	54
% students graduating within 6 years	70
Calendar	Semester
Student/faculty ratio	15:1
Profs interesting rating	82
Profs accessible rating	84

Most classes have 10–19 students.
Most lab/discussion sessions have 10–19 students.

MOST POPULAR MAJORS
Biology; Psychology; Registered Nursing/
Registered Nurse

STUDENTS SAY "..."

Academics

Located deep in the heart of Texas, Baylor is an educational powerhouse that helps undergraduates "achieve their academic potential" while simultaneously "guiding [and fostering] their moral and Christian values." The university seamlessly "integrates faith and learning" while providing an "uncommonly warm and open environment for any student." Yes, despite the fact that Baylor "is a big school," it still manages to maintain a "small community feel." And this sentiment clearly extends to the classroom. Undergrads gleefully explain that their professors "are always willing to help." What's more, "they actually care about you as an individual and they want you to succeed." One astounded freshman shares, "I heard during orientation that professors are known to invite their students to their home for dinner. I assumed this was mainly in upper-level classes. As a first semester freshman I've already had three offers." Of course, this friendliness doesn't mean that instructors go easy on their students. We've been assured that Baylor academics are "challenging." Thankfully, these professors also know how to make courses "fun and interesting." And they deliver "lectures [that] are understandable, realistic and applicable to both exams and real life." All in all, as another impressed freshman concludes, "Baylor is a school that pushes its students to grow, both intellectually and in their faith, in order to help them pursue the ultimate purpose for their life."

Life

Undergrads at Baylor are quite adept at finding "a good balance" between academics and social life. While they certainly take their schoolwork seriously, many students are quick to take advantage of opportunities outside the classroom as well. For starters, the university has a fairly sporty community and athletic events are quite popular on campus. As one sophomore business major shares, "Football games and tailgating are a must and the basketball games are fun too." Greek life is fairly active and fraternities and sororities certainly "have a strong presence." Many undergrads here are drawn to community service as well. One impressed freshman relays, "Volunteering is a big thing at Baylor, and many of the student organizations actively help out in the community." Undergrads also love the fact that there's "a bowling alley on campus," as well as "cheap movies" continually being screened. Baylor also hosts a number of great events such as "socials, dances...farmers markets, etc." Of course, there's plenty of adventure to be had when students are itching to get off-campus for a bit. For example, Baylor is located near a national park where students love to go for "hammocking, mountain biking, and hiking." And hometown Waco is "just an hour away from both Austin and Dallas so it's easy to make a weekend trip."

Student Body

When it comes to the typical Baylor student, it's probably not terribly surprising to learn that the majority are "most likely Christian." These "bright" and "studious" undergrads are not wholly defined by their faith, however, and many happily report that their peers are "eager to engage with...people of differing convictions." Indeed, a handful of undergrads asserts that "diversity is welcome and appreciated." Of course, that would be expected from a "respectful" and "courteous" student body. As one junior tells us, "There are so many different people here that summing us all up is impossible. Everyone can find someone who absolutely adores them and they become best friends. It's not hard to make friends at all." Hence, Baylor's "outgoing" undergrads seem to "have no problem adapting to college life and responsibilities."

FINANCIAL AID: 254-710-2611 • E-MAIL: ADMISSIONS@BAYLOR.EDU • WEBSITE: WWW.BAYLOR.EDU

THE PRINCETON REVIEW SAYS

Admissions

Very important factors considered include: rigor of secondary school record, class rank, standardized test scores. *Important factors considered include:* academic GPA, application essay, recommendation(s), extracurricular activities, talent/ability, character/personal qualities, level of applicant's interest. *Other factors considered include:* interview, alumni/ae relation, religious affiliation/commitment, volunteer work, work experience. SAT or ACT required. ACT with Writing recommended. TOEFL required of all international applicants. High school diploma is required and GED is accepted. *Academic units required:* 4 English, 4 math, 4 science, 2 science labs, 2 foreign language, 2 social studies, 1 history.

Financial Aid

Students should submit: FAFSA. Priority filing deadline is 3/1.The Princeton Review suggests that all financial aid forms be submitted as soon as possible after October 1. *Need-based scholarships/grants offered:* Federal Pell, FSEOG, State scholarships/grants, Private scholarships, College/university scholarship or grant aid from institutional funds. *Loan aid offered:* Direct Subsidized Stafford Loans, Direct Unsubsidized Stafford Loans, Direct PLUS loans, Federal Perkins Loans, Federal Nursing Loans, State Loans. Applicants will be notified of awards on a rolling basis beginning 3/15. Federal Work-Study Program available. Institutional employment available.

The Inside Word

Securing admission to Baylor is no proverbial walk in the park. Beyond assessing GPA, class rank and standardized test scores, admissions officers closely analyze applications to find students who demonstrate intellectual drive and curiosity. Moreover, they want undergrads who value their faith, demonstrate a commitment to service and a deep desire to become a Baylor Bear. We should also note that certain schools/programs (ex. School of Engineering and Computer Science) maintain additional requirements. Be sure to thoroughly investigate.

THE SCHOOL SAYS "..."

From the Admissions Office

"Baylor University is a private Christian university and a nationally ranked research institution. Baylor is the oldest continuously operating university in Texas and the largest Baptist university in the world. Students come from all fifty states and more than eighty foreign countries. Baylor's nationally recognized academic divisions offer 140 undergraduate degree programs, seventy-five master's degree programs, and forty-one doctoral degree programs. Baylor ranks in the top 10 percent of colleges and universities participating in the National Merit Scholarship program. Baylor is one of the select 10 percent of U.S. colleges and universities with a Phi Beta Kappa chapter. Baylor's undergraduate programs emphasize the central importance of vocation (calling) and service in students' lives, helping them explore their value and role in society. Baylor is a charter member of the Independent 529 Tuition Plan, a prepaid college tuition plan. Baylor's tuition is one of the lowest of any major private university in the Southwest and one of the least expensive in the nation. About 90 percent of Baylor students receive student financial assistance. The approximately 1,000-acre main campus adjoins the Brazos River near downtown Waco, a Central Texas city with a metro area population of 234,000. "

SELECTIVITY

Admissions Rating	89
# of applicants	32,136
% of applicants accepted	44
% of acceptees attending	24
# offered a place on the wait list	4,547
% accepting a place on wait list	22
% admitted from wait list	13

FRESHMAN PROFILE

Range SAT Critical Reading	560–650
Range SAT Math	580–670
Range SAT Writing	530–640
Range ACT Composite	25–30
Minimum paper TOEFL	540
Minimum internet-based TOEFL	76
% graduated top 10% of class	42
% graduated top 25% of class	75
% graduated top 50% of class	97

DEADLINES

Early action	
Deadline	11/1
Notification	1/15
Regular	
Deadline	2/1
Nonfall registration?	Yes

FINANCIAL FACTS

Financial Aid Rating	83
Annual tuition	$37,996
Room and board	$11,754
Required fees	$4,010
Books and supplies	$1,444
Average frosh need-based scholarship	$22,926
Average UG need-based scholarship	$21,228
% needy frosh rec. need-based scholarship or grant aid	100
% needy UG rec. need-based scholarship or grant aid	97
% needy frosh rec. non-need-based scholarship or grant aid	99
% needy UG rec. non-need-based scholarship or grant aid	92
% needy frosh rec. need-based self-help aid	81
% needy UG rec. need-based self-help aid	82
% frosh rec. any financial aid	98
% UG rec. any financial aid	93
% frosh need fully met	17
% ugrads need fully met	16
Average % of frosh need met	70
Average % of ugrad need met	65

BECKER COLLEGE

61 SEVER STREET, WORCESTER, MA 01609 • ADMISSIONS: 508-373-9400 • E-MAIL: ADMISSIONS@BECKER.EDU

CAMPUS LIFE

Quality of Life Rating	84
Fire Safety Rating	88
Green Rating	65
Type of school	Private
Affiliation	No Affiliation
Environment	City

STUDENTS

Total undergrad enrollment	2,148
% male/female	39/61
% from out of state	34
% frosh from public high school	65
% frosh live on campus	79
% ugrads live on campus	40
% African American	7
% Asian	2
% Caucasian	70
% Hispanic	9
% Native American	<1
% Pacific Islander	<1
% Two or more races	3
% Race and/or ethnicity unknown	7
% international	1
# of countries represented	23

SURVEY SAYS...

Students are happy
Students are friendly
Easy to get around campus

ACADEMICS

Academic Rating	70
% students returning for sophomore year	74
% students graduating within 4 years	17
% students graduating within 6 years	28
Calendar	Semester
Student/faculty ratio	17:1
Profs interesting rating	71
Profs accessible rating	69

Most classes have 20–29 students.
Most lab/discussion sessions have
10–19 students.

MOST POPULAR MAJORS

Game and Interactive Media Design;
Registered Nursing/Registered Nurse;
Business Administration and Management

STUDENTS SAY "..."

Academics

At Becker College, a private institution founded in 1784 in the second largest city in New England, undergrads truly feel that their school is dedicated to "helping students achieve their dreams." Students say that the college prides itself on providing a "personal education," one that helps you "push yourself to do your best." And it offers a "small, close-knit community" where everybody can get to know their peers. Academically, Becker allows students the opportunity to pursue a number of great disciplines. Of course, we'd be remiss if we didn't highlight the "outstanding" nursing program and the "very well established and highly successful pre-veterinary program." In addition, the college has "one of the best game design programs in the country." Inside the classroom, undergrads love that so many of their courses involve "one-on-one interaction and class discussions." There's no fear of languishing through boring lectures here! And, certainly, that can be attributed to "great" professors who go out of their way to "include real life examples" in their teaching. Perhaps even more essential, the instructors at Becker "are all very nice and genuinely care about their students' success." An animal care major shares that "all of my professors are very thorough and answer all my questions and concerns. They are easy to meet up with outside of classes." And a fellow animal care student summarizes her classroom experience by stating, "The professors dedicate a lot of their time to make sure that we are studying and working to the best of our abilities."

Life

Becker maintains "a 50/50 split between commuters and residents." However, it's certainly possible to seek out some fun on the weekends. Given Becker's amazing game design program, it's no surprise that "everybody plays video games here." Beyond simply cozying up with an X-Box, undergrads can also be found playing "Magic: The Gathering," and some ingenious students have even "made their own card games." Thankfully, even if you're not a gamer, you'll still be able to find activities. For example, many undergrads tend to congregate by "the pool tables in the student center." There are also plenty of clubs to join like the Lambing Club, fencing club, and dance team. And Becker even "sponsors trips every weekend." There is a moderate amount of alcohol consumption, but it doesn't seem to dominate campus life. A nursing student explains, "There are parties off campus, and I do enjoy going to them, but a lot of people choose not to drink." Finally, students enjoy taking advantage of the city of Worcester's many shopping and dining options.

Student Body

Becker undergrads tend to think very highly of their peers. And they assure us that anyone who chooses to attend can "make friends very quickly." This can certainly be attributed to the fact that "almost everyone is easy to talk to" as well as "easygoing." Even shy students can find their place here. The trick is simply to get involved. As one veterinarian science major explains, "Students fit in very well through sports teams and other activities and clubs outside the classroom." Despite having the adjective "nerd" bandied about, we're told that "the campus holds a diverse student body with many different interests." And, if "you play sports, video games, or share a love for animals, you'll fit in." Lastly, a nursing student shares, "what we all have in common is our dedication to our studies and our school. We all work hard in class."

FINANCIAL AID: 508-373-9440 • E-MAIL: FINANCIALAID@BECKER.EDU • WEBSITE: WWW.BECKER.EDU

THE PRINCETON REVIEW SAYS

Admissions

Very important factors considered include: rigor of secondary school record, academic GPA, standardized test scores. *Important factors considered include:* class rank, recommendation(s). *Other factors considered include:* application essay, interview, extracurricular activities, alumni/ae relation, volunteer work, work experience, level of applicant's interest. SAT or ACT required. ACT with or without writing accepted. SAT with or without Essay component accepted. TOEFL required of all international applicants. High school diploma is required and GED is accepted. *Academic units recommended:* 4 English, 3 math, 3 science, 2 science labs, 2 foreign language, 2 social studies, 2 history.

Financial Aid

Students should submit: FAFSA. Priority filing deadline is 3/15.The Princeton Review suggests that all financial aid forms be submitted as soon as possible after October 1. *Need-based scholarships/grants offered:* Federal Pell, FSEOG, State scholarships/grants, Private scholarships, College/university scholarship or grant aid from institutional funds. *Loan aid offered:* Direct Subsidized Stafford Loans, Direct Unsubsidized Stafford Loans, Direct PLUS loans, State Loans. Applicants will be notified of awards on a rolling basis beginning 3/15. Federal Work-Study Program available. Institutional employment available.

The Inside Word

Applicants interested in attending Becker must have taken a college preparatory curriculum. And, to be considered strong candidates, they need to have earned a minimum GPA of 3.0. While the essay and letter of recomendation are optional, Becker says that if submitted they are useful in considering each applicant's personal strengths and achievements.

THE SCHOOL SAYS " . . ."

From the Admissions Office

"Becker College offers master's, bachelor's and select associate's degrees in a range of disciplines, and adult learning programs. Becker College students are engaged socially, academically, and athletically. Our students receive a transformational learning experience that prepares them to thrive, contribute to, and lead in a global society. We emphasize global citizenship: knowledge of other world regions and cultures, familiarity with international issues, and cultivating skills to work effectively in cross-cultural environments. These skills are learned while engaging in all aspects of the college—from academics, community service, and student leadership, to campus activities, clubs, and social interaction. We also are committed to preparing students to be world ready for the rapidly changing and complex job market by offering unique, trans-disciplinary career pathways and learning experiences, and the development of the agile mindset in all graduates. We are proud of our 95 percent placement rate for employment or further study.

"Our admissions process reflects the Becker College philosophy that each student is a unique individual. Because of this, our requirements allow you to put your best foot forward and provide as much information as possible about who you are, what you hope to accomplish during your time at Becker College, and what you hope to do upon graduation.

"The admissions process is personal and unique for each applicant. To be considered for admission, applicants must submit a completed application along with an official high school transcript and official SAT/ACT test score results. Transfer students must submit an official college transcript. Admission requirements vary by program.

"Due to the rigorous admission standards for many of our programs, the most academically qualified applicants will be selected for admission."

SELECTIVITY

Admissions Rating	79
# of applicants	3,258
% of applicants accepted	67
% of acceptees attending	19
# offered a place on the wait list	0

FRESHMAN PROFILE

Range SAT Critical Reading	450–550
Range SAT Math	450–560
Range SAT Writing	430–540
Range ACT Composite	19–25
Minimum paper TOEFL	550
Average HS GPA	3.1

DEADLINES

Early decision	
Deadline	11/15
Notification	12/15
Early action	
Deadline	11/15
Notification	12/15
Regular	
Priority	2/15
Rolling	
Nonfall registration?	Yes

FINANCIAL FACTS

Financial Aid Rating	80
Annual tuition	$32,107
Room and board	$12,400
Required fees	$1,580
Books and supplies	$960
Average frosh need-based scholarship	$9,038
Average UG need-based scholarship	$8,410
% needy frosh rec. need-based scholarship or grant aid	75
% needy UG rec. need-based scholarship or grant aid	68
% needy frosh rec. non-need-based scholarship or grant aid	98
% needy UG rec. non-need-based scholarship or grant aid	94
% needy frosh rec. need-based self-help aid	93
% needy UG rec. need-based self-help aid	93
% frosh rec. any financial aid	100
% UG rec. any financial aid	88
% frosh need fully met	10
% ugrads need fully met	10
Average % of frosh need met	64
Average % of ugrad need met	63

BELLARMINE UNIVERSITY

2001 NEWBURG ROAD, LOUISVILLE, KY 40205 • ADMISSIONS: 502-272-8131 • TOLL-FREE: 800-274-4723 • FAX: 502-272-8002

CAMPUS LIFE

Quality of Life Rating	93
Fire Safety Rating	96
Green Rating	60*
Type of school	Private
Affiliation	Roman Catholic
Environment	Metropolis

STUDENTS

Total undergrad enrollment	2,651
% male/female	35/65
% from out of state	33
% frosh from public high school	74
% frosh live on campus	71
% ugrads live on campus	43
# of fraternities (% ugrad men join)	1 (1)
# of sororities (% ugrad women join)	1 (1)
% African American	4
% Asian	2
% Caucasian	85
% Hispanic	3
% Native American	<1
% Pacific Islander	<1
% Two or more races	3
% Race and/or ethnicity unknown	2
% international	1
# of countries represented	14

SURVEY SAYS...

Students are happy
Internships are widely available
School is well run
Students get along with local community
Students love Louisville, KY
Everyone loves the Knights
Alumni active on campus

ACADEMICS

Academic Rating	80
% students returning for sophomore year	81
% students graduating within 4 years	51
% students graduating within 6 years	67
Calendar	Semester
Student/faculty ratio	12:1
Profs interesting rating	86
Profs accessible rating	87

Most classes have 10–19 students.
Most lab/discussion sessions have
  10–19 students.

MOST POPULAR MAJORS
Psychology; Registered Nursing/Registered
Nurse; Kinesiology and Exercise Science

STUDENTS SAY "..."

Academics

Located at the edge of Louisville, this small Catholic university offers fifty majors and "seeks to benefit the public interest, to help create the future, and to improve the human condition." A "superb teaching staff," a recently renovated library, and an Academic Resource Center with free tutoring cohere to deliver a "challenging but rewarding" academic experience for students. The nursing program is a big draw here, as are Bellarmine's study abroad programs in sixty-eight countries, which more than a third of students avail themselves of. Generous financial aid only sweetens the pot. In line with its mission, Bellarmine University "seeks to train its students in the love of truth and equips them with the skills and tools necessary (e.g. critical thinking, problem solving) to live an enriched life."

The "insightful and dedicated" professors are almost always available to answer questions or concerns, and "want their students to pass their class with as much knowledge as possible." Because of the small class sizes ("I have one class with seven students," reports an actuarial science major), students are able to have one-on-one discussions with their professors. Most professors at Bellarmine "even provide their personal cell phones to students on their syllabi." This access to professors "really [establishes] an ability to grow closer to future employers and be willing to open up with them about issues, concerns, or ideas." Material is often taught through real world applications, and many teachers will even "help you find internships and jobs." Though students admit that some adjunct professors can be below par, "Bellarmine takes their course evaluations pretty seriously and assesses the situation quickly."

Life

People here are "very studious" during the week, but weekends offer plenty of options for socializing. A major hub of the city (Bardstown Road) is nearby, providing lots of little shops, restaurants, and bars, and the campus is close to the Louisville Zoological Garden, a park where students can often be found "playing and hanging out." The university also coordinates off-campus actives such as "Knight at the Movies" (the knight is Bellarmine's mascot), ice skating, and concerts, and students can take advantage of the Louisville Connections program, which offers "free tickets to events or places around Louisville, such as to Dracula at Actors Theatre, a day at Kentucky Kingdom, or a day horseback riding."

On campus, most people "hang around Cafe Ogle in between classes, sipping on coffee and working on their laptops." Bellarmine's men's basketball team draws huge crowds, and the school has "a niche, club or activity for everyone" (and "encourages and supports any club a student would like to create"). There are also events like "Late Knight Bingo, which is a huge Bingo party where students can win really awesome prizes," Homecoming, and "Ball on the Belle (a Halloween dance on the [steamboat] Belle of Louisville)." The campus itself is both beautiful and "small enough to be easily traversed if you only have 10 minutes between classes and need to be across campus."

Student Body

Though mostly white and from Kentucky and neighboring states, this is a socially wide-ranging group considering the small size of the student body, which naturally allows "blobbing of the social groups." The school is "welcoming to every single person and makes an effort to include everyone." "We are exposed to different cultures and customs from around the world seeing that our student body is so diverse," says a student. "I can't say I've ever met a stranger," says a student. Everyone is always willing to help and "comfort you with just a simple smile on their face." The strong athletic programs are never placed above academics, and "most all the athletes are also amazing students."

FINANCIAL AID: 502-452-8124 • E-MAIL: ADMISSIONS@BELLARMINE.EDU • WEBSITE: WWW.BELLARMINE.EDU

THE PRINCETON REVIEW SAYS

Admissions

Very important factors considered include: rigor of secondary school record, academic GPA, standardized test scores, recommendation(s), character/personal qualities, level of applicant's interest. *Important factors considered include:* class rank, extracurricular activities. *Other factors considered include:* application essay, interview, talent/ability, first generation, alumni/ae relation, geographical residence, state residency, racial/ethnic status, volunteer work, work experience. SAT or ACT required. ACT with or without writing accepted. SAT with or without Essay component accepted. TOEFL required of all international applicants. High school diploma is required and GED is accepted. *Academic units required:* 4 English, 3 math, 3 science, 2 science labs, 2 foreign language, 2 social studies, 1 history, 5 academic electives. *Academic units recommended:* 4 English, 4 math, 4 science, 2 science labs, 2 foreign language, 3 social studies, 2 history, 7 academic electives.

Financial Aid

Students should submit: FAFSA. Priority filing deadline is 2/1. The Princeton Review suggests that all financial aid forms be submitted as soon as possible after October 1. *Need-based scholarships/grants offered:* Federal Pell, FSEOG, State scholarships/grants, Private scholarships, College/university scholarship or grant aid from institutional funds. *Loan aid offered:* Direct Subsidized Stafford Loans, Direct Unsubsidized Stafford Loans, Direct PLUS loans, Federal Perkins Loans, College/university loans from institutional funds. Applicants will be notified of awards on a rolling basis beginning 3/15. Federal Work-Study Program available. Institutional employment available.

The Inside Word

Admissions at Bellarmine University is relatively competitive. However, as you would expect from their mission statement, the admissions committee takes a holistic approach to applications, and is looking for a well-rounded candidate whose qualifications reflect more than the sum total of a GPA and test scores. Recommendations and personal statements—which should present a strong picture of the student's educational goals—volunteer experiences, and extracurricular commitments, hold significant weight. Candidates with strong grades and diverse interests are likely to earn acceptance.

THE SCHOOL SAYS "..."

From the Admissions Office

"Bellarmine University prepares students for success through a liberal arts education, combined with training for mastery in a specialized area. We offer more than fifty majors in the arts and sciences, humanities, education, communication, business, environmental studies, nursing and health science, plus graduate programs in nursing, education, physical therapy, business and communication. We engage students in state-of-the-art classrooms and expand their horizons through internship and study abroad opportunities. Bellarmine delivers this world-class education just five miles from downtown Louisville, the nation's sixteenth largest city. The 175-acre campus is set in a safe, historic and eclectic neighborhood, and features a fitness center, tennis courts, athletic fields and two new dining halls. With more than fifty clubs and organizations, twenty NCAA Division II athletic teams, plus Division I men's lacrosse, Bellarmine offers a variety of recreational opportunities for all students. Students who reside on campus also find a Bellarmine difference in the living arrangements. From traditional residence halls to apartment-style and suite living arrangements, students have many housing options to choose from; the newest residence halls surround a Tuscan-style piazza. As Bellarmine attracts more residential students, the university has created more gathering spaces for them, such as the café on the ground floor of the Siena Primo residence hall. New learning communities cater to residents and commuters alike, offering opportunities for focused, collaborative studies on topics such as leadership, healthcare, science and technology."

SELECTIVITY

Admissions Rating	77
# of applicants	5,885
% of applicants accepted	84
% of acceptees attending	14

FRESHMAN PROFILE

Range SAT Critical Reading	495–590
Range SAT Math	500–610
Range ACT Composite	22–27
Minimum paper TOEFL	550
Minimum internet-based TOEFL	80
Average HS GPA	3.5
% graduated top 10% of class	25
% graduated top 25% of class	59
% graduated top 50% of class	85

DEADLINES

Early action	
Deadline	11/1
Notification	11/15
Regular	
Priority	2/1
Deadline	8/15
Nonfall registration?	Yes

APPLICANTS ALSO LOOK AT

Butler University; Centre College; Indiana University—Bloomington; Miami University; University of Kentucky

FINANCIAL FACTS

Financial Aid Rating	81
Annual tuition	$36,210
Room and board	$11,360
Required fees	$1,440
Books and supplies	$788
Average frosh need-based scholarship	$23,542
Average UG need-based scholarship	$22,364
% needy frosh rec. need-based scholarship or grant aid	100
% needy UG rec. need-based scholarship or grant aid	98
% needy frosh rec. non-need-based scholarship or grant aid	35
% needy UG rec. non-need-based scholarship or grant aid	33
% needy frosh rec. need-based self-help aid	66
% needy UG rec. need-based self-help aid	66
% frosh rec. any financial aid	100
% UG rec. any financial aid	91
Average cumulative indebtedness	$30,110
% frosh need fully met	23
% ugrads need fully met	21
Average % of frosh need met	77
Average % of ugrad need met	75

BELOIT COLLEGE

700 COLLEGE STREET, BELOIT, WI 53511 • ADMISSIONS: 608-363-2500 • FAX: 608-363-2075

STUDENTS SAY "..."

Academics

A small liberal arts college in southern Wisconsin, Beloit College offers students "small class sizes, [and] expansive study abroad opportunities" in an academic environment "that encourages debate and discovery." Beloit "embraces individuality" by giving students "freedom to study what they are passionate about." The student-designed "academic paths really can be customized to suit every student's needs, interests, and goals." One student explains that Beloit cultivates "critical thinkers who can put the liberal arts in practice." The college curriculum stresses "intensive essay writing and an emphasis on self identity." One molecular biology major characterizes this approach by explaining, "There is no such thing as a one-sided problem—at Beloit we ask the hard questions and approach solutions in a multidisciplinary manner that requires critical thinking, collaboration, and creativity." Beloiters describe their academic experiences as "nothing short of phenomenal." As one student explains, "My first day of classes teachers already knew my name by the time I sat down at the desk." Students benefit from "many one-on-one experiences, hands-on classes, and project-based learning." Because of the low student-to-faculty ratio and "motivated student body, it is possible to have close relationships with faculty that make for a more enriching college experience." And students relish those relationships, describing their professors as "easily accessible," "dynamic and knowledgeable." "They have different ways of making us learn and are generally nice and open," one student notes. Beloit professors also prove to be "very good resources for helping you with research, internships, and graduate school applications and program decisions." Students appreciate that their professors "bring unique perspectives to class material, and the small class size allows them the flexibility to tailor the courses to their students."

Campus Life

Beloit is "decorated by its open, welcoming community." Students say that "there is a lot of freedom for students to learn from their mistakes while living on campus and to make their own decisions. Students at Beloit are responsible for taking initiative in their decisions to learn, both in the classroom and out." Students report that there is a fair amount of "drinking on the weekend" but that "it's usually done pretty safely." Even though it is a small school, there is plenty on campus to keep students occupied: "Whether it's a Greek event, Black Lives Matter panel, new movie screenings, school sponsored trip to a haunted house or musical, or our professors' band is playing in the quad, there is always something going on." Sports and extracurricular activities are also popular as "everyone is a part of at least one club, and usually several." As spring rolls around students look forward "to spring day," a day without classes when students enjoy "giant inflatable bouncy houses, caricature artists, free junk food, and the martial arts demonstration."

Student Body

Many students celebrate the "outstanding diversity of the student body," including "a large international student population on campus and domestic students [who] come from all over the United States." Others point out that, "while there is diversity on campus, [. . .] the campus is also overwhelmingly white." Beloiters are predominantly liberal and "very engaged students and citizens, who are passionate about various causes and their academics." Most agree that students aren't afraid to address tough subjects and seek out "different opinions, backgrounds, and ideas that allow [them] to explore things outside of [their] comfort zone socially, personally, and intellectually." Even for "students who have felt out of place before" arriving at college, Beloit provides "a safe space to learn." "Beloit College students are a mixed bunch." One student explains, "[We're] unafraid to be different, and aesthetically unmatched by any other student body."

FINANCIAL AID: 608-363-2663 • E-MAIL: ADMISS@BELOIT.EDU • WEBSITE: WWW.BELOIT.EDU

THE PRINCETON REVIEW SAYS

Admissions

Very important factors considered include: rigor of secondary school record, academic GPA, application essay, recommendation(s). *Important factors considered include:* class rank, extracurricular activities, talent/ability. *Other factors considered include:* standardized test scores, interview, character/personal qualities, first generation, alumni/ae relation, volunteer work, work experience, level of applicant's interest. SAT or ACT required for some. ACT with or without writing accepted. SAT with or without Essay component accepted. High school diploma is required and GED is accepted. *Academic units recommended:* 4 English, 3 math, 3 science, 3 science labs, 3 foreign language, 4 social studies.

Financial Aid

Students should submit: FAFSA. Regular filing deadline is 3/1.The Princeton Review suggests that all financial aid forms be submitted as soon as possible after October 1. *Need-based scholarships/grants offered:* Federal Pell, FSEOG, State scholarships/grants, Private scholarships, College/university scholarship or grant aid from institutional funds. *Loan aid offered:* Direct Subsidized Stafford Loans, Direct Unsubsidized Stafford Loans, Direct PLUS loans, Federal Perkins Loans, College/university loans from institutional funds. Applicants will be notified of awards on a rolling basis beginning 3/1. Federal Work-Study Program available. Institutional employment available.

The Inside Word

Beloit wants to see a rigorous academic transcript but also emphasizes a holistic approach that focuses on getting to know the student behind the application. The admission office prefers to receive a letter of recommendation from a teacher who taught you during your junior yet, but it is most important to select someone who can provide the most insight to you as a student. Standardized test scores are optional for most applicants. Interviews can be arranged through Skype by contacting the school, and Beloit accepts ZeeMee. com profiles in an effort to get to know applicants better.

THE SCHOOL SAYS "..."

From the Admissions Office

"Beloiters spend four years challenged to explore their passions, excel in their studies, and apply the lessons of the classroom to the larger world, in their careers, and in service to others. That focus—putting the liberal arts into practice—has long set this college and its graduates apart. Study abroad, internships, research, service, and work opportunities are typical examples of the ways the Beloit experience extends beyond the classroom. Beloit students are more apt to value learning for its own sake and at the same time, understand the connection between college and the rest of their lives as citizens of the world.

"Beloit College uses the Common Application exclusively. Although students must submit test scores from the ACT or SAT, standardized test scores are less important than the strength of the academic program and performance, the essays, and recommendations. Beloit offers one binding early decision plan with a deadline of November 1 and notification by November 30; and two nonbinding early action plans with deadlines of either November 1 or December 1; notification is six weeks hence. Applicants who wish to be considered for merit scholarships are urged to apply under one of the early action plans. The preferred deadline for regular decision applicants in January 15."

SELECTIVITY	
Admissions Rating	86
# of applicants	3,552
% of applicants accepted	69
% of acceptees attending	16
# offered a place on the wait list	81
% accepting a place on wait list	40
% admitted from wait list	9

FRESHMAN PROFILE	
Range SAT Critical Reading	540–695
Range SAT Math	540–645
Range ACT Composite	24–30
Minimum paper TOEFL	550
Minimum internet-based TOEFL	80
Average HS GPA	3.4
% graduated top 10% of class	29
% graduated top 25% of class	64
% graduated top 50% of class	91

DEADLINES	
Early decision	
Deadline	11/1
Notification	11/30
Other ED	
Deadline	11/1
Other ED	
Notification	11/30
Early action	
Deadline	11/1
Notification	12/15
Regular	
Priority	1/15
Nonfall registration?	Yes

**APPLICANTS ALSO LOOK AT
AND OFTEN PREFER**
Carleton College

AND SOMETIMES PREFER
Grinnell College; Macalester College

AND RARELY PREFER
Ripon College

FINANCIAL FACTS	
Financial Aid Rating	89
Annual tuition	$44,590
Room and board	$7,890
Required fees	$460
Books and supplies	$1,000
Average frosh need-based scholarship	$31,060
Average UG need-based scholarship	$28,199
% needy frosh rec. need-based scholarship or grant aid	99
% needy UG rec. need-based scholarship or grant aid	98
% needy frosh rec. non-need-based scholarship or grant aid	52
% needy UG rec. non-need-based scholarship or grant aid	51
% needy frosh rec. need-based self-help aid	81
% needy UG rec. need-based self-help aid	79
% frosh rec. any financial aid	99
% UG rec. any financial aid	99
% UG borrow to pay for school	70
Average cumulative indebtedness	$31,308
% frosh need fully met	31
% ugrads need fully met	32
Average % of frosh need met	95
Average % of ugrad need met	94

BENNINGTON COLLEGE

OFFICE OF ADMISSIONS, BENNINGTON, VT 05201-6003 • ADMISSIONS: 802-440-4312 • FAX: 802-440-4320

STUDENTS SAY "..."

Academics
Bennington has a rep for "academic freedom" and creativity, driven by its Plan Process, which allows students to determine their own course of study, which "gives you agency in every aspect of your education." Faculty advisors and committees provide support and guidance throughout the process, and students receive "detailed, written evaluation" instead of grades (professors will provide letter grades at students' request, to help complete graduate school applications). One student praises the Plan Process for giving her the chance "to carve my own path for my education and have a close connection to my faculty." "Everyone at Bennington is encouraged and determined to be themselves and pursue their individual interests." Within Bennington's "tight community," "students are active participants in the educational process, learning to take initiative, self-advocate, and approach work with intention." The faculty "put their soul into the classes," which enjoy an 9:1 student/professor ratio. "My professors are engaging, brilliant, motivated, and present. I'm grateful to have them as my mentors." "Professors are well-informed, enthusiastic, and clearly love their jobs." Informally, "there is an unspoken rule that all professors go by their first names; this really fosters a friendly and equal relationship between teachers and students." "Classes are strongly discussion based" and the "small class sizes make it so you receive a lot of personalized attention in and out of class." While the college demonstrates "remarkable adherence to the real liberal arts (grammar, logic, and rhetoric)," Bennington provides a forward-looking "alternative education that puts an emphasis on personal and professional development." While some students feel that course "registration could be much smoother and less stressful," the classes themselves are "rigorous and intimate," and "the work assigned is almost always very interesting." In addition to their self-directed studies on the "beautiful campus" in Vermont, students love the school's annual seven-week Field Work Term, which places students in professional internships off-campus: "For our mandatory Field Work Term period, we have to find internships in the real world every year." The combination of the Field Work Term and the Plan Process, according to students, produces an "individualized education that actually means something." In short, according to its undergrads, "Bennington is about community living, cooperation, planning your life ahead, and designing your own education."

Life
"There's a small, tight-knit community here and it's not hard to have fun while carrying a great conversation anywhere on- or off-campus," says one student of life at Bennington. "Also, the place is gorgeous." There are no traditional dorms here: "The houses we live in are really great. Each house has a personality and unique communities are built in every house." Don't be fooled by the college's tiny size: Students report enjoying a stunning array of "gatherings at friends' houses, potlucks, dinners, drinks, movies, or open mics with friends," "plays, dance recitals, jazz improv sessions, poetry readings," "bands and concerts, art exhibits, rollerskating," and "dance parties." "The party scene is pretty wide," certainly wide enough to contain many different social motivations: "Drinking is popular, but there is very little peer pressure to drink and students who do not wish to partake have numerous things to do for fun." Bennington students tend to be more interested in intellectual engagement than keg parties: "I read widely and often and take pleasure in talking to my friends over a meal about the things we've been learning."

Student Body
"Students here are quirky, interesting, and self-aware." One reports that "my circles and I think about interconnectedness, interfaith spirituality, wellness, political activism, sustainability, music, body awareness, ritual, dance, feminism." "A typical Bennington student works hard, is passionate, takes some risks, has obscure taste in music, is willing to talk about important issues." Students describe themselves as "very alternative. Art school kids. We are a motley crew of rockers, flamboyant gays, science nerds, outdoorsy people." It's true that "we wear Birks, we're into tree-hugging, dodgeball is our favorite sport," and also that "students will find the right people at Bennington. We're very supportive of one another."

FINANCIAL AID: 802-440-4325 • E-MAIL: ADMISSIONS@BENNINGTON.EDU • WEBSITE: WWW.BENNINGTON.EDU

THE PRINCETON REVIEW SAYS

Admissions

Very important factors considered include: rigor of secondary school record, academic GPA, application essay, recommendation(s), interview, talent/ability, character/personal qualities. *Other factors considered include:* class rank, standardized test scores, extracurricular activities, volunteer work, work experience. SAT or ACT considered if submitted; SAT Subject Tests considered if submitted. ACT with or without writing accepted. TOEFL required of all international applicants. High school diploma is required and GED is accepted.

Financial Aid

Students should submit: FAFSA, Institution's own financial aid form, CSS/Financial Aid PROFILE, Noncustodial PROFILE. Regular filing deadline is 2/15. The Princeton Review suggests that all financial aid forms be submitted as soon as possible after October 1. *Need-based scholarships/grants offered:* Federal Pell, FSEOG, State scholarships/grants, Private scholarships, College/university scholarship or grant aid from institutional funds. *Loan aid offered:* Direct Subsidized Stafford Loans, Direct Unsubsidized Stafford Loans, Direct PLUS Loans. Applicants will be notified of awards on or about 3/26. Federal Work-Study Program available. Institutional employment available.

The Inside Word

As well as the Common Application, Bennington invites prospective students to submit their more open-ended Dimensional Application, which requires students to demonstrate original ideas, achievement, growth, and motivation in any way they choose. Interviews and campus visits are recommended if possible, SAT and ACT test scores are optional to the application, and students who choose the Dimensional Application are encouraged to submit thoughtful, creative supplemental materials.

THE SCHOOL SAYS ". . ."

From the Admissions Office

"At Bennington, your education is unified and fueled by your intellect and imagination, guided by a rigorous and ongoing conversation with your faculty, and shaped by your experience working in the world each year. Bennington is the only college to require that its students spend a term—every year—at work in the world. And its new Center for the Advancement of Public Action provides a unique opportunity for students to explore how the questions that matter to them come together with the questions that matter to the world. Rooted in an abiding faith in the talent, imagination, and responsibility of the individual, Bennington invites students to pursue and shape their own intellectual inquiries and, in doing so, to discover the profound interconnection of things.

"Submission of standardized test scores (the SAT, SAT Subject Tests, or the ACT) is optional."

SELECTIVITY

Admissions Rating	89
# of applicants	1,099
% of applicants accepted	63
% of acceptees attending	31
# offered a place on the wait list	17
% accepting a place on wait list	94
% admitted from wait list	31
# of early decision applicants	345
% accepted early decision	72

FRESHMAN PROFILE

Range SAT Critical Reading	590–730
Range SAT Math	550–670
Range SAT Writing	580–700
Range ACT Composite	26–32
Minimum paper TOEFL	577

DEADLINES

Early decision	
Deadline	11/15
Notification	12/20
Other ED	
Deadline	11/15
Other ED	
Notification	12/20
Early action	
Deadline	12/1
Notification	2/1
Regular	
Deadline	1/3
Notification	4/1
Nonfall registration?	Yes

APPLICANTS ALSO LOOK AT AND OFTEN PREFER
Bard College

AND SOMETIMES PREFER
New York University; Sarah Lawrence College

AND RARELY PREFER
Hampshire College; University of Vermont

FINANCIAL FACTS

Financial Aid Rating	84
Annual tuition	$49,440
Room and board	$14,520
Required fees	$660
Books and supplies	$1,000
Average frosh need-based scholarship	$33,135
Average UG need-based scholarship	$32,614
% needy frosh rec. need-based scholarship or grant aid	98
% needy UG rec. need-based scholarship or grant aid	99
% needy frosh rec. non-need-based scholarship or grant aid	10
% needy UG rec. non-need-based scholarship or grant aid	10
% needy frosh rec. need-based self-help aid	84
% needy UG rec. need-based self-help aid	86
% UG borrow to pay for school	73
Average cumulative indebtedness	$29,683
% frosh need fully met	10
% ugrads need fully met	12
Average % of frosh need met	77
Average % of ugrad need met	79

BENTLEY UNIVERSITY

175 FOREST STREET, WALTHAM, MA 02452 • ADMISSIONS: 781-891-2244 • FAX: 781-891-3414

STUDENTS SAY "..."

Academics

Bentley University boasts one of the country's top business programs that looks to send technically-skilled, globally-minded graduates into the real world (at a 98 percent job placement rate, no less). The curriculum at this just-outside-Boston school is heavily stacked with the liberal arts, and even though most everyone is here to get a business degree, there is "a vast number of perspectives, beliefs and strategies...that it is incredibly helpful in understanding course material as well as staying intellectually involved outside of the classroom." Still, the business classes are the core of a Bentley education, and they allow every student "to understand and be prepared for all aspects of the business world, including finance, marketing, accounting, operations, and statistics." There are "plenty of opportunities to incorporate liberal arts into your education and create a major and minor combination that best suits your interests."

Professors are "excited to teach and even more excited to engage in meaningful conversation with their students and peers." As students reach senior-level courses, teachers are "truly interested in helping to set you up with work and recommending you to some of their connections." A low teacher to student ratio further helps to create more personal relationships between professors and students. "All of my professors know my name," one student tells us. The alumni network is similarly useful and "easy to get involved in." A lot of the information that is taught is "also applied through case studies and working with local businesses," and group projects are common. Around 90 percent of students take advantage of the school's internship opportunities (the majority do so multiple times), and resources are plentiful all around: "There is always someone I can talk to if I feel the need," says one student.

Life

Weekdays are generally filled with class and homework, with "relaxation periods towards the end of the day and usually spent eating off campus or in a dorm room." During week nights, "there are a lot of group project meetings as many classes here have an emphasis on teamwork skills" and athletic games also receive a lot of support. A "multitude of extracurriculars" are there for the taking (many even have a business slant, such as the the Bentley Investment Group and Bentley Microfinance Group), and many students are active and "enjoy playing games like soccer or frisbee...on the green spaces." Additionally, there are always events going on "like guest speakers and games like trivia night in the student center." This is a pretty campus, and "daily fitness routines at the gym" are also on the schedule for most. Bentley organizes intramural sports, and going into Boston is a fun jaunt for those who can spare the time, with a free hourly shuttle making it easy to get to Harvard Square.

Student Body

Bentley is filled with "highly ambitious" students who find it refreshing to be surrounded by "people who want to be successful and are willing to put in the work to achieve success." The student body is predominantly white ("very preppy, a lot of pastel colors") with a relatively high guy to girl ratio, and "lots of students have money." Everyone in this "very cohesive and cooperative group of students" gets along and is friendly to each other. The college guarantees on-campus housing for all four years and most of the student body takes advantage, "creating a tight knit community" where there is "a big sense of belongingness." "It feels like living in a hotel with all of your friends," says a student.

FINANCIAL AID: 781-891-3441 • E-MAIL: UGADMISSION@BENTLEY.EDU • WEBSITE: WWW.BENTLEY.EDU

THE PRINCETON REVIEW SAYS

Admissions

Very important factors considered include: rigor of secondary school record, academic GPA, standardized test scores. *Important factors considered include:* application essay, recommendation(s), extracurricular activities, talent/ability, character/personal qualities, volunteer work, work experience. *Other factors considered include:* class rank, interview, first generation, alumni/ae relation, geographical residence, state residency, racial/ethnic status, level of applicant's interest. SAT or ACT required; SAT Subject Tests considered if submitted. ACT with or without writing accepted. SAT with or without Essay component accepted. TOEFL required of all international applicants. High school diploma is required and GED is accepted. *Academic units required:* 4 English, 4 math, 3 science, 2 science labs, 3 foreign language, 3 social studies. *Academic units recommended:* 4 English, 4 math, 4 science, 3 science labs, 4 foreign language, 4 social studies, and 2 units from above areas or other academic areas.

Financial Aid

Students should submit: FAFSA, CSS/Financial Aid PROFILE, Noncustodial PROFILE, Business/Farm Supplement. Regular filing deadline is 2/1.The Princeton Review suggests that all financial aid forms be submitted as soon as possible after October 1. *Need-based scholarships/grants offered:* Federal Pell, FSEOG, State scholarships/grants, Private scholarships, College/university scholarship or grant aid from institutional funds. *Loan aid offered:* Direct Subsidized Stafford Loans, Direct Unsubsidized Stafford Loans, Direct PLUS loans, State Loans. Applicants will be notified of awards on or about 3/31. Federal Work-Study Program available. Institutional employment available.

The Inside Word

If you think stacking your senior year electives with business classes in order to impress the Bentley admissions office, think again. Taking a broad array of classes that will challenge your skills, at AP level if possible, is your best approach. Whether in English, history/social sciences, math, lab sciences, and foreign language, the admission committee wants to see academic diversity. And be sure your grades and test scores are up to snuff, because you'll have plenty of competition.

THE SCHOOL SAYS "..."

From the Admissions Office

"Bentley is an internationally recognized business university known for integrating business with the arts and sciences. Students learn in an unmatched collection of high-tech learning labs and benefit from close working relationships with faculty who collaborate across disciplines. Bentley students are highly sought after by today's leading organizations because of their class-work with corporate clients, service-learning projects and valuable internship experiences.

"More than 98 percent of 2015 graduates were employed or enrolled in graduate school within six months of commencement. Their median annual salary was $53,000. This success was recognized by the Princeton Review in 2015 as Bentley was ranked number five nationally for 'Best Career Services.'

"Approximately 98 percent of freshmen live on campus. Students live and learn in a diverse environment that prepares them to thrive in today's diverse work world. International students representing nearly 100 countries are part of the Bentley community. There are more than 100 student organizations, as well as abundant intramurals, recreational sports, and twenty-three varsity teams in NCAA Divisions I and II. Bentley's location in Waltham, Massachusetts— minutes from Boston—puts the city's many resources within easy reach. Bentley's free shuttle makes regular trips to Harvard Square in Cambridge, just a subway ride from the heart of Boston. Boston also offers students many opportunities for internships and jobs after graduation."

SELECTIVITY

Admissions Rating	91
# of applicants	8,346
% of applicants accepted	42
% of acceptees attending	26
# offered a place on the wait list	1,898
% accepting a place on wait list	30
% admitted from wait list	16
# of early decision applicants	158
% accepted early decision	66

FRESHMAN PROFILE

Range SAT Critical Reading	540–640
Range SAT Math	600–690
Range SAT Writing	550–650
Range ACT Composite	26–30
Minimum paper TOEFL	577
Minimum internet-based TOEFL	90
% graduated top 10% of class	38
% graduated top 25% of class	72
% graduated top 50% of class	93

DEADLINES

Early decision	
Deadline	11/15
Regular	
Deadline	1/7
Nonfall registration?	Yes

APPLICANTS ALSO LOOK AT AND SOMETIMES PREFER

Babson College; Boston College; Boston University; Bryant University; Northeastern University; University of Connecticut; University of Massachusetts Amherst; Villanova University; Fordham University; New York University

FINANCIAL FACTS

Financial Aid Rating	87
Annual tuition	$42,550
Room and board	$14,520
Required fees	$1,535
Books and supplies	$1,200
Average frosh need-based scholarship	$30,356
Average UG need-based scholarship	$29,755
% needy frosh rec. need-based scholarship or grant aid	98
% needy UG rec. need-based scholarship or grant aid	98
% needy frosh rec. non-need-based scholarship or grant aid	25
% needy UG rec. non-need-based scholarship or grant aid	15
% needy frosh rec. need-based self-help aid	94
% needy UG rec. need-based self-help aid	96
% frosh rec. any financial aid	71
% UG rec. any financial aid	65
% UG borrow to pay for school	54
Average cumulative indebtedness	$29,547
% frosh need fully met	43
% ugrads need fully met	39
Average % of frosh need met	94
Average % of ugrad need met	93

BEREA COLLEGE

CPO 2220, BEREA, KY 40404 • ADMISSIONS: 859-985-3500 • FAX: 859-985-3512

STUDENTS SAY "..."

Academics

Kentucky's Berea College is one of the nation's few entirely tuition-free private colleges, providing a liberal arts education "to those who otherwise couldn't afford college but who are deserving of the opportunity." Berea is "truly a different world when it comes to the atmosphere of the college," and the "wonderful opportunity" offered to students is truly appreciated. The school takes a "holistic approach" to education and "expects a lot from students both in and outside of class," including labor (everyone is required to work at least ten hours per week) and convocations.

Professors take an active role in helping students learn: "If you miss a class, professors will email you to find out why." They "care about not just your learning but also about who you are as an individual" and "lively and passionate about their subjects, and it is very evident within their classrooms." "I've never felt more challenged than when I stepped foot in a Berea classroom," says a junior. The small student-to-faculty ratio gives professors the opportunity to get to know their students, and "[allows] them to adapt to their students' needs."

Dating back to 1855, the college is "very deeply rooted in Appalachian culture and history, but unafraid to address issues outside of that." The school gives low-income students the opportunity to pursue higher education while participating in a labor program, and so "produces well-rounded, hardworking students fully prepared for grad school or the workforce." "If the labor program is used to its fullest extent, each student has the opportunity to graduate with a fantastic résumé and many network connections," says a sophomore. It also offers "a huge scholarship to study abroad," of which many students take advantage.

Life

"Berea is a calm place" and "there isn't much going on unless you make something happen." Students are quite busy with studying and work, so "naps are rare" and "we usually don't sleep in because there is just so much to do." Most students are taking a full course load and then doing at least one or two extracurricular activities as well. "The town life is simply atrocious" but on campus, "student organizations are constantly holding events to keep Berea students occupied and having fun," including "movie nights, game nights, dances, [and] bowling." Heritage activities, such as Contra dancing, are big.

The town of Richmond is just a fifteen minute drive away (there is also a campus shuttle, and Lexington is a bit further), so getting out of small town life for some shopping or restaurant dining "is a must" from time to time. It is illegal to sell alcohol in the town of Berea, and it is against school rules to have alcohol on campus, so "there isn't a big party scene." There also happen to be "a lot of couples on campus," and "people take relationships seriously" here.

Student Body

Berea students are "creative" and "incredibly resilient" and almost everyone "comes from the Appalachian region [and] limited resources." Many tend to be first generation college students, and "most student's priorities are not in having the best material items or joining the best sorority." The most typical thing you'll see is "an overworked, but generally content student shuffling between classes and work." Also, "the one thing that ties us all together is the fact that we had to work so hard to get into Berea," says a freshman. ("You have to be either an outright nerd or a secret nerd to get [here].") As some have noticed, there "seems to be a great divide between traditional students and non-traditional."

FINANCIAL AID: 859-985-3310 • E-MAIL: ADMISSIONS@BEREA.EDU • WEBSITE: WWW.BEREA.EDU

THE PRINCETON REVIEW SAYS

Admissions

Very important factors considered include: interview. *Important factors considered include:* rigor of secondary school record, class rank, academic GPA, standardized test scores, application essay, character/personal qualities. *Other factors considered include:* recommendation(s), extracurricular activities, talent/ability, first generation, geographical residence, state residency, racial/ethnic status, volunteer work, work experience, level of applicant's interest. SAT or ACT required. ACT with or without writing accepted. SAT with or without Essay component accepted. TOEFL required of all international applicants. High school diploma is required and GED is accepted. *Academic units recommended:* 4 English, 3 math, 2 science, 2 science labs, 2 foreign language, 2 social studies.

Financial Aid

Students should submit: FAFSA. Regular filing deadline is 5/1.The Princeton Review suggests that all financial aid forms be submitted as soon as possible after October 1. *Need-based scholarships/grants offered:* Federal Pell, FSEOG, State scholarships/grants, Private scholarships, College/university scholarship or grant aid from institutional funds. *Loan aid offered:* Direct Subsidized Stafford Loans, Direct Unsubsidized Stafford Loans, Direct PLUS loans, College/university loans from institutional funds. Applicants will be notified of awards on a rolling basis beginning 11/1. Federal Work-Study Program available. Institutional employment available.

Inside Word

The Tuition Promise Scholarship that every student receives understandably attracts a lot of applicants. Competition among candidates is intense. It's also important to note, you may be too wealthy to get admitted here. Berea won't admit students whose parents can afford to send them elsewhere. Financially qualified applicants should apply as early as possible.

THE SCHOOL SAYS "..."

From the Admissions Office

"Since its founding in 1855, Berea College has provided a high quality, low-cost education to students of all races. As the first interracial and co-educational college in the South, Berea admits students with great academic promise but limited finanacial means. Over the past 150 years, Berea has evolved into one of the most distinctive colleges in the United States serving students primarily from the Appalachian region.

"All admitted students receive a Tuition Promise Scholarship, which completely covers the cost of tuition after other forms of grant & scholarship aid are applied. This leaves only minimal expenses for housing, meals, and other expenses. Students graduate with one of the lowest rates of student educational debt in the nation, and one in three students graduate debt free. In addition to the Scholarship, students receive a laptop computer and a paid-on campus job to assist with educational and personal expenses as well as gain valuable work experience before graduation.

"As a result of this combination of academic reputation and generous financial assistance, Berea attracts many more applicants than are able to be accepted, so admission is competitive. The best means of improving the chances for admission is to complete the application process as early as possible, preferably by October 31 of the senior year."

SELECTIVITY
Admissions Rating	94
# of applicants	1,637
% of applicants accepted	36
% of acceptees attending	72

FRESHMAN PROFILE
Range SAT Critical Reading	550–635
Range SAT Math	515–620
Range SAT Writing	500–605
Range ACT Composite	22–26
Minimum paper TOEFL	520
Minimum internet-based TOEFL	68
Average HS GPA	3.4
% graduated top 10% of class	24
% graduated top 25% of class	67
% graduated top 50% of class	96

DEADLINES
Regular Deadline	4/30
Nonfall registration?	No

FINANCIAL FACTS
Financial Aid Rating	60*
Annual tuition	$0
Room and board	$6,410
Required fees	$570
Books and supplies	$700
Average frosh need-based scholarship	$32,957
Average UG need-based scholarship	$27,810
% needy frosh rec. need-based scholarship or grant aid	100
% needy UG rec. need-based scholarship or grant aid	100
% needy frosh rec. non-need-based scholarship or grant aid	0
% needy UG rec. non-need-based scholarship or grant aid	0
% needy frosh rec. need-based self-help aid	100
% needy UG rec. need-based self-help aid	100
% frosh rec. any financial aid	100
% UG rec. any financial aid	100
% UG borrow to pay for school	68
Average cumulative indebtedness	$7,928
% frosh need fully met	0
% ugrads need fully met	0
Average % of frosh need met	96
Average % of ugrad need met	93

BOSTON COLLEGE

140 COMMONWEALTH AVENUE, CHESTNUT HILL, MA 02467-3809 • ADMISSIONS: 617-552-3100 • FAX: 617-552-0798

STUDENTS SAY "..."

Academics

Boston College, a small Jesuit school on the outskirts of Boston, "is all about educating the person as a whole." Its strong core curriculum ensures all students receive a "well-rounded" liberal arts education regardless of their chosen major. Boston College's well-respected education and business school attract a lot of students, and there are many other strong programs, including English and communication. Students think Boston College is a "great experience academically" and gush about their "phenomenal professors." A secondary education major student says, "Boston College's professors are truly exceptional and are devoted to undergraduate learning." They're "engaging, challenging, and understanding, [and] are genuinely interested in the student as a whole person." Boston College's "prestigious" academics come with "high expectations," but if students need help professors are "easily accessible outside of classes." Students "feel prepared for whatever is next" and note that their "well-connected" teachers and strong alumni network help with the job search. One student, who was drawn to Boston College because of its stellar reputation, finds it "even better than expected." Another adds, "I have always revered Boston College's academic and athletic reputation, and coming here, I have not been disappointed."

Life

Boston College's "gorgeous campus" and "perfect'" suburban location has created a very rich campus life and given the school a "strong community feel." There's "a superb sense of school spirit, which truly sets it apart." One student raves, "There is just so much school spirit and love for the university!" Boston College's "incredible sports teams" are well-supported by "superfans at every event." "There is also a large service component," to life at Boston College, which allows students "to serve the community in Boston and communities all around the world." Boston College offers a "plethora of extracurricular activities," and students think "there's a club or group for everyone here." The school has "great facilities" and "state-of-the-art resources." Dorms are generally well-reviewed, though students think the housing lottery could be more "fair." Students often go into Boston for all of its entertainment and cultural activities but are happy to return to their "close-knit college" where they "feel very at home."

Student Body

Boston College has gotten some flak for its "preppy," "white," and "homogenous" student body, and a communication student admits, "The school's nickname as 'J. Crew U.' isn't entirely unwarranted." Boston College could definitely use "greater racial diversity," but one student says that each year "the student body becomes more and more diverse." A student double-majoring in economics and German says, "Once you've settled in you'll find that it's not at all difficult to find a group of friends" no matter who you are. "There is a large religious/spiritual community," because of the school's Jesuit affiliation, but "it is only one group of many." Boston College's Division I ranking means there are plenty of athletes and sports fans. Students warn that Boston College is "not the place to go to class in your pajamas." People, particularly women, are "very well-dressed" and "stylish." Students say their peers are "really ambitious" and "hardworking." "The majority of students seem intelligent and academically driven as well as dedicated to and passionate about one or more extracurricular activities." Though people at Boston College are "academically oriented," they're "also into having a good time, and "have a work hard, play hard mentality." There's a moderate amount of drinking on campus and off, but students say that no matter what, everyone "definitely [has] school as a top priority."

FINANCIAL AID: 617-552-3300 • WEBSITE: WWW.BC.EDU

THE PRINCETON REVIEW SAYS

Admissions

Very important factors considered include: rigor of secondary school record, academic GPA, standardized test scores. *Important factors considered include:* class rank, application essay, recommendation(s), extracurricular activities, talent/ability, character/personal qualities, alumni/ae relation, religious affiliation/commitment, volunteer work. *Other factors considered include:* first generation, racial/ethnic status, work experience. SAT or ACT required; SAT Subject Tests considered if submitted. ACT with or without writing accepted. SAT with or without Essay component accepted. TOEFL required of all international applicants. High school diploma is required and GED is accepted. *Academic units recommended:* 4 English, 4 math, 4 science, 4 science labs, 4 foreign language, 4 social studies, 4 history.

Financial Aid

Students should submit: FAFSA, CSS/Financial Aid PROFILE, Noncustodial PROFILE, Business/Farm Supplement. Priority filing deadline is 2/1.The Princeton Review suggests that all financial aid forms be submitted as soon as possible after October 1. *Need-based scholarships/grants offered:* Federal Pell, FSEOG, State scholarships/grants, Private scholarships, College/university scholarship or grant aid from institutional funds. *Loan aid offered:* Direct Subsidized Stafford Loans, Direct Unsubsidized Stafford Loans, Direct PLUS loans, Federal Perkins Loans, Federal Nursing Loans, State Loans. Applicants will be notified of awards on or about 4/1. Federal Work-Study Program available. Institutional employment available.

The Inside Word

Boston College is one of many selective schools that eschew set admissions formulae. While a challenging high school curriculum and strong test scores are essential for any serious candidate, the college seeks students who are passionate and make connections between academic pursuits and extracurricular activities. The application process should reveal a distinct, mature voice and a student whose interest in education goes beyond the simple desire to earn an A.

THE SCHOOL SAYS "..."

From the Admissions Office

"Boston College students achieve at the highest levels with honors in the past ten years including two Rhodes scholarship winners, 173 Fulbrights, four Marshalls, eight Goldwaters, ten Beckmans, and five Truman Postgraduate Fellowship Programs. Junior Year Abroad and Scholar of the College Program offer students flexibility within the curriculum. Facilities opened in the past ten years include Stokes Hall, Cadigan Alumni Center, the Yawkey Athletics Center, the Hillside Cafe, and a new residence hall currently under construction slated to open in the Fall of 2016. Students enjoy the vibrant location in Chestnut Hill with easy access to the cultural and historical richness of Boston.

"Boston College requires freshman applicants to take the SAT with writing (or the ACT with the writing exam required). SAT Subject Tests are optional; but may be submitted if a student wishes to highlight a talent in a specific area."

SELECTIVITY

Admissions Rating	96
# of applicants	29,486
% of applicants accepted	29
% of acceptees attending	26
# offered a place on the wait list	7,072
% accepting a place on wait list	56
% admitted from wait list	9

FRESHMAN PROFILE

Range SAT Critical Reading	620–720
Range SAT Math	640–750
Range SAT Writing	640–730
Range ACT Composite	30–33
Minimum paper TOEFL	600
Minimum internet-based TOEFL	100
% graduated top 10% of class	79
% graduated top 25% of class	95
% graduated top 50% of class	99

DEADLINES

Early action	
Deadline	11/1
Notification	12/25
Regular	
Deadline	1/1
Notification	4/15
Nonfall registration?	Yes

APPLICANTS ALSO LOOK AT AND OFTEN PREFER

Brown University; Harvard College; University of Pennsylvania; Yale University; Duke University

AND SOMETIMES PREFER

Cornell University; Georgetown University; University of Notre Dame

AND RARELY PREFER

Boston University; Fordham University

FINANCIAL FACTS

Financial Aid Rating	94
Annual tuition	$50,480
Room and board	$13,818
Required fees	$816
Books and supplies	$1,250
Average frosh need-based scholarship	$34,324
Average UG need-based scholarship	$34,729
% needy frosh rec. need-based scholarship or grant aid	88
% needy UG rec. need-based scholarship or grant aid	87
% needy frosh rec. non-need-based scholarship or grant aid	3
% needy UG rec. non-need-based scholarship or grant aid	2
% needy frosh rec. need-based self-help aid	94
% needy UG rec. need-based self-help aid	93
% frosh rec. any financial aid	63
% UG rec. any financial aid	66
% frosh need fully met	100
% ugrads need fully met	100
Average % of frosh need met	100
Average % of ugrad need met	100

BOSTON UNIVERSITY

233 BAY STATE ROAD, BOSTON, MA 02215 • ADMISSIONS: 617-353-2300 • FAX: 617-353-9695

STUDENTS SAY "..."

Academics

Long recognized for offering both the breadth of a large research university and the depth of a private college, the "various schools and colleges within Boston University provide students with access to almost every imaginable program of study." In keeping with this, students report a wide variety of majors and concentrations, naming standout programs in engineering, education, and business administration. Professors are praised as much as is students' ability to choose them: BU professors are both "actively pursuing research in their field" and "engaging partners in my academic experience," and students find that professors' "interesting backgrounds...fuel class discussions in a variety of academic areas." Undergraduates also love the university's "location" as an "urban campus" in Boston's Back Bay, and benefit distinctly from BU's "opportunity access" when it comes to job placement. As a private university with a large student body, BU students also become the beneficiaries of the institution's "wealth," calling the experience one of "big campus resources with a small campus feel." The faculty and administration "are constantly striving to be better for the student's benefit" in delivering BU's unique curriculum, which is "equal parts liberal arts education and pre-professional experience." The university emphasizes "study abroad" and "research opportunities," which further broaden the possibilities of a BU education. Perhaps ideal for the student who desires a wide variety of choices in order to discover what comes next, "the range and diversity of opportunities at Boston University allows you to Be You."

Life

Continuing the theme of wide-ranging options, BU undergraduates divulge that student "life at BU is anything you want it to be." Because of BU's location in "the heart of Boston," "the city itself is like our campus," and BU undergrads can mingle freely with Boston's many other college students students in nearby Cambridge, Somerville, Allston, and Brookline. Students are rarely bored because "there's always something interesting going on on- and off-campus": campus life boasts "a lot of clubs and activities to get involved in," as well as "house parties," "BU hockey games," and "frat parties," while students' access to Boston spans everything from "a run along the Charles River" to "shopping on Newbury or in Harvard Square" to frequenting "plays and ballets and museums" and the many local "clubs and bars." Students strive to maximize the best of both sides of BU life, "prid[ing] themselves on being able to find balance in living strong academic lives and exciting social lives as well." Students seem satisfied with the choices they do end up making, reporting that BU life is "wonderful" and that "there is more to do than you will be able to find the time for."

Student Body

"There is a great sense of diversity, yet an overwhelming feeling of unity" within BU's large but closely connected undergraduate population. Students strongly resist the idea of a "typical student," asserting that "originality is valued highly at BU," as is "diversity of thought." "Because we are an international university," many students point out, "the student body is vastly diverse." Students have "a wide range of interests both inside and outside the classroom," and characterize themselves as "motivated, culturally-aware, intelligent, adventurous," "driven and involved," and "very passionate." BU undergrads find their peers "intellectually stimulating in conversations" and tend to group, as in most college experiences, around shared interests and experiences. One student echoes many of her classmates this way: "My life at BU is quite packed because I chose to make it that way."

FINANCIAL AID: 617-353-4176 • E-MAIL: ADMISSIONS@BU.EDU • WEBSITE: WWW.BU.EDU

THE PRINCETON REVIEW SAYS

Admissions

Very important factors considered include: rigor of secondary school record. *Important factors considered include:* class rank, academic GPA, standardized test scores, application essay, recommendation(s), level of applicant's interest. *Other factors considered include:* extracurricular activities, character/personal qualities, first generation, alumni/ae relation, geographical residence, state residency, racial/ethnic status, volunteer work, work experience. SAT or ACT required; SAT Subject Tests required for some. ACT with or without writing accepted. SAT with or without Essay component accepted. TOEFL required of all international applicants. High school diploma is required and GED is accepted. *Academic units required:* 4 English, 3 math, 3 science, 3 science labs, 2 foreign language, 3 social studies, 3 history. *Academic units recommended:* 4 English, 4 math, 4 science, 4 science labs, 4 foreign language, 4 social studies, 4 history.

Financial Aid

Students should submit: FAFSA, CSS/Financial Aid PROFILE, Noncustodial PROFILE. Regular filing deadline is 2/1.The Princeton Review suggests that all financial aid forms be submitted as soon as possible after October 1. *Need-based scholarships/grants offered:* Federal Pell, FSEOG, State scholarships/grants, Private scholarships, College/university scholarship or grant aid from institutional funds. *Loan aid offered:* Direct Subsidized Stafford Loans, Direct Unsubsidized Stafford Loans, Direct PLUS loans, Federal Perkins Loans, State Loans. Applicants will be notified of awards on a rolling basis beginning 4/1. Federal Work-Study Program available. Institutional employment available.

The Inside Word

BU can afford to stay competitive, and they strongly emphasize high school academic performance as the key indicator of a student's admissibility to the university. BU values students who take on a challenging high school curriculum (especially AP and IB classes, or whatever the most challenging courseload available is). The personal essay, recommendations, extracurricular activities, and standardized test scores (SAT or ACT plus SAT Writing) are also important factors in assessing applicants. Several undergraduate courses of study (mostly in medicine and the arts) require specific standardized test supplements; prospective students are encouraged to read BU's admissions requirements carefully before applying.

THE SCHOOL SAYS "..."

From the Admissions Office

"Boston University is a world-recognized, private teaching and research university committed to excellence in undergraduate education. Students study with distinguished faculty that include Fulbright Scholars, Pulitzer Prize winners, a MacArthur Fellow, Nobel Prize winners, and a former Poet Laureate. In ten undergraduate schools and colleges, BU offers students more than 250 programs of study, cutting-edge research with faculty mentors, internships in the United States and abroad, and one of the nation's most extensive study abroad programs. Housing is guaranteed for four years in a variety of on-campus residences, including high-rise buildings and historic brownstones. BU students are engaged with their campus community through over 450 student organizations, club and intramural sports, and twenty-three NCAA Division I sports teams. Students experience the city of Boston as an extension of campus for study, internships, employment, and cultural and recreational activities.

"Students also benefit from research and internship opportunities in the United States and abroad and a network of more than 300,000 alumni in 189 countries around the world. With more than 100 study abroad opportunities and classmates from over 100 countries, BU is truly a global university."

SELECTIVITY

Admissions Rating	94
# of applicants	54,781
% of applicants accepted	33
% of acceptees attending	20
# offered a place on the wait list	4,381
% accepting a place on wait list	51
% admitted from wait list	0
# of early decision applicants	1,643
% accepted early decision	43

FRESHMAN PROFILE

Range SAT Critical Reading	580–680
Range SAT Math	620–730
Range SAT Writing	600–690
Range ACT Composite	27–31
Average HS GPA	3.6
% graduated top 10% of class	58
% graduated top 25% of class	89
% graduated top 50% of class	99

DEADLINES

Early decision	
Deadline	11/1
Notification	12/15
Regular	
Priority	11/1
Deadline	1/3
Notification	4/1
Nonfall registration?	Yes

FINANCIAL FACTS

Financial Aid Rating	86
Annual tuition	$47,422
Room and board	$14,520
Required fees	$1,014
Books and supplies	$1,000
Average frosh need-based scholarship	$35,715
Average UG need-based scholarship	$32,397
% needy frosh rec. need-based scholarship or grant aid	100
% needy UG rec. need-based scholarship or grant aid	100
% needy frosh rec. non-need-based scholarship or grant aid	8
% needy UG rec. non-need-based scholarship or grant aid	5
% needy frosh rec. need-based self-help aid	88
% needy UG rec. need-based self-help aid	89
% frosh rec. any financial aid	54
% UG rec. any financial aid	54
% UG borrow to pay for school	53
Average cumulative indebtedness	$40,365
% frosh need fully met	40
% ugrads need fully met	30
Average % of frosh need met	93
Average % of ugrad need met	88

BOWDOIN COLLEGE

5000 COLLEGE STATION, BRUNSWICK, ME 04011-8441 • ADMISSIONS: 207-725-3100 • FAX: 207-725-3101

STUDENTS SAY "..."

Academics

Bowdoin College's "variety of equally high-quality academic programs," "the outdoorsy and welcoming culture of the campus," and beautiful scenery of hometown Brunswick, Maine make admission "an easy sell." At this small liberal arts college, people "are endlessly friendly, engaged and welcoming." Students agree "when you step onto campus, you get a very palpable feeling that people here care about each other." Undergrads praise Bowdoin's programs in government, science and music, and note that the college's small class sizes "foster closer and more intimate relationships with peers and faculty." The rigorous academic environment is "balanced with a strong sense of community on campus, a passion for issues of social, environmental, and racial justice, and a love of Maine." Professors are "top-notch" educators, who are "are clearly some of the best in their respective fields" and "manage a classroom well." The personable faculty "are all very accessible outside of the classroom and implore students to take time to reach out," offering students opportunities for "academic improvement and personal growth." Students say they often have a "a very difficult course load," but professors are "happy to help [them] understand the difficult course material." Overall students are "highly impressed" with their academic experience and "implore" first year students "to take time to reach out and make close connections" with faculty who will ensure everyone "[receives] the help they need to succeed in the classroom."

Life

The rigorous course load means that "students spend a lot of time with their academic work." But Bowdoin is a "cohesive community" whose students benefit from a "plethora of extracurriculars" (120 student organizations) and "athletic participation is substantial." Many students dedicate their free time to the outing club "and community service activities around Brunswick." Bowdoin benefits from being "close to the beach and located adjacent to the cute, bustling town of Brunswick." Parties at college houses ("old fraternities that were taken over by the school") are popular among first- and second-year students as juniors and seniors tend to "go to house parties in campus apartments or [at] off campus houses." The eight social houses are "sophomore residences and serve as a hub of social life on campus in a lot of ways—hosting fun but not scary-frat-y parties, bringing in speakers, and supporting a lot of events on campus." Popular Outing Club trips include "backpacking, canoeing, kayaking, camping, rafting, [and] surfing," and there is also skiing available at nearby Sugarloaf or Sunday River.

Student Body

Bowdoin students tell us "it's impossible to overemphasize the warmth of the student body." And they almost universally reject the stereotype that the student body is primarily "WASP, prep kids." Instead they describe the student body as "very spunky and diverse," politically liberal and friendly. "The Bowdoin 'hey!' is real," one student explains. "Everybody is so friendly that when you're walking across campus to class, you'll probably say 'hi' to at least seven people, and it won't be necessarily because you made awkward eye contact and felt you had to." Students are involved and tend to be busy. One student might "be on Residential Life Staff as an RA . . . be an economics major, LGBTQ leader, member of the hockey team, and work at the library simultaneously." While students are academically driven, "the atmosphere is hardly competitive," and people are more likely to be "competitive with [. . .] themselves." Overall, students are "highly motivated individuals who strive to learn about as many things as possible" and "keep themselves really busy with schoolwork, teams, clubs, and just hanging out."

BOWDOIN COLLEGE

THE PRINCETON REVIEW SAYS
Admissions
Very important factors considered include: rigor of secondary school record, class rank, academic GPA, application essay, recommendation(s), extracurricular activities, talent/ability, character/personal qualities. *Important factors considered include:* standardized test scores, first generation, alumni/ae relation. *Other factors considered include:* interview, geographical residence, state residency, racial/ethnic status. SAT or ACT considered if submitted; SAT Subject Tests considered if submitted. ACT with or without writing accepted. SAT with or without Essay component accepted. TOEFL required of all international applicants. High school diploma is required and GED is not accepted. *Academic units recommended:* 4 English, 4 math, 4 science, 3 science labs, 4 foreign language, 4 social studies.

Financial Aid
Students should submit: FAFSA, CSS/Financial Aid PROFILE, Noncustodial PROFILE, Business/Farm Supplement. Regular filing deadline is 2/15. The Princeton Review suggests that all financial aid forms be submitted as soon as possible after October 1. *Need-based scholarships/grants offered:* Federal Pell, FSEOG, State scholarships/grants, Private scholarships, College/university scholarship or grant aid from institutional funds. *Loan aid offered:* Direct Subsidized Stafford Loans, Direct Unsubsidized Stafford Loans, Federal Perkins Loans, State Loans. Applicants will be notified of awards on or about 3/20. Federal Work-Study Program available. Institutional employment available.

The Inside Word
Securing admission to Bowdoin is no easy feat. The college is need-blind and meets financial need without loans. Competition is definitely fierce, and it's imperative that applicants be near the top of their class. Admissions officers do take a holistic approach carefully analyzing academic success, course levels, school/community involvement, academic potential, writing samples, recommendations and character. The interview isn't required, but it can be helpful to the admission committee.

THE SCHOOL SAYS "..."
From the Admissions Office
"A Bowdoin education is best summed up by 'The Offer of the College':

'To be at home in all lands and all ages;
To count Nature a familiar acquaintance,
And Art an intimate friend;
To gain a standard for the appreciation of others' work
And the criticism of your own;
To carry the keys of the world's library in your pocket,
And feel its resources behind you in whatever task you undertake;
To make hosts of friends...
Who are to be leaders in all walks of life;
To lose yourself in generous enthusiasms
And cooperate with others for common ends—
This is the offer of the college for the best four years of your life.'

Adapted from the original 'Offer of the College'
by William DeWitt Hyde
President of Bowdoin College 1885–1917"

SELECTIVITY
Admissions Rating	98
# of applicants	6,790
% of applicants accepted	15
% of acceptees attending	50
# of early decision applicants	950
% accepted early decision	26

FRESHMAN PROFILE
Range SAT Critical Reading	690–765
Range SAT Math	685–770
Range SAT Writing	690–770
Range ACT Composite	31–34
Minimum paper TOEFL	600
Minimum internet-based TOEFL	100
% graduated top 10% of class	84
% graduated top 25% of class	98
% graduated top 50% of class	100

DEADLINES
Early decision	
Deadline	11/15
Notification	12/15
Regular	
Deadline	1/1
Notification	3/20
Nonfall registration?	No

APPLICANTS ALSO LOOK AT AND OFTEN PREFER
Brown University; Dartmouth College; Harvard College; Princeton University; Stanford University; Yale University

AND SOMETIMES PREFER
Amherst College; Williams College

AND RARELY PREFER
Middlebury College; Pomona College

FINANCIAL FACTS
Financial Aid Rating	99
Annual tuition	$47,744
Room and board	$13,142
Required fees	$468
Books and supplies	$836
Average frosh need-based scholarship	$42,165
Average UG need-based scholarship	$41,582
% needy frosh rec. need-based scholarship or grant aid	100
% needy UG rec. need-based scholarship or grant aid	100
% needy frosh rec. non-need-based scholarship or grant aid	0
% needy UG rec. non-need-based scholarship or grant aid	0
% needy frosh rec. need-based self-help aid	95
% needy UG rec. need-based self-help aid	96
% frosh rec. any financial aid	49
% UG rec. any financial aid	48
% UG borrow to pay for school	34
Average cumulative indebtedness	$20,883
% frosh need fully met	100
% ugrads need fully met	100
Average % of frosh need met	100
Average % of ugrad need met	100

BRADLEY UNIVERSITY

1501 WEST BRADLEY AVENUE, PEORIA, IL 61625 • ADMISSIONS: 309-677-1000 • FAX: 309-677-2797

STUDENTS SAY "..."

Academics

Academically, Bradley provides "the resources of a large university with the familiarity that comes from a small liberal arts school." Students love mid-sized Bradley in Illinois for the "size of the campus" and "the focus on small class sizes," as well as the Academic Exploration Program that helps unde-cided majors discover "what career fit[s] best for [their] personality and inter-ests." Bradley's "greatest strengths include the fabulous staff (professors and employees), the creative spirit, and the volunteer-oriented mindset." Bradley's Speech Team also gets high marks with proud students calling it the "best Speech Team in the nation." Students feel that "the individuals who go here are friendly and welcoming and so are the professors. They truly care about your academic standing and will help you do everything in your power to succeed." A recent graduate shares her experience: "While Bradley offers the academic choices of a larger university, it also provides students the guidance and men-toring of faculty that only a smaller university can provide." Another student emphasizes that "the single most satisfying experience for ambitious students is talking to the 300 companies at the annual fall job fair." Undergrads rave about the advantages Bradley provides coupled with the community and per-sonal attention that smaller schools tend to deliver.

Life

Nearly all students respond that Bradley "feels like home." Located in a resi-dential neighborhood on the west bluff of the Illinois River, the eighty-five-acre campus is just one mile from downtown Peoria, Illinois. The distinctive feel of Bradley comes from a blend of large school opportunities with the quality and personal attention of a small, private college. As one student puts it, the cam-pus is "extremely walkable so you can get anywhere in four minutes." What endears the university to most students is that it is able to provide outstanding resources and connections to big cities such as Chicago and St. Louis while maintaining the familiarity that comes from a small, liberal arts school. "Bradley always has something to do, but so does the city of Peoria" with its "festivals and great restaurants." On campus, there are "over [240] student organizations," and so "it is extremely easy for anyone to find their niche." Greek life "is really popular at Bradley and that unites people in a way." "Intramural sports are huge at Bradley as well," and it's a Division I school, so students can go "cheer on our Braves."

Student Body

At Bradley, students are "passionate and motivated," and the campus as a whole is "very welcoming and warm-hearted." A student sums it up: "There are phenomenal opportunities to volunteer and help people here. Bradley is a community of good people who are respectful and awesome." Another student feels that "the majority of students engage in Greek life" and that "it is cool to be involved in multiple student organizations and interest groups at Bradley." Another agrees that "one of Bradley's strengths is its size and how inclusive the students are" and that "everyone can find somewhere they belong." Still, a few comment that students here are "very privileged" and that the "student body, as well as the faculty and staff, need to become more diverse so that the univer-sity will be more well-rounded." Most students, however, would explain the Bradley "balance" this way: "Life at school is great . . . People are still very determined to do well in school, to get their degree," and "don't feel worried about finding a job after college, because [they] know that [they] have Bradley's faculty and staff to help [them] through that process."

FINANCIAL AID: 309-677-3089 • E-MAIL: ADMISSIONS@BRADLEY.EDU • WEBSITE: WWW.BRADLEY.EDU

THE PRINCETON REVIEW SAYS

Admissions

Very important factors considered include: rigor of secondary school record, academic GPA. *Important factors considered include:* class rank, standardized test scores. *Other factors considered include:* application essay, recommendation(s), interview, extracurricular activities, talent/ability, character/personal qualities, first generation, alumni/ae relation, geographical residence, racial/ethnic status, volunteer work, work experience, level of applicant's interest. SAT or ACT required. ACT with or without writing accepted. SAT with or without Essay component accepted. TOEFL required of all international applicants. High school diploma is required and GED is accepted. *Academic units required:* 4 English, 3 math, 2 science, 2 science labs, 2 social studies. *Academic units recommended:* 5 English, 4 math, 3 science, 3 science labs, 2 foreign language, 3 social studies, 2 history.

Financial Aid

Students should submit: FAFSA. Priority filing deadline is 3/1.The Princeton Review suggests that all financial aid forms be submitted as soon as possible after October 1. *Need-based scholarships/grants offered:* Federal Pell, FSEOG, State scholarships/grants, Private scholarships, College/university scholarship or grant aid from institutional funds. *Loan aid offered:* Direct Subsidized Stafford Loans, Direct Unsubsidized Stafford Loans, Direct PLUS loans, Federal Perkins Loans, Federal Nursing Loans. Applicants will be notified of awards on a rolling basis beginning 3/1. Federal Work-Study Program available. Institutional employment available.

The Inside Word

Due to Bradley's regional appeal, the vast majority of undergrads originate from Illinois. With an active eye toward broadening the student body's geographic demographics, the school presents an opportunity for out-of-staters seeking to attend an excellent university without having to endure the grueling admissions process of many private universities. Above-average students should find that gaining admission here is a relatively painless experience, with minimal admission requirements and three separate dates to apply (priority, standard, and rolling).

THE SCHOOL SAYS "..."

From the Admissions Office

"Bradley is a prestigious, private university in Peoria, Illinois, with 5,400 students. The university prepares students for immediate and substantial career success by offering resources not found at small colleges and more personalized experiences than large universities.

"Great academic variety leads to choices of majors, minors and graduate programs that are uncommon at most private universities. More than 185 academic programs are available in business, communications, education, engineering, fine and performing arts, health sciences, liberal arts, science and technology. Unique programs include entrepreneurship, game design, sports communication and physical therapy. Located less than three hours from Chicago, St. Louis and Indianapolis, the eighty-five-acre residential campus is located in a historic neighborhood just one mile from downtown Peoria, the largest metropolitan area in downstate Illinois.

"Bradley students develop leadership skills in more than 240 student organizations, with more than 60 dedicated to student leadership and community service. Students may also participate in the nation's most winning speech team, fraternities and sororities, and NCAA Division I athletics.

"Bradley graduates are well prepared for a career or direct entry to graduate school with 92 percent employed, continuing their education or pursuing other postgraduate experiences within six months of graduation. Seventy-seven percent of students reported having at least one career-related work experience before graduating, and 97 percent report having participated in an internship, practicum, undergraduate research, community service or study abroad.

"The Princeton Review rates Bradley's entrepreneurship program, internship opportunities and video game design programs as among the top in the nation."

SELECTIVITY

Admissions Rating	83
# of applicants	9,186
% of applicants accepted	66
% of acceptees attending	15
# offered a place on the wait list	0

FRESHMAN PROFILE

Range SAT Critical Reading	500–620
Range SAT Math	520–650
Range SAT Writing	470–610
Range ACT Composite	23–28
Minimum paper TOEFL	550
Minimum internet-based TOEFL	79
Average HS GPA	3.7
% graduated top 10% of class	22
% graduated top 25% of class	58
% graduated top 50% of class	89

DEADLINES

Regular	
Priority	2/1
Nonfall registration?	Yes

APPLICANTS ALSO LOOK AT AND OFTEN PREFER

Purdue University—West Lafayette; Northwestern University; University of Iowa

AND SOMETIMES PREFER

Butler University; DePaul University; Illinois Wesleyan University; Loyola University of Chicago; Marquette University; Saint Louis University; University of Illinois at Urbana-Champaign

AND RARELY PREFER

University of Missouri

FINANCIAL FACTS

Financial Aid Rating	83
Annual tuition	$31,110
Room and board	$9,700
Required fees	$370
Books and supplies	$1,200
Average frosh need-based scholarship	$17,808
Average UG need-based scholarship	$15,801
% needy frosh rec. need-based scholarship or grant aid	99
% needy UG rec. need-based scholarship or grant aid	96
% needy frosh rec. non-need-based scholarship or grant aid	14
% needy UG rec. non-need-based scholarship or grant aid	11
% needy frosh rec. need-based self-help aid	77
% needy UG rec. need-based self-help aid	80
% frosh rec. any financial aid	95
% UG rec. any financial aid	88
% UG borrow to pay for school	80
Average cumulative indebtedness	$28,093
% frosh need fully met	18
% ugrads need fully met	17
Average % of frosh need met	70
Average % of ugrad need met	67

BRANDEIS UNIVERSITY

415 SOUTH STREET, WALTHAM, MA 02454-9110 • ADMISSIONS: 781-736-3500 • FAX: 781-736-3536

CAMPUS LIFE

Quality of Life Rating	91
Fire Safety Rating	97
Green Rating	87
Type of school	Private
Affiliation	No Affiliation
Environment	City

STUDENTS

Total undergrad enrollment	3,621
% male/female	43/57
% from out of state	74
% frosh from public high school	57
% frosh live on campus	99
% ugrads live on campus	79
% African American	5
% Asian	13
% Caucasian	47
% Hispanic	7
% Native American	<1
% Pacific Islander	<1
% Two or more races	3
% Race and/or ethnicity unknown	5
% international	20
# of countries represented	54

SURVEY SAYS...

Lots of liberal students
Students are happy
Lab facilities are great
School is well run
Students are friendly
Diverse student types interact on campus
Students get along with local community
Students involved in community service
Students environmentally aware
Theater is popular
Active minority support groups

ACADEMICS

Academic Rating	89
% students returning for sophomore year	92
% students graduating within 4 years	80
% students graduating within 6 years	87
Calendar	Semester
Student/faculty ratio	10:1
Profs interesting rating	90
Profs accessible rating	86

Most classes have 10–19 students.

MOST POPULAR MAJORS
Biology; Economics; Psychology

STUDENTS SAY "..."

Academics

Located just outside Boston, Brandeis is a private liberal arts and research university that has "a little bit of everything." The school "gives students the freedom to explore both in and outside of the classroom" It has a (rightful) reputation for tough academics, particularly in the sciences, and this "pays off. Employers, grad schools, and certainly medical schools, know how tough the academics are." The school puts "a great importance on social justice and community," the latter of which "is unmatched" elsewhere. Academics at Brandeis are "stimulating," and even though a few professors at times can be "inconsistent and unreliable," the faculty on the whole is "extremely dedicated to their subjects" and "truly there for the students." "As a first-year student I was part of a class that was invited to the professor's house for a Thanksgiving pot luck dinner," says one. Getting some sort of outside help is necessary for the sciences, as "classes are often curved, and the competition is tough," but luckily professors are all available, and "all of the introductory classes break down into small groups once a week." People "care about their studies, but the atmosphere isn't competitive." Science-minded students are often impressed that there are "plenty of scientific research opportunities" for such a small school, and many students "find it difficult to choose classes because of all of the awesome course descriptions." Student services have expanded in recent years, and the Hiatt Career Center now offers "Graduate School Thursdays, alumni shadowing, mock interviews, and career fairs specifically themed toward 'green jobs,' government forums, and other student interests." Independence is a huge part of a Brandeis student's life, and the administration is good about "letting students take charge of their own educations." "We create our own experiences: independent study, clubs, and committees. Students own their experiences," says one student. "It is a wonderfully unique college experience with some of the nicest—and occasionally strangest—people you will ever meet."

Life

Because the school is situated in a small city immediately outside of college-rich Boston, it's able to have "sprawling lawns and an atmosphere of community and openness" while still being accessible to an urban cultural center. There is a "massive amount of extracurricular activities," so "there is always something to do," including a "Cheese Club that provides free cheese tasting," "arts outlets," and numerous organizations that place a "strong emphasis on volunteerism and social justice." "This is…a tremendous place to explore your passions—religiously, socially, and academically," says a student. There are "a ton" of theater, a cappella, and improv groups on campus, and if the campus events aren't enough to satiate your appetite for fun, "there are always ways to go and support other extracurricular groups on campus and see what they're all about." Still, one student warns, "If athletics are the center of your universe, then do not go to Brandeis."

Student Body

There are "few social lines that define the student body" at Brandeis, and "a lot of social life revolves around club life." Students are active here, and "it's not unheard of to find a neuroscience major who juggles DJing on WBRS, skydiving, and student government." This "intellectual and exciting" crew includes a "strong Jewish community," and almost everyone is "nerdy in a very, very cool way." People here are "really quirky and different," and most have secondary pursuits or hobbies outside of academics. "Whatever the students' passions and skills might be, everyone is incredibly motivated and driven toward achievement." Everyone is "fairly studious and encourages each other to study and do their best." Students seem to be friendly without fail. "If you stand in one place for too long on campus, you'll immediately find students approaching you asking if you're lost and how they can help," says a student.

FINANCIAL AID: 781-736-3700 • E-MAIL: ADMISSIONS@BRANDEIS.EDU • WEBSITE: WWW.BRANDEIS.EDU

THE PRINCETON REVIEW SAYS

Admissions

Very important factors considered include: rigor of secondary school record, class rank, academic GPA, character/personal qualities. *Important factors considered include:* application essay, recommendation(s), extracurricular activities, talent/ability, volunteer work, work experience, level of applicant's interest. *Other factors considered include:* standardized test scores, interview, first generation, alumni/ae relation, geographical residence, state residency, racial/ethnic status. SAT or ACT required. ACT with Writing required. TOEFL required of all international applicants. High school diploma is required and GED is accepted. *Academic units recommended:* 4 English, 4 math, 4 science, 2 science labs, 4 foreign language, 4 social studies.

Financial Aid

Students should submit: FAFSA, CSS/Financial Aid PROFILE, Noncustodial PROFILE. Regular filing deadline is 2/1.The Princeton Review suggests that all financial aid forms be submitted as soon as possible after October 1. *Need-based scholarships/grants offered:* Federal Pell, FSEOG, State scholarships/grants, Private scholarships, College/university scholarship or grant aid from institutional funds. *Loan aid offered:* Direct Subsidized Stafford Loans, Direct Unsubsidized Stafford Loans, Direct PLUS loans, Federal Perkins Loans, State Loans, College/university loans from institutional funds. Applicants will be notified of awards on or about 4/1. Federal Work-Study Program available. Institutional employment available.

The Inside Word

Admissions standards have risen at all top schools, and Brandeis is no exception: If you expect to get in here, you've got your work cut out for you. Your application should give evidence of both the ability and enthusiasm to handle demanding academics. A clear demonstration of writing ability will also help a lot.

THE SCHOOL SAYS "..."

From the Admissions Office

"Education at Brandeis is personal, combining the intimacy of a small liberal arts college and the intellectual power of a large research university. Classes are small and are taught by professors, 95 percent of whom hold the highest degree in their fields. They give students personal attention in state-of-the-art resources, giving them the tools to succeed in a variety of postgraduate endeavors.

"This vibrant, free-thinking, intellectual university was founded in 1948. Brandeis University reflects the values of the first Jewish Supreme Court Justice Louis Brandeis, which are passion for learning, commitment to social justice, respect for creativity and diversity, and concern for the world.

"Brandeis has an ideal location on the commuter rail right outside of downtown Boston; state-of-the-art sports facilities; and internships that complement interests in law, medicine, government, finance, business, and the arts.

"Brandeis meets 100 percent of demonstrated need for all admitted students."

SELECTIVITY

Admissions Rating	96
# of applicants	10,528
% of applicants accepted	34
% of acceptees attending	36
# offered a place on the wait list	1,553
% accepting a place on wait list	38
% admitted from wait list	4
# of early decision applicants	698
% accepted early decision	35

FRESHMAN PROFILE

Range SAT Critical Reading	600–700
Range SAT Math	650–770
Range SAT Writing	640–710
Range ACT Composite	29–32
Minimum paper TOEFL	600
Minimum internet-based TOEFL	100
Average HS GPA	4.0
% graduated top 10% of class	71
% graduated top 25% of class	91
% graduated top 50% of class	98

DEADLINES

Early decision	
Deadline	11/1
Notification	12/15
Regular	
Deadline	1/1
Notification	4/1
Nonfall registration?	Yes

FINANCIAL FACTS

Financial Aid Rating	90
Annual tuition	$47,702
Room and board	$13,856
Required fees	$1,596
Books and supplies	$1,000
Average frosh need-based scholarship	$38,299
Average UG need-based scholarship	$35,798
% needy frosh rec. need-based scholarship or grant aid	97
% needy UG rec. need-based scholarship or grant aid	94
% needy frosh rec. non-need-based scholarship or grant aid	8
% needy UG rec. non-need-based scholarship or grant aid	4
% needy frosh rec. need-based self-help aid	89
% needy UG rec. need-based self-help aid	94
% frosh rec. any financial aid	63
% UG rec. any financial aid	65
% UG borrow to pay for school	58
Average cumulative indebtedness	$30,850
% frosh need fully met	84
% ugrads need fully met	75
Average % of frosh need met	97
Average % of ugrad need met	85

BRIGHAM YOUNG UNIVERSITY (UT)

A-153 ASB, PROVO, UT 84602-1110 • ADMISSIONS: 801-422-2507 • FAX: 801-422-0005

CAMPUS LIFE

Quality of Life Rating	92
Fire Safety Rating	76
Green Rating	60*
Type of school	Private
Affiliation	Church of Jesus Christ of Latter-day Saints
Environment	City

STUDENTS

Total undergrad enrollment	30,221
% male/female	52/48
% from out of state	66
% frosh live on campus	79
% ugrads live on campus	19
% African American	<1
% Asian	2
% Caucasian	83
% Hispanic	6
% Native American	<1
% Pacific Islander	1
% Two or more races	4
% Race and/or ethnicity unknown	1
% international	3
# of countries represented	121

SURVEY SAYS...

Lots of conservative students
Students are happy
Classroom facilities are great
Great library
School is well run
Great financial aid
No one cheats
Students are friendly
Students are very religious
Students get along with local community
Students involved in community service
Very little drug use
Everyone loves the Cougars
Intramural sports are popular
Campus newspaper is popular

ACADEMICS

Academic Rating	83
% students returning for sophomore year	86
% students graduating within 4 years	31
% students graduating within 6 years	80
Calendar	Semester
Student/faculty ratio	20:1
Profs interesting rating	82
Profs accessible rating	80

Most classes have 10–19 students.

MOST POPULAR MAJORS

Business/Commerce; Exercise Physiology;
Elementary Education and Teaching

STUDENTS SAY "..."

Academics

Brigham Young University is a Mormon school that's "all about putting religion and education together" and learning "about secular subjects through spiritual eyes." The school provides a "high-quality" education in a "challenging" academic atmosphere. Students at Brigham Young strive for academic excellence. As one student explains, "Brigham Young pushes us to realize that our 'best' can be a lot better than we ever dreamed, and I love that!" The school offers a wide range of majors, and its education, business, and mathematics programs get great reviews, as does their language program. Classes are generally a "healthy mix of discussion and lecture," and the education classes in particular have "a lot of group work." The school doesn't focus only on classroom learning, however. "Hands-on experience, internships, and study abroad are highly encouraged," and many students take advantage of these opportunities. There are also "tons of undergraduate research opportunities." Professors are "passionate about what they're teaching," and they "really care about their students' success." Another adds, "Professors really do take a genuine interest in their students," and "the vast majority are also very willing to help out students individually." While students at Brigham Young appreciate the academic attention they receive from professors, they also like that it "is committed to spiritual and academic learning for the benefit and betterment of everyone" and that they're being taught to "pursue lifelong learning and service."

Life

Students at Brigham Young love the "atmosphere of spirituality that unites everyone" and "the kindness of those around you." Brigham Young provides a "safe environment," but students "still get to have real-world experiences." Recreationally, "there are multiple clubs across campus to fit the taste of different people," "tons of...performing events," and "fun student body activities, which are cheap." There are also "exceptional weekly devotions and forums." Brigham Young's athletics are well-supported and are a place where "students love to have fun." Students rave about the library and the "Adlab," but more than anything they appreciate that there are "good people everywhere you go."

Student Body Brigham Young has an extremely conservative "Honor Code" derived from the Mormon Church that requires, among other things, abstinence from drugs, alcohol, tobacco, coffee, and tea, as well as what the church considers "inappropriate" "sexual activity, including sex outside of marriage and homosexuality." The Honor Code is a plus for students seeking a like-minded peer group, such as this art education student who "didn't want to have to worry about walking in on my roommate sleeping with someone or have to hold her head up while she was puking her guts out into the toilet." The Honor Code also demands honesty and respect for others, which means the student body is "friendly, outgoing," and "concerned for others." Students are "smart and very confident in their intelligence," as well as "hardworking" and "goal-oriented." Mormon traditions mean that 25 percent of students are married, and people appreciate that "the school caters...really well to the average Latter-day Saint student coming in and working with those wanting to get married [or] go on missions." Marriage is definitely on many people's minds. A family studies major notes, "We are constantly encouraged to date." People generally think that "students mesh together well and it is easy to make new friends," though one concedes, "I can see how it could be hard to fit in if you are not used to the Mormon culture or beliefs."

BRIGHAM YOUNG UNIVERSITY (UT)

FINANCIAL AID: 801-422-4104 • E-MAIL: ADMISSIONS@BYU.EDU • WEBSITE: WWW.BYU.EDU

THE PRINCETON REVIEW SAYS

Admissions

Very important factors considered include: rigor of secondary school record, academic GPA, standardized test scores, interview, character/personal qualities, religious affiliation/commitment. *Important factors considered include:* application essay, recommendation(s), extracurricular activities, racial/ethnic status, volunteer work. *Other factors considered include:* talent/ability, first generation, geographical residence, state residency, work experience, level of applicant's interest. SAT or ACT required. ACT with or without writing accepted. SAT with or without Essay component accepted. TOEFL required of all international applicants. High school diploma is required and GED is accepted. *Academic units recommended:* 4 English, 4 math, 3 science, 2 foreign language, 2 history.

Financial Aid

Students should submit: FAFSA. Priority filing deadline is 4/15. The Princeton Review suggests that all financial aid forms be submitted as soon as possible after October 1. *Need-based scholarships/grants offered:* Federal Pell, Private scholarships, College/university scholarship or grant aid from institutional funds. *Loan aid offered:* Direct Subsidized Stafford Loans, Direct Unsubsidized Stafford Loans, Direct PLUS loans. Federal Work-Study Program available. Institutional employment available.

The Inside Word

An applicant pool of more than 10,000 necessitates a reliance on numbers, especially during the first round of cuts. Much of the matchmaking done at other schools isn't necessary here, as a highly self-selecting applicant pool typically precludes those who would make a poor fit. Still, admissions officers want to see at least respect (if not reverence) for LDS principles, without which survival here would be difficult indeed.

THE SCHOOL SAYS "..."

From the Admissions Office

"The mission of Brigham Young University—founded, supported, and guided by The Church of Jesus Christ of Latter-day Saints—is to assist individuals in their quest for perfection and eternal life. That assistance should provide a period of intensive learning in a stimulating setting where a commitment to excellence is expected and the full realization of human potential is pursued. All instruction, programs, and services at BYU, including a wide variety of extracurricular experiences, should make their own contribution toward the balanced development of the total person. Such a broadly prepared individual will not only be capable of meeting personal challenge and change but will also bring strength to others in the tasks of home and family life, social relationships, civic duty, and service to mankind.

"Freshman applicants are required to take either the ACT (with the optional writing section) or the SAT. The highest composite score will be used in admissions decisions."

SELECTIVITY

Admissions Rating	94
# of applicants	13,376
% of applicants accepted	48
% of acceptees attending	80

FRESHMAN PROFILE

Range SAT Critical Reading	570–680
Range SAT Math	580–68
Range SAT Writing	550–660
Range ACT Composite	27–31
Minimum paper TOEFL	500
Average HS GPA	3.8
% graduated top 10% of class	54
% graduated top 25% of class	85
% graduated top 50% of class	98

DEADLINES

Regular	
Priority	12/1
Deadline	2/1
Notification	2/28
Nonfall registration?	Yes

APPLICANTS ALSO LOOK AT AND SOMETIMES PREFER
University of Utah

FINANCIAL FACTS

Financial Aid Rating	78
Annual tuition	$5,150
Room and board	$7,330
Books and supplies	$992
Average frosh need-based scholarship	$4,908
Average UG need-based scholarship	$5,068
% needy frosh rec. need-based scholarship or grant aid	57
% needy UG rec. need-based scholarship or grant aid	80
% needy frosh rec. non-need-based scholarship or grant aid	69
% needy UG rec. non-need-based scholarship or grant aid	45
% needy frosh rec. need-based self-help aid	27
% needy UG rec. need-based self-help aid	30
% frosh rec. any financial aid	53
% UG rec. any financial aid	64
% UG borrow to pay for school	27
Average cumulative indebtedness	$15,720
% frosh need fully met	1
% ugrads need fully met	2
Average % of frosh need met	30
Average % of ugrad need met	34

BROWN UNIVERSITY

Box 1876, Providence, RI 02912 • Admissions: 401-863-2378 • Fax: 401-863-9300

STUDENTS SAY "..."

Academics

Interdisciplinary-focused Brown University in Providence, Rhode Island is entirely dedicated to undergraduate freedom, meaning students must take responsibility for designing their own courses of study via the Open Curriculum. Students sing the praises of the academic flexibility at this Ivy League institution and the accompanying emphasis on social action. "We would not be . . . strong students and teachers without a proper system in place to encourage that," says one undergrad. Those who roam these hallowed halls are "constantly questioning what could make the world and our school a better place." Every person "has their own interests and pursues it without any push from others," which is why Brown can be a "very intense" place to go to school—not because it's academically competitive, but "because there are so many people doing so much and fighting so hard for it."

Brown's faculty "are at the top of their fields and are working on research that pushes those fields forward." The "engaging, personal, and incredibly dedicated" professors are "the heart and soul of our strongest departments." They "care so much about what they do and connect with students on a very human level." Undergraduates come first here, and Brown encourages students to "explore their academic interests independently in order to experience everything that academics have to offer." "No other school I had looked at allowed students to completely build their own academic journey without any general requirements," says one student. Graduates tend to "not just go to the normative career options," and "career and internship placement has become a top priority of the new university administration."

Life

Life at Brown can be "exciting, but also filled with countless hours of study." Though academia reigns over the week, most people "go to house parties, sport parties, or downtown for the weekend," and there are "lectures, movie screenings, improv shows, dance performances, [and] a cappella showcases constantly." "Brown is generally a very happy place with many activities and events going on all the time," says a student. A great thing about these type of events is that "they are rarely exclusionary and the university is trusting of its students." Many here also do "intellectual activities or athletics over breaks," and "community clubs and special interest clubs (such as international student groups)" are extremely popular. Students also often go to the lounges in the dorms to watch movies with friends. The campus may be "beautiful," but when an off-campus breather is needed, students can easily walk one minute to Thayer Street and "enjoy restaurants and excellent dining" or walk twenty minutes to Providence Mall. Boston and New York are very close, but "Providence is busy enough that Brown never completely empties out."

Student Body

This "knowledgeable and inspiring" community is made up of people who are "very intelligent, care about global issues, and possess one or two quirks." The school "has a way of molding people into their best selves," and the most common trait is "a true zeal for whatever it is that we care most about." Although this is a liberal campus, there are "a handful of conservatives," and "the entire body has a general chilled-out vibe." There is "a prevailing intolerance of intolerance on campus," and the culture of activism "bespeaks an idealism and a strong moral code that drives a lot of the work students do on campus." "I've never experienced so many people willing to have a conversation about topics that usually make people uncomfortable or that people stray away," says one student.

FINANCIAL AID: 401-863-2721 • E-MAIL: ADMISSION_UNDERGRADUATE@BROWN.EDU • WEBSITE: WWW.BROWN.EDU

THE PRINCETON REVIEW SAYS

Admissions

Very important factors considered include: rigor of secondary school record, class rank, academic GPA, standardized test scores, application essays, recommendation(s), character/personal qualities, extracurricular activities. *Important factors considered include:* interview, first generation, alumni/ae relation, geographical residence, state residency, racial/ethnic status, volunteer work, work experience. ACT with or without Writing or SAT with or without Essay component plus two SAT Subject Tests required. High school diploma is required and GED is accepted. *Academic units required:* 4 English, 3 math, 3 science, 2 science labs, 3 foreign language, 2 history, 1 academic elective. *Academic units recommended:* 4 English, 4 math, 4 science, 3 science labs, 4 foreign language, 1 social studies, 2 history, 1 academic elective, 1 computer science, 1 visual/performing arts.

Financial Aid

Students should submit: FAFSA, CSS/Financial Aid PROFILE, Noncustodial PROFILE. Regular filing deadline is 2/1.The Princeton Review suggests that all financial aid forms be submitted as soon as possible after October 1. *Need-based scholarships/grants offered:* Federal Pell, FSEOG, State scholarships/grants, Private scholarships, College/university scholarship or grant aid from institutional funds. *Loan aid offered:* Direct Subsidized Stafford Loans, Direct Unsubsidized Stafford Loans, Direct PLUS loans, Federal Perkins Loans, College/university loans from institutional funds. Applicants will be notified of awards on or about 4/1. Federal Work-Study Program available. Institutional employment available.

The Inside Word

The cream of just about every crop applies to Brown, and, as at many selective schools, the acceptance rate tends to shrink each year. Gaining admission requires more than just a superior academic profile from high school. Candidates from states that are overrepresented in the applicant pool, such as New York, have to be particularly distinguished in order to have the best chance at admission. Brown accepts the Common Application, with additional writing supplements for all first-year students, and requires some additional statements from students who intend to study the sciences. Test scores (either the SAT plus two SAT Subject Tests or the ACT with or without Writing) are required.

THE SCHOOL SAYS "..."

From the Admissions Office

"Brown University is the nation's seventh oldest institution of higher education and the third oldest in New England. Since 1764, Brown has offered the best in liberal arts education, leading-edge scholarship and research, and opportunities for community-based service learning. Its flexible undergraduate curriculum involves more than 6,600 students in the design of their own studies, with nearly eighty concentrations in forty-four different academic areas and the option of independent study. The Warren Alpert Medical School of Brown University, Rhode Island's only medical school, provides over 500 students with medical instruction and clinical training at seven Brown-affiliated hospitals in and around Providence. Brown is one of eight members of the Ivy League."

SELECTIVITY

Admissions Rating	99
# of applicants	30,396
% of applicants accepted	9
% of acceptees attending	56
# of early decision applicants	3,043
% accepted early decision	20

FRESHMAN PROFILE

Range SAT Critical Reading	680–780
Range SAT Math	690–780
Range SAT Writing	690–780
Range ACT Composite	31–34
Minimum paper TOEFL	600
Minimum internet-based TOEFL	100
% graduated top 10% of class	91
% graduated top 25% of class	100
% graduated top 50% of class	100

DEADLINES

Early decision	
Deadline	11/1
Notification	12/15
Regular	
Deadline	1/1
Nonfall registration?	No

APPLICANTS ALSO LOOK AT AND OFTEN PREFER

Princeton University; Yale University; Stanford University; Harvard College

AND SOMETIMES PREFER

Columbia University; Cornell University; University of Pennsylvania

AND RARELY PREFER

Bowdoin College; Tufts University; Georgetown University; Oberlin College

FINANCIAL FACTS

Financial Aid Rating	95
Annual tuition	$50,224
Room and board	$13,200
Required fees	$1,142
Books and supplies	$1,540
Average frosh need-based scholarship	$42,109
Average UG need-based scholarship	$43,045
% needy frosh rec. need-based scholarship or grant aid	96
% needy UG rec. need-based scholarship or grant aid	96
% needy frosh rec. non-need-based scholarship or grant aid	0
% needy UG rec. non-need-based scholarship or grant aid	0
% needy frosh rec. need-based self-help aid	84
% needy UG rec. need-based self-help aid	89
% frosh rec. any financial aid	55
% UG rec. any financial aid	57
% UG borrow to pay for school	34
Average cumulative indebtedness	$22,197
% frosh need fully met	100
% ugrads need fully met	100
Average % of frosh need met	100
Average % of ugrad need met	100

BRYANT UNIVERSITY

1150 DOUGLAS PIKE, SMITHFIELD, RI 02917-1291 • ADMISSIONS: 401-232-6100 • FAX: 401-232-6731

CAMPUS LIFE

Quality of Life Rating	91
Fire Safety Rating	96
Green Rating	76
Type of school	Private
Affiliation	No Affiliation
Environment	Village

STUDENTS

Total undergrad enrollment	3,430
% male/female	59/41
% from out of state	88
% frosh from public high school	50
% frosh live on campus	95
% ugrads live on campus	82
# of fraternities (% ugrad men join)	5 (5)
# of sororities (% ugrad women join)	4 (11)
% African American	4
% Asian	5
% Caucasian	71
% Hispanic	7
% Native American	1
% Pacific Islander	1
% Two or more races	1
% Race and/or ethnicity unknown	2
% international	8
# of countries represented	72

SURVEY SAYS...

Students are happy
Great library
Career services are great
Internships are widely available
School is well run
Easy to get around campus
Lots of beer drinking
Hard liquor is popular
Everyone loves the Bulldogs
Intramural sports are popular

ACADEMICS

Academic Rating	79
% students returning for sophomore year	90
% students graduating within 4 years	76
% students graduating within 6 years	79
Calendar	Semester
Student/faculty ratio	13:1
Profs interesting rating	86
Profs accessible rating	85

Most classes have 30-39 students.
Most lab/discussion sessions have
fewer than 10 students.

MOST POPULAR MAJORS

Accounting; Finance; Marketing/Marketing
Management

STUDENTS SAY "..."

Academics

Located in Smithfield, Rhode Island, Bryant University is "small" New England school that "breaks the boundaries between liberal arts and business." "Bryant is primarily focused on business, but also encourages students to expand their world academically and professionally," one student explains. The university takes a "global view" to entrepreneurship, and Bryant students dream of "becoming the next CEO." "Classes are very small at Bryant, which means you get a lot of attention from your professors," an international business major explains. "Passionate" and with "real world experience in their field," professors here really "care about their students" and "are always willing to meet outside of class for extra help." The faculty make sure their lessons are both "fueled by discussion and meaningful readings" and "applicable to real situations." A Bryant education "prepares you to be a leader in today's world through countless team projects, leadership opportunities, and a strong value system." Above all, Bryant excels at "job placement" and the "well-connected" professors "have the resources to help students." "Students get great internships and experience that lead to a 98 percent placement rate in the workplace or grad school," one student explains. Students say that Bryant is "a place that builds character" and offers a "unique blend of business expertise with liberal arts subjects." While students really love the "close knit community" and the "beautiful campus," some students do wish for a greater focus on "sustainability," which "does not seem to be a major factor of the school." Still, one happy student sums the school up as "a supportive community of learners that is dedicated to challenging students in new and inventive ways."

Life

"Everyone's always busy" at Bryant and campus participation is the norm. As one accounting major says, "If you aren't in clubs, organizations or sports, [then] you aren't doing it right." Students tend to be in "several clubs" and "most students have work study jobs or internships" to bolster their job potential upon graduation. However, "Bryant students definitely believe in the 'work hard, play hard' motto." That means "study hard during the week" but "go out both weekend nights and a few weekday nights as well." "Because it is hard to get off campus, it does get kind of boring, so most people stay on campus to have fun and drink here." That said, some students do "go out to Providence or Boston to enjoy the city on weekends." "I would have to stress how career oriented this university is," one student says. "Students typically have more than one summer of internship experience before graduating and seniors frequently accept job offers during their fall semester." On campus, the university "constantly put[s] on events for students" including "Big Bingo, Laser Tag, musicians, comedians, and more." "Athletics are also a big part of life at Bryant," and students love "going to sporting events" and rooting for the Bulldogs.

Student Body

"A typical student here is from New England, majoring in business" and "involved in at least one organization on campus." The dress code is "very preppy" with students wearing "black Nike apparel" or else "nice clothes, even to class every day." While students do come from different backgrounds, "this is definitely an upper middle class school." "It's a school that has a bunch of wealthy white people promoting diversity," one student explains. However, "there has definitely been an increase in international students" in recent years. "The ethnic diversity is better than most business schools given the strong international program," another student confirms. Overall, Bryant students are "smart and driven" and "willing to meet new people." Students "fit in by finding groups they are interested in, and joining them."

FINANCIAL AID: 401-232-6020 • E-MAIL: ADMISSION@BRYANT.EDU • WEBSITE: WWW.BRYANT.EDU

THE PRINCETON REVIEW SAYS

Admissions

Very important factors considered include: rigor of secondary school record, academic GPA. *Important factors considered include:* class rank, standardized test scores, application essay, recommendation(s). *Other factors considered include:* interview, extracurricular activities, talent/ability, character/personal qualities, first generation, alumni/ae relation, geographical residence, state residency, racial/ethnic status, volunteer work, work experience, level of applicant's interest. SAT or ACT considered if submitted. ACT with or without writing accepted. TOEFL required of all international applicants. High school diploma is required and GED is accepted. *Academic units required:* 4 English, 4 math, 2 science, 2 science labs, 2 foreign language, 2 history. *Academic units recommended:* 4 English, 4 math, 3 science, 2 science labs, 2 foreign language, 3 history.

Financial Aid

Students should submit: FAFSA. Regular filing deadline is 2/15. The Princeton Review suggests that all financial aid forms be submitted as soon as possible after October 1. *Need-based scholarships/grants offered:* Federal Pell, FSEOG, State scholarships/grants, Private scholarships, College/university scholarship or grant aid from institutional funds. *Loan aid offered:* Direct Subsidized Stafford Loans, Direct Unsubsidized Stafford Loans, Direct PLUS loans, Federal Perkins Loans. Applicants will be notified of awards on or about 3/24. Federal Work-Study Program available. Institutional employment available.

The Inside Word

Bryant University seeks to combine business training with the best of a liberal arts education, and the admissions committee looks for students who will fit into that environment. There are no "cutoffs" or minimum score requirements for admissions, but the strongest applicants will have challenged themselves in high school by taking honors, AP, and IB courses when available. While interviews are not required, Bryant enjoys the opportunity to get to know prospective students on a more personal level. Interview notes are automatically added to your application file.

THE SCHOOL SAYS ". . ."

From the Admissions Office

"Bryant delivers an exceptional education for success in an age of unlimited global opportunity. The undergraduate curriculum is nationally recognized for innovation. From the very first semester, you'll find that Bryant's interdisciplinary studies and engaged learning are designed with your success in mind. Our world-class professors integrate theoretical and applied concepts in a broad range of majors from accounting to sociology, all complemented by rich co-curricular opportunities. A Bryant education speaks for itself—99 percent of our students are employed or enrolled in graduate school within six months of Commencement.

"At Bryant, you will discover your passion and create your own path as you develop the knowledge, skills, credentials, and qualities of character to become an active contributor who thinks in a global context. Uniquely dedicated to the integration of business and the liberal arts, and committed to an educational experience that blends knowledge and practice, Bryant students choose from nearly 100 courses of study.

"From attending a Bulldogs football game to practicing for a business competition, our students participate in more than 100 organizations and clubs.

"A globally focused education includes a diverse student body from seventy-two countries and thirty-six states.

"Our stunning, 435-acre campus in Smithfield, Rhode Island, is just fifteen minutes from downtown Providence, an hour from Boston, and three hours from New York City."

SELECTIVITY

Admissions Rating	82
# of applicants	6,705
% of applicants accepted	72
% of acceptees attending	19
# offered a place on the wait list	391
% accepting a place on wait list	30
% admitted from wait list	2
# of early decision applicants	186
% accepted early decision	67

FRESHMAN PROFILE

Range SAT Critical Reading	530–610
Range SAT Math	560–640
Range SAT Writing	510–610
Range ACT Composite	23–27
Minimum paper TOEFL	550
Minimum internet-based TOEFL	80
Average HS GPA	3.4
% graduated top 10% of class	24
% graduated top 25% of class	58
% graduated top 50% of class	90

DEADLINES

Early decision	
Deadline	11/1
Notification	12/15
Early action	
Deadline	11/15
Notification	1/15
Regular	
Deadline	2/1
Notification	3/15
Nonfall registration?	Yes

APPLICANTS ALSO LOOK AT AND OFTEN PREFER
Bentley University; Babson College

AND SOMETIMES PREFER
Providence College; Fairfield University

AND RARELY PREFER
Stonehill College; Quinnipiac University

FINANCIAL FACTS

Financial Aid Rating	84
Annual tuition	$40,564
Room and board	$14,975
Required fees	$398
Books and supplies	$1,300
Average frosh need-based scholarship	$9,008
Average UG need-based scholarship	$10,320
% needy frosh rec. need-based scholarship or grant aid	71
% needy UG rec. need-based scholarship or grant aid	76
% needy frosh rec. non-need-based scholarship or grant aid	75
% needy UG rec. non-need-based scholarship or grant aid	66
% needy frosh rec. need-based self-help aid	82
% needy UG rec. need-based self-help aid	87
% frosh rec. any financial aid	83
% UG rec. any financial aid	80
% frosh need fully met	50
% ugrads need fully met	50
Average % of frosh need met	51
Average % of ugrad need met	52

BRYN MAWR COLLEGE

101 NORTH MERION AVENUE, BRYN MAWR, PA 19010-2859 • ADMISSIONS: 610-526-5152 • FAX: 610-526-7471

STUDENTS SAY "..."

Academics

Bryn Mawr is all about "empowering women to achieve their dreams." The school has a "reputation for strong academics," and students confirm that work there is "no joke." Bryn Mawr is a small college, which means small classes. One student reports that most of hers have "around ten people," and another says her largest lecture class had forty students. This leads to "deep discussions [and] meaningful relationships [being] formed with peers and colleagues." Classes are "very interactive," and "great student-teacher relationships [are] established by the way classes are conducted." The faculty is "amazing and no doubt brilliant," and "they go a long way to make sure you don't only feel like students but also like a mini-family." An East Asian studies student says she feels "comfortable talking to faculty members/professors about anything." Students think one of the best parts about Bryn Mawr is the "amazing academic opportunities within the tri-co," and the "Quaker consortium": agreements that allow students to take classes at Haverford, Swarthmore, and the University of Pennsylvania. All of these great attributes combine to make Bryn Mawr a fantastic college experience. As one student puts it, Bryn Mawr "compels me to be extraordinary in an environment of equally extraordinary students."

Life

Academics are the focus of life at Bryn Mawr, but that doesn't mean students are "a bunch of nuns who sit around studying all day." "We do a lot of studying," a student explains, "but we also enjoy our time here." Not only are there "tons of school-sponsored activities," but there are opportunities to "go to a big party with tons of dancing and tons of people," at Bryn Mawr or at Haverford. "Meals here are really important," adds a student. "Dinner can be the only time we'll see each other, [which] can easily go on for an hour and a half." Bryn Mawr's "amazing food" probably has something to do with that. Bryn Mawr has an "absolutely beautiful campus," with great facilities, including a new gym with an "Olympic-sized swimming pool...TVs, large windows...and state-of-the-art machines that are built for women." Though Bryn Mawr has a suburban location, "the proximity and ease in traveling to Philadelphia, New York, and Washington, DC, is beyond fantastic." Students love Bryn Mawr's traditions, two of which are the Self-Government Association and the Honor Code. The Self-Government Association, the oldest student government in America, "allows...students to have an input on many aspects of how the college is run." The Honor Code, which every student must sign, emphasizes respect and integrity. The code creates "a strong community" and a safe one. One student says, "I don't lock my door!" Another adds, "You could lose a ring anywhere on campus and just send an e-mail out to the student body and have it back in the next few hours."

Student Body

"There is no typical student," at Bryn Mawr, "aside from women with a passion for learning and a commitment to excellence." A German student reports, "The variety of people here is enormous," and this "creates the...uniqueness that Bryn Mawr prides itself on." People's thoughts on racial diversity, however, "are kind of conflicting." One student explains, "Coming from a big city...Bryn Mawr did not seem very diverse, but my roommate came from a very small town and thought Bryn Mawr was extremely diverse." What students do agree on is that they're "friendly and welcoming," "creative," and "a little quirky." Though the intense workload means students are "very interested in... academics and work hard to get good grades," they "are also social" and "take time to build up strong friendships with other students." Students at Bryn Mawr really respect each other's individuality and love that their peers "have a purposive direction in regards to what they want to do with their future."

FINANCIAL AID: 610-526-5245 • E-MAIL: ADMISSIONS@BRYNMAWR.EDU • WEBSITE: WWW.BRYNMAWR.EDU

THE PRINCETON REVIEW SAYS

Admissions

Very important factors considered include: rigor of secondary school record, recommendation(s). *Important factors considered include:* academic GPA, application essay, extracurricular activities, character/personal qualities. *Other factors considered include:* class rank, standardized test scores, interview, talent/ability, first generation, alumni/ae relation, geographical residence, state residency, racial/ethnic status, volunteer work, work experience. ACT with or without writing accepted. TOEFL required of all international applicants. High school diploma is required and GED is accepted. *Academic units recommended:* 4 English, 3 math, 2 science, 1 science lab, 3 foreign language, 2 social studies, 2 history, 2 academic electives.

Financial Aid

Students should submit: FAFSA, CSS/Financial Aid PROFILE. Regular filing deadline is 3/1.The Princeton Review suggests that all financial aid forms be submitted as soon as possible after October 1. *Need-based scholarships/grants offered:* Federal Pell, FSEOG, State scholarships/grants, College/university scholarship or grant aid from institutional funds. *Loan aid offered:* Direct Subsidized Stafford Loans, Direct Unsubsidized Stafford Loans, Direct PLUS loans, Federal Perkins Loans. Federal Work-Study Program available. Institutional employment available.

The Inside Word

Bryn Mawr's student body is among the academically best in the nation. Outstanding preparation for graduate study draws an applicant pool that's well-prepared and intellectually curious. Interviews are strongly recommended but not required. If you're still unsure of how to stand out in the crowd, take advantage of Bryn Mawr's numerous on-campus and online opportunities to connect with current students.

THE SCHOOL SAYS "..."

From the Admissions Office

"Bryn Mawr's extraordinary academics, vibrant and diverse community, and focus on global leadership prepare students to challenge convention and take their places in the world. Every year 1,300 women from around the world gather on the college's historic campus to study with leading scholars, conduct advanced research, and expand the boundaries of what is possible. Consistently producing outstanding scholars, Bryn Mawr is ranked among the top fifteen of all colleges and universities in percentage of graduates who go on to earn a PhD, and is considered excellent preparation for the nation's top law, medical and business schools. More than 500 students collaborate with faculty on independent projects every year, and to augment an already strong curriculum, students may choose from more than 5,000 courses offered through nearby Haverford and Swarthmore colleges, as well as the University of Pennsylvania.

"Minutes outside of Philadelphia and only two hours by train from New York City and Washington, D.C., Bryn Mawr is recognized by many as one of the most stunning college campuses in the United States.

"Standardized test scores for U.S. applicants or U.S. permanent residents are not required. Non-U.S. citizens and Non-U.S. permanent residents are required to submit standardized test scores (SAT or ACT) as well as either the TOEFL or IELTS if their primary language is not English and/or their language of instruction over the last four years has not been English."

SELECTIVITY

Admissions Rating	94
# of applicants	2,890
% of applicants accepted	39
% of acceptees attending	35
# offered a place on the wait list	872
% accepting a place on wait list	49
% admitted from wait list	0
# of early decision applicants	279
% accepted early decision	50

FRESHMAN PROFILE

Range SAT Critical Reading	620–730
Range SAT Math	620–730
Range SAT Writing	630–730
Range ACT Composite	28–32
Minimum paper TOEFL	600
Minimum internet-based TOEFL	100
% graduated top 10% of class	63
% graduated top 25% of class	88
% graduated top 50% of class	98

DEADLINES

Early decision	
Deadline	11/15
Notification	12/15
Regular	
Deadline	1/15
Notification	4/1
Nonfall registration?	No

APPLICANTS ALSO LOOK AT AND OFTEN PREFER

Barnard College; Mount Holyoke College; Smith College; Wellesley College

AND SOMETIMES PREFER

Brown University; Cornell University; Grinnell College; Haverford College; New York University; Swarthmore College

FINANCIAL FACTS

Financial Aid Rating	96
Annual tuition	$47,640
Room and board	$15,370
Required fees	$1,150
Books and supplies	$1,000
Average frosh need-based scholarship	$38,311
Average UG need-based scholarship	$38,637
% needy frosh rec. need-based scholarship or grant aid	100
% needy UG rec. need-based scholarship or grant aid	100
% needy frosh rec. non-need-based scholarship or grant aid	5
% needy UG rec. non-need-based scholarship or grant aid	4
% needy frosh rec. need-based self-help aid	94
% needy UG rec. need-based self-help aid	91
% frosh rec. any financial aid	74
% UG rec. any financial aid	74
% UG borrow to pay for school	60
Average cumulative indebtedness	$22,914
% frosh need fully met	100
% ugrads need fully met	100
Average % of frosh need met	100
Average % of ugrad need met	100

BUCKNELL UNIVERSITY

OFFICE OF ADMISSION, 1 DENT DRIVE, LEWISBURG, PA 17837 • ADMISSIONS: 570-577-3000 • FAX: 570-577-3538

CAMPUS LIFE

Quality of Life Rating	89
Fire Safety Rating	94
Green Rating	94
Type of school	Private
Affiliation	No Affiliation
Environment	Village

STUDENTS

Total undergrad enrollment	3,569
% male/female	48/52
% from out of state	77
% frosh from public high school	64
% frosh live on campus	100
% ugrads live on campus	91
# of fraternities (% ugrad men join)	8 (42)
# of sororities (% ugrad women join)	8 (49)
% African American	3
% Asian	4
% Caucasian	77
% Hispanic	6
% Native American	<1
% Pacific Islander	0
% Two or more races	4
% Race and/or ethnicity unknown	<1
% international	5
# of countries represented	51

SURVEY SAYS...

Students are happy
Classroom facilities are great
Lab facilities are great
Great library
Career services are great
Internships are widely available
School is well run
Easy to get around campus
Recreation facilities are great
Lots of beer drinking
Hard liquor is popular
Everyone loves the Bison
Intramural sports are popular
Frats and sororities are popular
Alumni active on campus

ACADEMICS

Academic Rating	93
% students returning for sophomore year	93
% students graduating within 4 years	85
% students graduating within 6 years	90
Calendar	Semester
Student/faculty ratio	9:1
Profs interesting rating	92
Profs accessible rating	90

Most classes have 10–19 students.
Most lab/discussion sessions have
10–19 students.

MOST POPULAR MAJORS
Economics; Biology; Political Science and
Government

STUDENTS SAY "..."

Academics

Students choose Bucknell University, a private liberal arts school in central Pennsylvania, for its rep for "providing an excellent education, a small classroom setting with involved professors, and a close-knit community." The school packages a "great education and engineering school on a beautiful campus," where "the school spirit keeps students motivated to attend classes and try their hardest." Bucknell's academics provide "a well-rounded, interdisciplinary education" with a "strong focus on its undergraduates," who number over 3,500. The professors are "passionate about their area of study" and "truly care about us and encourage interaction outside of the classroom." They're "interesting, knowledgeable, and accessible." "The professors are at Bucknell because they want to work with students. It definitely shows in the classroom and during office hours." "There isn't one class where the professor doesn't know everyone's names within the first few weeks." Bucknell's culture fosters a "desire to develop its students as well-rounded, capable, intelligent and interesting individuals" who "are competent in both theory and practical application of coursework." The university's "well-respected engineering college" stands out among its academic offerings, as do Bucknell's small class sizes: "The ideal faculty to student ratio makes class time more meaningful and engaging. Our academics mean the perfect combination between challenging and fascinating." One student comments, "Unlike my friends at other universities, I honestly can't say that I have had a bad professor here." "The classes offered are extremely interesting and really instill a sense of passion and appreciation into what area you choose to study," and if you find an area of particular passion for you, "Bucknell offers many resources to its students that allow for success in whatever fields students would like to pursue." Indeed, Bucknell's undergrads are forward-looking, and many extol Bucknell's "unbelievable alumni network" and "retention rate," as well as its "research opportunities" and "high degree of job placement after school."

Life

If your ideal college experience includes "strong campus unity" with "opportunities for undergraduates, accessible professors, incredible athletic resources . . . engaging atmosphere," all on a "beautiful campus," Bucknell may deserve a close look. Students describe life at Bucknell as "a culture that fosters an eagerness to learn while simultaneously providing opportunities to engage and grow socially with an incredible student body." Students value both seriousness and fun, saying they "work hard play hard (and safe)," and that "everyone is very involved in various activities across campus. Students fit in well because everyone is part of many different groups." They feel "it's important to break out of your comfort zone, try new things, learn from your mistakes; you will be given opportunities of a lifetime at Bucknell, so take them." Bucknell's undergrads love "recreational sports of any kind" in the spaces between their ongoing "party, sleep, eat, study" cycle, and university-sponsored social highlights include "great events like cake decorating contests, canoe battleship, movie nights, and so many other fun events" on campus. "Bucknell has a reputation for being a party school, but there are plenty of students that do not party and live quite happily on this campus." "The school is good about getting artists and speakers here," so there's plenty to do besides drinking, but "house parties happen three to four times a week and the over twenty-one-year-olds go to the bars" as well. Overall, Bucknell is popular with its undergrads, who praise its "incredible opportunity, and incredible people."

Student Body

At Bucknell, "the way most students fit in is by joining Greek life." One student describes the student body as "very preppy, but all students are welcomed," and another as "a not very diverse but very open to diversity school!" "While most students may be geographically homogenous (tri-state area, Pennsylvania, Massachusetts)," one student believes that her school is distinctive "in that its people are extremely unique, and there is a lot of diversity of thought." Many students comment that the "white and wealthy" are prevalent at the university, and that the "campus looks like a country club."

FINANCIAL AID: 570-577-1331 • E-MAIL: ADMISSIONS@BUCKNELL.EDU • WEBSITE: WWW.BUCKNELL.EDU

THE PRINCETON REVIEW SAYS
Admissions
Very important factors considered include: rigor of secondary school record, academic GPA, standardized test scores, application essay, talent/ability, character/personal qualities. *Important factors considered include:* recommendation(s), extracurricular activities, volunteer work, work experience. *Other factors considered include:* class rank, first generation, alumni/ae relation, geographical residence, religious affiliation/commitment, racial/ethnic status. SAT or ACT required; SAT Subject Tests considered if submitted. ACT with or without writing accepted. SAT with or without Essay component accepted. TOEFL required of all international applicants. High school diploma is required and GED is accepted. *Academic units required:* 4 English, 3 math, 2 science, 2 foreign language, 2 social studies, 2 history, 1 academic elective. *Academic units recommended:* 4 English, 4 math, 2 science, 2 science labs, 4 foreign language, 2 social studies, 2 history, 1 academic elective.

Financial Aid
Students should submit: FAFSA, CSS/Financial Aid PROFILE. Regular filing deadline is 1/15. The Princeton Review suggests that all financial aid forms be submitted as soon as possible after October 1. *Need-based scholarships/grants offered:* Federal Pell, FSEOG, State scholarships/grants, Private scholarships, College/university scholarship or grant aid from institutional funds. *Loan aid offered:* Direct Subsidized Stafford Loans, Direct Unsubsidized Stafford Loans, Direct PLUS loans, Federal Perkins Loans. Applicants will be notified of awards on or about 4/1. Federal Work-Study Program available. Institutional employment available.

The Inside Word
A well-rounded, extremely polished application is non-negotiable for the hopeful Bucknell applicant, as the school gets more competitive every year. Admissions officers strive to consider all facets of the applications they receive—test scores, essays, recommendations, transcripts—so make sure you consider all of them carefully. In particular, the admission committee is looking for applicants who can demonstrate how they are bold, thoughtful, and compassionate leaders. Bucknell accepts the Common Application.

THE SCHOOL SAYS "..."
From the Admissions Office
"Bucknell University offers more than fifty majors and sixty-five minors in the College of Arts & Sciences, College of Engineering and School of Management. Your professors will be mentors and innovators in their fields who will challenge you to think critically, develop your ideas thoughtfully and apply what you learn. Bucknell is a residential university, so most students live on campus, but learning, service, research and recreation extend off campus. You will have the opportunity to volunteer as close as the local nursing home, community center and sustainable farm and as far away as New Orleans and Uganda. Every year, students also travel off campus to conduct research with faculty mentors. Destinations have included Alaska, Suriname, Australia and the Sudan.

"At Bucknell, you'll take advantage of career services such as advising, networking, mock interviews and employer fairs. You can explore your career options and network with alumni through summer internships with corporations, government organizations and non-profits locally, nationally and internationally. An externship program provides job-shadowing opportunities for sophomores.

"With its green spaces, brick buildings and striking vistas, Bucknell's 450-acre campus is a quintessential college environment in the heart of scenic central Pennsylvania. The restaurants and shops of downtown Lewisburg–including the Barnes & Noble at Bucknell University and the historic Campus Theatre–lie within walking distance of campus. The University is located within three-to four-hours' driving distance of Baltimore, New York City, Philadelphia, Pittsburgh and Washington, D.C."

SELECTIVITY
Admissions Rating	96
# of applicants	10,967
% of applicants accepted	25
% of acceptees attending	35
# offered a place on the wait list	2,427
% accepting a place on wait list	38
% admitted from wait list	6
# of early decision applicants	830
% accepted early decision	53

FRESHMAN PROFILE
Range SAT Critical Reading	590–680
Range SAT Math	620–710
Range SAT Writing	590–690
Range ACT Composite	28–32
Minimum paper TOEFL	600
Minimum internet-based TOEFL	100
Average HS GPA	3.5
% graduated top 10% of class	65
% graduated top 25% of class	91
% graduated top 50% of class	99

DEADLINES
Early decision	
Deadline	11/15
Notification	12/15
Regular	
Deadline	1/15
Notification	4/1
Nonfall registration?	No

APPLICANTS ALSO LOOK AT
AND OFTEN PREFER
Tufts University; Boston College

AND SOMETIMES PREFER
University of Rochester

AND RARELY PREFER
Lafayette College; Lehigh University

FINANCIAL FACTS
Financial Aid Rating	93
Annual tuition	$51,676
Room and board	$12,656
Required fees	$284
Books and supplies	$900
Average frosh need-based scholarship	$27,400
Average UG need-based scholarship	$25,000
% needy frosh rec. need-based scholarship or grant aid	89
% needy UG rec. need-based scholarship or grant aid	95
% needy frosh rec. non-need-based scholarship or grant aid	24
% needy UG rec. non-need-based scholarship or grant aid	22
% needy frosh rec. need-based self-help aid	100
% needy UG rec. need-based self-help aid	100
% frosh rec. any financial aid	62
% UG rec. any financial aid	62
% UG borrow to pay for school	52
Average cumulative indebtedness	$22,500
% frosh need fully met	91
% ugrads need fully met	91
Average % of frosh need met	91
Average % of ugrad need met	91

CALIFORNIA INSTITUTE OF TECHNOLOGY

1200 EAST CALIFORNIA BOULEVARD, PASADENA, CA 91125 • ADMISSIONS: 626-395-6341 • FAX: 626-683-3026

CAMPUS LIFE

Quality of Life Rating	89
Fire Safety Rating	90
Green Rating	91
Type of school	Private
Affiliation	No Affiliation
Environment	Metropolis

STUDENTS

Total undergrad enrollment	1,001
% male/female	61/39
% from out of state	63
% frosh from public high school	70
% frosh live on campus	100
% ugrads live on campus	86
% African American	1
% Asian	45
% Caucasian	27
% Hispanic	12
% Native American	<1
% Pacific Islander	0
% Two or more races	5
% Race and/or ethnicity unknown	<1
% international	8
# of countries represented	32

SURVEY SAYS...

Students always studying
Students are happy
Classroom facilities are great
Lab facilities are great
Great library
Internships are widely available
No one cheats
Students aren't religious
Easy to get around campus

ACADEMICS

Academic Rating	94
% students returning for sophomore year	97
% students graduating within 4 years	84
% students graduating within 6 years	91
Calendar	Semester
Student/faculty ratio	3:1
Profs interesting rating	69
Profs accessible rating	70

Most classes have 10–19 students.
Most lab/discussion sessions have
 10–19 students.

MOST POPULAR MAJORS
Mechanical Engineering; Physics; Computer
and Information Sciences

STUDENTS SAY ". . ."

Academics

Beyond arguably one of the most rigorous undergraduate educations in science out there, Caltech is a small, tight-knit community that is "geared towards training tomorrow's leaders and pioneers in the field of science." There may be a heavy emphasis on scientific learning and research, but "not to the point where students can do nothing else," as the core curriculum "exposes each student to a broad range of subjects" beyond the stereotypical fare. At Caltech, passionate researchers "work together to solve the problems of tomorrow, while enjoying great weather." Or to put it in the parlance of collegiate times: "Cross collaboration of ideas and ingenuity leads to epic-ness!" Academics are understandably "intense" at Caltech: "The work can be hell but you'll love what you learn." Fortunately, "classes are small and it's often easy to form tight bonds with the professors." The quality of teaching can vary—"just because they're Nobel Prize winners, does not make them good lecturers"—but the extremely low student to faculty ratio "makes it easier to interact on a personal basis with professors." "My academic experience here has been an extremely difficult whirlwind of humbling and fascinating knowledge," says a student. Much learning is done through the homework sets, on which students are encouraged to collaborate. The dedication Caltech has for training the researchers of tomorrow is renowned, and is evident in the accessibility to research for all students, even freshmen. The academic experience isn't just in the classroom; there are "lots of funding opportunities (for instance, the Housner and the MHF) for projects outside of the classroom." "One professor took me on for research after freshman year (we formulated an improved way to rank basketball players and teams), and I'm very good friends with him in what is now my junior year," says a mathematics major. Undergraduate student representation and self-government are happily welcomed here, and the school "really cares about the undergrads and wants to keep us happy." The school also does "a really good job of keeping students occupied and entertained while at the same time cramming a ridiculous amount of information into our heads."

Life

Modeled after the Oxford college system (and "very similar to Harry Potter"), the Caltech house system is the basis for undergraduate life, offering both a place to live and a social center for students. Freshmen are placed into one of eight houses after the first week of school, and "immediately are integrated into a close social network/safety net. Basically each student automatically gets ~100 friends." Each house has "a slightly different culture, and most people find that they identify strongly with at least one of the cultures"; as one student says, "My house has a tool room and turned down the housing office's offer to buy us a TV," says a senior electrical engineering major. In keeping with the one big happy family vibe, "undergraduates and grad students play Frisbee together, students and faculty play together in music groups, grad students go to undergraduate parties…and the students have a lot of unexploited trust from the faculty because of the Honor Code." Caltech has lots of fun traditions such as Halloween, when students "freeze pumpkins in liquid nitrogen and drop them off of Millikan library as a 'pumpkin-drop experiment.'" However, some feel that some of the new administrators "are trying to circumvent various student traditions and freedoms." The cherry on top of the Caltech sundae is "the fantastic SoCal weather, which is hard to beat anywhere in the world." Time is at a premium, but students "take trips to the beach and LA over the weekend; during the week, "[problem] sets and extracurriculars keep us pretty close to campus."

Student Body

"Everyone knows each other" at this "beautiful, small campus," and there's "no way around it": students here are "smart" and "nerdier than average," but "there is a wide range in personality within the student body." Most everyone has "an odd sense of humor and a serious hobby, whether it be MineCraft, building lasers, or rock climbing." There is "complete trust within the student body" at Caltech, and the house system provides "a family-like support network for students," which is a welcome respite from "extreme academic pressures."

CALIFORNIA INSTITUTE OF TECHNOLOGY

FINANCIAL AID: 626-395-6280 • E-MAIL: UGADMISSIONS@CALTECH.EDU • WEBSITE: ADMISSIONS.CALTECH.EDU

THE PRINCETON REVIEW SAYS

Admissions

Very important factors considered include: rigor of secondary school record, standardized test scores, application essay, recommendation(s), character/personal qualities. *Important factors considered include:* class rank, academic GPA, extracurricular activities. *Other factors considered include:* talent/ability, first generation, alumni/ae relation, racial/ethnic status, volunteer work, work experience. SAT or ACT required; SAT Subject Tests required. ACT with Writing required. SAT with Essay component required. TOEFL required of all international applicants. High school diploma or equivalent is not required. *Academic units required:* 3 English, 4 math, 2 science, 1 science lab, 1 social studies, 1 history. *Academic units recommended:* 4 English, 4 science, 3 foreign language, 3 social studies, 1 history.

Financial Aid

Students should submit: FAFSA, Institution's own financial aid form, CSS/Financial Aid PROFILE, State aid form, Noncustodial PROFILE, Business/Farm Supplement. Priority filing deadline is 3/2. The Princeton Review suggests that all financial aid forms be submitted as soon as possible after October 1. *Need-based scholarships/grants offered:* Federal Pell, FSEOG, State scholarships/grants, Private scholarships, College/university scholarship or grant aid from institutional funds. *Loan aid offered:* Direct Subsidized Stafford Loans, Direct Unsubsidized Stafford Loans, Direct PLUS loans, Federal Perkins Loans, College/university loans from institutional funds. Applicants will be notified of awards on a rolling basis beginning 4/15. Federal Work-Study Program available. Institutional employment available.

The Inside Word

Each Caltech application receives more than one read before it's presented to the admissions committee. This ensures that all candidates receive a thorough evaluation. The school values the unique drive and energy of its current students and desires applicants who display a similar combination of creativity and intellect. Stellar academic credentials are a must, and prospective students must display an aptitude for math and science.

THE SCHOOL SAYS "..."

From the Admissions Office

"Admission to the freshman class is based on many factors—some quantifiable, some not. What you say in your application is important! We do not offer interviews as part of the application, meaning that your essays and recommendation letters are particularly substantial in our review, especially given that faculty serve on the admissions committee. High school academic performance is very important, as is a demonstrated interest in math, science, and/or engineering. We are also interested in your character, maturity, and motivation, and we're proud of a selection process that incorporates all these aspects into each individual and thorough review. If you have any questions about the process or about Caltech in general, send us an email or give us a call. We'd like to hear from you!

"Freshman applicants must submit scores from either the SAT or ACT. All applicants must submit the SAT Math II Subject exam, as well as one of the science subject exams (either biology, chemistry. or physics.)"

SELECTIVITY

Admissions Rating	99
# of applicants	6,507
% of applicants accepted	9
% of acceptees attending	42
# offered a place on the wait list	615
% accepting a place on wait list	70
% admitted from wait list	0

FRESHMAN PROFILE

Range SAT Critical Reading	730–800
Range SAT Math	770–800
Range SAT Writing	730–790
Range ACT Composite	34–35
Minimum internet-based TOEFL	110
% graduated top 10% of class	99
% graduated top 25% of class	100
% graduated top 50% of class	100

DEADLINES

Early action	
Deadline	11/1
Notification	12/15
Regular	
Deadline	1/3
Notification	3/15
Nonfall registration?	No

APPLICANTS ALSO LOOK AT AND OFTEN PREFER

Massachusetts Institute of Technology

AND SOMETIMES PREFER

Princeton University; Stanford University; Harvard College

AND RARELY PREFER

Rensselaer Polytechnic Institute; Virginia Tech

FINANCIAL FACTS

Financial Aid Rating	96
Annual tuition	$43,710
Room and board	$13,371
Required fees	$1,680
Books and supplies	$1,323
Average frosh need-based scholarship	$37,873
Average UG need-based scholarship	$38,983
% needy frosh rec. need-based scholarship or grant aid	100
% needy UG rec. need-based scholarship or grant aid	100
% needy frosh rec. non-need-based scholarship or grant aid	1
% needy UG rec. non-need-based scholarship or grant aid	2
% needy frosh rec. need-based self-help aid	60
% needy UG rec. need-based self-help aid	67
% frosh rec. any financial aid	75
% UG rec. any financial aid	60
% UG borrow to pay for school	39
Average cumulative indebtedness	$20,677
% frosh need fully met	100
% ugrads need fully met	100
Average % of frosh need met	100
Average % of ugrad need met	100

CALIFORNIA STATE UNIVERSITY, STANISLAUS

ONE UNIVERSITY CIRCLE, TURLOCK, CA 95382 • ADMISSIONS: 209-667-3070 • FAX: 209-667-3788

CAMPUS LIFE

Quality of Life Rating	84
Fire Safety Rating	97
Green Rating	73
Type of school	Public
Affiliation	No Affiliation
Environment	Town

STUDENTS

Total undergrad enrollment	8,099
% male/female	36/64
% from out of state	<1
% frosh from public high school	96
% frosh live on campus	26
% ugrads live on campus	8
# of fraternities (% ugrad men join)	5 (7)
# of sororities (% ugrad women join)	11 (7)
% African American	2
% Asian	11
% Caucasian	24
% Hispanic	49
% Native American	<1
% Pacific Islander	1
% Two or more races	4
% Race and/or ethnicity unknown	5
% international	3
# of countries represented	22

SURVEY SAYS...
Lab facilities are great
Great library
Students are friendly

ACADEMICS

Academic Rating	67
% students returning for sophomore year	82
% students graduating within 4 years	16
% students graduating within 6 years	55
Calendar	Semester
Student/faculty ratio	20:1
Profs interesting rating	71
Profs accessible rating	68

Most classes have 20–29 students.
Most lab/discussion sessions have
20–29 students.

MOST POPULAR MAJORS
Business/Commerce; Psychology; Criminal
Justice/Safety Studies

STUDENTS SAY "..."

Academics

One of the members of California's noted state university system, Stanislaus "provides affordable education" that focuses on helping students prepare for their careers with a "professional, yet laid-back demeanor." This is "a great environment to be a part of," and the school "wants you to succeed, and they give you the info you need to succeed." Many of the students here live nearby, and the in-state tuition offers "rigorous" academics and "a great place to meet mentors and learn different approaches to life." Professors get mixed but mainly positive reviews; "some are excellent…go above and beyond," and are "wonderful at helping the students as much as they can," but others are just "fair," and "some should not be teaching." Registration could use some rejiggering; students say that the registration priority needs to change each semester, and the more popular departments could use "more of the same classes offered every semester, with multiple sections." Still, for higher-level classes, "small class sizes where you are able to get a lot of help from professors" are a huge boon. Nursing and business are some of "the strongest subjects that come out of here," and it is "very inexpensive for a fully accredited business degree" relative to many other schools. In developing well-prepared students, Stanislaus personnel are "attentive" on all fronts. "Very rarely are any of your classes taught by a graduate student or someone without a PhD," says a student. The accessibility of departments and staff is "always very easy," and "they are very informative with upcoming changes or events." Job placement is a huge end goal for Stanislaus State, and "helping students (especially veterans) during these rough economic times is a priority at CSU Stanislaus."

Life

Though Stan State offers "scenery as beautiful and varied as the students" and "awesome" weather, popular complaints are that "buildings need updating" and "there are too many geese on the grounds." The university's efforts to provide "a ton of organizations on campus" give the commuter students "a college experience like that of any other student living on campus." "It's nice that the school recognizes that we need a break sometimes and promote being a healthy individual, both mind and body," says one student. Events are regularly held in the quad, "student-run shows [such] as dance-offs or karaoke," and "music concerts are regularly held throughout the semesters, usually featuring guest artists or students." Turlock is "not the biggest town," but there is "easy access to the freeway," and local events and great places "keep everyone occupied." On campus, "there are lounges that you can play pool, darts, video games, etc.," and "Greek life is well-supported." The many commuter students mean that resident community on campus is "small and tightly knit"; there are a fair number of nontraditional students here as well, and they have no problems getting by. "I am an older student, and life on campus is great; everybody accepts me as just another student working toward my degree," one says.

Student Body

Perhaps due to the focus on future careers here, students are "motivated and excited to be at school." "I think we all know that with every class session we are that much closer to graduation," says one. Because the campus is so small, "a big portion of the student life is also Greek." Diversity is "rich" here, and there are "many different ethnicities and culture from all over." Though everyone is friendly and "easygoing," "typical students keep to themselves but does not hesitant to help another student if he or she asks for it," but even those who want to "can fit in almost anywhere, as most groups found around campus are very accepting."

FINANCIAL AID: 209-667-3336 • E-MAIL: OUTREACH_HELP_DESK@CSUSTAN.EDU • WEBSITE: WWW.CSUSTAN.EDU

THE PRINCETON REVIEW SAYS

Admissions

Very important factors considered include: rigor of secondary school record, academic GPA, standardized test scores. *Important factors considered include:* class rank. *Other factors considered include:* SAT or ACT required for some. ACT with or without writing accepted. SAT with or without Essay component accepted. TOEFL required of all international applicants. High school diploma is required and GED is accepted. *Academic units required:* 4 English, 3 math, 2 science, 2 science labs, 2 foreign language, 1 social studies, 1 history, 1 academic elective, 1 visual/performing arts. *Academic units recommended:* 4 English, 3 math, 2 science, 2 science labs, 2 foreign language, 1 social studies, 1 history, 1 academic elective, 1 visual/performing arts.

Financial Aid

Students should submit: FAFSA, State aid form. Priority filing deadline is 3/2. The Princeton Review suggests that all financial aid forms be submitted as soon as possible after October 1. *Need-based scholarships/grants offered:* Federal Pell, FSEOG, State scholarships/grants, Private scholarships, College/university scholarship or grant aid from institutional funds. *Loan aid offered:* Direct Subsidized Stafford Loans, Direct Unsubsidized Stafford Loans, Direct PLUS loans, Federal Perkins Loans. Applicants will be notified of awards on a rolling basis beginning 4/1. Federal Work-Study Program available. Institutional employment available.

The Inside Word

Like most state schools, Stanislaus State admissions practices are fairly straightforward. The university adheres to the eligibility index as defined by the California state system, so applicants who meet GPA and standardized test score minimums are automatically granted admission. Out-of-state candidates face more stringent requirements, as do those applying for highly competitive majors and programs.

THE SCHOOL SAYS "..."

From the Admissions Office

"For over fifty years, California State University, Stanislaus, has welcomed students from California's Central Valley and around the world. Stanislaus State continues to distinguish itself as an institution that provides top-quality degree programs with a high level of personal attention, offering over 100 undergraduate programs; twenty-four graduate programs, including a doctorate in educational leadership; seven credential programs; and six certificate programs. With a student-to-faculty ratio of 20 to 1, Stanislaus State demonstrates its commitment to individualized instruction over the more common lecture-hall style of many larger universities. The university enjoys an ideal location in the Northern San Joaquin Valley, a short distance from the San Francisco Bay Area, Monterey, Big Sur, the Sierra Nevada Mountains and the state capital of Sacramento. The main campus is located in the city of Turlock, a community that prides itself on its small-town atmosphere, clean living space, excellent schools and low crime rate. Degree programs in these disciplines have earned specialized accreditation: art, business administration, education, genetic counseling, music, nursing, psychology, public administration, social work and theater. The College of Business Administration and the College of Education, Kinesiology and Social Work have also earned prestigious state and national accreditation. Nearly $58 million in merit- and need-based grants and scholarships was awarded for the 2014–15 school year. Over 80 percent of undergraduates receive need-based aid, and more than $90 million in total financial assistance is awarded annually."

SELECTIVITY

Admissions Rating	75
# of applicants	7,080
% of applicants accepted	71
% of acceptees attending	25

FRESHMAN PROFILE

Range SAT Critical Reading	400–500
Range SAT Math	400–510
Range SAT Writing	400–500
Range ACT Composite	16–22
Minimum paper TOEFL	500
Minimum internet-based TOEFL	61
Average HS GPA	3.3

DEADLINES

Regular	
Priority	11/30
Deadline	11/30
Nonfall registration?	Yes

FINANCIAL FACTS

Financial Aid Rating	61
Annual in-state tuition	$5,472
Annual out-of-state tuition	$16,632
Room and board	$9,482
Required fees	$1,268
Books and supplies	$1,500
Average frosh need-based scholarship	$10,492
Average UG need-based scholarship	$9,870
% needy frosh rec. need-based scholarship or grant aid	86
% needy UG rec. need-based scholarship or grant aid	87
% needy frosh rec. non-need-based scholarship or grant aid	13
% needy UG rec. non-need-based scholarship or grant aid	10
% needy frosh rec. need-based self-help aid	76
% needy UG rec. need-based self-help aid	81
% frosh rec. any financial aid	85
% UG rec. any financial aid	84
% UG borrow to pay for school	56
Average cumulative indebtedness	$15,530
Average % of frosh need met	75
Average % of ugrad need met	76

CALVIN COLLEGE

3201 BURTON STREET SOUTHEAST, GRAND RAPIDS, MI 49546 • ADMISSIONS: 616-526-6106 • FAX: 616-526-6777

CAMPUS LIFE

Quality of Life Rating	91
Fire Safety Rating	82
Green Rating	80
Type of school	Private
Affiliation	Christian Reformed
Environment	City

STUDENTS

Total undergrad enrollment	3,869
% male/female	45/55
% from out of state	44
% frosh from public high school	49
% frosh live on campus	95
% ugrads live on campus	59
% African American	3
% Asian	4
% Caucasian	74
% Hispanic	4
% Native American	<1
% Pacific Islander	0
% Two or more races	4
% Race and/or ethnicity unknown	2
% international	10
# of countries represented	62

SURVEY SAYS...
Students are happy
Great library
Career services are great
School is well run
Students are very religious
Students love Grand Rapids, MI
Recreation facilities are great
Very little drug use

ACADEMICS

Academic Rating	81
% students returning for sophomore year	86
% students graduating within 4 years	57
% students graduating within 6 years	73
Calendar	Semester
Student/faculty ratio	13:1
Profs interesting rating	90
Profs accessible rating	91

Most classes have 20–29 students.
Most lab/discussion sessions have
10–19 students.

MOST POPULAR MAJORS
Business/Commerce; Engineering; Registered
Nursing/Registered Nurse

STUDENTS SAY "..."

Academics
Nestled in the heart of Grand Rapids, Calvin College manages to seamlessly integrate "Christian faith and learning." While Christian principles certainly permeate the campus, students stress that "religion [isn't] forced." Rather, the college simply "encourage[s] spiritual growth and provide[s] opportunities for spiritual, social, physical, and mental development." And though the academics are rigorous, undergrads have the benefit of learning in an "incredibly supportive and collaborative community." Students here also appreciate Calvin's emphasis on both "social justice and sustainability." Moreover, the college maintains a liberal arts focus and undergrads can explore numerous disciplines. Many individuals are especially quick to highlight the "amazing" science, education, and accounting programs. No matter their chosen courses of study, Calvin undergrads are likely to have great classroom experiences. As one nursing student brags, "The professors are what makes this school. They know everyone by name and help you to succeed." Additionally, undergrads make sure to note that their teachers "are engaged with the material while also being aware of individual student needs." A biochemistry major wholeheartedly agrees stating, "The professors are all very passionate about their field and they pass that on to the students." Importantly, students also find their instructors to be "very intelligent and well respected, but also very down-to-earth." As this satisfied literature major succinctly states, "I would say that faculty/student relationship is probably one of my favorite parts of Calvin."

Life
Life at Calvin is always abuzz with activity. As one sophomore psychology major shares, "The college puts on more than enough programs for students to attend during the weekend." For example, "carnivals and game nights...are pretty well attended and are an easy way for college students to have fun." Students also love taking in part in annual traditions such as "Jump into the Frozen Pond" which happens every February. We're even told that "you get a golden towel if you do it all four years!" Aside from testing their mettle in the cold, many undergrads also enjoy participating in dorm events like "floor dates" wherein "a given girl floor and guy floor do something together to get to know each other." Concerts are a fairly common occurrence as well—"FUN, Switchfoot, [and] Regina Spektor have all come in recent years." Students interested in a school with a hearty drinking culture might do best to look elsewhere, though. As one freshman reveals, "People more prone to partying seem frustrated with the campus' dry policies." However, he does quickly follow up by assuring they do "manage with off-campus events." And, of course, Grand Rapids offers "plenty of bars and clubs" for students of age.

Student Body
The typical Calvin undergrad can be categorized as "white, upper-middle class" and, not surprisingly, most Calvin students would describe themselves as religious or "spiritual." However, a knowledgeable senior insists, "We aren't limited by the fact that we are Christian, and being Christian doesn't make us all the same." In fact, "a great variety of students all with their different styles and personalities" can be found wandering Calvin's campus. A fellow senior stresses that "Calvin does a great job at recruiting students of different ethnic cultures and countries. Diversity is something that Calvin is very proud of!" A music education major agrees, stating, "There are a variety of people here: sporty people, nerds, musical people, math and science people, dancers, environmentally conscious people, etc." Thankfully, most students can also be described as "warm and welcoming," so "new students always seem to fit right in!"

FINANCIAL AID: 800-688-0122 • E-MAIL: ADMISSIONS@CALVIN.EDU • WEBSITE: WWW.CALVIN.EDU

THE PRINCETON REVIEW SAYS

Admissions

Very important factors considered include: rigor of secondary school record, academic GPA, standardized test scores, religious affiliation/commitment. *Important factors considered include:* application essay, recommendation(s), extracurricular activities, character/personal qualities. *Other factors considered include:* class rank, volunteer work, work experience, level of applicant's interest. SAT or ACT required for some. ACT with or without writing accepted. SAT with or without Essay component accepted. TOEFL required of all international applicants. High school diploma is required and GED is accepted. *Academic units required:* 3 English, 3 math, 2 science, 2 social studies, 3 academic electives. *Academic units recommended:* 4 English, 3 math, 2 science, 1 science lab, 2 foreign language, 3 social studies, 3 academic electives.

Financial Aid

Students should submit: FAFSA. Priority filing deadline is 2/15. The Princeton Review suggests that all financial aid forms be submitted as soon as possible after October 1. *Need-based scholarships/grants offered:* Federal Pell, FSEOG, State scholarships/grants, Private scholarships, College/university scholarship or grant aid from institutional funds. *Loan aid offered:* Direct Subsidized Stafford Loans, Direct Unsubsidized Stafford Loans, Direct PLUS loans, Federal Perkins Loans, State Loans, College/university loans from institutional funds. Applicants will be notified of awards on a rolling basis beginning 3/15. Federal Work-Study Program available. Institutional employment available.

The Inside Word

Admissions officers at Calvin are interested in candidates who will flourish within the school's academic and social community. Just as importantly, they seek applicants who are looking to deepen and affirm their faith. The college accepts roughly 75 percent of their applicant pool so students who maintain solid transcripts should not have too much difficulty getting in, though bear in mind that high acceptance rate is partially due to the self-selecting nature of Calvin's applicant cohort.

THE SCHOOL SAYS "..."

From the Admissions Office

"Calvin College is a top-ranked Christian liberal arts college that prepares students to lead with courageous conviction. Through rigorous academic study and intentional Christian community, students learn to think deeply, act justly and live wholeheartedly.

"At Calvin, we dare to pursue excellence in everything we take on. We don't settle for good enough…not in a lab, not in an art show, not even in a jump shot. It's a bold college path, but thousands of alumni will tell you it's a path worth traveling, no matter what sparks your passion.

"Here we believe that no one major has the upper hand in uncovering truths about God and the world. All are invited into the discovery. In fact, Calvin has had a liberal arts bent—a desire to explore all things—since its beginnings in 1876.

"Today's multi-faceted core curriculum allows students to chase the wonderings of philosophy, the intricacies of languages foreign and familiar, and the beauty of the world at a molecular level. Calvin offers 100+ majors and programs, with advanced courses that are compared to graduate-level experiences for their remarkable depth of learning.

"The meaningful work in your area of interest doesn't begin post-college, but right here during the Calvin experience—through in-depth research, fast-paced internships and the chance to present and publish alongside world-class faculty. Plus, with more than forty off-campus programs, Calvin empowers an impressive number of students to make global connections by studying abroad."

SELECTIVITY

Admissions Rating	84
# of applicants	3,824
% of applicants accepted	74
% of acceptees attending	33

FRESHMAN PROFILE

Range SAT Critical Reading	520–670
Range SAT Math	530–670
Range ACT Composite	23–30
Minimum paper TOEFL	550
Minimum internet-based TOEFL	80
Average HS GPA	3.7
% graduated top 10% of class	28
% graduated top 25% of class	56
% graduated top 50% of class	82

DEADLINES

Regular	
Deadline	8/15
Nonfall registration?	Yes

APPLICANTS ALSO LOOK AT AND OFTEN PREFER
Wheaton College (IL)

AND SOMETIMES PREFER
University of Michigan—Ann Arbor

FINANCIAL FACTS

Financial Aid Rating	82
Annual tuition	$30,425
Room and board	$9,690
Required fees	$235
Books and supplies	$1,100
Average frosh need-based scholarship	$19,240
Average UG need-based scholarship	$16,333
% needy frosh rec. need-based scholarship or grant aid	100
% needy UG rec. need-based scholarship or grant aid	99
% needy frosh rec. non-need-based scholarship or grant aid	13
% needy UG rec. non-need-based scholarship or grant aid	10
% needy frosh rec. need-based self-help aid	86
% needy UG rec. need-based self-help aid	90
% frosh rec. any financial aid	99
% UG rec. any financial aid	95
% UG borrow to pay for school	62
Average cumulative indebtedness	$31,236
% frosh need fully met	19
% ugrads need fully met	17
Average % of frosh need met	78
Average % of ugrad need met	74

CARLETON COLLEGE

100 SOUTH COLLEGE STREET, NORTHFIELD, MN 55057 • ADMISSIONS: 507-222-4190 • TOLL FREE: 800-995-2275 • FAX: 507-222-4526

CAMPUS LIFE

Quality of Life Rating	96
Fire Safety Rating	79
Green Rating	93
Type of school	Private
Affiliation	No Affiliation
Environment	Village

STUDENTS

Total undergrad enrollment	1,995
% male/female	49/51
% from out of state	82
% frosh from public high school	60
% frosh live on campus	100
% ugrads live on campus	96
% African American	4
% Asian	8
% Caucasian	63
% Hispanic	7
% Native American	<1
% Pacific Islander	<1
% Two or more races	5
% Race and/or ethnicity unknown	2
% international	10
# of countries represented	38

SURVEY SAYS...

Lots of liberal students
Students always studying
Students are happy
Classroom facilities are great
Great library
Internships are widely available
School is well run
No one cheats
Students are friendly
Diverse student types interact on campus
Students aren't religious
Students environmentally aware
Students love Northfield, MN
Easy to get around campus
Recreation facilities are great
Intramural sports are popular
College radio is popular
Active minority support groups

ACADEMICS

Academic Rating	98
% students returning for sophomore year	96
% students graduating within 4 years	91
% students graduating within 6 years	95
Calendar	Trimester
Student/faculty ratio	9:1
Profs interesting rating	98
Profs accessible rating	97

Most classes have 10–19 students.
Most lab/discussion sessions have 10–19 students.

MOST POPULAR MAJORS

Biology; Economics; Computer and Information Sciences

STUDENTS SAY "..."

Academics

Carleton College, with its low student-teacher ratio and small-town Minnesota setting, "is a rigorous school full of laid-back, outdoorsy students with a passion for learning and for developing strong community." With a trimester schedule and an emphasis on the liberal arts and interdisciplinary scholarship, Carleton also boasts strong programs in the sciences and social sciences. The school has a reputation for being "highly rigorous without the cut-throat competition that other elite institutions are known for"; many students use the words "challenging" and "collaborative" to describe this tight-knit, highly focused academic community. One student sums it up as an "Ivy League education without all the Ivy League pretensions." While academics are "challenging" and classes are "fairly fast-paced," the work is "worth every ounce of effort" and professors are almost universally praised as "friendly, accessible, supportive, and enthusiastic about teaching." Students "have no qualms about dropping in on office hours to chat" and have "been to many wonderful dinners at professors' homes." "Students help each other out a lot, too (even if it is just emotional support)." One student describes the school accurately with her reasons for choosing to attend: "I wanted to be at a place where I was challenged. I wanted to be surrounded by people who were smarter than me but also wanted to see me succeed." Finally, students report excellent resources for pursuing graduate study, and visible improvements within career services.

Life

Weekends at Carleton bustle with activity to help balance the intellectual challenges of weekday classes. As one student put it, "I often find myself attending a concert at the Cave, the student pub; going to a show one of my friends wrote at the Little Nourse Theater; taking a quick trip to the cities for Mall of America or an uptown excursion; or, most likely, having a surprisingly engaging and deep intellectual discussion with some friends at a party on a Friday night." Intramural sports such as broomball and ultimate Frisbee are "freakishly popular." Outdoor activities are very popular in the Arboretum, "an 800-acre forest where students go for runs, go snow-shoeing, or have camp fires." The campus even features Dacie Moses House, "a house for baking cookies 24/7." If you're looking to unwind with a less structured activity, "the drinking policy throughout Northfield is strict, but... it's relaxed here at Carleton," and most students report that while partying is an option, "there are just as many opportunities for substance-free activities. Even at parties, there is no pressure to drink." As Northfield is small and most students live in the dorms (a few wish for more off-campus living options), Carleton life tends to be campus-centric. "Carls" complain about very few things: the cold Minnesota weather, on-campus food options, and the accessibility of the health center. Overall, though, it's clear that students here feel well cared for.

Student Body

At Carleton, students are, "on the whole, pretty liberal" as well as "politically and environmentally aware," and "are highly interested in activism on the whole." Students note that they "spend the majority of the weekend studying but still find time for socializing and spending time on extracurriculars, but most students feel that they don't have enough 'down time.'" "Generally they are very welcoming, extremely kind (when walking around campus nearly everyone I pass will shoot me a smile), dedicated to their studies on weekdays but want to party on weekends, and kind of dorky." "There are so many clubs and organizations to get involved in, and so many people doing really interesting things outside of any structured class or club, that it is incredibly hard to not get involved in something or other." "Everyone loves to have meaningful conversations," "people are very self-aware, but not self-centered," and "the best part about that is that they all keep really open minds." Students feel that "Carleton has been ramping up diversity efforts in recent years," but could still stand a bit more improvement in that area.

FINANCIAL AID: 507-222-4138 • E-MAIL: ADMISSIONS@CARLETON.EDU • WEBSITE: WWW.CARLETON.EDU

THE PRINCETON REVIEW SAYS

Admissions

Very important factors considered include: rigor of secondary school record, class rank, academic GPA. *Important factors considered include:* standardized test scores, application essay, recommendation(s), extracurricular activities, talent/ability, character/personal qualities, alumni/ae relation, racial/ethnic status, volunteer work, work experience. *Other factors considered include:* interview, first generation, geographical residence, state residency. SAT or ACT required; SAT Subject Tests recommend. TOEFL required of all international applicants. High school diploma is required and GED is accepted. *Academic units recommended:* 4 English, 3 math, 3 science, 1 science lab, 3 foreign language, 3 social studies.

Financial Aid

Students should submit: FAFSA, CSS/Financial Aid PROFILE, Noncustodial PROFILE. Regular filing deadline is 2/15.The Princeton Review suggests that all financial aid forms be submitted as soon as possible after October 1. *Need-based scholarships/grants offered:* Federal Pell, FSEOG, State scholarships/grants, Private scholarships, College/university scholarship or grant aid from institutional funds. *Loan aid offered:* Direct Subsidized Stafford Loans, Direct Unsubsidized Stafford Loans, Direct PLUS loans, Federal Perkins Loans, State Loans, College/university loans from institutional funds. Applicants will be notified of awards on or about 3/31. Federal Work-Study Program available. Institutional employment available.

The Inside Word

Gaining admission to Carleton is highly competitive. While it is possible to get in without stellar high school grades and test scores if you show tremendous promise or have an exceptional talent, most successful applicants demonstrate all of these qualities. High school records are weighed most heavily here; standardized test scores are required, and your personal essay is also very important. Given the importance of community at Carleton, interviews are strongly recommended.

THE SCHOOL SAYS "..."

From the Admissions Office

"In an annual college freshmen survey, Carleton students identify themselves as everything from conservatives to liberals, with a majority of them falling in the moderate to liberal range. Although individualistic and energetic Carls take their academics seriously, they don't take themselves seriously. Participation in athletics, theater or music, religious events, or dining hall discussions marks the Carleton experience. The college recently opened two new LEED-certified, environmentally friendly residence halls and the new Weitz Center for Creativity, 134,000 square feet of performance, rehearsal, exhibition, teaching, and collaboration space. With nearly three-fifths of the student body receiving need-based grant aid, there is a broad socioeconomic representation across the student body. Nine percent of all students are international, and 16 percent come from traditionally underrepresented groups, and about 10 percent are first-generation students. A look at majors in the past decade shows that graduates cover all areas, with about one-third of them in each of the following: math/science, humanities and arts, and social sciences. More than two-thirds of all students will spend time earning class credits off campus; Carleton participates in programs worldwide from Asia to Africa. You can scuba dive off the Great Barrier Reef or walk the Great Wall of China. Within ten years of graduating, about 80 percent of alumni pursue graduate or professional degrees. Carleton ranks second among liberal arts colleges in the number of PhDs earned by its alumni."

SELECTIVITY

Admissions Rating	97
# of applicants	6,722
% of applicants accepted	21
% of acceptees attending	35
# offered a place on the wait list	1,350
% accepting a place on wait list	33
% admitted from wait list	4
# of early decision applicants	689
% accepted early decision	31

FRESHMAN PROFILE

Range SAT Critical Reading	660–750
Range SAT Math	660–770
Range SAT Writing	660–750
Range ACT Composite	29–33
Minimum paper TOEFL	600
% graduated top 10% of class	71
% graduated top 25% of class	96
% graduated top 50% of class	100

DEADLINES

Early decision	
Deadline	11/15
Notification	12/15
Regular	
Deadline	1/15
Notification	3/31
Nonfall registration?	No

APPLICANTS ALSO LOOK AT AND OFTEN PREFER
Williams College; Yale University

AND SOMETIMES PREFER
Bowdoin College

AND RARELY PREFER
Oberlin College; Macalester College

FINANCIAL FACTS

Financial Aid Rating	96
Room and board	$12,783
Required fees	$276
Books and supplies	$800
Average frosh need-based scholarship	$39,854
Average UG need-based scholarship	$36,482
% needy frosh rec. need-based scholarship or grant aid	100
% needy UG rec. need-based scholarship or grant aid	100
% needy frosh rec. non-need-based scholarship or grant aid	10
% needy UG rec. non-need-based scholarship or grant aid	14
% needy frosh rec. need-based self-help aid	97
% needy UG rec. need-based self-help aid	97
% frosh rec. any financial aid	54
% UG rec. any financial aid	56
% UG borrow to pay for school	41
Average cumulative indebtedness	$20,063
% frosh need fully met	100
% ugrads need fully met	100
Average % of frosh need met	100
Average % of ugrad need met	100

CARNEGIE MELLON UNIVERSITY

5000 FORBES AVENUE, PITTSBURGH, PA 15213 • ADMISSIONS: 412-268-2082 • FAX: 412-268-7838

STUDENTS SAY "..."

Academics

The dedicated students at Carnegie Mellon range from hard-core engineers to the artsiest of drama students, making this research university "a breeding ground for interdisciplinary collaboration." The school's motto—"my heart is in the work"—rings true for all on this Pittsburgh campus. Student say, "It is in our culture to stay up late, overload on classes, have more than one major, and to be extremely involved on campus." The university, founded by Andrew Carnegie in 1900, gives students the opportunity to become experts in their chosen field while also studying a broad range of coursework across disciplines. The difficulty of the classes and high expectations from your professors "will break you down, and you will have to build yourself up again." "We are in it together to defeat the class rather than ourselves," says a student. CMU's interdisciplinary environment is backed by the tremendous resources afforded students in whatever they choose, and the school "practically throws opportunities (internships, guidance)" at students. Though the course work is admittedly "stressful," the professors "are extremely knowledgeable and passionate about their subject[s]," and the "we're all in it together" mantra is a universal refrain. "Academically, you get challenged, but so does everyone else, so the work-heavy culture becomes a social thing," says a student. Though "there are some [professors] who are less reasonable grading-wise and/or are a bit boring in lecture," for the most part, they are "enthusiastic and very invested in the students' learning" and "will go as far as helping you pick out internships to apply for and giving advice on programs on campus and elsewhere." Much as its mission statement promises, CMU "provides excellent preparation for your future, especially [through] the career center." The residence life staff, RAs, and Housefellows are also "really committed to improving the social aspects of college." For those who know what they want, there are "unlimited opportunities to pursue your passions."

Life

Carnegie Mellon "students are unique for the amount of time they spend working on their studies," and most social activity "is based off of academics." "Carnegie Mellon offers endless opportunities for those who are willing to actively pursue it," and students find that there are "many clubs on campus that are constantly looking for new members." Despite the number of hours spent hitting the books, CMU has a decidedly non-competitive atmosphere: "Carnegie Mellon is filled with a bunch of high-achieving, non-competitive students that want to help each other." Discussions "are just at a higher level," and if students have to work late into a Friday evening, then so be it. Some at CMU "enjoy complaining about how stressed out we are, but that doesn't stop us from overloading on classes, signing up for more activities, or taking on more leadership positions." "You get to pick two: sleep, good grades, or a social life," goes the mantra. Still, in their spare time, "there is a massive video game 'community,'" as well as "not your typical Greek Life," which "is a great way to open up lots of experiences." The Pittsburgh location offers a "safe campus . . . but it is still within a city that offers many things to do," including free entry into area museums, "great restaurants, and sports teams."

Student Body

At Carnegie Mellon, everybody is "quirky in an endearing way." Basically, "there isn't really a norm except for the fact that you can be yourself." The mix of student interests and majors provides a curious but totally harmonious balance at every turn: "There are engineering students who can belt out any song from a musical and art students who are great at tennis. CMU students are diverse and unique and still able to come together to . . . create an environment where success is encouraged without risk of judgment." "We're all weird in our own way—we're either a scientist or artist so we can seem a strange bunch...eventually the labels artist or scientist fades, and you become friends with people from all over campus," says a student. Students "love their work and work hard, but also tend to be very involved in side projects, whether it be playing quidditch or creating a start-up." Basically, CMU is made up "an incredibly diverse bunch of nerds—in the best way possible;" they're "insanely driven," and "all have hidden talents."

FINANCIAL AID: 412-268-8186 • E-MAIL: UNDERGRADUATE-ADMISSIONS@ANDREW.CMU.EDU • WEBSITE: WWW.CMU.EDU

THE PRINCETON REVIEW SAYS

Admissions

Very important factors considered include: rigor of secondary school record, class rank, academic GPA, standardized test scores. *Important factors considered include:* application essay, recommendation(s), interview, extracurricular activities, talent/ability, character/personal qualities, first generation, alumni/ae relation, racial/ethnic status, volunteer work, work experience, level of applicant's interest. *Other factors considered include:* SAT or ACT required. ACT with Writing recommended. SAT with Essay component recommended. TOEFL required of all international applicants. High school diploma is required and GED is accepted. *Academic units required:* 4 English, 4 math, 3 science, 3 science labs, 2 foreign language, 3 academic electives. *Academic units recommended:* 4 English, 4 math, 3 science, 3 science labs, 2 foreign language, 3 academic electives.

Financial Aid

Students should submit: FAFSA, Institution's own financial aid form, CSS/Financial Aid PROFILE, Noncustodial PROFILE. Priority filing deadline is 2/15.The Princeton Review suggests that all financial aid forms be submitted as soon as possible after October 1. *Need-based scholarships/grants offered:* Federal Pell, FSEOG, State scholarships/grants, Private scholarships, College/university scholarship or grant aid from institutional funds. *Loan aid offered:* Direct Subsidized Stafford Loans, Direct Unsubsidized Stafford Loans, Direct PLUS loans, Federal Perkins Loans. Applicants will be notified of awards on or about 4/15. Federal Work-Study Program available. Institutional employment available.

The Inside Word

Don't be misled by Carnegie Mellon's acceptance rate. Although relatively high for a university of this caliber, the applicant pool is fairly self-selecting. If you haven't loaded up on demanding courses in high school, particularly if you're applying for any of CMU's technical colleges, you're not likely to be a serious contender. The admissions office explicitly states that it doesn't use formulas when making decisions. That said, a record of strong academic performance in the area of your intended major is key. Each of the school's six undergraduate colleges has varying academic and testing requirements, particularly in relation to SAT Subject Tests. Applications to schools in the College of the Fine Arts may also require an additional audition and/or portfolio requirement.

THE SCHOOL SAYS "..."

From the Admissions Office

"If you're looking for an intellectual environment that blends academic and artistic richness with classroom innovation, explore Carnegie Mellon. Consistently ranked as a top twenty-five institution, Carnegie Mellon is world-renowned for its unique approach to education and research. Left-brain and right-brain thinking unite within our collaborative culture, and is the foundation of learning at Carnegie Mellon. As a student, you will acquire a depth and breadth of knowledge while sharpening your problem-solving, critical thinking, creative and quantitative skills. You will develop sound critical judgment, resourcefulness and professional ethics through a collaborative and hands-on education. As a graduate, you will be one of the innovative leaders and problem-solvers of tomorrow. While a Carnegie Mellon education is marked by a strong focus on fundamental and versatile problem-solving skills in a particular discipline, your talents and interests don't remain confined to one area. The university respects academic diversity and provides opportunities for you to explore more than one field of study. Carnegie Mellon consists of seven colleges (six undergraduate): Carnegie Institute of Technology (engineering), College of Fine Arts, Dietrich College of Humanities and Social Sciences (combining liberal arts education with professional specializations), Tepper School of Business, Mellon College of Science, the School of Computer Science, and the Heinz College. Here, music, molecular science, acting, analysis, opera and organic chemistry weave in and out of the lives and minds of Carnegie Mellon students on a daily basis. The university's 150-acre main campus is located in the Oakland area of Pittsburgh, five miles from downtown."

SELECTIVITY

Admissions Rating	98
# of applicants	20,547
% of applicants accepted	24
% of acceptees attending	32
# offered a place on the wait list	5,526
% accepting a place on wait list	51
% admitted from wait list	0
# of early decision applicants	1,143
% accepted early decision	29

FRESHMAN PROFILE

Range SAT Critical Reading	650–740
Range SAT Math	710–800
Range SAT Writing	670–760
Range ACT Composite	31–34
Minimum internet-based TOEFL	102
Average HS GPA	3.8
% graduated top 10% of class	78
% graduated top 25% of class	95
% graduated top 50% of class	99

DEADLINES

Early decision	
Deadline	11/1
Notification	12/15
Regular	
Deadline	1/1
Notification	4/15
Nonfall registration?	No

FINANCIAL FACTS

Financial Aid Rating	83
Annual tuition	$51,196
Room and board	$12,960
Required fees	$844
Books and supplies	$2,400
Average frosh need-based scholarship	$31,926
Average UG need-based scholarship	$31,417
% needy frosh rec. need-based scholarship or grant aid	96
% needy UG rec. need-based scholarship or grant aid	96
% needy frosh rec. non-need-based scholarship or grant aid	19
% needy UG rec. non-need-based scholarship or grant aid	11
% needy frosh rec. need-based self-help aid	79
% needy UG rec. need-based self-help aid	85
% frosh need fully met	29
% ugrads need fully met	24
Average % of frosh need met	84
Average % of ugrad need met	82

CASE WESTERN RESERVE UNIVERSITY

WOLSTEIN HALL, CLEVELAND, OH 44106-7055 • ADMISSIONS: 216-368-4450 • FAX: 216-368-5111

CAMPUS LIFE

Quality of Life Rating	89
Fire Safety Rating	87
Green Rating	94
Type of school	Private
Affiliation	No Affiliation
Environment	Metropolis

STUDENTS

Total undergrad enrollment	5,121
% male/female	55/45
% from out of state	60
% frosh from public high school	70
% frosh live on campus	99
% ugrads live on campus	80
# of fraternities (% ugrad men join)	18 (34)
# of sororities (% ugrad women join)	9 (39)
% African American	5
% Asian	20
% Caucasian	52
% Hispanic	6
% Native American	<1
% Pacific Islander	<1
% Two or more races	4
% Race and/or ethnicity unknown	2
% international	11
# of countries represented	35

SURVEY SAYS...

Students are happy
Great library
Career services are great
Internships are widely available
School is well run
Great financial aid
Frats and sororities are popular

ACADEMICS

Academic Rating	87
% students returning for sophomore year	94
% students graduating within 4 years	63
% students graduating within 6 years	81
Calendar	Semester
Student/faculty ratio	11:1
Profs interesting rating	75
Profs accessible rating	81

Most classes have 10–19 students.
Most lab/discussion sessions have fewer than 10 students.

MOST POPULAR MAJORS

Mechanical Engineering; Biology; Biology

STUDENTS SAY "..."

Academics

Located in Cleveland, Ohio, Case Western Reserve University is mid-sized school that boasts "fantastic research opportunities," "an awesome environment," and "amazing financial aid." CWRU is "known as an outstanding engineering school" and "companies in the engineering field are aware of CWRU's excellence and rigor and are very eager to hire CWRU grads." "Our academics and academic reputation is phenomenal," one happy student boasts. The "well qualified and passionate" professors are "very involved in their fields" and "usually accessible and reasonable about their workload." "They all have connections within the research community or the private work sector." "Supplementary Instructors (past students who passed with an A) are also a great resource and host a variety of study sessions every week to go over material," one student brags. "We even get free tutoring (up to five hours a week). [The] academic load can be challenging, but if you take advantage of all the available resources around it's definitely manageable!" "It is possible to do well in class and be involved in clubs and sports." If there's an area that academics could improve, it's the liberal arts, as students in these majors report feeling their departments are sometimes overlooked. "Administration and advising could still use some work," one student says. "It is not always clear what path you should be taking in order to graduate, but if you ask enough people you can figure it out." Overall, CWRU "is very good at producing students prepared to excel in their career, especially within engineering, medicine, and business." The university "offers great scholarships and has fantastic research opportunities." A finance major reports she decided to attend because "it was affordable, prestigious, in an awesome environment, and the people here were all so genuine when I came to visit." All in all, students really feel that CWRU is a university on the rise. As a cognitive science and psychology student puts it, "If universities were stocks, I'd put all my money into Case Western."

Life

One student sums up the university as "nerdy but a lot of fun." Activities at Case reflect this "nerdy" nature. "One of our biggest campus events (which I help run) is a 10 day long game of tag known as Humans vs. Zombies," a sociology and theatre major says. On campus, "Case offers literally everything in the way of clubs, jobs, research, and things to do." Even though many students are "geeky," Greek life is also strong: "A lot of people are in fraternities or sororities (40 percent of campus and rising)." Students do seem to feel that one area of campus life needs improvement: "school spirit." "Few students could tell you the football team's record or who the basketball team is facing this weekend," one student says, elaborating that it isn't a surprise since the school is "academically focused." Off campus, there's always the entire city of Cleveland. Students love the "beautiful" campus as well as its "fantastic" "location in uptown Cleveland" near that city's "cultural center." The area close to campus "offers great museums and downtown has lots of attractions to check out."

Student Body

"Case definitely has a 'nerd school' reputation" but students want everyone to know that "we are not a group of loners that spend all their time in a lab or playing D&D." "You can find all sorts of people" here and overall the student body is "a quirky mish-mosh of quirky students all engaging with one another and doing their best to advance society in one form or another." "The typical student at Case Western is focused, hard-working, clever, quirky, and probably a little bit nerdy, but in the best way," one student explains. Students are high achievers; a typical student "works hard [and] studies a lot" yet always makes sure to find "time to socialize and invest their time in numerous groups, activities, and other endeavors." The "best way to fit in" is to get active by "joining student organizations, doing community service, jamming out to music in the residence halls, or doing a group study session."

FINANCIAL AID: 216-368-4530 • E-MAIL: ADMISSION@CASE.EDU • WEBSITE: WWW.CASE.EDU

THE PRINCETON REVIEW SAYS

Admissions

Very important factors considered include: rigor of secondary school record, class rank, academic GPA, standardized test scores, extracurricular activities. *Important factors considered include:* application essay, recommendation(s), interview, talent/ability, character/personal qualities, volunteer work, work experience, level of applicant's interest. *Other factors considered include:* first generation, alumni/ae relation, racial/ethnic status. SAT or ACT required; SAT Subject Tests considered if submitted. ACT with Writing required. SAT with Essay component required. TOEFL required of all international applicants. High school diploma is required and GED is accepted. *Academic units required:* 4 English, 3 math, 3 science, 2 science labs, 2 foreign language, 3 social studies. *Academic units recommended:* 4 math, 3 science labs, 3 foreign language, 4 social studies.

Financial Aid

Students should submit: FAFSA, Institution's own financial aid form, CSS/Financial Aid PROFILE, Noncustodial PROFILE. Priority filing deadline is 11/15. The Princeton Review suggests that all financial aid forms be submitted as soon as possible after October 1. *Need-based scholarships/grants offered:* Federal Pell, FSEOG, State scholarships/grants, Private scholarships, College/university scholarship or grant aid from institutional funds. *Loan aid offered:* Direct Subsidized Stafford Loans, Direct Unsubsidized Stafford Loans, Direct PLUS loans, Federal Perkins Loans, College/university loans from institutional funds. Applicants will be notified of awards on a rolling basis beginning 3/15. Federal Work-Study Program available. Institutional employment available.

The Inside Word

CWRU is a school with a growing profile, which means that the number of applications keeps increasing and competition is getting stiffer. Case uses a "single-door admission policy," meaning students apply to the whole school rather than individual departments. Once accepted, you can change majors without reapplying. Case accepts the Common Application and requires standardized test scores.

THE SCHOOL SAYS "..."

From the Admissions Office

"Challenging and innovative academic programs, next-level technology, experiential learning, real-world environments, and faculty mentors are at the core of the Case Western Reserve University experience. CWRU's faculty challenges and supports motivated students, and its partnerships with world-class cultural, educational, and scientific institutions ensure that your education extends beyond the classroom. CWRU offers more than seventy-five majors and minors and a single-door admission policy; once admitted to CWRU, you can major in any of our programs, or double and even triple major in several of them. Our student/faculty ratio, among the best in the nation, allows students to have close interaction with professors. Co-ops, internships, study abroad, and other opportunities bring theory to life in amazing settings, and 66 percent of students participate in research and independent study. SAGES, CWRU's four-year undergraduate core curriculum, connects students with faculty, peers and the community through small seminars that explore effective communication and analytical skills, and culminates in a Senior Capstone project. With 85 percent of students living on campus, CWRU has a residential feel unique to urban universities. First-year students live together in one of four themed residential colleges that involve resources from across Northeast Ohio: Cedar (arts), Juniper (world culture), Magnolia (sustainability), and Mistletoe (leadership through service). Admission Counselors consider all sections of the SAT, taking the best score for each section from multiple dates. The SAT (or ACT with writing) is used for evaluating applications for admission (and not used for course placement purposes)."

SELECTIVITY

Admissions Rating	94
# of applicants	22,807
% of applicants accepted	36
% of acceptees attending	15
# offered a place on the wait list	9,446
% accepting a place on wait list	54
% admitted from wait list	10
# of early decision applicants	341
% accepted early decision	32

FRESHMAN PROFILE

Range SAT Critical Reading	620–720
Range SAT Math	680–770
Range SAT Writing	620–720
Range ACT Composite	30–33
Minimum paper TOEFL	577
Minimum internet-based TOEFL	90
% graduated top 10% of class	71
% graduated top 25% of class	91
% graduated top 50% of class	99

DEADLINES

Early decision	
Deadline	11/1
Notification	12/15
Early action	
Deadline	11/1
Notification	12/15
Regular	
Deadline	1/15
Notification	3/20
Nonfall registration?	Yes

APPLICANTS ALSO LOOK AT AND OFTEN PREFER
Carnegie Mellon University

AND SOMETIMES PREFER
Boston University; Cornell University

FINANCIAL FACTS

Financial Aid Rating	91
Annual tuition	$44,156
Room and board	$13,850
Required fees	$404
Books and supplies	$1,200
Average frosh need-based scholarship	$29,932
Average UG need-based scholarship	$28,347
% needy frosh rec. need-based scholarship or grant aid	97
% needy UG rec. need-based scholarship or grant aid	97
% needy frosh rec. non-need-based scholarship or grant aid	25
% needy UG rec. non-need-based scholarship or grant aid	13
% needy frosh rec. need-based self-help aid	80
% needy UG rec. need-based self-help aid	85
% frosh rec. any financial aid	83
% UG rec. any financial aid	87
% UG borrow to pay for school	57
Average cumulative indebtedness	$28,562
% frosh need fully met	49
% ugrads need fully met	65
Average % of frosh need met	87
Average % of ugrad need met	84

CATAWBA COLLEGE

2300 WEST INNES STREET, SALISBURY, NC 28144 • ADMISSIONS: 704-637-4402 • FAX: 704-637-4222

STUDENTS SAY "..."

Academics

This small North Carolinian liberal arts school (associated with the United Church of Christ) offers students a well-rounded liberal arts education, a commitment to environmental sustainability, and classes structured around current events. Preparation for students entering their prospective fields is a focal point, and "professors go out of their way to make sure every student is involved in the learning process." Strong music, theatre, and environmental science programs are standouts of the seventy available academic fields of study at Catawba, which students say is "a strong community of teachers, faculty, and students with a common goal of excellence in education." All professors have a genuine passion for their subject matter, "always make sure the students understand the material," and "enjoy conversing with interested, engaged students both in and out of class." "Each one was always there when I needed advice or one on one help," says a student of the faculty, which cultivates a "family-oriented feeling." Small class sizes allow for close relationships with professors: "I go to class knowing they want me to succeed," says one student. "The professors at Catawba are fantastic," says another. "They truly care for your success, not just in the classroom, but in life." Life at school is "very lively and uplifting," and Catawba is constantly increasing its offerings to compete with other regional colleges; the school recently added a Winter Term to allow students the option of taking a single class between the fall and spring semesters, often incorporating travel into the curriculum. The buildings are admittedly "getting a little worn down and old," but renovations and improvements are underway.

Life

The vibe at Catawba is extremely relaxed ("[the] school is small [so] you're always on time everywhere"), and the grounds make it evident that "there is time and effort put into this beautiful campus." The college provides a lot of activities and opportunities for student involvement, and these are well-taken advantage of. "The student activities group is always doing something," which gives all students the "opportunity to find a place where they can grow." There is a 190-acre preserve that "encourages students to get out and enjoy nature" (and is also used by professors as a living classroom), and "the college and the town are very active together." Downtown Salisbury is close enough that students can visit relatively easily (many local businesses offer discounts to Catawba students), which is often necessary to the palate as everyone agrees that "the food could use major improvements." Outside of club activities, laying low is the pastime of choice here, and many nights are spent playing board games or watching movies; "going to the entertainment center to play pool or ping pong is also popular."

Student Body

A great deal of students here are "white, Christian, and southern", and around 85 percent percent of freshmen live on campus (though many will go on to live nearby as school progresses). There is an "equal mix of religious and sporty" among the roughly 1,300 students, who say that people tend to divide themselves by their primary field of study and "fit into their own groups but socialize outside of them." Closely related fields also have a tendency to form ties: "Biology and chemistry majors are often easy friends, as are theatre and English majors." Athletes are extremely well represented among the student population.

FINANCIAL AID: 704-637-4416 • E-MAIL: ADMISSION@CATAWBA.EDU • WEBSITE: WWW.CATAWBA.EDU

THE PRINCETON REVIEW SAYS

Admissions

Very important factors considered include: academic GPA, talent/ability, character/personal qualities, geographical residence. *Important factors considered include:* rigor of secondary school record, standardized test scores, extracurricular activities, volunteer work, work experience. *Other factors considered include:* class rank, application essay, interview, first generation, alumni/ae relation, state residency, religious affiliation/commitment, racial/ethnic status, level of applicant's interest. SAT or ACT required for some. ACT with or without writing accepted. TOEFL required of all international applicants. High school diploma is required and GED is accepted. *Academic units required:* 4 English, 3 math, 3 science, 3 social studies. *Academic units recommended:* 2 foreign language.

Financial Aid

Students should submit: FAFSA. Priority filing deadline is 3/15. The Princeton Review suggests that all financial aid forms be submitted as soon as possible after October 1. *Need-based scholarships/grants offered:* Federal Pell, FSEOG, State scholarships/grants, Private scholarships, College/university scholarship or grant aid from institutional funds. *Loan aid offered:* Direct Subsidized Stafford Loans, Direct Unsubsidized Stafford Loans, Direct PLUS loans, Federal Perkins Loans, State Loans, College/university loans from institutional funds. Applicants will be notified of awards on a rolling basis beginning 3/1. Federal Work-Study Program available. Institutional employment available.

The Inside Word

Since Catawba competes for students with several top regional schools, students who may not have been the highest achievers in high school but are ready to excel at the college level should put Catawba on their list. Catawba waves the application fee for students who apply online via the school's own application, and offers a test-optional application option for students with a 3.5 GPA or higher.

THE SCHOOL SAYS ". . ."

From the Admissions Office

"Catawba College prepares students for rewarding lives and careers helping them reach their highest potential as individuals. This attractive campus is centrally located in Salisbury, North Carolina, a short drive away from the mountains and Atlantic beaches. The community possesses a rich past and commitment to preserving its cultural and historic charm. In contrast, just forty-five minutes away is the much faster pace of Charlotte, North Carolina where shopping, transportation, and entertainment of all kinds are readily available.

"On campus, students study and socialize in a small college setting that offers strong traditions, excellent facilities, and beautiful surroundings. The high standards of quality set by Catawba's academic programs are matched by equally demanding sports and co-curricular programs. Students describe the community as caring and personable. They are also highly involved in campus activities ranging from the performing arts to homecoming and travel abroad. Faculty and staff are described by students as being important mentors. Whether in a state-of-the-art environmental science facility, attractive music and theatrical performance center, classroom, or one of the college's first-class athletic facilities, students report they feel as if they are among family when on campus.

"Perhaps the most important testimony to the attractiveness of Catawba is found in the words of its graduates who report numerous successful careers and rich memories of their time at school. Students applying for admission to Catawba College can apply test optional if they have a cumulative grade point average of a 3.5 or higher. Students interested in this option and those who meet the GPA requirement, must submit an Extracurricular & Leadership form found on the Catawba College website. For those students submitting test scores, Catawba accepts both ACT and SAT (students must submit the writing score of the SAT and ACT). Catawba does super score."

SELECTIVITY
Admissions Rating	89
# of applicants	3,117
% of applicants accepted	32
% of acceptees attending	31

FRESHMAN PROFILE
Range SAT Critical Reading	430–550
Range SAT Math	440–560
Range SAT Writing	410–510
Range ACT Composite	18–24
Minimum internet-based TOEFL	69
Average HS GPA	3.7
% graduated top 10% of class	13
% graduated top 25% of class	39
% graduated top 50% of class	73

DEADLINES
Regular	
Priority	3/1

APPLICANTS ALSO LOOK AT AND SOMETIMES PREFER
The University of North Carolina at Chapel Hill

AND RARELY PREFER
North Carolina State University; The University of North Carolina at Greensboro

FINANCIAL FACTS
Financial Aid Rating	83
Annual tuition	$29,333
Room and board	$10,487
Books and supplies	$1,400
Average frosh need-based scholarship	$6,984
Average UG need-based scholarship	$6,792
% needy frosh rec. need-based scholarship or grant aid	72
% needy UG rec. need-based scholarship or grant aid	78
% needy frosh rec. non-need-based scholarship or grant aid	98
% needy UG rec. non-need-based scholarship or grant aid	86
% needy frosh rec. need-based self-help aid	78
% needy UG rec. need-based self-help aid	78
% frosh rec. any financial aid	99
% UG rec. any financial aid	99
Average cumulative indebtedness	$28,961
% frosh need fully met	21
% ugrads need fully met	23
Average % of frosh need met	75
Average % of ugrad need met	72

THE CATHOLIC UNIVERSITY OF AMERICA

OFFICE OF UNDERGRADUATE ADMISSIONS, WASHINGTON, D.C. 20064 • ADMISSIONS: 202-319-5305 • FAX: 202-319-6533

CAMPUS LIFE

Quality of Life Rating	85
Fire Safety Rating	93
Green Rating	77
Type of school	Private
Affiliation	Roman Catholic
Environment	Metropolis

STUDENTS

Total undergrad enrollment	3,480
% male/female	47/53
% from out of state	97
% frosh from public high school	54
% frosh live on campus	92
% ugrads live on campus	57
# of fraternities (% ugrad men join)	1 (1)
# of sororities (% ugrad women join)	1 (1)
% African American	5
% Asian	3
% Caucasian	64
% Hispanic	13
% Native American	<1
% Pacific Islander	<1
% Two or more races	5
% Race and/or ethnicity unknown	4
% international	5
# of countries represented	78

SURVEY SAYS...

Students politically aware
Students are happy
Students are very religious
Students love Washington, DC
Great off-campus food

ACADEMICS

Academic Rating	82
% students returning for sophomore year	86
% students graduating within 4 years	62
% students graduating within 6 years	69
Calendar	Semester
Student/faculty ratio	7:1
Profs interesting rating	83
Profs accessible rating	82

Most classes have 10–19 students.
Most lab/discussion sessions have
10–19 students.

MOST POPULAR MAJORS

Architecture; Political Science and
Government; Registered Nursing/Registered
Nurse

STUDENTS SAY "..."

Academics

"DC is the perfect area for a university," and the students at Catholic University of America say "having a real campus just outside of Capitol Hill is fantastic," offering "tremendous perks," like "great access to internship and job opportunities." Students lament that their "stellar school [. . .] often gets lost among the power-players of Georgetown, GW, and American," but they argue that the opportunities for "collaborations with other universities" and "the numerous cultural offerings of the city" more than make up for it. Students praise "the small class sizes and individualized support from academic advisors," which "helps to foster a great working relationship" between students and faculty. These "world class researchers" "show a real interest in each student's success." "They are always willing to stay for a few minutes after class to talk" one student explains, "and are also always available at their office hours or via email and phone." Some professors even go as far as "[requiring] some sort of meeting with them outside of class to discuss course work and our progress in class." Attending a faith-based university where "Catholic Church teachings [are] ingrained throughout" is also important to some CUA students, who take pride in attending the "only school in the United States that is chartered by the Pope. Even so, "there is a wide variety of" religious sentiment at Catholic and "atheists [. . .] are tolerated quite well." Overall, students feel that "Catholic really strives to make our education as personal as possible."

Life

Washington, D.C., provides Catholic University students with "a surplus of activities," and the school plans plenty of "events to keep students on campus entertained." For the school's "large athletic population," CUA offers "varsity, club, and intramural sports teams." As a "highly competitive Division III school" CUA sends many of its teams "to the final rounds of NCAA tournaments" and "even those who are not a part of athletics tend to attend the events." Students say that belonging to a religious university means that community service "is more popular here than on other campuses," but most find a balance between school work, service and fun. An on-campus metro-stop means that "downtown D.C. is extremely accessible." This "wonderful city" "always offers new and exciting things to do. From going to the opera, ballet or symphony at the Kennedy Center, to a concert on U Street, to museums, to ice skating in the sculpture gardens," students always have something to fill their free time. Catholic isn't a dry campus and at some "events for upperclassmen (especially seniors), the university provides alcohol in moderation." Opinions are divided on the prevalence of drinking. Students who say that "there is a drinking culture on campus," also contend that they "don't feel any pressure" to partake if they don't want to. Others describe a student body where "a fair share enjoy some fun on the weekend, but it is not anything more than other colleges (in fact it is probably less)."

Student Body

Catholic University students are "largely white and Catholic" and are often "socially conservative," though there is "a small minority of liberal millennials." While some point to a lack of diversity, others argue that Catholic has "a good number of minority students for the size of our school." Most agree that the "student body seems to be very warm and welcoming." Many students identify a "big divide between the God Squad and the extreme party goers," but others say there is more overlap than meets the eye. "For example," one student told us, "I volunteer at masses but also occasionally go to parties with my friends and have a little fun." "Certainly, some people are more religious than others," and the average Catholic student "has a good mix of friends and a good balance on going out and doing school work."

FINANCIAL AID: 202-319-5307 • E-MAIL: CUA-ADMISSIONS@CUA.EDU • WEBSITE: WWW.CUA.EDU

THE PRINCETON REVIEW SAYS

Admissions

Very important factors considered include: rigor of secondary school record, academic GPA, recommendation(s), character/personal qualities. *Important factors considered include:* application essay, extracurricular activities, talent/ability, first generation, volunteer work. *Other factors considered include:* class rank, standardized test scores, interview, alumni/ae relation, geographical residence, racial/ethnic status, work experience, level of applicant's interest. SAT or ACT considered if submitted; SAT Subject Tests considered if submitted. ACT with or without writing accepted. SAT with or without Essay component accepted. TOEFL required of all international applicants. High school diploma is required and GED is accepted. *Academic units recommended:* 4 English, 3 math, 3 science, 1 science lab, 3 foreign language, 4 social studies, and 1 unit from above areas or other academic areas.

Financial Aid

Students should submit: FAFSA, CSS/Financial Aid PROFILE, Noncustodial PROFILE. Regular filing deadline is 4/10.The Princeton Review suggests that all financial aid forms be submitted as soon as possible after October 1. *Need-based scholarships/grants offered:* Federal Pell, FSEOG, State scholarships/grants, Private scholarships, College/university scholarship or grant aid from institutional funds. *Loan aid offered:* Direct Subsidized Stafford Loans, Direct Unsubsidized Stafford Loans, Direct PLUS loans, Federal Nursing Loans. Applicants will be notified of awards on a rolling basis beginning 3/20. Federal Work-Study Program available. Institutional employment available.

The Inside Word

The Catholic University of America's admission is fairly competitive. Certainly, the admission committee carefully assesses your GPA and the rigor of your course load, but standardized test scores are now optional. However, you must not slack on the other facets of your application as close attention is given to your personal statement and recommendations. Your extracurricular involvement is also vetted, and the university is especially on the lookout for candidates dedicated to community service.

THE SCHOOL SAYS " . . ."

From the Admissions Office

"The Catholic University of America's friendly atmosphere, rigorous academic programs, and emphasis on time-honored values attract students from all fifty states and more than forty-five foreign countries. Distinguished as the national university of the Catholic Church in the United States, CUA is the only institution of higher education established by the U.S. Catholic bishops; however, students from all religious traditions are welcome. Catholic University offers undergraduate degrees in seventy-eight major areas in nine schools of study. Students enroll in the schools of arts and sciences, social work, architecture, nursing, engineering, music, business and economics, philosophy, or theology and religious studies. Catholic University students can concentrate in areas of pre-professional study including law, dentistry, medicine, and veterinary studies. With the campus just minutes away from downtown via the Metrorail transit system, students enjoy a residential campus in an exciting city of historical monuments, theaters, festivals, restaurants, and parks. Students obtain internships throughout Washington, D.C., with the U.S. Congress, the Smithsonian Institution, NASA, the Kennedy Center, the National Institutes of Health, and many other prestigious organizations. Firsthand experience is a valuable component of a Catholic University education and the Office of Career Services offers comprehensive guidance to all students.

"Many students also take the opportunity to study abroad during their time at Catholic. With programs in fifty-two cities, including our own campus in Rome, students from all schools and majors can spend a semester or full year abroad. Politics majors even have the opportunity to complete a parliamentary internship in England, Ireland, or Brussels."

SELECTIVITY

Admissions Rating	81
# of applicants	5,991
% of applicants accepted	79
% of acceptees attending	19

FRESHMAN PROFILE

Range SAT Critical Reading	510–620
Range SAT Math	510–610
Range ACT Composite	22–28
Minimum paper TOEFL	550
Minimum internet-based TOEFL	80
Average HS GPA	3.4

DEADLINES

Early decision	
Deadline	11/15
Notification	12/20
Other ED Deadline	11/15
Other ED	
Notification	12/20
Early action	
Deadline	11/1
Notification	12/20
Regular	
Deadline	1/15
Nonfall registration?	Yes

APPLICANTS ALSO LOOK AT AND OFTEN PREFER
Boston College; University of Notre Dame

AND SOMETIMES PREFER
University of Virginia

AND RARELY PREFER
Fordham University; American University; The George Washington University

FINANCIAL FACTS

Financial Aid Rating	86
Annual tuition	$41,800
Room and board	$13,820
Required fees	$136
Books and supplies	$838
Average frosh need-based scholarship	$24,379
Average UG need-based scholarship	$22,976
% needy frosh rec. need-based scholarship or grant aid	98
% needy UG rec. need-based scholarship or grant aid	98
% needy frosh rec. non-need-based scholarship or grant aid	0
% needy UG rec. non-need-based scholarship or grant aid	0
% needy frosh rec. need-based self-help aid	80
% needy UG rec. need-based self-help aid	85
% frosh rec. any financial aid	94
% UG rec. any financial aid	89
% UG borrow to pay for school	58
Average cumulative indebtedness	$42,458
% frosh need fully met	43
% ugrads need fully met	42
Average % of frosh need met	79
Average % of ugrad need met	79

CENTENARY COLLEGE OF LOUISIANA

PO BOX 41188, SHREVEPORT, LA 71134-1188 • ADMISSIONS: 318-869-5131 • FAX: 318-869-5005

STUDENTS SAY "..."

Academics

As a small, private college with fewer than 1,000 students, Centenary College doesn't need to exaggerate the personal attention it can (and does) offer its undergraduates. "I have texted a pictured of my homework to one of my professors and they helped explain how to find the answer." Over and over again, students name their professors' close attention as the key to their success and satisfaction at Centenary: echoing the sentiment of many others, one says "the professors are the best part of Centenary." The faculty "wants to stay connected to their students," is "exciting and animated," "eager to help you succeed in their classes," and "extremely dedicated." The small class sizes are popular with both the "exceptionally supportive" faculty and the students, which fosters "a lot of personal attention as well as responsibility to show up to class." "Centenary is a small liberal arts school where the teachers know your name and are passionate about your success." However, slackers need not apply: "Most professors demand a lot out of students. There is no such thing as an easy class." The Centenary experience is also one that's well-oriented toward the future, and students praise their "easy access to the experiences I need for my major." They feel that Centenary's strength is founded on the "commitment it takes to its students" and that undergraduates "are the most important aspect" of the faculty and administration's pursuit of continuing excellence. "Centenary students pursue a personalized education" that is perhaps best encapsulated this way: "Small classes, passionate professors."

Life

Centenary's size as an "intimate and quaint campus" dominates students' depictions of their social life as much as it does their academic experience. The campus is "a close community and family" with "a plethora of organizations that allow for leadership opportunities," as well as "a surprisingly good Greek life for our size." Students are both academically serious and down for some good fun: "During the week students are always on top of school, come Thursday-Sunday it's all about the parties, frats and drinking, and Sunday is recovery and homework day." Politically, the student body is "pretty evenly split between liberal and conservative," though since the school is "United Methodist affiliated," there is a Christian emphasis on producing "moral, caring, and wise leaders." Many students participate in Centenary's "variety of sports, intramural or varsity," but non-athletes find plenty of social opportunities in the "alternative hang outs in dorm lobbies or at the religious life center, theatre, or library." Students love the "close-knit" vibe on campus, without feeling claustrophobic, reporting that undergrads "are quite close to each other here and it's easy to become fast friends with most anybody, so plenty of good old fashioned hanging out goes on."

Student Body

Centenary students "love to try new things," are "generally accepting of others," and "very committed to their interests." In terms of dividing their time between work and play, they're "highly involved socially and academically," and "able to balance both very well." Undergrads "have many interests and are encouraged to explore them together" "in a way that makes the whole campus hum harmoniously." They're happy on campus, reflecting that "Centenary campus life always has something going on" and that "overall life is pretty great at Centenary." When they want something different, there are also opportunities to "go off-campus to the Boardwalk or other places around Shreveport/Bossier" or enjoy "the local movie theater or shopping in downtown Shreveport." Students also let their minds take them to new frontiers, and depict that it's "usual to find people clustered talking about the problems of the world and offering ways to solve them." More than anything, Centenary students seem to like and value each other, and find their peers "becoming friends for life."

FINANCIAL AID: 318-869-5137 • E-MAIL: ADMISSIONS@CENTENARY.EDU • WEBSITE: WWW.CENTENARY.EDU

THE PRINCETON REVIEW SAYS

Admissions

Very important factors considered include: rigor of secondary school record, academic GPA, standardized test scores, application essay. *Important factors considered include:* class rank, recommendation(s), extracurricular activities, volunteer work. *Other factors considered include:* interview, talent/ability, character/personal qualities, alumni/ae relation, work experience. SAT or ACT required. ACT with or without writing accepted. TOEFL required of all international applicants. High school diploma is required and GED is accepted. *Academic units recommended:* 4 English, 3 math, 3 science, 2 foreign language, 3 social studies.

Financial Aid

Students should submit: FAFSA. Priority filing deadline is 2/15.The Princeton Review suggests that all financial aid forms be submitted as soon as possible after October 1. *Need-based scholarships/grants offered:* Federal Pell, FSEOG, State scholarships/grants, Private scholarships, College/university scholarship or grant aid from institutional funds. *Loan aid offered:* Direct Subsidized Stafford Loans, Direct Unsubsidized Stafford Loans, Direct PLUS loans, Federal Perkins Loans. Applicants will be notified of awards on a rolling basis beginning 3/15. Federal Work-Study Program available. Institutional employment available.

The Inside Word

Centenary prides itself on assessing applicants through a "holistic" review process that includes standard factors like GPA, high school courseload, a personal essay, recommendations, and especially a demonstrated record of balancing academic and extracurricular commitments. The school will accept applications after its February 15 deadline, but students seeking financial aid are strongly encouraged to apply by or before that deadline.

THE SCHOOL SAYS "..."

From the Admissions Office

"Just as a student's four-year experience at Centenary will be very personalized, so too is the application process. We pride ourselves on treating each applicant as an individual. We encourage all interested students to visit us—not only so they can see our campus and get a sense of the atmosphere, but also to provide us the opportunity to meet and get to know them.

"Consider Centenary for a life-changing experience. Our professors value your ideas and contributions and are passionate about teaching. We consider the Centenary Experience to be more than just a degree. You will live in a comprehensive learning environment that features connections to your academic, social, personal, and residential lives.

"Our students work and live within a strong community to create personalized, distinctive experiences, and enjoy a vibrant college life and graduate from Centenary prepared for their professional and personal lives.

"First-year applicants must submit either ACT or SAT scores. We recommend, but do not require, the ACT writing component."

SELECTIVITY

Admissions Rating	84
# of applicants	747
% of applicants accepted	67
% of acceptees attending	31

FRESHMAN PROFILE

Range SAT Critical Reading	490–590
Range SAT Math	490–610
Range ACT Composite	21–28
Minimum paper TOEFL	550
Average HS GPA	3.5

DEADLINES

Early action	
Deadline	12/1
Notification	1/15
Regular	
Priority	2/15
Deadline	8/1
Notification	4/1
Nonfall registration?	Yes

FINANCIAL FACTS

Financial Aid Rating	84
Average frosh need-based scholarship	$22,356
Average UG need-based scholarship	$21,136
% needy frosh rec. need-based scholarship or grant aid	100
% needy UG rec. need-based scholarship or grant aid	100
% needy frosh rec. non-need-based scholarship or grant aid	70
% needy UG rec. non-need-based scholarship or grant aid	74
% needy frosh rec. need-based self-help aid	63
% needy UG rec. need-based self-help aid	71
% frosh rec. any financial aid	100
% UG rec. any financial aid	99
% UG borrow to pay for school	68
Average cumulative indebtedness	$25,770
% frosh need fully met	24
% ugrads need fully met	22
Average % of frosh need met	68
Average % of ugrad need met	68

CENTRE COLLEGE

600 WEST WALNUT STREET, DANVILLE, KY 40422 • ADMISSIONS: 859-238-5350 • FAX: 859-238-5373

STUDENTS SAY "..."

Academics

Kentucky's Centre College is a private, liberal arts school armed with a "great national reputation." At the "small and personable" school it's rather easy to feel at home as you stroll around the campus. Additionally, undergrads truly appreciate that the college offers "great financial aid" as well as a "huge network in terms of postgraduate job search." Centre also aims to provide students with a global perspective and runs a robust study program. As one biology major gushes, "I have already been to Thailand, Cambodia and Hong Kong, and I will be leaving for Scotland for a semester in the fall." "Small classes" are another a hallmark of a Centre education, allowing for "a huge amount of one-on-one contact." And, perhaps most importantly, students rave about their "excellent" professors. Though they may be "tough" at times, we're also told that "their demands are worth the work!" An impressed religion major boasts, "In just two years I have had so many amazing professors who have altered the way I see the world in very meaningful and positive ways." By and large they are also "very accommodating and help students whenever they can." A psychology major supports this adding, "My professors are very attentive to my needs and are constantly reminding us that they're here to help, whether it's office hours or talking after class." And, even better, they "push you to be more than you ever thought you could be."

Life

Centre certainly adopts the stereotypical "work hard, play hard" mentality. Due to "rigorous academic courses" students are "always studying and doing homework." However, when time and schedule allow, they love to kick back. And there's a lot of which to take advantage! For starters "there are plenty of musical groups, athletic groups (intramural to D3 level), theatre groups, writing groups, art groups, student government groups and smaller niche groups for various interests." Moreover, "Greek life is a big part of Centre." This is partially attributed to the fact that "fraternities are the only ones allowed to host parties." Thankfully, it appears to be "a very open community," and we've been assured that all "parties are open to the entire campus." The Student Activities Council also hosts many "excellent events" such as "free midnight movies at the local theater" along with "really lively karaoke, poker night, etc." The performing arts center also manages to attract "top notch" musicians, dancers and comedians every year. Finally, though night life in hometown Danville "doesn't really exist," downtown Lexington "is only a 45-minute drive" and offers some great options for dining and entertainment.

Student Body

Centre seems to have cultivated a student body full of "passionate," "driven" and "intelligent" individuals. And undergrads certainly revel in the fact that you can find "a large sampling of people here." In other words, there "are nerds and athletes and drama kids and math whizzes." Impressively, "a lot of those lines blur" at Centre and it's not at all surprising to discover that "the quarterback is a drama major." Students say that the "typical student is white [and] comes from [a] middle to upper class family in either Lexington or Louisville" and "conservative," though others insist that the student body has "changed dramatically" in recent years. Fortunately, no matter their background or political leanings, students tend to be "open minded," and it's "very easy and comfortable to talk to just about anyone." "Everybody knows everybody," a contented psych major sums up. "And for the most part, everybody likes everybody. Centre is one big giant family."

FINANCIAL AID: 859-238-5365 • E-MAIL: ADMISSION@CENTRE.EDU • WEBSITE: WWW.CENTRE.EDU

THE PRINCETON REVIEW SAYS

Admissions

Very important factors considered include: rigor of secondary school record, academic GPA. *Important factors considered include:* class rank, standardized test scores, application essay, recommendation(s). *Other factors considered include:* interview, extracurricular activities, talent/ability, character/personal qualities, first generation, alumni/ae relation, geographical residence, racial/ethnic status, volunteer work, work experience. SAT or ACT required. ACT with Writing recommended. SAT with or without Essay component accepted. TOEFL required of all international applicants. High school diploma or equivalent is not required. *Academic units required:* 4 English, 3 math, 2 science, 2 science labs, 2 foreign language, 2 history. *Academic units recommended:* 4 math, 4 science, 4 foreign language, 2 social studies, 2 history, 1 visual/performing arts.

Financial Aid

Students should submit: FAFSA, Institution's own financial aid form. Regular filing deadline is 1/31.The Princeton Review suggests that all financial aid forms be submitted as soon as possible after October 1. *Need-based scholarships/grants offered:* Federal Pell, FSEOG, State scholarships/grants, Private scholarships, College/university scholarship or grant aid from institutional funds. *Loan aid offered:* Direct Subsidized Stafford Loans, Direct Unsubsidized Stafford Loans, Direct PLUS loans, Federal Perkins Loans, College/university loans from institutional funds. Applicants will be notified of awards on a rolling basis beginning 3/19. Federal Work-Study Program available. Institutional employment available.

The Inside Word

As Centre's reputation rises, earning a coveted acceptance becomes more and more competitive. A solid high school transcript full of challenging courses is a must. Standardized tests are also considered, though the school only uses the highest combination of scores. Make sure to include steady involvement in organizations and activities (including leadership roles) and work experience in your application. Lastly, students who are confident that Centre College is the school for them are highly encouraged to apply early admission.

THE SCHOOL SAYS " . . ."

From the Admissions Office

"Centre College offers its students a world of opportunities, highlighted by the nation's premier study abroad program. Approximately 85 percent of students study abroad at least once. CentreTerm programs explore an ever-increasing number of countries in January; in 2016, they included Argentina, Costa Rica, Ecuador, Egypt, Japan, India, Mexico, Morocco, New Zealand, Panama, Rwanda, Spain and Uganda. January 2017 destinations include Austria, Barbados, Brazil, Cuba, England, Ghana, Israel, Italy, Malaysia, Mexico and the Netherlands. In addition, there are nine permanent, semester-long residential programs: England, Scotland, Northern Ireland, France, Spain, Yucatan, China, and Japan. Centre's personalized approach means that most international study includes at least one Centre professor. Study abroad is so important that it is a component of the Centre Commitment: study abroad, an internship or research experience, and graduation in four years—guaranteed, or Centre will provide up to one more year of tuition for free. Centre's stellar academic reputation and exceptional commitment to remaining affordable lead to extraordinary success for our students: entrance to top graduate and professional schools, prestigious undergraduate and postgraduate fellowships (Rhodes, Fulbright, Goldwater, and Gates-Cambridge), and rewarding jobs. (On average, 95 percent are employed or in advanced study within one year of graduation.) Centre is a place where important conversations occur—in and out of the classroom. In 2012, for the second time in a dozen years, Centre's Norton Center for the Arts was the setting for the nation's only vice presidential debate. Even in years without a vice presidential debate, the Norton Center features an amazing array of high-profile arts performances and speakers, including the legendary Vienna Philharmonic, country music icon Dolly Parton, and Nobel prize–winner Elie Wiesel."

SELECTIVITY

Admissions Rating	89
# of applicants	2,716
% of applicants accepted	71
% of acceptees attending	19
# offered a place on the wait list	183
% accepting a place on wait list	23
% admitted from wait list	45
# of early decision applicants	100
% accepted early decision	68

FRESHMAN PROFILE

Range SAT Critical Reading	540–660
Range SAT Math	570–740
Range ACT Composite	26–31
Minimum paper TOEFL	580
Minimum internet-based TOEFL	90
Average HS GPA	3.6
% graduated top 10% of class	54
% graduated top 25% of class	84
% graduated top 50% of class	97

DEADLINES

Early decision	
Deadline	11/15
Notification	12/15
Early action	
Deadline	12/1
Notification	1/15
Regular	
Deadline	1/15
Notification	3/15
Nonfall registration?	No

APPLICANTS ALSO LOOK AT AND OFTEN PREFER
Davidson College

AND SOMETIMES PREFER
Kenyon College; Furman University

AND RARELY PREFER
University of Louisville

FINANCIAL FACTS

Financial Aid Rating	86
Annual tuition	$38,200
Room and board	$9,620
Books and supplies	$1,500
Average frosh need-based scholarship	$29,311
Average UG need-based scholarship	$26,886
% needy frosh rec. need-based scholarship or grant aid	100
% needy UG rec. need-based scholarship or grant aid	100
% needy frosh rec. non-need-based scholarship or grant aid	0
% needy UG rec. non-need-based scholarship or grant aid	0
% needy frosh rec. need-based self-help aid	62
% needy UG rec. need-based self-help aid	65
% frosh rec. any financial aid	97
% UG rec. any financial aid	96
% UG borrow to pay for school	55
Average cumulative indebtedness	$28,515
% frosh need fully met	37
% ugrads need fully met	31
Average % of frosh need met	87
Average % of ugrad need met	84

CHAMPLAIN COLLEGE

163 SOUTH WILLARD STREET BOX 670, BURLINGTON, VT 05402-0670 • ADMISSIONS: 802-860-2727 • FAX: 802-860-2767

CAMPUS LIFE

Quality of Life Rating	94
Fire Safety Rating	98
Green Rating	97
Type of school	Private
Affiliation	No Affiliation
Environment	Town

STUDENTS

Total undergrad enrollment	3,400
% male/female	59/41
% from out of state	78
% frosh live on campus	97
% ugrads live on campus	64
% African American	5
% Asian	2
% Caucasian	70
% Hispanic	5
% Native American	<1
% Pacific Islander	<1
% Two or more races	3
% Race and/or ethnicity unknown	14
% international	1
# of countries represented	27

SURVEY SAYS...

Students are happy
Classroom facilities are great
Career services are great
Internships are widely available
Class discussions encouraged
Students aren't religious
Students get along with local community
Students environmentally aware
Students love Burlington, VT
Great off-campus food

ACADEMICS

Academic Rating	81
% students returning for sophomore year	79
students graduating within 4 years	48
students graduating within 6 years	58
Calendar	Semester
Student/faculty ratio	13:1
Profs interesting rating	94
Profs accessible rating	84

Most classes have 10–19 students.
Most lab/discussion sessions have 10–19 students.

MOST POPULAR MAJORS

Game and Interactive Media Design;
Business/Commerce; Graphic Design

STUDENTS SAY "..."

Academics

The students at Champlain College in Burlington, Vermont, are "professional" and "career-minded," and name Champlain's "career-focused curriculum" as a primary reason for choosing the college. "Networking and the emphasis on internships at Champlain leads to a great deal of job placements relevant to your chosen major after (or before!) graduation," extols one student. Students love the "small class sizes," which "allow your professors and classmates to know, contribute and follow your success." They're also crazy about Champlain's "upside-down curriculum," which uniquely allows undergraduates to "take major-specific courses [their] first semester:" "I could begin major-related work on the first day." Game design, filmmaking, digital forensics, psychology, and marketing are all offered as majors, distinguishing Champlain's available courses of study to many applicants, with its "strong focus on major-specific skills, and field-applicable classwork." For the most part, students say the professors are "engaging, encouraging, and interesting" and "do all they can to help students understand the material and reach their full potential." Champlain works hard to produce graduates who know "how to survive and thrive in the business world" and "reach their highest level of satisfaction." Champlain is a "career-focused school that gives students the tools to succeed in the professional world." This career-conscious education is animated by Champlain's "engaging, encouraging, and interesting" professors, who "know your name," are "enthusiastic about the students' education," and "come from extremely professional backgrounds and add personal touches to their discussions that make students want to participate." In addition to academic curricula, Champlain's "LEAD program readies students for outside life," teaching life skills such as "financial sophistication" and fostering a "strong sense of community." For those interested in the burgeoning gaming industry, "Champlain's game major is also rigorous and unique, bringing students from amateurs to developing a game in a seemingly short four years." Champlain's greatest academic strength lies in "excellent professors, innovative classes," and an "inviting small-classroom environment."

Life

The small liberal arts college in cozy Burlington, Vermont, has a heavy academic focus on the video game industry, and skiing and gaming figure prominently into Champlain's social life. "There is a lot to do in town and on campus there are often events put on by clubs or the ASG. Every Thursday, a bus also takes students from campus to free bowling or to see a free movie at the movie theater." Students love Burlington—"full of endless opportunities for both outside and indoor activities"—and enjoy the shops and nightlife of Church Street. Both Champlain and Burlington "heavily promote sustainable living," and as such, students learn "an incredible amount about how to help and be aware of my community and ecosystem." For the dedicated skier/student, Champlain IDs will nab you discounted ski passes in the area, and "snow dictates class attendance in the spring." Overall, the outdoorsy will find plenty to love about Champlain and mantra seems to be, "Anything to be outside." Indoors, the "laid-back" social atmosphere tends toward "play[ing] video games rather often," and "there is an excellent music scene here in Burlington."

Student Body

Champlain's student population is summed up by one as "Champlain attracts a certain type: open, artistic, thoughtful, and intelligent," while another student is a little more blunt: "We are all nerdy in our own special way. It's a self-selective, "open-minded" population that's passionately adored by those who know what to expect: students "fit in well if they have researched the college before coming, as it is a small community within a larger community." There is "literally a bit of everything. Nerds, partiers, skiers, snowboarders, skateboarders and hippies." Another summarizes the Champlain student body as "everyone is incredibly friendly and supportive. I love that its large enough not to know everyone but small enough that it still feels like family." As a whole, Champlain students are "Motivated and engaged." They enjoy the social opportunities afforded by Burlington and Champlain, but "are also serious about doing big things and going far in life."

FINANCIAL AID: 802-860-2730 • E-MAIL: ADMISSION@CHAMPLAIN.EDU • WEBSITE: WWW.CHAMPLAIN.EDU

THE PRINCETON REVIEW SAYS
Admissions
Very important factors considered include: rigor of secondary school record, academic GPA, talent/ability. *Important factors considered include:* class rank, standardized test scores, application essay, recommendation(s), extracurricular activities, character/personal qualities, first generation, racial/ethnic status. *Other factors considered include:* alumni/ae relation, volunteer work, work experience. SAT or ACT required. ACT with or without writing accepted. SAT with or without Essay component accepted. TOEFL required of all international applicants. High school diploma is required and GED is accepted. *Academic units required:* 4 English, 3 math, 3 science, 3 science labs, 2 foreign language, 4 history, 4 academic electives. *Academic units recommended:* 4 math, 4 science, 4 foreign language.

Financial Aid
Students should submit: FAFSA. Regular filing deadline is 2/15. The Princeton Review suggests that all financial aid forms be submitted as soon as possible after October 1. *Need-based scholarships/grants offered:* Federal Pell, FSEOG, State scholarships/grants, Private scholarships, College/university scholarship or grant aid from institutional funds. *Loan aid offered:* Direct Subsidized Stafford Loans, Direct Unsubsidized Stafford Loans, Direct PLUS loans, Federal Perkins Loans. Applicants will be notified of awards on a rolling basis beginning 3/1. Federal Work-Study Program available. Institutional employment available.

The Inside Word
Don't neglect Champlain's special supplement to the Common Application, which allows you an opportunity to detail what you'd contribute to, and get out of, the Champlain community. For the BFA or BS programs in creative media, filmmaking, graphic design and digital media, game art and animation, and game design, prospective students must submit a portfolio of relevant creative work. Strong writing skills are important for all applicants.

THE SCHOOL SAYS "..."
From the Admissions Office
"Preparing students for the opportunities and challenges of an increasingly competitive world is not negotiable for us. When a student graduates from Champlain College, they can be confident that they are not only career-ready, but also life-ready. Students at Champlain College are immediately immersed in their prospective major and real-life internships via the Upside-Down Curriculum; they are challenged to think critically and further develop communication and writing abilities from the nationally acclaimed liberal arts core; and they will gain important skills such as financial sophistication, career management, and other life-building knowledge. It is an academic experience that is unparalleled, and our graduates are experiencing the benefits the day after graduation.

"However, in addition to academic preparation, going to college is about experiences, and there is no better college town in the East than Burlington, Vermont. Whether your interests are snowboarding and skiing, art and culture, music and expression, volunteering and community-building, or anything else, Burlington, Vermont, and our amazing campus have it covered. Champlain College students reside in historic Victorian mansions that overlook one of the country's most amazing natural vistas and are only steps from downtown Burlington.

"A Champlain College student is a student that feels optimistic about the future because she is taking control of it. It is a college environment of enrichment, support, and activity, and continually asks the question, what do you need to be successful upon graduation?

"We hope you can visit us soon and get a taste of the Champlain experience."

SELECTIVITY
Admissions Rating	80
# of applicants	5,587
% of applicants accepted	66
% of acceptees attending	15
# offered a place on the wait list	146
% accepting a place on wait list	10
% admitted from wait list	29
# of early decision applicants	478
% accepted early decision	79

FRESHMAN PROFILE
Range SAT Critical Reading	520–630
Range SAT Math	510–630
Range SAT Writing	490–600
Range ACT Composite	23–29
Minimum internet-based TOEFL	79
Average HS GPA	3.2
% graduated top 10% of class	10
% graduated top 25% of class	34
% graduated top 50% of class	77

DEADLINES
Nonfall registration?	Yes

FINANCIAL FACTS
Financial Aid Rating	80
Annual tuition	$37,436
Room and board	$14,050
Required fees	$100
Books and supplies	$1,000
Average frosh need-based scholarship	$19,068
Average UG need-based scholarship	$18,634
% needy frosh rec. need-based scholarship or grant aid	99
% needy UG rec. need-based scholarship or grant aid	98
% needy frosh rec. non-need-based scholarship or grant aid	11
% needy UG rec. non-need-based scholarship or grant aid	10
% needy frosh rec. need-based self-help aid	86
% needy UG rec. need-based self-help aid	83
% frosh rec. any financial aid	90
% UG rec. any financial aid	83
% UG borrow to pay for school	73
Average cumulative indebtedness	$33,236
% frosh need fully met	17
% ugrads need fully met	16
Average % of frosh need met	70
Average % of ugrad need met	68

CHAPMAN UNIVERSITY

ONE UNIVERSITY DRIVE, ORANGE, CA 92866 • ADMISSIONS: 714-997-6711 • FAX: 714-628-3404

CAMPUS LIFE
Quality of Life Rating	91
Fire Safety Rating	86
Green Rating	60*
Type of school	Private
Affiliation	Disciples of Christ
Environment	Metropolis

STUDENTS
Total undergrad enrollment	6,363
% male/female	40/60
% from out of state	26
% frosh from public high school	70
% frosh live on campus	91
% ugrads live on campus	34
# of fraternities (% ugrad men join)	9 (22)
# of sororities (% ugrad women join)	8 (40)
% African American	1
% Asian	10
% Caucasian	58
% Hispanic	14
% Native American	<1
% Pacific Islander	<1
% Two or more races	6
% Race and/or ethnicity unknown	5
% international	4
# of countries represented	83

SURVEY SAYS...
Students are happy
Classroom facilities are great
Internships are widely available
School is well run
Students love Orange, CA
Dorms are like palaces
Easy to get around campus
Frats and sororities are popular
College radio is popular

ACADEMICS
Academic Rating	81
% students returning for sophomore year	90
% students graduating within 4 years	65
% students graduating within 6 years	79
Calendar	4/1/4
Student/faculty ratio	14:1
Profs interesting rating	83
Profs accessible rating	84

Most classes have 10–19 students.
Most lab/discussion sessions have
10–19 students.

MOST POPULAR MAJORS
Business Administration; Psychology;
Communication Studies

STUDENTS SAY "..."

Academics

With its "small school" setting and So-Cal vibe, it's easy to see why students are charmed by Chapman. The university "truly emphasizes personal growth, campus involvement, and global citizenship," factors that undergrads here appreciate. There's also "great technology available" and a "gorgeous campus" to boot. Even better, "research and internship [opportunities]" abound. Chapman students also tend to rave about their "very engaging" professors, who make a concerted effort to "explain complex concepts in an understandable way." As a health sciences major shares, "These teachers aren't out to get you—they challenge you academically but are willing to help you if you're stuck or confused." It's quite obvious that "they're very dedicated and interested in the subject matters that they teach." Most importantly, they strive "to build meaningful relationships with students." And a biochemistry major boasts, "They offer so much help outside of the classroom and want to see you succeed. My overall academic experience has been wonderful."

Life

It's nearly impossible to not lead a "full and engaging" life here at Chapman. After all, there's simply too much of which to take advantage. To begin with, "the main campus provides concerts, plays, musical performances, art showings, and lectures, which are generally free for students." Additionally, "Dodge Film School has movie screenings...sometimes of movies that haven't come out yet." Chapman hosts plenty of "cool events like 'Yoga on the Lawn,' a winter festival or a chili cook off" as well. And we're also told that there's "a very large Greek presence." In fact, some undergrads insist that "Greek life can be instrumental in finding your group of friends." When the weekend rolls around, "there are usually house parties or people go to the local bars." However, many undergrads do complain that the parties tend to get shut down fairly early. Not surprisingly, students love attending school in Southern California. Chapman itself is located "right next to [Old Towne] Orange, which has many shops and restaurants where students love to walk around." Beyond that, "you can go to Disney, the beach, the Angels stadium, Los Angeles, San Diego or wherever else tickles your fancy."

Student Body

When asked to describe their peers, many Chapman undergrads quickly resort to adjectives such as "affluent," "Caucasian" and "attractive." And while there is definitely some truth to that, these students also encompass far more. Yes, walking around campus you'll also encounter individuals who are "kind, respectful, artistic, intelligent, and adventurous." For the most part, Chapman undergrads are a "driven" lot as well. Fortunately, there's not much cutthroat competition here. Indeed, we're told that students "love to work together to understand the subject material." A digital art and television product major explains further, "The mood of the student body is very collaborative. Everyone wants to socialize and be friendly and meet new people." While students are generally "accepting [of] diversity," they do tend to be "more conservative in political matters." Lastly, a sociology major sums up her peers by stating, "No matter what the interest is, whether it be Greek life, community service, their major, or even their social life, [students here] are motivated to succeed in their endeavors."

FINANCIAL AID: 714-997-6741 • E-MAIL: ADMIT@CHAPMAN.EDU • WEBSITE: WWW.CHAPMAN.EDU

THE PRINCETON REVIEW SAYS

Admissions

Very important factors considered include: rigor of secondary school record, class rank, academic GPA, standardized test scores, application essay, character/personal qualities. *Important factors considered include:* extracurricular activities, talent/ability, volunteer work. *Other factors considered include:* recommendation(s), interview, first generation, alumni/ae relation, geographical residence, state residency, racial/ethnic status, work experience. SAT or ACT required; SAT Subject Tests recommend. ACT with Writing required. TOEFL required of all international applicants. High school diploma is required and GED is accepted. *Academic units required:* 2 English, 2 math, 2 science, 1 science lab, 2 foreign language, 3 social studies. *Academic units recommended:* 4 English, 4 math, 4 science, 2 science labs, 4 foreign language, 4 social studies.

Financial Aid

Students should submit: FAFSA, State aid form. Priority filing deadline is 3/2. The Princeton Review suggests that all financial aid forms be submitted as soon as possible after October 1. *Need-based scholarships/grants offered:* Federal Pell, FSEOG, State scholarships/grants, Private scholarships, College/university scholarship or grant aid from institutional funds. *Loan aid offered:* Direct Subsidized Stafford Loans, Direct Unsubsidized Stafford Loans, Federal Perkins Loans. Applicants will be notified of awards on a rolling basis beginning 3/15. Federal Work-Study Program available. Institutional employment available.

Inside Word

Gaining admission to Chapman is certainly competitive. When reviewing applications, admissions officers tend to take a holistic approach. The rigor of an academic curriculum, grade trends, letters of recommendations, extracurricular activities and personal statements will all be closely evaluated. Chapman also considers an applicant's intended major and any academic or extracurricular experiences that reflect preparation (for that course of study). It should also be noted that certain majors have additional requirements. Applicants interested in studying in the arts or any major within Dodge College of Film & Media Arts will have additional application requirements. Students intending to pursue Film Production will need to apply by November 1, and those looking to pursue Pharmacy, Screen Acting or Theatre Performance have a priority deadline of November 1.

THE SCHOOL SAYS " . . . "

From the Admissions Office

"During our more than 150-year history, Chapman has evolved from a small, traditional liberal arts college into a vibrant and comprehensive midsized university distinguished for its extraordinary blend of liberal arts, science, and professional curriculum, including nationally recognized programs in health sciences, film and television production, business and economics, dance, music, theatre, writing, and teacher education. At Chapman, learning extends well beyond the classroom—our central Orange County, California, location offers countless cultural, educational, and career opportunities. Additionally, the temperate climate allows for a dynamic, outdoor-oriented lifestyle. Chapman's environment is involving, and we seek students who are willing to enter an atmosphere of healthy competition where their talents will be nurtured and actualized to the fullest—whether in the classroom, on the stage, or on the athletic field. We encourage prospective students to thoroughly investigate our broad spectrum of academic programs, so they may make a fully informed decision about how well Chapman fits with their interests and career goals.

"Chapman is a member of the Common Application. Applicants for freshman admission to Chapman University will be required to submit scores from either the SAT or the ACT including the ACT writing section."

SELECTIVITY

Admissions Rating	89
# of applicants	13,769
% of applicants accepted	47
% of acceptees attending	22

FRESHMAN PROFILE

Range SAT Critical Reading	550–640
Range SAT Math	550–650
Range SAT Writing	560–660
Range ACT Composite	25–30
Minimum paper TOEFL	550
Average HS GPA	3.7
% graduated top 10% of class	39
% graduated top 25% of class	79
% graduated top 50% of class	97

DEADLINES

Early action	
Deadline	11/1
Notification	12/20
Regular	
Deadline	1/15
Nonfall registration?	Yes

APPLICANTS ALSO LOOK AT AND OFTEN PREFER

Loyola Marymount University; University of San Diego; University of California—Los Angeles; University of Southern California; New York University

AND SOMETIMES PREFER

Pepperdine University

FINANCIAL FACTS

Financial Aid Rating	83
Annual tuition	$46,500
Room and board	$13,830
Required fees	$760
Books and supplies	$1,560
Average frosh need-based scholarship	$16,998
Average UG need-based scholarship	$16,096
% needy frosh rec. need-based scholarship or grant aid	93
% needy UG rec. need-based scholarship or grant aid	90
% needy frosh rec. non-need-based scholarship or grant aid	72
% needy UG rec. non-need-based scholarship or grant aid	66
% needy frosh rec. need-based self-help aid	86
% needy UG rec. need-based self-help aid	91
% UG borrow to pay for school	61
Average cumulative indebtedness	$27,837
% frosh need fully met	18
% ugrads need fully met	13
Average % of frosh need met	77
Average % of ugrad need met	72

CHRISTOPHER NEWPORT UNIVERSITY

1 AVENUE OF THE ARTS, NEWPORT NEWS, VA 23606-2998 • ADMISSIONS: 757-594-7015 • FAX: 757-594-7333

CAMPUS LIFE

Quality of Life Rating	95
Fire Safety Rating	96
Green Rating	60*
Type of school	Public
Affiliation	No Affiliation
Environment	City

STUDENTS

Total undergrad enrollment	5,051
% male/female	43/57
% from out of state	8
% frosh from public high school	70
% frosh live on campus	97
% ugrads live on campus	74
# of fraternities (% ugrad men join)	9 (20)
# of sororities (% ugrad women join)	8 (32)
% African American	8
% Asian	3
% Caucasian	74
% Hispanic	5
% Native American	<1
% Pacific Islander	<1
% Two or more races	5
% Race and/or ethnicity unknown	5
% international	<1
# of countries represented	32

SURVEY SAYS...

Students are happy
Classroom facilities are great
Lab facilities are great
Career services are great
School is well run
Students are friendly
Diverse student types interact on campus
Students are very religious
Students get along with local community
Students involved in community service
Dorms are like palaces
Easy to get around campus
Recreation facilities are great

ACADEMICS

Academic Rating	81
% students returning for sophomore year	88
students graduating within 4 years	57
students graduating within 6 years	70
Calendar	Semester
Student/faculty ratio	15:1
Profs interesting rating	90
Profs accessible rating	96
Most classes have 10–19 students.	

MOST POPULAR MAJORS
Psychology; Biology; Speech Communication and Rhetoric

STUDENTS SAY "..."

Academics
Christopher Newport was an English seaman and captain of "the largest of the three ships that brought the Jamestown settlers to the New World." Over 400 years later, Christopher Newport University "is Virginia's up and coming prestigious university," providing "a private school education and experience at a public school cost." "CNU is the perfect size" at "just over 5,000 students." Students enjoy "close relationships between teachers and students" and "small classes and easily accessible professors." Most of the professors "are enthusiastic about their material" and "will work you until you sweat...but this is not necessarily a bad thing." CNU is a university where "professors actually HAVE office hours in which you can see them without appointment to receive extra help." As is true at any school, "some are better than others." One English major says that while the professors are "very approachable" and "care about the students," "I can't say I've had very many who just strike me with awe and inspiration." Students have positive things to say about the administration and the "interactive president" who "runs CNU with excellence." "From the deans to the custodial staff, everyone at CNU is held to a high standard and each seems to genuinely enjoy his/her job." Students rave about the weather, the "absolutely beautiful" campus, and the "always delicious" dining hall food. Students do feel the dining food, while tasty, can be "overpriced" and the dining facilities are "a tad small" and "crowded." Some students feel the school could add more majors, but note "every year CNU seems to be adding more." Perhaps that's because "CNU's motto is 'Students first'" and the university responds to student needs. From the "friendly atmosphere" and "amazing professors" to the "good financial aid" and "great classes," CNU is a school that feels like a "second home" while also being "a gateway to opportunities in all areas of life."

Life
CNU students are very active on campus and "almost every student is involved in some type of club or organization." "We have SO MANY clubs (literally more than 200) and students are always creating new clubs," meaning "there is something for everyone." "From a capella to ballroom dancing to ping pong to politics or finance, you are actually going to find something (or many things!) that you love," one student explains. CNU is a dry campus, which means there is no alcohol allowed on campus, even for students who are over twenty-one. So unlike a lot of universities, "the party scene isn't exactly a big part of college life," although students note that "drinking is somewhat common off campus." "The Greek presence at CNU is very widespread," and "the school does an excellent job of getting speakers and events on campus." "There isn't much to do in the town on weekends" so "for fun people go to CNU hockey games, Virginia Beach (forty minutes away), beaches on the James River near campus (five minutes away), house parties, concerts at the Norva in Norfolk...[participate in] intramural sports, and hundreds of clubs." Overall, students are happy with life on CNU's "beautiful campus." Life is "laid back" and fosters a "unique and positive culture." "I am able to see new faces every day, but still see friendly faces in the crowd as well," one student says.

Student Body
The number one description of students at CNU is "friendly." This is a school where "people will always find something in common with one another" and people form "intentional relationships that last a lifetime." The typical student is a "studious, middle class Caucasian; friendly, sociable," and many are "rich white kids from NOVA [who] love big white columns." Although "there needs to be greater diversity at the university," "CNU is not Pleasantville, we have plenty of diversity in socioeconomic backgrounds, styles, and ways of thinking." One student warns that "atheist/agnostic" students might find an "overbearing prevalence of Christian organizations." Other students love the "strong moral values" on campus and say, "People of all different races, religions, and interests interact on a daily basis." Students here care "about their academic career" and "are very friendly and always willing to help others." At the end of the day, "everyone here is really cool and everyone is so nice!"

FINANCIAL AID: 757-594-7170 • E-MAIL: ADMIT@CNU.EDU • WEBSITE: WWW.CNU.EDU

THE PRINCETON REVIEW SAYS

Admissions

Very important factors considered include: rigor of secondary school record, academic GPA. *Important factors considered include:* class rank, standardized test scores, application essay, recommendation(s), interview, extracurricular activities, talent/ability, character/personal qualities, level of applicant's interest. *Other factors considered include:* first generation, alumni/ae relation, geographical residence, state residency, volunteer work, work experience. SAT or ACT required for some. ACT with or without writing accepted. SAT with or without Essay component accepted. TOEFL required of all international applicants. High school diploma is required and GED is accepted. *Academic units required:* 4 English, 4 math, 4 science, 3 foreign language, 4 social studies, 2 academic electives, 1 visual/performing arts, and 4 units from above areas or other academic areas. *Academic units recommended:* 4 English, 4 math, 4 science, 3 science labs, 3 foreign language, 4 social studies, 2 academic electives, 1 visual/performing arts, and 4 units from above areas or other academic areas.

Financial Aid

Students should submit: FAFSA. Priority filing deadline is 3/1.The Princeton Review suggests that all financial aid forms be submitted as soon as possible after October 1. *Need-based scholarships/grants offered:* Federal Pell, FSEOG, State scholarships/grants, Private scholarships, College/university scholarship or grant aid from institutional funds. *Loan aid offered:* Direct Subsidized Stafford Loans, Direct Unsubsidized Stafford Loans, Direct PLUS Loans. Applicants will be notified of awards on a rolling basis beginning 3/1. Federal Work-Study Program available. Institutional employment available.

The Inside Word

Alongside the Honors Program, CNU boasts a unique President's Leadership Program for "high achieving students identified for their academic and leadership potential." Interviews are required for both programs. Christopher Newport University is one of the more selective universities in the state, so students will want to bring their A game to their applications.

THE SCHOOL SAYS ". . ."

From the Admissions Office

"Christopher Newport University wants you to thrive academically. Even more so, we want you to lead a life of significance. That's why our undergraduate experience—one that combines cutting-edge academics, stellar leadership opportunities, and high-impact service initiatives—inspires great leaders for the twenty-first century. Honoring the best of the liberal arts and sciences, our curriculum shapes hearts and minds for a lifetime of service. We seek students of honor who will make the world a better place. Fifty percent of our students score between 1070 and 1230 on the SAT (critical reading and math), and students must live on campus through their junior year. Our contemporary, state-of-the-art residential facilities win rave reviews from students and parents alike.

"Here you will study alongside distinguished professors, and over the last five years, we have added more than 100 tenure-track Ph.D.s to our faculty. Outside the classroom, you will gain hands-on experience through internships with top organizations like NASA and the Thomas Jefferson National Accelerator Facility.

"At CNU, you will enjoy countless opportunities to develop leadership skills. Make an impact through the President's Leadership Program; design a challenging curriculum in the Honors Program; team with faculty on groundbreaking research; take your studies overseas by studying abroad; and share your talents through 200-plus student organizations. We are also home to one of the most successful NCAA Division III programs in the nation with student-athletes who excel both in the classroom and on the field of play.

"Explore our campus further to discover opportunities as rich as your imagination."

SELECTIVITY

Admissions Rating	86
# of applicants	7,366
% of applicants accepted	60
% of acceptees attending	28
# offered a place on the wait list	1,566
% accepting a place on wait list	35
% admitted from wait list	42
# of early decision applicants	487
% accepted early decision	77

FRESHMAN PROFILE

Range SAT Critical Reading	540–630
Range SAT Math	530–620
Range SAT Writing	510–600
Range ACT Composite	23–27
Minimum paper TOEFL	530
Minimum internet-based TOEFL	71
Average HS GPA	3.8
% graduated top 10% of class	17
% graduated top 25% of class	53
% graduated top 50% of class	88

DEADLINES

Early decision	
Deadline	11/15
Notification	12/15
Early action	
Deadline	12/1
Notification	1/15
Regular	
Priority	11/15
Deadline	2/1
Notification	3/15
Nonfall registration?	Yes

APPLICANTS ALSO LOOK AT AND OFTEN PREFER
University of Virginia; The College of William & Mary

AND SOMETIMES PREFER
Virginia Tech; James Madison University; George Mason University

FINANCIAL FACTS

Financial Aid Rating	80
Average frosh need-based scholarship	$6,535
Average UG need-based scholarship	$6,567
% needy frosh rec. need-based scholarship or grant aid	66
% needy UG rec. need-based scholarship or grant aid	64
% needy frosh rec. non-need-based scholarship or grant aid	49
% needy UG rec. non-need-based scholarship or grant aid	32
% needy frosh rec. need-based self-help aid	74
% needy UG rec. need-based self-help aid	80
% frosh rec. any financial aid	71
% UG rec. any financial aid	59
% UG borrow to pay for school	60
Average cumulative indebtedness	$29,710
% frosh need fully met	6
% ugrads need fully met	15
Average % of frosh need met	68
Average % of ugrad need met	68

CITY UNIVERSITY OF NEW YORK—BARUCH COLLEGE

UNDERGRADUATE ADMISSIONS, 151 EAST 25TH STREET, NEW YORK, NY 10010 • ADMISSIONS: 646-312-1400 • FAX: 646-312-1363

CAMPUS LIFE

Quality of Life Rating	82
Fire Safety Rating	60*
Green Rating	62
Type of school	Public
Affiliation	No Affiliation
Environment	Metropolis

STUDENTS

Total undergrad enrollment	15,254
% male/female	51/49
% from out of state	3
% frosh from public high school	89
% ugrads live on campus	2
% African American	9
% Asian	32
% Caucasian	23
% Hispanic	22
% Native American	<1
% Pacific Islander	<1
% Two or more races	2
% Race and/or ethnicity unknown	0
% international	11
# of countries represented	174

SURVEY SAYS...

Students are happy
Great library
Career services are great
Students love New York, NY
Very little drug use
Active minority support groups

ACADEMICS

Academic Rating	80
% students returning for sophomore year	91
% students graduating within 4 years	42
% students graduating within 6 years	70
Calendar	Semester
Student/faculty ratio	17:1
Profs interesting rating	80
Profs accessible rating	71

Most classes have 20–29 students.
Most lab/discussion sessions have 20–29 students.

MOST POPULAR MAJORS
Accounting; Finance

STUDENTS SAY "..."

Academics

One of the City University of New York's senior colleges, Baruch College's schools (Weissman School of Arts and Sciences, School of Public Affairs, and the Zicklin School of Business, which is the largest of the three) are located in Manhattan and take full advantage of being in "the greatest city of the world:" Students here have access to "internships, big companies, and...Wall Street." Low in-state (as well as reasonable out-of-state) tuition means that many here "go to school while already working in interesting and impressive positions," and have come to Baruch purely "to improve themselves," which increases the level of maturity in the classroom. There is a wide variety of courses ("especially [for] those interested in business"), and the school offers ad-hoc majors, which allows students to design programs that will support their career goals.

Though this is not a research university, there are a "vast amount of resources" that are available to the students here. The education system is "well organized and up to date with the current world," and Baruch is tied with many companies in New York, which "creates even more opportunities for internships as well as job opportunities." "Some of my business professors came from leading huge corporations, and their anecdotes about their prior work helps students internalize the material," says one student. There is "an impressive number of career-developing programs on campus that are free of charge and readily available to all students," and "it is clear that the professors at Baruch have first-hand experience in the material they are teaching to students."

Life

As a commuter school most students go to classes and go home, but "there are great clubs and events always happening" for those that do hang around, and the "lounges are usually packed." "It is all about how much time and effort you put into finding things to do," says a student. Most students are working part-time or full time while taking courses here, but find plenty to do in between classes, from "hanging out in the club area with the clubs, playing in the game room, working out in the gym, or taking classes in our trading floor." There is so much student activity around Baruch that it is often hard to contain, and "there is always something going on and always free food around campus."

Though most do not get the typical on-campus college experience, all agree that "for the price and the benefits associated with the school the tradeoff is worth it." This is New York City, which means "you can practically do ANYTHING with your day." Museums are free for students, and "of course the shopping and food are amazing." The school's Newman Vertical Campus on Lexington Ave is a hive of activity, and though elevator crowding is a problem, when a student's eyes look at the breathtaking view of the building, "It makes you feel proud to be a Baruchi!"

Student Body

Students come from all over the world and Baruch is "full of bright and ambitious minds;" being a student here "means you learn to interact with peers from all over the world." "My fellow peers have a good sense of where they want to steer their careers and exactly what they want to do after college," says one student. Baruch is "full of first generation college graduates," and the school is a real microcosm of NYC: "the hustle and bustle, crowds, everyone has somewhere to go, and everyone has a dream they hope will one day be fulfilled." This is a very unique commuter school and in that "it has such an involved student body" where "there is a sense of community through clubs and extracurriculars."

FINANCIAL AID: 646-312-1360 • E-MAIL: ADMISSIONS@BARUCH.CUNY.EDU • WEBSITE: WWW.BARUCH.CUNY.EDU

THE PRINCETON REVIEW SAYS

Admissions

Very important factors considered include: rigor of secondary school record, academic GPA, standardized test scores. *Important factors considered include:* application essay, recommendation(s). *Other factors considered include:* interview, extracurricular activities, talent/ability, character/personal qualities, work experience. SAT or ACT required; SAT Subject Tests considered if submitted. ACT with or without writing accepted. TOEFL required of all international applicants. High school diploma is required and GED is accepted. *Academic units required:* 4 English, 3 math, 2 science, 2 science labs, 2 foreign language, 4 social studies. *Academic units recommended:* 2 foreign language, 1 academic elective.

Financial Aid

Students should submit: FAFSA, State aid form. Priority filing deadline is 4/15.The Princeton Review suggests that all financial aid forms be submitted as soon as possible after October 1. *Need-based scholarships/grants offered:* Federal Pell, FSEOG, State scholarships/grants, Private scholarships, College/university scholarship or grant aid from institutional funds. *Loan aid offered:* Direct Subsidized Stafford Loans, Direct Unsubsidized Stafford Loans, Direct PLUS loans, Federal Perkins Loans. Applicants will be notified of awards on a rolling basis beginning 4/15. Federal Work-Study Program available. Institutional employment available.

The Inside Word

Admissions have grown steadily more competitive in recent years, especially for students seeking undergraduate business degrees. Today, Baruch receives nearly fifteen applications for every slot in its freshman class. Your math scores on standardized tests count more heavily here than verbal scores.

THE SCHOOL SAYS "..."

From the Admissions Office

"Baruch College is in the heart of New York City. As an undergraduate, you will join a vibrant learning community of students and scholars in the middle of an exhilarating city full of possibilities. Baruch is a place where theory meets practice. You can network with city leaders; secure business, cultural, and nonprofit internships; access the music, art, and business scene; and meet experts who visit our campus. You will take classes that bridge business, arts, science, and social policy, learning from professors who are among the best in their fields. One third of our freshmen participate in learning communities, which offer incoming students small, interdisciplinary classes and an opportunity to get to know our faculty through class room discussion and planned field trips throughout the city. Baruch offers thirty-one majors and fifty-five minors in three schools: the School of Public Affairs, the Weissman School of Arts and Science, and the Zicklin School of Business. Highly qualified undergraduates may apply to the Baruch College Honors program, which offers scholarships, small seminars and honors courses. Students may also study abroad through programs in more than thirty countries. Our seventeen-floor Newman Vertical Campus serves as the college's hub. Here you will find the atmosphere and resources of a traditional college campus, but in a lively urban setting. Our classrooms have state-of-the-art technology, and our library was named the top college library in the nation. Baruch also has a simulated trading floor for students who are interested in Wall Street. You can also enjoy a three-level athletics and recreation complex, which features a twenty-five-meter indoor pool as well as a performing arts complex. In 2013, Baruch College opened the 25th Street Pedestrian Plaza, providing outdoor space for major student actives like Freshmen Convocation, Winter Carnival and Spring Fling, as well as an informal setting for students to gather on a nice day. The college is now offering housing at 1760 3rd Avenue (in Manhattan, on the Upper East Side). The state-of-the-art residences are equipped with a concierge, high tech gym, laundry facility that texts when your clothes are dry, and a very chill lounge to study or relax with your friends. The building is just blocks away from Central Park, and Serendipity. Baruch's selective admission standards, strong academic programs, top national honors, as well as its internship and job-placement opportunities make it an exceptional educational value."

SELECTIVITY

Admissions Rating	91
# of applicants	19,864
% of applicants accepted	32
% of acceptees attending	23

FRESHMAN PROFILE

Range SAT Critical Reading	520–630
Range SAT Math	580–690
Minimum paper TOEFL	550
Minimum internet-based TOEFL	80
Average HS GPA	3.3
% graduated top 10% of class	48
% graduated top 25% of class	78
% graduated top 50% of class	93

DEADLINES

Early decision	
Deadline	12/13
Notification	1/7
Other ED	
Deadline	12/13
Other ED	
Notification	1/7
Regular	
Priority	12/1
Deadline	2/1
Notification	5/1
Nonfall registration?	Yes

APPLICANTS ALSO LOOK AT AND OFTEN PREFER
Brooklyn College; Queens College

AND SOMETIMES PREFER
University at Albany–SUNY; Hunter College

FINANCIAL FACTS

Financial Aid Rating	80
Annual in-state tuition	$6,330
Annual out-of-state tuition	$16,800
Required fees	$531
Books and supplies	$1,363
Average frosh need-based scholarship	$7,559
Average UG need-based scholarship	$6,870
% needy frosh rec. need-based scholarship or grant aid	99
% needy UG rec. need-based scholarship or grant aid	97
% needy frosh rec. non-need-based scholarship or grant aid	5
% needy UG rec. non-need-based scholarship or grant aid	2
% needy frosh rec. need-based self-help aid	31
% needy UG rec. need-based self-help aid	41
% frosh rec. any financial aid	67
% UG rec. any financial aid	53
% frosh need fully met	15
% ugrads need fully met	10
Average % of frosh need met	65
Average % of ugrad need met	58

CITY UNIVERSITY OF NEW YORK—BROOKLYN COLLEGE

2900 BEDFORD AVENUE, BROOKLYN, NY 11210 • ADMISSIONS: 718-951-5001 • FAX: 718-951-4506

STUDENTS SAY "..."

Academics

Brooklyn College "is the perfect representative of Brooklyn as a borough and [of] success in the community," an institution that, like its home borough, "educates its students in an environment that reflects diversity, opportunity (study abroad, research, athletics, employment), and support." "Lauded as one of the best senior colleges in CUNY" and boasting "a beautiful campus," Brooklyn College entices a lot of bright students looking for an affordable, quality, undergraduate experience as well as some attracted by the school's relatively charitable admissions standards. It's easier to get in here than to stay in; Brooklyn College is "an academically challenging and rigorous school" that "feels a lot more competitive than one would anticipate." Professors "are fabulous" and "really passionate about the subjects that they teach and their students' career paths," although there are some "grumpy and nasty professors" that might best be avoided. Students are especially sanguine about special programs here, such as the various honors programs, in which "you will meet tons of highly intelligent people. Honors classes boast very good in-class discussions and highly vibrant, enthusiastic students. Non-honors classes are more run-of-the-mill but still very good academically." The school also works hard to provide "constant and innumerable job opportunities available to students and the Magner Center, which helps students find jobs and internships, and [to] help them prepare for the real world through résumé writing workshops [and] job interview workshops." There are also "many financial awards available."

Life

"Apart from all the clubs and athletics on campus, most people come for class and then leave" at Brooklyn College because "we are a commuter school, so it has to be this way. All social activities happen off campus." There are "pretty nice places to hang out around campus for the occasional coffee," and "there are a lot of student organizations and a lot of activities done to help enhance student life on campus," but the "immediate surroundings of the Brooklyn College campus are generally not where you would want to stay for hours," and "on weekends the campus usually is dead." That said, "the campus is quite beautiful, and the quad during spring time is usually a nice place to sit and relax." Furthermore, "New York City hotspots are a twenty- to forty-minute [subway] ride away," and Brooklyn itself is "a great place to live" where "there are always fun things happening."

Student Body

"The typical student at Brooklyn College is hardworking, from the NY metro area, and a commuter." Many "hold part-time jobs and pay at least part of their own tuition, so they are usually in a rush because they have a lot more responsibility on their shoulders than the average college student." Like Brooklyn itself, "the student body is very diversified," with everyone from "an aspiring opera singer to quirky film majors to single mothers looking for a better life for their children," and so "no student can be described as being typical. Everyone blends in as normal, and little segregation is noticed (if it exists)." Students here represent more than 100 nations and speak nearly as many languages. There are students who "come from Long Island to North Carolina, from Connecticut to even Hong Kong."

CITY UNIVERSITY OF NEW YORK—BROOKLYN COLLEGE

FINANCIAL AID: 718-951-5051 • E-MAIL: ADMINQRY@BROOKLYN.CUNY.EDU • WEBSITE: WWW.BROOKLYN.CUNY.EDU

THE PRINCETON REVIEW SAYS

Admissions

Very important factors considered include: rigor of secondary school record, academic GPA, standardized test scores. *Important factors considered include: Other factors considered include:* SAT or ACT required. ACT with or without writing accepted. TOEFL required of all international applicants. High school diploma is required and GED is accepted. *Academic units recommended:* 4 English, 3 math, 3 science, 3 foreign language, 4 social studies, 4 academic electives.

Financial Aid

Students should submit: FAFSA. Priority filing deadline is 4/1.The Princeton Review suggests that all financial aid forms be submitted as soon as possible after October 1. *Need-based scholarships/grants offered:* Federal Pell, FSEOG, State scholarships/grants, Private scholarships, College/university scholarship or grant aid from institutional funds. *Loan aid offered:* Direct Subsidized Stafford Loans, Direct Unsubsidized Stafford Loans, Direct PLUS loans, Federal Perkins Loans. Applicants will be notified of awards on a rolling basis beginning 5/1. Federal Work-Study Program available. Institutional employment available.

The Inside Word

Brooklyn College doesn't set the bar inordinately high; students with less-than-stellar high school records can receive a chance to prove themselves here. Once they get in, though, they had better be prepared to work; Brooklyn College typically loses about 20 percent of its freshman class each year, and six-year graduation rates rarely exceed 50 percent. Getting into Brooklyn College is one thing; surviving its academic challenges is a whole other thing entirely.

THE SCHOOL SAYS ". . ."

From the Admissions Office

"Brooklyn College is a premier public liberal arts college. For the last five years it has been consistently designated as one of America's Best Value Colleges by The Princeton Review and, in 2009, was cited as one of the top fifty Best Value Public Colleges in the nation. Respected nationally for its rigorous academic standards, the college has increased both the size and academic quality of its student body. It takes pride in such innovative programs as its award-winning Freshman Year College; the Honors Academy, which houses six programs for high achievers; and its nationally recognized core curriculum. Its School of Education is ranked among the top twenty in the country for graduates who go on to be considered among the best teachers in New York City. Brooklyn College's strong academic reputation has attracted an outstanding faculty of nationally renowned teachers and scholars. Among the awards they have won are Pulitzers, Guggenheims, Fulbrights, and many National Institutes of Health grants.

"The student body consists of more than 16,000 undergraduate and graduate students who represent the ethnic and cultural diversity of the borough. The college's accessibility by subway or bus allows students to further enrich their educational experience through New York City's many cultural events and institutions. In recent years, student achievements have been acknowledged with Fulbright and Truman Scholarships and an Emmy Award. In 2010 we received our third Rhodes Scholarship in eleven years.

"The Brooklyn College campus, considered to be among the most beautiful in the nation, is in the midst of an ambitious program of expansion and renewal. A new residence hall has opened two blocks from the campus. It includes such amenities as single, as well as shared, rooms, Wi-Fi throughout, community lounges, a fitness center, and kitchenettes in every room. The dazzling library is the most technologically advanced educational and research facility in the CUNY system. Opened in 2009, the West Quad Building has state-of-the-art student services and is home to the physical education department. A separate fitness center, basketball and handball courts, and a competition pool is open for use by students and staff. Ground has been broken for a new performing arts center, followed in the coming years with a new science complex."

SELECTIVITY

Admissions Rating	88
# of applicants	20,324
% of applicants accepted	37
% of acceptees attending	18

FRESHMAN PROFILE

Range SAT Critical Reading	470–570
Range SAT Math	500–610
Minimum paper TOEFL	500
Average HS GPA	3.3
% graduated top 10% of class	18
% graduated top 25% of class	50
% graduated top 50% of class	78

DEADLINES

Regular	
Priority	2/1
Nonfall registration?	Yes

FINANCIAL FACTS

Financial Aid Rating	89
Annual in-state tuition	$6,330
Required fees	$508
Average frosh need-based scholarship	$3,400
Average UG need-based scholarship	$3,400
% needy frosh rec. need-based scholarship or grant aid	64
% needy UG rec. need-based scholarship or grant aid	82
% needy frosh rec. non-need-based scholarship or grant aid	23
% needy UG rec. non-need-based scholarship or grant aid	24
% needy frosh rec. need-based self-help aid	68
% needy UG rec. need-based self-help aid	77
% frosh rec. any financial aid	80
% UG rec. any financial aid	79
% UG borrow to pay for school	30
Average cumulative indebtedness	$15,306
% frosh need fully met	74
% ugrads need fully met	82
Average % of frosh need met	88
Average % of ugrad need met	89

CITY UNIVERSITY OF NEW YORK—CITY COLLEGE

160 CONVENT AVENUE, WILLE ADMINISTRATION BUILDING, NEW YORK, NY 10031 • ADMISSIONS: 212-650-6977 • FAX: 212-650-6417

STUDENTS SAY "..."

Academics

As the first school of the City University of New York system, CCNY "stands for growth, education, and creativity." Many students choose the school due to its "astonishingly low cost" and proximity to home, and its practicality is backed up by "rigorous academic programs." "I fell in love with the school during open house, and it's the exact way I imagined after enrolling," says a student. The university has also made substantial new investments in science and medicine, and it is the only public college in New York City to offer engineering and architecture degrees, which is a huge draw for the school (but there is "no coddling here in the engineering school," warns one student). A "multitude" of classes are taught by "awesome professors with experience and wonderful careers" who "are available outside of the class" and "exhibit great love for the materials they teach." Generally, professors "go above and beyond" to ensure that students are able to grasp what they are learning. "My professors devote time and effort to making sure students understand the material being taught," confirms a student. The diversity in the student body, as well as the faculty and administration, "is profound," which "helps many people interact with different people from different cultures and come together to get through each semester in college." No matter their background, all here "take our education and future careers seriously." "There are a lot of talented people in the school overall," says a student, not to mention the "strong ties to research collaborators and institutions." Professors "will make you learn and work for the A," but "It has overall been a very rewarding experience," according to a student.

Life

Since so many students work and live full lives outside of classes, most students commute home each night. "The campus is nice, and there's a lot to do, but there's very little 'campus life,'" according to one student. CCNY has "amazing events," but "sometimes it's hard to partake due to our employment and fiscal priorities." The clubs "are always having shows, fairs, and other types of events offered to all students." People are "very respectful and helpful," and "a new student will always be able to find help." The library and cafeteria are both popular hangout spots, and "there is a gym, both for workout and for sports." Let's also not forget where the school is located: "It isn't hard to find fun around New York City." Harlem "is very historic," and "there are great places to eat around City College." The radio station WCCR "always has a ton of people having fun, hanging out, and playing music."

Student Body

The diversity at CCNY is not just ethnic—it is also political, economic, academic, age, and every other means of categorization—which means that there is no typical student. This large group of "diverse students seeking excellence" all feel like they fit in because "we each have something to bring to the table." On any average day, "you can walk through the college and see people of all ages and races interacting with each other." Students "live busy lives," and the vast majority "works and goes to school at the same time." Most students are commuters, and many are "immigrant or come from an immigrant family," but "most identify first and foremost as New Yorkers." Many subscribe to clubs and other extracurriculars "to fit in and make friends." Most CCNY students are not looking for the "typical college experience," but rather are interested "in the intellectual and emotional growth that comes with higher education."

FINANCIAL AID: 212-650-5819 • E-MAIL: ADMISSIONS@CCNY.CUNY.EDU • WEBSITE: WWW.CCNY.CUNY.EDU

THE PRINCETON REVIEW SAYS

Admissions

Very important factors considered include: rigor of secondary school record, academic GPA. *Important factors considered include:* standardized test scores. *Other factors considered include:* application essay, recommendation(s). SAT or ACT required. TOEFL required of all international applicants. High school diploma is required and GED is accepted. *Academic units recommended:* 4 English, 3 math, 2 science, 2 science labs, 3 foreign language, 4 social studies, 1 visual/performing arts.

Financial Aid

Students should submit: FAFSA, State aid form. Priority filing deadline is 3/15. The Princeton Review suggests that all financial aid forms be submitted as soon as possible after October 1. *Need-based scholarships/grants offered:* Federal Pell, FSEOG, State scholarships/grants, College/university scholarship or grant aid from institutional funds. *Loan aid offered:* Direct Subsidized Stafford Loans, Direct Unsubsidized Stafford Loans, Direct PLUS Loans. Applicants will be notified of awards on a rolling basis beginning 4/1. Federal Work-Study Program available. Institutional employment available.

The Inside Word

City College is one of the toughest CUNY schools get into, with an admissions rate of about 33 percent (some schools and programs within can be lower). Selective freshman programs—such as the honors college—may require a supplemental paper application, letters of recommendation, and/or a personal statement. The good news is that students can apply online to as many as six CUNY colleges with one application.

THE SCHOOL SAYS ". . ."

From the Admissions Office

"City is an old school with new ideas. Founded in 1847, we take pride in our tradition, eagerly embrace the present, and ride the cutting edge of the future. CCNY has one of the most diverse student bodies in any college of America, and is a mirror image of New York City. Our mission emphasizes access and excellence in undergraduate and graduate education and research, and opportunities for internships and study abroad abound. Whether you are looking for preparation for an exciting career or graduate and doctoral studies, City College offers the path to your future. We offer over 100 undergraduate and graduate degrees in architecture, education, engineering, the arts and humanities, the social sciences and science, as well as a unique BS/MD program. High achieving students interested in any discipline also may have the opportunity to participate including the Macaulay Honors College and the CCNY Honors Program.

"We are seeking students who will thrive at City both academically and personally, while contributing to the community inside and outside of the classroom. Candidates will be considered on the basis of overall strength of academic preparation (a minimum of sixteen academic units must have been completed), grades in individual subjects, overall high school average, and SAT or ACT scores. Applicants who have taken the General Equivalency Diploma (GED) examination must submit test scores and can be eligible provided they have attained a score of at least 3250 or higher. City College admits a small number of academically exceptional high school students upon the completion of their high school junior year. Students enter as matriculated students into the college's Honors program. Applicants generally are from the upper 10 percent of their high school class.

"All freshmen applying to The Bernard and Anne Spitzer School of Architecture are required to submit a Creative Challenge form; freshmen applying to The Grove School of Engineering are required to submit a supplemental application form; and freshmen applying to the Sophie Davis School of Biomedical Education are required to submit two separate applications."

SELECTIVITY

Admissions Rating	82
# of applicants	24,735
% of applicants accepted	40
% of acceptees attending	17

FRESHMAN PROFILE

Range SAT Critical Reading	460–590
Range SAT Math	510–640
Range SAT Writing	450–580
Minimum paper TOEFL	500
Minimum internet-based TOEFL	61

DEADLINES

Regular	
Priority	2/1
Nonfall registration?	Yes

FINANCIAL FACTS

Financial Aid Rating	91
Annual in-state tuition	$6,330
Annual out-of-state tuition	$16,800
Room and board	$11,516
Required fees	$410
Books and supplies	$1,364
Average frosh need-based scholarship	$8,224
Average UG need-based scholarship	$8,145
% needy frosh rec. need-based scholarship or grant aid	91
% needy UG rec. need-based scholarship or grant aid	96
% needy frosh rec. non-need-based scholarship or grant aid	54
% needy UG rec. non-need-based scholarship or grant aid	61
% needy frosh rec. need-based self-help aid	44
% needy UG rec. need-based self-help aid	61
% frosh rec. any financial aid	80
% UG rec. any financial aid	79
% frosh need fully met	74
% ugrads need fully met	82
Average % of frosh need met	84
Average % of ugrad need met	83

CITY UNIVERSITY OF NEW YORK—HUNTER COLLEGE

695 PARK AVENUE, ROOM N203, NEW YORK, NY 10065 • ADMISSIONS: 212-772-4490 • FAX: 212-650-3472

CAMPUS LIFE

Quality of Life Rating	84
Fire Safety Rating	97
Green Rating	93
Type of school	Public
Environment	Metropolis

STUDENTS

Total undergrad enrollment	16,550
% male/female	36/64
% from out of state	3
% frosh from public high school	70
# of fraternities	2
# of sororities	2
% African American	11
% Asian	28
% Caucasian	33
% Hispanic	21
% Native American	<1
% Pacific Islander	0
% Two or more races	0
% Race and/or ethnicity unknown	0
% international	6
# of countries represented	151

SURVEY SAYS...

Great financial aid
Diverse student types interact on campus
Students love New York, NY

ACADEMICS

Academic Rating	72
% students returning for sophomore year	82
% students graduating within 4 years	25
% students graduating within 6 years	54
Calendar	Semester
Student/faculty ratio	13:1
Profs interesting rating	69
Profs accessible rating	70

Most classes have 20–29 students.

MOST POPULAR MAJORS

Psychology; English; Chemistry

STUDENTS SAY "..."

Academics

Hunter boasts an "outstanding" reputation based in part on its ability to offer "a solid education at an affordable price" and "exposure to New York City." Students who like to challenge the status quo will find a home here. In Hunter classrooms, "diversity of thought is not only tolerated, but encouraged." Those classes can be "very tough," forcing students to "work hard to keep good grades." Some students groan that professors here "teach at a fast pace," but students who pay attention will find that their educators generally "know the subjects that they are teaching very well." While there are some "very tedious professors," most students find that professors are "intellectually challenged by brilliant instructors." A few students wish there were more tenured professors on staff and say that part-time educators "would care more if they were paid more." Yet many departments win praise, including the "highly respected" psychology department, which is "affiliated with most of the prestigious hospitals in New York City," as well as challenging English and nursing programs. Maybe most important is that students will get a sense for what their education will mean outside of school. These professors "bring to the table their vast experiences in their field of expertise and have never hesitated to educate on what to expect when we are outside of the classroom, often offering a practical aspect to what in many classrooms are strictly academic discussions."

Life

On one hand, being located in Manhattan means that Hunter has immediate access to almost anything in arts, culture, music, and nightlife that an urban adventurer can imagine. On the other hand, "Hunter is largely a commuter school, so there is not much campus life at night or on the weekends," a situation one student calls "miserable." Students won't get a typical college life here. "Nobody lives on campus at Hunter," and "most people who attend school at Hunter work part-time or full-time, have apartments, pay bills, and go to school full-time." That is not to say there is no excitement at Hunter. You just "have to make an effort for things to happen and to gather people because they need to make time from their schedules to meet up." Those who put in the effort will find that the city is their oyster. One student notes that whether it is food or music or entertainment, "anything that's not academic-related you can find easily from blocks away," while another notes, "New York is a tourist haven," so there is no shortage of things to do. But again, it won't come to you. Be prepared to make things happen. "The only way to make friends is to dorm (which is nearly impossible) or to hang around campus joining fraternities and clubs." If you're a commuter student or work full-time, as many Hunter students do, "socializing is nearly impossible."

Student Body

New York City is one of the most diverse metropolitan areas in the world, so it should come as no surprise that "there is no typical student at Hunter." This cultural melting pot of a region means "the diversity here is real and comes in all forms, most especially diversity of thought and opinion." One student notes that "all of my classrooms contain a mix of every ethnicity and nationality, all ages, all types of people." Even with this wide array of cultures, "somehow, [students] all manage to fit in and get along with one another." Students here also vary wildly in age, with older attendees common in most classrooms. "Most students work full- or part-time while juggling a full-time schedule," which can make it "extremely difficult to make friends, because it's a commuter school." This also means that "there's little sense of school identity." However, for those who involve themselves with other students, "as long as you are not too shy, it is easy to make friends around here."

City University of New York—Hunter College

FINANCIAL AID: 212-772-4820 • E-MAIL: ADMISSIONS@HUNTER.CUNY.EDU • WEBSITE: WWW.HUNTER.CUNY.EDU

THE PRINCETON REVIEW SAYS

Admissions

Very important factors considered include: rigor of secondary school record, academic GPA, standardized test scores, application essay. *Important factors considered include: Other factors considered include:* SAT or ACT required. TOEFL required of all international applicants. High school diploma is required and GED is accepted. *Academic units required:* 2 English, 2 math, 1 science, 1 science lab. *Academic units recommended:* 4 English, 3 math, 2 science, 2 foreign language, 4 social studies, 1 academic elective, 1 visual/performing arts.

Financial Aid

Students should submit: FAFSA, State aid form. Priority filing deadline is 5/1. The Princeton Review suggests that all financial aid forms be submitted as soon as possible after October 1. *Need-based scholarships/grants offered:* Federal Pell, State scholarships/grants, College/university scholarship or grant aid from institutional funds. *Loan aid offered:* Direct Subsidized Stafford Loans, Direct Unsubsidized Stafford Loans, Direct PLUS loans, Federal Perkins Loans, State Loans, College/university loans from institutional funds. Applicants will be notified of awards on a rolling basis beginning 5/15. Federal Work-Study Program available. Institutional employment available.

The Inside Word

Getting into Hunter is consistently getting harder, with the admissions office getting in excess of 30,000 applications a year. Applicants should be prepared to present strong grades that meet the school's admissions formula. (Hunter officials do not divulge the formula.) Programs fill up fast, so applying early is essential. Wait too long and thousands of students will have gotten in line in front of you.

THE SCHOOL SAYS "..."

From the Admissions Office

"Located in the heart of Manhattan, Hunter offers students the stimulating learning environment and career-building opportunities you might expect from a college that's been a part of the world's most exciting city since 1870. The largest college in the City University of New York, Hunter pulses with energy. Hunter's vitality stems from a large, highly diverse faculty and student body. Its schools—Arts and Sciences, Education, Nursing, Social Work and Public Health—provide an affordable first-rate education. Undergraduates have extraordinary opportunities to conduct high level research with renowned faculty, and to participate in credit-bearing internships in media, the arts, government and many other fields. The college's high standards and special programs ensure a challenging education. Several specialized programs for first-year students keep classmates together as they pursue courses in the liberal arts, pre–health science, pre-nursing, premed, or honors. A range of honors programs is available for students with strong academic records, including the highly competitive tuition-free Macaulay Honors College for entering freshmen and the Thomas Hunter Honors Program, which offers small classes with personalized mentoring by outstanding faculty. Qualified students also benefit from Hunter's participation in minority science research and training programs, the prestigious Andrew W. Mellon Minority Undergraduate Program, and many other passports to professional success.

"Applicants for the entering class are required to take either the SAT or the ACT."

SELECTIVITY

Admissions Rating	84
# of applicants	28,041
% of applicants accepted	39
% of acceptees attending	20

FRESHMAN PROFILE

Range SAT Critical Reading	520–620
Range SAT Math	540–640
Minimum paper TOEFL	500

DEADLINES

Regular	
Deadline	3/15
Nonfall registration?	Yes

FINANCIAL FACTS

Financial Aid Rating	84
Annual in-state tuition	$6,330
Annual out-of-state tuition	$16,800
Room and board	$8,655
Required fees	$450
Average frosh need-based scholarship	$8,713
Average UG need-based scholarship	$7,202
% needy frosh rec. need-based scholarship or grant aid	89
% needy UG rec. need-based scholarship or grant aid	82
% needy frosh rec. non-need-based scholarship or grant aid	89
% needy UG rec. non-need-based scholarship or grant aid	14
% needy frosh rec. need-based self-help aid	21
% needy UG rec. need-based self-help aid	22
% frosh rec. any financial aid	91
% UG rec. any financial aid	94
% frosh need fully met	20
% ugrads need fully met	13
Average % of frosh need met	73
Average % of ugrad need met	72

CITY UNIVERSITY OF NEW YORK—QUEENS COLLEGE

65-30 KISSENA BOULEVARD, QUEENS, NY 11367 • ADMISSIONS: 718-997-5600 • FAX: 718-997-5617

CAMPUS LIFE

Quality of Life Rating	83
Fire Safety Rating	97
Green Rating	84
Type of school	Public
Affiliation	No Affiliation
Environment	Metropolis

STUDENTS

Total undergrad enrollment	16,100
% male/female	44/56
% from out of state	2
% frosh from public high school	65
% frosh live on campus	1
% ugrads live on campus	2
# of fraternities (% ugrad men join)	6 (1)
# of sororities (% ugrad women join)	6 (1)
% African American	9
% Asian	27
% Caucasian	29
% Hispanic	28
% Native American	0
% Pacific Islander	0
% Two or more races	1
% Race and/or ethnicity unknown	0
% international	5
# of countries represented	170

SURVEY SAYS...

Students love Flushing, NY
Great library
Diverse student types interact on campus
Very little drug use

ACADEMICS

Academic Rating	73
% students returning for sophomore year	85
% students graduating within 4 years	28
% students graduating within 6 years	58
Calendar	Semester
Student/faculty ratio	14:1
Profs interesting rating	69
Profs accessible rating	66
Most classes have 20–29 students.	

MOST POPULAR MAJORS

Accounting; Psychology; Economics

STUDENTS SAY "..."

Academics

Located in New York's "most diverse borough," Queens College "offers high quality academics for a very reasonable price." As one student puts it, "Queens is about getting a valuable and quality education that does not drain you financially for the future." In keeping with the fact that the majority of QC students live off campus in a variety of nearby communities, one of the school's strengths is helping students become "the best you can be so you can give back to the community." One student even goes as far as to say that QC is "considered the Harvard of CUNY." The Macaulay Honors College and the Aaron Copeland School of Music both get high marks, with students saying that QC as a whole "provides a strong liberal arts education to give [students] well-rounded knowledge and skills." Professors generally "genuinely care about [students'] grades and well-being;" as one student puts it, "They won't let me fall behind." But while "most professors genuinely care for [students'] success," it's inevitable that they will "vary in terms of quality." As one student puts it, "Many of my professors just lecture and don't interact too much, however, some are very involved and passionate." Students appreciate the "challenging yet interesting courses" but some lament that for the coveted courses, "you have to really run and register for those classes like it's a competition."

Life

Though the school opened the Summit Apartments, its first residence hall, in 2009, the majority of QC students still commute; as one student observes, "Even though the Summit Apartments can only house 500 students, it still remains pretty empty throughout the semesters." Since "most students come here to go to class and then head home or to their job afterwards," many QC students say that it's difficult to foster much sense of a school community—"the sense of community could use some work." But others counter, saying that, "I would not expect a school composed mostly of commuters to bond as much as we do." Outside of class, it's "very hard to be bored," especially "being so close to the city, there are a lot of activities to do around the area." Many students explore Queens, which is accessible via a free QC shuttle. For those who live on campus, or those commuters who stick around after class, as one student puts it, "We have clubs for everything, and if there isn't a club for something you like you could always start [one] up." One thing that students agree helps unite QC as a community is student government: "Student government provides us with events and carnivals during both the fall and spring semesters. It brings people together."

Student Body

Diversity is key at Queens College, where, as one student puts it, "We have a very diverse campus, so no minority is really ever a minority." "If one were to ask me to name every ethnicity, nationality, and religious group on campus, I would not even know where to begin," says another. QC "has a very friendly student body" and some says that "the friendships and bonds you make from taking transit together, or sharing stories is special in [its] own way." Others note that "there is not much of an established social life" and that "if you want to make friends here you really have to work for it." Many students "have part-time jobs," some students "are parents, and have to take care of their children"—"Of course, many people are straight out of high school [too], but even these people usually spend a lot of time off campus." Students describe their peers as "career-minded and focused;" they "love to have fun, but they [are] still focused on their studies and their futures."

CITY UNIVERSITY OF NEW YORK—QUEENS COLLEGE

FINANCIAL AID: 718-997-5123 • E-MAIL: VINCENT.ANGRISANI@QC.CUNY.EDU • WEBSITE: WWW.QC.CUNY.EDU

THE PRINCETON REVIEW SAYS

Admissions

Very important factors considered include: rigor of secondary school record, academic GPA, standardized test scores. *Other factors considered include:* SAT or ACT required; SAT Subject Tests recommend. ACT with or without writing accepted. TOEFL required of all international applicants. High school diploma is required and GED is accepted. *Academic units required:* 4 English, 3 math, 2 science, 2 science labs, 3 foreign language, 4 social studies. *Academic units recommended:* 3 science, 3 science labs.

Financial Aid

Students should submit: FAFSA, Institution's own financial aid form, State aid form. Priority filing deadline is 2/15.The Princeton Review suggests that all financial aid forms be submitted as soon as possible after October 1. *Need-based scholarships/grants offered:* Federal Pell, FSEOG, State scholarships/grants, Private scholarships, College/university scholarship or grant aid from institutional funds. *Loan aid offered:* Direct Subsidized Stafford Loans, Direct Unsubsidized Stafford Loans, Direct PLUS loans, Federal Perkins Loans. Applicants will be notified of awards on a rolling basis beginning 3/1. Federal Work-Study Program available. Institutional employment available.

The Inside Word

Queens College looks for students with a B average (or better) or a GED score of at least 3500 to be a strong candidate for admission; the school encourages a high school education that includes a full range of language arts and science courses. Standardized test scores are also a requirement. Exceptional applicants should look into Macaulay Honors College, which provides free tuition and other benefits (including a study grant and a free laptop) to gifted students.

THE SCHOOL SAYS " . . . "

From the Admissions Office

"Queens College prepares students to become the leaders of tomorrow by offering a rigorous education in the liberal arts and sciences under the guidance of an outstanding faculty dedicated to teaching and scholarship. Our students graduate with the skills that employers and the best graduate schools are looking for: a critical, problem-solving intelligence, the ability to express ideas clearly, an aptitude for the latest technologies, and an appreciation of different cultures.

"Queens College has over 170 programs, and is recognized nationally for the excellence of its academic offerings. We have more computer science majors than any other university in New York City, and rank third in New York State for the number of accounting and business students we graduate. Our acclaimed Aaron Copland School of Music offers talented students a fine liberal arts education and conservatory-level training. We're the ideal choice for aspiring educators—no school in the metropolitan area has graduated more teachers, counselors, and principals than QC. Our tuition is among the most affordable in the nation.

"Located in the most exciting city in the world, QC provides a vibrant student life experience for students who live on or off campus. We have over 100 student clubs, 19 NCAA Division II teams, and numerous intramural and recreation programs. Our students represent 170 countries, which creates an extraordinarily diverse and welcoming campus community. With programs such as honors, internships, service-learning, and study abroad, QC offers countless opportunities for personal and professional growth."

SELECTIVITY

Admissions Rating	83
# of applicants	18,416
% of applicants accepted	40
% of acceptees attending	21

FRESHMAN PROFILE

Range SAT Critical Reading	460–570
Range SAT Math	510–610
Range SAT Writing	440–560
Minimum paper TOEFL	500
Minimum internet-based TOEFL	62
Average HS GPA	3.5

DEADLINES

Regular	
Notification	2/1
Nonfall registration?	Yes

FINANCIAL FACTS

Financial Aid Rating	94
Annual in-state tuition	$6,330
Annual out-of-state tuition	$16,800
Room and board	$14,168
Required fees	$608
Books and supplies	$1,364
Average frosh need-based scholarship	$5,011
Average UG need-based scholarship	$4,379
% needy frosh rec. need-based scholarship or grant aid	87
% needy UG rec. need-based scholarship or grant aid	85
% needy frosh rec. non-need-based scholarship or grant aid	4
% needy UG rec. non-need-based scholarship or grant aid	3
% needy frosh rec. need-based self-help aid	14
% needy UG rec. need-based self-help aid	31
% frosh rec. any financial aid	85
% UG rec. any financial aid	55
% frosh need fully met	81
% ugrads need fully met	96
Average % of frosh need met	96
Average % of ugrad need met	96

THE BEST 381 COLLEGES ■ 163

CLAREMONT MCKENNA COLLEGE

888 COLUMBIA AVENUE, CLAREMONT, CA 91711 • ADMISSIONS: 909-621-8088 • FAX: 909-621-8516

CAMPUS LIFE
Quality of Life Rating	99
Fire Safety Rating	88
Green Rating	86
Type of school	Private
Affiliation	No Affiliation
Environment	Town

STUDENTS
Total undergrad enrollment	1,301
% male/female	52/48
% from out of state	56
% frosh live on campus	100
% ugrads live on campus	97
# of fraternities (% ugrad men join)	(0)
# of sororities (% ugrad women join)	(0)
% African American	4
% Asian	10
% Caucasian	43
% Hispanic	12
% Native American	<1
% Pacific Islander	<1
% Two or more races	8
% Race and/or ethnicity unknown	6
% international	17
# of countries represented	31

SURVEY SAYS...
Students are happy
Great library
Career services are great
Internships are widely available
Class discussions encouraged
School is well run
Great financial aid
No one cheats
Students are friendly
Diverse student types interact on campus
Students aren't religious
Great food on campus
Dorms are like palaces
Easy to get around campus
Lots of beer drinking
Everyone loves the Stags
Campus newspaper is popular
Alumni active on campus

ACADEMICS
Academic Rating	96
% students returning for sophomore year	96
% students graduating within 4 years	80
Calendar	Semester
Student/faculty ratio	8:1
Profs interesting rating	98
Profs accessible rating	99

Most classes have 10–19 students.

MOST POPULAR MAJORS
Economics; Political Science and Government; Psychology

STUDENTS SAY ". . ."
Academics
Students at Claremont McKenna really love their school. With its "phenomenal academics," "brilliant professors," "amazing career services center," and "perfect weather," it's no wonder CMC students are "the happiest students in America." Claremont McKenna is known for its government and economics majors, but philosophy, international relations, and the Keck Science program also get high marks. CMC is a part of the Claremont College Consortium, so if students are looking for something that CMC doesn't have, they can probably find it at one of the four sister schools. Students rave about Claremont's emphasis on "professionalism" and all of the "great research and internship opportunities." The workload is heavy, and professors set "high expectations," so "students spend their weeks slaving over their papers, books, readings, research projects, problem sets, etc." Despite the intense workload, students love their professors. "Professors are absolute geniuses in their field," one student gushes. They're "helpful and encouraging," "incredibly accessible," and even "willing to Skype on the weekends to answer questions." "This sounds corny," one student admits, "this really is a place where professors become like family." Students spend a "good deal of out-of-classroom time" with their teachers. "When you take both academics and quality of life into account," a cognitive neuroscience major says, "I can't believe I almost went to an Ivy over this place."

Life
Life is good at Claremont McKenna. The "constantly beaming California sun and the close vicinity to both mountains and beaches" mean students spend their time outdoors when they can. But even when students are lounging in the sun or playing Frisbee, they're not really taking a break. The "conversation doesn't end in the classroom," a student explains, and the "intellectual culture… really allows for twenty-four-hour learning." While Claremont McKenna has the campus and "community-life and identity of a small school" it "still [has] the resources of the other four C's." Even without the other schools students feel "completely pampered" because "the school cares about its students so much." A Spanish major says, "The relationship between the students and the administration is excellent here," and the "student government and Dean of Students Office…subsidize incredible off-campus trips and on-campus parties." One of the best things about Claremont McKenna is the Marian Miner Cook Athenaeum, which hosts prestigious guest lecturers four nights a week. One student wisely asks, "Where else could you have dinner with Jesse Jackson, Mitt Romney, etc.?" Students agree, "There's a niche for everyone, and the welcoming, accepting atmosphere makes fitting in easy."

Student Body
"Claremont McKenna doesn't accept students who aren't amazing." "Amazing" means a "really smart" person who's "incredibly motivated and career-driven." It's "a tight-knit community of driven, competitive, and intelligent people who know how to be successful and have a great time." "A lot of kids are political and well-informed"; most are "active on campus," very into sports, and involved with internships or clubs. But even though the environment is "academically strict, the students…rarely fit the 'nerdy' stereotype." Students are extremely well-rounded; they "know how to lead a discussion…clock hours in the library, play a varsity or club sport, and hold a leadership position in a club or organization," and they also know how to throw "a great party on Saturday night."

CLAREMONT MCKENNA COLLEGE

FINANCIAL AID: 909-621-8356 • E-MAIL: ADMISSION@CMC.EDU • WEBSITE: WWW.CMC.EDU

THE PRINCETON REVIEW SAYS

Admissions

Very important factors considered include: rigor of secondary school record, class rank, academic GPA, standardized test scores, recommendation(s), extracurricular activities, character/personal qualities. *Important factors considered include:* application essay, talent/ability. *Other factors considered include:* interview, first generation, alumni/ae relation, geographical residence, racial/ethnic status, volunteer work, work experience. SAT or ACT required; SAT Subject Tests required for some. ACT with Writing required. TOEFL required of all international applicants. High school diploma is required and GED is accepted. *Academic units required:* 4 English, 3 math, 2 science, 2 science labs, 3 foreign language, 1 social studies, 1 history. *Academic units recommended:* 4 English, 4 math, 3 science, 3 science labs, 3 foreign language, 1 social studies, 1 history.

Financial Aid

Students should submit: FAFSA, CSS/Financial Aid PROFILE, State aid form, Noncustodial PROFILE, Business/Farm Supplement. Regular filing deadline is 2/1. The Princeton Review suggests that all financial aid forms be submitted as soon as possible after October 1. *Need-based scholarships/grants offered:* Federal Pell, FSEOG, State scholarships/grants, Private scholarships, College/university scholarship or grant aid from institutional funds. *Loan aid offered:* Direct Subsidized Stafford Loans, Direct Unsubsidized Stafford Loans, Direct PLUS loans, Federal Perkins Loans, College/university loans from institutional funds. Applicants will be notified of awards on or about 4/1. Federal Work-Study Program available. Institutional employment available.

The Inside Word

Although applicants have to possess exemplary academic qualifications to gain admission to Claremont McKenna, the importance of making a good match shouldn't be underestimated. Colleges of such small size and selectivity devote much more energy to determining whether the candidate as an individual fits instead of whether a candidate has the appropriate test scores.

THE SCHOOL SAYS "..."

From the Admissions Office

"CMC offers a first-rate liberal arts education where students can acquire a broad experience across a range of disciplines from the humanities to the social sciences to the sciences, but where they can also pursue an unusually rich spectrum of courses in economics, public affairs, and international relations. CMC's mission is clear: To educate students for meaningful, productive, and responsible lives of leadership. By combining the intellectual breadth of liberal arts with the more pragmatic concerns of public affairs, CMC students gain the vision, skills, and values necessary for leadership in all sectors of society.

"Applicants must take the SAT Test or ACT both with writing. We will use the highest scores from the SAT or ACT. SAT Subject Tests are not required unless home-schooled."

SELECTIVITY

Admissions Rating	98
# of applicants	6,043
% of applicants accepted	11
% of acceptees attending	50
# offered a place on the wait list	614
% accepting a place on wait list	57
% admitted from wait list	11
# of early decision applicants	675
% accepted early decision	26

FRESHMAN PROFILE

Range SAT Critical Reading	660–750
Range SAT Math	690–770
Range SAT Writing	680–760
Range ACT Composite	30–33
Minimum paper TOEFL	600
Minimum internet-based TOEFL	100
% graduated top 10% of class	78
% graduated top 25% of class	97
% graduated top 50% of class	100

DEADLINES

Early decision	
Deadline	11/1
Notification	12/15
Regular	
Deadline	1/1
Notification	4/1
Nonfall registration?	No

FINANCIAL FACTS

Financial Aid Rating	96
Average frosh need-based scholarship	$38,850
Average UG need-based scholarship	$40,438
% needy frosh rec. need-based scholarship or grant aid	97
% needy UG rec. need-based scholarship or grant aid	98
% needy frosh rec. non-need-based scholarship or grant aid	58
% needy UG rec. non-need-based scholarship or grant aid	45
% needy frosh rec. need-based self-help aid	88
% needy UG rec. need-based self-help aid	91
% frosh rec. any financial aid	43
% UG rec. any financial aid	45
% frosh need fully met	100
% ugrads need fully met	91
Average % of frosh need met	100
Average % of ugrad need met	100

CLARK UNIVERSITY

950 MAIN STREET, WORCESTER, MA 01610-1477 • ADMISSIONS: 508-793-7431 • FAX: 508-793-8821

STUDENTS SAY "..."

Academic

In Worcester, Massachusetts, Clark University is an "offbeat, academically rigorous and social justice oriented" institution, which is precisely why the students here love it so much. Indeed, they proudly assert that their school's agenda is all about "challenging convention and changing the world." Additionally, the university truly nurtures its undergrads and provides a "place where students can focus on their education [both] inside and outside the classroom in a progressive, enlightened, empowering setting." And many individuals also value the fact that they're able to "engage in [serious], hands-on . . . research" as undergraduates. Academically, the university has a "strong biology program," a "good reputation for its psychology program" and also maintains an impressive "focus on sustainability and global issues." Moreover, the school manages to attract "very intelligent" and "passionate" professors who "are legitimately interested in their students' academic progress and overall achievement and well-being." To illustrate this point, an international development major shares, "Professors make a point to get to know the class, even in a big lecture hall. They hold office hours, hand out cell phone numbers, and do their best to be available." Ultimately, "Clark University is a place where you can feel comfortable to explore who you are and what you want to be."

Life

It's nearly impossible for students to be bored at Clark. Indeed, there "is almost an endless number of clubs from Model UN, to yoga, to All Kinds of Girls, to the International Students Association, to Hillel." Additionally, there are numerous "events every week including [activities] like CUFS movie screenings, Big Prize Bingo, and outing club trips." Clarkies also tend to have a creative and artistic bent. Therefore, "you will see more students at an a cappella concert or improv comedy show than a basketball game." And when the weekend rolls around, it's quite common for students to attend "parties at various houses." These get-togethers are "relatively laid back" and we're told that students "consume substances in a responsible, casual manner." When undergrads are angling to get off campus, the surrounding "Worcester community is full of cultural attractions and amazing restaurants." Even better, since Worcester "is a college town . . . it's very easy to mingle with students from neighboring institutions." All in all, a psychology major concludes that Clark provides "a low-pressure social environment [where] you can decide to go to a lecture on the latest political issues, go to one of the many delicious restaurants [near campus] or [attend] a house party."

Student Body

Admittedly, Clark students "don't like to categorize themselves or others." As one sociology student emphatically states, "No two students are alike at Clark, we come from all over the world and each have a different story and perspective." A psychology major quickly agrees sharing, "Clark takes pride in the fact that it has no 'typical' student to represent it. Everyone here is a unique fruit, and the thing that seemingly unifies us all is the ability to think outside the box, challenge convention, and 'change the world.'" Nonetheless, the vast majority of undergrads here tend to identify as "Democrats" and often prove to be both "environmentally aware" as well as "politically correct." They are also "passionate, involved in many clubs and campus activities, social, and active in the community." And while students here certainly "take their academics seriously, [they] don't take [themselves] too seriously." In other words, undergrads don't need to worry about being in a competitive environment. Then again, that's just what you'd expect from a "sweet" student body that's "sympathetic toward one another."

CLARK UNIVERSITY

THE PRINCETON REVIEW SAYS

Admissions

Very important factors considered include: rigor of secondary school record, academic GPA, recommendation(s). *Important factors considered include:* application essay, extracurricular activities, talent/ability, character/personal qualities, volunteer work. *Other factors considered include:* class rank, standardized test scores, interview, first generation, alumni/ae relation, geographical residence, racial/ethnic status, work experience, level of applicant's interest. SAT or ACT considered if submitted. ACT with or without writing accepted. SAT with or without Essay component accepted. TOEFL required of all international applicants. High school diploma is required and GED is accepted. *Academic units recommended:* 4 English, 3 math, 3 science, 2 science labs, 2 foreign language, 2 social studies, 2 history.

Financial Aid

Students should submit: FAFSA, CSS/Financial Aid PROFILE, Noncustodial PROFILE. Regular filing deadline is 2/1.The Princeton Review suggests that all financial aid forms be submitted as soon as possible after October 1. *Need-based scholarships/grants offered:* Federal Pell, FSEOG, State scholarships/grants, College/university scholarship or grant aid from institutional funds. *Loan aid offered:* Direct Subsidized Stafford Loans, Direct Unsubsidized Stafford Loans, Direct PLUS loans, Federal Perkins Loans, State Loans. Applicants will be notified of awards on or about 3/31. Federal Work-Study Program available. Institutional employment available.

The Inside Word

Admissions officers at Clark take a holistic approach to the application process. After all, they are striving to uncover individuals who will add to and enhance the vibrancy of the campus. Moreover, since Clark encourage hands-on research, study abroad and fieldwork, they are looking for candidates who are excited by the idea of taking their education beyond the classroom. While the college aims to accept students with A and B averages, they definitely appreciate applicants who show steady academic improvement each successive year. And they are charmed by students who demonstrate heartfelt commitment to their communities and social causes.

SELECTIVITY

Admissions Rating	90
# of applicants	8,045
% of applicants accepted	55
% of acceptees attending	15
# offered a place on the wait list	670
% accepting a place on wait list	47
% admitted from wait list	4
# of early decision applicants	48
% accepted early decision	73

FRESHMAN PROFILE

Range SAT Critical Reading	560–670
Range SAT Math	560–670
Range SAT Writing	560–670
Range ACT Composite	26–30
Minimum paper TOEFL	550
Average HS GPA	3.7
% graduated top 10% of class	44
% graduated top 25% of class	77
% graduated top 50% of class	99

DEADLINES

Early decision	
Deadline	11/1
Notification	12/15
Early action	
Deadline	11/1
Notification	12/15
Regular	
Deadline	1/15
Notification	4/1
Nonfall registration?	Yes

APPLICANTS ALSO LOOK AT AND OFTEN PREFER
Boston College; Boston University

AND SOMETIMES PREFER
Skidmore College; Syracuse University

AND RARELY PREFER
University of Vermont

FINANCIAL FACTS

Financial Aid Rating	92
Annual tuition	$42,800
Room and board	$8,450
Required fees	$350
Books and supplies	$800
Average frosh need-based scholarship	$27,747
Average UG need-based scholarship	$26,628
% needy frosh rec. need-based scholarship or grant aid	98
% needy UG rec. need-based scholarship or grant aid	98
% needy frosh rec. non-need-based scholarship or grant aid	39
% needy UG rec. non-need-based scholarship or grant aid	40
% needy frosh rec. need-based self-help aid	78
% needy UG rec. need-based self-help aid	82
% frosh rec. any financial aid	91
% UG rec. any financial aid	89
% frosh need fully met	59
% ugrads need fully met	65
Average % of frosh need met	93
Average % of ugrad need met	95

CLARKSON UNIVERSITY

HOLCROFT HOUSE, POTSDAM, NY 13699 • ADMISSIONS: 315-268-6480 • FAX: 315-268-7647

STUDENTS SAY "..."

Academics

Located in northern New York (with additional facilities in Beacon and Schenectady), Clarkson University is best known for its strong business and engineering programs, and its exceptional record of career placement for graduates thanks to its "amazing reputation with a large range of companies." The science and tech programs "prepare engineering-centric minds for the future of the ever-advancing technological world," and the school is constantly "keeping a responsible eye on ways to positively influence a 'green' and sustainable future." A competitive Honors Program and excellent scholarships only sweeten the deal. As one sophomore puts it, "Golden Knights = Golden Education." Professors "have been in their field for years and try to give you the best information they can." "Many of my professors have become advisors, friends, and great mentors," says one student. "A lot of the math and science professors are foreign" and can be hard to understand, but "the TAs are usually very good" and the higher level courses in particular "really show the brilliance of the staff here." The curriculum is "challenging" and goes beyond theory to real world application, and everything is taught through the lens of the "sustainability mindset." The workload is "heavy," but you "always have something applicable to take from every class."

Clarkson being a medium-sized school, "you meet tons of people and get to form good connections with most," and the excellent alumni network is buoyed by the many internships and co-ops that are readily available. "I know that if I obtain a degree I will have little to no trouble getting a job," says a civil engineering major. Facilities are the source of many complaints here, as "nearly all of the academic and recreational buildings could use a major overhaul."

Life

Clarkson is "a good size—not so small as to be clique-y, not so big that you get lost among thousands of other students," and there are several nearby schools that help to diversify the faces students see each day. Though it's proximate to Canada and the Adirondacks, there is "not much to do in Potsdam" for fun without "freezing to death in the cold weather," so "most entertainment lies in campus attractions and campus organizations." People partake in a lot of winter sports such as hiking and skiing, or they "just stay in and play Cards Against Humanity, or rent an academic building and watch a movie on the big screen."

For a STEM major there is "much pressure put on you by the workload," so students study for the most of the week—"sleepless nights are commonplace and being in more clubs than you should be able to handle is normal"—then decompress with "sports, clubs or other activities in their free time." There is "a good attempt at late night programs by res life, but often times you'll end up at a party." Greek life "thrives on weekends" and the Division I hockey games are "a great event where the whole community—both school and town—gather together and cheer as loudly as possible."

Student Body

The "small town atmosphere" of Clarkson is home to a group of "strongly motivated" students and people who "are always there by your side trying to push you to always do your best." The number of students creates a community where "everyone seems to know one another and you rarely see a unknown face." Though the majority of students fit the description "nerdy white male," Clarkson is a "very academically and socially diverse" school for its size; "you don't always have to hang out with the 'smart' people, but you aren't surrounded by dumb people either." Religion rarely matters; "whether you're a PS4, XBox One, PC, or Nintendo player is much more important." "We're all a little quirky here," confesses one student.

FINANCIAL AID: 315-268-6480 • E-MAIL: ADMISSION@CLARKSON.EDU • WEBSITE: WWW.CLARKSON.EDU

THE PRINCETON REVIEW SAYS

Admissions

Very important factors considered include: rigor of secondary school record, academic GPA. *Important factors considered include:* class rank, standardized test scores, recommendation(s), extracurricular activities, volunteer work. *Other factors considered include:* application essay, talent/ability, character/personal qualities, first generation, alumni/ae relation, work experience, level of applicant's interest. SAT or ACT required; SAT Subject Tests recommend. ACT with or without writing accepted. SAT with or without Essay component accepted. TOEFL required of all international applicants. High school diploma is required and GED is accepted. *Academic units required:* 4 English, 3 math, 1 science, and 4 units from above areas or other academic areas. *Academic units recommended:* 4 math, 4 science.

Financial Aid

Students should submit: FAFSA, State aid form. Regular filing deadline is 3/1. The Princeton Review suggests that all financial aid forms be submitted as soon as possible after October 1. *Need-based scholarships/grants offered:* Federal Pell, FSEOG, State scholarships/grants, Private scholarships, College/university scholarship or grant aid from institutional funds. *Loan aid offered:* Direct Subsidized Stafford Loans, Direct Unsubsidized Stafford Loans, Direct PLUS loans, Federal Perkins Loans, College/university loans from institutional funds. Applicants will be notified of awards on a rolling basis beginning 3/14. Federal Work-Study Program available. Institutional employment available.

The Inside Word

Clarkson wants students with a strong background in science and math who also have a curiosity for applying technology and science in the real world. Show them that you're interested in being involved outside the classroom. Students with solid transcripts will have a good shot at admission. Serious candidates should interview anyway; if you have a strong application and strong desire to come here, it could help you get some scholarship money.

THE SCHOOL SAYS "..."

From the Admissions Office

"Clarkson University is the institution of choice for 4,300 enterprising students from diverse backgrounds who embrace challenge and thrive in a rigorous, highly collaborative learning environment. Our 640-wooded-acre main campus is adjacent to the six-million-acre Adirondack Park, which offers exceptional outdoor recreation and a living laboratory for field research and environmental studies.

"Clarkson's programs in engineering, business, the sciences, liberal arts, and the health professions emphasize team-based learning as well as immersion in sustainability principles, creative problem solving and leadership skills. Clarkson is also on the leading edge of today's emerging technologies and fields of study offering innovative, boundary-spanning degree programs in engineering and management, digital arts and sciences, environmental science and policy, and the health professions among others.

"At Clarkson, students and faculty work closely together in a supportive and personalized environment. Students are encouraged to participate in faculty-mentored research projects from their first year, and to take advantage of co-ops and study abroad programs. Our collaborative and hands-on approach to education translates into remarkably successful careers and meaningful contributions to society; our placement rates into students' career choice are among the highest in the country. Alumni experience accelerated career growth. One in five alumni are already a CEO, president, or vice president of a company.

"Applicants are required to take the ACT with writing section optional or the SAT. We will use the student's best scores from either test. SAT Subject Tests are recommended but not required."

SELECTIVITY

Admissions Rating	87
# of applicants	6,906
% of applicants accepted	68
% of acceptees attending	17
# offered a place on the wait list	56
% accepting a place on wait list	18
% admitted from wait list	60
# of early decision applicants	180
% accepted early decision	81

FRESHMAN PROFILE

Range SAT Critical Reading	520–630
Range SAT Math	560–660
Range SAT Writing	490–600
Range ACT Composite	24–30
Minimum paper TOEFL	550
Minimum internet-based TOEFL	80
Average HS GPA	3.7
% graduated top 10% of class	36
% graduated top 25% of class	72
% graduated top 50% of class	95

DEADLINES

Early decision	
Deadline	12/1
Notification	1/1
Regular	
Deadline	1/15
Nonfall registration?	Yes

APPLICANTS ALSO LOOK AT AND OFTEN PREFER

Rensselaer Polytechnic Institute; Rochester Institute of Technology; Syracuse University

AND SOMETIMES PREFER

St. Lawrence University; University of Rochester; Worcester Polytechnic Institute

AND RARELY PREFER

Cornell University; Drexel University; Ithaca College; Northeastern University

FINANCIAL FACTS

Financial Aid Rating	86
Average frosh need-based scholarship	$31,060
Average UG need-based scholarship	$29,663
% needy frosh rec. need-based scholarship or grant aid	99
% needy UG rec. need-based scholarship or grant aid	99
% needy frosh rec. non-need-based scholarship or grant aid	14
% needy UG rec. non-need-based scholarship or grant aid	14
% needy frosh rec. need-based self-help aid	82
% needy UG rec. need-based self-help aid	82
% frosh rec. any financial aid	97
% UG rec. any financial aid	97
% UG borrow to pay for school	84
Average cumulative indebtedness	$29,000
% frosh need fully met	20
% ugrads need fully met	21
Average % of frosh need met	89
Average % of ugrad need met	90

CLEMSON UNIVERSITY

105 SIKES HALL, CLEMSON, SC 29634-5124 • ADMISSIONS: 864-656-2287 • FAX: 864-656-2464

CAMPUS LIFE

Quality of Life Rating	95
Fire Safety Rating	96
Green Rating	60*
Type of school	Public
Affiliation	No Affiliation
Environment	Village

STUDENTS

Total undergrad enrollment	18,016
% male/female	53/47
% from out of state	35
% frosh from public high school	89
% frosh live on campus	98
% ugrads live on campus	41
# of fraternities (% ugrad men join)	26 (10)
# of sororities (% ugrad women join)	17 (15)
% African American	7
% Asian	2
% Caucasian	83
% Hispanic	3
% Native American	<1
% Pacific Islander	<1
% Two or more races	3
% Race and/or ethnicity unknown	1
% international	1
# of countries represented	84

SURVEY SAYS...

Students are happy
Great library
Career services are great
Internships are widely available
School is well run
Great financial aid
Students are friendly
Students are very religious
Students get along with local community
Students involved in community service
Students environmentally aware
Recreation facilities are great
Lots of beer drinking
Everyone loves the Tigers
Intramural sports are popular
Campus newspaper is popular
Alumni active on campus

ACADEMICS

Academic Rating	78
% students returning for sophomore year	93
% students graduating within 4 years	61
% students graduating within 6 years	82
Calendar	Semester
Student/faculty ratio	18:1
Profs interesting rating	81
Profs accessible rating	90

Most classes have 10–19 students.
Most lab/discussion sessions have 20–29 students.

MOST POPULAR MAJORS

Engineering; Business/Commerce; Biology

STUDENTS SAY "..."

Academics

Located in South Carolina, legendary sports stronghold Clemson University is "all about supporting its academics as well as its athletic teams." This public university is an ACC school that can provide "many opportunities to each student, no matter the major." The "incredible energy" surrounding Clemson academics, sports, and culture yields "a ton of school spirit," and it is apparent from the first step on campus that "the students love Clemson, and professors love Clemson students." The size and Southern charm offer students the best of both worlds: the "friendly atmosphere of a small town college, with the advantages and opportunities of a huge university," including study abroad, myriad research opportunities, and Division I athletics. "No other place makes a student feel so instantly welcomed and at home while making you feel like you are a part of something bigger than yourself." Most of the professors are "very engaging" and "supportive advisers" who relate interesting real-life examples to their lectures. "Professors are willing to delve deep into subjects that they are interested in and love student input and involvement," says a student. They are "lively and make the material interesting to learn" and "put teaching first," and the resulting atmosphere is "enriching and expansive." There is no competitive streak among students, only a desire to succeed, and the whole campus is "full of encouragement, support, and building relationships with those around you." Unsurprisingly, the school is "full of traditions," and it has "a great balance between sports, organizations, and study." The Clemson alumni network is internationally strong. "Clemson is one big family; [you] immediately bond with other Clemson people you meet around the world," one student says. "There is something in these hills that is something special, and you will know it immediately once you become a member of the Clemson Family."

Life

One of the greatest strengths of Clemson University is its heritage, which "resonates with any person who has ever had the privilege to call this campus home." The school is all about uniting more than 18,000 strangers into "a supportive family grounded in a shared passion for excellence." "Students at Clemson are very interested in Clemson," says a student. "What I mean by that is the students create their own lives and communities within the school." There are "plenty of opportunities" to become involved and active on campus, whether "through sports or academic organizations." Greek life is also "rather popular," but not every student joins. Study abroad is strongly encouraged. The school is nestled next to the mountains, and "there are a ton of trails owned by Clemson University" for students to hike and bike. Varsity sports are massively well-attended, and intramural sports are "huge"; "there are always pickup games on Bowman Field." On weekends, many students go downtown to the bars, "where there is a smaller, intimate setting, but still fun and exciting."

Student Body

While the majority of students are Southern and white, students of all backgrounds are bonded "by their sheer love of Clemson." The school spirit bleeds into everyone's demeanor, and this overwhelmingly happy and "very active" bunch "honestly try to include and befriend everyone." They are "very friendly, family oriented, athletic, and well put together." Many are also religious ("mostly Christian") and "go on mission trips and volunteer locally in the community." Most students here are down with Clemson athletics and "are willing to cheer for whatever sport is going on."

FINANCIAL AID: 864-656-2280 • E-MAIL: CUADMISSIONS@CLEMSON.EDU • WEBSITE: WWW.CLEMSON.EDU

THE PRINCETON REVIEW SAYS

Admissions

Very important factors considered include: rigor of secondary school record, class rank, academic GPA, standardized test scores, state residency. *Important factors considered include:* alumni/ae relation. *Other factors considered include:* application essay, recommendation(s), extracurricular activities, talent/ability. SAT or ACT required. ACT with Writing required. TOEFL required of all international applicants. High school diploma is required and GED is accepted. *Academic units required:* 4 English, 3 math, 3 science, 3 science labs, 2 foreign language, 1 social studies, 1 history, 2 academic electives, 1 computer science, 1 visual/performing arts, and 1 unit from above areas or other academic areas. *Academic units recommended:* 4 math, 4 science labs, 3 foreign language.

Financial Aid

Students should submit: FAFSA. Priority filing deadline is 4/1.The Princeton Review suggests that all financial aid forms be submitted as soon as possible after October 1. *Need-based scholarships/grants offered:* Federal Pell, FSEOG, State scholarships/grants, Private scholarships, College/university scholarship or grant aid from institutional funds, Federal Nursing Scholarships. *Loan aid offered:* Direct Subsidized Stafford Loans, Direct Unsubsidized Stafford Loans, Direct PLUS loans, Federal Perkins Loans, State Loans, College/university loans from institutional funds. Applicants will be notified of awards on a rolling basis beginning 4/1. Federal Work-Study Program available. Institutional employment available.

The Inside Word

With its Southern charm, competitive Division I athletics, and Greek life, Clemson will be an ideal fit for many types of students. But don't think that Clemson doesn't take its academics seriously. Admissions are competitive, and a good GPA and test scores will be needed for all who apply. For the SAT, the middle 50 percent of recently admitted students have test scores ranging from 1160 to 1310 (not including the writing section). For the ACT, the middle 50 percent score range is 26 to 30 for the composite.

THE SCHOOL SAYS "..."

From the Admissions Office

"One of the country's most selective public research universities, Clemson University was founded with a mission to be a high seminary of learning dedicated to teaching, research, and service. Nearly 120 years later, these three concepts remain at the heart of this university and provide the framework for an exceptional educational experience for Clemson students.

"At Clemson, professors take the time to get to know students and to explore innovative ways of teaching. Exceptional teaching is one reason Clemson's retention and graduation rates rank among the highest in the country among public universities. Exceptional teaching is also why Clemson continues to attract an increasingly talented student body. The class rank and SAT scores of Clemson's incoming freshman are among the highest of the nation's public research universities.

"Clemson offers over 250 student clubs and organizations; the spirit that students show for this university is unparalleled.

"Midway between Charlotte, North Carolina, and Atlanta, Georgia, Clemson University is located on 1,400 acres of beautiful rolling hills within the foothills of the Blue Ridge Mountains and along the shores of Lake Hartwell.

"Applicants are required to take the SAT or the ACT with the writing section. The best combined scores from SAT test will be used in the admissions process. We do not, however, combine sub scores from the ACT in order to create a new composite score."

SELECTIVITY

Admissions Rating	92
# of applicants	22,396
% of applicants accepted	51
% of acceptees attending	30
# offered a place on the wait list	2,249
% accepting a place on wait list	35
% admitted from wait list	99

FRESHMAN PROFILE

Range SAT Critical Reading	560–660
Range SAT Math	590–690
Range ACT Composite	27–31
Minimum paper TOEFL	550
Average HS GPA	4.0
% graduated top 10% of class	56
% graduated top 25% of class	86
% graduated top 50% of class	98

DEADLINES

Regular	
Priority	12/1
Deadline	5/1
Nonfall registration?	Yes

APPLICANTS ALSO LOOK AT AND SOMETIMES PREFER

Georgia Institute of Technology; University of Virginia; University of Georgia

AND RARELY PREFER

Auburn University; Florida State University; North Carolina State University; University of Maryland–College Park; University of South Carolina–Columbia; College of Charleston

FINANCIAL FACTS

Financial Aid Rating	82
Annual in-state tuition	$13,022
Annual out-of-state tuition	$31,940
Room and board	$8,718
Required fees	$860
Books and supplies	$1,308
Average frosh need-based scholarship	$10,776
Average UG need-based scholarship	$8,946
% needy frosh rec. need-based scholarship or grant aid	92
% needy UG rec. need-based scholarship or grant aid	81
% needy frosh rec. non-need-based scholarship or grant aid	71
% needy UG rec. non-need-based scholarship or grant aid	52
% needy frosh rec. need-based self-help aid	67
% needy UG rec. need-based self-help aid	75
% frosh rec. any financial aid	87
% UG rec. any financial aid	71
% UG borrow to pay for school	49
Average cumulative indebtedness	$30,270
% frosh need fully met	21
% ugrads need fully met	17
Average % of frosh need met	61
Average % of ugrad need met	55

COE COLLEGE

1220 FIRST AVENUE NE, CEDAR RAPIDS, IA 52402 • ADMISSIONS: 319-399-8500 • FAX: 319-399-8816

CAMPUS LIFE

Quality of Life Rating	86
Fire Safety Rating	87
Green Rating	76
Type of school	Private
Affiliation	Presbyterian
Environment	City

STUDENTS

Total undergrad enrollment	1,416
% male/female	42/58
% from out of state	55
% frosh live on campus	90
% ugrads live on campus	86
# of fraternities (% ugrad men join)	5 (18)
# of sororities (% ugrad women join)	4 (28)
% African American	6
% Asian	3
% Caucasian	74
% Hispanic	9
% Native American	<1
% Pacific Islander	<1
% Two or more races	3
% Race and/or ethnicity unknown	3
% international	1
# of countries represented	20

SURVEY SAYS...

Students are happy
Career services are great
Great financial aid
Easy to get around campus
Lots of beer drinking

ACADEMICS

Academic Rating	82
% students returning for sophomore year	77
% students graduating within 4 years	60
% students graduating within 6 years	67
Calendar	Quarter
Student/faculty ratio	11:1
Profs interesting rating	83
Profs accessible rating	88

Most classes have fewer than 10 students.
Most lab/discussion sessions have
 10–19 students.

MOST POPULAR MAJORS

Biology; Business Administration; Psychology

STUDENTS SAY "..."

Academics

Located in Cedar Rapids, Iowa, Coe College is a small school with a "tight-knit community feel" that provides "something different for everyone." "Coe has a very warm and friendly atmosphere" that works for "the betterment of each individual Kohawk through experiences, in and out of the classroom, as well as creating a mature adult prepared for the 'real-world.'" Students who need financial help shouldn't worry, because the "financial aid rocks!" Students love "the small class sizes that allow you to have a personable experience with each of your professors." The low teacher/student ratio also comes with "excellent, intelligent, helpful, and caring professors" who "all have great abundances of knowledge and all teach in different ways." "I honestly have not had a bad instructor," a chemistry major tells us. "They give you their home phone and cell phone numbers and invite you to call them. No teaching assistants here." A sociology student boasts of "relationships with my professors, and [I] feel that they invest in me and want me to succeed." Although the students rate their professors highly, they didn't feel the same way about the classrooms the professors teach in. Students have complained about the state of campus buildings in the past, but the school has invested in significant improvements in recent years. For many, the school is "an ideal size." "Big without being too big." One student lists Coe's strengths up as "the small class sizes, the community atmosphere, the involvement of students, study abroad programs, physics, and athletics." Coe has "the ability [to make] literally anyone feel comfortable."

Life

Although Coe is located in Iowa's second largest city, the college has a four-year residency requirement, and "people often fall victim to the 'Coe bubble,'" one student warns. "A lot of people are not familiar with the city and refuse to venture out. Most people I know enjoy alcohol on the weekends." While Coe isn't located "in the best neighborhood to go out in, we do have bars that are within blocks from our campus [that] are attended a lot on the weekends by students." Like many colleges, drinking is a common social activity. "In all honesty, Coe's students typically do drink alcohol—both on campus and off campus at the Cedar Rapids bars." However, other students see a variety of activities available. "There are parties, lots of video games, people playing intramural sports, Friday after class events…something for everyone." "For fun students go to SAC events like free midnight movies, tie-dying, dance socials in the pub, quarter bowling night, ice skating." The school hosts a regular talent show, Blindspot, which is so named because it's "open for students to perform without judgment." When asked what the school could improve on, the students were unanimous in their complaint: "The food is something we all wish would improve." To compound matters, "students are required to have a meal plan," and there aren't many options for "alternative diets such as vegan and vegetarian."

Student Body

"About one-third of [Coe's] student body is athletes," but "there really isn't a particular social group or type of personality that this school is known for, so it's easy to fit in with one—or any—group on campus." "The average students are exactly that: average," a student explains. "It is a very typical representation of the Midwest. There are very few students (I'd say less than ten people in the entire population on campus) [who] do not truly fit in anywhere." "While Greek organizations maintain a significant presence in numbers," Greek life doesn't dominate the school: "They don't organize for significant events or provide any clear distinction from other students." Students at Coe "are friendly," a trait helped by an "orientation [that] creates a forced interaction [and] gets people mingling." "There is not a typical student at Coe," one student says, "because each student is treated uniquely and takes a unique set of classes."

FINANCIAL AID: 319-399-8540 • E-MAIL: ADMISSION@COE.EDU • WEBSITE: WWW.COE.EDU

THE PRINCETON REVIEW SAYS

Admissions

Very important factors considered include: academic GPA, standardized test scores. *Important factors considered include:* class rank. *Other factors considered include:* rigor of secondary school record, application essay, interview, extracurricular activities, talent/ability, character/personal qualities, first generation, alumni/ae relation, racial/ethnic status, volunteer work, level of applicant's interest. SAT or ACT required. ACT with or without writing accepted. SAT with or without Essay component accepted. TOEFL required of all international applicants. High school diploma is required and GED is accepted. *Academic units recommended:* 4 English, 3 math, 3 science, 1 science lab, 2 foreign language, 3 social studies, 2 academic electives.

Financial Aid

Students should submit: FAFSA. Priority filing deadline is 3/1. The Princeton Review suggests that all financial aid forms be submitted as soon as possible after October 1. *Need-based scholarships/grants offered:* Federal Pell, FSEOG, State scholarships/grants, Private scholarships, College/university scholarship or grant aid from institutional funds. *Loan aid offered:* Direct Subsidized Stafford Loans, Direct Unsubsidized Stafford Loans, Direct PLUS loans, Federal Perkins Loans, College/university loans from institutional funds. Applicants will be notified of awards on a rolling basis. Federal Work-Study Program available. Institutional employment available.

The Inside Word

About 400 new students begin their college journey at Coe College each fall, and classes average a mere sixteen students. Despite its small size, Coe has the largest undergraduate writing center in the country, and many students enjoy its help. If you're seeking an intimate college experience with quality academics—Coe is one of the smallest colleges to contain a Phi Beta Kappa chapter—you would do well to consider Coe.

THE SCHOOL SAYS ". . ."

From the Admissions Office

"A Coe education begins to pay off right away. In fact, ninety-eight percent of last year's graduating class were either working or in graduate school within one year of graduation. Our graduates do so well because of our student-centered approach to learning and required hands-on experience which may be satisfied through an internship, research project, practicum experience or off-campus study. In recent years Coe students have interned at places like the Chicago Board of Trade, Mayo Clinic and Rockwell Collins. Others have completed research on Coe's campus through the National Science Foundation's Research Experiences for Undergraduates program or the Department of Business and Economics' Spellman Summer Research Program. Still others have combined travel with an internship in South Africa or student teaching in Tanzania for an unforgettable off-campus experience. Coe College is one of the few liberal arts institutions in the country to require hands-on learning for graduation."

SELECTIVITY

Admissions Rating	85
# of applicants	3,457
% of applicants accepted	63
% of acceptees attending	17

FRESHMAN PROFILE

Range SAT Critical Reading	515–625
Range SAT Math	495–640
Range SAT Writing	520–608
Range ACT Composite	22–27
Minimum paper TOEFL	520
Minimum internet-based TOEFL	68
Average HS GPA	3.6
% graduated top 10% of class	27
% graduated top 25% of class	55
% graduated top 50% of class	88

DEADLINES

Early decision	
Deadline	11/15
Notification	12/1
Early action	
Deadline	12/10
Notification	1/20
Regular	
Priority	12/10
Deadline	3/1
Nonfall registration?	Yes

APPLICANTS ALSO LOOK AT AND OFTEN PREFER
University of Iowa

AND SOMETIMES PREFER
Luther College

FINANCIAL FACTS

Financial Aid Rating	86
Average frosh need-based scholarship	$29,510
Average UG need-based scholarship	$26,770
% needy frosh rec. need-based scholarship or grant aid	100
% needy UG rec. need-based scholarship or grant aid	100
% needy frosh rec. non-need-based scholarship or grant aid	14
% needy UG rec. non-need-based scholarship or grant aid	15
% needy frosh rec. need-based self-help aid	82
% needy UG rec. need-based self-help aid	81
% frosh rec. any financial aid	99
% UG rec. any financial aid	99
% UG borrow to pay for school	74
Average cumulative indebtedness	$35,009
% frosh need fully met	20
% ugrads need fully met	21
Average % of frosh need met	85
Average % of ugrad need met	83

COLBY COLLEGE

4000 MAYFLOWER HILL, WATERVILLE, ME 04901-8848 • ADMISSIONS: 207-859-4800 • FAX: 207-859-4828

CAMPUS LIFE

Quality of Life Rating	90
Fire Safety Rating	98
Green Rating	99
Type of school	Private
Affiliation	No Affiliation
Environment	Village

STUDENTS

Total undergrad enrollment	1,857
% male/female	48/52
% from out of state	88
% frosh from public high school	49
% frosh live on campus	100
% ugrads live on campus	95
% African American	3
% Asian	6
% Caucasian	62
% Hispanic	6
% Native American	<1
% Pacific Islander	<1
% Two or more races	5
% Race and/or ethnicity unknown	9
% international	11
# of countries represented	74

SURVEY SAYS...

Students always studying
Students are happy
Classroom facilities are great
Great library
School is well run
Great financial aid
Students are friendly
Students aren't religious
Great food on campus
Lots of beer drinking

ACADEMICS

Academic Rating	92
% students returning for sophomore year	93
% students graduating within 4 years	88
Calendar	4/1/4
Student/faculty ratio	9:1
Profs interesting rating	95
Profs accessible rating	99

Most classes have 10–19 students.
Most lab/discussion sessions have 10–19 students.

MOST POPULAR MAJORS
Biology; Economics; English

STUDENTS SAY "..."

Academics

Nestled in the liberal arts college corridor of Maine, Colby is a classic New England college, full of socially-conscious, outdoorsy students and where self-motivated projects are encouraged. The school is willing to give students the time and resources to develop their own ideas and pursuits: There are "amazing support systems" in place for all students, and "tons of opportunities to forge your own path and get ample support from the college," which fosters a community of "well-rounded, kind, thoughtful, and critically-thinking citizens." Professors are "brilliant and always available," and it is as common to have professors invite students over for dinner as a class. They "truly will go above and beyond to help a student who demonstrates willingness to work hard and engage." All professors are available for office hours during the week and are "willing to talk with students about the work, or just have a chat." Students are made "to get out of their comfort zone and learn through hands on experience and research"; for example, in the Education department, "research and other information presented inside of the classroom are complemented by experiences outside of the classroom in the greater Waterville community." "Every single one of my classes has had a component that has surprised me in its interesting content that I have never considered or known about," says a student. An active alumni network and a recent new president only further helps Colby in "implementing changes that the student body wants and needs." The administration "has always listened to student groups and there is a respect for their opinions that often result in policy changes where they are needed," and there is a tremendous level of involvement throughout campus. Colby "is an extended family that looks out for every student and promotes the exploration and development of new ideas and interests."

Life

As a result of their broad interests and workloads, Colby students are "usually fairly busy (in a good way)." Most weekends there is a pretty large social scene and virtually all social events happen on the "gorgeous" campus, as "Mayflower Hill is its own little thriving community." Walking around you'll see "people playing Frisbee on Miller Lawn, slack-lining near Johnson Pond during the fall and spring, sledding on Chapel Hill, and skating or playing hockey on Johnson Pond in the winter." Getting off campus "isn't the easiest" but everyone is allowed to have a car so more likely than not you will find someone on campus that can take you anywhere. As you may know, Maine is "absolutely beautiful," and "all four seasons have something great to offer." In the winter, people ski most weekends and in the summer they often go to Colby's waterfront lake property to swim. Most everyone lives on campus, so "people are always around when you're looking for something to do." When a student turns twenty-one the social scene "becomes a lot better, with both bar nights and pub nights (at the on-campus pub)." Despite the fact that everybody is very busy, "it's a very happy atmosphere here. People have great discussions over dinner."

Student Body

Colby is a place for "forward-thinking, friendly, quirky, social, active people." The joke on campus is that "everyone is J.O.B.: just outside of Boston," but in addition to the New England crew ("the perfect mixture of preppy outdoorsmen"), a substantial portion of the student body hails from outside of New England. Most Colby students are "quite fit" and enjoy the outdoors; almost all are involved in "either a varsity sport, club sport, or some other club that fits their interests."

COLBY COLLEGE

FINANCIAL AID: 207-859-4832 • E-MAIL: ADMISSIONS@COLBY.EDU • WEBSITE: WWW.COLBY.EDU

THE PRINCETON REVIEW SAYS

Admissions

Very important factors considered include: rigor of secondary school record, academic GPA, recommendation(s), character/personal qualities. *Important factors considered include:* class rank, standardized test scores, application essay, extracurricular activities, talent/ability, racial/ethnic status. *Other factors considered include:* interview, first generation, alumni/ae relation, geographical residence, state residency, volunteer work, work experience, level of applicant's interest. SAT or ACT required for some; SAT Subject Tests required for some. ACT with Writing recommended. TOEFL required of all international applicants. High school diploma or equivalent is not required. *Academic units recommended:* 4 English, 3 math, 2 science, 2 science labs, 3 foreign language, 2 social studies.

Financial Aid

Students should submit: FAFSA, CSS/Financial Aid PROFILE, Business/Farm Supplement. Regular filing deadline is 2/1. The Princeton Review suggests that all financial aid forms be submitted as soon as possible after October 1. *Need-based scholarships/grants offered:* Federal Pell, FSEOG, State scholarships/grants, Private scholarships, College/university scholarship or grant aid from institutional funds. *Loan aid offered:* Direct Subsidized Stafford Loans, Direct Unsubsidized Stafford Loans, Direct PLUS loans, Federal Perkins Loans, State Loans. Applicants will be notified of awards on or about 4/1. Federal Work-Study Program available. Institutional employment available.

The Inside Word

Colby continues to be both very selective and successful in converting admits to enrollees, which makes for a perpetually challenging admissions process. Currently, less than 30 percent of applicants are accepted (more than 60 percent of whom graduated in the top 10 percent of their class), so hit those books and ace those exams to stand a fighting chance. One thing that could set you apart from the pack? An interest in other cultures. Nearly seventy percent of Colby students study abroad—in fact, for some degrees it's required.

THE SCHOOL SAYS " . . ."

From the Admissions Office

"Founded in 1813, Colby is one of America's most selective colleges. Serving only undergraduates, Colby's rigorous program is rooted in deep exploration of ideas and close interaction with world-class faculty scholars—a recipe for transformative academic experiences. Students pursue their intellectual passions by choosing among fifty-seven majors or developing their own. Colby students in all disciplines take advantage of research opportunities and collaboration with professors that often result in coauthoring peer-reviewed articles or co-presenting research at conferences. Nearly 70 percent of students study abroad in more than sixty countries. The College facilitates internships as well as a unique four-year program that uses a sequence of activities to prepare students for careers and advanced study. The alumni network also offers graduates resources and connections as they set out to make a profound impact on the world. Co-curricular and campus-life programs connect learning opportunities to student life. The College's exceptional campus facilities, including the finest college art museum in the country and state-of-the-art academic buildings and labs, are enhanced by Maine's unique natural resources, which enrich the academic program. Students enjoy easy access to world-class research institutions and a wealth of civic engagement experiences in the local community. A national leader in sustainability and environmental education, Colby was one of the first colleges in the country to achieve carbon neutrality. As part of its long-standing commitment to accessibility for the most academically qualified applicants, the College meets 100 percent of calculated need and includes grants—not loans—in financial aid packages."

SELECTIVITY

Admissions Rating	95
# of applicants	7,593
% of applicants accepted	23
% of acceptees attending	30
# offered a place on the wait list	1,497
# of early decision applicants	576
% accepted early decision	50

FRESHMAN PROFILE

Range SAT Critical Reading	630–720
Range SAT Math	640–740
Range SAT Writing	630–730
Range ACT Composite	29–32
Minimum internet-based TOEFL	100
% graduated top 10% of class	63
% graduated top 25% of class	93
% graduated top 50% of class	97

DEADLINES

Early decision	
Deadline	11/15
Notification	12/15
Regular	
Deadline	1/1
Notification	4/1
Nonfall registration?	Yes

APPLICANTS ALSO LOOK AT AND OFTEN PREFER

Harvard College; Amherst College; Brown University; Cornell University; Dartmouth College; Bowdoin College; Middlebury College

AND SOMETIMES PREFER

Bates College; Boston College

AND RARELY PREFER

Connecticut College; Dickinson College

FINANCIAL FACTS

Financial Aid Rating	96
Annual tuition	$47,060
Room and board	$12,610
Required fees	$2,060
Books and supplies	$700
Average frosh need-based scholarship	$44,991
Average UG need-based scholarship	$43,468
% needy frosh rec. need-based scholarship or grant aid	100
% needy UG rec. need-based scholarship or grant aid	100
% needy frosh rec. non-need-based scholarship or grant aid	2
% needy UG rec. non-need-based scholarship or grant aid	2
% needy frosh rec. need-based self-help aid	65
% needy UG rec. need-based self-help aid	72
% frosh rec. any financial aid	45
% UG rec. any financial aid	40
Average cumulative indebtedness	$23,343
% frosh need fully met	100
% ugrads need fully met	100
Average % of frosh need met	100
Average % of ugrad need met	100

COLGATE UNIVERSITY

13 OAK DRIVE, HAMILTON, NY 13346 • ADMISSIONS: 315-228-7401 • FAX: 315-228-7544

STUDENTS SAY ". . ."

Academics

Colgate University is known for its "very rigorous academic curriculum" and "invaluable" professors who "are the glue that hold the university together." Many students say they chose Colgate because they wanted "a small liberal arts school that had the opportunities and resources of a larger institution" combined with a "heavily involved alumni network" that "makes the Colgate connection a truly valuable resource." All agree that, at Colgate, you're "more than just a number" and that "there is no [shortage] of caring professors that are meaningfully invested in your academic success." As intimidating as it might seem to have, "internationally influential" professors, a history and political science double major assures that "classes are enjoyable and the professors are accessible." A junior adds, "One of the wonderful things about Colgate is that these relationships start as early as freshman year. Students do not have to wait until their senior year to build fantastic relationships with the faculty." However, another student grumbles, "Course selection is very stressful, and freshmen often get slighted." Any complaints about the faculty centered on "teaching styles" not meshing with individual students' "learning style." "However, there are a plethora of resources available to students to succeed despite any of their problems." "Colgate allowed me to become the person I always wanted to be, but didn't know I was capable of being," sings one senior whose sentiment is widely echoed.

Life

Colgate University "has an amazing campus with people who work hard and have goals but also know how to have a really fun time." Students say the campus is "breathtaking," and they value "its small size and intimate nature." A philosophy major says, "Colgate is great because you can't walk 200 feet without a professor, student, or faculty member acknowledging you by name, yet you're constantly meeting new people and having new experiences. There is never a dull moment at Colgate." Students say, "Colgate strives for the perfect combination of academics and extracurriculars," and they feel the university "does a great job at helping us balance those and gives us opportunities to get involved in all the groups and events around campus." In addition to a plethora of clubs, students are actively involved in Greek life and Division I athletics. A junior says, "I loved how Colgate was located in the middle of nowhere" because "everything revolved around the campus," but in case you're worried about isolation, another student adds, "Colgate brings a lot of interesting speakers to the campus, which helps provide for a more rounded liberal arts experience." Students praise the administration, saying, "It is easy for students to contact the administration and thus have their voices directly heard by the community. The president holds drop-in office hours for students every week and takes notes on what students say during the session."

Student Body

Colgate boasts a "happy and enthusiastic student body" with a typical student that "is athletic, smart, engaged, and down to earth." They "enjoy having fun, but spend time in the library as well." Many say "the typical Colgate student is a preppy New Englander, who can be found almost always wearing Patagonia and Sperrys." However, this stereotype seems to be becoming less apt as there is "great diversity under the surface." As long as students are "not afraid to do what they love, they will find their niche and fit in." Fraternities and sororities as well as partying in general are popular: "Greek life does have a huge presence in the social life at Colgate," but "it is not exclusive to just those who are members." Most students mentioned the recent changes in the school's alcohol policies. Some tout it as the impetus for "initiatives to expand the amount of alternatives to partying on weekends." Others cited it as "the biggest issue on campus right now" between the students and administration. Despite the "country club atmosphere," a computer science major says, "When you're stranded in Hamilton, New York, for four years you'll inevitably end up fitting in regardless whether you are the typical student or not."

COLGATE UNIVERSITY

THE PRINCETON REVIEW SAYS

Admissions

Very important factors considered include: rigor of secondary school record, class rank, academic GPA. *Important factors considered include:* standardized test scores, application essay, recommendation(s), extracurricular activities, talent/ability, character/personal qualities. *Other factors considered include:* first generation, alumni/ae relation, geographical residence, racial/ethnic status, volunteer work, work experience. SAT or ACT required. ACT with or without writing accepted. TOEFL required of all international applicants. High school diploma is required and GED is accepted. *Academic units required:* 4 English, 3 math, 3 science, 2 science labs, 3 foreign language, 3 social studies. *Academic units recommended:* 4 English, 4 math, 4 science, 4 science labs, 4 foreign language, 4 social studies.

Financial Aid

Students should submit: CSS/Financial Aid PROFILE, Noncustodial PROFILE. Regular filing deadline is 1/15.The Princeton Review suggests that all financial aid forms be submitted as soon as possible after October 1. *Need-based scholarships/grants offered:* Federal Pell, FSEOG. *Loan aid offered:* Direct Subsidized Stafford Loans, Direct Unsubsidized Stafford Loans, Direct PLUS loans, Federal Perkins Loans. Applicants will be notified of awards on or about 3/26. Federal Work-Study Program available. Institutional employment available.

The Inside Word

Admission to this upstate New York gem is some of the most competitive around. You will need to arm yourself with excellent scores, grades, recommendations, and extracurricular activities. However, Colgate is also looking for that extra ingredient which might not translate from the common app alone and is always seeking increased diversity across the board.

THE SCHOOL SAYS "..."

From the Admissions Office

"Colgate provides an environment where students can appreciate, celebrate, and learn about their own cultures as well as those of the people around them. The class of 2019 represents one of Colgate's most diverse class years yet. Of the class of 2019, 29 percent self-identified as being from multicultural backgrounds, and 7 percent are international students. Colgate's student body also includes students from forty-nine states, the District of Columbia, and forty-eight countries. Students and faculty alike are drawn to Colgate by the quality of its academic programs. Faculty initiative has given the university a rich mix of learning opportunities that includes a liberal arts core, fifty-four academic concentrations, and a wealth of Colgate faculty-led, off-campus study programs in the United States and abroad. But there is more to Colgate than academic life, including a full complement of living options set within a campus described as one of the most beautiful in the country. The Trudy Fitness Center is an integral component of Colgate's Wellness Initiative, which encourages healthy, purposeful, and balanced lifestyles within the community. A center for community service builds upon the tradition of Colgate students interacting with the surrounding community in meaningful ways. Colgate students become extraordinarily devoted alumni, contributing significantly to career networking and exploration programs on and off campus. Ten new professional networks bring current students and alumni together for powerful career connections that last long after graduation. For students in search of a busy and varied campus life, Colgate is a place to learn and grow."

SELECTIVITY
Admissions Rating	97
# of applicants	8,724
% of applicants accepted	27
% of acceptees attending	32
# offered a place on the wait list	1,896
% accepting a place on wait list	48
% admitted from wait list	5
# of early decision applicants	829
% accepted early decision	47

FRESHMAN PROFILE
Range SAT Critical Reading	620–720
Range SAT Math	630–730
Range ACT Composite	30–33
Average HS GPA	3.7
% graduated top 10% of class	75
% graduated top 25% of class	94
% graduated top 50% of class	99

DEADLINES
Early decision	
Deadline	11/15
Notification	12/15
Regular	
Deadline	1/15
Notification	4/1
Nonfall registration?	No

APPLICANTS ALSO LOOK AT AND OFTEN PREFER
Cornell University; Dartmouth College; Middlebury College

AND SOMETIMES PREFER
Brown University; Boston College; Washington University in St. Louis

AND RARELY PREFER
Colby College; Bucknell University; Bates College; Lehigh University; Lafayette College

FINANCIAL FACTS
Financial Aid Rating	99
Annual tuition	$51,635
Room and board	$13,075
Required fees	$320
Books and supplies	$1,040
Average frosh need-based scholarship	$43,321
Average UG need-based scholarship	$41,428
% needy frosh rec. need-based scholarship or grant aid	100
% needy UG rec. need-based scholarship or grant aid	99
% needy frosh rec. non-need-based scholarship or grant aid	0
% needy UG rec. non-need-based scholarship or grant aid	0
% needy frosh rec. need-based self-help aid	66
% needy UG rec. need-based self-help aid	74
% frosh rec. any financial aid	38
% UG rec. any financial aid	38
% frosh need fully met	100
% ugrads need fully met	100
Average % of frosh need met	100
Average % of ugrad need met	100

COLLEGE OF THE ATLANTIC

105 EDEN STREET, BAR HARBOR, ME 04609 • ADMISSIONS: 207-288-5015 • FAX: 207-288-4126

CAMPUS LIFE
Quality of Life Rating	95
Fire Safety Rating	97
Green Rating	99
Type of school	Private
Affiliation	No Affiliation
Environment	Rural

STUDENTS
Total undergrad enrollment	338
% male/female	30/70
% from out of state	78
% frosh from public high school	67
% frosh live on campus	100
% ugrads live on campus	50
% African American	1
% Asian	3
% Caucasian	72
% Hispanic	5
% Native American	0
% Pacific Islander	0
% Two or more races	2
% Race and/or ethnicity unknown	1
% international	17
# of countries represented	40

SURVEY SAYS...
Lots of liberal students
Students always studying
Students are happy
Internships are widely available
Class discussions encouraged
Great financial aid
No one cheats
Students are friendly
Students aren't religious
Students get along with local community
Students environmentally aware
Students love Bar Harbor, ME
Great food on campus
Dorms are like palaces
Easy to get around campus
Theater is popular

ACADEMICS
Academic Rating	94
% students returning for sophomore year	80
% students graduating within 4 years	57
% students graduating within 6 years	71
Calendar	Trimester
Student/faculty ratio	10:1
Profs interesting rating	98
Profs accessible rating	95

Most classes have 10–19 students.
Most lab/discussion sessions have
fewer than 10 students.

MOST POPULAR MAJORS
Ecology; Humanities/Humanistic Studies;
Multi-/Interdisciplinary Studies

STUDENTS SAY "..."

Academics
At this tiny Bar Harbor school, students "don't just take classes": they immerse themselves in experiences and in "an intimate, friendly community" of do-ers and critical thinkers. The college offers one self-designed major, human ecology, which takes an interdisciplinary approach to learning; this means "your undergraduate experience really is what you make of it." As a result, students are involved in outside projects in many areas that COA might not have many classes in. You also see "an interesting blend of subjects—physics, life drawing, environmental policy might all be found in one senior thesis." This unique educational model helps students "merge [their] talents/interests in a meaningful and applicable way," and allows for graduate-level research and real-world work experience at the undergraduate level. Students can't say enough about their professors, who "foster an environment open to discussion." If they do not know the answer to a question, "they are likely to admit it and research" the answer for you. "It's hard for me to talk to friends at other schools because it's not popular to love your college and academics as much as I do," says a student. Conversations extend outside classrooms all of the time; COA "is a college and a community that demands cognizance, compassion, and trust." There is a tremendous amount of academic freedom here, as well as "the ability to self-govern as a community"; COAers all recognize "the trust and responsibility the institution places in all students to create their own academic path between and among traditional majors." Self-motivated learning is everything here, and College of the Atlantic is for "idealists with elbow grease." Students can try their hand at numerous internship, residency, and study abroad opportunities, as the school "endeavors to make education a verb, and apply it to positively impact the world." Professors are deeply invested in their roles as educators, and "pour their hearts into this." "They expect our best and help us achieve it," says a student. "I am challenged and encouraged in equal parts."

Life
The housing and food here get rave reviews, and "many great conversations about the state of the world take place in houses, at meals, and just about anywhere else." The "active Outing Club" offers plenty of opportunities for students to kayak in Frenchman Bay and explore their "backyard" (Acadia National Park) or "other incredible natural areas of Maine." "It's hard to get bored when you live in such a beautiful landscape," says a student. COA students strive to be conscious of how their actions affect their social, political, and natural environments, and "there's definitely a hippie aesthetic." "We are constantly thinking about the latest environmental/social justice issue and thoughtful debates about these subjects happen at every meal." For fun, most students will "host potlucks with friends, spend time outdoors, and dance (with exceptional skill) together." Contra dancing ("one of the best things ever") is "alive and well in Maine and at COA!" "Reading parties, movie screenings, philosophical debates, and playback theatre companies" are also common, and "evenings often finish with singing, fiddles and guitars."

Student Body
Students at COA are typically "down to earth, progressive, and passionate about improving the world around them." Or, to put it another way: "Brilliant and a little weird." While the student body may be small (with a pretty skewed gender ratio at about 70 percent female), there's a great deal of diversity within the student body, both culturally (there is a huge international student population) and socioeconomically. "Nobody has the opportunity to hang out with people just like them"; instead students say, "We learn to be with each other, to share space." The four-year, straight through plan is not always typical here, and students "often leave for months or years and come back with experiences that enhance their and everyone else's education."

FINANCIAL AID: 207-288-5015 • E-MAIL: INQUIRY@COA.EDU • WEBSITE: WWW.COA.EDU

THE PRINCETON REVIEW SAYS

Admissions

Very important factors considered include: rigor of secondary school record, application essay, recommendation(s). *Important factors considered include:* class rank, academic GPA, interview, extracurricular activities, talent/ability, character/personal qualities, volunteer work, work experience. *Other factors considered include:* standardized test scores, first generation, alumni/ae relation, geographical residence, state residency, racial/ethnic status, level of applicant's interest. SAT or ACT considered if submitted; SAT Subject Tests considered if submitted. ACT with or without writing accepted. TOEFL required of all international applicants. High school diploma is required and GED is accepted. *Academic units required:* 4 English, 3 math, 2 science, 2 science labs, 2 social studies. *Academic units recommended:* 4 math, 3 science, 2 foreign language, 2 history, 1 academic elective.

Financial Aid

Students should submit: FAFSA, Institution's own financial aid form, Noncustodial PROFILE, Business/Farm Supplement. Regular filing deadline is 2/15. The Princeton Review suggests that all financial aid forms be submitted as soon as possible after October 1. *Need-based scholarships/grants offered:* Federal Pell, FSEOG, State scholarships/grants, Private scholarships, College/university scholarship or grant aid from institutional funds. *Loan aid offered:* Direct Subsidized Stafford Loans, Direct Unsubsidized Stafford Loans, Direct PLUS loans, Federal Perkins Loans. Applicants will be notified of awards on or about 4/1. Federal Work-Study Program available.

The Inside Word

Don't let COA's high acceptance rate fool you: the self-selecting applicant pool is comprised of dedicated and successful students. Standardized test scores are optional, but encouraged for applicants from nontraditional programs or alternative grading systems.

THE SCHOOL SAYS "..."

From the Admissions Office

"College of the Atlantic is a small, interdisciplinary college on Maine's Mount Desert Island. All students design their own major in human ecology—an educational approach that integrates knowledge from across academic disciplines and personal experience to investigate, and ultimately improve, the relationships between humans and our natural, social, and built environments. COA prepares students to become independent thinkers, challenge conventional wisdom, deal with pressing environmental and social issues, and engage passionately and thoughtfully to transform the world around them into a better place.

"Our campus is located on the shore of Frenchman Bay, a short walk from the mountains and trails of Acadia National Park—an ideal location for learning in the field. Many students spend time working or conducting research in the national park or on the college's organic farms and offshore island research stations on Mount Desert Rock and Great Duck Island. In addition to having numerous opportunities for research and field study, all COA students complete an internship and a capstone senior project.

"We look for students seeking a rigorous, hands-on, self-directed academic experience and meaningful engagement in a dynamic community of scholars. The best way to experience COA's unique approach to education, governance, and community life is to visit campus. While you're here, make time to sit in on classes, connect with faculty and current students, sample a homemade meal in the dining hall, and explore the national park."

SELECTIVITY

Admissions Rating	89
# of applicants	400
% of applicants accepted	76
% of acceptees attending	27
# offered a place on the wait list	35
% accepted early decision	80

FRESHMAN PROFILE

Range SAT Critical Reading	590–680
Range SAT Math	540–630
Range SAT Writing	580–670
Range ACT Composite	28–32
Minimum paper TOEFL	567
Minimum internet-based TOEFL	86
Average HS GPA	3.6
% graduated top 10% of class	26
% graduated top 25% of class	47
% graduated top 50% of class	95

DEADLINES

Early decision	
Deadline	12/1
Notification	12/15
Regular	
Deadline	2/1
Notification	4/1
Nonfall registration?	Yes

APPLICANTS ALSO LOOK AT AND OFTEN PREFER

Bowdoin College; Middlebury College

AND SOMETIMES PREFER

Colby College; Hampshire College; Bard College

AND RARELY PREFER

Green Mountain College; University of Maine

FINANCIAL FACTS

Financial Aid Rating	96
Annual tuition	$42,993
Room and board	$9,747
Required fees	$549
Books and supplies	$600
Average frosh need-based scholarship	$36,362
Average UG need-based scholarship	$32,640
% needy frosh rec. need-based scholarship or grant aid	100
% needy UG rec. need-based scholarship or grant aid	99
% needy frosh rec. non-need-based scholarship or grant aid	1
% needy UG rec. non-need-based scholarship or grant aid	1
% needy frosh rec. need-based self-help aid	97
% needy UG rec. need-based self-help aid	99
% frosh rec. any financial aid	98
% UG rec. any financial aid	97
% frosh need fully met	36
% ugrads need fully met	31
Average % of frosh need met	97
Average % of ugrad need met	94

COLLEGE OF CHARLESTON

66 GEORGE STREET, CHARLESTON, SC 29424 • ADMISSIONS: 843-953-5670 • FAX: 843-953-6322

CAMPUS LIFE

Quality of Life Rating	92
Fire Safety Rating	97
Green Rating	85
Type of school	Public
Affiliation	No Affiliation
Environment	City

STUDENTS

Total undergrad enrollment	10,468
% male/female	37/63
% from out of state	35
% frosh from public high school	75
% frosh live on campus	90
% ugrads live on campus	31
# of fraternities (% ugrad men join)	14 (19)
# of sororities (% ugrad women join)	13 (24)
% African American	7
% Asian	2
% Caucasian	80
% Hispanic	5
% Native American	<1
% Pacific Islander	<1
% Two or more races	4
% Race and/or ethnicity unknown	1
% international	1
# of countries represented	60

SURVEY SAYS...

Students are happy
Great library
Students love Charleston, SC
Great off-campus food
Easy to get around campus
Lots of beer drinking

ACADEMICS

Academic Rating	74
% students returning for sophomore year	79
% students graduating within 4 years	56
% students graduating within 6 years	68
Calendar	Semester
Student/faculty ratio	15:1
Profs interesting rating	76
Profs accessible rating	79

Most classes have 20–29 students.
Most lab/discussion sessions have
20–29 students.

MOST POPULAR MAJORS

Business Administration and Management;
Biology; Psychology

STUDENTS SAY "..."

Academics

Situated on a "beautiful, historic campus" in one of the South's most charming cities, it's no wonder that College of Charleston has such satisfied undergraduates. Indeed, students report that a "welcoming" vibe permeates the school and it's truly evident that the "supportive staff [want] to see...their students [succeed]." Many undergraduates also appreciate that the school is generous with scholarships and provides "lots of opportunities for travel and research." Students benefit from "small class sizes" and "a student-teacher ratio of 15:1." By and large, professors here are quite "passionate about their subject [matter]" and their enthusiasm is often infectious. Most instructors "encourage discussion" and seem to really "love student involvement both inside and outside of the classroom." Undergrads also happily report that many professors make themselves "accessible" and are "happy to talk to any students who are interested in their class." And one political science major even brags that "every teacher I've had has known the name of every student." Finally, this blissful sophomore concludes, "The College of Charleston consistently provides great academics, meaningful experiences to engage with the city, and fantastic people who want to do fantastic things."

Life

Life at College of Charleston is simultaneously "stressful [and] fun." Therefore, these undergrads very quickly adopt the work-hard-play-hard mentality so popular among college students everywhere. Thankfully, there's plenty to take advantage of when they want to kick back. To begin with, fraternities and sororities are "a big part of campus life." Indeed, "people are always excited for Greek events; although only 20 percent of [undergrads] are active members it [still maintains a visible] presence." Moreover, students admit that C of C does have a healthy drinking culture. As one political science major shares, "House parties in cramped historic homes are popular, as are the bars downtown." However, a psychology major quickly follows up by emphatically stating, "While there are quite a few parties that go on, none are really out of hand. People stay safe and watch out for each other mostly." Of course, opportunities and activities outside of the party scene abound. Students with a penchant for the outdoors can enjoy "going to the beach, kayaking, sailing, rock climbing, surfing, and hiking." And the "Cougar Activities Board always [hosts] great [events]." Finally, students simply adore their adopted hometown. "There's so much history here in Charleston, you're guaranteed to learn something new all the time." The city is also home to "hundreds of renowned restaurants" and many "festival, concert" and "shopping" options.

Student Body

When walking around C of C's campus, one could easily be forgiven for thinking that the typical student here is "a young white female who comes from a wealthy family and is into sorority life." However, don't be fooled! The college is actually home to "a wide array of people from different places in life." A sophomore tells us, "We have a diverse student body of preppy southern belles, hipsters, sorority girls, frat stars, skater boys, and beach bums." Indeed, there's a range of personalities, "and you can find someone like you." Importantly, looking beyond stereotypes and broad social categorization, the College of Charleston seems to attract a student body that's "smart, well-rounded, and willing to work hard." And while "there are definitely cliques," many undergrads are able to hop around differing social groups with ease. Perhaps this can be attributed to the fact that, "in general, the typical student absorbs the Charleston spirit: they're friendly, open, and generally happy."

FINANCIAL AID: 843-953-5540 • E-MAIL: ADMISSIONS@COFC.EDU • WEBSITE: WWW.COFC.EDU

THE PRINCETON REVIEW SAYS

Admissions

Very important factors considered include: rigor of secondary school record, academic GPA, standardized test scores. *Important factors considered include:* class rank, talent/ability, character/personal qualities, first generation, state residency. *Other factors considered include:* application essay, recommendation(s), extracurricular activities, alumni/ae relation, geographical residence, racial/ethnic status, volunteer work, work experience, level of applicant's interest. SAT or ACT required. ACT with or without writing accepted. SAT with or without Essay component accepted. TOEFL, IELTS, SAT, or ACT required of all international applicants. High school diploma is required and GED is accepted. *Academic units required:* 4 English, 4 math, 3 science, 3 science labs, 3 foreign language, 2 social studies, 1 history, 3 academic electives, 1 visual/performing arts, and 1 unit from above areas or other academic areas. *Academic units recommended:* 4 English, 4 math, 2 history, 1 computer science.

Financial Aid

Students should submit: FAFSA. Priority filing deadline is 3/1.The Princeton Review suggests that all financial aid forms be submitted as soon as possible after October 1. *Need-based scholarships/grants offered:* Federal Pell, FSEOG, State scholarships/grants, Private scholarships, College/university scholarship or grant aid from institutional funds. *Loan aid offered:* Direct Subsidized Stafford Loans, Direct Unsubsidized Stafford Loans, Direct PLUS loans, Federal Perkins Loans. Applicants will be notified of awards on a rolling basis beginning 4/10. Federal Work-Study Program available. Institutional employment available.

The Inside Word

When it comes to assessing applicants, admissions officers at the College of Charleston try to take the holistic approach shared by many liberal arts schools. Of course, a candidate's GPA, standardized tests and class rank hold the most weight. Successful applicants are typically in the top 20 percent of their class and consistently earn A's and B's. Beyond academics, leadership and extracurricular experience will also help bolster an application. Above all, the admissions committee wants students who will contribute to a vibrant campus life.

THE SCHOOL SAYS ". . ."

From the Admissions Office

"To succeed in our increasingly complex world, college graduates must be able to think creatively, explore new ideas, compete, collaborate, and meet the challenges of our global society. At the College of Charleston, students find out about themselves, their lives and the lives of others. They discover how to shape their future, and they prepare to create change and opportunity. Founded in 1770, the College of Charleston's mission is to provide students with a first-class education in the arts and sciences, education and business. Students have 130 majors and minors from which to choose—and they often choose to combine several—and complement their academic courses with overseas study, research and internships for a truly customized education.

"Approximately 10,000 undergraduates choose the college for its small-college feel blended with the advantages and diversity of an urban, mid-sized university. The College, home to students from forty-nine states and fifty-five countries, provides a creative and intellectually stimulating environment where students are challenged and guided by a committed and caring full-time faculty of 565 distinguished teacher-scholars, all in an incomparable historic setting. The city of Charleston serves as a living and learning laboratory for student experiences in business, science, teaching, the humanities, languages and the arts. At the same time, students and faculty are engaged with the community in partnerships to improve education, enhance the business community and enrich the overall quality of life in the region. In the great liberal arts tradition, a College of Charleston education focuses on discovery and personal growth, as well as preparation for life, work and service to our society."

SELECTIVITY

Admissions Rating	81
# of applicants	11,722
% of applicants accepted	77
% of acceptees attending	25
# offered a place on the wait list	172

FRESHMAN PROFILE

Range SAT Critical Reading	520–610
Range SAT Math	510–600
Range ACT Composite	23–28
Minimum paper TOEFL	570
Minimum internet-based TOEFL	80
Average HS GPA	3.9
% graduated top 10% of class	21
% graduated top 25% of class	54
% graduated top 50% of class	90

DEADLINES

Early action	
Deadline	11/1
Notification	1/1
Regular	
Priority	2/1
Deadline	4/1
Nonfall registration?	Yes

APPLICANTS ALSO LOOK AT AND OFTEN PREFER

University of Georgia; The University of North Carolina at Chapel Hill; College of William and Mary; University of Virginia

AND SOMETIMES PREFER

Clemson University; Elon University; University of Miami; University of South Carolina–Columbia

FINANCIAL FACTS

Financial Aid Rating	80
Annual in-state tuition	$10,900
Annual out-of-state tuition	$28,444
Room and board	$11,629
Required fees	$460
Books and supplies	$1,224
Average frosh need-based scholarship	$3,317
Average UG need-based scholarship	$3,176
% needy frosh rec. need-based scholarship or grant aid	71
% needy UG rec. need-based scholarship or grant aid	68
% needy frosh rec. non-need-based scholarship or grant aid	78
% needy UG rec. non-need-based scholarship or grant aid	47
% needy frosh rec. need-based self-help aid	70
% needy UG rec. need-based self-help aid	75
% frosh rec. any financial aid	53
% UG rec. any financial aid	47
% frosh need fully met	22
% ugrads need fully met	18
Average % of frosh need met	58
Average % of ugrad need met	57

COLLEGE OF THE HOLY CROSS

ADMISSIONS OFFICE, ONE COLLEGE STREET, WORCESTER, MA 01610-2395 • ADMISSIONS: 508-793-2443 • FAX: 508-793-3888

CAMPUS LIFE

Quality of Life Rating	84
Fire Safety Rating	97
Green Rating	86
Type of school	Private
Affiliation	Roman Catholic
Environment	City

STUDENTS

Total undergrad enrollment	2,916
% male/female	50/50
% from out of state	62
% frosh from public high school	51
% frosh live on campus	99
% ugrads live on campus	91
# of fraternities (% ugrad men join)	(0)
# of sororities (% ugrad women join)	(0)
% African American	3
% Asian	5
% Caucasian	70
% Hispanic	10
% Native American	<1
% Pacific Islander	<1
% Two or more races	3
% Race and/or ethnicity unknown	5
% international	2
# of countries represented	15

SURVEY SAYS...

Students are happy
Students involved in community service
Alumni active on campus

ACADEMICS

Academic Rating	91
% students returning for sophomore year	96
% students graduating within 4 years	89
% students graduating within 6 years	92
Calendar	Semester
Student/faculty ratio	9:1
Profs interesting rating	93
Profs accessible rating	96

Most classes have 10–19 students.
Most lab/discussion sessions have fewer than 10 students.

MOST POPULAR MAJORS

Economics; Political Science and Government; Psychology

STUDENTS SAY "..."

Academics

This small, Jesuit liberal arts school in Massachusetts operates under a selfless mission statement of "men and women for others." The school's strong academic tradition marries with "countless opportunities to learn through internships, speaker series," "strong student life," and "small classes" to focus on shaping the student as a whole person. Academics at Holy Cross are "rigorous, and the main priority of students on campus"; a caring faculty and administration foster "an incredible learning environment for students," and through their experiences, students receive "a broad-based foundation to be successful in variety of careers." "From the acceptance letter alone, I knew that my entire application was read thoroughly and that my character was closely examined," says one happy student. At Holy Cross, "you're more than just a number in the classroom and on the field." Professors here are "dedicated to creating an exciting learning environment." They are "always accessible and more than happy to help," and they "get to know you on an individual and personal level." Students are encouraged "to reflect on their experiences and continue to better himself/herself as a whole person." "There are endless opportunities despite the fact that it is a small college," one student says. "It is a place where like in the parable of the mustard seed one can grow." In addition to a "fantastic alumni network" spread across several fields in various industries, there is a strong science program that includes plenty of research opportunities. The college "demands enormous amounts of work from its students, but puts them in a great position to succeed." "Holy Cross equips their students with an intangible set of skills that not only prepares them for a job, but for life," says a student.

Life

Holy Cross has "a multitude" of groups and activities available to its students, as well as a plethora of community service opportunities. Everyone loves "going to sporting events, especially football and basketball." Though the "exceptionally beautiful" campus has a lot of fans, all agree that the college "could update some of the residence halls," and there have been complaints about the lack of dining options, which the school has addressed with upgrades to its Main Dining Hall. The community among freshman dorms is "outstanding," and "many of the friends you make your first year will stay with you for years to come." During the week and on Sundays, "people take their work very seriously," and the library is generally pretty full, but parties are popular on weekends, and "that nerdy chem major you see working hard all week can turn into the girl riding the mechanical bull at a local bar." For those who choose to abstain from the party circuit, "SGA-sponsored events such as karaoke or dances are a blast." Worcester is a fun little town (and Boston a free weekend shuttle ride away), and the restaurants in the area are "amazing."

Student Body

Many students here are "preppy" and from New England, and most all of this "uncommonly friendly" lot is "studious with an activity or two that defines their interests and what they do during the weekend"; in fact, it is rare "to find someone with no extracurricular responsibilities." Everyone tends to be "very put together" and "generally articulate," and "there is a tremendous sense of community." There is "a diverse set of interests" among the whole student body. In general, "all love being here." "If you want to do well academically, have fun on the weekend...study hard and play hard, then you will fit in at Holy Cross."

FINANCIAL AID: 508-793-2265 • E-MAIL: ADMISSIONS@HOLYCROSS.EDU • WEBSITE: WWW.HOLYCROSS.EDU

THE PRINCETON REVIEW SAYS

Admissions

Very important factors considered include: rigor of secondary school record, academic GPA, recommendation(s), interview. *Important factors considered include:* class rank, application essay, extracurricular activities, character/personal qualities. *Other factors considered include:* standardized test scores, talent/ability, first generation, alumni/ae relation, geographical residence, state residency, religious affiliation/commitment, racial/ethnic status, volunteer work, work experience, level of applicant's interest. SAT or ACT considered if submitted; SAT Subject Tests considered if submitted. ACT with or without writing accepted. TOEFL required of all international applicants. High school diploma is required and GED is accepted. *Academic units recommended:* 4 English, 4 math, 4 science, 2 science labs, 4 foreign language, 2 social studies, 2 history.

Financial Aid

Students should submit: FAFSA, CSS/Financial Aid PROFILE, Noncustodial PROFILE, Business/Farm Supplement. Regular filing deadline is 2/1.The Princeton Review suggests that all financial aid forms be submitted as soon as possible after October 1. *Need-based scholarships/grants offered:* Federal Pell, FSEOG, State scholarships/grants, Private scholarships, College/university scholarship or grant aid from institutional funds. *Loan aid offered:* Direct Subsidized Stafford Loans, Direct Unsubsidized Stafford Loans, Direct PLUS loans, Federal Perkins Loans. Applicants will be notified of awards on or about 4/1. Federal Work-Study Program available. Institutional employment available.

The Inside Word

Admission to Holy Cross is competitive; therefore, a demanding high school course load is required to be a viable candidate. The college values effective communication skills—it thoroughly evaluates each applicant's personal statement and short essay responses. Interviews are important, especially for those applying early decision. Students who graduate from a Jesuit high school might find themselves at a slight advantage.

THE SCHOOL SAYS "..."

From the Admissions Office

"When applying to Holy Cross, two areas deserve particular attention. First, the essay should be developed thoughtfully, with correct language and syntax in mind. That essay reflects for the Admissions Committee how you think and how you can express yourself. Second, activity beyond the classroom should be clearly defined. Since Holy Cross has only 2,800 students, the chance for involvement/participation is exceptional. The committee reviews many applications for academically qualified students. A key difference in being accepted is the extent to which a candidate participates in-depth beyond the classroom—don't be modest; define who you are. Interviews are highly recommended and are used as part of the evaluation process.

"Standardized test scores (i.e., SAT, SAT Subject Tests, and ACT) are optional. Students may submit their scores if they believe the results paint a fuller picture of their achievements and potential, but those students who don't submit scores will not be at a disadvantage in admissions decisions."

SELECTIVITY

Admissions Rating	92
# of applicants	6,595
% of applicants accepted	37
% of acceptees attending	30
# offered a place on the wait list	1,307
% accepting a place on wait list	38
% admitted from wait list	2
# of early decision applicants	442
% accepted early decision	75

FRESHMAN PROFILE

Range SAT Critical Reading	600–690
Range SAT Math	620–690
Range SAT Writing	610–700
Range ACT Composite	28–31
Minimum paper TOEFL	600
Minimum internet-based TOEFL	100
% graduated top 10% of class	61
% graduated top 25% of class	89
% graduated top 50% of class	100

DEADLINES

Early decision	
Deadline	12/15
Other ED Deadline	12/15
Regular	
Deadline	1/15
Nonfall registration?	No

FINANCIAL FACTS

Financial Aid Rating	94
Annual tuition	$48,295
Room and board	$13,225
Required fees	$645
Books and supplies	$700
Average frosh need-based scholarship	$34,015
Average UG need-based scholarship	$33,714
% needy frosh rec. need-based scholarship or grant aid	85
% needy UG rec. need-based scholarship or grant aid	84
% needy frosh rec. non-need-based scholarship or grant aid	3
% needy UG rec. non-need-based scholarship or grant aid	3
% needy frosh rec. need-based self-help aid	90
% needy UG rec. need-based self-help aid	93
% frosh rec. any financial aid	61
% UG rec. any financial aid	56
% UG borrow to pay for school	59
Average cumulative indebtedness	$25,613
% frosh need fully met	100
% ugrads need fully met	100
Average % of frosh need met	100
Average % of ugrad need met	100

THE COLLEGE OF IDAHO

2112 CLEVELAND BOULEVARD, CALDWELL, ID 83605-4432 • ADMISSIONS: 208-459-5305 • FAX: 208-459-5757

CAMPUS LIFE

Quality of Life Rating	93
Fire Safety Rating	88
Green Rating	68
Type of school	Private
Affiliation	No Affiliation
Environment	Town

STUDENTS

Total undergrad enrollment	1,039
% male/female	49/51
% from out of state	25
% frosh live on campus	94
% ugrads live on campus	59
# of fraternities (% ugrad men join)	3 (17)
# of sororities (% ugrad women join)	4 (18)
% African American	2
% Asian	2
% Caucasian	66
% Hispanic	14
% Native American	1
% Pacific Islander	1
% Two or more races	3
% Race and/or ethnicity unknown	4
% international	7
# of countries represented	46

SURVEY SAYS...

Students politically aware
Students are happy
School is well run
No one cheats
Students are friendly
Diverse student types interact on campus
Great food on campus
Easy to get around campus
Lots of beer drinking
Everyone loves the Yotes
Intramural sports are popular
Theater is popular
Alumni active on campus

ACADEMICS

Academic Rating	83
% students returning for sophomore year	82
% students graduating within 4 years	54
% students graduating within 6 years	68
Calendar	Semester
Student/faculty ratio	10:1
Profs interesting rating	96
Profs accessible rating	95

Most classes have 10–19 students.
Most lab/discussion sessions have
10–19 students.

MOST POPULAR MAJORS

Biology; Business Administration and
Management; Psychology

STUDENTS SAY "..."

Academics

A small liberal arts school, The College of Idaho is "like a diamond in the rough." Students tell us, "You'd be surprised at the very high quality this little school offers!" The small class sizes and low student-to-teacher ratio promote the school's emphasis on "individual learning" and a "personalized education plan." The academic experience at The College of Idaho is "incredibly rigorous but also very rewarding." Though the school has a "well-developed" liberal arts core, students also describe the biology and premed programs as "fantastic." Courses are "challenging," "fascinating," and "great preparation for both graduate school and the professional world." The small school environment provides a "sense of community" and allows students to develop "strong working relationships" with their professors. Students tell us their professors are "attentive," "very accessible," and "passionate about what they teach." One graduating senior described the school as "an academic gold mine of some of the most published and highly regarded professors and researchers in the field." The "personal teaching" approach the professors at The College of Idaho take makes them "consistently recognized nationally and internationally for their contributions to the academic community and to their students." The administration is "involved with the students" and "effective" though "the professors are what make The College of Idaho great." Also great is the fact that the school is "cost competitive" and offers "generous scholarships." As one freshman tells us, "My school is way more than a place for me to learn. My teachers have become more like guardians for my education, and my peers...my second family."

Life

Life in Caldwell can be "pretty quiet" but Boise, the capital, is only about a thirty-minute drive away, and the school regularly hosts trips into the city. However, the campus "strives" and "mostly succeeds" in making up for the town by sponsoring many activities on campus. A student tells us, "On campus there is always something going on...I rarely have a night where there isn't something that I could do for fun." The College of Idaho offers a variety of extracurricular activities. The school's Program Council "puts on great events all year long." Such events as movie and bowling nights are open to all students and are often offered free of charge. Students at The College of Idaho also tend to be very interested in clubs and club-sponsored events. With a multitude of clubs to join, there is a club "for all personality types." One student tells us, "Whether it is attending a theater or band concert, an athletic event, or a club meeting, there are plenty of ways to get involved." Students describe their school life as "great overall," and because the school is so small, "any major campus-sponsored activity brings us all together as one, giant, friendly social club."

Student Body

Students tell us, The College of Idaho has "students from many walks of life" and a "student body full of individuals." While a majority of the student body is "white, middle-class, and right out of high school," students at The College of Idaho promote an "atmosphere of learning from others no matter their background." Many students tell us that there really isn't a "typical student," which isn't so surprising given its large international student population. Each student at The College of Idaho is "an active participant in the campus community." One junior tells us students are, "overly involved" and "extremely busy with clubs, campus activities, athletics, and academics." Students are "hardworking but social," "intelligent," and "well-rounded." According to one sophomore, "though [we are all] different, the commonality of going to C of I brings us together."

FINANCIAL AID: 208-459-5307 • E-MAIL: ADMISSION@COLLEGEOFIDAHO.EDU • WEBSITE: WWW.COLLEGEOFIDAHO.EDU

THE PRINCETON REVIEW SAYS

Admissions

Very important factors considered include: academic GPA. *Important factors considered include:* rigor of secondary school record, standardized test scores, application essay, recommendation(s), character/personal qualities, alumni/ae relation. *Other factors considered include:* class rank, interview, extracurricular activities, talent/ability, first generation, volunteer work, work experience, level of applicant's interest. SAT or ACT considered if submitted. ACT with or without writing accepted. SAT with or without Essay component accepted. TOEFL required of all international applicants. High school diploma is required and GED is accepted. *Academic units recommended:* 4 English, 3 math, 2 science, 2 foreign language, 2 social studies, 2 history, 4 academic electives.

Financial Aid

Students should submit: FAFSA. Priority filing deadline is 2/1. The Princeton Review suggests that all financial aid forms be submitted as soon as possible after October 1. *Need-based scholarships/grants offered:* Federal Pell, FSEOG, State scholarships/grants, Private scholarships, College/university scholarship or grant aid from institutional funds. *Loan aid offered:* Direct Subsidized Stafford Loans, Direct Unsubsidized Stafford Loans, Direct PLUS loans, Federal Perkins Loans. Applicants will be notified of awards on or about 3/15. Federal Work-Study Program available. Institutional employment available.

The Inside Word

The admissions committee at The College of Idaho is looking for students who have taken high school seriously. Candidates who demonstrate reasonable academic success and a variety of extracurricular activities will be handed the keys to a quality academic program and a unique college experience, one that stresses self-confidence and social responsibility.

THE SCHOOL SAYS "..."

From the Admissions Office

"Founded in 1891, The College of Idaho is the state's oldest private liberal arts college. The C of I has a legacy of academic exellence, a winning athletics tradition, and a history of producing successful graduates, including severn Rhodes Scholars, fourteen Masrhall, Truman, and Goldwater Scholars, three governors, four NFL players, Academy Award and Pulitzer Prize winners, and countless business leaders and innovators. The College's distinctive PEAK Curriculum challenges students to attain competencies in the four knowledge peaks—the humanities, natural sciences, social sciences, and a professional field—empowering them to earn a major and three minors in four years. C of I students have small classes taught by outstanding professors, with a diverse student body of approximately 1,100 and and 11-to-1 student-to-faculty ratio. C of I students also enjoy competitive NAIA athletics programs, outstanding visual and performing arts activities, and a beautiful residential campus in Caldwell, located just thirty miles from downtown Boise and minutes from world-class outdoor recreation opportunities. The College of Idaho is nationally recognized as one of America's top liberal arts schools, as well as for its outstanding combination of academic quality and economic value. Scholarships and financial aid abound, as do opportunities for undergraduate research, study abroad experiences, internships, and leadership development. The C of I is test-optional for admissoin. All students—whether they submit test scores or not—are considered based upon high schoocol academic records, co-curricular activities, community involvement, writing ability, recommendations, and other personal achievements. To learn more, visit www.collegeofidaho.edu."

SELECTIVITY

Admissions Rating	72
# of applicants	955
% of applicants accepted	90
% of acceptees attending	23

FRESHMAN PROFILE

Range SAT Critical Reading	450–590
Range SAT Math	470–600
Range SAT Writing	450–570
Range ACT Composite	20–26
Minimum paper TOEFL	550
Minimum internet-based TOEFL	79
Average HS GPA	3.5
% graduated top 10% of class	23
% graduated top 25% of class	27
% graduated top 50% of class	25

DEADLINES

Early action	
Deadline	11/16
Notification	12/21
Regular	
Priority	11/15
Deadline	2/16
Nonfall registration?	Yes

APPLICANTS ALSO LOOK AT AND OFTEN PREFER
University of Idaho

AND RARELY PREFER
Brigham Young University (UT)

FINANCIAL FACTS

Financial Aid Rating	85
Annual tuition	$26,670
Room and board	$8,990
Required fees	$755
Books and supplies	$1,200
Average frosh need-based scholarship	$3,831
Average UG need-based scholarship	$5,243
% needy frosh rec. need-based scholarship or grant aid	100
% needy UG rec. need-based scholarship or grant aid	100
% needy frosh rec. non-need-based scholarship or grant aid	37
% needy UG rec. non-need-based scholarship or grant aid	100
% needy frosh rec. need-based self-help aid	81
% needy UG rec. need-based self-help aid	63
% frosh rec. any financial aid	99
% UG rec. any financial aid	100
% UG borrow to pay for school	70
Average cumulative indebtedness	$30,865
% frosh need fully met	25
% ugrads need fully met	20
Average % of frosh need met	87
Average % of ugrad need met	92

THE COLLEGE OF NEW JERSEY

PO BOX 7718, EWING, NJ 08628-0718 • ADMISSIONS: 609-771-2131 • FAX: 609-637-5174

CAMPUS LIFE

Quality of Life Rating	87
Fire Safety Rating	98
Green Rating	90
Type of school	Public
Affiliation	No Affiliation
Environment	Village

STUDENTS

Total undergrad enrollment	6,758
% male/female	41/59
% from out of state	6
% frosh from public high school	70
% frosh live on campus	95
% ugrads live on campus	60
# of fraternities (% ugrad men join)	11 (14)
# of sororities (% ugrad women join)	13 (11)
% African American	6
% Asian	10
% Caucasian	66
% Hispanic	12
% Native American	<1
% Pacific Islander	<1
% Two or more races	<1
% Race and/or ethnicity unknown	5
% international	<1
# of countries represented	32

SURVEY SAYS...

Students are happy
Great library
Career services are great
Students are friendly
Easy to get around campus

ACADEMICS

Academic Rating	83
% students returning for sophomore year	95
% students graduating within 4 years	72
% students graduating within 6 years	85
Calendar	Semester
Student/faculty ratio	13:1
Profs interesting rating	81
Profs accessible rating	84

Most classes have 20–29 students.
Most lab/discussion sessions have 10–19 students.

MOST POPULAR MAJORS

Biology; Psychology; Business Administration and Management

STUDENTS SAY "..."

Academics

The College of New Jersey is a small public college dedicated to education and to the pursuit of passions, all at an affordable price. Each of TCNJ's "excellent" seven schools offers "an awesome range of classes to choose from" (it is "one of the best schools in the area for future teachers," in particular), and the academic environment "is an open and honest one." On top of all that, "the campus is gorgeous, the students are friendly, and you can't beat the price!" "The College of New Jersey is a community unlike any I have ever been a part of; everyone is proud to be a part of and to contribute to the TCNJ culture," says a satisfied student.

Professors are always available in and out of the "small classes," and they "are truly interested in the progress and well-being of their students." Though the classes for liberal learning requirements are "stressful," teachers want their students to do well and "are eager to help and answer questions." "There has never been a moment where I have felt unsupported in my academic endeavors or felt that I could not reach out for help," says a student. A few students warn that some requirements become hard to fill because "there are only a few options that fit the topic, and everyone is trying to get into those classes."

One of TCNJ's greatest strengths is the Freshman Year Seminar Program. Freshman students choose a class that they are interested in (ranging from "a class on Bruce Springsteen, to one about Harry Potter, to one about the meaning of life"), and then live on a floor with all of the students in that class. "This is a wonderful opportunity to build community and to ensure that students are surrounded by people with similar interests and academic goals."

Life

Life at TCNJ is "calm and enjoyable." Students refer to the school as an "island of suburban housing," which works well in terms of building community, but the atmosphere does tend to cut students off from the outside world (especially freshmen, who aren't allowed cars). Students keep busy with their studies, organizations, and "many great events the school hosts," but "they also enjoy spending time with friends and having a good time together." "A lot of people party. A lot of people don't party. Most people love it here," sums up a student simply. While the local origins of the students means that some students do go home on weekends, "almost every weekend, the school organizes a trip to nearby Princeton, NYC, or Philadelphia" for those who stick around. "The school actually sends out a weekly calendar listing all of the events being held on campus that week," says a student. Students do warn about housing; as selection for upper-class housing is done strictly by a lottery system, "several do not get housing" each year, and some of the freshmen that do get their guaranteed housing find that their dorms are "ancient, dirty, and falling apart."

Student Body

People "are serious about their education here," and students describe themselves as "quite diverse." There is "always a group for somebody": "I don't know anyone that feels like they don't fit in, and if they do feel that way, it's because they aren't putting in the effort to do so," says a student. Everyone is on campus for a reason, whether it's major-/career-specific or "simply to gain leadership or life experiences," and all are "self-motivated, personable, and goal-oriented." While students are accepting of minorities, "the majority is most certainly still white." On the whole, "students are very happy and friendly and therefore make it much easier to fit in and make friends."

FINANCIAL AID: 609-771-2211 • E-MAIL: TCNJINFO@TCNJ.EDU • WEBSITE: WWW.TCNJ.EDU

THE PRINCETON REVIEW SAYS

Admissions

Very important factors considered include: rigor of secondary school record, class rank, standardized test scores, extracurricular activities, volunteer work. *Important factors considered include:* application essay, recommendation(s), talent/ability, character/personal qualities, geographical residence, state residency. *Other factors considered include:* academic GPA, first generation, alumni/ae relation, racial/ethnic status, work experience, level of applicant's interest. SAT or ACT required. ACT with or without writing accepted. SAT with or without Essay component accepted. TOEFL required of all international applicants. High school diploma is required and GED is accepted. *Academic units required:* 4 English, 4 math, 4 science, 2 science labs, 2 foreign language, 2 social studies.

Financial Aid

Students should submit: FAFSA, CSS/Financial Aid PROFILE. Regular filing deadline is 10/1.The Princeton Review suggests that all financial aid forms be submitted as soon as possible after October 1. *Need-based scholarships/grants offered:* Federal Pell, FSEOG, State scholarships/grants, Private scholarships, College/university scholarship or grant aid from institutional funds, Federal Nursing Scholarships. *Loan aid offered:* Direct Subsidized Stafford Loans, Direct Unsubsidized Stafford Loans, Direct PLUS loans, Federal Perkins Loans, Federal Nursing Loans. Applicants will be notified of awards on a rolling basis beginning 6/1. Federal Work-Study Program available. Institutional employment available.

The Inside Word

TCNJ accepts a high percentage of its 10,000 applicants, but that figure is deceiving; this is a self-selecting applicant pool, and those with no chance of acceptance simply don't bother. Admissions are as competitive as you would expect at a school that offers state residents a small-college experience and a highly respected degree for bargain-basement prices. TCNJ's admissions staff examines every component of a student's application, but none more carefully than the high school transcript. Students should apply a soon as possible once the application becomes available.

THE SCHOOL SAYS "..."

From the Admissions Office

"The College of New Jersey is one of the United States' great higher education success stories. With a long history as New Jersey's preeminent teacher of teachers, the college has grown into a new role as educator of the nation's best students in a wide range of fields. The College of New Jersey has created a culture of constant questioning—a place where knowledge is not merely received but reconfigured. In small classes, students and faculty members collaborate in a rewarding process: As they seek to understand fundamental principles, apply key concepts, reveal new problems, and pursue new lines of inquiry, students gain a fluency of thought in their disciplines. The college's 289-acre tree-lined campus is a union of vision, engineering, beauty, and functionality. Neoclassical Georgian Colonial architecture, meticulous landscaping, and thoughtful design merge in a dynamic system, constantly evolving to meet the needs of TCNJ students. About half of TCNJ's entering class will be academic scholars, with large numbers of National Merit finalists and semifinalists. The College of New Jersey is bringing together the best ideas from around the nation and building a new model for public undergraduate education on one campus."

SELECTIVITY

Admissions Rating	89
# of applicants	11,290
% of applicants accepted	49
% of acceptees attending	26
# offered a place on the wait list	1,837
% accepting a place on wait list	29
% admitted from wait list	18
# of early decision applicants	600
% accepted early decision	69

FRESHMAN PROFILE

Range SAT Critical Reading	550–640
Range SAT Math	570–670
Range SAT Writing	550–650
Range ACT Composite	26–30
Minimum paper TOEFL	550
Minimum internet-based TOEFL	90
% graduated top 10% of class	39
% graduated top 25% of class	79
% graduated top 50% of class	97

DEADLINES

Early decision	
Deadline	11/1
Notification	12/1
Regular	
Priority	11/1
Deadline	2/1
Nonfall registration?	Yes

APPLICANTS ALSO LOOK AT AND OFTEN PREFER

New York University; Rutgers; The State University of New Jersey–New Brunswick; University of Delaware; Villanova University

AND SOMETIMES PREFER

Boston University; Penn State University Park

AND RARELY PREFER

Stevens Institute of Technology

FINANCIAL FACTS

Financial Aid Rating	78
Annual in-state tuition	$10,879
Annual out-of-state tuition	$21,810
Room and board	$12,498
Required fees	$4,587
Books and supplies	$1,200
Average frosh need-based scholarship	$14,316
Average UG need-based scholarship	$12,074
% needy frosh rec. need-based scholarship or grant aid	37
% needy UG rec. need-based scholarship or grant aid	39
% needy frosh rec. non-need-based scholarship or grant aid	31
% needy UG rec. non-need-based scholarship or grant aid	27
% needy frosh rec. need-based self-help aid	66
% needy UG rec. need-based self-help aid	75
% frosh rec. any financial aid	70
% UG rec. any financial aid	62
% frosh need fully met	8
% ugrads need fully met	11
Average % of frosh need met	42
Average % of ugrad need met	46

COLLEGE OF THE OZARKS

OFFICE OF ADMISSIONS, POINT LOOKOUT, MO 65726 • ADMISSIONS: 417-690-2636 • FAX: 417-335-2618

CAMPUS LIFE

Quality of Life Rating	92
Fire Safety Rating	89
Green Rating	70
Type of school	Private
Affiliation	Interdenominational
Environment	Rural

STUDENTS

Total undergrad enrollment	1,452
% male/female	47/53
% from out of state	19
% frosh from public high school	74
% frosh live on campus	92
% ugrads live on campus	82
% African American	1
% Asian	1
% Caucasian	93
% Hispanic	2
% Native American	<1
% Pacific Islander	<1
% Two or more races	2
% Race and/or ethnicity unknown	0
% international	2
# of countries represented	16

SURVEY SAYS...

Lots of conservative students
Students are happy
Career services are great
School is well run
Students are friendly
Diverse student types interact on campus
Students are very religious
Students get along with local community
Recreation facilities are great
Very little drug use
Campus newspaper is popular

ACADEMICS

Academic Rating	80
% students returning for sophomore year	73
% students graduating within 4 years	63
% students graduating within 6 years	73
Calendar	Semester
Student/faculty ratio	14:1
Profs interesting rating	84
Profs accessible rating	81

Most classes have 10–19 students.
Most lab/discussion sessions have
10–19 students.

MOST POPULAR MAJORS

Elementary Education and Teaching; Business
Administration and Management; Agricultural
Business and Management

STUDENTS SAY "..."

Academics

The appeal of College of the Ozarks is simple: "It's a tuition-free, small, Christ-oriented college!" Students come here so they can "graduate debt-free" and get "a free education consisting of hard work and Christian qualities." The school's slogan is "Hard Work U," and students are expected to work hard while receiving a "Christian education" in a "positive environment." The school "works to instill patriotic, academic, Christian, cultural, and vocational morals to all students." An example is how "we are strongly encouraged to respect war veterans and thank them for their service as much as possible." C of O is about "hard work and God!!!" This can sometimes come at a price, as students suggest there could be "more toler-ance for those who think differently." "It seems that some of the new policies and expectations aim to isolate the school from mainstream higher education and I don't agree with that," a mathematics and computer science major says. Students who share the school's values will find "a great place to receive an amazing educa-tion, form lifelong relationships, and deepen [their] faith." C of O professors are "dedicated, intelligent leaders" who "are challenging, but willing to help each student understand in a way that works best for them." "I am willing to brag on for hours on most of my professors," and English major says. "I have never had profes-sors more eager to teach not have I had professors so eager to help you succeed," says another student. Overall, "College of the Ozarks cares for nothing but its stu-dents" and focuses on making them "well rounded citizens rather than making money." One happy Business Administration major explains their decision to attend this way: "As soon as I came through the gates, I saw how beautiful it was. On our tour, EVERYTHING exceeded my expectations. That's when I knew College of the Ozarks was where I wanted to be."

Life

Students enjoy the "safety and the strictness of an alcohol-free campus." As a Christian school, "we have really strict policies about alcohol and drugs" and "although some students party, most do not." Instead, students "participate in school activities or clubs for fun" and "spend any free time outdoors playing games when the weather is nice." The school works hard to organize events on campus "such as dances, competitions, and a variety of other student events." "The school is constantly planning hay rides, drive in movies, and other events," a Nursing student explains. As a school with a strongly religious student body, many students participate in "Bible studies either on or off campus." "Come midnight campus is like a ghost town," perhaps in part because "many students hold jobs in addition to their 'on-campus 15-hour-a-week job.'" While "some of the buildings are very old and sketchy," "in a few years that won't be the case because they have plans of renovation and construction." Students really love "the week-long freshman orien-tation," which leaves incoming students "familiar with the whole campus/campus opportunities" as well as giving them "a solid group of friends." Another student explains that "this entire place is one huge family and you are never bored."

Student Body

The typical C of O student is "hard working," "white, traditional," and a "Christian conservative." "Most of our students" come from a "mid-western small town," especially around the Ozarks. "Students fit in by being hard workers" and are fre-quently described as "very friendly." "Very laid-back, but very driven; an interest-ing dynamic," one student explains. Since students come from "a similar back-ground" they "have no reason to disagree with one another." This means that the school luckily "doesn't have a lot of drama." On the other hand, "C of O is NOT diverse at all," and "one of the most conservative places you will find in the [United States]." The traditional religious values mean "a typical student at C of O is responsible and respectful to authority" while following "high moral standards." If you share those values, you'll find fellow students who are "very friendly, polite, eager to serve and help, and well informed." "There isn't your typical separation of upper and lower class men," one student explains. "It is a privilege to get into this college and we treat everyone like they deserve to be here."

FINANCIAL AID: 417-690-3292 • E-MAIL: ADMISS4@COFO.EDU • WEBSITE: WWW.COFO.EDU

THE PRINCETON REVIEW SAYS

Admissions

Very important factors considered include: rigor of secondary school record, class rank, interview, character/personal qualities. *Important factors considered include:* academic GPA, standardized test scores, recommendation(s), geographical residence, volunteer work, work experience, level of applicant's interest. *Other factors considered include:* extracurricular activities, talent/ability, first generation, alumni/ae relation, state residency, religious affiliation/commitment. SAT or ACT required. ACT with Writing required. SAT with or without Essay component accepted. TOEFL required of all international applicants. High school diploma is required and GED is accepted. *Academic units required:* 4 English, 3 math, 2 science, 1 science lab, 3 history. *Academic units recommended:* 2 foreign language, 3 social studies.

Financial Aid

Students should submit: FAFSA. Priority filing deadline is 2/15. The Princeton Review suggests that all financial aid forms be submitted as soon as possible after October 1. *Need-based scholarships/grants offered:* Federal Pell, FSEOG, State scholarships/grants, Private scholarships, College/university scholarship or grant aid from institutional funds. *Loan aid offered:* Applicants will be notified of awards on or about 7/1. Federal Work-Study Program available. Institutional employment available.

The Inside Word

C of O was founded "to provide the advantages of a Christian education for youth of both sexes, especially those found worthy, but who are without sufficient means to procure such training." The tuition-free education, which requires students to work fifteen hours a week on campus, means that applicants will need to demonstrate their financial need. The school's slogan of "Hard Work U" is not an empty phrase. Applicants will want to showcase a hard work ethic when applying.

THE SCHOOL SAYS "..."

From the Admissions Office

"College of the Ozarks is unique because of its no-tuition, work-study program, but also because it strives to educate the head, the heart, and the hands. At C of O, there are high expectations of students—the college stresses character development as well as study and work. An education from 'Hard Work U.' offers many opportunities, not the least of which is the chance to graduate debt-free. Life at C of O isn't all hard work and no play, however. There are many opportunities for fun. The nearby resort town of Branson, Missouri, offers ample opportunities for recreation and summer employment, and Table Rock Lake, only a few miles away, is a terrific spot to swim, sun, and relax. Numerous on-campus activities such as Mudfest, Luau Night, dances, and holiday parties give students lots of chances for fun without leaving the college. At 'Hard Work U.,' we work hard, but we know how to have fun, too.

"Applicants are required to submit scores from the ACT or the SAT. We will use the student's best scores from either test. Writing scores are not required."

SELECTIVITY
Admissions Rating	96
# of applicants	3,122
% of applicants accepted	12
% of acceptees attending	89
# offered a place on the wait list	865
% accepting a place on wait list	99
% admitted from wait list	0

FRESHMAN PROFILE
Range SAT Critical Reading	455–498
Range SAT Math	495–561
Range SAT Writing	485–534
Range ACT Composite	21–25
Minimum paper TOEFL	550
Minimum internet-based TOEFL	79
Average HS GPA	3.6
% graduated top 10% of class	23
% graduated top 25% of class	61
% graduated top 50% of class	91

DEADLINES
Regular Priority	2/15
Nonfall registration?	No

APPLICANTS ALSO LOOK AT AND OFTEN PREFER
Missouri State University

AND SOMETIMES PREFER
Southwest Baptist University

FINANCIAL FACTS
Financial Aid Rating	90
Annual tuition	$0
Room and board	$6,500
Required fees	$430
Books and supplies	$1,000
Average frosh need-based scholarship	$14,336
Average UG need-based scholarship	$14,917
% needy frosh rec. need-based scholarship or grant aid	100
% needy UG rec. need-based scholarship or grant aid	100
% needy frosh rec. non-need-based scholarship or grant aid	7
% needy UG rec. non-need-based scholarship or grant aid	12
% needy frosh rec. need-based self-help aid	93
% needy UG rec. need-based self-help aid	87
% frosh rec. any financial aid	100
% UG rec. any financial aid	100
% UG borrow to pay for school	7
Average cumulative indebtedness	$5,339
% frosh need fully met	22
% ugrads need fully met	36
Average % of frosh need met	86
Average % of ugrad need met	89

College of Saint Benedict/Saint John's University

37 South College Ave, St. Joseph, MN 56374 • Admissions: 320-363-5055 • Fax: 320-363-5650

CAMPUS LIFE

Quality of Life Rating	91
Fire Safety Rating	97
Green Rating	89
Type of school	Private
Affiliation	Roman Catholic
Environment	Village

STUDENTS

Total undergrad enrollment	3,685
% male/female	47/53
% from out of state	18
% frosh from public high school	75
% frosh live on campus	100
% ugrads live on campus	90
% African American	3
% Asian	4
% Caucasian	80
% Hispanic	6
% Native American	1
% Pacific Islander	<1
% Two or more races	1
% Race and/or ethnicity unknown	0
% international	5
# of countries represented	27

SURVEY SAYS...

Students are happy
Great library
Career services are great
School is well run
Students are friendly
Great food on campus
Campus newspaper is popular
Alumni active on campus

ACADEMICS

Academic Rating	82
% students returning for sophomore year	88
% students graduating within 4 years	73
% students graduating within 6 years	81
Calendar	Semester
Student/faculty ratio	12:1
Profs interesting rating	86
Profs accessible rating	88

Most classes have 10–19 students.
Most lab/discussion sessions have
10–19 students.

MOST POPULAR MAJORS

Business Administration and Management;
Psychology; Biology

STUDENTS SAY "..."

Academics

Minnesota's College of Saint Benedict (for women) and Saint John's University (for men) are two Catholic liberal arts colleges that share one academic program and classes, but retain separate dorms, campuses, and traditions. Students come to this "beautiful, friendly environment" and leave with "a well-rounded education...ready to take on the world." The Benedictine values "are upheld by every student in everyday life" and help breed graduates that are "all about service and making an impact in the world." "This school is a must for any student who wants to feel accepted and a part of a rich community, while at the same time receiving an education that is second to none," says one junior. Professors truly take to heart the feedback they receive from their students, are "extremely dedicated and passionate," and "are willing to work...on projects outside of class even if it means extra work for them." They "are interested in us figuring things out for ourselves" and are "big on [students] being prepared for class so more time can be spend discussing or practicing material instead of lecturing." The ultimate testament to faculty involvement: "At CSB/SJU, I have never had a professor that has struggled to know my name (besides the fact that I am a twin)." Discussion is "lively" (particularly in upper division courses), and students "are offered many great opportunities to further our experiences and education." The open environment "does what it can to help students feel comfortable and learn."

The school provides "excellent scientific and business opportunities" and "endless connections with not only other schools across the nation, but.... across the world" that aid in post-undergraduate employment or continued education opportunities. The "incredible" study abroad program sees a large number of students take advantage of it at some point in their college careers.

Life

The school "really makes sure your transition into your first semester runs smoothly" and that students "have a lot of options for meeting new people." The Student Activities and Leadership Development Office plans "large campus events such as orientation and Thanksgiving dinners," and also has an "inspired leaders series" of after-hours classes taught by professors that promote leadership on campus. On weekends, students often take adventure trips (like "California Surfing trips, Boundary Waters canoe trips, and Colorado climbing trips") with the school's Peer Resource Program.

School pride is "ridiculous" at CSB/SJU and athletic events "are the high points for entertainment," especially against rival St. Thomas. For fun, students take advantage of the school's "rich recreational abilities" both in the arboretum and on nearby waterways, where "ice fishing, fishing, hiking, and hanging out at the beach are popular." "The warm months of the year are awesome with the lake/raft open. It feels like a summer camp," says a student. Many students "do go out on the weekends" to parties or bars, but there is an "outstanding campus programming board" that plans events every weekend on campus as an alternative to drinking. "As long as you can step out that door and make good use of your time, you'll have an amazing time," assures a sophomore.

Student Body

Most of the "Johnnies" and "Bennies" here are "from Minnesota or the surrounding states," are "hard-working, fun-loving," and "believe in the importance of education." Not surprisingly, the majority are Catholic and take "'Minnesota Nice' to a whole new level": "Expect to have doors open for you [and] people smile and greet you on occasion when you're passing by." People have no trouble finding a friend group with related interests via "the many clubs and activities that are offered." "Everyone fits like a puzzle piece" and students "commonly have social issues that they are passionate about, such as gender equality, sustainability, [or] health and wellness."

FINANCIAL AID: 320-363-5388 • E-MAIL: ADMISSIONS@CSBSJU.EDU • WEBSITE: WWW.CSBSJU.EDU

THE PRINCETON REVIEW SAYS

Admissions

Very important factors considered include: rigor of secondary school record, academic GPA, standardized test scores, extracurricular activities. *Important factors considered include:* class rank, application essay, recommendation(s), alumni/ae relation. *Other factors considered include:* interview, talent/ability, character/personal qualities, first generation, geographical residence, volunteer work, work experience. SAT or ACT required. ACT with or without writing accepted. SAT with or without Essay component accepted. TOEFL required of all international applicants. High school diploma is required and GED is accepted. *Academic units required:* 4 English, 3 math, 2 science, 2 science labs, 2 social studies, 4 academic electives. *Academic units recommended:* 2 foreign language.

Financial Aid

Students should submit: FAFSA, Institution's own financial aid form. Priority filing deadline is 3/15.The Princeton Review suggests that all financial aid forms be submitted as soon as possible after October 1. *Need-based scholarships/ grants offered:* Federal Pell, FSEOG, State scholarships/grants, College/university scholarship or grant aid from institutional funds. *Loan aid offered:* Direct Subsidized Stafford Loans, Direct Unsubsidized Stafford Loans, Direct PLUS loans, Federal Perkins Loans, State Loans. Applicants will be notified of awards on a rolling basis beginning 3/15. Federal Work-Study Program available. Institutional employment available.

The Inside Word

Students with decent grades and a few extracurricular activities that "show promise of community contribution" shouldn't have any problem getting into CSB/SJU. You may apply to CSB/SJU using the Common Application or by using the school's CSBSJU GET INspired application—the school doesn't have a preference.

THE SCHOOL SAYS ". . ."

From the Admissions Office

"The College of Saint Benedict (CSB), for women, and Saint John's University (SJU), for men, are nationally recognized Catholic liberal arts colleges and ranked as two of the top three Catholic colleges in the nation. They share one academic program, and students attend classes together on both campuses. This integrated learning experience combines a challenging academic program with extensive opportunities for international study, leadership, service learning, spiritual growth and cultural and athletic involvement. We provide students access to the resources of not one, but two nationally leading liberal arts colleges through a common undergraduate curriculum, identical degree requirements, and a single academic calendar. We are committed to the development of the whole person, meeting the unique needs of both women and men in single-gender and co-educational experiences—experiences that could not be provided by traditional single-sex colleges and would not typically be provided by co-educational colleges. The colleges are part of a centuries-old Benedictine tradition of faith, learning, and community. Hospitality, community, stewardship and service to the common good are bedrock Benedictine values expressed throughout the curriculum and the co-curriculum. We are part of a Catholic intellectual tradition committed to openness, intellectual inquiry, and the lively engagement of faith and reason. The colleges are committed to global learning and connection. We provide international study programs on six continents and are annually ranked among the top three baccalaureate colleges nationally in the number of students completing semester-long study abroad. More than half of all students study abroad before they graduate–an international study participation rate significantly higher than the national average for liberal arts colleges. More than 200 academic courses have an international component or global emphasis. One-third of our faculty has led a study abroad program. We enroll nearly 200 students from more than thirty countries, creating an enriching and culturally diverse global experience on campus. CSB/SJU annually rank first or second among Minnesota's private colleges for the number of undergraduate international students."

SELECTIVITY

Admissions Rating	80
# of applicants	3,465
% of applicants accepted	74
% of acceptees attending	36

FRESHMAN PROFILE

Range SAT Critical Reading	480–570
Range SAT Math	450–580
Range SAT Writing	470–550
Range ACT Composite	22–28
Minimum paper TOEFL	550
Minimum internet-based TOEFL	80
Average HS GPA	3.5
% graduated top 10% of class	27
% graduated top 25% of class	55
% graduated top 50% of class	89

DEADLINES

Early action	
Deadline	11/15
Notification	12/15
Regular	
Priority	11/15
Notification	4/1
Nonfall registration?	Yes

APPLICANTS ALSO LOOK AT AND OFTEN PREFER

St. Olaf College; University of Minnesota–Twin Cities Campus; University of Wisconsin–Madison

FINANCIAL FACTS

Financial Aid Rating	87
Annual tuition	$39,850
Room and board	$10,229
Required fees	$996
Books and supplies	$1,000
Average frosh need-based scholarship	$29,032
Average UG need-based scholarship	$27,019
% needy frosh rec. need-based scholarship or grant aid	98
% needy UG rec. need-based scholarship or grant aid	99
% needy frosh rec. non-need-based scholarship or grant aid	95
% needy UG rec. non-need-based scholarship or grant aid	95
% needy frosh rec. need-based self-help aid	94
% needy UG rec. need-based self-help aid	94
% frosh rec. any financial aid	95
% UG rec. any financial aid	94
% UG borrow to pay for school	71
Average cumulative indebtedness	$39,588
% frosh need fully met	38
% ugrads need fully met	37
Average % of frosh need met	92
Average % of ugrad need met	90

THE COLLEGE OF WILLIAM & MARY

OFFICE OF ADMISSIONS, PO BOX 8795, WILLIAMSBURG, VA 23187-8795 • ADMISSIONS: 757-221-4223 • FAX: 757-221-1242

CAMPUS LIFE

Quality of Life Rating	94
Fire Safety Rating	91
Green Rating	76
Type of school	Public
Affiliation	No Affiliation
Environment	Village

STUDENTS

Total undergrad enrollment	6,301
% male/female	44/56
% from out of state	30
% frosh from public high school	77
% frosh live on campus	100
% ugrads live on campus	74
# of fraternities (% ugrad men join)	17 (26)
# of sororities (% ugrad women join)	13 (34)
% African American	7
% Asian	8
% Caucasian	59
% Hispanic	9
% Native American	<1
% Pacific Islander	0
% Two or more races	4
% Race and/or ethnicity unknown	6
% international	6
# of countries represented	54

SURVEY SAYS...

Students are happy
Lab facilities are great
Great library
Career services are great
Internships are widely available
School is well run
No one cheats
Students are friendly
Diverse student types interact on campus
Students involved in community service
Students environmentally aware
Recreation facilities are great

ACADEMICS

Academic Rating	89
% students returning for sophomore year	96
% students graduating within 4 years	82
% students graduating within 6 years	90
Calendar	Semester
Student/faculty ratio	12:1
Profs interesting rating	89
Profs accessible rating	93

MOST POPULAR MAJORS
Business, English, Psychology

STUDENTS SAY "..."

Academics

Students at The College of William & Mary are extraordinarily happy with their overall experience and with their academics in particular. One student sums up the school's vibe by saying, "William & Mary achieves a remarkable balance between the dynamic, progressive academics of a liberal arts college and the strong sense of history and tradition one would expect from America's second-oldest school." "There are endless and amazing" opportunities here, with an emphasis on undergraduate research that makes W&M unique among small liberal arts schools. "Professors will engage you outside of the classroom and give you the opportunity to conduct your own research project, even in a non-science curriculum." Many "are often in newspapers and magazines and have relevant and copious work experience in the subjects they're teaching." Across the board, "professors are one of the best things about W&M." They "are always accessible for extra help," and "they also really take the time to get to know their students outside of the classroom." In the classroom, "William & Mary professors truly know how to balance lecture with discussion. Especially in traditionally lecture-based subjects, like history, professors devote a lot of class time to discussion to understand what students think." Slackers take note: "Professors expect a lot of work outside of class," and "classes usually require a good amount of reading, especially for the humanities." All this hard work is very rewarding, though, with many upperclassmen and graduating seniors expressing how well-prepared they feel for the "real-world," and one student says that the professors "have upended the way I thought about their subject, opening completely new veins of inquiry."

Life

When students describe campus life at W&M, the word community comes up—a lot. And this community "is made up of incredibly involved, dedicated, and supportive students who have big dreams and big fun," who say: "We study hard, but we know how to have fun, too." Alma Mater Productions (AMP), the college programming board, "sponsors a lot of different events that are well-attended, including...comedians, music artists, movies, etc." Student organizations are also very strong, from intramural sports, some form of which "almost everyone plays," to arts organizations such as "the William & Mary Symphony Orchestra, three university choirs, the Middle Eastern Music Ensemble, an Early Music Ensemble, an Appalachian string band, a small chamber orchestra, eleven a cappella groups and...two all-student theater companies." "On the weekends, there is always a party to go to" and "the Greek community is very inclusive." Off campus, students enjoy the charms of Colonial Williamsburg, theme park Busch Gardens, Jamestown Beach on the James River, and "great outlet shopping!" Despite a few gripes about parking (which are common on a small campus), students are generally happy with their facilities, with the library and the business school receiving special mention.

Student Body

Students are quick to note that there's a generalization that the "T.W.A.M.P., or Typical William & Mary Person...is the person [who] does all their reading, shows up to class every day, and is a nerd," but most are equally quick to cast this stereotype aside. The real T.W.A.M.P., they tell us, is "open-minded, outgoing, charismatic, driven, dedicated, caring, and unique." The school is full of "well-rounded people who are in touch with their inner nerd," and "intellectual people who care about the world find the zaniest ways to have fun." "Students fit in many social circles," and students credit the close bonding that happens in freshmen dorms for this inclusivity. "You will often see the members of the football team in the library as much as any other student," and "everyone is involved with at least one other thing outside of class, and often...about ten other things." "Students are an eclectic bunch united by our thirst for knowledge and overwhelming Tribe Pride."

FINANCIAL AID: 757-221-2420 • E-MAIL: ADMISSION@WM.EDU • WEBSITE: WWW.WM.EDU

THE PRINCETON REVIEW SAYS

Admissions

Very important factors considered include: rigor of secondary school record, class rank, academic GPA, standardized test scores, application essay, recommendation(s), extracurricular activities, talent/ability, character/personal qualities, state residency, volunteer work, work experience. *Important factors considered include: Other factors considered include:* interview, first generation, alumni/ae relation, geographical residence, racial/ethnic status. SAT or ACT required; SAT Subject Tests considered if submitted. ACT with or without writing accepted. SAT with or without Essay component accepted. TOEFL required of all international applicants. High school diploma or equivalent is not required. *Academic units recommended:* 4 English, 4 math, 4 science, 3 science labs, 4 foreign language, 4 social studies.

Financial Aid

Students should submit: FAFSA, CSS/Financial Aid PROFILE.The Princeton Review suggests that all financial aid forms be submitted as soon as possible after October 1. *Need-based scholarships/grants offered:* Federal Pell, FSEOG, State scholarships/grants, Private scholarships, College/university scholarship or grant aid from institutional funds. *Loan aid offered:* Direct Subsidized Stafford Loans, Direct Unsubsidized Stafford Loans, Direct PLUS loans, Federal Perkins Loans. Federal Work-Study Program available. Institutional employment available.

The Inside Word

The volume of applications at W&M is extremely high; thus, admission is ultra-competitive. Only very strong students from out of state should apply. The large applicant pool necessitates a labor-intensive candidate evaluation process; each admissions officer reads roughly 150 application folders per week during the peak review season. But this is one admissions committee that moves fast without sacrificing a thorough holistic review. There probably isn't a tougher public college admissions committee in the country.

THE SCHOOL SAYS "..."

From the Admissions Office

"William & Mary is the nation's second-oldest college and preeminent small public university. Yes, we have one of the lowest student/faculty ratio (twelve to one) of any public university. We're also known for having one of the most successful undergraduate business programs in the United States, a model United Nations team that perennially vies for the world championship, and extensive opportunities for undergraduate research. Students at William & Mary follow in the footsteps of alumni ranging from Thomas Jefferson, James Monroe, and John Tyler to Comedy Central's Jon Stewart, Academy Award nominee Glenn Close, Chancellor and former Secretary of Defense Robert Gates, and Super Bowl-winning Pittsburg Steeler's coach Mike Tomlin. In short, William & Mary offers a top-rated educational experience at a comparatively low cost and in the company of interesting people from a broad variety of backgrounds. If you are an academically strong, involved student looking for a challenge in a great campus community, William & Mary may well be the place for you."

SELECTIVITY

Admissions Rating	96
# of applicants	14,952
% of applicants accepted	34
% of acceptees attending	29
# offered a place on the wait list	3,552
% accepting a place on wait list	47
% admitted from wait list	11
# of early decision applicants	1,070
% accepted early decision	50

FRESHMAN PROFILE

Range SAT Critical Reading	630–730
Range SAT Math	630–730
Range SAT Writing	620–720
Range ACT Composite	28–32
Minimum paper TOEFL	600
Minimum internet-based TOEFL	100
Average HS GPA	4.2
% graduated top 10% of class	81
% graduated top 25% of class	96
% graduated top 50% of class	100

DEADLINES

Early decision	
Deadline	11/1
Notification	12/1
Regular	
Deadline	1/1
Notification	4/1
Nonfall registration?	No

APPLICANTS ALSO LOOK AT AND SOMETIMES PREFER

Duke University; Georgetown University; University of Virginia; The University of North Carolina at Chapel Hill; Cornell University; Princeton University; Dartmouth College; Vanderbilt University

FINANCIAL FACTS

Financial Aid Rating	82
% needy frosh rec. need-based scholarship or grant aid	0
% needy UG rec. need-based scholarship or grant aid	0
% needy frosh rec. non-need-based scholarship or grant aid	0
% needy UG rec. non-need-based scholarship or grant aid	0
% needy frosh rec. need-based self-help aid	0
% needy UG rec. need-based self-help aid	0
% frosh rec. any financial aid	54
% UG rec. any financial aid	53

THE COLLEGE OF WOOSTER

847 COLLEGE AVENUE, WOOSTER, OH 44691 • ADMISSIONS: 330-263-2322 • FAX: 330-263-2621

STUDENTS SAY "..."

Academics

The College of Wooster is small, personable "tight-knit community" that offers "a truly stellar education" to those who attend. Mentoring is a huge focal point of Wooster's academics, and the "resources are endless" for those looking to take advantage of things like "numerous opportunities for research and internships." Independent study is a highlight of the undergraduate experience, and the school "teaches research and how to apply skills learned to the outside world." This "very open school" challenges its student to succeed both in and out of the classroom, and "the staff pushes [the college] to change with the times in the classroom and around the campus."

Professors at Wooster are "hidden gems" who are all "very passionate about their subjects" and their goal "to shape their students into lifelong learners." "It's as if your professor is your colleague on your quest for eternal knowledge," says a freshman. These intimate ties between student and professor are "what makes Wooster such an incredible place." "My professors, both past and present, know more than just my name," says a student. "My success is a product of my professors' enthusiasm towards their subject matter and our futures," says another. The work may be "challenging," but it "teaches students how to write exceptionally," and there is "plenty of help from professors, TAs, [and] peer tutoring." "Collaborative work and experience" are stressed, and classes are set up "in a way that allows people to learn from their peers as well as their professors."

Research plays a "huge" role at Wooster, especially with senior year Independent Study, when students are given the opportunity to work with a faculty mentor on a project in any topic they are passionate about—and "they can do so much with it." The institution is also aware of the effort that students must put in to have success and "is realistic in its expectations for students' learning." "Wooster is a community of learners working together to help one another reach their full potential and goals," says a sophomore chemistry major.

Life

"The character of the campus community is friendly beyond measure" at this "dazzling" campus. People are usually "busy in the library doing homework or working on their Independent Studies," but everyone finds time for (typically multiple) extracurriculars, which "run the gamut of recreational pastimes." "We have just as many students in our music ensembles as we do that play sports," says a student. People enjoy using the weekends to relieve the stress of a rigorous academic schedule, and the majority enjoy "social drinking" at the fraternity or program houses, or going to the on-campus club called "the Underground" on Friday nights.

For those who choose not to party, there are "many other recreational activities for those who are not in sports or who do not enjoy drinking," and the college "is very good at bringing in entertainment," such as "comedians, professional music artists, and forum speakers which are all free to students." A student run weekly flyer, *The Pot*, helps "keep students up to date on all of the campus events happening." A lot of the time, though, "students will just hang out together and relax."

Student Body

"The life force of this school is really our fantastic student body," says a student. This "unparalleled" community is made up of "quite a range of people," but most are "quirky," "friendly," "open-minded," and "liberal." It's also a "very involved" student body ("school spirit is huge at Wooster"), so a typical COW kid "tends to be in a hodgepodge of sports, clubs, music groups, etc. that suit their fancy." There are "very few social cliques" and everyone is friendly and "willing to interact with one another." Students here are "very accepting of different personalities, beliefs, and ways of life."

FINANCIAL AID: 800-877-3688 • E-MAIL: ADMISSIONS@WOOSTER.EDU • WEBSITE: WWW.WOOSTER.EDU

THE PRINCETON REVIEW SAYS

Admissions

Very important factors considered include: rigor of secondary school record, academic GPA. *Important factors considered include:* class rank, standardized test scores, application essay, recommendation(s), interview, extracurricular activities, character/personal qualities, level of applicant's interest. *Other factors considered include:* talent/ability, first generation, alumni/ae relation, geographical residence, state residency, racial/ethnic status, volunteer work, work experience. SAT or ACT required. ACT with Writing recommended. SAT with Essay component recommended. TOEFL required of all international applicants. High school diploma is required and GED is accepted. *Academic units required:* 4 English, 3 math, 3 science, 2 science labs, 2 foreign language, 3 social studies, 1 academic elective.

Financial Aid

Students should submit: FAFSA, Institution's own financial aid form, CSS/Financial Aid PROFILE. Priority filing deadline is 2/15. The Princeton Review suggests that all financial aid forms be submitted as soon as possible after October 1. *Need-based scholarships/grants offered:* Federal Pell, FSEOG, State scholarships/grants, Private scholarships, College/university scholarship or grant aid from institutional funds, United Negro College Fund. *Loan aid offered:* Direct Subsidized Stafford Loans, Direct Unsubsidized Stafford Loans, Direct PLUS loans, Federal Perkins Loans. Applicants will be notified of awards on a rolling basis beginning 3/15. Federal Work-Study Program available. Institutional employment available.

The Inside Word

The College of Wooster is a small, selective liberal arts school in a region of the country where there are quite a few small, selective liberal arts schools. For the most part, only solid students get past the gatekeepers here, and you should expect a thorough review of your application. Nevertheless, the admit rate is high. Stiff competition from similar institutions means the school will occasionally admit students who don't have stellar academic records.

THE SCHOOL SAYS "..."

From the Admissions Office

"The College of Wooster is America's premier college for mentored undergraduate research. Our mission is to graduate educated, not merely trained, people; to produce responsible, independent thinkers, rather than specialists in any given field. Our commitment to independence is especially evident in IS, the college's distinctive program in which every senior works one-to-one with a faculty mentor to complete a project in the major. IS comes from 'independent study,' but, in reality, it is an intellectual collaboration of the highest order and permits every student the freedom to pursue something in which he or she is passionately interested. IS is the centerpiece of an innovative curriculum. More than just the project itself, the culture that sustains IS—and, in turn, is sustained by IS—is an extraordinary college culture. The same attitudes of student initiative, openness, flexibility, and individual support enrich every aspect of Wooster's vital residential college life."

SELECTIVITY

Admissions Rating	88
# of applicants	5,748
% of applicants accepted	55
% of acceptees attending	18
# offered a place on the wait list	726
% accepting a place on wait list	9
% admitted from wait list	15
# of early decision applicants	130
% accepted early decision	65

FRESHMAN PROFILE

Range SAT Critical Reading	540–670
Range SAT Math	560–680
Range SAT Writing	540–650
Range ACT Composite	25–30
Minimum internet-based TOEFL	81
Average HS GPA	3.7
% graduated top 10% of class	46
% graduated top 25% of class	70

DEADLINES

Early decision	
Deadline	11/1
Notification	11/15
Other ED	
Deadline	1/15
Notification	2/1
Early action	
Deadline	11/15
Notification	12/31
Regular	
Deadline	2/15
Notification	4/1
Nonfall registration?	Yes

FINANCIAL FACTS

Financial Aid Rating	90
Annual tuition	$44,520
Room and board	$10,650
Required fees	$430
Books and supplies	$1,000
Average frosh need-based scholarship	$29,714
Average UG need-based scholarship	$29,842
% needy frosh rec. need-based scholarship or grant aid	97
% needy UG rec. need-based scholarship or grant aid	98
% needy frosh rec. non-need-based scholarship or grant aid	23
% needy UG rec. non-need-based scholarship or grant aid	14
% needy frosh rec. need-based self-help aid	73
% needy UG rec. need-based self-help aid	81
% frosh rec. any financial aid	99
% UG rec. any financial aid	99
% UG borrow to pay for school	62
Average cumulative indebtedness	$27,946
% frosh need fully met	60
% ugrads need fully met	50
Average % of frosh need met	95
Average % of ugrad need met	92

COLORADO COLLEGE

14 EAST CACHE LA POUDRE STREET, COLORADO SPRINGS, CO 80903 • ADMISSIONS: 719-389-6344 • FAX: 719-389-6816

STUDENTS SAY ". . ."

Academics
Students are drawn to Colorado College for its unique "Block Plan," in which students take one intensive class at a time. The academic year is structured as eight blocks of three to five weeks each, punctuated by five-day "block breaks." Students find the Block Plan empowers them to participate in "a strongly immersive approach to education," reporting that "the classes are very challenging, but after cramming in a semester's worth of calculus in four weeks, you basically feel like you can conquer anything." "Colorado College abhors mediocrity; either you succeed more than you ever thought possible, or fail in spectacular ways." Academically, students "love the class sizes and classes. I feel fully invested in each class I take here." The "intense and exhausting" pace of block classes bonds students and professors: "My professors have given me more opportunities for growth and cared more than I ever imagined they would. I have yet to have a professor whose home I haven't been to and family I haven't met." "In my last block the professor was spending the whole morning afternoon—and evening—with us!" "My professors appear to be geniuses in their respective fields...I have been amazed at the extent to which the block plan allows each student to delve into their course material." The "small classes" "do away with student anonymity" and "foster excellent discussion and intellectual growth." Students also appreciate the "internship opportunities" and "preparation for post-graduation" offered by the school, often in concert with the "ability to study off campus or abroad." Colorado College undergrads see their objective as "pursuing excellence through diverse and rich viewpoints" and "immersion in a dynamic array of intellectual endeavors." "My school emphasizes an attitude of working diligently, so that free time can be appreciated to its fullest." "They genuinely value the college's "great support system and connections," which make "opportunities to learn off campus" "accessible." "The shared values of intellectual engagement, physical and mental health, passion, and a sense of adventure define Colorado College's spirit."

Life
Students call the Colorado College experience one of "focused study in a Rocky Mountain environment." "Looking at Pikes Peak is a constant reminder about how beautiful of a state we are in." "Outdoor activities are a big thing here," and indeed, another student observes that "slacklining, doing homework in the sun, and playing guitar on the lawn all happen when it's nice out. Sledding and skiing down campus hills, snowball fights, and fire pits happen in the winter." Despite this athletic emphasis, "people are pretty accepting [of] what you like doing for fun" and "the common slang is 'you do you'... Another thing I like is there is no peer pressure to get involved with substances." "You really don't have to leave campus if you don't want to," but if you do, downtown Colorado Springs "is only about a ten minute walk from campus, and there are many interesting restaurants to dine at for special occasions or a fun night out." "Life at school is very busy," and CC students like it that way: "People think about how to have fun after intense weeks or blocks." In sum, a "Colorado College experience is" one of "non-competitive, non-judgmental, intellectual and physical adventure on the Block Plan in the little warm nest of the Rockies."

Student Body
Colorado College undergrads respect each other, saying that "everyone here is very intelligent" and "almost everyone was a valedictorian or salutatorian." In equal measure, "CC students have passion for academic and outdoor pursuits," as evidenced by one student's depiction of "intellectual discussion about our impact on nature while rock climbing." Students do say things like, "CC is great but there are rich hippies everywhere," and the school "is not very diverse, which is one of the main improvements I would like to see in the future." That said, students see well beyond themselves: "The typical student is well-traveled, intelligent...quirky, outdoorsy, and a bit of a hipster." CC students "are usually very accepting and friendly," as well as "largely involved with their community, environment and academics" and "very vocal about their opinions."

COLORADO COLLEGE

FINANCIAL AID: 719-389-6651 • E-MAIL: ADMISSION@COLORADOCOLLEGE.EDU • WEBSITE: WWW.COLORADOCOLLEGE.EDU

THE PRINCETON REVIEW SAYS

Admissions

Very important factors considered include: rigor of secondary school record. *Important factors considered include:* class rank, academic GPA, standardized test scores, application essay, recommendation(s), interview, extracurricular activities. *Other factors considered include:* talent/ability, character/personal qualities, first generation, alumni/ae relation, religious affiliation/commitment, racial/ethnic status, volunteer work, work experience, level of applicant's interest. SAT or ACT required for some; SAT Subject Tests required for some. ACT with or without writing accepted. SAT with or without Essay component accepted. High school diploma or equivalent is not required. *Academic units required:* 4 English.

Financial Aid

Students should submit: FAFSA, CSS/Financial Aid PROFILE, Noncustodial PROFILE. Regular filing deadline is 2/15. The Princeton Review suggests that all financial aid forms be submitted as soon as possible after October 1. *Need-based scholarships/grants offered:* Federal Pell, FSEOG, State scholarships/grants, Private scholarships, College/university scholarship or grant aid from institutional funds. *Loan aid offered:* Direct Subsidized Stafford Loans, Direct Unsubsidized Stafford Loans, Direct PLUS loans, Federal Perkins Loans. Applicants will be notified of awards on or about 3/15. Federal Work-Study Program available. Institutional employment available.

The Inside Word

Admission at Colorado College is highly competitive, with over 95 percent of the student body accepted for fall 2014 graduated in the top quarter of their high school class. The rigor of the block program requires students to demonstrate self-motivation and commitment to both academics and extracurriculars, and strong writing skills are considered essential to the application. CC has a "test flexible" policy that allows applicants to submit the combination of scores that will best support their application. Interviews and arts supplements are non-required application options; students who feel their strengths will be showcased by these options should carefully consider them.

THE SCHOOL SAYS " . . ."

From the Admissions Office

"Students enter Colorado College for the opportunity to study intensely in small learning communities. Groups of students work closely with one another and faculty in discussion-based classes and hands-on labs. CC encourages a well-rounded education, combining the academic rigor of a traditional liberal arts college, with the focus and flexibility of the block plan. Rich programs in athletics, community service, student government, and the arts balance an engaged student life. The college encourages students to push themselves academically, and many continue their studies at the best graduate and professional schools in the nation. Because roughly 81 percent of students study abroad while at CC, the college has been recognized as a national leader in international education. The block plan allows classes to incorporate field study into the curriculum, whether studying winter field ecology at the CC Cabin or Dante and Michelangelo in Italy. Its location at the base of the Rockies makes CC a great choice for students who enjoy backpacking, hiking, climbing, and skiing.

"Colorado College adopted a flexible testing policy, beginning with the 2015 class. We require that applicants submit either the SAT Reasoning Test or ACT or elect a third option, including three exams of the applicant's choice, chosen from a list of acceptable exams."

SELECTIVITY

Admissions Rating	97
# of applicants	8,062
% of applicants accepted	17
% of acceptees attending	42
# offered a place on the wait list	1,119
% accepting a place on wait list	21
% admitted from wait list	10
# of early decision applicants	875
% accepted early decision	30

FRESHMAN PROFILE

Range SAT Critical Reading	630–710
Range SAT Math	620–710
Range SAT Writing	620–700
Range ACT Composite	28–32
% graduated top 10% of class	68
% graduated top 25% of class	91
% graduated top 50% of class	100

DEADLINES

Early decision	
Deadline	11/15
Notification	12/15
Early action	
Deadline	11/15
Notification	12/18
Regular	
Priority	1/15
Deadline	1/15
Notification	4/1
Nonfall registration?	Yes

FINANCIAL FACTS

Financial Aid Rating	96
Annual tuition	$48,576
Room and board	$11,215
Required fees	$420
Books and supplies	$1,248
Average frosh need-based scholarship	$45,232
Average UG need-based scholarship	$40,539
% needy frosh rec. need-based scholarship or grant aid	97
% needy UG rec. need-based scholarship or grant aid	96
% needy frosh rec. non-need-based scholarship or grant aid	31
% needy UG rec. non-need-based scholarship or grant aid	19
% needy frosh rec. need-based self-help aid	71
% needy UG rec. need-based self-help aid	76
% frosh rec. any financial aid	57
% UG rec. any financial aid	54
% UG borrow to pay for school	37
Average cumulative indebtedness	$22,068
% frosh need fully met	100
% ugrads need fully met	99
Average % of frosh need met	100
Average % of ugrad need met	100

COLORADO STATE UNIVERSITY

1062 CAMPUS DELIVERY, FORT COLLINS, CO 80523-1062 • ADMISSIONS: 970-491-6909 • FAX: 970-491-7799

CAMPUS LIFE

Quality of Life Rating	95
Fire Safety Rating	88
Green Rating	99
Type of school	Public
Affiliation	No Affiliation
Environment	City

STUDENTS

Total undergrad enrollment	24,433
% male/female	49/51
% from out of state	21
% frosh live on campus	95
% ugrads live on campus	27
# of fraternities (% ugrad men join)	24 (9)
# of sororities (% ugrad women join)	18 (12)
% African American	2
% Asian	2
% Caucasian	73
% Hispanic	11
% Native American	1
% Pacific Islander	<1
% Two or more races	2
% Race and/or ethnicity unknown	4
% international	4
# of countries represented	66

SURVEY SAYS...

Students are happy
Career services are great
School is well run
Students get along with local community
Students love Fort Collins, CO
Great off-campus food
Recreation facilities are great
Campus newspaper is popular

ACADEMICS

Academic Rating	74
% students returning for sophomore year	87
% students graduating within 4 years	41
% students graduating within 6 years	68
Calendar	Semester
Student/faculty ratio	16:1
Profs interesting rating	76
Profs accessible rating	78

Most classes have 10–19 students.
Most lab/discussion sessions have
20–29 students.

MOST POPULAR MAJORS

Mechanical Engineering; Biology; Psychology

STUDENTS SAY "..."

Academics

Colorado State University provides its 30,000 students with numerous academic resources that guide them toward academic success. Even in light of its size, there is "open communication" between students and the administration, and "the institution strives to prepare students with hands-on experience while they are students so they can be prepared in the real world." This "hidden gem" offers a "wonderful education, friendly people, and awesome culture," along with "excellent" green efforts, a strong engineering program, and myriad research opportunities. CSU also cares about its students becoming active members in the community ("Social responsibility, ethics, and sustainability play a large part in our education at CSU," one student says), and the school is quite connected with its hometown of Fort Collins.

Most professors are "willing to help you however way they can"; their feedback is "honest and beneficial for students." "Our professors genuinely care, and they leave their legacy on campus by helping students network and make an impact in the community," says a student. For those in need of extra assistance, there is free tutoring offered for classes in the College of Natural Sciences and College of Liberal Arts. Even though it is a large campus, the school has "so many ways to meet people and create communities on campus that really help you succeed." Green is god here; no matter what aspect of the university you look at, "everyone is concerned with how their actions affect the environment," and "many majors look toward educating their students about job opportunities in the green job force." As for the working world, "an education at CSU is valued and therefore opens up many career opportunities." The college also "does a great job or bringing resources to campus through speakers, panels, and career fairs."

Life

"People enjoy each other here; they enjoy life here." "Bike-friendly" Fort Collins offers a "big-city, small-town life that is green but not pretentious." When everyone is done with the various meetings they have that evening, they "most likely enjoy some great food in our Old Town then head to the nice nightlife in the area." "Fort Collins is such a fun town with fabulous food and many things to do. There is always something to do around here: go to a concert, go shopping, spend a day in the mountains," says a student. "Living in Colorado encourages us to be better students so we can go outside and enjoy why we live in this beautiful state." People are "definitely more outdoors-oriented"; year-round sports are expected—on the weekends "lots of people will rock-climb, trail-run, bike, ski, snowboard, or ice-climb"—and "the gym is always busy." Once in a while, students go to Denver or Boulder "just to try something new," such as malls, the aquarium, or attending sports games—though CSU football gets some criticism from students due to its performance. Basically, life is "usually hectic, yet productive."

Student Body

CSU is "probably the friendliest campus I visited," according to many students. Rams are "chill and outgoing," "well-rounded, physically fit," and "place an emphasis on grades." They are "laid-back but serious about studies," and they "want to succeed, but also like to have fun outside of class." Most are "generally very involved either in the campus community or the Fort Collins community whether it is with service, jobs, or community events." Everyone here "finds their comfort zone in some way or another, and it seems to work for everyone."

COLORADO STATE UNIVERSITY

FINANCIAL AID: 970-491-6321 • E-MAIL: ADMISSIONS@COLOSTATE.EDU • WEBSITE: WWW.COLOSTATE.EDU

THE PRINCETON REVIEW SAYS

Admissions

Very important factors considered include: rigor of secondary school record, academic GPA. *Important factors considered include:* class rank, standardized test scores, application essay, recommendation(s). *Other factors considered include:* extracurricular activities, talent/ability, character/personal qualities, first generation, alumni/ae relation, geographical residence, volunteer work, work experience. SAT or ACT required. ACT with or without writing accepted. SAT with or without Essay component accepted. TOEFL required of all international applicants. High school diploma is required and GED is accepted. *Academic units required:* 4 English, 4 math, 3 science, 2 science labs, 1 foreign language, 2 social studies, 1 history, 2 academic electives. *Academic units recommended:* 4 English, 4 math, 3 science, 2 science labs, 2 foreign language, 2 social studies, 1 history, 2 academic electives.

Financial Aid

Students should submit: FAFSA, CSS/Financial Aid PROFILE, Noncustodial PROFILE. Priority filing deadline is 3/1. The Princeton Review suggests that all financial aid forms be submitted as soon as possible after October 1. *Need-based scholarships/grants offered:* Federal Pell, FSEOG, State scholarships/grants, Private scholarships, College/university scholarship or grant aid from institutional funds. *Loan aid offered:* Direct Subsidized Stafford Loans, Direct Unsubsidized Stafford Loans, Direct PLUS loans, Federal Perkins Loans. Applicants will be notified of awards on a rolling basis beginning 3/1. Federal Work-Study Program available. Institutional employment available.

The Inside Word

Colorado State University admits about eight out of ten applicants; the primary task of its admissions office is to determine who not to admit. Certain majors and programs are more competitive and impose additional admissions qualifications. Art and design programs, for example, require a portfolio review; programs in art, biomedical sciences, business, computer science, engineering, and technical journalism impose higher GPA and standardized test score floors than the school's other programs.

THE SCHOOL SAYS " . . ."

From the Admissions Office

"As one of the nation's premier research universities, Colorado State offers more than 150 undergraduate programs of study in eight colleges. Students come here from fifty states and eighty-five countries, and they appreciate the quality and breadth of the university's academic offerings. But Colorado State is more than just a place where students can take their scholarship to the highest level. It's also a place where they can gain invaluable experience in the fields of their choice, whether they're immersing themselves in professional internships, studying on the other side of the globe or teaming up with faculty on groundbreaking research projects. In addition to an outstanding experiential learning environment, Colorado State students enjoy a sense of community that's unusual for a large university. They develop meaningful relationships with faculty members who bring out their best work, and they live and learn with diverse peers who value their ideas and expand their perspectives. These types of connections lead to countless opportunities for social networking and professional accomplishments. By the time our students graduate from Colorado State, they have the knowledge, practical experience, and interpersonal skills they need to make a significant contribution to their world.

"Although academic performance is a primary factor in admissions decisions, Colorado State's holistic review process also recognizes personal qualities and experiences that have the potential to enrich the university and the Fort Collins community. To apply, students may submit the Common Application or the Colorado State University application for admission."

SELECTIVITY

Admissions Rating	78
# of applicants	18,556
% of applicants accepted	81
% of acceptees attending	32

FRESHMAN PROFILE

Range SAT Critical Reading	520–620
Range SAT Math	520–630
Range ACT Composite	22–28
Minimum paper TOEFL	550
Minimum internet-based TOEFL	79
Average HS GPA	3.6
% graduated top 10% of class	19
% graduated top 25% of class	48
% graduated top 50% of class	83

DEADLINES

Early action	
Deadline	12/1
Notification	2/1
Regular	
Deadline	2/1
Nonfall registration?	Yes

APPLICANTS ALSO LOOK AT AND OFTEN PREFER

Arizona State University; University of Arizona; University of Colorado Boulder; University of Denver; University of Oregon

FINANCIAL FACTS

Financial Aid Rating	82
Annual in-state tuition	$8,301
Annual out-of-state tuition	$25,010
Room and board	$10,794
Required fees	$2,257
Books and supplies	$1,140
Average frosh need-based scholarship	$7,274
Average UG need-based scholarship	$7,162
% needy frosh rec. need-based scholarship or grant aid	75
% needy UG rec. need-based scholarship or grant aid	67
% needy frosh rec. non-need-based scholarship or grant aid	38
% needy UG rec. non-need-based scholarship or grant aid	27
% needy frosh rec. need-based self-help aid	68
% needy UG rec. need-based self-help aid	74
% frosh rec. any financial aid	76
% UG rec. any financial aid	67
% UG borrow to pay for school	57
Average cumulative indebtedness	$23,347
% frosh need fully met	32
% ugrads need fully met	23
Average % of frosh need met	64
Average % of ugrad need met	82

COLUMBIA UNIVERSITY

212 HAMILTON HALL MC 2807, NEW YORK, NY 10027 • ADMISSIONS: 212-854-2522 • FAX: 212-894-1209

CAMPUS LIFE
Quality of Life Rating	95
Fire Safety Rating	85
Green Rating	96
Type of school	Private
Affiliation	No Affiliation
Environment	Metropolis

STUDENTS
Total undergrad enrollment	6,102
% male/female	52/48
% from out of state	67
% frosh from public high school	57
% frosh live on campus	100
% ugrads live on campus	94
# of fraternities (% ugrad men join)	17 (8)
# of sororities (% ugrad women join)	11 (10)
% African American	12
% Asian	22
% Caucasian	34
% Hispanic	12
% Native American	2
% Pacific Islander	0
% Two or more races	0
% Race and/or ethnicity unknown	4
% international	14
# of countries represented	87

SURVEY SAYS...
Students always studying
Students are happy
Great library
Career services are great
Internships are widely available
Great financial aid
Students love New York, NY
Great off-campus food
Easy to get around campus
Theater is popular
Campus newspaper is popular
Active minority support groups

ACADEMICS
Academic Rating	94
% students returning for sophomore year	99
% students graduating within 4 years	89
% students graduating within 6 years	96
Calendar	Semester
Student/faculty ratio	6:1
Profs interesting rating	79
Profs accessible rating	79

Most classes have 10–19 students.

MOST POPULAR MAJORS
Political Science and Government; English;
Engineering

STUDENTS SAY "..."

Academics

The Ivy League's Columbia University has an international rep as "an elite institution in the greatest city in the world." The hallmark of a Columbia education has to be its Core Curriculum, which "values intellectualism over single-minded pre-professionalism" and "ensures that students can understand and analyze the foundations of Western thought and contemporary society." "The experience of collective intellectual growth might not be unique to Columbia, but I think the Core is the only program in the nation that requires its participants to interact with each other as much as they do with the texts. The intellectual corpus created by the Core is absolutely my favorite thing about Columbia." For the most part, classes are "thought-provoking," and "professors are invested in the students and are extremely accessible." One student complains, "I don't like the fact that I have graduate students teaching some of my intro classes." Another student confesses, "Not every class has been a home run, but the ones that have been truly knock it out of the park." Good grades take some hard work. "Although it is difficult to get an A, it is definitely not uncommon." Students feel that "Columbia provides amazing access to New York and will definitely change the way that you think about the world."

Life

"Student life here is strongly influenced by New York City. Since the city offers millions of activities, fun can range from spending the day at the Met to going to an underground rave downtown, it's really up to each person." Situated in the Upper Manhattan neighborhood of Morningside Heights, Columbia "offers so many free and discounted tickets to museums and cultural events, there's always something fun to get out and do." All you have to do is get on the subway. Students feel that Columbia "has a complete campus inside New York City, so each student is free to choose whether they want to take advantage of the urban setting or just stay on campus and have a more traditional campus experience." Undergrads have access to a vast array of "research positions, internships, externships, and study abroad experiences." Students want to point out that since they live in New York City, there's no one typical activity that students take part in. Instead, "there's a ton of things to do around campus, but then a lot of people will also go downtown to a comedy show or to a new bar or to a Broadway show." The general consensus is that "the opportunities are just endless."

Student Body

The "unparalleled" student body "encompasses multiple political views" and is also "very active politically." "Students fit in by learning to accept that they are different and that others may disagree with them on any number of issues." One student opines, "Because the right-wing portion of the student body is a minority, it is also more outspoken and thus pretty visible on campus." Another comments, "Being religious and/or conservative on this campus is tough." "In terms of socioeconomic status, ethnicity, religion, age, and sexual preference, this school has everything. You will never feel as if you don't belong." A student sums it up this way: "We fit in because of our diversity." As for relaxation, "everyone has their own fun on the weekends. There seems to be a nice equal mix between those who go to parties, those who go out into the city, those who stay in with friends or do work, etc. The campus really accommodates . . . everyone." Students at Columbia "do all sorts of different things but the unifying factor is how passionate about what they study everyone is."

FINANCIAL AID: 212-854-3711 • WEBSITE: WWW.UNDERGRAD.ADMISSIONS.COLUMBIA.EDU

THE PRINCETON REVIEW SAYS

Admissions

Very important factors considered include: rigor of secondary school record, class rank, academic GPA, standardized test scores, application essay, recommendation(s), character/personal qualities. *Important factors considered include:* extracurricular activities, talent/ability. *Other factors considered include:* interview, alumni/ae relation, geographical residence, racial/ethnic status, volunteer work, work experience. ACT with Writing required. TOEFL required of all international applicants. High school diploma is required and GED is accepted. *Academic units recommended:* 4 English, 4 math, 4 science, 4 science labs, 4 foreign language, 4 history, 4 academic electives.

Financial Aid

Students should submit: FAFSA, CSS/Financial Aid PROFILE, Noncustodial PROFILE. Regular filing deadline is 3/1.The Princeton Review suggests that all financial aid forms be submitted as soon as possible after October 1. *Need-based scholarships/grants offered:* Federal Pell, FSEOG, State scholarships/grants, Private scholarships, College/university scholarship or grant aid from institutional funds. *Loan aid offered:* Direct Subsidized Stafford Loans, Direct Unsubsidized Stafford Loans, Direct PLUS loans, Federal Perkins Loans, College/university loans from institutional funds. Applicants will be notified of awards on or about 4/1. Federal Work-Study Program available. Institutional employment available.

The Inside Word

There's no magic formula or pattern to guide students who are seeking admission to Columbia University. Excellent grades in rigorous classes may not be enough, and many great candidates are rejected each year. Admissions officers take a holistic approach to evaluating applications, and they pay extra attention to personal accomplishments in non-academic activities as they look to build a diverse class that will greatly contribute to the university.

THE SCHOOL SAYS "..."

From the Admissions Office

"Columbia maintains an intimate college campus within one of the world's most vibrant cities. After a day exploring New York City you come home to a traditional college campus within an intimate neighborhood. Nobel Prize–winning professors will challenge you in class discussions and meet one-on-one afterward. The Core Curriculum attracts intensely free-minded scholars, and connects all undergraduates. Science and engineering students pursue cutting-edge research in world-class laboratories with faculty members at the forefront of scientific discovery. Classroom discussions are only the beginning of your education. Ideas spill out from the classrooms, electrifying the campus and Morningside Heights. Friendships formed in the residence halls solidify during a game of Frisbee on the South Lawn or over bagels on the steps of Low Library. From your first day on campus, you will be part of our diverse community.

"Columbia offers extensive need-based financial aid and meets the full need of every student admitted as a first-year with grants instead of loans. Parents with calculated incomes below $60,000 are not expected to contribute any income or assets to tuition, room, board and mandatory fees and families with calculated incomes between $60,000 and $100,000 and with typical assets have a significantly reduced contribution. Parents earning over $100,000 can still qualify for significant financial aid. To support students pursuing study abroad, research, internships and community service opportunities, Columbia offers the opportunity to apply for additional funding and exemptions from academic year and summer work expectations. A commitment to diversity—of every kind—is a long-standing Columbia hallmark. We believe cost should not be a barrier to pursuing your educational dreams."

SELECTIVITY

Admissions Rating	99
# of applicants	36,250
% of applicants accepted	6
% of acceptees attending	63
# of early decision applicants	3,337
% accepted early decision	19

FRESHMAN PROFILE

Range SAT Critical Reading	700–790
Range SAT Math	700–800
Range SAT Writing	700–790
Range ACT Composite	32–35
Minimum paper TOEFL	600

DEADLINES

Early decision	
Deadline	11/1
Notification	12/15
Regular	
Deadline	1/1
Notification	4/1
Nonfall registration?	No

APPLICANTS ALSO LOOK AT AND OFTEN PREFER
Massachusetts Institute of Technology; Yale University; Stanford University; Harvard College

AND SOMETIMES PREFER
University of Pennsylvania; Princeton University

AND RARELY PREFER
Brown University; Cornell University; Dartmouth College; New York University

FINANCIAL FACTS

Financial Aid Rating	97
Annual tuition	$50,526
Room and board	$12,860
Required fees	$2,474
Books and supplies	$1,200
Average frosh need-based scholarship	$47,895
Average UG need-based scholarship	$49,348
% needy frosh rec. need-based scholarship or grant aid	97
% needy UG rec. need-based scholarship or grant aid	97
% needy frosh rec. non-need-based scholarship or grant aid	1
% needy UG rec. non-need-based scholarship or grant aid	1
% needy frosh rec. need-based self-help aid	78
% needy UG rec. need-based self-help aid	86
% frosh rec. any financial aid	55
% UG rec. any financial aid	60
% UG borrow to pay for school	27
Average cumulative indebtedness	$8,093
% frosh need fully met	100
% ugrads need fully met	100
Average % of frosh need met	100
Average % of ugrad need met	100

CONNECTICUT COLLEGE

270 MOHEGAN AVENUE, NEW LONDON, CT 06320 • ADMISSIONS: 860-439-2200 • FAX: 860-439-4301

CAMPUS LIFE
Quality of Life Rating	86
Fire Safety Rating	60*
Green Rating	80
Type of school	Private
Affiliation	No Affiliation
Environment	Town

STUDENTS
Total undergrad enrollment	1,918
% male/female	38/62
% from out of state	82
% frosh from public high school	50
% frosh live on campus	100
% ugrads live on campus	99
% African American	4
% Asian	4
% Caucasian	71
% Hispanic	9
% Native American	<1
% Pacific Islander	<1
% Two or more races	3
% Race and/or ethnicity unknown	3
% international	6
# of countries represented	43

SURVEY SAYS...
Students are happy
Career services are great
Internships are widely available
No one cheats
Students aren't religious
Students environmentally aware
Hard liquor is popular

ACADEMICS
Academic Rating	92
% students returning for sophomore year	90
% students graduating within 4 years	79
% students graduating within 6 years	83
Calendar	Semester
Student/faculty ratio	9:1
Profs interesting rating	85
Profs accessible rating	82

Most classes have 10–19 students.
Most lab/discussion sessions have 10–19 students.

MOST POPULAR MAJORS
Economics; Psychology; Biology

STUDENTS SAY "..."

Academics
Located in eastern Connecticut, the picturesque Connecticut College is a classic private New England liberal arts school that shows a "great commitment to being sustainable, to promoting community service, and to learning." The college provides "great academic, extracurricular, and athletic opportunities to all students," and the "beloved" honor code makes for "a close-knit, supportive community." A strong focus on interdisciplinary education, small classes, and self-scheduled exams give students the autonomy to truly tailor their learning around their interests. The academics are "rigorous but continuously relevant, interesting, and enlightening." Most classes are discussion-based, which "allows students to express their own opinions while hearing from their fellow students and professors." Though there are a few bad apples, most professors are always accessible ("especially outside of their office hours") and are "constantly bringing learning outside of the classroom, whether it be within a residence hall, a restaurant, museum, or gallery downtown, or within their own homes." "All of my professors are incredibly engaging and obviously here to excite students about their studies," says a student. Other high points include the "approachability of the staff," excellent career office and internship opportunities, and strong residential programs and academic centers that "help students with a myriad of topics." Connecticut College assures that no student will go through school with "your typical major/minor pairing"; with certificate programs, tons of research opportunities, independent studies and more, every student "has a completely unique and entirely interdisciplinary experience here."

Life
"Life as a student is all about balancing your school work with your extracurricular activities and choosing which events you want to attend," says one. The residential programs lay a great groundwork for student life, and much of the fun on campus "is through social events through the dorms." It helps that "everyone knows one another—between offices, custodial staff, campus safety, and students." There are a wide range of activities to get involved with (everything from athletics, to arts, to activism, to community service, etc.), as well as "numerous faculty-led discussions and speakers every week." Most activities that take place on campus make it "lively and interesting." The campus as a whole is "very friendly, and you are always surrounded by familiar faces," though the relationship with the town of New London is "something that can always be improved upon." For fun, students "attend each others' events, attend social functions in the student center, grab some coffee at one of our coffee shops, and generally hang out with each other." The library is "a very social place during the week," and though students work very hard, they "know how to have a good time on the weekends"—every Saturday there is a well-attended dance put on by the Student Activities Council. Day trips to Boston and New York are also common.

Student Body
Many students at Conn are generally "smart, probably upper-class, well-dressed, and white," though the school "embraces diversity." The common theme among all Conn students in "their active involvement both on campus and off and their desire to be challenged in all aspects of their educations." Students fit in by "showing an interest in their studies, but also carrying on an active social life." It is fairly easy to find one's niche within the community, and "while it might take a semester to become adjusted, there are many groups, teams, and other resources...that help freshmen find a place here."

FINANCIAL AID: 860-439-2058 • E-MAIL: ADMISSION@CONNCOLL.EDU • WEBSITE: WWW.CONNCOLL.EDU

THE PRINCETON REVIEW SAYS

Admissions

Very important factors considered include: rigor of secondary school record, class rank, academic GPA, character/personal qualities. *Important factors considered include:* application essay, recommendation(s), interview, extracurricular activities, talent/ability, racial/ethnic status, volunteer work, work experience. *Other factors considered include:* standardized test scores, first generation, alumni/ae relation, geographical residence, state residency, religious affiliation/commitment, level of applicant's interest. SAT or ACT considered if submitted; SAT Subject Tests considered if submitted. ACT with or without writing accepted. SAT with or without Essay component accepted. High school diploma is required and GED is accepted.

Financial Aid

Students should submit: FAFSA, CSS/Financial Aid PROFILE, Noncustodial PROFILE. Priority filing deadline is 2/15.The Princeton Review suggests that all financial aid forms be submitted as soon as possible after October 1. *Need-based scholarships/grants offered:* Federal Pell, FSEOG, State scholarships/grants *Loan aid offered:* Direct Subsidized Stafford Loans, Direct Unsubsidized Stafford Loans, Direct PLUS loans, Federal Perkins Loans. Applicants will be notified of awards on or about 4/1. Federal Work-Study Program available. Institutional employment available.

The Inside Word

Connecticut College is the archetypal selective New England college, and admissions officers are judicious in their decisions. Competitive applicants will have pursued a demanding course load in high school. Admissions officers look for students who are curious and who thrive in challenging academic environments. Since Connecticut College has a close-knit community, personal qualities are also closely evaluated, and interviews are important.

THE SCHOOL SAYS "..."

From the Admissions Office

"Connecticut College has all the hallmarks of the best liberal arts colleges: small classes; stellar teaching; close faculty-student relationships; more than 40 majors in the arts, sciences, humanities and social sciences; and plentiful co-curricular activities.

"A rigorous new curriculum, called Connections, gives students a chance to tailor their academic experiences around a problem they want to solve. It puts them in classes and conversations with people who are asking big questions similar to their own, and teaches them to look at the issues from many different angles. It demands that they understand what's going on in the world right outside their doors and across the globe. And it teaches them to grapple with and synthesize complex ideas in today's increasingly interconnected world.

"What sets this college apart is its active, outward-focused vision of 'liberal arts in action.' Interdisciplinary classes, programs, centers and majors foster critical think-ing and problem solving. Students connect theory to the real world via community service, community learning, student-faculty research, international experiences and campus leadership. More than half of students study away and more than 70 percent do a college-funded summer internship in the United States or abroad.

"Liberal arts in action also means living under a ninety-three-year-old Honor Code, with self-scheduled exams, a student-run Honor Council, and a student voice in campus decision making. The campus community is close and supportive; there is no Greek life. About 30 percent of students are varsity athletes competing in the New England Small College Athletic Conference (NCAA Division III)."

SELECTIVITY

Admissions Rating	90
# of applicants	5,182
% of applicants accepted	40
% of acceptees attending	23
# offered a place on the wait list	1,306
% accepting a place on wait list	49
% admitted from wait list	10
# of early decision applicants	347
% accepted early decision	70

FRESHMAN PROFILE

Range SAT Critical Reading	610–700
Range SAT Math	610–700
Range SAT Writing	610–698
Range ACT Composite	28–31
% graduated top 10% of class	49
% graduated top 25% of class	79
% graduated top 50% of class	99

DEADLINES

Early decision	
Deadline	11/15
Notification	12/15
Regular	
Deadline	1/1
Notification	3/31
Nonfall registration?	Yes

APPLICANTS ALSO LOOK AT AND OFTEN PREFER

Bates College; Bowdoin College; Colby College; Hamilton College; Tufts University; Wesleyan University

AND SOMETIMES PREFER

Boston College; Brandeis University; Skidmore College

AND RARELY PREFER

Oberlin College; The George Washington University; Carleton College

FINANCIAL FACTS

Financial Aid Rating	94
Room and board	$13,615
Required fees	$325
Average frosh need-based scholarship	$37,224
Average UG need-based scholarship	$35,847
% needy frosh rec. need-based scholarship or grant aid	96
% needy UG rec. need-based scholarship or grant aid	95
% needy frosh rec. non-need-based scholarship or grant aid	0
% needy UG rec. non-need-based scholarship or grant aid	0
% needy frosh rec. need-based self-help aid	91
% needy UG rec. need-based self-help aid	89
% frosh rec. any financial aid	59
% UG rec. any financial aid	54
% UG borrow to pay for school	47
Average cumulative indebtedness	$34,098
% frosh need fully met	100
% ugrads need fully met	100
Average % of frosh need met	100
Average % of ugrad need met	100

The Cooper Union for the Advancement of Science and Art

30 Cooper Square, New York, NY 10003 • Admissions: 212-353-4120 • Fax: 212-353-4342

STUDENTS SAY "..."

Academics

Gifted students clamor for a spot at The Cooper Union for the Advancement of Science and Art. The small school has continued its tradition of hefty discounts with a universal half-tuition scholarship that can be a huge selling point. However, the rigorous and "very reputable" academic programs are the main reason to attend this unique New York City college. "An institution of the highest caliber," Cooper Union has a narrow academic focus, conferring degrees only in fine arts, architecture, engineering. Cooper Union's "engineering program is considered one of the best in the nation"; there are "plenty of opportunities for independent study in your field," and "lab facilities are incredible." Individual learning is emphasized, and the student-to-teacher ratio is excellent: "The freshman year courses have about twenty to twenty-five students in each, while the courses in later years have as few as five students in a class." When it comes to the teaching staff, adjunct faculty gets mixed reviews, while "full-time professors are really great. They have great experience, like what they do, like the students, [and] are really accessible and happy to help." "Professors vary widely in their teaching methods"; yet most are "very accessible, friendly, [and] expect a high level of quality for work." Unfortunately, if you don't like your instructor, you're out of luck because "there are only a few professors in each department, meaning students have the same professor over and over again."

Life

Located in New York City's East Village, Cooper Union offers "an opportunity to live in one of the most energetic and dynamic cities in the world." Unfortunately, "there isn't time for anything other than your classes." To meet the school's high academic demands and "spine-breaking workload," "the typical schedule for any Cooper student who hopes to survive is go to class, study and do homework, sleep for a few hours, and repeat." At Cooper Union, there are few Greek organizations, no dormitories for upperclassmen, and "no recreational facilities or cafeterias on campus" (although there is a cafe with snacks and gathering space). Students are the first to admit that "the social life is rather limited," and "weekends are more often spent in the lab or library than at parties." However, those who make time for a little recreation say, "There are plenty of parties happening in the Village and at NYU that students can attend"—not to mention, plenty of "comedy clubs, movies, bowling, lounges, and bars" throughout New York City. Art students, though also self-professed workaholics, may also make time to "go to art openings of fellow students, professors, and friends, party, [or] play a lot of music." However, most students say that when they "sacrifice a few hours of sleep to do something enjoyable, it usually includes just hanging out with friends."

Student Body

Cooper Union's campus is largely comprised of "three distinct types of students," each delineated by major field: art, architecture, and engineering. Typical art students are "alternative kids" with the "just-rolled-out-of-bed look" while future architects are "very sleek" and fashionable, but "never leave their studio." The more "socially awkward" engineers are also largely like-minded. One says, "If you have some obscure technological passion, someone in the engineering school is guaranteed to be as passionate." According to some, "Artists hang out with artists, engineers with engineers, architects with architects." However, most Cooper Union students laugh off stereotypes, telling us the school is filled with "very unique, interesting people," eager to learn and cross-pollinate between departments. A current student reassures us, "Of course, the odds are high that a group of electrical engineers will end up talking about video games, but there seems to be a broad spectrum of personalities present here." Across the board, students in every major are serious about their studies, and most of Cooper's selective admits are "super intelligent, super creative, and/or just super hardworking."

THE COOPER UNION FOR THE ADVANCEMENT OF SCIENCE AND ART

FINANCIAL AID: 212-353-4130 • E-MAIL: ADMISSIONS@COOPER.EDU • WEBSITE: WWW.COOPER.EDU

THE PRINCETON REVIEW SAYS

Admissions

Very important factors considered include: rigor of secondary school record, academic GPA, standardized test scores, talent/ability, level of applicant's interest. *Important factors considered include:* application essay, extracurricular activities, character/personal qualities. *Other factors considered include:* class rank, recommendation(s), interview, first generation, racial/ethnic status, volunteer work, work experience. SAT or ACT required; SAT Subject Tests required for engineering applicants only. ACT with Writing recommended. SAT with Essay component recommended. TOEFL required of all international applicants. High school diploma is required and GED is accepted. *Academic units required:* 4 English, 1 math, 1 science, 1 social studies, 1 history, 8 academic electives. *Academic units recommended:* 4 English, 4 math, 4 science, 3 science labs, 2 foreign language, 4 social studies.

Financial Aid

Students should submit: FAFSA. Regular filing deadline is 5/1.The Princeton Review suggests that all financial aid forms be submitted as soon as possible after October 1. *Need-based scholarships/grants offered:* Federal Pell, FSEOG, State scholarships/grants, Private scholarships, College/university scholarship or grant aid from institutional funds. *Loan aid offered:* Direct Subsidized Stafford Loans, Direct Unsubsidized Stafford Loans, Direct PLUS loans, Federal Perkins Loans, College/university loans from institutional funds. Applicants will be notified of awards with admissions packets. Federal Work-Study Program available. Institutional employment available.

The Inside Word

The admission rate to Cooper Union is extremely competitive. In recent years, only about 15 percent of applicants have been accepted to the undergraduate program. The fine arts (BFA) program is usually the most competitive of Cooper's three schools, though all admits must be academically accomplished and top of their high school class. Depending on whether you plan to pursue engineering, art, or architecture, admissions requirements and applications deadlines vary.

THE SCHOOL SAYS "..."

From the Admissions Office

"Each of Cooper Union's three schools—architecture, art and engineering—adheres strongly to preparation for its profession and is committed to a problem-solving philosophy of education in a small, scholarship environment. A rigorous curriculum and group projects reinforce this unique atmosphere in higher education and contribute to a strong sense of community and identity in each school. With McSorley's Ale House and the Joseph Papp Public Theatre nearby, Cooper Union remains at the heart of the city's tradition of free speech, enlightenment, and entertainment. Cooper's Great Hall has hosted national leaders, from Abraham Lincoln to Booker T. Washington, from Mark Twain to Samuel Gompers, from Susan B. Anthony to Betty Friedan, and more recently, President Bill Clinton and President Barack Obama. In fall of 2009, we opened the doors of our new academic building. Designed by Pritzker Prize–winning architect, Thom Mayne, the new building was designed to enhance and encourage more interaction between students in all three schools. We're seeking students who have a passion to study our professional programs. Cooper Union students are independent thinkers, following the beat of their own drum. Many of our graduates become world-class leaders in the disciplines of architecture, fine arts, design, and engineering.

"For art and architecture applicants, SAT scores are considered after the home test and portfolio work. For engineering applicants, high school grades and the SAT and SAT Subject Test scores are the most important factors considered in admissions decisions."

SELECTIVITY

Admissions Rating	98
# of applicants	3,258
% of applicants accepted	13
% of acceptees attending	55
# offered a place on the wait list	315
% accepting a place on wait list	97
% admitted from wait list	4
# of early decision applicants	228
% accepted early decision	30

FRESHMAN PROFILE

Range SAT Critical Reading	610–720
Range SAT Math	630–790
Range SAT Writing	600–720
Range ACT Composite	31–34
Minimum paper TOEFL	600
Minimum internet-based TOEFL	100
Average HS GPA	3.5
% graduated top 10% of class	85
% graduated top 25% of class	90
% graduated top 50% of class	95

DEADLINES

Early decision	
Deadline	12/1
Notification	12/23
Other ED	
Deadline	12/1
Other ED	
Notification	12/23
Regular	
Priority	12/1
Deadline	1/9
Notification	4/1
Nonfall registration?	No

APPLICANTS ALSO LOOK AT AND OFTEN PREFER
Columbia University; Cornell University

AND SOMETIMES PREFER
Carnegie Mellon University

FINANCIAL FACTS

Financial Aid Rating	97
Annual tuition	$40,800
Room and board	$15,560
Required fees	$1,850
Books and supplies	$1,650
Average frosh need-based scholarship	$20,143
Average UG need-based scholarship	$12,603
% needy frosh rec. need-based scholarship or grant aid	84
% needy UG rec. need-based scholarship or grant aid	81
% needy frosh rec. non-need-based scholarship or grant aid	100
% needy UG rec. non-need-based scholarship or grant aid	100
% needy frosh rec. need-based self-help aid	54
% needy UG rec. need-based self-help aid	60
% frosh rec. any financial aid	100
% UG rec. any financial aid	100
% UG borrow to pay for school	34
Average cumulative indebtedness	$4,125
% frosh need fully met	100
% ugrads need fully met	100
Average % of frosh need met	92
Average % of ugrad need met	92

CORNELL COLLEGE

600 FIRST STREET SW, MOUNT VERNON, IA 52314-1098 • ADMISSIONS: 319-895-4215 • FAX: 319-895-4451

STUDENTS SAY "..."

Academics

Cornell College, a small liberal arts school in Iowa, employs a unique one-course-at-a-time program, allowing students to focus on just one course (or "block") each month, providing an "intense, thorough, and complete immersion." Though students agree that this "series of experiences" "doesn't give you any time to think about anything but the class you're in right then," it allows for personalized curricula design, and areas like the humanities "work perfectly with the block plan." Students also "always know when to find people," which makes it easy to get together. Some classes may not be the most challenging, but "upper-level courses are very engaging and fulfilling." "You could have hours and hours of homework one block and practically none the next," says a student. The block plan makes it very easy to gain off-campus field experience or do international study, and it's "easier to try off-campus opportunities." Administration is generally "excellent at taking a personal interest in each student," though some note, "There is not much transparency at the administrative level," which can be "out of touch" at times. The registrar is "the most dreaded office on campus," with residence life a close second. On the classroom side, professors "know how to motivate and encourage their students," and though "you may get a bad apple maybe once a year," they're "not only knowledgeable but dedicated." "The personal attention you can receive from any given professor, if you seek them out, is especially rewarding," says a student. All in all, students love the block structure and the sense of community it creates, as "no matter what it is you may want to do, you can find someone to do it with you." One student claims he "cannot imagine learning any other way."

Life

Since Cornell is very campus-focused, the school makes sure there's a large variety of campus organizations and "many events going on almost every weekend." Though there's definitely a "small-town quiet," Cedar Rapids and Iowa City are both only a twenty-minute drive away, and "ice climbing, rock-climbing, paddling, and hiking" are popular outdoor pastimes. It's also "fairly easy to start up a new club or group." In addition, the school provides winter and spring breaks as well as five "block breaks," which last four and a half days and give students the opportunity to travel, go skiing or camping, and so on. The cold weather can cause problems here, in both a locked-in feel and the possibility for accidents, and students are encouraged to "bring snow boots!" Many here tend to have a love-hate relationship with sports; while athletics are a huge boon, "the athletes and the non-athletes are seldom friends." Much like the curriculum, lunchtimes are pretty unique, and students all eat in a common cafeteria, naturally falling into a somewhat "high school" habit of eating at the same tables every day. Most people stay on campus for entertainment and socializing, "creating a cohesive community." Parties do take place on weekends, and "drinking is popular on campus but never forced," but in general, "people are more interested in just having a good conversation with their peers."

Student Body

There's "a great diversity of interests" in people who attend Cornell, and the "super busy" students have a hard time defining a more common characteristic than the fact that almost all are driven and involved. Some division into typical groups does occur—"the cafeteria design and Greek life are very conducive to this problem"—but "even group to group there is always mingling because you never know who will be in your next class." Since the classes are so small and "you see the same people four hours a day for three and a half weeks," people are generally accepting, and "you have to be really, really strange here to stick out." As one freshman says, "The only intolerance I've seen is toward the consistently indolent."

FINANCIAL AID: 319-895-4216 • E-MAIL: ADMISSION@CORNELLCOLLEGE.EDU • WEBSITE: WWW.CORNELLCOLLEGE.EDU

THE PRINCETON REVIEW SAYS

Admissions

Very important factors considered include: rigor of secondary school record, academic GPA, character/personal qualities. *Important factors considered include:* class rank, application essay, recommendation(s), extracurricular activities, talent/ability, volunteer work, work experience. *Other factors considered include:* standardized test scores, interview, first generation, alumni/ae relation, geographical residence, state residency, racial/ethnic status, level of applicant's interest. SAT or ACT optional; SAT Subject Tests considered if submitted. ACT with or without writing accepted. Proof of English proficiency required of all international applicants. High school diploma is required and GED is accepted. *Academic units recommended:* 4 English, 3 math, 3 science, 2 foreign language, 3 social studies, 1 academic elective.

Financial Aid

Students should submit: FAFSA. The Princeton Review suggests that all financial aid forms be submitted as soon as possible after October 1. *Need-based scholarships/grants offered:* Federal Pell, FSEOG, State scholarships/grants, Private scholarships, College/university scholarship or grant aid from institutional funds. *Loan aid offered:* Direct Subsidized Stafford Loans, Direct Unsubsidized Stafford Loans, Direct PLUS loans, Federal Perkins Loans. Federal Work-Study Program available. Institutional employment available.

The Inside Word

Given Cornell's relatively unique approach to study, it's no surprise that the admissions committee here focuses attention on both academic and personal strengths. Cornell's small, highly self-selected applicant pool is chock-full of students with solid self-awareness, motivation, and discipline.

THE SCHOOL SAYS "..."

From the Admissions Office

"Cornell College, a highly selective liberal arts college in Mount Vernon, Iowa, is recognized as one of the colleges featured in *Colleges That Change Lives*. Characterized by the life-changing academic immersion of its One Course At A Time curriculum, this distinctive approach allows students to focus on a single academic subject per eighteen-day block. It lays the foundation for a student's entire Cornell education through transformative intellectual partnerships and close-knit learning communities that bring out the best in our ambitious students. The One Course curriculum mirrors the pace of most working environments where employees are expected to handle tight deadlines and high expectations on every project, every day. Since there is never more than one course to focus on, faculty can take entire classes on field trips for a day or an entire block. Cornell's residential campus attracts a student body from forty-five states and eighteen foreign countries. Together, they experience a vast array of off-campus opportunities designed to take them into the world to fulfill their academic and personal goals, as well as a lineup of speakers and entertainment options that brings the world to them. Cornell College is frequently cited as a 'Best Buy.' Ninety-three percent of Cornell graduates complete their degrees in four years, and 55 percent go on to complete an advanced degree."

SELECTIVITY

Admissions Rating	84
# of applicants	1,934
% of applicants accepted	71
% of acceptees attending	20
# offered a place on the wait list	13
% accepting a place on wait list	15
% admitted from wait list	100
# of early decision applicants	63
% accepted early decision	60

FRESHMAN PROFILE

Range SAT Critical Reading	510–660
Range SAT Math	500–640
Range SAT Writing	490–630
Range ACT Composite	23–29
Minimum paper TOEFL	550
Minimum internet-based TOEFL	79
Average HS GPA	3.4
% graduated top 10% of class	22
% graduated top 25% of class	45
% graduated top 50% of class	88

DEADLINES

Early decision	
Deadline	11/1
Notification	12/15
Early action	
Deadline	12/1
Notification	2/1
Regular	
Priority	12/1
Deadline	2/1
Nonfall registration?	Yes

APPLICANTS ALSO LOOK AT AND SOMETIMES PREFER

Beloit College; Coe College; Colorado College; Knox College; Kalamazoo College

FINANCIAL FACTS

Financial Aid Rating	85
Annual tuition	$37,500
Room and board	$8,500
Required fees	$225
Books and supplies	$1,164
Average frosh need-based scholarship	$25,076
Average UG need-based scholarship	$26,007
% needy frosh rec. need-based scholarship or grant aid	100
% needy UG rec. need-based scholarship or grant aid	99
% needy frosh rec. non-need-based scholarship or grant aid	33
% needy UG rec. non-need-based scholarship or grant aid	11
% needy frosh rec. need-based self-help aid	78
% needy UG rec. need-based self-help aid	85
% frosh rec. any financial aid	99
% UG rec. any financial aid	98
% UG borrow to pay for school	74
Average cumulative indebtedness	$30,790
% frosh need fully met	23
% ugrads need fully met	16
Average % of frosh need met	80
Average % of ugrad need met	88

CORNELL UNIVERSITY

UNDERGRADUATE ADMISSIONS, 410 THURSTON AVENUE, ITHACA, NY 14850 • ADMISSIONS: 607-255-5241 • FAX: 607-255-0659

CAMPUS LIFE

Quality of Life Rating	92
Fire Safety Rating	89
Green Rating	99
Type of school	Private
Affiliation	No Affiliation
Environment	Town

STUDENTS

Total undergrad enrollment	14,315
% male/female	48/52
% from out of state	65
% frosh live on campus	100
% ugrads live on campus	55
# of fraternities (% ugrad men join)	47 (33)
# of sororities (% ugrad women join)	18 (34)
% African American	6
% Asian	18
% Caucasian	41
% Hispanic	12
% Native American	<1
% Pacific Islander	<1
% Two or more races	4
% Race and/or ethnicity unknown	8
% international	10
# of countries represented	82

SURVEY SAYS...

Students always studying
Students are happy
Classroom facilities are great
Lab facilities are great
Great library
Career services are great
Internships are widely available
School is well run
Great financial aid
Students environmentally aware
Great food on campus
Great off-campus food
Lots of beer drinking
Campus newspaper is popular
Alumni active on campus

ACADEMICS

Academic Rating	91
% students returning for sophomore year	97
% students graduating within 4 years	86
% students graduating within 6 years	93
Calendar	Semester
Student/faculty ratio	9:1
Profs interesting rating	81
Profs accessible rating	79

Most classes have 10–19 students.
Most lab/discussion sessions have 10–19 students.

MOST POPULAR MAJORS

Biology; Hotel/Motel Administration/Management; Labor and Industrial Relations

STUDENTS SAY "..."

Academics

The westernmost of the Ivies, Cornell University provides its students with a prestigious education, paired with "an unwavering commitment to leave a positive impact on the world." The school is "more than a bunch of books and exams—it's an experience that challenges students to break free from their comfort zones." Seven different undergraduate colleges (including one of the premier Hotel Administration schools in the nation) "really make it feel small and specialized," and "top notch faculty." The university is "a place where any person can find instruction in any study (and it won't feel like work)," as it allows its students to explore any kind of interest they may have (ranging from Punk Rock as a literary genre to particle physics) while "also offering an incredible amount of depth within each department." There are endless opportunities to "pursue other topics, enhance your knowledge of things that you're already interested in, and try completely random things that you'd never even heard of before." Professors are "experts in their field, almost always conducting their own research, and are enthusiastic about passing their knowledge on to their students."

"[Since] being in Ithaca, you're kind of in the middle of nowhere," there are plenty of reasons to focus on your studies, but "Cornell as an administration keeps the faculty, research, and access to the most recent information so up-to-date that this campus is as connected as any place in the world." Between balancing those amazing resources and the community feel, the Cornell bigwigs get a lot of applause, as they have "proven time and time again that they care, both on an individual and system-wide level." Great internships, a strong alumni network, and "boundless opportunities after graduation" round out the "definition of amazing" that is Cornell University. "I was intimidated to go here, but now I will say that I cannot imagine going anywhere else," says a junior.

Life

As they say, "Ithaca is gorges," so hiking and outdoor activities are big pastimes. The "absolutely gorgeous campus" in the Finger Lakes region allows students to "truly, purely enjoy their time here" by "experiencing the natural beauties of Upstate New York, along with the eccentricity of surrounding town." "I think it sums up the Cornell experience to say that at dinner a few nights ago, our conversation included the presidential debate, Macbeth, sex, cantaloupes, sex WITH cantaloupes, drone strikes in Pakistan, the iPhones, and invasive parasitic species in Southeast Asia," says a freshman. The school's infrastructure is "intense"—"we have our own dairy so that we can make our own milk, for goodness sake"—and "there's just so much going on at every moment [that] the hard part is choosing what it is you want to do." Many admit that various aspects of Cornell life can cause stress—the upperclass housing lottery, course enrollment system, workload, and difficulty studying abroad all get singled out—but students are able to discern when to kick back and enjoy themselves. Fun can range anywhere from "an awesome party in Collegetown to a movie night in the dorm while ordering insomnia cookies," but "it's definitely acceptable to turn down weekend plans because you have too much work to do."

Student Body

With so many different colleges within Cornell, there is "a plethora of diverse students" here, but the underlying commonality between all students is "ambition and ability." "From farm kids and pre-med students to engineers and hotelies, Cornell is home to all sorts of students," says one. "You'll find yourself with a roommate who was on Team USA, a friend who was a firefighter, and a classmate who's backpacked around the world." The integration of people with eclectic interests "[inspires] others to become active students," which is easily enough done at a university with hundreds upon hundreds of student organizations. "Everyone's smart and that's just accepted," but "a competitive environment isn't created." Cornellians are "very committed to academics but always know how to put books aside and relax." Most do research and volunteer work, and many "are involved in some form of Greek life."

FINANCIAL AID: 607-255-5147 • E-MAIL: ADMISSIONS@CORNELL.EDU • WEBSITE: WWW.CORNELL.EDU

THE PRINCETON REVIEW SAYS

Admissions

Very important factors considered include: rigor of secondary school record, academic GPA, standardized test scores, application essay, recommendation(s), extracurricular activities, talent/ability, character/personal qualities. *Important factors considered include:* class rank. *Other factors considered include:* interview, first generation, alumni/ae relation, geographical residence, state residency, racial/ethnic status, volunteer work, work experience. SAT or ACT required; SAT Subject Tests required for some. ACT with or without writing accepted. TOEFL required of all international applicants. High school diploma or equivalent is not required. *Academic units required:* 4 English, 3 math. *Academic units recommended:* 3 science, 3 science labs, 3 foreign language, 3 social studies, 3 history.

Financial Aid

Students should submit: FAFSA, CSS/Financial Aid PROFILE, Noncustodial PROFILE. Regular filing deadline is 2/15.The Princeton Review suggests that all financial aid forms be submitted as soon as possible after October 1. *Need-based scholarships/grants offered:* Federal Pell, FSEOG, State scholarships/grants, Private scholarships, College/university scholarship or grant aid from institutional funds. *Loan aid offered:* Direct Subsidized Stafford Loans, Direct Unsubsidized Stafford Loans, Direct PLUS loans, Federal Perkins Loans, College/university loans from institutional funds. Applicants will be notified of awards on or about 4/1. Federal Work-Study Program available. Institutional employment available.

The Inside Word

Gaining admission to Cornell is a tough coup regardless of your intended field of study, but some of the university's seven schools are more competitive than others. If you're thinking of trying to "backdoor" your way into one of the most competitive schools—by gaining admission to a less competitive one, then transferring after one year—be aware that you will have to resubmit the entire application and provide a statement outlining your academic plans. It's not impossible to accomplish, but Cornell works hard to discourage this sort of maneuvering.

THE SCHOOL SAYS "..."

From the Admissions Office

"Cornell University, an Ivy League school and land-grant college located in the scenic Finger Lakes region of central New York, provides an outstanding education to students in seven small to midsize undergraduate colleges: Agriculture and Life Sciences; Architecture, Art, and Planning; Arts and Sciences; Engineering; Hotel Administration; Human Ecology; and Industrial and Labor Relations. Cornellians come from all fifty states and more than 120 countries, and they pursue their academic goals in more than 100 departments. The College of Arts and Sciences, one of the smallest liberal arts schools in the Ivy League, offers more than forty majors, most of which rank near the top nationwide. Applied programs in the other six colleges also rank among the best in the world. Other special features of the university include a world-renowned faculty; over 4,000 courses available to all students; an extensive undergraduate research program; superb research, teaching, and library facilities; a large, diverse study abroad program; and more than 800 student organizations and thirty-four varsity sports. Cornell's campus is one of the most beautiful in the country; students pass streams, rocky gorges, and waterfalls on their way to class. First-year students make their home on North Campus, a living-learning community that features a special advising center, faculty-in-residence, a fitness center, and traditional residence halls as well as theme-centered buildings such as Ecology House. Cornell University invites applications from all interested students and uses the Common Application exclusively with a short required Cornell Supplement. Students applying for admissions will submit scores from the SAT or ACT (with writing). We also require SAT Subject Tests. Subject test requirements are college-specific."

SELECTIVITY

Admissions Rating	97
# of applicants	41,900
% of applicants accepted	15
% of acceptees attending	50
# offered a place on the wait list	3,583
% accepting a place on wait list	62
% admitted from wait list	4
# of early decision applicants	4,560
% accepted early decision	26

FRESHMAN PROFILE

Range SAT Critical Reading	650–750
Range SAT Math	680–780
Range ACT Composite	30–34
Minimum paper TOEFL	600
Minimum internet-based TOEFL	100
% graduated top 10% of class	89
% graduated top 25% of class	97
% graduated top 50% of class	100

DEADLINES

Early decision	
Deadline	11/1
Regular	
Deadline	1/2
Nonfall registration?	No

FINANCIAL FACTS

Financial Aid Rating	96
Average frosh need-based scholarship	$39,787
Average UG need-based scholarship	$38,377
% needy frosh rec. need-based scholarship or grant aid	98
% needy UG rec. need-based scholarship or grant aid	98
% needy frosh rec. non-need-based scholarship or grant aid	0
% needy UG rec. non-need-based scholarship or grant aid	0
% needy frosh rec. need-based self-help aid	88
% needy UG rec. need-based self-help aid	92
% frosh rec. any financial aid	60
% UG rec. any financial aid	57
% UG borrow to pay for school	43
Average cumulative indebtedness	$24,394
% frosh need fully met	100
% ugrads need fully met	100
Average % of frosh need met	100
Average % of ugrad need met	100

CREIGHTON UNIVERSITY

2500 CALIFORNIA PLAZA, OMAHA, NE 68178 • ADMISSIONS: 402-280-2703 • FAX: 402-280-2685

CAMPUS LIFE

Quality of Life Rating	90
Fire Safety Rating	96
Green Rating	86
Type of school	Private
Affiliation	Roman Catholic Jesuit
Environment	Metropolis

STUDENTS

Total undergrad enrollment	4,163
% male/female	43/57
% from out of state	75
% frosh from public high school	51
% frosh live on campus	95
% ugrads live on campus	60
# of fraternities (% ugrad men join)	5 (30)
# of sororities (% ugrad women join)	7 (46)
% African American	2
% Asian	10
% Caucasian	71
% Hispanic	8
% Native American	<1
% Pacific Islander	<1
% Two or more races	4
% Race and/or ethnicity unknown	1
% international	3
# of countries represented	33

SURVEY SAYS...

Students are happy
Career services are great
School is well run
Students are friendly
Students are very religious
Students get along with local community
Students involved in community service
Easy to get around campus
Recreation facilities are great
Everyone loves the Bluejays

ACADEMICS

Academic Rating	84
% students returning for sophomore year	90
% students graduating within 4 years	72
% students graduating within 6 years	79
Calendar	Semester
Student/faculty ratio	11:1
Profs interesting rating	83
Profs accessible rating	86

Most classes have 10–19 students.
Most lab/discussion sessions have
10–19 students.

MOST POPULAR MAJORS

Nursing; Biology; Psychology

STUDENTS SAY "..."

Academics

The voices echoing from this Omaha school are resoundingly pleased with their choice to attend "a great Jesuit university focused on academics and creating well-rounded students." Students are also active outside the classroom, getting "involved" in the campus and local community, and the school makes sure it churns a student out as a complete package: "academically, socially, culturally, faith-filled, and service-oriented." Creighton wants to form students who are driven inside the classroom but "want to find deeper meanings in all that they do to enact change in the world." Though classes are tough, the typical class size is small, which "makes discussion possible in nearly every class." Likewise, professors are extraordinarily helpful and "know how to present material in an interesting manner for the most part." Professors are all "exceptional" and really run the gamut "from quirky nerds to outspoken rebels to hilarious Jesuit priests." Many students come here for medical school, allied health, or business school. There are also a variety of services offered, such as a tutoring program called "The Study," where students get help from other students on a one-on-one basis. "Students at Creighton learn to enjoy the process, rather than just the product," says one. Both the teaching staff and administration are highly accessible; office hours don't seem to stop, and every Wednesday morning the much-loved president has breakfast with a different group of students to listen to their concerns and to talk about how life at Creighton is going. "At Creighton students come first, and it is as simple as that!" chirps a happy junior.

Life

"While academics are a huge part of our schooling, they are not all-encompassing," says a student. Community service happily takes up a lot of students' time, and there are fall break and spring break service trips all over the United States. Sports, both intercollegiate and intramural, are huge on and off campus; Omaha and the Old Market have plenty of music venues, bowling, shopping, and restaurants (a good thing, because the food at Creighton is universally despised and "needs to be improved drastically"). Students would like to see some more options for getting off campus, though; the difficulty and cost of living off campus means on-campus housing is in high demand. The Greek community at Creighton "is not as intense as at state schools," but students in sororities or fraternities hold many leadership positions on campus. Weeknights are mainly for studying, but house parties are available on weekends, and "the bar scene is where many students spend their nights off." The school and student government do an excellent job of providing plenty of activities that are enjoyed by all, such as ice skating, weekly movies, and "mock TV shows like the 'Price is Right,'" and no one has any problem with peer pressure. "It is very easy to be productive and involved but still be able to find time for fun," says a biology and Spanish major.

Student Body

The typical student is white and from the Midwest, and most are "outgoing and friendly," which is probably why atypical students have no problems fitting in. And the "old brick road that runs down the middle of campus (called the mall) provides excellent opportunities to meet new people." "It doesn't matter where you came from or why you're here" as "most students have the same values, which allows the community to feel connected." "Everyone is interconnected through someone; there are very few degrees of separation between individuals," one student says, though others claim that there's no shortage of cliques. Creighton students are incredibly balanced in their work and play and are "over-the-top involved" with activities and community service while maintaining full academic loads. The school is very involved in study abroad programs, so there are a fair number of international students in each class. "I've never been in a place where so many people will hold the door open for me to walk through, if that gives any indication of the type of student here," says a student.

FINANCIAL AID: 402-280-2731 • E-MAIL: ADMISSIONS@CREIGHTON.EDU • WEBSITE: WWW.CREIGHTON.EDU

THE PRINCETON REVIEW SAYS

Admissions

Very important factors considered include: rigor of secondary school record, academic GPA. *Important factors considered include:* standardized test scores, application essay. *Other factors considered include:* class rank, recommendation(s), extracurricular activities, talent/ability, character/personal qualities, first generation, racial/ethnic status, volunteer work, level of applicant's interest. SAT or ACT required. ACT with or without writing accepted. SAT with or without Essay component accepted. TOEFL required of all international applicants. High school diploma is required and GED is accepted. *Academic units required:* 4 English, 3 math, 2 science, 1 science lab, 2 foreign language, 2 social studies, 3 academic electives. *Academic units recommended:* 4 English, 4 math, 3 science, 2 science labs, 3 foreign language, 4 social studies, 3 academic electives.

Financial Aid

Students should submit: FAFSA, Institution's own financial aid form. Priority filing deadline is 3/1.The Princeton Review suggests that all financial aid forms be submitted as soon as possible after October 1. *Need-based scholarships/grants offered:* Federal Pell, FSEOG, State scholarships/grants, Private scholarships, College/university scholarship or grant aid from institutional funds. *Loan aid offered:* Direct Subsidized Stafford Loans, Direct Unsubsidized Stafford Loans, Direct PLUS loans, Federal Perkins Loans, Federal Nursing Loans. Applicants will be notified of awards on a rolling basis beginning 3/15. Federal Work-Study Program available. Institutional employment available.

The Inside Word

Creighton's lack of name recognition and its location can handicap its search for quality students, occasionally forcing the school to lower the bar to fill its incoming classes, so the school's loss could well be your gain. For those comfortable in a Jesuit school, Creighton offers bright, hardworking students a great opportunity at a quality education.

THE SCHOOL SAYS "..."

From the Admissions Office

"Students come to Creighton University for the opportunities of a lifetime. Creighton's nine schools and colleges deliver powerful education that connects renowned programs in arts and sciences, law and business with eight health professions programs (dentistry, medicine, nursing, pharmacy, occupational and physical therapy, public health and emergency medical services) all on the same walkable campus. Creighton's rigorous academics and commitment to Jesuit, Catholic ideals and values create an environment that fosters academic excellence, social justice and personal growth. More than 8,000 undergraduate, graduate and professional students come to Creighton each year to find their place in the world through lives of leadership and service.

"Creighton's 4,000+ undergraduates find new possibilities through personalized advising, a strong focus on leadership skills and opportunities for undergraduate research. The Center for Undergraduate Research and Scholarship (CURAS) ensures that undergraduates work directly with faculty researchers, present at national conferences and publish in scholarly journals. And not all learning takes place in the classroom or lab. Creighton business students find abundant internship opportunities (the University is within walking distance of four Fortune 500 company headquarters) and all Creighton students find life-changing experiences through community service opportunities. Creighton students, contributed over one million hours of service locally, regionally, nationally and internationally last year."

"At Creighton, you get it all—national professors of the year; a 98 percent placement rate within eight months of graduation; an 11:1 student-to-faculty ratio; 50 plus undergraduate majors; BIG EAST athletic competition; 200 plus clubs and organizations and more—because Creighton University is the complete package."

SELECTIVITY

Admissions Rating	87
# of applicants	9,747
% of applicants accepted	70
% of acceptees attending	16
# offered a place on the wait list	0

FRESHMAN PROFILE

Range SAT Critical Reading	510–630
Range SAT Math	540–650
Range SAT Writing	510–620
Range ACT Composite	24–29
Minimum paper TOEFL	550
Minimum internet-based TOEFL	80
Average HS GPA	3.8
% graduated top 10% of class	37
% graduated top 25% of class	68
% graduated top 50% of class	92

DEADLINES

Regular	
Priority	12/1
Deadline	2/15
Nonfall registration?	Yes

APPLICANTS ALSO LOOK AT AND OFTEN PREFER
University of Notre Dame

AND SOMETIMES PREFER
Boston College; University of Iowa

AND RARELY PREFER
Iowa State University; Marquette University; Santa Clara University; University of Kansas

FINANCIAL FACTS

Financial Aid Rating	85
Annual tuition	$34,810
Room and board	$10,294
Required fees	$1,612
Books and supplies	$1,200
Average frosh need-based scholarship	$21,566
Average UG need-based scholarship	$21,823
% needy frosh rec. need-based scholarship or grant aid	100
% needy UG rec. need-based scholarship or grant aid	96
% needy frosh rec. non-need-based scholarship or grant aid	22
% needy UG rec. non-need-based scholarship or grant aid	18
% needy frosh rec. need-based self-help aid	81
% needy UG rec. need-based self-help aid	82
% frosh rec. any financial aid	99
% UG rec. any financial aid	97
% UG borrow to pay for school	57
Avg indebtedness	$33,792
% frosh need fully met	28
% UG need full met	27
Avg % frosh need met	85
Avg % UG need met	81

DARTMOUTH COLLEGE

6016 McNUTT HALL, HANOVER, NH 03755 • ADMISSIONS: 603-646-2875 • FAX: 603-646-1216

CAMPUS LIFE

Quality of Life Rating	94
Fire Safety Rating	89
Green Rating	94
Type of school	Private
Affiliation	No Affiliation
Environment	Village

STUDENTS

Total undergrad enrollment	4,289
% male/female	51/49
% from out of state	97
% frosh from public high school	55
% frosh live on campus	100
% ugrads live on campus	88
# of fraternities (% ugrad men join)	17 (46)
# of sororities (% ugrad women join)	11 (44)
% African American	7
% Asian	14
% Caucasian	48
% Hispanic	8
% Native American	2
% Pacific Islander	<1
% Two or more races	5
% Race and/or ethnicity unknown	7
% international	8
# of countries represented	70

SURVEY SAYS...

Students are happy
Classroom facilities are great
Lab facilities are great
Great library
Internships are widely available
Students are friendly
Students aren't religious
Easy to get around campus
Recreation facilities are great
Lots of beer drinking
Frats and sororities are popular
Campus newspaper is popular
Alumni active on campus

ACADEMICS

Academic Rating	96
% students returning for sophomore year	99
% students graduating within 4 years	88
Calendar	Semester
Student/faculty ratio	7:1
Profs interesting rating	90
Profs accessible rating	94

Most classes have 10–19 students.

MOST POPULAR MAJORS

Economics; Psychology; Political Science and Government

STUDENTS SAY "..."

Academics

Tucked away in bucolic New Hampshire, Dartmouth College manages to strike a nice "balance between the intimacy of a college [and] the opportunity of a university." Students feel fortunate that the administration places an "emphasis on pursuing passions, and making the college experience your own." And while Dartmouth certainly maintains a "competitive" atmosphere, students here truly appreciate that "no one really talks about their grades openly." Indeed, it's "generally understood that everyone is smart." A neuroscience major tells us that academically, "Dartmouth puts a huge focus on the undergraduate students, and I have found my professors to be available and engaging in nearly every instance. My classes are all challenging, but they are very discussion based and tend to be small, which keeps me working hard and interested in the material." And an impressed Middle Eastern studies major interjects, "I came to Dartmouth for the professors, but they were far beyond anything I could have hoped for. Not only are they great lecturers and accomplished scholars, they go out of their way to be available outside of the classroom, and to forge relationships beyond what is expected or necessary." When it comes down to it, "Dartmouth is considered to be a combination of Hogwarts and Disney World because it is known for its community and intelligent students and faculty, who also are personable and know how to have fun."

Life

There's no getting around it; at Dartmouth, the "Greek system is the main source of social activity." However, if you're wary of fraternities and sororities, fret not. A biology major reveals that a "very large percentage of students are involved which makes the Greek houses quite diverse and representative of the student body as a whole." Indeed, fraternities "are very inclusive" and while students definitely drink "there really isn't any pressure to." Further, plenty of social options exist beyond the party scene. "On any given night, you can do anything from see a hockey game to the early premiere of some cool new movie at the Hop[kins Center for the Arts], you can go to a dance party or just play cards or jam out on guitar or something... there are so many options to do whatever you're interested in doing." Dartmouth undergrads also love convening with nature. "Outdoorsy activities are huge here. The Appalachian Trail literally runs right through our campus. The Dartmouth Outing Club is the oldest and largest college outing club, and many students (even students who never did so before college) get involved with hiking, canoeing, rock climbing, and so forth." And a philosophy major concludes, "Whether it's skating on Occom Pond, going on a hike, going kayaking, apple picking, thrift shopping... there are boundless opportunities to do anything that interests you, and it means that whatever you're doing in your free time is always something really awesome."

Student Body

Undergrads here emphatically insist that it's "hard to define a typical student because at Dartmouth literally every type of person is represented." Of course, if pressed, they might reluctantly admit that the average student comes across as "preppy, academically goal oriented but also extremely social." And, as you might expect, undergrads also report that their peers are certainly very "smart." Fortunately, they "do not boast about their intellectual capacity." A happy senior tells us that "the common denominator is that Dartmouth students are very involved." Indeed, "whether it's with a club sports team, a cappella group, community service project, academic research, or a Greek house, Dartmouth students manage to do a lot of things in the course of the day." One incredulous sophomore concurs, adding that his friends "are always studying and participating in some extracurricular activity and you wonder how they have time to sleep and then you will see them out at a frat too. Then they show up at class the next morning with all of the work completed and they seem like a magician." Finally a junior concludes, "It's a small enough school that there is a sense of community that's always present, but large enough that everyone can find their own niche and their own area of the school and the community that caters to them perfectly."

FINANCIAL AID: 800-443-3605 • E-MAIL: ADMISSIONS.REPLY@DARTMOUTH.EDU • WEBSITE: WWW.DARTMOUTH.EDU

THE PRINCETON REVIEW SAYS

Admissions

Very important factors considered include: rigor of secondary school record, class rank, academic GPA, standardized test scores, application essay, recommendation(s), extracurricular activities, character/personal qualities. *Important factors considered include:* talent/ability, volunteer work. *Other factors considered include:* interview, first generation, alumni/ae relation, geographical residence, racial/ethnic status. SAT or ACT required. ACT with Writing required. TOEFL required of all international applicants. High school diploma or equivalent is not required. *Academic units recommended:* 4 English, 4 math, 4 science, 4 foreign language, 4 social studies.

Financial Aid

Students should submit: FAFSA, CSS/Financial Aid PROFILE, Noncustodial PROFILE, Business/Farm Supplement. Regular filing deadline is 2/1.The Princeton Review suggests that all financial aid forms be submitted as soon as possible after October 1. *Need-based scholarships/grants offered:* Federal Pell, FSEOG, State scholarships/grants, Private scholarships, College/university scholarship or grant aid from institutional funds. *Loan aid offered:* Direct Subsidized Stafford Loans, Direct Unsubsidized Stafford Loans, Direct PLUS loans, Federal Perkins Loans, State Loans, College/university loans from institutional funds. Applicants will be notified of awards on or about 4/2. Federal Work-Study Program available. Institutional employment available.

The Inside Word

Competition to secure a coveted acceptance letter from Dartmouth is fierce. After all, the majority of admitted students are in the top of their respective high school classes. Therefore, academic success is mandatory for any serious contender as is a schedule chock-full of honors, AP and/or IB courses. Of course, admissions officers are looking for well-rounded students so extracurricular activities, personal statements and recommendations will also be closely assessed. Finally, it's important to know that Dartmouth is a need-blind institution.

THE SCHOOL SAYS "..."

From the Admissions Office

"With its focus on undergraduate education and a flexible year-round academic calendar that encourages travel and research, Dartmouth is uniquely positioned to help students pursue their interests, prepare for a career and make an impact on the world. All classes are taught by members of the faculty, over 1,000 students per year pursue independent study for credit, and almost two-thirds of students participate in study abroad programs.

"Dartmouth opened the Class of 1978 Life Sciences Center in the fall of 2011, and the Black Family Visual Arts Center opened in the fall of 2012. These new facilities are designed to expand Dartmouth's commitment to undergraduate research and further the college's collaboration between faculty and students.

"On campus, students participate in nearly 400 student organizations, including thirty-four intercollegiate varsity teams, over forty different community service projects, and more than fifty performing groups. Dartmouth's hometown of Hanover offers an active political scene, a vibrant arts community, and unparalleled outdoors and recreational opportunities (including our own ski mountain!).

"To help all Dartmouth students take advantage of the Dartmouth Experience, the college practices need-blind admission for all applicants, meets the full demonstrated need for all admitted students, and offers free tuition and no loan requirements for all students whose annual family incomes are below $100,000.

"Dartmouth's admissions process is designed to identify students who will thrive in a challenging and flexible academic environment, who value community, and who will take advantage of the college's undergraduate focus."

SELECTIVITY
Admissions Rating	98
# of applicants	19,296
% of applicants accepted	12
% of acceptees attending	52
# offered a place on the wait list	1,855
% accepting a place on wait list	61
% admitted from wait list	0
# of early decision applicants	1,682
% accepted early decision	28

FRESHMAN PROFILE
Range SAT Critical Reading	680–780
Range SAT Math	680–770
Range SAT Writing	690–790
Range ACT Composite	30–34
Minimum paper TOEFL	600
Minimum internet-based TOEFL	250
% graduated top 10% of class	93
% graduated top 25% of class	99
% graduated top 50% of class	100

DEADLINES
Early decision	
Deadline	11/1
Notification	12/15
Regular	
Deadline	1/1
Notification	4/10
Nonfall registration?	No

FINANCIAL FACTS
Financial Aid Rating	96
Annual tuition	$48,120
Room and board	$14,238
Required fees	$1,386
Books and supplies	$1,260
Average frosh need-based scholarship	$44,666
Average UG need-based scholarship	$42,263
% needy frosh rec. need-based scholarship or grant aid	98
% needy UG rec. need-based scholarship or grant aid	95
% needy frosh rec. non-need-based scholarship or grant aid	0
% needy UG rec. non-need-based scholarship or grant aid	0
% needy frosh rec. need-based self-help aid	90
% needy UG rec. need-based self-help aid	93
% frosh rec. any financial aid	58
% UG rec. any financial aid	54
% frosh need fully met	100
% ugrads need fully met	100
Average % of frosh need met	100
Average % of ugrad need met	100

DAVIDSON COLLEGE

PO Box 7156, Davidson, NC 28035-7156 • Admissions: 704-894-2230 • Fax: 704-894-2016

CAMPUS LIFE

Quality of Life Rating	88
Fire Safety Rating	60*
Green Rating	60*
Type of school	Private
Affiliation	Presbyterian
Environment	Village

STUDENTS

Total undergrad enrollment	1,784
% male/female	50/50
% from out of state	75
% frosh from public high school	47
% frosh live on campus	100
% ugrads live on campus	94
# of fraternities (% ugrad men join)	8 (39)
# of sororities (% ugrad women join)	6 (70)
% African American	7
% Asian	5
% Caucasian	68
% Hispanic	8
% Native American	1
% Pacific Islander	0
% Two or more races	4
% Race and/or ethnicity unknown	1
% international	6
# of countries represented	42

SURVEY SAYS...

Students politically aware
Students always studying
Students are happy
School is well run
No one cheats
Students involved in community service
Students love Davidson, NC
Alumni active on campus

ACADEMICS

Academic Rating	90
% students returning for sophomore year	96
% students graduating within 4 years	90
% students graduating within 6 years	93
Calendar	Semester
Student/faculty ratio	10:1
Profs interesting rating	84
Profs accessible rating	86

Most classes have 10–19 students.
Most lab/discussion sessions have
10–19 students.

MOST POPULAR MAJORS

Biology; Political Science and Government;
Psychology

STUDENTS SAY "..."

Academics

This small school north of Charlotte, North Carolina, cultivates an environment "that is very open to change and improvement" and empowers students to "be better people and make a difference in the world." The administration works hard to create an on-campus community and constantly makes efforts "to support and improve Davidson," all while keeping students happy and their minds full. "I have never witnessed people so eager to come do their job every day. [Professors] are almost too willing to help," says a student. There is also a trickle-down effect because even the student body is supportive and "eager to watch you succeed." The school offers a classic liberal arts education, encouraging students to take classes in all areas, and "all of these people come out smarter than they came in." "If I could spend twenty years being educated by this administration and these professors, I would," says a very happy junior. School is the number one priority for all of the students here, and while academics are all-consuming, time-wise, they are also "fascinating and rewarding." Without a doubt, Davidson is a tough school—"99 percent of us left our 4.0 GPAs back in high school," claims a student—and professors don't believe in grade inflation or curving grades, but they do readily make themselves available outside of class for help or discussion. There is a lot of work, but it "is accompanied by even more resources with which it can be successfully managed." One student testimonial: "My calculus teacher last semester has office hours in the student union, and he invited the whole class over to his house for chicken dinner—twice!" The dedication of the staff is contagious, and "though the work is rigorous, time spent in school never feels wasted."

Life

Davidson "possesses an intense study culture, and people hit the books regularly; it's cool to be smart." One of the many wonderful things about Davidson "is that academics voluntarily leave the classroom." "It's not uncommon to hear people discussing their current academic topics at lunch or in the gym." Basketball is a huge common ground for the student body at large; "Everyone enjoys being a part of the underdog/Cinderella story." Weeks are devoted to study, as well as extracurricular activities—"you see your friends because you are doing homework together or eating meals together, not because you're vegging out." Of course, even Davidson students need to kick back, and there are always plenty of parties to be found on the weekends. Fraternities and eating houses (the Davidson version of sororities) are popular. Fortunately, "there really is no pressure to drink. You can go out and dance and have a great time or have movie nights with friends," says a student. The combination of the idyllic atmosphere and the workload "can make it hard to stay up-to-date on current events, yet most students remain well-informed."

Student Body

Davidson is "an amalgamation of all types of people, religiously, ethnically, politically, economically, etc.," all "united under the umbrella of intellectual curiosity" and their devotion to the school as a community. The typical Davidson student is "probably white," but in the past few years, admissions has been making progress in racially diversifying the campus, which students agree upon as necessary. Though there are plenty of Southern, preppy, athletic types to fit the brochure examples, there are many niches for every type of "atypical" student. "There are enough people that one can find a similar group to connect with, and there are few enough people that one ends up connecting with dissimilar [people] anyway," says a student. Everyone here is smart and well-rounded; admissions "does a good job...so if you're in you'll probably make the cut all the way through the four years." Most students have several extracurriculars to round out their free time, and they have a healthy desire to enjoy themselves when the books shut. "During the week we work hard. On the weekends we play hard. We don't do anything halfway," says a senior. Though the majority of students lean to the left, there's a strong conservative contingent, and there are no real problems between the two.

FINANCIAL AID: 704-894-2232 • E-MAIL: ADMISSION@DAVIDSON.EDU • WEBSITE: WWW.DAVIDSON.EDU

THE PRINCETON REVIEW SAYS

Admissions

Very important factors considered include: rigor of secondary school record, recommendation(s), character/personal qualities, volunteer work. *Important factors considered include:* standardized test scores, application essay, interview, extracurricular activities, talent/ability. *Other factors considered include:* class rank, academic GPA, alumni/ae relation. SAT or ACT required. ACT with Writing recommended. SAT with Essay component recommended. TOEFL required of all international applicants. High school diploma is required and GED is not accepted. *Academic units required:* 4 English, 3 math, 2 science, 2 foreign language, and 2 units from above areas or other academic areas. *Academic units recommended:* 4 math, 4 science, 4 foreign language, and 4 units from above areas or other academic areas.

Financial Aid

Students should submit: FAFSA, CSS/Financial Aid PROFILE, Noncustodial PROFILE, Business/Farm Supplement. Regular filing deadline is 2/15.The Princeton Review suggests that all financial aid forms be submitted as soon as possible after October 1. *Need-based scholarships/grants offered:* Federal Pell, FSEOG, State scholarships/grants, Private scholarships, College/university scholarship or grant aid from institutional funds. *Loan aid offered:* Direct Subsidized Stafford Loans, Direct Unsubsidized Stafford Loans, Direct PLUS Loans. Applicants will be notified of awards on or about 4/1. Federal Work-Study Program available. Institutional employment available.

The Inside Word

The combination of Davidson's low acceptance rate and high yield really packs a punch. Prospective applicants beware: Securing admission at this prestigious school is no easy feat. Admitted students are typically at the top of their high school classes and have strong standardized test scores. Candidates with leadership experience generally garner the favor of admissions officers. The college takes its honor code seriously and, as a result, seeks out students of demonstrated reputable character.

THE SCHOOL SAYS "..."

From the Admissions Office

"Davidson College is one of the nation's premier academic institutions, a college of the liberal arts and sciences respected for its intellectual vigor, the high quality of its faculty and students, and the achievements of its alumni. Davidson is distinguished by its strong honor code, close collaboration between professors and students, an environment that encourages both intellectual growth and community service, and a commitment to international education. Davidson places great value on student participation in extracurricular activities, intercollegiate athletics, and intramural sports. The college has a strong regional identity, grounded in traditions of civility and mutual respect, and has historic ties to the Presbyterian Church. The college has a strong commitment to making a Davidson education affordable. The college doesn't include student loans in its financial aid packages. Through the Davidson Trust, 100 percent of demonstrated financial need for domestic student is met with a combination of grants and student employment.

"Applicants are required to complete and submit scores from the SAT and/or the ACT. SAT Subject Tests (mathematics and one of your choice) are recommended. Davidson will utilize the scores that place the student in the greatest possible light."

SELECTIVITY

Admissions Rating	96
# of applicants	5,382
% of applicants accepted	22
% of acceptees attending	43
# of early decision applicants	638
% accepted early decision	48

FRESHMAN PROFILE

Range SAT Critical Reading	630–720
Range SAT Math	630–720
Range SAT Writing	610–720
Range ACT Composite	29–32
Minimum paper TOEFL	600
Minimum internet-based TOEFL	100
Average HS GPA	4.0
% graduated top 10% of class	55
% graduated top 25% of class	91
% graduated top 50% of class	91

DEADLINES

Early decision	
Deadline	11/15
Notification	12/15
Regular	
Deadline	1/2
Notification	4/1
Nonfall registration?	No

APPLICANTS ALSO LOOK AT AND OFTEN PREFER

Princeton University; Swarthmore College; Williams College; Stanford University

AND SOMETIMES PREFER

Vanderbilt University; University of Virginia; The University of North Carolina at Chapel Hill

AND RARELY PREFER

Colgate University; Emory University

FINANCIAL FACTS

Financial Aid Rating	96
Annual tuition	$46,501
Room and board	$13,153
Required fees	$465
Books and supplies	$1,000
Average frosh need-based scholarship	$37,846
Average UG need-based scholarship	$40,140
% needy frosh rec. need-based scholarship or grant aid	99
% needy UG rec. need-based scholarship or grant aid	99
% needy frosh rec. non-need-based scholarship or grant aid	34
% needy UG rec. non-need-based scholarship or grant aid	32
% needy frosh rec. need-based self-help aid	62
% needy UG rec. need-based self-help aid	70
% frosh rec. any financial aid	52
% UG rec. any financial aid	52
% UG borrow to pay for school	27
Average cumulative indebtedness	$19,929
% frosh need fully met	100
% ugrads need fully met	100
Average % of frosh need met	100
Average % of ugrad need met	100

DEEP SPRINGS COLLEGE

APPLICATIONS COMMITTEE, DYER, NV 89010 • ADMISSIONS: 760-872-2000 • FAX: 760-872-4466

STUDENTS SAY "..."

Academics

The "three pillars" of a Deep Springs education—"labor, academics, and self-governance"—combine to produce "unparalleled challenges" that run the gamut "from fixing a hay baler in the middle of the night to puzzling over a particularly difficult passage of Hegel." That's what the twenty-eight men who attend Deep Springs tell us. These unique undergraduates basically run their own school, work the ranch where it is located, and complete a rigorous curriculum, an itinerary that "creates an environment of intense growth and responsibility." Class work occurs in a seminar format in which "teachers participate similarly to students." Classes "aren't so much a transfer of information from professor to student as they are a time for the entire class to push the boundaries of collective thought as far as possible." Composition and public speaking are the only required courses; all others are chosen by the student body and taught by a faculty of three long-term professors (one each in the humanities, social sciences, and natural sciences) and one to three visiting scholars or artists. The system relies on a commitment to self-determination, which means "how successful Deep Springs is as an institution depends upon the manner in which its students are engaging with its project." While the size of the school inevitably means that "lab and library facilities are not what they might be," students tell us that the overall Deep Springs experience compensates for any shortcomings. A student explains: "Mistakes and flaws are seen as pedagogy in action. See a broken fence or heater? Fix it, or learn to fix it. The mechanical skills we pick up during the process of taking responsibility for our livelihood are surely valuable, but the self-confidence and that emerges from learning to do things one never could have thought possible is the essence of a Deep Springer's education."

Life

At Deep Springs, where "the desert sun rises slowly," everyday student life is totally unlike other colleges because "no one drinks, everyone helps run the ranch in some way, and no one can be totally self-absorbed (unless he's out hiking in the desert)." Instead, students immerse themselves in the Deep Springs way. As one student explains, "Life is very intellectual but also in constant relationship to the natural beauty of the desert and the operation of the College's farm and ranch." Conversations tend to revolve around "what work needs to be done, what decisions need to be made, [and] which classes are most interesting," or, as one student put its, "Sunsets. Hegel. Welding. Jane Austen." Fun at Deep Springs, where days are "marked by an extreme busyness," is "self generated": "'Fun' is hard to come by, and one has to learn how to enjoy people, work, and engagement." Students do occasionally take a break, however: "Fun just means something a little different . . . Half-naked dances to Miley Cyrus, fully naked soccer, or fully clothed conversations on anything from Kierkegaard to Kanye West ensure that there really isn't a dull moment in the Valley." Also, occasionally "there are 'boojies'," a kind of hectic dance party in the Rumpus Room of the dorm, " or students will "go to the dunes a valley over for a bit of late-night naked surfing down the sand." Undergrads concede that Deep Springs "life can be intense:" There is "a whirlwind of activity from labor to class to meals to labor again to meetings to a few precious hours of sleep. But where many students would find such a lifestyle stressful and unsustainable, we find it meaningful and valuable" and that keeps undergrads energized and motivated."

Student Body

"It is impossible to characterize a 'typical' student, as there are only twenty-eight," students understandably warn, but they add that "we all are hardworking and are committed to a life of service." Undergrads are also predictably "outdoorsy," "interested in the arts," "motivated, and responsible," as "it takes a unique type of person to even consider Deep Springs, much less succeed and thrive in such an environment." As one student puts it, "The typical student at Deep Springs is committed to the life of the intellect and committed to finding education in our labor program. Most of the students here believe that a life of service, informed by discourse and labor, is a necessary notion to understand in today's world."

FINANCIAL AID: 760-872-2000 • E-MAIL: APCOM@DEEPSPRINGS.EDU • WEBSITE: WWW.DEEPSPRINGS.EDU

THE PRINCETON REVIEW SAYS

Admissions

Very important factors considered include: application essay, interview, character/personal qualities, level of applicant's interest. *Important factors considered include:* rigor of secondary school record, academic GPA, extracurricular activities, volunteer work, work experience. *Other factors considered include:* class rank, standardized test scores, recommendation(s), talent/ability, first generation, racial/ethnic status. SAT or ACT required for some. ACT with or without writing accepted. High school diploma or equivalent is not required.

Financial Aid

*Students should submit:*The Princeton Review suggests that all financial aid forms be submitted as soon as possible after October 1.

The Inside Word

Students will be hard-pressed to find a school with a more personal or thorough application process than Deep Springs. Given the intimate and collegial atmosphere of the school, matchmaking is the top priority. Candidates are evaluated by a body composed of students, faculty, and staff members. The application is writing intensive; finalists are expected to spend several days on campus, during which they will undergo a lengthy interview.

THE SCHOOL SAYS "..."

From the Admissions Office

"Founded in 1917, Deep Springs College lies isolated in a high desert valley of eastern California, thirty miles from the nearest town. Its enrollment is limited to twenty-eight students, each of whom receives a full scholarship that covers tuition and room and board, and is valued at more than $50,000 per year. Students engage in rigorous academics, govern themselves, and participate in the operation of our ranch and farm.

"Given our small size, statistics must be viewed with context. Nonetheless, we have compiled data from the past five years to give some perspective on the characteristics of our students.

"The Applications Committee (ApCom) receives between 180 and 250 applications each year. Between thirteen and fifteen applicants are invited to enroll; ten are added to a wait-list. After two years at Deep Springs, students generally transfer to other schools to complete their studies. Students regularly attend Yale, University of Chicago, and Brown, and also have recently chosen several other schools including Cornell, Evergreen, Harvard, Reed, Stanford, Swarthmore, and UC Berkeley.

"Despite its small size, Deep Springs is a diverse community. In the past five years, 30 percent of Deep Springs students have been people of color. More than 11 percent of students have identified as LGBT. International students have made up about 20 percent of the Student Body. In each year, at least one student has spent between one semester and two years enrolled at another college before attending Deep Springs."

SELECTIVITY

Admissions Rating	99
# of applicants	200
% of applicants accepted	10
% of acceptees attending	84
# offered a place on the wait list	5
% accepting a place on wait list	100
% admitted from wait list	100

FRESHMAN PROFILE

Range SAT Critical Reading	740–800
Range SAT Math	670–740
% graduated top 10% of class	100
% graduated top 25% of class	100
% graduated top 50% of class	100

DEADLINES

Regular	
Deadline	11/7
Notification	4/15
Nonfall registration?	No

APPLICANTS ALSO LOOK AT AND RARELY PREFER

Harvard College; Swarthmore College; University of Chicago; Cornell University; Stanford University; Yale University

FINANCIAL FACTS

Financial Aid Rating	60*
Annual tuition	$0
Books and supplies	$1,200
Average frosh need-based scholarship	$0
% needy frosh rec. need-based scholarship or grant aid	0
% needy UG rec. need-based scholarship or grant aid	0
% needy frosh rec. non-need-based scholarship or grant aid	0
% needy UG rec. non-need-based scholarship or grant aid	0
% needy frosh rec. need-based self-help aid	0
% needy UG rec. need-based self-help aid	0
% frosh rec. any financial aid	100
% UG rec. any financial aid	100
Average % of frosh need met	0
Average % of ugrad need met	0

DENISON UNIVERSITY

Box H, Granville, OH 43023 • Admissions: 740-587-6276 • Fax: 740-587-6306

CAMPUS LIFE
Quality of Life Rating	89
Fire Safety Rating	96
Green Rating	91
Type of school	Private
Affiliation	No Affiliation
Environment	Village

STUDENTS
Total undergrad enrollment	2,282
% male/female	43/57
% from out of state	72
% frosh from public high school	66
% frosh live on campus	99
% ugrads live on campus	99
# of fraternities (% ugrad men join)	9 (21)
# of sororities (% ugrad women join)	9 (34)
% African American	7
% Asian	4
% Caucasian	66
% Hispanic	10
% Native American	<1
% Pacific Islander	<1
% Two or more races	4
% Race and/or ethnicity unknown	2
% international	8
# of countries represented	34

SURVEY SAYS...
Students are happy
Classroom facilities are great
Lab facilities are great
Career services are great
Internships are widely available
Class discussions encouraged
School is well run
Great financial aid
Easy to get around campus
Lots of beer drinking
Hard liquor is popular

ACADEMICS
Academic Rating	91
% students returning for sophomore year	89
% students graduating within 4 years	78
% students graduating within 6 years	80
Calendar	Semester
Student/faculty ratio	10:1
Profs interesting rating	89
Profs accessible rating	92

Most classes have 10–19 students.

MOST POPULAR MAJORS
Economics; Psychology; Biology

STUDENTS SAY "..."

Academics

For those seeking out "a small, liberal arts school with quality academics as well as a penchant for producing students who are well-rounded citizens," Denison University deserves a closer look. The school is "set in a beautiful and very safe town" in suburban Central Ohio near Columbus, and offers "an intelligent and welcoming community ready and willing to help others" as well as "a great support system." Denison offers a campus filled with "continuous construction of new facilities," including academic, residential, and recreational spaces, where "students have diverse opportunities to explore their talents and improve their skills through campus jobs, clubs, internships, and the election of double majors and minors that don't necessarily fit together." "The classes are challenging," and "the academics are competitive and foster interesting class selection." One student also admits, "General education requirements, although somewhat tedious, provide opportunities for students to grow in areas that they normally would not consider investing their time in."

The crown jewels of the school's academic life seem to be the professors who are "tough, but usually fair." One student raves, "At Denison, we have professors that can make a poem out of a picture and a mountain out of a math problem. We are so privileged to be surrounded by scholars who are passionate about teaching and learning what they love." Students get a chance to form close bonds with their professors thanks to the "small student-to-faculty ratio" as well as the high accessibility of the professors outside of the classroom. According to one student, "As far as professor availability goes, I see my professors on campus so often that I'm starting to suspect they sleep in their offices..." Students keep it all in perspective and recognize that "although academics are certainly important here, Denison teaches you how to shape what you know so that you become a more curious, passionate, and interesting individual."

Life

"Life here is a big blur of class, athletics, parties, and down time." That seems to be the general consensus among students at this school. In other words, "whether you enjoy sports, Greek life, service or quidditch it can all be found at Denison!" Students highlight that "There's a good party scene, largely dominated by fraternities, but there are more and more non-Greek options" and "at least 50 percent of the campus is out partying on any given Friday or Saturday night." Offering another perspective, one student notes, "Parties happen every weekend, but there are plenty of people who prefer to chill with friends in the dorm rooms and just watch movies." For those interested in exploring life off campus, "Granville is small but cute, [and] there's plenty to eat at a good price," and "some cute shops." "Many also choose Columbus for clubbing, the alternative and bucolic Homestead for random parties, or even the Broadway area in Granville for dining in the ten-ish big restaurant options, drinking at Brew's, or just studying in River Road or Village Coffee Co. coffee shops. Whit's Frozen Custard is great too."

Student Body

Denison students generally agree that "we have a reputation as a WASP-y, East-Coast-in-Ohio school, but that is slowly changing." And while many students at Denison can be described as "tall, good-looking, and dressed in Vineyard Vines, J. Crew, or RL," one student explains, "At first, most students will feel like preppy New Englanders, but if you don't conform to this image it's still easy to find friends." This would include the environmentalists who "are a pretty big presence on campus now." At Denison, many seem to agree, "Students are also extremely involved, almost everyone is involved in at least two to three clubs or activities, and many people hold some sort of leadership role." Ultimately, "Denison is a place for real people who love caring about each other and learning, [and] if you don't like having a close-knit group of people there to support you, then don't go to Denison."

FINANCIAL AID: 800-336-4766 • E-MAIL: ADMISSIONS@DENISON.EDU • WEBSITE: WWW.DENISON.EDU

THE PRINCETON REVIEW SAYS

Admissions

Very important factors considered include: rigor of secondary school record, academic GPA, application essay, recommendation(s). *Important factors considered include:* interview, extracurricular activities, talent/ability, level of applicant's interest. *Other factors considered include:* class rank, standardized test scores, character/personal qualities, first generation, alumni/ae relation, geographical residence, state residency, racial/ethnic status, volunteer work, work experience. SAT or ACT considered if submitted. ACT with or without writing accepted. SAT with or without Essay component accepted. TOEFL required of all international applicants. High school diploma is required and GED is accepted. *Academic units required:* 4 English, 4 math, 4 science, 3 foreign language, 2 social studies, 1 history, 1 academic elective.

Financial Aid

Students should submit: FAFSA. Priority filing deadline is 3/15.The Princeton Review suggests that all financial aid forms be submitted as soon as possible after October 1. *Need-based scholarships/grants offered:* Federal Pell, FSEOG, State scholarships/grants, Private scholarships, College/university scholarship or grant aid from institutional funds. *Loan aid offered:* Direct Subsidized Stafford Loans, Direct Unsubsidized Stafford Loans, Direct PLUS loans, Federal Perkins Loans, College/university loans from institutional funds. Applicants will be notified of awards on a rolling basis beginning 3/28. Federal Work-Study Program available. Institutional employment available.

The Inside Word

Admission to Denison is pretty straightforward. The school "suggests" an interview, meaning you should do one if at all possible. It's a great way to demonstrate your interest in the school, which improves your chances of admission, especially if your grades, test scores, and overall profile put you on the admit/reject borderline. Denison offers and alternative test-optional application process for high-achieving students.

THE SCHOOL SAYS "..."

From the Admissions Office

"Denison University is a leading national residential liberal arts college located just outside Columbus, Ohio. The college balances a rigorous and relevant academic experience founded on perceptive mentorship by dedicated faculty at the cutting edge of their research, with robust co-curricular and extra-curricular programming, which includes athletics, performing and fine arts and more than 170 student-run organizations, providing abundant opportunities for students to develop leadership qualities and nurture friendships that will last throughout their lives. Wellness and academic support programs serve the whole student, promoting academic accomplishment as well as resilience, balance and well being.

"Denison students are comprehensively prepared for lifetimes of civic and personal success, expanding their skills and expertise through extensive research opportunities and innovative career programming. The college is creating the gold standard in supporting students transitioning to life after college, through meaningful alumni networking, innovative programs that establish discrete capabilities related to vocations, and well-paid summer internships in their field of interest, which help them to establish relationships and forge skills directly related to their future careers. Proof of their student success is provided on an interactive webpage, 'The Denison Difference,' which reports graduate placement in careers, graduate schools and service opportunities. Denison students have been granted more than 150 Fulbright and other international post-graduate scholarships, and in recent years have garnered 100 percent acceptance rates to both medical and law school programs. The college's distinguished alumni claim both Rhodes Scholar and a Gates Cambridge Scholar honors."

SELECTIVITY

Admissions Rating	90
# of applicants	6,110
% of applicants accepted	48
% of acceptees attending	22
# offered a place on the wait list	515
% accepting a place on wait list	85
% admitted from wait list	5
# of early decision applicants	246
% accepted early decision	88

FRESHMAN PROFILE

Range SAT Critical Reading	580–680
Range SAT Math	580–680
Range ACT Composite	26–31
Minimum paper TOEFL	599
Average HS GPA	3.6
% graduated top 10% of class	55
% graduated top 25% of class	23
% graduated top 50% of class	96

DEADLINES

Early decision	
Deadline	11/15
Regular	
Priority	11/15
Deadline	1/15
Notification	3/15
Nonfall registration?	Yes

APPLICANTS ALSO LOOK AT AND OFTEN PREFER

University of Michigan–Ann Arbor; University of Richmond

AND SOMETIMES PREFER

Kenyon College; Oberlin College; Boston College; Vanderbilt University; Northwestern University; Gettysburg College

AND RARELY PREFER

Case Western Reserve University; Bucknell University; DePauw University; Dickinson College; Miami University

FINANCIAL FACTS

Financial Aid Rating	88
Books and supplies	$650
Average frosh need-based scholarship	$33,696
Average UG need-based scholarship	$34,812
% needy frosh rec. need-based scholarship or grant aid	100
% needy UG rec. need-based scholarship or grant aid	100
% needy frosh rec. non-need-based scholarship or grant aid	93
% needy UG rec. non-need-based scholarship or grant aid	93
% needy frosh rec. need-based self-help aid	78
% needy UG rec. need-based self-help aid	77
% frosh rec. any financial aid	99
% UG rec. any financial aid	98
% UG borrow to pay for school	50
Average cumulative indebtedness	$28,146
% frosh need fully met	21
% ugrads need fully met	22
Average % of frosh need met	90
Average % of ugrad need met	92

DePaul University

One East Jackson Boulevard, Chicago, IL 60604-2287 • Admissions: 312-362-8300 • Fax: 312-362-5749

CAMPUS LIFE

Quality of Life Rating	92
Fire Safety Rating	99
Green Rating	86
Type of school	Private
Affiliation	Roman Catholic
Environment	Metropolis

STUDENTS

Total undergrad enrollment	15,961
% male/female	47/53
% from out of state	23
% frosh from public high school	78
% frosh live on campus	70
% ugrads live on campus	17
# of fraternities (% ugrad men join)	10 (3)
# of sororities (% ugrad women join)	16 (6)
% African American	8
% Asian	8
% Caucasian	55
% Hispanic	18
% Native American	<1
% Pacific Islander	<1
% Two or more races	4
% Race and/or ethnicity unknown	4
% international	3
# of countries represented	84

SURVEY SAYS...

Students are happy
Classroom facilities are great
Career services are great
School is well run
Students love Chicago, IL
Great off-campus food
Recreation facilities are great

ACADEMICS

Academic Rating	73
% students returning for sophomore year	84
% students graduating within 4 years	0
Calendar	Semester
Student/faculty ratio	16:1
Profs interesting rating	79
Profs accessible rating	79

Most classes have 20–29 students.
Most lab/discussion sessions have
20–29 students.

MOST POPULAR MAJORS

Accounting; Finance; Psychology

STUDENTS SAY "..."

Academics

DePaul University's urban setting means this Chicago school is "all about integrating the opportunities of the city into the classroom," offering students "the essentials in order for a student to succeed in the business field." Here, the "dedicated" teaching staff's "extensive experience outside of the classroom... really brings valuable information into the classroom." That experience proves beneficial to career-focused students because it "encourages students to become critical life thinkers so that they are not just prepared for a job, but have the skills to become present in all life decisions." This real-world focus in classroom studies and its "extensive school of commerce curriculum" is part of what has given DePaul a "strong academic reputation." Internship and career-placement opportunities both during school and after graduation result in, according to some graduates, students who are "some of the hardest working and driven college students around." The multiple colleges of DePaul University "stress engaging with other students, working collaboratively, combining previous knowledge with new learning, and being an active participant in one's education." Students praise the easy access provided by the urban setting and its accompanying public transportation, and like the "practical real world experience" brought to the table by the educators here—though some note "there are ones that are tougher graders," so applicants should be prepared to work.

Life

The school's location in downtown Chicago, one of the largest and most vibrant cities in the United States, means that "there is a plethora of choices of things to do" and plenty of transportation to get to them. Students "are always going to the museums, the art institute, Navy pier, shopping on Michigan Ave, the zoo, the beach, etc.," and "in the summer the outdoor concerts and food tasting events take over Grant Park." Throw in "the lakefront, bars and restaurants, sports teams (pro and collegiate)," along with "cultural venues [and] free public events," and it's no wonder students say they "never get bored." Sports fanatics will especially find more than enough to keep themselves busy outside of class. If the wealth of riches that is Chicago professional sports is not enough—the Bulls, Blackhawks, White Sox, Cubs, and Bears all play here—"having DePaul in the Big East conference brings great college basketball to Chicago," too. For those who prefer to stay on campus in this "simply amazing" city, DePaul has a strong Greek scene. The bottom line is, life at DePaul is all about location, location, location, so "the internships, classes, and social life are centered around the city."

Student Body

There is no nailing down the typical DePaul student. "It's like a melting pot of experience and people from all over the world that come to be a part of the DePaul environment," a "unique blend of all kinds of students" who are "like a giant mixed bag of Jelly Bellys...every student is so different you have a little bit of everything." One student goes so far as to suggest it's "possibly the most diverse school in the country." Though attendees "come from all walks of life" and "individuality is promoted strongly," virtually anyone "can fit in easily if they want." "Every student has a place where they feel comfortable," one student says, "and it is hard to find a student that doesn't fit in here." If there is a tie that binds, it is that DePaul students are "kind and friendly," "outgoing and respectful," a group who "study hard to get where they're going but still find time to socialize." Hard work is a common trait. "The majority of students seem to hold outside employment," a student notes, "which brings a strong real world emphasis to the class from staff and students alike." But hard workers aside, the typical DePaul student? "There is no typical anything."

FINANCIAL AID: 312-362-8091 • E-MAIL: ADMISSION@DEPAUL.EDU • WEBSITE: WWW.DEPAUL.EDU

THE PRINCETON REVIEW SAYS

Admissions

Very important factors considered include: rigor of secondary school record, academic GPA, standardized test scores. *Important factors considered include:* class rank, recommendation(s), extracurricular activities, talent/ability, character/personal qualities, volunteer work, work experience, level of applicant's interest. *Other factors considered include:* application essay, interview, first generation, alumni/ae relation, geographical residence, state residency, religious affiliation/commitment, racial/ethnic status. SAT or ACT recommend. ACT with or without writing accepted. SAT with or without Essay component accepted. TOEFL required of all international applicants. High school diploma is required and GED is accepted. *Academic units required:* 4 English, 3 math, 3 science, 2 science labs, and 2 units from above areas or other academic areas. *Academic units recommended:* 4 English, 3 math, 3 science, 2 science labs, 2 foreign language, and 2 units from above areas or other academic areas.

Financial Aid

Students should submit: FAFSA. Priority filing deadline is 3/1.The Princeton Review suggests that all financial aid forms be submitted as soon as possible after October 1. *Need-based scholarships/grants offered:* Federal Pell, FSEOG, State scholarships/grants, Private scholarships, College/university scholarship or grant aid from institutional funds. *Loan aid offered:* Direct Subsidized Stafford Loans, Direct Unsubsidized Stafford Loans, Direct PLUS loans, Federal Perkins Loans. Applicants will be notified of awards on a rolling basis beginning 3/15. Federal Work-Study Program available. Institutional employment available.

The Inside Word

DePaul's reputation as one of the most diverse schools in the country is not mere hyperbole, it's a truth expressed by student after student, and by the actions of the administration itself. The school actively seeks out minority students both as freshmen and transfers, and in an effort to surmount tuition-related obstacles works with local community colleges so students can meet their requirements at a lower cost before transferring to DePaul. Standardized test scores are optional. Students who do not submit test scores will be required to send responses to several short essay questions.

THE SCHOOL SAYS "..."

From the Admissions Office

"The nation's largest Catholic university, DePaul University is nationally recognized for its innovative academic programs that embrace a comprehensive learn-by-doing approach. DePaul has two residential locations. The Lincoln Park Campus is home to the College of Liberal Arts and Social Sciences, the College of Science and Health, the College of Education, the School of Music, The Theatre School and the extensive John T. Richardson Library. The Loop location, located in Chicago's downtown—a world-class center for business, government, law, and culture—is home to DePaul's Driehaus College of Business, College of Communication, College of Law, College of Computing and Digital Media, and School for New Learning."

SELECTIVITY

Admissions Rating	80
# of applicants	19,628
% of applicants accepted	72
% of acceptees attending	18

FRESHMAN PROFILE

Range SAT Critical Reading	520–620
Range SAT Math	490–610
Range ACT Composite	22–28
Minimum paper TOEFL	550
Minimum internet-based TOEFL	80
Average HS GPA	3.6
% graduated top 10% of class	20
% graduated top 25% of class	54
% graduated top 50% of class	87

DEADLINES

Early action	
Deadline	11/15
Notification	1/15
Regular	
Priority	11/15
Deadline	2/1
Notification	3/15
Nonfall registration?	Yes

FINANCIAL FACTS

Financial Aid Rating	79
Annual tuition	$35,680
Room and board	$12,873
Required fees	$681
Books and supplies	$1,104
Average frosh need-based scholarship	$10,969
Average UG need-based scholarship	$12,001
% needy frosh rec. need-based scholarship or grant aid	90
% needy UG rec. need-based scholarship or grant aid	85
% needy frosh rec. non-need-based scholarship or grant aid	86
% needy UG rec. non-need-based scholarship or grant aid	67
% needy frosh rec. need-based self-help aid	73
% needy UG rec. need-based self-help aid	77
% frosh rec. any financial aid	98
% UG rec. any financial aid	87
% UG borrow to pay for school	68
Average cumulative indebtedness	$29,932
% frosh need fully met	11
% ugrads need fully met	8
Average % of frosh need met	65
Average % of ugrad need met	61

DePauw University

204 East Seminary, Greencastle, IN 46135 • Admissions: 765-658-4006 • Fax: 765-658-4007

STUDENTS SAY "..."

Academics

Serious-minded students are drawn to DePauw University for its "small classes," "encouraging" professors, and the "individual academic attention" they can expect to receive. Academically, DePauw is "demanding but rewarding," and "requires a lot of outside studying and discipline" in order to keep up. Professors' "expectations are very high," which means "you can't slack off and get good grades." Be prepared to pull your "fair share of all-nighters." Fortunately, DePauw professors are more than just stern taskmasters. Though they pile on the work, they "are always helpful and available" to students in need. When things get overwhelming, "they are very understanding and will cut you a break if you really deserve" it. As a result, students come to know their professors "on a personal level," making DePauw the kind of school where it is "common [for students] to have dinner at a professor's house." Beyond stellar professors, DePauw's other academic draws include "extraordinary" study abroad opportunities and a "wonderful" alumni network great for "connections and networking opportunities." Alums also "keep our endowment pretty high, making it easy for the school to give out merit scholarships," which undergraduates appreciate. Student opinion regarding the administration ranges from ambivalent to slightly negative. One especially thorny issue is class registration; you "rarely" get into all the classes you want.

Life

Few schools are as Greek as DePauw, but students are quick to point out that "it is by no means *Animal House*." The Greek system here is more holistic than that. It "promotes not only social activities but also philanthropic events." That's not to say there aren't lots of frat parties here. There are. But "the administration has cracked down big time" on the larger frat parties, and "now there are just small parties in apartments and dorms." One recently issued rule is that freshmen "will not be allowed on Greek property until after rush, which is the first week of second semester." In addition to administrative regulation, students exercise their own self-restraint; for the typical undergraduate, "the week is mostly reserved for studying." Beyond the frats and sororities, "there is always a theater production, athletic event, or organization-sponsored event going on," and popular bands occasionally perform on campus. It's a good thing so much is happening at the school because off-campus entertainment options are scarce: "If there is really any fun to be had, it's not in Greencastle." The situation could be greatly improved if there were just a few "more restaurants and stores in the town or a nearby town." As things stand, however, students "have to go to Indianapolis (forty-five miles) to go shopping, watch a good movie, eat at a good restaurant, etc."

Student Body

The typical DePauw student is "upper middle class," "a little preppy, a little athletic," and "hardworking;" students "[party] hard on weekend," and "usually become[s] involved with the Greek system." Students describe their peers as "driven" and wearing "polos and pearls." They "have all had multiple internships, international experience, and [have held] some type of leadership position." Though these folks may seem "overcommitted," they "always get their work done." For those who don't fit this mold, don't fret; most students seem to be "accepting of the different types" of people on campus. Diversity on campus is augmented through the school's partnership with the Posse Foundation, which brings in urban (though not necessarily minority) "students from Chicago and NYC every year." These students are described as "leaders on campus" and "take real initiative to hold their communities together."

Financial Aid: 765-658-4030 • E-mail: admission@depauw.edu • Website: www.depauw.edu

THE PRINCETON REVIEW SAYS

Admissions

Very important factors considered include: rigor of secondary school record, academic GPA, standardized test scores. *Important factors considered include:* class rank, application essay, recommendation(s). *Other factors considered include:* interview, extracurricular activities, talent/ability, character/personal qualities, first generation, alumni/ae relation, geographical residence, state residency, volunteer work, work experience, level of applicant's interest. SAT or ACT required. ACT with or without writing accepted. TOEFL required of all international applicants. High school diploma is required and GED is accepted. *Academic units recommended:* 4 English, 4 math, 2 science labs.

Financial Aid

Students should submit: FAFSA, CSS/Financial Aid PROFILE. Regular filing deadline is 2/1.The Princeton Review suggests that all financial aid forms be submitted as soon as possible after October 1. *Need-based scholarships/grants offered:* Federal Pell, FSEOG, State scholarships/grants, Private scholarships, College/university scholarship or grant aid from institutional funds. *Loan aid offered:* Direct Subsidized Stafford Loans, Direct Unsubsidized Stafford Loans, Direct PLUS loans, Federal Perkins Loans, College/university loans from institutional funds. Applicants will be notified of awards on a rolling basis beginning 3/10. Federal Work-Study Program available. Institutional employment available.

The Inside Word

Prospective applicants should not be deceived by DePauw's high acceptance rate. The students who are accepted and choose to enroll here have the academic goods to justify their admission. Many of them are accepted by more "competitive" schools and still choose DePauw. DePauw's generous financial aid packages have a lot to do with students' choice to enroll.

THE SCHOOL SAYS "..."

From the Admissions Office

"DePauw University is nationally recognized for intellectual and experiential challenges that link liberal arts education with life's work, preparing graduates for uncommon professional success, service to others and personal fulfillment. DePauw graduates count among their ranks a Nobel Laureate, a vice president and United States congressman, Pulitzer Prize-winning and Newbery Award-winning authors, and a number of CEOs and humanitarian leaders. Our students demonstrate a love for learning, a willingness to serve others, the reason and judgment to lead, an interest in engaging worlds and cultures unknown to them, the courage to question their assumptions and a strong commitment to community. Pre-professional and career exploration are encouraged through Winter Term, when more than 700 students pursue their own off-campus experiential learning opportunities. Other innovative programs include Honor Scholars, Environmental Fellows, Media Fellows and Science Research Fellows, affording selected students additional seminar and internship opportunities. The University offers a new approach to music education in the entrepreneurial 21CM program in the School of Music.

"Freshman applicants are required to submit scores of the writing section of the SAT or the ACT."

SELECTIVITY

Admissions Rating	90
# of applicants	5,282
% of applicants accepted	57
% of acceptees attending	17
# of early decision applicants	52
% accepted early decision	88

FRESHMAN PROFILE

Range SAT Critical Reading	530–640
Range SAT Math	560–660
Range SAT Writing	520–630
Range ACT Composite	25–29
Minimum paper TOEFL	560
Average HS GPA	3.9
% graduated top 10% of class	48
% graduated top 25% of class	83
% graduated top 50% of class	97

DEADLINES

Early decision	
Deadline	11/1
Notification	1/1
Other ED	
Deadline	11/1
Other ED	
Notification	1/1
Early action	
Deadline	12/1
Notification	1/31
Regular	
Deadline	2/1
Nonfall registration?	Yes

APPLICANTS ALSO LOOK AT AND OFTEN PREFER
Indiana University Bloomington; Vanderbilt University; University of Notre Dame

AND SOMETIMES PREFER
University of Illinois at Urbana-Champaign; Miami University; Denison University

AND RARELY PREFER
Hanover College

FINANCIAL FACTS

Financial Aid Rating	87
Annual tuition	$43,950
Room and board	$11,700
Required fees	$728
Books and supplies	$900
Average frosh need-based scholarship	$31,067
Average UG need-based scholarship	$30,895
% needy frosh rec. need-based scholarship or grant aid	100
% needy UG rec. need-based scholarship or grant aid	100
% needy frosh rec. non-need-based scholarship or grant aid	24
% needy UG rec. non-need-based scholarship or grant aid	19
% needy frosh rec. need-based self-help aid	75
% needy UG rec. need-based self-help aid	80
% frosh need fully met	33
% ugrads need fully met	27
Average % of frosh need met	89
Average % of ugrad need met	89

DICKINSON COLLEGE

PO Box 1773, Carlisle, PA 17013-2896 • Admissions: 717-245-1231 • Fax: 717-245-1442

STUDENTS SAY "..."

Academics

Students feel that Dickinson "excels in sustainability and global education," and that their professors "go out of their way to make sure students understand the material and are doing well in their classes. It is not uncommon to walk by a professor's office and see it filled with students asking questions." But be warned, those who did not do the reading, for "many Dickinson classes are discussion based so arriving to class prepared is essential for academic success." Professors are both "tremendously accessible," "very engaging," and "come with all sorts of life experiences and connections in their respective fields to get students to interact with people in the areas they are studying." Classes are often "discussion-based," and "really give you an opportunity to engage and grow into the topic." Students feel that Dickinson "stresses the importance of a global mindset" alongside "an increasing sense of sustainability and a small community feel." Some students feel that their fellow classmates fail to "participate at a meaningful level." They cite its unique combination of being a small liberal arts school with a global perspective and an emphasis on sustainability as their reasons for attending, and say that Dickinson provides them "with the resources to develop and broaden your personal strengths" to better become "engaged within the local community and on a global scale."

Life

The social scene at Dickinson "revolves around sports even though it's a D-III school." Greek life plays a "small role" in the social scene too, and students claim men no longer feel "pressured to rush." The typical student "drinks two to three nights per week," though "activities outside of classes are limited because the town is small and stuck in the 1700s when it was built. However, there are a few great restaurants and take out places within close walking distance of campus." The dorms could "be improved," but the "administration is aware of this and there are various improvements currently happening as well as plans for future residential hall development." The dining service could use some work, but overall the food is "not terrible." It's a work hard, play hard campus at Dickinson, "the library will be full all day Saturday and Sunday and then everyone clears out to go hang out—either parties or other campus activities." Carlisle "has a charming downtown area right next to campus" and, as for the campus, well "it is so breathtakingly beautiful," and "not only is it pleasing to the eye, but I knew as soon as I set foot on campus that I would be able to achieve my academic goals while at Dickinson for undergrad. The study abroad program is phenomenal and continues to exceed expectations."

Student Body

Dickinson has a "unique community" full of "talented students and professors that encourage each other to pursue their passions," although it "needs to improve diversity." In general the student body is "middle class, friendly, not necessarily aware of others outside his or her demographic but willing to learn about others, engaged in campus life, athletic." There are "a lot of students who are clearly very privileged. There are also a large number of students who may or may not be but don't flaunt it, a relatively high percentage of foreign students, and a fair number of students from rural Pennsylvania and similar areas. A lot of people are remarkably intelligent," and practically everyone is "friendly and agreeable." "Involved" and "engaged" are two words that come up a lot. Students at Dickinson "have very diverse interests, but the one thing they all have in common is that they are passionate about something."

FINANCIAL AID: 717-245-1308 • E-MAIL: ADMISSIONS@DICKINSON.EDU • WEBSITE: WWW.DICKINSON.EDU

THE PRINCETON REVIEW SAYS

Admissions

Very important factors considered include: rigor of secondary school record, academic GPA, application essay, recommendation(s), extracurricular activities, talent/ability, character/personal qualities, volunteer work, level of applicant's interest. *Important factors considered include:* class rank, standardized test scores, interview, alumni/ae relation, geographical residence, state residency, racial/ethnic status, work experience. *Other factors considered include:* first generation. SAT or ACT recommend; SAT Subject Tests considered if submitted. ACT with or without writing accepted. SAT with or without Essay component accepted. TOEFL required of all international applicants. High school diploma is required and GED is accepted. *Academic units required:* 4 English, 3 math, 3 science, 2 science labs, 2 foreign language, 2 social studies, 2 academic electives. *Academic units recommended:* 3 foreign language.

Financial Aid

Students should submit: FAFSA, CSS/Financial Aid PROFILE, State aid form, Noncustodial PROFILE. Regular filing deadline is 2/1.The Princeton Review suggests that all financial aid forms be submitted as soon as possible after October 1. *Need-based scholarships/grants offered:* Federal Pell, FSEOG, State scholarships/grants, Private scholarships, College/university scholarship or grant aid from institutional funds. *Loan aid offered:* Direct Subsidized Stafford Loans, Direct Unsubsidized Stafford Loans, Direct PLUS loans, Federal Perkins Loans, College/university loans from institutional funds. Applicants will be notified of awards on or about 3/20. Federal Work-Study Program available. Institutional employment available.

The Inside Word

The applicant pool for small liberal arts colleges has become increasingly competitive in recent years, and Dickinson is no exception. For admission here, you'll want to be the stereotypical well-rounded student, with a solid GPA in challenging classes, and broad extracurricular involvement.

THE SCHOOL SAYS ". . ."

From the Admissions Office

"Dickinson is a nationally recognized liberal arts college chartered in 1783 in Carlisle, Pennsylvania. Devoted to its revolutionary roots, the college maintains the mission of founder Benjamin Rush—to provide a useful education in the liberal arts and sciences. Dickinson has a robust academic program, offering forty-three majors plus minors, certificates, independent research, and internships. Our innovative programs range from neuroscience to security studies, and develop intellectual independence by actively engaging in research, fieldwork, lab work in state-of-the-art science programs and other experiential opportunities. The newest addition to our curriculum, a certificate in social innovation & entrepreneurship, is evidence of our emphasis on being responsive in today's ever-changing economy. Dickinson's global curriculum includes international business and management, international studies, thirteen languages, and many globally oriented courses. Dickinson offers one of the world's most respected study abroad programs, and more than half of Dickinson's students study in more than forty programs in twenty-five countries on six continents. Dickinson is recognized as a leader among educational institutions committed to sustainability and green initiatives. The Center for Sustainability Education integrates sustainability into its academics, facilities, operations, and campus culture. Dickinson has received the highest awards from the Association for the Advancement of Sustainability in Higher Education, Sierra Club, Sustainable Endowments Institute, The Princeton Review, and Second Nature. Dickinson alumni are at the top of their fields as business leaders, professional artists and writers, sports agents and athletes, doctors and researchers. And many of them used their liberal arts foundation to forge their own paths. Our graduate school partnerships enable our students to enter top programs with greater ease and reflect the high regard in which Dickinson is held."

SELECTIVITY

Admissions Rating	91
# of applicants	6,031
% of applicants accepted	47
% of acceptees attending	26
# offered a place on the wait list	848
% accepting a place on wait list	31
% admitted from wait list	0
# of early decision applicants	406
% accepted early decision	77

FRESHMAN PROFILE

Range SAT Critical Reading	590–680
Range SAT Math	600–700
Range SAT Writing	590–690
Range ACT Composite	27–30
Minimum internet-based TOEFL	90

DEADLINES

Early decision	
Deadline	11/15
Notification	12/15
Early action	
Deadline	12/1
Notification	2/15
Regular	
Deadline	2/1
Notification	3/20
Nonfall registration?	No

APPLICANTS ALSO LOOK AT AND OFTEN PREFER

Franklin and Marshall College; Connecticut College; Colby College; Middlebury College; Skidmore College

AND SOMETIMES PREFER

Gettysburg College; Hamilton College; American University; Lafayette College; Trinity College (CT); Bucknell University

FINANCIAL FACTS

Financial Aid Rating	94
Annual tuition	$50,730
Room and board	$12,794
Required fees	$450
Books and supplies	$1,130
Average frosh need-based scholarship	$36,639
Average UG need-based scholarship	$35,343
% needy frosh rec. need-based scholarship or grant aid	98
% needy UG rec. need-based scholarship or grant aid	97
% needy frosh rec. non-need-based scholarship or grant aid	7
% needy UG rec. non-need-based scholarship or grant aid	7
% needy frosh rec. need-based self-help aid	91
% needy UG rec. need-based self-help aid	90
% frosh rec. any financial aid	81
% UG rec. any financial aid	76
% UG borrow to pay for school	55
Average cumulative indebtedness	$28,108
% frosh need fully met	88
% ugrads need fully met	84
Average % of frosh need met	99
Average % of ugrad need met	99

DREW UNIVERSITY

OFFICE OF COLLEGE ADMISSIONS, MADISON, NJ 07940-1493 • ADMISSIONS: 973-408-3739 • FAX: 973-408-3068

CAMPUS LIFE

Quality of Life Rating	86
Fire Safety Rating	92
Green Rating	86
Type of school	Private
Affiliation	Methodist
Environment	Village

STUDENTS

Total undergrad enrollment	1,450
% male/female	39/61
% from out of state	32
% frosh from public high school	67
% frosh live on campus	87
% ugrads live on campus	76
% African American	10
% Asian	6
% Caucasian	56
% Hispanic	10
% Native American	<1
% Pacific Islander	<1
% Two or more races	4
% Race and/or ethnicity unknown	9
% international	5
# of countries represented	30

SURVEY SAYS...

Class discussions encouraged
Theater is popular
Students are happy

ACADEMICS

Academic Rating	82
% students returning for sophomore year	85
% students graduating within 4 years	63
% students graduating within 6 years	67
Calendar	Semester
Student/faculty ratio	10:1
Profs interesting rating	81
Profs accessible rating	82

Most classes have 10–19 students.
Most lab/discussion sessions have 10–19 students.

MOST POPULAR MAJORS

Psychology; Business; Economics

STUDENTS SAY "..."

Academics

Drew University features three major draws, according to current students: a gorgeous campus, a prime location (less than an hour from New York City by train), and strong academics. As at many schools, "some majors...are stronger than others," and introductory classes tend to be large lectures, but "class sizes, especially in upper-level courses, are generally small," which allows for "meaningful discussions." Though some say the administration "tends to be aloof," this obviously isn't a problem with the faculty. Students say professors are "very approachable, accommodating, and enthusiastic about what they teach." "They are quite engaging...have PhDs in the field that they teach, and...seem genuinely interested in helping us improve." "They're always there when students want extra help and are very understanding." One happy English major tells us, "My professors have really encouraged me to pursue the most out of my education here. One provided me with the opportunity to read my original poetry in NYC with distinguished poets. Another has influenced my decision to write a senior thesis. Within my major, I feel like part of a family. All of my professors know me, and I think they truly care about my performance." A neuroscience major raves, "Science professors will be acting out the material or showing demos of the material." Study abroad opportunities also abound, and the proximity to New York City gives students amazing internship opportunities.

Life

Life at Drew is typical of life on other small, Northeastern campuses, with a balanced blend of school-sponsored events, student clubs, and "of course, like any other college, students drink and party once the weekend comes, but it's not the only focus here." Students also enjoy heading off campus to nearby Morristown, and "trips to NYC are funded to go to museums, the outlet mall, basketball games, etc." Also on campus is the Shakespeare Theatre of New Jersey, and students are happy to take advantage of work-study opportunities there, as well as performances. On campus, there are a lot of "activities—at least one every night," and "facilities and living councils are constantly making improvements." "Students tend to try and get their money's worth by participating in as many opportunities as they can," and whether it's "environmental film screenings, a lecture by Anderson Cooper, or free food from the Polish Culture Club, there is always something you can become involved in." "There are lots of alcohol-free events planned for the weekends," "for example, sometimes performers like musicians or comedians come and perform, or sometimes there are guests." Club Drew, "a club [night] once a month on campus with a DJ," is well-attended.

Student Body

"A typical student at Drew is smart, driven," and "hardworking, but still parties at least once a week." "Talkative," "outgoing," and "social" also come up a lot when Drew students describe themselves. While some say "the typical Drew student is white, American, [and] from the East Coast," "we have an abundance of students from diverse ethnic backgrounds," and "there's a lot of different types of people, from jocks to hipsters." "There are jocks, theater junkies, musicians, premed students, international students, political science enthusiasts, and everything else." "It's mind-boggling how different the... undergraduates are," but "with an outstanding number of clubs and other social groups, literally any student can find a group of people to click with," and students suggest "to get the best experience out of Drew...you need to get involved."

FINANCIAL AID: 973-408-3112 • E-MAIL: CADM@DREW.EDU • WEBSITE: WWW.DREW.EDU

THE PRINCETON REVIEW SAYS

Admissions

Very important factors considered include: rigor of secondary school record, academic GPA, interview. *Important factors considered include:* application essay, recommendation(s), extracurricular activities, talent/ability, character/personal qualities. *Other factors considered include:* class rank, standardized test scores, alumni/ae relation, racial/ethnic status, volunteer work, work experience, level of applicant's interest. SAT or ACT considered if submitted. ACT with or without writing accepted. SAT with or without Essay component accepted. TOEFL required of all international applicants. High school diploma or equivalent is not required. *Academic units recommended:* 4 English, 3 math, 2 science, 2 foreign language, 2 social studies, 2 history, 3 academic electives.

Financial Aid

Students should submit: FAFSA. Regular filing deadline is 2/15.The Princeton Review suggests that all financial aid forms be submitted as soon as possible after October 1. *Need-based scholarships/grants offered:* Federal Pell, FSEOG, State scholarships/grants, Private scholarships, College/university scholarship or grant aid from institutional funds. *Loan aid offered:* Direct Subsidized Stafford Loans, Direct Unsubsidized Stafford Loans, Direct PLUS loans. Applicants will be notified of awards on or about 3/25. Federal Work-Study Program available. Institutional employment available.

The Inside Word

Drew takes a holistic approach to evaluating applications, so you definitely want to showcase more than just your GPA (though that's also important). Drew's applicant pool has grown significantly in recent years, so presenting yourself as not only a great student but also a great fit with the school will help you stand out from the pack. The school is test optional.

THE SCHOOL SAYS "..."

From the Admissions Office

"Drew's educational philosophy is built on fostering deep connections between its students and its faculty members, between its curriculum and its world and between its classrooms and real-world, hands-on experiences. Drew students are assigned a faculty mentor the summer before their first year, even before they take their first class. Faculty mentors and students collaborate on class schedules, discuss potential majors/minors, arrange internships and apply for jobs and/or graduate schools throughout and beyond a student's four years at Drew. Drew's location on a beautiful, wooded campus outside New York City makes possible an education that ties the classroom to the city, evident in its New York City programs on Wall Street, at the United Nations, on the contemporary art scene and on communications and media. Drew's Center for Civic Engagement combines the curricular with real-world learning opportunities in local communities—bringing to life Drew's motto 'Freely you have received; freely give.' Civic Scholars attend seminars on civic engagement, perform internships with multiple nonprofit/government agencies and take community-based classes that link their academic interests with their work in the community.

"Drew's location in a dynamic metropolitan area provides excellent internship opportunities, which often lead to employment. Over the last few years, Drew students have interned at employers such as CBS Sports, CNN, Entertainment Weekly, GoldmanSachs, Lincoln Center, Michael Kors, the New York Police Department and the United Nations. Six months after graduation, 94 percent of respondents from Drew's Class of 2014 were working or in graduate/professional school. They are employed at organizations such as Google, Coca-Cola, Chubb Insurance, Merrill Lynch, the Federal Trade Commission, ING Financial Partners, Morgan Stanley, Novartis and Prudential, and are attending graduate programs at Harvard, Duke, Princeton and Columbia, among others."

SELECTIVITY

Admissions Rating	83
# of applicants	3,025
% of applicants accepted	70
% of acceptees attending	17
# of early decision applicants	63
% accepted early decision	47

FRESHMAN PROFILE

Range SAT Critical Reading	500–620
Range SAT Math	490–620
Range SAT Writing	490–610
Range ACT Composite	22–29
Minimum paper TOEFL	550
Minimum internet-based TOEFL	80
Average HS GPA	3.6
% graduated top 10% of class	27
% graduated top 25% of class	65
% graduated top 50% of class	88

DEADLINES

Early decision	
Deadline	11/15
Notification	12/15
Regular	
Deadline	2/15
Notification	3/25
Nonfall registration?	Yes

FINANCIAL FACTS

Financial Aid Rating	82
Annual tuition	$45,552
Room and board	$12,672
Required fees	$832
Books and supplies	$1,128
Average frosh need-based scholarship	$32,459
Average UG need-based scholarship	$31,323
% needy frosh rec. need-based scholarship or grant aid	100
% needy UG rec. need-based scholarship or grant aid	100
% needy frosh rec. non-need-based scholarship or grant aid	9
% needy UG rec. non-need-based scholarship or grant aid	7
% needy frosh rec. need-based self-help aid	79
% needy UG rec. need-based self-help aid	80
% frosh rec. any financial aid	98
% UG rec. any financial aid	95
% UG borrow to pay for school	69
Average cumulative indebtedness	$24,345
% frosh need fully met	16
% ugrads need fully met	14
Average % of frosh need met	79
Average % of ugrad need met	76

DREXEL UNIVERSITY

3141 CHESTNUT STREET, PHILADELPHIA, PA 19104 • ADMISSIONS: 215-895-2400 • FAX: 215-895-1285

STUDENTS SAY ". . ."

Academics

By far the biggest draw for students seems to be Drexel University's cooperative education program that "gives students the opportunity to gain hands-on experience and develop professionally in their field of study." The co-op program is "an amazing experience" and "really sets [Drexel] apart." The program "offers real-world work experience and contacts at up to three local and/or national companies before graduation—and in this economy, it's all in who you know!" The co-op really helps students get "an excellent job after graduation." "Drexel University has diversified from its roots," and the school is "no longer being about just engineering. [Drexel] has set out to educate students to prepare them for careers in all industries." Students enjoy a "great campus location" in Philadelphia and the school "prides itself on innovative technologies that value sustainability, progressive learning that encourages constant change, and opportunities for invaluable experience." Although most of the professors "are very knowledgeable in their field" and offer "hands-on learning combined with direct application," many students say that "too many professors speak English as a second language" and "have difficulty communicating to their students." Students also pinpoint the "red tape" and "bureaucracy" as frustrating, saying that it bogs down the school. "Drexel is unfortunately run too much like a business sometimes," one student explains. "It can be difficult to get through the red tape that ties up departments." Some students also see the tuition as "outrageous." Although "some facilities are old and need work," Drexel is good about "dumping money into improving facilities" and most are "top-quality." One student proudly says, "Drexel is a great school," and it "is only going upward from here."

Life

Drexel University is located "right in the heart" of Philadelphia, one of the country's largest and most vibrant cities. Consequently, much of student life involves exploring this unique city. "It is so easy to learn how to use the subway and go into the heart of the city. It's so much fun to check out new locations, go shopping, and try out some of the best restaurants in town." Students love "the comedy club in center city [and] the bars in Old City," and they often head to a "Phillies, Flyers, or 76ers game." "The music scene in Philadelphia is great," and "the Philadelphia Museum of Art is just a twenty-minute walk from campus." In addition to having the entire city of Philadelphia at your disposal, the University of Pennsylvania is "right across the street." "If you're into partying, there's always a party going on, if not, head over to UPenn or Temple," one student advises. On campus, "Greek life is a big part of Drexel's community." If there's a downside to Drexel life, it's that there's "very little school spirit." "The basketball team is all the school spirit that exists; there isn't any besides that," a student explains. But as soon as you step off campus, "there are countless other things to do too, like museums, operas, and musicals."

Student Body

"There is no such thing as a typical Drexel student," one student declares. "Our campus is incredibly diverse in every way." "Drexel is a mixing bowl" and "very multicultural." "Everyone is different, and we all interact with each other and fit in [with] all different groups." "There are so many different people from everywhere, and it's amazing. Black, white, gay, straight: it just makes the college life here diverse and exciting." "Most students get involved in one or more student organizations" to fit in. Students are also very hardworking and "busy with classes and studies." "Everyone is focused on careers after college, but people still like to have fun on the weekends." "We're generally pretty mellow people," a chemical engineering student explains. "[We] work hard, but don't get too uptight about grades and classes."

FINANCIAL AID: 215-895-1600 • E-MAIL: ENROLL@DREXEL.EDU • WEBSITE: WWW.DREXEL.EDU

THE PRINCETON REVIEW SAYS

Admissions

Very important factors considered include: rigor of secondary school record, class rank, academic GPA, standardized test scores. *Important factors considered include:* application essay, recommendation(s), character/personal qualities. *Other factors considered include:* interview, extracurricular activities, talent/ability, first generation, alumni/ae relation, volunteer work, work experience, level of applicant's interest. SAT or ACT required. ACT with or without writing accepted. TOEFL required of all international applicants. High school diploma is required and GED is accepted. *Academic units required:* 3 math, 1 science, 1 science lab. *Academic units recommended:* 1 foreign language.

Financial Aid

Students should submit: FAFSA, CSS/Financial Aid PROFILE. Priority filing deadline is 3/1.The Princeton Review suggests that all financial aid forms be submitted as soon as possible after October 1. *Need-based scholarships/grants offered:* Federal Pell, FSEOG, State scholarships/grants, Private scholarships, College/university scholarship or grant aid from institutional funds. *Loan aid offered:* Direct Subsidized Stafford Loans, Direct Unsubsidized Stafford Loans, Direct PLUS loans, Federal Perkins Loans, State Loans. Applicants will be notified of awards on a rolling basis beginning 3/15. Federal Work-Study Program available. Institutional employment available.

The Inside Word

Drexel University's nationally recognized co-op program provides unique hands-on experience for students with companies in and around Philadelphia to help them in their post-college employment. Given the current state of the economy, that's a huge boost for prospective applicants, especially in the engineering fields that Drexel still specializes in.

THE SCHOOL SAYS "..."

From the Admissions Office

"Drexel University has maintained a reputation for academic excellence since its founding in 1891. Through Drexel Co-op, students have the opportunity to test-drive their degree in paid full-time positions where they can earn up to 18 months of workplace experience before graduation with employers such as *Fortune* 500 companies, major pharmaceutical companies, and top design firms, as well as nonprofit agencies and government organizations. More than 1,500 employers in thirty-three states and forty international locations participate in the Drexel Co-op program. The average six-month co-op salary is more than $16,000.

"Drexel offers more than 80 undergraduate majors and over twenty accelerated degree programs. Accelerated degree options include the BA/BS/JD in law; BA/BS/MD in medicine; BS/DPT in physical therapy; BS/MS in computing and informatics; and BS/MBA in business.

"Qualified students can apply to the Honors program, which is open to students in every academic discipline. The Honors program offers special living communities designed for the exceptional student and opportunities for social activities, traveling, and independent projects. The STAR (Students Tackling Advanced Research) Scholars program invites qualified students to participate in faculty-mentored research projects in their chosen fields as early as the freshman year.

"Drexel also has an active Study Abroad program in more than two dozen countries around the world. Freshman Frontiers: First Term in Dublin, Drexel's newest option for studying abroad, is a selective program that enables students in qualifying majors to study at the Dublin Business School and School of Arts for the first term of their freshman year."

SELECTIVITY

Admissions Rating	83
# of applicants	47,477
% of applicants accepted	76
% of acceptees attending	8

FRESHMAN PROFILE

Range SAT Critical Reading	530–630
Range SAT Math	560–670
Range SAT Writing	520–630
Range ACT Composite	24–29
Minimum paper TOEFL	550
Average HS GPA	3.5
% graduated top 10% of class	29
% graduated top 25% of class	61
% graduated top 50% of class	90

DEADLINES

Early action	
Deadline	11/1
Notification	12/15
Regular	
Deadline	1/15
Nonfall registration?	Yes

FINANCIAL FACTS

Financial Aid Rating	79
Annual tuition	$44,646
Room and board	$14,367
Required fees	$2,405
Books and supplies	$2,053
Average frosh need-based scholarship	$28,234
Average UG need-based scholarship	$21,813
% needy frosh rec. need-based scholarship or grant aid	100
% needy UG rec. need-based scholarship or grant aid	94
% needy frosh rec. non-need-based scholarship or grant aid	11
% needy UG rec. non-need-based scholarship or grant aid	3
% needy frosh rec. need-based self-help aid	78
% needy UG rec. need-based self-help aid	86
% frosh need fully met	22
% ugrads need fully met	20
Average % of frosh need met	62
Average % of ugrad need met	56

DUKE UNIVERSITY

2138 CAMPUS DRIVE, DURHAM, NC 27708-0586 • ADMISSIONS: 919-684-3214 • FAX: 919-681-1661

STUDENTS SAY ". . ."

Academics

Duke University is "all about academic excellence complemented by highly competitive Division I sports and an enriching array of extracurricular activities," making the university "an exciting, challenging, and enjoyable place to be." Undergraduates choose Duke because they "are passionate about a wide range of things, including academics, sports, community service, research, and fun." And because the school seems equally committed to accommodating all of those pursuits; as one student puts it, "Duke is for the Ivy League candidate who is a little bit more laid-back about school and overachieving (but just a bit) and a lot more into the party scene." Academics "are very difficult in the quantitative majors (engineering, math, statistics, economics, premed)" and "much easier in the non-quantitative majors," but there's an "across-the-board excellence in all departments from humanities to engineering." In all areas, there's a "supportive environment in which the faculty, staff, and students are willing to look out for the other person and help them succeed." It's the norm to have large study groups, and "the review sessions, peer tutoring system, writing center, and academic support center are always helpful when students are struggling with anything from math homework to creating a résumé." Professors' "number-one priority is teaching undergraduates," and their love of discussion means they "would rather that the students lead the class as opposed to them leading the class." "There are a few who make me want to stay at Duke forever," says a student. Because "the school has a lot of confidence in its students," it offers them "seemingly limitless opportunities."

Life

Life at Duke "is very relaxed," and "you can either be a part of nothing, or you can be so over-committed that it's not even funny." Because "the student union and other organizations provide entertainment all the time, from movies to shows to campus-wide parties," there's "a wealth of on-campus opportunities to get involved." Indeed, weekends are for relaxing, and "people usually stay on campus for fun," because hometown Durham "has a few quirky streets and squares with restaurants, shops, clubs, etc., but to really do much you have to go to Raleigh or Chapel Hill," each twenty to thirty minutes away by car. The perception that "Durham is pretty dangerous" further dampens students' enthusiasm for the city. Undergrads' fervor for Blue Devils sports, on the other hand, can be boundless; sports, "especially basketball, are a huge deal here," and undergrads "will paint themselves completely blue and wait in line on the sidewalk in K-ville for three days to jump up and down in Cameron Indoor Stadium." Greek life "plays a big role in the social scene here," but "almost all the parties are open, so it definitely isn't hard to get into a party." Though it's a "very party-heavy school," a lot of people "just do their own thing—have a movie night, go exploring, go skiing or to the beach for a weekend." Still, the social scene can be "a little too intense" at times.

Student Body

The typical Duke student "is someone who cares a lot about his or her education but at the same time won't sacrifice a social life for it." Life involves "getting a ton of work done first and then finding time to play and have fun." The typical student here is studious but social, athletic but can never be seen in the gym, job hunting but not worrying, and so on and so forth." Everyone is "incredibly focused," but "that includes social success as well." Students tend to be "focused on graduating and obtaining a lucrative and prosperous career," and although they "go out two to three times a week," they're "always looking polished." An "overwhelming number" are athletes, "not just varsity athletes…but athletes in high school or generally active people. Duke's athletic pride attracts this kind of person." The student body "is surprisingly ethnically diverse, with a number of students of Asian, African, and Hispanic descent," and "every type of person finds a welcoming group where he or she fits in."

FINANCIAL AID: 919-684-6225 • E-MAIL: UNDERGRAD-ADMISSIONS@DUKE.EDU • WEBSITE: WWW.DUKE.EDU

THE PRINCETON REVIEW SAYS

Admissions

Very important factors considered include: rigor of secondary school record, class rank, academic GPA, standardized test scores, application essay, recommendation(s), extracurricular activities, talent/ability, character/personal qualities. *Important factors considered include: Other factors considered include:* interview, first generation, alumni/ae relation, geographical residence, state residency, religious affiliation/commitment, racial/ethnic status, volunteer work, work experience. ACT with Writing required. High school diploma is required and GED is not accepted. *Academic units recommended:* 4 English, 3 math, 3 science, 3 foreign language, 3 social studies.

Financial Aid

Students should submit: FAFSA, CSS/Financial Aid PROFILE, Noncustodial PROFILE, Business/Farm Supplement. Regular filing deadline is 3/1. The Princeton Review suggests that all financial aid forms be submitted as soon as possible after October 1. *Need-based scholarships/grants offered:* Federal Pell, FSEOG, State scholarships/grants, Private scholarships, College/university scholarship or grant aid from institutional funds. *Loan aid offered:* Direct Subsidized Stafford Loans, Direct Unsubsidized Stafford Loans, Direct PLUS loans, Federal Perkins Loans, College/university loans from institutional funds. Applicants will be notified of awards on or about 4/1. Federal Work-Study Program available. Institutional employment available.

The Inside Word

Duke is an extremely selective undergraduate institution, which affords the school the luxury of rejecting many qualified applicants. You'll have to present an exceptional record just to be considered; to make the cut, you'll have to impress the admissions office that you can contribute something unique and valuable to the incoming class. Being one of the best basketball players in the nation (male or female) helps a lot, but even athletes have to show academic excellence to get in the door here.

THE SCHOOL SAYS "..."

From the Admissions Office

"Duke University offers an interesting mix of tradition and innovation, undergraduate college and major research university, Southern hospitality and international presence, and athletic prowess and academic excellence. Students come to Duke from all over the United States and the world and from a range of racial, ethnic, and socioeconomic backgrounds. They enjoy contact with a world-class faculty through small classes and independent study. More than forty majors are available in the arts and sciences and engineering; arts and sciences students may also design their own curriculum through Program II. Certificate programs are available in a number of interdisciplinary areas. Special academic opportunities include the Focus Program and seminars for first-year students, study abroad, study at the Duke Marine Laboratory and Duke Primate Center, the Duke in New York and Duke in Los Angeles arts programs, and several international exchange programs. While admission to Duke is highly selective, applications of U.S. citizens and permanent residents are evaluated without regard to financial need and the university pledges to meet 100 percent of the demonstrated need of all admitted U.S. students and permanent residents. A limited amount of financial aid is also available for foreign citizens, and the university will meet the full demonstrated financial need for those admitted students as well.

"Applicants must take either the ACT with the writing exam, or the SAT plus two SAT Subject Tests (mathematics Subject Test required for applicants to the Pratt School of Engineering)."

SELECTIVITY

Admissions Rating	98
# of applicants	30,546
% of applicants accepted	12
% of acceptees attending	45
# of early decision applicants	2,439
% accepted early decision	31

FRESHMAN PROFILE

Range SAT Critical Reading	670–760
Range SAT Math	690–790
Range SAT Writing	680–780
Range ACT Composite	31–34
% graduated top 10% of class	90
% graduated top 25% of class	8
% graduated top 50% of class	2

DEADLINES

Early decision	
Deadline	11/1
Notification	12/15
Regular	
Priority	12/20
Deadline	1/2
Notification	4/1
Nonfall registration?	No

APPLICANTS ALSO LOOK AT AND OFTEN PREFER

Princeton University; Yale University; Stanford University; Harvard College

AND SOMETIMES PREFER

University of Pennsylvania; Brown University; Cornell University; Dartmouth College

AND RARELY PREFER

Georgetown University; University of Virginia; The University of North Carolina at Chapel Hill; Northwestern University

FINANCIAL FACTS

Financial Aid Rating	95
Annual tuition	$45,800
Room and board	$13,290
Required fees	$1,443
Books and supplies	$1,345
Average frosh need-based scholarship	$36,348
Average UG need-based scholarship	$39,275
% needy frosh rec. need-based scholarship or grant aid	85
% needy UG rec. need-based scholarship or grant aid	87
% needy frosh rec. non-need-based scholarship or grant aid	11
% needy UG rec. non-need-based scholarship or grant aid	8
% needy frosh rec. need-based self-help aid	84
% needy UG rec. need-based self-help aid	89
% frosh need fully met	100
% ugrads need fully met	100
Average % of frosh need met	100
Average % of ugrad need met	100

DUQUESNE UNIVERSITY

600 FORBES AVENUE, PITTSBURGH, PA 15282 • ADMISSIONS: 412-396-6222 • FAX: 412-396-6223

CAMPUS LIFE

Quality of Life Rating	90
Fire Safety Rating	99
Green Rating	82
Type of school	Private
Affiliation	Roman Catholic
Environment	Metropolis

STUDENTS

Total undergrad enrollment	5,961
% male/female	38/62
% from out of state	26
% frosh live on campus	92
% ugrads live on campus	56
# of fraternities (% ugrad men join)	(17)
# of sororities (% ugrad women join)	(23)
% African American	5
% Asian	2
% Caucasian	81
% Hispanic	3
% Native American	<1
% Pacific Islander	<1
% Two or more races	3
% Race and/or ethnicity unknown	1
% international	4
# of countries represented	47

SURVEY SAYS...

Students are happy
Students love Pittsburgh, PA
Frats and sororities are popular

ACADEMICS

Academic Rating	77
% students returning for sophomore year	85
% students graduating within 4 years	63
% students graduating within 6 years	72
Calendar	Semester
Student/faculty ratio	14:1
Profs interesting rating	76
Profs accessible rating	77

Most classes have 10–19 students.
Most lab/discussion sessions have 10–19 students.

MOST POPULAR MAJORS
Nursing Science; Pharmacy; Biology

STUDENTS SAY "..."

Academics

At Duquesne, a private Catholic university in Pittsburgh, students are "thoughtful, dedicated to success, morally and spiritually driven, diverse, and are not only interested in serving our community within the Pittsburgh region, but strive to make a difference in areas around the globe." There is "an unspoken respect between students that promotes unity and success throughout the campus." The school is "very focused on providing a friendly yet professional, scholarly Catholic education" and "serving students by serving [G]od is the [school's] motto," though other faiths are welcome, too. Students say that their school is "all about growth of the student through mind, body, and spirit—the whole person, you are not just a number." With small class sizes, "it's easy to get to know the professor one-on-one and it's easier to become close to other students because you see them so frequently." While professors receive mixed reviews, most "are very thorough in their teaching and pride themselves in their work" and are "passionate and helpful." Duquesne "wants students to be successful" and does everything it can "to make [students into] the best teachers, nurses, lawyer, musicians, etc. that we can be. They give us an immense amount of resources on campus and throughout the community and city of Pittsburgh to excel in our careers."

Life

With Duquesne University situated "[in] the heart of the city of Pittsburgh, the only thing that limits what you can do is winter weather and your course load." The nearby South Side area of downtown Pittsburgh is "a great place to go on the weekends." For sports enthusiasts, "the Consol Energy Center is a block from campus for hockey games, and for baseball and football fans, both the Steelers and Pirates stadiums are easy to get to as well." "We have a loop bus on the weekend that will take us to other areas of the city." On campus, "the university provides a plethora of fun activities for students to do in their down time, and our hundreds of student organizations and athletic teams allow students to get involved in the school when they are not busy studying or socializing." Though there are no Greek houses on campus, Greek life is an integral part of the social scene. While roughly a quarter of the student body is affiliated with a frat or sorority, students admit that it can feel like "Duquesne University consists mainly of Greek life or athletes." "Duquesne also features a solid intramural sports program" and "lots of students enjoy intramural sports on campus."

Student Body

"The majority of students at Duquesne are white upper middle class" and the "style of Duquesne is very preppy." "Everyone is very courteous and polite," though some students say it's "not the most diverse place." Others counter that "Duquesne has a wide variety of students from many backgrounds that mesh well into a studious and fun student body. All students bring something valuable to the campus." Underscoring the sense of community here, "the student body at Duquesne is a warm and welcoming group of people, highlighting its Catholic-style approach to education." Most students seem to agree that their "peers at Duquesne University are thoughtful, dedicated to success, morally and spiritually-driven, diverse, and are not only interested in serving our community within the Pittsburgh region, but strive to make a difference in areas around the globe."

FINANCIAL AID: 412-396-6607 • E-MAIL: ADMISSIONS@DUQ.EDU • WEBSITE: WWW.DUQ.EDU

THE PRINCETON REVIEW SAYS

Admissions

Very important factors considered include: rigor of secondary school record, academic GPA. *Important factors considered include:* standardized test scores. *Other factors considered include:* class rank, application essay, recommendation(s), interview, extracurricular activities, talent/ability, character/personal qualities, first generation, alumni/ae relation, racial/ethnic status, volunteer work, work experience, level of applicant's interest. SAT or ACT required for some. ACT with or without writing accepted. SAT with or without Essay component accepted. High school diploma is required and GED is accepted. *Academic units recommended:* 4 English, 2 math, 2 science, 2 foreign language, 2 social studies, 4 academic electives.

Financial Aid

Students should submit: FAFSA. Priority filing deadline is 5/1.The Princeton Review suggests that all financial aid forms be submitted as soon as possible after October 1. *Need-based scholarships/grants offered:* Federal Pell, FSEOG, State scholarships/grants, Private scholarships, College/university scholarship or grant aid from institutional funds, United Negro College Fund. *Loan aid offered:* Direct Subsidized Stafford Loans, Direct Unsubsidized Stafford Loans, Direct PLUS loans, Federal Perkins Loans, Federal Nursing Loans. Applicants will be notified of awards on a rolling basis beginning 3/1. Federal Work-Study Program available. Institutional employment available.

The Inside Word

Different academic programs have different minimum requirements for applicant GPAs and standardized test scores. Scores are optional for applicants for liberal arts, business, and music majors, though these students must have a minimum cumulative GPA of 3.0 within a college preparatory curriculum to be considered for admission.

THE SCHOOL SAYS ". . ."

From the Admissions Office

"Duquesne University is a private, Catholic institution long known for its rich, diverse liberal arts studies and schools of pharmacy, law, sciences, music, education, nursing, business, health sciences and leadership. Founded in 1878 by the Congregation of the Holy Spirit (the Spiritans), Duquesne University has grown to become an educational and economic powerhouse that serves nearly 10,000 students across nine schools of study. Our students enjoy a secure fifty-acre campus and can take advantage of a variety of opportunities for athletics and arts, as well as nearly 200 student organizations. Approximately 3,700 students live in seven residence halls. Campus amenities include the multi-level Power Center, which houses a recreation and fitness center, a Barnes & Noble bookstore with a Starbucks café, and The Red Ring, a full-service restaurant. In an ecumenical atmosphere open to diversity, students of all races, cultures and religious traditions are valued and supported. Located just steps away from downtown Pittsburgh, Duquesne University is readily accessible to the business, entertainment and shopping centers of the city. The university's central location also provides a perfect laboratory for off-campus learning and community service. Duquesne students gain practical experience through fieldwork, research projects and internships at Pittsburgh's major corporations and health care systems."

SELECTIVITY

Admissions Rating	81
# of applicants	7,354
% of applicants accepted	76
% of acceptees attending	26
# of early decision applicants	185
% accepted early decision	74

FRESHMAN PROFILE

Range SAT Critical Reading	520–600
Range SAT Math	520–610
Range SAT Writing	500–600
Range ACT Composite	23–28
Minimum paper TOEFL	575
Minimum internet-based TOEFL	90
Average HS GPA	3.7
% graduated top 10% of class	23
% graduated top 25% of class	54
% graduated top 50% of class	86

DEADLINES

Early decision	
Deadline	11/1
Notification	11/15
Other ED	
Deadline	11/1
Other ED	
Notification	11/15
Early action	
Deadline	12/1
Notification	1/15
Regular	
Priority	11/1
Deadline	7/1
Nonfall registration?	Yes

APPLICANTS ALSO LOOK AT AND OFTEN PREFER
University of Pittsburgh—Pittsburgh Campus

AND SOMETIMES PREFER
West Virginia University

FINANCIAL FACTS

Financial Aid Rating	79
Annual tuition	$33,778
Room and board	$11,418
Books and supplies	$1,400
Average frosh need-based scholarship	$18,586
Average UG need-based scholarship	$17,645
% needy frosh rec. need-based scholarship or grant aid	100
% needy UG rec. need-based scholarship or grant aid	97
% needy frosh rec. non-need-based scholarship or grant aid	100
% needy UG rec. non-need-based scholarship or grant aid	95
% needy frosh rec. need-based self-help aid	99
% needy UG rec. need-based self-help aid	86
% frosh rec. any financial aid	99
% UG rec. any financial aid	96
% UG borrow to pay for school	73
Average cumulative indebtedness	$38,437
% frosh need fully met	19
% ugrads need fully met	17
Average % of frosh need met	76
Average % of ugrad need met	73

EARLHAM COLLEGE

801 NATIONAL ROAD WEST, RICHMOND, IN 47374-4095 • ADMISSIONS: 765-983-1600 • FAX: 765-983-1560

STUDENTS SAY ". . ."

Academics

Given Earlham's Quaker roots, it's no surprise that undergraduates find the college to be "welcoming and accepting." Located in Richmond, Indiana, this small school of 1,000 also "places a strong emphasis on community building and social justice," two facets valued by the student body as well. To that end, Earlham also endeavors to take into account the thoughts and feelings of its undergrads. As a psychology major explains, "I really appreciate how much input students get in campus decisions such as hiring, and that all important decisions are made by consensus." Academically, Earlham works diligently to arm students with "cultural awareness" and the ability to "think critically." It also "emphasizes a global perspective, a tolerance of dissenting opinions, and an open mind." Classrooms are graced by "amazing" professors, who "have such interesting perspectives and know a lot within their fields." As one thrilled student quickly interjects, "I actually enjoy having classes and my professors always make any topic worth listening to...even classes like the Diversity of Mathematics." And a grateful English major adds, "Earlham has professors who really engage and care for the students. I have had professors who have invited me to dinner to discuss course work and life in general. I am so thankful for such opportunities."

Life

Many Earlham undergrads are quite dedicated to their studies. Therefore, throughout the week, they can frequently be found hitting the books. Of course, they also love to let loose every now and again. Like most colleges, clubs are "popular" at Earlham and students can participate in everything "ranging from dance to slacklining." Additionally, "the Student Activities Board...throws weekly events, such as bingo, a talent show, or Halloween dances. RAs [also] have programs, and there are various musical acts brought in as well." Beyond clubs and organizations, the campus also features "amazing" woods with "great trails" and undergrads often head out there to "walk around and hang out." And while there is definitely some partying to be found, it doesn't necessarily dominate the social scene. Lastly, when undergrads are itching to break away from campus life, "Dayton, Cincinnati, [and] Indianapolis, are not too far a drive."

Student Body

Earlham undergrads quite happily report that their peers are "passionate, involved, friendly, self-possessed, and generally very liberal." They also love that the college seems to yield a "very diverse" student body. As an English major states, "We have students from different countries, socioeconomic backgrounds, and many other identity categories." And a theater student adds, "This is the school where everyone fits in. We have students of all genders, sexualities, multiple religions, races, and ethnicities. No one is marginalized because of these things." It's important to note that "the school is a sanctuary for students who identify with some part of the LGBTQ spectrum." Many undergrads here are also "socially aware," "environmentally concerned" and "involved with social justice issues." And most students seem to be genuinely interested in "learning more for the sake of learning than for getting a well-paying job or all A's." As a content psych major confidently concludes, "There is no typical student at Earlham [since] everyone is recognized not as a stereotype or part of some group, but rather as individuals who have a lot to offer to the table because of their unique background."

FINANCIAL AID: 765-983-1217 • E-MAIL: ADMISSIONS@EARLHAM.EDU • WEBSITE: WWW.EARLHAM.EDU

THE PRINCETON REVIEW SAYS

Admissions

Very important factors considered include: rigor of secondary school record, academic GPA, application essay. *Important factors considered include:* recommendation(s), extracurricular activities, character/personal qualities. *Other factors considered include:* class rank, standardized test scores, interview, talent/ability, alumni/ae relation, racial/ethnic status, volunteer work, work experience. SAT or ACT considered if submitted. ACT with Writing required. SAT with Essay component required. TOEFL required of all international applicants. High school diploma is required and GED is accepted. *Academic units required:* 4 English, 3 math, 3 science, 2 science labs, 2 foreign language, 2 social studies, 2 history. *Academic units recommended:* 4 math, 4 science, 4 foreign language, 2 social studies, 2 history.

Financial Aid

Students should submit: FAFSA. Priority filing deadline is 3/1.The Princeton Review suggests that all financial aid forms be submitted as soon as possible after October 1. *Need-based scholarships/grants offered:* Federal Pell, FSEOG, State scholarships/grants, Private scholarships, College/university scholarship or grant aid from institutional funds. *Loan aid offered:* Direct Subsidized Stafford Loans, Direct Unsubsidized Stafford Loans, Direct PLUS loans, Federal Perkins Loans, State Loans, College/university loans from institutional funds. Applicants will be notified of awards on a rolling basis beginning 3/15. Federal Work-Study Program available. Institutional employment available.

Inside Word

Gaining admission to Earlham is a competitive process. After all, the college is pretty selective; a strong high school transcript replete with challenging courses is a must. That said, admissions officers strive to create a diverse student body and seek out applicants with a broad range of life experiences and intellectual interests. Candidates who demonstrate concern for issues surrounding peace, social justice and social responsibility and who embrace differences will likely have an edge. Finally, we should note that Earlham is test-optional school.

THE SCHOOL SAYS "..."

From the Admissions Office

"Earlham is an academically distinguished liberal arts college. Students seek out the College for its richly collaborative and experiential approach to teaching and learning. The majority of Earlham students study abroad and engage in undegraduate research. Student academic interests are spread evenly among the natural sciences, social sciences, humanities and arts. Earlham has recently invested more than $60 million in its academic facilities. The College ranks among the top 2 percent of all colleges in graduates who earn a Ph.D., and acceptance rates to medical and law and other professional schools schools are exceptionally high. The Center for Integrated Learning assists students in pursuing their passions and in finding internships. Earlham is renowned as an accepting and welcoming academic community, embracing individual and cultural differences. Shaped by Quaker perspectives, Earlham's values are rooted in a commitment to caring for the world we inhabit, improving human society, promoting global education, seeking peaceful and just transformation of conflicts, affirming the equality of all persons, and maintaining high ethical standards of personal conduct. Not surprisingly, Earlham graduates give importance to not only being successful but to pursuing meaningful work and contributing to their communities. While it limits enrollment, Earlham attracts students from almost all fifty states and nearly eighty different nations. There are over sixty student organizations and sixteen intercollegiate sports as well as an equestrian program. The College's student body is attractively diverse, multi-talented, and brings positive energy to student life and a drive to make a difference in a rapidly changing world."

SELECTIVITY

Admissions Rating	89
# of applicants	2,549
% of applicants accepted	62
% of acceptees attending	16
# offered a place on the wait list	336
# of early decision applicants	10
% accepted early decision	100

FRESHMAN PROFILE

Range SAT Critical Reading	550–700
Range SAT Math	560–690
Range SAT Writing	530–680
Range ACT Composite	25–31
Minimum paper TOEFL	550
Minimum internet-based TOEFL	80
Average HS GPA	3.6
% graduated top 10% of class	43
% graduated top 25% of class	71
% graduated top 50% of class	92

DEADLINES

Early decision	
Deadline	11/1
Notification	12/1
Early action	
Deadline	1/15
Notification	2/15
Regular	
Priority	12/1
Deadline	2/15
Notification	4/1
Nonfall registration?	Yes

APPLICANTS ALSO LOOK AT AND OFTEN PREFER
Oberlin College

AND SOMETIMES PREFER
Grinnell College

FINANCIAL FACTS

Financial Aid Rating	86
Annual tuition	$43,500
Room and board	$9,120
Required fees	$890
Books and supplies	$1,200
Average frosh need-based scholarship	$31,777
Average UG need-based scholarship	$29,460
% needy frosh rec. need-based scholarship or grant aid	97
% needy UG rec. need-based scholarship or grant aid	99
% needy frosh rec. non-need-based scholarship or grant aid	29
% needy UG rec. non-need-based scholarship or grant aid	24
% needy frosh rec. need-based self-help aid	84
% needy UG rec. need-based self-help aid	90
% frosh rec. any financial aid	98
% UG rec. any financial aid	96
% UG borrow to pay for school	60
Average cumulative indebtedness	$25,784
% frosh need fully met	18
% ugrads need fully met	16
Average % of frosh need met	93
Average % of ugrad need met	92

ECKERD COLLEGE

4200 FIFTY-FOURTH AVENUE SOUTH, ST. PETERSBURG, FL 33711 • ADMISSIONS: 727-864-8331 • FAX: 727-866-2304

STUDENTS SAY "..."

Academics

Located on Florida's Gulf Coast in St. Petersburg, Eckerd College is a small liberal arts college that prepares students to be "well-rounded, educated people for the 'real world', rather than for just one job." Indeed, 40 percent of all students will go on to pursue advanced degrees, and the school's "academics are top notch and continue to impress," particularly the constantly expanding, "hands on" science department, which "really flourishes." Also of note is the study abroad program, of which many students take advantage.

Eckerd is "all about having small class sizes in order to maximize learning and personal connections to professors." Professors are "always approachable on an academic and personal level" and "make the classes fun and interesting." There is a "level of genuine care" from the teachers; according to a senior, "If I have a question, it gets answered, simple as that." "Not once has an email been ignored that I have sent to a professor," echoes a junior. Class discussion is very important (many classes have a sizeable participation grade), and faculty encourages opposing views, creating "an environment where it is easy for everybody to openly express their opinions without judgment."

The mentor program assigns students to professors in the field of their major(s), their job being "to help guide the student through choosing classes and registration, or anything else." The "quirky" liberal arts curriculum turns out graduates that "are not pigeonholed into the skills associated with their major, but [who] have developed a wide range of abilities which make them attractive to employers."

Life

The school's heartstoppingly beautiful location on the waterfront gives it a feel of being "like summer camp with an enriching academic experience"; as a senior asks (rhetorically): "How can you beat a dorm that overlooks the bay?" The dorms "are beautiful so there is no need to live off campus," and the school's yellow bike program allows students to "just pick up the yellow bikes and ride wherever you need" (though some students think there should be "more dedication through internal action to the environmental principles it espouses").

There are "eclectic options of student activities" at Eckerd, and since there is no Greek life, the Campus Activities crew is allotted "a crazy amount of money to have fun events on campus, such as cookouts, dances, casino nights, and an actual carnival brought onto campus." Obviously marine activities are popular, and for fun, people "go to the beach, go downtown, [and borrow] paddleboards/kayaks at the waterfront." People love to go to downtown St. Pete, and there are many famous restaurants nearby (good thing, as the cafeteria food is "definitely our weakest point," according to many students).

There's a definite party streak here, and "pot and beer are not strangers to Eckerd parties," which typically take place outside. Still, it's "a very no-pressure environment" for those who choose not to partake, and "there is a very 'free as a bird' mentality'" here so "people rarely feel trapped." Life at this school is generally relaxed but busy. It matches the atmosphere of the location," says a freshman.

Student Body

This "barefooted and brainy" brood "has a wide variety of students who all fit different niches." "It isn't unheard of to see people in three-piece suits sitting with what we might call modern-day hippies," says a student. The "very relaxed" crowd adopts a "laid back Florida attitude," and every student is "friendly, approachable and has a general positive attitude about being here at Eckerd." Most everyone is "pretty liberal" and "has a strong interest in environmental sustainability."

FINANCIAL AID: 727-864-8334 • E-MAIL: ADMISSIONS@ECKERD.EDU • WEBSITE: WWW.ECKERD.EDU

THE PRINCETON REVIEW SAYS

Admissions

Very important factors considered include: rigor of secondary school record, academic GPA. *Important factors considered include:* standardized test scores, application essay, recommendation(s), interview, extracurricular activities, talent/ability, character/personal qualities. *Other factors considered include:* class rank, first generation, alumni/ae relation, volunteer work, work experience, level of applicant's interest. SAT or ACT required. ACT with or without writing accepted. High school diploma is required and GED is accepted. *Academic units recommended:* 4 English, 3 math, 3 science, 2 science labs, 2 foreign language, 2 social studies, 1 history, 3 academic electives.

Financial Aid

Students should submit: FAFSA. Priority filing deadline is 3/1.The Princeton Review suggests that all financial aid forms be submitted as soon as possible after October 1. *Need-based scholarships/grants offered:* Federal Pell, FSEOG, State scholarships/grants, Private scholarships, College/university scholarship or grant aid from institutional funds. *Loan aid offered:* Direct Subsidized Stafford Loans, Direct Unsubsidized Stafford Loans, Direct PLUS loans, Federal Perkins Loans, College/university loans from institutional funds. Applicants will be notified of awards on a rolling basis beginning 2/20. Federal Work-Study Program available. Institutional employment available.

The Inside Word

Most of the applicants Eckerd admits come from the top quarter of their high school classes. However, competition from other small liberal arts schools of roughly the same caliber or better is stiff. As a result, Eckerd is a relatively easy admit for B-plus students with decent standardized test scores (the school gives more weight in its decisions to courses and grades than to SAT and ACT scores, however). The admissions process here is rolling, which means that applying early will help your chances. Eckerd can afford to be more selective later on in the admissions cycle, especially for candidates who profess an interest in its most esteemed programs (for example, marine science), so those with serious interest should consider Eckerd's early admission policy.

THE SCHOOL SAYS "..."

From the Admissions Office

"Eckerd, a coeducational college of liberal arts and sciences, has a diverse student body from forty-eight states and thirty-three countries. Located on 188 acres of waterfront property in St. Petersburg, Florida, we take advantage of our spectacular mile of campus waterfront along the Gulf of Mexico for outdoor laboratories in biology, marine science and environmental studies as well as for an array of intramural, club and intercollegiate sports and water recreation. Offerings in the arts and humanities, including lectures and classes by Nobel Prize-winner Elie Wiesel, inspire creativity and foster critical thinking and self-awareness. Eckerd is dedicated to minimizing its operational footprint and maximizing sustainable practices. Eckerd's Community Garden contributes to our 'Eat Local' initiative, and our Yellow Community Bike Program is designed to increase bicycle use on campus and decrease car traffic. In addition to being 'green,' Eckerd students are service-oriented, volunteering more than 70,000 hours annually in the Tampa Bay community and across the globe. Eckerd's innovative 4-1-4 calendar gives students the opportunity to study abroad during the January Winter Term or semester-long programs. Nearly 70 percent of our graduates have spent at least one term overseas, many at Eckerd study centers in London, China and Latin America. A recent successful fundraising campaign made it possible for a renaissance in the sciences at Eckerd. In addition to the new, 55,000 square-foot James Center for Molecular and Life Sciences, the college is significantly upgrading equipment, labs and classrooms for the environmental studies, math, physics, computer science and behavioral sciences departments. We venture together in the Eckerd experience to think beyond the conventional questions, methods and solutions. At Eckerd College, we ThinkOUTside."

SELECTIVITY
Admissions Rating	80
# of applicants	4,135
% of applicants accepted	73
% of acceptees attending	12
# offered a place on the wait list	51
% accepting a place on wait list	16
% admitted from wait list	6

FRESHMAN PROFILE
Range SAT Critical Reading	500–610
Range SAT Math	500–600
Range ACT Composite	23–28
Minimum paper TOEFL	550
Minimum internet-based TOEFL	79
Average HS GPA	3.4

DEADLINES
Early action	
Deadline	11/15
Notification	12/15
Nonfall registration?	Yes

FINANCIAL FACTS
Financial Aid Rating	85
Annual tuition	$39,684
Room and board	$10,920
Required fees	$336
Books and supplies	$1,200
Average frosh need-based scholarship	$23,984
Average UG need-based scholarship	$23,726
% needy frosh rec. need-based scholarship or grant aid	100
% needy UG rec. need-based scholarship or grant aid	100
% needy frosh rec. non-need-based scholarship or grant aid	0
% needy UG rec. non-need-based scholarship or grant aid	0
% needy frosh rec. need-based self-help aid	99
% needy UG rec. need-based self-help aid	100
% frosh rec. any financial aid	97
% UG rec. any financial aid	95
% frosh need fully met	22
% ugrads need fully met	19
Average % of frosh need met	85
Average % of ugrad need met	83

ELON UNIVERSITY

100 CAMPUS DRIVE, ELON, NC 27244-2010 • ADMISSIONS: 336-278-3566 • FAX: 336-278-7699

CAMPUS LIFE

Quality of Life Rating	92
Fire Safety Rating	94
Green Rating	93
Type of school	Private
Affiliation	No Affiliation
Environment	Town

STUDENTS

Total undergrad enrollment	5,903
% male/female	41/59
% from out of state	72
% frosh from public high school	58
% frosh live on campus	99
% ugrads live on campus	62
# of fraternities (% ugrad men join)	10 (18)
# of sororities (% ugrad women join)	12 (39)
% African American	6
% Asian	2
% Caucasian	82
% Hispanic	5
% Native American	<1
% Pacific Islander	<1
% Two or more races	2
% Race and/or ethnicity unknown	1
% international	2
# of countries represented	49

SURVEY SAYS...

Students are happy
Classroom facilities are great
Great library
Career services are great
Internships are widely available
School is well run
Dorms are like palaces
Easy to get around campus
Recreation facilities are great
Lots of beer drinking
Hard liquor is popular
Intramural sports are popular
Frats and sororities are popular
Theater is popular

ACADEMICS

Academic Rating	84
% students returning for sophomore year	90
% students graduating within 4 years	79
% students graduating within 6 years	83
Calendar	4/1/4
Student/faculty ratio	12:1
Profs interesting rating	91
Profs accessible rating	90

Most classes have 10–19 students.
Most lab/discussion sessions have 10–19 students.

MOST POPULAR MAJORS

Business Administration and Management; Communication; Psychology

STUDENTS SAY "..."

Academics

Elon University boasts "a beautiful campus" and "one of the best study abroad programs in the country." Although located in the small town of Elon, North Carolina, the school has an "emphasis on global awareness" and "encourages awareness and action [on] global issues" while producing "global leaders" that will "make the world a better place." The global focus is displayed in the "phenomenal" study abroad program that is hugely popular with students. "Seventy[-two] percent of our student body has been abroad," one student explains. "I got the chance to study in Los Angeles, Turkey and Dubai. Those trips were the best part about going to Elon." The "small classes" really "facilitate relationships with professors" and there are "incredible opportunities for hands-on engagement and close mentorship." "The relationships between students and professors is so strong and personal, and has really shaped my college experience," one happy student says. Professors are described as "enthusiastic," "engaging," "kind" and "very experienced." "Professors know their students names and are genuinely interested in their success throughout their time at Elon," one student explains. Classes are often "discussion based" and this makes the classrooms "atmospheres for thoughtful discussions and learning." The school goes out of the way to connect students with the faculty. "The sense of community is heightened by the amazing traditions at Elon," a strategic communications major explains, "including College Coffee, where students and professors get to mix and mingle over free pastries and coffee every Tuesday morning." Like the professors, the staff and administration are "engaged and friendly." "Elon pays attention to the WHOLE student—not just grades, athletics, or involvement" and academics here are "all about connections, whether between individuals, groups, or simply concepts." A human service studies student says, "I have been pushed by my professors, peers, and mentors to become my best student, leader, and person since stepping on this campus." One biochemistry major puts it more simply: "You [could] never create a more perfect university if you tried."

Life

One word sums up life at Elon: "BUSY." Students here are "engaged" and "over-involved with everything, and extend ourselves too far at times." "Over-commitment IS the norm, and students are professionals in training rather than kids," one student clarifies. "It's kind of the Elon 'joke' that every student here is involved in at least two extracurricular activities" and the student body "wants to make an impact in real world." Still, students "work hard and play hard" at Elon. "Parties happen every weekend" and "Greek life dominates the social scene." That said, "recently, the social scene for non-Greeks has definitely increased with club sports teams and other student organizations throwing open parties." There is a real "lack of activism and advocacy on campus" despite the global focus of the school. Elon is "mainly a walking campus," but off campus there is "no way to get [anywhere] without a car." That isn't much of a problem since "there is very little to do off-campus" as the town of Elon is small with under 10,000 people. Luckily, plenty happens on campus including "movie nights, Bingo, concerts, and other fun events."

Student Body

There is a "strong sense of community" among the Elon student body. This is not a campus where people walk around with "their head down listening to music. You'll always see people you know walking to class since we do have a tight-knit community." The average student is "preppy, conservative," "upper middle/upper class," "white" and "likes to party." There is not much "socioeconomic/racial diversity" and, despite being a Southern school, most students are "usually Northern kids." Students "fit in with organizations they become involved in," which is easy since almost every student "is involved in several on-campus organizations" and "feels a genuine sense of belonging and appreciation across campus."

FINANCIAL AID: 336-278-7640 • E-MAIL: ADMISSIONS@ELON.EDU • WEBSITE: WWW.ELON.EDU

THE PRINCETON REVIEW SAYS

Admissions

Very important factors considered include: rigor of secondary school record, academic GPA, standardized test scores, application essay. *Important factors considered include:* recommendation(s), extracurricular activities, talent/ability, alumni/ae relation, volunteer work, work experience. *Other factors considered include:* class rank, character/personal qualities, first generation, geographical residence, state residency, racial/ethnic status, level of applicant's interest. SAT or ACT required. ACT with or without writing accepted. SAT with or without Essay component accepted. TOEFL required of all international applicants. High school diploma is required and GED is accepted. *Academic units required:* 4 English, 3 math, 3 science, 1 science lab, 2 foreign language, 1 social studies, 2 history. *Academic units recommended:* 4 English, 4 math, 3 science, 1 science lab, 3 foreign language, 1 social studies, 2 history.

Financial Aid

Students should submit: FAFSA, Institution's own financial aid form, CSS/Financial Aid PROFILE. Priority filing deadline is 2/15.The Princeton Review suggests that all financial aid forms be submitted as soon as possible after October 1. *Need-based scholarships/grants offered:* Federal Pell, FSEOG, State scholarships/grants, Private scholarships, College/university scholarship or grant aid from institutional funds. *Loan aid offered:* Direct Subsidized Stafford Loans, Direct Unsubsidized Stafford Loans, Direct PLUS loans, Federal Perkins Loans. Applicants will be notified of awards on a rolling basis beginning 3/30. Federal Work-Study Program available. Institutional employment available.

The Inside Word

Elon receives about 10,000 applications each year for the 1,500 spots in the first year class. As such, competition is stiff and prospective students will need to stand out beyond the usual strong grades and scores. The school looks for students with strong leadership skills, a desire to be involved on campus life, and a history of co-curricular activities.

THE SCHOOL SAYS "..."

From the Admissions Office

"Elon offers the resources of a large university in a close-knit community atmosphere. The university's 5,782 undergraduates choose from more than 60 majors. Graduate programs are offered in business administration, law, management, education, interactive media, physical therapy and physician assistant studies. The National Survey of Student Engagement recognizes Elon among the nation's most effective universities in promoting hands-on learning. Academic and co-curricular activities are seamlessly blended, especially in the Elon Experiences: study abroad, internships, service, leadership and undergraduate research. Participation is among the highest in the nation; 72 percent of graduating seniors have studied abroad, 86 percent have internship experiences and 86 percent have participated in service. Elon's 4-1-4 academic calendar allows students to devote January to global study or to explore innovative on-campus courses. Elon's historic 620-acre campus is recognized as one of the most beautiful in the country. New additions include two major residential neighborhoods—the Global Neighborhood and The Station at Mill Point; the Gerald L. Francis Center, home of the School of Health Sciences; the three-story Elon Town Center, which includes Elon's Barnes & Noble bookstore, a pizzeria and ice cream shop; the international themed Lakeside Dining Hall, including the Winter Garden Café food court; and Alumni Field House and Hunt Softball Park for Elon's NCAA Division I Phoenix athletics. The athletics programs compete in the Colonial Athletic Association. First-year applicants are required to take the SAT or ACT. Only the highest scores will be considered in the admission decision."

SELECTIVITY

Admissions Rating	88
# of applicants	10,256
% of applicants accepted	57
% of acceptees attending	26
# offered a place on the wait list	2,718
% accepting a place on wait list	38
% admitted from wait list	3
# of early decision applicants	504
% accepted early decision	86

FRESHMAN PROFILE

Range SAT Critical Reading	550–640
Range SAT Math	560–650
Range SAT Writing	550–650
Range ACT Composite	25–29
Minimum paper TOEFL	550
Minimum internet-based TOEFL	79
Average HS GPA	4.0
% graduated top 10% of class	24
% graduated top 25% of class	58
% graduated top 50% of class	90

DEADLINES

Early decision	
Deadline	11/1
Notification	12/1
Early action	
Deadline	11/10
Notification	12/20
Regular	
Priority	11/10
Deadline	1/10
Notification	3/20
Nonfall registration?	Yes

FINANCIAL FACTS

Financial Aid Rating	79
Annual tuition	$31,773
Room and board	$10,998
Required fees	$399
Books and supplies	$900
Average frosh need-based scholarship	$13,546
Average UG need-based scholarship	$14,124
% needy frosh rec. need-based scholarship or grant aid	86
% needy UG rec. need-based scholarship or grant aid	89
% needy frosh rec. non-need-based scholarship or grant aid	45
% needy UG rec. non-need-based scholarship or grant aid	47
% needy frosh rec. need-based self-help aid	78
% needy UG rec. need-based self-help aid	80
% frosh rec. any financial aid	63
% UG rec. any financial aid	61
% UG borrow to pay for school	43
Average cumulative indebtedness	$31,622
% frosh need fully met	15
% ugrads need fully met	17
Average % of frosh need met	60
Average % of ugrad need met	60

EMERSON COLLEGE

120 BOYLSTON STREET, BOSTON, MA 02116-4624 • ADMISSIONS: 617-824-8600 • FAX: 617-824-8609

CAMPUS LIFE

Quality of Life Rating	88
Fire Safety Rating	94
Green Rating	65
Type of school	Private
Affiliation	No Affiliation
Environment	Metropolis

STUDENTS

Total undergrad enrollment	3,789
% male/female	40/60
% from out of state	76
% frosh from public high school	68
% frosh live on campus	99
% ugrads live on campus	58
# of fraternities (% ugrad men join)	5 (2)
# of sororities (% ugrad women join)	3 (3)
% African American	3
% Asian	4
% Caucasian	67
% Hispanic	11
% Native American	<1
% Pacific Islander	<1
% Two or more races	5
% Race and/or ethnicity unknown	6
% international	5
# of countries represented	60

SURVEY SAYS...

Lots of liberal students
Students are happy
Class discussions encouraged
Students aren't religious
Students love Boston, MA
Easy to get around campus
College radio is popular
Theater is popular

ACADEMICS

Academic Rating	78
% students returning for sophomore year	89
% students graduating within 4 years	77
% students graduating within 6 years	80
Calendar	Semester
Student/faculty ratio	13:1
Profs interesting rating	81
Profs accessible rating	71

Most classes have 10–19 students.
Most lab/discussion sessions have
10–19 students.

MOST POPULAR MAJORS

Cinematography and Film/Video Production;
Theatre/Theater

STUDENTS SAY "..."

Academics

"Perfectly situated in the heart of Boston," Emerson's campus sits "in close proximity to a plethora of other academic institutions and culture." Emerson is "the number one school for film/television/media production." The combination of a "very active" alumni network and plentiful "industry connections" greatly help students in their post-college careers. Emerson fosters a "creative atmosphere" where people have "passion for [their] craft" and "strive to do their best." As one student puts it, "Emerson is a specialized school for people who are passionate and know exactly what they want to do with that passion." The faculty and students are "creative and professional," and the experience of attending Emerson "is like a mini version of what the film industry or the business world looks like." In general, "the facilities are awesome, especially the TV studios." However, the most common complaint was the state of the dining facilities, with feedback ranging from "not very good" to "makes me feel sick every time." Students also wish there were "more study abroad programs." Academics are "very hands-on rather than learning theory." The professors "are knowledgeable and passionate about their crafts," and have plenty of experience "working in their field of study." As with any school, "professors obviously vary depending on the subject," however, the school's size makes it "pretty easy to avoid the bad professors just through word of mouth." Overall, "Emerson is an inclusive, accepting, and progressive school that fosters creativity and provides a positive environment to learn and grow." As one happy student declares, "Emerson College is the greatest decision I have ever made!"

Life

Emerson does not have a "normal campus where kids walk around in their pjs." Students here are constantly active. "Life at school is a combination of running to classes, running to projects, and running to clubs," one student reports. "No matter what your major is, there's an abundance of extracurricular opportunities" and the "clubs and organizations are awesome and incredibly professional." The college puts on "a lot of activities on weekends on campus," and students here are "very social beings and love to get involved in everything—from summer internships to student orgs to the Quidditch World Cup team." Due to Emerson's "extremely strict rules regarding drugs and alcohol," "you have to take a train to get to any parties." Luckily, "Emerson is right in the middle of Boston" providing "many opportunities to experience the real world, see live music, study in the park, go to a free movie pre-screening, eat out, [or] explore new neighborhoods."

Student Body

Emerson students are "creative, innovative, friendly, and passionate." Although students say racial diversity could be improved, the school is "very LGBTQ friendly" and has a "large LGBT community." The most common word used to describe students was "hipster," specifically "hipsters who have a love affair with cigarettes and black coffee." This can make some non-hipster students feel "out of place," but most students "are friendly and are very open-minded." There is also a strong "nerdy" vibe to campus. "I have not met anybody who hates Doctor Who," one student says. Another describes the student body as "artsy, nerdy, funny, weird, cool, hipster, chill, creative, smart...the list is endless. We all fit in." Despite the "very artsy" student body and general "liberal" views, students can be "apathetic and uninformed when it comes to politics." One thing is for sure though, the students at Emerson "work hard." A visual media arts major even declares them "the most dedicated and ambitious students of all time." Since "everyone here does cool things," when you attend Emerson your creative sparks fly and "you too will begin to do cool things."

FINANCIAL AID: 617-824-8655 • E-MAIL: ADMISSION@EMERSON.EDU • WEBSITE: WWW.EMERSON.EDU

THE PRINCETON REVIEW SAYS

Admissions

Very important factors considered include: academic GPA, standardized test scores. *Important factors considered include:* rigor of secondary school record, class rank, application essay, recommendation(s), extracurricular activities, talent/ability, character/personal qualities. *Other factors considered include:* first generation, alumni/ae relation, geographical residence, racial/ethnic status, volunteer work, work experience. SAT or ACT required; SAT Subject Tests considered if submitted. ACT with Writing required. TOEFL required of all international applicants. High school diploma is required and GED is accepted. *Academic units required:* 4 English, 3 math, 3 science, 3 foreign language, 3 social studies. *Academic units recommended:* 4 English, 3 math, 3 science, 3 foreign language, 3 social studies, 4 academic electives.

Financial Aid

Students should submit: FAFSA, CSS/Financial Aid PROFILE, Noncustodial PROFILE, Business/Farm Supplement. Priority filing deadline is 3/1.The Princeton Review suggests that all financial aid forms be submitted as soon as possible after October 1. *Need-based scholarships/grants offered:* Federal Pell, FSEOG, State scholarships/grants, Private scholarships, College/university scholarship or grant aid from institutional funds. *Loan aid offered:* Direct Subsidized Stafford Loans, Direct Unsubsidized Stafford Loans, Direct PLUS loans, Federal Perkins Loans, State Loans. Applicants will be notified of awards on or about 4/1. Federal Work-Study Program available. Institutional employment available.

The Inside Word

From its location in Boston's theatre district to its large alumni network, Emerson is the perfect school for students interested in communications, theater, and television, among other academic offerings. Jobs and internship opportunities abound in those fields, helping students jumpstart their careers upon graduation. If you are applying in cinematography or the performing arts, be prepared to complete an artistic review with your application.

THE SCHOOL SAYS "..."

From the Admissions Office

"Emerson College is the nation's only four-year, liberal arts institution devoted exclusively to the study of communication and the arts. For over 130 years Emerson has educated the most innovative and creative minds in the fields of marketing, visual and media arts, entrepreneurship, publishing and writing, journalism, performing arts, and speech pathology and audiology. Guided by an award-winning faculty, Emerson students are provided with the real-world experience, professional-grade facilities, and foundational liberal arts knowledge they need to be at the cutting edge of their ever-changing industries.

"Located in the heart of Boston's Theatre District, Emerson's main campus is home to award-winning literary journals, sound treated television studios, and several digital editing and audio post-production suites. The Tufte Performance and Production Center houses a theater design/technology center, makeup lab, and costume shop. There are several programs to observe speech and hearing therapy, a professional marketing focus group room, digital newsroom, and the Paramount Center, which includes a sound stage, scene shop, rehearsal studios, black box theatre, and film screening room.

"Emerson has nearly eighty student organizations and performance groups as well as fourteen NCAA Division III teams. The college also sponsors programs in Los Angeles and Washington, D.C.; study abroad in the Netherlands, Taiwan, and Czech Republic; and course cross-registration with the six-member Boston ProArts Consortium. The tightly-knit network of 28,000 alumni and the connections that Emerson students make on campus follow them into their post-graduate life, paving the way to collaborative projects, internships, and career opportunities across the globe."

SELECTIVITY

Admissions Rating	90
# of applicants	8,709
% of applicants accepted	49
% of acceptees attending	20
# offered a place on the wait list	1,569
% accepting a place on wait list	22
% admitted from wait list	3

FRESHMAN PROFILE

Range SAT Critical Reading	580–680
Range SAT Math	560–650
Range SAT Writing	580–670
Range ACT Composite	26–30
Minimum paper TOEFL	550
Minimum internet-based TOEFL	80
Average HS GPA	3.7
% graduated top 10% of class	37
% graduated top 25% of class	73
% graduated top 50% of class	95

DEADLINES

Early action	
Deadline	11/1
Notification	12/15
Regular	
Deadline	1/15
Notification	4/1
Nonfall registration?	Yes

APPLICANTS ALSO LOOK AT AND OFTEN PREFER
University of Southern California

AND SOMETIMES PREFER
Northeastern University; New York University; Boston University; Chapman University; Syracuse University

AND RARELY PREFER
American University; Fordham University; Ithaca College; University of Massachusetts Amherst

FINANCIAL FACTS

Financial Aid Rating	85
Annual tuition	$42,144
Room and board	$16,320
Required fees	$764
Average frosh need-based scholarship	$19,175
Average UG need-based scholarship	$17,140
% needy frosh rec. need-based scholarship or grant aid	91
% needy UG rec. need-based scholarship or grant aid	87
% needy frosh rec. non-need-based scholarship or grant aid	23
% needy UG rec. non-need-based scholarship or grant aid	15
% needy frosh rec. need-based self-help aid	93
% needy UG rec. need-based self-help aid	94
% frosh need fully met	16
% ugrads need fully met	14
Average % of frosh need met	68
Average % of ugrad need met	59

EMORY UNIVERSITY

EMORY UNIVERSITY, 1390 OXFORD ROAD NE, ATLANTA, GA 30322 • ADMISSIONS: 404-727-6036 • FAX: 404-727-4303

STUDENTS SAY "..."

Academics

As one of the South's top universities, Emory is a "prestigious, mid-size university where students are excited to be learning, living, and engaging beside world-renowned faculty and impassioned peers." With its plethora of students from the East Coast, one student describes the school as "a Northeastern school in the South that focuses on research, while encouraging cooperation and diversity among its [students]." The academics are "rigorous" but "it's hard to meet an Emory student who only focuses on school work and isn't involved in any additional organizations." The "eccentric students living on each other's energy while being pushed academically" appreciate that at Emory, it's "about pushing yourself beyond academics to understand how you can succeed in your career, your community and the world." Pre-professional programs, especially in the health fields, get high marks and overall, professors are "dedicated to their material and care if their students do well," while the classes are "challenging and thought-provoking." As one student puts it, "I never thought I would enjoy managerial accounting, but my professor's passion for the subject has allowed me to absorb the information easily and in a fun manner." Some say that the "general education requirements can be a pain" but concede that those courses "have pushed me to explore new things." Even for undergraduates, "there are a lot of research opportunities" and "great opportunities to connect with faculty and staff."

Life

As one student observes, "although located in the south, the large amount of New York/New Jersey students make [Emory] have almost a Northeastern feel without the harsh winters." Described as "welcoming and hardworking," the students insist that though "classes often stress [us] out, no one ever seems too down, as the community here seems to lift everyone's spirits." "There is always something going on on campus to fill the day," and many students draw attention to an event called "Wonderful Wednesday in Asbury Circle where student organizations set up tables around the circle and showcase their events happening, throw out free tee shirts, and even hand out food." Depending on your preference, "There are always cool things going on in Atlanta if you don't want to spend your weekend on Frat Row." At Emory, students say there is "a strong community that is aided by Greek life and athletics, but not dominated by them." The consensus is that "life at Emory tends to be what you make it" but as one student underscores, "I've never been bored here, not for a single second." Students take advantage of Atlanta's food scene, as well as the "Experience Shuttles that go to different locations around Atlanta each Saturday." One student points out that "Atlanta might be the festival capital of the world because it feels like there is a different festival every weekend which are always sure to be fun."

Student Body

"Most Emory students are intelligent, academically engaged, socially and environmentally aware, and quirky and fun. We don't get riled up about football games; we get riled up about elections and social issues." Students say that Emory is "extremely diverse" and "brings together students from all different cultures, races, religions, and backgrounds." Most agree that "We're able to have fun while still working hard." There is a decided lack of competition and an emphasis on collaboration: "While everyone here is determined to achieve their goals, they're going to work together to do it rather than compete with each other." With the plethora of clubs and organizations on campus, one student appreciated that there are "a lot of extracurricular activities that aren't intimidating to incoming students" and generally there's "a student body that seems to be all on the same wavelength."

FINANCIAL AID: 404-727-6039 • E-MAIL: ADMISSION@EMORY.EDU • WEBSITE: APPLY.EMORY.EDU

THE PRINCETON REVIEW SAYS

Admissions

Very important factors considered include: academic GPA, recommendation(s), extracurricular activities, talent/ability, character/personal qualities. *Important factors considered include:* rigor of secondary school record, standardized test scores, application essay, volunteer work. *Other factors considered include:* class rank, interview, first generation, alumni/ae relation, geographical residence, state residency, racial/ethnic status, work experience. SAT or ACT required; SAT Subject Tests considered if submitted. ACT with Writing required. SAT with Essay component required. TOEFL required of all international applicants. High school diploma is required and GED is not accepted. *Academic units recommended:* 4 English, 4 math, 4 science, 2 science labs, 4 foreign language, 2 social studies, 2 history, 1 visual/performing arts.

Financial Aid

Students should submit: FAFSA, CSS/Financial Aid PROFILE, Noncustodial PROFILE. Regular filing deadline is 3/1.The Princeton Review suggests that all financial aid forms be submitted as soon as possible after October 1. *Need-based scholarships/grants offered:* Federal Pell, FSEOG, Private scholarships, College/university scholarship or grant aid from institutional funds. *Loan aid offered:* Direct Subsidized Stafford Loans, Direct Unsubsidized Stafford Loans, Direct PLUS loans, Federal Perkins Loans, Federal Nursing Loans, State Loans, College/university loans from institutional funds. Applicants will be notified of awards on or about 4/1. Federal Work-Study Program available. Institutional employment available.

The Inside Word

Early decision applications to Emory have surged in the past several years, leading students to question whether they want to join the early word crowd— perhaps increasing their chances of admission—or take their chances with regular admission. Those hoping for admission should aim for a 3.75 (or better) GPA and polish up your writing skills and extracurricular activities.

THE SCHOOL SAYS "..."

From the Admissions Office

"Emory is an inquiry-driven, ethically engaged, and diverse community whose members work collaboratively for positive transformation in the world through courageous leadership in teaching, research scholarship, health care, and social action. The university is internationally recognized for its outstanding liberal arts colleges, superb professional schools, and leading health care system. Emory is noted as one of the most diverse selective universities in the country.

"Emory offers a distinctive undergraduate experience with programs in the humanities, sciences, business, and nursing allowing students to explore their interests and talents in the classroom and in the field. Entering freshman may apply to Emory College, a four-year liberal arts education within the heart of a major research university. Students may also apply to Oxford College where student spend the first two years on Emory's original campus thirty-eight miles east of Atlanta. Emory provides a rich setting for learning from excellent teaching in small classes to lectures from prominent scholars to opportunities for study abroad, research, and internships.

"Emory students balance hard work with having fun. With 70 percent of students living on campus, the community is enhanced by a close-knit living environment. The campus life thrives on constant activity, and students are encouraged to get involved, share opinions, and flourish. Emory is a dynamic place that is constantly in a state of sustainable growth and improvement. Take a look at all Emory has to offer—you'll see why Emory students feel inspired to do more with what they learn here."

SELECTIVITY

Admissions Rating	97
# of applicants	20,492
% of applicants accepted	24
% of acceptees attending	28
# offered a place on the wait list	3,809
% accepting a place on wait list	50
% admitted from wait list	2
# of early decision applicants	2,437
% accepted early decision	30

FRESHMAN PROFILE

Range SAT Critical Reading	620–720
Range SAT Math	650–770
Range SAT Writing	640–730
Range ACT Composite	29–33
Minimum paper TOEFL	600
Average HS GPA	3.7
% graduated top 10% of class	83
% graduated top 25% of class	96
% graduated top 50% of class	99

DEADLINES

Early decision	
Deadline	11/1
Notification	12/15
Regular	
Deadline	1/1
Notification	4/1
Nonfall registration?	No

APPLICANTS ALSO LOOK AT AND OFTEN PREFER

Washington University in St. Louis; Duke University; The University of North Carolina at Chapel Hill; Georgia Institute of Technology

AND SOMETIMES PREFER

Dartmouth College; Wake Forest University

AND RARELY PREFER

Drexel University; DePauw University

FINANCIAL FACTS

Financial Aid Rating	94
Annual tuition	$45,700
Room and board	$13,130
Required fees	$614
Books and supplies	$1,224
Average frosh need-based scholarship	$38,283
Average UG need-based scholarship	$37,657
% needy frosh rec. need-based scholarship or grant aid	90
% needy UG rec. need-based scholarship or grant aid	91
% needy frosh rec. non-need-based scholarship or grant aid	32
% needy UG rec. non-need-based scholarship or grant aid	29
% needy frosh rec. need-based self-help aid	95
% needy UG rec. need-based self-help aid	95
% frosh rec. any financial aid	55
% UG rec. any financial aid	54
% frosh need fully met	100
% ugrads need fully met	93
Average % of frosh need met	100
Average % of ugrad need met	97

THE EVERGREEN STATE COLLEGE

2700 EVERGREEN PARKWAY NORTHWEST, OLYMPIA, WA 98505 • ADMISSIONS: 360-867-6170 • FAX: 360-867-5114

CAMPUS LIFE

Quality of Life Rating	88
Fire Safety Rating	90
Green Rating	88
Type of school	Public
Affiliation	No Affiliation
Environment	City

STUDENTS

Total undergrad enrollment	3,872
% male/female	45/55
% from out of state	25
% frosh live on campus	74
% ugrads live on campus	23
% African American	5
% Asian	3
% Caucasian	65
% Hispanic	10
% Native American	2
% Pacific Islander	<1
% Two or more races	8
% Race and/or ethnicity unknown	6
% international	<1
# of countries represented	22

SURVEY SAYS...

Lots of liberal students
Students are happy
Internships are widely available
No one cheats
Students aren't religious
Students environmentally aware
Active minority support groups

ACADEMICS

Academic Rating	71
% students returning for sophomore year	66
% students graduating within 4 years	41
% students graduating within 6 years	54
Calendar	Quarter
Student/faculty ratio	22:1
Profs interesting rating	92
Profs accessible rating	70

Most classes have 20–29 students.

MOST POPULAR MAJORS

Social Sciences; Liberal Arts and Sciences;
Natural Sciences

STUDENTS SAY ". . ."

Academics

"Keeping education in its purest form alive and well in the heart of the Northwest," The Evergreen State College offers "a unique approach" to academics. The school provides an "interactive environment—with a diverse, enriching learning method," which allows students "to focus on [their] passions and explore them in detail." Everyone creates their own educational paths and directs the pace of their own learning. As a few students say admiringly, "I feel a sense of freedom with the academics at Evergreen." "I have more power as a student." Greatly appreciated is the flexibility found within the curriculum. "I was excited about building my own major." "No self-motivated student will leave Evergreen unsatisfied." Students work collaboratively here and support one another in their endeavors. "It's not about grades or competition; it's about self-improvement and personal fulfillment." Evaluations are used to view student progress, with "interdisciplinary education over declared majors" being the focus. "Your classes are all interconnected, so it's easy to link what you're doing into a defined path." "My transcript says more about me than A's, B's, and C's possibly could." "The philosophy...definitely lowers the stress I experience around academics." Professors assist students in innumerable ways and are "very intimately involved in the education of their students." "At Evergreen, in order to have a great experience you need to be able to talk to your professors and engage with them." "I have not met a professor yet who was not willing to rework their mode of teaching to better serve the class." The educational atmosphere is highly interactive. Most every student "actively engages the material with field work, undergraduate research, and extended trips." "Class time is spent doing workshops, seminars, or a led discussion where everyone participates." "Even the science programs involve large portions of discussion and peer collaboration." As one undergraduate describes slyly, "My professors have been A++, if Evergreen assigned grades."

Life

Evergreen has a "booming extracurricular life"; students enjoy the "thriving local art and music scene, very hip and fresh," in Olympia as well as easily accessible Seattle or Portland. "The Flaming Eggplant, the student-run cafe, is simply the cheapest and most delicious place on the planet," as well as a very popular hangout. The Student Activities office has no shortage of options for undergraduates here, with "more than fifty different clubs and student groups." Physical activity is popular, and the recreational center has racquetball, a pool, a rock-climbing wall, and various places to exercise. There is "no shortage of local hiking, backpacking, and biking opportunities." "Hikes in the woods, down to the beach, or up to the bluff are very common as well as late-night stargazing." The physical surroundings are viewed with much admiration at Evergreen. "Our campus is set back in this magical forest with these winding paths down to the beach. There are tree forts, giant sculptures, dream catchers in the trees, hidden drum circles, and music everywhere." As one student describes fondly, "To me, it is reminiscent of Thoreau's solitude in nature."

Student Life

The "kindness and awareness of the community" is frequently said by students to be one of the most valued aspects of their experience here. "Articulate" and "inquisitive" undergraduates are evident in large numbers. "Students tend to be very politically aware and active with very liberal points of view" and are "mostly peaceful relaxed people" amidst an "open-minded social environment." The dorms are divided into different themes, and "the residential staff is professional and keeps the housing community functioning and safe." "The campus police are pretty awesome people," as well. Evergreen is respected by students throughout the college for its "forward-thinking" administration and faculty, with a "dedication to sustainability" being clearly evident around the campus.

FINANCIAL AID: 360-867-6205 • E-MAIL: ADMISSIONS@EVERGREEN.EDU • WEBSITE: WWW.EVERGREEN.EDU

THE PRINCETON REVIEW SAYS

Admissions

Very important factors considered include: rigor of secondary school record, academic GPA, application essay. *Important factors considered include:* standardized test scores, first generation, level of applicant's interest. *Other factors considered include:* recommendation(s), interview, extracurricular activities, volunteer work, work experience. SAT or ACT required. ACT with or without writing accepted. SAT with or without essay component accepted. TOEFL required of all international applicants. High school diploma is required and GED is accepted. *Academic units required:* 4 English, 3 math, 2 science, 2 science labs, 2 foreign language, 3 social studies, 1 academic elective, and 1 unit from above areas or other academic areas.

Financial Aid

Students should submit: FAFSA. Priority filing deadline is 3/1.The Princeton Review suggests that all financial aid forms be submitted as soon as possible after October 1. *Need-based scholarships/grants offered:* Federal Pell, FSEOG, state scholarships/grants, private scholarships, college/university scholarship or grant aid from institutional funds. *Loan aid offered:* Direct Subsidized Stafford Loans, Direct Unsubsidized Stafford Loans, Direct PLUS loans, Federal Perkins Loans, college/university loans from institutional funds. Applicants will be notified of awards on a rolling basis beginning 4/1. Federal Work-Study Program available. Institutional employment available.

The Inside Word

Students at Evergreen are commonly some of the strongest performers from their high schools, although the admissions department considers a variety of traits from applicants (including strength of character) when considering prospective undergraduates. The school's unique and self-directed academic curriculum favors those students who can adequately handle the responsibility of creating and developing their own educational path.

THE SCHOOL SAYS "..."

From the Admissions Office

"Evergreen is a public arts and sciences college nationally recognized for its full-time interdisciplinary studies programs. Students work closely with faculty to study an issue or theme from the perspective of several academic disciplines. They apply what's learned to real world issues, complete projects in groups, and discuss concepts in seminars that typically involve a faculty member and twenty to twenty-five students. The emphasis on seminars, interdisciplinary problem solving, and collaboration means students are well prepared for graduate school and the world of work. Our students tend to be politically active, environmentally savvy, and more concerned about social justice than competition and personal gain.

"All applicants are encouraged to complete a Free Application for Federal Student Aid (FAFSA). Evergreen's priority financial aid deadline is March 1, though applicants may submit the form later and may be awarded aid if funds are still available.

"Freshman applicants are required to submit test scores from either the SAT or ACT tests. The student's best composite score will be used in the admissions process."

SELECTIVITY
Admissions Rating	71
# of applicants	1,744
% of applicants accepted	98
% of acceptees attending	35

FRESHMAN PROFILE
Range SAT Critical Reading	490–630
Range SAT Math	450–560
Range SAT Writing	460–590
Range ACT Composite	20–26
Minimum paper TOEFL	550
Minimum internet-based TOEFL	79
Average HS GPA	3.0
% graduated top 10% of class	9
% graduated top 25% of class	25
% graduated top 50% of class	64

DEADLINES
Regular	
Priority	2/1
Nonfall registration?	Yes

APPLICANTS ALSO LOOK AT AND OFTEN PREFER
Western Washington University; University of Washington; University of California, Santa Cruz; Lewis & Clark College

AND SOMETIMES PREFER
Hampshire College; Portland State University; University of Puget Sound; Seattle University; Willamette University

AND RARELY PREFER
Colorado State; Eckerd College; University of Montana; Humboldt State University; Warren Wilson College

FINANCIAL FACTS
Financial Aid Rating	78
Annual out-of-state tuition	$21,927
Room and board	$9,492
Required fees	$693
Books and supplies	$1,050
Average frosh need-based scholarship	$8,832
Average UG need-based scholarship	$9,936
% needy frosh rec. need-based scholarship or grant aid	85
% needy UG rec. need-based scholarship or grant aid	84
% needy frosh rec. non-need-based scholarship or grant aid	3
% needy UG rec. non-need-based scholarship or grant aid	1
% needy frosh rec. need-based self-help aid	67
% needy UG rec. need-based self-help aid	76
% frosh rec. any financial aid	61
% UG rec. any financial aid	65
% UG borrow to pay for school	56
Average cumulative indebtedness	$21,131
% frosh need fully met	9
% ugrads need fully met	6
Average % of frosh need met	56
Average % of ugrad need met	62

FAIRFIELD UNIVERSITY

1073 NORTH BENSON ROAD, FAIRFIELD, CT 06824-5195 • ADMISSIONS: 203-254-4100 • FAX: 203-254-4199

STUDENTS SAY "..."

Academics

As a Jesuit school, Fairfield University seeks to "educate the mind, body and spirit both inside and outside the classroom." "An academically strong school with great post-graduate career support," Fairfield students are encouraged to "make a difference in the world." Certainly, one of Fairfield's greatest assets is its "small class sizes." This allows for a "space where everyone's opinion has an opportunity to be heard and respected" during class lectures. Undergrads also highly value their core curriculum and point to the strong business and nursing programs as stalwarts of the university. Best of all, Fairfield manages to attract professors that are "second to none." The vast majority are "extraordinarily dedicated and compassionate about teaching." More importantly, they "take a vested interest in their students. And, as one thrilled (and perhaps relieved) marketing major shares, "Their doors are always open and they are always willing to help students in any way they can."

Life

Academics often come first at Fairfield: "Students are extremely dedicated to their studies and you are never alone in the library no matter what day of the week or time of day." That said, these undergrads definitely still carve out time to kick back and relax. To begin with, the university sponsors "a ton of activities" from "karaoke [to] bingo nights." We're told that "the most popular events [include]… PrezBall, our kind of homecoming dance, Midnight Breakfast, ShamJam for St. Patricks day, and ClamJam at the end of the year." Additionally, "sporting events are usually well attended." Thursday night through the weekend, a number of undergrads can be spotted heading "out to parties at the Townhouses on campus where the juniors live." Fortunately, as mentioned above, there are plenty of social alternatives and no real pressure to drink. Students also frequently "take the shuttle bus right into the town of Fairfield which has so many cute shops and restaurants." And, when the weather permits, these undergrads love to head to the beach which is "less than three miles" from campus. Finally, when they're itching to get a little further away, they can simply "take the bus to the train station and hop on the Metro-North to New York City."

Student Body

While the student body here is predominantly caucasian, we're told that "for a small school" there's "incredible" geographic diversity. Students come "from all over the U.S. and [around] the world as well," and no matter where they're from, they're "friendly and welcoming." As one happy undergrad further explains, "People are constantly opening and holding doors for other people, offering help to others, and much more. The students here are truly kind." They're also "incredibly motivated and driven to meet their goals." A mass communications major rushes to comment on this sharing, "My peers are excited to not only learn in their field of study, but also in vast array of core classes we are required to take." And while one theater students quietly laments that the "social scene is a little cliquey," in the same breath she rushes to assure us that "it is not hard to make friends." A business/management major agrees with the latter and adds, "It's scary how quickly and easily I was able to feel accepted and welcomed by the people who go here. I was able to find a group of people and in the year and half that I've been here I know consider them my second family."

FINANCIAL AID: 203-254-4125 • E-MAIL: ADMIS@FAIRFIELD.EDU • WEBSITE: WWW.FAIRFIELD.EDU

THE PRINCETON REVIEW SAYS

Admissions

Very important factors considered include: rigor of secondary school record, academic GPA, application essay, recommendation(s). *Important factors considered include:* interview, extracurricular activities, talent/ability, character/personal qualities, first generation, volunteer work, work experience, level of applicant's interest. *Other factors considered include:* class rank, standardized test scores, alumni/ae relation, geographical residence, racial/ethnic status. SAT or ACT considered if submitted. ACT with or without writing accepted. SAT with or without Essay component accepted. TOEFL required of all international applicants. High school diploma is required and GED is not accepted. *Academic units required:* 4 English, 3 math, 3 science, 2 science labs, 2 foreign language, 2 social studies, 2 history. *Academic units recommended:* 4 English, 4 math, 4 science, 4 foreign language, 2 social studies, 2 history.

Financial Aid

Students should submit: FAFSA, CSS/Financial Aid PROFILE, Noncustodial PROFILE, Business/Farm Supplement. Regular filing deadline is 2/15. The Princeton Review suggests that all financial aid forms be submitted as soon as possible after October 1. *Need-based scholarships/grants offered:* Federal Pell, FSEOG, State scholarships/grants, Private scholarships, College/university scholarship or grant aid from institutional funds, Federal Nursing Scholarships. *Loan aid offered:* Direct Subsidized Stafford Loans, Direct Unsubsidized Stafford Loans, Direct PLUS loans, Federal Perkins Loans, Federal Nursing Loans. Applicants will be notified of awards on a rolling basis beginning 4/1. Federal Work-Study Program available. Institutional employment available.

The Inside Word

When it comes to selecting applicants, Fairfield strives to take a thorough and well-rounded approach. The being said, your high school academic record will be of primary importance. Beyond your grades, admissions officers will closely assess how challenging your high school curriculum was. And they will also consider your extracurricular participation to glean how you may contribute to campus life. Finally, Fairfield is a test-optional school.

THE SCHOOL SAYS "..."

From the Admissions Office

"Fairfield University welcomes students of unique promise into a learning and living community that will give them a solid intellectual foundation and the confidence they need to reach their individual goals. Students at Fairfield benefit from the deep-rooted Jesuit commitment to education of the whole person—mind, body, and spirit, and our admission policies are consistent with that mission. When considering an applicant, Fairfield looks at measures of academic achievement, students' curricular and extracurricular activities, their life skills and accomplishments, and the degree to which they have an appreciation for Fairfield's mission and outlook. In keeping with its holistic review process, Fairfield is a test optional institution. Students choosing not to submit test scores do not have to submit any additional documents, but are encouraged to schedule a campus interview. Fairfield University students are challenged to be creative and active members of a community in which diversity is encouraged and honored. The university community is committed to excellence in educating, serving, inspiring and training students in a wide variety of disciplines and fields. Students can complement their classroom performance with a rich array of study abroad, internship and research opportunities. Our location is ideal, offering a picturesque 200-acre campus in the coastal community of Fairfield, Connecticut, just an hour away from the cultural, intellectual and economic opportunities of New York City. On campus, students participate in a vast array of activities, including varsity and intramural athletics, performing arts groups and an extremely active student government. All of this prepares our graduates for a rich and fulfilling future, whether students pursue a career, service opportunities or graduate study. In our most recent survey of graduates of the Class of 2015 six months after graduation, 97 percent of students were employed full time, in graduate school or pursuing a service opportunity."

SELECTIVITY

Admissions Rating	82
# of applicants	10,767
% of applicants accepted	65
% of acceptees attending	14
# offered a place on the wait list	2,573
% accepting a place on wait list	34
% admitted from wait list	11
# of early decision applicants	137
% accepted early decision	91

FRESHMAN PROFILE

Range SAT Critical Reading	540–630
Range SAT Math	560–640
Range SAT Writing	550–640
Range ACT Composite	25–29
Minimum paper TOEFL	550
Minimum internet-based TOEFL	80
Average HS GPA	3.4
% graduated top 10% of class	31
% graduated top 25% of class	69
% graduated top 50% of class	97

DEADLINES

Early decision	
Deadline	11/15
Notification	12/15
Other ED	
Deadline	1/15
Other ED	
Notification	2/15
Early action	
Deadline	11/1
Notification	12/20
Regular	
Deadline	1/15
Notification	4/1
Nonfall registration?	Yes

APPLICANTS ALSO LOOK AT AND OFTEN PREFER

Boston College

FINANCIAL FACTS

Financial Aid Rating	85
Annual tuition	$44,250
Room and board	$13,520
Required fees	$625
Books and supplies	$1,150
Average frosh need-based scholarship	$25,764
Average UG need-based scholarship	$24,472
% needy frosh rec. need-based scholarship or grant aid	98
% needy UG rec. need-based scholarship or grant aid	98
% needy frosh rec. non-need-based scholarship or grant aid	13
% needy UG rec. non-need-based scholarship or grant aid	13
% needy frosh rec. need-based self-help aid	82
% needy UG rec. need-based self-help aid	83
% frosh rec. any financial aid	92
% UG rec. any financial aid	78
% UG borrow to pay for school	68
Average cumulative indebtedness	$38,780
% frosh need fully met	27
% ugrads need fully met	30
Average % of frosh need met	80
Average % of ugrad need met	78

FLAGLER COLLEGE

74 KING STREET, ST. AUGUSTINE, FL 32085-1027 • ADMISSIONS: 800-304-4208 • FAX: 904-826-0094

STUDENTS SAY ". . ."

Academics

For those seeking "an excellent education in a beautiful location," Flagler College is a small comprehensive liberal arts school in Florida that offers a "comfortable atmosphere," "tons of history and culture," and "a perfect ratio of professors to student." The school's strong education program is a huge draw here, but there are plenty of other strong programs in Flagler's twenty-five available majors. Hard workers get noticed, and there are plenty of opportunities to excel outside of the classroom, which "has been the most valuable aspect," according to one student.

The faculty here is "extremely enthusiastic about their jobs" and "very knowledgeable in their fields," though "there are a few that I don't think have real direction," says a student. Nevertheless, most are "always willing to meet and discuss work outside of the classroom," and the fact that "it is pretty easy to get to know the professors within your major on a personal basis makes things a lot easier and comfortable." This close-knit community breeds an environment where every person actively wants "to share experiences and knowledge with the faculty and other students." Class time is treated as an "intellectual journey," wherein one main question or discussion topic is introduced, and students explore every aspect of it using the professor as the tour guide. "This system the professors at Flagler College have evokes curiosity from all students, leaving very little room for confusion."

Aside from the "ample help from teachers," the "personable" administration is "good at communicating to all students via school e-mail." The attendance policy can be tough on some students—"you only get a certain number of absences, excused or unexcused, before you get dropped from a course"—but most still know that this tough love is in place to help students be "encouraged in a way that leads to excellent work." The best classes are the ones with eight or so people in them, as "you really lean on each other throughout the semester."

Life

Life is "pretty chill at Flagler," where "homework usually isn't too bad most of the time." As far as making friends, this "relaxed," happy lot has no problems. "Attend a few of the many social activities that Flagler College offers. It's really easy to make friends there!" suggests one student. On the first Friday of the month, all the art galleries "throw their doors wide open and serve treats," and the "casual and quaint" tourist-centric town of St. Augustine "is an awesome place to spend your time, walking around, going out to eat, and doing a little bit of shopping." Campus activities tend to "die around 7:00 P.M.," and many students tend to live nearby off campus (due to Flagler College residential rules, which restrict interdorm visiting, drugs, and alcohol).

Sunny days mean "the pool and West lawn are the places to be," and on weekends, "many times we drive to Jacksonville and go out at night there." Biking, beach volleyball, and walking along the sand dunes are just some of the beachy pastimes here, where "the beach mentality triumphs, including surfer culture." The campus itself "is beautiful, we sometimes even compare it to Hogwarts," says a student.

Student Body

Your typical Flagler student is "easygoing and very laid-back" ("How can you not be with the beach five miles away?" asks a student) as well as "super nice and friendly." It's not difficult to fit in at Flagler College, because "there is a crowd for everybody, despite the small size of the student body," even if this student body as a whole is a bit "homogenous." All students provide different viewpoints and "seem to be very respectful of others' views." There are quite a few surfers and artistic types, and even these groups are "very motivated and ready to broaden their education."

FINANCIAL AID: 904-819-6225 • E-MAIL: ADMISS@FLAGLER.EDU • WEBSITE: WWW.FLAGLER.EDU

THE PRINCETON REVIEW SAYS

Admissions

Very important factors considered include: rigor of secondary school record. *Important factors considered include:* academic GPA, standardized test scores, application essay, recommendation(s), extracurricular activities, talent/ability, character/personal qualities, alumni/ae relation, volunteer work. *Other factors considered include:* first generation, geographical residence, state residency, racial/ethnic status, work experience, level of applicant's interest. SAT or ACT required. ACT with Writing recommended. SAT with Essay component recommended. TOEFL required of all international applicants. High school diploma is required and GED is accepted. *Academic units required:* 4 English, 3 math, 2 science, 1 science lab, 3 social studies, 1 history, 2 academic electives. *Academic units recommended:* 4 English, 4 math, 4 science, 2 science labs, 2 foreign language, 4 social studies, 4 history.

Financial Aid

Students should submit: FAFSA, State aid form. Priority filing deadline is 3/1. The Princeton Review suggests that all financial aid forms be submitted as soon as possible after October 1. *Need-based scholarships/grants offered:* Federal Pell, FSEOG, State scholarships/grants, Private scholarships, College/university scholarship or grant aid from institutional funds. *Loan aid offered:* Direct Subsidized Stafford Loans, Direct Unsubsidized Stafford Loans, Direct PLUS loans, Federal Perkins Loans. Applicants will be notified of awards on a rolling basis beginning 3/1. Federal Work-Study Program available. Institutional employment available.

The Inside Word

Several high-profile programs, a desirable location, and a small, incoming freshman class all conspire to drive down Flagler's admissions rate. Still, Flagler is not top-tier when it comes to selectivity, and strong candidates should meet little resistance from the admissions office. About half of the incoming freshmen graduated in the top quarter of their classes, so make sure you build a strong application with harder courses and strong grades.

THE SCHOOL SAYS ". . ."

From the Admissions Office

"Flagler College is an independent, four-year, coeducational, residential institution located in picturesque St. Augustine. A famous historic tourist center in northeast Florida, it is located to the south of Jacksonville and north of Daytona Beach. Flagler students have ample opportunity to explore the rich cultural heritage and international flavor of St. Augustine, and there's always time for a relaxing day at the beach, about four miles from campus. The annual cost for tuition, room, and board at Flagler is about the same as state universities. The small student body helps to keep one from becoming 'just a number.' Flagler serves a predominately full-time student body and seeks to enroll students who can benefit from the type of educational experience the college offers. Because of the college's mission and distinctive characteristics, some students may benefit more from an educational experience at Flagler than others. The college's admission standards and procedures are designed to select from among the applicants those students most likely to succeed academically, to contribute significantly to the student life program at Flagler, and to become graduates of the college. Flagler College provides an exceptional opportunity for a private education at an extremely affordable cost.

"All applicants to Flager College must submit either their SAT or ACT scores."

SELECTIVITY

Admissions Rating	87
# of applicants	5,260
% of applicants accepted	50
% of acceptees attending	25
# offered a place on the wait list	48
% accepting a place on wait list	42
% admitted from wait list	100
# of early decision applicants	532
% accepted early decision	53

FRESHMAN PROFILE

Range SAT Critical Reading	490–588
Range SAT Math	470–560
Range SAT Writing	480–570
Range ACT Composite	21–26
Minimum paper TOEFL	550
Minimum internet-based TOEFL	75
Average HS GPA	3.5

DEADLINES

Early decision	
Deadline	11/1
Notification	12/15
Regular	
Priority	11/1
Deadline	3/1
Notification	3/31
Nonfall registration?	Yes

APPLICANTS ALSO LOOK AT AND RARELY PREFER

Rollins College; Florida Southern College; Eckerd College

FINANCIAL FACTS

Financial Aid Rating	80
Annual tuition	$17,500
Room and board	$10,015
Books and supplies	$1,000
Average frosh need-based scholarship	$9,324
Average UG need-based scholarship	$9,477
% needy frosh rec. need-based scholarship or grant aid	100
% needy UG rec. need-based scholarship or grant aid	97
% needy frosh rec. non-need-based scholarship or grant aid	8
% needy UG rec. non-need-based scholarship or grant aid	6
% needy frosh rec. need-based self-help aid	91
% needy UG rec. need-based self-help aid	92
% frosh rec. any financial aid	88
% UG rec. any financial aid	87
% UG borrow to pay for school	67
Average cumulative indebtedness	$28,897
% frosh need fully met	15
% ugrads need fully met	12
Average % of frosh need met	58
Average % of ugrad need met	57

FLORIDA SOUTHERN COLLEGE

111 LAKE HOLLINGSWORTH DRIVE, LAKELAND, FL 33801 • ADMISSIONS: 800-274-4131 • FAX: 863-680-4120

STUDENTS SAY "..."

Academics

Florida Southern College, a small suburban school between Tampa and Orlando, offers more than fifty majors, a tight-knit community, and a core educational structure based on the premise of engaged learning. "Everyone is very involved and loves advancing the school," to the point where "it's hard not to get involved with events just about [every] day." The entire population is "striving to have the best community, student body, and school possible," and FSC constantly "asks [students] what they can do to improve and then follows through with those suggestions." FSC offers a Four-Year Graduation Guarantee that says that if students follow certain guidelines and still do not graduate within that given time, the school will cover tuition until they graduate. Internships are also guaranteed, and all students have the opportunity to study abroad for one to two weeks at no additional cost through the Junior Journey program. The theatre program is a sizable draw, and the arts receive unabashed support from all: "Every single school theatre show sells out every night."

"Most professors are some of the best people I've ever met, let alone the best educators," says one student. They "do a great job sharing their enthusiasm with their students" and provide lots of opportunities such as internships, volunteer events, and research opportunities that students "would not be able to get if [they] did not have such involved and motivated teachers." "If you are late to class or not coming to class your professors will 100 percent be texting you to make sure everything is okay and to help you out if you need anything," says a student. Experiential learning goes along with class discussions and lectures, and with smaller class sizes, "it is easier for professors to slow down and focus on specific areas and students."

Life

Florida Southern College "is not just great for classes; regular life here is top notch as well." Facilities and resources get rave reviews. The wellness center offers "a spectacular amount of gym equipment," the library is stocked thousands of books and movies, "dorms are nice and usually spacious," and the student lounge is a great place "to just chill out and play games, whether it be ping-pong, pool, foosball, or simply watching TV." FSC's prime location means "a lot of kids also have passes to Disney and Universal," where they can blow off steam for the day. Downtown Lakeland itself ("the perfect college town") is "very fun to go to," especially the first Friday of every month when the city puts on big events.

On campus, the main dining hall is a popular spot at night ("steak AND shrimp every Saturday!!"), and with over eighty clubs and activities, such as "Winter Wonderland, Southern Takeover (a big concert), comedy shows, [and] service events," means "there is never a dull moment." "There are so many different ways to get involved on campus and it's so easy to do," confirms a student. Greek life is "a very big experience" here, and its members "tend to participate in intramurals, community service, and fundraisers."

Student Body

Only a couple thousand undergraduates roam this "beautiful" campus, but they make a "colorful and diverse" group. Friend groups "are not usually confined to the people within a major or hall," and students assure that if you are involved in any organizations, "you know almost everyone on campus. You can recognize anyone that you walk past." Each student brings his or her own culture and background to the table, and many say "it's amazing to see such diversity yet a sense of togetherness within the student body." Athletes, Greeks, and people involved in the arts do tend to be more inclusive, but "everyone feels like family."

FINANCIAL AID: 863-680-4140 • E-MAIL: FSCADM@FLSOUTHERN.EDU • WEBSITE: WWW.FLSOUTHERN.EDU

THE PRINCETON REVIEW SAYS

Admissions

Very important factors considered include: rigor of secondary school record, academic GPA. *Important factors considered include:* standardized test scores, application essay, recommendation(s), extracurricular activities, talent/ability, character/personal qualities, level of applicant's interest. *Other factors considered include:* class rank, interview, first generation, alumni/ae relation, religious affiliation/commitment, racial/ethnic status, volunteer work, work experience. SAT or ACT required. ACT with or without writing accepted. SAT with or without Essay component accepted. TOEFL required of all international applicants. High school diploma is required and GED is accepted. *Academic units required:* 4 English, 3 math, 2 science, 2 science labs, 3 social studies, 3 history, 1 academic elective. *Academic units recommended:* 2 foreign language.

Financial Aid

Students should submit: FAFSA, Institution's own financial aid form. Regular filing deadline is 7/1.The Princeton Review suggests that all financial aid forms be submitted as soon as possible after October 1. *Need-based scholarships/ grants offered:* Federal Pell, FSEOG, State scholarships/grants, Private scholarships, College/university scholarship or grant aid from institutional funds, Federal Nursing Scholarships. *Loan aid offered:* Direct Subsidized Stafford Loans, Direct Unsubsidized Stafford Loans, Direct PLUS loans, Federal Perkins Loans. Applicants will be notified of awards on a rolling basis beginning 3/1. Federal Work-Study Program available. Institutional employment available.

The Inside Word

Grades and test scores are the most important admission criteria here, but extracurricular activities, community service, and leadership experience also count for a lot. Admissions officers are on the lookout for applicants who demonstrate intellectual curiosity and a desire to succeed. Without a doubt, the strongest candidates are those who have challenged themselves by taking honors, advanced placement, or IB courses.

THE SCHOOL SAYS "..."

From the Admissions Office

"Florida Southern is a friendly, vibrant, and energetic campus, offering dynamic engaged learning opportunities that include guaranteed internships, student-faculty collaborative research and performance, service learning, and study abroad. An innovative program—the Junior Journey—guarantees all students the opportunity to study domestically or overseas during their junior year at no cost for the trip other than minimal course credit charges. FSC offers more than fifty majors in fields such as art, biology, business, chemistry, communication, education, marine biology, music and theater performance, nursing, and psychology. Pre-professional programs include pre-medicine, pre-pharmacy, pre-dentistry, and pre-law. The college is known for its great faculty, small classes (thirteen to one student/faculty), and personalized attention. The college has a state-of-the art technology center, as well as contemporary residence halls with scenic views of Lake Hollingsworth. Our involved student population enjoys rich and varied student life programming that includes championship NCAA Division II events in nineteen sports, intramurals, more than eighty clubs and organizations, an extensive Greek system, and an elaborate and diverse selection of weekend activities. The college's popular lakefront program features free kayaks, canoes, and paddleboats. FSC is home to the world's largest single-site collection of structures designed by Frank Lloyd Wright, which provides a stunning setting for living and academic learning communities. Ninety-six percent of graduates report landing jobs in their fields or continuing their studies at top-tier graduate and professional schools within six months of graduation."

SELECTIVITY

Admissions Rating	89
# of applicants	6,190
% of applicants accepted	45
% of acceptees attending	25
# offered a place on the wait list	0
# of early decision applicants	173
% accepted early decision	41

FRESHMAN PROFILE

Range SAT Critical Reading	520–620
Range SAT Math	530–610
Range SAT Writing	500–600
Range ACT Composite	24–29
Minimum paper TOEFL	550
Average HS GPA	3.7
% graduated top 10% of class	24
% graduated top 25% of class	59
% graduated top 50% of class	91

DEADLINES

Early decision	
Deadline	12/1
Notification	12/15
Early action	
Notification	Regular
Priority	3/1
Nonfall registration?	Yes

FINANCIAL FACTS

Financial Aid Rating	83
Average frosh need-based scholarship	$20,621
Average UG need-based scholarship	$18,952
% needy frosh rec. need-based scholarship or grant aid	100
% needy UG rec. need-based scholarship or grant aid	99
% needy frosh rec. non-need-based scholarship or grant aid	62
% needy UG rec. non-need-based scholarship or grant aid	68
% needy frosh rec. need-based self-help aid	3
% needy UG rec. need-based self-help aid	6
% frosh rec. any financial aid	99
% UG rec. any financial aid	98
% UG borrow to pay for school	73
Average cumulative indebtedness	$29,254
% frosh need fully met	29
% ugrads need fully met	27
Average % of frosh need met	75
Average % of ugrad need met	52

FLORIDA STATE UNIVERSITY

PO Box 3062400, Tallahassee, FL 32306-2400 • Admissions: 850-644-6200 • Fax: 850-644-0197

STUDENTS SAY "..."

Academics

Florida State University is "a large, sports-oriented, research-intensive state school that has a niche for everybody, as long as you are willing to search." In addition to its strong academics, students tended to choose FSU for its "sports teams"—the Florida State Seminoles—the "great weather," and the fact that it's "a place with great traditions." "Florida State is a school that is so rooted in tradition it is extremely hard not to proudly call yourself a True Seminole." FSU is also "affordable" for in-state students with "excellent scholarships." "The tight vicinity of the campus [causes] the student body to be a close-unit of individuals." "FSU's reputation as a small-school feel in a big university was what drew me in," says an accounting and finance student. Reviews of the professors are mixed, as is common at many large universities. "About one-fourth of the professors are no good at teaching, about half of them are decent or good, and about one-fourth are great," one student explains. Another attests, "I have had wonderful professors that have eyes, ears, and heart to a world beyond my own, and have shown me that anything is achievable if I try hard enough." Students do wish for "smaller class sizes" and "more discussions in class." If the students have one common complaint, it's "parking!," which is "always a huge hassle." Students also wish for better sustainability, recycling, and green programs. "FSU has traditionally been all about the humanities, and it's great that we're expanding into other areas, but we shouldn't forget our main focus," one student says. An English major sums up FSU: "Florida State University is a school where students are asked to uphold the garnet and gold and to live intentionally in the direction of leadership, academics, and service."

Life

"Sports is basically your whole life here," claims one student. While a university as large as FSU—the population is 40,000 plus—has students of many types, athletics and "school spirit" are what "bring everyone together" at FSU. "Everyone likes to socialize and party, usually off campus, like at bars or houses." Greek life is also "very prominent" FSU has a reputation as a party school, and "many students go out on the weekend or even sometimes during the week. The use of alcohol and marihuana is very common." "The majority of FSU students gets rowdy almost every night of the week," confirms another. However, one student claims that "FSU is a recovering party school." Since its heyday in the mid-nineties, FSU has calmed down a bit, but you can still find thriving parties and clubs any day of the week." "People go to Wakulla Springs to swim or to Bear Paw to go around the river during the weekends." Although "Tallahassee is one of the most boring cities I have ever been to," "the nightlife is...very important in Tallahassee; there are many bars and clubs to attend." "My life at Florida State is busy," one political science student explains. "I am always on the move, from class, to student government, Greek life, internships at the capital, and nightlife. I think people at FSU are constantly thinking about how they can better themselves and the university."

Student Body

Your average FSU student is a "football fan, partier, into academics and community service, [and] passionate." Students tend to be "extremely involved," whether it's in athletics, "Greek life or community service, or one of the other hundreds of groups and clubs here at FSU." "Greek [life] is a huge part of campus, but you are fine if you are not in one." Although "the majority of students are Caucasians," "students of all races and religions work together here to make FSU an enjoyable environment," and "the school continues to become more diverse each year." No matter what their background, every FSU student has "a colossal amount of school spirit and loves to go out and support the team."

FLORIDA STATE UNIVERSITY

FINANCIAL AID: 850-644-5716 • E-MAIL: ADMISSIONS@ADMIN.FSU.EDU • WEBSITE: WWW.FSU.EDU

THE PRINCETON REVIEW SAYS

Admissions

Very important factors considered include: rigor of secondary school record, academic GPA. *Important factors considered include:* standardized test scores, talent/ability, state residency. *Other factors considered include:* class rank, application essay, recommendation(s), extracurricular activities, character/personal qualities, first generation, alumni/ae relation, geographical residence, volunteer work, work experience. SAT or ACT required. ACT with Writing required. SAT with Essay component required. TOEFL required of all international applicants. High school diploma is required and GED is accepted. *Academic units required:* 4 English, 4 math, 3 science, 2 science labs, 2 foreign language, 1 social studies, 2 history, 3 academic electives. *Academic units recommended:* 4 English, 4 math, 4 science, 2 science labs, 4 foreign language, 2 social studies, 2 history, 3 academic electives.

Financial Aid

Students should submit: FAFSA, State aid form. The Princeton Review suggests that all financial aid forms be submitted as soon as possible after October 1. *Need-based scholarships/grants offered:* Federal Pell, FSEOG, State scholarships/grants, Private scholarships, College/university scholarship or grant aid from institutional funds. *Loan aid offered:* Direct Subsidized Stafford Loans, Direct Unsubsidized Stafford Loans, Direct PLUS loans, Federal Perkins Loans. Applicants will be notified of awards on a rolling basis beginning 4/5. Federal Work-Study Program available. Institutional employment available.

The Inside Word

With 25,000 applications to process annually, FSU must rely on a formula-driven approach to triage its applicant pool. With the exception of applicants to special programs, only borderline candidates receive a truly thorough review; all others are either clearly in or clearly out based on grades, curriculum, and test scores. Candidates for programs in fine arts, creative arts, and performing arts must undergo a more rigorous review that includes a portfolio or audition.

THE SCHOOL SAYS "..."

From the Admissions Office

"The Florida State University is an internationally recognized teaching and research institution committed to preparing our students for a life that balances knowledge, creativity, leadership, and contribution. Designated as a Carnegie Research University (very high research activity), Florida State offers more than 320 undergraduate, graduate, and professional degree programs, including medicine and law. Our students have the opportunity to conduct research alongside Nobel laureates and Pulitzer Prize winners, Guggenheim Fellows, members of the National Academy of Sciences and American Academy of Arts and Sciences, and other globally recognized teachers and researchers. Through the efforts of our Office of Undergraduate Research, students partner with faculty who share their academic interests, and who encourage them to design and conduct original research projects. Through the Office of National Fellowships, Florida State has become a leader among the state's public universities by setting records in the award of national fellowships and scholarships for our students. We offer state-of-the-art teaching techniques in our technologically enhanced classrooms and wireless networking community. Our innovative student services include a comprehensive campus-wide leadership learning program, a center for community and global-based learning through service, and an award-winning career center. World-class cultural events, championship athletics, extensive recreational facilities, and a friendly, close-knit University community enrich student life and extend learning well beyond the classroom. Our diverse student body hails from all fifty states and more than 130 countries, and our numerous international programs throughout the world include year-round programs in Florence, Italy; London, England; Panama City, Panama; and Valencia, Spain."

SELECTIVITY

Admissions Rating	89
# of applicants	29,828
% of applicants accepted	56
% of acceptees attending	37

FRESHMAN PROFILE

Range SAT Critical Reading	560–640
Range SAT Math	560–640
Range SAT Writing	560–640
Range ACT Composite	25–29
Minimum paper TOEFL	550
Minimum internet-based TOEFL	80
Average HS GPA	3.9
% graduated top 10% of class	38
% graduated top 25% of class	75
% graduated top 50% of class	97

DEADLINES

Regular	
Deadline	1/15
Nonfall registration?	Yes

FINANCIAL FACTS

Financial Aid Rating	80
Annual in-state tuition	$4,640
Annual out-of-state tuition	$19,806
Room and board	$10,264
Required fees	$1,867
Books and supplies	$1,000
Average frosh need-based scholarship	$8,203
Average UG need-based scholarship	$7,917
% needy frosh rec. need-based scholarship or grant aid	94
% needy UG rec. need-based scholarship or grant aid	90
% needy frosh rec. non-need-based scholarship or grant aid	76
% needy UG rec. non-need-based scholarship or grant aid	66
% needy frosh rec. need-based self-help aid	61
% needy UG rec. need-based self-help aid	65
% frosh rec. any financial aid	96
% UG rec. any financial aid	87
% UG borrow to pay for school	52
Average cumulative indebtedness	$22,912
% frosh need fully met	14
% ugrads need fully met	9
Average % of frosh need met	62
Average % of ugrad need met	61

FORDHAM UNIVERSITY

441 EAST FORDHAM ROAD, BRONX, NY 10458 • ADMISSIONS: 718-817-4000 • FAX: 718-367-9404

CAMPUS LIFE

Quality of Life Rating	90
Fire Safety Rating	96
Green Rating	60*
Type of school	Private
Affiliation	Roman Catholic
Environment	Metropolis

STUDENTS

Total undergrad enrollment	8,855
% male/female	44/56
% from out of state	55
% frosh from public high school	55
% frosh live on campus	77
% ugrads live on campus	55
% African American	4
% Asian	10
% Caucasian	59
% Hispanic	14
% Native American	<1
% Pacific Islander	<1
% Two or more races	3
% Race and/or ethnicity unknown	2
% international	7
# of countries represented	68

SURVEY SAYS...

Students are happy
Students love Bronx, NY
Easy to get around campus
College radio is popular
Theater is popular

ACADEMICS

Academic Rating	82
% students returning for sophomore year	91
% students graduating within 4 years	75
% students graduating within 6 years	81
Calendar	Semester
Student/faculty ratio	14:1
Profs interesting rating	79
Profs accessible rating	77

Most classes have 10–19 students.
Most lab/discussion sessions have 10–19 students.

MOST POPULAR MAJORS

Communication and Media Studies; Business Administration and Management; Social Sciences

STUDENTS SAY "..."

Academics

With campuses in the Bronx and Manhattan boroughs of New York City, Fordham "is a reputable and challenging school" that promotes "Jesuit values in the capital of the world." Students can't rave enough about the location in America's most famous city. "New York is my campus" is a common refrain. The school provides "a holistic Jesuit education with and emphasis on justice and the care of the whole person while taking advantage of the resources of New York City," a philosophy and classical languages major says. Just as NYC is America's great melting pot, "Fordham is a place where everyone is encouraged to feel welcome and at home." Despite being located in such a large city, the university itself is "a tight knit community with tons of opportunities for education and personal growth."

The "fantastic and engaging" professors "are knowledgeable and available." Professors here "maintain their own research and careers outside of teaching" and bring "real world experience" to classes. As at any university, professors can be "hit or miss," but overall students find the professors to be "very engaging and accessible to their students." "Though they vary in teaching technique, all care about my success in their class," one happy student says. "Open discussions" are often promoted in class. Students also praise "the alumni network and the spirit of camaraderie" that the school engenders. Fordham provides a "rigorous but rewarding" education. "Fordham is a difficult university and requires student to spend a great deal of time on academic pursuits," a political science major says, "but this workload included practical and experiential learning in New York City. This is a school where students are interested in "making a difference in the world." And the university works to develop "each student into a well-rounded student through the liberal arts core, volunteerism, and internships."

Life

"The students at Fordham are overall very independent" and students each do their own thing. Many "are very active in clubs and activities, whether they are leadership activities, sports, or multicultural clubs, etc." Others are "indifferent about" Fordham life, and instead spend their time in New York City. They "love going into Manhattan to explore and discover new eateries, neighborhoods," "go to concerts, Broadway shows, sports games," or any of the other million activities that NYC offers. There is something of a social divide between commuter students and residents, with the latter being understandably more involved on campus. Many students combine their love of Fordham and the Big Apple, being "outgoing and studious while also into going out and exploring New York City." As one student says, "We're in New York City, but the highlight of the Fordham experience is Pugsley's pizza at 2:00 A.M."

Student Body

While the "stereotypical" Fordham student "is a white, Catholic middle-to-upper class person who is just like any other average college student," the school is more diverse than its reputation. "Fordham often gets the rep that it's a bunch of Polo wearing and Coach toting students, but that couldn't be more incorrect," a communications major confirms. This is especially true at the Lincoln Center campus, where "there is a HUGE LGBTQ community that is extremely vocal and inclusive." While the Lincoln Center campus is "very artsy," the Rose Hill campus in the Bronx "has more 'bros'" and less diversity. "There is a great sense of solidarity and community" among "minority students" and those who "stand out more." Students describe themselves as "studious, fun, open-minded, passionate" as well as "well rounded-athletic, academic, social." Many are "from the Tri-State area," but "every walk of life, expression, and style is represented." "Everyone is nice and supports each other, but there is not much interaction between the groups," one student says. The nightlife and bar scene is "very prevalent in the Bronx (Rose Hill Campus)." As one might expect from a NYC school, students care about their appearance. As one student says, it's "one of the most well-dressed campuses that I've been to!"

FINANCIAL AID: 718-817-3800 • E-MAIL: ENROLL@FORDHAM.EDU • WEBSITE: WWW.FORDHAM.EDU

THE PRINCETON REVIEW SAYS

Admissions

Very important factors considered include: rigor of secondary school record, academic GPA, standardized test scores. *Important factors considered include:* application essay, recommendation(s), extracurricular activities, talent/ability, character/personal qualities, volunteer work. *Other factors considered include:* class rank, first generation, alumni/ae relation, geographical residence, racial/ethnic status, work experience, level of applicant's interest. SAT or ACT required; SAT Subject Tests considered if submitted. ACT with Writing required. SAT with or without Essay component accepted. TOEFL required of all international applicants. High school diploma is required and GED is accepted. *Academic units required:* 4 English, 3 math, 3 science, 2 foreign language, 3 social studies. *Academic units recommended:* 4 English, 4 math, 4 science, 4 foreign language, 4 social studies.

Financial Aid

Students should submit: FAFSA, CSS/Financial Aid PROFILE, State aid form, Noncustodial PROFILE, Business/Farm Supplement. Regular filing deadline is 2/10.The Princeton Review suggests that all financial aid forms be submitted as soon as possible after October 1. *Need-based scholarships/grants offered:* Federal Pell, FSEOG, State scholarships/grants, Private scholarships, College/university scholarship or grant aid from institutional funds. *Loan aid offered:* Direct Subsidized Stafford Loans, Direct Unsubsidized Stafford Loans, Direct PLUS loans, Federal Perkins Loans. Applicants will be notified of awards on a rolling basis beginning 3/31. Federal Work-Study Program available. Institutional employment available.

The Inside Word

Fordham applicants have to choose between the two campuses: Lincoln Center in Manhattan and Rose Hill in the Bronx. Students tell us that the campuses have different feels, and the majority of majors are available on both. However, a few majors are specific to each campus, such as dance at Lincoln Center and chemistry at Rose Hill. Students who have a good sense of what they want to major in should make sure to check the list of majors on each campus before applying.

THE SCHOOL SAYS ". . ."

From the Admissions Office

"Fordham University offers a distinctive, values-centered educational experience that is rooted in the Jesuit tradition of intellectual rigor and personal attention. Located in New York City, Fordham offers to students the unparalleled educational, cultural and recreational advantages of one of the world's greatest cities. Fordham has two residential campuses in New York—the tree-lined, eighty-five-acre Rose Hill campus in the Bronx, and the cosmopolitan Lincoln Center campus in the heart of Manhattan's performing arts center. The university's state-of-the-art facilities and buildings include one of the most technologically advanced libraries in the country. Fordham offers a variety of majors, concentrations and programs that can be combined with an extensive career planning and placement program. More than 2,600 organizations in the New York metropolitan area offer students internships that provide hands-on experience and valuable networking opportunities in fields such as business, communications, medicine, law and education.

"Applicants are required to take SAT or the ACT with the writing section. SAT Subject Tests are recommended but not required."

SELECTIVITY

Admissions Rating	91
# of applicants	42,811
% of applicants accepted	48
% of acceptees attending	11
# offered a place on the wait list	8,184
% accepting a place on wait list	32
% admitted from wait list	1

FRESHMAN PROFILE

Range SAT Critical Reading	580–670
Range SAT Math	590–680
Range SAT Writing	590–680
Range ACT Composite	27–31
Minimum paper TOEFL	575
Minimum internet-based TOEFL	90
Average HS GPA	3.6
% graduated top 10% of class	46
% graduated top 25% of class	79
% graduated top 50% of class	97

DEADLINES

Early decision	
Deadline	11/1
Notification	12/20
Early action	
Deadline	11/1
Notification	12/20
Regular	
Priority	11/1
Deadline	1/1
Notification	4/1
Nonfall registration?	Yes

FINANCIAL FACTS

Financial Aid Rating	83
Annual tuition	$46,120
Room and board	$16,350
Required fees	$1,197
Books and supplies	$1,012
Average frosh need-based scholarship	$25,614
Average UG need-based scholarship	$23,883
% needy frosh rec. need-based scholarship or grant aid	98
% needy UG rec. need-based scholarship or grant aid	97
% needy frosh rec. non-need-based scholarship or grant aid	24
% needy UG rec. non-need-based scholarship or grant aid	19
% needy frosh rec. need-based self-help aid	68
% needy UG rec. need-based self-help aid	70
% frosh rec. any financial aid	90
% UG rec. any financial aid	80
% frosh need fully met	32
% ugrads need fully met	27
Average % of frosh need met	82
Average % of ugrad need met	76

FRANKLIN & MARSHALL COLLEGE

PO Box 3003, Lancaster, PA 17604-3003 • Admissions: 717-291-3953 • Fax: 717-291-4389

STUDENTS SAY "..."

Academics

Established in 1787, Franklin & Marshall College is a little liberal arts gem located in south central Pennsylvania. With around 2,200 students, F&M offers numerous opportunities for academic exploration and expansion, and there is "a great balance between a strong and competitive academic culture, talented and successful athletic teams, and a vibrant social life." The school offers numerous interdisciplinary majors and minors, "does an excellent job of making sure you know how to write," and a collaborative learning experience that extends beyond the classroom through research opportunities and the College Houses (residential communities).

The rigorous academics are "demanding and challenging" gauntlets thrown down by professors that are "esteemed published scholars in their respective fields." "You'll work hard but you'll learn a lot," says a student. Small classes offer plenty of face and advice time with these scholars: "Whether it be for class selection or post graduate paths, they are always there to help." "The support for a student here is absolutely astonishing," says another. The classroom setting at F&M is completely different from the traditional lecture halls of bigger schools, and students "often have round tables for close discussion with…professors." Students love the fact that academic and personal growth are equally important, and the environment is shaped by "people who are active both in school and extracurriculars, and who get excited about both." "Someone said to me the other week that you're not taking advantage of what F&M has to offer if you haven't been to a professor's office and discussed something other than class," says a student. The professors at F&M all have "a certain level of uniqueness" in them, but students appreciate that they all possess a great level of understanding. "My professors have managed to get me engaged in areas that have always seemed like a bore to me."

Life

Athletic teams are "highly competitive and are very active in the local community," and there is a "large emphasis" on fraternity and sorority life and sports teams at F&M. There is always something to do on weekends, between "[staying] in or [going] to the cinemas to watch movies with your roommates, [hanging] out in frat parties or [attending] events run by an organization for alternative options for frat parties." Club organizations are wildly popular, and "campus is not big, so getting around takes about ten minutes no matter where you are." "We all really get into our extracurricular activities," says a student.

Off-campus, downtown Lancaster offers plenty of entertainment and dining options (such as the Central Market), and a mall is just fifteen minutes away. College Houses often take "really fun field trips" and in the spring and fall the Barnstormers (the minor league baseball team), is a popular destination for students.

Student Body

These "smart overachievers who work hard" are also "some of the nicest people you'll ever meet." Though mostly white, there is an "amazing diversity" on campus, with a bent towards "slightly preppy, but very open-minded." Many F&M students are on a varsity sports team as well as a member of a sorority or fraternity, and a typical student "is probably involved in three to five clubs and is trying out for theater, an a capella group, or another organization." Students categorically study hard, and "fill our free time with fun and meaningful clubs and community service."

FINANCIAL AID: 717-291-3991 • E-MAIL: ADMISSION@FANDM.EDU • WEBSITE: WWW.FANDM.EDU

THE PRINCETON REVIEW SAYS

Admissions

Very important factors considered include: rigor of secondary school record, class rank, academic GPA, character/personal qualities. *Important factors considered include:* standardized test scores, application essay, recommendation(s), interview, extracurricular activities, talent/ability, volunteer work. *Other factors considered include:* alumni/ae relation, geographical residence, racial/ethnic status, work experience, level of applicant's interest. SAT or ACT considered if submitted. ACT with or without writing accepted. TOEFL required of all international applicants. High school diploma is required and GED is accepted. *Academic units required:* 4 English, 3 math, 2 science, 2 science labs, 2 foreign language, 1 social studies, 2 history, 1 visual/performing arts. *Academic units recommended:* 4 math, 3 science, 3 science labs, 4 foreign language, 3 social studies, 3 history.

Financial Aid

Students should submit: FAFSA, CSS/Financial Aid PROFILE, Noncustodial PROFILE. Regular filing deadline is 2/15. The Princeton Review suggests that all financial aid forms be submitted as soon as possible after October 1. *Need-based scholarships/grants offered:* Federal Pell, FSEOG, State scholarships/grants, Private scholarships, College/university scholarship or grant aid from institutional funds. *Loan aid offered:* Direct Subsidized Stafford Loans, Direct Unsubsidized Stafford Loans, Direct PLUS loans, Federal Perkins Loans, College/university loans from institutional funds. Applicants will be notified of awards on or about 4/1. Federal Work-Study Program available.

The Inside Word

While admission at F&M is competitive, the admissions committee does show some flexibility. The college allows students who feel that standardized test scores don't reflect their true academic capacity to submit two graded writing samples to replace the test scores. Applicants are also encouraged to include nontraditional materials, such as art portfolios or recordings of musical performances, in their applications. Finally, F&M offers a "Spring Option," in which students can elect to start classes in the spring semester after spending the fall abroad, or pursuing a "challenging program in consultation with an experienced faculty advisor at F&M."

THE SCHOOL SAYS ". . ."

From the Admissions Office

"The hallmarks of a Franklin & Marshall education are individual attention and a supportive community. Our faculty members challenge you to achieve your best and engage you personally on a level you will not find at other institutions. We have one professor for every nine students, and two-thirds of our students collaborate on a research project or other directed study directly with a faculty member. Here are three more things you should know about F&M: 1) Our professors do not confine learning to classrooms and labs. They take you into the field and the local community to teach you how to *do* what students at other institutions may only read about. 2) We have College Houses, not dorms. Our five College Houses, which bring together first-year students into smaller groups, are student-governed spaces where you socialize, learn, and stretch your intellect. Based in each house are a faculty mentor and an administrative counselor to guide you. 3) No one gets lost. The depth and breadth of student activities and experiences provide everyone with a place to belong. Our students find a strong sense of self, and they find their 'homes' in clubs, athletic teams, their College Houses, fraternities and sororities, the performing and musical arts, and the other strong communities they have the freedom to create for themselves."

SELECTIVITY

Admissions Rating	93
# of applicants	7,146
% of applicants accepted	32
% of acceptees attending	26
# offered a place on the wait list	1,944
# of early decision applicants	555
% accepted early decision	61

FRESHMAN PROFILE

Range SAT Critical Reading	580–670
Range SAT Math	630–730
Range ACT Composite	28–31
Minimum paper TOEFL	600
% graduated top 10% of class	48
% graduated top 25% of class	80
% graduated top 50% of class	97

DEADLINES

Early decision	
Deadline	11/15
Notification	12/15
Regular	
Deadline	1/15
Notification	4/1
Nonfall registration?	Yes

APPLICANTS ALSO LOOK AT AND OFTEN PREFER

University of Pennsylvania; Cornell University; Haverford College; Hamilton College

AND SOMETIMES PREFER

Bucknell University; Colgate University; Lehigh University; Lafayette College; Dickinson College

FINANCIAL FACTS

Financial Aid Rating	96
Annual tuition	$50,300
Room and board	$12,770
Required fees	$100
Books and supplies	$1,200
Average frosh need-based scholarship	$43,342
Average UG need-based scholarship	$41,659
% needy frosh rec. need-based scholarship or grant aid	100
% needy UG rec. need-based scholarship or grant aid	99
% needy frosh rec. non-need-based scholarship or grant aid	20
% needy UG rec. non-need-based scholarship or grant aid	22
% needy frosh rec. need-based self-help aid	93
% needy UG rec. need-based self-help aid	95
% frosh rec. any financial aid	51
% UG rec. any financial aid	53
% UG borrow to pay for school	51
Average cumulative indebtedness	$26,162
% frosh need fully met	100
% ugrads need fully met	100
Average % of frosh need met	100
Average % of ugrad need met	100

FRANKLIN W. OLIN COLLEGE OF ENGINEERING

OLIN WAY, NEEDHAM, MA 02492-1245 • ADMISSIONS: 781-292-2222 • FAX: 781-292-2210

CAMPUS LIFE

Quality of Life Rating	95
Fire Safety Rating	91
Green Rating	68
Type of school	Private
Affiliation	No Affiliation
Environment	Town

STUDENTS

Total undergrad enrollment	370
% male/female	50/50
% from out of state	86
% frosh live on campus	100
% ugrads live on campus	100
% African American	<1
% Asian	16
% Caucasian	53
% Hispanic	5
% Native American	<1
% Pacific Islander	0
% Two or more races	7
% Race and/or ethnicity unknown	11
% international	8
# of countries represented	13

SURVEY SAYS...

Lots of liberal students
Students always studying
Students are happy
Classroom facilities are great
Lab facilities are great
Career services are great
Internships are widely available
Class discussions encouraged
School is well run
Great financial aid
No one cheats
Students are friendly
Diverse student types interact on campus
Students get along with local community
Great food on campus
Dorms are like palaces
Easy to get around campus
Very little drug use
Campus newspaper is popular

ACADEMICS

Academic Rating	98
% students returning for sophomore year	91
% students graduating within 4 years	76
% students graduating within 6 years	93
Calendar	Semester
Student/faculty ratio	8:1
Profs interesting rating	99
Profs accessible rating	92

Most classes have 20–29 students.

MOST POPULAR MAJORS

Engineering; Electrical and Electronics
Engineering; Mechanical Engineering

STUDENTS SAY "..."

Academics

If the "hands-on approach to engineering, friendly students, small and intimate setting, [and reputation as] academically one of the best schools in the nation" don't win you over, perhaps the fact that "Olin is constantly changing curriculum to try and better fit students' needs" will. New England's Olin College of Engineering takes a real-world approach to engineering education, focusing on "hands-on, project-based learning, and close relations with peers and professors. It's totally different from just about every other undergraduate institution." Olin recognizes that students don't want to become engineers because they "have a passion for learning how to solve differential equations thirty-five different ways"; they become engineers "to tackle big problems and solve them effectively. But to do so," this student recognizes, "I need to be an effective communicator, an influential team member, and a capable thinker." And that is what sets Olin apart. "The professors want to make sure I actually learn the important aspects of the class. They don't grade me on when I turned things in or my spelling mistakes, they grade on my thoughts and the quality of my work." In addition, "Olin doesn't have tenure for professors, nor is it a major research institution, so the professors that are here love teaching. This shows inside and outside the classroom, as these professors care so much more about each student's learning than their own career path." But be warned, if this approach sounds easy, it's not. Olin's is a "rigorous, intense school that cranks out top-notch employable engineers that are well-rounded and able to accomplish anything thrown at them."

Life

The devotion to real-world learning at Olin means "people think a lot about self-improvement and learning." The academic focus causes some to "get overwhelmed with the amount of work," but for most this "uniquely awesome" group of students manages to find plenty of ways to keep themselves busy, even during down time. "For fun, we often go on adventures and try and get out and about ... A good number of kids find odd, interesting activities to do such as river rafting or spelunking." Theater, music, the arts, Ultimate Frisbee and other activities draw plenty of interest—as does becoming a trapeze artist. That's right, "we are also a circus school. Unicycling, juggling, and fire arts are some of the biggest activities on campus." It should come as no surprise that this engineering-focused school has a rich geek culture, with video games, Doctor Who clubs, and even Pokemon proving popular among the student body. Throw in paintball, laser tag, parties and more, and there is no shortage of things to do. And if you're still having trouble? "It's also always good to keep an eye on our Carpe Diem mailing list, on which students will give notice of fun things happening around campus—from free food, to movie nights, games, dance lessons, Midnight Math, theatre, the student newspaper, paintball, art parties, and much more."

Student Body

"Olin is a vibrant community of students who are passionate about what they do and who love to get their hands dirty solving real-world problems," a whole campus made up of "awesome, smart people who are very supportive and involved and never sleep!" This student body is "not very athletic," but they are "very smart and find projects and work to be fun and often do them out of class." Typical Olin students are "usually found constantly working on various fun and interesting projects." There may be cliques here, just like at any school, but "everyone is nice to one another." Students here recognize that "everyone has quirks, but that is what makes us interesting. What makes Olin awesome is that the quirks are accepted and celebrated here instead of picked on." All in all, this "geeky" and "quirky" group "are not segregated or shunned, anyone can talk and hang out with anyone, no matter age, race, socioeconomic background, gender, orientation, what have you." As one student puts it, "It really feels like a big family here."

FRANKLIN W. OLIN COLLEGE OF ENGINEERING

FINANCIAL AID: 781-292-2343 • E-MAIL: INFO@OLIN.EDU • WEBSITE: WWW.OLIN.EDU

THE PRINCETON REVIEW SAYS

Admissions

Very important factors considered include: rigor of secondary school record, academic GPA, application essay, recommendation(s), interview, extracurricular activities, talent/ability, character/personal qualities, level of applicant's interest. *Important factors considered include:* class rank, standardized test scores, racial/ethnic status, volunteer work. *Other factors considered include:* first generation, alumni/ae relation, geographical residence, state residency, work experience. SAT or ACT required; SAT Subject Tests considered if submitted. ACT with Writing required. SAT with Essay component required. High school diploma is required and GED is accepted. *Academic units recommended:* 4 English, 4 math, 4 science, 3 science labs, 2 foreign language, 2 social studies, 2 history.

Financial Aid

Students should submit: FAFSA. Regular filing deadline is 2/15. The Princeton Review suggests that all financial aid forms be submitted as soon as possible after October 1. *Need-based scholarships/grants offered:* Federal Pell, FSEOG, College/university scholarship or grant aid from institutional funds. *Loan aid offered:* Direct Subsidized Stafford Loans, Direct Unsubsidized Stafford Loans, Direct PLUS Loans. Applicants will be notified of awards on or about 3/21. Institutional employment available.

The Inside Word

Brains are not enough to get into Olin. Social skills, depth, and the ability to communicate are taken seriously by admissions. Olin boasts many students who have turned down offers from schools like MIT and Cal Tech for just this reason. It is a unique school that looks for passion, creativity, and a spirit of adventure in its students. If you're a reclusive genius, you will be at a disadvantage in this pool of applicants.

THE SCHOOL SAYS "..."

From the Admissions Office

"We are a vibrant community of talented, confident, energetic students and faculty and we are looking for students who are not only academically accomplished but also like adventure, thrive on creativity and have an entrepreneurial streak—and come from every kind of cultural, economic and geographic background imaginable. The Olin Tuition Scholarship, valued at more than $80,000, is awarded to every enrolled student to recognize their achievements and is complemented by our policy of meeting full demonstrated need—meaning finances should never stand in the way of an Olin education.

"Our admission process is like no other. It's done in two stages; first students apply using the Common Application; then from our exceptionally talented and academically gifted applicant pool we invite about 240 students to attend one of three Candidates' Weekends. We seek to get to know our applicants' personal qualities (like risk-taking, creativity, passion and team spirit) during these weekends of getting acquainted through group activities and interviews. Admission is then offered to candidates who possess the greatest promise of contributing to—and benefiting from—the Olin experience. Following the Candidates' Weekends admission is offered to approximately 135 students.

"We require either the SAT or ACT with Writing score, and we honor the best score combination on the SAT or best composite score achieved on the ACT."

SELECTIVITY

Admissions Rating	98
# of applicants	1,075
% of applicants accepted	11
% of acceptees attending	64
# offered a place on the wait list	57
% accepting a place on wait list	82
% admitted from wait list	28

FRESHMAN PROFILE

Range SAT Critical Reading	710–800
Range SAT Math	730–800
Range SAT Writing	680–770
Range ACT Composite	32–35
Average HS GPA	3.9

DEADLINES

Regular	
Deadline	1/1
Notification	3/21
Nonfall registration?	No

APPLICANTS ALSO LOOK AT AND OFTEN PREFER

Massachusetts Institute of Technology; Stanford University; California Institute of Technology; Princeton University; Yale University

AND SOMETIMES PREFER

Carnegie Mellon University; University of California—Berkeley; Harvey Mudd College

AND RARELY PREFER

Rose-Hulman Institute of Technology; Worcester Polytechnic Institute

FINANCIAL FACTS

Financial Aid Rating	96
Annual tuition	$45,000
Room and board	$15,600
Required fees	$525
Books and supplies	$300
Average frosh need-based scholarship	$42,883
Average UG need-based scholarship	$40,374
% needy frosh rec. need-based scholarship or grant aid	100
% needy UG rec. need-based scholarship or grant aid	100
% needy frosh rec. non-need-based scholarship or grant aid	100
% needy UG rec. non-need-based scholarship or grant aid	100
% needy frosh rec. need-based self-help aid	81
% needy UG rec. need-based self-help aid	88
% frosh rec. any financial aid	100
% UG rec. any financial aid	100
% UG borrow to pay for school	43
Average cumulative indebtedness	$19,196
% frosh need fully met	97
% ugrads need fully met	97
Average % of frosh need met	100
Average % of ugrad need met	99

FURMAN UNIVERSITY

3300 POINSETT HIGHWAY, GREENVILLE, SC 29613 • ADMISSIONS: 864-294-2034 • FAX: 864-294-2018

CAMPUS LIFE

Quality of Life Rating	93
Fire Safety Rating	90
Green Rating	97
Type of school	Private
Affiliation	No Affiliation
Environment	City

STUDENTS

Total undergrad enrollment	2,731
% male/female	43/57
% from out of state	72
% frosh from public high school	59
% frosh live on campus	98
% ugrads live on campus	96
# of fraternities (% ugrad men join)	7 (33)
# of sororities (% ugrad women join)	7 (58)
% African American	5
% Asian	2
% Caucasian	78
% Hispanic	4
% Native American	<1
% Pacific Islander	0
% Two or more races	2
% Race and/or ethnicity unknown	2
% international	6
# of countries represented	54

SURVEY SAYS...

Students always studying
Students are happy
Classroom facilities are great
Lab facilities are great
Great library
Internships are widely available
School is well run
Great financial aid
No one cheats
Students are very religious
Students environmentally aware
Students love Greenville, SC
Great off-campus food
Recreation facilities are great

ACADEMICS

Academic Rating	86
% students returning for sophomore year	89
% students graduating within 4 years	79
% students graduating within 6 years	83
Calendar	Semester
Student/faculty ratio	11:1
Profs interesting rating	88
Profs accessible rating	96

MOST CLASSES HAVE 20–29 STU-
DENTS. MOST POPULAR MAJORS
Political Science and Government; Business/
Commerce; Health Professions

STUDENTS SAY "..."

Academics

Students can't stop talking about Furman University's "beautiful campus" and "warm, but challenging, academic community." This combination of brains and beauty is what makes Furman "an ideal choice" for four years. "Furman is about academic excellence through engaged learning," says one undergrad. Expect to hear "engaged" used "ad nauseum" on campus, but students claim that such a term "truly describes the kind of personal education available" thanks to "small class sizes," professors "who love to teach and enjoy getting to know their students," and "numerous" academic and extracurricular opportunities. Furman's science programs are "especially" challenging. Professors here are "very qualified (sometimes overqualified), passionate about what they teach, and are not easy graders." That said, they're "very willing to help their students." Students praise the administration, which is "really accessible." In the words of one undergrad, "They work with students to solve problems and genuinely care about making Furman a better school and not just a higher-ranking institution." However, some students find that the administration can be "very conservative in their thinking about student on-campus social life." Ultimately, while "Furman is not for the academically faint-of-heart," there's pride in knowing that "you're receiving a great education that will help you after you graduate."

Life

With so many students reporting that Furman's campus is "absolutely gorgeous," it's a wonder they ever leave it. However, "the surrounding city of Greenville is great," and its "thriving, small-town feel" brings in plenty of students on the weekends. Life at school is "busy, but so much fun." Students here spend "a lot of time thinking about academics, classes, and their future," but they also "invest a lot of time in their relationships with their friends." The school's "inclusive, close-knit community" is complemented with "lots of interesting things to do on campus, from music concerts to improv shows to sports games." "Weeknights are mostly spent studying," says one undergrad, which makes the library "a popular social spot." However, once the weekend rolls around, students spend their nights "out on the town." "There are tons of bars, restaurants, and clubs for people to go to" in Greenville, while those looking for a "party" can head for "fraternity houses." While the university "is not as crazy party-wise as larger schools," students "can find a party if they want to." Mostly though, students are happy to "meet up with friends for meals, coffee, or just to hang out."

Student Body

Many find that Furman is something of a "country club" when it comes to its student body, not just "because it is private and somewhat expensive," but also because the "typical" student is "wealthy, white, conservative, and preppy." Some find that "the majority of the student body is obsessed with being as 'generic' and 'normal' as possible, so that any student who does not fit the norm, be it due to a difference in religion or clothing style, will find it harder to fit in." However, others have found that there's more to the student body than first meets the eye. As one undergrad says, "The longer I stay at Furman, the more I realize that many students don't fit the stereotype." One thing that everyone seems to agree on is that everyone is "very accepting" and "very committed to their academic pursuits." That said, some wouldn't mind seeing the school "improve by attracting a more diverse student body, as well as lowering the cost of tuition."

FINANCIAL AID: 864-294-2204 • E-MAIL: ADMISSIONS@FURMAN.EDU • WEBSITE: WWW.FURMAN.EDU

THE PRINCETON REVIEW SAYS

Admissions

Very important factors considered include: rigor of secondary school record. *Important factors considered include:* class rank, academic GPA, application essay, extracurricular activities, character/personal qualities. *Other factors considered include:* standardized test scores, recommendation(s), interview, talent/ability, first generation, alumni/ae relation, racial/ethnic status, volunteer work, work experience, level of applicant's interest. SAT or ACT recommend. ACT with Writing recommended. TOEFL required of all international applicants. High school diploma is required and GED is accepted. *Academic units required:* 4 English, 3 math, 2 science, 2 science labs, 2 foreign language, 3 social studies. *Academic units recommended:* 4 English, 4 math, 3 science, 2 science labs, 3 foreign language, 4 social studies.

Financial Aid

Students should submit: FAFSA, Institution's own financial aid form, CSS/Financial Aid PROFILE, State aid form. Regular filing deadline is 1/15. The Princeton Review suggests that all financial aid forms be submitted as soon as possible after October 1. *Need-based scholarships/grants offered:* Federal Pell, FSEOG, State scholarships/grants, Private scholarships, College/university scholarship or grant aid from institutional funds. *Loan aid offered:* Direct Subsidized Stafford Loans, Direct Unsubsidized Stafford Loans, Direct PLUS loans, Federal Perkins Loans, State Loans. Applicants will be notified of awards on or about 4/1. Federal Work-Study Program available. Institutional employment available.

The Inside Word

Chances are, if you're applying to Furman, you already have a good idea if you can get in or not. Furman's applicant pool is highly self-selected, meaning that the university's high acceptance rate doesn't equate to easy admission; in fact, it's the direct opposite, as applicants are typically very strong. Looking for a way to stand out from the crowd? Let the admissions committee know how valuable you are through your extracurriculars—sports, community service, and artistic endeavors will go a long way in making your case.

THE SCHOOL SAYS "..."

From the Admissions Office

"Furman University is a private liberal arts university that seeks and cultivates engaged, well-rounded, and passionate students. With 2,700 undergraduates from forty-six states and fifty-four countries, Furman's academic community prepares its students for meaningful lives of service and leadership through engaged learning, a process characterized by small classes, a close-knit community, student-faculty research, internships, and faculty-led study. With emphasis on a collaborative educational experience, Furman challenges students to put into practice the theories and methods learned from a distinguished and active faculty. Furman offers eighteen NCAA Division I men's and women's athletic teams, a nationally competitive music program, and hundreds of organizations and clubs. The stunning campus is located just minutes from vibrant downtown Greenville, noted as one of America's most livable cities, and the foothills of the Blue Ridge Mountains, where hiking and other adventure sports abound. Nearby are also some of the nation's most picturesque beaches and coastal towns. The admission committee believes that a student's potential for success is not determined solely by standardized test scores. Rather, it is interested in getting to know the whole student—one who seeks leadership, service, commitment to the community, and civic engagement. Therefore, Furman does not require prospective students to submit test scores unless the student determines the scores best represent academic ability and accomplishment. If a student chooses not to submit standardized test scores, then the university recommends that the student to participate in a formal interview as part of the application."

SELECTIVITY

Admissions Rating	87
# of applicants	5,043
% of applicants accepted	65
% of acceptees attending	21
# offered a place on the wait list	208
% accepting a place on wait list	51
% admitted from wait list	14
# of early decision applicants	126
% accepted early decision	94

FRESHMAN PROFILE

Range SAT Critical Reading	550–660
Range SAT Math	550–660
Range SAT Writing	550–660
Range ACT Composite	25–30
% graduated top 10% of class	39
% graduated top 25% of class	71
% graduated top 50% of class	92

DEADLINES

Early decision	
Deadline	11/1
Notification	11/15
Other ED	
Deadline	11/1
Other ED	
Notification	11/15
Early action	
Deadline	11/15
Notification	12/20
Regular	
Deadline	1/15
Notification	3/1
Nonfall registration?	No

APPLICANTS ALSO LOOK AT AND OFTEN PREFER

The University of North Carolina at Chapel Hill

FINANCIAL FACTS

Financial Aid Rating	86
Annual tuition	$45,632
Room and board	$12,080
Required fees	$380
Books and supplies	$1,200
Average frosh need-based scholarship	$32,120
Average UG need-based scholarship	$33,774
% needy frosh rec. need-based scholarship or grant aid	100
% needy UG rec. need-based scholarship or grant aid	100
% needy frosh rec. non-need-based scholarship or grant aid	100
% needy UG rec. non-need-based scholarship or grant aid	100
% needy frosh rec. need-based self-help aid	71
% needy UG rec. need-based self-help aid	71
% frosh rec. any financial aid	98
% UG rec. any financial aid	94
% UG borrow to pay for school	37
Average cumulative indebtedness	$32,594
% frosh need fully met	26
% ugrads need fully met	28
Average % of frosh need met	79
Average % of ugrad need met	79

George Mason University

4400 University Drive, Fairfax, VA 22030-4444 • Admissions: 703-993-2400 • Fax: 703-993-4622

STUDENTS SAY "..."

Academics

When describing George Mason University, current students are quick to quote the school motto: This is a place "where innovation is tradition." One student expands on that, saying, "Mason provides a space for students to achieve academic excellence; expand their knowledge of the diverse cultures, practices, and beliefs that surround them; and be prepared to enter the real-world as a global citizen." Diversity of the student body and proximity to Washington, D.C., are major selling points at this large public university, so it's no surprise that government, global affairs, and communication are popular majors. The faculty is "extremely knowledgeable and experienced" here, and "most try to learn your name." The Robinson Professors program brings "distinguished" professors in the liberal arts and sciences to campus, and students highly recommend classes taught by these professors. "They are experts in their fields, know what they are talking about, and have real life experiences they bring into the classroom." As well, "adjunct professors can be a great strength" because many of them are practicing professionals in D.C., and they "bring stories and examples from the real-world into our classroom." "For example, my professor for my Conflict 300 course is one of the main peace facilitators in the Georgian/South Ossetian conflict...when she returned from this conference [between the two countries], she told us everything and we got to see how the material and techniques we were studying are actually applied in our field." Students are equally satisfied with the school's administration: "The school will take action immediately to fix any problems that arise."

Life

Students at GMU never seem to be bored. Campus life is "filled with classes, friends, and work." On-campus activities are very popular, and there are many offered, including the university's ambassador program and intramural sports, such as underwater hockey and even quidditch. Just a few of the regular events on campus include "movies playing in our Johnson Center Cinema that are in between theater and DVD release, there are local bands playing live in the Rathskeller, the HIV/AIDS Awareness Fashion Show, drag competitions, University dances and highlighter parties." Greek life is there for those who want it: "We're not a 'fratty' school by any means, but the Greek community is very active and they do party." The campus is "beautiful," and "there are new housing buildings going up and even new academic buildings" (which is good news, since the two things students want to see improve are parking and housing availability). Students love living close to D.C. without the "hassle of city living," but when they want to head downtown, "it's very easy to get into the city by taking the Mason-to-Metro shuttle to the Vienna Metro Station, hopping on the Orange Line and then taking the Metro into the heart of the city!" Many students have internships in the city, including those "on Capitol Hill." "The music scene and bars are fantastic as well!"

Student Body

"Diversity is off the charts" at GMU, and many students describe their school as "a melting pot." As one student puts it, "There are so many different nationalities represented, so many stories, so many languages spoken. At the same time, it didn't take me long to find a good group of friends that were interested in hanging out and just having a good time together." "The typical GMU student is always busy—between coursework and extracurricular activities we're very involved on campus and are also into other activities, such as having jobs or internships." "Mason students are also politically active and global citizens." While a majority of students come from Virginia, there are also "students from over 130 countries, so everyone adds their own personal flavor to our student body." In spite of all these different backgrounds and cultures, "There are many student organizations that successfully create programs and events to unite students."

FINANCIAL AID: 703-993-2353 • E-MAIL: ADMISSIONS@GMU.EDU • WEBSITE: WWW.GMU.EDU

THE PRINCETON REVIEW SAYS
Admissions
Very important factors considered include: rigor of secondary school record, academic GPA. *Important factors considered include:* class rank, standardized test scores, talent/ability, character/personal qualities. *Other factors considered include:* application essay, recommendation(s), extracurricular activities, first generation, alumni/ae relation, volunteer work, work experience, level of applicant's interest. SAT or ACT required for some. ACT with or without writing accepted. SAT with or without Essay component accepted. TOEFL required of all international applicants. High school diploma is required and GED is accepted. *Academic units required:* 4 English, 3 math, 2 science, 2 science labs, 2 foreign language, 3 social studies, 3 academic electives. *Academic units recommended:* 4 English, 4 math, 3 science, 3 science labs, 3 foreign language, 4 social studies, 5 academic electives.

Financial Aid
Students should submit: FAFSA. Priority filing deadline is 3/1. The Princeton Review suggests that all financial aid forms be submitted as soon as possible after October 1. *Need-based scholarships/grants offered:* Federal Pell, FSEOG, State scholarships/grants, Private scholarships, College/university scholarship or grant aid from institutional funds. *Loan aid offered:* Direct Subsidized Stafford Loans, Direct Unsubsidized Stafford Loans, Direct PLUS loans, Federal Perkins Loans, Federal Nursing Loans. Applicants will be notified of awards on a rolling basis beginning 4/1. Federal Work-Study Program available. Institutional employment available.

The Inside Word
GMU is a popular college choice for two key reasons: Its proximity to Washington, D.C., and the fact that its applicant pool isn't as competitive as those of University of Virginia and The College of William & Mary, the two flagships of the Virginia state system. GMU's quality faculty and impressive facilities make it worth consideration, especially if you're looking for a school in the D.C. area and affordability is a factor.

THE SCHOOL SAYS "..."
From the Admissions Office
"George Mason University is an innovative and entrepreneurial institution with global distinction in a range of academic fields. Located just outside Washington, D.C., our beautiful residential campus boasts a diverse student population, which gives our students the benefit of growing from a wide range of ideas and perspectives. As the largest public research institution in Virginia, Mason enrolls nearly 34,000, with students in over 200 degree programs at the undergraduate, master's, doctoral, and professional levels. With strong undergraduate and graduate degree programs, our students are routinely recognized with national and international scholarships and awards. Our connection to the D.C. area results in engaged and dedicated faculty members who are at the top of their respective fields, and who are regular contributors on all of the major national news networks, including frequent appearances on National Public Radio. This connectivity extends to our students, who take advantage of our unparalleled internship and research opportunities, and who secure careers at national and international companies and organizations, ranging from National Geographic to the White House. At Mason, we pride ourselves on being among the most innovative universities in the world. Many of our degree programs are the first of their kind, including the first Ph.D. program in biodefense, the first D.C.-based undergraduate program in Conflict Analysis and Resolution, the first dedicated Cybersecurity Engineering program in the region, and one of the most innovative performing arts management programs in the United States. Mason is at the forefront of the emerging field of biotechnology, is a leader in the performing arts, and holds a preeminent position in the fields of economics, electronic journalism, and history, just to name a few. "

SELECTIVITY
Admissions Rating	82
# of applicants	21,981
% of applicants accepted	69
% of acceptees attending	21
# offered a place on the wait list	1,884
% accepting a place on wait list	50
% admitted from wait list	37

FRESHMAN PROFILE
Range SAT Critical Reading	520–620
Range SAT Math	520–630
Range ACT Composite	23–29
Minimum paper TOEFL	570
Minimum internet-based TOEFL	80
Average HS GPA	3.7
% graduated top 10% of class	21
% graduated top 25% of class	56
% graduated top 50% of class	92

DEADLINES
Early action	
Deadline	11/1
Notification	12/15
Regular	
Priority	11/1
Deadline	1/15
Nonfall registration?	Yes

APPLICANTS ALSO LOOK AT AND SOMETIMES PREFER
James Madison University; The George Washington University; University of Virginia; Virginia Tech; University of Maryland–College Park

FINANCIAL FACTS
Financial Aid Rating	79
Annual in-state tuition	$7,976
Annual out-of-state tuition	$28,622
Room and board	$10,510
Required fees	$2,976
Books and supplies	$1,150
Average frosh need-based scholarship	$6,540
Average UG need-based scholarship	$6,092
% needy frosh rec. need-based scholarship or grant aid	77
% needy UG rec. need-based scholarship or grant aid	76
% needy frosh rec. non-need-based scholarship or grant aid	35
% needy UG rec. non-need-based scholarship or grant aid	17
% needy frosh rec. need-based self-help aid	76
% needy UG rec. need-based self-help aid	77
% frosh rec. any financial aid	70
% UG rec. any financial aid	59
% UG borrow to pay for school	58
Average cumulative indebtedness	$27,373
% frosh need fully met	5
% ugrads need fully met	5
Average % of frosh need met	64
Average % of ugrad need met	57

THE GEORGE WASHINGTON UNIVERSITY

2121 I STREET NORTHWEST, SUITE 201, WASHINGTON, D.C. 20052 • ADMISSIONS: 202-994-6040 • FAX: 202-994-0325

CAMPUS LIFE

Quality of Life Rating	85
Fire Safety Rating	60*
Green Rating	95
Type of school	Private
Affiliation	No Affiliation
Environment	Metropolis

STUDENTS

Total undergrad enrollment	11,157
% male/female	44/56
% from out of state	97
% frosh from public high school	70
% frosh live on campus	98
% ugrads live on campus	60
# of fraternities (% ugrad men join)	12 (23)
# of sororities (% ugrad women join)	9 (27)
% African American	6
% Asian	10
% Caucasian	56
% Hispanic	8
% Native American	<1
% Pacific Islander	<1
% Two or more races	4
% Race and/or ethnicity unknown	5
% international	10
# of countries represented	122

SURVEY SAYS...

Career services are great
Students love Washington, DC
Dorms are like palaces
Lots of beer drinking
Hard liquor is popular
Campus newspaper is popular

ACADEMICS

Academic Rating	83
% students returning for sophomore year	94
% students graduating within 4 years	76
% students graduating within 6 years	83
Calendar	Semester
Student/faculty ratio	13:1
Profs interesting rating	84
Profs accessible rating	74

Most classes have 10–19 students.
Most lab/discussion sessions have 20–29 students.

MOST POPULAR MAJORS

International Relations and Affairs; Business Administration and Management; Psychology

STUDENTS SAY "..."

Academics

Get ready for "hands-on learning in an environment unlike any other" at George Washington University, where a location "four blocks away from the White House, down the street from the State Department, and near nearly all world headquarters" means "connections and opportunity" for undergraduates. Students call it "the perfect place to study international affairs" and praise the "amazing journalism program," the excellent political communications major, the political science program ("What political science major would pass up the chance to go toe-to-toe with protestors every week at the rallies outside the White House and Congress?"), the sciences (benefiting from the region's many research operations), and other departments too numerous to name. As one student puts it, "GW is a place where everyone can find their niche. Whether you are a politically active campaign volunteer, a hip-hop dancer, or a future Broadway actor, there is a place for you at GW." The school places a premium on hiring "professors of practice," teachers who "are either currently working in their field or just retired to teach." The faculty includes "former ambassadors, governors on the Federal Reserve Board, and CNN correspondents." These instructors emphasize "a balance between theory and practice that provides a foundation of knowledge and pragmatism from which students can feel prepared to enter any sector of work after school." The resulting education "gets students prepared for post-college life through an emphasis on internships and career-focused classes," putting "a lot of emphasis on acclimation to the real world." GWU has a new Science and Engineering Hall, the largest science facility at a university in DC.

Life

"Life at GW is about independence," students report. "There are no real cafeterias" on campus, "you have to rely on your own feet for transportation, and there is very little regulation in dorms." As a result, "there is little school spirit, but that fact alone seems to tie everyone together." The campus isn't entirely dead; there are frat parties ("which are hard to attend for non-member males and easy to attend for women"), the "occasional dorm-room party, which is usually small," and "apartment parties off campus" for upperclassmen. Campus organizations offer all sorts of events, and the school hosts a veritable who's who of guest speakers on a regular basis. Students love the school's Midnight Monument Tour, held "during the warmer parts of the year," during which "students walk the five blocks to the National Mall at 2:00 A.M. and tour the monuments. It is an awesome experience." Still, most students prefer to spend free time exploring D.C. on their own. The city provides "so much to do…it's overwhelming: monuments, free museums, fairs, every major sports franchise, and lots of student specials on the above things." D.C.'s upscale Georgetown neighborhood is nearby for "shopping, dining, seeing movies, etc.," while culturally diverse Adams Morgan is great for shopping, ethnic dining, and live music. Students have access to all of DC with a metro stop on campus.

Student Body

Though "GW students are often stereotyped as spoiled and wealthy Northeastern kids," and a few students here concede that there's some basis for the stereotype, most would also add that "white, preppy, fraternity/sorority members" who "like nice labels on their clothing" neither define nor dominate the campus population. "The reality is that there's tremendous diversity here of all stripes—geographic, religious, political, racial, and intellectual," with "students from dozens of countries and all fifty states." "GW is truly a national and even international school," one student writes. "I love walking out of the library and hearing conversations happening in a half-dozen languages." The school has always been a popular destination for Jewish students. There is also "a huge LGBT group on campus, with very little discrimination." Nearly everyone here is "incredibly driven," "combining classes with an internship, maybe a sport, and usually a few extracurriculars."

FINANCIAL AID: 202-994-6620 • E-MAIL: GWADM@GWU.EDU • WEBSITE: WWW.GWU.EDU

THE PRINCETON REVIEW SAYS

Admissions

Very important factors considered include: academic GPA, rigor of secondary school record. *Important factors considered include:* application essay, recommendation(s), extracurricular activities, talent/ ability, volunteer and work experience. *Other factors considered include:* character/personal qualities, interview, alumni/ae relation, geographic residence, SAT or ACT required for some (writing not required). TOEFL required for most international applicants. High school diploma or GED required. *Academic units required:* 4 English, 2 math, 2 science, 1 science lab, 2 foreign language, 2 social studies. *Academic units recommended:* 4 English, 4 math, 4 science, 4 foreign language, 4 social studies.

Financial Aid

Students should submit: FAFSA, CSS/Financial Aid PROFILE. Regular filing deadline is 2/1.The Princeton Review suggests that all financial aid forms be submitted as soon as possible after October 1. *Need-based scholarships/grants offered:* Federal Pell, FSEOG, State scholarships/grants, College/university scholarship or grant aid from institutional funds. *Loan aid offered:* Direct Subsidized Stafford Loans, Direct Unsubsidized Stafford Loans, Direct PLUS loans, Federal Perkins Loans. Applicants will be notified of awards with admissions decisions. Federal Work-Study Program available. Institutional employment available.

The Inside Word

With more than 25,000 applications to process annually, GW could be forgiven if it gave student essays only a perfunctory glance. The school insists, however, that essays are carefully reviewed. Take note and proceed accordingly. Application rates have surged throughout the past decade. This school is only getting more popular, so applicants should be prepared to bring their A-game.

THE SCHOOL SAYS "..."

From the Admissions Office

"GW students are excited about putting knowledge into action so they can change the world and improve the human experience. At many universities, the edge of campus is the real world, but not at GW, where our campus and Washington, D.C., are seamless. We look for bright and diverse students who are ambitious, energetic, and self-motivated. GW is close to the centers of thought and action in every discipline offered. We offer outstanding academics, strong tradition, faculty connections and provide students with the best research, internship, service, and job opportunities in Washington, D.C. A generous scholarship and financial assistance program attracts top students from all parts of the country and the world."

"Tuition is fixed until a student graduates, up to five years or ten full semesters."

SELECTIVITY

Admissions Rating	92
# of applicants	19,837
% of applicants accepted	46
% of acceptees attending	28
# offered a place on the wait list	3,827
% accepting a place on wait list	35
% admitted from wait list	5
# of early decision applicants	1,034
% accepted early decision	69

FRESHMAN PROFILE

Range SAT Critical Reading	590–690
Range SAT Math	600–700
Range SAT Writing	600–690
Range ACT Composite	27–31
Minimum paper TOEFL	550
% graduated top 10% of class	56
% graduated top 25% of class	86
% graduated top 50% of class	98

DEADLINES

Early decision I	
Deadline	11/1
Notification	12/15
Early decision II	
Deadline	1/1
Notification	2/15
Regular	
Deadline	1/1
Notification	4/1
Nonfall registration?	Yes

APPLICANTS ALSO LOOK AT AND OFTEN PREFER

University of California—Berkeley; Emory University; Georgetown University; University of Southern California; University of Virginia

AND SOMETIMES PREFER

Northeastern University; Boston University; American University; New York University

FINANCIAL FACTS

Financial Aid Rating	83
Annual tuition	$51,875
Room and board	$12,500
Required fees	$75
Books and supplies	$1,275
Average frosh need-based scholarship	$27,843
Average UG need-based scholarship	$29,917
% needy frosh rec. need-based scholarship or grant aid	96
% needy UG rec. need-based scholarship or grant aid	94
% needy frosh rec. non-need-based scholarship or grant aid	63
% needy UG rec. non-need-based scholarship or grant aid	34
% needy frosh rec. need-based self-help aid	75
% needy UG rec. need-based self-help aid	80
% UG borrow to pay for school	51
Average cumulative indebtedness	$33,081
% frosh need fully met	47
% ugrads need fully met	52
Average % of frosh need met	89
Average % of ugrad need met	88

GEORGETOWN UNIVERSITY

THIRTY-SEVENTH AND O STREETS, NORTHWEST, WASHINGTON, D.C. 20057 • ADMISSIONS: 202-687-3600 • FAX: 202-687-5084

STUDENTS SAY ". . ."

Academics

This moderately sized elite academic establishment stays true to its Jesuit foundations by educating its students with the idea of "cura personalis," or "care for the whole person." The "well-informed" student body perpetuates upon itself, creating an atmosphere full of vibrant intellectual life, that is "also balanced with extracurricular learning and development." "Georgetown is...a place where people work very, very hard without feeling like they are in direct competition," says an international politics major. Located in Washington, D.C., there's a noted School of Foreign Service here, and the access to internships is a huge perk for those in political or government programs. In addition, the proximity to the nation's capital fetches "high-profile guest speakers," with many of the most powerful people in global politics speaking regularly, as well as a large number of adjunct professors who, either are currently working in government, or have retired from high-level positions.

Georgetown offers a "great selection of very knowledgeable professors, split with a good proportion of those who are experienced in realms outside of academia (such as former government officials) and career academics," though there are a few superstars who might be "somewhat less than totally collegial." Professors tend to be "fantastic scholars and teachers" and are "generally available to students," as well as often being "interested in getting to know you as a person (if you put forth the effort to talk to them and go to office hours)." Though Georgetown has a policy of grade deflation, meaning "A's are hard to come by," there are "a ton of interesting courses available," and TAs are used only for optional discussion sessions and help with grading. The academics "can be challenging or they can be not so much (not that they are ever really easy, just easier);" it all depends on the courses you choose and how much you actually do the work. The school administration is well-meaning and "usually willing to talk and compromise with students," but the process of planning activities can be full of headaches and bureaucracy, and the administration itself "sometimes is overstretched or has trouble transmitting its message." Nevertheless, "a motivated student can get done what he or she wants."

Life

Students are "extremely well aware of the world around them," from government to environment, social to economic, and "Georgetown is the only place where an argument over politics, history, or philosophy is preceded by a keg stand." Hoyas like to have a good time on weekends, and parties at campus and off-campus apartments and townhouses "are generally open to all comers and tend to have a somewhat networking atmosphere; meeting people you don't know is a constant theme." With such a motivated group on such a high-energy campus, "people are always headed somewhere, it seems—to rehearsal, athletic practice, a guest speaker, [or] the gym." Community service and political activism are particularly popular, as is basketball. Everything near Georgetown is in walking distance, including the world of D.C.'s museums, restaurants, and stores, and "grabbing or ordering late night food is a popular option."

Student Body

There are "a lot of wealthy students on campus," and preppy-casual is the fashion de rigueur; this is "definitely not a 'granola' school," but students from diverse backgrounds are typically welcomed by people wanting to learn about different experiences. Indeed, everyone here is well-traveled and well-educated, and there are "a ton of international students." "You better have at least some interest in politics or you will feel out-of-place," says a student. The school can also be "a bit cliquish, with athletes at the top," but there are "plenty of groups for everybody to fit into and find their niche," and "there is much crossover between groups."

FINANCIAL AID: 202-687-4547 • E-MAIL: GUADMISS@GEORGETOWN.EDU • WEBSITE: WWW.GEORGETOWN.EDU

THE PRINCETON REVIEW SAYS

Admissions

Very important factors considered include: rigor of secondary school record, class rank, academic GPA, standardized test scores, application essay, recommendation(s), talent/ability, character/personal qualities, first generation. *Important factors considered include:* interview, extracurricular activities, volunteer work. *Other factors considered include:* alumni/ae relation, geographical residence, state residency, racial/ethnic status, work experience. SAT or ACT required; SAT Subject Tests recommend. ACT with or without writing accepted. TOEFL required of all international applicants. High school diploma is required and GED is accepted.

Financial Aid

Students should submit: FAFSA, CSS/Financial Aid PROFILE, Business/Farm Supplement. Priority filing deadline is 2/1.The Princeton Review suggests that all financial aid forms be submitted as soon as possible after October 1. *Need-based scholarships/grants offered:* Federal Pell, FSEOG, State scholarships/grants, Private scholarships, College/university scholarship or grant aid from institutional funds. *Loan aid offered:* Direct Subsidized Stafford Loans, Direct Unsubsidized Stafford Loans, Direct PLUS loans, Federal Perkins Loans, Federal Nursing Loans. Applicants will be notified of awards on or about 4/1. Federal Work-Study Program available. Institutional employment available.

The Inside Word

It was always tough to get admitted to Georgetown, but in the early 1980s Patrick Ewing and the Hoyas created a basketball sensation that catapulted the place into position as one of the most selective universities in the nation. There has been no turning back since. GU receives over twelve applications for every space in the entering class, and the academic strength of the pool is impressive. Virtually 80 percent of the entire student body took AP courses in high school. Candidates who are wait-listed should hold little hope for an offer of admission; over the past several years Georgetown has taken very few off their lists.

THE SCHOOL SAYS "..."

From the Admissions Office

"Georgetown was founded in 1789 by John Carroll, who concurred with his contemporaries Benjamin Franklin and Thomas Jefferson in believing that the success of the young democracy depended upon an educated and virtuous citizenry. Carroll founded the school with the dynamic Jesuit tradition of education, characterized by humanism and committed to the assumption of responsibility and action. Georgetown is a national and international university, enrolling students from all fifty states and over 100 foreign countries. Undergraduate students are enrolled in one of four undergraduate schools: the College of Arts and Sciences, School of Foreign Service, Georgetown School of Business, and Georgetown School of Nursing and Health Studies. All students share a common liberal arts core and have access to the entire university curriculum.

"Applicants must submit scores from SAT or the ACT. Three SAT Subject Tests are highly recommended."

SELECTIVITY

Admissions Rating	98
# of applicants	19,478
% of applicants accepted	17
% of acceptees attending	47
# offered a place on the wait list	2,188
% accepting a place on wait list	57
% admitted from wait list	12

FRESHMAN PROFILE

Range SAT Critical Reading	660–750
Range SAT Math	660–750
Range ACT Composite	30–34
% graduated top 10% of class	89
% graduated top 25% of class	98
% graduated top 50% of class	100

DEADLINES

Early action	
Deadline	11/1
Notification	12/15
Regular	
Deadline	1/10
Notification	4/1
Nonfall registration?	No

APPLICANTS ALSO LOOK AT AND OFTEN PREFER

University of Pennsylvania; Duke University

AND SOMETIMES PREFER

Cornell University; University of Virginia; University of Notre Dame; Northwestern University

AND RARELY PREFER

Boston College; Tufts University; New York University; The George Washington University

FINANCIAL FACTS

Financial Aid Rating	93
Average frosh need-based scholarship	$42,794
Average UG need-based scholarship	$40,104
% needy frosh rec. need-based scholarship or grant aid	89
% needy UG rec. need-based scholarship or grant aid	97
% needy frosh rec. non-need-based scholarship or grant aid	40
% needy UG rec. non-need-based scholarship or grant aid	30
% needy frosh rec. need-based self-help aid	79
% needy UG rec. need-based self-help aid	9
% UG borrow to pay for school	38
Average cumulative indebtedness	$23,067
% frosh need fully met	100
Average % of frosh need met	100
Average % of ugrad need met	100

GEORGIA INSTITUTE OF TECHNOLOGY

OFFICE OF UNDERGRADUATE ADMISSIONS, ATLANTA, GA 30332-0320 • ADMISSIONS: 404-894-4154 • FAX: 404-894-9511

CAMPUS LIFE

Quality of Life Rating	72
Fire Safety Rating	96
Green Rating	98
Type of school	Public
Affiliation	No Affiliation
Environment	Metropolis

STUDENTS

Total undergrad enrollment	15,142
% male/female	66/34
% from out of state	34
% frosh live on campus	98
% ugrads live on campus	53
# of fraternities (% ugrad men join)	40 (25)
# of sororities (% ugrad women join)	16 (30)
% African American	7
% Asian	19
% Caucasian	51
% Hispanic	7
% Native American	<1
% Pacific Islander	<1
% Two or more races	4
% Race and/or ethnicity unknown	2
% international	11
# of countries represented	95

SURVEY SAYS...

Students politically aware
Recreation facilities are great
Students love Atlanta, GA
Great off-campus food
Everyone loves the Yellow Jackets
Career services are great

ACADEMICS

Academic Rating	67
% students returning for sophomore year	97
% students graduating within 4 years	40
% students graduating within 6 years	85
Calendar	Semester
Student/faculty ratio	19:1
Profs interesting rating	67
Profs accessible rating	66

Most classes have 10–19 students.
Most lab/discussion sessions have
20–29 students.

MOST POPULAR MAJORS

Mechanical Engineering; Industrial
Engineering; Computer and Information
Sciences

STUDENTS SAY "..."

Academics

The Georgia Institute of Technology—Georgia Tech for short—"challenges its students academically while providing a culturally diverse environment, all culminating in preparation for life after college." Students warn that the school "is extremely challenging, academically. If you don't like learning it's probably not for you." They also point out that "since Georgia Tech is a research school, most professors are more concerned about their own research than the quality of their teaching. You're basically teaching yourself the entire subject in order to prepare for an almost impossible exam," although students also add that "while many of the professors at Georgia Tech are focused on their research, there are teachers who truly care about their students and the learning process." As one student advises, "a lot of classes seem to be more about getting the right professor: Some are bad teachers, some are inaccessible, but some are so good that their classes fill up seconds after registration opens." And while "classes are challenging," they're also "interesting" so all of that hard work is "not too bad. If you're organized and get help when you need it, you'll be okay, because we have tons of free tutoring on campus...If you need help with anything, there are countless different places that offer tutoring. The best resource is usually fellow students. Because everyone knows how tough of a school it is, there is a spirit of camaraderie here that you don't find anywhere else." Students also appreciate that Tech "is one of the only schools in the country that offers the BS distinction for liberal arts majors because we [get] such a rigorous grounding in math and science." Finally, students note that "career services are outstanding."

Life

One Georgia Tech engineer sums up the typical student itinerary this way: "Study, study, drink. Repeat." As another student puts it, "there is a saying here that between good grades, a social life, and sleep, you can only have two." That's why "basically people bust their [butts] during the week, and when the weekends arrive they're prepared to let loose a bit." Fortunately, "Georgia Tech has a little something for everyone. Salsa club on weekends, musical groups, intramural sports—even a skydiving club!" Other options include "a 'good enough' NCAA Division I sports program, a good social scene," a welcoming Greek community, "and for everyone else, there's the city of Atlanta right at your doorstep. You're just a short ride away from movies, shopping, the Fox Theatre, the High Museum of Art, Piedmont Park, and one of the best club and bar scenes in the South," centered mainly in the neighborhoods of Buckhead and Midtown. For those without cars in this driving city, transportation comes in the form of "a 'Tech Trolley' that takes a route around midtown, and a 'Stinger Shuttle' that goes to the MARTA [Atlanta's subway] station, giving students access to the airport, downtown (although that is walkable), and Lenox Square Mall." With more than "300 organizations already on campus," students seeking leadership experience can most likely find it, and they can find other students with like-minded interests.

Student Body

"The greatest strength of Georgia Tech is its diversity," undergrads report. "Students, activities, opportunities, teachers—all are diverse." One observes that the school hosts "the full range of stereotypes, from the fraternity boys with their croackies and boat shoes to the socially challenged nerds who stay in their rooms 24/7 programming computers. But no matter what, you know everyone is highly intelligent. Many times it is the students who have the best grades who are the drunkest." One student explains, "Unlike at high school, no one looks down upon you if you know the entire periodic table, if you can do differential equations, or you can speak three languages; rather, you are respected." One sore spot: Men outnumber women here by greater than a two to one ratio. The situation is most pronounced in engineering (three to one) and computer (more than four to one) disciplines. Women actually outnumber men in the liberal arts and science colleges.

FINANCIAL AID: 404-894-4160 • E-MAIL: ADMISSION@GATECH.EDU • WEBSITE: WWW.GATECH.EDU

THE PRINCETON REVIEW SAYS

Admissions

Very important factors considered include: rigor of secondary school record, academic GPA, extracurricular activities. *Important factors considered include:* standardized test scores, application essay, talent/ability, character/personal qualities, geographical residence, state residency, volunteer work, work experience. *Other factors considered include:* recommendation(s), interview, first generation, alumni/ae relation, racial/ethnic status. SAT or ACT required; SAT Subject Tests considered if submitted. ACT with Writing required. SAT with Essay component recommended. High school diploma is required and GED is accepted. *Academic units required:* 4 English, 4 math, 4 science, 2 science labs, 2 foreign language, 3 social studies.

Financial Aid

Students should submit: FAFSA, Institution's own financial aid form, CSS/Financial Aid PROFILE. Regular filing deadline is 2/15.The Princeton Review suggests that all financial aid forms be submitted as soon as possible after October 1. *Need-based scholarships/grants offered:* Federal Pell, FSEOG, State scholarships/grants, Private scholarships, College/university scholarship or grant aid from institutional funds, United Negro College Fund. *Loan aid offered:* Direct Subsidized Stafford Loans, Direct Unsubsidized Stafford Loans, Direct PLUS loans, Federal Perkins Loans, State Loans, College/university loans from institutional funds. Applicants will be notified of awards on or about 4/15. Federal Work-Study Program available. Institutional employment available.

The Inside Word

Students considering Georgia Tech shouldn't be deceived by the acceptance rate. Georgia Tech is a demanding school, and its applicant pool is largely self-selecting. While admissions counselors have begun to implement a more well-rounded approach to the admissions process, grades and test scores are still where candidates make their mark.

THE SCHOOL SAYS "..."

From the Admissions Office

"Georgia Tech consistently ranks among the nation's top public universities producing leaders in engineering, computing, business, architecture, and the sciences while remaining one of the best college buys in the country. The 400-acre campus is nestled in the heart of the fun, dynamic and progressive city of Atlanta. Recent campus improvements yielded new state-of-the art academic and research buildings, apartment-style housing, phenomenal social and recreational facilities, and the most extension fiber-optic cable system on any college campus.

"Georgia Tech has a great academic reputation, and our graduates are well-prepared to meet today's challenges. A unique advantage many students find is Georgia Tech's strong emphasis on undergraduate students. Undergraduates can gain practical work experience through our co-op and internship programs and can begin doing research as early as their freshman year. Students can also gain an international perspective through study abroad, work abroad, or the international plan. In addition, Georgia Tech has added the Clough Undergraduate Center, a state-of-the-art facility that includes forty-one classrooms, two 300-plus seat auditoriums, group study rooms, presentation rehearsal studios, a rooftop garden, and a café.

"With a Division I ACC sports program and access to Atlanta's music, theater, and other cultural venues, Georgia Tech offers its diverse and passionate student body a unique combination of top academics in a thriving and vibrant setting. We encourage you to come visit campus and see why Georgia Tech continues to attract the nation's most motivated, interesting, and creative students."

SELECTIVITY
Admissions Rating	97
# of applicants	27,277
% of applicants accepted	32
% of acceptees attending	35
# offered a place on the wait list	3,397
% accepting a place on wait list	60
% admitted from wait list	2

FRESHMAN PROFILE
Range SAT Critical Reading	630–730
Range SAT Math	680–770
Range SAT Writing	640–730
Range ACT Composite	30–33
Average HS GPA	4.0
% graduated top 10% of class	81
% graduated top 25% of class	96
% graduated top 50% of class	99

DEADLINES
Early action	
Deadline	10/15
Notification	1/10
Regular	
Priority	10/15
Deadline	1/10
Notification	3/14
Nonfall registration?	Yes

APPLICANTS ALSO LOOK AT AND OFTEN PREFER
University of California–Berkeley; University of Florida; University of Georgia; University of Michigan–Ann Arbor; University of Virginia; The University of Texas at Austin

AND SOMETIMES PREFER
Cornell University; North Carolina State University; Purdue University—West Lafayette; Stanford University; and University of Illinois at Urbana-Champaign

AND RARELY PREFER
University of California–Irvine

FINANCIAL FACTS
Financial Aid Rating	81
Average frosh need-based scholarship	$7,953
Average UG need-based scholarship	$10,108
% needy frosh rec. need-based scholarship or grant aid	86
% needy UG rec. need-based scholarship or grant aid	86
% needy frosh rec. non-need-based scholarship or grant aid	53
% needy UG rec. non-need-based scholarship or grant aid	61
% needy frosh rec. need-based self-help aid	66
% needy UG rec. need-based self-help aid	65
% frosh rec. any financial aid	63
% UG rec. any financial aid	72
% UG borrow to pay for school	40
Average cumulative indebtedness	$25,182
% frosh need fully met	35
% ugrads need fully met	24
Average % of frosh need met	84
Average % of ugrad need met	74

GETTYSBURG COLLEGE

ADMISSIONS OFFICE, GETTYSBURG, PA 17325-1484 • ADMISSIONS: 717-337-6100 • FAX: 717-337-6145

CAMPUS LIFE
Quality of Life Rating	94
Fire Safety Rating	91
Green Rating	80
Type of school	Private
Affiliation	Lutheran
Environment	Village

STUDENTS
Total undergrad enrollment	2,454
% male/female	47/53
% from out of state	74
% frosh from public high school	70
% frosh live on campus	100
% ugrads live on campus	94
# of fraternities (% ugrad men join)	9 (31)
# of sororities (% ugrad women join)	6 (33)
% African American	3
% Asian	2
% Caucasian	79
% Hispanic	5
% Native American	<1
% Pacific Islander	0
% Two or more races	2
% Race and/or ethnicity unknown	3
% international	5
# of countries represented	36

SURVEY SAYS...
Students always studying
Students are happy
Classroom facilities are great
Lab facilities are great
Great library
Career services are great
Internships are widely available
School is well run
Great financial aid
Great food on campus
Easy to get around campus
Recreation facilities are great
Lots of beer drinking
Frats and sororities are popular
Alumni active on campus

ACADEMICS
Academic Rating	94
% students returning for sophomore year	91
% students graduating within 4 years	80
Calendar	Semester
Student/faculty ratio	10:1
Profs interesting rating	86
Profs accessible rating	93
Most classes have 10–19 students.	

MOST POPULAR MAJORS
Psychology; Political Science and Government; Business/Commerce

STUDENTS SAY "..."

Academics

Personal and intellectual growth is at the heart of the Gettysburg College experience. Students eagerly praise the school's "friendly, community-oriented atmosphere," and competent, caring professors. "The faculty takes a developed interest in the students' academics and successes, [and] the campus offers countless opportunities for leadership, self-discovery, and the like." In fact, first-year students are surprised to find that "by the first day, the professor knows each student by name and why they're taking the class." With uniformly small class sizes and an emphasis on discussion in the classroom, "professors at Gettysburg make sure that students understand why they are learning the things that they are, and there is a lot of emphasis put on putting 'theory into practice' outside of the classroom." "Many professors go above and beyond, making themselves available to aid students." A current student shares, "My Intro to Chemistry professor would be at the Science Center until 11:00 P.M. before an exam, helping everyone study." Academic opportunities—such as the "amazing study abroad program"—are ample at Gettysburg. Plus, as an exclusively undergraduate institution, Gettysburg "allows for opportunities (i.e., research, publications) that many do not get" at larger universities. In this "nurturing environment," the "administration knows students by name" and even the "registrar, transportation services, off-campus studies, and library staff are lovely and do everything they can to help you." In particular, "President Riggs (a Gettysburg alum and former faculty member) is a phenomenal community leader and makes a sincere effort to connect with students, faculty, and staff."

Life

Enthusiastic and overcommitted, most students at Gettysburg are pursuing "a major and a minor or a double-major, and a majority are involved in at least several college organizations (whether it's a community service group, sports team, or Greek organization)." With so much on their plate, it is no surprise that "the students at Gettysburg buckle down and work hard" during the week. Socially, "life at Gettysburg is very Greek-oriented," and, come the weekend, "frat hopping" is "popular on this campus." Not your style? No worries: Greek life may be "huge" on campus; "However, that does not mean that that is the only thing to do." For students looking for alternate activities, the school hosts "movie nights, plays, and musical performances." Many students also "love going to our theme parties and Happy Hours at the Attic, our on-campus nightclub," while others "get together with friends and watch movies or go out for coffee." For a relaxing respite, "The surrounding area and town is beautiful, so one of my favorite things to do is just walk around out on the battlefields or through town." In addition, "people also like to get off campus traveling to bigger city areas like Baltimore, Harrisburg, D.C., and even Philly and New York City."

Student Body

Academics come first at Gettysburg, where "the student body is extremely intelligent and motivated and serious about their work." When they're not studying, "Gettysburg's student body is very involved" in the school and local community, and "volunteering is very popular." "Each student—in one way or another—takes part in community service during their time at Gettysburg." Demographically, "most of the student body is...middle-class, white, and from the Northeast." And, lest we forget, the Gettysburg student body is also well known for its uniform "tendency to wear preppy clothes." A current student elaborates, "Open up a J. Crew magazine and find the most attractive models in it and you have a typical Gettysburg College student." While some say the student body has a "cookie-cutter" feel to it, others remind us that "while Gettysburg has a reputation for being mostly white, upper-class students, there is diversity all around if you are willing to open up your eyes and see it."

FINANCIAL AID: 717-337-6611 • E-MAIL: ADMISS@GETTYSBURG.EDU • WEBSITE: WWW.GETTYSBURG.EDU

THE PRINCETON REVIEW SAYS

Admissions

Very important factors considered include: rigor of secondary school record, class rank, academic GPA, recommendation(s). *Important factors considered include:* standardized test scores, application essay, interview, extracurricular activities, talent/ability, character/personal qualities, volunteer work. *Other factors considered include:* first generation, alumni/ae relation, geographical residence, racial/ethnic status, work experience, level of applicant's interest. SAT or ACT required; SAT Subject Tests considered if submitted. ACT with or without writing accepted. SAT with or without Essay component accepted. TOEFL required of all international applicants. High school diploma is required and GED is accepted. *Academic units required:* 4 English, 3 math, 3 science, 3 science labs, 3 foreign language, 3 social studies, 3 history. *Academic units recommended:* 4 English, 4 math, 4 science, 4 science labs, 4 foreign language, 4 social studies, 4 history.

Financial Aid

Students should submit: FAFSA, CSS/Financial Aid PROFILE. Regular filing deadline is 2/1.The Princeton Review suggests that all financial aid forms be submitted as soon as possible after October 1. *Need-based scholarships/grants offered:* Federal Pell, FSEOG, State scholarships/grants, Private scholarships, College/university scholarship or grant aid from institutional funds. *Loan aid offered:* Direct Subsidized Stafford Loans, Direct Unsubsidized Stafford Loans, Direct PLUS loans, Federal Perkins Loans, College/university loans from institutional funds. Applicants will be notified of awards on or about 4/1. Federal Work-Study Program available. Institutional employment available.

The Inside Word

Prospective Gettysburg students can register for an account on the school's website to view Gettysburg events in their area or connect with students on campus. To really get a feel for Gettysburg, however, many students say a campus visit is a must. If you're lucky enough to gain admission to this competitive liberal arts school, a campus visit might be just the thing to seal the deal.

THE SCHOOL SAYS ". . ."

From the Admissions Office

"Four major goals of Gettysburg College to best prepare students to enter the real world, include, first, to accelerate the intellectual development of our first-year students by integrating them more quickly into the intellectual life of the campus; second, to use interdisciplinary courses combining the intellectual approaches of various fields; third, to encourage students to develop an international perspective through course work, study abroad, association with international faculty, and a variety of extracurricular activities; and fourth, to encourage students to develop (1) a capacity for independent study by ensuring that all students work closely with individual faculty members on an extensive project during their undergraduate years and (2) the ability to work with their peers by making the small group a central feature in college life.

"Gettysburg College strongly recommends that freshman applicants submit scores from the SAT. Students may also choose to submit scores from the ACT (with or without the writing component) in lieu of the SAT."

SELECTIVITY

Admissions Rating	92
# of applicants	6,386
% of applicants accepted	40
% of acceptees attending	28
# of early decision applicants	444
% accepted early decision	68

FRESHMAN PROFILE

Range SAT Critical Reading	600–670
Range SAT Math	610–680
% graduated top 10% of class	56
% graduated top 25% of class	82
% graduated top 50% of class	98

DEADLINES

Early decision	
Deadline	11/15
Notification	12/15
Regular	
Priority	1/15
Deadline	1/15
Notification	4/1
Nonfall registration?	Yes

APPLICANTS ALSO LOOK AT AND OFTEN PREFER
Colgate University

AND SOMETIMES PREFER
Bucknell University

AND RARELY PREFER
Muhlenberg College

FINANCIAL FACTS

Financial Aid Rating	94
Annual tuition	$49,140
Room and board	$11,730
Books and supplies	$500
Average frosh need-based scholarship	$33,314
Average UG need-based scholarship	$33,139
% needy frosh rec. need-based scholarship or grant aid	96
% needy UG rec. need-based scholarship or grant aid	95
% needy frosh rec. non-need-based scholarship or grant aid	55
% needy UG rec. non-need-based scholarship or grant aid	50
% needy frosh rec. need-based self-help aid	87
% needy UG rec. need-based self-help aid	86
% frosh rec. any financial aid	60
% UG rec. any financial aid	60
% UG borrow to pay for school	61
Average cumulative indebtedness	$30,544
% frosh need fully met	88
% ugrads need fully met	87
Average % of frosh need met	90
Average % of ugrad need met	90

GONZAGA UNIVERSITY

502 EAST BOONE AVENUE, SPOKANE, WA 99258 • ADMISSIONS: 509-313-6572 • FAX: 509-313-5780

STUDENTS SAY "..."

Academics

Gonzaga University "has a strong Jesuit Catholic tradition and has sustained an environment of academic excellence." By far, the two most commonly cited strengths are the basketball team and the "awesome community!" Gonzaga is a "close-knit community." "At Gonzaga, we are one big family," one student says. "Everyone is incredibly friendly," and there's "a great sense of school spirit and a family-like environment." "Not to mention being able to cheer in one of the most intimidating basketball stadiums in the United States." "It is a family here, and you really get to know your professors," one student explains. "Everyone here is interconnected, and basketball is wonderful too! It's a way we all come together." Students also believe "the Jesuit mission of Gonzaga sets it apart from other schools." Gonzaga "is a socially competent, caring institution" where you'll "be constantly challenged to be your best, make lifelong relationships, and develop a critical understanding of the world around you." The professors get mixed reviews: "It is about a 50 percent chance of getting a good professor." "Professors are good in general, but adjunct faculty is typically hired at the last minute and not good," one student explains. "Many of the professors for the core requirements are very religious and not especially open to new ideas." "Gonzaga tries to get students to think about the world in a holistic way—understanding how everything is interrelated—and finding our purpose in that." Students think the "registration processes" and "cafeteria food" could "use some improvement," and "because Gonzaga is a smaller school, it is at times difficult to arrange your schedule due to limited availability of classes and time constraints."

Life

Students at Gonzaga are "devoted equally to...academics and social life." "People generally just want to socialize," one student explains. "Everyone for the most part does do their work, but there is definitely an emphasis on developing relationships." "The party scene is lively" at Gonzaga although students caution "we're not *that* big of a party school." During basketball season, Gonzaga basketball becomes "a way of life," and "basketball games and waiting in line for tickets are the largest social experience on campus." "*Everyone* goes to the basketball games. It's practically required to graduate." This leads some students to wish there was "less focus on men's basketball." Because the school is located in rainy Spokane, Washington, "the worst thing about Gonzaga is the weather, which the school can't really do anything about." Still, many students "stay active through sports" and enjoy the outdoors, "whether that's skiing, hiking, rafting, climbing, wake boarding, or just soaking up some rays." "People often snowboard at Mount Spokane, or if they are feeling adventurous, they drive the hour to Canada or hour to Montana." At Gonzaga, students "read, Rage, Repent, Repeat. We wake up, work out, eat, and make memories."

Student Body

Although Gonzaga students stress the college's tight-knit community, many feel that while "the university claims to be accepting of all beliefs, opinions, and lifestyles," "in reality that's just not the case." "It is a community for sure, but really only if you're white and upper middle class, and the Jesuit Catholic mission can sometimes be troublesome for those of us with liberal and non-mainstream Catholic beliefs," explains one student. "Even feminism is kind of seen as taboo here." Others insist that "everyone here seems to blend well together," and "no matter your background, you are accepted here." Students study "hard through the week" but have "a lot of fun on weekends." Students describe themselves as "friendly, very open," "mostly preppy," "conventionally minded," "well-mannered," "religious," and tending to come "from a good family." Gonzaga has "a mostly Caucasian population," and "diversity is a huge issue, and Gonzaga could definitely improve how it treats students of diverse backgrounds." It should be no shock that "the typical student is a huge basketball fan" with "extreme school spirit."

FINANCIAL AID: 509-313-6582 • E-MAIL: ADMISSIONS@GONZAGA.EDU • WEBSITE: WWW.GONZAGA.EDU

THE PRINCETON REVIEW SAYS

Admissions

Very important factors considered include: rigor of secondary school record, academic GPA, character/personal qualities, first generation. *Important factors considered include:* standardized test scores, application essay, recommendation(s), extracurricular activities, talent/ability. *Other factors considered include:* interview, alumni/ae relation, racial/ethnic status, volunteer work, work experience, level of applicant's interest. SAT or ACT required. ACT with or without writing accepted. SAT with or without Essay component accepted. TOEFL required of all international applicants. High school diploma is required and GED is not accepted. *Academic units required:* 4 English, 3 math, 3 science, 3 science labs, 2 foreign language, 2 social studies, 2 history, 2 academic electives. *Academic units recommended:* 4 English, 4 math, 4 science, 4 science labs, 3 foreign language, 3 social studies, 3 history, 3 academic electives.

Financial Aid

Students should submit: FAFSA. Priority filing deadline is 2/1. The Princeton Review suggests that all financial aid forms be submitted as soon as possible after October 1. *Need-based scholarships/grants offered:* Federal Pell, FSEOG, State scholarships/grants, Private scholarships, College/university scholarship or grant aid from institutional funds. *Loan aid offered:* Direct Subsidized Stafford Loans, Direct Unsubsidized Stafford Loans, Direct PLUS loans, Federal Perkins Loans, Federal Nursing Loans, College/university loans from institutional funds. Applicants will be notified of awards on a rolling basis beginning 3/1. Federal Work-Study Program available. Institutional employment available.

The Inside Word

Gonzaga is a great example of how a high-profile athletic program can transform a competitive school into a highly competitive one. During the past decade, Gonzaga's admit rate has decreased substantially while class rank, standardized test scores, and high school GPA have all increased measurably.

THE SCHOOL SAYS "..."

From the Admissions Office

"Education at Gonzaga is not comparable to an academic 'assembly line'; rather, it is person-to-person and face-to-face. This personal quality is also true of our admission and financial aid processes. Therefore, allow us to know you beyond the boundaries of your college application. Visit campus, phone us, e-mail us—let us see the person behind the data. Good luck with your college search and your applications. Go Zags!

"All sections of the SAT will be accepted, but the essay section will not receive universal consideration. If taken, the essay score may be considered in cases where more information specific to writing ability would be helpful in decision making."

SELECTIVITY

Admissions Rating	87
# of applicants	6,729
% of applicants accepted	73
% of acceptees attending	27
# offered a place on the wait list	332
% accepting a place on wait list	39
% admitted from wait list	0

FRESHMAN PROFILE

Range SAT Critical Reading	540–640
Range SAT Math	550–650
Range ACT Composite	25–29
Minimum paper TOEFL	550
Average HS GPA	3.7
% graduated top 10% of class	39
% graduated top 25% of class	71
% graduated top 50% of class	95

DEADLINES

Early action	
Deadline	11/15
Notification	1/15
Regular	
Priority	11/15
Deadline	2/1
Notification	3/15
Nonfall registration?	Yes

APPLICANTS ALSO LOOK AT AND OFTEN PREFER

University of Washington; Cal Poly San Luis Obispo

AND SOMETIMES PREFER

Santa Clara University; Seattle University; University of Portland

AND RARELY PREFER

Washington State University; University of Oregon

FINANCIAL FACTS

Financial Aid Rating	85
Annual tuition	$38,980
Room and board	$11,158
Required fees	$750
Books and supplies	$1,092
Average frosh need-based scholarship	$20,411
Average UG need-based scholarship	$20,609
% needy frosh rec. need-based scholarship or grant aid	100
% needy UG rec. need-based scholarship or grant aid	100
% needy frosh rec. non-need-based scholarship or grant aid	22
% needy UG rec. non-need-based scholarship or grant aid	19
% needy frosh rec. need-based self-help aid	67
% needy UG rec. need-based self-help aid	70
% frosh rec. any financial aid	99
% UG rec. any financial aid	98
% UG borrow to pay for school	65
Average cumulative indebtedness	$29,459
% frosh need fully met	26
% ugrads need fully met	23
Average % of frosh need met	79
Average % of ugrad need met	78

GORDON COLLEGE

255 GRAPEVINE ROAD, WENHAM, MA 01984 • ADMISSIONS: 978-867-4218 • FAX: 978-867-4682

STUDENTS SAY "..."

Academics

A small, liberal arts school just north of Boston, Gordon College truly does an outstanding job of providing a "strong community" for its student body. The school endeavors to develop "well-rounded Christian leaders who will have a positive influence on the world." And, to that end, it does a good job of attracting students who are "not just looking to get a degree to get jobs that pay well;" many Gordon undergrads hope to use their education to "make a difference." These same undergrads also greatly appreciate Gordon's "unbeatable" financial aid packages. Importantly, the college also offers a wide range of academic departments. Students are especially quick to highlight the "very strong music education program" as well as the "good mathematics program." They're also full of praise for their professors who "really try to work with the students and their learning styles, making class time valuable and enjoyable." An accounting major further explains, "They all love to have personal interaction with students and seeks to help us in the best way possible." Gordon professors also "challenge...student[s] to think independently and research what they are learning." And this social work and sociology student happily sums up her academic experience stating, "I love the way my classes are run, and I value the education I am getting."

Life

Get ready for your calendar to fill up at Gordon! A psychology major shares, "There is usually some kind of event going on...every weekend sponsored by one of the [school's] organizations or clubs." Of course, it's essential to point out that the college maintains a "dry campus," hence "on-campus activities tend to be a very wholesome kind of fun." And, naturally, "faith-based discussions and events are prominent on campus" as well. "When the weather is nice," many Gordon students can be found "on the quad doing homework, playing Frisbee or soccer." The college also maintains "a beautiful forest on campus with lakes to swim in and running trails." And the Campus Events Council organizes a number of concerts throughout the year involving "both famous and local bands." Outside of organized events there's "a lot of dialogue, laughing, movie-watching, game playing, etc." The surrounding area also offers plenty of entertainment options. Students frequently head "to the beach, downtown Salem, or to one of the malls around here for fun." Additionally, "Boston is about a half hour away, and people can take the commuter rail in which is not too far."

Student Body

Given that Gordon is a religious college, it's not surprising that undergrads here define the typical student as "a white evangelical Christian who comes from an upper middle class family." Many are "interested in what is trending in Evangelical subculture—and might be radical enough to listen to Beyoncé, but nothing more than that." In other words, you're likely to encounter a number of "Christian hipsters" with "moderate political views" and "a strong interest in social justice." A sociology major does caution that "generally you can find a place here if you are white and straight. If not, [it's] tough." However, a linguistics major does counter that "students can find their niche no matter where their interests and coursework may take them." Some say that community is a priority for the Gordon administration: "The school works very hard to make sure everyone feels accepted and everyone has a friend or someone [with whom] to talk."

GORDON COLLEGE

FINANCIAL AID: 978-867-4246 • E-MAIL: ADMISSIONS@GORDON.EDU • WEBSITE: WWW.GORDON.EDU

THE PRINCETON REVIEW SAYS

Admissions

Very important factors considered include: rigor of secondary school record, academic GPA, standardized test scores, recommendation(s), interview, extracurricular activities, talent/ability, character/personal qualities, religious affiliation/commitment. *Important factors considered include:* class rank, application essay, first generation, alumni/ae relation, volunteer work, work experience, level of applicant's interest. *Other factors considered include:* geographical residence, racial/ethnic status. SAT or ACT required; SAT Subject Tests considered if submitted. ACT with Writing required. TOEFL required of all international applicants. High school diploma is required and GED is accepted. *Academic units required:* 4 English, 2 math, 2 science, 1 science lab, 2 foreign language, 2 social studies, 5 academic electives. *Academic units recommended:* 4 English, 3 math, 3 science, 1 science lab, 4 foreign language, 2 social studies, 5 academic electives.

Financial Aid

Students should submit: FAFSA. Priority filing deadline is 3/1. The Princeton Review suggests that all financial aid forms be submitted as soon as possible after October 1. *Need-based scholarships/grants offered:* Federal Pell, FSEOG, State scholarships/grants, Private scholarships, College/university scholarship or grant aid from institutional funds. *Loan aid offered:* Direct Subsidized Stafford Loans, Direct Unsubsidized Stafford Loans, Direct PLUS loans, Federal Perkins Loans, State Loans. Applicants will be notified of awards on a rolling basis beginning 2/15. Federal Work-Study Program available. Institutional employment available.

The Inside Word

Gaining admission to Gordon is somewhat competitive. Admissions officers closely review high school transcripts for academic promise. Therefore, a solid college prep curriculum is a must. Applicants must also demonstrate a strong commitment to Christianity as well. In fact, students must submit a Christian faith reference in addition to an academic reference. Applicants with deep ties to their religious beliefs are likely the strongest candidates. Finally, it's required that students sit for admissions interview, but accomodations can be made if you are unable to visit campus.

THE SCHOOL SAYS "..."

From the Admissions Office

"There are three core distinctions that—taken together—set Gordon College apart from other academically rigorous liberal arts institutions:

"Gordon's mission. Gordon graduates men and women distinguished by intellectual maturity and Christian character, committed to lives of service, and prepared for leadership worldwide. With a liberal arts education in the tradition of New England's best colleges, our students gain the qualities most sought by employers—the ability to think critically, reason analytically, communicate persuasively and—even more importantly—to act morally. The Gordon Commission. This is the essence of our experience—to stretch the mind, deepen the faith and elevate the contribution Gordon students and graduates make to the world around us. We stretch the mind through a challenging education that is both broad and deep, and one that offers the freedom to ask and explore tough questions. We deepen the faith by integrating Christian beliefs and practice into all aspects of our educational experience. We elevate the contribution—to the common good, to our communities, to developing the next generation of thoughtful Christian leaders—through programs and outreach that emphasize service over self and that span the globe.

"Gordon's Location. Boston is the global "hub" of higher education—this is where the world comes to study. We are strategically located in the proximity of the cultural centers of education (Boston), finance (New York) and politics (Washington). Boston also has a reputation as a leader in developing talent—which means greater opportunity for students who study here."

SELECTIVITY

Admissions Rating	82
# of applicants	1,832
% of applicants accepted	93
% of acceptees attending	26
# offered a place on the wait list	7
% accepting a place on wait list	0
# of early decision applicants	27
% accepted early decision	85

FRESHMAN PROFILE

Range SAT Critical Reading	480–620
Range SAT Math	470–610
Range SAT Writing	460–620
Range ACT Composite	23–29
Minimum internet-based TOEFL	85
Average HS GPA	3.6
% graduated top 10% of class	26
% graduated top 25% of class	61
% graduated top 50% of class	83

DEADLINES

Early decision	
Deadline	10/15
Notification	11/1
Early action	
Deadline	11/15
Notification	12/1
Regular	
Priority	2/1
Deadline	8/1
Nonfall registration?	Yes

FINANCIAL FACTS

Financial Aid Rating	82
Annual tuition	$34,528
Room and board	$10,412
Required fees	$1,532
Books and supplies	$800
Average frosh need-based scholarship	$22,952
Average UG need-based scholarship	$18,906
% needy frosh rec. need-based scholarship or grant aid	100
% needy UG rec. need-based scholarship or grant aid	100
% needy frosh rec. non-need-based scholarship or grant aid	14
% needy UG rec. non-need-based scholarship or grant aid	12
% needy frosh rec. need-based self-help aid	84
% needy UG rec. need-based self-help aid	86
% frosh rec. any financial aid	99
% UG rec. any financial aid	99
% UG borrow to pay for school	82
Average cumulative indebtedness	$35,169
% frosh need fully met	16
% ugrads need fully met	15
Average % of frosh need met	74
Average % of ugrad need met	70

GOUCHER COLLEGE

1021 DULANEY VALLEY ROAD, BALTIMORE, MD 21204-2794 • ADMISSIONS: 410-337-6100 • FAX: 410-337-6354

STUDENTS SAY "..."

Academics

This small innovative Maryland college is centered around the 3Rs: relationships, resilience, and reflection. With only around 1,450 students, Goucher College is a "close community that cares deeply about social justice, activism, broadening horizons, and making a difference," and there is a strong emphasis on environmental awareness, "opening one's eyes to the world around them, and exploring and learning through traveling" (as evidenced by the mandatory study abroad requirement). The truly liberal arts curriculum at this "education rich place" is buttressed by an excellent advising system and the Academic Center for Excellence, and around three-quarters of all students go on to graduate or professional school. Since Goucher is a "small but mighty" school, there are "many ways in which staff and faculty work together to make sure that you stand out from the crowd and become more marketable."

Professors "try hard to ensure the best education and the best learning environment for each individual"; they "have a lot of work experience that they bring to the classroom," and most professors are still working in addition to teaching or are very involved in research (that undergraduate students have a chance to be a part of). Classes come with "great variety," and are usually under ten people, so "the culture for group discussions is really kind of built in." They are designed to encompass multiple perspectives of a subject, so that "students can get a full picture." Professors "understand in order for us to digest the material, we NEED to discuss it," and they are "always available to talk or help" so students can keep up with the sometimes demanding academics. As one student puts it, "You come to Goucher to go to school...you will have to be committed to your studies if you want to succeed."

Life

Each day students typically have a mix of classes, club meetings/events, athletic practices, work (many students have jobs on- or off-campus), and socializing, and the school is very good about allowing students "to balance their lives between academic and non-academic activities." Each semester has a theme with various events associated with it; a recent theme was "mindfulness," which incorporated several speakers and a yoga class. Students are "generally really laid back about dining" and spend long periods of time in the dining halls and at the cafe socializing. Pickup games of Frisbee are common on the Quad, and "of course, people like to head out into the woods for a walk" (the school also boasts two labyrinths).

People here are "very school-oriented," so while they like to have fun on weekend nights, "the library is full on Sundays." Parties are relatively infrequent, and "usually consist of small get-togethers in the dorms." There is a mall within walking distance, and Baltimore is fifteen-minute drive (or free shuttle) away. This socially conscious school offers "a ton of community service initiatives" and works closely with the surrounding Towson and Baltimore communities.

Student Body

Goucher is "a great place for unique and quirky people": "We're all very confident, and we all have an individual sense of who we are." "You're bound to find someone on this campus with the same interests as you, no matter what those interests are," says a student. Even with strong personalities, everyone here connects well and brings a "broad range" of perspectives to the table, but some say the school is "slightly segmented in terms of students that could be considered athletic, social, quirky, [and] alternative." A large number of international students attend this "globally-minded" school. There is "a political consciousness" across all students, who have "a certain openness and degree of maturity" beyond their college years.

FINANCIAL AID: 410-337-6141 • E-MAIL: ADMISSIONS@GOUCHER.EDU • WEBSITE: WWW.GOUCHER.EDU

THE PRINCETON REVIEW SAYS

Admissions

Very important factors considered include: rigor of secondary school record, academic GPA. *Important factors considered include:* application essay, recommendation(s), extracurricular activities, talent/ability, volunteer work. *Other factors considered include:* class rank, standardized test scores, interview, character/personal qualities, first generation, alumni/ae relation, geographical residence, state residency, racial/ethnic status, work experience, level of applicant's interest. SAT or ACT considered if submitted. ACT with Writing required. SAT with or without Essay component accepted. TOEFL required of all international applicants. High school diploma is required and GED is accepted. *Academic units required:* 4 English, 3 math, 2 science, 2 science labs, 2 foreign language, 3 social studies, 2 academic electives. *Academic units recommended:* 4 English, 4 math, 3 science, 3 science labs, 4 foreign language, 3 social studies, 2 academic electives.

Financial Aid

Students should submit: FAFSA, CSS/Financial Aid PROFILE, Noncustodial PROFILE. Priority filing deadline is 2/1. The Princeton Review suggests that all financial aid forms be submitted as soon as possible after October 1. *Need-based scholarships/grants offered:* Federal Pell, FSEOG, State scholarships/grants, Private scholarships, College/university scholarship or grant aid from institutional funds. *Loan aid offered:* Direct Subsidized Stafford Loans, Direct Unsubsidized Stafford Loans, Direct PLUS loans, Federal Perkins Loans, College/university loans from institutional funds. Applicants will be notified of awards on or about 3/1. Federal Work-Study Program available. Institutional employment available.

The Inside Word

Goucher College is the first college in the nation to create an application option requesting student-submitted videos as the decisive factor for admission. Students can choose not to submit transcripts, test scores, and other traditional application materials. Instead, applicants can send Goucher a straightforward, two-minute video about how they see themselves flourishing at the college.

THE SCHOOL SAYS "..."

From the Admissions Office

"Goucher is a small coeducational liberal arts college with a big view of the world. Located just north of Baltimore, MD, the college is redefining the meaning of a liberal arts education and preparing its graduates for the jobs of the future. Goucher provides students with a broad-based education: they learn how to think creatively and critically, how to process new information and experiences, and how to use these tools to solve problems and become effective lifelong learners. One way the college helps its students achieve their goals is by focusing on a new set of the 3Rs: relationships, resilience, and reflection. Goucher understands faculty and peer relationships are a prerequisite for learning, resilience is a stronger predictor of success than intelligence, and students must be able to reflect on how they learn best in order to continue acquiring knowledge after graduation. The college serves a bright and motivated student population of almost 1,500, representing forty-four states and thirty-eight countries. Innovation drives the college's methods both inside and outside the classroom. Goucher was the first college in the nation to implement an undergraduate study abroad requirement, as well as the first create an application option requesting student-submitted videos as the decisive factor for admission. The college believes in complementing rigorous curriculum with abundant opportunities for hands-on experience in the world. Goucher students put their education into action through collaborative research with faculty, service-learning programs that support local communities, unique internships, and, of course, international study."

SELECTIVITY

Admissions Rating	80
# of applicants	3,577
% of applicants accepted	78
% of acceptees attending	14
# offered a place on the wait list	61
% accepting a place on wait list	72
% admitted from wait list	16
# of early decision applicants	44
% accepted early decision	84

FRESHMAN PROFILE

Range SAT Critical Reading	500–630
Range SAT Math	480–590
Range SAT Writing	500–610
Range ACT Composite	23–28
Minimum paper TOEFL	550
Average HS GPA	3.2
% graduated top 10% of class	22
% graduated top 25% of class	47
% graduated top 50% of class	84

DEADLINES

Early decision	
Deadline	11/15
Notification	12/15
Early action	
Deadline	12/1
Notification	2/1
Regular	
Priority	2/1
Deadline	8/1
Notification	4/1
Nonfall registration?	Yes

FINANCIAL FACTS

Financial Aid Rating	84
Annual tuition	$42,600
Room and board	$12,300
Required fees	$816
Books and supplies	$1,200
Average frosh need-based scholarship	$29,973
Average UG need-based scholarship	$28,963
% needy frosh rec. need-based scholarship or grant aid	100
% needy UG rec. need-based scholarship or grant aid	99
% needy frosh rec. non-need-based scholarship or grant aid	17
% needy UG rec. non-need-based scholarship or grant aid	13
% needy frosh rec. need-based self-help aid	81
% needy UG rec. need-based self-help aid	84
% frosh rec. any financial aid	99
% UG rec. any financial aid	93
% UG borrow to pay for school	65
Average cumulative indebtedness	$32,190
% frosh need fully met	22
% ugrads need fully met	22
Average % of frosh need met	80
Average % of ugrad need met	80

GREEN MOUNTAIN COLLEGE

ONE BRENNAN CIRCLE, POULTNEY, VT 05764-1199 • ADMISSIONS: 802-287-8000 • FAX: 802-287-8099

CAMPUS LIFE
Quality of Life Rating	87
Fire Safety Rating	97
Green Rating	99
Type of school	Private
Affiliation	Methodist
Environment	Rural

STUDENTS
Total undergrad enrollment	597
% male/female	49/51
% from out of state	85
% frosh live on campus	98
% ugrads live on campus	85
% African American	4
% Asian	1
% Caucasian	53
% Hispanic	3
% Native American	1
% Pacific Islander	0
% Two or more races	1
% Race and/or ethnicity unknown	33
% international	3
# of countries represented	12

SURVEY SAYS...
Lots of liberal students
Students are happy
Class discussions encouraged
Students are friendly
Students aren't religious
Students environmentally aware
Easy to get around campus
Lots of beer drinking
Campus newspaper is popular

ACADEMICS
Academic Rating	82
% students returning for sophomore year	66
% students graduating within 4 years	34
% students graduating within 6 years	38
Calendar	Semester
Student/faculty ratio	14:1
Profs interesting rating	96
Profs accessible rating	92

Most classes have 10–19 students.
Most lab/discussion sessions have 10–19 students.

MOST POPULAR MAJORS
Environmental Studies; Parks, Recreation and Leisure Studies; Agroecology and Sustainable Agriculture

STUDENTS SAY "..."

Academics
Green Mountain College, located in Poultney, Vermont, is a small, private, liberal arts college in the Vermont countryside. One of the goals of Green Mountain is its active focus on sustainability and teaching all of their incoming students to live "responsibly" as global citizens. In fact, the college has a set of thirty-seven credit, core classes known as the Environmental Liberal Arts, which combines a liberal arts education with a strong focus on the environment. With most students saying that their class sizes "are usually around fifteen to thirty students," they really feel like they get to know their professors "not only as academic instructors, but as people," and most rave that they really bond with a majority of their teachers, saying they "haven't really met any professor that I can't connect with in some way." Since a lot of professors get to really know their students, most students say they have no problem getting personal letters from professors when they are "ready to apply for a job/internship/graduate school, because they know...you and what you've done with your time here." The students love that the school promotes a great education with a focus on teaching students how to be themselves "while learning in dynamic and hands-on ways"; this comes through an emphasis that an education doesn't just come from a classroom, but from real world experience as well.

Life
Being located in the Vermont country, Green Mountain College offers its students a great experience for those who love to experience nature. Its location at the foot of the Green Mountains makes it ideal for students who enjoy spending their free time "skiing, snowboarding, camping, [and] hiking." Incoming freshman and transfer students can register for one of the pre-orientation "Wilderness Challenges," where these new people bond together over a five day adventure focused on such activities as rock-climbing, canoeing, and yoga. During the school year, the student run College Programming Board does "a great job with providing concerts and other events on campus" for those wishing to stay nearby. The college isn't located right next to a big city, so many make their own fun on campus. Students also say that there are options to get away such as "a few charming...restaurants on Main Street," but in general, "there is not much to do around town." However, for those students who are willing to take a drive, the ski resort town of Killington is nearby—about forty minutes away—which students call "a huge plus."

Student Body
The student population at Green Mountain College likes to think of itself as a "very tight-knit community," with a "typical" student being "very outgoing [and] friendly." Many students here "want to make a positive impact on the world in some way or another," especially in the area of sustainability. Though many students agree that certainly a certain type of student attends Green Mountain, it's hard to nail down that typical student description. One student clarifies that there are "no [frat] bros, no sorority girls," but explains that the vast majority are happy to live "amongst other weird, happy, wonderful people while learning about sustainability," which is clear in the projects that students take on for the betterment of campus. Students led the way in preparing and funding an engineering study for the college's biomass plant and recently built a solar powered garage that houses an electric vehicle.

FINANCIAL AID: 802-287-8210 • E-MAIL: ADMISS@GREENMTN.EDU • WEBSITE: WWW.GREENMTN.EDU

THE PRINCETON REVIEW SAYS

Admissions

Very important factors considered include: academic GPA, recommendation(s). *Important factors considered include:* rigor of secondary school record, class rank, standardized test scores, application essay, interview, extracurricular activities, volunteer work, level of applicant's interest. *Other factors considered include:* talent/ability, character/personal qualities, alumni/ae relation, religious affiliation/commitment, racial/ethnic status, work experience. SAT or ACT required for some; SAT Subject Tests considered if submitted. ACT with or without writing accepted. TOEFL required of all international applicants. High school diploma is required and GED is accepted. *Academic units required:* 4 English, 3 math, 3 science, 2 science labs, 1 foreign language, 3 social studies, 1 history, 5 academic electives. *Academic units recommended:* 4 math, 4 science, 2 foreign language, 2 history.

Financial Aid

Students should submit: FAFSA. Priority filing deadline is 3/1. The Princeton Review suggests that all financial aid forms be submitted as soon as possible after October 1. *Need-based scholarships/grants offered:* Federal Pell, FSEOG, State scholarships/grants, Private scholarships, College/university scholarship or grant aid from institutional funds. *Loan aid offered:* Direct Subsidized Stafford Loans, Direct Unsubsidized Stafford Loans, Direct PLUS Loans. Applicants will be notified of awards on a rolling basis beginning 11/1. Federal Work-Study Program available. Institutional employment available.

The Inside Word

Green Mountain College has twenty-six majors to choose from. Because the student population sits at about 600 students, it should be known that applications are accepted throughout the year and that Green Mountain has a test-optional policy, so it is not mandatory that applicants supply their ACT or SAT scores, but if students choose not to, they have to fill out the college's Insight Portfolio and provide a graded writing sample that was written within the last two years. For those interested in financial aid, there are numerous programs that the college offers, and 94 percent of all GMC students receive financial aid and about 90 percent receive institutional support. Academic-based scholarships are awarded on a rolling basis as well.

THE SCHOOL SAYS " . . . "

From the Admissions Office

"Green Mountain College was named the number one 'Coolest School' by *Sierra* magazine. GMC is a liberal arts college that is on the forefront of sustainability education.

"While we are proud of our national recognition for sustainability, three-quarters of our students do not major in environmental studies, but rather select a liberal arts major that they are passionate about—education, business, art, psychology, biology, etc. The student body is united by a sense of social responsibility and penchant for service. Diversity thrives at Green Mountain College. The academic community is highly engaged and provides a truthful and authentic scholarly environment.

"GMC's working farm is a special attraction for students from all majors. It provides a visible model of sustainability and produces a significant quantity of food for the college community. Students can also major in sustainable agriculture and food production and/or earn twelve credits over the summer in farm life ecology, a 'field and table' intensive.

"The college is committed to and guarantees graduation in four years for students who meet academic requirements. An entrepreneurial spirit carries throughout the entire community resulting in a one of kind graduation."

SELECTIVITY

Admissions Rating	79
# of applicants	825
% of applicants accepted	66
% of acceptees attending	24

FRESHMAN PROFILE

Range SAT Critical Reading	480–590
Range SAT Math	460–530
Range SAT Writing	430–580
Range ACT Composite	18–24
Minimum paper TOEFL	500
Minimum internet-based TOEFL	61

DEADLINES

Early action	
Deadline	11/1
Notification	12/14
Regular	
Priority	3/1
Nonfall registration?	Yes

FINANCIAL FACTS

Financial Aid Rating	83
Annual tuition	$33,898
Room and board	$11,492
Required fees	$1,442
Average frosh need-based scholarship	$29,878
Average UG need-based scholarship	$26,168
% needy frosh rec. need-based scholarship or grant aid	100
% needy UG rec. need-based scholarship or grant aid	100
% needy frosh rec. non-need-based scholarship or grant aid	14
% needy UG rec. non-need-based scholarship or grant aid	11
% needy frosh rec. need-based self-help aid	82
% needy UG rec. need-based self-help aid	84
% frosh rec. any financial aid	96
% UG rec. any financial aid	94
% UG borrow to pay for school	74
Average cumulative indebtedness	$38,701
% frosh need fully met	21
% ugrads need fully met	17
Average % of frosh need met	83
Average % of ugrad need met	79

GRINNELL COLLEGE

1103 PARK STREET, GRINNELL, IA 50112-1690 • ADMISSIONS: 641-269-3600 • FAX: 641-269-4800

STUDENTS SAY "..."

Academics

Founded in 1846, Grinnell College is a small private liberal arts college in Iowa where innovative intellectual discourse is central to learning. Guided by a commitment to academic rigor and a "commitment to social justice," the school stresses self-governance ("Self-Gov is Love") and the "very supportive" student body has the power to make change on campus. "Grinnell operates on self-governance which means the students are held accountable for their actions by their fellow students rather than being cited by RAs or school officials," says a student.

Learning at Grinnell "can be characterized as entering into a dialogue with professors and classmates." The curriculum stresses the methodology as well as the content of a given discipline; professors "expect students to be able to evaluate scholarship critically and come to their own conclusions." Faculty here are "incredibly diverse" and "eager to teach in a small liberal arts college," and "they all are willing to meet outside of class and leave their schedule open to help you."

Grinnell is one of the few schools without required general education courses, and students here "are truly free to explore their passions without feeling obligated to study things they don't enjoy." The school encourages students "to try a bit of everything" whether or not it's related to their major, and is "wonderful about bringing in important speakers to help you learn outside of the classroom." However, the school's size means there aren't as many classes offered as larger universities, and "some classes are only offered in either the spring or fall semester." Still, the school dedicates tons of resources for students, and "individual needs, especially academics related ones, are always met." The college also heavily subsidizes "spring break volunteer trips, conference travel costs, student groups, unpaid internships, trips to job-shadow alumni, and so much more."

Life

"Fun predominates in the academic community and support systems" as well as in nonacademic ways. After being hard workers during the week, "almost everyone likes to go out on weekends and let loose a little bit," whether "in a traditional party environment with beer and drinking games on weekends, or something as goofy as a weekly Nerf gun battle in our science facility on Friday nights (yes, there's a club for that)." There are in fact many different organizations run by students, and "there's always some sort of performance going on." Popular movies are shown for free on campus, and concerts and themed dance parties are held. "Even though we are located in a small town in Iowa, most students don't feel the urge to hit a bus or car to Des Moines, Chicago or the Twin Cities every weekend," assures a student. "We make our own amusements; surprisingly little property destruction results of this boredom compared to other college towns I know." Grinnellians are "very passionate about wellness, respect and being politically correct," and this translates into a lot of talks, dialogues and activities to promote all three of these aspects. "If you have an opinion be prepared to defend it," says a student. There are of course some social divisions (notably athletes and non-athletes), but "not in a harmful way." "People love to dance here. People love to deconstruct social constructions here." It's "an amazing mix of silly times and very smart people."

Student Body

Grinnell is a school filled with an "odd bunch" of students who are "genuinely interested in developing relationships with each other and a connection with the greater world." All "have a quality about them that is a little bit awkward and silly and most people feel comfortable expressing this." "You can always find someone who really understands your brand of crazy," says a junior. This group of "socially conscious scholars" is traditionally "liberal, very intelligent," and "willing to critically think about every issue or belief mostly in constructive ways." There is no set formula for fitting in; "almost everyone finds people that they are comfortable with here." Grinnell is also home to a large international student population, hailing from more than eighty countries.

FINANCIAL AID: 641-269-3250 • E-MAIL: ADMISSION@GRINNELL.EDU • WEBSITE: WWW.GRINNELL.EDU

THE PRINCETON REVIEW SAYS

Admissions

Very important factors considered include: rigor of secondary school record, class rank, academic GPA, recommendation(s). *Important factors considered include:* standardized test scores, application essay, extracurricular activities, talent/ability. *Other factors considered include:* interview, character/personal qualities, first generation, alumni/ae relation, geographical residence, state residency, racial/ethnic status, volunteer work, work experience, level of applicant's interest. SAT or ACT required. ACT with or without writing accepted. SAT with or without Essay component accepted. TOEFL required of all international applicants. High school diploma is required and GED is accepted. *Academic units recommended:* 4 English, 4 math, 3 science, 3 science labs, 3 foreign language, 3 social studies, 3 history.

Financial Aid

Students should submit: FAFSA, CSS/Financial Aid PROFILE, Noncustodial PROFILE. Regular filing deadline is 2/1. The Princeton Review suggests that all financial aid forms be submitted as soon as possible after October 1. *Need-based scholarships/grants offered:* Federal Pell, FSEOG, State scholarships/grants, Private scholarships, College/university scholarship or grant aid from institutional funds. *Loan aid offered:* Direct Subsidized Stafford Loans, Direct Unsubsidized Stafford Loans, Direct PLUS loans, Federal Perkins Loans, College/university loans from institutional funds. Applicants will be notified of awards on or about 4/1. Federal Work-Study Program available. Institutional employment available.

The Inside Word

Grinnell's admissions process is refreshingly straightforward. Students need to be able to thrive academically as well as demonstrate an ability to take an active role in their education as you'll be responsible for co-creating your curriculum with your advisor, and you'll have to find your voice in a self-governing residential community. Grinnell is extremely selective, so you'll have to give it your all. An interview isn't required here, but do it anyway.

THE SCHOOL SAYS ". . ."

From the Admissions Office

"Grinnell College is a place where independence of thought and social conscience are instilled. Grinnell is a college with the resources of a school ten times its size, a faculty that reads like a Who's Who of Teaching, and a learning environment where debate does not end in the classroom and often begins in the dining hall.

"Grinnellians are committed to learning, respect for themselves and others, contributing to global social good, willing collaboration, and the courage to try.

"We look for students who show strong potential, have the courage to try new things, demonstrate a willingness to speak out and share their opinions, and bring different perspectives to our international campus in the middle of Iowa. Grinnell College is filled with students who are serious about learning but are not always serious."

SELECTIVITY

Admissions Rating	97
# of applicants	6,414
% of applicants accepted	25
% of acceptees attending	28
# offered a place on the wait list	1,224
% accepting a place on wait list	39
% admitted from wait list	4
# of early decision applicants	316
% accepted early decision	53

FRESHMAN PROFILE

Range SAT Critical Reading	640–740
Range SAT Math	660–770
Range ACT Composite	30–33
% graduated top 10% of class	81
% graduated top 25% of class	96
% graduated top 50% of class	100

DEADLINES

Early decision	
Deadline	11/15
Regular	
Deadline	1/15
Nonfall registration?	No

FINANCIAL FACTS

Financial Aid Rating	96
Annual tuition	$48,322
Room and board	$11,980
Required fees	$436
Books and supplies	$900
Average frosh need-based scholarship	$37,426
Average UG need-based scholarship	$38,612
% needy frosh rec. need-based scholarship or grant aid	99
% needy UG rec. need-based scholarship or grant aid	99
% needy frosh rec. non-need-based scholarship or grant aid	16
% needy UG rec. non-need-based scholarship or grant aid	10
% needy frosh rec. need-based self-help aid	83
% needy UG rec. need-based self-help aid	87
% frosh rec. any financial aid	88
% UG rec. any financial aid	87
% UG borrow to pay for school	59
Average cumulative indebtedness	$15,982
% frosh need fully met	100
% ugrads need fully met	100
Average % of frosh need met	100
Average % of ugrad need met	100

GROVE CITY COLLEGE

100 CAMPUS DRIVE, GROVE CITY, PA 16127-2104 • ADMISSIONS: 724-458-2100 • FAX: 724-458-3395

CAMPUS LIFE
Quality of Life Rating	87
Fire Safety Rating	93
Green Rating	69
Type of school	Private
Affiliation	Presbyterian
Environment	Rural

STUDENTS
Total undergrad enrollment	2,444
% male/female	50/50
% from out of state	48
% frosh from public high school	62
% frosh live on campus	98
% ugrads live on campus	96
# of fraternities (% ugrad men join)	10 (18)
# of sororities (% ugrad women join)	8 (19)
% African American	1
% Asian	2
% Caucasian	92
% Hispanic	1
% Native American	<1
% Pacific Islander	0
% Two or more races	3
% Race and/or ethnicity unknown	0
% international	1
# of countries represented	14

SURVEY SAYS...
Lots of conservative students
Students always studying
Students are happy
Classroom facilities are great
Career services are great
School is well run
Students are very religious
Very little drug use
Intramural sports are popular
Theater is popular

ACADEMICS
Academic Rating	81
% students returning for sophomore year	89
% students graduating within 4 years	80
% students graduating within 6 years	85
Calendar	Semester
Student/faculty ratio	13:1
Profs interesting rating	80
Profs accessible rating	90

Most classes have 10–19 students.
Most lab/discussion sessions have
20–29 students.

MOST POPULAR MAJORS
Mechanical Engineering; Biology; General
Literature

STUDENTS SAY ". . ."

Academics

Students avow that Grove City is "a great option for someone who wants to learn from a Christian perspective." Located near Pittsburgh, this "small, conservative, independent" college is renowned for its "great spiritual atmosphere," providing a "very high-quality and competitive education," and has "a high rate of graduate school acceptance and job placement." One student mentions, "Grove City College keeps traditional values and top-of-the-line academics at the heart of everything it does." All courses are taught by professors, who are seen as "tough but fair and willing to help out their students." "You probably will not do well in most classes if you just do the minimum." Grade competition is almost a pastime for some, but others effectively juggle studies and other activities. "Some people like to over-exaggerate the difficulty of the academics. It is definitely challenging, but very doable." Professors "encourage students to learn and think for themselves, rather than trying to indoctrinate them into a particular ideology." "We are typically religious and conservative in beliefs, but that doesn't mean we're not open-minded." Still, undergraduates believe instructors "are equipping them spiritually and socially to live successful, godly lives." Notes a student, "I am able to learn from people who truly love what they do and do it because they love God." "I've truly grown leaps and bounds in my spiritual life," marvels another thrilled undergraduate.

Life

"Fun outside of class is what you make it" at Grove City College. Seemingly everyone is involved in multiple organizations and extracurricular activities. Academic groups, social clubs, intramural sports...all are popular, as are opportunities "for spiritual growth through campus ministries, student-initiated small groups, and local churches." "The community is wonderful, and it is a very uplifting place to be," although many students do long for a bit more personal freedom. As one student says, "While the rules at GCC are certainly strict, they are very clearly articulated," although another asserts they "are not as strict as made out to be. Really they are quite lax compared to other conservative Christian colleges." The school's rules can lead to interaction between the sexes becoming somewhat complex. There are relatively firm "inter-visitation rules" between men and women, and students would like "more areas to spend time coed." Registration has reportedly become "quicker and easier" and is "pretty fair as to who gets into classes." The cafeteria does "an excellent job providing a variety of healthy food options," and the food "is amazing compared to most other college campuses." Even though Grove City is a smaller school, "the parking situation for students is very ideal" and "not far from the dorms and academic buildings." Students are effusive in their admiration for the physical surroundings, describing them as "pretty and well-maintained, "enchanting," and "quiet and laid-back." "I always feel safe," another reports. The town itself is small, but has "good churches, a neat old theater, nice restaurants, and a great sense of community."

Student Body

Embraced by some students, rejected by others, the moniker of a "Grover" is said to describe "a studious person, desiring to be involved in as much as possible while striving to still perform excellently in academics." Furthermore, many here describe themselves as "very type-A." "Most students are extremely conscious of their grades." At the same time, others profess to handle everything with more perspective. "Grove City can be stressful, but only if you let it!" What is universal at Grove City is this: everyone is described as "dedicated, motivated, conscientious, and responsible." Many undergrads "generally have a strong Christian faith and are excited about the opportunities to deepen that faith at college;" however, "people from all walks can further their education, grow relationships, and learn true humility and service." "The unity of the campus body is one of the greatest assets to our school," and Grove City does a "phenomenal job of integrating all freshmen or transfer students."

FINANCIAL AID: 724-458-3300 • E-MAIL: ADMISSIONS@GCC.EDU • WEBSITE: WWW.GCC.EDU

THE PRINCETON REVIEW SAYS

Admissions

Very important factors considered include: rigor of secondary school record, academic GPA, standardized test scores, application essay, interview, character/personal qualities, level of applicant's interest. *Important factors considered include:* recommendation(s), extracurricular activities. *Other factors considered include:* class rank, talent/ability, first generation, alumni/ae relation, geographical residence, state residency, religious affiliation/commitment, racial/ethnic status, volunteer work, work experience. SAT or ACT required. ACT with or without writing accepted. SAT with or without Essay component accepted. TOEFL required of all international applicants. High school diploma is required and GED is accepted. *Academic units recommended:* 4 English, 3 math, 3 science, 2 science labs, 3 foreign language, 3 social studies, 2 history.

Financial Aid

Students should submit: Institution's own financial aid form. Regular filing deadline is 4/15. The Princeton Review suggests that all financial aid forms be submitted as soon as possible after October 1. *Need-based scholarships/grants offered:* State scholarships/grants, Private scholarships, College/university scholarship or grant aid from institutional funds. *Loan aid offered:* State and private loans. First-time freshman applicants will be notified of rewards on a rolling basis beginning 3/15. Institutional employment available.

The Inside Word

Gaining entrance into Grove City College is difficult and highly competitive. Students must have outstanding personal characteristics, and they need to be prepared for a strenuous but workable course load. Christian values are of utmost importance at GCC, and the school values students who seek out surroundings based on those principles. Interviews and recommendations are highly valued as components of the admission process.

THE SCHOOL SAYS "..."

From the Admissions Office

"A good college education doesn't have to cost a fortune. For decades, Grove City College has offered a quality education at costs among the lowest nationally. Since the 1990s, increased national academic acclaim has come to Grove City College. Grove City College is a place where professors teach; you will not see graduate assistants or teacher's aides in the classroom. Our professors are also active in the total life of the campus. More than 150 student organizations on campus afford opportunity for a wide variety of cocurricular activities. Outstanding scholars and leaders in education, science, and international affairs visit the campus each year. The environment at Grove City College is friendly, secure, and dedicated to high standards.

"There is a fresh spiritual vitality on campus that touches every aspect of your college life. In the classroom, we don't shy away from discussing all points of view, however we adhere to Christ's teaching as relevant guidance for living. Come visit and learn more."

SELECTIVITY

Admissions Rating	87
# of applicants	1,541
% of applicants accepted	81
% of acceptees attending	44
# offered a place on the wait list	160
% accepting a place on wait list	93
% admitted from wait list	37
# of early decision applicants	282
% accepted early decision	84

FRESHMAN PROFILE

Range SAT Critical Reading	536–655
Range SAT Math	640–654
Range ACT Composite	24–29
Minimum paper TOEFL	550
Minimum internet-based TOEFL	79
Average HS GPA	3.7
% graduated top 10% of class	40
% graduated top 25% of class	68
% graduated top 50% of class	91

DEADLINES

Early decision	
Deadline	11/15
Notification	12/15
Regular	
Deadline	2/1
Notification	3/15
Nonfall registration?	Yes

APPLICANTS ALSO LOOK AT AND OFTEN PREFER
Penn State University Park

AND SOMETIMES PREFER
University of Pittsburgh–Pittsburgh Campus;
Wheaton College (IL)

FINANCIAL FACTS

Financial Aid Rating	78
Annual tuition	$16,154
Room and board	$8,802
Books and supplies	$1,000
Average frosh need-based scholarship	$7,594
Average UG need-based scholarship	$7,103
% needy frosh rec. need-based scholarship or grant aid	100
% needy UG rec. need-based scholarship or grant aid	98
% needy frosh rec. non-need-based scholarship or grant aid	14
% needy UG rec. non-need-based scholarship or grant aid	9
% needy frosh rec. need-based self-help aid	52
% needy UG rec. need-based self-help aid	66
% frosh rec. any financial aid	77
% UG rec. any financial aid	79
% UG borrow to pay for school	57
Average cumulative indebtedness	$36,997
% frosh need fully met	14
% ugrads need fully met	9
Average % of frosh need met	56
Average % of ugrad need met	52

GUILFORD COLLEGE

5800 WEST FRIENDLY AVENUE, GREENSBORO, NC 27410 • ADMISSIONS: 336-316-2100 • FAX: 336-316-2954

STUDENTS SAY "..."

Academics

Guilford's legendarily "accepting culture" arises through the incorporation of a number of core tenets that include "diversity, equality, community, stewardship, etc." The school is "a place where you can express yourself free from judgment," and "impacts every aspect of your life and continues to carry you as part of its family even after you graduate." Students are given the opportunity to make all of their own choices, and the school works at "providing support for those decisions," and heavily promotes the idea "that doing things the hard way is usually worth it."

The Quaker college is known for being green (to put it mildly), and the administration works to raise "student and individual awareness of the environment and everyday life through education and service learning." The level of engagement of the students is matched only by the school's willingness to listen; student involvement is in everything from policy changes to food options, and "can be one person's efforts or many." "I know someone who campaigned for getting coffee in the cafeteria's ice cream selection, and this year we had a trial run that seems to have gone over well," says a sophomore. Still, a few students do think the administration could let up on "parenting the students."

Professors are able to "create an environment that invites discussion of materials from different perspectives" that "[pushes] and [supports] you at the same time." The "intensity of academic learning" means that "your absence in a class does not go unnoticed," unsurprising at a place where teachers are called by their first name ("which is really awesome"). The small scale class sizes "really allow for individual attention and academic growth." Most classrooms are arranged with the desks in a circle and the classes are "highly interactive"; every class "is filled with questions for the class to answer, even simple questions."

Life

Fun at this "socially intriguing" comes in many forms: walking in the woods, hiking, community service, the local art and music scene. "It's always felt like more of a village than an institution," says one student. Relaxation is taken very seriously after a week of hard work (Guilford is "writing heavy" and "the library and its resources are used a great deal"), and "lying down by the lake and playing music or watching movies with friends is almost mandatory." Bars in Greensboro are also an option, but if students can't get there "the school does a good job at hosting activities around campus, which can help the slower weekends." There is admittedly "a lot of weed, but it's totally fine if you aren't into smoking or drinking."

People on this "beautiful" campus are very socially and politically aware, and "someone ...is always planning protests or creating petitions." Food options are a sore spot for Guilford students, and "there's also sometimes an athletic divide." Students are "really active" in groups and organizations, and there is "lots of talk of oppression, gender issues, and race in the social sciences and humanities."

Student Body

This is one "funky community of diverse people," all of whom "seem to share some appreciation for the outdoors and nuttier aspects of life." "Hippies or athletes" covers the majority of the student body (as does "liberal"), and there are many "refreshingly weird individuals" who've "taken their time at Guilford as an opportunity to redefine themselves." "We color outside of the lines in innovative and interesting ways," says one student. Friend groups tend to be in cliques, but are "still very friendly with other groups"; as one junior puts it, "There's a lot of varying interests but some wires tend to be the same across the board... like being culturally aware, or fighting against the oppression of minorities."

FINANCIAL AID: 336-316-2354 • E-MAIL: ADMISSION@GUILFORD.EDU • WEBSITE: WWW.GUILFORD.EDU

THE PRINCETON REVIEW SAYS

Admissions

Very important factors considered include: rigor of secondary school record, academic GPA, application essay. *Important factors considered include:* class rank, standardized test scores, recommendation(s), extracurricular activities, character/personal qualities, volunteer work. *Other factors considered include:* interview, talent/ability, first generation, alumni/ae relation, geographical residence, state residency, religious affiliation/commitment, racial/ethnic status, work experience, level of applicant's interest. SAT or ACT recommend. ACT with or without writing accepted. TOEFL required of all international applicants. High school diploma is required and GED is accepted. *Academic units recommended:* 4 English, 3 math, 3 science, 2 foreign language, 3 social studies, 3 history.

Financial Aid

Students should submit: FAFSA. Priority filing deadline is 2/15. The Princeton Review suggests that all financial aid forms be submitted as soon as possible after October 1. *Need-based scholarships/grants offered:* Federal Pell, FSEOG, State scholarships/grants, Private scholarships, College/university scholarship or grant aid from institutional funds. *Loan aid offered:* Direct Subsidized Stafford Loans, Direct Unsubsidized Stafford Loans, Direct PLUS loans, Federal Perkins Loans. Applicants will be notified of awards on a rolling basis beginning 2/15. Federal Work-Study Program available. Institutional employment available.

The Inside Word

Getting into Guilford College goes beyond the numbers. Guilford is looking for students who demonstrate strong drive and personal motivation. Applicants to the school should have a solid high school record and good extracurricular activities (preferably of the tree-hugging and/or varsity sports variety). While a Quaker connection couldn't hurt, the school is more interested in your character and personal qualities and level of interest in the school. The admissions essay is your chance to make your case.

THE SCHOOL SAYS "..."

From the Admissions Office

"Guilford is proud to be included for the twenty-fifth consecutive year in The Princeton Review's *Best Colleges* edition. Guilford can best be described by its academic rigor, preparation for graduate school and careers, and its commitment to service in a caring, socially aware and supportive community.

"This is a campus that celebrates all walks of life. Guilford brings together students from many different religious, socioeconomic, geographic, and ethnic backgrounds. You can be yourself here and that's a great feeling. Open-mindedness is embraced, especially in the classrooms, living spaces, and social settings on campus where you will challenge others and be challenged yourself.

"There is no stereotypical Guilford student. Our students have many passions including athletics and intramurals, community service, social justice and multiculturalism. However the bond that ties them together is the academic curriculum that prepares them for life and a career. The Guilford experience is truly a transformative one."

SELECTIVITY

Admissions Rating	83
# of applicants	3,001
% of applicants accepted	62
% of acceptees attending	19
# offered a place on the wait list	0

FRESHMAN PROFILE

Range SAT Critical Reading	450–590
Range SAT Math	460–580
Range SAT Writing	430–560
Range ACT Composite	19–26
Minimum paper TOEFL	550
Average HS GPA	3.1
% graduated top 10% of class	12
% graduated top 25% of class	34
% graduated top 50% of class	71

DEADLINES

Early decision	
Deadline	11/15
Early action	
Deadline	11/15
Notification	12/15
Regular	
Priority	11/15
Deadline	2/15
Nonfall registration?	Yes

APPLICANTS ALSO LOOK AT AND SOMETIMES PREFER

Earlham College; The University of North Carolina at Chapel Hill; Goucher College; Elon University

FINANCIAL FACTS

Financial Aid Rating	83
Annual tuition	$33,050
Room and board	$9,370
Required fees	$380
Average frosh need-based scholarship	$26,997
Average UG need-based scholarship	$19,797
% needy frosh rec. need-based scholarship or grant aid	91
% needy UG rec. need-based scholarship or grant aid	92
% needy frosh rec. non-need-based scholarship or grant aid	96
% needy UG rec. non-need-based scholarship or grant aid	56
% needy frosh rec. need-based self-help aid	76
% needy UG rec. need-based self-help aid	72
% frosh rec. any financial aid	98
% UG rec. any financial aid	86
% frosh need fully met	5
% ugrads need fully met	5
Average % of frosh need met	83
Average % of ugrad need met	84

HAMILTON COLLEGE

OFFICE OF ADMISSION, CLINTON, NY 13323 • ADMISSIONS: 315-859-4421 • FAX: 315-859-4457

STUDENTS SAY "..."

Academics

Upstate New York liberal arts school Hamilton College offers fine academics and an open curriculum that give students "preparation for the future that goes far beyond exam-taking strategies." The focus on writing and speaking, the lack of core requirements, and the small class sizes put a "keen focus on students as unique individuals with different abilities and aspirations." "Hamilton allows you the freedom to be anyone, but gives you the direction to become the best person you can become," says a student. The school's "mix of old-school practices with liberal thinking" allows students to become "true intellectuals beyond the basics of academia." "Hamilton College is all about learning how to think and then conveying those ideas into writing," says a student. The professors at Hamilton are "brilliant but they do not flaunt it and instead defer to class discussions." Professors are also "always available outside of class to discuss anything further." "Their extensive office hours are when you can really connect with them," says one student. In using their "ability to bring classes to life," professors demonstrate their interest in "comprehension of the material beyond grades." The open curriculum allows for classes to be "extremely productive," because "people want to be there learning and talking about what interests them." "I know when I enroll in a class that the people I take that class with are truly interested in the class (just as I am)," says one student. "They aren't there to fulfill a requirement." Though the campus itself is large, the undergraduate population is fewer than 2,000, so class sizes are downright tiny (which is "excellent"), and if you can't get in to a class, "all you have to do is talk to the professors, and they'll usually make room for you." Research opportunities are plentiful, and facilities (such as labs) "are well-equipped." The administration "does what they can to adhere to the needs and wants of the students."

Life

The "beautiful campus" is located in the middle of relatively nowhere, but students are creative in that they "very successfully compensate for our isolated location with themed parties, clubs, and other eclectic activities." Students are "incredibly devoted" to their school work, but they are also devoted to having a good time. "A typical Hamilton student loves to learn on the weekdays, and drink...on the weekends (but gets to bed early enough to study the following afternoon!)." Still, there are plenty of people on campus who prefer to remain sober, though "whether that is a choice or due to lack of confidence in finding parties, I don't know." More often than not, "Hamiltonians aren't strictly about working themselves to death." People who have cars (a huge plus) can go downtown or into New Hartford in their free time, but "most students spend most of their time on campus." Often, students just catch the van that travels around the area and "go to the movies or the mall and just hang out with friends." Hamilton has "a very intellectually stimulating academic environment," and "it is not at all uncommon to find a whole dorm room debating about an economic theory that only one of them actually learned about in class."

Student Body

"The typical student at Hamilton was a top student at his/her high school; is very invested in at least one activity on campus; works hard during the week but makes the most of weekends; is invested in maintaining health and fitness; and has big dreams for his/her future." "'Preppy' seems to be the common connection between a lot of students," but "for a school in the middle of Central New York, [Hamilton has] a remarkably varied student population." Students are often characteristically preppy, athletic "light siders," or artsy "dark siders," "but things aren't really that black and white, and there is typically a place for everyone as long as you look." Everyone is "exceptionally nice," and "people here aren't afraid to be themselves." "Everyone is passionate about their academics as well as their activities outside the classroom."

FINANCIAL AID: 800-859-4413 • E-MAIL: ADMISSION@HAMILTON.EDU • WEBSITE: WWW.HAMILTON.EDU

THE PRINCETON REVIEW SAYS

Admissions

Very important factors considered include: rigor of secondary school record, class rank, academic GPA. *Important factors considered include:* standardized test scores, application essay, recommendation(s), interview, extracurricular activities, character/personal qualities. *Other factors considered include:* talent/ability, first generation, alumni/ae relation, geographical residence, racial/ethnic status, volunteer work, work experience, level of applicant's interest. SAT or ACT required. TOEFL required of all international applicants. High school diploma is required and GED is accepted. *Academic units recommended:* 4 English, 3 math, 3 science, 3 foreign language, 3 social studies.

Financial Aid

Students should submit: FAFSA, Institution's own financial aid form, CSS/Financial Aid PROFILE, State aid form, Noncustodial PROFILE, Business/Farm Supplement. Regular filing deadline is 2/15. The Princeton Review suggests that all financial aid forms be submitted as soon as possible after October 1. *Need-based scholarships/ grants offered:* Federal Pell, FSEOG, State scholarships/grants, Private scholarships, College/university scholarship or grant aid from institutional funds. *Loan aid offered:* Direct Subsidized Stafford Loans, Direct Unsubsidized Stafford Loans, Direct PLUS loans, Federal Perkins Loans, College/university loans from institutional funds. Applicants will be notified of awards on or about 4/1. Federal Work-Study Program available. Institutional employment available.

The Inside Word

Similar to any prestigious liberal arts schools, Hamilton takes a well-rounded, personal approach to admissions. They rely heavily on academic achievement and intellectual promise, but in a mission to create a talented and diverse incoming class, admissions officers also strive to attain a complete, accurate profile of each candidate. Standardized tests are required and students may choose which scores to submit from an approved menu that includes the ACT, SAT, and SAT Subject Tests. The admissions team at Hamilton also strongly recommends interviews either on or off campus with alumni volunteers.

THE SCHOOL SAYS "..."

From the Admissions Office

"There is no one Hamilton student, just as there is no one Hamilton experience, but the promise we make to our students is the same: At Hamilton, our open curriculum enables you to study what interests you, our welcoming and unpretentious student body will accept you for who you are and what you believe, and our devoted network of alumni and career center professionals will help you find your future. Our faculty will expect your full attention and participation academically, and you will learn to expect a lot from yourself.

"We are also committed to ensuring that a Hamilton education is available to all deserving students, so for those unable to pay our fees, we make an additional promise: We will review your application without considering your financial circumstances (which is known as 'need-blind' admission) and then, once you are admitted, we will meet your full demonstrated need for all four years.

"We ask you for a pledge in return: We expect you to work to your ability, be open to new ideas, and contribute your talents to our community."

SELECTIVITY

Admissions Rating	96
# of applicants	5,434
% of applicants accepted	25
% of acceptees attending	35
# offered a place on the wait list	958
% accepting a place on wait list	38
% admitted from wait list	13
# of early decision applicants	616
% accepted early decision	38

FRESHMAN PROFILE

Range SAT Critical Reading	650–740
Range SAT Math	650–730
Range SAT Writing	650–750
Range ACT Composite	31–33
% graduated top 10% of class	77
% graduated top 25% of class	96
% graduated top 50% of class	100

DEADLINES

Early decision	
Deadline	11/15
Notification	12/15
Regular	
Deadline	1/1
Notification	4/1
Nonfall registration?	Yes

APPLICANTS ALSO LOOK AT AND OFTEN PREFER

Middlebury College; Bowdoin College; Dartmouth College; Williams College; Brown University; Amherst College

AND SOMETIMES PREFER

Colgate University; Wesleyan University

AND RARELY PREFER

Skidmore College; Bates College

FINANCIAL FACTS

Financial Aid Rating	96
Annual tuition	$49,010
Room and board	$12,570
Required fees	$490
Books and supplies	$1,300
Average frosh need-based scholarship	$40,802
Average UG need-based scholarship	$41,170
% needy frosh rec. need-based scholarship or grant aid	100
% needy UG rec. need-based scholarship or grant aid	100
% needy frosh rec. non-need-based scholarship or grant aid	0
% needy UG rec. non-need-based scholarship or grant aid	0
% needy frosh rec. need-based self-help aid	85
% needy UG rec. need-based self-help aid	82
% frosh rec. any financial aid	53
% UG rec. any financial aid	48
% UG borrow to pay for school	39
Average cumulative indebtedness	$17,654
% frosh need fully met	100
% ugrads need fully met	100
Average % of frosh need met	100
Average % of ugrad need met	100

HAMPDEN-SYDNEY COLLEGE

PO BOX 667, HAMPDEN-SYDNEY, VA 23943-0667 • ADMISSIONS: 434-223-6120 • FAX: 434-223-6346

CAMPUS LIFE

Quality of Life Rating	84
Fire Safety Rating	88
Green Rating	71
Type of school	Private
Affiliation	Presbyterian
Environment	Rural

STUDENTS

Total undergrad enrollment	1,087
% male/female	100/0
% from out of state	29
% frosh from public high school	73
% frosh live on campus	100
% ugrads live on campus	95
# of fraternities (% ugrad men join)	11 (34)
# of sororities (% ugrad women join)	(0)
% African American	6
% Asian	1
% Caucasian	81
% Hispanic	2
% Native American	<1
% Pacific Islander	0
% Two or more races	6
% Race and/or ethnicity unknown	3
% international	0
# of countries represented	11

SURVEY SAYS...

Lots of conservative students
Students are happy
Great library
Great financial aid
No one cheats
Recreation facilities are great
Lots of beer drinking
Everyone loves the Tigers
Intramural sports are popular
Frats and sororities are popular
Alumni active on campus

ACADEMICS

Academic Rating	83
% students returning for sophomore year	83
% students graduating within 4 years	57
% students graduating within 6 years	63
Calendar	Semester
Student/faculty ratio	10:1
Profs interesting rating	90
Profs accessible rating	97

Most classes have 10–19 students.

MOST POPULAR MAJORS

Economics; History; Business/Managerial Economics

STUDENTS SAY "..."

Academics

Something of an anomaly in higher education today, Hampden-Sydney is a small, all-male liberal arts school "focus[ed] on forming good men." The Virginian college offers "a close-knit community of professors and students," one where "tradition and opportunity" abound. It's also highly "concerned with the character of the students it produces." Additionally, Hampden-Sydney undergrads tout the strong bonds of brotherhood that form here; one only needs to look at the "extensive alumni network" for evidence. Academically, the college places an "emphasis on rhetorical ability and classical knowledge." And undergrads are quick to praise the "strong government and economics departments" as well as the great "reputation for pre-med students." Undergrads also appreciate the bevy of discussion based courses, which can be partially be attributed to "small" class sizes. One English major explains the benefits: "This method of learning has allowed me to be a far better and more engaged student than I was in high school."

Thankfully, students also give the professors themselves high marks. They report that their teachers are "engaging and intelligent" and "accessible" to boot! Perhaps even more importantly, they seem to "genuinely care about the success of their students." Or, as one cool psych major eloquently expresses, Hampden-Sydney professors are simply "the bomb.com."

Life

While Hampden-Sydney students can be a studious bunch, they also strive to find a good work and life balance. A biology major elaborates, "During the week, you'll hear students at lunch talking about their classes, making plans to study together, etc. On weekends, however, our two favorite activities come into play: alcohol and girls." More specifically, many students here happily embrace the Greek system. Indeed, we're told that "fraternity life is popular and consumes 99 percent of the social scene." Hampden-Sydney undergrads also love to support their sports teams, especially when it comes to football. Of course, these games also provide students with an excuse to host their historic tailgates. A foreign affairs major explains, "Our tailgates are incredible; students dress in coat and tie and drink whiskey and beer while connected with Hampden-Sydney men of generations past." Beyond tailgating, it's also "common for each [student] organization to have multiple balls or formals." Thankfully, there are plenty of activities to participate in for those not interested in the party scene. We're told that "paintball, fly fishing, archery [and] outdoors club" are all quite popular. And lest you think that these students' idea of fun is devoid of intellectual activity, a government major assures us that "I constantly find myself in conversation with my peers on the subject of politics, philosophy, religion, and business."

Student Body

When pushed to classify their peers, many Hampden-Sydney undergrads will admit that "the typical student is white, conservative, from a middle to upper middle class family" and "Southern." However, undergrads quickly counter that "all students are respectful of each other and there are no tensions between different types of students." Moreover, behind the "preppy" facades, you'll find "quality young men that have good morals and show concern for others." Indeed, these "students are friendly and able to be picked out of a crowd for their gentlemanly behavior." Hampden-Sydney students also describe their classmates as possessing "strong communication skills." And, just as vital, they "know how to have a good time but also know when to work hard." Many find common ground with their peers by getting involved with some "athletic team/club . . . as well as other outdoor activities." And a number of students love to go "hunting and fishing." Overall, "the brotherhood is strong, and can be felt when one walks on campus." Rest assured that "there's always a place for someone" at Hampden-Sydney.

FINANCIAL AID: 434-223-6119 • E-MAIL: HSAPP@HSC.EDU • WEBSITE: WWW.HSC.EDU

THE PRINCETON REVIEW SAYS

Admissions

Very important factors considered include: rigor of secondary school record, academic GPA, standardized test scores, application essay, recommendation(s), character/personal qualities. *Important factors considered include:* class rank, extracurricular activities. *Other factors considered include:* interview, talent/ability, first generation, alumni/ae relation, volunteer work, work experience, level of applicant's interest. SAT or ACT required. ACT with or without writing accepted. SAT with or without Essay component accepted. TOEFL required of all international applicants. High school diploma is required and GED is accepted. *Academic units required:* 4 English, 3 math, 2 science, 1 science lab, 2 foreign language, 1 social studies, 1 history, 3 academic electives. *Academic units recommended:* 4 math, 3 science, 3 foreign language.

Financial Aid

Students should submit: FAFSA, State aid form. Priority filing deadline is 3/1. The Princeton Review suggests that all financial aid forms be submitted as soon as possible after October 1. *Need-based scholarships/grants offered:* Federal Pell, FSEOG, State scholarships/grants, Private scholarships, College/university scholarship or grant aid from institutional funds. *Loan aid offered:* Direct Subsidized Stafford Loans, Direct Unsubsidized Stafford Loans, Direct PLUS loans, Federal Perkins Loans, College/university loans from institutional funds. Applicants will be notified of awards on or about 3/15. Federal Work-Study Program available. Institutional employment available.

The Inside Word

Hampden-Sydney provides undergrads with a competitive academic environment. Therefore, admissions officers are looking for students who enrolled in demanding college prep courses and earned solid grades. Moreover, on-campus interviews are highly encouraged; we recommend scheduling one if at all possible. Finally, those applicants who are convinced that Hampden-Sydney is their top choice should consider applying early.

THE SCHOOL SAYS "..."

From the Admissions Office

"The spirit of Hampden-Sydney is its sense of community. As one of only 1,120 students, you will be in small classes and find it easy to get extra help or inspiration from professors when you want it. Many of our professors live on campus and enjoy being with students in the snack bar as well as in the classroom. They give you the best, most personal education as possible. A big bonus of small-college life is that everybody is invited to go out for everything, and you can be as much of a leader as you want to be. From athletics to debating to publications to fraternity life, this is part of the process that produces a well-rounded Hampden-Sydney graduate.

"Hampden-Sydney College requires either the SAT or ACT standardized test with essay."

SELECTIVITY

Admissions Rating	86
# of applicants	3,683
% of applicants accepted	55
% of acceptees attending	15
# of early decision applicants	108
% accepted early decision	35

FRESHMAN PROFILE

Range SAT Critical Reading	500–620
Range SAT Math	500–610
Range SAT Writing	460–580
Range ACT Composite	21–27
Minimum paper TOEFL	600
Minimum internet-based TOEFL	100
Average HS GPA	3.4
% graduated top 10% of class	12
% graduated top 25% of class	37
% graduated top 50% of class	77

DEADLINES

Early decision	
Deadline	11/15
Notification	12/15
Early action	
Deadline	1/15
Notification	2/15
Regular	
Deadline	3/1
Notification	4/15
Nonfall registration?	Yes

APPLICANTS ALSO LOOK AT AND OFTEN PREFER
Virginia Tech; University of Virginia

AND SOMETIMES PREFER
James Madison University

AND RARELY PREFER
Randolph-Macon College

FINANCIAL FACTS

Financial Aid Rating	84
Annual tuition	$39,920
Room and board	$13,060
Required fees	$1,810
Books and supplies	$1,000
Average frosh need-based scholarship	$28,626
Average UG need-based scholarship	$28,086
% needy frosh rec. need-based scholarship or grant aid	100
% needy UG rec. need-based scholarship or grant aid	100
% needy frosh rec. non-need-based scholarship or grant aid	16
% needy UG rec. non-need-based scholarship or grant aid	14
% needy frosh rec. need-based self-help aid	83
% needy UG rec. need-based self-help aid	80
% frosh rec. any financial aid	100
% UG rec. any financial aid	99
% UG borrow to pay for school	65
Average cumulative indebtedness	$33,153
% frosh need fully met	20
% ugrads need fully met	18
Average % of frosh need met	77
Average % of ugrad need met	78

HAMPTON UNIVERSITY

OFFICE OF ADMISSIONS, HAMPTON, VA 23668 • ADMISSIONS: 757-727-5328 • FAX: 757-727-5095

CAMPUS LIFE

Quality of Life Rating	80
Fire Safety Rating	72
Green Rating	60*
Type of school	Private
Affiliation	No Affiliation
Environment	City

STUDENTS

Total undergrad enrollment	3,419
% male/female	34/66
% from out of state	73
% frosh from public high school	90
% frosh live on campus	98
% ugrads live on campus	62
# of fraternities (% ugrad men join)	6 (5)
# of sororities (% ugrad women join)	3 (4)
% African American	94
% Asian	<1
% Caucasian	2
% Hispanic	1
% Native American	<1
% Pacific Islander	0
% Two or more races	0
% Race and/or ethnicity unknown	0
% international	2
# of countries represented	33

SURVEY SAYS...

Lots of liberal students
Students are happy
Students are very religious
Campus newspaper is popular

ACADEMICS

Academic Rating	75
% students returning for sophomore year	77
% students graduating within 4 years	39
% students graduating within 6 years	60
Calendar	Semester
Student/faculty ratio	12:1
Profs interesting rating	70
Profs accessible rating	66

Most classes have fewer than 10 students.

MOST POPULAR MAJORS

Psychology; Business Administration and Management; Biology

STUDENTS Say ". . ." Academics

Virginia's Hampton University is one of the world's top historically black universities, offering students a progressive education in business, the sciences, and the liberal arts. This "school of tradition, family values, and excellent education" is well-known for its focus on STEM programs and its five-year MBA program, and proudly forces its students to be at the top of their game. "My school exudes and strives for a standard of excellence in any and every aspect," says a junior political science major of the oft-quoted motto "The Standard of Excellence."

Professors "are at the top of their field," and the majority of the faculty members provide office hours "where students can have more one-to-one assistance" on lecture topics on which they may need more clarification. "My professors have not only been teachers in the classroom, but in my personal life as well," says a student. "I have been taught how to use the communication and research skills that I have obtained outside of the classroom." In addition, the university provides "a plethora of outside resources" such as paid internships, undergraduate research, and job shadowing opportunities.

The "historically rich" institution is "supportive of its legacy being upheld by all that pass through" while at the same time making individuals aware of their own legacies and "supporting them in their professional and academic endeavors through all available resources." Alumni connections abound in such an environment, and there are plenty of "excellent career planning tools," internships, and careers available to students "during and after their tenure at Hampton." There is "an immense amount of clout and history behind Hampton University's walls." Though the campus is undoubtedly "beautiful" (and sits right on the water), many agree that some of the facilities (especially the dorms) could use renovation. In recent years, three new dorms were constructed and historic halls were modernized.

Life

Hampton does an excellent job of "blending past traditions with modern times," and Homecoming and Spring Fest are two important events for Hampton. On the "closed" campus, there is an "unlimited [number] of activities for students to participate in." During Organization Week, the student center has a two hour "12–2" period, during which "students are able to be social during the day," and many students love to "catch a Friday movie" night there as well, or hang out with friends in the new waterfront dining hall.

Hampton is small and "not a college town." and since "the University is really the only thing around," having a car is useful. Monday through Friday campus life is "mostly academic and extracurricular," with students mostly focused on class and the various clubs that they may be involved in. On the weekends students attend on and off campus parties, or go to "kickbacks," which are "a more low key version of a party." "Student life is lacking as far as dorm life," so many students "often interact with the students from NSU, ODU, and William & Mary." For the most part, "everyone on campus has the same mindset, a unanimous goal, and that's to graduate and strive for a successful life."

Student Body

The typical student here is an African-American "go-getter" who is "trying to make something of themselves." He or she is "poised, considerate, and self-sufficient" and "knows how to act and dress in the appropriate setting and time." "Hampton students have a certain attitude about themselves, you can always tell a Hamptonian. Once you have been Hamptonized, there is no going back," explains one student cryptically. This "driven," "hardworking" crowd gets along fairly well, and there are no issues of isolation "unless one chooses that lifestyle." Students are almost without fail "outgoing and involved in many organizations within the school and the community."

FINANCIAL AID: 757-727-5332 • E-MAIL: ADMIT@HAMPTONU.EDU • WEBSITE: WWW.HAMPTONU.EDU

THE PRINCETON REVIEW SAYS

Admissions

Very important factors considered include: rigor of secondary school record, academic GPA, application essay, character/personal qualities. *Important factors considered include:* class rank, recommendation(s). *Other factors considered include:* extracurricular activities, talent/ability, alumni/ae relation, volunteer work, work experience, level of applicant's interest. SAT or ACT required for some. ACT with or without writing accepted. SAT with or without Essay component accepted. TOEFL required of all international applicants. High school diploma is required and GED is accepted. *Academic units required:* 4 English, 3 math, 2 science, 2 science labs, 2 social studies, 6 academic electives. *Academic units recommended:* 2 foreign language.

Financial Aid

Students should submit: FAFSA. Priority filing deadline is 2/15. The Princeton Review suggests that all financial aid forms be submitted as soon as possible after October 1. *Need-based scholarships/grants offered:* Federal Pell, FSEOG, State scholarships/grants, Private scholarships, College/university scholarship or grant aid from institutional funds, United Negro College Fund. *Loan aid offered:* Direct Subsidized Stafford Loans, Direct Unsubsidized Stafford Loans, Direct PLUS loans, Federal Perkins Loans, Federal Nursing Loans. Applicants will be notified of awards on a rolling basis beginning 4/15. Federal Work-Study Program available.

The Inside Word

Hampton University allows for early action admissions, meaning that students can receive an early decision without having to commit to attending the school. Around a quarter of HU's applicant pool pursues this option. You would be wise to follow suit; the school is bound to be more lenient early in the process than later, when it has already admitted many qualified students.

THE SCHOOL SAYS "..."

From the Admissions Office

"Hampton attempts to provide the environment and structures most conducive to the intellectual, emotional, and aesthetic enlargement of the lives of its members. The university gives priority to effective teaching and scholarly research while placing the student at the center of its planning. Hampton will ask you to look inwardly at your own history and culture and examine your relationship to the aspirations and development of the world."

SELECTIVITY

Admissions Rating	83
# of applicants	10,258
% of applicants accepted	69
% of acceptees attending	13

FRESHMAN PROFILE

Range SAT Critical Reading	470–540
Range SAT Math	470–550
Range ACT Composite	19–24
Minimum paper TOEFL	525
Average HS GPA	3.2
% graduated top 10% of class	20
% graduated top 25% of class	45
% graduated top 50% of class	90

DEADLINES

Early action	
Deadline	11/1
Notification	12/15
Regular	
Priority	3/1
Nonfall registration?	Yes

APPLICANTS ALSO LOOK AT AND OFTEN PREFER
Spelman College

AND SOMETIMES PREFER
Howard University; University of Maryland–College Park; Virginia Tech

FINANCIAL FACTS

Financial Aid Rating	80
Annual tuition	$20,526
Room and board	$10,176
Required fees	$2,586
Books and supplies	$1,100
Average frosh need-based scholarship	$5,138
Average UG need-based scholarship	$5,120
% needy frosh rec. need-based scholarship or grant aid	95
% needy UG rec. need-based scholarship or grant aid	92
% needy frosh rec. non-need-based scholarship or grant aid	83
% needy UG rec. non-need-based scholarship or grant aid	53
% needy frosh rec. need-based self-help aid	81
% needy UG rec. need-based self-help aid	78
% frosh rec. any financial aid	39
% UG rec. any financial aid	43
% UG borrow to pay for school	77
Average cumulative indebtedness	$32,463
% frosh need fully met	37
% ugrads need fully met	54
Average % of frosh need met	39
Average % of ugrad need met	43

HANOVER COLLEGE

PO Box 108, HANOVER, IN 47243-0108 • ADMISSIONS: 800-213-2178 • FAX: 812-866-7098

STUDENTS SAY "..."

Academics

Hanover College is a school that is brimming with opportunity. And with its "beautiful" campus and emphasis on "gaining real-life skills and making life-long connections," it's easy to understand why students are drawn here. The vast majority of classes at Hanover are "small and discussion based," and many also place "a heavy focus on writing." While the academics can be challenging, students eagerly report that "many of the harder classes have tutors for that specific class." Additionally, the Learning Center is always "willing to go over things with you, edit papers and more." Importantly, it's evident that Hanover professors "love what they teach...and that excitement often carries over to the student." Indeed, they excel at "bring[ing] the material to life...and easily keep the attention of the class." Just as essential, Hanover professors are also known to be "caring and down to earth" and "devoted to their students." And, as this ecstatic art history major concludes, "Most of the professors on staff are part of the best people you will ever meet in life."

Life

While some undergrads grumble that "life at Hanover is pretty slow," others steadfastly argue that "there are SO many things [with which] to be involved." For starters, students can participate in "over sixty organizations" including "Adopt A Grandparent, Circle K Community Service, Best Buddies, and so many more." Additionally, individuals who enjoy the arts will be delighted to hear that both "the theater department and the improv group...never disappoint [and] the choir and band concerts [are] always very enjoyable [as well]." For those that are more athletically inclined, we're told that "when it's warm out, students go hiking, play wiffleball, or...sand volleyball." Many undergrads also gravitate to the Student Activities Center which offers "game tables, [a] theater room, televisions [and] study spots." And, in the evenings, "chances are some club always has something planned—be it a movie showing [or] a poetry night!" Hanover also has a relatively robust party scene. Indeed, undergrads inform us that "Greek life is big on... campus." And while there "are only four frats...they are a [major] part of [the] social life." Finally, when students are looking for a break from the campus routine, they often head to nearby Madison or Louisville, which is a mere "forty-minute drive [away]" and the closest major city.

Student Body

Hanover is home to a "small, pretty laid back and surprising[ly] interesting community." Indeed, while undergrads here admit that ethnic diversity "is still an issue," they happily point out that you'll find a wide array of personality types. Of course, the "majority of the students are committed to their academics and [strive to find] a balance between work and play." Many Hanover undergrads "are also extremely passionate about the things in which they invest their time, whatever that may be, and encourage that passion in others." It's important to note that the college's small size does make it "[easy] for cliques...to form." However, we're assured "it is also quite easy to break into the cliques if you are really interested in hanging out with certain groups of people." This social ease can be attributed to the fact that Hanover features some of the "friendliest individuals that Indiana has to offer." In fact, you are virtually guaranteed "to see a smiling face or to get a hello anywhere you walk on campus, whether it be from a fellow student or a faculty member." As one satisfied economics major sums up, "We are all about making everyone feel welcome and making Hanover College home."

FINANCIAL AID: 812-866-7029 • E-MAIL: ADMISSION@HANOVER.EDU • WEBSITE: WWW.HANOVER.EDU

THE PRINCETON REVIEW SAYS

Admissions

Very important factors considered include: rigor of secondary school record, class rank, academic GPA. *Important factors considered include:* standardized test scores, recommendation(s), talent/ability. *Other factors considered include:* application essay, interview, extracurricular activities, character/personal qualities, first generation, alumni/ae relation, geographical residence, state residency, racial/ethnic status, volunteer work, work experience, level of applicant's interest. SAT or ACT required. ACT with Writing recommended. TOEFL required of all international applicants. High school diploma is required and GED is not accepted. *Academic units required:* 4 English, 3 math, 3 science, 2 science labs, 2 foreign language, 2 social studies, 2 history, 2 academic electives. *Academic units recommended:* 4 English, 4 math, 4 science, 3 science labs, 4 foreign language, 3 social studies, 3 history, 3 academic electives, 1 visual/performing arts.

Financial Aid

Students should submit: FAFSA. Regular filing deadline is 3/1. The Princeton Review suggests that all financial aid forms be submitted as soon as possible after October 1. *Need-based scholarships/grants offered:* Federal Pell, FSEOG, State scholarships/grants, Private scholarships, College/university scholarship or grant aid from institutional funds. *Loan aid offered:* Direct Subsidized Stafford Loans, Direct Unsubsidized Stafford Loans, Direct PLUS loans, College/university loans from institutional funds. Applicants will be notified of awards on or about 3/1. Federal Work-Study Program available. Institutional employment available.

The Inside Word

Similar to many liberal arts college, Hanover takes a holistic approach to the admissions process. Certainly, the school closely evaluates your high school curriculum as well as your GPA. Standardized test scores are also considered, though they hold less weight than your transcript. Beyond academics, admissions officers look at your extracurricular participation and community activities. Letters of recommendation and a writing sample will also be important. Further, expect Hanover to assess the strength of your high school. And, lastly, ethnic, cultural and geographic diversity will likely come into play.

THE SCHOOL SAYS "..."

From the Admissions Office

"Since our founding in 1827, we have been committed to providing students with a personal, rigorous, and well-rounded liberal arts education. Part of the college search process is finding that school that proves to be a good match. For those who see the value in an education that demands engagement and who see college as a time for exploration and involvement, they will find that Hanover is all they could hope for and more.

"The admission process serves as an introduction to the personal education that students receive at Hanover College. Every application is considered individually with emphasis being placed on a student's high school curriculum and the student's academic performance in that curriculum. While we realize that not every high school has the same course offerings, we expect students to have selected a college preparatory curriculum as challenging as possible within his or her particular high school or academic setting.

"Hanover College accepts both the SAT and ACT. Students taking the ACT are required to take the optional writing section. For students who have taken one or both of the tests multiple times, we will use the highest sub scores when calculating a student's score on either test for admission and scholarship purposes."

SELECTIVITY

Admissions Rating	83
# of applicants	3,355
% of applicants accepted	61
% of acceptees attending	15
# offered a place on the wait list	0

FRESHMAN PROFILE

Range SAT Critical Reading	480–610
Range SAT Math	470–610
Range SAT Writing	460–570
Range ACT Composite	22–27
Minimum paper TOEFL	550
Minimum internet-based TOEFL	80
Average HS GPA	3.6
% graduated top 10% of class	20
% graduated top 25% of class	54
% graduated top 50% of class	92

DEADLINES

Early action	
Deadline	12/1
Notification	12/20
Regular	
Nonfall registration?	Yes

APPLICANTS ALSO LOOK AT AND OFTEN PREFER

Butler University; DePauw University

AND SOMETIMES PREFER

Indiana University Bloomington; Miami University; Centre College; Wittenberg University; Wabash College

AND RARELY PREFER

Kenyon College; Earlham College

FINANCIAL FACTS

Financial Aid Rating	85
Annual tuition	$33,744
Room and board	$10,452
Required fees	$770
Books and supplies	$1,200
Average frosh need-based scholarship	$25,014
Average UG need-based scholarship	$23,479
% needy frosh rec. need-based scholarship or grant aid	100
% needy UG rec. need-based scholarship or grant aid	100
% needy frosh rec. non-need-based scholarship or grant aid	25
% needy UG rec. non-need-based scholarship or grant aid	17
% needy frosh rec. need-based self-help aid	74
% needy UG rec. need-based self-help aid	82
% frosh rec. any financial aid	100
% UG rec. any financial aid	100
% UG borrow to pay for school	76
Average cumulative indebtedness	$28,526
% frosh need fully met	31
% ugrads need fully met	24
Average % of frosh need met	82
Average % of ugrad need met	80

HARVARD COLLEGE

86 BRATTLE STREET, CAMBRIDGE, MA 02138 • ADMISSIONS: 617-495-1551 • FAX: 617-495-8821

STUDENTS SAY "..."

Academics

Bully to those who get the chance to be a part of the "dynamic universe" that is Harvard College, who find themselves in an "amazing irresistible hell" that pushes them to the extremes of their intellect and ability. Unsurprisingly, the legendarily "very difficult" school attracts some of the country's most promising youth, who rise to the occasion in almost every aspect of their life on campus, not just the classroom. Harvard's recent financial aid enhancements have increased the number of applications by a landslide, but even after getting past the admissions hurdle, "people find ways to make everything (especially clubs and even partying) competitive." Happily, this streak is more of a "latent competition," as there are more than enough opportunity and resources to go around. "It is impossible to 'get the most out of Harvard' because Harvard offers so much," says one student. Much like the students, the professors at this "beautiful, fun, historic, and academically alive place" in Cambridge, Massachusetts, are among "the brightest minds in the world," and "the level of achievement is unbelievable." Some of the larger introductory classes are taught by teaching fellows (TFs), meaning "you do have to go to office hours to get to know your big lecture class professors on a personal level," but once your figurative underclass dues are paid, the access to "incredible" and "every so often, fantastic" professors is perfectly within reach. Top it off with Grade-A internship and employment opportunities, a good old alumni network, and a crimson pedigree for your résumé, and you may just end up agreeing with the Harvard student who refers to his experience as "rewarding beyond anything else I've ever done." Though the administration can be "waaaaay out of touch with students" and "reticent to change," it at least "does a good job of watching over its freshmen through extensive advising programs," and students all have faith that their best interests are being kept in mind.

Life

Cambridge and Boston are nothing if not college towns, and students never lack for options if they just want to "go see a play, a concert, hit up a party, go to the movies, or dine out." Students quickly learn when to hit the books and when to hit the streets, so "studying becomes routine." "There is a vibrant social atmosphere on campus and between students and the local community." As one student puts it, "Boredom does not exist here. There are endless opportunities and endless passionate people to do them with." "Basically, if you want to do it, Harvard either has it or has the money to give to you so you can start it." "Partying in a more traditional setting is available at Harvard, but is not a prevalent aspect of the school's social life. While there is a pub on campus that provides an excellent venue to hang out and play a game of pool or have a reasonably priced drink," and parties happen on weekends at Harvard's finals clubs, there's no real pressure for students to partake if they're not interested.

Student Body

Much as you might expect, ambition and achievement are the ties that bind at Harvard, and "Everyone is great for one reason or another," says a student. Most every student can be summed up with the same statement: "Works really hard. Doesn't sleep. Involved in a million extracurriculars." Diversity is found in all aspects of life, from ethnicities to religion to ideology, and "there is a lot of tolerance and acceptance at Harvard for individuals of all races, religions, socioeconomic backgrounds, life styles, etc."

FINANCIAL AID: 617-495-1581 • E-MAIL: COLLEGE@FAS.HARVARD.EDU • WEBSITE: WWW.COLLEGE.HARVARD.EDU

THE PRINCETON REVIEW SAYS

Admissions

Very important factors considered include: Important factors considered include: Other factors considered include: rigor of secondary school record, academic GPA, standardized test scores, application essay, recommendation(s), interview, extracurricular activities, talent/ability, character/personal qualities, first generation, alumni/ae relation, geographical residence, racial/ethnic status, volunteer work, work experience. SAT or ACT required. ACT with Writing required. High school diploma or equivalent is not required. *Academic units recommended:* 4 English, 4 math, 4 science, 4 foreign language, 3 social studies, 2 history.

Financial Aid

Students should submit: FAFSA, CSS/Financial Aid PROFILE, Noncustodial PROFILE, Business/Farm Supplement. Regular filing deadline is 3/1. The Princeton Review suggests that all financial aid forms be submitted as soon as possible after October 1. *Need-based scholarships/grants offered:* Federal Pell, FSEOG, State scholarships/grants, Private scholarships, College/university scholarship or grant aid from institutional funds. *Loan aid offered:* Direct Subsidized Stafford Loans, Direct Unsubsidized Stafford Loans, Direct PLUS loans, Federal Perkins Loans, State Loans, College/university loans from institutional funds. Applicants will be notified of awards on or about 4/1. Federal Work-Study Program available. Institutional employment available.

The Inside Word

It just doesn't get any tougher than this. Candidates to Harvard face dual obstacles—an awe-inspiring applicant pool and, as a result, admissions standards that defy explanation in quantifiable terms. Harvard denies admission to the vast majority, and virtually all of them are top students. It all boils down to splitting hairs, which is quite hard to explain and even harder for candidates to understand. Rather than being as detailed and direct as possible about the selection process and criteria, Harvard keeps things close to the vest—before, during, and after. They even refuse to admit that being from lesser populated states like South Dakota is an advantage. Thus the admissions process does more to intimidate candidates than to empower them. Moving to a common application seemed to be a small step in the right direction, but with the current explosion of early decision applicants and a super-high yield of enrollees, things aren't likely to change dramatically.

THE SCHOOL SAYS "..."

From the Admissions Office

"The admissions committee looks for energy, ambition, and the capacity to make the most of opportunities. Academic ability and preparation are important, and so is intellectual curiosity—but many of the strongest applicants have significant, non-academic interests and accomplishments, as well. There is no formula for admission, and applicants are considered carefully, with attention to future promise.

"Freshman applicants may submit the SAT. The ACT with writing component is also accepted. All students must also submit three SAT Subject Tests of their choosing."

SELECTIVITY

Admissions Rating	99
# of applicants	37,307
% of applicants accepted	6
% of acceptees attending	80
# offered a place on the wait list	0

FRESHMAN PROFILE

Range SAT Critical Reading	700–800
Range SAT Math	700–800
Range SAT Writing	710–790
Range ACT Composite	32–35
Average HS GPA	4.1
% graduated top 10% of class	95
% graduated top 25% of class	99
% graduated top 50% of class	100

DEADLINES

Early action	
Deadline	11/1
Notification	12/16
Regular	
Deadline	1/1
Notification	4/1
Nonfall registration?	No

FINANCIAL FACTS

Financial Aid Rating	96
Annual tuition	$41,632
Room and board	$15,381
Required fees	$3,646
Books and supplies	$1,000
Average frosh need-based scholarship	$48,671
Average UG need-based scholarship	$46,409
% needy frosh rec. need-based scholarship or grant aid	100
% needy UG rec. need-based scholarship or grant aid	99
% needy frosh rec. non-need-based scholarship or grant aid	0
% needy UG rec. non-need-based scholarship or grant aid	0
% needy frosh rec. need-based self-help aid	71
% needy UG rec. need-based self-help aid	85
% frosh rec. any financial aid	54
% UG rec. any financial aid	56
% UG borrow to pay for school	24
Average cumulative indebtedness	$16,723
% frosh need fully met	100
% ugrads need fully met	100
Average % of frosh need met	100
Average % of ugrad need met	100

HARVEY MUDD COLLEGE

301 Platt Boulevard, Claremont, CA 91711-5990 • Admissions: 909-621-8011 • Fax: 909-607-7046

CAMPUS LIFE
Quality of Life Rating	91
Fire Safety Rating	84
Green Rating	60*
Type of school	Private
Affiliation	No Affiliation
Environment	Town

STUDENTS
Total undergrad enrollment	804
% male/female	54/46
% from out of state	58
% frosh from public high school	59
% frosh live on campus	100
% ugrads live on campus	99
% African American	2
% Asian	21
% Caucasian	44
% Hispanic	10
% Native American	<1
% Pacific Islander	0
% Two or more races	6
% Race and/or ethnicity unknown	4
% international	12

SURVEY SAYS...
Lots of liberal students
Students always studying
Students are happy
Classroom facilities are great
Internships are widely available
School is well run
No one cheats
Students are friendly
Students aren't religious
Great food on campus
Easy to get around campus

ACADEMICS
Academic Rating	97
% students graduating within 4 years	90
% students graduating within 6 years	94
Calendar	Semester
Student/faculty ratio	8:1
Profs interesting rating	98
Profs accessible rating	97

Most classes have 10–19 students.
Most lab/discussion sessions have 10–19 students.

MOST POPULAR MAJORS
Engineering; Computer and Information Sciences; Mathematics

STUDENTS SAY "..."

Academics

Harvey Mudd College, according to its mission statement, "seeks to educate engineers, scientists, and mathematicians well versed in all of these areas and in the humanities and the social sciences so that they may assume leadership in their fields with a clear understanding of the impact of their work on society." As a result, its students "really understand their impact on both their global and campus communities." Breadth is also instilled in a Harvey Mudd education through its membership in the "Claremont Colleges," a five-college consortium that includes Pomona and Claremont McKenna, and because of this, its "students are more well-rounded than most in the sciences and get to pursue their passions outside of the STEM fields." Students also praise the "broad core curriculum at Harvey Mudd," which "produces scientists who can rise to meet interdisciplinary challenges within the sciences" and facilitates "great post-grad opportunities." Classes are hard but rewarding: "The brutal work fosters an extremely collaborative environment where people focus not on the grade they get but the learning behind it." "Academics are perfect. Could not ask for more rigorous and interesting learning." HMC undergrads demonstrate a "commitment to" Harvey Mudd's "honor code," which requires students "to conduct themselves with honesty and integrity both personally and academically and to respect the rights of others." This ethic, as well as support systems like "the proctor mentor system in the dorms," which positions RAs to act as resources to students "without all of the policing," creates a "tight community" on campus. "There is no segregation based on class year, major, race, academic ability, dorm or anything. Everyone is respectful, smart, aware, supportive, and unique." Professors are almost universally reported to be "incredible," "truly dedicated to undergraduate teaching," and "always willing to spend hours outside of class answering questions." HMC's small classes and lack of graduate programs focuses faculty attention on undergrads: "My only 'large' class as a freshman is an intro to CS Class of 100 students and by the fifth day the professor knew all 100 names." Overall, "the work at HMC is very challenging, but I have had the best support system; from the Academic Excellence tutors providing help for all required core classes to the professors who are readily accessible and enthusiastic helpers."

Life

Students agree that Harvey Mudd enables tremendous growth, which isn't always easy: "You feel really smart before Mudd, you feel really stupid during Mudd, and after Mudd you feel like a genius." Socially speaking, "conversations at dinner are probably really weird and nerdy from an outsiders point of view," and "people care about ...lots of other serious issues along with more frivolous ones." Many appreciate that "campus-wide parties are funded by the college, ensuring that they are safe and well-funded," and these include "a foam party, where a dorm courtyard is filled with soap foam," and "a holiday party where (literally) tons of snow are trucked in." There's plenty to do on campus, but "Claremont Village is within a 20-minute walk," and "it takes about an hour and a half to get to LA's Union Station from Mudd, and downtown LA and Little Tokyo are both accessible from there." "A lot of students do drink, but there is honestly never any pressure. I don't drink at all and I have never felt any pressure to do anything I wasn't comfortable with." One student sums up the HMC life this way: "Work really, really hard, play hard."

Student Body

"Harvey Mudd has a strong community of talented students that build each other up." Many HMC students offer similar praise for the college's "small, tight knit community in which everyone looks after one another." The "typical student is friendly, outgoing, and passionate about their (sometimes slightly weird) interests," and "it's really easy to form close friendships, whether in your dorm or through study groups." "Everyone at the school is extremely enthusiastic about learning," and the college's culture promotes lots of intellectual bonding amongst "nerds, but the kind that can hold conversations." "Most people are top of their class from high school, so freshman year, everyone is a bit cocky (but Mudd humbles you really quickly)." Undergrads value that "the honor code works very well, and students are pretty much always eager to help one another."

FINANCIAL AID: 909-621-8055 • E-MAIL: ADMISSION@HMC.EDU • WEBSITE: WWW.HMC.EDU

THE PRINCETON REVIEW SAYS

Admissions

Very important factors considered include: rigor of secondary school record, academic GPA, application essay, recommendation(s), talent/ability, character/personal qualities. *Important factors considered include:* class rank, standardized test scores, extracurricular activities, first generation. *Other factors considered include:* interview, alumni/ae relation, geographical residence, state residency, racial/ethnic status, volunteer work, work experience, level of applicant's interest. SAT or ACT required; SAT Subject Tests required. TOEFL required of all international applicants. High school diploma or equivalent is not required. *Academic units required:* 4 English, 4 math, 3 science, 1 history. *Academic units recommended:* 4 English, 4 math, 4 science, 2 science labs, 2 foreign language, 2 social studies, 2 history, 2 academic electives.

Financial Aid

Students should submit: FAFSA, CSS/Financial Aid PROFILE, State aid form, Noncustodial PROFILE, Business/Farm Supplement. Regular filing deadline is 2/1. The Princeton Review suggests that all financial aid forms be submitted as soon as possible after October 1. *Need-based scholarships/grants offered:* Federal Pell, FSEOG, State scholarships/grants, Private scholarships, College/university scholarship or grant aid from institutional funds. *Loan aid offered:* Direct Subsidized Stafford Loans, Direct Unsubsidized Stafford Loans, Direct PLUS loans, Federal Perkins Loans, College/university loans from institutional funds. Applicants will be notified of awards on or about 4/1. Federal Work-Study Program available. Institutional employment available.

The Inside Word

Harvey Mudd is as rigorous in admissions as it is in its education, so serious applicants are well advised to demonstrate big chops in their high school STEM courseload, without sacrificing attention to humanities and extracurriculars. Applicants should carefully review HMC's eligibility requirements for high school transcripts, as well as its standardized testing requirements, and remember that the college is competitive enough that admission is no guarantee even for highly qualified applicants.

THE SCHOOL SAYS "..."

From the Admissions Office

"HMC is a wonderfully unusual combination of a liberal arts college and research institute. Our students love math and science, want to live and learn deeply in an intimate climate of cooperation and trust, thrive on innovation and discovery, and enjoy rigorous coursework in arts, humanities, and social sciences in addition to a technical curriculum. At least a year of research or our innovative clinic program is required (or guaranteed, if you prefer). The resources at HMC are astounding, and all are accessible to undergraduates: labs, shops, work areas, and most importantly, faculty. You'll find the professors and student body stimulating and supportive—they'll challenge you inside and outside the classroom, and share your love of learning and collaboration. They'll also share your love of fun and sense of humor (math jokes and all). In addition, we benefit from the unique consortium that is the Claremont Colleges.

"In the final analysis, our graduates are prepared well for whatever their next steps will be. They can see relationships between disparate fields of study and investigation, are resourceful, know how to work in teams, and are able to articulate their ideas to both lay-people and specialized experts. A wide range of companies are eager to hire our seniors, and HMC sends the highest proportion of graduates to Ph.D. programs of any undergraduate college in the country."

SELECTIVITY

Admissions Rating	98
# of applicants	3,678
% of applicants accepted	14
% of acceptees attending	37
# offered a place on the wait list	596
% accepting a place on wait list	67
% admitted from wait list	4
# of early decision applicants	377
% accepted early decision	17

FRESHMAN PROFILE

Range SAT Critical Reading	678–770
Range SAT Math	740–800
Range SAT Writing	680–760
Range ACT Composite	33–35
Minimum paper TOEFL	600
Minimum internet-based TOEFL	100
% graduated top 10% of class	88
% graduated top 25% of class	99
% graduated top 50% of class	100

DEADLINES

Early decision	
Deadline	11/15
Notification	12/15
Regular	
Deadline	1/1
Notification	4/1
Nonfall registration?	No

APPLICANTS ALSO LOOK AT AND OFTEN PREFER

California Institute of Technology; Massachusetts Institute of Technology

AND SOMETIMES PREFER

Cornell University; University of California—Berkeley

AND RARELY PREFER

University of California—San Diego

FINANCIAL FACTS

Financial Aid Rating	96
Annual tuition	$48,315
Room and board	$15,833
Required fees	$279
Books and supplies	$800
Average frosh need-based scholarship	$40,188
Average UG need-based scholarship	$35,637
% needy frosh rec. need-based scholarship or grant aid	98
% needy UG rec. need-based scholarship or grant aid	97
% needy frosh rec. non-need-based scholarship or grant aid	21
% needy UG rec. non-need-based scholarship or grant aid	12
% needy frosh rec. need-based self-help aid	55
% needy UG rec. need-based self-help aid	72
% frosh rec. any financial aid	84
% UG rec. any financial aid	76
% frosh need fully met	100
% ugrads need fully met	100
Average % of frosh need met	100
Average % of ugrad need met	100

HAVERFORD COLLEGE

370 WEST LANCASTER AVENUE, HAVERFORD, PA 19041 • ADMISSIONS: 610-896-1350 • FAX: 610-896-1338

STUDENTS SAY "..."

Academics

Founded in 1833, Haverford College in Pennsylvania is "small, but exceptionally vibrant and engaging," offering a "solid academic experience" under one of the country's oldest and most revered honor codes. Though founded by Quakers, the school is nonsectarian, but the community aspect of its founders remains, creating what one student calls "a challenging, interesting environment with the best people I know." The teacher education program is one of the most notable, but there is a strong emphasis on writing and a "breadth of amazing programs" for everyone else. The real love affair is with Haverford's "awesome, invested" professors, who "lead a group of idealistic students to point—but never force—us into a better way of thinking." They want to put in the time to get to know you, and the small size of the school "allows for plenty of opportunities for collaborating with faculty and staff and building a relationship." "You are more than just a face in a classroom of many; you are a unique person that has something to offer," says a student. "My 'big intro lecture course' has forty-one students," says another. "My professor still knows me by name, and we have long conversations when we pass on Founder's Green." The school's learning environment stresses "engaging in hard and honest conversations with your peers," and "students have a lot of power" through their roles in the administration of the college. "I love the amount of independence and autonomy [the school] gives to its students," says a student. Because of the kind of student this attracts, "we wind up with a really conscientious student body invested in the school." The resources available to students here are incredible, as well. You can get "credit for research" (there is plenty of research here in every department), and if you want to go off campus for research, "you can get funding for that as well."

Life

The culture of "trust, concern, and respect" created by the Honor Code carries over into the rest of this "awesome, at times idiosyncratic, place where community thrives and cliques are very loose if existent at all." "The honor code unifies everyone." "Being able to take an exam in your own room, sitting relaxed on your bed because your professor trusts you not to look at your books is one of the luxuries of being here," says a student. People study hard here, but they take a break over the weekend at a party or two "before cracking the books again. Athletics are also "really important" for much of the student body—most here are athletic, even if it's not at a varsity level—and some of the male sports teams "function like fraternities" (which do not exist at HC). Because it's a small place, "sometimes it feels like everyone knows your business," but everyone is so insanely nice that "the social scene is great" and the only thing you'll hear complaints about is the food. Students govern themselves and the happenings at the school through the "Plenaries" that happen twice a year, when the majority of the student body must be present. New York and Philadelphia are both easily accessible by train, and "Suburban Square (the local outdoor shopping center) is a great place to hang out, get coffee, or even go shopping."

Student Body

Everyone is "passionate," "people are always up for intellectual discussion," and "everyone works very hard." Students here were all motivated enough to get in and "want to succeed for themselves and not to appease others." Students describe other students as having "hearts of gold and giant brains that they put to use to change the world for the better." "It's a small school full of nice kids—not naive (well, sometimes naive), just genuinely compassionate and interested in other people, whether or not that's 'cool,'" says a student. Though all are bound by "intellectual passion and interests outside of academics," diversity otherwise on campus "lacks a little." Still, "the great thing about Haverford is that, although we have a variety of students from all different social circles, everyone is a touch awkward." This is a fact that the "nerdy and ridiculously friendly" students embrace. "I feel like I could potentially become friends with anyone on campus," says a student.

FINANCIAL AID: 610-896-1350 • E-MAIL: ADMISSION@HAVERFORD.EDU • WEBSITE: WWW.HAVERFORD.EDU

THE PRINCETON REVIEW SAYS

Admissions

Very important factors considered include: rigor of secondary school record, academic GPA, application essay, recommendation(s), extracurricular activities, character/personal qualities. *Important factors considered include:* class rank, standardized test scores, talent/ability, volunteer work, work experience. *Other factors considered include:* interview, first generation, alumni/ae relation, geographical residence, racial/ethnic status, level of applicant's interest. ACT with or without writing accepted. SAT with or without Essay component accepted. TOEFL required of all international applicants. High school diploma or equivalent is not required. *Academic units recommended:* 4 English, 3 math, 3 science, 3 science labs, 3 foreign language, 3 social studies.

Financial Aid

Students should submit: FAFSA, CSS/Financial Aid PROFILE, Noncustodial PROFILE, Business/Farm Supplement. Regular filing deadline is 2/1. The Princeton Review suggests that all financial aid forms be submitted as soon as possible after October 1. *Need-based scholarships/grants offered:* Federal Pell, FSEOG, State scholarships/grants, College/university scholarship or grant aid from institutional funds. *Loan aid offered:* Direct Subsidized Stafford Loans, Direct Unsubsidized Stafford Loans, Direct PLUS Loans. Applicants will be notified of awards on or about 4/1. Federal Work-Study Program available. Institutional employment available.

The Inside Word

Haverford's applicant pool is an impressive and competitive lot (only about one-quarter of applicants get in). Intellectual curiosity is paramount, and applicants are expected to keep a demanding academic schedule in high school. Additionally, the college places a high value on ethics, as evidenced by its honor code. The admissions office seeks students who will reflect and promote Haverford's ideals.

THE SCHOOL SAYS "..."

From the Admissions Office

"Haverford strives to be a college in which integrity, honesty, and concern for others are dominant forces. The college does not have many formal rules; rather, it offers an opportunity for students to govern their affairs and conduct themselves with respect and concern for others. Each student is expected to adhere to the honor code as it is adopted each year by the Students' Association. Haverford's Quaker roots show most clearly in the relationship of faculty and students, in the emphasis on integrity, in the interaction of the individual and the community, and through the college's concern for the uses to which its students put their expanding knowledge. Haverford's 1,200 students represent a wide diversity of interests, backgrounds, and talents. They come from public, parochial, and independent schools across the United States, Puerto Rico, and thirty-nine foreign countries. Students of color are an important part of the Haverford community.

"Haverford College meets 100 percent of the demonstrated need of all admitted students and seeks to minimize or eliminate debt for our graduates. Students with family income below $60,000 will not have any loans included in their financial aid package; students with family income above this level will have loans ranging from $1,500 to $3,000 per year. And our need-blind admission policy means that an application for financial aid has no bearing on the admission decision for U.S. citizens and eligible non-citizens."

SELECTIVITY

Admissions Rating	98
# of applicants	3,467
% of applicants accepted	25
% of acceptees attending	41
# offered a place on the wait list	883
% accepting a place on wait list	40
% admitted from wait list	3
# of early decision applicants	323
% accepted early decision	46

FRESHMAN PROFILE

Range SAT Critical Reading	660–760
Range SAT Math	660–770
Range SAT Writing	670–770
Range ACT Composite	31–34
Minimum internet-based TOEFL	100
% graduated top 10% of class	96
% graduated top 25% of class	100
% graduated top 50% of class	100

DEADLINES

Early decision	
Deadline	11/15
Notification	12/15
Regular	
Deadline	1/15
Notification	4/1
Nonfall registration?	No

FINANCIAL FACTS

Financial Aid Rating	99
Annual tuition	$50,564
Room and board	$13,900
Average frosh need-based scholarship	$47,009
Average UG need-based scholarship	$45,390
% needy frosh rec. need-based scholarship or grant aid	98
% needy UG rec. need-based scholarship or grant aid	97
% needy frosh rec. non-need-based scholarship or grant aid	0
% needy UG rec. non-need-based scholarship or grant aid	0
% needy frosh rec. need-based self-help aid	91
% needy UG rec. need-based self-help aid	91
% frosh rec. any financial aid	51
% UG rec. any financial aid	51
% UG borrow to pay for school	28
Average cumulative indebtedness	$14,750
% frosh need fully met	100
% ugrads need fully met	100
Average % of frosh need met	100
Average % of ugrad need met	100

HILLSDALE COLLEGE

33 East College Street, Hillsdale, MI 49242 • Admissions: 517-607-2327 • Fax: 517-607-2223

STUDENTS SAY "..."

Academics

Hillsdale College is home to "Socratic-style lectures," and "a very strong reputation nationally [for taking] the idea of pursuing truth and liberty seriously." Professors "hold the students to a very high (yet not unattainable) standard of quality in their work and contributions to discussion." As one student explains, "I loved the idea of going to a school where a class on the U.S. Constitution was part of the core curriculum, where the student/professor ratio was ten to one… it was small enough that would never just be another number." Students feel that "Hillsdale has a very strong core curriculum, ensuring that students are proficiently educated in a variety of subject matter as well as advanced in their major field of study" and "promotes a high academic standard, ensuring that success is earned, not granted." While there has been a trend in recent years "against the economics/business/accounting department and the sciences in favor of less technical education," students find that because Hillsdale notably takes no government funding, it "remains one of two truly free institutions in the nation … uninfluenced by the whims of politicians and biased policymakers," and makes up for this via privately funded scholarships. Students reported that they came to Hillsdale to "study 'the good, the true, and the beautiful' with others, both professors and fellow students, who would be equally dedicated to pursuit of these things."

Life

"There isn't, frankly, a ton to 'do' in the area," but "Hillsdale students are good company, and going out to dinner with some good friends, attending a sorority or fraternity function if you're a member, going to an informal reading group at a professor's house, seeing the visiting theater performance or a student performance, taking the occasional road trip to Ann Arbor or a fancy mall—these are kinds of things the Hillsdale students I know do in their spare time." "If given the opportunity, students will often travel to Ann Arbor to get foods like Chipotle," and most students feel they "have yet to be bored." Some students think that the town of Hillsdale is "uninspiring," but others "love the quaint, small town feel. Other than the plethora of on-campus events, Hillsdale township boasts a movie theater, bowling alley, skating rink, and a recently upgraded bar with nightly music." Students at Hillsdale appreciate "the self-sustaining religious sincerity" on campus. Students note that "time management is ESSENTIAL" and that "relaxing on the weekend usually consists of drinking because there isn't really anything else to do," while noting furthermore that "since the administration is strict on drinking and partying, people often host parties at off campus houses and drink there."

Student Body

"The students here are incredible, but very religious. This makes them believe that certain people (homosexuals, those of different religions) are wrong, and somewhat inferior." The typical student is a "straight-laced Christian" and "conservative" with people "fitting in groups formed through shared interest and religious beliefs." There is, however, "room for all ideas," although "some strange, narrow-minded fundamentalists still get admitted to the school," but "they choose to remain in their own circles." The admissions process at Hillsdale is blind, therefore making "racial diversity…irrelevant." At Hillsdale, "the rigor of classes combined with Midwestern disingenuousness creates an incredibly fluid intellectual climate, with minimal competitive nastiness and little egocentric fear." "Swing dance club is very popular as well as the College Republicans." Students at Hillsdale "often fall into three categories (Greek, athlete, or intellectual); these categories overlap all the time and there is no animosity between them." Some students feel that "Hillsdale isn't as conservative as it sometimes claims to be."

FINANCIAL AID: 517-607-2350 • E-MAIL: ADMISSIONS@HILLSDALE.EDU • WEBSITE: WWW.HILLSDALE.EDU

THE PRINCETON REVIEW SAYS

Admissions

Very important factors considered include: rigor of secondary school record, academic GPA, standardized test scores, application essay, interview, extracurricular activities, character/personal qualities, level of applicant's interest. *Important factors considered include:* recommendation(s), volunteer work, work experience. *Other factors considered include:* talent/ability, alumni/ae relation. SAT or ACT required; SAT Subject Tests recommend. ACT with or without writing accepted. SAT with or without Essay component accepted. High school diploma is required and GED is accepted. *Academic units required:* 4 English, 3 math, 3 science, 2 social studies, 3 history. *Academic units recommended:* 4 English, 4 math, 4 science, 2 science labs, 3 foreign language, 4 social studies, 4 history.

Financial Aid

Students should submit: Institution's own financial aid form. Priority filing deadline is 5/1. The Princeton Review suggests that all financial aid forms be submitted as soon as possible after October 1. *Need-based scholarships/grants offered:* Private scholarships, College/university scholarship or grant aid from institutional funds. *Loan aid offered:* College/university loans from institutional funds. Applicants will be notified of awards on a rolling basis beginning 12/1. Institutional employment available.

Inside Word

Don't let Hillsdale's high acceptance rate fool you. The academic profile of incoming freshmen is tremendous and only serious, solid candidates should bother applying here. Even though you don't have to be politically conservative to get in, a passionate and well-reasoned essay singing the praises of free-market economics or defending traditional values certainly can't hurt you.

THE SCHOOL SAYS "..."

From the Admissions Office

"Personal attention is a hallmark at Hillsdale. Small classes are combined with teaching professors who make their students a priority. The academic environment at Hillsdale will actively engage you as a student. Extracurricular activities abound at Hillsdale with the more than 100 clubs and organizations that offer excellent leadership opportunities. From athletics and the fine arts, to Greek life and community volunteer programs, you will find it difficult not to be involved in our thriving campus community. In addition, numerous study abroad programs, a 685-acre biological station in northern Michigan, and the Washington-Hillsdale Internship Program (WHIP) are just a few of the unique off-campus opportunities available to you at Hillsdale.

"Our strength as a college is found in our mission and in our curriculum. The core curriculum at Hillsdale contains the essence of the classical liberal arts education. Through it you are introduced to the history, the philosophical and theological ideas, the works of literature, and the scientific discoveries that set Western Civilization apart. As explained in our mission statement, 'the college considers itself a trustee of modern man's intellectual and spiritual inheritance from the Judeo-Christian faith and Greco-Roman culture, a heritage finding its clearest expression in the American experiment of self-government under law.'

"We seek students who are ambitious, intellectually active and who are ready to become leaders worthy of this heritage in their personal as well as professional lives.

"Applicants can meet admissions requirements by submitting the results of the SAT, or the ACT (writing section optional). We will use the student's best composite/combined score in the evaluation process. The SAT Subject Tests in literature and U.S. history are also recommended."

SELECTIVITY

Admissions Rating	91
# of applicants	1,859
% of applicants accepted	50
% of acceptees attending	40
# offered a place on the wait list	79
% accepting a place on wait list	19
% admitted from wait list	40
# of early decision applicants	168
% accepted early decision	60

FRESHMAN PROFILE

Range SAT Critical Reading	620–750
Range SAT Math	580–660
Range SAT Writing	610–730
Range ACT Composite	27–31
Minimum paper TOEFL	560
Minimum internet-based TOEFL	83
Average HS GPA	3.8

DEADLINES

Early decision	
Deadline	11/1
Notification	12/1
Regular	
Priority	1/1
Deadline	4/1
Nonfall registration?	Yes

APPLICANTS ALSO LOOK AT AND OFTEN PREFER

United States Naval Academy; Grove City College; Northwestern University; United States Air Force Academy

AND SOMETIMES PREFER

Albion College; Calvin College

AND RARELY PREFER

Knox College; Colorado College

FINANCIAL FACTS

Financial Aid Rating	85
Annual tuition	$23,840
Room and board	$9,760
Required fees	$752
Books and supplies	$1,200
Average frosh need-based scholarship	$7,554
Average UG need-based scholarship	$7,905
% needy frosh rec. need-based scholarship or grant aid	65
% needy UG rec. need-based scholarship or grant aid	61
% needy frosh rec. non-need-based scholarship or grant aid	80
% needy UG rec. non-need-based scholarship or grant aid	82
% needy frosh rec. need-based self-help aid	0
% needy UG rec. need-based self-help aid	66
% frosh rec. any financial aid	97
% UG rec. any financial aid	98
% UG borrow to pay for school	48
Average cumulative indebtedness	$28,636
% frosh need fully met	36
% ugrads need fully met	40
Average % of frosh need met	60
Average % of ugrad need met	65

HOBART AND WILLIAM SMITH COLLEGES

629 SOUTH MAIN STREET, GENEVA, NY 14456 • ADMISSIONS: 315-781-3622 • FAX: 315-781-3914

STUDENTS SAY ". . ."

Academics

According to one of its undergraduates, Hobart and William Smith Colleges offer students a "commitment to fostering growth of character and the ability to succeed in our chosen field" along "with a well-rounded education." These small, residential colleges in Geneva, New York provide an education of both depth and breadth, prioritizing "the liberal arts opportunity to explore majors before being locked into a program track." "The students, staff, and faculty really embrace the idea of the liberal arts education here," which means that "connections are made across disciplines, borders, and generations." Students highly value "the small student to faculty ratio, which allows teachers to hold students to a high level of competency and foster good relationships with each student." HWS's "small class sizes allow for more discussion-based classes, which enhance the overall learning experience." "Professors are always accessible, and a good number of them reach out to their students as opposed to simply expecting students to take initiative for help. They easily become friends with students and keep in touch with and mentor them after graduation." These professors show themselves to be "very respectful while simultaneously maintaining high standards of work," and one student comments, "I've never had a professor that did not inspire me while here." Another student declares, "Basically every single class I have walked out of I have called my mom or dad to discuss some wild new set of information I learned that I hadn't known before. That's a pretty awesome thing." Another appreciates how "I absolutely love what I've done in my studies here and how my mind has morphed in turn for the better." Many students call HWS "an extremely well-rounded college," with "superb academic, career, extracurricular and athletics opportunities for all its students." It's one of the "only small liberal arts colleges in the country with an architecture program," and overall, "there are endless opportunities while attending the school and post-graduation."

Life

Plenty of students engage with the colleges' offerings in "athletics, leadership and entrepreneurship, study abroad opportunities, alum network and connections," but they also like to have fun. "Students at HWS are very eclectic and are all involved in many different things, making fitting in easy." Indeed, "students fit in by getting involved in various organizations on campus such as athletics, fraternities, clubs and extracurriculars." "People love hanging out on campus for the most part, but they do enjoy excursions off campus, whether it be a quick dinner in downtown Geneva or Canandaigua (15 minutes away), or…a weekend getaway in Rochester or Syracuse." "The Finger Lakes are home to some of the best wineries in the United States. Wine tours, exploring the local lakes, and hiking trails and gorges take up a lot of students' time during the warm months." "We do not have sororities on campus," but "we do have fraternities," and "the majority of students do drink and party, but there are plenty of campus-sponsored events for those not looking for that kind of weekend activity." "Nightlife on campus can range from a small get together at an apartment or a big party in either the fraternity houses, bigger theme houses, or off campus." Some students say while "the nightlife on campus isn't as widespread as other places, it is still just as lively."

Student Body

Hobart and William Smith Colleges' motto is "Preparing Students to Lead Lives of Consequence," and its undergrads take this statement of purpose to heart. "A strong sense of community defines Hobart and William Smith Colleges," and those communities include "Geneva, NY in the smallest sense of the word and defining what it means to be a global citizen in the biggest sense of the word." One student marvels that "when I came to campus, people around me asked 'what can we do for you?' rather than 'what can you do for us?' and that has stayed true during my four years here." The typical HWS student is "outgoing," "extremely involved," and an "academically driven and social person." "You often hear about the stereotypical rich, preppy 'Smithie' or 'Hobart bro.' And while of course they exist, they are not the only type of student here, nor are they the majority."

FINANCIAL AID: 315-781-3315 • E-MAIL: ADMISSIONS@HWS.EDU • WEBSITE: WWW.HWS.EDU

THE PRINCETON REVIEW SAYS

Admissions

Very important factors considered include: rigor of secondary school record, academic GPA. *Important factors considered include:* application essay, recommendation(s), interview, extracurricular activities, character/personal qualities, volunteer work, work experience. *Other factors considered include:* class rank, standardized test scores, talent/ability, first generation, alumni/ae relation, geographical residence, state residency, racial/ethnic status, level of applicant's interest. SAT or ACT required for some; SAT Subject Tests considered if submitted. ACT with or without writing accepted. SAT with or without Essay component accepted. TOEFL required of all international applicants. High school diploma is required and GED is accepted. *Academic units required:* 4 English, 3 math, 3 science, 2 science labs, 2 foreign language, 2 social studies, 2 academic electives. *Academic units recommended:* 3 foreign language, 3 social studies, 4 academic electives.

Financial Aid

Students should submit: FAFSA, CSS/Financial Aid PROFILE, State aid form, Noncustodial PROFILE. Regular filing deadline is 2/1. The Princeton Review suggests that all financial aid forms be submitted as soon as possible after October 1. *Need-based scholarships/grants offered:* Federal Pell, FSEOG, State scholarships/grants, Private scholarships, College/university scholarship or grant aid from institutional funds. *Loan aid offered:* Direct Subsidized Stafford Loans, Direct Unsubsidized Stafford Loans, Direct PLUS loans, Federal Perkins Loans. Federal Work-Study Program available. Institutional employment available.

The Inside Word

Hobart and William Smith Colleges have a selective acceptance rate of 50 percent, which hovers in the mid-range for small liberal arts colleges of distinction. Prospective students should demonstrate a real appetite for challenge in their applications. Serious applicants are well advised to include at least two years of a foreign language and some AP classes on their transcripts. HWS is standardized test optional.

THE SCHOOL SAYS " . . ."

From the Admissions Office

"Hobart and William Smith Colleges seek students with a sense of adventure and a commitment to the life of the mind. Inside the classroom, students find the academic climate to be rigorous, with a faculty that is deeply involved in teaching and working with them. Outside, they discover a supportive community that helps to cultivate a balance and hopes to foster an integration among academics, extracurricular activities, and social life. Hobart and William Smith, as coordinate colleges, have an awareness of gender differences and equality and are committed to respect and a celebration of diversity.

"Hobart and William Smith Colleges are test optional. Students may submit the SAT, ACT, or no standardized tests at all."

SELECTIVITY

Admissions Rating	88
# of applicants	4,488
% of applicants accepted	57
% of acceptees attending	25
# offered a place on the wait list	622
% accepting a place on wait list	29
% admitted from wait list	12
# of early decision applicants	389
% accepted early decision	82

FRESHMAN PROFILE

Range SAT Critical Reading	570–670
Range SAT Math	600–670
Range ACT Composite	26–30
Minimum paper TOEFL	550
Minimum internet-based TOEFL	80
Average HS GPA	3.4
% graduated top 10% of class	30
% graduated top 25% of class	65
% graduated top 50% of class	92

DEADLINES

Early decision	
Deadline	11/15
Notification	12/15
Regular	
Deadline	2/1
Notification	4/1
Nonfall registration?	Yes

APPLICANTS ALSO LOOK AT AND OFTEN PREFER
Trinity College (CT); Colgate University

AND SOMETIMES PREFER
St. Lawrence University; Skidmore College

AND RARELY PREFER
State University of New York at Geneseo

FINANCIAL FACTS

Financial Aid Rating	89
Annual tuition	$48,586
Room and board	$12,583
Required fees	$1,091
Books and supplies	$1,300
Average frosh need-based scholarship	$29,520
Average UG need-based scholarship	$28,981
% needy frosh rec. need-based scholarship or grant aid	99
% needy UG rec. need-based scholarship or grant aid	99
% needy frosh rec. non-need-based scholarship or grant aid	25
% needy UG rec. non-need-based scholarship or grant aid	18
% needy frosh rec. need-based self-help aid	73
% needy UG rec. need-based self-help aid	80
% frosh rec. any financial aid	90
% UG rec. any financial aid	88
% UG borrow to pay for school	61
Average cumulative indebtedness	$34,504
% frosh need fully met	67
% ugrads need fully met	62
Average % of frosh need met	80
Average % of ugrad need met	78

HOFSTRA UNIVERSITY

100 HOFSTRA UNIVERSITY, HEMPSTEAD, NY 11549 • ADMISSIONS: 516-463-6700 • FAX: 516-463-5100

CAMPUS LIFE

Quality of Life Rating	83
Fire Safety Rating	98
Green Rating	78
Type of school	Private
Affiliation	No Affiliation
Environment	City

STUDENTS

Total undergrad enrollment	6,824
% male/female	46/54
% from out of state	36
% frosh live on campus	69
% ugrads live on campus	47
# of fraternities (% ugrad men join)	15 (8)
# of sororities (% ugrad women join)	12 (9)
% African American	8
% Asian	9
% Caucasian	57
% Hispanic	14
% Native American	<1
% Pacific Islander	1
% Two or more races	2
% Race and/or ethnicity unknown	4
% international	4
# of countries represented	53

SURVEY SAYS...

Students are happy
Great library
Easy to get around campus
Recreation facilities are great

ACADEMICS

Academic Rating	77
% students returning for sophomore year	80
% students graduating within 4 years	49
% students graduating within 6 years	60
Calendar	Semester
Student/faculty ratio	13:1
Profs interesting rating	72
Profs accessible rating	71

Most classes have 10–19 students.
Most lab/discussion sessions have
 20–29 students.

MOST POPULAR MAJORS

Biology; Psychology; Accounting

STUDENTS SAY "..."

Academics

From the instant you set foot on Hofstra University's "beautiful" campus, you can sense the "comforting and welcoming" vibe that permeates the school. Undergrads here happily report that their college is "full of opportunities" to develop "socially as well as intellectually." Many are also quick to note that the university provides "really great services for people with disabilities." And students value Hofstra's "proximity to New York City [which] makes it ideal for [landing]…internships and [jobs]."

Academically, undergrads especially love to highlight the "impressive" Lawrence Herbert School of Communications, which is flush with some rather unique opportunities. For example, as one amazed students explains, Hofstra's radio station— WRHU—"is the ONLY college radio station to be a flagship station for a professional sports team. We are the radio home for the New York Islanders." Across all courses of study, Hofstra undergrads benefit from "small" class sizes. In turn, this gives students "a better opportunity to connect with their professors and advisors" than they'd have in large lectures. And, speaking of professors, the university consistently hires instructors who are "very knowledgeable and passionate about their subjects." It's also quite evident that they "really care about their students and want them to succeed." Finally, as one thrilled dance major sums up, "I could not put together a better university if I tried."

Life

It's not uncommon for Hofstra students to spend the majority of their week hitting the books. Fortunately, when they need a distraction from studying, there is plenty of fun to be had! To begin with, the student body is fairly athletic. As one psychology major shares, "Our sports team[s] have dedicated followings, from quidditch to volleyball." Moreover, "there are so many amazing clubs that offer so much to their members and provide community outreach and volunteer opportunities." Undergrads also love partaking in events such as "trivia night, [and] coffee house, which presents student-based music and comedy performances." "A lot of students also participate in Hofstra Versus Zombies…once every semester." When undergrads truly need a break, they often consider heading to the beach, which is a mere "ten miles [away]." And, of course, undergrads here absolutely love that New York City is so accessible. A physician assistant student explains, "There is…a direct train to NYC only fifteen minutes away and Hofstra provides a shuttle to the train station." All in all, you have to work pretty hard to be bored here.

Student Body

The "student body at Hofstra is a unique mixture of commuters and residential students." The school manages to attract both individuals from the surrounding Long Island area as well as undergrads who come all the way from China. No matter where they hail from, Hofstra students gladly report that, for the most part, their peers are "very friendly." As an English major further explains, "I can walk up to just about anyone and start a conversation on anything from the weather to Plato and Socrates." An industrial engineering student concurs, assuring us that students "are really helpful; whenever you need anything, they [are] there for you even if they haven't gotten to know you yet." And, perhaps most importantly, undergrads here "are notorious for their work ethic and ability to juggle internships, academics, and getting involved on campus." Finally, one confident psych student assures us that, "with over 200 clubs, everyone is able to find their niche and join a friend group."

HOFSTRA UNIVERSITY

FINANCIAL AID: 516-463-8000 • E-MAIL: ADMISSION@HOFSTRA.EDU • WEBSITE: WWW.HOFSTRA.EDU

THE PRINCETON REVIEW SAYS

Admissions

Very important factors considered include: rigor of secondary school record, class rank, academic GPA, application essay, recommendation(s). *Important factors considered include:* interview, extracurricular activities, talent/ability, character/personal qualities. *Other factors considered include:* standardized test scores, first generation, alumni/ae relation, geographical residence, racial/ethnic status, volunteer work, work experience, level of applicant's interest. SAT or ACT considered if submitted; SAT Subject Tests considered if submitted. ACT with Writing recommended. SAT with Essay component recommended. TOEFL required of all international applicants. High school diploma is required and GED is accepted. *Academic units required:* 4 English, 3 math, 3 science, 1 science lab, 2 foreign language, 3 social studies. *Academic units recommended:* 4 math, 4 science, 2 science labs, 3 foreign language, 4 social studies.

Financial Aid

Students should submit: FAFSA, State aid form. Priority filing deadline is 2/15. The Princeton Review suggests that all financial aid forms be submitted as soon as possible after October 1. *Need-based scholarships/grants offered:* Federal Pell, FSEOG, State scholarships/grants, Private scholarships, College/university scholarship or grant aid from institutional funds, United Negro College Fund. *Loan aid offered:* Direct Subsidized Stafford Loans, Direct Unsubsidized Stafford Loans, Direct PLUS loans, Federal Perkins Loans, State Loans, College/university loans from institutional funds. Applicants will be notified of awards on a rolling basis beginning 3/1. Federal Work-Study Program available. Institutional employment available.

The Inside Word

Hofstra admissions officers take a comprehensive look at each applicant's transcript to assess academic ability and potential. ACT or SAT scores are required for international applicants, home-schooled students, individuals applying for Hofstra's Trustee Scholarship, and candidates interested in dual degree programs—but standardized tests are optional for everyone else.

THE SCHOOL SAYS "..."

From the Admissions Office

"The value of a Hofstra degree is recognized across the country and around the globe.

"At Hofstra University, we will know your name. We provide you with the resources and advantages of a large university, but the personal attention of a small college. Hofstra offers 158 undergraduate program options in the liberal arts and sciences with schools of engineering, business, communication, education, medicine and law; a diverse undergraduate student body that comes from forty-six U.S. states and fifty-three countries; seventeen Division I sports; thirty-five residence halls; eighteen eateries and cafes; a Fall Festival that has featured world-famous; and an alumni network of more than 131,000 who have been where you are now, and have become leaders in their fields.

"We're less than an hour from New York City, which means easy access to the adventure, cultural life and resources of an international metropolis, and internships at global giants in every industry.

"On-campus experiential learning includes more than 200 pre-professional, social and academic clubs, and state-of-the-art facilities. Hofstra also recognizes the value of bringing once-in-a-lifetime learning opportunities to our campus, most notably by hosting presidential debates in 2008 and 2012.

"Our faculty are scholars, artists, and scientists who are passionate about their work and dedicated to teaching and training the next generation of leaders—including you. Your future is full of hope and possibilities. The Hofstra experience allows you to imagine, design, and create both the journey and the destination."

SELECTIVITY

Admissions Rating	85
# of applicants	27,991
% of applicants accepted	61
% of acceptees attending	10
# offered a place on the wait list	612
% accepting a place on wait list	32
% admitted from wait list	62

FRESHMAN PROFILE

Range SAT Critical Reading	540–620
Range SAT Math	550–640
Range ACT Composite	24–29
Minimum paper TOEFL	550
Minimum internet-based TOEFL	80
Average HS GPA	3.6
% graduated top 10% of class	27
% graduated top 25% of class	63
% graduated top 50% of class	91

DEADLINES

Early action	
Deadline	11/15
Notification	12/15
Nonfall registration?	Yes

APPLICANTS ALSO LOOK AT AND OFTEN PREFER

New York University; Syracuse University; Boston University; Northeastern University

AND SOMETIMES PREFER

State University of New York—Stony Brook University; Penn State University Park; Fordham University; Drexel University; State University of New York—Binghamton University

AND RARELY PREFER

Quinnipiac University; St. John's University; University of Massachusetts Amherst

FINANCIAL FACTS

Financial Aid Rating	81
Annual tuition	$39,400
Room and board	$13,950
Required fees	$1,060
Books and supplies	$1,000
Average frosh need-based scholarship	$19,719
Average UG need-based scholarship	$16,820
% needy frosh rec. need-based scholarship or grant aid	96
% needy UG rec. need-based scholarship or grant aid	94
% needy frosh rec. non-need-based scholarship or grant aid	18
% needy UG rec. non-need-based scholarship or grant aid	15
% needy frosh rec. need-based self-help aid	81
% needy UG rec. need-based self-help aid	76
% frosh rec. any financial aid	96
% UG rec. any financial aid	91
% UG borrow to pay for school	70
% frosh need fully met	23
% ugrads need fully met	21
Average % of frosh need met	66
Average % of ugrad need met	61

HOLLINS UNIVERSITY

Box 9707, Roanoke, VA 24020-1707 • Admissions: 540-362-6401 • Fax: 540-362-6218

STUDENTS SAY ". . ."

Academics

"Tiny," all-female Hollins University "drips in" "unique traditions" and offers "an intimate atmosphere" that "feels like a community or family, not an institution." Students assure us that "a Hollins education is inspiring and nothing short of life-changing." There are fabulous opportunities to study abroad. Double-majors are mundane. Among the thirty or so majors available here, the "strong English program" is especially notable. The creative writing program in particular is "one of the nation's best." Classes are small and extremely "interactive." "The discussions in class will start slowly," observes an English major, "but they'll suddenly be out of the teacher's control the next minute." "Don't go if you didn't do the readings," adds a physics major. "Professors pour so much time into their students," relates a studio art major. They "want to hear from their students" and "are always more than willing to help." The staff in the financial aid office, on the other hand, can sometimes be "unwilling to help."

Life

Students at Hollins "adore the school." Life on this "gorgeous" and "peaceful" campus is "a unique amalgam of individualistic zaniness and required academic hustle and bustle." "People are very concerned about homework." "Sleepless nights during weekdays" aren't uncommon. At the same time, the student community is "hugely strong." "Hollins really embodies the concept of sisterhood." "Everyone comes together for" a throng of "crazy and not-so-crazy traditions." "It isn't uncommon to put on odd costumes or break into songs or see seniors in decorated robes. It's hard to explain these things other than to say, 'it's a Hollins thing.'" In the fall, the school president cancels morning classes and declares Tinker Day. "Everyone dresses up in wacky costumes, everything from a wetsuit to a prom dress, and hikes Tinker Mountain." Ring Night ("the best weekend of your life") and faculty Christmas caroling are a couple other noteworthy traditions. Hollins is also home to "amazing extracurriculars" including "a great horseback riding program." "There is a high level of student involvement" across the board, and "there is always something happening on campus." Lectures, concerts, and recitals are abundant. The theater program "is excellent, and the shows are always worth going to." "There are several subcultures people can fit into"—everything from intercollegiate athletics to a surprisingly strong anime contingent. "If you want to attend frat parties and keggers, it is very easy with the number of coed universities nearby," but "this isn't the typical 'party school.'" "Life at Hollins is walking down the dorm hall with all the dorm doors open and girls running down the hall to each other's rooms to talk and have fun or do homework together," explains one student. "The friends we make here are still going to be our sisters long after we have gone out into the world to accomplish what our experience at Hollins gave us the courage to do." "The dorms are hospitable but old." "Every now and then, the food is great and wonderful" but, for the gourmand, meals here general have some room for improvement.

Student Body

The women of Hollins describe themselves as "empowered, enthusiastic," "worldly, aware," "strong, and confident." "There are all sorts at Hollins: horse girls, anime girls, art majors, writers, filmmakers, bio students, dancers, feminists, scientists." The gay and transgender population is "large." "The glory of Hollins is that there is seldom a stereotype," agrees another student. "There is no mold that any student must fit, regardless of what activities and groups you are involved in. It is a place to be yourself." "Odd ducks" proliferate. "You name it; you see it (minus males, that is)." "Everyone is so different, and everyone is so amazingly tolerant of everyone's differences." However, some students can be "cliquey and exclusive." "Most people are involved in several clubs and organizations so it's easy to have a very diverse group of friends," describes one student.

FINANCIAL AID: 540-362-6332 • E-MAIL: HUADM@HOLLINS.EDU • WEBSITE: WWW.HOLLINS.EDU

THE PRINCETON REVIEW SAYS

Admissions

Very important factors considered include: academic GPA, standardized test scores. *Important factors considered include:* application essay, recommendation(s). *Other factors considered include:* rigor of secondary school record, class rank, interview, extracurricular activities, talent/ability, character/personal qualities, first generation, alumni/ae relation, volunteer work, work experience, level of applicant's interest. SAT or ACT required. ACT with or without writing accepted. TOEFL required of all international applicants. High school diploma is required and GED is accepted. *Academic units required:* 4 English, 3 math, 3 science, 2 foreign language, 3 social studies.

Financial Aid

Students should submit: FAFSA, State aid form. Priority filing deadline is 2/15. The Princeton Review suggests that all financial aid forms be submitted as soon as possible after October 1. *Need-based scholarships/grants offered:* Federal Pell, FSEOG, State scholarships/grants, Private scholarships, College/university scholarship or grant aid from institutional funds. *Loan aid offered:* Direct Subsidized Stafford Loans, Direct Unsubsidized Stafford Loans, Direct PLUS loans, Federal Perkins Loans, College/university loans from institutional funds. Applicants will be notified of awards on a rolling basis beginning 3/1. Federal Work-Study Program available. Institutional employment available.

The Inside Word

While the overall stats at Hollins are solid, the admit rate is high, and gaining admission won't be terrifically difficult if you have decent test scores and above-average grades. Keep in mind, though, that the applicants here are a highly self-selecting group and the admissions staff is able to take a long look at everyone who applies. Consequently, your best bet is to demonstrate a sincere desire to be a part of the unique milieu on this campus.

THE SCHOOL SAYS "..."

From the Admissions Office

"Hollins University's slogan, 'Women who are going places start at Hollins,' endures because it captures what this independent liberal arts institution means to its students. Hollins has been a motivating force for women to go places creatively, intellectually, and geographically since it was founded over 170 years ago. As Hollins graduate and Pulitzer Prize-winner Annie Dillard said, Hollins is a place 'where friendships thrive, minds catch fire, careers begin, and hearts open to a world of possibility.'

"Hollins offers majors in twenty-seven fields. While perhaps best known for its creative writing discipline, the university features strong programs in the visual and performing arts and the social and physical sciences. Hollins also has an innovative general education program called Education Through Skills and Perspectives (ESP). In ESP, students acquire knowledge across the curriculum. One of the most sought-after programs at Hollins is the Batten Leadership Institute, a comprehensive curricular program designed to maximize each student's leadership style and potential and teach her skills she will use both now and in the future. It is the only program of its kind in the nation.

"Hollins was among the first colleges in the nation to offer an international study abroad program. Today, more than 40 percent of Hollins' students—many times the national average—study abroad. Internship opportunities are another of Hollins' distinctions. Thanks to an active, dedicated network of alumnae and friends of the university, 65 percent of Hollins seniors put their education to work with a diverse group of organizations.

"Hollins' slogan underscores the most important question each student is asked from the moment she arrives until the day she leaves, and it is asked by her professors, her peers, and especially by herself: 'Where do you want to go?'"

SELECTIVITY

Admissions Rating	85
# of applicants	2,233
% of applicants accepted	61
% of acceptees attending	14
# offered a place on the wait list	0
# of early decision applicants	11
% accepted early decision	91

FRESHMAN PROFILE

Range SAT Critical Reading	500–630
Range SAT Math	460–570
Range SAT Writing	490–590
Range ACT Composite	20–27
Minimum paper TOEFL	550
Minimum internet-based TOEFL	80
Average HS GPA	3.6
% graduated top 10% of class	23
% graduated top 25% of class	36
% graduated top 50% of class	93

DEADLINES

Early decision	
Deadline	11/1
Notification	11/15
Early action	
Deadline	12/1
Notification	12/15
Regular	
Priority	2/1
Nonfall registration?	Yes

FINANCIAL FACTS

Financial Aid Rating	83
Annual tuition	$36,200
Room and board	$12,800
Required fees	$685
Books and supplies	$600
Average frosh need-based scholarship	$30,113
Average UG need-based scholarship	$28,509
% needy frosh rec. need-based scholarship or grant aid	100
% needy UG rec. need-based scholarship or grant aid	100
% needy frosh rec. non-need-based scholarship or grant aid	100
% needy UG rec. non-need-based scholarship or grant aid	100
% needy frosh rec. need-based self-help aid	61
% needy UG rec. need-based self-help aid	65
% frosh rec. any financial aid	100
% UG rec. any financial aid	99
% frosh need fully met	18
% ugrads need fully met	18
Average % of frosh need met	84
Average % of ugrad need met	83

HOWARD UNIVERSITY

2400 SIXTH STREET NORTHWEST, WASHINGTON, D.C. 20059 • ADMISSIONS: 202-806-2700 • FAX: 202-806-4467

CAMPUS LIFE
Quality of Life Rating	79
Fire Safety Rating	98
Green Rating	60*
Type of school	Private
Affiliation	No Affiliation
Environment	Metropolis

STUDENTS
Total undergrad enrollment	7,013
% male/female	33/67
% from out of state	95
% frosh from public high school	80
% frosh live on campus	93
% ugrads live on campus	59
# of fraternities (% ugrad men join)	10 (4)
# of sororities (% ugrad women join)	8 (6)
% African American	91
% Asian	2
% Caucasian	1
% Hispanic	<1
% Native American	1
% Pacific Islander	<1
% Two or more races	0
% Race and/or ethnicity unknown	0
% international	4
# of countries represented	86

SURVEY SAYS...
Lots of liberal students
Students are very religious
Frats and sororities are popular
College radio is popular
Campus newspaper is popular

ACADEMICS
Academic Rating	77
% students returning for sophomore year	85
% students graduating within 4 years	42
Calendar	Semester
Student/faculty ratio	10:1
Profs interesting rating	69
Profs accessible rating	65

Most classes have fewer than 10 students.
Most lab/discussion sessions have
10–19 students.

MOST POPULAR MAJORS
Journalism; Radio and Television; Biology

STUDENTS SAY "..."

Academics

Noted for "outstanding achievements as an institution as well as the accomplishments of a great majority of its alumni," Howard University takes great pride in preparing students "to compete on a local and global level." With "inspiring faculty and a perspective that cannot be found anywhere else," the school "breeds pride and excellence" and is a "formidable force in producing African American intellectuals." "Howard University is more than a place to get an education, it is a once-in-a-lifetime experience that not only strengthens your mind, but also your spirit and pride in who you are as a person and who you have the potential to become," says an appreciative student. Other undergrads add, "I wanted the experience of attending a Historically Black College," with a rich tradition and history. "Once you become a Bison" you experience "the sense of being a part of such a tremendous legacy." Students here believe that a Howard education is wonderful preparation for life in today's competitive employment environment. "Howard pushes you and teaches patience." Professors are admired for being able to "bridge the gap between the real world and the textbook;" "It is up to you to apply information outside of class through internships and supplementary experiences." They are "supportive and helpful," have "a genuine interest in their subject," and they make sure "course material is appropriate." Discussions are encouraged, which "helps to solidify understanding...I am able to have a voice in the class and share my opinion." Networking opportunities are abundant, and job placement upon graduation is high.

Life

A common theme heard throughout Howard University is how "students are very tight-knit and supportive of one another." "Dormitories are lively," and "life is fast-paced." School events are normally a "major part of the social calendar," and there is great encouragement for students "to be involved in campus organizations and student government." While there are many Greeks on campus, "the main focus of our Greek Life is community service. Any social event or gathering that is hosted by the Greeks normally has most of all of the proceeds going to a charity or community service project." There are also "student-run organizations that work in the community," providing "opportunities to be a part of something bigger than you." Students obviously love taking advantage of all of the opportunities the Washington, D.C., area provides. The Metro is a popular form of transportation, with the station "very easily accessible from the main Howard University campus." Many locations are Metro-accessible, but you must be cognizant of operating hours.

Student Body

At Howard University, there is at least one commonality everyone can agree on: Students are busy. "At any given time a student at Howard can be found taking a full course load, working, and interning." Extracurricular activities and community service are also on the plate of many Howard undergraduates. Students are often described as "friendly, outgoing, stylish, and fashionable." The campus exudes "a culture of achievement and encouragement;" "most students are very goal-oriented and driven." "A Howardite is very career-oriented and knows what he or she wants to do after graduation." Students here are also "very socially conscious." Geographic diversity is prevalent, and "Howard students are educated to think on a global scale." "Students are very accepting of each other and their backgrounds;" "We are an ever-changing, comprehensive, innovative, and supportive community." Meaningful conversation is prevalent, with many "discussions surrounding social and political issues." "Howard represents the best of the educated and progressive African American community."

FINANCIAL AID: 202-806-2840 • E-MAIL: ADMISSION@HOWARD.EDU • WEBSITE: WWW.HOWARD.EDU

THE PRINCETON REVIEW SAYS

Admissions

Very important factors considered include: rigor of secondary school record, class rank, academic GPA, standardized test scores. *Important factors considered include: Other factors considered include:* application essay, recommendation(s), extracurricular activities, talent/ability, first generation, alumni/ae relation, volunteer work, work experience, level of applicant's interest. SAT or ACT required. ACT with Writing recommended. TOEFL required of all international applicants. High school diploma is required and GED is accepted. *Academic units required:* 4 English, 3 math, 2 science, 2 science labs, 2 foreign language, 2 social studies, 4 academic electives.

Financial Aid

Students should submit: FAFSA. Regular filing deadline is 5/1. The Princeton Review suggests that all financial aid forms be submitted as soon as possible after October 1. *Need-based scholarships/grants offered:* Federal Pell, FSEOG, State scholarships/grants, Private scholarships, College/university scholarship or grant aid from institutional funds, Federal Nursing Scholarships. *Loan aid offered:* Direct Subsidized Stafford Loans, Direct Unsubsidized Stafford Loans, Direct PLUS loans, Federal Perkins Loans, Federal Nursing Loans, State Loans, College/university loans from institutional funds. Applicants will be notified of awards on a rolling basis beginning 2/16. Federal Work-Study Program available. Institutional employment available.

The Inside Word

Howard attracts quite a significant number of applicants, and the school maintains a high rate of graduation for those who do gain admittance. While standardized testing is certainly a primary part of evaluating those looking to enroll, this does not preclude other students from seeking entrance; proven ability from high school and the capacity to handle higher learning in a diligent, responsible manner is also highly valued.

THE SCHOOL SAYS "..."

From the Admissions Office

"Since its founding, Howard has stood among the few institutions of higher learning where blacks and other minorities have participated freely in a truly comprehensive university experience. Thus, Howard has assumed a special responsibility in preparing its students to exercise leadership wherever their interests and commitments take them. Howard has issued approximately 111,233 degrees, diplomas, and certificates to men and women in the professions, the arts and sciences, and the humanities. The university has produced and continues to produce a high percentage of the nation's African American professionals in the fields of medicine, dentistry, pharmacy, engineering, nursing, architecture, religion, law, music, social work, education, and business. There are more than 10,036 students from across the nation and approximately eighty-five countries and territories attending the university. Their varied customs, cultures, ideas, and interests contribute to Howard's international character and vitality. More than 1,598 faculty members represent the largest concentration of black scholars in any single institution of higher education.

"All applicants who have never been to college are required to submit scores from either the SAT or the ACT (with the writing component)."

SELECTIVITY

Admissions Rating	89
# of applicants	13,760
% of applicants accepted	48
% of acceptees attending	22

FRESHMAN PROFILE

Range SAT Critical Reading	500–610
Range SAT Math	490–610
Range SAT Writing	490–600
Range ACT Composite	21–27
Minimum paper TOEFL	550
Average HS GPA	3.3
% graduated top 10% of class	26
% graduated top 25% of class	55
% graduated top 50% of class	86

DEADLINES

Early action	
Deadline	11/1
Notification	12/20
Regular	
Priority	2/15
Deadline	2/15
Nonfall registration?	Yes

APPLICANTS ALSO LOOK AT AND OFTEN PREFER

Hampton University; Spelman College

AND SOMETIMES PREFER

University of Maryland–College Park; The George Washington University

FINANCIAL FACTS

Financial Aid Rating	73
Annual tuition	$22,737
Room and board	$13,814
Required fees	$1,233
Books and supplies	$3,000
Average frosh need-based scholarship	$5,729
Average UG need-based scholarship	$7,291
% needy frosh rec. need-based scholarship or grant aid	62
% needy UG rec. need-based scholarship or grant aid	63
% needy frosh rec. non-need-based scholarship or grant aid	57
% needy UG rec. non-need-based scholarship or grant aid	47
% needy frosh rec. need-based self-help aid	72
% needy UG rec. need-based self-help aid	75
% frosh rec. any financial aid	96
% UG rec. any financial aid	96
% frosh need fully met	12
% ugrads need fully met	9
Average % of frosh need met	13
Average % of ugrad need met	13

ILLINOIS INSTITUTE OF TECHNOLOGY

10 WEST THIRTY-THIRD STREET, CHICAGO, IL 60616 • ADMISSIONS: 312-567-3025 • FAX: 312-567-6939

CAMPUS LIFE

Quality of Life Rating	80
Fire Safety Rating	83
Green Rating	62
Type of school	Private
Affiliation	No Affiliation
Environment	Metropolis

STUDENTS

Total undergrad enrollment	2,991
% male/female	70/30
% from out of state	21
% frosh from public high school	90
% frosh live on campus	71
% ugrads live on campus	64
# of fraternities (% ugrad men join)	7 (11)
# of sororities (% ugrad women join)	3 (15)
% African American	6
% Asian	13
% Caucasian	33
% Hispanic	16
% Native American	<1
% Pacific Islander	<1
% Two or more races	2
% Race and/or ethnicity unknown	4
% international	26
# of countries represented	74

SURVEY SAYS...

Students love Chicago, IL
Very little drug use
Diverse student types interact on campus
Easy to get around campus

ACADEMICS

Academic Rating	77
% students returning for sophomore year	92
% students graduating within 4 years	38
% students graduating within 6 years	73
Calendar	Semester
Student/faculty ratio	13:1
Profs interesting rating	69
Profs accessible rating	67

Most classes have 10–19 students.
Most lab/discussion sessions have
20–29 students.

MOST POPULAR MAJORS

Architecture; Mechanical Engineering;
Computer and Information Sciences

STUDENTS SAY "..."

Academics

Minutes from downtown Chicago, Illinois Institute of Technology is a "beautiful green oasis in a bustling city." This career oriented school prepares students to "[make] the jump from student to professional" with a curriculum "strongly based on applied learning" and access "to student research at all levels." But IIT "caters to those individuals that want to pursue careers in areas of STEM," the curriculum "puts an equal emphasis on the life sciences and doesn't discount humanities." And while most come for the school's "historic reputation," particularly in engineering and architecture, students don't dismiss the value of the school's diversity. "The size and diversity of Illinois Tech is perfect," one student argues, "small enough for individual attention, but large enough for various resources to be available. Working with students from around the world gives you a unique perspective that is useful after college as well." Many students offer hot and cold reviews of the faculty. "I have had some really fantastic professors who are engaging and make the material genuinely interesting," one student explains. "However, I've had the exact opposite too." Others say that their "professors are very willing to help... but [they]want you to think for yourself." Most agree that IIT "is a very academic based institution with mostly excellent professors, especially in upper level classes. Academics here are challenging but rewarding." "Like any school we have our good teachers and our bad teachers. For the most part, they try to be engaging and interesting." Others are quick to point out that many of IIT professors "also work in the field" and, therefore, they "apply topics studied in the lectures to the real world" and "their lectures are very current with the solutions and technologies that are actually being used."

Life

Students enjoy "playing chess," "video/tabletop gaming, movie watching," but many report that "life at school is work and study everyday with a few breaks in between." Or as one jocular student puts it, "This school is nerd school." While some prefer a lifestyle that is "simple and sorted," these academically driven students also enjoy playing intramural sports and exploring the many museums, restaurants and cultural attractions of the city. Between the workload, the "very strict" on campus alcohol policies and "mostly small apartments" in Chicago "that get packed quickly," students say "there doesn't seem to be much partying going on at this school." But many students emphasize the important role that Greek life plays in their lives. "The brotherhoods and sisterhoods on-campus can be a serious life-saver," one student explains, "for those struggling socially, mentally, emotionally, and academically. Most people who go Greek refer to it as the best decision they made while at school, and those who don't join immediately often wish they did. Yes, it's that good."

Student Body

"The students at IIT are absolute nerds, and we all say that with pride." IIT "students study hard, focus for the future, bathe in the diversity of campus life, and are able to enjoy all events/programs that IIT and Chicago has to offer." Many students highlight an interest in "innovation and in aspiring creativity." IIT has "a very heavily male demographic" of "quiet introverts" who value teamwork and hail from around the world. Roughly half of the total IIT student body are international students, which provides "a variety of perspectives and cultures present in classroom discussions and clubs. Students largely describe one another as "warm, accepting, welcoming, and friendly." Overwhelmingly, "Illinois Tech students are serious about their studies, have a great eye for design and architecture, and love to have a good time especially when there is free food involved, which is often the case."

FINANCIAL AID: 312-567-7219 • E-MAIL: ADMISSION@IIT.EDU • WEBSITE: WWW.IIT.EDU

THE PRINCETON REVIEW SAYS

Admissions

Very important factors considered include: rigor of secondary school record, academic GPA, standardized test scores. *Important factors considered include:* class rank, recommendation(s). *Other factors considered include:* application essay, interview, extracurricular activities, talent/ability, character/personal qualities, first generation, alumni/ae relation, volunteer work, work experience, level of applicant's interest. SAT or ACT required; SAT Subject Tests considered if submitted. ACT with or without writing accepted. TOEFL required of all international applicants. High school diploma is required and GED is accepted. *Academic units required:* 4 English, 4 math, 3 science, 2 science labs, 2 foreign language, 2 social studies. *Academic units recommended:* 4 English, 4 math, 3 science, 2 science labs, 2 foreign language, 2 social studies, 2 history, 1 computer science, 1 visual/performing arts.

Financial Aid

Students should submit: FAFSA. Priority filing deadline is 2/1. The Princeton Review suggests that all financial aid forms be submitted as soon as possible after October 1. *Need-based scholarships/grants offered:* Federal Pell, FSEOG, State scholarships/grants, Private scholarships, College/university scholarship or grant aid from institutional funds. *Loan aid offered:* Direct Subsidized Stafford Loans, Direct Unsubsidized Stafford Loans, Direct PLUS loans, Federal Perkins Loans. Applicants will be notified of awards on a rolling basis beginning 3/15. Federal Work-Study Program available. Institutional employment available.

The Inside Word

Competition to get in includes students worthy of top tech schools like MIT and CalTech, so only those who feel confident they can handle the rigorous curriculum bother applying, making the admissions pools self-selecting. It would be smart to emphasize work ethic and career goals to win over admission officers at this academically demanding and career driven school. Extracurriculars and leadership roles always look good, but you should especially highlight any STEM-based activities outside the classroom.

THE SCHOOL SAYS "..."

From the Admissions Office

"IIT is committed to providing students a distinctive and relevant education through hands-on learning, dedicated teachers, small class sizes, and undergraduate research opportunities. Classes are taught by senior faculty—not teaching assistants—who foster our culture of innovation with their own firsthand research experience. Students are immersed in our interdisciplinary approach to learning through the team-based, creative problem-solving experience of the Interprofessional Projects Program (IPROs). The Office of Undergraduate Research provides mentored collaborative research experiences for undergraduates. Our entrepreneurship program challenges students to develop start-up technology companies. University Technology Park at IIT, a business incubator located on campus, supports this challenge by providing numerous opportunities to work with companies at every stage of growth, from conception to sophistication. The Leadership Academy teaches leadership skills that advance students in their personal and professional development.

"IIT's location in the world-class city of Chicago gives students priceless access to the professional world through internships and employment. The university's own diverse student population mirrors the global work environment faced by all graduates.

"First year students applying for admission into the entering class are required to submit an SAT or ACT score. We will use the student's best scores from either test. Subject tests are accepted, but not required. It is highly recommended that transfer applicants have completed thirty credit hours and have taken calculus and/or physics. Both first-year and transfer students are evaluated for significant merit based scholarships upon admission."

SELECTIVITY

Admissions Rating	89
# of applicants	4,403
% of applicants accepted	53
% of acceptees attending	21

FRESHMAN PROFILE

Range SAT Critical Reading	520–650
Range SAT Math	630–730
Range SAT Writing	520–640
Range ACT Composite	25–30
Minimum paper TOEFL	550
Minimum internet-based TOEFL	80
Average HS GPA	4.0
% graduated top 10% of class	56
% graduated top 25% of class	70
% graduated top 50% of class	98

DEADLINES

Regular	
Priority	12/1
Deadline	8/1
Nonfall registration?	Yes

APPLICANTS ALSO LOOK AT AND OFTEN PREFER

Northwestern University; University of Michigan—Ann Arbor; Case Western University; Carnegie Mellon University

AND SOMETIMES PREFER

University of Illinois—Urbana-Champaign; Purdue University—West Lafayette; Loyola University Chicago; Marquette University; Rensselaer Polytechnic Institute

AND RARELY PREFER

University of Illinois—Chicago; Bradley University; DePaul University

FINANCIAL FACTS

Financial Aid Rating	82
Annual uition	$43,,500
Room and board	$11,898
Required fees	$1,714
Books and supplies	$1,250
Average frosh need-based scholarship	$32,136
Average UG need-based scholarship	$29,733
% needy frosh rec. need-based scholarship or grant aid	100
% needy UG rec. need-based scholarship or grant aid	99
% needy frosh rec. non-need-based scholarship or grant aid	19
% needy UG rec. non-need-based scholarship or grant aid	10
% needy frosh rec. need-based self-help aid	63
% needy UG rec. need-based self-help aid	76
% frosh rec. any financial aid	100
% UG rec. any financial aid	99
% UG borrow to pay for school	59
Average cumulative indebtedness	$30,569
% frosh need fully met	22
% ugrads need fully met	13
Average % of frosh need met	83
Average % of ugrad need met	75

ILLINOIS WESLEYAN UNIVERSITY

PO Box 2900, Bloomington, IL 61702-2900 • Admissions: 309-556-3031 • Fax: 309-556-3820

STUDENTS SAY "..."

Academics

Located in Bloomington, Illinois Wesleyan University is a community that "invites you to make the most of your education and is ready to bend over backwards to ensure you enjoy your experience." Though the school doesn't have that big of a reputation outside the Midwest "despite its excellent education," it is an underrated gem that is "always trying to give students opportunities that are beyond what most schools can give." It truly is "a small school that oozes big opportunities."

Professors are "brilliant and accessible" "insightful" individuals who are "the best in their field." "The exuberance they have for their subject area and their students is very evident." Many of them are involved in research and "often include students in helping them," while others are involved in other ways; for example, "the mayor of Bloomington is also a political science professor—how cool is that!" "There have been a few life-changing professors who I am so grateful to have taken their class," says a business administration major.

Facilities and the career center are excellent, there are numerous opportunities for community engagement and research, and "there are so many resources and programs that help students who are seeking any type of support, whether it be academic, moral, or health." Wesleyan also "does a great job getting students ready for graduate school," and faculty "put [a lot of] effort into the information being taught, and really try and relate it to real life."

The school has a reputation for "overinvolved students who travel abroad, are the president of three clubs, and still maintain excellent grades." "IWU pushes us to excel academically while encouraging us to pursue our passions outside of our schoolwork," says a student. Overall, IWU is "a friendly community where your professors become mentors, your classmates become lifelong friends, and you graduate prepared to make a real difference in the world."

Life

As with many colleges, there's a strong weekday-weekend divide: "There is a fair trade of work and play." Sunday through Wednesday nights, "people are studying, going to meetings for clubs, maybe going to an event or two," but come the weekend, students "will go to parties at fraternity houses or off-campus houses, or go to the bars." Bloomington-Normal also has a variety of "great restaurants" and shopping venues which "are fun places to go to on the weekends," and neighboring ISU offers "some of that big college town culture can be found in the area."

The Office of Student Activities "does a great job having entertainment available for students" and almost every weekend a free event is held in the student center, "whether that be a concert, comedian, movie, or other entertainment." There is a "plethora of study groups" ("People are very receptive to getting work done together"), "great opportunities for intellectual discussions" at the coffee shop, and "students are always in food areas discussing, reading, or doing homework." "We have a weird obsession with the Game Show network as well here," confesses a student. "Buncha dorks. We know it and we own it!"

Student Body

The typical Wesleyan student "has a major that they take great pride in studying" and "often compare workloads to bond." Students here are "very academically focused" ("it's very rare to find students who don't try") but are also aware that "having a social life is important as well." Most everyone is "very liberal and rather artistic" and "very involved with many different activities." While there are noticeable groups such as "athletes, Greek life, and theater kids" which mainly stick together, "everyone has friends in other departments and organizations." There is "lots of competition on campus for internships and research opportunities," but "everyone is very helpful when it comes to informing others of opportunities." A "large percentage" of the campus is Greek life-affiliated.

FINANCIAL AID: 309-556-3096 • E-MAIL: IWUADMIT@IWU.EDU • WEBSITE: WWW.IWU.EDU

THE PRINCETON REVIEW SAYS

Admissions

Very important factors considered include: rigor of secondary school record, academic GPA, interview. *Important factors considered include:* class rank, standardized test scores, application essay, extracurricular activities, talent/ability, character/personal qualities. *Other factors considered include:* recommendation(s), first generation, alumni/ae relation, geographical residence, state residency, racial/ethnic status, volunteer work, work experience, level of applicant's interest. SAT or ACT required. ACT with or without writing accepted. SAT with or without Essay component accepted. TOEFL required of all international applicants. High school diploma is required and GED is accepted. *Academic units recommended:* 4 English, 3 math, 3 science, 2 science labs, 3 foreign language, 2 social studies.

Financial Aid

Students should submit: FAFSA, Institution's own financial aid form. Priority filing deadline is 3/1. The Princeton Review suggests that all financial aid forms be submitted as soon as possible after October 1. *Need-based scholarships/grants offered:* Federal Pell, FSEOG, State scholarships/grants, Private scholarships, College/university scholarship or grant aid from institutional funds. *Loan aid offered:* Direct Subsidized Stafford Loans, Direct Unsubsidized Stafford Loans, Direct PLUS loans, Federal Perkins Loans, Federal Nursing Loans, College/university loans from institutional funds. Applicants will be notified of awards on a rolling basis beginning 3/1. Federal Work-Study Program available. Institutional employment available.

The Inside Word

There's no application fee at IWU, and the school accepts the Common Application, so there are few reasons not to apply to IWU if you're even slightly interested in attending. Those applying to any of the creative arts school may be required to submit additional materials such as a portfolio. Don't expect to breeze through, though. You won't get into this highly selective college without a solid academic profile or a compelling story.

THE SCHOOL SAYS "..."

From the Admissions Office

"Illinois Wesleyan University attracts a wide variety of students who are interested in pursuing diverse fields such as vocal performance, biology, psychology, German, physics, or business administration. At IWU, students are not forced into either/or choices. Rather, they are encouraged to pursue multiple interests simultaneously—a philosophy that is in keeping with the spirit and value of a liberal arts education. The distinctive 4-4-1 calendar allows students to follow their interests each school year in two semesters followed by an optional month-long class in May. May term opportunities include classes on campus; research collaboration with faculty; travel and study in such places as Australia, China, South Africa, and Europe; as well as local, national, and international internships. Study abroad is very popular, with one out of every two students enjoying a travel experience.

"The IWU mission statement reads in part: 'A liberal education at Illinois Wesleyan fosters creativity, critical thinking, effective communication, strength of character, and a spirit of inquiry; it deepens the specialized knowledge of a discipline with a comprehensive world view. It affords the greatest possibilities for realizing individual potential while preparing students for democratic citizenship and life in a global society…The university, through its policies, programs, and practices, is committed to diversity, social justice, and environmental sustainability. A tightly knit, supportive university community, together with a variety of opportunities for close interaction with excellent faculty, both challenges and supports students in their personal and intellectual development.'"

SELECTIVITY

Admissions Rating	87
# of applicants	3,744
% of applicants accepted	62
% of acceptees attending	39
# offered a place on the wait list	193
% accepting a place on wait list	21
% admitted from wait list	53

FRESHMAN PROFILE

Range ACT Composite	25–30
Minimum paper TOEFL	550
Minimum internet-based TOEFL	80
Average HS GPA	3.7
% graduated top 10% of class	34
% graduated top 25% of class	69
% graduated top 50% of class	97

DEADLINES

Early action	
Deadline	11/15
Notification	1/15
Regular	
Nonfall registration?	Yes

APPLICANTS ALSO LOOK AT AND OFTEN PREFER

University of Notre Dame; Northwestern University

AND SOMETIMES PREFER

University of Illinois at Urbana-Champaign; Washington University in St. Louis

FINANCIAL FACTS

Financial Aid Rating	87
Annual tuition	$42,290
Room and board	$9,796
Required fees	$200
Books and supplies	$800
Average frosh need-based scholarship	$26,251
Average UG need-based scholarship	$24,220
% needy frosh rec. need-based scholarship or grant aid	100
% needy UG rec. need-based scholarship or grant aid	100
% needy frosh rec. non-need-based scholarship or grant aid	15
% needy UG rec. non-need-based scholarship or grant aid	11
% needy frosh rec. need-based self-help aid	76
% needy UG rec. need-based self-help aid	83
% frosh rec. any financial aid	100
% UG rec. any financial aid	100
% UG borrow to pay for school	69
Average cumulative indebtedness	$35,219
% frosh need fully met	45
% ugrads need fully met	41
Average % of frosh need met	87
Average % of ugrad need met	85

INDIANA UNIVERSITY—BLOOMINGTON

300 NORTH JORDAN AVENUE, BLOOMINGTON, IN 47405-1106 • ADMISSIONS: 812-855-0661 • FAX: 812-855-5102

STUDENTS SAY "..."

Academics

Indiana University—Bloomington focuses on creating well-rounded students who will be successful in and after college. This large state school challenges its students academically, but it "creates a fun collegiate environment, as well." "Academics and school spirit are its specialties!" says one student. The institution offers excellent financial aid and numerous opportunities for graduate and undergraduate students across all departments to conduct research, adding to "the perfect combination of excellent undergraduate teaching, Division I athletic teams backed by a passionate sense of school spirit, and a lively social scene." The "many excellent professors" here "really care about what they do," and they really "know what they're talking about." They "clearly want what's best for their students," and "the learning environment they create is excellent." "I have been very impressed with the individual attention I have received—mostly due to the level of commitment by professors to their students," says one student. The "rigorous and competitive classroom environment" gives students "the knowledge to be successful in our futures through great faculty, facilities, and tradition." Most professors at IU have professional experiences, and therefore "can bring their subjects to life." The "world-renowned business program" and the education and journalism schools are standouts here, but students say that all of the "school systems are great and easy to access," which makes "communicating with students/professors easy." Even with 40,000 people on campus, the administration gives student groups "much freedom of planning," and this warm environment allows students to "collaborate academically and non-academically as one community." This autonomy grants students the chance to explore "anything we want, whenever, but [find] the key thing we'll love through many opportunities and great programs."

Life

This "best-kept secret of the Midwest" is located in "the vibrant city of Bloomington," where "the restaurants off campus are amazing," with "many options to choose from." During the week, people "work really hard," and the campus is very active, with "a good number of students working out or running." There is "always something going on and something to do on campus that will fit the need of any student." Weekends generally start on Thursday night and go through Saturday night, when "house parties are popular," and the Greek system, although it only encompasses roughly 20 percent of the campus, "provides a strong social scene." The legendary IU basketball team is "starting to really rebuild its legacy," and attending games is common. There are also "free movies at the Union on weekends," and just "a very fun social scene" in general. Looking around the "beautiful" campus, you can see people jogging, and if the weather's really nice, you can find people lying outside on the grass and on benches snoozing."

Student Body

With such a large student body, "You are destined to find someone who you 'click' with." "It's unheard of that a student won't be able to fit in somewhere," says one. Typical is hard to nail down with tens of thousands of people, but many here are "very respectful of one another and ready to help out a fellow Hoosier" and "very lively and fun," and each student manages to have "an equal balance of school and social life." International students (often attracted by the business and music schools) are "accepted and encouraged to attend IU." Most students can be called "hard workers who also know how to have fun on the weekends."

INDIANA UNIVERSITY—BLOOMINGTON

FINANCIAL AID: 812-855-0321 • E-MAIL: IUADMIT@INDIANA.EDU • WEBSITE: WWW.IUB.EDU

THE PRINCETON REVIEW SAYS

Admissions

Very important factors considered include: rigor of secondary school record, class rank, GPA, standardized test scores. *Important factors considered include:* application essay. *Other factors considered include:* recommendation(s), interview, extracurricular activities, talent/ability, character/personal qualities, first generation, alumni/ae relation, geographical residence, state residency, racial/ethnic status, volunteer work, work experience. SAT or ACT required. TOEFL required of all international applicants. High school diploma is required and GED is accepted. *Academic units required:* 4 English, 3 science, 2 science labs, 2 foreign language, 3 social studies.

Financial Aid

Students should submit: FAFSA. Priority filing deadline is 3/10. The Princeton Review suggests that all financial aid forms be submitted as soon as possible after October 1. *Need-based scholarships/grants offered:* Federal Pell, FSEOG, State scholarships/grants, Private scholarships, College/university scholarship or grant aid from institutional funds. *Loan aid offered:* Direct Subsidized Stafford Loans, Direct Unsubsidized Stafford Loans, Direct PLUS loans, Federal Perkins Loans, Federal Nursing Loans, College/university loans from institutional funds. Applicants will be notified of awards on a rolling basis beginning in March. Federal Work-Study Program available. Institutional employment available.

The Inside Word

Above-average high school performers (defined by both grade point average and test scores) should meet little resistance from the IU admissions office. Students will have the opportunity to meet admissions representatives at numerous recruiting events held in many locations throughout the country or during a campus visit. Rolling admission favors those who apply early in the process. IU's music program is highly competitive; admission hinges upon a successful audition.

THE SCHOOL SAYS "..."

From the Admissions Office

"Indiana University, one of America's great teaching and research universities, extends learning and teaching beyond the traditional classroom. When visiting campus, students and parents typically describe IU as 'what college should be like.' Students bring diverse experiences, beliefs, and backgrounds from all fifty states and 126 countries to a campus often cited as one of the most beautiful in the nation. IU offers a quintessential college experience. Students enjoy the advantages, opportunities, and resources of a large school, while still receiving personal attention and support. Because of the outstanding academic and cultural resources, students have the best of both worlds.

"Indiana offers more than 5,000 courses and 200+ undergraduate majors—many nationally and internationally known—including programs in the arts, sciences, humanities, and social sciences as well as highly rated Schools of Business, Music, Education, Media, Public and Environmental Affairs, and Public Health. Students customize academic programs with double and individualized majors, internships, and research opportunities, utilizing state-of-the-art technology. Representatives from more than 1,500 businesses, government agencies, and not-for-profit organizations come to campus yearly to recruit IU students.

"IUB requires the SAT and/or ACT. The writing sections determine possible credit, placement, or exemption from writing requirements. Students must submit a complete application for admission (including official transcript and test scores) by November 1 for maximum consideration for IU Achievement and Selective Scholarships."

SELECTIVITY

Admissions Rating	85
# of applicants	34,483
% of applicants accepted	78
% of acceptees attending	29
# offered a place on the wait list	1,843
% accepting a place on wait list	21
% admitted from wait list	7

FRESHMAN PROFILE

Range SAT Critical Reading	520–630
Range SAT Math	540–660
Range SAT Writing	510–620
Range ACT Composite	24–30
Minimum paper TOEFL	550
Minimum internet-based TOEFL	79
Average HS GPA	3.6
% graduated top 10% of class	34
% graduated top 25% of class	68
% graduated top 50% of class	95

DEADLINES

Early action	
Deadline	11/1
Regular	
Priority	2/1
Nonfall registration?	Yes

FINANCIAL FACTS

Financial Aid Rating	82
Annual in-state tuition	$9,087
Annual out-of-state tuition	$32,945
Required fees	$1,301
Books and supplies	$1,230
Average frosh need-based scholarship	$11,891
Average UG need-based scholarship	$10,575
% needy frosh rec. need-based scholarship or grant aid	77
% needy UG rec. need-based scholarship or grant aid	80
% needy frosh rec. non-need-based scholarship or grant aid	16
% needy UG rec. non-need-based scholarship or grant aid	15
% needy frosh rec. need-based self-help aid	62
% needy UG rec. need-based self-help aid	63
% frosh rec. any financial aid	72
% UG rec. any financial aid	75
% UG borrow to pay for school	48
Average cumulative indebtedness	$27,681
% frosh need fully met	26
% ugrads need fully met	24
Average % of frosh need met	66
Average % of ugrad need met	66

INDIANA UNIVERSITY OF PENNSYLVANIA

1011 SOUTH DRIVE, INDIANA, PA 15705 • ADMISSIONS: 724-357-2230 • FAX: 724-357-6281

STUDENTS SAY

Academics
Indiana University of Pennsylvania maintains a simple way of doing things—provide students with an "inexpensive" education replete with "respected" programs. And the university has certainly delivered on those promises. Indeed, from the "good business school" to the "great writing program," undergrads have their pick of some truly stellar academic departments. Special praise is reserved for IUP's "fantastic" communications media program in which students have access to "a full-fledged commercial radio station (WIUP-FM), television studio (IUP-TV), two photography studios, a print studio, a full audio lab, a full motion capture/video game lab, and a huge center dedicated for media production and research (CMPR)." Beyond amazing facilities, undergrads at IUP have the privilege of learning from "great," "knowledge-able" professors. Most instructors here work to ensure that "discussion[s are] a big part of [the classroom] . . . experience." Moreover, it's clearly evident that they're "passionate about what they do." As a journalism and public relations major explains, "My professors really care about their subjects and take the time to thoroughly explain concepts and ideas to students." And a thrilled nursing major sums it up: "[Professors] feel like family and express that they genuinely care about the students outside of just the classroom situation. They see [us] as more than just students and aim to help us get the most out of IUP resources and time."

Life
It's quite easy to lead a full (and busy!) life at IUP. After all, "there are many opportunities to get involved on campus." Students can participate in "everything from National Honors Societies to sports teams, and everything in between." While some students admit that "drinking is a large part of [social life]" at IUP, others insist that there "are great alternatives to partying." These include "bingo on Friday nights, the incredible theatre productions, as well as multiple art galleries on campus." We're also told that "Indiana, PA is very much a college town." And when students want to take a break from campus life, they often head to Philadelphia Street, "a bustling center of bars and restaurants . . . almost all of the businesses on Philly Street are very welcoming to students." Many undergrads love taking advantage of "dollar bowling night" as well. And students yearning to get a little farther away can take advantage of IUP's "really great entertainment network," which frequently organizes trips to "Pirates games, Penguins games, Steeler[s'] games, museums [and] concerts." All in all, it's easy to get out and about and Pittsburgh is only about an hour's drive away.

Student Body
Many undergrads at Indiana University of Pennsylvania steadfastly assert that there's "no typical student here." As a geology and applied math double-major explains, "The variety of majors offered here attracts many different people with different interests and goals in life. Whatever you are looking for here, you will most likely find it." A nutrition major concurs adding, "There is [a] large mix of personalities on campus. From jock, preppy, intellectual, band member, religious etc. Because of this, everyone can fit in with at least one type of group." That being said, it can often feel as though the vast majority of students are "white, Christian, straight, and from an upper-middle class family in central or western PA." A pre-med student bemoans, "IUP has very little diversity, and the towns these students come from also have very little diversity. It can be tough being different sometimes." Thankfully, however, the majority of undergrads here are "friendly" and "helpful" and "open to meeting new people."

FINANCIAL AID: 724-357-2218 • E-MAIL: ADMISSIONS-INQUIRY@IUP.EDU • WEBSITE: WWW.IUP.EDU

THE PRINCETON REVIEW SAYS

Admissions

Very important factors considered include: academic GPA. *Important factors considered include:* rigor of secondary school record, standardized test scores. *Other factors considered include:* class rank, application essay, recommendation(s), interview, extracurricular activities, talent/ability, character/personal qualities, first generation, volunteer work, work experience, level of applicant's interest. SAT or ACT required. ACT with or without writing accepted. SAT with or without Essay component accepted. TOEFL required of all international applicants. High school diploma is required and GED is accepted. *Academic units required:* 4 English, 3 math, 3 science, 2 science labs. *Academic units recommended:* 2 foreign language, 3 social studies, 2 history.

Financial Aid

Students should submit: FAFSA. Priority filing deadline is 4/15. The Princeton Review suggests that all financial aid forms be submitted as soon as possible after October 1. *Need-based scholarships/grants offered:* Federal Pell, FSEOG, State scholarships/grants, Private scholarships, College/university scholarship or grant aid from institutional funds, United Negro College Fund. *Loan aid offered:* Direct Subsidized Stafford Loans, Direct Unsubsidized Stafford Loans, Direct PLUS loans, Federal Perkins Loans. Applicants will be notified of awards on a rolling basis beginning 3/14. Federal Work-Study Program available. Institutional employment available.

The Inside Word

Admissions officers at Indiana University of Pennsylvania pay closest attention to academic preparation and performance when considering applications. Officers typically only consider personal statements, recommendations and extracurricular participation for applicants on the border of eligibility. Finally, IUP operates on the basis of rolling admissions (with the exception of the speech language pathology and audiology program). Therefore, it is advantageous to apply as early as possible.

THE SCHOOL SAYS " . . ."

From the Admissions Office

"At IUP, we look at each applicant as an individual, not as a number. That means we'll review your application materials very carefully. When reviewing applications, the admissions committee's primary focus is on the student's high school record and SAT or ACT scores. We're always happy to speak with prospective students. Call us toll-free at 800-422-6830 or 724-357-2230, or e-mail us at admissions-inquiry@iup.edu.

"Students applying for admission are required to take the SAT or ACT."

SELECTIVITY

Admissions Rating	71
# of applicants	9,566
% of applicants accepted	88
% of acceptees attending	30

FRESHMAN PROFILE

Range SAT Critical Reading	430–530
Range SAT Math	430–530
Range SAT Writing	410–520
Minimum paper TOEFL	500
Minimum internet-based TOEFL	61
% graduated top 10% of class	8
% graduated top 25% of class	26
% graduated top 50% of class	62

DEADLINES

Nonfall registration?	Yes

APPLICANTS ALSO LOOK AT AND OFTEN PREFER
Penn State University Park; Westminster College (PA); Duquesne University

AND SOMETIMES PREFER
West Virginia University; University of Delaware; James Madison University

AND RARELY PREFER
Ohio University—Athens

FINANCIAL FACTS

Financial Aid Rating	79
Annual in-state tuition	$7,060
Annual out-of-state tuition	$17,650
Room and board	$11,880
Required fees	$2,876
Books and supplies	$1,100
Average frosh need-based scholarship	$6,645
Average UG need-based scholarship	$5,944
% needy frosh rec. need-based scholarship or grant aid	67
% needy UG rec. need-based scholarship or grant aid	65
% needy frosh rec. non-need-based scholarship or grant aid	43
% needy UG rec. non-need-based scholarship or grant aid	24
% needy frosh rec. need-based self-help aid	90
% needy UG rec. need-based self-help aid	90
% frosh rec. any financial aid	80
% UG rec. any financial aid	81
% UG borrow to pay for school	82
Average cumulative indebtedness	$36,514
% frosh need fully met	9
% ugrads need fully met	8
Average % of frosh need met	62
Average % of ugrad need met	57

IOWA STATE UNIVERSITY

100 ENROLLMENT SERVICES, AMES, IA 50011-2011 • ADMISSIONS: 515-294-5836 • FAX: 515-294-2592

CAMPUS LIFE

Quality of Life Rating	93
Fire Safety Rating	92
Green Rating	98
Type of school	Public
Affiliation	No Affiliation
Environment	Town

STUDENTS

Total undergrad enrollment	30,034
% male/female	57/43
% from out of state	31
% frosh from public high school	93
% frosh live on campus	94
% ugrads live on campus	41
# of fraternities (% ugrad men join)	36 (12)
# of sororities (% ugrad women join)	25 (20)
% African American	3
% Asian	3
% Caucasian	76
% Hispanic	5
% Native American	<1
% Pacific Islander	<1
% Two or more races	2
% Race and/or ethnicity unknown	5
% international	7
# of countries represented	116

SURVEY SAYS...

Students are happy
Great library
Internships are widely available
School is well run
Students love Ames, IA
Easy to get around campus
Recreation facilities are great
Lots of beer drinking
Everyone loves the Cyclones
Intramural sports are popular
Alumni active on campus

ACADEMICS

Academic Rating	74
% students returning for sophomore year	87
% students graduating within 4 years	41
% students graduating within 6 years	71
Calendar	Semester
Student/faculty ratio	19:1
Profs interesting rating	70
Profs accessible rating	71

Most classes have 20–29 students.
Most lab/discussion sessions have 20–29 students.

MOST POPULAR MAJORS

Mechanical Engineering; Kinesiology and Exercise Science; Finance

STUDENTS SAY "..."

Academics

More than 28,000 undergrads come together in Ames to get degrees in more than 100 majors, successfully giving off "a small-school feel with a big-university atmosphere." Science and technology are the main draws at this research university, but this "welcoming and friendly environment" treats all of its students well, regardless of their academic path. Professors, academic advisers, and other staff are all "very willing to help you academically and personally," and the Cyclone Nation is all about "engaging students not only in the classroom, but in the whole college experience." Professors "do what they can" for their students, focusing on experiences outside the classroom. It's also clear to students that the professors "truly love what they teach and bring passion to their lectures," working hard "to make students truly know what they want to spend the rest of their life doing." "Iowa State is all about preparing you for an actual career through hands-on teaching," says a student. Though lecture classes in the early college years can run large, the classroom experience (both in and out) only improves as students specialize. "I've been given the opportunity to work on an independent research project with a faculty mentor, which has been a really rewarding opportunity," says one student. All of the administration, "all the way up to our president and provost," is "dedicated to making student life at Iowa State the main priority." One of the school's greatest strengths is its ability to get students involved in internships, making it "extremely easy to find a job in your area of study"; every year, there are "very large engineering, agriculture, and business/LAS career fairs [that] allow students to find internships and full-time jobs easily." Even if one of your classes isn't the greatest, there "are many computer labs, help sessions, and teacher's assistants to go to for extra help."

Life

Iowa State is all about having "a big college experience (the athletics, the clubs, the shows, the educational opportunities, the school spirit) in a small college town"; indeed, Ames' support of the university "gives it a very at home and smaller feel than it actually is." During the week, students "mostly focus on classes and schoolwork." The weekends provide more of a chance to cut loose, whether that's a free event on campus, hanging out in each others' rooms and playing video games, partying, or playing an intramural sport (basketball, flag football, broomball, and others are "very popular"). "Winning an intramural championship t-shirt is very important and highly coveted on campus," says one student. There are "hundreds of clubs and activities for any of your interests," and the campus "will host bands quite a bit, and also a lot of late-night activities such as bingo, hypnotist shows, speakers, and lots of food." If you can't find what you want on campus, go off campus into downtown Ames, which is "full of fast-food and chain restaurants, bars, movie theaters, a mall, as well as locally owned businesses, restaurants, and novelty shops." Most students live on campus for their first two years, but off campus is "still very close to campus... so it's very comfortable and relatively cheap."

Student Body

Understandably, most students here are from the Midwest: "corn fed and bred," as they say. There is "some diversity," but "most of the students are white, and the second largest group is Asian." These "humble," "extremely friendly" students "care about the community and get involved with as many activities as possible." "If someone gets off of the campus and city bus system without thanking the bus driver, it's practically a sin," says a student. Although total enrollment is at about 35,000 (including graduate students), "students make it feel like a small town where everyone is a member of the Cyclone family."

IOWA STATE UNIVERSITY

FINANCIAL AID: 515-294-2223 • E-MAIL: ADMISSIONS@IASTATE.EDU • WEBSITE: WWW.IASTATE.EDU

THE PRINCETON REVIEW SAYS

Admissions

Very important factors considered include: rigor of secondary school record, class rank, academic GPA, standardized test scores. *Other factors considered include:* application essay, recommendation(s), interview, extracurricular activities, talent/ability, character/personal qualities, geographical residence, state residency, volunteer work, work experience. SAT or ACT required. ACT with or without writing accepted. SAT with or without Essay component accepted. TOEFL required of all international applicants. High school diploma is required and GED is accepted. *Academic units required:* 4 English, 3 math, 3 science, 2 science labs, 2 foreign language, 2 social studies. *Academic units recommended:* 4 English, 4 math, 4 science, 3 science labs, 3 foreign language, 4 social studies.

Financial Aid

Students should submit: FAFSA. Priority filing deadline is 3/1. The Princeton Review suggests that all financial aid forms be submitted as soon as possible after October 1. *Need-based scholarships/grants offered:* Federal Pell, FSEOG, State scholarships/grants, College/university scholarship or grant aid from institutional funds. *Loan aid offered:* Direct Subsidized Stafford Loans, Direct Unsubsidized Stafford Loans, Direct PLUS loans, Federal Perkins Loans, College/university loans from institutional funds. Applicants will be notified of awards on a rolling basis beginning 4/1. Federal Work-Study Program available. Institutional employment available.

The Inside Word

Admission to ISU is formula-driven and based on: ACT composite score; high school GPA; high school percentile rank; and number of high school courses completed in the core subject areas. The formula, known as the Regent Admission Index (RAI), is as follows: RAI = (2 × ACT composite score) + (1 × percentile high school rank) + (20 × high school grade point average) + (5 × number of years of high school courses completed in the core subject areas). Anyone earning an RAI score of at least 245 is automatically admitted; the admissions office reviews applicants scoring below 245 individually to determine which will also be admitted. An alternate RAI is calculated for schools who do not use class rank.

THE SCHOOL SAYS "..."

From the Admissions Office

"Iowa State University offers all the advantages of a major university along with the friendliness and warmth of a residential campus. There are more than 100 undergraduate programs of study in the Colleges of Agriculture and Life Sciences, Business, Design, Human Sciences, Engineering, Liberal Arts and Sciences, and Veterinary Medicine. Our 1,800 faculty members include Rhodes Scholars, Fulbright Scholars, and National Academy of Sciences and National Academy of Engineering members. Recognized for its high quality of life, Iowa State has taken practical steps to make the university a place where students feel like they belong. Iowa State has been recognized for the high quality of campus life and the exemplary out-of-class experiences offered to its students. Along with a strong academic experience, students also have opportunities for further developing their leadership skills and interpersonal relationships through any of the more than 800 student organizations, sixty intramural sports, and a multitude of arts and recreational activities."

SELECTIVITY

Admissions Rating	79
# of applicants	19,164
% of applicants accepted	87
% of acceptees attending	37

FRESHMAN PROFILE

Range SAT Critical Reading	460–620
Range SAT Math	500–640
Range ACT Composite	22–28
Minimum paper TOEFL	530
Minimum internet-based TOEFL	71
Average HS GPA	3.5
% graduated top 10% of class	22
% graduated top 25% of class	54
% graduated top 50% of class	91

DEADLINES

Nonfall registration?	Yes

APPLICANTS ALSO LOOK AT AND OFTEN PREFER

University of Illinois at Urbana-Champaign;
University of Minnesota—Twin Cities Campus;
University of Wisconsin—Madison; Purdue University—West Lafayette

AND RARELY PREFER

Baylor University

FINANCIAL FACTS

Financial Aid Rating	83
Annual in-state tuition	$6,648
Annual out-of-state tuition	$19,768
Room and board	$8,070
Required fees	$1,088
Books and supplies	$1,034
Average frosh need-based scholarship	$8,389
Average UG need-based scholarship	$7,059
% needy frosh rec. need-based scholarship or grant aid	98
% needy UG rec. need-based scholarship or grant aid	98
% needy frosh rec. non-need-based scholarship or grant aid	46
% needy UG rec. non-need-based scholarship or grant aid	45
% needy frosh rec. need-based self-help aid	66
% needy UG rec. need-based self-help aid	75
% frosh rec. any financial aid	88
% UG rec. any financial aid	79
% UG borrow to pay for school	64
Average cumulative indebtedness	$27,571
% frosh need fully met	35
% ugrads need fully met	33
Average % of frosh need met	82
Average % of ugrad need met	80

ITHACA COLLEGE

ITHACA COLLEGE, OFFICE OF ADMISSION, ITHACA, NY 14850-7002 • ADMISSIONS: 607-274-3124 • FAX: 607-274-1900

STUDENTS SAY "..."

Academics

"Small class sizes" that afford plenty of "personal attention," "outstanding" scholarships, and cross-registration with nearby Cornell University are a few great reasons to choose Ithaca College, a smallish school in central New York that offers many of the resources you would expect to find at a much larger university. "You are able to be a part of a community and get the chance to pursue interests that are not necessarily a part of your chosen course of study," relates an English major. "We have loads of opportunities to do and try a wide variety of things." The vast multitude of academic offerings includes "one of the best communication schools in the country." Also notable are "strong" majors in music, business, and drama; a "highly competitive" six-year doctorate program in physical therapy; and the cinema and photography program. Professors are "really engaging and understand how to present the material so that it is relevant and meaningful." On the whole, faculty members are "really passionate about their fields and have a genuine interest in getting students excited about their passions." By far, the most common academic complaint about academics at Ithaca concerns registration, which can be trying. Some say, "the buildings—inside and out—are a bit outdated." Overall the campus is known for its picturesque beauty. "People aren't kidding when they say 'Ithaca is Gorges (gorgeous),'" promises one student.

Life

The number of extracurricular choices is "considerable" at Ithaca College. At the same time, "the school is small enough for anyone to get involved." There are "speakers and events offered on campus." There's also a nearly professional-quality college radio station. Many students "are part of an athletic team or participate in intramural athletics." For relaxation, students often "hang out on the quad," throwing Frisbees or "playing music on the lawns on tie-dye sheets." The social situation at Ithaca is "nothing like the party scene you'd find at a larger university," but "there are some good parties" now and then. While the campus is a little "isolated," students also frequently manage to attend frat parties at Cornell and generally "enjoy the social scene" the nearby Ivy offers. "The town of Ithaca is quaint but lively." There's "a good music scene and a lot of cool stores." When the weather is nice, "there's always some festival," or at least it seems that way. "If you're an outdoorsy person," the wooded and rocky surrounding area is a wonderland of activity. "The hiking here is unbelievable," and few other schools offer the opportunity to "go cliff jumping on a hot Saturday." On the negative side, winters are cold as a matter of course, and "the cold and rain do hinder activities." Students joke, be prepared to get your exercise walking between classes; "the hills here will kill you."

Student Body

The typical undergrad here is "genuine," "easygoing," "always busy," "well-dressed," and has a "sunny disposition despite the gray skies." Beyond those qualities, the population is "a wide mix of hipsters, jocks, theater kids, music students," and "crunchy granola hippies." "People of all kinds fit in here." "Everyone finds their niche." Cliques are often based loosely on academics. "Ithaca is not so much one community as a whole," explains one student. "Instead, each school (music, communications, business, etc.) is its own community." Ethnic diversity and other kinds of diversity are "not entirely unheard of." However, people are "usually from the Northeast," and "the population of students that fit into the typical suburban, upper-middle-class family is definitely significant." Politically, "students at Ithaca tend to be liberal." Some students tell us that you'll find "a lot of people are environmentally and socially conscious" here who want "to change the world."

FINANCIAL AID: 607-274-3131 • E-MAIL: ADMISSION@ITHACA.EDU • WEBSITE: WWW.ITHACA.EDU

THE PRINCETON REVIEW SAYS

Admissions

Very important factors considered include: rigor of secondary school record, academic GPA, level of applicant's interest. *Important factors considered include:* application essay, recommendation(s), extracurricular activities, talent/ability, character/personal qualities. *Other factors considered include:* class rank, standardized test scores, interview, first generation, alumni/ae relation, volunteer work, work experience. SAT or ACT considered if submitted; SAT Subject Tests considered if submitted. ACT with or without writing accepted. SAT with or without Essay component accepted. TOEFL required of all international applicants. High school diploma is required and GED is accepted. *Academic units required:* 4 English, 3 math, 3 science, 2 foreign language, 3 social studies, 1 academic elective. *Academic units recommended:* 4 English, 4 math, 4 science, 3 foreign language, 4 social studies, 1 academic elective.

Financial Aid

Students should submit: FAFSA, CSS/Financial Aid PROFILE. Priority filing deadline is 2/1. The Princeton Review suggests that all financial aid forms be submitted as soon as possible after October 1. *Need-based scholarships/grants offered:* Federal Pell, FSEOG, State scholarships/grants, Private scholarships, College/university scholarship or grant aid from institutional funds. *Loan aid offered:* Direct Subsidized Stafford Loans, Direct Unsubsidized Stafford Loans, Direct PLUS loans, Federal Perkins Loans. Applicants will be notified of awards on a rolling basis beginning 2/15. Federal Work-Study Program available. Institutional employment available.

The Inside Word

Ithaca's admissions profile continues to be on the rise with a good deal of highly competitive applicants. Programs requiring an audition (for example, music) or portfolio review (for example, art) are among Ithaca's most demanding for admission. If you want to pursue the six-year clinical doctorate in physical therapy, focus on completing substantial math and science coursework in high school.

THE SCHOOL SAYS "..."

From the Admissions Office

"Located in central New York's Finger Lakes region, Ithaca College offers more than 100 majors in its Schools of Business, Communications, Health Sciences and Human Performance, Humanities and Sciences, and Music.

"Whether you dream of becoming a media mogul, nonprofit hero, groundbreaking scientist, or brilliant composer—Ithaca College will make you ready. Our dedicated professors are experts in their fields and will make you an expert in yours by providing hands-on experience from day one. Experiment in a lab, light up the stage, take risks in the stock market—whatever your interests, you'll dive in right away to turn classroom theory into well-practiced skill.

"From our vibrant campus community to the world beyond, you'll find exciting opportunities to expand your mind and enhance your education. Nearly 200 student organizations provide the perfect place to create award-winning projects, volunteer, philosophize, and connect. Add more valuable skills with a fast-paced internship or enlightening study-abroad program, including our semester-long options in New York City, L.A., and London. From campus life to life experience, Ithaca College will make you ready for your career and anything that comes your way.

"To learn more, visit ithaca.edu/ready."

SELECTIVITY

Admissions Rating	84
# of applicants	16,519
% of applicants accepted	67
% of acceptees attending	16
# offered a place on the wait list	1,286
% accepting a place on wait list	14
% admitted from wait list	18
# of early decision applicants	189
% accepted early decision	92

FRESHMAN PROFILE

Range SAT Critical Reading	550–640
Range SAT Math	550–630
Range SAT Writing	560–640
Range ACT Composite	24–29
Minimum paper TOEFL	550
Minimum internet-based TOEFL	80
% graduated top 10% of class	23
% graduated top 25% of class	63
% graduated top 50% of class	91

DEADLINES

Early decision	
Deadline	11/1
Notification	12/15
Early action	
Deadline	12/1
Notification	2/1
Regular	
Deadline	2/1
Notification	4/15
Nonfall registration?	Yes

APPLICANTS ALSO LOOK AT
AND OFTEN PREFER
Boston University; New York University

AND SOMETIMES PREFER
Penn State—University Park

AND RARELY PREFER
Fordham University

FINANCIAL FACTS

Financial Aid Rating	85
Annual tuition	$40,658
Room and board	$14,674
Books and supplies	$1,537
Average frosh need-based scholarship	$25,597
Average UG need-based scholarship	$24,760
% needy frosh rec. need-based scholarship or grant aid	97
% needy UG rec. need-based scholarship or grant aid	98
% needy frosh rec. non-need-based scholarship or grant aid	30
% needy UG rec. non-need-based scholarship or grant aid	15
% needy frosh rec. need-based self-help aid	91
% needy UG rec. need-based self-help aid	91
% frosh rec. any financial aid	96
% UG rec. any financial aid	93
% UG borrow to pay for school	72
Average cumulative indebtedness	$39,771
% frosh need fully met	52
% ugrads need fully met	41
Average % of frosh need met	90
Average % of ugrad need met	85

JAMES MADISON UNIVERSITY

SONNER HALL, MSC 0101, HARRISONBURG, VA 22807 • ADMISSIONS: 540-568-5681 • FAX: 540-568-3332

STUDENTS SAY "..."

Academics

James Madison University has a reputation as "a school that values education, respect, and integrity." The university boasts "one of the best BA programs for musical theater on the East Coast," and an "amazing" business school. A communication major says, "James Madison offered a positive, enriching, and supportive learning environment," and most students agree that JMU is an "inspiring environment filled with students striving to be productive members of society." A senior says, "I found the JMU environment to be comfortable and conducive to learning," and it seems clear that "JMU is all about taking your academics seriously." Professors get consistently high marks for being "available to help" and "interested in student achievement." Although they're often described as "challenging," students say professors are "willing to facilitate your education in any way possible" and "are very down to earth, approachable, and huge supporters of discussion-based classes." Like any large university, there are "some professors you want to avoid," and students grumble that "registering for classes, if you don't have priority, is a pain." It's worth noting, however, that "classrooms and facilities are always well kept and very up-to-date with all the best teaching technology."

Life

Located in Virginia's Shenandoah Valley, JMU is known for its "beautiful" campus, and students rave about the "benefits of walking in the mountains." An English major says, "The moment I walked on campus I was captured by the student spirit and how beautiful it is." School spirit is generally high, and students say, "There's a huge sense of JMU pride, everyone loves the Dukes!" A senior adds, "We have so much pride for our school. There is a friendly, collaborative ambiance here that is unparalleled anywhere else." The university is known for its Southern hospitality, and one student describes the student body as "the 'door-holding freaks of America' because even when people are several feet away, we stand there to hold the door for them." There are numerous ways to get involved on campus, and the "sheer number of student activities is stellar." Students rave about the "personal involvement that JMU offer(s)," and say, "They make you feel like a part of the campus, not just another number." Food services and facilities get high marks across the board, and most agree that the "administration and faculty are always willing to talk to students and point them in the right direction," noting that one of "the greatest strengths of the school is the ability to get any sort of assistance when needed." Regardless, there are complaints about traffic on campus, and many feel, "the school could improve on parking, by a long shot."

Student Body

At JMU, "the typical student is friendly, smart, open-minded, and fun." Students describe themselves as "excellent [at] maintaining a round, balanced life," and say, "Everyone seems relaxed and knows how to have fun but keep their school work a priority." One student jokes that the typical student is "probably a girl considering our ratio seems like eighty to twenty at times," and another concurs, "more males would be nice." Students tend to be "white from the upper- to middle-class," and an International Affairs major says, "Although we do have all types here, most people consist of your typical prep wearing Uggs and a North Face." Some complain, "There is party atmosphere here that can seem dominating," and say, "If you do not go out and party you stand out." Others note, however, "Greek life is small," and parties "are usually open to everyone," adding that partying isn't "all students here think about. People will get together and drink for fun, but it isn't a necessity." A sophomore says, "On the weekends, students can go to downtown Harrisonburg to the various restaurants and shops," or enjoy on-campus movies at a reduced rate. Still others take advantage of the "great places to hike and spend time outdoors" and JMU's easy accessibility to nearby ski resorts.

FINANCIAL AID: 540-568-7820 • E-MAIL: ADMISSIONS@JMU.EDU • WEBSITE: WWW.JMU.EDU

THE PRINCETON REVIEW SAYS

Admissions

Very important factors considered include: rigor of secondary school record, academic GPA. *Important factors considered include:* standardized test scores. *Other factors considered include:* application essay, recommendation(s). SAT or ACT required. ACT with or without writing accepted. SAT with or without Essay component accepted. TOEFL required of all international applicants. High school diploma is required and GED is accepted. *Academic units required:* 4 English, 4 math, 2 social studies, 2 history.

Financial Aid

Students should submit: FAFSA. Priority filing deadline is 3/1. The Princeton Review suggests that all financial aid forms be submitted as soon as possible after October 1. *Need-based scholarships/grants offered:* Federal Pell, FSEOG, State scholarships/grants, Private scholarships, College/university scholarship or grant aid from institutional funds. *Loan aid offered:* Direct Subsidized Stafford Loans, Direct Unsubsidized Stafford Loans, Direct PLUS loans, Federal Perkins Loans. Applicants will be notified of awards on a rolling basis beginning 4/1. Federal Work-Study Program available. Institutional employment available.

The Inside Word

At JMU admissions are competitive, but the admissions staff insists that they're not searching for a "magic combination" of test scores and GPA. Admissions officers review each application individually and are most interested in the quality of an applicant's secondary school education, followed by performance and test scores. The personal statement is a vehicle for conveying information an applicant deems important but doesn't appear elsewhere in the application, as such it's optional.

THE SCHOOL SAYS "..."

From the Admissions Office

"James Madison University's philosophy of inclusiveness—known as 'all together one'—means that students become a part of a real community that nurtures its own to learn, grow, and succeed. Our professors, many of whom have a wealth of real-world experience, pride themselves on making teaching their top priority. We take seriously the responsibility to maintain an environment that fosters learning and encourages students to excel in and out of the classroom. Our rich variety of educational, social, and extracurricular activities include more than 100 innovative and traditional undergraduate majors and programs, a well-established study abroad program, a cutting-edge information security program, more than 350 student clubs and organizations, and an expanded 280,000-square-foot, state-of-the-art recreation center. The university's picturesque, self-contained campus is located in the heart of the Shenandoah Valley, a four-season area that's easy to call home. Great food, fun times, exciting intercollegiate athletics, and rigorous academics all combine to create the unique James Madison experience. From the library to the residence halls and from our outstanding honors program to our highly successful career placement program, the university is committed to equipping our students with the tools they need to achieve their dreams."

SELECTIVITY

Admissions Rating	82
# of applicants	21,439
% of applicants accepted	73
% of acceptees attending	28
# offered a place on the wait list	2,500
% accepting a place on wait list	48
% admitted from wait list	42

FRESHMAN PROFILE

Range SAT Critical Reading	520–610
Range SAT Math	520–610
Range ACT Composite	23–27
Minimum paper TOEFL	550
% graduated top 10% of class	23
% graduated top 25% of class	41
% graduated top 50% of class	97

DEADLINES

Early action	
Deadline	11/1
Notification	1/15
Regular	
Deadline	1/15
Notification	4/1
Nonfall registration?	No

APPLICANTS ALSO LOOK AT AND OFTEN PREFER
University of Virginia; Virginia Tech

AND SOMETIMES PREFER
University of Delaware; George Mason University

FINANCIAL FACTS

Financial Aid Rating	83
Annual in-state tuition	$5,724
Annual out-of-state tuition	$20,848
Room and board	$9,396
Required fees	$4,294
Books and supplies	$976
Average frosh need-based scholarship	$7,861
Average UG need-based scholarship	$7,080
% needy frosh rec. need-based scholarship or grant aid	53
% needy UG rec. need-based scholarship or grant aid	51
% needy frosh rec. non-need-based scholarship or grant aid	9
% needy UG rec. non-need-based scholarship or grant aid	10
% needy frosh rec. need-based self-help aid	76
% needy UG rec. need-based self-help aid	70
% frosh rec. any financial aid	59
% UG rec. any financial aid	56
% UG borrow to pay for school	100
Average cumulative indebtedness	$25,677
% frosh need fully met	78
% ugrads need fully met	68
Average % of frosh need met	40
Average % of ugrad need met	43

JOHNS HOPKINS UNIVERSITY

3400 NORTH CHARLES STREET, BALTIMORE, MD 21218 • ADMISSIONS: 410-516-8171 • FAX: 410-516-6025

CAMPUS LIFE
Quality of Life Rating	91
Fire Safety Rating	98
Green Rating	92
Type of school	Private
Affiliation	No Affiliation
Environment	Metropolis

STUDENTS
Total undergrad enrollment	5,386
% male/female	51/49
% from out of state	88
% frosh from public high school	57
% frosh live on campus	99
% ugrads live on campus	52
# of fraternities (% ugrad men join)	11 (17)
# of sororities (% ugrad women join)	11 (26)
% African American	6
% Asian	23
% Caucasian	40
% Hispanic	13
% Native American	<1
% Pacific Islander	<1
% Two or more races	5
% Race and/or ethnicity unknown	3
% international	10
# of countries represented	65

SURVEY SAYS...
Students always studying
Students are happy
Lab facilities are great
Great library
School is well run
Easy to get around campus
Recreation facilities are great

ACADEMICS
Academic Rating	91
% students returning for sophomore year	97
% students graduating within 4 years	88
% students graduating within 6 years	94
Calendar	4/1/4
Profs interesting rating	78
Profs accessible rating	76

Most classes have 10–19 students.

MOST POPULAR MAJORS
Bioengineering and Biomedical Engineering;
Neuroscience; Public Health

STUDENTS SAY "..."

Academics

Johns Hopkins University in Baltimore might have a rep for STEM, but undergrads say JHU offers a diversity of strong programs, including in music and political science, in which students "[can] study anything and still be taught by the highest of experts." Students say that the academics here are "beyond compare" and rave about the interdisciplinary studies, hands-on engagement, and an "availability of resources, research, internship, and job opportunities [that] are unmatched." With 5,300 undergrads, Hopkins is "small enough for strong interactions among students" and large enough for "unparalleled opportunities to pursue research, form strong relationships with professors, and learn from an outstanding group of peers." While most students major in STEM fields, they "come from various backgrounds and have vastly different experiences," and every student here is "overwhelmingly passionate about what they do and aspires to make an impact in their field." Students have the ability to design their own curriculum, and professors "make themselves very accessible to their students for coffee chats, career advice or even just to give life advice." Though there are a few duds in the bunch (and "some TAs sometimes don't speak the best English"), most instructors are "more than willing to push class topics beyond the confines of the textbook to expose us to the implications of the topics discussed in class." Students appreciate that Hopkins posts what other students think of courses so each person "can see what classes appear 'better' and so professors can gain feedback and improve." Classes are "rigorous but very cooperative" and teach you "how to approach any problem fearlessly." The strong alumni network helps with job placement, and the school "gives out a lot of money to undergrads with good ideas through the Wilson Fellowship." Professors are eager ("almost giddy even") to take undergraduates under their wings and show them how to do research, and these opportunities are available regardless of your major: "One of my art history major friends curated his own exhibit in a gallery downtown (with work from several world-renowned artists) as his research project," says a student.

Life

There's a saying about the "Hopkins 500"—that "it's the same 500 people who are social and go out to parties and bars." In reality, "it's probably closer to one thousand but it's always the same people you see out," and the library doesn't necessarily die down just because it's a weekend night; "some of the students prefer to study all the time." Though life can get stressful, "most students at Hopkins are the type that thrive under pressure." The majority of student life "revolves around clubs and organizations," and throughout the week (as well as on weekends), students will also attend "concerts, symposiums with famous guest speakers or explore what Baltimore has to offer, such as its "a great music and food scene." Nearby Mount Vernon "has fantastic culture and food," and Fells Point and Federal Hill are known for their nightlife; Orioles and Ravens games are also popular. Thanks to the city's relatively low cost of living, students "tend to go out and eat at nice restaurants without paying too much money." During lacrosse season, some people will go the games and "get really involved in the season."

Student Body

This group of "ambitious workhorses" are "very intellectually curious and smart" and "want to be on the forefront of innovation." The typical Hopkins student "works really hard, and knows how to cut loose as well." Though many students are interested in the sciences, everyone at Johns Hopkins "brings something unique to the school whether it is their love for art, school spirit at sporting events or their desire to find a cure for cancer." The demographics include "a lot of international people and people from various backgrounds." There may be "a lot of introverts," but "people are very nice and helpful," and everyone is "invested in the livelihood of the Hopkins community."

FINANCIAL AID: 410-516-8028 • E-MAIL: GOTOJHU@JHU.EDU • WEBSITE: WWW.JHU.EDU

THE PRINCETON REVIEW SAYS

Admissions

Very important factors considered include: rigor of secondary school record, academic GPA, application essay, recommendation(s), character/personal qualities. *Important factors considered include:* class rank, standardized test scores, extracurricular activities, talent/ability. *Other factors considered include:* interview, first generation, alumni/ae relation, geographical residence, state residency, racial/ethnic status, volunteer work, work experience. SAT or ACT required. ACT with or without writing accepted. SAT with or without Essay component accepted. TOEFL required of all international applicants. High school diploma or equivalent is not required. *Academic units recommended:* 4 English, 4 math, 4 science, 4 foreign language, 2 social studies, 2 history.

Financial Aid

Students should submit: FAFSA, CSS/Financial Aid PROFILE, Noncustodial PROFILE. The Princeton Review suggests that all financial aid forms be submitted as soon as possible after October 1. *Need-based scholarships/grants offered:* Federal Pell, FSEOG, State scholarships/grants, Private scholarships, College/university scholarship or grant aid from institutional funds. *Loan aid offered:* Direct Subsidized Stafford Loans, Direct Unsubsidized Stafford Loans, Direct PLUS loans, Federal Perkins Loans, College/university loans from institutional funds. Applicants will be notified of awards on or about 4/1. Federal Work-Study Program available. Institutional employment available.

The Inside Word

Top schools like Hopkins receive more and more applications every year and, as a result, grow harder and harder to get into. With more than 20,000 applicants, Hopkins can be highly selective and look for individuals who will thrive in the Hopkins community. Counselors utilize a holistic approach to admissions and in particular are looking for applicants who can demonstrate their academic character, their impact outside of the classroom, and how they engage with their communities.

THE SCHOOL SAYS "..."

From the Admissions Office

"Johns Hopkins University is a place where ambitious, talented, and creative students thrive. Here, students in all majors embrace a spirit of learning through exploration and discovery. We offer students the freedom to pursue their intellectual passions, the opportunity to learn from academic leaders, and the chance to make an impact right away. With no core curriculum, students are able—and encouraged—to build the academic path that is right for them, with guidance from staff and administrators to help them find their way. Our students can combine their interests—academic and otherwise—in ways that are meaningful to them, and often discover new passions while they're here. Double majoring and majoring or taking classes across disciplines are common practices; in addition, over 97 percent of students have at least one career-related experience as undergraduates. Studying abroad is also a common option. Outside of the classroom, students are active and engaged on a lively campus, involved in activities from dance or singing groups to international service organizations. The admissions committee approaches applications from a holistic perspective, evaluating the 'whole student.' In addition to looking at a student's academic achievement and intellectual curiosity, we seek to admit students who are excited about learning and living at Johns Hopkins. We look for students who will bring something to the campus community while taking advantage of all Johns Hopkins has to offer."

SELECTIVITY

Admissions Rating	99
# of applicants	24,716
% of applicants accepted	13
% of acceptees attending	40
# offered a place on the wait list	2,752
% accepting a place on wait list	63
% admitted from wait list	11
# of early decision applicants	1,866
% accepted early decision	29

FRESHMAN PROFILE

Range SAT Critical Reading	690–760
Range SAT Math	710–790
Range SAT Writing	690–770
Range ACT Composite	32–34
Minimum paper TOEFL	600
Average HS GPA	3.9
% graduated top 10% of class	92
% graduated top 25% of class	99
% graduated top 50% of class	100

DEADLINES

Early decision	
Deadline	11/1
Notification	12/15
Regular	
Deadline	1/1
Notification	4/1
Nonfall registration?	No

APPLICANTS ALSO LOOK AT AND OFTEN PREFER

University of Pennsylvania; Princeton University; Massachusetts Institute of Technology; Yale University; Harvard College

AND SOMETIMES PREFER

Cornell University; Northwestern University

AND RARELY PREFER

Washington University in St. Louis

FINANCIAL FACTS

Financial Aid Rating	93
Annual Tuition	$50,410
Room and board	$14,976
Required fees	$500
Average frosh need-based scholarship	$38,946
Average UG need-based scholarship	$36,687
% needy frosh rec. need-based scholarship or grant aid	94
% needy UG rec. need-based scholarship or grant aid	92
% needy frosh rec. non-need-based scholarship or grant aid	33
% needy UG rec. non-need-based scholarship or grant aid	20
% needy frosh rec. need-based self-help aid	80
% needy UG rec. need-based self-help aid	84
% frosh rec. any financial aid	63
% UG rec. any financial aid	57
% UG borrow to pay for school	42
Average cumulative indebtedness	$24,702
% frosh need fully met	100
% ugrads need fully met	100
Average % of frosh need met	100
Average % of ugrad need met	100

JUNIATA COLLEGE

1700 MOORE STREET, HUNTINGDON, PA 16652 • ADMISSIONS: 814-641-3420 • FAX: 814-641-3100

CAMPUS LIFE

Quality of Life Rating	89
Fire Safety Rating	88
Green Rating	66
Type of school	Private
Affiliation	Church of Brethren
Environment	Village

STUDENTS

Total undergrad enrollment	1,570
% male/female	44/56
% from out of state	34
% frosh from public high school	80
% frosh live on campus	99
% ugrads live on campus	82
% African American	3
% Asian	4
% Caucasian	73
% Hispanic	4
% Native American	<1
% Pacific Islander	0
% Two or more races	2
% Race and/or ethnicity unknown	6
% international	8
# of countries represented	29

SURVEY SAYS...
Students are happy
Lab facilities are great
Great financial aid
Students are friendly
Students environmentally aware
Easy to get around campus

ACADEMICS

Academic Rating	84
% students returning for sophomore year	86
% students graduating within 4 years	67
% students graduating within 6 years	73
Calendar	Semester
Student/faculty ratio	13:1
Profs interesting rating	90
Profs accessible rating	87

Most classes have 10–19 students.
Most lab/discussion sessions have 10–19 students.

MOST POPULAR MAJORS
Biology; Physical Sciences; Business/Commerce

STUDENTS SAY "..."

Academics

Juniata College is a private liberal arts college located in Huntingdon, Pennsylvania. The college is named after the Juniata River. The school has "excellent science programs," and a few students say that there need to be "more resources [for] non-science programs." However, even students not majoring in science get access to some great facilities, with theater students exclaiming, "The theater program is unlike any other in country" and praising their new Halbritter Center for the Performing Arts. At Juniata, students can choose one of the many majors offered, or they can design their own under the Program of Emphasis. Many students do so, about 30 percent, which allows each student to choose which classes would best fit their intended area of study. All students have the option of working with two faculty advisors. The "outstanding education" is built on a bedrock of strong faculty members who offer "superior education through meaningful personal interaction." Most class sizes tend to be fairly small, and though some classes are "tough to get in to because there is only one professor for a certain subject," many agree that they love the attention that each professor gives and that the teachers "really go out of their way" to help students succeed and "value student success as much as the student does." Success, however, doesn't come without a price at Juniata, with a large amount of the students agreeing that their "good grades do not come without effort," but that the class load is "challenging, but not overwhelming."

Life

Students seem to agree that there "isn't much to do in the town" of Huntingdon, but Juniata College makes up for it by making sure there is "always something to do" on campus. There are so many activities and groups on campus that some say, "It feels like you're missing out if you go home for the weekend." There are a "lot of traditions such as Storming of the Arch, Mountain Day, and Madrigal" that have been around the campus for decades and help bring students together. For instance, during Mountain Day, classes are canceled, and students and faculty are shuttled to a state park near the school where there are lunches, nature walks, and various games being played, and neither group knows when exactly it is going to be until the morning of the event. While there might be a lot of activities to do on campus, "if you want to party you can find one." If you want to just relax with your fellow students, "Raystown Lake is only twenty minutes away," where many students like to go and relax. Back on campus, many students seem to think that the "dorms and food" need improvement, but believe that the academic experience they receive outweighs those inconveniences.

Student Body

Students tend to describe themselves as "driven" and "passionately interested in their subjects," though they also take pride in their "laid-back" attitudes, saying they "know how to balance fun and work." During the week students "tend to buckle down and get their work done." A lot of "exchange students from around the world" that come to Juniata College to pursue their education. Students agree that "everyone fits in somewhere" at Juniata College because "people are accepted not despite their differences, but because of them."

FINANCIAL AID: 814-641-3141 • E-MAIL: ADMISSIONS@JUNIATA.EDU • WEBSITE: WWW.JUNIATA.EDU

THE PRINCETON REVIEW SAYS

Admissions

Very important factors considered include: rigor of secondary school record, academic GPA, standardized test scores, application essay, recommendation(s), character/personal qualities. *Important factors considered include:* interview, extracurricular activities, talent/ability, first generation, volunteer work. *Other factors considered include:* alumni/ae relation, geographical residence, state residency, racial/ethnic status, level of applicant's interest. SAT or ACT recommend. ACT with or without writing accepted. TOEFL required of all international applicants. High school diploma is required and GED is accepted. *Academic units required:* 4 English, 3 math, 3 science, 2 science labs, 1 social studies, 3 history.

Financial Aid

Students should submit: FAFSA. Priority filing deadline is 2/15. The Princeton Review suggests that all financial aid forms be submitted as soon as possible after October 1. *Need-based scholarships/grants offered:* Federal Pell, FSEOG, State scholarships/grants, Private scholarships, College/university scholarship or grant aid from institutional funds. *Loan aid offered:* Direct Subsidized Stafford Loans, Direct Unsubsidized Stafford Loans, Direct PLUS loans, Federal Perkins Loans, College/university loans from institutional funds. Applicants will be notified of awards on a rolling basis beginning 3/1. Federal Work-Study Program available. Institutional employment available.

The Inside Word

High school seniors who are interested in Juniata must apply either by November 15 for early decision or by Feburary 15 for regular decision. Interested applicants can submit their SAT or ACT scores, but standardized test scores are not required. This is in addition to the required essays that are part of the application process. For those looking to save some money, there is no application fee for anyone who applies to Juniata via the website. They also provide incoming freshman with Inbound Retreats each August, which allows them to sign up for one of thirty-eight different retreats and get an idea of what college life is like, but without having to go to class.

THE SCHOOL SAYS ". . ."

From the Admissions Office

"Juniata's unique approach to learning has a flexible, student-centered focus. With the help of two advisors, more than half of Juniata's students designed their own Program of Emphasis (POE)—it's like a major but better. Those who choose a more traditional academic journey still benefit from the assistance of two faculty advisors and interdisciplinary collaboration between multiple academic departments. In addition, all students benefit from the recent, significant investments in academic facilities that help students actively learn by doing. For example, the new Halbritter Center for the Performing Arts houses an innovative theater program where theater professionals work side-by-side with students. The Sill Business Incubator provides $5,000 in seed capital to students with a desire to start their own business. The LEED-certified Raystown Environmental Studies Field Station, located on nearby Raystown Lake, gives unparalleled, hands-on study opportunities to students. And the von Liebig Center for Science provides opportunities for student/faculty research surpassing those available at even large universities. As the 2003 Middle States Accreditation Team noted, 'Juniata is truly a student-centered college. There is a remarkable cohesiveness in this commitment—faculty, students, trustees, staff, and alumni, each from their own vantage point, describe a community in which the growth of the student is central.' This cohesiveness creates a dynamic learning environment that enables students to think and grow intellectually, to evolve in their academic careers, and to graduate as active, successful participants in the global community. Freshman applicants may submit the SAT (or the ACT with or without the writing component). We will use their best scores from either test. "

SELECTIVITY

Admissions Rating	83
# of applicants	2,604
% of applicants accepted	77
% of acceptees attending	18
# offered a place on the wait list	40
# of early decision applicants	111
% accepted early decision	87

FRESHMAN PROFILE

Range SAT Critical Reading	510–630
Range SAT Math	510–620
Range SAT Writing	480–600
Range ACT Composite	23–29
Minimum paper TOEFL	550
Minimum internet-based TOEFL	79
Average HS GPA	3.7
% graduated top 10% of class	30
% graduated top 25% of class	58
% graduated top 50% of class	91

DEADLINES

Early decision	
Deadline	11/15
Notification	12/23
Other ED	
Deadline	11/15
Notification	12/23
Regular	
Deadline	2/15
Notification	2/1
Nonfall registration?	Yes

APPLICANTS ALSO LOOK AT AND OFTEN PREFER
Gettysburg College

AND SOMETIMES PREFER
Allegheny College; Susquehanna University

FINANCIAL FACTS

Financial Aid Rating	85
Annual tuition	$41,390
Room and board	$11,590
Required fees	$780
Books and supplies	$1,000
Average frosh need-based scholarship	$26,702
Average UG need-based scholarship	$26,136
% needy frosh rec. need-based scholarship or grant aid	99
% needy UG rec. need-based scholarship or grant aid	98
% needy frosh rec. non-need-based scholarship or grant aid	18
% needy UG rec. non-need-based scholarship or grant aid	15
% needy frosh rec. need-based self-help aid	82
% needy UG rec. need-based self-help aid	84
% frosh rec. any financial aid	100
% UG rec. any financial aid	100
% UG borrow to pay for school	71
Average cumulative indebtedness	$35,774
% frosh need fully met	25
% ugrads need fully met	22
Average % of frosh need met	83
Average % of ugrad need met	82

KALAMAZOO COLLEGE

1200 ACADEMY STREET, KALAMAZOO, MI 49006 • ADMISSIONS: 269-337-7166 • FAX: 269-337-7390

STUDENTS SAY "..."

Academics

If you are looking for a "unique" school with "close knit" community and a study abroad program that "is bar none," look no further than Kalamazoo. Founded in 1833, this Michigan school is known for its flexible "K Plan," which "allows students to design their own schedules with only a few universal requirements." "The curriculum is writing intensive and prepares students for a broad spectrum of jobs that may be available," one economics major explains. Because of its intimate size, Kalamazoo College is a place where students "feel like a name rather than a number." The school's "smart, demanding, [and] supportive" professors are "one of the best things about the school." They "take the time to get to know you" by being "really accessible" and wanting "you to come to their office hours to talk with them." The professors at Kalamazoo have real world experience in their fields and bring these "interesting experiences into the classroom to be discussed broken apart piece by piece and put back together in a meaningful and productive way." "As at any college, there are some mediocre or bad professors," one student cautions, "but I have had far more great experiences than poor ones." Kalmazoo's education goes beyond just academics. As one student explains, "We learn skills that not only prepare us for careers in the future, but also how to be better people." A psychology major sums up Kalamazoo as "a place that encompasses social justice, challenging, yet enriching academics, inside a liberal atmosphere."

Life

Kalamazoo students can't say enough about "the sense of community at this school" that students guarantee is "something that you won't be able to find at most other schools." "A welcoming spirit" abounds in this "home-like environment where everyone knows and loves everyone." Because of the school's size, "students are heavily invested in their education and engaged in campus life." Students enjoy strolling around the "Ivy League-style campus" and "club involvement is huge." Downtown Kalamazoo is right off campus, giving students access to urban amenities like "quality restaurants" and "a nice movie theater." However, another student cautions that "the downtown is basic and many shops and restaurants fall outside of a student budget." Consequently, "campus is the social hub." Kalamazoo fosters an intellectually active community and much of student life revolves around "discussing issues surrounding social justice or politics." The "work hard, play hard mentality" can be seen through the numerous parties—"more than you'd expect for such a small, academic school." However, there is something for everyone on campus as "the school puts on lots of events for those who wish to avoid partying."

Student Body

"Liberal kids dominate" at Kalamazoo, but students stress that "everyone who goes to K can find a different niche to fit in to." Although "a large percentage of students do come from Michigan or the Midwest," the student body includes many foreign students, and the majority of students study abroad. "It's no secret that everyone at K is weird," one happy student explains. "But the good thing is that we're all weird in different ways. And we're all awesome weirdos." As another student explains, "K is all about taking the smart and slightly quirky people from high school and putting them together in an environment that involves hard work and worldly experience." If there is one thing that Kalamazoo students have in common, it is creativity. Students are "creative in their schoolwork, hobbies, extracurricular activities, fashions, basically anything."

KALAMAZOO COLLEGE

FINANCIAL AID: 269-337-7192 • E-MAIL: ADMISSION@KZOO.EDU • WEBSITE: WWW.KZOO.EDU

THE PRINCETON REVIEW SAYS

Admissions

Very important factors considered include: rigor of secondary school record, academic GPA, extracurricular activities. *Important factors considered include:* application essay, recommendation(s). *Other factors considered include:* standardized test scores, interview, talent/ability, character/personal qualities, first generation, alumni/ae relation, geographical residence, state residency, racial/ethnic status, volunteer work, work experience, level of applicant's interest. SAT or ACT considered if submitted. ACT with or without writing accepted. SAT with Essay component required. TOEFL required of all international applicants. High school diploma is required and GED is accepted. *Academic units required:* 4 English, 3 math, 3 science, 3 foreign language, 2 social studies, 2 history. *Academic units recommended:* 4 English, 4 math, 4 science, 4 foreign language, 2 social studies, 2 history.

Financial Aid

Students should submit: FAFSA. Priority filing deadline is 2/15. The Princeton Review suggests that all financial aid forms be submitted as soon as possible after October 1. *Need-based scholarships/grants offered:* Federal Pell, FSEOG, State scholarships/grants, Private scholarships, College/university scholarship or grant aid from institutional funds. *Loan aid offered:* Direct Subsidized Stafford Loans, Direct Unsubsidized Stafford Loans, Direct PLUS loans, Federal Perkins Loans. Applicants will be notified of awards on a rolling basis beginning 3/23. Federal Work-Study Program available. Institutional employment available.

The Inside Word

The "K-Plan," which focuses on a broad liberal arts education and engagement with other cultures, is central to the Kalamazoo education. Consequently, college admissions officers are on the lookout for students that show the creativity, ambition, and motivation to thrive at Kalamazoo. Students with artistic backgrounds will want to emphasize that in their application. Admissions are competitive here, so applicants will be expected to have strong test scores and high school grades.

THE SCHOOL SAYS "..."

From the Admissions Office

"It is rare to find the purposeful integration and high participation rate of experiential education that is found at Kalamazoo College. During the past fifty years, 85 percent of our graduates have formally studied in another country while 80 percent have completed an internship or externship, and 100 percent complete a senior project. Our students often pursue international internships and senior project experiences, in addition to their planned study abroad terms. Also, Kalamazoo is one of the few selective liberal arts colleges to be found in a city—the Kalamazoo metro area has a population of approximately 225,000 with the advantage of being near a university of nearly 30,000 students. It is a diverse and vibrant community with wonderful access to the arts, athletics, service-learning, and social activism opportunities. We do more in four years so students can do more in a lifetime.

"Emphasis in admission is placed on a student's high school experience including GPA, course selection, and co-curricular involvement."

SELECTIVITY	
Admissions Rating	88
# of applicants	2,455
% of applicants accepted	72
% of acceptees attending	21
# offered a place on the wait list	228
% accepting a place on wait list	28
# of early decision applicants	37
% accepted early decision	84

FRESHMAN PROFILE	
Range SAT Critical Reading	530–660
Range SAT Math	540–690
Range SAT Writing	510–650
Range ACT Composite	26–30
Minimum paper TOEFL	550
Minimum internet-based TOEFL	84
Average HS GPA	3.8
% graduated top 10% of class	40
% graduated top 25% of class	79
% graduated top 50% of class	97

DEADLINES	
Early decision	
Deadline	11/1
Notification	12/1
Early action	
Deadline	11/1
Notification	12/20
Regular	
Priority	11/15
Deadline	2/15
Notification	4/1
Nonfall registration?	No

**APPLICANTS ALSO LOOK AT
AND OFTEN PREFER**
Georgetown University

AND SOMETIMES PREFER
Albion College

FINANCIAL FACTS	
Financial Aid Rating	89
Annual tuition	$42,510
Room and board	$8,886
Required fees	$336
Books and supplies	$720
Average frosh need-based scholarship	$29,445
Average UG need-based scholarship	$28,294
% needy frosh rec. need-based scholarship or grant aid	97
% needy UG rec. need-based scholarship or grant aid	98
% needy frosh rec. non-need-based scholarship or grant aid	28
% needy UG rec. non-need-based scholarship or grant aid	20
% needy frosh rec. need-based self-help aid	75
% needy UG rec. need-based self-help aid	81
% frosh rec. any financial aid	98
% UG rec. any financial aid	97
% UG borrow to pay for school	61
Average cumulative indebtedness	$28,764
% frosh need fully met	58
% ugrads need fully met	47
Average % of frosh need met	94
Average % of ugrad need met	92

KANSAS STATE UNIVERSITY

119 ANDERSON HALL, MANHATTAN, KS 66506 • ADMISSIONS: 785-532-6250 • FAX: 785-532-6393

CAMPUS LIFE

Quality of Life Rating	99
Fire Safety Rating	60*
Green Rating	60*
Type of school	Public
Affiliation	No Affiliation
Environment	Town

STUDENTS

Total undergrad enrollment	19,859
% male/female	52/48
% from out of state	18
% frosh from public high school	80
% frosh live on campus	74
% ugrads live on campus	23
# of fraternities (% ugrad men join)	28 (0)
# of sororities (% ugrad women join)	16 (0)
% African American	4
% Asian	1
% Caucasian	78
% Hispanic	7
% Native American	<1
% Pacific Islander	<1
% Two or more races	3
% Race and/or ethnicity unknown	1
% international	6
# of countries represented	107

SURVEY SAYS...

Students are happy
Great library
Career services are great
Internships are widely available
School is well run
Great financial aid
Students are friendly
Diverse student types interact on campus
Students are very religious
Students get along with local community
Students love Manhattan, KS
Great food on campus
Great off-campus food
Easy to get around campus
Recreation facilities are great
Everyone loves the Wildcats
Intramural sports are popular
Alumni active on campus
Active minority support groups

ACADEMICS

Academic Rating	70
% students returning for sophomore year	83
% students graduating within 4 years	29
% students graduating within 6 years	62
Calendar	Semester
Student/faculty ratio	19:1
Profs interesting rating	78
Profs accessible rating	86
Most classes have 20–29 students.	

MOST POPULAR MAJORS

Business Administration and Management;
Animal Sciences; Mechanical Engineering

STUDENTS SAY "..."

Academics

Despite its large size, Kansas State University "still has a small-town, welcoming feeling" and "a family atmosphere that the whole university buys into." With such a strong focus on community, students say that "you'll usually be only a few degrees of separation from any other person." The long history of K-State (students wear purple all the time, since "there's a lot of Wildcat pride across campus") is "something that you can't get anywhere else." Some facilities "could receive a boost," though, as "there are a lot of great buildings on campus, but there are some classrooms that need an update." At the end of the day, K-State "is all about putting students first, and they put you first as soon as you become a freshman." And the faculty is no exception: "K-State's professors commit beyond the classroom. Not only are they catalysts for my learning, they push me as a person and always give me the support I need in the most genuine way," and "they focus on not just lecturing info to you, they also use class discussion, even in large lectures, as a way for them to see that you understand what is being taught. I haven't had one professor not include some sort of class discussion into class time."

Life

Manhattan, Kansas, is "the perfect college town—not too big, not too small." There are lots of student discounts, "delicious restaurants, and quirky gift shops," and on the weekends you will find most students in the beloved Aggieville, the local entertainment district. Overall, "Manhattan is a great place to live, both as a student and a graduate. The university works well with the community, and vice versa. Students are not looked down upon, and it is a great college town." A lot of the social life at K-State "revolves around the sporting events," especially football, with many students "reserving their Saturdays to watch our team." Outside of sports, students hit up Aggieville, as well as "the many [Union Program Council] Events held on campus," such as "one dollar movies on the weekends, dances within the residence halls, and crafts at the union." The school has more than 475 student organizations to get involved in, from religious organizations to athletic clubs; "there is something for everyone here at K-State, and if we don't have it, start it."

Student Body

"Community is extremely important here" is the general consensus that rings out amongst the Wildcat populace of K-State. And, since most people at this are Kansans, there is a strong Midwestern vibe amongst these "down-to-earth, family-oriented people," all of whom "consider success in college a very important aspect of their lives." Everyone is "pumped about our sports and traditions"—football is understandably big here—and most people can be found "wearing purple and excited for the next sporting event!" "Many" students at K-State "have a Church background." While some feel that the students here are "not exactly the most modern thinkers," nearly all agree that the students are "very friendly and approachable."

KANSAS STATE UNIVERSITY

FINANCIAL AID: 785-532-6420 • E-MAIL: K-STATE@K-STATE.EDU • WEBSITE: WWW.K-STATE.EDU

THE PRINCETON REVIEW SAYS

Admissions

Very important factors considered include: rigor of secondary school record, class rank, academic GPA, standardized test scores. *Other factors considered include:* recommendation(s). SAT or ACT recommend. ACT with or without writing accepted. SAT with or without Essay component accepted. High school diploma is required and GED is accepted. *Academic units required:* 4 English, 3 math, 3 science, 3 social studies, 3 academic electives.

Financial Aid

Students should submit: FAFSA. Priority filing deadline is 3/1. The Princeton Review suggests that all financial aid forms be submitted as soon as possible after October 1. *Need-based scholarships/grants offered:* Federal Pell, FSEOG, State scholarships/grants, Private scholarships, College/university scholarship or grant aid from institutional funds. *Loan aid offered:* Direct Subsidized Stafford Loans, Direct Unsubsidized Stafford Loans, Direct PLUS loans, Federal Perkins Loans, College/university loans from institutional funds. Applicants will be notified of awards on a rolling basis beginning 4/1. Federal Work-Study Program available. Institutional employment available.

The Inside Word

Though K-State is chock full of strong students, admission is refreshingly straightforward. Completion of the pre-college curriculum is required, and if you're a Kansas student, you must obtain at least a 2.0 GPA on these courses. Nonresidents must obtain at least a 2.5 GPA. You will then need to get either a 21 ACT composite score, a 980 when combining the critical reading and math sections of the SAT, or rank in the top third of your high school class. A cumulative GPA of at least 2.0 must also be achieved on all attempted college work. These basic requirements will qualify your admission. In other words, you're in!

THE SCHOOL SAYS "..."

From the Admissions Office

"In addition to strong academic programs and exceptional faculty, Kansas State University is home to a one-of-a-kind family atmosphere. Take K-State Proud, a student-led, nationally recognized philanthropy that allows students to create scholarships for their peers. So far, the campaign has raised more than $1 million.

"Members of the K-State family come from all fifty states and more than 100 countries. K-Staters find their footing through K-State First, a first-year experience program that helps freshmen establish a strong foundation through shared courses, learning communities, mentors and a common book program. It's easy for students to customize their college experiences to fit individual personalities and interests. Kansas State University offers more than 250 majors and options, and 475 student organizations and clubs—with the option to create your own. One prominent student organization, the Black Student Union, won the Clarence Wine Award for Outstanding Big 12 Council of the Year for the eighth time in the past eleven years. Each year, the university awards $26 million in scholarships and $230 million in financial aid. We're proud to offer students a multitude of ways to find success, including undergraduate research opportunities. Kansas State University undergraduates have researched everything from sustainable energy to musical lyrics. The university's numerous research facilities and centers offer invaluable resources for students to explore and discover. As the university pushes forward to become a Top 50 public research university by 2025, there has never been a better time to be a K-Stater."

SELECTIVITY

Admissions Rating	74
# of applicants	9,178
% of applicants accepted	95
% of acceptees attending	42

FRESHMAN PROFILE

Range SAT Critical Reading	470–600
Range SAT Math	480–640
Range SAT Writing	440–580
Range ACT Composite	22–28
Average HS GPA	3.5
% graduated top 10% of class	22
% graduated top 25% of class	47
% graduated top 50% of class	75

DEADLINES

Nonfall registration?	Yes

FINANCIAL FACTS

Financial Aid Rating	84
Annual in-state tuition	$8,517
Annual out-of-state tuition	$22,596
Room and board	$8,430
Required fees	$833
Books and supplies	$856
Average frosh need-based scholarship	$4,363
Average UG need-based scholarship	$4,298
% needy frosh rec. need-based scholarship or grant aid	54
% needy UG rec. need-based scholarship or grant aid	56
% needy frosh rec. non-need-based scholarship or grant aid	72
% needy UG rec. non-need-based scholarship or grant aid	49
% needy frosh rec. need-based self-help aid	69
% needy UG rec. need-based self-help aid	77
% UG borrow to pay for school	58
Average cumulative indebtedness	$25,799
% frosh need fully met	19
% ugrads need fully met	16
Average % of frosh need met	78
Average % of ugrad need met	77

KENYON COLLEGE

KENYON COLLEGE, ADMISSION OFFICE, GAMBIER, OH 43022-9623 • ADMISSIONS: 740-427-5776 • FAX: 740-427-5770

CAMPUS LIFE

Quality of Life Rating	90
Fire Safety Rating	89
Green Rating	80
Type of school	Private
Affiliation	Episcopal, but non-denominational in practice
Environment	Rural

STUDENTS

Total undergrad enrollment	1,698
% male/female	45/55
% from out of state	83
% frosh from public high school	51
% frosh live on campus	100
% ugrads live on campus	100
# of fraternities (% ugrad men join)	7 (18)
# of sororities (% ugrad women join)	4 (20)
% African American	4
% Asian	4
% Caucasian	73
% Hispanic	7
% Native American	<1
% Pacific Islander	0
% Two or more races	4
% Race and/or ethnicity unknown	3
% international	5
# of countries represented	41

SURVEY SAYS...

Lots of liberal students
Students always studying
Students are happy
Classroom facilities are great
Lab facilities are great
Class discussions encouraged
No one cheats
Students are friendly
Students aren't religious
Recreation facilities are great
Lots of beer drinking
Hard liquor is popular
Theater is popular
Campus newspaper is popular

ACADEMICS

Academic Rating	96
% students returning for sophomore year	93
% students graduating within 4 years	84
% students graduating within 6 years	88
Calendar	Semester
Student/faculty ratio	10:1
Profs interesting rating	97
Profs accessible rating	97
Most classes have 10–19 students.	

MOST POPULAR MAJORS
Economics; Psychology; English

STUDENTS SAY "..."

Academics

This tiny midwestern liberal arts mainstay is Ohio's oldest private college, and is filled with "uniquely quirky and motivated" students and faculty alike. The school's "academic vigor" and intense focus on writing (it is known as "The Writers' College") are two of Kenyon's hallmarks, and the curriculum provides "a well-rounded liberal arts education in which emphasis [is] placed on critical thinking and class discussion." "Even though I don't want to be an English major, I think any college that values writing as much as Kenyon does has its priorities straight," says a student of the highly valued workforce skill.

The school "really knows how to offer a huge diversity of programs and activities to a very small campus," and "it is honestly hard to find a professor who is not thrilled by the content that they are teaching." The faculty is a deeply caring bunch who "love learning just as much as the students" and challenge them to succeed, and they make it known that "your voice is valued in class discussion." "I once met with a professor for an hour every day leading up to the final because I was so nervous about it, and he hardly batted an eye at taking that much time out of his day for only one student," says a sophomore.

"Small, individualized class sizes" make it so that classes are "terrifically interesting," and "out of class work is always meaningful." Students don't compete with each other when it comes to grades so "the cooperative learning environment makes it less stressful," and though "you will spend the vast majority of your time studying … it is also extremely rewarding." The "relatively" open curriculum allows students to take courses that they are truly interested in, and "there is a wide variety of options available in terms of classes" for students to develop new passions.

Life

People come to this "small campus with a big sense of community" because they know it will be a good fit, and it shows in the satisfaction levels here. "I stepped on campus and noticed two things: everyone was happy and the campus was gorgeous," says one of many happy students. The school is a place for "smart, forward-thinking students who study hard but also understand the necessity of taking breaks and having a good time on weekends." People at Kenyon are taught "to see, discuss, and connect the dots"; "Even though I'm not a philosophy major I feel just as at home in those conversations as I do when I discuss Mahler or the next big party," says a student.

The "utterly pastoral" campus is "absolutely lovely"; "It's like going to school in a Marlowe poem—and with all of the English majors running around, most people know who Marlowe is," says a student. The town of Gambier is "in the middle of nowhere, so campus can get to be claustrophobic at times," but it provides its fair share of entertainment. "Greeks throw great parties [and] intramurals are popular, as are activist groups for everything from gender awareness to Palestine," and the nearby Kokosing Gap Trail is oft-used. The KAC (Kenyon Athletic Center) is unparalleled for a Division III school, and the "dining hall has an amazing commitment to local food." Partying on Wednesdays and the weekends "is a typical activity to unwind after a challenging week of academics."

Student Body

The word most often used to describe Kenyon students in "quirky." There are a variety of types, but "most people have a quirk or five." There are "a lot of hipster students and then a good selection of athletes" at Kenyon, but everyone "tends to be extremely friendly, well-rounded, and smart." Everyone is seriously involved in academics and extracurriculars, and "you're either a jack of all trades here or a master of four." There aren't really many cliques; "someone on the football team could just as easily be in the community choir or quiz bowl club."

KENYON COLLEGE

FINANCIAL AID: 740-427-5240 • E-MAIL: ADMISSIONS@KENYON.EDU • WEBSITE: WWW.KENYON.EDU

THE PRINCETON REVIEW SAYS

Admissions

Very important factors considered include: rigor of secondary school record, academic GPA, application essay, recommendation(s), character/personal qualities. *Important factors considered include:* class rank, standardized test scores, interview, extracurricular activities, talent/ability, level of applicant's interest. *Other factors considered include:* first generation, alumni/ae relation, geographical residence, state residency, racial/ethnic status, volunteer work, work experience. SAT or ACT required; SAT Subject Tests considered if submitted. ACT with or without writing accepted. TOEFL required of all international applicants. High school diploma is required and GED is accepted. *Academic units required:* 4 English, 4 math, 3 science, 3 science labs, 3 foreign language, 3 social studies, 3 academic electives. *Academic units recommended:* 4 English, 4 math, 4 science, 3 science labs, 4 foreign language, 3 social studies, 3 academic electives, and 1 unit from above areas or other academic areas.

Financial Aid

Students should submit: FAFSA, CSS/Financial Aid PROFILE, Noncustodial PROFILE. Regular filing deadline is 2/15. The Princeton Review suggests that all financial aid forms be submitted as soon as possible after October 1. *Need-based scholarships/grants offered:* Federal Pell, FSEOG, State scholarships/grants, Private scholarships, College/university scholarship or grant aid from institutional funds. *Loan aid offered:* Direct Subsidized Stafford Loans, Direct Unsubsidized Stafford Loans, Direct PLUS loans, Federal Perkins Loans, College/university loans from institutional funds. Federal Work-Study Program available. Institutional employment available.

The Inside Word

In terms of admissions selectivity, Kenyon is of the first order of selective, small, Midwestern, liberal arts schools. Kenyon shares a lot of application and admit overlap with other schools in this niche, and the choice for many students comes down to "best fit." As Kenyon is a writing-intensive institution, applicants should expect that all written material submitted to the school in the admissions process will be scrutinized. Revise and proofread accordingly.

THE SCHOOL SAYS "..."

From the Admissions Office

"Students and alumni alike think of Kenyon as a place that fosters 'learning in the company of friends.' While faculty expectations are rigorous and the work challenging, the academic atmosphere is cooperative, not competitive. Indications of intellectual curiosity and passion for learning, more than just high grades and test scores, are what we look for in applications. Important as well are demonstrated interests in non-academic pursuits, whether in athletics, the arts, writing, or another passion. Life in this small college community is fueled by the talents and enthusiasm of our students, so the admission staff seeks students who have a range of talents and interests.

"The high school transcript, recommendations, and the personal statement are of primary importance in reviewing preparedness and fit. Standardized tests (SAT or ACT) are of secondary importance."

SELECTIVITY
Admissions Rating	95
# of applicants	7,076
% of applicants accepted	24
% of acceptees attending	29
# offered a place on the wait list	2,876
% accepting a place on wait list	35
% admitted from wait list	2
# of early decision applicants	428
% accepted early decision	58

FRESHMAN PROFILE
Range SAT Critical Reading	630–730
Range SAT Math	610–690
Range SAT Writing	620–720
Range ACT Composite	28–32
Minimum internet-based TOEFL	100
Average HS GPA	4.0
% graduated top 10% of class	61
% graduated top 25% of class	54
% graduated top 50% of class	97

DEADLINES
Early decision	
Deadline	11/15
Notification	12/15
Regular	
Priority	1/15
Deadline	1/15
Notification	4/1
Nonfall registration?	No

APPLICANTS ALSO LOOK AT AND RARELY PREFER
Skidmore College; Earlham College; Case Western Reserve University; Miami University; Dickinson College; Connecticut College; The College of Wooster

FINANCIAL FACTS
Financial Aid Rating	92
Annual tuition	$49,220
Room and board	$12,130
Required fees	$1,980
Books and supplies	$1,900
Average frosh need-based scholarship	$40,319
Average UG need-based scholarship	$39,628
% needy frosh rec. need-based scholarship or grant aid	97
% needy UG rec. need-based scholarship or grant aid	96
% needy frosh rec. non-need-based scholarship or grant aid	26
% needy UG rec. non-need-based scholarship or grant aid	17
% needy frosh rec. need-based self-help aid	83
% needy UG rec. need-based self-help aid	80
% frosh rec. any financial aid	53
% UG rec. any financial aid	42
% UG borrow to pay for school	36
Average cumulative indebtedness	$27,000
% frosh need fully met	64
% ugrads need fully met	63
Average % of frosh need met	100
Average % of ugrad need met	100

KNOX COLLEGE

2 EAST SOUTH STREET, CAMPUS BOX 148, GALESBURG, IL 61401 • ADMISSIONS: 309-341-7100 • FAX: 309-341-7070

STUDENTS SAY "..."

Academics

Students say that Knox College enjoys a "great academic reputation" for its dedication to providing a "well-rounded liberal arts program" that "values independent initiative," while "staying in tune with its roots as a progressive and accessible institution." The college has a saying about students having "the freedom to flourish." The institution gives everyone "the appropriate space to grow on their own." "I knew that I would be allowed to be myself, choose the classes that I felt would have the most influence on my education and prepare me for the future." Students are highly encouraged to take classes outside of their majors. Undergraduates are "commonly studying two vastly different subjects and allowing them to merge into one interdisciplinary interest." Knox does have "one of the best creative writing programs in the country," as well as the Peace Corps Preparatory Program—offered solely through Knox. The academic trimester system, comprised of three classes each term, provides students with "a semester's worth of course work in a ten-week period." Many in the student body believe that this arrangement "promotes better study habits and more attention focused on each class," which are "tough and require a lot of time studying, reading, writing, and thinking." "You don't come to Knox if you want to shy away from class discussion," and professors "concentrate on the student having good critical thinking skills." Students are pleased to find that "you are academically challenged without fierce competition." "I've never had an easy professor, but I've always had reasonable ones." Projects and presentations are common; if tests are given, there is an honor code, and "they trust you not to cheat." The faculty and administration are spoken of highly, and they "not only encourage the students to take charge and make change, but they listen and act on the student body's opinions."

Life

Popular manners of relaxation and recreation include intramural sports, campus organizations, and "artistic expression, be it poetry, visual art, performance art, music." Students "go to parties, play games, dance, etc., just like any other college campus. The difference is, our fraternity parties are open to the entire campus and do not serve alcohol." Parties here "are places where you generally know everyone there, you have a good time and no one steals your coat or purse." Undergrads here are also very creative. "When we want to do something fun we typically organize it ourselves." A much-anticipated event is "Flunk Day, a day every spring when classes are canceled and the entire campus goes out on the lawn and plays games, eats great food and enjoys free entertainment." Union Board "brings films, entertainers, concerts, and other groups to campus, including Second City," and the Gizmo is "one of the best places to socialize and eat some late night food." Wandering off-campus a bit is also fun. Undergrads say "Galesburg is a charming town...you just have to look a little bit." "McGillacuddy's has amazing burgers, and Knox's music department hosts Jazz Nights there on Thursdays." Students enjoy the town's intimate, relaxing atmosphere: "Good coffee shops, a really nice park with a lake, and many beautiful old historic buildings," and "an annual Chocolate Festival." A twenty-four-hour diner is nearby, and "students can also drive to Peoria or take the train to Chicago."

Student Body

Knox is praised throughout the campus for its "support for first-generation college students, which really reflects Knox's history and values." "You'll meet a lot of people very fast, and by the end of your first term you'll already be good friends with a pretty big portion of the student body." Many undergrads portray themselves as "weird," with variations on a common theme: "We call it the 'Knox awkward.'" "The smart but sort of socially awkward kids in high school," what they describe as their social "Knoxwardness." "Everyone at Knox is a little eccentric, but we embrace each other's differences." "Students fit in by being themselves, no matter who they are." As one student perceptively notes, there is a "highly diverse combination of creative, intellectual minds here. It's as if every person here is some highly distinctive character from an artsy film." Another puts it a bit more succinctly: "Thank you college admission gods."

FINANCIAL AID: 309-341-7149 • E-MAIL: ADMISSION@KNOX.EDU • WEBSITE: WWW.KNOX.EDU

THE PRINCETON REVIEW SAYS

Admissions

Very important factors considered include: rigor of secondary school record, academic GPA, application essay. *Important factors considered include:* class rank, recommendation(s), interview, character/personal qualities. *Other factors considered include:* standardized test scores, extracurricular activities, talent/ability, first generation, alumni/ae relation, geographical residence, racial/ethnic status, volunteer work, level of applicant's interest. SAT or ACT recommend; SAT Subject Tests considered if submitted. ACT with or without writing accepted. TOEFL required of all international applicants. High school diploma is required and GED is accepted. *Academic units recommended:* 4 English, 4 math, 4 science, 2 science labs, 3 foreign language, 2 social studies, 2 history, 1 academic elective.

Financial Aid

Students should submit: FAFSA, Institution's own financial aid form. Priority filing deadline is 2/1. The Princeton Review suggests that all financial aid forms be submitted as soon as possible after October 1. *Need-based scholarships/grants offered:* Federal Pell, FSEOG, State scholarships/grants, Private scholarships, College/university scholarship or grant aid from institutional funds. *Loan aid offered:* Direct Subsidized Stafford Loans, Direct Unsubsidized Stafford Loans, Direct PLUS loans, Federal Perkins Loans, College/university loans from institutional funds. Applicants will be notified of awards on a rolling basis beginning 2/15. Federal Work-Study Program available. Institutional employment available.

The Inside Word

Knox draws students from nearly fifty countries and almost fifty states—with a student body of only 1,400, diversity is hugely important here. Admission standards are high, and prospective students are viewed both qualitatively and quantitatively. Three out of every four freshman were ranked in the top quarter of their high school classes.

THE SCHOOL SAYS "..."

From the Admissions Office

"The Knox experience is one that empowers you to experience your education in the classroom, in the real world, and through an ever-expanding network of personal and professional peers. Understanding that college should be a place where you explore your academic passions and where your talents are nourished, Knox gives you the freedom to flourish. At Knox, you'll discover how to learn and think for yourself, and to discover what you want to do with the knowledge and ideas you develop. By providing you with opportunities to both explore and 'do,' a Knox education is designed to give you the agility to pursue your chosen career path—even as it changes over time. Working with your faculty advisor from your first day on campus, you'll identify educational goals and a personal educational plan to achieve them. Your plan will include a broad foundation in the liberal arts and a primary area of specialization plus a second major or minor. You'll enhance what you learn in the classroom through internships, independent research, service projects, study abroad, and other hands-on learning experiences. You'll learn by doing, which will give you perspectives that can only be found by putting your knowledge into practice. Your Knox education proceeds along a course you set for yourself. As a result, your aspirations are met and our nation and the global community gain from citizens who are able to think for themselves, understand our complex and interdependent world, and act on their principles."

SELECTIVITY

Admissions Rating	85
# of applicants	3,445
% of applicants accepted	64
% of acceptees attending	18
# offered a place on the wait list	123
% accepting a place on wait list	19
% admitted from wait list	13

FRESHMAN PROFILE

Range SAT Critical Reading	580–630
Range SAT Math	590–660
Range SAT Writing	580–630
Range ACT Composite	23–29
Minimum paper TOEFL	550
Minimum internet-based TOEFL	80
% graduated top 10% of class	34
% graduated top 25% of class	67
% graduated top 50% of class	97

DEADLINES

Early action	
Deadline	11/1
Notification	11/30
Regular	
Deadline	1/15
Notification	3/30
Nonfall registration?	No

APPLICANTS ALSO LOOK AT AND SOMETIMES PREFER

University of Illinois at Urbana-Champaign; Illinois Wesleyan University

AND RARELY PREFER

Loyola University of Chicago; Northwestern University; Bradley University; Grinnell College; DePauw University

FINANCIAL FACTS

Financial Aid Rating	87
Annual tuition	$41,094
Room and board	$9,012
Required fees	$753
Average frosh need-based scholarship	$32,565
Average UG need-based scholarship	$29,393
% needy frosh rec. need-based scholarship or grant aid	99
% needy UG rec. need-based scholarship or grant aid	98
% needy frosh rec. non-need-based scholarship or grant aid	10
% needy UG rec. non-need-based scholarship or grant aid	11
% needy frosh rec. need-based self-help aid	88
% needy UG rec. need-based self-help aid	86
% frosh rec. any financial aid	99
% UG rec. any financial aid	98
% UG borrow to pay for school	60
Average cumulative indebtedness	$32,644
% frosh need fully met	23
% ugrads need fully met	26
Average % of frosh need met	91
Average % of ugrad need met	88

LAFAYETTE COLLEGE

118 MARKLE HALL, EASTON, PA 18042 • ADMISSIONS: 610-330-5100 • FAX: 610-330-5355

STUDENTS SAY "..."

Academics

Lafayette College is "a small, prestigious liberal arts school" that offers a "warm, community feel." Even before you decide to attend, "walking around campus left me with a cozy, at-home feeling," one psychology major gushes. Thanks to the "top-quality engineering education," many students say, "Lafayette is your classic liberal arts college with a twist" and point to the "vast array of research" and "study abroad opportunities" available to undergrads. The college "prides itself on student/faculty relationships." A geology major proclaims when professors are "good, they're great. Even the 'bad' professors, however, take the time to know each student and are usually available outside of class." An international affairs major says, "Whether you're an engineer, a premed student, or an art major, there is a great academic program and an embracing group of people waiting for you at Lafayette." Overall the professors get high marks because "their office doors are always open," and "are invested in seeing [students] not only graduate but also do well." The focus on undergraduate education provides "maximum opportunities and makes resumes and applications for graduate school and jobs look fierce!" Students go so far as to claim, "It's not very common to hear that someone doesn't like one of their professors at Lafayette." Generally, "classes are challenging but manageable, if you put in the time."

Life

At Lafayette, the "campus is gorgeous," and students say you feel the "close atmosphere of the school" after "immediately walking onto the campus." Overall students feel, "the campus community is very supportive," and a civil engineering major says, "The family atmosphere adds to the education and makes Lafayette feel more like home than school." With "over 200 clubs and organizations on campus," there "is something that will fit everyone's lifestyle and hobbies," and when it comes to their Division I athletics, "students radiate school pride." Lafayette boasts a "great career center due to the close ties alumni have with the college," and career services are offered to students during all four years of their undergraduate study. The administration actively requests "student forums and opinions when decisions need to be made." While some say "the facilities are first rate" and improving, others lament "the arts, while growing, are still fairly small." Lafayette has welcomed a new President and there are changes on the way. Within the last year, the food provider has been replaced and offerings have "improved tremendously."

Student Body

Lafayette students are "passionate and driven" and "tend to be athletic, very preppy, and serious about their education." A sophomore says the typical student is "white middle to upper-middle class students from the tri-state area," but another adds, "Recent years have brought in a number of different types of people." "More lower income, international, and non-white students have joined" the Lafayette community. Regardless, some students point out that it can be "a very self-segregated campus." "These cliques are not unique to Lafayette, but they are present." Just under 30 percent of the student body is "involved with Greek life," and some feel that those "not involved in Greek life or sports can be isolated"; however, many students have felt a change occurring in recent years with Lafayette "trying to add more living learning community (LLCs) to create a social living space outside the Greek system." On weekends, most students stay on campus, and "very rarely is there a weekend where something isn't going on." Organizations are always "sponsoring fun events, including Condom Bingo, which is a fan favorite. And if you're into the party scene, it isn't too hard to stumble into one."

LAFAYETTE COLLEGE

FINANCIAL AID: 610-330-5055 • E-MAIL: ADMISSIONS@LAFAYETTE.EDU • WEBSITE: WWW.LAFAYETTE.EDU

THE PRINCETON REVIEW SAYS

Admissions

Very important factors considered include: rigor of secondary school record, academic GPA. *Important factors considered include:* class rank, standardized test scores, application essay, recommendation(s), interview, extracurricular activities, talent/ability, character/personal qualities. *Other factors considered include:* first generation, alumni/ae relation, geographical residence, racial/ethnic status, volunteer work, work experience, level of applicant's interest. SAT or ACT required; SAT Subject Tests recommend. ACT with or without writing accepted. SAT with or without Essay component accepted. TOEFL required of all international applicants. High school diploma or equivalent is not required. *Academic units recommended:* 4 English, 3 math, 2 science, 2 science labs, 2 foreign language, 5 academic electives.

Financial Aid

Students should submit: FAFSA, CSS/Financial Aid PROFILE, Noncustodial PROFILE. Regular filing deadline is 3/1. The Princeton Review suggests that all financial aid forms be submitted as soon as possible after October 1. *Need-based scholarships/grants offered:* Federal Pell, FSEOG, State scholarships/grants, Private scholarships, College/university scholarship or grant aid from institutional funds. *Loan aid offered:* Direct Subsidized Stafford Loans, Direct Unsubsidized Stafford Loans, Direct PLUS loans, Federal Perkins Loans, College/university loans from institutional funds. Applicants will be notified of awards on or about 4/1. Federal Work-Study Program available. Institutional employment available.

The Inside Word

Like all elite institutions, Lafayette College takes into account a variety of factors when evaluating prospective students. While emphasis is placed on scores, high school record, rigor of courses, and other numbers, the admissions committee also values a commitment to social awareness and potential for leadership as exhibited through extracurricular activities such as community service. In fact, service is a big part of the Lafayette community.

THE SCHOOL SAYS "..."

From the Admissions Office

"Located seventy miles from Manhattan and sixty miles from Center City Philadelphia, Lafayette provides university-size resources in an exclusively undergraduate, student-centered college.

"Our rallying cry is the Marquis de Lafayette's family motto, Cur Non ('Why not?'). It means anything is possible here—with Lafayette's muscle and energy, no dream is too wild or ambitious to make happen. All the experiences students need to create their edge are built into their four years. It's an unparalleled platform from which to find their way forward into a complex, rapidly changing world.

"There are nearly fifty majors to choose from in the humanities, social sciences, natural sciences, and engineering. The faculty are accomplished professor-mentors who are dedicated to connecting with students on both a professional and a personal level.

"While remaining dedicated to programs in which students learn to think critically, to communicate effectively, and to relate seemingly unconnected ideas, Lafayette also is dedicated to providing an education that is valuable in its relevance, in which students cross disciplinary, cultural, and international boundaries to connect in meaningful ways with faculty, with each other, and with the world. This high-impact education—with a distinctive cross-disciplinary orientation, high-level research, rigorous small-class discussion, field experiences, community-based learning projects, and global studies—attracts active, engaged learners who achieve a notable career advantage. In recent years, 95 percent or more of Lafayette's graduating classes have been employed, in graduate school, in an internship, or in service work within six months of graduation."

SELECTIVITY

Admissions Rating	95
# of applicants	7,465
% of applicants accepted	30
% of acceptees attending	30
# offered a place on the wait list	1,532
% accepting a place on wait list	28
% admitted from wait list	1
# of early decision applicants	704
% accepted early decision	49

FRESHMAN PROFILE

Range SAT Critical Reading	580–670
Range SAT Math	620–710
Range SAT Writing	590–690
Range ACT Composite	27–31
Minimum paper TOEFL	550
Minimum internet-based TOEFL	80
Average HS GPA	3.5
% graduated top 10% of class	70
% graduated top 25% of class	93
% graduated top 50% of class	98

DEADLINES

Early decision	
Deadline	11/15
Notification	12/15
Regular	
Deadline	1/15
Notification	4/1
Nonfall registration?	Yes

APPLICANTS ALSO LOOK AT AND OFTEN PREFER

Princeton University; Boston College; Tufts University; Cornell University; Johns Hopkins University

AND SOMETIMES PREFER

Bucknell University; Colgate University

FINANCIAL FACTS

Financial Aid Rating	95
Annual tuition	$46,590
Room and board	$13,920
Required fees	$420
Books and supplies	$1,000
Average frosh need-based scholarship	$39,316
Average UG need-based scholarship	$37,495
% needy frosh rec. need-based scholarship or grant aid	95
% needy UG rec. need-based scholarship or grant aid	93
% needy frosh rec. non-need-based scholarship or grant aid	33
% needy UG rec. non-need-based scholarship or grant aid	23
% needy frosh rec. need-based self-help aid	88
% needy UG rec. need-based self-help aid	93
% frosh rec. any financial aid	61
% UG rec. any financial aid	58
% UG borrow to pay for school	55
Average cumulative indebtedness	$31,154
% frosh need fully met	100
% ugrads need fully met	100
Average % of frosh need met	100
Average % of ugrad need met	100

LAKE FOREST COLLEGE

555 NORTH SHERIDAN ROAD, LAKE FOREST, IL 60045 • ADMISSIONS: 847-735-5000 • FAX: 847-735-6291

CAMPUS LIFE

Quality of Life Rating	90
Fire Safety Rating	82
Green Rating	60*
Type of school	Private
Affiliation	No Affiliation
Environment	Village

STUDENTS

Total undergrad enrollment	1,572
% male/female	44/56
% from out of state	36
% frosh from public high school	70
% frosh live on campus	89
% ugrads live on campus	74
# of fraternities (% ugrad men join)	3 (19)
# of sororities (% ugrad women join)	4 (21)
% African American	7
% Asian	5
% Caucasian	58
% Hispanic	17
% Native American	<1
% Pacific Islander	0
% Two or more races	3
% Race and/or ethnicity unknown	3
% international	8
# of countries represented	76

SURVEY SAYS...

Students are happy
Great library
Career services are great
Internships are widely available
Great financial aid
Easy to get around campus
Recreation facilities are great

ACADEMICS

Academic Rating	89
% students returning for sophomore year	85
% students graduating within 4 years	66
% students graduating within 6 years	72
Calendar	Semester
Student/faculty ratio	12:1
Profs interesting rating	90
Profs accessible rating	93

Most classes have 10–19 students.
Most lab/discussion sessions have
10–19 students.

MOST POPULAR MAJORS

Business/Commerce; Speech Communication
and Rhetoric; Biology

STUDENTS SAY "..."

Academics

Lake Forest provides a broad-ranging general education curriculum. One student points out, "The teachers really challenge you and generally are really nice and easy to access." The academic breadth at Lake Forest College is both challenging and inspiring. Another student adds, "The small school size means administration can help you, and they actually do. The class sizes and teachers won't let anyone hide or get away with spotty work." The emphasis is giving each student an individual and well-rounded education in the liberal arts, and this cross-disciplinary education is accessible because of the attentive faculty and staff. A current student tells us, "Lake Forest is a solid college with great financial aid." Another facet of the learning experience that Lake Forest students appreciate is that the college provides and promotes numerous opportunities outside of the classroom. Studying abroad, internships, community service, and career development are all encouraged and presented across campus. Overall, the impression is that of "the world is at your fingertips and your campus experience should allow you to sample many options and explore and create in a supportive environment." Lake Forest's professors are by far its strongest asset. A sophomore tells us, "They're accessible, highly knowledgeable in their designated areas of expertise, and have very high expectations for student performance. Additionally, they encourage us as students to learn by doing as opposed to simply lecturing."

Life

When students consider Lake Forest, a word that might come to mind is "balance." One student explains, "The town of Lake Forest is not at all a college town, and you'd be hard-pressed to find anything more than a grocery store and a few places to eat. However, almost everything you need is on campus." The beautiful 107-acre campus is located thirty miles north of downtown Chicago, providing access to the city with the respite of a more laid-back town along the shore of Lake Michigan. "Chicago is a huge asset both socially and academically," says one student. "[It] is ever-changing and does not get dull." The school offers transit passes for a discounted price, and students visit the city often. A ten-minute walk will easily get you into the main part of town, and it is an easy train ride to Chicago, but equally attractive is that in the same ten minutes you can walk to the beach and enjoy the shores of Lake Michigan. A freshman describes, "Lake Michigan, and a beautiful beach, is only half a mile from campus, and the campus is beautiful especially in the fall and after the first snowfall." Another student sums it up nicely, saying, "At Lake Forest College, students get a world-class education and the skills they need to succeed in life while immersed in a school-spirit-rich campus lifestyle that doesn't compare to any other school."

Student Body

Student organizations are very strong at Lake Forest, and, therefore, there are always student-run events on campus that are frequented by the student body. "A typical Lake Forest student is usually pretty involved whether it is in a sport, club, theater, or music," says one sophomore. "Everyone usually finds a group that they fit into with friends with similar interests." Another student adds, "Everyone is different, and everyone fits in." Like any college, students say they can get "stressed out, but [are] generally upbeat. At this school it is considered normal to be in a thousand different clubs and extracurricular activities and to attend campus events and campus parties." A sophomore explains, "Life at my school can be very challenging because your classes will push you. However, there is still time for fun, and you will see a good number of your peers at social events on campus. One of the most common is the ACPs (All Campus Parties) that are held on Fridays and hosted by various student organizations." In the end, it all comes back to balance—and at Lake Forest students can cultivate the many experiences available into one productive adult life.

FINANCIAL AID: 847-735-5103 • E-MAIL: ADMISSIONS@LAKEFOREST.EDU • WEBSITE: WWW.LAKEFOREST.EDU

THE PRINCETON REVIEW SAYS

Admissions

Very important factors considered include: rigor of secondary school record, application essay, interview, extracurricular activities, talent/ability, character/personal qualities. *Important factors considered include:* academic GPA. *Other factors considered include:* class rank, standardized test scores, recommendation(s), first generation, alumni/ae relation, geographical residence, volunteer work, work experience, level of applicant's interest. SAT or ACT recommend. ACT with or without writing accepted. TOEFL required of all international applicants. High school diploma is required and GED is accepted. *Academic units required:* 4 English, 3 math, 3 science, 3 science labs, 2 foreign language, 2 social studies, 2 history, 3 academic electives. *Academic units recommended:* 4 English, 4 math, 4 science, 4 science labs, 4 foreign language, 2 social studies, 2 history, 3 academic electives, and 1 unit from above areas or other academic areas.

Financial Aid

Students should submit: FAFSA. Regular filing deadline is 5/1. The Princeton Review suggests that all financial aid forms be submitted as soon as possible after October 1. *Need-based scholarships/grants offered:* Federal Pell, FSEOG, State scholarships/grants, Private scholarships, College/university scholarship or grant aid from institutional funds. *Loan aid offered:* Direct Subsidized Stafford Loans, Direct Unsubsidized Stafford Loans, Direct PLUS loans, Federal Perkins Loans, College/university loans from institutional funds. Applicants will be notified of awards on a rolling basis beginning 3/1. Federal Work-Study Program available. Institutional employment available.

The Inside Word Lake Forest is small enough to give each application it receives close and careful consideration. Solid high school performers should have little difficulty gaining admission, but keep in mind that Lake Forest has a prep-school-at-the-college-level feel and likes to assess the whole candidate, not just grades and test scores. In fact, test scores are optional.

THE SCHOOL SAYS "..."

From the Admissions Office

"Our beautiful 107-acre campus is ideally located on Chicago's North Shore near Lake Michigan. Lake Forest College gives every student direct access to superb faculty and a powerful network of alumni who help our graduates begin careers. This access provides every student with a valuable edge on a bright future.

"Our flexible curriculum supports double majors and minors, and students are also offered unparalleled internships in Chicago, great lab research experiences, championship athletics, and study-abroad opportunities. Students learn in a rigorous academic environment in small class settings where professors do all of the teaching and advising. Career-building internships are plentiful in the Chicago area, and students can pursue up to three for credit. Study abroad is encouraged, and students can also spend a semester living and interning in Chicago.

"The student body is comprised of students from nearly every state and eighty-one countries around the world and together they form a diverse learning community that prepares them to succeed in today's global society.

"Developing career goals—and a plan of action to achieve them—is a fundamental goal of the Career Advancement Center and the College community as a whole. Students have access to programs, resources, career advisors, and a powerful network of alumni throughout their four years.

"Our outcomes are hard to match: More than 90 percent of our graduates had jobs, graduate school, or other opportunities secured within six months of graduation, well above the national average."

SELECTIVITY

Admissions Rating	87
# of applicants	3,373
% of applicants accepted	55
% of acceptees attending	19
# of early decision applicants	58
% accepted early decision	67

FRESHMAN PROFILE

Range SAT Critical Reading	480–610
Range SAT Math	500–600
Range SAT Writing	460–580
Range ACT Composite	22–28
Minimum paper TOEFL	550
Minimum internet-based TOEFL	83
Average HS GPA	3.7
% graduated top 10% of class	39
% graduated top 25% of class	64
% graduated top 50% of class	91

DEADLINES

Early decision	
Deadline	11/15
Early action	
Deadline	11/15
Regular	
Priority	2/15
Nonfall registration?	Yes

APPLICANTS ALSO LOOK AT AND OFTEN PREFER

University of Illinois at Urbana-Champaign

FINANCIAL FACTS

Financial Aid Rating	87
Annual tuition	$43,392
Room and board	$9,810
Required fees	$724
Books and supplies	$1,000
Average frosh need-based scholarship	$31,865
Average UG need-based scholarship	$30,270
% needy frosh rec. need-based scholarship or grant aid	100
% needy UG rec. need-based scholarship or grant aid	100
% needy frosh rec. non-need-based scholarship or grant aid	0
% needy UG rec. non-need-based scholarship or grant aid	0
% needy frosh rec. need-based self-help aid	90
% needy UG rec. need-based self-help aid	88
% frosh rec. any financial aid	94
% UG rec. any financial aid	95
% frosh need fully met	21
% ugrads need fully met	26
Average % of frosh need met	85
Average % of ugrad need met	83

LAWRENCE UNIVERSITY

711 EAST BOLDT WAY, APPLETON, WI 54911-5699 • ADMISSIONS: 920-832-6500 • FAX: 920-832-6782

CAMPUS LIFE
Quality of Life Rating	92
Fire Safety Rating	83
Green Rating	70
Type of school	Private
Affiliation	No Affiliation
Environment	City

STUDENTS
Total undergrad enrollment	1,561
% male/female	45/55
% from out of state	71
% frosh live on campus	99
% ugrads live on campus	96
# of fraternities (% ugrad men join)	4 (20)
# of sororities (% ugrad women join)	4 (14)
% African American	3
% Asian	5
% Caucasian	70
% Hispanic	7
% Native American	<1
% Pacific Islander	<1
% Two or more races	4
% Race and/or ethnicity unknown	1
% international	11
# of countries represented	42

SURVEY SAYS...
Lots of liberal students
Students are happy
Class discussions encouraged
School is well run
Great financial aid
No one cheats
Students are friendly
Students aren't religious
Students environmentally aware
Great food on campus
Easy to get around campus

ACADEMICS
Academic Rating	92
% students returning for sophomore year	89
% students graduating within 4 years	63
% students graduating within 6 years	76
Calendar	Trimester
Student/faculty ratio	9:1
Profs interesting rating	94
Profs accessible rating	94
Most classes have fewer than 10 students.	

MOST POPULAR MAJORS
Music Performance; Biology; Psychology

STUDENTS SAY "..."

Academics

The minute you step foot onto the campus of Lawrence University, you immediately sense that the school is comprised of a "beautifully warm and positive community." Soon after, you realize that it deftly manages to balance this supportive nature with a "weird, quirky vibe." And students couldn't be happier about the combination. Of course, it also doesn't hurt that Lawrence is "very helpful" when it comes to financial aid. Undoubtedly, the university really strives to make higher education "affordable." Looking beyond financials, many undergraduates are drawn to Lawrence for its "world-class" music conservatory. They also really value the fact that LU "encourages creativity and exploration." In fact, students can even "create [their] own major or design [their] own class." Another hallmark of a Lawrence education is professor "accessibility." As one extremely satisfied student states, "There is not a professor here who wouldn't at the very least get coffee or lunch upon request." After all, since LU "is an undergraduate-only school, professors really are here for their students. There's an extraordinary amount of support and academic enthusiasm [from them]."

Life

Life at Lawrence certainly moves at a hectic pace. In fact, there's usually so much activity buzzing through campus that undergrads often "argue with each other about who has a busier schedule." As one junior happily explains, "There's so much going on at any given time that [students] rarely want to leave even for a weekend. There are (free) concerts, speakers, parties, musicals/plays, movie showings, get togethers, game nights, club meetings, and a whole ton of other events." An economics major rushes to add, "Students [also] go on backpacking trips, cross-country skiing...[and] volunteer at the Boys & Girls Club." There's even "an active swing dance community!" Of course, Lawrence's stellar music program means that "conservatory concerts, shows, and recitals... account for [a large portion] of the night life." And if the aforementioned options don't excite you, a knowing senior assures us, "Everyone [is able to have] fun in their own way—from ultimate frisbee... to raising sea urchins." Moreover, trivia nights are another extremely popular activity at Lawrence. An English major shares, "LU is home to the Great Midwestern Trivia Contest, 48 straight hours of trivia in which teams both on and off campus compete, mostly for bragging rights. It's a lot of crazy fun and sleep deprivation." Finally, if you're looking to escape the confines of the university, the "campus is surrounded by some great shops, coffee shops, and restaurants."

Student Body

When asked to reflect on their peers, one of the first words that springs to mind for many LU students is "intellectual." As one impressed freshman explains, "at any given time there will [be] plenty of conversations going on about Plato, conservation, politics, or art." However, if you're looking beyond book smarts, many LU undergrads say you'll be hard pressed to find an adjective or category that could easily encompass all of these students. A relieved freshman reports, "You'll find all sorts of people here—homebodies who like to study all the time, partygoers, musicians, athletes, scientists, gamers, you name it, we have it. There will always be someone here that you can fit in with, and it's wonderful." And a thrilled senior brags, "Talk to any student for 15 minutes and you'll learn something fascinating and unexpected—even the people you thought you would never get along with." Additionally, these "motivated" and "independent" undergrads typically maintain "a variety of interests and passions" and tend to be "open-minded [and] liberal." All in all, as a linguistics and German double major confidently summarizes, "If you are at all a social person, you will have no trouble making friends within your dorm, classes, or extracurricular [activities]."

FINANCIAL AID: 920-832-6583 • E-MAIL: ADMISSIONS@LAWRENCE.EDU • WEBSITE: WWW.LAWRENCE.EDU

THE PRINCETON REVIEW SAYS

Admissions

Very important factors considered include: rigor of secondary school record, class rank, academic GPA, talent/ability, character/personal qualities. *Important factors considered include:* application essay, recommendation(s), interview, extracurricular activities. *Other factors considered include:* standardized test scores, first generation, alumni/ae relation, geographical residence, racial/ethnic status, volunteer work, work experience, level of applicant's interest. SAT or ACT considered if submitted; SAT Subject Tests considered if submitted. ACT with or without writing accepted. SAT with or without Essay component accepted. High school diploma is required and GED is not accepted. *Academic units recommended:* 4 English, 3 math, 3 science, 2 foreign language, 2 social studies, 2 history.

Financial Aid

Students should submit: FAFSA, CSS/Financial Aid PROFILE, Noncustodial PROFILE. Priority filing deadline is 2/1. The Princeton Review suggests that all financial aid forms be submitted as soon as possible after October 1. *Need-based scholarships/grants offered:* Federal Pell, FSEOG, State scholarships/grants, Private scholarships, College/university scholarship or grant aid from institutional funds. *Loan aid offered:* Direct Subsidized Stafford Loans, Direct Unsubsidized Stafford Loans, Direct PLUS loans, Federal Perkins Loans. Applicants will be notified of awards on a rolling basis beginning 3/1. Federal Work-Study Program available. Institutional employment available.

The Inside Word

Lawrence University takes a holistic approach to the admissions game. The school does its best to look beyond numbers and get a full sense of each applicant. Admissions officers pay close attention to the types of classes candidates have taken and the activities pursued. They also consider a student's background. Interviews are highly important so it would behoove applicants to sit for one. Finally, those who are test averse can breathe a sigh of relief; submitting SAT and/or ACT scores is optional.

THE SCHOOL SAYS " . . ."

From the Admissions Office

"Lawrence believes college should not be a one-size-fits-all experience, and that you'll learn best when you're educated as a unique individual. Within our college of liberal arts and sciences and our conservatory of music—both devoted exclusively to undergraduate education—you'll have unparalleled opportunities to collaborate closely with your professors in small classes (93 percent have fewer than twenty students in them; 67 percent have total enrollments of one). Our 1,500 students come from nearly every state and about fifty countries to enjoy the distinctive benefits of this engaged—and engaging—community. It's a close-knit, residential, 24/7 campus filled with smart and talented people who are pursuing an astonishing variety of academic and extracurricular interests. Our picturesque, residential campus is nestled on the banks of the Fox River in Appleton, Wisconsin, (metro population: 236,000), one of the fastest growing metropolitan areas in the Midwest. Björklunden, our 441-acre estate on more than one mile of pristine Lake Michigan shoreline (two hours north of campus), provides educational and recreational opportunities for students to enhance their on-campus learning experiences.

"We seek students who are intellectual, imaginative, and innovative: qualities best quantified from a thorough review of your curriculum, academic performance, essay, activities, and recommendations. Accordingly, Lawrence considers—but does not require—the ACT and the SAT in our review of applications for admission and scholarship."

SELECTIVITY

Admissions Rating	89
# of applicants	3,014
% of applicants accepted	68
% of acceptees attending	19
# offered a place on the wait list	249
% accepting a place on wait list	28
% admitted from wait list	10
# of early decision applicants	12
% accepted early decision	92

FRESHMAN PROFILE

Range SAT Critical Reading	560–690
Range SAT Math	610–730
Range SAT Writing	580–690
Range ACT Composite	26–32
Minimum paper TOEFL	577
Minimum internet-based TOEFL	90
Average HS GPA	3.6
% graduated top 10% of class	42
% graduated top 25% of class	77
% graduated top 50% of class	97

DEADLINES

Early action I	
Deadline	11/1
Notification	12/15
Early action II	
Deadline	12/1
Notification	1/25
Regular	
Deadline	1/15
Notification	4/1
Nonfall registration?	Yes

APPLICANTS ALSO LOOK AT AND SOMETIMES PREFER
Beloit College; Grinnell College

AND RARELY PREFER
Kalamazoo College; Knox College

FINANCIAL FACTS

Financial Aid Rating	89
Annual tuition	$44,544
Room and board	$9,654
Required fees	$300
Average frosh need-based scholarship	$31,540
Average UG need-based scholarship	$29,622
% needy frosh rec. need-based scholarship or grant aid	96
% needy UG rec. need-based scholarship or grant aid	99
% needy UG rec. non-need-based scholarship or grant aid	0
% needy frosh rec. need-based self-help aid	80
% needy UG rec. need-based self-help aid	80
% frosh rec. any financial aid	97
% UG rec. any financial aid	97
% UG borrow to pay for school	62
Average cumulative indebtedness	$33,343
% frosh need fully met	46
% ugrads need fully met	45
Average % of frosh need met	97
Average % of ugrad need met	95

LE MOYNE COLLEGE

1419 SALT SPRINGS RD., SYRACUSE, NY 13214-1301 • ADMISSIONS: 315-445-4300 • FAX: 315-445-4711

Academics

Founded in 1946, Syracuse's Le Moyne College is a 3,500-student private college that "combines Jesuit teachings and traditions while engaging all students into their own development as an individual, part of the community and the world as a whole." Those who go to Le Moyne cite the "unparalleled" feeling of community and that the constant sense that the "personable and endearing administrators" "actually care about you" as the best part of their time here, and the "focus on community service" helps drive the foundational Jesuit principles home.

One of Le Moyne's greatest strengths is the amount of help available to students. "Between office hours, the Academic Support Center and friendly upperclassmen, your questions will be answered!" promises a student. "Small intimate class sizes" mean that "professors are always willing to help students," and nothing is taught by TAs so "it is easy to foster a personal connection with you professors." Classes are "intellectually challenging," the honors program is "very worthwhile," and the majority of professors really "try to bring the material to life." They "bring in outside information that connects with the material we are learning, which I find helps spark discussions with every person in the class." "I have learned so much in so little time. And I have evolved a thirst for more," says a freshman chemistry major.

Strong nursing and business programs stand out in this "active learning community," as does the desire to keep the college "a place of high moral values." Some of the facilities on school such as the science labs or library "could be renovated," but luckily nearly all the classrooms are accessible within buildings connected by tunnels and hallways, eliminating the need to travel outside from class to class (a huge benefit in the freezing, and long, Central NY winters).

Life

Life in Syracuse "offers so many opportunities," and students revel in their four years in a "perfect community—small, generous, and service oriented." Almost all students are required to live on campus all four years, which creates "a cozy campus with a homey atmosphere" (not to mention beautiful). Parking is definitely on students' wish lists, but the dining facilities receive rare high marks: "The food is great and there is a good variety."

The school keeps students pleasantly busy, and "offers a lot of activities around the campus [so] you will never get bored." Le Moyne offers "free tickets to concerts and SU basketball games" and "puts on a lot of fun events such as movie nights...comedy improv groups, and other performers." "Partying is a big factor here," and students often head up to Syracuse or to the campus bar on weekends. However, there is "a pretty sizable portion of students who don't like to go out" and there are always programs going on at night, such as "a snow tubing trip, bowling trip, and an on-campus Pinterest Live! Event...in addition to Trivia Night at the on-campus pub, of course!"

Student Body

Many students come from cities and small towns in New York State, are "family-oriented,""Catholic," and "most likely white." Everyone is "extremely friendly," though Le Moyne has a great deal of cliques, although "one can create friends easily" and said cliques "interact far more fluidly" than in high school. Most are "usually dressed nicely and seem prepared for class," and do the standard work during the week, go out on weekends routine. "A lot of students here are athletes as well," and many "bond over sports, or the performing arts." The "wide range" of people on campus means there are "many who are up all night partying non-stop from Thursday until Sunday, then there are those who still grab coloring books and sit down to watch Disney movies for fun."

Financial Aid: 315-445-4400 • E-mail: admission@lemoyne.edu • Website: www.lemoyne.edu

THE PRINCETON REVIEW SAYS

Admissions

Very important factors considered include: rigor of secondary school record, academic GPA. *Important factors considered include:* class rank, application essay, recommendation(s), interview, extracurricular activities, talent/ability, work experience. *Other factors considered include:* standardized test scores, character/personal qualities, alumni/ae relation, geographical residence, state residency, volunteer work, level of applicant's interest. SAT or ACT required for some. ACT with or without writing accepted. SAT with or without Essay component accepted. TOEFL required of all international applicants. High school diploma is required and GED is accepted. *Academic units required:* 4 English, 3 math, 3 science, 3 foreign language, 4 social studies. *Academic units recommended:* 4 math, 4 science, 3 science labs.

Financial Aid

Students should submit: FAFSA, State aid form. Priority filing deadline is 2/15. The Princeton Review suggests that all financial aid forms be submitted as soon as possible after October 1. *Need-based scholarships/grants offered:* Federal Pell, FSEOG, State scholarships/grants, Private scholarships, College/university scholarship or grant aid from institutional funds. *Loan aid offered:* Direct Subsidized Stafford Loans, Direct Unsubsidized Stafford Loans, Direct PLUS loans, Federal Perkins Loans. Applicants will be notified of awards on or about 3/15. Federal Work-Study Program available. Institutional employment available.

The Inside Word

As a younger college, Le Moyne sees slightly lower application numbers than many other small private colleges in the Northeast. While a strong college prep record and good SAT or ACT scores are required (as well as one letter of recommendation from a guidance/college counselor or three letters of recommendation from clergy, coaches, employers, teachers, etc.), those who have decent academic record should have no trouble getting in.

THE SCHOOL SAYS "..."

From the Admissions Office

"Learning, leadership and service are the hallmarks of a Le Moyne College education. Those values are evident in the College's recently reconfigured Core Curriculum, a series of courses steeped in the Jesuit tradition and designed to develop the intellectual skills that are critical for success in the 21st century. The intent of the Core Curriculum is to do more than provide knowledge in specific disciplines, though. It was created to stretch the minds of our students, to remove barriers to their ways of thinking, and to help them discover new approaches to life's challenges. At the center of the Le Moyne experience is a commitment to social justice and to providing students with the best possible preparation for life and work.

"Le Moyne students can choose from more than thirty undergraduate majors as well as pre-professional studies and graduate programs in business administration, education, nursing and physician assistant studies. Whatever field they choose to pursue, Le Moyne graduates are prepared to lead successful lives of leadership and service to others.

"Beyond the academics, Le Moyne students have the opportunity to grow and explore on a campus with dynamic new academic, athletic and social spaces at a cost that is remarkably affordable. (More than 90 percent of undergrads receive some form of financial aid.). With over eighty clubs and organizations, students are sure to find an activity that interests them while forming life-long friendships. Our picturesque 160-acre campus in the heart of New York state enhances Le Moyne's outstanding programs."

SELECTIVITY

Admissions Rating	81
# of applicants	6,877
% of applicants accepted	62
% of acceptees attending	15
# offered a place on the wait list	198
% accepting a place on wait list	12
% admitted from wait list	4

FRESHMAN PROFILE

Range SAT Critical Reading	480–580
Range SAT Math	500–590
Range ACT Composite	21–25
Minimum paper TOEFL	550
Minimum internet-based TOEFL	79
Average HS GPA	3.5
% graduated top 10% of class	22
% graduated top 25% of class	55
% graduated top 50% of class	88

DEADLINES

Early action	
Deadline	11/15
Notification	12/15
Regular	
Priority	2/1
Nonfall registration?	Yes

APPLICANTS ALSO LOOK AT AND SOMETIMES PREFER

Syracuse University; State University of New York–University at Buffalo; State University of New York at Geneseo; State University of New York at Binghamton; State University of New York—University at Albany; Siena College; Nazareth College; Ithaca College

FINANCIAL FACTS

Financial Aid Rating	83
Annual tuition	$31,260
Room and board	$12,540
Required fees	$990
Books and supplies	$1,300
Average frosh need-based scholarship	$20,903
Average UG need-based scholarship	$19,583
% needy frosh rec. need-based scholarship or grant aid	100
% needy UG rec. need-based scholarship or grant aid	100
% needy frosh rec. non-need-based scholarship or grant aid	16
% needy UG rec. non-need-based scholarship or grant aid	13
% needy frosh rec. need-based self-help aid	78
% needy UG rec. need-based self-help aid	80
% frosh rec. any financial aid	88
% UG rec. any financial aid	91
% UG borrow to pay for school	88
Average cumulative indebtedness	$34,941
% frosh need fully met	27
% ugrads need fully met	24
Average % of frosh need met	80
Average % of ugrad need met	76

LEHIGH UNIVERSITY

27 MEMORIAL DRIVE WEST, BETHLEHEM, PA 18015 • ADMISSIONS: 610-758-3100 • FAX: 610-758-4361

STUDENTS SAY ". . ."

Academics

Located in Pennsylvania's Lehigh Valley, Lehigh University offers students a long history of traditions, more than 100 majors and programs, and "the ability to collaborate with other students across different fields of study." The coursework here is difficult—"keeping even the brightest students on their toes"—but "the kinship formed through the struggle and triumph are irreplaceable." Research opportunities can be found in plenty, study abroad is wildly popular, and a strong engineering school and business school do "an amazing job making sure everyone gets high-paying internships junior year and jobs after college" (in fact, 96 percent of students are employed or in graduates school within six months of graduation).

The professors are "very intellectual beings who are also very interesting as people": "knowledgeable, available, and some are even awakening." They are incredibly accessible, and "always give students their emails, mail boxes, phone numbers, and sometimes even cell phone numbers." "Make sure to get to know them outside of the classroom since they often give out career advice," advises a student. The cross-disciplinary programs that Lehigh offers (such as the IDEAS program, which integrates arts and engineering) are "beyond what many other institutions provide." Resources are in good supply at Lehigh; for example, there are tutors "consistently available to assist students in any subject they are struggling with." In addition to having world class facilities, students are "encouraged by those around them to become involved in research," which is just one component in the awesome "return on investment" that so many speak of as the great perk of attending Lehigh.

Life

This is a truly beautiful school and "a great compact campus that you can walk" the entirety of. There is "never a dull moment" because everyone here is "always working on a project or a class or something they're independently creating." Over 150 different clubs and organizations make it easy to get involved, and Lehigh is "big into Greek life." There are "so many events, guest speakers, athletic competitions, student groups, and alcohol-free/drug-free After Dark events" that students can't even conceive of doing it all. It's also not unusual for groups of friends to plan activities at this collaborative school: "In the past few weeks I've had snowball fights, gone hiking, eaten dinner with friends, and gone ice skating."

Lehigh is a both-ends-of-the candle school, and typically students to spend "countless hours" in the library and then relax by going out at night; "even the kids who are in the hardest classes and wake up at 7:00 A.M. to study are going hard at these parties." "Everyone gets a true college experience," says a student. Not only are students double and sometimes triple majors in various fields, but "many are also varsity athletes, have multiple minors, and are heavily involved in some type of organization or club on campus."

Student Body

The student body at Lehigh is "extremely hard working, both academically and socially." "We work hard and have fun doing it," says a student. This group is "fairly affluent" and a majority of the students are from New Jersey, New York, and Pennsylvania, but "Lehigh prides itself on its search for diversity." The utter respect that Mountain Hawks have for their fellow students is admirable: "The best part about the people around me is the common bond of intelligence," says a student. "No matter what another student is doing, whether it be marching band, or joining a fraternity or a sorority, I know that every student on this campus is an intellectual."

FINANCIAL AID: 610-758-3181 • E-MAIL: ADMISSIONS@LEHIGH.EDU • WEBSITE: WWW.LEHIGH.EDU

THE PRINCETON REVIEW SAYS

Admissions

Very important factors considered include: rigor of secondary school record, recommendation(s). *Important factors considered include:* standardized test scores, application essay, extracurricular activities, talent/ability, character/personal qualities, volunteer work, level of applicant's interest. *Other factors considered include:* class rank, academic GPA, interview, first generation, alumni/ae relation, geographical residence, racial/ethnic status, work experience. SAT or ACT required; SAT Subject Tests recommend. ACT with Writing required. SAT with Essay component required. TOEFL required of all international applicants. High school diploma or equivalent is not required. *Academic units required:* 4 English, 3 math, 2 science, 2 science labs, 2 foreign language, 2 social studies, 3 academic electives.

Financial Aid

Students should submit: FAFSA, CSS/Financial Aid PROFILE, Noncustodial PROFILE. Deadlines vary with admission options. The Princeton Review suggests that all financial aid forms be submitted as soon as possible after October 1. *Need-based scholarships/grants offered:* Federal Pell, FSEOG, State scholarships/grants, College/university scholarship or grant aid from institutional funds. *Loan aid offered:* Direct Subsidized Stafford Loans, Direct Unsubsidized Stafford Loans, Direct PLUS loans, College/university loans from institutional funds. Applicants will be notified of awards at time of admission. Federal Work-Study Program available. Institutional employment available.

The Inside Word

Competition for spots in Lehigh's freshmen class is perennially increasing. Students should be sure to start their applications early, be well prepared with scores and grades, as well as demonstrate their talents and passions through volunteer opportunities, work experience, or extracurricular activities. Prospective students should visit campus and make contact with the admissions staff. Interviews are recommended but not required.

THE SCHOOL SAYS "..."

From the Admissions Office

"Lehigh is a premier private residential research university. The majority of our students—undergraduate and graduate—live on campus, allowing research and discovery to happen almost anywhere. We are a top tier national research university and have earned a reputation for an entrepreneurial and interdisciplinary approach to learning. This learning is connected to real-world applications and reinforced with cutting edge academic research and hands–on experiences. Lehigh's beautifully wooded campus spans 2,358 acres, making it one of the largest private campuses in the country. More than 7,000 students call this hillside university 'home.' With three distinguished undergraduate colleges (Arts & Sciences, Business, and Engineering), Lehigh strikes the perfect balance: students can expect a personalized experience while benefiting from the resources, opportunities and environment of an internationally recognized research university. The Lehigh community is guided by a common set of core values: integrity, equitable community, academic freedom, intellectual curiosity and leadership.

"Today, our global alumni community includes more than 78,000 loyal graduates. Nearly 96 percent of last year's graduates are employed or in graduate school just six months after leaving campus.

"Located in Pennsylvania's scenic Lehigh Valley, home to about 800,000 people, the campus is in close proximity to both New York City and Philadelphia. Our campus is on South Mountain in Bethlehem and consists of three contiguous areas: Asa Packer Campus (most academic and residential buildings), Mountaintop Campus and the Murray H. Goodman Campus (Division I athletic complex)."

SELECTIVITY

Admissions Rating	94
# of applicants	12,843
% of applicants accepted	30
% of acceptees attending	32
# offered a place on the wait list	4,232
% accepting a place on wait list	44
% admitted from wait list	0
# of early decision applicants	999
% accepted early decision	58

FRESHMAN PROFILE

Range SAT Critical Reading	590–680
Range SAT Math	640–740
Range ACT Composite	29–32
Minimum paper TOEFL	570
Minimum internet-based TOEFL	90
% graduated top 10% of class	60
% graduated top 25% of class	89
% graduated top 50% of class	98

DEADLINES

Early decision	
Deadline	11/15
Notification	12/15
Regular	
Deadline	1/1
Notification	4/1
Nonfall registration?	Yes

APPLICANTS ALSO LOOK AT AND OFTEN PREFER

University of Pennsylvania; Johns Hopkins University; Cornell University; Boston College

AND SOMETIMES PREFER

Bucknell University

AND RARELY PREFER

Drexel University; Boston University

FINANCIAL FACTS

Financial Aid Rating	91
Annual tuition	$47,920
Room and board	$12,690
Required fees	$400
Books and supplies	$1,000
Average frosh need-based scholarship	$34,998
Average UG need-based scholarship	$34,878
% needy frosh rec. need-based scholarship or grant aid	96
% needy UG rec. need-based scholarship or grant aid	98
% needy frosh rec. non-need-based scholarship or grant aid	16
% needy UG rec. non-need-based scholarship or grant aid	15
% needy frosh rec. need-based self-help aid	94
% needy UG rec. need-based self-help aid	95
% frosh rec. any financial aid	57
% UG rec. any financial aid	62
% UG borrow to pay for school	54
Average cumulative indebtedness	$34,940
% frosh need fully met	51
% ugrads need fully met	63
Average % of frosh need met	95
Average % of ugrad need met	97

LEWIS & CLARK COLLEGE

0615 SOUTHWEST PALATINE HILL ROAD, PORTLAND, OR 97219-7899 • ADMISSIONS: 503-768-7040 • FAX: 503-768-7055

CAMPUS LIFE

Quality of Life Rating	92
Fire Safety Rating	87
Green Rating	99
Type of school	Private
Affiliation	No Affiliation
Environment	City

STUDENTS

Total undergrad enrollment	2,209
% male/female	39/61
% from out of state	89
% frosh from public high school	75
% frosh live on campus	98
% ugrads live on campus	70
% African American	2
% Asian	6
% Caucasian	66
% Hispanic	10
% Native American	1
% Pacific Islander	<1
% Two or more races	4
% Race and/or ethnicity unknown	6
% international	5
# of countries represented	80

SURVEY SAYS...

Lots of liberal students
Students are happy
Classroom facilities are great
Great library
Career services are great
Students aren't religious
Students environmentally aware
Students love Portland, OR
Great off-campus food
Easy to get around campus
Campus newspaper is popular

ACADEMICS

Academic Rating	91
% students returning for sophomore year	83
% students graduating within 4 years	66
% students graduating within 6 years	72
Calendar	Semester
Student/faculty ratio	12:1
Profs interesting rating	92
Profs accessible rating	92

Most classes have 10–19 students.
Most lab/discussion sessions have 20–29 students.

MOST POPULAR MAJORS

Psychology; Biology; International Relations and Affairs

STUDENTS SAY ". . ."

Academics

While living in Portland, Oregon, you may "get rained on a lot," that doesn't stop many students from extolling about the otherwise "wonderful," "perfect," "ideal," and "exciting" location. This "suburban-hilltop liberal arts college" sits in an "absolutely beautiful" spot "next to a huge forest, [with] downtown only twenty minutes away." Besides the setting, students are lured by the school's "strong outdoors program," "great study abroad opportunities," as well as the promise of "a very green and liberal school." "Lewis & Clark is a utopia for thinkers and outdoors lovers alike. While challenging academically, the emphasis on a holistic education means that students are encouraged to explore all that Portland and the beautiful Northwest has to offer." Professors are noted for their support and "are devoted to their students in a way that wouldn't be possible in a larger school." "Lewis & Clark has professors that care so much, and if you want to put the effort into building relationships with them you will get so much from the education." Students give excellent marks for the "seasoned professors in upper-level classes." However, one student feels that "some of the temporary staff are less excellent."

Life

Life is full, and friends are plentiful at Lewis & Clark. "It's beautiful, small, and an overall friendly place with students who really take education seriously." Community supported agriculture (CSA) is taken seriously here, too. "Many are very concerned about living a healthy and sustainable life style" and are "very active gardeners and composters." The small campus is "beautiful and enjoyable to study and live in." "It feels intimate without feeling claustrophobic." When the weather is nice, "people try to find every excuse to be outside." "They generally enjoy hiking, skiing, camping, and many other activities that bring them closer to nature." Although partying exists, it is not at the forefront here. "Parties are frequent, but hardly out of control." "A lot of students are involved in student-run organizations such as a cappella, theatrical improv, open mic nights, and their own bands. Many people are advocates, and lots of students give significant amounts of their time to assist their communities." With Portland easily accessible using the school's "free shuttle that goes from campus to downtown," escaping campus is "extremely easy." "There are so many fun things to do downtown—concerts, coffee shops, restaurants, and a ton of funky antique shops that are perfect to explore on a nice day. The Pearl District, Hawthorne Boulevard, and of course the Saturday Market are all fun places to go check out." Athletics are popular at Lewis & Clark, and students speak proudly of their teams. Although some students point out of lack of fans cheering them on at games and meets, one classmate puts it into perspective. "L&C was one of the only colleges to really support me being [a part] of the athletic department as a varsity basketball player and the music department as a classical double bass player. I didn't want to go to a college that would force me to choose between my two passions. L&C has allowed me to grow as an athlete, musician, and as a student; not a lot of colleges can do that."

Student Body

To generalize, "students are usually athletes or hippies." There seems to be some divide between the two groups, but most everyone is "very liberal, engaged in a variety of issues, and smart." One student describes the school as being "full of people that you'd actually want to make friends with." Another says classmates are "genuine" and "really independent." "Most kids are more than willing to try something adventurous, and most take advantage of the fact that our student body has students coming from all over the country and world." Students tend to value "freedom of expression and thought, and an open environment in which to discuss differences." The fact that many students have traveled or lived in another country enriches the classroom experience. Classmates "constantly have stories about their time abroad," and "it is also very difficult to find someone who has never traveled abroad."

FINANCIAL AID: 503-768-7090 • E-MAIL: ADMISSIONS@LCLARK.EDU • WEBSITE: WWW.LCLARK.EDU

THE PRINCETON REVIEW SAYS

Admissions

Very important factors considered include: rigor of secondary school record, academic GPA. *Important factors considered include:* class rank, standardized test scores, application essay, recommendation(s), extracurricular activities, talent/ability, character/personal qualities, volunteer work, work experience. *Other factors considered include:* interview, first generation, alumni/ae relation, geographical residence, racial/ethnic status, level of applicant's interest. SAT or ACT required for some. ACT with or without writing accepted. SAT with or without Essay component accepted. TOEFL required of all international applicants. High school diploma is required and GED is accepted. *Academic units recommended:* 4 English, 4 math, 3 science, 2 science labs, 2 foreign language, 3 social studies, 1 visual/performing arts.

Financial Aid

Students should submit: FAFSA, CSS/Financial Aid PROFILE. Priority filing deadline is 2/15. The Princeton Review suggests that all financial aid forms be submitted as soon as possible after October 1. *Need-based scholarships/grants offered:* Federal Pell, FSEOG, State scholarships/grants, Private scholarships, College/university scholarship or grant aid from institutional funds. *Loan aid offered:* Direct Subsidized Stafford Loans, Direct Unsubsidized Stafford Loans, Direct PLUS loans, Federal Perkins Loans. Applicants will be notified of awards on a rolling basis beginning 3/15. Federal Work-Study Program available. Institutional employment available.

The Inside Word

If you have your heart set on L&C, make sure you tell that to the admissions committee. While grades and SAT scores are certainly important, L&C is also interested in students who will take advantage of the school's unique philosophy and educational environment. So make sure your application essay and interview emphasizes why L&C is the right fit for both you and the school.

THE SCHOOL SAYS "..."

From the Admissions Office

"Our record number of applicants in recent years cite a variety of reasons for choosing Lewis & Clark. Many mention the multiple educational opportunities available to our students, including a small arts and sciences college with a twelve to one student/faculty ratio; a location only six miles from dynamic downtown Portland; a setting in the heart of the Pacific Northwest, with more than eighty trips per year offered by our College Outdoors Program; and a gateway to the rest of the world—nearly 60 percent of our graduates included an overseas program in their curriculum. Since 1962, more than 11,749 students and 282 faculty members have participated in 861 programs in sixty-eight countries on six continents. Our curriculum has undergone a total review to better prepare graduates going into the twenty-first century and now includes a robust and fast-expanding Center for Entrepreneurship."

SELECTIVITY

Admissions Rating	90
# of applicants	7,368
% of applicants accepted	63
% of acceptees attending	14
# offered a place on the wait list	775
% accepting a place on wait list	29
% admitted from wait list	0
# of early decision applicants	65
% accepted early decision	86

FRESHMAN PROFILE

Range SAT Critical Reading	600–720
Range SAT Math	590–670
Range SAT Writing	580–630
Range ACT Composite	27–31
Minimum paper TOEFL	575
Minimum internet-based TOEFL	91
Average HS GPA	3.9
% graduated top 10% of class	48
% graduated top 25% of class	82
% graduated top 50% of class	97

DEADLINES

Early decision	
Deadline	11/1
Notification	12/15
Early action	
Deadline	11/1
Notification	12/31
Regular	
Priority	1/15
Deadline	3/1
Notification	4/1
Nonfall registration?	Yes

FINANCIAL FACTS

Financial Aid Rating	85
Annual tuition	$44,744
Room and board	$11,218
Required fees	$360
Books and supplies	$1,050
Average frosh need-based scholarship	$29,808
Average UG need-based scholarship	$29,836
% needy frosh rec. need-based scholarship or grant aid	98
% needy UG rec. need-based scholarship or grant aid	99
% needy frosh rec. non-need-based scholarship or grant aid	10
% needy UG rec. non-need-based scholarship or grant aid	6
% needy frosh rec. need-based self-help aid	89
% needy UG rec. need-based self-help aid	93
% frosh rec. any financial aid	94
% UG rec. any financial aid	91
% UG borrow to pay for school	57
Average cumulative indebtedness	$26,257
% frosh need fully met	27
% ugrads need fully met	22
Average % of frosh need met	90
Average % of ugrad need met	89

Louisiana State University

1146 Pleasant Hall, Baton Rouge, LA 70803 • Admissions: 225-578-1175 • Fax: 225-575-4433

STUDENTS SAY "..."

Academics

At Louisiana State University's flagship campus, you'll find "outstanding academics combined with a great college life." Some students here opt for only the latter as for many, "LSU is about football and partying." "Those who wish to apply themselves," however, "have ample opportunity and resources," and they can learn almost anything, since "the greatest strength of LSU by far is its diversity. [You] can come to LSU for sports, music...science, economics, or nearly any sort of humanities discipline you are interested in." Areas of strength include programs in premedical science, engineering, agriculture, and mass communications. The school is huge, which means "somewhere within that huge number is someone that you can get along with," but also it is easy to "get lost in the crowd," especially in intro-level classes. However, "once you get into classes that are smaller and more geared toward your chosen major, you are able to develop more of a one-on-one relationship with your professors." Fortunately "many administrative tasks" (such as "bills and registration") "can be completed online, and computers are available all across campus for students who don't have personal computers," making the bureaucracy somewhat easier to navigate. The school also offers academic lifelines such as "free tutoring all day long. The tutors are students who have already taken [the] courses."

Life

LSU is a big enough school to offer something for everyone, and undergrads here enjoy countless activities within a variety of subcultures. Most divisions, however, dissolve on game day, when tailgating is raised to the level of "an art form." A freshman reports, "On Saturdays during football season everyone is on campus before the game with friends, beer, and barbeque." Fans "come from all over and stay out all day. It's the one day when it doesn't matter who you are, as long as you're wearing purple and gold." Other entertainment options (for those of age) include Thursday nights at the bars of Tigerland, "a street with three popular college bars right next to each other," and parties wherever and whenever possible. The Greek system here is "highly influential," but students note, "This isn't the kind of school where a student doesn't have a social life if he or she isn't Greek." For the more aesthetically inclined, "LSU has an amazing art center—The Shaw Center—complete with a theater and fancy sushi bar on the top floor, which looks over the Mississippi River." Undergrads report "the beauty of our campus is amazing. The 100-plus-year-old oaks and the Italian Renaissance architecture wow any visitor to LSU's campus."

Student Body

The typical student at LSU "studies moderately—enough to get the grade he or she desires in a class"—and "frequently spends time with friends, possibly going to parties or places that serve alcohol." Mixed in is "a good number of atypical students who study more and do not go partying over the weekends. These students find fulfillment in their own interests regardless of what others think." While "conservative frat boys and sorority girls dominate the campus," the school is home to a diverse population including "many from foreign countries and other ethnic groups." There are even a few who "don't give a damn about LSU football"—hey, at a school this big, anything's possible. The student body also includes a substantial population of legacies.

LOUISIANA STATE UNIVERSITY

FINANCIAL AID: 225-578-3103 • E-MAIL: ADMISSIONS@LSU.EDU • WEBSITE: WWW.LSU.EDU

THE PRINCETON REVIEW SAYS

Admissions

Very important factors considered include: rigor of secondary school record, academic GPA, standardized test scores. *Important factors considered include:* talent/ability. *Other factors considered include:* class rank, application essay, recommendation(s), extracurricular activities, first generation, alumni/ae relation. SAT or ACT required. ACT with or without writing accepted. TOEFL required of all international applicants. High school diploma is required and GED is accepted. *Academic units required:* 4 English, 4 math, 4 science, 2 foreign language, 3 social studies, 1 history, 1 visual/performing arts.

Financial Aid

Students should submit: FAFSA, Institution's own financial aid form. Priority filing deadline is 4/1. The Princeton Review suggests that all financial aid forms be submitted as soon as possible after October 1. *Need-based scholarships/ grants offered:* Federal Pell, FSEOG, State scholarships/grants, Private scholarships, College/university scholarship or grant aid from institutional funds. *Loan aid offered:* Direct Subsidized Stafford Loans, Direct Unsubsidized Stafford Loans, Direct PLUS loans, Federal Perkins Loans, College/university loans from institutional funds. Applicants will be notified of awards on a rolling basis beginning 12/15. Federal Work-Study Program available. Institutional employment available.

The Inside Word

If you've got the right numbers, getting in to LSU is 1-2-3. Guaranteed admission requirements include completion of nineteen core units, 1030 SAT or 22 ACT, and a 3.0 academic GPA. Students who don't meet these requirements should submit supporting documentation and a letter outlining their qualifications for admission with their initial application.

THE SCHOOL SAYS "..."

From the Admissions Office

"LSU, one of only twenty-one universities nationwide designated as a land-grant, sea-grant, and space-grant institution, also holds the Carnegie Foundation's 'very high research activity' university designation.

"LSU's instructional programs include around 200 undergraduate and graduate or professional degrees. Outside of the classroom, residential colleges, service-learning opportunities, and more than 300 registered student organizations contribute to an exciting and meaningful college experience.

"Louisiana State University offers the Southern hospitality of a small community while providing the benefits of a large, technologically advanced institution.

"Freshman applicants are required to take the SAT or ACT; ACT with writing component required for Honors College applicants. LSU will use the best scores from either SAT or ACT, when making admission decisions."

SELECTIVITY
Admissions Rating	82
# of applicants	16,580
% of applicants accepted	77
% of acceptees attending	45

FRESHMAN PROFILE
Range SAT Critical Reading	500–600
Range SAT Math	510–630
Range ACT Composite	23–28
Minimum paper TOEFL	550
Minimum internet-based TOEFL	79
Average HS GPA	3.5
% graduated top 10% of class	25
% graduated top 25% of class	54
% graduated top 50% of class	82

DEADLINES
Regular	
Priority	11/15
Deadline	4/15
Nonfall registration?	Yes

FINANCIAL FACTS
Financial Aid Rating	83
Annual in-state tuition	$7,552
Annual out-of-state tuition	$24,715
Room and board	$11,200
Required fees	$2,162
Books and supplies	$1,500
Average frosh need-based scholarship	$10,405
Average UG need-based scholarship	$10,097
% needy frosh rec. need-based scholarship or grant aid	95
% needy UG rec. need-based scholarship or grant aid	87
% needy frosh rec. non-need-based scholarship or grant aid	4
% needy UG rec. non-need-based scholarship or grant aid	3
% needy frosh rec. need-based self-help aid	67
% needy UG rec. need-based self-help aid	73
% frosh rec. any financial aid	95
% UG rec. any financial aid	81
% frosh need fully met	26
% ugrads need fully met	22
Average % of frosh need met	72
Average % of ugrad need met	68

LOYOLA MARYMOUNT UNIVERSITY (CA)

ONE LMU DRIVE, SUITE 100, LOS ANGELES, CA 90045-8350 • ADMISSIONS: 310-338-2750 • FAX: 310-338-2797

CAMPUS LIFE

Quality of Life Rating	95
Fire Safety Rating	89
Green Rating	93
Type of school	Private
Affiliation	Roman Catholic
Environment	Metropolis

STUDENTS

Total undergrad enrollment	6,259
% male/female	44/56
% from out of state	24
% frosh from public high school	48
% frosh live on campus	94
% ugrads live on campus	51
# of fraternities (% ugrad men join)	9 (22)
# of sororities (% ugrad women join)	12 (37)
% African American	6
% Asian	11
% Caucasian	45
% Hispanic	21
% Native American	<1
% Pacific Islander	<1
% Two or more races	8
% Race and/or ethnicity unknown	<1
% international	9
# of countries represented	74

SURVEY SAYS...

Students are happy
Classroom facilities are great
Great library
Career services are great
School is well run
Students involved in community service
Students environmentally aware
Students love Los Angeles, CA
Great off-campus food
Easy to get around campus
Recreation facilities are great

ACADEMICS

Academic Rating	83
% students returning for sophomore year	91
% students graduating within 4 years	70
% students graduating within 6 years	79
Calendar	Semester
Student/faculty ratio	11:1
Profs interesting rating	82
Profs accessible rating	93

Most classes have 10–19 students.
Most lab/discussion sessions have 10–19 students.

MOST POPULAR MAJORS
Speech Communication and Rhetoric; Psychology; English

STUDENTS SAY "..."

Academics

Loyola Marymount University is a private, Jesuit liberal arts college in Los Angeles that focuses on educating every aspect of a person through learning, leadership, and service. There is "a constant presence of LMU's mission statement and if the student is willing to achieve something it can and will be achieved here." The school's Jesuit ideals "are all carried out and expressed by students, staff, and faculty" and there is an emphasis placed on social justice and each student's larger role in the world beyond the borders of the "beautiful" campus.

Classroom discussion is "apparent in all classes:" even those that are lecture-based have a separate lab section devoted to intelligent conversation. The small class sizes make students "feel comfortable approaching...professors with questions and conversation." Professors "have a wealth of experience and share many stories and ethical dilemmas during class." They also "deeply care about their students... and encourage outside interaction." "Every professor I have had has been easily accessible, has known my name, and has given me a fair challenge to expand my academic prowess in the subject," says a student.

One of the greatest strengths of LMU is the networking (aided by the L.A. location and "the happiness that pervades...being in Southern California"); the school is "constantly connecting students with opportunities both on and off campus to gain experience and leadership qualities." Students are wholly committed to the ideal of "bettering yourself both personally and academically in order to give back to the greater community"; "it does not matter what cultural background you may come from, there is something at LMU for you to engage in."

Life

Loyola Marymount is "beautiful," with its "stunning views of LA, landscapes, classrooms, and people." "Happy people, beautiful campus" does seem to sum up life at LMU, which is "a melting pot of pretty people, a beautiful environment, LA culture, and education for the whole person." The school does not lack for SoCal things to do: "go to the beach, go shopping, go touristing into nearby Los Angeles, go hiking, try new food, party, [and] tan." Since the weather is "always sunny and warm," people are outside "24/7 all year round." LMU provides buses and discounted tickets to many LA attractions. "Being at LMU is like living at a resort, but all the students work hard and earn their place," says a student.

A unique thing to LMU is that there is "both a strong Greek life presence and an even stronger service organization presence." These organizations "are well known in the LA area" and "most people join either a service organization, Greek organization, or a leadership position in housing or school administration." Life at LMU is "fulfilling," and "many opportunities for bettering your life present themselves frequently."

Student Body

The typical LMU student is "very active on campus" and engaged in many activities while balancing school, internships, and volunteering. Demographically, there is a "substantial [number] of upper-class, white students," but "there is plenty of diversity to go around." Although Greek life is "a large portion" of this campus, there are no Greek houses, and "everyone is very inclusive so finding a group of friends is not an issue of concern." People here are "genuine" and this place "will push you to do more than just attend classes, [which] is how you meet people." "I cannot imagine someone who is involved in anything in campus not fitting in," says a student.

FINANCIAL AID: 310-338-2753 • E-MAIL: ADMISSIONS@LMU.EDU • WEBSITE: WWW.LMU.EDU

THE PRINCETON REVIEW SAYS

Admissions

Very important factors considered include: academic GPA. *Important factors considered include:* rigor of secondary school record, standardized test scores, application essay, talent/ability, character/personal qualities. *Other factors considered include:* class rank, recommendation(s), extracurricular activities, first generation, alumni/ae relation. SAT or ACT required; SAT Subject Tests considered if submitted. ACT with or without writing accepted. SAT with or without Essay component accepted. TOEFL required of all international applicants. High school diploma is required and GED is accepted. *Academic units recommended:* 4 English, 3 math, 2 science, 2 science labs, 3 foreign language, 3 social studies, 1 academic elective.

Financial Aid

Students should submit: FAFSA. Priority filing deadline is 2/1. The Princeton Review suggests that all financial aid forms be submitted as soon as possible after October 1. *Need-based scholarships/grants offered:* Federal Pell, FSEOG, State scholarships/grants, Private scholarships, College/university scholarship or grant aid from institutional funds. *Loan aid offered:* Direct Subsidized Stafford Loans, Direct Unsubsidized Stafford Loans, Direct PLUS loans, Federal Perkins Loans, College/university loans from institutional funds. Applicants will be notified of awards on a rolling basis beginning 1/31. Federal Work-Study Program available. Institutional employment available.

The Inside Word

LMU's admission staff reviews each application individually. There's no minimum GPA or minimum test scores required for admission, and the school strives to consider the student's range of experiences and character. Nonetheless, the academic record is the single most important factor in an admissions decision. For interested students, the school offers an early action program, though students admitted through this program aren't required to attend.

THE SCHOOL SAYS "..."

From the Admissions Office

"Loyola Marymount University is a diverse Jesuit university devoted to excellence in undergraduate education and the preparation of students for lives of leadership and service. LMU's picturesque campus overlooks Los Angeles, the Pacific Ocean, and the burgeoning tech hub of Silicon Beach, offering unparalleled opportunities for ambitious students who seek a transformative undergraduate experience.

"LMU features small classes taught by dedicated, award-winning professors where students experience the personal attention and deep intellectual engagement that are the hallmarks of Jesuit education. Nationally-ranked programs in a broad range of areas—including entrepreneurship, film, finance, theatre, and engineering—are paired with a vibrant campus life and innovative career and professional development programs.

"LMU invites men and women of diverse backgrounds and talents to experience our challenging and engaging courses, beautiful campus, and welcoming community – all set against the backdrop of a world-class city."

SELECTIVITY

Admissions Rating	89
# of applicants	13,288
% of applicants accepted	51
% of acceptees attending	20
# offered a place on the wait list	2,037
% accepting a place on wait list	25
% admitted from wait list	35

FRESHMAN PROFILE

Range SAT Critical Reading	550–640
Range SAT Math	560–660
Range SAT Writing	550–650
Range ACT Composite	25–30
Minimum paper TOEFL	550
Minimum internet-based TOEFL	80
Average HS GPA	3.8
% graduated top 10% of class	44
% graduated top 25% of class	76
% graduated top 50% of class	93

DEADLINES

Early action	
Deadline	11/1
Notification	12/20
Regular	
Deadline	1/15
Nonfall registration?	Yes

APPLICANTS ALSO LOOK AT AND OFTEN PREFER

University of California–Los Angeles; University of California–Berkeley; University of Southern California

AND SOMETIMES PREFER

University of California–Santa Barbara

AND RARELY PREFER

University of California–Irvine

FINANCIAL FACTS

Financial Aid Rating	83
Annual tuition	$41,876
Room and board	$14,470
Required fees	$693
Books and supplies	$1,764
Average frosh need-based scholarship	$20,271
Average UG need-based scholarship	$19,970
% needy frosh rec. need-based scholarship or grant aid	97
% needy UG rec. need-based scholarship or grant aid	95
% needy frosh rec. non-need-based scholarship or grant aid	16
% needy UG rec. non-need-based scholarship or grant aid	12
% needy frosh rec. need-based self-help aid	76
% needy UG rec. need-based self-help aid	80
% frosh rec. any financial aid	92
% UG rec. any financial aid	87
% UG borrow to pay for school	56
Average cumulative indebtedness	$30,487
% frosh need fully met	23
% ugrads need fully met	19
Average % of frosh need met	68
Average % of ugrad need met	66

LOYOLA UNIVERSITY CHICAGO

1032 WEST SHERIDAN ROAD, CHICAGO, IL 60660 • ADMISSIONS: 773-508-3075 • FAX: 773-508-8926

STUDENTS SAY "..."

Academics

Standing tall alongside the shore of Lake Michigan eight miles north of downtown Chicago, Loyola University "provides the best of both worlds: an integrated campus and a taste of the city life." The undergraduate campus is located next to Lake Michigan, and the surrounding area is "gorgeous." The academic programs are "rigorous and fascinating," and the school offers "significant financial assistance and plenty of scholarships." The school's location "allows Loyola to attract top-notch faculty while giving students of all disciplines the opportunity to find something that interests them." Built on strong Jesuit values, Loyola cares deeply about social justice ("set the world on fire" is a common credo) and "developing intellectual and socially responsible students." "My school is about preparing students for careers and being aware of problems around us," says a student.

"The majority of the professors [are] excellent." The professors "find a good balance in their teaching methods that allow students to engage the material and engage other students in the classroom." "They are the kind of teachers that one remembers for a long time," says a student. "Many bring in business professionals to relate our classroom material to the real world," and "the work is challenging, but not overbearing." "I've had several professors who I would go out of my way to take again," says a student. "The academics make everyone work hard, regardless of natural ability, but it pays off every time."

The "well-known academic integrity of the school" provides a great reputation in Chicago, and the "connections and opportunities" the school provides to students seeking jobs and internships are numerous. Since the curriculum is centered on being well-rounded, "students can build an education that will serve them well in the future." "Loyola challenges its students to be the best they can be, no matter what their major or background is."

Life

"What's great about Loyola is that it is very future-focused, but it never forgets about the present either," says a student. Students at this school are quite involved, and they "find a good core group of people that they work together within classes, clubs, organizations, and/or athletics." "Community service opportunities" abound, as do plenty of study abroad opportunities, and students "go on trips that involve doing out of the ordinary activities," including skiing and skydiving.

Chicago is "a gold mine" of recreational opportunities, though students admit that the "social atmosphere of the campus is very dull." "Basically, the biggest hobby around here is exploring Chicago. We go out every weekend, just looking for things to do and always finding them," says a student. "Many students drink, but not all." The campus itself is "very relaxed, a sort of oasis in a bustling city," and there is even a beach right off campus on Lake Michigan, so "clearly, it does not feel much like a city most of the time."

Student Body

This group of "witty, hardworking, smart, and outgoing" people are all "studious and fairly involved but able to have fun." The typical student "comes from an upper-middle-class family, has some faith background, and balances school with social life well." Many are from local suburbs of Chicago ("being in the city, many Loyola students are fashionable and like to experiment with clothing") and care about "enjoying the city." "It is very easy to fit in because of how accepting people are," and "there is a real feel of family." Students "normally fit in the best in activities or the freshmen residence halls." Many students comment that there seems to be a lot of pre-med students here. Most everyone is "involved in some extracurricular or another," and many students have a job as well.

LOYOLA UNIVERSITY CHICAGO

FINANCIAL AID: 773-508-7704 • E-MAIL: ADMISSION@LUC.EDU • WEBSITE: WWW.LUC.EDU

THE PRINCETON REVIEW SAYS

Admissions

Very important factors considered include: rigor of secondary school record, academic GPA, standardized test scores. *Important factors considered include:* recommendation(s), extracurricular activities, character/personal qualities, volunteer work, level of applicant's interest. *Other factors considered include:* class rank, interview, talent/ability, first generation, alumni/ae relation, geographical residence, state residency, work experience. SAT or ACT required. ACT with or without writing accepted. TOEFL or IELTS required of all international applicants. High school diploma is required and GED is accepted. *Academic units required:* 4 English, 3 math, 3 science, 2 foreign language, 2 social studies, 1 history. *Academic units recommended:* 4 English, 4 math, 3 science, 2 foreign language, 2 social studies, 2 history, 3 academic electives.

Financial Aid

Students should submit: FAFSA. Priority filing deadline is 3/1. The Princeton Review suggests that all financial aid forms be submitted as soon as possible after October 1. *Need-based scholarships/grants offered:* Federal Pell, FSEOG, State scholarships/grants, Private scholarships, College/university scholarship or grant aid from institutional funds. *Loan aid offered:* Direct Subsidized Stafford Loans, Direct Unsubsidized Stafford Loans, Direct PLUS loans, Federal Perkins Loans, Federal Nursing Loans. Applicants will be notified of awards on a rolling basis beginning 2/15. Federal Work-Study Program available. Institutional employment available.

The Inside Word

Loyola is fairly conventional when it comes to admissions policies. Successful candidates usually have a combination of strong grades, success in a tough college preparatory curriculum, and solid extracurricular activities. The school adheres to Jesuit teaching, so applicants with significant volunteer work should impress admissions officers.

THE SCHOOL SAYS " . . ."

From the Admissions Office

"At Loyola University Chicago, a world-class city serves as the backdrop for a world-class education. Loyola offers a choice of more than eighty majors and minors, with extensive program options that allow students to explore and develop their unique talents. The Core Curriculum at Loyola solidifies student credentials by emphasizing lifelong skills and values while providing students the opportunity to complete a second major or add a minor. The University frequently enhances its undergraduate academic programming by modifying and adding new majors in emerging fields. For example, Loyola's new Engineering Science Department includes majors in Biomedical, Computer, and Environmental Engineering which offer hands-on learning opportunities starting freshman year. Loyola's Institute for Environmental Sustainability offers degree program options in environmental studies, environmental policy, and environmental science with concentrations such as conservation and restoration. Housed in a state-of-the-art and LEED-certified facility, the Institute features a greenhouse, biodiesel lab, collaborative research labs, and the largest geothermal facility in the Chicago region. Loyola continues to open new facilities and renovate existing buildings. The University recently completed a $100 million renovation campaign to revolutionize the student on-campus experience. Loyola has gained a new sports arena, a new student union, a revamped fitness center, and two new, cutting-edge residence halls. One of these, San Francisco Hall, is a green residence aimed at cultivating sustainable living. Between Loyola's two main campuses, students benefit from a traditional campus feel as well as a vibrant, urban atmosphere. For more information about undergraduate academics, housing, student life, financial aid, scholarship opportunities, and more, visit LUC.edu/undergrad."

SELECTIVITY

Admissions Rating	85
# of applicants	21,555
% of applicants accepted	71
% of acceptees attending	14

FRESHMAN PROFILE

Range SAT Critical Reading	520–630
Range SAT Math	518–630
Range SAT Writing	520–630
Range ACT Composite	24–29
Minimum paper TOEFL	550
Minimum internet-based TOEFL	79
Average HS GPA	3.7
% graduated top 10% of class	33
% graduated top 25% of class	70
% graduated top 50% of class	92

DEADLINES

Regular	
Priority	12/1
Nonfall registration?	Yes

APPLICANTS ALSO LOOK AT AND OFTEN PREFER

DePaul University; Indiana University Bloomington; Marquette University; Northwestern University; Saint Louis University; University of ChicagoUniversity of Illinois at Urbana-Champaign; University of Iowa; University of Michigan–Ann Arbor; University of Minnesota–Twin Cities Campus; University of Wisconsin–Madison

AND SOMETIMES PREFER

Boston College; Boston University; Bradley University; Fordham University

AND RARELY PREFER

Butler University; University of Missouri

FINANCIAL FACTS

Financial Aid Rating	82
Annual tuition	$40,052
Room and board	$13,770
Required fees	$1,332
Books and supplies	$1,200
Average frosh need-based scholarship	$20,960
Average UG need-based scholarship	$19,243
% needy frosh rec. need-based scholarship or grant aid	98
% needy UG rec. need-based scholarship or grant aid	95
% needy frosh rec. non-need-based scholarship or grant aid	11
% needy UG rec. non-need-based scholarship or grant aid	9
% needy frosh rec. need-based self-help aid	82
% needy UG rec. need-based self-help aid	83
% frosh rec. any financial aid	97
% UG rec. any financial aid	88
% UG borrow to pay for school	71
Average cumulative indebtedness	$31,750
% frosh need fully met	14
% ugrads need fully met	13
Average % of frosh need met	80
Average % of ugrad need met	79

LOYOLA UNIVERSITY IN MARYLAND

4501 NORTH CHARLES STREET, BALTIMORE, MD 21210 • ADMISSIONS: 410-617-5012 • FAX: 410-617-2176

CAMPUS LIFE

Quality of Life Rating	92
Fire Safety Rating	94
Green Rating	76
Type of school	Private
Affiliation	Roman Catholic
Environment	Village

STUDENTS

Total undergrad enrollment	4,068
% male/female	42/58
% from out of state	82
% frosh from public high school	51
% frosh live on campus	98
% ugrads live on campus	81
% African American	6
% Asian	4
% Caucasian	78
% Hispanic	9
% Native American	<1
% Pacific Islander	<1
% Two or more races	2
% Race and/or ethnicity unknown	<1
% international	<1
# of countries represented	37

SURVEY SAYS...

Students are happy
Classroom facilities are great
Great library
Career services are great
Internships are widely available
Class discussions encouraged
School is well run
Students are very religious
Students involved in community service
Dorms are like palaces
Easy to get around campus
Recreation facilities are great
Lots of beer drinking
Hard liquor is popular

ACADEMICS

Academic Rating	86
% students returning for sophomore year	87
% students graduating within 4 years	76
% students graduating within 6 years	81
Calendar	Semester
Student/faculty ratio	11:1
Profs interesting rating	91
Profs accessible rating	90

Most classes have 20–29 students.
Most lab/discussion sessions have
10–19 students.

MOST POPULAR MAJORS

Business Administration and Management;
Psychology; Communication

STUDENTS SAY ". . ."

Academics

The Jesuits have a long history of excellence in higher education, and that tradition is richly reflected in the academic programs at Loyola University in Maryland. The undergraduate experience is built around Loyola's "fantastic core curriculum," which ensures "a solid foundation in the natural sciences, English, history, philosophy and theology." Through the core, students across disciplines "take some awesome classes that will completely change your perspective on the world." Jesuit values and philosophy are emphasized in the coursework, yet the school strikes the "right balance between religion, spirituality, and the everyday life of college students." No matter what field you choose to study, "the academics are outstanding and the coursework is challenging." A true teaching university, Loyola professors use "different learning techniques to cater to everyone's different learning styles." Professors "actually know each of their students by name." Serving as both personal and academic mentors, Loyola professors "get to know you personally, take time out of their office hours to have intellectual discussions, show you how to learn and how to teach, and help you out when you are having difficulties." The relationship can even extend off campus, as it's "fairly common for professors to give out their personal cell phone numbers or to even invite the class to their home for dinner." There's extensive "academic support" and tutoring for students in every discipline, and the "Career Center is open for students starting at day one." Though some would like to see a "larger variety of classes" for undergraduates, many praise the "excellent study abroad program," which offers the opportunity to spend a year in one of fourteen countries.

Life

Loyola students juggle school, service, spirituality, and social life with extraordinary flair. Monday through Friday, most undergraduates are "insanely busy doing loads of homework, projects, reading, community service, clubs, lectures, [and] sports." Of particular note, Loyola offers "amazing opportunities to get involved in the Baltimore community through service." In fact, the school uses "Baltimore city as an extension of the classroom," where students learn about real life, rather than living in a college bubble. On the weekends, things slow down around campus, though students can partake of the "numerous speakers, movies, events, or sporting events" hosted by the university. In addition, "a lot of people go out to bars on Fridays and Saturdays," because "there is no Greek life" on campus and Loyola's strict alcohol policies make it difficult to throw parties. Loyola students can be found out and about in Baltimore, "going out to eat, catching an Orioles game, attending a concert at the BSO, [or] walking around the harbor." "Most students live on campus" during the school year, enjoying a surprisingly comfortable lifestyle in Loyola's cushy dormitories. If you score a spot in one of the suites, you and your roommates will "have full kitchens in your dorm by sophomore year."

Student Body

In addition to being predominantly Catholic, "many of the students are white, from New York or New Jersey, and come from private high schools." You'll see plenty of "Uggs, North Face, pearls, and J. Crew" around campus. Although "the student body may appear homogenous," students insist that "everyone can fit in well if you get past the initial stereotypes and immerse yourself in the opportunities Loyola has to offer." On that note, students "try to live out the core values of the university and enjoy being a contributing member of school community." Here, students "care about their academics and do well in school, but they also try to balance that with extracurriculars and their spiritual life." On the whole, the campus "really welcoming and trustworthy," with a "great sense of community." With so many ways to get involved, most students "find their niche at Loyola very quickly."

THE PRINCETON REVIEW SAYS

Admissions

Very important factors considered include: rigor of secondary school record, academic GPA, application essay, recommendation(s), character/personal qualities. *Important factors considered include:* extracurricular activities, talent/ability, volunteer work. *Other factors considered include:* class rank, standardized test scores, first generation, alumni/ae relation, geographical residence, racial/ethnic status, work experience, level of applicant's interest. SAT or ACT considered if submitted. ACT with or without writing accepted. TOEFL required of all international applicants. High school diploma is required and GED is accepted. *Academic units required:* 4 English, 3 math, 3 science, 3 foreign language, 2 social studies, 2 history. *Academic units recommended:* 4 English, 4 math, 4 science, 4 foreign language, 3 social studies, 3 history, 1 computer science, 1 visual/performing arts.

Financial Aid

Students should submit: FAFSA, CSS/Financial Aid PROFILE, Noncustodial PROFILE. Regular filing deadline is 2/15. The Princeton Review suggests that all financial aid forms be submitted as soon as possible after October 1. *Need-based scholarships/grants offered:* Federal Pell, FSEOG, State scholarships/grants, Private scholarships, College/university scholarship or grant aid from institutional funds. *Loan aid offered:* Direct Subsidized Stafford Loans, Direct Unsubsidized Stafford Loans, Direct PLUS loans, Federal Perkins Loans, College/university loans from institutional funds. Applicants will be notified of awards on or about 3/15. Federal Work-Study Program available. Institutional employment available.

The Inside Word

Loyola University in Maryland considers a student's academic record to be among the most important factors in an admissions decision. Successful students usually rank in the top quarter of their classes. Although Loyola will consider standardized test scores if you submit them, the SAT or ACT are optional for all first-year applicants. If you decide to apply without taking the SAT, Loyola asks that you submit an additional personal essay or recommendation.

THE SCHOOL SAYS "..."

From the Admissions Office

"To make a wise choice about your college plans, you will need to find out more. We extend to you these invitations. Question-and-answer periods with an admissions counselor are helpful to prospective students. An appointment should be made in advance. Admission office hours are 9:00 A.M. to 5:00 P.M., Monday through Friday. College day programs and Saturday information programs are scheduled during the academic year. These programs include a video about Loyola, a general information session, a discussion of various majors, a campus tour, and lunch. Summer information programs can help high school juniors to get a head start on investigating colleges. These programs feature an introductory presentation about the university and a campus tour."

SELECTIVITY

Admissions Rating	87
# of applicants	13,867
% of applicants accepted	61
% of acceptees attending	12
# offered a place on the wait list	2,347
% accepting a place on wait list	18
% admitted from wait list	35

FRESHMAN PROFILE

Range SAT Critical Reading	550–650
Range SAT Math	560–640
Range ACT Composite	25–29
Minimum paper TOEFL	550
Minimum internet-based TOEFL	79
Average HS GPA	3.4
% graduated top 10% of class	26
% graduated top 25% of class	62
% graduated top 50% of class	91

DEADLINES

Early action	
Deadline	11/1
Notification	1/15
Regular	
Priority	11/1
Deadline	1/15
Notification	3/15
Nonfall registration?	Yes

APPLICANTS ALSO LOOK AT AND OFTEN PREFER

Boston College; Georgetown University; University of Notre Dame

AND SOMETIMES PREFER

Villanova University; College of the Holy Cross

AND RARELY PREFER

Providence College; Fordham University

FINANCIAL FACTS

Financial Aid Rating	94
Annual tuition	$43,800
Room and board	$14,200
Required fees	$1,400
Books and supplies	$1,250
Average frosh need-based scholarship	$21,995
Average UG need-based scholarship	$22,245
% needy frosh rec. need-based scholarship or grant aid	89
% needy UG rec. need-based scholarship or grant aid	89
% needy frosh rec. non-need-based scholarship or grant aid	33
% needy UG rec. non-need-based scholarship or grant aid	29
% needy frosh rec. need-based self-help aid	96
% needy UG rec. need-based self-help aid	95
% frosh rec. any financial aid	75
% UG rec. any financial aid	70
% UG borrow to pay for school	61
Average cumulative indebtedness	$34,375
% frosh need fully met	92
% ugrads need fully met	90
Average % of frosh need met	93
Average % of ugrad need met	92

LOYOLA UNIVERSITY NEW ORLEANS

6363 ST. CHARLES AVENUE, NEW ORLEANS, LA 70118-6195 • ADMISSIONS: 504-865-3240 • FAX: 504-865-3383

CAMPUS LIFE
Quality of Life Rating	95
Fire Safety Rating	98
Green Rating	79
Type of school	Private
Affiliation	Roman Catholic
Environment	City

STUDENTS
Total undergrad enrollment	2,691
% male/female	40/60
% from out of state	59
% frosh from public high school	57
% frosh live on campus	84
% ugrads live on campus	49
# of fraternities (% ugrad men join)	4 (9)
# of sororities (% ugrad women join)	4 (21)
% African American	17
% Asian	4
% Caucasian	51
% Hispanic	16
% Native American	1
% Pacific Islander	<1
% Two or more races	4
% Race and/or ethnicity unknown	5
% international	3
# of countries represented	42

SURVEY SAYS...
Students are happy
Great library
Career services are great
Internships are widely available
Class discussions encouraged
School is well run
Great financial aid
Diverse student types interact on campus
Students get along with local community
Students involved in community service
Students environmentally aware
Students love New Orleans, LA
Great off-campus food
Easy to get around campus
Campus newspaper is popular
Active minority support groups

ACADEMICS
Academic Rating	81
% students returning for sophomore year	77
% students graduating within 4 years	54
% students graduating within 6 years	66
Calendar	Semester
Student/faculty ratio	12:1
Profs interesting rating	87
Profs accessible rating	87

Most classes have 10–19 students.
Most lab/discussion sessions have 10–19 students.

MOST POPULAR MAJORS
Music Management; Research and Experimental Psychology; Public Relations, Advertising, and Applied Communication

STUDENTS SAY "..."

Academics

A warm private school in the heart of a big, vibrant city, Loyola University New Orleans excels at "helping everyone find their niche" through a well-rounded academic program and an "emphasis on individual success." Not an ivory tower, Loyola strives "to provide students with the skills needed for a professional career." To that end, professors "know how to relate the classroom lessons to real life," in addition to promoting service learning and "hands-on experiences," both on and off campus. Furthering the Jesuit ideal of "educating the person as a whole," there is a "focus on ethics in every single class," and the coursework will "challenge you so that you are ready to think critically about the world." Students are particularly proud of the school's strong mass communications major, while others point out that Loyola's "music industry program is something that's not really available at any college unless it's a music conservatory." Described as "engaging and reliable," Loyola professors are "very passionate about their subjects, which helps them bring the class and content to life." Most important, the faculty expresses "genuine concern" for students, "always looking to help you excel" and "providing help outside of class time." A current student writes, "My professors from freshman year still remember my name and will occasionally contact me about internships, etc." This supportiveness is visible throughout the school and defines the Loyola experience: Here, "students, faculty, and staff have a great relationship, and there is a general sense of goodwill among the Loyola community."

Life

"Loyola, being so small, can make each student feel like they belong" and there is a "great sense of community" within the undergraduate college. You'll often see students "sitting out on benches talking with their friends between classes" or getting together to "hang out in the quad on nice days." For fun, "there are always events and activities" on campus. In fact, students say you never know what to expect: "Coming to the residential dorms one may find a barbecue, a Quidditch match, or even a band playing." In their downtime, Loyola students love to study or stroll in Audubon Park, located just across the street from the school, or "take walks around New Orleans," an "awesome" city to explore. On the weekends, many go out to "enjoy local cuisine" or "shop in little boutiques" along Magazine Street and St. Charles Avenue, and "because New Orleans is such a cultural hub, there is always something fun going on," especially for those who love nightlife. A student says, "In New Orleans, people will take any opportunity they have to celebrate—holidays, birthdays, building demolitions. You name it, we'll celebrate it." Taking a cue from their upbeat surroundings, many students "head to local bars either to party or to see their friends play in bands." On that note, "art is definitely an emphasis on our campus. You can specifically notice the appreciation and commitment to music through events on campus, performances, renowned speakers, and conversations regarding music."

Students

According to their classmates, the typical Loyola undergrad is "very intelligent, open-minded, [and] politically and environmentally aware." As students, they are generally "hardworking" and committed to their major, though most are open-minded and "ready to try new things." On this "welcoming and accepting" campus, "students feel no need to 'fit in.' The diversity is so high here that it's almost impossible to stand out." In fact, "at Loyola and in New Orleans, differences are celebrated," and "Students of all religions, nationalities, races and genders interact in a friendly and respectful manner." A current student elaborates, "The student population is reflective of the city population in that no one is really afraid to be themselves." While many students are attracted to the school's religious affiliation, "one of the greatest things about my school is how welcoming it is towards other cultures, religions, and ways of life even though it is a Catholic university." Nonetheless, locals note, "Loyola could improve with the integration of on-campus students and commuters."

FINANCIAL AID: 504-865-3231 • E-MAIL: ADMIT@LOYNO.EDU • WEBSITE: WWW.LOYNO.EDU

THE PRINCETON REVIEW SAYS

Admissions

Very important factors considered include: rigor of secondary school record, academic GPA, standardized test scores. *Important factors considered include:* application essay, recommendation(s), extracurricular activities, talent/ability. *Other factors considered include:* class rank, interview, character/personal qualities, alumni/ae relation, geographical residence, racial/ethnic status, volunteer work, work experience, level of applicant's interest. SAT or ACT required; SAT Subject Tests considered if submitted. ACT with or without writing accepted. SAT with or without Essay component accepted. TOEFL required of all international applicants. High school diploma is required and GED is accepted. *Academic units required:* 4 English, 2 math, 2 science, 2 social studies. *Academic units recommended:* 4 English, 3 math, 3 science, 1 science lab, 2 foreign language, 2 social studies.

Financial Aid

Students should submit: FAFSA. Priority filing deadline is 3/1. The Princeton Review suggests that all financial aid forms be submitted as soon as possible after October 1. *Need-based scholarships/grants offered:* Federal Pell, FSEOG, State scholarships/grants, Private scholarships, College/university scholarship or grant aid from institutional funds, United Negro College Fund. *Loan aid offered:* Direct Subsidized Stafford Loans, Direct Unsubsidized Stafford Loans, Direct PLUS loans, Federal Perkins Loans. Applicants will be notified of awards on a rolling basis beginning 3/1. Federal Work-Study Program available. Institutional employment available.

The Inside Word

Admission to Loyola is competitive. In the most recent admissions cycle, the average entering student had a high school GPA of 3.66. In addition to reviewing your GPA, Loyola also evaluates students based on their standardized test scores, class rank, extracurricular activities, and personal statement. Volunteer work and community service will serve your application to any school well, but they're especially helpful at this Jesuit institution.

THE SCHOOL SAYS "..."

From the Admissions Office

"Chartered in 1912, Loyola University New Orleans is one of twenty-eight Jesuit colleges in the United States. It celebrates the rich history of that Jesuit tradition, including the commitment to social justice and education of the whole person—body, mind, and spirit.

"Though it celebrates tradition, Loyola commits to continued innovation both in art and science. To create state-of-the-art space for increasingly important STEM training, Loyola recently completed a $94 million update to Monroe Hall that added two floors and 114,000 square feet to the building. The renovated space features smart classrooms; chemistry, physics and biology laboratories; a 3,000-square-foot rooftop greenhouse; design, elements, and art studio spaces; a screen printing room; a darkroom; and new technologies like 3D printers. This year Loyola also celebrates new major programs: Digital Filmmaking, Computer Information Systems, Popular and Commercial Music, and Business Analytics.

"Additionally, Loyola was among the top producers of Fulbright Students and Scholars in the U.S. for the 2015–2016 academic year. The university's Mass Communication program also won a record ninety-three awards, including The Maroon's Pacemaker Award, known as 'the Pulitzer for college journalism.' Our STEM students have the opportunity to engage in scholarly research at the undergraduate level on topics ranging from developmental biology to ecosystem ecology, and an undergraduate just won a national 2016 Goldwater Scholarship.

"Loyola students continue to excel because the university invests in their future, providing excellent facilities, internships, rich student life, study abroad programs, service learning initiatives, a robust honors program, and abundant experiential learning opportunities."

SELECTIVITY

Admissions Rating	75
# of applicants	3,591
% of applicants accepted	90
% of acceptees attending	21

FRESHMAN PROFILE

Range SAT Critical Reading	520–620
Range SAT Math	480–610
Range ACT Composite	22–28
Minimum paper TOEFL	550
Minimum internet-based TOEFL	79
Average HS GPA	3.5
% graduated top 10% of class	8
% graduated top 25% of class	20
% graduated top 50% of class	39

DEADLINES

Early action	
Deadline	11/15
Notification	12/19
Regular	
Priority	12/1
Nonfall registration?	Yes

APPLICANTS ALSO LOOK AT AND OFTEN PREFER

Saint Louis University; University of Miami; Boston University; Fordham University

AND SOMETIMES PREFER

Louisiana State University; Tulane University; Xavier University of Louisiana; Loyola University Chicago

FINANCIAL FACTS

Financial Aid Rating	83
Annual tuition	$36,938
Room and board	$12,964
Required fees	$1,566
Books and supplies	$1,224
Average frosh need-based scholarship	$29,994
Average UG need-based scholarship	$26,814
% needy frosh rec. need-based scholarship or grant aid	100
% needy UG rec. need-based scholarship or grant aid	99
% needy frosh rec. non-need-based scholarship or grant aid	11
% needy UG rec. non-need-based scholarship or grant aid	10
% needy frosh rec. need-based self-help aid	83
% needy UG rec. need-based self-help aid	79
% frosh rec. any financial aid	92
% UG rec. any financial aid	92
% frosh need fully met	13
% ugrads need fully met	12
Average % of frosh need met	80
Average % of ugrad need met	73

LYNCHBURG COLLEGE

1501 LAKESIDE DRIVE, LYNCHBURG, VA 24501 • ADMISSIONS: 434-544-8300 • FAX: 434-544-8653

STUDENTS SAY ". . ."

Academics

Located in the foothills of the Blue Ridge Mountains, Lynchburg College "is not just a school, but a family that allows its students to learn and have fun doing it." Students describe this "small" school as having a "friendly atmosphere" and being "truly a home away from home." LC is "all about getting the job done" in "fostering and preparing the next generation of leaders." The school is especially known for its "great Nursing program." "The smaller size of the school allows for your education to be much more intimate and personal," a Biomedical Sciences student explains. "The small size of the school makes it easy to establish a relationship with your professors" and makes "it easy to get to know classmates." Professors are "very organized," "very professional," and "always willing to stop and clarify" while also trying "their best to make the class interesting and fun." At LC, you "can tell that these teachers take their job very serious and want to see their students succeed in this world." Some students say they have "mixed feelings" about the professors, as "some have been great and others not so much." The most common area of complaint is the "quality of cafeteria food," which "could be more varied" and does not do much "to accommodate vegans and vegetarians." Overall, students gave high marks to the administration. They especially praised the "communication between the Dean of Students and the actual students" and noted that the "administration truly takes the time to understand its students." One student was simply amazed at "how absolutely EVERY SINGLE PERSON who attends or works at this school is so involved." At the end of the day, LC is a college that doesn t only educate you, but "instills values and a sense of family that lasts far longer than any career you will ever have."

Life

LC is a school where "hard work is required, and fun on the weekends is encouraged." "We like to have fun, but we definitely know how to buckle down and get serious when it comes to our education," an Education major explains. "The amount of student involvement [is] astonishing" at LC. "A typical student at LC is someone who is in no less than four clubs/activities with some form of officer position in at least one or two of them," one student explains. "Life revolves around school and athletics around here" and "either Greek, clubs, or a sports team involvement is expected here at LC." Greek life is big on campus, although "Greek organizations are not the stereotypical kind you see on TV. We are all supportive of each other, play intramurals, hang out, and do community service together." Some students suggest that the student body is mainly divided between "Greeks" and "athletes," "but there is not much overlap between these groups." Off campus activities include "hiking, river rafting" as well as "many shopping options." On campus, the "very active Student Activities Board" works hard to provide students with an array of "events, concerts, and discounted opportunities throughout the city."

Student Body

Most of the students at LC are "Caucasian, upper class, prep," and from either Virginia or "the upper east coast." "Everyone is pretty laid back" and students are "not super academically inclined, but passionate about the major/ career path they choose." One student sums up the typical student: "Friendly. Amazing. Smart." Although LC "is mostly White Virginians, students come from all socioeconomic statuses and walks of life." Students do wish for more "international students and diversity on campus," and say "it would be nice to have students from other areas of the States." "LC is an extremely accepting campus," an Environmental Studies major says, and "students of all kinds are able to work together." As noted above, students are "deeply involved" on campus and in student organizations. This means students are "able to connect with a lot of people on campus" and "somehow everyone seems to find their place and everyone fits in."

FINANCIAL AID: 434-544-8229 • E-MAIL: ADMISSIONS@LYNCHBURG.EDU • WEBSITE: WWW.LYNCHBURG.EDU

THE PRINCETON REVIEW SAYS

Admissions

Very important factors considered include: rigor of secondary school record, academic GPA, standardized test scores. *Important factors considered include:* interview. *Other factors considered include:* class rank, application essay, recommendation(s), extracurricular activities, talent/ability, character/personal qualities, volunteer work, work experience, level of applicant's interest. SAT or ACT required. ACT with or without writing accepted. SAT with or without Essay component accepted. TOEFL required of all international applicants. High school diploma is required and GED is accepted. *Academic units required:* 4 English, 3 math, 3 science, 2 science labs, 2 foreign language, 2 social studies, 2 history. *Academic units recommended:* 4 English, 4 math, 4 science, 2 science labs, 3 foreign language, 2 social studies, 2 history, 1 academic elective.

Financial Aid

Students should submit: FAFSA, State aid form. Priority filing deadline is 3/1. The Princeton Review suggests that all financial aid forms be submitted as soon as possible after October 1. *Need-based scholarships/grants offered:* Federal Pell, FSEOG, State scholarships/grants, Private scholarships, College/university scholarship or grant aid from institutional funds. *Loan aid offered:* Direct Subsidized Stafford Loans, Direct Unsubsidized Stafford Loans, Direct PLUS loans, Federal Perkins Loans. Applicants will be notified of awards on a rolling basis beginning 3/5. Federal Work-Study Program available. Institutional employment available.

Inside Word

LC uses a rolling admission, so students can apply at any time following junior year. LC recommends applying at the start of the fall semester of senior year. Transcripts and SAT or ACT scores are required, while a college essay and a letter of recommendation are strongly recommended but not required. Applicants lucky enough to be admitted are automatically considered for academic scholarships.

THE SCHOOL SAYS "..."

From the Admissions Office

"Lynchburg College gives students and alumni opportunities for life in the classroom and careers. LC offers a wealth of opportunities that prepare students for success in life.

"Throughout their years at LC, students discover new things about themselves and their interests. LC provides a challenging curriculum of liberal arts, sciences, and professional programs that develops broad-based understanding and specialized knowledge, leading to fulfilling careers.

"LC students connect with the world from their early days at the College. They benefit from personal interaction with expert faculty. A vibrant campus life helps students forge meaningful connections with each other and with alumni who have exceled in countless career paths.

"LC students and alumni achieve excellence in the classroom, where they consistently earn places in competitive graduate programs; athletics, including multiple national and conference championships; and in the global workforce.

"LC students express high satisfaction with their school, giving it high marks in all five benchmarks of the National Survey of Student Engagement, which measures how colleges engage their students in activities related to learning and personal development. These areas include student-faculty interaction, supportive campus environment, level of academic challenge, active and collaborative learning, and enriching education experiences.

"From the moment prospective students step onto this beautiful campus, they begin to appreciate the Lynchburg College experience. Students and families are invited to attend one of the many visit events throughout the year."

SELECTIVITY

Admissions Rating	78
# of applicants	4,916
% of applicants accepted	69
% of acceptees attending	15

FRESHMAN PROFILE

Range SAT Critical Reading	460–570
Range SAT Math	450–550
Range SAT Writing	430–540
Range ACT Composite	19–24
Minimum paper TOEFL	550
Minimum internet-based TOEFL	78
Average HS GPA	3.4

DEADLINES

Early decision	
Deadline	11/15
Notification	12/15
Early action	
Deadline	10/15
Notification	11/1
Nonfall registration?	Yes

FINANCIAL FACTS

Financial Aid Rating	84
Annual tuition	$34,610
Room and board	$9,590
Required fees	$945
Books and supplies	$1,000
Average frosh need-based scholarship	$23,854
Average UG need-based scholarship	$22,871
% needy frosh rec. need-based scholarship or grant aid	100
% needy UG rec. need-based scholarship or grant aid	99
% needy frosh rec. non-need-based scholarship or grant aid	22
% needy UG rec. non-need-based scholarship or grant aid	14
% needy frosh rec. need-based self-help aid	72
% needy UG rec. need-based self-help aid	81
% frosh rec. any financial aid	80
% UG rec. any financial aid	74
% frosh need fully met	26
% ugrads need fully met	18
Average % of frosh need met	78
Average % of ugrad need met	76

MACALESTER COLLEGE

1600 GRAND AVENUE, ST. PAUL, MN 55105 • ADMISSIONS: 651-696-6357 • FAX: 651-696-6724

STUDENTS SAY "..."

Academics

Macalester College in Minnesota is an academic powerhouse; it "opens myriad doors for students to work incredibly hard at what they love and, through research, explore avenues of interest they may not have previously considered." The school attracts a high quality of "academic-minded" students because of the generous financial aid and places an emphasis on internationalism; the college also strongly encourages students to follow their interests in developing extracurricular student organizations. "Student organizations are provided exceptional guidance and funding from the college," says a student. The atmosphere is "academically challenging without feeling competitive," and Macalester is all about "finding the balance between serious academics, service, and fun." The "genuine, resourceful, accessible, and friendly" professors "are exceptional mentors" who "share the excitement they have about their particular fields." "I have found a lot of variety both in the teaching styles of my instructors and class topics, which is something I really appreciate about my major and Macalester in general," says one student. When professors can, they "change lecture to discussion," "add various different types of course materials," and generally keep students engaged. There is also a lot of interdisciplinary work and collaborations between professors in order to "help develop new courses, research topics, and even academic majors." Personal relationships are incredibly important to the faculty here, and professors "invest their time in the success of each student." Though there's "a definite depth to courses provided," the small size of the school means that "the variety within departments could be sparse." Being in the Twin Cities, there are "a lot of opportunities for volunteering and internships," and non-achievements, whether in sports, arts, or community service, are given "equal recognition." "There is an awareness about the world, our place in it, and how our choices affect it. There is an earnest desire to learn and listen to differing perspectives," says a student.

Life

This "unique international community in the middle of a frozen metropolis" ("I wish I could pick up the entire campus and move it to a warmer climate") has an "ideal" placement in a "beautiful" residential neighborhood dotted with restaurants and shops, with quick access to two major cities. At Mac, "there is so much to do on campus that you're never bored." "So many organizations, so little time!" says a student. With more than 120 organizations, "it's hard to find the time to get involved in everything, but very easy to find something to do." For more casual fun, people "go out into St. Paul and Minneapolis, go to dances on campus, go to house parties off campus, or just hang out and watch movies or have conversations." Parties "only happen on the weekend, and they are nonexistent around midterms or finals"; "Often people end up talking about Marxism or feminist theory at parties anyway." "You know you're at Macalester when the football team had its first winning season in decades, but our poetry slam team [are] national defending champions." Deep conversations about politics, spirituality, and identity are frequent, and "class and school invade all aspects of life here."

Student Body

Macalester is full of "intelligent," "left-wing," "self-driven students who want to participate in academics, politics, and social issues." There is a "simultaneous light-heartedness and intensity" to Macalester students, and everyone here is "eager to converse and debate with peers who may have a very different background from them." "The socioeconomic range is huge, as is the geographical diversity with international students composing 19 percent of the student body." "The experience of sitting in a class of twenty with students from eight different countries discussing the cultural implications of translation is one that can only be found at Macalester," says a student. "It would be easier to define the typical kid who is not at Mac: bro/fraternity-type guys and ditsy, sorority girls," says one student. "Mainstream people without their own opinions don't make it here."

FINANCIAL AID: 651-696-6214 • E-MAIL: ADMISSIONS@MACALESTER.EDU • WEBSITE: WWW.MACALESTER.EDU

THE PRINCETON REVIEW SAYS

Admissions

Very important factors considered include: rigor of secondary school record, academic GPA. *Important factors considered include:* standardized test scores, application essay, recommendation(s), extracurricular activities, character/personal qualities. *Other factors considered include:* class rank, interview, talent/ability, first generation, alumni/ae relation, racial/ethnic status, volunteer work, work experience. SAT or ACT required; SAT Subject Tests considered if submitted. ACT with or without writing accepted. SAT with or without Essay component accepted. TOEFL required of all international applicants. High school diploma or equivalent is not required. *Academic units recommended:* 4 English, 3 math, 3 science, 3 science labs, 3 foreign language, 3 social studies.

Financial Aid

Students should submit: FAFSA, CSS/Financial Aid PROFILE, Noncustodial PROFILE. Regular filing deadline is 3/1. The Princeton Review suggests that all financial aid forms be submitted as soon as possible after October 1. *Need-based scholarships/grants offered:* Federal Pell, FSEOG, State scholarships/grants, Private scholarships, College/university scholarship or grant aid from institutional funds. *Loan aid offered:* Direct Subsidized Stafford Loans, Direct Unsubsidized Stafford Loans, Direct PLUS loans, State Loans, College/university loans from institutional funds. Applicants will be notified of awards on or about 4/1. Federal Work-Study Program available. Institutional employment available.

The Inside Word

To say that Macalester's star is on the rise is to put it very mildly. The number of applicants to the school continues to increase. Accordingly, it has grown substantially more difficult to gain admission here within a very short period of time. Candidates need to put their best foot forward in their applications; two-thirds of the current first year class ranked in the top 10 percent of their high school classes.

THE SCHOOL SAYS "..."

From the Admissions Office

"Macalester has been preparing students for world citizenship and providing an integrated international education for over six decades. The United Nations flag has flown on campus since 1950 and 18 percent of the students are citizens of another country, with over ninety countries represented on campus. Over 60 percent of Mac students study abroad, going to nearly fifty countries all over the world each year. Graduates enter the workforce or graduate school with respected scholarship and real experience in a global community, prepared to succeed in their chosen fields. Mac students thrive in a rigorous academic environment, supported by accomplished faculty who love to teach. Located in a friendly residential neighborhood in the heart of a vibrant metropolitan area, Macalester offers unusually broad, easily accessible internship opportunities to add valuable experience, connections and practice at getting things done, often leading to job opportunities after graduation. Two out of three Mac students complete an internship at a Twin Cities business, law firm, hospital, financial institution, museum, theater, state government, research lab, environmental agency, or nonprofit group (and more), all within a few miles of campus. Students rave about the food at Mac, which includes vegetarian fare, food for meat lovers, plenty of variety and entrées from around the world. A new athletic and recreation center opened in the fall of 2009, including a large fitness center, indoor track, gymnasium, natatorium, field house, gathering spaces, juice bar, atrium and more. Athletic teams frequently earn the highest cumulative GPA in the nation. Macalester meets the full demonstrated need for every admitted student, providing broad socioeconomic representation in the student body."

SELECTIVITY

Admissions Rating	94
# of applicants	6,030
% of applicants accepted	39
% of acceptees attending	25
# offered a place on the wait list	350
% accepting a place on wait list	51
% admitted from wait list	0
# of early decision applicants	227
% accepted early decision	53

FRESHMAN PROFILE

Range SAT Critical Reading	620–730
Range SAT Math	620–740
Range SAT Writing	630–720
Range ACT Composite	29–32
Minimum paper TOEFL	600
Minimum internet-based TOEFL	100
% graduated top 10% of class	65
% graduated top 25% of class	95
% graduated top 50% of class	100

DEADLINES

Early decision	
Deadline	11/15
Notification	12/15
Regular	
Deadline	1/15
Notification	3/30
Nonfall registration?	No

APPLICANTS ALSO LOOK AT AND OFTEN PREFER

Swarthmore College; University of Chicago

AND SOMETIMES PREFER

Pomona College; Brown University

AND RARELY PREFER

Oberlin College; Kenyon College

FINANCIAL FACTS

Financial Aid Rating	97
Annual tuition	$50,418
Room and board	$11,266
Required fees	$221
Books and supplies	$1,123
Average frosh need-based scholarship	$37,273
Average UG need-based scholarship	$35,887
% needy frosh rec. need-based scholarship or grant aid	99
% needy UG rec. need-based scholarship or grant aid	99
% needy frosh rec. non-need-based scholarship or grant aid	6
% needy UG rec. non-need-based scholarship or grant aid	5
% needy frosh rec. need-based self-help aid	89
% needy UG rec. need-based self-help aid	93
% frosh rec. any financial aid	79
% UG rec. any financial aid	79
% UG borrow to pay for school	69
Average cumulative indebtedness	$21,544
% frosh need fully met	100
% ugrads need fully met	100
Average % of frosh need met	100
Average % of ugrad need met	100

MANHATTAN COLLEGE

MANHATTAN COLLEGE PARKWAY, RIVERDALE, NY 10471 • ADMISSIONS: 718-862-7200 • FAX: 718-862-8019

STUDENTS SAY "..."

Academics

This traditional Catholic college is located in the Riverdale section of the Bronx, just 30 minutes north of Manhattan and all of its resources. Manhattan College's nearly 4,000 students form a tight community, and that "carries a lot of weight in its alumni and its quality of education." The library is open 24 hours, there are "many resources to help you get an internship or a job," and the proximity of a world hub nearby truly influences every aspect of life at school: "To have New York City just around the corner is such a great environment to study in, it makes you truly motivated and [exposes you] to many situations you most likely would not been exposed to at other universities throughout the country." There is a real sense that the administration "does a great job in providing its students with a great balance between social life and academics."

The professors get to know students personally, so "you aren't just another number in their class. You get the help and education you deserve and pay for." "My professors are great at helping to clarify any problems, easy to talk to, pioneers in their field, and overall just want to see me succeed," says one mechanical engineering major. The faculty is well-equipped in their subject content, and "best of all, they present it in a way that makes it interesting to the average 20-year-old." The small class sizes makes for regular discussions, and the vast swath of cultures, backgrounds, and ethnicities also means "there is always someone who can paint a picture of a different culture in every class-room."

Life

The college's size "allows you to make connections quickly and make friends easily;" the "surrounding area gives endless social possibilities" and the quad is usually full of people relaxing and hanging out. Van Cortlandt Park is right next door, and "there are many great places to eat around the neighborhood" (which is good, as "the dining options are very limited" on campus). On weekdays, most people stick to "a basic schedule of going to classes, meals, the gym, and library to study," but on the weekends the hair comes down. "Whether it's going to a sporting event, going to one of the local bars or personally going to see a Broadway show, people usually take their time off to do things off campus," says a student of the relaxed attitude at the end of the day. Manhattan (the borough) is a constant lure, so "very frequently we head to the city to explore and have fun"; discount tickets to New York sports teams given out by Student Activities are "an extremely popular activity that a lot of students partake in."

Student Body

The "fairly diverse student body" cops to feeling more like a family, and "the vibe on campus is definitely very open and friendly." There is "a wonderful representation of commuter students who are from all areas of NYC," but the majority of students live on campus and "embrace the urban area outside of the campus." "Because of the size...you'll see people you know all the time and sometimes have time to stop and have a conversation," says one student. A fair number of athletes make up the population, and there are quite a few engineers to be found, but all mix seamless. Everyone "reaches out to or helps anyone who is struggling in classes or even personal issues," and students are "very dedicated to the school." "Once a Jasper, always a Jasper."

FINANCIAL AID: 718-862-7100 • E-MAIL: ADMIT@MANHATTAN.EDU • WEBSITE: WWW.MANHATTAN.EDU

THE PRINCETON REVIEW SAYS

Admissions

Very important factors considered include: rigor of secondary school record, class rank, academic GPA, standardized test scores. *Important factors considered include:* application essay, recommendation(s). *Other factors considered include:* interview, extracurricular activities, talent/ability, character/personal qualities, first generation, alumni/ae relation, geographical residence, volunteer work, work experience, level of applicant's interest. SAT or ACT required. ACT with Writing recommended. High school diploma is required and GED is accepted in some circumstances. *Academic units required:* 4 English, 3 math, 2 science, 2 science labs, 2 foreign language, 3 social studies, 2 academic electives. *Academic units recommended:* 4 English, 4 math, 4 science, 4 science labs, 3 foreign language, 4 social studies.

Financial Aid

Students should submit: FAFSA. Regular filing deadline is 4/1. The Princeton Review suggests that all financial aid forms be submitted as soon as possible after October 1. *Need-based scholarships/grants offered:* Federal Pell, FSEOG, State scholarships/grants, Private scholarships, College/university scholarship or grant aid from institutional funds. *Loan aid offered:* Direct Subsidized Stafford Loans, Direct Unsubsidized Stafford Loans, Direct PLUS loans, Federal Perkins Loans. Applicants will be notified of awards on a rolling basis beginning 2/15. Federal Work-Study Program available. Institutional employment available.

The Inside Word

Manhattan College admission is all done on a rolling basis, though priority is given to those who apply before March 1. With nearly two-thirds of applicants gaining admission, students with a solid academic background (emphasis on rigorous courses) and decent SAT scores shouldn't find any problems getting in.

THE SCHOOL SAYS "..."

From the Admissions Office

"We are a Lasallian Catholic college offering a transformative education that touches your mind and heart. We strive to promote faith, respect, education, community and social action. Manhattan College promises great value by consistently ranking among schools with the best return on investment and highest graduate salaries. In Riverdale, the greatest city in the world is at the doorstep of campus. In a quiet neighborhood in the Bronx, located ten miles from the bustling streets of midtown Manhattan, students enjoy a traditional college campus that's just a short subway ride from the endless opportunities available in NYC. Our professors often use the city as a classroom with field trips to Wall Street, museums and other world-famous locations.

"We have 3,500 students and a student-to-faculty ratio of 12:1, so our students enjoy the benefits of a small college with close faculty interaction. With more than forty majors and twenty graduate programs across six distinct schools, Manhattan College has big academic opportunities. Our students take what they learn in the classroom and apply it to the real world through internships, service-learning projects and study abroad.

"Founded on the principles of John Baptist de La Salle, patron saint of teachers, the College strives to promote faith, respect, quality education, community and social justice in all that we do. One example, The Lasallian Outreach Volunteer Experience (L.O.V.E.), provides service and social-justice travel experiences. Some offer immersion experiences: the chance to live in solidarity with the poor, experience an unfamiliar culture and learn about issues of social justice. Others involve more hands-on service work, such as helping rebuild in New Orleans post-Hurricane Katrina."

SELECTIVITY

Admissions Rating	81
# of applicants	8,313
% of applicants accepted	67
% of acceptees attending	16
# offered a place on the wait list	423
% accepting a place on wait list	28
% admitted from wait list	74
# of early decision applicants	73
% accepted early decision	93

FRESHMAN PROFILE

Range SAT Critical Reading	490–580
Range SAT Math	500–610
Range SAT Writing	480–590
Range ACT Composite	22–27
Minimum paper TOEFL	550
Minimum internet-based TOEFL	80
Average HS GPA	89.8
% graduated top 10% of class	23
% graduated top 25% of class	51
% graduated top 50% of class	84

DEADLINES

Early decision	
Deadline	11/15
Notification	12/31
Regular	
Priority	3/1
Nonfall registration?	Yes

APPLICANTS ALSO LOOK AT AND SOMETIMES PREFER
Fordham University

FINANCIAL FACTS

Financial Aid Rating	81
Annual Tuition	$36,900
Room and board	$15,010
Required fees	$1,955
Average frosh need-based scholarship	$21,362
Average UG need-based scholarship	$14,451
% needy frosh rec. need-based scholarship or grant aid	0
% needy UG rec. need-based scholarship or grant aid	0
% needy frosh rec. non-need-based scholarship or grant aid	12
% needy UG rec. non-need-based scholarship or grant aid	12
% needy frosh rec. need-based self-help aid	73
% needy UG rec. need-based self-help aid	64
% frosh rec. any financial aid	88
% UG rec. any financial aid	86
% UG borrow to pay for school	80
Average cumulative indebtedness	$40,220
% frosh need fully met	44
% ugrads need fully met	13
Average % of frosh need met	80
Average % of ugrad need met	69

MARIST COLLEGE

3399 NORTH ROAD, POUGHKEEPSIE, NY 12601-1387 • ADMISSIONS: 845-575-3226 • FAX: 845-575-3215

STUDENTS SAY "..."

Academics

Marist College is a comprehensive college with liberal arts tradition located "on the Hudson River" that is gaining a national reputation. The students enjoy the "small class sizes," "Catholic underpinning" (the school was founded as a Catholic school but is no longer officially associated with the church), and "proximity to New York City." Located in Poughkeepsie, NY, Marist is only "an hour and a half away from NYC," providing plenty of opportunities for internships, jobs, and excursions to the greatest city in the world. Students also boast about the "excellent alumni network" and "very strong study abroad program." "Marist just feels like home the moment you pull on to campus," one student says. "You can receive a great education here along with the beautiful view it offers," a Business Administration major explains. "Marist is about opportunity" and the school provides an "enriching community with a variety of clubs, courses, and activities for all students to enjoy." "Marist revolves around progressively learning to obtain jobs for the immediate future" and students graduate "prepared for the workplace." An example of this is the Computer Science program that offers the opportunity for "joint study with IBM." "The partnership with IBM has allowed our school to work side by side with some of the biggest leaders in the technology industry," one student explains. The Fashion Program is also very strong and popular with students. The staff of "incredibly knowledgeable and engaging" professors are "very hands on." "Classes are capped at about twenty-five students," and "most professors are willing to work one-on-one with you to ensure you will progress academically." "Professors generally demonstrate enthusiasm for material, with a soundly deliberate approach to relaying it to students," a Computer Science major clarifies. The faculty really "care about students" and "encourage students to go see them if you are falling behind or have any personal issues." "We are go-getters and a growing college," one happy student says while another sums up Marist thusly: "Marist College is the complete package—academics and extracurricular keep me busy and having fun."

Life

Although Marist students are "hard workers," "life at Marist is often very relaxing because of its atmosphere and location." Students love to be outside on their "spectacular" "sprawling green campus" that is located "on the beautiful Hudson River." "When the weather is nice you can find the campus littered with all ages and classes enjoying the sun and the open campus areas," a student explains. The location provides students with the best of both worlds. They live in a gorgeous campus and can go to the lovely city of Poughkeepsie "for shopping, hiking, apple picking, or just walking around our rich community." On the other hand, all the big cities pleasures of NYC are just "a train ride away" and students regularly go down for "day or weekend trips to the city." Some students wish there was "bigger Greek life" on campus. On campus, sporting events are popular and the college provides events for students such as "movies, shows, bingo, and open mic." When not at a campus event or going to "historical sites in the Hudson Valley," students like to "go out to parties," "hang out with friends," or attend "random cookie nights in a dorm."

Student Body

Many Marist students "come from the tri-state area," especially Long Island, "but there is also a great variation of people from all over the world with many personalities." The average student is "preppy," "friendly," "well off" and "ready to meet new people." Students are active on campus, and most "join a club, sports team, or Greek life." Students do think that "the diversity could be expanded a little." The school's fashion program seems to influence school style, as many remark that the student body is "nicely dressed" and "up with the latest fashion trends." Some say the school is "very clique based," but that "students find their clique." "Students typically fit in well, even those who differ from the typical student." "Marist is where the nice people go," one Psychology major says. "The students at Marist are the kind of people who hold the door for you and say 'god bless you' when you sneeze."

FINANCIAL AID: 845-575-3230 • E-MAIL: ADMISSION@MARIST.EDU • WEBSITE: WWW.MARIST.EDU

THE PRINCETON REVIEW SAYS

Admissions

Very important factors considered include: rigor of secondary school record, academic GPA. *Important factors considered include:* class rank, application essay, recommendation(s), extracurricular activities, talent/ability, character/personal qualities, geographical residence, state residency, volunteer work, work experience. *Other factors considered include:* standardized test scores, first generation, alumni/ae relation, racial/ethnic status, level of applicant's interest. SAT or ACT considered if submitted. ACT with or without writing accepted. SAT with or without Essay component accepted. TOEFL required of all international applicants. High school diploma is required and GED is accepted. *Academic units required:* 4 English, 3 math, 3 science, 2 science labs, 2 foreign language, 2 social studies, 1 history, 2 academic electives. *Academic units recommended:* 4 math, 4 science, 3 science labs, 3 foreign language.

Financial Aid

Students should submit: FAFSA. Regular filing deadline is 5/1. The Princeton Review suggests that all financial aid forms be submitted as soon as possible after October 1. *Need-based scholarships/grants offered:* Federal Pell, FSEOG, State scholarships/grants, Private scholarships, College/university scholarship or grant aid from institutional funds. *Loan aid offered:* Direct Subsidized Stafford Loans, Direct Unsubsidized Stafford Loans, Direct PLUS Loans. Applicants will be notified of awards on a rolling basis beginning 4/1. Federal Work-Study Program available. Institutional employment available.

The Inside Word

Marist College says they accepted about 40 percent of the students who applied last year, and the average student had a recalculated GPA between 88 and 93. Students who are worried their grades and test scores are not robust enough should know that Marist admires applicants who indicate they will be active participants and leaders on campus and in the academic community. Students with special talents, such as artistic or athletic ones, should emphasize those as well.

THE SCHOOL SAYS "..."

From the Admissions Office

"Marist is a 'hot school' among prospective students. Applications are up over 50 percent since 2007. Meanwhile, the number of seats available for the freshman class remains at about 1,100, making for a very competitive admission process. Our recommendations: keep your grades up, participate in community service, and exercise leadership in the classroom, extracurricular endeavors, and your community. We encourage a campus visit. When prospective students see Marist—our beautiful location on the Hudson River, top-quality facilities, the close interaction between students and faculty, and the fact that everyone really enjoys their time here—they want to become a part of the Marist College community. We'll help you in the transition to college through an innovative first-year program that provides mentors for every student. You'll also learn how to use technology in whatever field you choose. Marist invests in the student experience. A new academic building for music programs and Student Center has dramatically improved performances and club space, and students call the new Grand Dining Hall 'Hogwarts on the Hudson.' We emphasize three aspects of a true Marist experience: excellence in education, community, and service to others. Just seventy-five miles north of New York City, Marist's location allows students the opportunity complete an internship in the city, network with professionals, plan a fun day trip, and get practical work experience through our Marist in Manhattan program. At Marist, you'll get a premium education, develop your skills, have fun and make lifelong friends, have the opportunity to gain valuable experience through our great internship and study abroad programs, including our branch campus in Florence, Italy, and be ahead of the competition for graduate school or a career."

SELECTIVITY

Admissions Rating	89
# of applicants	9,213
% of applicants accepted	45
% of acceptees attending	29
# offered a place on the wait list	3,645
% accepting a place on wait list	33
% admitted from wait list	9
# of early decision applicants	216
% accepted early decision	94

FRESHMAN PROFILE

Range SAT Critical Reading	520–620
Range SAT Math	530–630
Range SAT Writing	520–630
Range ACT Composite	23–28
Minimum paper TOEFL	550
Minimum internet-based TOEFL	80
Average HS GPA	3.3
% graduated top 10% of class	26
% graduated top 25% of class	61
% graduated top 50% of class	87

DEADLINES

Early decision	
Deadline	11/15
Notification	12/15
Early action	
Deadline	11/15
Notification	1/15
Regular	
Deadline	2/1
Notification	4/1
Nonfall registration?	Yes

APPLICANTS ALSO LOOK AT AND OFTEN PREFER
Villanova University; Boston University

AND SOMETIMES PREFER
Loyola University Maryland

FINANCIAL FACTS

Financial Aid Rating	80
Annual tuition	$33,250
Room and board	$14,850
Required fees	$550
Books and supplies	$1,000
Average frosh need-based scholarship	$17,763
Average UG need-based scholarship	$16,304
% needy frosh rec. need-based scholarship or grant aid	72
% needy UG rec. need-based scholarship or grant aid	71
% needy frosh rec. non-need-based scholarship or grant aid	97
% needy UG rec. non-need-based scholarship or grant aid	84
% needy frosh rec. need-based self-help aid	82
% needy UG rec. need-based self-help aid	83
% frosh rec. any financial aid	66
% UG rec. any financial aid	64
% UG borrow to pay for school	71
Average cumulative indebtedness	$34,865
% frosh need fully met	18
% ugrads need fully met	17
Average % of frosh need met	66
Average % of ugrad need met	64

MARLBORO COLLEGE

PO Box A, Marlboro, VT 05344-0300 • Admissions: 802-258-9236 • Fax: 802-451-7555

STUDENTS SAY "..."

Academics

Teeny tiny Marlboro College in Vermont offers a "self-driven, free, and intimate academic climate" with a "rustic feel." With an average class size of just five students, the school is all about creating a serious academic setting "where students are on equal footing with teachers and decide their own academic paths." "I dictate my own academics at Marlboro; I have the freedom to seriously study most anything," says one student. Marlboro's unique academic system, culminating in the Plan of Concentration, is "incredibly exciting"; through this curriculum, students "can focus right in, very specifically, on the particular books or ideas that interest them most." The "incredibly sharp-witted and compassionate" faculty members at Marlboro "have strong personalities," and relationships with professors are "really intimate (in a good way)." "By the end of a class—provided you participate—they know you well, and you know them well," says a student. There's definitely "a relaxed, humorous atmosphere that manages to coexist with the intense academics, somehow." Discussions can run deep, and "there are few classes here in which the professor talks more than the students do." There are also more than 400 tutorials in a year at Marlboro, which are typically reserved for juniors and seniors; most are one-on-one, and depend on students taking charge of a subject, preparing for and leading a weekly meeting with the faculty member and completing a piece of research or production. In addition, there is a "town-meeting-style community government" in place and "lots of energy from staff going into projects outside the classroom." Though no student lacks for attention or academic assistance, some admit that resources can be spread thin in some areas, including the "limited in number" professors; accessible as they are, some subject areas only have one professor, which means that "if you don't get along with the professor in your department you can either suck it up, or choose a different major." However, all of the "ingenious" professors are "great and really flexible. They just want to help." Grades, "while something that happen," are not considered important—instead the work students produce "is for our own pleasure and pride."

Life

With just a couple hundred students enrolled, there aren't a lot of redundancies or waste. The dining hall is a central meeting place, and many students "hang out there for hours talking." People also spend a lot of time in the library, which is open 24 hours and "functions as some people's second home." In this "intellectual yet casual atmosphere," everybody "seems to be reading constantly," and students "talk about books a lot, or articles, or things people have read on the internet." "Class materials get inside people's heads, and they seem to want to share it." Parties do occur on weekends, though it's not a huge scene; "It's common to see people talk about epistemology while they're drunk and dance while they're sober." "We party a bit, play lots of video games, watch a lot of movies, and sometimes go into town," says one student. Athletics aren't really very big (other than nearby hiking), and "most of time we like *talking* to each other." People are "constantly philosophizing [on] the state of things."

Student Body

Marlboro is "a place where 'the weird kids' from high schools all across the nation congregate and make beautiful music together (often literally)." "There is no typical student. That's the point," says one. Students here are "functionally eccentrics," "quirky," and "ready to pursue their own passions." There is a "high level of LGBTQ tolerance," and most students here are "usually politically mindful and open to challenging his or her perspectives." "It's kind of crazy, and everyone likes each other," says a student. There are people of all sorts, "from suits to rainbows, dreadlocks to comb-overs, you get the point." Essentially, "there is nothing too weird for Marlboro."

FINANCIAL AID: 802-258-9312 • E-MAIL: ADMISSIONS@MARLBORO.EDU • WEBSITE: WWW.MARLBORO.EDU

THE PRINCETON REVIEW SAYS

Admissions

Very important factors considered include: application essay, interview. *Important factors considered include:* rigor of secondary school record, academic GPA, recommendation(s), extracurricular activities, talent/ability, character/personal qualities, level of applicant's interest. *Other factors considered include:* class rank, standardized test scores, first generation, volunteer work, work experience. SAT or ACT considered if submitted. ACT with or without writing accepted. SAT with or without Essay component accepted. TOEFL required of all international applicants. High school diploma is required and GED is accepted. *Academic units recommended:* 4 English, 3 math, 3 science, 2 foreign language, 2 social studies, 2 history, 2 academic electives.

Financial Aid

Students should submit: FAFSA. Priority filing deadline is 3/1. The Princeton Review suggests that all financial aid forms be submitted as soon as possible after October 1. *Need-based scholarships/grants offered:* Federal Pell, FSEOG, State scholarships/grants, Private scholarships, College/university scholarship or grant aid from institutional funds. *Loan aid offered:* Direct Subsidized Stafford Loans, Direct Unsubsidized Stafford Loans, Direct PLUS Loans. Applicants will be notified of awards on a rolling basis beginning 3/1. Federal Work-Study Program available. Institutional employment available.

The Inside Word

Don't be misled by Marlboro's acceptance rate—this isn't the type of school that attracts many applications from students unsure of whether they belong at Marlboro. Most applicants are qualified both in terms of academic achievement and sincere intellectual curiosity. The school seeks candidates "with intellectual promise, a high degree of self-motivation, self-discipline, personal stability, social concern, and the ability and desire to contribute to the college community." These are the qualities you should stress on your application.

THE SCHOOL SAYS "..."

From the Admissions Office

"Marlboro College is distinguished by its curriculum, praised in higher education circles as unique; it is known for its self-governing philosophy, in which each student, faculty, and staff has an equal vote on many issues affecting the community; and it is recognized for its sixty-nine year history of offering a rigorous, exciting, self-designed course of study taught in very small classes and individualized study with faculty. Marlboro's size also distinguishes it from most other schools. With 200 students and a student/faculty ratio of four to one, it is one of the nation's smallest liberal arts colleges. Few other schools offer a program where students have such close interaction with faculty, and where community life is inseparable from academic life. The self-designed, self-directed Plan of Concentration that occupies their last two years at Marlboro, allows students to develop their own unique academic work by defining a problem, setting clear limits on an area of inquiry, and analyzing, evaluating, and reporting on the outcome of a significant project. A Marlboro education teaches you to think for yourself, articulate your thoughts, express your ideas, believe in yourself, and do it all with the clarity, confidence, and self-reliance necessary for later success, no matter what postgraduate path you take."

SELECTIVITY

Admissions Rating	77
# of applicants	144
% of applicants accepted	94
% of acceptees attending	26
# of early decision applicants	3
% accepted early decision	100

FRESHMAN PROFILE

Range SAT Critical Reading	580–760
Range SAT Math	510–600
Range SAT Writing	580–660
Minimum paper TOEFL	577
Minimum internet-based TOEFL	90
Average HS GPA	3.2
% graduated top 10% of class	17
% graduated top 25% of class	33
% graduated top 50% of class	67

DEADLINES

Early decision	
Deadline	11/15
Notification	12/1
Early action	
Deadline	1/15
Notification	2/1
Regular	
Priority	3/1
Nonfall registration?	Yes

APPLICANTS ALSO LOOK AT AND OFTEN PREFER
Reed College

AND SOMETIMES PREFER
College of the Atlantic; Bard College; The Evergreen State College

AND RARELY PREFER
Bennington College; University of Vermont

FINANCIAL FACTS

Financial Aid Rating	81
Annual tuition	$39,086
Room and board	$10,802
Required fees	$944
Books and supplies	$1,200
Average frosh need-based scholarship	$29,231
Average UG need-based scholarship	$25,443
% needy frosh rec. need-based scholarship or grant aid	100
% needy UG rec. need-based scholarship or grant aid	99
% needy frosh rec. non-need-based scholarship or grant aid	0
% needy UG rec. non-need-based scholarship or grant aid	0
% needy frosh rec. need-based self-help aid	100
% needy UG rec. need-based self-help aid	99
% frosh rec. any financial aid	98
% UG rec. any financial aid	94
% UG borrow to pay for school	83
Average cumulative indebtedness	$36,805
% frosh need fully met	0
% ugrads need fully met	0
Average % of frosh need met	78
Average % of ugrad need met	79

MARQUETTE UNIVERSITY

PO BOX 1881, MILWAUKEE, WI 53201-1881 • ADMISSIONS: 414-288-7302 • FAX: 414-288-3764

CAMPUS LIFE

Quality of Life Rating	87
Fire Safety Rating	98
Green Rating	85
Type of school	Private
Affiliation	Roman Catholic-Jesuit
Environment	Metropolis

STUDENTS

Total undergrad enrollment	8,334
% male/female	47/53
% from out of state	67
% frosh from public high school	60
% frosh live on campus	94
% ugrads live on campus	52
# of fraternities (% ugrad men join)	10 (4)
# of sororities (% ugrad women join)	13 (9)
% African American	4
% Asian	6
% Caucasian	73
% Hispanic	10
% Native American	<1
% Pacific Islander	<1
% Two or more races	4
% Race and/or ethnicity unknown	<1
% international	4
# of countries represented	39

SURVEY SAYS...

Students are happy
Great library
Career services are great
School is well run
Easy to get around campus
Lots of beer drinking
Everyone loves the Golden Eagles

ACADEMICS

Academic Rating	78
% students returning for sophomore year	90
% students graduating within 4 years	58
% students graduating within 6 years	80
Calendar	Semester
Student/faculty ratio	15:1
Profs interesting rating	74
Profs accessible rating	82

Most classes have 10–19 students.
Most lab/discussion sessions have
10–19 students.

MOST POPULAR MAJORS

Biomedical Sciences; Registered Nursing/
Registered Nurse; Mechanical Engineering

STUDENTS SAY " . . ."

Academics

A highly regarded Jesuit school, Marquette University "seeks to provide a well-rounded education based upon excellence, faith, leadership and service." Undergrads here truly value how the university is able to seamlessly integrate "the classroom [with] the greater Milwaukee area through applied programs, service learning and social activities." Marquette also manages to foster "great relationships with many of companies in the area (and in other states) and those companies come [here when] looking for interns to hire." As if that wasn't enough, the university's size is also a fantastic asset. A biomedical science major explains, "There's a real sense of community. It's a big enough school so you don't know everyone, but small enough so that you feel important."

Academically, the school's physical therapy, physician's assistant and business programs are all quite "strong" and very "highly" regarded. Fortunately, no matter your major, Marquette undergrads are privy to "enthusiastic" professors who seem to "genuinely care about [their] students." A nursing student agrees adding, "I've seen professors send students home to rest when they are sick, offer study sessions outside of class, lend students a book if they bought the wrong one, etc." Many professors also have ample professional experience. Therefore, they're able to bring "real world" insight directly into classroom. Overall, though "classes are difficult" professors "push you to do your best and you definitely come out learning a lot."

Life

If there's one notion that undergrads here make abundantly clear, it's that there is never a shortage of fun to be had at Marquette. Whether it's "a sorority or fraternity event, a get-together at your friend's, a concert at the Rave…a school sponsored event such as discounted tickets to the Broadway musical showing downtown, or free admission to the Olympic training ice rink off campus (skates included!)—there is ALWAYS something to do." Naturally, given that Marquette is part of the Big East Conference, the campus maintains a healthy "basketball culture." Students also love the fact that there are "a multitude of opportunities to get involved with community service." Additionally, Marquette offers groups "for everything from knitting to dancing to sailing… [as well as] club sports…[and] various martial arts and Quidditch." During the warmer months, it's not uncommon to see students simply "studying [outside] or playing catch/Frisbee [on] the quad." Finally, undergrads love the fact that the campus is a mere "five minutes away from downtown [Milwaukee]." This makes it easy for students to explore all the city has to offer from restaurants and shops to museums and cultural festivals.

Student Body

Given Marquette's location, it's not surprising that the majority of students hail "from the Midwest" with "a [hefty] number…from the Chicago area" in particular. And though "many students come from wealthy families, there are a large portion of people that attend Marquette due to generous scholarships." Thankfully, no matter your geographic heritage or economic status, undergrads assure us that you'll find a "friendly" student body. And though it's a Jesuit university, "Marquette welcomes students of all backgrounds [and] promotes unity among students of all faiths and cultural communities." More importantly, when pressed to describe and define their peers, undergrads assert that their fellow students are "down to earth, kind, funny [and] hardworking." They are also extremely "concerned about others and about social issues [as well]." Additionally, most students tend to be "very upbeat and passionate about everything that has to do with Marquette." Lastly, a political science major gushes, "This place felt like home right away because of how many genuine people are here."

MARQUETTE UNIVERSITY

FINANCIAL AID: 414-288-7390 • E-MAIL: ADMISSIONS@MARQUETTE.EDU • WEBSITE: WWW.MARQUETTE.EDU

THE PRINCETON REVIEW SAYS

Admissions

Very important factors considered include: rigor of secondary school record, academic GPA. *Important factors considered include:* standardized test scores, application essay, extracurricular activities, volunteer work. *Other factors considered include:* class rank, recommendation(s), talent/ability, character/personal qualities, first generation, alumni/ae relation, racial/ethnic status, work experience. SAT or ACT required. ACT with or without writing accepted. SAT with or without Essay component accepted. TOEFL required of all international applicants. High school diploma is required and GED is accepted. *Academic units required:* 4 English, 2 science labs. *Academic units recommended:* 4 English, 3 science labs, 2 foreign language, 3 social studies, 2 history.

Financial Aid

Students should submit: FAFSA. The Princeton Review suggests that all financial aid forms be submitted as soon as possible after October 1. *Need-based scholarships/grants offered:* Federal Pell, FSEOG, State scholarships/grants, Private scholarships, College/university scholarship or grant aid from institutional funds. *Loan aid offered:* Direct Subsidized Stafford Loans, Direct Unsubsidized Stafford Loans, Direct PLUS loans, Federal Perkins Loans, Federal Nursing Loans, State Loans, College/university loans from institutional funds. Applicants will be notified of awards on a rolling basis beginning 3/5. Federal Work-Study Program available. Institutional employment available.

The Inside Word

Marquette's admissions officers do not take their job lightly. Each application is read by at least two individuals before any decisions are made. When evaluating a candidate, officers first look to assess the high school transcript. They make a note of grade trends and pay close attention to how challenging an applicant's course load was. Marquette also considers the highest composite SAT and/or ACT score. Next, they take into account an applicant's personal statement along with his/her extracurricular activities. Finally, the school weighs the evaluation submitted by the guidance counselor.

SELECTIVITY

Admissions Rating	84
# of applicants	20,486
% of applicants accepted	74
% of acceptees attending	12
# offered a place on the wait list	3,681
% accepting a place on wait list	31
% admitted from wait list	93

FRESHMAN PROFILE

Range SAT Critical Reading	530–640
Range SAT Math	540–660
Range SAT Writing	510–640
Range ACT Composite	24–30
Minimum paper TOEFL	530
Minimum internet-based TOEFL	78
% graduated top 10% of class	34
% graduated top 25% of class	68
% graduated top 50% of class	94

DEADLINES

Regular	
Priority	12/1
Deadline	12/1
Nonfall registration?	Yes

APPLICANTS ALSO LOOK AT AND OFTEN PREFER

University of Illinois at Urbana-Champaign;
University of Notre Dame

AND SOMETIMES PREFER

University of Wisconsin–Madison; University of Minnesota–Twin Cities Campus

AND RARELY PREFER

Loyola University Chicago; Saint Louis University

FINANCIAL FACTS

Financial Aid Rating	83
Annual tuition	$38,000
Required fees	$470
Books and supplies	$1,008
Average frosh need-based scholarship	$21,049
Average UG need-based scholarship	$18,681
% needy frosh rec. need-based scholarship or grant aid	98
% needy UG rec. need-based scholarship or grant aid	98
% needy frosh rec. non-need-based scholarship or grant aid	13
% needy UG rec. non-need-based scholarship or grant aid	12
% needy frosh rec. need-based self-help aid	80
% needy UG rec. need-based self-help aid	81
% frosh rec. any financial aid	100
% UG rec. any financial aid	99
% UG borrow to pay for school	62
Average cumulative indebtedness	$37,048
% frosh need fully met	25
% ugrads need fully met	26
Average % of frosh need met	77
Average % of ugrad need met	78

MASSACHUSETTS INSTITUTE OF TECHNOLOGY

77 MASSACHUSETTS AVENUE, CAMBRIDGE, MA 02139 • ADMISSIONS: 617-253-3400 • FAX: 617-258-8304

CAMPUS LIFE
Quality of Life Rating	81
Fire Safety Rating	93
Green Rating	89
Type of school	Private
Affiliation	No Affiliation
Environment	City

STUDENTS
Total undergrad enrollment	4,527
% male/female	54/46
% from out of state	90
% frosh from public high school	65
% frosh live on campus	100
% ugrads live on campus	94
# of fraternities (% ugrad men join)	25 (48)
# of sororities (% ugrad women join)	7 (36)
% African American	6
% Asian	25
% Caucasian	37
% Hispanic	15
% Native American	<1
% Pacific Islander	<1
% Two or more races	6
% Race and/or ethnicity unknown	2
% international	10
# of countries represented	96

SURVEY SAYS...
Students always studying
Students are happy
Classroom facilities are great
Lab facilities are great
Great library
Career services are great
Internships are widely available
School is well run
No one cheats
Students aren't religious
Students love Cambridge, MA
Dorms are like palaces
Recreation facilities are great
Very little drug use
Campus newspaper is popular
Alumni active on campus

ACADEMICS
Academic Rating	98
% students returning for sophomore year	98
% students graduating within 4 years	82
% students graduating within 6 years	92
Calendar	4/1/4
Student/faculty ratio	3:1
Profs interesting rating	77
Profs accessible rating	81

Most classes have fewer than 10 students.
Most lab/discussion sessions have
10–19 students.

MOST POPULAR MAJORS
Computer Science; Mechanical Engineering;
Mathematics

STUDENTS SAY "..."

Academics
Massachusetts Institute of Technology, the East Coast mecca of engineering, science, and mathematics, "is the ultimate place for information overload, endless possibilities, and expanding your horizons." The "amazing collection of creative minds" includes enough Nobel laureates to fill a jury box as well as brilliant students who are given substantial control of their educations; one explains, "The administration's attitude toward students is one of respect. As soon as you come on campus, you are bombarded with choices." Students need to be able to manage a workload that "definitely push[es you] beyond your comfort level." A chemical engineering major elaborates: "MIT is different from many schools in that its goal is not to teach you specific facts in each subject. MIT teaches you how to think, not about opinions but about problem solving. Facts and memorization are useless unless you know how to approach a tough problem." Professors here range from "excellent teachers who make lectures fun and exciting" to "dull and soporific" ones, but most "make a serious effort to make the material they teach interesting by throwing in jokes and cool demonstrations." "Access to an amazing number of resources, both academic and recreational," "research opportunities for undergrads with some of the nation's leading professors," and a rock-solid alumni network complete the picture. If you ask "MIT alumni where they went to college, most will immediately stick out their hand and show you their 'brass rat' (the MIT ring, the second most recognized ring in the world)."

Life
At MIT, "it may seem...like there's no life outside problem sets and studying for exams," but "there's always time for extracurricular activities or just relaxing" for those "with good time-management skills" or the "ability to survive on [a] lack of sleep." Options range from "building rides" (recent projects have included a motorized couch and a human-sized hamster wheel) "to partying at fraternities to enjoying the largest collection of science fiction novels in the United States at the MIT Science Fiction Library." Students occasionally find time to "pull a hack," which is a prank, "like the life-size Wright brothers' plane that appeared on top of the Great Dome for the one-hundredth anniversary of flight." Undergrads tell us, "MIT has great parties—a lot of Wellesley, Harvard, and BU students come to them," but also that "there are tons of things to do other than party" here. "Movies, shopping, museums, and plays are all possible with our location near Boston. There are great restaurants only [blocks] away from campus, too...From what I can tell, MIT students have way more fun on the weekends than their Cambridge counterparts [at] Harvard."

Student Body
"There actually isn't one typical student at MIT," students here assure us, explaining that "hobbies range from building robots and hacking to getting wasted and partying every weekend. The one thing students all have in common is that they are insanely smart and love to learn. Pretty much anyone can find the perfect group of friends to hang out with at MIT." "Most students do have some form of 'nerdiness'" (like telling nerdy jokes, being an avid fan of *Star Wars*, etc.), but "contrary to MIT's stereotype, most MIT students are not geeks who study all the time and have no social skills. The majority of the students here are actually quite 'normal.'" The "stereotypical student [who] looks techy and unkempt...only represents about 25 percent of the school." The rest include "multiple-sport standouts, political activists, fraternity and sorority members, hippies, clean-cut business types, LARPers, hackers, musicians, and artisans. There are people who look like they stepped out of an Abercrombie & Fitch catalog and people who dress in all black and carry flashlights and multi-tools. Not everyone relates to everyone else, but most people get along, and it's almost a guarantee that you'll fit in somewhere.

MASSACHUSETTS INSTITUTE OF TECHNOLOGY

FINANCIAL AID: 617-253-4917 • E-MAIL: ADMISSIONS@MIT.EDU • WEBSITE: WEB.MIT.EDU

THE PRINCETON REVIEW SAYS

Admissions

Very important factors considered include: character/personal qualities. *Important factors considered include:* rigor of secondary school record, academic GPA, standardized test scores, application essay, recommendation(s), interview, extracurricular activities, talent/ability. *Other factors considered include:* class rank, first generation, geographical residence, racial/ethnic status, volunteer work, work experience. SAT or ACT required; SAT Subject Tests required. ACT with or without writing accepted. SAT with or without Essay component accepted. High school diploma or equivalent is not required. *Academic units recommended:* 4 English, 4 math, 4 science, 2 foreign language, 2 social studies.

Financial Aid

Students should submit: FAFSA, CSS/Financial Aid PROFILE, Noncustodial PROFILE, Business/Farm Supplement. Regular filing deadline is 2/15. The Princeton Review suggests that all financial aid forms be submitted as soon as possible after October 1. *Need-based scholarships/grants offered:* Federal Pell, FSEOG, State scholarships/grants, Private scholarships, College/university scholarship or grant aid from institutional funds. *Loan aid offered:* Direct Subsidized Stafford Loans, Direct Unsubsidized Stafford Loans, Direct PLUS loans, Federal Perkins Loans, College/university loans from institutional funds. Applicants will be notified of awards on or about 3/15. Federal Work-Study Program available. Institutional employment available.

The Inside Word

MIT has one of the nation's most competitive admissions processes. The school's applicant pool is so rich it turns away numerous qualified candidates each year. Put your best foot forward and take consolation in the fact that rejection doesn't necessarily mean that you don't belong at MIT, but only that there wasn't enough room for you the year you applied. Your best chance to get an edge: Find ways to stress your creativity, a quality that MIT's admissions director told *USA TODAY* is lacking in many prospective college students.

THE SCHOOL SAYS "..."

From the Admissions Office

"The students who come to the Massachusetts Institute of Technology are some of America's—and the world's—best and most creative. As graduates, they leave here to make real contributions—in science, technology, business, education, politics, architecture, and the arts. From any class, many will go on to do work that is historically significant. These young men and women are leaders, achievers, and producers. Helping such students make the most of their talents and dreams would challenge any educational institution. MIT gives them its best advantages: a world-class faculty, unparalleled facilities, and remarkable opportunities. In turn, these students help to make the institute the vital place it is. They bring fresh viewpoints to faculty research: More than three-quarters participate in the Undergraduate Research Opportunities Program, developing solutions for the world's problems in areas such as energy, the environment, cancer, and poverty. They play on MIT's thirty-three intercollegiate teams as well as in its fifty-plus music, theater, and dance groups. To their classes and to their out-of-class activities, they bring enthusiasm, energy, and individual style."

SELECTIVITY

Admissions Rating	99
# of applicants	18,306
% of applicants accepted	8
% of acceptees attending	73
# offered a place on the wait list	652
% accepting a place on wait list	88
% admitted from wait list	9

FRESHMAN PROFILE

Range SAT Critical Reading	680–780
Range SAT Math	750–800
Range SAT Writing	690–780
Range ACT Composite	33–35
Minimum internet-based TOEFL	90
% graduated top 10% of class	98
% graduated top 25% of class	100
% graduated top 50% of class	100

DEADLINES

Early action	
Deadline	11/1
Notification	12/20
Regular	
Deadline	1/1
Notification	3/20
Nonfall registration?	No

APPLICANTS ALSO LOOK AT AND OFTEN PREFER
Harvard College

AND SOMETIMES PREFER
Princeton University; Yale University; Stanford University

AND RARELY PREFER
California Institute of Technology; Cornell University; Duke University; University of Pennsylvania; Columbia University

FINANCIAL FACTS

Financial Aid Rating	95
Annual tuition	$46,400
Room and board	$13,730
Required fees	$304
Books and supplies	$1,000
Average frosh need-based scholarship	$39,882
Average UG need-based scholarship	$39,775
% needy frosh rec. need-based scholarship or grant aid	96
% needy UG rec. need-based scholarship or grant aid	96
% needy frosh rec. non-need-based scholarship or grant aid	2
% needy UG rec. non-need-based scholarship or grant aid	1
% needy frosh rec. need-based self-help aid	82
% needy UG rec. need-based self-help aid	87
% frosh rec. any financial aid	86
% UG rec. any financial aid	76
% UG borrow to pay for school	32
Average cumulative indebtedness	$23,485
% frosh need fully met	100
% ugrads need fully met	100
Average % of frosh need met	100
Average % of ugrad need met	100

MAYNOOTH UNIVERSITY

International Office, Maynooth, Co Kildare, Ireland • Admissions: +353 1-708-3868 • Fax: +353 1-708-6113

CAMPUS LIFE

Quality of Life Rating	92
Fire Safety Rating	89
Green Rating	73
Type of school	Public
Affiliation	No Affiliation

STUDENTS

Total undergrad enrollment	8,573
% male/female	43/57
% frosh live on campus	18
% ugrads live on campus	3
% African American	0
% Asian	0
% Caucasian	0
% Hispanic	0
% Native American	0
% Pacific Islander	0
% Two or more races	0
% Race and/or ethnicity unknown	0
% international	0
# of countries represented	90

SURVEY SAYS...

Students are happy
Classroom facilities are great
School is well run
Students are friendly
Recreation facilities are great
Lots of beer drinking

ACADEMICS

Academic Rating	66
% students returning for sophomore year	88
% students graduating within 4 years	0
% students graduating within 6 years	82
Calendar	Semester
Student/faculty ratio	25:1
Profs interesting rating	81
Profs accessible rating	78

Most classes have 20–29 students.

MOST POPULAR MAJORS

Liberal Arts and Sciences; Business/
Commerce; Multi-/Interdisciplinary Studies

STUDENTS SAY "..."

Academics

In emerald Ireland, just outside of Dublin, there lies the country's second-oldest and fastest growing university, Maynooth University. The school's town location and its relatively small size give off a "community atmosphere," and "modern and up-to-date" facilities and a "beautiful campus" make it "a nice environment to study in" with a "great history" to back it up. "The academic standard at Maynooth is impeccable, with lecturers, lecture halls, tutors, and labs of the finest stature," says a science major. There's a wide selection of classes available at Maynooth, and course content "is generally well-explained, with tutorials and support centers available." Professors "are without exception experts in their field" and "continually encouraging us to engage in discussions, to ask questions, and to develop not only a well-informed but independent way of thinking." "Almost all my lecturers are great orators that bring their subjects to life, creating a genuine interest among their students," says a Spanish major. Add to that the fact that they're "very, very, very approachable outside of class" ("There is always someone that you can approach for help and guidance"), and students are happy to receive "the best learning experience possible." Administration is responsive to student concerns, and there's a "friendliness of everyone on campus, from the president right down to the cleaners." The services the school provides are all "brilliant," from the library to the residence services. People also all love the "great" online class system, Moodle, which allows you to upload assignments and download class notes. "You are given every little or big piece of help you require or request to ensure you can achieve your highest grades," says a student. "In my six months here, I have yet to hear a disgruntled word aimed at the campus or the staff."

Life

Maynooth is a "very vibrant town" that "has all facilities needed by third-level students (including clubs, pubs, and pizzerias)." The student body "isn't too big," and the majority "keep on top of college work, participate in a club or society or two, and enjoy a night in the pub with their friends." There's a "vast amount" of clubs and societies, which means "there's always somewhere for you to go, whether it's the Play-Doh society or the Harry Potter appreciation society—we got it all!" The student union also "hosts concerts and social events regularly," and everyone enjoys the "good mood" of their compatriots. "For fun, the nightlife is key," and "every Wednesday and Thursday [are] party nights," when people go to the nightclubs or bars, play card games, drink beers, and "hang out with...mates." The school consists of two connected campuses, which "combine the old with the new." "South campus covered in snow is like a scene from Hogwarts in Harry Potter, [and] then "the north campus is modern." For those who live on campus, "everything is just at your fingertips," including a free gym. The university has completed a major extension to the library and is developing additional academic, research, and residence facilities as part of its Campus Master Plan.

Student Body

Look around Maynooth, and for the most part you'll just see a whole bunch of "your normal average twenty-year-old Irish girl [or] boy," though there's "a great mix of both city students and those from a rural background," as well as international, traditional, and "mature" students. "Individuality is very much encouraged" here, and in the midst of this "bubbly," "friendly" group is "a good place to make new friends." "Being Irish, we all like to have the 'craic' with people, meaning have fun," says a student. This group is also very "trustworthy," and "you can leave your laptop in the library for hours, and no one would ever take it."

E-MAIL: INTERNATIONAL.OFFICE@NUIM.IE • WEBSITE: WWW.NUIM.IE/INTERNATIONAL

THE PRINCETON REVIEW SAYS

Admissions

Very important factors considered include: rigor of secondary school record, academic GPA, standardized test scores. *Important factors considered include: Other factors considered include:* class rank, application essay, recommendation(s), talent/ability, character/personal qualities, volunteer work, work experience, level of applicant's interest. SAT or ACT required. ACT with Writing recommended. TOEFL required of all international applicants. *Academic units required:* 4 English, 4 math, and 16 units from above areas or other academic areas. *Academic units recommended:* 4 English, 4 math, 4 science, 4 foreign language, 4 social studies, 4 history, 4 computer science, and 4 units from above areas or other academic areas.

Financial Aid

Students should submit: FAFSA. Regular filing deadline is 6/1. The Princeton Review suggests that all financial aid forms be submitted as soon as possible after October 1. *Need-based scholarships/grants offered: Loan aid offered:* Direct Subsidized Stafford Loans, Direct Unsubsidized Stafford Loans, Direct PLUS Loans. Applicants will be notified of awards on a rolling basis beginning 3/1. Federal Work-Study Program available. Institutional employment available.

THE SCHOOL SAYS "..."

From the Admissions Office

"Maynooth University is pleased to be one of the few international universities to be included in The Princeton Review Best Colleges series. You do not require a visa to study in Ireland as a U.S. citizen, and the fees for Maynooth University are comparable to most in-state tuition fees in the US. So, for the price of your flights, you could get an international university experience for nearly the same price as staying at home!

"Degrees awarded by Irish Universities are internationally recognized as being of high quality. From September 2016 Maynooth University will implement a new undergraduate curriculum, a model unlike any other in the Irish university sector, and which is similar to a U.S. Liberal Arts curriculum. The new curriculum model features greatly increased flexibility, giving students the ability to specialize immediately or explore options in first year and specialize later. It will be possible for students to combine subjects across the humanities and sciences; broaden their perspective by taking a 10-credit elective stream, a short course outside of their core subject(s); pursue both major and minor subjects within an honours degree; or study a modern language alongside any degree. The revisions also include a greater emphasis on experiential learning, including expanded study abroad, work placement and volunteer opportunities.

"The International Office offers full support to all international students during the application process and once you arrive on campus. Maynooth University is very popular with U.S. students studying in Ireland and the campus is known as one of the friendliest in Ireland."

SELECTIVITY

Admissions Rating	79
# of applicants	14,256
% of applicants accepted	20
% of acceptees attending	93

FRESHMAN PROFILE

Minimum paper TOEFL	550
Minimum internet-based TOEFL	80
Average HS GPA	3.4

DEADLINES

Regular	
Deadline	7/1
Nonfall registration?	No

FINANCIAL FACTS

Financial Aid Rating	60*
Avg annual tuition (EU citizens)	$7,488
Avg annual tuition (non-EU citizens)	$14,553
Room and board	$6,841
% needy frosh rec. need-based scholarship or grant aid	0
% needy UG rec. need-based scholarship or grant aid	0
% needy frosh rec. non-need-based scholarship or grant aid	0
% needy UG rec. non-need-based scholarship or grant aid	0
% needy frosh rec. need-based self-help aid	0
% needy UG rec. need-based self-help aid	0

McGILL UNIVERSITY

845 SHERBROOKE STREET WEST, MONTREAL, QC H3A 0G4, CANADA • ADMISSIONS: 514-398-3910 • FAX: 514-398-4193

CAMPUS LIFE
Quality of Life Rating	89
Fire Safety Rating	79
Green Rating	60*
Type of school	Public
Affiliation	No Affiliation
Environment	Metropolis

STUDENTS
Total undergrad enrollment	25,081
% male/female	42/58
% from out of state	37
% frosh live on campus	51
% ugrads live on campus	12
# of fraternities (% ugrad men join)	8 (0)
# of sororities (% ugrad women join)	4 (0)
% African American	0
% Asian	0
% Caucasian	0
% Hispanic	0
% Native American	0
% Pacific Islander	0
% Two or more races	0
% Race and/or ethnicity unknown	0
% international	0
# of countries represented	136

SURVEY SAYS...
Lots of liberal students
Students are happy
Students aren't religious
Students love Montreal, QC
Great off-campus food
Lots of beer drinking

ACADEMICS
Academic Rating	74
Calendar	Semester
Student/faculty ratio	16:1
Profs interesting rating	69
Profs accessible rating	65

Most classes have 10–19 students.
Most lab/discussion sessions have 20–29 students.

MOST POPULAR MAJORS
Political Science and Government;
Psychology; Business/Commerce

STUDENTS SAY "..."

Academics

A world class school in a great city (Montreal), McGill University has "a nearly unparalleled reputation" around North America and the world, and gives students "the tools [they] need, a positive environment," and the space for them to make their own opportunities. The school is known for "embracing the internationality of all the students"; those who attend pay "a fraction of the cost that a top private school in the U.S. would cost," and a McGill degree "opens the most doors for graduating students." It is "everything you want to learn and do, found in 19th century buildings and snow." The faculty is generally "high caliber" but the quality can vary slightly. "I've had drone-ish philosophy profs and some teachers whose enthusiasm, intelligence and wit made even discussing Judith Butler for the fiftieth time fascinating, some teachers who shut off after class and a few who became ersatz therapists/mothers," says one junior. Academics tend to be theoretical and "old-school," containing rigorous, structured curricula, and there is a good deal of active research going on by the faculty, which "makes lectures up-to-date and continuously changing." Professors are also "always eager to take on students for independent research projects and lab assistance, as long as students make an effort." Students do admit that the school struggles with a fair amount of "bureaucratic redundancy," but agree that the school is "a facility that works very hard in order to ensure its students' success not only within its educational system, but also in preparing them for the outside world." "McGill does not baby you, and that makes you more responsible for yourself," says a student.

Life

The size of the school means "there are many social as well as academic opportunities." Admittedly "it takes a lot of work to have time to play," but students manage just fine. "People are at the library after a night of partying," says one. Most people "take school seriously and work really hard," but also love to go out when they're through. "How many McGill students does it take to screw in a lightbulb?" asks a student. "One, just don't ask them to do it Thursday, Friday, or Saturday."

Every McGill student has an abiding love for Montreal, which provides "a bilingual environment in a major metropolitan city." "McGill is very much a Montreal school... it's not uncommon for students to start renting an apartment their first year." Not to mention one other aspect: "The legal drinking age of 18 was unimportant to me when I applied, but very quickly I discovered its value," says a student. The bar and club scene in Montreal is "famous and with good reason," and Thursday is campus bar night. "The music scene and making dinners" for large groups of friends are also wildly popular activities.

The Macdonald Campus of McGill is actually "quite different" from the much larger downtown campus: the "community is smaller, in a scenic area (between the waterfront and a forest)" and there is a "different atmosphere [and a] different social life." McGill is also close to lots of good ski hills, which gives plenty of opportunities for students to leave Montreal, as well. "You have much more freedom to do what you want and there are endless places to visit, during the day and at night," says a junior finance major.

Student Body

McGill has "an incredibly diverse student body" in terms of nationalities, though "ethnicity-wise, the vast majority of the students are Caucasian." The student body "doesn't usually form cliques"; people "appreciate each other's differences" and all are "hard-working, engaged and interested in the world around them." "There's no way to not fit in with an undergrad population so large- you'll find your people," assures one student. Many American students are surprised at the "international flavor" and autonomy of the native Quebecois, but catch on by their second year. However, "it can be hard for outsiders to break into the local Quebec students' social circles, especially for non-French speakers."

FINANCIAL AID: 514-398-6013 • E-MAIL: ADMISSIONS@MCGILL.CA • WEBSITE: WWW.MCGILL.CA

THE PRINCETON REVIEW SAYS

Admissions

Very important factors considered include: rigor of secondary school record, academic GPA, standardized test scores. *Important factors considered include:* class rank. *Other factors considered include:* recommendation(s). ACT with Writing required. TOEFL required of all international applicants. High school diploma is required and GED is not accepted. *Academic units recommended:* 4 English, 4 math, 3 science, 3 science labs, 3 foreign language, 2 social studies, 2 history.

Financial Aid

Students should submit: Institution's own financial aid form. Regular filing deadline is 6/30. The Princeton Review suggests that all financial aid forms be submitted as soon as possible after October 1. *Need-based scholarships/grants offered:* Private scholarships, College/university scholarship or grant aid from institutional funds. *Loan aid offered:* College/university loans from institutional funds. Applicants will be notified of awards on a rolling basis beginning 3/1. Institutional employment available.

The Inside Word

Admission to McGill is highly competitive and decisions are based on an applicant's academic record. Extracurricular activities aren't significant in the admissions decision but may pertain to entrance scholarships. Applicants from the United States are required to submit standardized test scores, and minimum test score requirements are published on the McGill website.

THE SCHOOL SAYS "..."

From the Admissions Office

"McGill processes more than 30,000 online applications a year. Very few programs are available to non-Quebec students for January admission; consult the website for details.

"Applicants may submit results from of the SAT (plus at least two appropriate SAT Subject Tests). The ACT is accepted in lieu of the SAT and SAT Subject Test combination. Please note that certain programs can require specific SAT Subject Tests."

SELECTIVITY

Admissions Rating	90
# of applicants	24,651
% of applicants accepted	56
% of acceptees attending	35

FRESHMAN PROFILE

Range SAT Critical Reading	640–740
Range SAT Math	650–720
Range SAT Writing	650–730
Range ACT Composite	29–32
Minimum paper TOEFL	577
Minimum internet-based TOEFL	90

DEADLINES

Regular	
Deadline	1/15
Nonfall registration?	Yes

APPLICANTS ALSO LOOK AT AND OFTEN PREFER

University of Toronto; New York University

AND SOMETIMES PREFER

Columbia University; Harvard College; University of California–Berkeley

FINANCIAL FACTS

Financial Aid Rating	72
Average UG need-based scholarship	$4,750
% needy frosh rec. need-based scholarship or grant aid	0
% needy UG rec. need-based scholarship or grant aid	63
% needy frosh rec. non-need-based scholarship or grant aid	0
% needy UG rec. non-need-based scholarship or grant aid	31
% needy frosh rec. need-based self-help aid	0
% needy UG rec. need-based self-help aid	89
% UG rec. any financial aid	28

MERCER UNIVERSITY—MACON

ADMISSIONS OFFICE, MACON, GA 31207-0001 • ADMISSIONS: 478-301-2650 • FAX: 478-301-2828

CAMPUS LIFE

Quality of Life Rating	86
Fire Safety Rating	89
Green Rating	60*
Type of school	Private
Affiliation	No Affiliation
Environment	City

STUDENTS

Total undergrad enrollment	2,899
% male/female	50/50
% from out of state	19
% frosh live on campus	92
% ugrads live on campus	69
# of fraternities (% ugrad men join)	11 (23)
# of sororities (% ugrad women join)	7 (26)
% African American	18
% Asian	8
% Caucasian	58
% Hispanic	5
% Native American	<1
% Pacific Islander	<1
% Two or more races	4
% Race and/or ethnicity unknown	3
% international	4
# of countries represented	37

SURVEY SAYS...

Students are happy
Internships are widely available
School is well run
Great financial aid
Students are very religious
Easy to get around campus
Recreation facilities are great
Everyone loves the Mercer Bears
Intramural sports are popular
Frats and sororities are popular
Active minority support groups

ACADEMICS

Academic Rating	81
% students returning for sophomore year	87
% students graduating within 4 years	47
% students graduating within 6 years	61
Calendar	Semester
Student/faculty ratio	13:1
Profs interesting rating	82
Profs accessible rating	86

Most classes have 10–19 students.
Most lab/discussion sessions have 20–29 students.

MOST POPULAR MAJORS

Engineering; Business/Commerce; Biology

STUDENTS SAY "..."

Academics

Mercer University is a Georgia institution anchored in Macon, consisting of a dozen colleges and schools and offering "big school opportunities with a small school environment." The "active and welcoming atmosphere" offers "easy access to study resources" and an administration that "is there for the students." "They are a wonderful support system," says one. Mercer focuses on cultivating a passion for service in both the world and one's immediate surroundings, and many say that the best part about the school is "the community that it builds with the surrounding area." Students are proud to say that their school "upholds integrity, spirit, academia" and "everyone at Mercer has incredible school spirit and really loves being there."

The professors here are "phenomenal," allowing students to think for themselves and arrive at their own conclusions, "leading the discussions in as unbiased a manner as possible," and "playing devil's advocate when necessary." Everyone receives a "small liberal arts classroom experience," tests are geared toward an understanding past the lectures in order "to make sure students truly comprehend the material," and it is common for students and professors to chat about goals and aspirations in casual conversation. "My professors are some of my greatest cheerleaders, supporters, and mentors," says one student. "I have gotten to know them on a personal level, and they have done the same with me."

The holistic approach to general education taken by Mercer is applauded by students, who "are expected to interact every day" and therefore feel prepared to enter the workforce as "well-rounded thinkers." Various courses also have supplemental instruction (SI) where a previous student will assist students for seventy minutes, for three nights a week. "The greatest strength of MU is the value it places on students," says one of a school that "[encourages] participation in every facet of the university."

Life

The "beautiful" campus is small so students "are all very connected in classes and extracurriculars." QuadWorks is the school's main organizer of events, putting on movies, game nights, socials, and other activities that get students involved, and students attend a lot of sporting events: "Fall is football, winter is basketball (which is probably the most popular), baseball is in the spring." Athletics and Greek life are very popular; for those not playing sports at the collegiate level, "there are intramural sports and club sports that you can be a part of." Though studying takes up a good deal of time and "Mercer is a real working campus" as far as students with jobs go, there are plenty of Netflix and card game nights.

Macon is "a vibrant town" with a good music scene and a nearby downtown that boasts restaurants, theaters, bars (the campus is dry), and shopping; students head here often. Mercer is also rich in traditional ceremonies for students to participate in such as a "pilgrimage to Penfield (the original site of the university), the annual Christmas tree lighting ceremony, and Founders Day."

Student Body

Mercer University has students of all ethnic backgrounds and goals, though most everyone is southern, "studies a lot," and is "involved in at least one campus organization, a campus job, and some kind of regular commitment to community service." A significant portion of students come from a "conservative Christian background" but "cultural backgrounds and demographic differences have very little effect on students' relationships." "There are numerous cultural/ethnic organizations that each student can be a part of without feeling excluded," says a student. In addition to the excellent town-gown relations between Mercer and Macon, students also "think about helping others and giving back" both locally (building local homes, accounting classes to help the underprivileged manage their finances) and internationally (through Mercer On Mission programs).

FINANCIAL AID: 478-301-2670 • E-MAIL: ADMISSIONS@MERCER.EDU • WEBSITE: WWW.MERCER.EDU

THE PRINCETON REVIEW SAYS

Admissions

Very important factors considered include: rigor of secondary school record, academic GPA, standardized test scores, level of applicant's interest. *Important factors considered include:* application essay, extracurricular activities, talent/ability, character/personal qualities, volunteer work. *Other factors considered include:* class rank, recommendation(s), interview, alumni/ae relation, work experience. SAT or ACT required. ACT with or without writing accepted. SAT with or without Essay component accepted. TOEFL or IELTS required of all international applicants. High school diploma is required and GED is accepted. *Academic units required:* 4 English, 4 math, 3 science, 2 science labs, 2 foreign language, 1 social studies, 2 history.

Financial Aid

Students should submit: FAFSA, State aid form. Priority filing deadline is 3/1. The Princeton Review suggests that all financial aid forms be submitted as soon as possible after October 1. *Need-based scholarships/grants offered:* Federal Pell, FSEOG, State scholarships/grants, College/university scholarship or grant aid from institutional funds, Federal Nursing Scholarships. *Loan aid offered:* Direct Subsidized Stafford Loans, Direct Unsubsidized Stafford Loans, Direct PLUS loans, Federal Perkins Loans, Federal Nursing Loans, College/university loans from institutional funds. Applicants will be notified of awards on a rolling basis beginning 3/15. Federal Work-Study Program available. Institutional employment available.

The Inside Word

For those considering Mercer, readiness to work hard should not be taken lightly. Students report that transfers end up dropping out after a semester, even after coming from a major university. The admissions policy is seen as lenient, yet the work certainly isn't. It may not seem difficult to get into Mercer, but graduating is another matter.

THE SCHOOL SAYS "..."

From the Admissions Office

"For many high school seniors, the college search can be a stressful process. As an admissions counseling staff, we are committed to helping each and every student that we meet to identify their best personal 'fit' for a college or university. During this process, many find that Mercer is the right place for their higher education journey. At Mercer, each student is matched with a personal admissions counselor. This counselor remains his or her primary point of contact from application through enrollment. We get to know our applicants through personal contact, high school visits, regional receptions, college fairs, and our numerous campus visitation programs. Our counselors work closely with students and their families through the application, financial aid, housing, orientation, and other enrollment processes to ensure that students make a smooth transition from high school to college. This makes for a truly enjoyable and informed admissions experience for all involved.

"Mercer University begins accepting applications for undergraduate admission on August 1. We encourage high school seniors to submit their completed applications (including official transcripts and test scores; IELTS or TOEFL for international students) before our priority application deadline of October 15 to be considered for the University's most prestigious scholarships. Our regular decision deadline is February 1. We evaluate applications on a rolling basis throughout the academic year."

SELECTIVITY

Admissions Rating	83
# of applicants	4,559
% of applicants accepted	67
% of acceptees attending	27

FRESHMAN PROFILE

Range SAT Critical Reading	550–650
Range SAT Math	560–660
Range SAT Writing	530–625
Range ACT Composite	24–30
Minimum paper TOEFL	550
Minimum internet-based TOEFL	80
Average HS GPA	3.8
% graduated top 10% of class	45
% graduated top 25% of class	73
% graduated top 50% of class	95

DEADLINES

Early action	
Deadline	10/15
Notification	11/15
Regular	
Priority	2/1
Deadline	4/1
Notification	Rolling
Nonfall registration?	Yes

APPLICANTS ALSO LOOK AT AND OFTEN PREFER

University of Georgia; Emory University; Georgia Institute of Technology

AND SOMETIMES PREFER

Vanderbilt University; University of North Carolina at Chapel Hill; Auburn University; Furman University, Florida State University

AND RARELY PREFER

Clemson University

FINANCIAL FACTS

Financial Aid Rating	88
Annual tuition	$34,150
Room and board	$10,678
Required fees	$300
Books and supplies	$1,200
Average frosh need-based scholarship	$25,648
Average UG need-based scholarship	$24,770
% needy frosh rec. need-based scholarship or grant aid	100
% needy UG rec. need-based scholarship or grant aid	99
% needy frosh rec. non-need-based scholarship or grant aid	33
% needy UG rec. non-need-based scholarship or grant aid	28
% needy frosh rec. need-based self-help aid	54
% needy UG rec. need-based self-help aid	57
% frosh rec. any financial aid	99
% UG rec. any financial aid	97
% UG borrow to pay for school	69
Average cumulative indebtedness	$26,321
% frosh need fully met	47
% ugrads need fully met	41
Average % of frosh need met	89
Average % of ugrad need met	85

MIAMI UNIVERSITY (OH)

301 SOUTH CAMPUS AVENUE, OXFORD, OH 45056 • ADMISSIONS: 513-529-2531

STUDENTS SAY "..."

Academics

Attending school at Miami University may be "the iconic college experience." Located in Oxford, Ohio, "a quaint college town" with a "beautiful red brick campus," which students describe as "gorgeous" and "astoundingly beautiful," the school "has a rich tradition and history" that "is committed to its image as a premier undergraduate institution." The "prestige" of the business school affords many promising opportunities both during school and after graduation. Students agree, "Miami really prepares students for the real world after college." "A degree from Miami is worth a lot to many employers." "Miami University students are recruited by companies, and that provides great leverage when looking for internships and jobs." The curriculum as a whole offers "a challenging academic workload" that truly tests a student's abilities as well as "prepares students for the workplace after graduation while also giving them the opportunity to thrive while on campus." This "devotion to excellent undergraduate instruction" is backed by "an extremely strong orientation program, a dedicated student affairs department, and an overwhelming amount of student involvement in co-curricular activities." Smaller classrooms that allow for "engaging" discussion are more highly valued than large lectures, which may be "hard to sit through." Professors are a "mixed bag." "If you get the right ones, it makes all the difference." A student in the Honors Program calls the experience "phenomenal. It offers the ability to grow as a student and person through both in and out of class experiences."

Life

Miami University offers "a vibrant social atmosphere." With more than 16,000 students on campus Miami may be "the perfect size," where you "can see everyone...but still meet many new people." With a "plethora of student activities," "Miami makes it possible to find groups or organizations that can fit any student's interest, and many tend to help in propelling graduates into jobs or programs once they leave the campus." "Greek life is everywhere you look," according to one student who posits "it often seems as though everyone is because of how visible they are on campus," though statistics indicate only about one-third of undergraduates go Greek. On the partying front, "if you are looking to drink, you will certainly find it here if you want." "Miami students can find a wealth of great bars and clubs uptown—many of which are eighteen-plus, allowing freshmen and sophomores to enjoy the dance floors and bars that make up almost all of the nightlife." The campus also "offers a lot of alternative programs for students who wish to avoid alcohol." "Late night programming is offered through Miami, as well as athletic events and other cultural events." Among sports, "hockey is really popular." Students tend to be happy with life at Miami. "There is a ton to do on and off campus. The town is quaint, but it is mainly a college town, so it's like an extension of the school. Nightlife is pretty big here, but so are academics and activities. Students definitely are actively thinking about their futures, and they take academics seriously."

Student Body

The typical student is "very involved on campus, is concerned about his or her academics, and wants to make a good impression on others. We care about how we present ourselves, but in a good way." Another student says, "The typical student is very academically focused, challenge-driven, competitive, extraverted, and demonstrates a preference for dressing well." Several students commented that students tend to "look and dress alike." "It can be very cliquish, especially in the Greek community." Anyone can fit in though, it's "all about finding your niche on campus which is generally done through people in your major, and especially student organizations." Miami tends to attract students who are "white, upper-middle-class, and Christian. The campus lacks diversity socioeconomically, ethnically, and religiously; however, the student body is generally accepting of all students no matter the background." One student relishes the challenge "to find diversity even in people who look similar and [has] grown because of it."

MIAMI UNIVERSITY (OH)

FINANCIAL AID: 513-529-0001 • E-MAIL: ADMISSION@MIAMIOH.EDU • WEBSITE: WWW.MIAMIOH.EDU

THE PRINCETON REVIEW SAYS

Admissions

Very important factors considered include: rigor of secondary school record, academic GPA, standardized test scores, application essay, recommendation(s), talent/ability, character/personal qualities. *Other factors considered include:* extracurricular activities, first generation, alumni/ae relation, geographical residence, state residency, volunteer work, work experience. SAT or ACT required. Demonstrated English proficiency required of all international applicants. High school diploma is required and GED is accepted. *Academic units recommended:* 4 English, 4 math, 3 science, 2 foreign language, 2 social studies, 1 history, 1 visual/performing arts.

Financial Aid

Students should submit: FAFSA. The Princeton Review suggests that all financial aid forms be submitted as soon as possible after October 1. *Need-based scholarships/grants offered:* Federal Pell, FSEOG, State scholarships/grants, Private scholarships, College/university scholarship or grant aid from institutional funds. *Loan aid offered:* Direct Subsidized Stafford Loans, Direct Unsubsidized Stafford Loans, Direct PLUS loans, Federal Perkins Loans, College/university loans from institutional funds. Applicants will be notified of awards on a rolling basis. Federal Work-Study Program available. Institutional employment available.

The Inside Word

Getting into Miami University isn't easy. High grades and ACT scores are a good start, and there is more you can do to better your odds. Admissions officers favor students who have challenged themselves academically, are active in their schools, lead student organizations or other activities, and volunteer in their community.

THE SCHOOL SAYS ". . ."

From the Admissions Office

"At Miami, you'll find a level of involvement—in your classes, in your research, in your extracurricular activities—that you won't find at other schools. What sets Miami apart as a Public Ivy is the ability to give students a personalized small-college experience within the excitement and opportunities of a midsize university, all at a public school cost. With more than 100 majors to choose from, and a liberal arts foundation that allows students to explore different areas of interest, finding your true passion—in and out of the classroom—is at the heart of what the Miami University experience is all about. This deep level of engagement is reflected in the 90 percent freshman to sophomore retention rate and Miami's 80 percent graduation rate, which is among the top for public universities across the country. Miami's reputation for producing outstanding leaders with real-world experience makes us a target school for top global firms, leads to acceptance rates into law and medical school which far exceed the national averages, and result in impressive placement rates for graduates. According to surveys and national data, 95.5 percent of Miami University students who graduated in 2014–2015 were employed or in school by fall 2015. Students also benefit from small class sizes—66 percent of undergraduate classes have fewer than thirty students—and personal attention from faculty members in the classroom, through research opportunities, and through faculty mentoring programs. Outside of the classroom, students can participate in over 475 student organizations, attend social and cultural events, or get involved with one of the most extensive intramural and club sports program in the country."

SELECTIVITY

Admissions Rating	88
# of applicants	27,454
% of applicants accepted	65
% of acceptees attending	21
# offered a place on the wait list	3,269
% accepting a place on wait list	28
% admitted from wait list	0
# of early decision applicants	1,030
% accepted early decision	71

FRESHMAN PROFILE

Range SAT Critical Reading	550–650
Range SAT Math	590–690
Range SAT Writing	540–650
Range ACT Composite	26–30
Minimum paper TOEFL	550
Minimum internet-based TOEFL	80
Average HS GPA	3.8
% graduated top 10% of class	36
% graduated top 25% of class	68
% graduated top 50% of class	94

DEADLINES

Early decision	
Deadline	11/15
Notification	12/15
Early action	
Deadline	12/1
Notification	2/1
Regular	
Deadline	2/1
Notification	3/15
Nonfall registration?	Yes

APPLICANTS ALSO LOOK AT AND OFTEN PREFER
Boston College; Northwestern University

AND SOMETIMES PREFER
University of Wisconsin–Madison

AND RARELY PREFER
Ohio University–Athens; Xavier University (OH)

FINANCIAL FACTS

Financial Aid Rating	81
Annual in-state tuition	$13,533
Annual out-of-state tuition	$30,233
Room and board	$11,644
Required fees	$754
Books and supplies	$1,140
Average frosh need-based scholarship	$10,176
Average UG need-based scholarship	$8,754
% needy frosh rec. need-based scholarship or grant aid	88
% needy UG rec. need-based scholarship or grant aid	87
% needy frosh rec. non-need-based scholarship or grant aid	18
% needy UG rec. non-need-based scholarship or grant aid	12
% needy frosh rec. need-based self-help aid	72
% needy UG rec. need-based self-help aid	78
% frosh need fully met	22
% ugrads need fully met	17
Average % of frosh need met	60
Average % of ugrad need met	58

MICHIGAN TECHNOLOGICAL UNIVERSITY

1400 TOWNSEND DRIVE, HOUGHTON, MI 49931 • ADMISSIONS: 906-487-2335 • FAX: 906-487-2125

STUDENTS SAY "..."

Academics

Michigan Technological University has "very high standards when it comes to education" and offers "serious study in a beautiful (often snowy) environment." It boasts a "really good reputation as an engineering school," and it's no secret that "engineering is a part of everybody's life." All agree, "Michigan Tech provides an atmosphere that nurtures learning" and "puts students first when it comes to their learning experience by providing hands-on experience." The university offers "lots of internship and co-op opportunities" and "pathways for career development and professional advancement." Students say that the courses are "challenging" and that the university "pushes students to excel academically." Professors are "generally interesting and helpful," but some can be "dull." A junior says, "Concentrated courses are great, but [general education courses] are huge, impersonal, and just plain awful," and another student adds, "The experience gets better with more time you put into your program, the professors become more interactive, and the experience becomes more meaningful."

Life

Michigan Tech "is in a small town in the middle of the deep North woods," which makes "the sense of community remarkable." Students say that campus is "incredibly safe," that "the atmosphere is very friendly," and that "there are a lot of opportunities to get involved." A physics major notes, "You start to see people you know everywhere on campus. It is really easy to find a friend and talk to someone." Enhancing the "strong student community" are "over 200 clubs" and a variety of "winter activities to be a part of." Many students take advantage of "free access to Mont Ripley," the university's own ski hill and the oldest one in Michigan. A freshman says, "We have broomball, Winter Carnival, and lots of campus-wide events!" Many students agree, "The administration in every department works hard to answer questions and help out as much as possible, which is really great when you're a freshman," but some feel there's a "gap between [the] administration and students," particularly when it comes to spending. There are complaints about dorm food, leading a junior to say, "I would like to see some more selection and variation between dining halls," and students feel there's a need for "more parking spots close to campus." While "the library is a great place to study," some "of the classrooms are dated" and could use technological updating.

Student Body

At Michigan Tech, the typical student "is smart and a little more introspective than average," but still "great at balancing school and hanging out." Most students "are looking to get a good education and are fairly laid-back," and the student body consists of "down-to-earth friendly people," who "work hard during the week and look forward to relaxing and having fun on the weekends." It's no secret that "the ratio is a little guy-heavy" and that, because of this, "girls get doors opened for them across campus." Students tend to be "white and male," and a junior acknowledges, "There's little diversity ethnically, but everyone feels welcome." A chemical engineering major says, "You have to be a little bit of a nerd to fit in," and another student agrees, "I think most people think about classes first, hanging out second." It's common for students to "stay in and play video games," but there's also a large contingent of "outdoorsy people." A sophomore says, "Winters are long and cold up here," and students take advantage of the plentiful snow by "hiking, biking, four-wheeling, skiing, [and] snowmobiling." Students look forward to Winter Carnival, "a long weekend off from classes where students build giant, impressive snow sculptures, play broomball, [and] stay out all night," and for fun they enjoy "house parties and moderate drinking/merrymaking [to] warm up the cold winters."

FINANCIAL AID: 906-487-2622 • E-MAIL: MTU4U@MTU.EDU • WEBSITE: WWW.MTU.EDU

THE PRINCETON REVIEW SAYS

Admissions

Very important factors considered include: academic GPA, standardized test scores. *Important factors considered include:* rigor of secondary school record. *Other factors considered include:* class rank, application essay, recommendation(s), extracurricular activities, talent/ability, character/personal qualities, volunteer work. SAT or ACT required. ACT with or without writing accepted. SAT with or without Essay component accepted. TOEFL required of all international applicants. High school diploma is required and GED is accepted. *Academic units required:* 3 English, 3 math, 2 science. *Academic units recommended:* 4 English, 4 math, 3 science, 2 foreign language, 3 social studies, 2 academic electives, 1 computer science.

Financial Aid

Students should submit: FAFSA. Priority filing deadline is 3/1. The Princeton Review suggests that all financial aid forms be submitted as soon as possible after October 1. *Need-based scholarships/grants offered:* Federal Pell, FSEOG, State scholarships/grants, Private scholarships, College/university scholarship or grant aid from institutional funds. *Loan aid offered:* Direct Subsidized Stafford Loans, Direct Unsubsidized Stafford Loans, Direct PLUS loans, Federal Perkins Loans, College/university loans from institutional funds. Applicants will be notified of awards on a rolling basis beginning 3/15. Federal Work-Study Program available. Institutional employment available.

The Inside Word

Michigan Tech strives to enroll bright, adventurous students. Students aren't required to submit recommendations from teachers, although they may submit a "High School Counselor Information Page" if they would like their counselor to share information regarding their high school performance. Applicants to the Visual and Performing Arts Department degree programs are required to submit supplemental materials, including an essay.

THE SCHOOL SAYS "..."

From the Admissions Office

"At Michigan Tech, our students create the future. Our unique Enterprise Program lets students work on real industry problems such as building a satellite, designing advanced robotics systems, developing better alternative fuels, and planning a public transit system. Through student groups like Engineers Without Borders and the campus-wide Make a Difference Day, our students impact lives in our community and around the world.

"Students can choose from over 120 degree programs in engineering; forest resources; computing; technology; business; economics; mathematics; natural, physical and environmental sciences; arts; humanities; and social sciences. We offer exciting degree programs in growing fields such as biomedical engineering, wildlife ecology and management, and pre-health professions.

"Outside of the classrooms and labs, students enjoy our golf course, ski hill, cross-country ski trails and recreational forest, and a safe, friendly, small-town atmosphere in beautiful Upper Michigan. Located on the Keweenaw Waterway, the campus is only minutes from Lake Superior. During Winter Carnival, students build huge snow statues and play broomball, the most popular game on campus. There are varsity and intramural sports, including football, men's and women's basketball, tennis, cross-country, nordic skiing, track and field, soccer, volleyball, and hockey. The Huskies hockey team made the NCAA finals in 2015.

"We recommend that students applying for admission take the SAT or the ACT."

SELECTIVITY

Admissions Rating	84
# of applicants	5,386
% of applicants accepted	75
% of acceptees attending	31

FRESHMAN PROFILE

Range SAT Critical Reading	545–665
Range SAT Math	565–690
Range SAT Writing	505–625
Range ACT Composite	24–29
Minimum paper TOEFL	550
Minimum internet-based TOEFL	79
Average HS GPA	3.7
% graduated top 10% of class	28
% graduated top 25% of class	62
% graduated top 50% of class	92

DEADLINES

Regular	
Priority	1/15
Nonfall registration?	Yes

APPLICANTS ALSO LOOK AT AND SOMETIMES PREFER

University of Michigan–Ann Arbor; University of Minnesota–Twin Cities Campus; University of Wisconsin–Madison; University of Illinois at Urbana-Champaign; Purdue University–West Lafayette

FINANCIAL FACTS

Financial Aid Rating	81
Annual in-state tuition	$13,986
Annual out-of-state tuition	$29,950
Room and board	$9,857
Required fees	$300
Books and supplies	$1,200
Average frosh need-based scholarship	$9,417
Average UG need-based scholarship	$7,728
% needy frosh rec. need-based scholarship or grant aid	85
% needy UG rec. need-based scholarship or grant aid	79
% needy frosh rec. non-need-based scholarship or grant aid	84
% needy UG rec. non-need-based scholarship or grant aid	74
% needy frosh rec. need-based self-help aid	78
% needy UG rec. need-based self-help aid	84
% frosh rec. any financial aid	97
% UG rec. any financial aid	91
% UG borrow to pay for school	73
Average cumulative indebtedness	$35,741
% frosh need fully met	22
% ugrads need fully met	19
Average % of frosh need met	81
Average % of ugrad need met	73

MIDDLEBURY COLLEGE

THE EMMA WILLARD HOUSE, MIDDLEBURY, VT 05753-6002 • ADMISSIONS: 802-443-3000 • FAX: 802-443-2056

STUDENTS SAY "..."

Academics

One of the most highly regarded liberal arts colleges in the United States, Middlebury College in Vermont is about "creating a person both socially and intellectually prepared for the world." The school has "a high level of global thinking and language acquisition in such a rural place," and there is an "emerging focus on creativity and entrepreneurship." When teaching students to develop communication, writing, creativity, and critical thinking skills, the school "allows you to develop these skills in whatever subject or subjects that one is most passionate about." Students' needs and choices are "of very high priority" to the administration, and there is "institutional support for whatever absurd idea might strike you." Professors are, on the whole, "truly top-notch"; not only are they "brilliant academics, but they are also adept teachers and classroom leaders." They come here because they want to teach undergraduates and research; "Middlebury expects both; most professors deliver." "Several of my professors have given out their cell phone numbers after particularly difficult lectures to make sure that students can figure things out," says one. "It's almost impossible to actually be 'invisible.'" The overall academic experience is "very intense" ("If you haven't done the reading, prepare to be called out for it"), but "students reliably enjoy their classes."

Life

Empty hours at Middlebury are in short supply; "If you've got free time in your day at Middlebury, you're doing something wrong," says a student. However, after all that reading, "at the end of the day, we all just like to get together and hit up the Snow Bowl to go skiing." "Vermont does make a difference," says one student of Middlebury's location near mountains, lakes, and ski trails, and its focus on "how important the outdoor experience is for the school." Drinking is "fairly prevalent" on Fridays and Saturdays, but "not during the week." It's a healthy culture, and "public safety does a good job of keeping things safe while not being overly intrusive." The dorms are "gorgeous," and there is even one called the Chateau, modeled after the largest chateau in Fontainebleau, France. The number of activities available are admirable, and "most people actually choose not to go into cities on weekends because they would hate to miss what's going on on-campus that weekend."

Student Body

The pervasive atmosphere at Middlebury is "super friendly and caring," and there is not only the pressure to work hard, but "also the encouragement to make sure students succeed." Students "compete with themselves, not their classmates." With a happy population, beautiful environs, and not a single student going unchallenged, the school encompasses "a perfect blend of intellectual curiosity, responsible living, and fun." As one student eloquently puts it, it's a bunch of "bright kids doing too many things—all of them good, none related to sleep." This "engaged, active," "preppy" student body "doesn't take themselves too seriously but do take serious initiative." A typical go-getter student "pursues at least one major, a minor, and is the star of at least one sports team or special interest group, but usually more." Social life can be "very centered around athletic teams," but these "well-read, outgoing," and "well-rounded students from stable backgrounds" always end up connecting with people they can relate with easily. "You will struggle to find time to spend with all the different friends you will make," says a student. Social ease is a common trait among MiddKids, and most students "know how to hold a conversation and [are] open to new experiences."

FINANCIAL AID: 802-443-5158 • E-MAIL: ADMISSIONS@MIDDLEBURY.EDU • WEBSITE: WWW.MIDDLEBURY.EDU

THE PRINCETON REVIEW SAYS

Admissions

Very important factors considered include: rigor of secondary school record, class rank, academic GPA, extracurricular activities, talent/ability, character/personal qualities. *Important factors considered include:* standardized test scores, application essay, recommendation(s), racial/ethnic status. *Other factors considered include:* interview, first generation, alumni/ae relation, geographical residence, volunteer work, work experience, level of applicant's interest. ACT with or without writing accepted. SAT with or without Essay component accepted. TOEFL required of all international applicants. High school diploma or equivalent is not required. *Academic units recommended:* 4 English, 4 math, 3 science, 3 science labs, 4 foreign language, 3 social studies.

Financial Aid

Students should submit: FAFSA, Institution's own financial aid form, CSS/Financial Aid PROFILE, Noncustodial PROFILE. Regular filing deadline is 2/1. The Princeton Review suggests that all financial aid forms be submitted as soon as possible after October 1. *Need-based scholarships/grants offered:* Federal Pell, FSEOG, State scholarships/grants, Private scholarships, College/university scholarship or grant aid from institutional funds. *Loan aid offered:* Direct Subsidized Stafford Loans, Direct Unsubsidized Stafford Loans, Direct PLUS loans, College/university loans from institutional funds. Applicants will be notified of awards on or about 4/1. Federal Work-Study Program available. Institutional employment available.

The Inside Word

Middlebury gives you options in standardized testing. The school will accept either the ACT or the SAT or three SAT Subject Tests (the tests must be in three different subject areas, however). Middlebury is extremely competitive; improve your chances of admission by crafting a standardized test profile that shows you in the best possible light.

THE SCHOOL SAYS "..."

From the Admissions Office

"The successful Middlebury candidate excels in a variety of areas including academics, athletics, the arts, leadership, and service to others. These strengths and interests permit students to grow beyond their traditional 'comfort zones' and conventional limits. Our classrooms are as varied as the Green Mountains, the Metropolitan Museum of Art, or the great cities of Russia and Japan. Outside the classroom, students informally interact with professors in activities such as intramural basketball games and community service. At Middlebury, students develop critical-thinking skills, enduring bonds of friendship, and the ability to challenge themselves.

"Middlebury's Commons system is the backbone of student residential life at the College. The residence halls are grouped into 'living-learning communities,' or Commons, which combine the academic, social, and residential components of college life. They also foster close relationships between the student residents and the faculty and staff who are part of their Commons.

"Middlebury offers majors and programs in forty-six different fields, with particular strengths in languages, international studies, environmental studies, literature and creative writing, and the sciences. Opportunities for engaging in individual research with faculty abound at Middlebury."

SELECTIVITY

Admissions Rating	97
# of applicants	8,891
% of applicants accepted	17
% of acceptees attending	38
# offered a place on the wait list	1,304
% accepting a place on wait list	41
% admitted from wait list	6
# of early decision applicants	961
% accepted early decision	33

FRESHMAN PROFILE

Range SAT Critical Reading	630–750
Range SAT Math	640–750
Range SAT Writing	650–760
Range ACT Composite	29–33

DEADLINES

Early decision	
Deadline	11/1
Regular	
Deadline	1/1
Nonfall registration?	Yes

APPLICANTS ALSO LOOK AT AND OFTEN PREFER

Amherst College; Dartmouth College; Harvard College; Williams College; Princeton University

AND SOMETIMES PREFER

Brown University; Yale University; Stanford University; Duke University; Pomona College

AND RARELY PREFER

Bowdoin College; Colby College; Colgate University; Hamilton College

FINANCIAL FACTS

Financial Aid Rating	99
Tuition	$47,418
Room and board	$13,628
Required fees	$410
Books and supplies	$1,000
Average frosh need-based scholarship	$42,741
Average UG need-based scholarship	$41,778
% needy frosh rec. need-based scholarship or grant aid	100
% needy UG rec. need-based scholarship or grant aid	98
% needy frosh rec. non-need-based scholarship or grant aid	0
% needy UG rec. non-need-based scholarship or grant aid	0
% needy frosh rec. need-based self-help aid	94
% needy UG rec. need-based self-help aid	92
% frosh rec. any financial aid	48
% UG rec. any financial aid	42
% UG borrow to pay for school	41
Average cumulative indebtedness	$17,797
% frosh need fully met	100
% ugrads need fully met	100
Average % of frosh need met	100
Average % of ugrad need met	100

MILLS COLLEGE

5000 MacArthur Boulevard, Oakland, CA 94613 • Admissions: 510-430-2135 • Fax: 510-430-3298

STUDENTS SAY ". . ."

Academics

Mills College in Oakland, California, is a small women's institution with a "rigorous academic program" defined as "the epitome of a liberal arts education." "I was drawn to the small class sizes, the beauty of the campus, and the wonderfully articulate and confident women that I came in contact with." With approximately 1,000 undergraduates and fairly small class sizes, it is no wonder that professors "know almost all of [their students] individually." As one student attests, "Even in introductory lecture classes, you can get to know your professors." Another student concurs, "Not only am I on a first-name basis with all of my professors, I have their personal phone numbers and e-mail addresses! I feel that I matter here!" Students have high praise for the faculty. "The professors are amazing. They are extremely smart and totally accessible." "Professors are interesting and insightful and promote lively discussions in class. Standards are high and challenging. Topics are very relevant to today's issues." "Mills College is all about empowering its students and creating an environment that encourages hard work and social and political awareness." "There is great support for students with disabilities or special needs." "The library and several computer labs make it easy to find a place to get things done."

Life

"School life is pretty academically focused. Little time is spent off campus if you live on campus because social interaction usually involves study groups. There is little to no real partying on campus, though you can find it off campus if you are looking for it." "The beauty of the campus" is a significant plus for many students. Situated on 135 acres, the school has plenty of natural areas, and the atmosphere is relaxing and peaceful, which means it is very conducive to studying. "Mills exceeds expectations in creating an intimate and welcoming environment as well as in promoting student activism." Students agree that Mills is a special place. "The atmosphere at Mills is incredible! It is academic, empowering, creative, and always intellectually stimulating." Students here seem to know how to balance their schedules and how to appreciate the education they are receiving. Mills "offers a very rigorous education that is stimulating yet fun." But this enthusiasm for their school does not carry over to campus life on the weekends when "it sort of turns into a ghost town." Students also warn, "If you're looking for a party school, look elsewhere." You do not have to go very far for entertainment. "Many students love the Berkeley and San Francisco nightlife."

Student Body

Here's how some Mills students describe themselves and their peers: "The typical student is female, academically inclined, and individualistic (possesses few stereotypically mainstream qualities)." "Students are typically politically active in some way, and many have one or two causes they know really well. Students are inquisitive and very intent on doing well academically. We don't party very much. We're also very welcoming." At Mills College, "the students are really diverse; pretty much everyone is different. In order to fit in, all you have to do is be yourself." This diversity is what seems to set it apart from most other schools. "It's a unique group of people, and the school is not everyone's cup of tea." One student clarifies, "Mills is full of 'nontraditional' students from all over the world. I didn't want to be in a place where everyone was on the same track, with the same agenda. I wanted to be in a place where every other person would have their own cause, their own independent ideas." This "very open-minded environment" sets Mills apart from most other colleges in how students "embrace diversity and gender equality in hopes of creating a better world." With a wide range of ages and backgrounds, the traditional student is anything but traditional.

FINANCIAL AID: 510-430-2000 • E-MAIL: ADMISSION@MILLS.EDU • WEBSITE: WWW.MILLS.EDU/UNDERGRAD

THE PRINCETON REVIEW SAYS

Admissions

Very important factors considered include: rigor of secondary school record. *Important factors considered include:* academic GPA, application essay, recommendation(s), extracurricular activities, character/personal qualities. *Other factors considered include:* interview, talent/ability, first generation, alumni/ae relation, geographical residence, state residency, racial/ethnic status, volunteer work, work experience. SAT or ACT not used. TOEFL required of all international applicants. High school diploma is required and GED is accepted. *Academic units required:* 4 English, 3 math, 2 science, 2 science labs, 2 foreign language, 2 social studies, 2 history. *Academic units recommended:* 4 English, 4 math, 4 science, 2 science labs, 4 foreign language, 4 social studies, 4 history, 2 visual/performing arts.

Financial Aid

Students should submit: FAFSA, State aid form. Regular filing deadline is 2/15. The Princeton Review suggests that all financial aid forms be submitted as soon as possible after October 1. *Need-based scholarships/grants offered:* Federal Pell, FSEOG, State scholarships/grants, Private scholarships, College/university scholarship or grant aid from institutional funds. *Loan aid offered:* Direct Subsidized Stafford Loans, Direct Unsubsidized Stafford Loans, Direct PLUS loans, Federal Perkins Loans, College/university loans from institutional funds. Applicants will be notified of awards on a rolling basis beginning 3/1. Federal Work-Study Program available. Institutional employment available.

Inside Word

Mills strives to create a diverse community of students and welcomes older, nontraditional undergraduates. In fact, 17 percent of the Mills undergraduate population is older than twenty-three. Admissions interviews, though not required, are highly encouraged and can be conducted via Skype or FaceTime.

THE SCHOOL SAYS ". . ."

From the Admissions Office

"Mills offers a challenging liberal arts curriculum that encourages you to think creatively, prepares you to take well-calculated risks, and equips you to put your passions into practice. We are driven by our determination to improve ourselves and the world around us and to work smarter by working together. Here you will be encouraged to stand out by standing up for your ideas and empowered to find your voice and make a statement in your career and your community.

"At Mills, you'll ask thoughtful questions, generate new ideas, and share your opinions in an inclusive community that welcomes women from all ages and backgrounds. With mentoring from accomplished professors and an 10:1 student-faculty ratio, you will learn how to examine every side of an argument so that you can succeed in every type of situation. Where most people see problems, you'll see possibilities as you gain the confidence to speak up and the power to create your own path.

"Mills has been educating creative, independent women since 1852, two years after California became a state. Since then, we have been ranked as one of the top colleges in the West. Our 135-acre campus in the heart of the San Francisco Bay Area has been home to more than 20,000 alumnae who have gone on to excel as authors, composers, scientists, lawyers, professors, ambassadors, news anchors, governors, congresswomen, and activists."

SELECTIVITY

Admissions Rating	86
# of applicants	1,119
% of applicants accepted	75
% of acceptees attending	49
# offered a place on the wait list	0

FRESHMAN PROFILE

Range SAT Critical Reading	530–670
Range SAT Math	500–620
Range SAT Writing	530–650
Range ACT Composite	24–30
Minimum paper TOEFL	550
Minimum internet-based TOEFL	80
Average HS GPA	3.7
% graduated top 10% of class	28
% graduated top 25% of class	68
% graduated top 50% of class	96

DEADLINES

Early action	
Deadline	11/15
Notification	12/1
Regular	
Priority	1/15
Nonfall registration?	Yes

APPLICANTS ALSO LOOK AT AND OFTEN PREFER

Santa Clara University; University of California–Santa Barbara; University of California–Berkeley; University of California–Davis; University of California–Irvine; University of California–Los Angeles

AND SOMETIMES PREFER

University of Puget Sound; Occidental College

AND RARELY PREFER

Pepperdine University; Scripps College

FINANCIAL FACTS

Financial Aid Rating	83
Annual tuition	$44,322
Room and board	$13,528
Required fees	$1,298
Books and supplies	$1,514
Average frosh need-based scholarship	$36,050
Average UG need-based scholarship	$33,036
% needy frosh rec. need-based scholarship or grant aid	91
% needy UG rec. need-based scholarship or grant aid	90
% needy frosh rec. non-need-based scholarship or grant aid	96
% needy UG rec. non-need-based scholarship or grant aid	97
% needy frosh rec. need-based self-help aid	81
% needy UG rec. need-based self-help aid	89
% frosh rec. any financial aid	100
% UG rec. any financial aid	92
% UG borrow to pay for school	79
Average cumulative indebtedness	$33,329
% frosh need fully met	23
% ugrads need fully met	14
Average % of frosh need met	94
Average % of ugrad need met	80

MILLSAPS COLLEGE

1701 NORTH STATE STREET, JACKSON, MS 39210 • ADMISSIONS: 601-974-1050 • FAX: 601-974-1059

CAMPUS LIFE

Quality of Life Rating	89
Fire Safety Rating	90
Green Rating	74
Type of school	Private
Affiliation	Methodist
Environment	Metropolis

STUDENTS

Total undergrad enrollment	771
% male/female	51/49
% from out of state	55
% frosh from public high school	55
% frosh live on campus	97
% ugrads live on campus	87
# of fraternities (% ugrad men join)	6 (59)
# of sororities (% ugrad women join)	6 (63)
% African American	11
% Asian	4
% Caucasian	74
% Hispanic	2
% Native American	1
% Pacific Islander	0
% Two or more races	1
% Race and/or ethnicity unknown	3
% international	4
# of countries represented	16

SURVEY SAYS...

Students are happy
Career services are great
Class discussions encouraged
School is well run
No one cheats
Students get along with local community
Easy to get around campus
Lots of beer drinking
Frats and sororities are popular
Campus newspaper is popular

ACADEMICS

Academic Rating	85
% students returning for sophomore year	80
% students graduating within 4 years	62
Calendar	Semester
Student/faculty ratio	9:1
Profs interesting rating	94
Profs accessible rating	95

Most classes have 10–19 students.
Most lab/discussion sessions have
10–19 students.

MOST POPULAR MAJORS
Biology; Psychology; Business Administration
and Management

STUDENTS SAY ". . ."

Academics

Millsaps is a small college, so students "get a lot of personal attention." It is a "school where everybody knows your name," as well as "a place where every student has to work hard to stay above water; excellence is the norm, not the exception." What makes Millsaps unique is how it "breaks the mold by providing superb education as well as fun, combining the two in ways so subtle that a student may not even realize they're learning!" The school "offers great courses taught by charismatic professors" who "bring the material to life...through their innovative teaching methods." "Classes are not easy but the quality of learning is top notch." "Professors always encourage students to discuss class material and voice their opinions and questions about it. They encourage you to form your own ideas." These "friendly and approachable" professors "continue to teach outside of the classroom." "They welcome one-on-one time...to further develop understanding." Students have praise for the education they are receiving saying, "coming out of Millsaps I will be fully prepared for grad school. My professors not only lecture, but they turn the material into hands-on learning opportunities," and "I seriously respect my school's standard of excellence in hiring people who are wonderful at their jobs." Besides "great professors," the school offers "a prestigious business school," "abundant study abroad programs," and "strong Southern hospitality and heritage." The school's small size provides opportunities to receive "a top-notch education, while also getting to play sports and be in clubs." Although Millsaps may not be affordable for everyone, it "strives to be generous with scholarships." One student was pleased to report, "They offered the most financial assistance by far." Although student surveys were mostly positive, like this one: "Millsaps College provides the ideal learning atmosphere for liberal arts studies where they teach us how to think and not what to think," there were complaints about "the internet and networking capabilities," and "the cafeteria is an area where great improvement is needed."

Life

"Students at Millsaps think about their classwork first and foremost. After that, we think about hanging out with friends and having fun." The campus is "so beautiful and filled with cozy spots that many students spend a lot of their time outside." "While most schools have 'the quad' where students hang out between classes, Millsaps has 'The Bowl.' It is a beautiful area of grass and trees in the center of campus." But one student notes that there is still room for improvement. "The campus is beautiful, but the insides of the buildings need a serious upgrade. Every time I walk into a building, I feel like I've been transported back to the seventies." Although "most of the upperclassmen dorms are amazing," the "freshman dorms are a little sketchy." On campus "there are concerts and fun days all throughout the semester." "There are parties at the fraternity houses, and...some really cool things to do from concerts to oxygen bars to laser tag." "I would definitely call it a 'party school,' despite the tough academics." "There is a lot of partying on the weekends but almost everyone still manages to get studying finished." Students also point out, "We don't have to drink to have fun at Millsaps, though. You can always find a friend to hang out with, go to the movies, shop, or find a new great place to eat. The Millsaps curriculum even makes study groups fun (for the most part), believe it or not." Off campus, students venture into Jackson where "there are great restaurants."

Student Body

Is there a typical Millsaps student? Some students think so: "The typical student at Millsaps was an over-involved, cool nerd in high school. We throw ourselves into sports, clubs, Greek life, and community service like it's our job. It's how we thrive." "Students fit in by being involved in Greek life and other organizations." "A typical student is involved in many activities from sports to community service clubs. Student interests are diverse, and the student body in general is very friendly and interactive." Another student disagrees, "There is no 'typical student' really—the most common thread is a desire to change the world (usually, with a stop at graduate school)."

FINANCIAL AID: 800-352-1050 • E-MAIL: ADMISSIONS@MILLSAPS.EDU • WEBSITE: WWW.MILLSAPS.EDU

THE PRINCETON REVIEW SAYS

Admissions

Very important factors considered include: rigor of secondary school record, academic GPA, standardized test scores, character/personal qualities. *Important factors considered include:* class rank, application essay, recommendation(s), extracurricular activities, talent/ability. *Other factors considered include:* interview, volunteer work, work experience. SAT or ACT required. ACT with or without writing accepted. TOEFL required of all international applicants. High school diploma is required and GED is accepted. *Academic units required:* 4 English, 3 math, 3 science, 2 science labs, 1 foreign language, 2 social studies, 2 history, 1 academic elective. *Academic units recommended:* 4 English, 4 math, 4 science, 2 science labs, 2 foreign language, 2 social studies, 2 history, 2 academic electives.

Financial Aid

Students should submit: FAFSA. Priority filing deadline is 3/1. The Princeton Review suggests that all financial aid forms be submitted as soon as possible after October 1. *Need-based scholarships/grants offered:* Federal Pell, FSEOG, State scholarships/grants, Private scholarships, College/university scholarship or grant aid from institutional funds. *Loan aid offered:* Direct Subsidized Stafford Loans, Direct Unsubsidized Stafford Loans, Direct PLUS loans, Federal Perkins Loans, College/university loans from institutional funds. Applicants will be notified of awards on a rolling basis beginning 3/15. Federal Work-Study Program available. Institutional employment available.

The Inside Word

Millsaps' trademark friendliness begins during the admissions process. The school encourages prospective students to get in touch with an admissions counselor to ask questions, arrange a visit, or connect you with a current student. For early action admission or scholarships, students need to apply in January. After that, the school admits students on a rolling basis.

THE SCHOOL SAYS "..."

From the Admissions Office

"Students at Millsaps College choose their own paths, propelled by individual interests and goals. Guided by teachers and mentors who know them well, Millsaps students are elevated by countless opportunities to put ideas into motion. Through broad exploration of the humanities, sciences, socials sciences, and business, students pursue individualized academic programs, gaining exposure to new disciplines, new points of view, and new possibilities. At Millsaps, every course is taught at the honors level. Of the faculty members, 94percent hold the highest degree attainable in their discipline. And, with a student-teacher ratio of 9:1 and an average class size of fourteen, professors expect students to actively participate in their educations. Millsaps College is one of the few liberal arts colleges in the country with both a Phi Beta Kappa Chapter (the first in Mississippi) and an AACSB-accredited business program at the Else School of Management. Millsaps' new Compass Curriculum will guide the course planning for all incoming first-year students to find their best path to graduation and beyond. The Compass Curriculum will challenge students and engage them in the exploration of knowledge domains focuses on four key Student Learning Outcomes: Thinking and Reasoning, Communication, Integrative and Collaborative Learning, and Problem Solving and Creative Practice."

SELECTIVITY

Admissions Rating	87
# of applicants	2,861
% of applicants accepted	57
% of acceptees attending	14

FRESHMAN PROFILE

Range SAT Critical Reading	510–640
Range SAT Math	520–630
Range ACT Composite	23–29
Minimum paper TOEFL	550
Minimum internet-based TOEFL	80
Average HS GPA	3.7

DEADLINES

Early action	
Deadline	11/15
Notification	1/15
Regular	
Priority	2/1
Deadline	7/1
Nonfall registration?	Yes

APPLICANTS ALSO LOOK AT AND OFTEN PREFER
University of Mississippi

AND SOMETIMES PREFER
Rhodes College

AND RARELY PREFER
Texas Christian University; Furman University

FINANCIAL FACTS

Financial Aid Rating	85
Annual tuition	$31,872
Room and board	$11,878
Required fees	$2,110
Books and supplies	$1,100
Average frosh need-based scholarship	$25,280
Average UG need-based scholarship	$23,363
% needy frosh rec. need-based scholarship or grant aid	100
% needy UG rec. need-based scholarship or grant aid	100
% needy frosh rec. non-need-based scholarship or grant aid	26
% needy UG rec. non-need-based scholarship or grant aid	20
% needy frosh rec. need-based self-help aid	70
% needy UG rec. need-based self-help aid	75
% frosh rec. any financial aid	100
% UG rec. any financial aid	98
% frosh need fully met	34
% ugrads need fully met	28
Average % of frosh need met	87
Average % of ugrad need met	80

Missouri University of Science and Technology

300 West 13th Street; 106 Parker Hall, Rolla, MO 65409-1060 • Admissions: 573-341-4165 • Fax: 573-341-4082

CAMPUS LIFE

Quality of Life Rating	87
Fire Safety Rating	88
Green Rating	83
Type of school	Public
Affiliation	No Affiliation
Environment	Village

STUDENTS

Total undergrad enrollment	6,841
% male/female	77/23
% from out of state	19
% frosh from public high school	85
% ugrads live on campus	40
# of fraternities (% ugrad men join)	23 (21)
# of sororities (% ugrad women join)	5 (19)
% African American	3
% Asian	3
% Caucasian	77
% Hispanic	3
% Native American	<1
% Pacific Islander	<1
% Two or more races	0
% Race and/or ethnicity unknown	3
% international	4
# of countries represented	38

SURVEY SAYS...

Students are happy
Career services are great
Internships are widely available
School is well run
Lots of beer drinking

ACADEMICS

Academic Rating	74
% students graduating within 4 years	23
% students graduating within 6 years	63
Calendar	Semester
Student/faculty ratio	18:1
Profs interesting rating	77
Profs accessible rating	77

Most classes have 20–29 students.
Most lab/discussion sessions have
10–19 students.

MOST POPULAR MAJORS

Civil Engineering; Electrical and Electronics
Engineering; Mechanical Engineering

STUDENTS SAY ". . ."

Academics

Top performers in science and technology will find a home at Missouri S&T, because here "students are exposed to just about every different type of engineering," making it "one of the best universities that prepares engineers for industry." Unsurprisingly, this does not come without challenge. Classes can be "very tough and intimidating," where "it's not uncommon to have a 55 percent or less average on a test." Students ready for the rigorous academics should "not expect to be babied at all" because "the professors are there to challenge you." The aim is to "prepare students to find a job in the real world and help us to get the experience to succeed in it." Students who have run the gauntlet say "the quality of education and availability of resources here is second to none." That education comes via "hands-on learning, small class sizes, and caring professors" who are "some of the smartest professors in the world." Though they challenge their students, they don't leave them out to dry. "All of the professors have office hours, whether open or by appointment," students note. Indeed, "the accessibility of instructors and other faculty/staff" at this small school is seen as a strength. Yes, "this school definitely is willing to challenge their students," but numbers-crunching engineers will find value in their education, because S&T "comes in the top three schools in average starting salary for graduates, and won't guarantee a huge debt burden."

Life

Missouri University of Science and Technology may be "a small school in the middle of Missouri," but "our range of student organizations is mind-boggling." You name the club and it probably exists, as well as school activities ranging from "scavenger hunts, video game nights, cooking classes, viewing parties, dance lessons, and much more." Of course, in a school where "all of the students are always worrying about that next exam in calculus or dreading their lab in the afternoon," it is not surprising that studying is as big a pastime as hanging out. Here, "academics are everyone's top priority." When not studying, "drinking is pretty big on weekends." Other activities include "playing sports, video games, and working out." Downtown Rolla isn't a thriving Mecca of activity because "there's not so much to do in the town," however, "someone always has something going on." St. Louis is close enough for day trips, and there are a slew of student organizations to occupy downtime. "Virtually every student is either heavily involved in a diverse group of these student organizations or devotes much of their time to design teams or research." Generally, if you're at S&T and are not kept busy, it's probably because you don't want to be busy.

Student Body

Imagine a less stereotypical Big Bang Theory and you're close to the mark. The typical student may be "a little nerdy," "those kids that didn't fit in during high school" but who "now can be themselves." A typical S&T student "is someone who never really had to study in high school to get good grades, but they are working hard here to maintain that standard." While most S&T students are smart—"we came here primarily to learn," one attendee notes—they are not introverted or antisocial. The "very friendly" people on campus "live together in harmony." Indeed, "everyone can find a place to fit in" thanks to the "over 212 student organizations." While about half of the students here are from Missouri or nearby states, the others "are from the edges of the nation and even some foreign countries, which is astounding considering our small enrollment size." Education is the priority for those who attend, so meeting people is simple because "it is really easy just to strike up a conversation with someone." The like-minded atmosphere makes socializing easy. "We are all nerds, so we adapt to the social environment once we are introduced."

MISSOURI UNIVERSITY OF SCIENCE AND TECHNOLOGY

FINANCIAL AID: 573-341-4282 • E-MAIL: ADMISSIONS@MST.EDU • WEBSITE: WWW.MST.EDU

THE PRINCETON REVIEW SAYS

Admissions

Very important factors considered include: rigor of secondary school record, class rank, academic GPA, standardized test scores. *Important factors considered include:* recommendation(s). *Other factors considered include:* application essay, interview, extracurricular activities, talent/ability, character/personal qualities, volunteer work, work experience, level of applicant's interest. SAT or ACT required. ACT with or without writing accepted. TOEFL required of all international applicants. High school diploma is required and GED is accepted. *Academic units required:* 4 English, 4 math, 3 science, 1 science lab, 2 foreign language, 3 social studies, 1 visual/performing arts.

Financial Aid

Students should submit: FAFSA. Priority filing deadline is 2/1. The Princeton Review suggests that all financial aid forms be submitted as soon as possible after October 1. *Need-based scholarships/grants offered:* Federal Pell, FSEOG, State scholarships/grants, Private scholarships, College/university scholarship or grant aid from institutional funds. *Loan aid offered:* Federal Loans, State Loans, College/university loans from institutional funds. Federal Work-Study Program available. Institutional employment available.

The Inside Word

Winning admission to Missouri University of Science and Technology is largely a numbers game, as it often is with other leading public universities. Expect to have to meet class rank and standardized test cutoffs, along with distribution requirements, in order to be granted admission. And apply early if possible. The pool of applicants is competitive, and is made up of students of similar caliber. Get off to an early start and you'll have an advantage.

THE SCHOOL SAYS "..."

From the Admissions Office

"Missouri University of Science and Technology is one of the nation's top technological universities and offers strong academics in humanities, social sciences, education, business and other degree programs. Our fifteen engineering programs and computing and science programs are nationally and internationally renowned. With 8,642 students from all states in the US and over sixty other countries, Missouri S&T provides a 'big campus' feel of diversity and student engagement on a medium-sized campus.

"S&T offers rigorous academics, exceptional graduation and placement rates, excellent access to co-ops and internships, experiential learning for all undergraduates, affordable tuition combined with generous scholarship programs, and a 3.8 percent loan default rate as a result of superior career outcomes for our students.

"S&T students are successful due to a combination of outstanding academics and easy access to personal and professional growth. The vast majority of courses are taught by tenured professors engaged in cutting-edge research and scholarship, in a faculty culture that values undergraduate education and 'hands-on' learning and personal attention, which extends back to our founding in 1870. S&T sponsors over 200 student clubs, and students enjoy outdoor activities among the area's scenic parks, lakes and riverways.

"Widely recognized as one of the nation's best universities, Missouri S&T provides an outstanding education, at a reasonable cost with exceptional student outcomes."

SELECTIVITY

Admissions Rating	85
# of applicants	3,592
% of applicants accepted	88
% of acceptees attending	47
# offered a place on the wait list	0

FRESHMAN PROFILE

Range SAT Critical Reading	520–660
Range SAT Math	560–640
Range ACT Composite	25–31
Minimum internet-based TOEFL	79
Average HS GPA	3.71
% graduated top 10% of class	44
% graduated top 25% of class	74
% graduated top 50% of class	94

DEADLINES

Regular	
Deadline	Rolling
Notification	Rolling
Nonfall registration?	Yes

APPLICANTS ALSO LOOK AT AND OFTEN PREFER

University of Missouri; Truman State University; University of Illinois at Urbana-Champaign; Iowa State University

AND SOMETIMES PREFER

University of Kansas; Purdue University–West Lafayette; Kansas State University

FINANCIAL FACTS

Financial Aid Rating	87
Annual	
Annual out-of-state tuition	$24,810
Room and board	$9,464
Required fees	$1,342
Books and supplies	$830
Average frosh need-based scholarship	$9,488
Average UG need-based scholarship	$7,460
% needy frosh rec. need-based scholarship or grant aid	95
% needy UG rec. need-based scholarship or grant aid	91
% needy frosh rec. non-need-based scholarship or grant aid	28
% needy UG rec. non-need-based scholarship or grant aid	33
% needy frosh rec. need-based self-help aid	17
% needy UG rec. need-based self-help aid	29
% frosh rec. any financial aid	91
% UG rec. any financial aid	85
% frosh need fully met	96
% ugrads need fully met	94
Average % of frosh need met	28
Average % of ugrad need met	36

MONMOUTH UNIVERSITY (NJ)

ADMISSION, MONMOUTH UNIVERSITY, WEST LONG BRANCH, NJ 07764-1898 • ADMISSIONS: 732-571-3456 • FAX: 732-263-5166

CAMPUS LIFE

Quality of Life Rating	88
Fire Safety Rating	98
Green Rating	80
Type of school	Private
Affiliation	No Affiliation
Environment	Village

STUDENTS

Total undergrad enrollment	4,693
% male/female	42/58
% from out of state	14
% frosh from public high school	85
% frosh live on campus	82
% ugrads live on campus	46
# of fraternities (% ugrad men join)	8 (16)
# of sororities (% ugrad women join)	8 (15)
% African American	5
% Asian	3
% Caucasian	74
% Hispanic	11
% Native American	<1
% Pacific Islander	<1
% Two or more races	2
% Race and/or ethnicity unknown	3
% international	1
# of countries represented	23

SURVEY SAYS...

Students are happy
Great library
Great off-campus food

ACADEMICS

Academic Rating	72
% students returning for sophomore year	83
% students graduating within 4 years	51
% students graduating within 6 years	67
Calendar	Semester
Student/faculty ratio	14:1
Profs interesting rating	74
Profs accessible rating	75

Most classes have 20–29 students.
Most lab/discussion sessions have
10–19 students.

MOST POPULAR MAJORS

Business Administration and Management;
Communication; Education

STUDENTS SAY "..."

Academics

Monmouth University in New Jersey is a small liberal arts school that provides an environment and experience where students truly learn and gain marketable life skills. Students here are all about "getting a good education in a suburban area that will prepare you for your intended career," and there is "an incredible combination of a laid back persona with professionalism." A "great internship program," excellent scholarships, and a five-year master's program are just a few of the school's draws, and the school "takes strong pride in its education, professors, students, athletics along with everything else, and will settle for nothing but the best."

Most of the professors at Monmouth "really care about student success" and "are friendly and easily accessible outside the classroom," though many students say there is a contingent that phones in their lectures. "I've had professors that are really hands-on and stray from the typical slideshow and...do in-class presentations, while I've had other professors read off the PowerPoint the whole time," says a senior.

Due to the small class sizes, "it's difficult to go into a classroom unnoticed," so "teachers are able to focus on you and help." Additionally, "[students] aren't lost in a crowd" and "Monmouth really tries to create a community-feel among all the students." For those needing extra help, there is "a wonderful Center for Student Services in which a tutor can be reached, a writing center to help with papers, [and] a math center." "I enjoy almost all of my classes and love the relaxed nature of the university as a whole," says a student.

Life

The "small, classy campus" is "in a great location" in central New Jersey, and makes for "a very comfortable place to be." The beach is only a mile away (which one student says "reminds me paradise is only down the street"), so on a nice day "everyone will be soaking up the sun." Regardless of tanning temptations, "everyone is also really focused on school and wants to succeed." The ground maintenance here is "impeccable," and "the landscaping is always groomed and gorgeous." Students at Monmouth "are very serious about their school work and about their sport if they are an athlete, but they also want to have fun." Once the weekend hits, "everyone does their own thing." Commuters go home, "sports teams have parties, fraternities and sororities have joint parties, and "a lot of students attend games and support our athletic teams" (Monmouth is a Division I school). Campus safety is a priority for the school, and is reflected in the community. "I feel as if other students on campus are always looking out for one another in addition to our safety department, the MUPD, and the blue light system on campus," says a freshman. The university holds "a good number" of events on campus for students, as well, and "there are things to do in the local area that students do for entertainment."

Student Body

Most of the students here are "white, upper-middle class" and hail from nearby areas, so Monmouth can be "somewhat of a suitcase school," but there is still a close knit community where "you know just about everyone." People here are "friendly and fun-loving, but also seriously committed to their studies," and with the popularity of clubs and fraternities and sororities (Greek life "has gone 'viral' in the past few years"), all students "can fit in SOMEWHERE." It doesn't hurt that the university has a set of required general education courses that every student has to take before they graduate, so "it is easy for people from all majors to meet and socialize."

MONMOUTH UNIVERSITY (NJ)

FINANCIAL AID: 732-571-3463 • E-MAIL: ADMISSION@MONMOUTH.EDU • WEBSITE: WWW.MONMOUTH.EDU

THE PRINCETON REVIEW SAYS

Admissions

Very important factors considered include: rigor of secondary school record, academic GPA, standardized test scores. *Important factors considered include:* application essay, recommendation(s), extracurricular activities, volunteer work, work experience. *Other factors considered include:* character/personal qualities, alumni/ae relation. SAT or ACT required. ACT with or without writing accepted. SAT with or without Essay component accepted. TOEFL required of all international applicants. High school diploma is required and GED is accepted. *Academic units required:* 4 English, 3 math, 2 science, 1 science lab, 2 history, 5 academic electives. *Academic units recommended:* 2 foreign language, 2 social studies.

Financial Aid

Students should submit: FAFSA. Regular filing deadline is 6/30. The Princeton Review suggests that all financial aid forms be submitted as soon as possible after October 1. *Need-based scholarships/grants offered:* Federal Pell, FSEOG, State scholarships/grants, Private scholarships, College/university scholarship or grant aid from institutional funds, Federal Nursing Scholarships. *Loan aid offered:* Direct Subsidized Stafford Loans, Direct Unsubsidized Stafford Loans, Direct PLUS loans, Federal Perkins Loans, State Loans, College/university loans from institutional funds, private loans. Applicants will be notified of awards on a rolling basis beginning 2/15. Federal Work-Study Program available. Institutional employment available. Off-campus job opportunities are good.

Inside Word

B students with slightly above-average SAT or ACT scores should find little impediment to gaining admission to Monmouth. The school's national stature is on the rise, resulting in more competitive applicant base, but Monmouth must still compete with a lot of heavy hitters for top regional students.

THE SCHOOL SAYS " . . ."

From the Admissions Office

"As the region's premier private coastal university, Monmouth University attracts students looking for a personalized learning environment that will ignite their curiosity and prepare them for life after college.

"Students benefit from an intellectually challenging academic experience built on a strong liberal arts foundation and learning experiences that are both high impact and immersive, extending beyond the classroom. Our breathtaking coastal campus provides a safe, suburban setting in one of the world's largest metropolitan regions, ideally positioned to help our students develop and pursue their career interests while enjoying rich cultural opportunities.

Monmouth University's student life features active student clubs and organizations, including eight sororities and eight fraternities, and dozens of academic/leadership honor societies, reflecting our spirit and community. Monmouth's twenty-three NCAA Division I athletic teams attract lively support from students and other members of the campus and local communities while instilling university pride.

"At Monmouth, our dedication to connecting the campus to support student growth is unmatched. We invest the resources to enable critical learning outcomes, and go above-and-beyond to support personal growth and development. Our campus-wide culture of teaching excellence immerses students in a demanding college experience that enhances their capacity to think and learn. Students benefit from small class sizes that foster collaborative learning and research opportunities with faculty and peers that know you by name.

"As leaders in academic, interpersonal, and career success, we are driven to influence progress by graduating people of purpose with the critical thinking skills required for global relevance and impact."

SELECTIVITY

Admissions Rating	76
# of applicants	8,486
% of applicants accepted	78
% of acceptees attending	17
# offered a place on the wait list	0
# of early decision applicants	3,897
% accepted early decision	80

FRESHMAN PROFILE

Range SAT Critical Reading	480–570
Range SAT Math	470–550
Range SAT Writing	440–560
Range ACT Composite	20–25
Minimum paper TOEFL	550
Minimum internet-based TOEFL	79
Average HS GPA	3.3
% graduated top 10% of class	14
% graduated top 25% of class	39
% graduated top 50% of class	77

DEADLINES

Early action	
Deadline	12/1
Notification	1/15
Regular	
Priority	12/1
Deadline	3/1
Nonfall registration?	Yes

FINANCIAL FACTS

Financial Aid Rating	80
Annual tuition	$34,664
Room and board	$13,038
Required fees	$700
Books and supplies	$1,234
Average frosh need-based scholarship	$11,806
Average UG need-based scholarship	$12,164
% needy frosh rec. need-based scholarship or grant aid	68
% needy UG rec. need-based scholarship or grant aid	50
% needy frosh rec. non-need-based scholarship or grant aid	94
% needy UG rec. non-need-based scholarship or grant aid	95
% needy frosh rec. need-based self-help aid	87
% needy UG rec. need-based self-help aid	84
% frosh rec. any financial aid	99
% UG rec. any financial aid	96
% UG borrow to pay for school	77
Average cumulative indebtedness	$31,487
% frosh need fully met	13
% ugrads need fully met	14
Average % of frosh need met	66
Average % of ugrad need met	64

MONTANA TECH OF THE UNIVERSITY OF MONTANA

1300 WEST PARK STREET, BUTTE, MT 59701 • ADMISSIONS: 406-496-4256 • FAX: 406-496-4710

STUDENTS SAY "..."

Academics Even if Montana Tech of the University of Montana weren't one of the only tech institutes in the state, its excellent science programs and reputation for developing high quality engineers to send out into the workforce would keep its classrooms filled. Located in Butte, the school "stresses the importance of knowing present technologies" and offers "hands-on experience" and "great internship opportunities" to assure great engineers after graduating (the job placement rate for many major approaches 100 percent). The "high education at lower cost school model" is well-known particularly within the mining and petroleum industries, though the (very few) students who choose a major outside of STEM typically have "limited opportunities for advancement."

For the most part, professors "have industry experience and can teach based on their personal experiences," but everyone agrees that there are "always a few bad apples" in the mix. Luckily, the size of the classrooms is small "so you have more one on one time with your instructor." The curriculum offers "ample opportunities for intellectual growth," focusing on "quantitative learning" in order to send students off with "degrees that actually accomplish things and impact the world." Students are "challenged by professors to work their hardest and to do the best that they can." "It is very easy to stand out in a very good way," says one sophomore. "If you are willing to put in the effort, the professors are more than happy to help you find internships, school jobs, and research opportunities."

The school also has "some of the most cutting edge technology at its disposal." This same equipment "can be accessed by most students no matter major or education level." Workloads "can be grueling," but interestingly (unlike many other engineering schools), the academics are "hardly competitive" as "most students attend MT Tech with the idea that they will be guaranteed a decent paying job as long as they graduate."

Life

The "historically fascinating" mining town town of Butte is "old as dirt and full of rich history," as well as "very community oriented." There are "festivals and community activities often" in the summer months; during the stretched out winter months, "temperatures are often bitter cold, and the sun shines for less than 150 days of the year." Fortunately, there are a host of rampantly popular activities in the surrounding mountains, such as "hunting, skiing, snowboarding, biking, [and] hiking."

During the school year, people generally go to class and do their homework in the evenings and then "blow off steam at bars and/or parties on the weekends." There's also a weekly movie night on campus, and campus entertainment "does its best to bring in musicians, speakers and comedians." Intramural sports are popular, as are student clubs and Frisbee golf, and there is "plenty of bar hopping nearby." Overall, MT Tech is "very calm and a great place to learn."

Student Body

The school is small enough that life borders on "knowing everyone on campus, at least [by] names," buoyed by the fact that many locals attend Montana Tech. The typical student is "a hardworking Montanan who most likely grew up on a farm/ranch and carries that hard work ethic into their studies." As expected, most students are engineers and most students "enjoy outdoor activities, as well as gaming." The gender breakdown is far from equal and not always comfortable for women; there are "a lot of guys at Tech and not so many girls." "A lot of racial diversity, but I feel like a woman in a sea of men," says one female undergraduate. The student body tends to skew a bit older, and there is also a "very large Arabic population" here due to the world-class petroleum engineering department. Despite the "bitterly cold weather" in the long winter, people are "warm and friendly."

MONTANA TECH OF THE UNIVERSITY OF MONTANA

FINANCIAL AID: 406-496-4213 • E-MAIL: ENROLLMENT@MTECH.EDU • WEBSITE: WWW.MTECH.EDU

THE PRINCETON REVIEW SAYS

Admissions

Very important factors considered include: class rank, academic GPA, standardized test scores. *Important factors considered include: Other factors considered include:* SAT or ACT required. ACT with Writing recommended. TOEFL required of all international applicants. High school diploma is required and GED is accepted. *Academic units required:* 4 English, 3 math, 2 science, 2 science labs, 3 social studies, and 2 units from above areas or other academic areas. *Academic units recommended:* 4 math.

Financial Aid

Students should submit: FAFSA. Priority filing deadline is 3/1. The Princeton Review suggests that all financial aid forms be submitted as soon as possible after October 1. *Need-based scholarships/grants offered:* Federal Pell, FSEOG, State scholarships/grants, Private scholarships, College/university scholarship or grant aid from institutional funds. *Loan aid offered:* Direct Subsidized Stafford Loans, Direct Unsubsidized Stafford Loans, Direct PLUS loans, Federal Perkins Loans, College/university loans from institutional funds. Applicants will be notified of awards on a rolling basis beginning 3/15. Fed

Inside Word

Montana Tech is a godsend for students who are strong academically but not likely to be offered admission to nationally renowned technical institutes. In fact, because of its small size and relatively remote location, Montana Tech is a good choice for anyone leaning toward a technical career. You would be hard-pressed to find many other places as low-key and personal in the realm of academia.

THE SCHOOL SAYS "..."

From the Admissions Office

"Characterize Montana Tech by listening to what employers say. They tell us Tech graduates stand out with an incredible work ethic and top-notch technical skills. Last year, 176 companies held on-campus interviews and attended Montana Tech's career fairs competing for our students and graduates. The beneficiaries: the students! Montana Tech has had a ten-year annual average placement rate of 92 percent including acceptance into professional and graduate programs. Learning takes place in a personalized environment, in first-class academic facilities, and in the heart of the Rocky Mountains. Outdoor recreation provides a great balance to the rigors of the course work at Montana Tech. We are a small school where our students receive a terrific education, and in the end, get great jobs! The SAT (or the ACT with the writing section) is recommended for all student applying for admission. Students who do not take the tests with the writing component may be required to take an additional English placement test from college before they enroll."

SELECTIVITY

Admissions Rating	77
# of applicants	952
% of applicants accepted	90
% of acceptees attending	52

FRESHMAN PROFILE

Range SAT Critical Reading	490–590
Range SAT Math	540–630
Range SAT Writing	450–560
Range ACT Composite	22–27
Minimum paper TOEFL	525
Minimum internet-based TOEFL	71
Average HS GPA	3.5
% graduated top 10% of class	24
% graduated top 25% of class	57
% graduated top 50% of class	85

DEADLINES

Nonfall registration?	Yes

APPLICANTS ALSO LOOK AT AND OFTEN PREFER

Michigan Technological University

FINANCIAL FACTS

Financial Aid Rating	81
Annual in-state tuition	$6,797
Annual out-of-state tuition	$20,512
Room and board	$8,562
Books and supplies	$1,050
Average frosh need-based scholarship	$5,678
Average UG need-based scholarship	$5,485
% needy frosh rec. need-based scholarship or grant aid	90
% needy UG rec. need-based scholarship or grant aid	89
% needy frosh rec. non-need-based scholarship or grant aid	10
% needy UG rec. non-need-based scholarship or grant aid	5
% needy frosh rec. need-based self-help aid	73
% needy UG rec. need-based self-help aid	80
% frosh rec. any financial aid	72
% UG rec. any financial aid	67
% frosh need fully met	21
% ugrads need fully met	12
Average % of frosh need met	68
Average % of ugrad need met	63

MORAVIAN COLLEGE

1200 MAIN STREET, BETHLEHEM, PA 18018 • ADMISSIONS: 610-861-1320 • FAX: 610-625-7930

STUDENTS SAY "..."

Academics

Located in Bethlehem, Pennsylvania in the Lehigh Valley, a short drive from both Philadelphia and New York City, Moravian College is the sixth oldest college in the United States. Bethlehem is "a beautiful town," and students like the "small atmosphere" at this campus of 1,800 and the "old time and historic feel [of] the college," as well as Moravian College's "warm community, and small classes." In particular, students praise the "fabulous" nursing and music programs here. Students love that the class sizes, which are most frequently under twenty students, "allow you to get to know your professors one-on-one and on a first name basis." Moravian College feels like "a family" of students "pursuing their passions together," says a music education major. "The professors are fantastic," a biology major attests. They are "extremely good at taking complex topics and making them understandable for students of any major or background" and "they are always willing to talk to students and help them out." My "professors are passionate about the subject they teach," notes a transfer student, and "they are always willing to help if I don't understand the material." They "make learning hands on and entertaining," says another. Students come to "class every day ready and excited to learn." "The community we have here," says a chemistry major, "is pretty unbelievable."

Life

Campus life is described as "welcoming and friendly." For "a small school" Moravian College has "many opportunities to be involved in groups on campus." "We have everything from Greek life to student government to the German club," notes a biology major. There are more than eighty clubs and organizations focusing on everything from the environment to politics to performing arts. "There is a club or organization for everyone on campus," says one student. There are also a variety of campus events, including new movies that "run every week, club meetings, intramural sports teams, and bingo." Moravian College also offers "great food with many healthy options" as well as "a large, clean, up-to-date gym" for health-conscious and athletic students. Moravian College students live in "suite-style" dorms "where students have the option to live in a single room while being part of a small group that shares a kitchen," which allows for some "independence." Many students "enjoy going to parties on Thursdays and Saturdays at the fraternities on campus." And "there are many accessible places off campus to eat, drink, bowl, swim, take a nice walk, etc." Bethlehem was also named by Money magazine as one of the country's "Best Places to Live," and there is plenty to do in the historic city, which has a thriving music and arts scene, as well as restaurants, bars, and shops.

Student Body

Moravian College students hail from twenty-four states and fourteen countries. The typical student here is "friendly" and "spends their weekdays in the libraries and their weekends on the town." Students are involved "in something, whether that's a sport, fraternity/sorority, or general club." They are "active," "self-reliant," "outgoing," "helpful, and encouraging of others." "The majority of students are white guys or girls from middle class backgrounds," but "students mix and fit in together regardless of religion/race/gender." Many students "are athletes" and those who aren't "are extremely involved in activities such as student government, music, art or community service." A computer science major notes the "wide variety of students. Some religious, some not, some involved with alternative lifestyles, some not" and says "there is a group for almost everyone" at Moravian College. "The large majority of students here are very diverse and involved in many different clubs, teams, and organizations and therefore have friends in all of these places," says a public health major. At Moravian College "the football team isn't just friends with the football team and members of Greek life aren't just friends with members of their chapter, the friend groups here are very diverse." And students, a psychology major notes, have a "love for the school through the thick and thin."

FINANCIAL AID: 610-861-1330 • E-MAIL: ADMISSIONS@MORAVIAN.EDU • WEBSITE: WWW.MORAVIAN.EDU

THE PRINCETON REVIEW SAYS

Admissions

Very important factors considered include: rigor of secondary school record, class rank, academic GPA, character/personal qualities, alumni/ae relation, level of applicant's interest. *Important factors considered include:* standardized test scores, application essay, recommendation(s), extracurricular activities, talent/ability, first generation, volunteer work. *Other factors considered include:* interview, geographical residence, work experience. SAT or ACT required; SAT Subject Tests considered if submitted. ACT with or without writing accepted. SAT with or without Essay component accepted. TOEFL required of all international applicants. High school diploma is required and GED is accepted. *Academic units required:* 4 English, 3 math, 3 science, 2 science labs, 2 foreign language, 4 social studies. *Academic units recommended:* 4 math.

Financial Aid

Students should submit: FAFSA, Institution's own financial aid form. Priority filing deadline is 3/1. The Princeton Review suggests that all financial aid forms be submitted as soon as possible after October 1. *Need-based scholarships/grants offered:* Federal Pell, FSEOG, State scholarships/grants, Private scholarships, College/university scholarship or grant aid from institutional funds, United Negro College Fund, Federal Nursing Scholarships. *Loan aid offered:* Direct Subsidized Stafford Loans, Direct Unsubsidized Stafford Loans, Direct PLUS loans, Federal Perkins Loans, Federal Nursing Loans, State Loans. Applicants will be notified of awards on a rolling basis beginning 2/25. Federal Work-Study Program available. Institutional employment available.

The Inside Word

Admissions officers at Moravian College will accept both the Common Application and Moravian College's own Online Application. Admission is based on an all-inclusive view of the student, including academics, extracurriculars, and character, with an emphasis on challenging courses, recommendations, and community activism. The nursing program requires a combined SAT score of 1500 or above, with no section less than 500; an ACT score of 23 or above; and a 3.3 GPA. Moravian also strongly encourages a campus visit, though it is not required.

THE SCHOOL SAYS "..."

From the Admissions Office

"America's sixth-oldest college, Moravian College emphasizes the deliberate integration of a broad-based liberal arts curriculum with hands-on learning experiences to effectively prepare its students, not just for jobs, but for successful careers. Moravian College excels at transforming good students into highly competent graduates that are ready to enter the workplace with confidence or shine in graduate school. Students benefit from Moravian College's strong academic majors, opportunities for internships, undergraduate research and scholarship, and programs that foster a deeper enjoyment of life. The 12:1 student-faculty ratio means students get personal attention from a scholarly and dedicated faculty who ensure their success. The proof is in the results, 97 percent of students who earn a bachelor's degree, do so in four years. Moravian College issues a MacBook Pro laptop and an iPad to all incoming freshmen to enhance learning and help students gain the 21st-century knowledge and skills that will be transferrable over numerous careers. The College offers fifty programs of study; business, education, health professions, social and biological sciences are among the most popular. Moravian College's strong athletics, music, and art programs, and more than eighty clubs and organizations offer healthy physical and creative outlets for every student.

"Located in historic Bethlehem, Pa., Moravian College has long history of educating and developing leaders in many fields. Students leave Moravian College with the skills, knowledge, and support necessary to more deeply enjoy life, work, and their role in the world. More than 90 percent of its graduates are employed or attending graduate school within ten months of graduation."

SELECTIVITY

Admissions Rating	77
# of applicants	2,737
% of applicants accepted	75
% of acceptees attending	26
# offered a place on the wait list	0

FRESHMAN PROFILE

Range SAT Critical Reading	470–580
Range SAT Math	460–510
Range SAT Writing	430–550
Range ACT Composite	19–23
Minimum paper TOEFL	550
Minimum internet-based TOEFL	80
Average HS GPA	3.4
% graduated top 10% of class	10
% graduated top 25% of class	38
% graduated top 50% of class	72

DEADLINES

Regular	
Priority	3/1
Deadline	3/1
Nonfall registration?	Yes

FINANCIAL FACTS

Financial Aid Rating	83
Annual tuition	$37,251
Room and board	$11,636
Required fees	$881
Average frosh need-based scholarship	$25,311
Average UG need-based scholarship	$23,208
% needy frosh rec. need-based scholarship or grant aid	100
% needy UG rec. need-based scholarship or grant aid	98
% needy frosh rec. non-need-based scholarship or grant aid	8
% needy UG rec. non-need-based scholarship or grant aid	8
% needy frosh rec. need-based self-help aid	92
% needy UG rec. need-based self-help aid	93
% frosh rec. any financial aid	99
% UG rec. any financial aid	98
% frosh need fully met	10
% ugrads need fully met	11
Average % of frosh need met	77
Average % of ugrad need met	72

MOUNT HOLYOKE COLLEGE

NEWHALL CENTER, SOUTH HADLEY, MA 01075 • ADMISSIONS: 413-538-2023 • FAX: 413-538-2409

CAMPUS LIFE

Quality of Life Rating	93
Fire Safety Rating	88
Green Rating	92
Type of school	Private
Affiliation	No Affiliation
Environment	Town

STUDENTS

Total undergrad enrollment	2,099
% male/female	0/100
% from out of state	75
% frosh from public high school	65
% frosh live on campus	100
% ugrads live on campus	95
% African American	6
% Asian	10
% Caucasian	45
% Hispanic	8
% Native American	<1
% Pacific Islander	<1
% Two or more races	4
% Race and/or ethnicity unknown	1
% international	26
# of countries represented	69

SURVEY SAYS...

Lots of liberal students
Students always studying
Students are happy
Classroom facilities are great
Lab facilities are great
Great library
Class discussions encouraged
School is well run
No one cheats
Students are friendly
Diverse student types interact on campus
Students environmentally aware
Great food on campus
Dorms are like palaces
Easy to get around campus
Recreation facilities are great
Alumni active on campus
Active minority support groups

ACADEMICS

Academic Rating	96
% students returning for sophomore year	90
% students graduating within 4 years	78
% students graduating within 6 years	85
Calendar	Semester
Student/faculty ratio	10:1
Profs interesting rating	98
Profs accessible rating	95

Most classes have 10–19 students.
Most lab/discussion sessions have 10–19 students.

MOST POPULAR MAJORS

English; Economics; Psychology

STUDENTS SAY "..."

Academics

Situated in breathtaking western Massachusetts, Mount Holyoke is one of the nation's premier colleges for women. Undergrads here quickly tout the school's ability to both foster an incredibly "collaborative and inclusive atmosphere" and embrace "student uniqueness and diversity." Indeed, from day one of their first year, undergrads sense that Mount Holyoke "genuinely wants the best for each of its students and is willing to work for that." Undergrads also love that the college is able to pair a "rigorous liberal arts education with...career experience." And many students are quick to take advantage of the college's "great study abroad opportunities" as well. Of course, don't bother attending if you expect to slack off! After all, professors routinely "push students to go further than they expected." And these students wouldn't have it any other way. A satisfied junior expounds, "My educational experience has been characterized by small classes of passionate, intelligent students sharing in informed discussion led by inspiring professors who are leaders in their academic fields. It is this classroom experience that has kept me so invested in and excited about my coursework for the past three years." Truly, Mount Holyoke is "a place for impassioned women to invest emotionally and intellectually in their education and emerge as capable leaders, activists, and citizens."

Life

Students here are a pretty active lot. As such, they frequently enjoy engaging in "outdoor activities like hiking and apple picking as well as a broad range of athletics." However, if you don't fancy yourself the sporty type, fear not. There "are also many clubs to fit nearly every hobby from singing to community service." Certainly, students can participate in everything "from midnight howling and fandom-themed groups to the Roosevelt Institute, NARAL, and equestrian clubs." And a number of students are "active in social justice [groups]." It's also quite common for these undergrads to simply sit around and engage in "very intellectual conversations...about politics, subjects brought up in their classes, or maybe just a lively debate about a book or a movie." On the weekends, many students head "off-campus to nearby college towns such as Northampton and Amherst to socialize because...South Hadley is fairly quiet without many options." Fortunately, "bars, music venues, and really good restaurants" are only "a short (free) bus ride away." And, of course, "there's always plenty going on with...the other colleges in the Five College Consortium: from lectures to theatre to concerts to exhibits to parties."

Student Body

Mount Holyoke, as a proud sophomore excitedly shares, "attracts bright, ambitious students from around the world, women who are committed both to their own success and to working for the common good." Indeed, the undergrads here are incredibly impressed with their peers. And it's completely understandable why! As a history major declares, "The typical woman is very confident and very intelligent. She's driven to do well in her courses as well as with extracurriculars. She doesn't take 'no' for an answer and stands up for what she believes in." Students also happily report "the student body is racially and ethnically diverse, internationally representative, inclusive of many sexual orientations and gender identities, and embraces this variety in student organizations and general social life." And Mount Holyoke undergrads feel very fortunate that this affords them the opportunity to "get to meet people they might never have met otherwise." Most importantly, students here "are very friendly and loving which helps create a close and welcoming community."

FINANCIAL AID: 413-538-2291 • E-MAIL: ADMISSION@MTHOLYOKE.EDU • WEBSITE: WWW.MTHOLYOKE.EDU

THE PRINCETON REVIEW SAYS

Admissions

Very important factors considered include: rigor of secondary school record, class rank, academic GPA, application essay, recommendation(s). *Important factors considered include:* interview, extracurricular activities, talent/ability, character/personal qualities, volunteer work, work experience. *Other factors considered include:* standardized test scores, first generation, alumnae relation, geographical residence, racial/ethnic status, level of applicant's interest. SAT or ACT considered if submitted; SAT Subject Tests required for some. ACT with or without writing accepted. SAT with or without Essay component accepted. TOEFL required of all international applicants. High school diploma is required and GED is accepted. *Academic units recommended:* 4 English, 3 science labs, 3 history, 1 academic elective.

Financial Aid

Students should submit: FAFSA, CSS/Financial Aid PROFILE, Noncustodial PROFILE. Regular filing deadline is 3/1. The Princeton Review suggests that all financial aid forms be submitted as soon as possible after October 1. *Need-based scholarships/grants offered:* Federal Pell, FSEOG, State scholarships/grants, Private scholarships, College/university scholarship or grant aid from institutional funds. *Loan aid offered:* Direct Subsidized Stafford Loans, Direct Unsubsidized Stafford Loans, Direct PLUS loans, Federal Perkins Loans, State Loans, College/university loans from institutional funds. Applicants will be notified of awards on or about 4/1. Federal Work-Study Program available. Institutional employment available.

The Inside Word

Competition to gain admission to Mount Holyoke is tight. Therefore, a strong academic record is a must. Candidates should have taken a rigorous course-load, complete with honors, AP, and/or IB classes. The college also values strong writing skills so expect essays/personal statements to be closely assessed. While interviews are not required they are strongly recommended; it is in an applicant's best interest to schedule one. Conversely, with the exception of home-schooled students, standardized tests are optional.

THE SCHOOL SAYS "..."

From the Admissions Office

"The majority of students who choose Mount Holyoke do so because it is an outstanding research liberal arts college. After a semester or two, they start to appreciate the distinctive advantages of a women's college, even though most never thought they'd attend a women's college when they started their college search. They appreciate the remarkable array of opportunities that are available—for academic achievement, career exploration, internships, study abroad, and leadership—and the impressive, creative accomplishments of their peers. If you're looking for a college that will challenge you to be your best, most powerful self and to fulfill your potential, Mount Holyoke should be at the top of your list.

"Submission of standardized test scores is optional for most applicants to Mount Holyoke College. However, the TOEFL is required of students whose primary language is not English, and the SAT Subject Tests are required for home-schooled students."

SELECTIVITY
Admissions Rating	93
# of applicants	3,858
% of applicants accepted	50
% of acceptees attending	27
# offered a place on the wait list	785
% accepting a place on wait list	58
% admitted from wait list	2
# of early decision applicants	321
% accepted early decision	50

FRESHMAN PROFILE
Range SAT Critical Reading	620–730
Range SAT Math	610–735
Range SAT Writing	630–720
Range ACT Composite	29–32
Minimum internet-based TOEFL	100
Average HS GPA	3.8
% graduated top 10% of class	58
% graduated top 25% of class	90
% graduated top 50% of class	97

DEADLINES
Early decision	
Deadline	11/15
Notification	1/1
Other ED	
Deadline	1/1
Notification	2/1
Regular	
Deadline	1/15
Notification	4/1
Nonfall registration?	Yes

APPLICANTS ALSO LOOK AT AND OFTEN PREFER
Bowdoin College; Brown University

AND SOMETIMES PREFER
Amherst College; Barnard College; Bryn Mawr College; Grinnell College; Macalester College

FINANCIAL FACTS
Financial Aid Rating	96
Annual tuition	$45,680
Room and board	$13,440
Required fees	$186
Average frosh need-based scholarship	$32,332
Average UG need-based scholarship	$31,101
% needy frosh rec. need-based scholarship or grant aid	100
% needy UG rec. need-based scholarship or grant aid	99
% needy frosh rec. non-need-based scholarship or grant aid	28
% needy UG rec. non-need-based scholarship or grant aid	20
% needy frosh rec. need-based self-help aid	85
% needy UG rec. need-based self-help aid	88
% frosh rec. any financial aid	81
% UG rec. any financial aid	80
% UG borrow to pay for school	69
Average cumulative indebtedness	$25,339
% frosh need fully met	100
% ugrads need fully met	100
Average % of frosh need met	100
Average % of ugrad need met	100

MUHLENBERG COLLEGE

2400 WEST CHEW STREET, ALLENTOWN, PA 18104-5596 • ADMISSIONS: 484-664-3200 • FAX: 484-664-3032

STUDENTS SAY "..."

Academics

Students who attend Muhlenberg College in Allentown, Pennsylvania are welcomed into a "close-knit" community and are privy to "a well-rounded liberal arts education." And while the academics are certainly "rigorous," undergraduates here love the fact it's "[not] a cutthroat atmosphere." Importantly, students have their pick of many terrific disciplines, from the "amazing theater department" to the "extremely strong" education and science programs. Undergrads are also happy to champion their "dedicated" professors who understand how to create and foster "engaging courses." They also value the fact that Muhlenberg instructors "really take the time to get to know you and answer your questions." As one satisfied student interjects, "My professors so far have all been amazing and truly want me to succeed." Finally, as an international studies and Spanish double major sums up, "Muhlenberg is a place where someone can pursue theater AND chemistry, play a varsity sport AND lead a volunteer organization, work individually with a professor AND befriend a dining services worker."

Life

It's quite easy to lead a full and fulfilling life at Muhlenberg. To begin with, the "school offers tons of free activities over the weekends, from movie showings to Stuff-A-Plush." Undergrads here also love to take advantage of the college's strong performing arts scene. Indeed, "a cappella groups are very popular at Muhlenberg." Additionally, given "the large theater department," it's virtually guaranteed that "there's always a show in production." Sports are equally popular and we're told that "football and basketball games have good attendance records." While there's a modest amount of drinking, the college doesn't have a crazy party scene. As a biology major shares, "There's a few bars and clubs in the area that offer college nights on Thursdays which is fun. Every now and then the fraternities will host parties. A lot of people frequent the sports houses' parties on the weekends. But a lot of people also just chill and watch a movie." From time to time, the school hosts theme parties "like flapper-era zombies or a speakeasy (with a live jazz band!)" as well. Lastly, undergrads enjoy Allentown's public parks which provide "great areas to hike, explore, bird-watch, read or take a jog." And they periodically capitalize on Muhlenberg's relatively close proximity to both Philadelphia and New York.

Student Body

Strolling around the Muhlenberg campus, you'll probably pass by a number of students who are "white, upper-middle class [and] from New Jersey." Thankfully, though that might seem to define the typical undergrad here, there's much more to these students. Indeed, many individuals assert that their peers are extremely "hardworking" and "friendly." A French and education double-major explains, "Most people are involved with many different aspects of campus life, and these aspects tend not to be 'cliquey' because of the crossover. For example, there are many football players who are members of a cappella groups or who take dance." Importantly, we're also told that "being nice is kind of important" at Muhlenberg. An English major qualifies, "If someone doesn't hold the door open for the person behind them, they're basically made to wear a scarlet letter and deemed a pariah." And, finally, a biology major sums up his peers by stating, "There is a place for everyone on campus. We have a huge theater program, yet almost 30 percent of our school participates in athletics, so you can see there are all extremes and everything in between."

FINANCIAL AID: 484-664-3175 • E-MAIL: ADMISSION@MUHLENBERG.EDU • WEBSITE: WWW.MUHLENBERG.EDU

THE PRINCETON REVIEW SAYS

Admissions

Very important factors considered include: rigor of secondary school record, academic GPA, character/personal qualities. *Important factors considered include:* class rank, standardized test scores, application essay, recommendation(s), interview, extracurricular activities, talent/ability, volunteer work, work experience. *Other factors considered include:* first generation, alumni/ae relation, racial/ethnic status, level of applicant's interest. SAT or ACT required for some. ACT with Writing required. TOEFL required of all international applicants. High school diploma is required and GED is accepted. *Academic units required:* 4 English, 3 math, 2 science, 2 science labs, 2 foreign language, 2 history, 1 academic elective. *Academic units recommended:* 4 English, 4 math, 3 science, 3 science labs, 4 foreign language, 2 social studies, 2 history, 1 academic elective.

Financial Aid

Students should submit: FAFSA, Institution's own financial aid form, CSS/Financial Aid PROFILE, State aid form, Noncustodial PROFILE, Business/Farm Supplement. Regular filing deadline is 2/15. The Princeton Review suggests that all financial aid forms be submitted as soon as possible after October 1. *Need-based scholarships/grants offered:* Federal Pell, FSEOG, State scholarships/grants, Private scholarships, College/university scholarship or grant aid from institutional funds. *Loan aid offered:* Direct Subsidized Stafford Loans, Direct Unsubsidized Stafford Loans, Direct PLUS loans, Federal Perkins Loans. Applicants will be notified of awards on or about 4/1. Federal Work-Study Program available. Institutional employment available.

The Inside Word

Admissions officers at Muhlenberg endeavor to get a strong sense of each candidate. After all, they are on the hunt for students who will thrive at and complement the college. Of course, that being said, academic records are of primary concern. And a strong performance in college prep courses is a must. Applicants wary of standardized tests rejoice; submission of ACT or SAT scores is optional here. However, those students who choose not to send in their scores will be required to submit an additional statement. They'll also have to sit for an interview with a member of the admission staff (which is recommended regardless).

THE SCHOOL SAYS "..."

From the Admissions Office

"Listening to our own students, we've learned that most picked Muhlenberg mainly because it has a long-standing reputation for being academically demanding on one hand but personally supportive on the other. We expect a lot from our students, but we also expect a lot from ourselves in providing the challenge and support they need to stretch, grow, and succeed. It's not unusual for professors to put their home phone numbers on the course syllabus and encourage students to call them at home with questions. Upperclassmen are helpful to underclassmen. 'We really know about collegiality here,' says an alumna who now works at Muhlenberg. 'It's that kind of place.' The supportive atmosphere and strong work ethic produce lots of successes. The premed and pre-law programs are very strong, as are programs in theater arts, English, psychology, the sciences, business, and accounting. 'When I was a student here,' recalls Dr. Walter Loy, now a professor emeritus of physics, 'we were encouraged to live life to its fullest, to do our best, to be honest, to deal openly with others, and to treat everyone as an individual. Those are important things, and they haven't changed at Muhlenberg.'

"Students have the option of submitting SAT or ACT scores (including the writing sections) or submitting a graded paper with teacher's comments and grade on it from junior or senior year and interviewing with a member of the admissions staff."

SELECTIVITY

Admissions Rating	90
# of applicants	5,015
% of applicants accepted	48
% of acceptees attending	24
# offered a place on the wait list	1,690
% accepting a place on wait list	19
% admitted from wait list	13
# of early decision applicants	354
% accepted early decision	81

FRESHMAN PROFILE

Range SAT Critical Reading	560–660
Range SAT Math	560–660
Range SAT Writing	560–660
Range ACT Composite	25–31
Minimum paper TOEFL	550
Minimum internet-based TOEFL	80
Average HS GPA	3.3
% graduated top 10% of class	41
% graduated top 25% of class	71
% graduated top 50% of class	94

DEADLINES

Early decision	
Deadline	2/15
Other ED	
Deadline	2/15
Regular	
Priority	2/15
Deadline	2/15
Notification	3/15
Nonfall registration?	Yes

APPLICANTS ALSO LOOK AT AND OFTEN PREFER

Bucknell University; Villanova University

AND SOMETIMES PREFER

Dickinson College

FINANCIAL FACTS

Financial Aid Rating	89
Annual tuition	$47,825
Room and board	$11,090
Required fees	$485
Books and supplies	$1,300
Average frosh need-based scholarship	$28,024
Average UG need-based scholarship	$26,007
% needy frosh rec. need-based scholarship or grant aid	90
% needy UG rec. need-based scholarship or grant aid	91
% needy frosh rec. non-need-based scholarship or grant aid	75
% needy UG rec. non-need-based scholarship or grant aid	68
% needy frosh rec. need-based self-help aid	71
% needy UG rec. need-based self-help aid	73
% frosh rec. any financial aid	89
% UG rec. any financial aid	88
% UG borrow to pay for school	57
Average cumulative indebtedness	$30,527
% frosh need fully met	31
% ugrads need fully met	33
Average % of frosh need met	93
Average % of ugrad need met	93

NAZARETH COLLEGE

4245 EAST AVENUE, ROCHESTER, NY 14618-3790 • ADMISSIONS: 585-389-2860 • FAX: 585-389-2826

STUDENTS SAY "..."

Academics

Nazareth is a small private college with a range of professional undergraduate majors not usually offered by liberal arts schools—many students note that the physical therapy program was what drew them to the college. The music education and health sciences majors receive particularly high praise, with some students calling out art, history, and psychology as well. The small class sizes—cited by many students as one of the best things about Nazareth—allow for "very close relationships with our professors" and "most professors try to make class as interactive as possible," though "of course like [at] any other school you may end up with a sub par teacher." The vast majority "take an interest in getting to know their students and are very open to helping students outside of the classroom," and "most are very easy to communicate and collaborate with, especially if [a student is] interested in research." Particularly in upper-level courses, "professors have the students' best interests in mind and always teach their classes with passion." Classes are mixed between lectures and discussions, depending on course of study, and students are strongly encouraged to pursue internships during their undergraduate studies.

Life

Nazareth offers a host of activities on campus, but students enjoy the surrounding city of Rochester as well. On weekends, many head off campus to bars and "amazing restaurants" (a good thing, since the majority of students report that they'd love to see dining hall food improve). The school also arranges for discounted tickets and transportation to concerts and sporting events. On campus, there are "mixers" (dances), Hunger Games theme nights, laser tag, bingo, and comedians. Many clubs are service-oriented, and working out is popular. Students report that the school's policies around alcohol and parties are strict and free "on-campus activities...cater to students who prefer alcohol and drug-free activities," but that plenty of parties occur off-campus for those interested. Nazareth's location makes it the rare school that keeps both residential and commuter students happy, with positive town-gown relations. Students also enjoy school-subsidized "inexpensive trips to...New York City or Montreal for the weekend."

Student Body

Nazareth has a low male-to-female ratio, and the typical student is "an upper middle class white girl," but "there are also many international students and students from the inner city. There are cliques, but most people get along from all walks of life." "They value education but also make time for social activities." While many students are from New York, there is a visible international community on campus. Male students are generally described as either athletes or theater majors. Most students are involved in "at least one club, sport, job, or activity," and anecdotally, "student athletes are almost a quarter of the student body...Every student finds their own little niche though," because "there's something for everyone here." "Students are often close with those in their major and/or those they work with." The vast majority are "friendly and easy-going," and students are very clear that "the more you get involved the better your college experience will be."

FINANCIAL AID: 585-389-2310 • E-MAIL: ADMISSIONS@NAZ.EDU • WEBSITE: WWW.NAZ.EDU

THE PRINCETON REVIEW SAYS

Admissions

Very important factors considered include: rigor of secondary school record, class rank, academic GPA, application essay, recommendation(s). *Important factors considered include:* interview, extracurricular activities, talent/ability, character/personal qualities, geographical residence, state residency, racial/ethnic status, volunteer work, work experience, level of applicant's interest. *Other factors considered include:* standardized test scores, first generation, alumni/ae relation. SAT or ACT considered if submitted; SAT Subject Tests considered if submitted. ACT with or without writing accepted. TOEFL required of all international applicants. High school diploma is required and GED is accepted. *Academic units required:* 4 English, 3 math, 3 science, 2 science labs, 3 foreign language, 3 social studies. *Academic units recommended:* 4 English, 4 math, 4 science, 4 foreign language, 4 social studies.

Financial Aid

Students should submit: FAFSA, State aid form. Priority filing deadline is 2/15. The Princeton Review suggests that all financial aid forms be submitted as soon as possible after October 1. *Need-based scholarships/grants offered:* Federal Pell, FSEOG, State scholarships/grants, Private scholarships, College/university scholarship or grant aid from institutional funds. *Loan aid offered:* Direct Subsidized Stafford Loans, Direct Unsubsidized Stafford Loans, Direct PLUS loans, Federal Perkins Loans, Federal Nursing Loans. Applicants will be notified of awards on a rolling basis beginning 2/1. Federal Work-Study Program available. Institutional employment available.

The Inside Word

Nazareth has a fairly high acceptance rate, meaning solid students with good test scores shouldn't sweat over getting accepted here. Admissions officers review each applicant's Common Application, high school transcript, recommendations, and essay; SAT scores are optional. Art, music, and theatre programs require additional application materials.

THE SCHOOL SAYS "..."

From the Admissions Office

"Preparing students for a world of rapid change, and for careers yet to be defined, is the focus at Nazareth. College graduates must have relevant knowledge, exceptional critical thinking skills, a global mindset, and work experience. These four foundations of a Nazareth education prepare you for the future. Our unusually broad array of high-caliber academics for a small college includes more than sixty majors, such as education; math and sciences; business and management; visual arts, music, theatre, foreign languages, and other humanities; and a diverse mix of health programs. Expect small classes, personal attention, friendliness, and our nationally recognized community service work. Our uncommon core curriculum is student-focused and integrated with your career goals. We promote global dexterity through coursework, foreign-language houses, events, a diverse campus community, and dozens of opportunities to travel, study, intern, and experience life overseas. Our College stands out for its Fulbright scholars, selected to teach around the world, and for its commitment to developing student leaders through the 2015 Clinton Global Initiative University. Nazareth is coeducational and independent, located on 150 beautifully landscaped acres in a suburb of Rochester, which is New York's third-largest city and rich in culture and entertainment. New facilities include Peckham Hall math/science building with state-of-the-art labs and, opening in 2015, a renovated Wellness and Rehabilitation Institute with extensive clinic and collaboration spaces. Students attend free theatre, music, dance, and international performances at the Nazareth College Arts Center. Our athletes boast one of the highest graduation rates in NCAA Division III."

SELECTIVITY

Admissions Rating	79
# of applicants	3,677
% of applicants accepted	76
% of acceptees attending	19
# offered a place on the wait list	60
% accepting a place on wait list	2
% admitted from wait list	0
# of early decision applicants	275
% accepted early decision	87

FRESHMAN PROFILE

Range SAT Critical Reading	480–580
Range SAT Math	490–590
Range SAT Writing	460–580
Range ACT Composite	22–27
Minimum paper TOEFL	550
Minimum internet-based TOEFL	79
Average HS GPA	89.0
% graduated top 10% of class	27
% graduated top 25% of class	58
% graduated top 50% of class	86

DEADLINES

Early decision	
Deadline	11/15
Notification	12/15
Regular	
Priority	12/1
Deadline	2/1
Nonfall registration?	Yes

FINANCIAL FACTS

Financial Aid Rating	84
Annual tuition	$31,024
Room and board	$13,150
Required fees	$1,400
Books and supplies	$1,100
Average frosh need-based scholarship	$18,752
Average UG need-based scholarship	$16,424
% needy frosh rec. need-based scholarship or grant aid	100
% needy UG rec. need-based scholarship or grant aid	100
% needy frosh rec. non-need-based scholarship or grant aid	45
% needy UG rec. non-need-based scholarship or grant aid	35
% needy frosh rec. need-based self-help aid	95
% needy UG rec. need-based self-help aid	95
% UG borrow to pay for school	84
Average cumulative indebtedness	$38,853
% frosh need fully met	40
% ugrads need fully met	32
Average % of frosh need met	84
Average % of ugrad need met	80

NEW COLLEGE OF FLORIDA

5800 BAY SHORE ROAD, SARASOTA, FL 34243-2109 • ADMISSIONS: 941-487-5000 • FAX: 941-487-5001

STUDENTS SAY "..."

Academics

New College of Florida, a uniquely small and unconventional public institution, "provides challenging courses for highly self-motivated students who want a large amount of control over their academic choices." It's all about "self-directed learning" here (working closely with faculty advisers, "the student decides what he or she is going to learn and how she is going to learn it") that leaves undergrads "free to do what they please—with their bodies, their studies, their behavior—but while also being held to high academic standards." Those who can balance the intellectual freedom NCF offers with the academic accountability it demands, wind up with "a rounded education that enables them to critically and pragmatically examine and understand the world in which we live...and weird parties." The academics "are undeniably awesome" at NCF, while the small-school setting and the student body "encourage a love of learning, whether it be academic, political, or hobby-related." It's the sort of school where "it is very popular for groups of students to get together to talk about class readings outside of the classroom, usually at the college coffee shop, as a means of socializing." NCF undergrads receive "narrative evaluations instead of grades. These evaluations give advice and help us to become better students." Many here "love having written evaluations in which our process and progress are documented, not only the final outcome. The evaluations force students to fully participate and the professors to pay close attention." All students must write a senior thesis to graduate; reports one undergrad, "recently we had a survey...on which one of the sections dealt with the possibility of making the senior thesis optional. There was an overwhelming response that this was unacceptable. I think that says a lot about how proud we are of our academic standards."

Life

Having fun "in a glorified retirement community requires ingenuity of the New College student population," but "thankfully, most grew up in suburban Florida" and so are used to a slower pace. It helps that the campus is near Lido and Siesta Beaches, "where [students] enjoy unlimited swimming, sunning, and Frisbee playing," and that "downtown Sarasota isn't that bad either," since it's home to a number of "ethnic eateries. Thai food, in particular, seems to have a cult following on campus—with constant debate as to which restaurant is the best or most authentic and student events that advertise Thai food are bound to pull in dozens of followers." On campus, students enjoy everything "from club meetings to public speakers to 'hip' bands playing shows. There's usually something to do and usually free food to be found!" There are also "school-wide parties every Friday and Saturday night in a courtyard outside of the dorms. Different students get to decide the theme of each dance party and the music to be played. Most on-campus students never leave campus during the weekend because of these dance parties."

Student Body

New College students share "a few things in common: Most...are friendly, passionate about the things they believe in, very hard workers, liberal, and most of all, try to be open to new experiences." The students are "largely middle-class, white, and liberal. There are of course exceptions, but the school is rather small,'" there is "a fairly strong [LGBTQ] community here, and many transgendered people who have decided to make New College their coming-out grounds. The student body is generally aware of gender issues and respectful of {LGBTQ} people of all types." There are even "some Republicans on campus. Maybe four. I'm not sure. We're not the type of school that generally attracts heavy right-wingers."

FINANCIAL AID: 941-487-5000 • E-MAIL: ADMISSIONS@NCF.EDU • WEBSITE: WWW.NCF.EDU

THE PRINCETON REVIEW SAYS

Admissions

Very important factors considered include: rigor of secondary school record, academic GPA, application essay. *Important factors considered include:* class rank, standardized test scores, recommendation(s), extracurricular activities, character/personal qualities, volunteer work, work experience, level of applicant's interest. *Other factors considered include:* talent/ability, first generation, alumni/ae relation, geographical residence, state residency. SAT or ACT required; SAT Subject Tests considered if submitted. ACT with Writing required. SAT with Essay component required. TOEFL required of all international applicants. High school diploma is required and GED is accepted. *Academic units required:* 4 English, 4 math, 3 science, 2 science labs, 2 foreign language, 3 social studies, 2 academic electives. *Academic units recommended:* 4 English, 4 math, 4 science, 2 science labs, 4 foreign language, 4 social studies, 4 academic electives.

Financial Aid

Students should submit: FAFSA. Priority filing deadline is 2/15. The Princeton Review suggests that all financial aid forms be submitted as soon as possible after October 1. *Need-based scholarships/grants offered:* Federal Pell, FSEOG, State scholarships/grants, Private scholarships, College/university scholarship or grant aid from institutional funds. *Loan aid offered:* Direct Subsidized Stafford Loans, Direct Unsubsidized Stafford Loans, Direct PLUS Loans. Applicants will be notified of awards on a rolling basis beginning 3/15. Federal Work-Study Program available. Institutional employment available.

The Inside Word

New College isn't your typical public school. The tiny student body allows admissions officers here to review each application carefully; expect a thorough going over of your essays, recommendations, and extracurricular activities. Iconoclastic students tend to thrive here, and the admissions staff knows that. Don't be afraid to let your freak flag fly; it won't get you in here if your academics aren't top flight, but it certainly won't hurt you either.

THE SCHOOL SAYS "..."

From the Admissions Office

"Deep curiosity, inspired individualism, civic-mindedness, and a dash of quirkiness. New College students collaborate with their professors to build a program of courses, seminars, and independent and group projects to meet their individual needs and interests. The result? A remarkably rigorous and engaging education (with highly affordable tuition). New College students apply theories and methods they learn in the classroom to research and creative work of their own design. While learning to organize and execute large projects, they sharpen their critical thinking—a skillset that serves them well in grad school and the world beyond higher education. The social atmosphere is relaxed and intellectually playful; the campus celebrates creativity, service, and the value of the individual. New College welcomes admitted students to visit "in depth"—arrange to talk and tour, attend a class, perhaps lunch with a current student at the student-run Four Winds Cafe before making the decision to enroll. Application Materials (November 1 Priority Deadline): Common Application (with essay and fee/fee waiver), official transcript(s), recommendation, and SAT or ACT scores. Some Florida public college transfers can have exam scores waived—please inquire. International applicants and applicants with materials from abroad, should inquire about additional materials needed. Financial Aid (November 1 Priority FAFSA Deadline): If you seek need-based grants and/or federal student loans, please complete the Free Application for Federal Student Aid. In addition to packaging need-based aid, the College offers scholarship funding to nearly all of its entering students."

SELECTIVITY

Admissions Rating	89
# of applicants	1,655
% of applicants accepted	61
% of acceptees attending	26
# offered a place on the wait list	178
% accepting a place on wait list	29
% admitted from wait list	59

FRESHMAN PROFILE

Range SAT Critical Reading	610–720
Range SAT Math	560–660
Range SAT Writing	570–670
Range ACT Composite	27–31
Minimum paper TOEFL	560
Minimum internet-based TOEFL	83
Average HS GPA	4.0
% graduated top 10% of class	43
% graduated top 25% of class	79
% graduated top 50% of class	97

DEADLINES

Regular	
Priority	11/1
Deadline	4/15
Nonfall registration?	No

APPLICANTS ALSO LOOK AT AND OFTEN PREFER

Florida State University; University of Central Florida; University of Florida; University of Miami; University of South Florida; Rollins College

AND SOMETIMES PREFER

Grinnell College; University of Chicago; New York University; Eckerd College

AND RARELY PREFER

Warren Wilson College; Yale University

FINANCIAL FACTS

Financial Aid Rating	87
Annual in-state tuition	$6,916
Annual out-of-state tuition	$29,944
Room and board	$8,932
Books and supplies	$1,200
Average frosh need-based scholarship	$9,832
Average UG need-based scholarship	$8,752
% needy frosh rec. need-based scholarship or grant aid	91
% needy UG rec. need-based scholarship or grant aid	92
% needy frosh rec. non-need-based scholarship or grant aid	16
% needy UG rec. non-need-based scholarship or grant aid	12
% needy frosh rec. need-based self-help aid	79
% needy UG rec. need-based self-help aid	82
% frosh rec. any financial aid	100
% UG rec. any financial aid	98
% UG borrow to pay for school	48
Average cumulative indebtedness	$14,929
% frosh need fully met	48
% ugrads need fully met	37
Average % of frosh need met	89
Average % of ugrad need met	83

NEW JERSEY INSTITUTE OF TECHNOLOGY

OFFICE OF UNIVERSITY ADMISSIONS, NEWARK, NJ 07102 • ADMISSIONS: 973-596-3300 • FAX: 973-596-3461

CAMPUS LIFE

Quality of Life Rating	77
Fire Safety Rating	99
Green Rating	60*
Type of school	Public
Affiliation	No Affiliation
Environment	Metropolis

STUDENTS

Total undergrad enrollment	8,008
% male/female	76/24
% from out of state	8
% frosh from public high school	85
% frosh live on campus	51
% ugrads live on campus	23
# of fraternities	19
# of sororities	4
% African American	9
% Asian	22
% Caucasian	33
% Hispanic	22
% Native American	<1
% Pacific Islander	<1
% Two or more races	3
% Race and/or ethnicity unknown	6
% international	4
# of countries represented	83

SURVEY SAYS...

Very little drug use
Different types of students interact
Easy to get around campus

ACADEMICS

Academic Rating	69
% students returning for sophomore year	88
% students graduating within 4 years	23
% students graduating within 6 years	61
Calendar	Semester
Student/faculty ratio	17:1
Profs interesting rating	65
Profs accessible rating	65
Most classes have 20–29 students.	

MOST POPULAR MAJORS

Mechanical Engineering; Civil Engineering; Architecture

STUDENTS SAY "..."

Academics

A well-respected school within the state's public university system, New Jersey Institute of Technology is "all about putting your best work forward so that you can achieve what you want in life after graduation." As "an affordable tech school with many good returns in the future," NJIT is "a place where opportunities are widely available and where you can stand out, as long as you work hard." Students agree that course loads are heavy across the board, regardless of academic department. "The work load is very rigorous" and "everyone studies all the time." The engineering, architecture, and computer science departments earn high praise, with one student proclaiming that NJIT "produces the most useful engineers on the planet." The professors earn mixed reviews, with some undergrads noting that "many of the professors...are hired for their research skills and not for their teaching" and that while their professors are "very educated," some "have difficulty explaining [material] to students." Others students counter that their "professors are experts in their field. They give insightful tips on how to solve certain problems based on experience," and they are "very accessible out of class." "NJIT is all about STEM" and "is on the cutting edge of science and technology as well as research."

Life

With its "very dedicated students" who "take their work seriously," it can sometimes seem like there's little time for fun at NJIT. There is also a visible commuter population, "making weekends very empty," as one student puts it. But even students who "are constantly studying" need a break, and luckily "there are always campus events." For those who want to venture a little farther, "New York is a 15-minute train ride away." Students are mixed on the school's Newark location, with some reporting that "NJIT isn't in the best area," though the campus feels safe because "not only do we have police, but also [security] guards that are stationed all over campus." Video games are popular and students flock to a dedicated game room to engage in friendly competitions. Says one computer science major, "Video games are what most people use to [socialize], but at the end of the day, most of the time is spent studying." Greek life is a small presence on campus, though with NJIT's roughly 8:2 men to women ratio, Greek events "tend to be sausage fests. The girls there are generally from other colleges and universities in the area."

Student Body

With its "diverse, inquisitive, and talented" student body, NJIT is full of "[hard-working] students who strive to make changes to make the school better each year." Students say that they are "all here to learn and succeed" and when groups of friends hang out, "[half] the time these groups are playing multiplayer games on their computers, trying to relax. The other half of the time they can be found studying together for an exam they have in common." Some students complain that, "There [are] not enough choices for entertainment" while others say that "if I want relax [I] just bring my laptop." The soccer field is a popular place to play sports and if "you have some free time people go to the gym or to the green and hang out, there is usually an event going on in the mid-campus." But whether it's a complicated engineering project or a marathon video game session, NJIT students proudly proclaim "We do it with passion!"

FINANCIAL AID: 973-596-3479 • E-MAIL: ADMISSIONS@NJIT.EDU • WEBSITE: WWW.NJIT.EDU

THE PRINCETON REVIEW SAYS

Admissions

Very important factors considered include: rigor of secondary school record, class rank, standardized test scores. *Important factors considered include:* academic GPA. *Other factors considered include:* application essay, recommendation(s), interview, extracurricular activities, talent/ability, character/personal qualities, alumni/ae relation, geographical residence, state residency, religious affiliation/commitment, racial/ethnic status, volunteer work, work experience, level of applicant's interest. SAT or ACT required. TOEFL required of all international applicants. High school diploma is required and GED is accepted. *Academic units required:* 4 English, 4 math, 2 science, 2 science labs. *Academic units recommended:* 2 foreign language, 1 social studies, 1 history, 2 academic electives.

Financial Aid

Students should submit: FAFSA. Priority filing deadline is 3/15. The Princeton Review suggests that all financial aid forms be submitted as soon as possible after October 1. *Need-based scholarships/grants offered:* Federal Pell, FSEOG, State scholarships/grants, Private scholarships, College/university scholarship or grant aid from institutional funds, United Negro College Fund. *Loan aid offered:* Direct Subsidized Stafford Loans, Direct Unsubsidized Stafford Loans, Direct PLUS loans, Federal Perkins Loans, State Loans. Applicants will be notified of awards on a rolling basis beginning 12/15. Federal Work-Study Program available. Institutional employment available.

The Inside Word

The NJIT admission committee looks for applicants who can handle rigorous academics. Qualified candidates will be in the top 25 percent of their graduating class or have a minimum 3.0 GPA, with especially strong grades in math, science, and English. The essay section score of the SAT is used to determine first-year English class placement rather than admission. Applicants for interior design, industrial design, digital design, and architecture majors are required to submit a portfolio of creative work along with the regular application requirements.

THE SCHOOL SAYS "..."

From the Admissions Office

"Talented high school graduates from across the nation come to NJIT to prepare for leadership roles in architecture, business, engineering, medical, legal, science, and technological fields. Students experience a public research university conducting over $100 million in research that maintains a small-college atmosphere at a modest cost. Our attractive forty-five-acre campus is just minutes from New York City and less than an hour from the Jersey shore. Students find an outstanding faculty and a safe, diverse, and caring learning and residential community. NJIT's academic environment challenges and prepares students for rewarding careers and full-time advanced study after graduation. The campus is computing-intensive.

"Students applying for admission to NJIT may provide scores from either the SAT or the ACT. Writing sample scores will not be used for admission purposes, but are used for placement in first-year courses. SAT Subject Test scores are not required for any major."

SELECTIVITY

Admissions Rating	86
# of applicants	6,045
% of applicants accepted	61
% of acceptees attending	30

FRESHMAN PROFILE

Range SAT Critical Reading	510–620
Range SAT Math	580–670
Range SAT Writing	500–620
Minimum paper TOEFL	550
Minimum internet-based TOEFL	79
Average HS GPA	3.6
% graduated top 10% of class	31
% graduated top 25% of class	59
% graduated top 50% of class	87

DEADLINES

Regular	
Deadline	3/1
Nonfall registration?	Yes

APPLICANTS ALSO LOOK AT AND OFTEN PREFER

Drexel University; Rensselaer Polytechnic Institute; The College of New Jersey

AND SOMETIMES PREFER

Penn State University Park; Virginia Tech; Worcester Polytechnic Institute; Stevens Institute of Technology

FINANCIAL FACTS

Financial Aid Rating	80
Annual in-state tuition	$13,434
Annual out-of-state tuition	$27,652
Room and board	$13,296
Required fees	$2,904
Books and supplies	$2,600
Average frosh need-based scholarship	$12,902
Average UG need-based scholarship	$11,981
% needy frosh rec. need-based scholarship or grant aid	88
% needy UG rec. need-based scholarship or grant aid	84
% needy frosh rec. non-need-based scholarship or grant aid	59
% needy UG rec. non-need-based scholarship or grant aid	43
% needy frosh rec. need-based self-help aid	77
% needy UG rec. need-based self-help aid	85
% frosh rec. any financial aid	87
% UG rec. any financial aid	72
% UG borrow to pay for school	62
Average cumulative indebtedness	$37,195
% frosh need fully met	13
% ugrads need fully met	9
Average % of frosh need met	61
Average % of ugrad need met	58

NEW YORK UNIVERSITY

665 BROADWAY, NEW YORK, NY 10012 • ADMISSIONS: 212-998-4500 • FAX: 212-995-4902

CAMPUS LIFE

Quality of Life Rating	87
Fire Safety Rating	98
Green Rating	70
Type of school	Private
Affiliation	No Affiliation
Environment	Metropolis

STUDENTS

Total undergrad enrollment	24,985
% male/female	43/57
% from out of state	64
% frosh from public high school	59
% frosh live on campus	85
% ugrads live on campus	44
# of fraternities (% ugrad men join)	23 (7)
# of sororities (% ugrad women join)	14 (6)
% African American	5
% Asian	20
% Caucasian	36
% Hispanic	12
% Native American	<1
% Pacific Islander	<1
% Two or more races	4
% Race and/or ethnicity unknown	9
% international	15
# of countries represented	139

SURVEY SAYS...

Students are happy
Internships are widely available
Students love New York, NY
Great off-campus food
Hard liquor is popular
Theater is popular

ACADEMICS

Academic Rating	81
% students returning for sophomore year	92
% students graduating within 4 years	72
% students graduating within 6 years	82
Calendar	Semester
Student/faculty ratio	10:1
Profs interesting rating	81
Profs accessible rating	76

Most classes have 10–19 students.
Most lab/discussion sessions have
fewer than 10 students.

MOST POPULAR MAJORS

Liberal Arts and Sciences; Drama and
Dramatics/Theatre Arts; Business/Commerce

STUDENTS SAY "..."

Academics

"Location, location, location" in "the most amazing city on earth," along with "great facilities" and "top-notch faculty," makes New York University an excellent choice for those seeking "an untraditional college experience" in "a paradise for the independent and motivated." With more than 20,000 students and ten distinct schools offering more than 230 areas of study, NYU "is about diversity. Students are from all over the world; they come from different cultures, and they have different talents and interests. Similarly, NYU offers endless opportunities for students, no matter what their interests or ambitions are." The school offers huge opportunities to participate in research, pursue an internship, or begin a career in the arts (although "you have to be active and willing to find these opportunities"). Given the school's size, many students are "actually quite surprised by the accessibility of both the faculty and administration." Although "this is not the kind of school where students really get to know all of their teachers, as it is unlikely that a student will have a professor more than once," those who make the effort report that "it is so easy to meet with [professors] outside of class, and I still get e-mails from professors about internships, jobs, and scholarship recommendations." Many here also tout the "great study abroad programs."

Life

"Living in New York City is the biggest part of going to school at New York University," NYU students agree. The school's New York City campus is located in the heart of Greenwich Village, one of the city's major nightlife destinations, so "there is always something to do at any hour of the day," usually within walking distance of the school. One student reports, "Every weekend there are tons of things to do, both at NYU and in New York City. NYU really takes advantage of its location, so a lot of the programming provided by residence life or the student resource center is engaging you in the city that has become your new home." Living in the Big Apple means that "on any given day you can go to a museum, concert, sporting event, or theater performance . . . and a lot of the times, NYU will foot the bill if you go to an event in the city with your RA or with a club." The location also provides plenty of internship opportunities, which is good because "the vast majority of students at NYU are interested in interning and finding jobs through that gateway." The school has an atypical campus; it surrounds Washington Square Park, a busy public square where students love to relax when the weather is accommodating.

Student Body

"There is no typical student at NYU," where an undergraduate student body of more than 20,000 and a broad range of academic interests ensure a broad demographic. "Each school at NYU attracts a different group," students tell us. "The Tisch School of the Arts attracts a very out-there group of actors and the like." "Hipsters are pretty pervasive throughout all schools except Stern"; although "every school has people who break those stereotypes. [Even so,] few students can find ways to not fit in because of the huge number of students" at the university. Throughout NYU, "students tend to be incredibly motivated and ambitious." Students insist that "it is also important to note that NYU students are very accepting of each other's differences," an important factor at a school that brings together "students of all different backgrounds, ethnicities, and gender identities and makes them coexist within the university."

FINANCIAL AID: 212-998-4444 • E-MAIL: ADMISSIONS@NYU.EDU • WEBSITE: WWW.NYU.EDU

THE PRINCETON REVIEW SAYS

Admissions

Very important factors considered include: rigor of secondary school record, class rank, academic GPA, standardized test scores, talent/ability. *Important factors considered include:* application essay, recommendation(s), extracurricular activities, character/personal qualities. *Other factors considered include:* interview, first generation, alumni/ae relation, geographical residence, racial/ethnic status, volunteer work, work experience, level of applicant's interest. ACT with Writing required. TOEFL required of all international applicants. High school diploma is required and GED is accepted. *Academic units required:* 4 English, 3 math, 3 science, 3 science labs, 3 foreign language, 3 social studies, 3 history. *Academic units recommended:* 4 English, 4 math, 4 science, 4 science labs, 4 foreign language, 4 social studies, 4 history.

Financial Aid

Students should submit: FAFSA, CSS/Financial Aid PROFILE, Noncustodial PROFILE. Regular filing deadline is 2/15. The Princeton Review suggests that all financial aid forms be submitted as soon as possible after October 1. *Need-based scholarships/grants offered:* Federal Pell, FSEOG, State scholarships/grants, Private scholarships, College/university scholarship or grant aid from institutional funds, Federal Nursing Scholarships. *Loan aid offered:* Direct Subsidized Stafford Loans, Direct Unsubsidized Stafford Loans, Direct PLUS loans, Federal Perkins Loans, Federal Nursing Loans, College/university loans from institutional funds. Applicants will be notified of awards on a rolling basis beginning 4/1. Federal Work-Study Program available. Institutional employment available.

The Inside Word

Undergraduates must apply to one of NYU's undergraduate schools and colleges: the College of Arts and Science; the Polytechnic School of Engineering, the Liberal Studies Program; the Stern School of Business; the College of Nursing; the Gallatin School of Individualized Study; the Silver School of Social Work; the Steinhardt School of Culture, Education, and Human Development; the Tisch School of the Arts; or the School of Professional Studies. This is different from the application process at some universities and obviously requires some forethought. Remember that this is a highly competitive university; if your application doesn't reflect a serious interest in your intended area of study, your chances of gaining admission will be diminished.

THE SCHOOL SAYS ". . ."

From the Admissions Office

"NYU is the largest independent research university in the United States and one of just nineteen private universities in the prestigious Association of American Universities. Founded in 1831 by Albert Gallatin, it is now one the most influential universities in the world. NYU's degree-granting campuses in New York, Abu Dhabi, and Shanghai are complemented by global centers in Accra, Berlin, Buenos Aires, Florence, London, Madrid, Paris, Prague, Sydney, Tel Aviv, and Washington, D.C. Throughout this global network, NYU students benefit from an exceptionally rich academic climate fostered by a faculty of renowned, award-winning scholars—many of whom have won Nobel Prizes and MacArthur Genius Grants, as well as Emmy, Oscar, and Grammy Awards. As a result, NYU attracts more students from outside the United States than any other American university while sending more of its own students abroad than any other American institution. More than 4,000 courses allow students to explore their interests in distinctly urban settings."

SELECTIVITY

Admissions Rating	93
# of applicants	50,804
% of applicants accepted	35
% of acceptees attending	33
# of early decision applicants	7,016
% accepted early decision	32

FRESHMAN PROFILE

Range SAT Critical Reading	610–710
Range SAT Math	630–740
Range SAT Writing	620–720
Range ACT Composite	28–32
Minimum internet-based TOEFL	100
Average HS GPA	3.7

DEADLINES

Early decision	
Deadline	11/1
Notification	12/15
Regular	
Deadline	1/1
Notification	4/1
Nonfall registration?	No

FINANCIAL FACTS

Financial Aid Rating	74
Annual tuition	$43,746
Room and board	$16,782
Required fees	$2,424
Books and supplies	$1,070
Average frosh need-based scholarship	$31,488
Average UG need-based scholarship	$24,246
% needy frosh rec. need-based scholarship or grant aid	90
% needy UG rec. need-based scholarship or grant aid	88
% needy frosh rec. non-need-based scholarship or grant aid	1
% needy UG rec. non-need-based scholarship or grant aid	0
% needy frosh rec. need-based self-help aid	83
% needy UG rec. need-based self-help aid	81
% frosh need fully met	11
% ugrads need fully met	5
Average % of frosh need met	72
Average % of ugrad need met	58

NORTH CAROLINA STATE UNIVERSITY

BOX 7103, RALEIGH, NC 27695 • ADMISSIONS: 919-515-2434 • FAX: 919-515-5039

STUDENTS SAY "..."

Academics

The "largest and most diverse" of North Carolina's public university system, NC State provides undergrads with a "high level education" and "great value." The campus rings with a "welcoming, down-to-earth" vibe and "Wolfpack pride" is certainly infectious. Moreover, the university maintains "opportunities to fit every single type of person no matter their interest." Academically, NC State is home to a stellar engineering school that students contend is "the best engineering program in the state of North Carolina." It offers "world-renowned faculty who conduct innovative and cutting edge research in a plethora of scientific fields." Undergrads also like to emphasize the "exceptionally rigorous" design program which is "small and personal." And we'd certainly be remiss if we didn't mention the "fantastic business school" and "great entrepreneurship program" it has developed. Inside the classroom, students find their professors to be "very enthusiastic about what they teach" and appreciate that they truly "challenge you to think." As one satisfied junior adds, "My professors are extremely knowledgeable about the course material and bring in practical demonstrations to bring the lecture to life." And just as important, "professors love to discuss future professional development plans with undergraduate students." All in all, it's highly evident that "professors and TAs here love their jobs." Simply put, "they want you to succeed."

Life

Students proffer that NC State's campus is always abuzz with activity. As one excited senior quickly shares, "There's always something to do for fun—spanking the UNC Tarheels at football, painting the Free Expression Tunnel, stalking American Idol winner Scotty McCreery, and people-watching at the State Fair are just a few examples." Athletics are extremely popular here and it often feels as though "basketball games and football games are almost required [viewing]." And, naturally, these contests are accompanied by "a large tailgate culture." Additionally, the university "sponsors many different programs, ranging from concerts to a movie at the campus cinema every weekend." And there are "quite a few service and community oriented activities that go on around campus, such as Shack-A-Thon for Habitat for Humanity and the Krispy Kreme Challenge for children's hospitals." Students also love to take advantage of the surrounding area. As one freshman tells us, "Hillsborough Street has a lot of fun restaurants to go to when we want to go out and do things. Also, there [are] lots of [places] to go to the movies and shop right outside of campus." Indeed, the "Raleigh-area is full of things to do from concerts, bars, shows, restaurants, museums, malls, etc." As another freshman sums up life at NC State, "The problem isn't finding something to do, it is finding time to do it all [while] manag[ing] to stay on task and put aside time to study."

Student Body

When you first step onto the campus of NC State, "first impressions might make it seem like everyone there is a sorority girl or a frat guy who all wear cowboy boots and come from rural NC." However, "if you look closely [you'll see a] very diverse campus with lots of opportunities." Indeed, you'll find a range from "hipster to farm boy" and everything in between. Of course, no matter the easy or convenient characterization, most undergrads agree that their peers are "welcoming" and "friendly." Students tell us that "fitting in is super easy and getting involved with any of the many programs on campus help[s] with meeting new people and making friends!" And while most students are "devoted to academics," they all still manage to "go out and have fun." Additionally, undergrads say their peers "are service oriented and always think of creative ways to give back." Finally, as one junior reveals, "NCSU is huge, so every person can find a spot—and when you do, you find a family. To me, it doesn't feel like a large school. I see someone I know walking on campus every day. I don't know anyone, particularly those that began their education living on campus, that hasn't found their niche."

NORTH CAROLINA STATE UNIVERSITY

FINANCIAL AID: 919-515-2421 • E-MAIL: UNDERGRAD_ADMISSIONS@NCSU.EDU • WEBSITE: WWW.NCSU.EDU

THE PRINCETON REVIEW SAYS

Admissions

Very important factors considered include: rigor of secondary school record, class rank, academic GPA, standardized test scores. *Important factors considered include: Other factors considered include:* application essay, extracurricular activities, talent/ability, character/personal qualities, first generation, alumni/ae relation, geographical residence, state residency, racial/ethnic status, volunteer work, work experience. SAT or ACT required; SAT Subject Tests considered if submitted. ACT with or without writing accepted. SAT with or without Essay component accepted. High school diploma is required and GED is accepted. *Academic units required:* 4 English, 4 math, 3 science, 1 science lab, 2 foreign language, 1 social studies, 1 history. *Academic units recommended:* 4 English, 4 math, 3 science, 1 science lab, 2 foreign language, 1 social studies, 1 history.

Financial Aid

Students should submit: FAFSA. Priority filing deadline is 3/1. The Princeton Review suggests that all financial aid forms be submitted as soon as possible after October 1. *Need-based scholarships/grants offered:* Federal Pell, FSEOG, State scholarships/grants, Private scholarships, College/university scholarship or grant aid from institutional funds, United Negro College Fund. *Loan aid offered:* Direct Subsidized Stafford Loans, Direct Unsubsidized Stafford Loans, Direct PLUS loans, Federal Perkins Loans, State Loans, College/university loans from institutional funds. Applicants will be notified of awards on a rolling basis beginning 4/1. Federal Work-Study Program available. Institutional employment available.

The Inside Word

As one of the nation's top research universities, NC State maintains a competitive admissions process. Successful applicants take a rigorous courseload and often have a B-plus average or better. Admissions officers also closely weigh GPA, class rank and standardized test scores. Extracurricular activities are of secondary importance.

THE SCHOOL SAYS ". . ."

From the Admissions Office

"NC State is arguably the most popular university in the state, with more NC students seeking admission than at any other college or university. More than 20,000 students from across the nation seek one of the 4,250 available freshman spaces. Students choose NC State for its strong and varied academic programs, national reputation for excellence, low cost, location in Raleigh and the Research Triangle Park area, and very friendly atmosphere. Our students like the excitement of a large campus and the many opportunities it offers, such as Cooperative Education, Study Abroad, extensive honors programming, and theme residence halls. Each year, hundreds of NC State graduates are accepted into medical or law schools or other areas of advanced professional study. More corporate and government entities recruit graduates from NC State than from any other university in the United States."

SELECTIVITY

Admissions Rating	91
# of applicants	21,099
% of applicants accepted	50
% of acceptees attending	40
# offered a place on the wait list	2,433
% accepting a place on wait list	42
% admitted from wait list	2

FRESHMAN PROFILE

Range SAT Critical Reading	570–650
Range SAT Math	590–680
Range SAT Writing	540–630
Range ACT Composite	27–31
Minimum paper TOEFL	563
Minimum internet-based TOEFL	85
Average HS GPA	3.7
% graduated top 10% of class	51
% graduated top 25% of class	87
% graduated top 50% of class	99

DEADLINES

Early action	
Deadline	10/15
Notification	1/30
Regular	
Priority	10/15
Deadline	1/15
Nonfall registration?	Yes

APPLICANTS ALSO LOOK AT AND OFTEN PREFER

The University of North Carolina at Chapel Hill

FINANCIAL FACTS

Financial Aid Rating	85
Annual in-state tuition	$6,407
Annual out-of-state tuition	$23,926
Room and board	$10,635
Required fees	$2,473
Books and supplies	$1,082
Average frosh need-based scholarship	$10,186
Average UG need-based scholarship	$9,913
% needy frosh rec. need-based scholarship or grant aid	93
% needy UG rec. need-based scholarship or grant aid	90
% needy frosh rec. non-need-based scholarship or grant aid	21
% needy UG rec. non-need-based scholarship or grant aid	13
% needy frosh rec. need-based self-help aid	70
% needy UG rec. need-based self-help aid	72
% frosh rec. any financial aid	75
% UG rec. any financial aid	68
% UG borrow to pay for school	55
Average cumulative indebtedness	$17,461
% frosh need fully met	24
% ugrads need fully met	24
Average % of frosh need met	80
Average % of ugrad need met	78

NORTHEASTERN UNIVERSITY

360 HUNTINGTON AVENUE, BOSTON, MA 02115 • ADMISSIONS: 617-373-2200 • FAX: 617-373-8780

CAMPUS LIFE
Quality of Life Rating	94
Fire Safety Rating	94
Green Rating	95
Type of school	Private
Affiliation	No Affiliation
Environment	Metropolis

STUDENTS
Total undergrad enrollment	17,990
% male/female	50/50
% from out of state	70
% frosh live on campus	99
% ugrads live on campus	48
# of fraternities (% ugrad men join)	18 (8)
# of sororities (% ugrad women join)	14 (12)
% African American	4
% Asian	12
% Caucasian	49
% Hispanic	7
% Native American	<1
% Pacific Islander	<1
% Two or more races	4
% Race and/or ethnicity unknown	6
% international	19
# of countries represented	121

SURVEY SAYS...
Students are happy
Career services are great
Internships are widely available
Students love Boston, MA
Great off-campus food
Dorms are like palaces
Easy to get around campus
Recreation facilities are great

ACADEMICS
Academic Rating	83
% students returning for sophomore year	97
% students graduating within 4 years	0
% students graduating within 6 years	84
Calendar	Semester
Student/faculty ratio	14:1
Profs interesting rating	76
Profs accessible rating	75

Most classes have 10–19 students.
Most lab/discussion sessions have 10–19 students.

MOST POPULAR MAJORS
Engineering; Health Services; Business/Commerce

STUDENTS SAY "..."

Academics

Boston's Northeastern University is all about "experiential learning, a global outlook, high standard academics and the balance of success with a happy life." The major draw is the school's signature co-op program, where students spend up to three six- month periods working full time (usually for pay) while living in the residence halls and maintaining full-time student status. "In an uncertain economy, the world-class co-op program really gives students a leg up in finding a career," says a student. A strong honors program (members of which share living quarters in a specialized Living Learning Community) adds to the list of Northeastern's benefits. From "the first day that you are on campus, the school is asking how everything you're doing affects your resume," says a student.

The professors are often actually professionals in their field, so that students can "learn from firsthand accounts and experiences." They are "very research- oriented," and proponents of "using innovation and modern technology for the students' advantage." "My professors all come from a variety of backgrounds, have fascinating research projects, and love to teach," says a student. They "always organize extra lectures, speakers, and events for students who are really interested in the course."

Aside from the co-op program, the study abroad program, the "variety of majors and classes," the "elite classroom experience.," and the "great programs available for freshman" all draw applause. However, some students do wish that there was "less red-tape," as "a lot of things get lost in the 'Northeastern shuffle'." Still, there is good advising available and "everything is well-organized." "Northeastern University encourages learning through a creative and diverse environment that allows students to broaden their view on life and helps their transition into the working world." "What other school allows you to travel abroad for internships and multiple summers and semesters but still allows you to graduate on time?" asks a student.

Life

This "urban university with a campus feeling" has the city of Boston as its backyard, which "always has something for students of all ages to do." The location is "prime" and the public transport is easy; in fact, Northeastern has four separate subway stops. "It's safe and offers a wide variety of activities from night clubs to the theater to sports"; the Museum of Fine Arts is down the street, the Red Sox are around the block and for students of age, "Boston's best bars are down the corner."

"Here the focus is on academics, co-op, and student organizations." People do like to go out on occasion, but "since there aren't many parties at NU, they mostly go to BU, Harvard, and MIT." There is some Greek life at Northeastern (but no houses), and "different sororities and fraternities often interact together for various events like Homecoming." The student groups on campus put on "tons of events and programs," and people are "pretty into" the ever-present hockey and basketball games.

Student Body

Students at Northeastern are smart and here to learn. With so many people taking part in different co-ops and study abroad programs, it can be hard to pin down anything as "typical" at Northeastern, and "diversity is growing every year." "At any given time, around one third of students are working full time," which means that despite the very accepting student body, it can sometimes be "difficult to make friends as everyone is always coming and going." Unsurprisingly, people here are "hard-working and focused on making money as well as getting a job after graduation."

FINANCIAL AID: 617-373-3190 • E-MAIL: ADMISSIONS@NEU.EDU • WEBSITE: WWW.NORTHEASTERN.EDU/ADMISSIONS

THE PRINCETON REVIEW SAYS

Admissions

Very important factors considered include: rigor of secondary school record, academic GPA, standardized test scores, application essay, recommendation(s). *Important factors considered include:* extracurricular activities, talent/ability, character/personal qualities, volunteer work, work experience. *Other factors considered include:* class rank, interview, first generation, geographical residence, racial/ethnic status, level of applicant's interest. SAT or ACT required. ACT with or without writing accepted. SAT with or without Essay component accepted. TOEFL required of all international applicants. High school diploma is required and GED is accepted. *Academic units required:* 4 English, 3 math, 3 science, 2 science labs, 2 foreign language, 3 social studies, 2 history. *Academic units recommended:* 4 math, 4 science.

Financial Aid

Students should submit: FAFSA, CSS/Financial Aid PROFILE, Noncustodial PROFILE. Priority filing deadline is 2/15. The Princeton Review suggests that all financial aid forms be submitted as soon as possible after October 1. *Need-based scholarships/grants offered:* Federal Pell, FSEOG, State scholarships/grants, Private scholarships, College/university scholarship or grant aid from institutional funds. *Loan aid offered:* Direct Subsidized Stafford Loans, Direct Unsubsidized Stafford Loans, Direct PLUS loans, Federal Perkins Loans, Federal Nursing Loans, State Loans. Applicants will be notified of awards on or about 4/1. Federal Work-Study Program available. Institutional employment available.

The Inside Word

Applicants to Northeastern are evaluated based on their secondary school performance, with the difficulty of courses given emphasis, and you should go beyond minimum graduation requirements for high school to show broad intellectual curiosity. The committee recommends having strong standardized test scores.

THE SCHOOL SAYS " . . ."

From the Admissions Office

"There's a certain energy about Northeastern University. It comes from our bright, ambitious students, exhibiting a strong sense of purpose in the classroom and while working or studying abroad. In the heart of Boston—the ultimate college city—and across the globe, Northeastern students challenge themselves intellectually, investigate career options, participate in community service, and graduate both personally and professionally prepared for their future careers and graduate school. A Northeastern education is like no other, integrating rigorous classroom learning with real-world experiences—through opportunities to study, work, research, and serve on seven continents. Our students learn how to apply their knowledge, to solve problems, and to make a difference in the world—before they graduate."

SELECTIVITY

Admissions Rating	95
# of applicants	50,523
% of applicants accepted	28
% of acceptees attending	19
# of early decision applicants	773
% accepted early decision	31

FRESHMAN PROFILE

Range SAT Critical Reading	660–740
Range SAT Math	680–770
Range SAT Writing	640–730
Range ACT Composite	31–34
Minimum internet-based TOEFL	92
% graduated top 10% of class	70
% graduated top 25% of class	94
% graduated top 50% of class	99

DEADLINES

Early decision	
Deadline	11/1
Notification	12/15
Early action	
Deadline	11/1
Notification	12/31
Regular	
Deadline	1/1
Notification	4/1
Nonfall registration?	Yes

FINANCIAL FACTS

Financial Aid Rating	85
Annual tuition	$44,620
Room and board	$13,210
Required fees	$420
Average frosh need-based scholarship	$32,339
Average UG need-based scholarship	$25,281
% needy frosh rec. need-based scholarship or grant aid	98
% needy UG rec. need-based scholarship or grant aid	94
% needy frosh rec. non-need-based scholarship or grant aid	47
% needy UG rec. non-need-based scholarship or grant aid	35
% needy frosh rec. need-based self-help aid	89
% needy UG rec. need-based self-help aid	87
% frosh need fully met	100
% ugrads need fully met	37
Average % of frosh need met	100
Average % of ugrad need met	85

NORTHWESTERN UNIVERSITY

PO Box 3060, Evanston, IL 60208-3060 • Admissions: 847-491-7271

STUDENTS SAY "..."

Academics

"The strength of the school is its range." Northwestern students agree, vowing their school "has everything": "Intelligent but laid-back students, excel[lence] in academic fields," "great extracurriculars and good parties," "strong [Big Ten] sports spirit," and "so many connections and opportunities during and after graduation." Undergrads here brag of "nationally acclaimed programs for almost anything anyone could be interested in, from engineering to theater to journalism to music," and report "everything is given fairly equal weight. Northwestern students and faculty do not show a considerable bias" toward specific fields. The school accomplishes all this while maintaining a manageable scale. While its relatively small size allows for good student-professor interaction, it has "all the perks" of a big school, including "many opportunities" for research and internships. Be aware, however, "Northwestern is not an easy school. It takes hard work to be average here." If you "learn from your failures quickly and love to learn for the sake of learning rather than the grade," students say it is quite possible to stay afloat and even to excel. Helping matters are numerous resources established by administrators and professors, including tutoring programs such as Northwestern's Gateway Science Workshop. Those who take advantage of these opportunities find the going much easier than those who don't.

Life

There are two distinct sections of the Northwestern campus. The North Campus is where "you can find a party every night of the week" and "the Greek scene is strong." The South Campus, about a one-mile trek from the action to the north, is "more artsy and has minimal partying on weeknights," but is closer to town so "it is easy" to "buy dinner, see a show at the movies, and go shopping. People who live on North Campus have a harder time getting motivated to go into Evanston and tap into all that is offered." As one South Campus resident puts it, "South Campus is nice and quiet in its own way. I enjoy reading and watching movies here, and the quietude is appreciated when study time rolls around. But for more exciting fun, a trip north is a must." Regardless of where students live, extracurriculars are "incredible here. There is a group for every interest, and the groups are amazingly well-managed by students alone. This goes hand-in-hand with how passionate students at Northwestern are about what they love." Many students "are involved in plays, a cappella groups, comedy troupes, and other organizations geared toward the performing arts. Activism is also very popular, with many involved in political groups, human-rights activism, and volunteering." In addition, Northwestern's membership in the Big Ten means students "attend some of the best sporting events in the country." Chicago, of course, "is a wonderful resource. People go into the city for a wide variety of things—daily excursions, jobs, internships, nights out, parties, etc."

Student Body

The typical Northwestern student "was high school class president with a 4.0, swim team captain, and on the chess team." So it makes sense everyone here "is an excellent student who works hard" and "has a leadership position in at least two clubs, plus an on-campus job." Students also tell us "there's [a] great separation between North Campus (think: fraternities, engineering, state school mentality) and South Campus (think: closer to Chicago and its culture, arts and letters, liberal arts school mentality). Students segregate themselves depending on background and interests, and it's rare for these two groups to interact beyond a superficial level." The student body here includes sizeable Jewish, Indian, and East-Asian populations.

FINANCIAL AID: 847-491-7400 • E-MAIL: UG-ADMISSION@NORTHWESTERN.EDU • WEBSITE: WWW.NORTHWESTERN.EDU

THE PRINCETON REVIEW SAYS

Admissions

Very important factors considered include: rigor of secondary school record, class rank, academic GPA, standardized test scores. *Important factors considered include:* application essay, recommendation(s), extracurricular activities, talent/ability, character/personal qualities. *Other factors considered include:* interview, first generation, alumni/ae relation, racial/ethnic status, volunteer work, work experience, level of applicant's interest. SAT or ACT required; SAT Subject Tests recommend. ACT with Writing required. TOEFL required of all international applicants. High school diploma or equivalent is not required. *Academic units recommended:* 4 English, 3 math, 2 science, 2 science labs, 2 foreign language, 2 social studies, 2 history, 1 academic elective.

Financial Aid

Students should submit: FAFSA, CSS/Financial Aid PROFILE, Noncustodial PROFILE. Regular filing deadline is 3/5. The Princeton Review suggests that all financial aid forms be submitted as soon as possible after October 1. *Need-based scholarships/grants offered:* Federal Pell, FSEOG, State scholarships/grants, College/university scholarship or grant aid from institutional funds. *Loan aid offered:* Direct Subsidized Stafford Loans, Direct Unsubsidized Stafford Loans, Direct PLUS loans, Federal Perkins Loans, College/university loans from institutional funds. Applicants will be notified of awards on or about 4/15. Federal Work-Study Program available. Institutional employment available.

The Inside Word

Northwestern is among the nation's most expensive undergraduate institutions, a fact that dissuades some qualified students from applying. The school is working to attract more low-income applicants by increasing the number of full scholarships available for students whose family income is less than $45,000. Low-income students who score well on the ACT may receive a letter from the school encouraging them to apply. Even if you don't receive this letter, you should consider applying if you've got the goods—you may be pleasantly surprised by the offer you receive from the financial aid office.

THE SCHOOL SAYS ". . ."

From the Admissions Office

"Consistent with its dedication to excellence, Northwestern provides both an educational and an extracurricular environment that enables its undergraduate students to become accomplished individuals and informed and responsible citizens. To the students in all its undergraduate schools, Northwestern offers liberal learning and professional education to help them gain the depth of knowledge that will empower them to become leaders in their professions and communities. Furthermore, Northwestern fosters in its students a broad understanding of the world in which we live as well as excellence in the competencies that transcend any particular field of study: writing and oral communication, analytical and creative thinking and expression, and quantitative and qualitative methods of thinking.

"Applicants are required to take the SAT or the ACT with the writing section."

SELECTIVITY

Admissions Rating	98
# of applicants	32,122
% of applicants accepted	13
% of acceptees attending	48
# offered a place on the wait list	2,614
% accepting a place on wait list	55
% admitted from wait list	2
# of early decision applicants	3,102
% accepted early decision	35

FRESHMAN PROFILE

Range SAT Critical Reading	690–760
Range SAT Math	710–800
Range ACT Composite	31–34
% graduated top 10% of class	91
% graduated top 25% of class	100
% graduated top 50% of class	100

DEADLINES

Early decision	
Deadline	11/1
Notification	12/15
Regular	
Deadline	1/1
Notification	4/1
Nonfall registration?	Yes

APPLICANTS ALSO LOOK AT AND OFTEN PREFER

Yale University; Harvard College

AND SOMETIMES PREFER

Princeton University; Stanford University; University of Chicago

AND RARELY PREFER

DePaul University; Purdue University–West Lafayette; Marquette University

FINANCIAL FACTS

Financial Aid Rating	93
Annual tuition	$50,424
Room and board	$15,489
Required fees	$431
Books and supplies	$1,620
Average frosh need-based scholarship	$42,088
Average UG need-based scholarship	$40,208
% needy frosh rec. need-based scholarship or grant aid	98
% needy UG rec. need-based scholarship or grant aid	97
% needy frosh rec. non-need-based scholarship or grant aid	0
% needy UG rec. non-need-based scholarship or grant aid	0
% needy frosh rec. need-based self-help aid	75
% needy UG rec. need-based self-help aid	78
% frosh need fully met	100
% ugrads need fully met	100
Average % of frosh need met	100
Average % of ugrad need met	100

OBERLIN COLLEGE

101 NORTH PROFESSOR STREET, OBERLIN, OH 44074 • ADMISSIONS: 440-775-8411 • FAX: 440-775-6905

CAMPUS LIFE

Quality of Life Rating	86
Fire Safety Rating	78
Green Rating	98
Type of school	Private
Affiliation	No Affiliation
Environment	Rural

STUDENTS

Total undergrad enrollment	2,961
% male/female	45/55
% from out of state	92
% frosh from public high school	60
% frosh live on campus	100
% ugrads live on campus	77
% African American	5
% Asian	4
% Caucasian	70
% Hispanic	7
% Native American	<1
% Pacific Islander	<1
% Two or more races	6
% Race and/or ethnicity unknown	1
% international	7
# of countries represented	

SURVEY SAYS...

Students environmentally aware
Lots of liberal students
Students politically aware
Lab facilities are great
Great library
Students aren't religious
Easy to get around campus
Theater is popular
Active minority support groups

ACADEMICS

Academic Rating	93
% students returning for sophomore year	94
% students graduating within 4 years	76
% students graduating within 6 years	88
Calendar	4/1/4
Student/faculty ratio	8:1
Profs interesting rating	91
Profs accessible rating	87

Most classes have 10–19 students.
Most lab/discussion sessions have fewer than 10 students.

MOST POPULAR MAJORS
English; Biology; History

STUDENTS SAY "..."

Academics

Oberlin College, a school "for laid-back people who enjoy learning and expanding social norms, allows each and every student to have the undergrad experience for which he or she is looking, all the while challenging the students to change themselves and the world for the better." Oberlin is a place where students "focus on learning for learning's sake rather than making money in a career." As one student explains, "I didn't plan on becoming a scholar when I entered Oberlin....As fate would have it, I ended up loving my college classes and professors. Now I hope to be a professor of religion." At Oberlin, "academics are very highly valued, but balanced with a strong interest in the arts and a commitment to society." Some might suggest Oberlin puts the "liberal" in "liberal arts," and the school's staunchest supporters agree, stressing the school's emphasis on open-mindedness and the belief that "one person can change the world." Among the school's offerings, "the sciences, English, politics, religion, music, environmental studies, and East-Asian studies are particularly noteworthy." The presence of a prestigious music school imbues the entire campus community. One undergrad writes, "Oberlin's greatest strength is the combination of the college and the conservatory. They are not separated, so students mix with each other all the time." Professors here—the "heart and soul of the school"—are dedicated teachers who "treat you more like collaborators and realize that even with their PhDs, they can learn and grow from you, as well as you from them." They are "excellent instructors and fantastic people" who are "focused on learning instead of deadlines." Undergrads also appreciate "a cooperative learning environment" in which "students bond over studying together for difficult exams."

Life

Life during the week at Oberlin can be "pretty bland," as "almost everyone has to crack the books and study it up." It's not always bland, though. Some here manage to find time for the many "events [going on] each weekend—operas, plays, organ pumps, etc.," or "rally to stage to help the oppressed." Thursday afternoons at Oberlin mean "Classical Thursdays," an event during which "you get free beer from the college if you bring a professor to the on-campus pub." Another feature of campus life is "the musical scene, which has its heart in the conservatory. All of the other arts—performing, studio, whatever—are intertwined with the talent in the conservatory." On weekends, "people let loose and drink beer. Not everyone does this every weekend. Some don't do it at all," and "there is absolutely no pressure on those who don't." There are also "tons of student-produced social events like parties, fundraisers, concerts, dances, etc.," keeping students "very connected to each other and to what's going on in the community." Hometown Oberlin "is a small town, and about all there is to do there is go out for pizza or Chinese, see a movie for two or three dollars at the Apollo, or go to the Feve, the bar in town."

Student Body

"If you're a liberal, artsy, indie loner who likes to throw around the phrase 'heteronormative white privilege,'" then Oberlin might be the place for you. "We're like the Island of Misfit Toys, but together we make a great toy chest." "We're all different and unusual, which creates a common bond between students." "Musicians, jocks, science geeks, creative writing majors, straight, bi, questioning, queer, and trans [students]," all have their place here, alongside "straight-edge, international, local, and joker students." Oberlin has a reputation for a left-leaning and active student body. One undergrad observes, "They are less active politically than they would like to think, but still more active than most people elsewhere." Another adds, "Most students are very liberal, but the moderates and (few) Republicans have a fine time of it. Every student has different interests and isn't afraid to talk about them." Some here worry, "Oberlin's student body is becoming more and more mainstream each year."

FINANCIAL AID: 440-775-8142 • E-MAIL: COLLEGE.ADMISSIONS@OBERLIN.EDU • WEBSITE: WWW.OBERLIN.EDU

THE PRINCETON REVIEW SAYS

Admissions

Very important factors considered include: rigor of secondary school record, class rank, academic GPA, standardized test scores. *Important factors considered include:* application essay, recommendation(s), extracurricular activities, talent/ability, character/personal qualities, first generation. *Other factors considered include:* interview, alumni/ae relation, racial/ethnic status, volunteer work, work experience, level of applicant's interest. SAT or ACT required. ACT with Writing recommended. TOEFL required of all international applicants. High school diploma is required and GED is accepted. *Academic units required:* 4 English, 3 math, 3 science, 3 foreign language, 3 social studies. *Academic units recommended:* 4 math, 4 science.

Financial Aid

Students should submit: FAFSA, Institution's own financial aid form, CSS/Financial Aid PROFILE, Noncustodial PROFILE. Regular filing deadline is 2/15. The Princeton Review suggests that all financial aid forms be submitted as soon as possible after October 1. *Need-based scholarships/grants offered:* Federal Pell, FSEOG, State scholarships/grants, Private scholarships, College/university scholarship or grant aid from institutional funds, United Negro College Fund. *Loan aid offered:* Direct Subsidized Stafford Loans, Direct Unsubsidized Stafford Loans, Federal Perkins Loans, College/university loans from institutional funds. Applicants will be notified of awards on or about 4/1. Federal Work-Study Program available. Institutional employment available.

The Inside Word

Oberlin's music conservatory is one of the most elite programs in the nation. Aspiring music students should expect stiff competition for one of the 600 available slots. Other applicants won't have a much easier time of it. Oberlin is a highly selective institution that attracts a highly competitive applicant pool. Your personal statement could be the make-or-break factor here.

THE SCHOOL SAYS "..."

From the Admissions Office

"Oberlin College, located in northeast Ohio, is a liberal arts college of intense energy and creativity, built on a foundation of academic, artistic, and musical excellence. The only institution in the United States where a top-ranked liberal arts college and a world-renowned conservatory of music share a seamless student culture and campus, Oberlin also boasts an art museum that is known as one of the best in the country. Noted for its sustainability initiatives and achievements, Oberlin has been recognized as one of the 'greenest' institutions in the USA and continues to challenge itself and its students to find better and more efficient ways to be environmentally responsible. Oberlin's flexible curriculum honors the individual and prepares students to tackle the complex challenges that face our planet and society. In fact, the majority of Oberlin's 2900 students continue on to prestigious fellowships and PhD programs. Oberlin has been on the front lines of changing the world for almost two centuries, often serving as the prototype for progress even in the face of strong resistance, beginning with its admission of students of color in 1835—the first in the nation to adopt this practice as policy. With its longstanding commitments to access, diversity, and inclusion, and with limitless opportunities for scholarly and cultural exploration, Oberlin is the ideal laboratory in which to debate, study, and grow."

SELECTIVITY

Admissions Rating	95
# of applicants	7,227
% of applicants accepted	33
% of acceptees attending	34
# of early decision applicants	431
% accepted early decision	62

FRESHMAN PROFILE

Range SAT Critical Reading	640–730
Range SAT Math	620–720
Range SAT Writing	640–730
Range ACT Composite	28–32
Minimum paper TOEFL	600
Average HS GPA	3.6
% graduated top 10% of class	61
% graduated top 25% of class	91
% graduated top 50% of class	100

DEADLINES

Early decision	
Deadline	11/15
Notification	12/15
Regular	
Deadline	1/15
Notification	4/1
Nonfall registration?	No

APPLICANTS ALSO LOOK AT AND OFTEN PREFER

Swarthmore College; Brown University; Wesleyan University; Yale University; Stanford University

AND SOMETIMES PREFER

Vassar College; Williams College; Grinnell College; Carleton College; Macalester College; Northwestern University

AND RARELY PREFER

Connecticut College

FINANCIAL FACTS

Financial Aid Rating	95
Annual tuition	$49,928
Room and board	$13,630
Required fees	$636
Books and supplies	$930
Average frosh need-based scholarship	$33,248
Average UG need-based scholarship	$31,071
% needy frosh rec. need-based scholarship or grant aid	96
% needy UG rec. need-based scholarship or grant aid	99
% needy frosh rec. non-need-based scholarship or grant aid	81
% needy UG rec. non-need-based scholarship or grant aid	73
% needy frosh rec. need-based self-help aid	79
% needy UG rec. need-based self-help aid	89
% frosh rec. any financial aid	61
% UG rec. any financial aid	60
% frosh need fully met	100
% ugrads need fully met	100
Average % of frosh need met	100
Average % of ugrad need met	100

OCCIDENTAL COLLEGE

1600 CAMPUS ROAD, LOS ANGELES, CA 90041-3314 • ADMISSIONS: 323-259-2700 • FAX: 323-341-4875

CAMPUS LIFE

Quality of Life Rating	91
Fire Safety Rating	81
Green Rating	90
Type of school	Private
Affiliation	No Affiliation
Environment	Metropolis

STUDENTS

Total undergrad enrollment	2,112
% male/female	43/57
% from out of state	52
% frosh from public high school	60
% frosh live on campus	100
% ugrads live on campus	82
# of fraternities (% ugrad men join)	4 (12)
# of sororities (% ugrad women join)	4 (21)
% African American	5
% Asian	13
% Caucasian	49
% Hispanic	15
% Native American	<1
% Pacific Islander	<1
% Two or more races	9
% Race and/or ethnicity unknown	2
% international	5
# of countries represented	28

SURVEY SAYS...

Lots of liberal students
Students are happy
Students are friendly
Students aren't religious
Students environmentally aware
Great food on campus
Great off-campus food
Campus newspaper is popular

ACADEMICS

Academic Rating	91
% students returning for sophomore year	93
% students graduating within 4 years	82
Calendar	Semester
Student/faculty ratio	10:1
Profs interesting rating	90
Profs accessible rating	89

Most classes have 10–19 students.
Most lab/discussion sessions have
10–19 students.

MOST POPULAR MAJORS

Economics; International Relations and
Affairs; Biology

STUDENTS SAY "..."

Academics

An "intellectual, accepting, beautiful" liberal arts college in northeast Los Angeles, Occidental is "perfect for hard-working and involved students who not only want to be challenged academically, but also want to be pushed to learn more about the world around them." At this small school, classes are "intellectually stimulating," spearheaded by professors who "encourage critical analysis, ask interesting questions, and allow students to create informed opinions about the subject." The faculty and staff "really encourage students to take a proactive role in their education," giving them the freedom to "experiment with a wide range of courses." A current undergrad enthuses, "I love the interdisciplinary aspect of academics. I can really tailor my coursework to what I am interested in." In the classroom, Oxy professors "find ways to connect the lectures to the real world," and many are "very willing to have students help them with their research," providing valuable hands-on experience to undergraduates. Students further augment their coursework through numerous extracurricular and off-campus opportunities, including study abroad, academic conferences, and the school's popular "UN internship program." "Courses are challenging," but Oxy "professors want to see you succeed," and the favorably low student-to-faculty ratio means "there are plenty of opportunities to get extra help on the tough material." In fact, most professors "go the extra mile to make themselves available" and "are invested in cultivating real relationships with students."

Life

"People are really passionate about their extracurricular activities and internships"·at Occidental, where most students are "busy from dawn to dusk, and loving it." Clubs and intramural sports, "from quidditch to women's rugby," are popular across campus, and "Greek life is getting bigger and bigger every year." On campus, "there are frequently guest speakers, dialogues, and workshops," and on the weekends, the school organizes "dances, trivia nights, movie screenings, fashion shows, concerts, food tastings, beer gardens, and many other events." When it comes to parties, the alcohol policy is "strict" (even students of legal age are "forbidden from drinking in their dorms"), so most campus get-togethers are small and subdued. Off campus, "house parties are a huge source of fun on the weekends," as are "music shows, bars, and clubs" in surrounding L.A. When they don't have anything planned, students "listen to and make music, watch movies, have impromptu dance parties, and do wacky things." You can't beat having the "intimacy of a small college with Los Angeles as your backyard," and students love the fact that Oxy is "not isolated from the surrounding community like many other college campuses." In their free time, many take advantage of the Southern California setting to "go to the beach, go shopping in L.A., go out to eat in Eagle Rock, [and] go hiking." "Having a car definitely helps" if you want to explore the surrounding city, though "the school has a 'Bengal Bus' system that provides free rides to areas close to campus."

Students

Oxy students are "well rounded," "socially and politically conscious," and "excited to be at Occidental." Though they take academics seriously, "people at Oxy are concerned with much, much more than their education. They are focused on academically succeeding, sure, but they are also concerned with social issues, identity, meeting new people, having fun, and gathering a variety of other skills to help them succeed in life outside of Oxy." Many note the "overwhelmingly left-wing atmosphere" on campus, admitting that the people and their viewpoints can feel a little "homogeneous" at times. However, "every student at Oxy treats all persons equally, regardless of sexual orientation, gender identity, or religious views," and most are readily "accepting of different opinions." With such a tiny enrollment, it's easy to find "a good niche of close friends at Oxy," and "if you're involved on campus, expect your friend group to continually grow." Despite the rigors of the academic program, "there is a communal desire to help each other succeed."

FINANCIAL AID: 323-259-2548 • E-MAIL: ADMISSION@OXY.EDU • WEBSITE: WWW.OXY.EDU

THE PRINCETON REVIEW SAYS

Admissions

Very important factors considered include: rigor of secondary school record, academic GPA, application essay, recommendation(s). *Important factors considered include:* class rank, standardized test scores, extracurricular activities, character/personal qualities, volunteer work, work experience. *Other factors considered include:* interview, talent/ability, first generation, alumni/ae relation, geographical residence, racial/ethnic status, level of applicant's interest. SAT or ACT required. ACT with Writing recommended. SAT with Essay component recommended. TOEFL required of all international applicants. High school diploma is required and GED is accepted. *Academic units recommended:* 4 English, 3 math, 3 science, 3 foreign language, 2 social studies, 3 history.

Financial Aid

Students should submit: FAFSA, CSS/Financial Aid PROFILE, State aid form, Noncustodial PROFILE. Regular filing deadline is 2/1. The Princeton Review suggests that all financial aid forms be submitted as soon as possible after October 1. *Need-based scholarships/grants offered:* Federal Pell, FSEOG, State scholarships/grants, Private scholarships, College/university scholarship or grant aid from institutional funds. *Loan aid offered:* Direct Subsidized Stafford Loans, Direct Unsubsidized Stafford Loans, Direct PLUS loans, Federal Perkins Loans, College/university loans from institutional funds. Applicants will be notified of awards on or about 4/1. Federal Work-Study Program available. Institutional employment available.

The Inside Word

The admissions team at Occidental does not use any minimums or formulas when evaluating an applicant's eligibility for the incoming class. In addition to academic achievement, they place a lot of weight on essays and recommendations in their mission to create a diverse incoming class. A demanding course load in high school is essential for competitive candidates, but successful applicants will also show what makes them unique, from volunteer experiences to artistic talent.

THE SCHOOL SAYS "..."

From the Admissions Office

"Here's what our students tell us:

'The professors have all been just amazing. They're all very willing to coordinate times to meet and discuss how you feel about a class and what you want to get out of it.'

'I realize the caliber of discussion that occurs at Oxy is not easily matched. I've developed very strong relationships with many professors, and that's something I believe is unique to Oxy.'

'The program has been awesome. Whether you want to go to med school or grad school, it's a great experience. The professors really want you to succeed.'

'I've been working with postdoctoral researchers as an undergraduate. It's very rewarding. Oxy challenges me both inside and outside the classroom.'

'Occidental opened my eyes to different beliefs, values, and ideas. Discussions in class are much more interesting, because you consider things you might not have thought about before.'

'Oxy's close-knit community and its size make me feel this is a place I can call home.'

'Oxy instills curiosity and makes students want to go out and learn a subject on their own. I've gotten a broader sense of self and have been able to fulfill my learning goals.'

"Occidental requires all applicants (including international students) to take either the SAT or ACT with the writing component. SAT Subject Tests are recommended but not required."

SELECTIVITY

Admissions Rating	92
# of applicants	5,911
% of applicants accepted	45
% of acceptees attending	20
# offered a place on the wait list	705
% accepting a place on wait list	51
% admitted from wait list	7
# of early decision applicants	255
% accepted early decision	41

FRESHMAN PROFILE

Range SAT Critical Reading	600–690
Range SAT Math	600–690
Range SAT Writing	605–690
Range ACT Composite	28–31
Minimum paper TOEFL	600
Average HS GPA	3.6
% graduated top 10% of class	55
% graduated top 25% of class	90
% graduated top 50% of class	99

DEADLINES

Early decision	
Deadline	11/15
Notification	12/15
Regular	
Deadline	1/15
Notification	3/25
Nonfall registration?	No

APPLICANTS ALSO LOOK AT AND OFTEN PREFER

University of California–Berkeley; University of California–Los Angeles; University of Southern California

AND SOMETIMES PREFER

Claremont McKenna College

FINANCIAL FACTS

Financial Aid Rating	95
Annual tuition	$48,690
Room and board	$13,946
Required fees	$558
Books and supplies	$1,244
Average frosh need-based scholarship	$37,998
Average UG need-based scholarship	$35,814
% needy frosh rec. need-based scholarship or grant aid	90
% needy UG rec. need-based scholarship or grant aid	91
% needy frosh rec. non-need-based scholarship or grant aid	32
% needy UG rec. non-need-based scholarship or grant aid	35
% needy frosh rec. need-based self-help aid	86
% needy UG rec. need-based self-help aid	85
% frosh rec. any financial aid	72
% UG rec. any financial aid	74
% UG borrow to pay for school	55
Average cumulative indebtedness	$29,947
% frosh need fully met	100
% ugrads need fully met	99
Average % of frosh need met	100
Average % of ugrad need met	100

OHIO NORTHERN UNIVERSITY

525 SOUTH MAIN STREET, ADA, OH 45810 • ADMISSIONS: 419-772-2260 • FAX: 419-772-2821

STUDENTS SAY "..."

Academics

Many students are attracted to Ohio Northern University's "prestigious" Raabe College of Pharmacy, a "six-year program" that "is focused on developing the next generation of clinical pharmacists who are well rounded leaders, clinicians, and members of society." But this comprehensive university offers its 2,900 students lots of other outstanding academic options: "The accounting program is highly ranked," "it has a great political science program that has sent many students to graduate school and politics," and "the engineering college is great." An ONU education provides practical applications for knowledge as well as theoretical ones, with a "wonderful incorporation of current events and timeless business principles." Students are also drawn to ONU's "good financial aid" and "varsity sports," with one athlete noting that ONU "was my most affordable option of Division III schools where I could play soccer and receive a quality education." Undergrads feel that their "renowned faculty" "are outstanding and all influential in the field," but also that their "professors are very friendly and down to earth" and that they "are real and treat students like people not as if they are beneath them, so it is easier to understand material." In addition to academic performance, "professors care about the student's well-being and future endeavors" and "they are always available to help." "It's great that even though there are 170-plus senior pharmacy majors, the professors still know my name." ONU's "classes are tough, no doubt about it," but "my overall academic experience has been above and beyond anything I could've expected." As a whole, students call ONU "a top-notch education with a family-like atmosphere that is very conducive for learning and excelling in many disciplines."

Life

ONU's hometown of Ada, OH, is a "small town," but one with "good places to eat and a movie theatre." There's also a "big town," Columbus, "fifteen minutes away with a lot of attractions so always something to do if you have the time to drive." "Because we are in a small town, the students bond together to find fun things to do," including D3 athletics and "pick-up sports games," "fraternity house parties and local bars (The Regal Beagle and The Cask Room)," as well as "several university-sponsored events throughout the year." Socializing and academics mix freely: "People love hanging out with each other, especially when they are trying to get things done." Social life can be a "mixed bag" of "students who spend all of their time focused on school" and "a good number of students who enjoy having a good time and hanging out with friends"; still "people here are very relaxed—you do what you want and everyone is fine with you being who you are." "Students usually party on the weekends," but "hard drugs are rare." Dorm life is also popular: "It's easy to have fun in the dorms, especially during winter."

Student Body

As you might expect, "in a small town, students must get along because there are high chances they will see one another again," so at ONU, "everyone is very caring toward each other." The typical ONU student "is committed to academics, to service, and has leadership potential," and students appreciate that "everyone here finds a supportive group of friends." Many students are Midwestern and "some denomination of Christian," with a majority of ONU's population hailing from "in-state, some surrounding states and internationals." Students see themselves as involved and conscientious: ONU students often belong to "several clubs and organizations," are "always willing to help or mentor younger students, and very concerned about academic success." One undergrad offers this bit of advice: "Most students are friends with other people in the same activities that they're involved in, so join something you're interested in and don't be shy!"

OHIO NORTHERN UNIVERSITY

FINANCIAL AID: 419-772-2272 • E-MAIL: ADMISSIONS-UG@ONU.EDU • WEBSITE: WWW.ONU.EDU

THE PRINCETON REVIEW SAYS

Admissions

Very important factors considered include: rigor of secondary school record, academic GPA, standardized test scores. *Important factors considered include:* class rank, application essay, recommendation(s), interview, extracurricular activities. *Other factors considered include:* talent/ability, character/personal qualities, first generation, alumni/ae relation, volunteer work, level of applicant's interest. SAT or ACT required. ACT with or without writing accepted. TOEFL required of all international applicants. High school diploma is required and GED is accepted. *Academic units required:* 4 English, 2 math, 2 science, 2 science labs, 2 social studies, 2 history, 4 academic electives. *Academic units recommended:* 4 English, 4 math, 3 science, 2 science labs, 2 foreign language, 3 social studies, 2 history, 4 academic electives, 1 computer science, 1 visual/performing arts.

Financial Aid

Students should submit: FAFSA. Priority filing deadline is 4/15. The Princeton Review suggests that all financial aid forms be submitted as soon as possible after October 1. *Need-based scholarships/grants offered:* Federal Pell, FSEOG, State scholarships/grants, Private scholarships, College/university scholarship or grant aid from institutional funds. *Loan aid offered:* Direct Subsidized Stafford Loans, Direct Unsubsidized Stafford Loans, Direct PLUS loans, Federal Perkins Loans, State Loans, College/university loans from institutional funds. Applicants will be notified of awards on a rolling basis beginning 3/1. Federal Work-Study Program available. Institutional employment available.

The Inside Word

ONU's well-regarded pharmacy school is without question the most competitive of the university's program, and has a Dec. 1 application deadline; Arts & Sciences, Business, and Engineering students may apply on a rolling basis. Strong high school transcripts and standardized test scores will assist any application, and particularly those seeking merit-based financial aid. Applicants are evaluated holistically, so in addition to GPAs and test scores, admissions counselors will also consider high school leadership and community service activities.

THE SCHOOL SAYS "..."

From the Admissions Office

"The purpose of Ohio Northern is to help students develop into self-reliant, mature men and women capable of clear and logical thinking and sensitive to the higher values of truth, beauty, and goodness. ONU selects its student body from among those students possessing characteristics congruent with the institution's objectives. Generally, a student must be prepared to use the resources of the institution to achieve personal and educational goals.

"Students applying for admission are urged to submit scores for the SAT or the ACT with the writing section. The student's best composite scores will be used for scholarship purposes.

"The Office of Admissions highly encourages a campus visit. To schedule a visit, please visit www.onu.edu/admissions/visit_us or call 888-408-4668."

SELECTIVITY	
Admissions Rating	84
# of applicants	3,337
% of applicants accepted	69
% of acceptees attending	27

FRESHMAN PROFILE	
Range SAT Critical Reading	520–620
Range SAT Math	530–650
Range SAT Writing	510–600
Range ACT Composite	23–29
Minimum paper TOEFL	480
Minimum internet-based TOEFL	54
Average HS GPA	3.7
% graduated top 10% of class	35
% graduated top 25% of class	62
% graduated top 50% of class	90

DEADLINES	
Regular	
Priority	12/1
Deadline	8/15
Nonfall registration?	Yes

APPLICANTS ALSO LOOK AT AND SOMETIMES PREFER
Miami University; Wittenberg University; The Ohio State University–Columbus

FINANCIAL FACTS	
Financial Aid Rating	63
Annual tuition	$27,500
Room and board	$10,910
Required fees	$550
Books and supplies	$1,800
% needy frosh rec. need-based scholarship or grant aid	0
% needy UG rec. need-based scholarship or grant aid	0
% needy frosh rec. non-need-based scholarship or grant aid	0
% needy UG rec. non-need-based scholarship or grant aid	0
% needy frosh rec. need-based self-help aid	0
% needy UG rec. need-based self-help aid	0

THE BEST 381 COLLEGES ■ 419

THE OHIO STATE UNIVERSITY—COLUMBUS

STUDENT ACADEMIC SVCS. BLDG. 281 WEST LANE AVE., COLUMBUS, OH 43210 • ADMISSIONS: 614-292-3980 • FAX: 614-292-4818

CAMPUS LIFE

Quality of Life Rating	89
Fire Safety Rating	60*
Green Rating	96
Type of school	Public
Affiliation	No Affiliation
Environment	Metropolis

STUDENTS

Total undergrad enrollment	45,289
% male/female	52/48
% from out of state	17
% frosh from public high school	85
% frosh live on campus	94
% ugrads live on campus	26
# of fraternities	42
# of sororities	25
% African American	6
% Asian	6
% Caucasian	71
% Hispanic	4
% Native American	<1
% Pacific Islander	<1
% Two or more races	3
% Race and/or ethnicity unknown	3
% international	7
# of countries represented	112

SURVEY SAYS...

Students are happy
Great library
Career services are great
School is well run
Students love Columbus, OH
Great food on campus
Recreation facilities are great
Lots of beer drinking
Everyone loves the Buckeyes
Alumni active on campus

ACADEMICS

Academic Rating	75
% students returning for sophomore year	94
% students graduating within 4 years	59
% students graduating within 6 years	83
Calendar	Semester
Student/faculty ratio	19:1
Profs interesting rating	74
Profs accessible rating	77

Most classes have 20–29 students.
Most lab/discussion sessions have 20–29 students.

MOST POPULAR MAJORS
Psychology; Finance; Communication

STUDENTS SAY " . . ."

Academics

Opportunities abound at The Ohio State University in Columbus, Ohio. Located "in a growing city," OSU has the distinction of being one of the largest schools in the United States. The "amazing opportunities" that come from such a large campus extend beyond the classrooms, "both academically and socially." "Everywhere you turn, there are always new and exciting things to be doing and learning." But the school's above-average size should not intimidate students. "OSU has a great way of breaking down the large school into much smaller communities." Established in 1870, "Ohio State has traditions like [nowhere] else. The feeling you get by being a Buckeye is truly one of a kind." What makes OSU special is how it "combines the love of tradition with the excellence of modern facilities and technology." "Ohio State really wants to offer students the most it can, including providing some state-of-the-art facilities and unique opportunities on campus to engage in the community. The school is very committed to bringing Ohio State students into the world as educated individuals." Students have many decisions to make when choosing from all the "very prestigious majors and classes" available. Student opinions about professors vary. One student says, "Some are better than others." Another is more enthusiastic about the faculty: "My academic experience has been great! I have admired and become very close to many professors, and I feel as though I have taken something away from every class I have taken." Overall, most students feel they "can learn a great deal here and take away an abundance of knowledge." Although "some of the big lectures are hard to keep up with…there is always free tutoring to help students get caught up."

Life

"Ohio State is a sports fan's paradise. [The] campus is bursting with Buckeye spirit, and it's infectious." "There may not be another school in the country that is as excited, spirited, and proud of literally everything they do like Ohio State is." "Not only do students love attending games, but we also have so many intramural sports that students get involved in for fun. You really never need to leave campus because there is always something fun happening." Plus, "there is a large city to explore as well. People who love sports, theater, and the arts will never run out of activities." Taking advantage of these options is easy because "students ride the city bus for free." Still, students feel the need to be careful and are concerned about "on and off campus safety." For some, the sheer number of choices can be overwhelming. "There are so many opportunities that it is easy to get lost in everything you feel you should be doing." Another student wonders if the school is doing its best to get messages out to everyone. "There have been occasions where things are not communicated to the entire student body as a whole, most likely due to the large student population. Sometimes I feel like I miss out on interesting and exciting things because I just wasn't made aware it was available." One student strongly recommends a visit to the school before you apply: "You will know as soon as you step on campus if it's the perfect fit for you!"

Student Body

Many students had good things to say about how the large amount of diversity positively affects life on campus. "Students here are open to different types of people—there is little or no discrimination. Diversity is valued here." "We have people from all different backgrounds, all different ethnicities. Students embrace the diversity and learn about new cultures and meet new people!" Somehow, Ohio State manages to bring everyone together. "The one common thing that seems to unite [us] is the love for our institution. Not everyone is a sports fan, but everyone bleeds scarlet and gray about something on this campus, whether it be sports, their research, or their classes." While at Ohio State, many students take advantage of the vast opportunity to travel to further broaden their world knowledge. "Studying abroad is something a lot of students do to learn more about other types of people, but there are also students here from so many places that a student can learn a lot by just making friends from different geographical areas."

THE OHIO STATE UNIVERSITY—COLUMBUS

FINANCIAL AID: 614-292-0300 • E-MAIL: ASKABUCKEYE@OSU.EDU • WEBSITE: WWW.OSU.EDU

THE PRINCETON REVIEW SAYS

Admissions

Factors considered include: rigor of secondary school record, class rank, academic GPA, standardized test scores, application essay, extracurricular activities, talent/ability, first generation, volunteer work, work experience, recommendation(s), character/personal qualities, geographical residence, state residency, racial/ethnic status. SAT or ACT required. ACT with or without writing accepted. SAT with or without Essay component accepted. TOEFL required of all international applicants. High school diploma is required and GED is accepted. *Academic units required:* 4 English, 3 math, 3 science, 3 science labs, 2 foreign language, 2 social studies, 1 academic elective, 1 visual/performing arts. *Academic units recommended:* 4 English, 4 math, 3 science, 3 science labs, 3 foreign language, 3 social studies, 1 academic elective, 1 visual/performing arts.

Financial Aid

Students should submit: FAFSA. Priority filing deadline is 2/1. The Princeton Review suggests that all financial aid forms be submitted as soon as possible after October 1. *Need-based scholarships/grants offered:* Federal Pell, FSEOG, State scholarships/grants, Private scholarships, College/university scholarship or grant aid from institutional funds. *Loan aid offered:* Direct Subsidized Stafford Loans, Direct Unsubsidized Stafford Loans, Direct PLUS loans, Federal Perkins Loans, Federal Nursing Loans, State Loans, College/university loans from institutional funds. Applicants will be notified of awards by late Feb. Federal Work-Study Program available. Institutional employment available.

The Inside Word

Standards are high at OSU, which attracts a huge number of applicants. But OSU is still worth a shot for the average student. Applications are reviewed with an eye for more than just grades and class rank, and the university's great reputation and affordable cost make it a good choice for anyone looking at large schools.

THE SCHOOL SAYS "..."

From the Admissions Office

"How will you make your mark? More importantly: Where's the best environment to get started? Ohio State has the breadth and depth to take you wherever your goals lead, an environment rich in experiences and unexpected opportunities. It's a leading public institution for research with study abroad programs in over fifty countries. You'll be in contact with world-class faculty, studying in world-class facilities, living in a smart and thriving city. Ohio State students who've made their mark say it's because they went to Ohio State. We're looking to add the best and brightest to make their mark in this year's class. Will it be you?"

SELECTIVITY
Admissions Rating	91
# of applicants	40,240
% of applicants accepted	49
% of acceptees attending	30
# offered a place on the wait list	1,556
% accepting a place on wait list	20
% admitted from wait list	100

FRESHMAN PROFILE
Range SAT Critical Reading	560–670
Range SAT Math	610–720
Range SAT Writing	560–660
Range ACT Composite	27–31
Minimum paper TOEFL	550
Minimum internet-based TOEFL	79
% graduated top 10% of class	62
% graduated top 25% of class	95
% graduated top 50% of class	99

DEADLINES
Early action	
Deadline	1/11
Regular	
Deadline	2/1
Notification	3/31
Nonfall registration?	Yes

APPLICANTS ALSO LOOK AT AND OFTEN PREFER
University of Michigan–Ann Arbor; Northwestern University; University of Wisconsin–Madison; University of Notre Dame

AND SOMETIMES PREFER
Miami University; University of Cincinnati; Case Western Reserve University

AND RARELY PREFER
Ohio University–Athens; University of Dayton

FINANCIAL FACTS
Financial Aid Rating	82
Annual in-state tuition	$$10,037
Annual out-of-state tuition	$27,365
Room and board	$11,666
Books and supplies	$1,234
Average frosh need-based scholarship	$11,071
Average UG need-based scholarship	$9,633
% needy frosh rec. need-based scholarship or grant aid	90
% needy UG rec. need-based scholarship or grant aid	83
% needy frosh rec. non-need-based scholarship or grant aid	9
% needy UG rec. non-need-based scholarship or grant aid	5
% needy frosh rec. need-based self-help aid	77
% needy UG rec. need-based self-help aid	87
% frosh rec. any financial aid	89
% UG rec. any financial aid	79
% UG borrow to pay for school	55
Average cumulative indebtedness	$27,400
% frosh need fully met	29
% ugrads need fully met	19
Average % of frosh need met	74
Average % of ugrad need met	68

OHIO UNIVERSITY—ATHENS

CHUBB HALL 120, 1 OHIO UNIVERSITY, ATHENS, OH 45701 • ADMISSIONS: 740-593-4100 • FAX: 740-593-0560

CAMPUS LIFE

Quality of Life Rating	80
Fire Safety Rating	86
Green Rating	94
Type of school	Public
Affiliation	No Affiliation
Environment	Village

STUDENTS

Total undergrad enrollment	23,513
% male/female	41/59
% from out of state	15
% frosh from public high school	83
% frosh live on campus	96
% ugrads live on campus	46
# of fraternities (% ugrad men join)	19 (8)
# of sororities (% ugrad women join)	12 (11)
% African American	5
% Asian	1
% Caucasian	83
% Hispanic	3
% Native American	<1
% Pacific Islander	<1
% Two or more races	3
% Race and/or ethnicity unknown	1
% international	3
# of countries represented	78

SURVEY SAYS...

Students politically aware
Recreation facilities are great
Students are friendly
Students are happy
Lots of beer drinking
Hard liquor is popular

ACADEMICS

Academic Rating	69
% students returning for sophomore year	79
% students graduating within 4 years	48
% students graduating within 6 years	67
Calendar	Trimester
Student/faculty ratio	18:1
Profs interesting rating	67
Profs accessible rating	66

Most classes have 20–29 students.
Most lab/discussion sessions have 10–19 students.

MOST POPULAR MAJORS

Speech Communication and Rhetoric; Journalism; Psychology

STUDENTS SAY ". . ."

Academics

"Academically, OHIO has something for everyone, from astrophysics to the history of rock and roll," students at this large state-run university boast. And students have an equally wide range of choices when it comes to committing themselves to academics; "You can take advantage of the vast amount of knowledge and resources directly available, or you can forget studies and party," students tell us. Those seeking a challenge will have no trouble finding it here, however; OHIO boasts "a strong engineering faculty," a noteworthy aviation program offered within the university's demanding college of engineering and technology, an "excellent and very selective early childhood education program," and "one of the best journalism schools in the country"—the E.W. Scripps School of Journalism—which offers "frequent opportunities to learn and grow outside the classroom with guest speakers and special events." The Scripps College houses "a great communications school" offering great hands-on experience; one student informs us that "Southeast Ohio depends on our college television and radio station for their news, weather, and high school sports." As at any large university, unassertive students are in danger of getting lost in the crowd, but those who make the effort to seek out faculty and administrators assure us that "the school is very supportive of the students. I have close relationships with multiple professors, and I think that they generally take a strong interest in the students."

Life

"Ohio University has a beautiful campus with lots of character, both in academia and nightlife," students here report. Though many students remain independent, Greek organizations play a major role in the life of the campus, providing service to the community and serving as a social catalyst. Some undergraduates assure us that the school "truly lives up to its reputation as a party school. It is never hard to find a party on any given night, whether in the dorms or off campus." One undergrad writes, "A nationwide reputation as a party school is not something I'm proud of," but most accept things as they are, noting that "Ohio University is a school where everyone can find a group of people doing whatever they're particularly interested in," which is to say that partying is hardly the only option here. College athletics are a big draw (especially football, men's basketball, and women's volleyball), as are such annual events as Homecoming and the school is host to literally hundreds of student clubs and organizations serving interests of every variety. Hometown Athens is a typical small college town with access to a wide variety of outdoor activities. The closest cities of note—Columbus, Ohio, and Charleston, West Virginia—are each about a ninety-minute drive from the OHIO campus.

Student Body

The OHIO student body "is pretty homogenous," with a large contingent of undergrads who are "white, middle- to upper-class, and from Ohio." "We have a small minority population, especially in the undergraduate programs," one student concedes, "but it's easy to interact with other cultures if you seek them out." Students here "try to get involved in community service, especially those involved in Greek life," and they are "generally friendly." One student observes that "students totally devoted to their schoolwork are atypical here." Yet, it should be noted that OHIO students have succeeded in claiming a number of nationally competitive academic awards in recent years, with *The Chronicle of Higher Education* having recognized Ohio University as being among the nation's top producers of U.S. Fulbright Students.

FINANCIAL AID: 740-593-4141 • E-MAIL: ADMISSIONS@OHIO.EDU • WEBSITE: WWW.OHIO.EDU

THE PRINCETON REVIEW SAYS

Admissions

Very important factors considered include: rigor of secondary school record, academic GPA, standardized test scores. *Important factors considered include:* class rank, application essay, first generation. *Other factors considered include:* recommendation(s), extracurricular activities, talent/ability, character/personal qualities, alumni/ae relation, geographical residence, state residency, volunteer work, work experience. SAT or ACT required. ACT with Writing recommended. SAT with Essay component recommended. High school diploma is required and GED is accepted. *Academic units required:* 4 English, 4 math, 3 science, 2 foreign language, 3 social studies, 4 academic electives, and 1 unit from above areas or other academic areas. *Academic units recommended:* 4 English, 4 math, 3 science, 2 foreign language, 3 social studies, 4 academic electives, 1 visual/performing arts.

Financial Aid

Students should submit: FAFSA. The Princeton Review suggests that all financial aid forms be submitted as soon as possible after October 1. *Need-based scholarships/grants offered:* Federal Pell, FSEOG, State scholarships/grants, Private scholarships, College/university scholarship or grant aid from institutional funds. *Loan aid offered:* Direct Subsidized Stafford Loans, Direct Unsubsidized Stafford Loans, Direct PLUS loans, Federal Perkins Loans. Federal Work-Study Program available. Institutional employment available.

The Inside Word

Admissions requirements vary from school to school at Ohio University. The Honors Tutorial College is most selective (you should be in the top 10 percent of your graduating class and earn at least a 30/1300 on your ACT/SAT for best consideration), followed by the journalism school (top 15 percent, 25/1140), the business college (top 20 percent, 24/1100), media arts and studies, engineering, and visual communication. Admissions decisions are made through holistic review; those on the cusp should get in if they've demonstrated academic improvement during their junior and senior years and show evidence of academic preparation.

THE SCHOOL SAYS "..."

From the Admissions Office

"Ohio University offers a welcoming campus and more than 250 outstanding academic programs that make a degree from OHIO an instant advantage. Our dedicated professors do more than just teach—they serve as mentors and advisors who prepare students for success. Ohio University's recently launched initiative, The OHIO Guarantee, may be of particular interest to families facing budgetary challenges: It enables Athens Campus undergraduate students to pay a single "fixed" rate that covers tuition, room and meal plan, and fees for four years. In addition, Ohio University is home to an Honors Tutorial College that offers high-ability students distinctive, tutorial-based learning opportunities that mirror the instructional model used for centuries at British universities such as Cambridge and Oxford.

"Students can enhance their educational experiences with adventures beyond the classroom. Education abroad opportunities can range from studying the plays of Shakespeare in London to retail merchandising in China. Students also can participate in meaningful research and internships, community service, and more than 500 student organizations. OHIO's picturesque campus—among the most beautiful in the nation—features learning communities that create a welcoming environment for first-year students. Friendships are forged as students with diverse backgrounds study, learn, and socialize together.

"Many students proudly cheer on Ohio University's athletics teams. The Bobcats have garnered increasing national attention in recent years, with the football team winning back-to-back bowl games and the men's basketball team reaching the Sweet 16 round of the NCAA Tournament. Swimming and diving, volleyball, and other sports round out the athletic program. Many students participate in club and intramural sports or learn to rappel, kayak, or canoe through OHIO's Outdoor Pursuits Program."

SELECTIVITY

Admissions Rating	79
# of applicants	21,000
% of applicants accepted	74
% of acceptees attending	28
# offered a place on the wait list	0

FRESHMAN PROFILE

Range SAT Critical Reading	490–600
Range SAT Math	500–610
Range SAT Writing	470–590
Range ACT Composite	22–26
Average HS GPA	3.5
% graduated top 10% of class	16
% graduated top 25% of class	43
% graduated top 50% of class	81

DEADLINES

Regular	
Priority	12/1
Nonfall registration?	Yes

AND SOMETIMES PREFER

The Ohio State University–Columbus; Miami University; University of Cincinnati; University of Dayton

FINANCIAL FACTS

Financial Aid Rating	77
Annual out-of-state tuition	$19,566
Room and board	$10,734
Books and supplies	$990
Average frosh need-based scholarship	$6,768
Average UG need-based scholarship	$6,424
% needy frosh rec. need-based scholarship or grant aid	93
% needy UG rec. need-based scholarship or grant aid	76
% needy frosh rec. non-need-based scholarship or grant aid	13
% needy UG rec. non-need-based scholarship or grant aid	14
% needy frosh rec. need-based self-help aid	99
% needy UG rec. need-based self-help aid	98
% frosh rec. any financial aid	92
% UG rec. any financial aid	75
% UG borrow to pay for school	66
Average cumulative indebtedness	$28,083
% frosh need fully met	31
% ugrads need fully met	25
Average % of frosh need met	51
Average % of ugrad need met	45

OHIO WESLEYAN UNIVERSITY

61 SOUTH SANDUSKY STREET, DELAWARE, OH 43015 • ADMISSIONS: 740-368-3020 • FAX: 740-368-3314

STUDENTS SAY ". . ."

Academics

To some, Ohio Wesleyan University offers the best of both worlds: the "smaller school" experience of a "liberal arts education" along with the "fantastic financial aid," "scholarship money," and "opportunity to play a collegiate sport" available at a "global" university. OWU offers eighteen different pre-professional majors in areas like pre-medicine and pre-engineering, along with "enriching" programs called out by students in "psychology," "economics," "Black World Studies," and others. In addition, the university facilitates special programs like "the undergraduate research program, SSRP, that allows only Ohio Wesleyan students to work with a professor over the summer," which entrusts undergrads with "a rare opportunity to get paid to do research almost always one-on-one with a PhD, where at any other school you'll be working with lab techs and graduate students." Another crown jewel of the OWU academic experience is the "Theory to Practice opportunities," which challenge students to design their own project applications "for grants through the school that allow you to do your own research [and] travel to gain new experience." Similarly, OWU's "Travel-Learning Courses" create "many opportunities to go abroad" for students with intellectual wanderlust, and with such a global focus, OWU also attracts "many international students" to its Ohio campus. The faculty participates in this global citizenship as well: "The professors are very diverse, like the students here, bringing different perspectives and knowledge to campus." They're also committed to their students, who find that professors are "good at engaging the student is classroom discussions" and "will go out of their way to help you. I have had numerous professors support me in applying for grants, applying for research experiences at other universities, as well as jobs." Students report that "a major benefit of going to a smaller school is that I am on a first-name basis with multiple professors, and even text them if I need help with something," and that they've "had professors stay until 6pm just to make sure I understood a concept." An OWU education also builds a foundation for the future: the university boasts "strong career services" and "OWU alums are very dedicated to helping provide employment to students post graduation."

Life

OWU's "close knit community" is forged through common-interest bonds: "Most students are nerds/passionate about something. They usually fit in by finding people interested in the same things they are." The prototypical OWU student is "extremely involved in clubs/organizations," but has lots of choices of what to join: there's an "amazing club and Greek Life," "varsity sports," "jobs on campus," and "SLUs (small living units)," described as "intentional communities centered around various mission statements." All of this adds up to a robust "overall community" and "great campus culture" that "make OWU an even better school to attend. The majority of students stay on campus because of the community and friendships that they have formed." That said, a lot of students "go to class and study during the week like its [their] job," "and every night do homework followed by Netflix." "In general, everyone is in study groups during the week and watching movies with friends when free," then "weekends are spent with friends at a frat, sorority, or sport house." "Drinking does occur, as does drug usage," but "it's not a huge party school," and "many people are devoted strongly to their academics."

Student Body

OWU is populated by enthusiastic joiners of all different stripes, and students love the "very culturally diverse" atmosphere of the school. "I've never met so many people that are religiously and culturally different in a single place. It's amazing!" Because "we only have around 1800 students" and "students and faculty alike push for acceptance of everyone," it's "very easy to make friends in this type of environment." Students extol each other as "friendly and smart", as well as "outgoing, overcommitted in student organizations, and driven," and love that "it is impossible to judge or peg people" because "everyone here is from all over with different backgrounds." At OWU, "everyone fits in somewhere."

OHIO WESLEYAN UNIVERSITY

FINANCIAL AID: 740-368-3050 • E-MAIL: OWUADMIT@OWU.EDU • WEBSITE: WWW.OWU.EDU

THE PRINCETON REVIEW SAYS

Admissions

Very important factors considered include: rigor of secondary school record, academic GPA, application essay, recommendation(s), interview, character/personal qualities. *Important factors considered include:* class rank, standardized test scores, extracurricular activities, talent/ability. *Other factors considered include:* first generation, alumni/ae relation, geographical residence, racial/ethnic status, volunteer work, work experience, level of applicant's interest. SAT or ACT required for some. ACT with or without writing accepted. SAT with or without Essay component accepted. TOEFL required of all international applicants. High school diploma is required and GED is accepted. *Academic units required:* 4 English, 3 math, 3 science, 2 foreign language, 3 social studies. *Academic units recommended:* 4 English, 4 math, 4 science, 3 foreign language, 4 social studies.

Financial Aid

Students should submit: FAFSA. Priority filing deadline is 2/15. The Princeton Review suggests that all financial aid forms be submitted as soon as possible after October 1. *Need-based scholarships/grants offered:* Federal Pell, FSEOG, State scholarships/grants, Private scholarships, College/university scholarship or grant aid from institutional funds. *Loan aid offered:* Direct Subsidized Stafford Loans, Direct Unsubsidized Stafford Loans, Direct PLUS loans, Federal Perkins Loans, College/university loans from institutional funds. Federal Work-Study Program available. Institutional employment available.

The Inside Word

For students with a high school GPA of 3.0 or higher at the end of junior year, OWU no longer requires SAT or ACT scores. Students with high scores are certainly advised to submit them, they may be required for some scholarship and honors programs. Well-roundedness is a must for any serious applicant. OWU offers both Early Decision and Early Admission options.

THE SCHOOL SAYS ". . ."

From the Admissions Office

"Ohio Wesleyan University, a national liberal arts university with a major international presence, is remarkable for the broad range of its academic and pre-professional programs, the international dimensions of its curriculum, an emphasis on community through leadership and service, and its unwavering commitment to focus on linking theory and practice in every field of study. The university is located in Delaware, Ohio, just north of Columbus, the capital city.

"OWU's Theory-to-Practice initiative includes competitive university-funded grants that allow students to propose and conduct original research, serve meaningful internships, and participate in service opportunities and cultural immersion throughout the world. Travel-Learning Courses augment classroom theory with international travel and study in multiple fields in countries throughout the world. The university offers eighty-six majors, far more than most institutions of its size.

"For the past five consecutive years, the university has been honored with the President's Honor Roll Award for Community Service, with Distinction; OWU was one of three colleges nationwide to win the 2009 President's Award for Excellence in General Community Service.

"Ohio Wesleyan has twenty-three varsity athletic teams: eleven men's and twelve women's. OWU boasts more team championships and Academic All-America® scholar-athletes than any other school in the North Coast Athletic Conference and has won Division III national championships in men's soccer (two), women's soccer (two), and men's basketball, with individual national titles in several other sports.

"Applicants may submit the SAT or the ACT. Best scores from either test will be considered in the application review."

SELECTIVITY

Admissions Rating	80
# of applicants	3,949
% of applicants accepted	75
% of acceptees attending	0
# of early decision applicants	78
% accepted early decision	56

FRESHMAN PROFILE

Range SAT Critical Reading	510–630
Range SAT Math	510–620
Range SAT Writing	480–610
Range ACT Composite	22–28
Minimum paper TOEFL	550
Average HS GPA	3.4
% graduated top 10% of class	23
% graduated top 25% of class	52
% graduated top 50% of class	84

DEADLINES

Early decision	
Deadline	11/15
Notification	11/30
Early action	
Deadline	1/15
Regular	
Priority	1/15
Deadline	3/1
Notification	3/1
Nonfall registration?	Yes

APPLICANTS ALSO LOOK AT AND OFTEN PREFER

Denison University; Miami University; The College of Wooster; The Ohio State University–Columbus; Wittenberg University

AND SOMETIMES PREFER

Kenyon College; Ohio University–Athens

AND RARELY PREFER

Oberlin College

FINANCIAL FACTS

Financial Aid Rating	85
Annual tuition	$42,910
Room and board	$11,540
Required fees	$320
Books and supplies	$1,300
Average frosh need-based scholarship	$28,970
Average UG need-based scholarship	$27,864
% needy frosh rec. need-based scholarship or grant aid	100
% needy UG rec. need-based scholarship or grant aid	100
% needy frosh rec. non-need-based scholarship or grant aid	21
% needy UG rec. non-need-based scholarship or grant aid	19
% needy frosh rec. need-based self-help aid	80
% needy UG rec. need-based self-help aid	83
% UG borrow to pay for school	67
Average cumulative indebtedness	$33,810
% frosh need fully met	23
% ugrads need fully met	22
Average % of frosh need met	79
Average % of ugrad need met	79

PENNSYLVANIA STATE UNIVERSITY—UNIVERSITY PARK

201 SHIELDS BUILDING, BOX 3000, UNIVERSITY PARK, PA 16802-3000 • ADMISSIONS: 814-865-5471 • FAX: 814-863-7590

CAMPUS LIFE

Quality of Life Rating	94
Fire Safety Rating	98
Green Rating	95
Type of school	Public
Affiliation	No Affiliation
Environment	Town

STUDENTS

Total undergrad enrollment	40,742
% male/female	54/46
% from out of state	31
% ugrads live on campus	34
# of fraternities (% ugrad men join)	56 (18)
# of sororities (% ugrad women join)	27 (19)
% African American	4
% Asian	6
% Caucasian	69
% Hispanic	6
% Native American	<1
% Pacific Islander	<1
% Two or more races	3
% Race and/or ethnicity unknown	2
% international	11
# of countries represented	110

SURVEY SAYS...

Students are happy
Classroom facilities are great
Great library
Career services are great
Internships are widely available
School is well run
Students get along with local community
Students love University Park, PA
Great off-campus food
Recreation facilities are great
Lots of beer drinking
Hard liquor is popular
Everyone loves the Nittany Lions
Intramural sports are popular
Campus newspaper is popular
Alumni active on campus

ACADEMICS

Academic Rating	77
% students returning for sophomore year	93
% students graduating within 4 years	64
% students graduating within 6 years	86
Calendar	Semester
Student/faculty ratio	16:1
Profs interesting rating	77
Profs accessible rating	79

Most classes have 20–29 students.
Most lab/discussion sessions have 20–29 students.

MOST POPULAR MAJORS

Business, Management, Marketing; Engineering; Communication

STUDENTS SAY "..."

Academics

Immense "pride and a sense of community" pervade every aspect of life at Penn State. Students love the remarkable "school spirit" and "strong family feel" on this vibrant campus, and they are equally proud of the "quality education" they receive. An affordable public institution, PSU offers "highly regarded programs across a wide range of academic colleges," including a "prestigious undergrad business school," top engineering and education majors, and the competitive Schreyer Honors College, which participants describe as "the finest honors program in the nation." "Classes freshman year are mostly lectures," which can be "intimidating" for new students. Fortunately, "even in lectures with hundreds of students, many professors still make an effort to get to know their class and have plenty of office hours to make themselves more accessible." Plus, the academic experience becomes more individualized as you move through the system. A current student shares, "As I have gotten into my majors, my classes are down to about fifteen to forty people and there are a lot more discussions. I know all of my professors personally now." Academics are often described as "rigorous" and "competitive," but most students are able to stay afloat; here, "professors will challenge you, but it's nothing that a hard-working student can't handle." Job-seeking seniors praise the career center, as well as the school's fantastic alumni connections, saying, "The Penn State networking web is incredible!" Not to mention, the school's enviable "location within driving distance to Philadelphia, Washington, and New York" makes it easier to score a job at graduation.

Life

If you are looking for the "full college experience," you'll find "the perfect mix of great academics, social life, and sports" at Penn State. While "the library is usually filled with students" during the week, "everyone counts down the days till the weekend, then its party, party, party." Throughout fall semester, football is a campus-wide obsession; "game days are super exciting and unifying for the student population," which turns out in large numbers to tailgate and cheer at Beaver Stadium. In addition to sports, "Greek Life dominates the social scene," though students also flock to the many bars in downtown State College. A current student jokes, "Nothing brings the Penn State community together like stumbling around downtown with 3,000 other drunken students." Those looking for a mellower night out will find "on-campus concerts, stand up comedians, craft nights, sporting events, and other ways of having fun without drugs or alcohol." Others like to "go out to the local avenue and try new eateries, and walk around campus and enjoy the scenery." In addition to the "killer social life," there are hundreds of clubs and student groups; of particular note, many students "fit in by joining THON, the largest student-run philanthropy in the world, that raises money for children with pediatric cancer." No matter what your interests, "between football games, Late Nights at the HUB, festivities downtown, movies, shows at Eisenhower Auditorium or the Penn State Theatre, concerts at the BJC...there is something for everyone."

Students

With a total enrollment of more than 40,000, "Penn State is the passion and pride of a large and diverse student body." Demographically, the school draws heavily from the Northeast; in particular, there are "lots of kids from the tri-state area," and most could be described as "athletic, suburban, and friendly middle-class." While some note that "the percentage of minorities and foreign students is low," they also say, "pretty much every student will find somewhere to fit in." Especially during the first year, "there are many opportunities to meet new people," and "mostly everyone is friendly," making it easy to form bonds and build relationships. The best way to make friends is to "try different clubs and find your niche"; from Greek organizations to sports, most Penn Staters have "a great enthusiasm for extracurricular and philanthropic involvement." On that note, most undergrads "take their education seriously," but achieve a "good balance of school and social life."

PENNSYLVANIA STATE UNIVERSITY—UNIVERSITY PARK

FINANCIAL AID: 814-865-6301 • E-MAIL: ADMISSIONS@PSU.EDU • WEBSITE: WWW.PSU.EDU

THE PRINCETON REVIEW SAYS

Admissions

Very important factors considered include: academic GPA, standardized test scores. *Important factors considered include:* rigor of secondary school record. *Other factors considered include:* class rank, application essay, extracurricular activities, talent/ability, character/personal qualities, alumni/ae relation, geographical·residence, state residency, volunteer work, work experience. SAT or ACT required. ACT with or without writing accepted. SAT with or without Essay component accepted. TOEFL required of all international applicants. High school diploma is required and GED is accepted. *Academic units required:* 4 English, 3 math, 3 science, 2 foreign language, 3 social studies. *Academic units recommended:* 3 foreign language.

Financial Aid

Students should submit: FAFSA. Priority filing deadline is 2/15. The Princeton Review suggests that all financial aid forms be submitted as soon as possible after October 1. *Need-based scholarships/grants offered:* Federal Pell, FSEOG, State scholarships/grants, Private scholarships, College/university scholarship or grant aid from institutional funds. *Loan aid offered:* Direct Subsidized Stafford Loans, Direct Unsubsidized Stafford Loans, Direct PLUS loans, Federal Perkins Loans, College/university loans from institutional funds. Federal Work-Study Program available. Institutional employment available.

The Inside Word

Though the school does not have any minimum requirements for an incoming student's GPA or standardized test scores, high school GPA is by far the most important factor in PSU admissions. According to the school's website, high school grades account for two-thirds of the final admissions decision. Other factors, like standardized test scores, make up the remaining third. PSU is a popular choice for Pennsylvania residents and admits on a rolling basis; prospective students should submit their applications as early as possible.

THE SCHOOL SAYS " . . . "

From the Admissions Office

"Unique among large public universities, Penn State combines the more than 40,000 student setting of its University Park campus with twenty academically and administratively integrated undergraduate locations across Pennsylvania.

"Ranging in size from 600 to 4,000 students, most of Penn State's residential and commuter locations offer the first two years of baccalaureate instruction as well as a limited number of two- and four-year degree programs. These small-college settings focus on the needs of new students by offering smaller classes and close interaction with faculty. More than half of the undergraduates who complete their studies at University Park start at another Penn State campus.

"Applicants are qualified for review for any of Penn State's campuses, with preferences considered in the order requested. Choice of location and entrance difficulty are based, in part, on demand. Due to its popularity, the University Park campus is the most competitive for admission. Freshman applicants may submit the results from the SAT or the ACT with the writing component."

SELECTIVITY

Admissions Rating	89
# of applicants	53,472
% of applicants accepted	51
% of acceptees attending	28
# offered a place on the wait list	1,473
% accepting a place on wait list	100
% admitted from wait list	98

FRESHMAN PROFILE

Range SAT Critical Reading	530–630
Range SAT Math	560–670
Range SAT Writing	540–640
Range ACT Composite	25–29
Minimum paper TOEFL	550
Minimum internet-based TOEFL	80
Average HS GPA	3.6
% graduated top 10% of class	41
% graduated top 25% of class	82
% graduated top 50% of class	98

DEADLINES

Regular	
Priority	11/30
Nonfall registration?	Yes

APPLICANTS ALSO LOOK AT AND OFTEN PREFER

Carnegie Mellon University; Cornell University; Lehigh University; University of Michigan–Ann Arbor; University of Maryland–College Park

AND SOMETIMES PREFER

Emory University; Georgetown University; Harvard College; Johns Hopkins University; University of Virginia

FINANCIAL FACTS

Financial Aid Rating	77
Annual in-state tuition	$16,572
Annual out-of-state tuition	$30,404
Room and board	$10,920
Required fees	$942
Books and supplies	$1,840
Average frosh need-based scholarship	$7,052
Average UG need-based scholarship	$7,144
% needy frosh rec. need-based scholarship or grant aid	43
% needy UG rec. need-based scholarship or grant aid	51
% needy frosh rec. non-need-based scholarship or grant aid	47
% needy UG rec. non-need-based scholarship or grant aid	36
% needy frosh rec. need-based self-help aid	72
% needy UG rec. need-based self-help aid	81
% frosh rec. any financial aid	66
% UG rec. any financial aid	67
% UG borrow to pay for school	56
Average cumulative indebtedness	$35,972
% frosh need fully met	8
% ugrads need fully met	8
Average % of frosh need met	58
Average % of ugrad need met	59

PEPPERDINE UNIVERSITY

24255 PACIFIC COAST HIGHWAY, MALIBU, CA 90263 • ADMISSIONS: 310-456-4392 • FAX: 310-506-4861

STUDENTS SAY ". . ."

Academics
A small private college overlooking the Pacific Ocean, Pepperdine is an "amazingly beautiful" place to get an education. With about 3,500 undergraduates and an excellent teacher/student ratio, Pepperdine and its "smaller class sizes make it beyond easy to form personal yet academic relationships with your professors." Although "academics are quite challenging," professors "take their role as a mentor seriously. They invite classes over for meals, meet students for coffee, and are eager to help you move in the direction of your dreams." While universally supportive, professors get mixed reviews regarding the ability to keep your attention: Some professors "are very lively and exciting, while some are boring and you would rather take a nap." Career and internship opportunities naturally grow out of the school's prime location, strong alumni network, and regional ties. "Professors are well-connected with both corporations and the surrounding community," and there are "endless internship and volunteer opportunities" in the region. Plus, "Pepperdine's International Program is consistently ranked as one of the best," offering "programs in Florence, London, Shanghai, Buenos Aires...the list goes on! Anyone who is looking forward to studying abroad should definitely look into our programs." Pepperdine is affiliated with the Church of Christ, and Christian values are "prevalent but not overwhelming" in academic curriculum; all students, regardless of their background, are required to attend the "mandatory Convocation program"—a series of chapels, Bible studies, and speakers, designed to promote spirituality. While there's a conservative slant among the higher-ups, Pepperdine's administration is "much more moderate than what you would find at other small, Christian schools."

Life
Pepperdine students gloat about their school's perfect location in Malibu, California, where "there is a 360-degree view of the Pacific Ocean, and students can walk to the beach." The "campus is surrounded by national parks and beach," so nature lovers enjoy "countless opportunities for hiking, swimming, running, waterfall jumping, camping, [and] rock-climbing." "The close proximity to LA, Santa Monica, Hollywood, and the Pacific Coast Highway make it easy for students to find things to do." Students say that a car is a necessity. Fortunately, "there are enough students with cars to hitch a ride," if you don't have your own set of wheels. Alcohol is prohibited at Pepperdine, and "the dry campus policy is strictly enforced." Therefore, "people have to go off campus to drink and party." "The people who party can do so without it affecting the people who don't at all." While the campus is undeniably dreamy, students would like to see the school "improve is the student health facilities and workout facilities"—as well as provide more student parking.

Student Body
"Academics, service, athletics, and social events are all a big part of the life of a typical student." During college, "the typical Pepperdine student is involved in two service projects, spends their spring break building homes in Central America, has huge career goals, is involved in a performing arts group, looks forward to new student orientation all year, and studies abroad as a sophomore." Pepperdine students are also good about "being healthy and eating well and exercising right." It can feel "as if all the popular kids across all the different high schools across America convened in Malibu." However, students tell us "there is a lot more diversity" at Pepperdine today. You get a nice mix of "art majors to the science kids to the surfers to the hardcore studiers to the philosophy majors." Most students come from "a Christian background whether or not they are religious now," and some students are strongly religious and conservative. "Finding alternative viewpoints may be tough," but most students are "fairly open-minded" and "extremely nice."

FINANCIAL AID: 310-506-4301 • E-MAIL: ADMISSION-SEAVER@PEPPERDINE.EDU • WEBSITE: WWW.PEPPERDINE.EDU

THE PRINCETON REVIEW SAYS

Admissions

Very important factors considered include: rigor of secondary school record, academic GPA, application essay, extracurricular activities, talent/ability, character/personal qualities, religious affiliation/commitment. *Important factors considered include:* standardized test scores, recommendation(s), volunteer work. *Other factors considered include:* first generation, alumni/ae relation, racial/ethnic status, work experience. SAT or ACT required. ACT with or without writing accepted. SAT with or without Essay component accepted. TOEFL required of all international applicants. High school diploma is required and GED is accepted.

Financial Aid

Students should submit: FAFSA. Priority filing deadline is 2/15. The Princeton Review suggests that all financial aid forms be submitted as soon as possible after October 1. *Need-based scholarships/grants offered:* Federal Pell, FSEOG, State scholarships/grants, Private scholarships, College/university scholarship or grant aid from institutional funds, United Negro College Fund. *Loan aid offered:* Direct Subsidized Stafford Loans, Direct Unsubsidized Stafford Loans, Direct PLUS loans, Federal Perkins Loans, College/university loans from institutional funds. Applicants will be notified of awards on or about 4/15. Federal Work-Study Program available. Institutional employment available.

The Inside Word

Admission to Pepperdine is highly selective. The school generally receives over 9,900 applications for the incoming class of fewer than 1,000 students. Decisions are made based on a student's academic record, standardized test scores, and two letters of recommendation—one personal and the other academic. Students affiliated with the Church of Christ are eligible for special Church of Christ scholarships; to be considered, applicants must submit a letter of recommendation from a church leader.

THE SCHOOL SAYS "..."

From the Admissions Office

"As a selective university, Pepperdine seeks students who show promise of academic achievement at the collegiate level. However, we also seek students who are committed to serving the university community, as well as others with whom they come into contact. We look for community-service activities, volunteer efforts, and strong leadership qualities, as well as a demonstrated commitment to academic studies and an interest in the liberal arts.

"Seaver College of Pepperdine University requires freshman applicants to submit scores from either the SAT Reasoning Test (including the writing portion) or the ACT (including the writing test). The scores are evaluated in conjunction with the grade point average in specific courses completed."

SELECTIVITY
Admissions Rating	91
# of applicants	9,923
% of applicants accepted	38
% of acceptees attending	20

FRESHMAN PROFILE
Range SAT Critical Reading	550–650
Range SAT Math	550–670
Range SAT Writing	550–650
Range ACT Composite	25–30
Minimum paper TOEFL	550
Minimum internet-based TOEFL	80
Average HS GPA	3.6
% graduated top 10% of class	48
% graduated top 25% of class	80
% graduated top 50% of class	97

DEADLINES
Regular	
Deadline	1/5
Notification	4/1
Nonfall registration?	Yes

APPLICANTS ALSO LOOK AT AND OFTEN PREFER
University of Southern California; University of California–Los Angeles; University of San Diego; University of California–San Diego; Loyola Marymount University

AND SOMETIMES PREFER
Vanderbilt University; New York University

AND RARELY PREFER
Occidental College

FINANCIAL FACTS
Financial Aid Rating	85
Annual tuition	$49,770
Room and board	$14,330
Required fees	$252
Books and supplies	$1,500
Average frosh need-based scholarship	$32,440
Average UG need-based scholarship	$37,026
% needy frosh rec. need-based scholarship or grant aid	99
% needy UG rec. need-based scholarship or grant aid	97
% needy frosh rec. need-based self-help aid	99
% needy UG rec. need-based self-help aid	71
% frosh rec. any financial aid	94
% UG rec. any financial aid	81
% UG borrow to pay for school	57
Average cumulative indebtedness	$34,820
% frosh need fully met	16
% ugrads need fully met	21
Average % of frosh need met	73
Average % of ugrad need met	77

PITZER COLLEGE

1050 NORTH MILLS AVENUE, CLAREMONT, CA 91711-6101 • ADMISSIONS: 909-621-8129 • FAX: 909-621-8770

STUDENTS SAY ". . ."

Academics

Pitzer College is "small, personal, and unique," but because students have access to the classes and "excellent resources" at four other local colleges through the Claremont Consortium, "you can choose to make your college experience as large or as small as you want!" Pitzer doesn't have a lot of requirements, so there's a high degree of academic freedom and flexibility, including the opportunity to create your own major. Students gush about the level of "student autonomy," calling Pitzer "a challenging school that allows students to become effective leaders." Emphasis is on "social responsibility" and "intercultural understanding," and classes "are constantly being connected to present society and how you can pursue social issues through your field of study." "Professors are as zesty and zany as they are brilliant and intriguing" and they "encourage respectful dialogue inside and outside the classroom." Generally, "emphasis [is] on discussion; besides intro courses you won't find many lecture classes." "Pitzer is all about analytical thinking and learning to think beyond the material in front of you. Professors won't settle for summary; be prepared to form and argue your own opinions." Students are very positive about their professors, calling them "life changing" and "dedicated and enthusiastic." A history major says professors "demand a lot from their students," and a political science major adds that "they want to know each of their students individually and help them out as much as they can."

Life

Pitzer's location means great weather, which means "year-round outdoor activities." "Everyday walking through campus you'll see classes being held outside on the grass, students lying in hammocks reading, students studying while laying out by the pool, or students fixing old bikes at the Green Bike Program (a student-run club, promoting green transportation by providing bikes for the community)." Pitzer students love the "very laid-back and easy-going environment," but find the school is still able to enforce "a serious education." The College Consortium means there's always something going on, whether it's a "speaker series, dances, parties, or concerts," and there's "no shortage of things to do." Students report an "average" amount of drinking and drug use, and a few noted that though there's "a lot of pot smoking" they "never felt pressured" to take part. The five colleges "sponsor parties...with kegs, deejays, etc.," though the big parties usually take place at the other colleges, or off campus. Pitzer is "close enough to Los Angeles to head in for concerts, museums, shopping, etc., [and] many students do camping trips in Southern California [or] head to the beach." There's also a campus organization, Pitzer Outdoor Adventures (POA), that "funds students each week to basically go out on epic adventures. Want gas money for surfing? Okay! Want some funds for a back packing trip? Done!" A leader of POA admits with the school funding adventures, it "doesn't get much better."

Student Body

"The one thing all Pitzer students do have in common is awareness and community involvement. Every student on this campus has a strong voice." Pitzer students are hard workers and "passionate thinkers," "intelligent, chill, accepting, and friendly." Though Pitzer is small, "there is such a wide variety of people [that] you'll find a place where you fit in," and a sociology student adds that, "You only really don't fit in if you're unfriendly and mean." "At Pitzer, there are countless ways to meet people...and if you can't find something at Pitzer you can definitely find it at one of the other Claremont Colleges." Pitzer has a reputation as a "hippie" (and sometimes "hipster") school, but students say the "diversity among personalities is growing rapidly." One student says that Pitzer students "are a collection of creative people who, in their different ways, like to think outside of the box."

FINANCIAL AID: 909-621-8208 • E-MAIL: ADMISSION@PITZER.EDU • WEBSITE: WWW.PITZER.EDU

THE PRINCETON REVIEW SAYS

Admissions

Very important factors considered include: rigor of secondary school record, academic GPA, application essay, character/personal qualities. *Important factors considered include:* recommendation(s), extracurricular activities, talent/ability, volunteer work. *Other factors considered include:* class rank, first generation, alumni/ae relation, geographical residence, racial/ethnic status, work experience, level of applicant's interest. SAT or ACT considered if submitted. ACT with or without writing accepted. SAT with or without Essay component accepted. TOEFL required of all international applicants. High school diploma is required and GED is accepted. *Academic units required:* 4 English, 3 math, 3 science, 3 science labs, 3 foreign language, 3 social studies, 1 history, 1 visual/performing arts.

Financial Aid

Students should submit: FAFSA, CSS/Financial Aid PROFILE, State aid form, Noncustodial PROFILE. Regular filing deadline is 2/1. The Princeton Review suggests that all financial aid forms be submitted as soon as possible after October 1. *Need-based scholarships/grants offered:* Federal Pell, FSEOG, State scholarships/grants, Private scholarships, College/university scholarship or grant aid from institutional funds. *Loan aid offered:* Direct Subsidized Stafford Loans, Direct Unsubsidized Stafford Loans, Direct PLUS loans, Federal Perkins Loans, College/university loans from institutional funds. Applicants will be notified of awards on or about 4/1. Federal Work-Study Program available. Institutional employment available.

The Inside Word

This is a place where applicants can feel confident in letting their thoughts flow freely on admissions essays. Not only does the committee read them (a circumstance more rare in college admissions that one is led to believe), but they've also set up the process to emphasize them! Thus, what you have to say for yourself will go much further than numbers in determining your suitability for Pitzer.

THE SCHOOL SAYS "..."

From the Admissions Office

"Pitzer is about opportunities. It's about possibilities. The students who come here are looking for something different from the usual 'take two courses from column A, two courses from column B, and two courses from column C.' That kind of arbitrary selection doesn't make a satisfying education at Pitzer. So we look for students who want to have an impact on their own education, who want the chief responsibility—with help from their faculty advisors—in designing their own futures.

"Pitzer's admission policy uses a test-optional policy. Students in the top 10 percent of their class or those who have an unweighted academic GPA of 3.5 or higher are not required to submit test scores. Others are allowed to choose from a variety of choices, including standardized tests (i.e., the SAT and ACT with the writing component)."

SELECTIVITY

Admissions Rating	97
# of applicants	4,149
% of applicants accepted	13
% of acceptees attending	48
# offered a place on the wait list	1,021
% accepting a place on wait list	88
% admitted from wait list	3
# of early decision applicants	405
% accepted early decision	29

FRESHMAN PROFILE

Range SAT Critical Reading	620–720
Range SAT Math	630–720
Range ACT Composite	29–32
Minimum paper TOEFL	520
Minimum internet-based TOEFL	70
Average HS GPA	3.9

DEADLINES

Early decision	
Deadline	11/15
Notification	12/18
Regular	
Deadline	1/1
Notification	4/1
Nonfall registration?	No

APPLICANTS ALSO LOOK AT AND OFTEN PREFER

Claremont McKenna College; Scripps College; University of California–Berkeley; University of California–Los Angeles; Occidental College; University of Southern California

AND SOMETIMES PREFER

Boston University; Colorado College; Whitman College; Lewis & Clark College; New York University

FINANCIAL FACTS

Financial Aid Rating	97
Annual tuition	$48,400
Room and board	$15,210
Required fees	$270
Average frosh need-based scholarship	$42,479
Average UG need-based scholarship	$40,220
% needy frosh rec. need-based scholarship or grant aid	100
% needy UG rec. need-based scholarship or grant aid	100
% needy frosh rec. non-need-based scholarship or grant aid	7
% needy UG rec. non-need-based scholarship or grant aid	7
% needy frosh rec. need-based self-help aid	90
% needy UG rec. need-based self-help aid	88
% frosh rec. any financial aid	34
% UG rec. any financial aid	41
% UG borrow to pay for school	37
Average cumulative indebtedness	$21,951
% frosh need fully met	100
% ugrads need fully met	100
Average % of frosh need met	100
Average % of ugrad need met	100

POMONA COLLEGE

333 NORTH COLLEGE WAY, CLAREMONT, CA 91711-6312 • ADMISSIONS: 909-621-8134 • FAX: 909-621-8952

STUDENTS SAY "..."

Academics

At Pomona College in Claremont, you can get "an academically rigorous education" in a "low-stress California atmosphere." At this prestigious liberal arts school, "The professors are, for the most part, fantastic—engaging, creative, and sharp," and "all classes are taught by professors, not grad students or TAs." With small class sizes in every department, "there is an emphasis on collaborative learning," and "many professors are great discussion leaders and really motivate students to get involved in class." Students have the advantage of "getting to know professors outside the classroom, in any setting, from office hours, to Thanksgiving dinner at their homes." Illustrating how personal the experience can be, a student tells us, "Today, I had a class with seven people in it, then lunch with a physics professor, and then a personal tutorial with a philosophy professor." Another student adds, "Between department barbecues, parties, and weekend retreats, by the time you're an upperclassman, you will know most of the professors in your major department quite well." In complement to the intimate academic atmosphere, Pomona "offers the resources of a large university" through the Claremont College consortium, which offers joint events and cross-registration with four adjoining colleges. Among other programs, "Pomona pays for students to take otherwise unpaid internship positions." Students praise Pomona's "efficiency in taking care of administrative tasks such as financial aid and registration," adding that the administration "is very good at responding to what students want."

Life

Pomona students are "ridiculously happy" about their lot in life, and why shouldn't they be? They're living in a "perfect world full of intelligent, engaging, and open individuals, amazing academics, brilliant opportunities to get involved in, and enough sunshine to make anyone happy to be alive." The weather is a key aspect of the experience, and "on a nice day, everyone heads outside in shorts and t-shirts to do their class work." On any given day, "you'll see people setting up telescopes outside the dorms at night to try to get a glimpse of the stars, you'll find people practicing ukulele on our quad, you'll see students filming for a project in the dining halls, [or] you'll see someone riding around campus on a bamboo bike." "Many people are involved in intramural sports," and students love "hiking, skiing, and going to the beach year round." There are many beautiful beaches in the area, and "Joshua Tree is only an hour and a half away, so there are camping trips there just about every weekend." Though the school is small, there are four other undergraduate colleges in the Claremont Consortium, and Pomona students can "take their classes, eat at their dining halls, go to their parties, swim in their pools, and generally share in a great experience." When it's time to blow off steam, "there are large 5C-sponsored parties that people go to and enjoy."

Student Body

At Pomona, only a quarter or so of students are from California, yet the California attitude reigns supreme. Here, you'll find a number of "tree-hugging, rock-climbing, Tom's shoes-wearing" undergraduates, with most students generally falling within the "liberal, upper-middle-class, hipster-athlete" continuum. Students report a "decent level of diversity and a strong international community." Studious and talented, Pomona undergraduates "excel in the classroom and usually have some sort of passion that they pursue outside of the classroom." "Underneath our sundresses and rainbow flip-flops, we're all closet nerds—everybody is really passionate about something or other." At Pomona, "you will meet the football player who got a perfect score on his SAT or the dreadlocked hippie who took multivariable calculus when he was sixteen." Dress code is uniformly casual, and "flip-flops, polo, or tank tops and shorts" are the unofficial uniform.

FINANCIAL AID: 909-621-8205 • E-MAIL: ADMISSIONS@POMONA.EDU • WEBSITE: WWW.POMONA.EDU

THE PRINCETON REVIEW SAYS

Admissions

Very important factors considered include: rigor of secondary school record, class rank, academic GPA, standardized test scores, application essay, recommendation(s), extracurricular activities, talent/ability, character/personal qualities. *Important factors considered include:* interview. *Other factors considered include:* first generation, alumni/ae relation, racial/ethnic status, volunteer work, work experience. ACT with Writing recommended. TOEFL required for international applicants from non English speaking schools. High school diploma or equivalent is not required. *Academic units required:* 4 English, 4 math, 2 science, 2 science labs, 3 foreign language, 2 social studies. *Academic units recommended:* 4 English, 4 math, 4 science, 3 science labs, 4 foreign language, 4 social studies.

Financial Aid

Students should submit: FAFSA, CSS/Financial Aid PROFILE, Noncustodial PROFILE, Business/Farm Supplement. Regular filing deadline is 3/1. The Princeton Review suggests that all financial aid forms be submitted as soon as possible after October 1. *Need-based scholarships/grants offered:* Federal Pell, FSEOG, State scholarships/grants, Private scholarships, College/university scholarship or grant aid from institutional funds. *Loan aid offered:* Direct Subsidized Stafford Loans, Direct Unsubsidized Stafford Loans, Direct PLUS loans, College/university loans from institutional funds. Applicants will be notified of awards on or about 4/1. Federal Work-Study Program available. Institutional employment available.

The Inside Word

For first-year applicants, Pomona College offers regular decision admissions, as well as two binding early decision programs. Admissions officials evaluate a student's academic record carefully, examining the rigor of high school coursework, class rank, and grade point average. Ninety-two percent of Pomona admits rank in the top 10 percent of their class. Students are strongly encouraged to visit campus and meet with admissions staff, though it's not required.

THE SCHOOL SAYS "..."

From the Admissions Office

"Pomona College is a place for adventurous, creative students, who have talent and passion and are prepared to dream big and work hard in order to make a difference in the world.

"Pomona students enjoy both the advantages of a small college, where professors teach every class, and the opportunities and resources of a larger university, with more than 7,000 students.

"The founding member of the Claremont Colleges, Pomona is one of five adjacent undergraduate colleges and two graduate institutions that make up this unique, Oxford-style consortium. Students may supplement Pomona's extensive curricular offerings with classes at any of the other Claremont Colleges, each no more than a few minutes' walk away.

"Pomona's Southern California location provides its students with rich educational resources, exciting opportunities for both scientific and community-based research, and geographic and cultural diversity."

SELECTIVITY

Admissions Rating	98
# of applicants	8,099
% of applicants accepted	10
% of acceptees attending	48
# offered a place on the wait list	842
% accepting a place on wait list	58
% admitted from wait list	5
# of early decision applicants	1,187
% accepted early decision	15

FRESHMAN PROFILE

Range SAT Critical Reading	670–760
Range SAT Math	690–770
Range SAT Writing	680–770
Range ACT Composite	30–34
Minimum paper TOEFL	600
Minimum internet-based TOEFL	100
% graduated top 10% of class	92
% graduated top 25% of class	100
% graduated top 50% of class	100

DEADLINES

Early decision	
Deadline	11/1
Notification	12/15
Regular	
Deadline	1/1
Notification	4/1
Nonfall registration?	No

APPLICANTS ALSO LOOK AT AND OFTEN PREFER

Princeton University; Yale University; Stanford University; Harvard College; Brown University

AND SOMETIMES PREFER

Williams College; Brown University; University of California–Berkeley; MIT; Duke University; Columbia University

FINANCIAL FACTS

Financial Aid Rating	99
Annual tuition	$47,280
Room and board	$15,150
Required fees	$340
Books and supplies	$900
Average frosh need-based scholarship	$45,689
Average UG need-based scholarship	$42,064
% needy frosh rec. need-based scholarship or grant aid	100
% needy UG rec. need-based scholarship or grant aid	100
% needy frosh rec. non-need-based scholarship or grant aid	0
% needy UG rec. non-need-based scholarship or grant aid	0
% needy frosh rec. need-based self-help aid	100
% needy UG rec. need-based self-help aid	100
% frosh rec. any financial aid	57
% UG rec. any financial aid	56
% UG borrow to pay for school	39
Average cumulative indebtedness	$13,381
% frosh need fully met	100
% ugrads need fully met	100
Average % of frosh need met	100
Average % of ugrad need met	100

PORTLAND STATE UNIVERSITY

OFFICE OF ADMISSIONS AND RECORDS, PORTLAND, OR 97207-0751 • ADMISSIONS: 503-725-3511 • FAX: 503-725-5525

CAMPUS LIFE

Quality of Life Rating	87
Fire Safety Rating	73
Green Rating	98
Type of school	Public
Affiliation	No Affiliation
Environment	Metropolis

STUDENTS

Total undergrad enrollment	21,980
% male/female	46/54
% from out of state	166
% frosh from public high school	85
% ugrads live on campus	10
# of fraternities (% ugrad men join)	3 (1)
# of sororities (% ugrad women join)	3 (1)
% African American	3
% Asian	8
% Caucasian	59
% Hispanic	11
% Native American	1
% Pacific Islander	1
% Two or more races	5
% Race and/or ethnicity unknown	4
% international	7
# of countries represented	94

SURVEY SAYS...

Lots of liberal students
Students environmentally aware
Students love Portland, OR
Recreation facilities are great

ACADEMICS

Academic Rating	69
% students returning for sophomore year	70
students graduating within 4 years	14
students graduating within 6 years	41
Calendar	Semester
Student/faculty ratio	21:1
Profs interesting rating	74
Profs accessible rating	66

Most classes have 10–19 students.
Most lab/discussion sessions have 10–19 students.

MOST POPULAR MAJORS
Psychology; Business/Commerce; Social Sciences

STUDENTS SAY "..."

Academics

Portland State University's motto is "let knowledge serve the city," and students echo this philosophy, saying their school "has a strong focus on civic engagement and sustainability." "PSU is a great learning environment in the heart of the city" and a "good value" for your tuition dollars. It's also "a green-minded urban school" that's "training students to be good community members." "There is a wealth of courses" on offer here, with degrees in social work, a range of business majors, and the hard sciences all receiving praise. "Classes are usually pretty small," and professors "promote lots of in-class discussion and are readily available to meet outside of class as well." "They really care about the student's success, and they really help broaden our scope of learning [and] thinking critically." Adjunct professors are "very connected to the community and their particular areas of expertise." Overall, students are happy with their instructors, saying, "Most professors are engaging and truly want to challenge you and help you succeed." They "are well-educated [and] well-versed in current issues and research." There's "the occasional dud thrown into the mix," though. Generally, "they are prepared and are passionate about the classes they teach. They have a wealth of experiences to bring to classroom," and they're "easily accessible for questions or further assistance, students just need to reach out."

Life

The city of Portland is a big draw for PSU students. "The campus is extraordinarily beautiful and ideally located." Outdoor activities are big here: "There's skiing, hiking, camping, [and] fishing." "The downtown area has plenty of microbrew pubs, nightlife, eateries, and theaters." "The people are friendly, and the city is gorgeous and easy to navigate. You can go to the beach or to the mountain in about two hours, and there are many things to do outdoors. There are great parks throughout the city." "The public transportation is outstanding." It's bike- and vegan-friendly. "There are lots of activist and awareness-raising events going on all the time, and lots of students are involved in volunteering (on and off campus)." Because PSU has a large nontraditional undergraduate population and the majority of students live off campus, the sense of community extends beyond the school and into the city. "There are a lot of things to do on campus, and there are different groups on campus that promote going out into the community at large and helping out." "Because the student body is so big and really diverse, PSU has tons of programs/clubs/groups that help make you feel more involved with your school. PSU is also committed to sustainability: Any new buildings are made with the latest green technology, and recycling is a big deal."

Student Body

"It is difficult to define the typical PSU student, because there are so many of us from so many different backgrounds," one student says, and diversity does indeed seem to be the name of the game at PSU. Students describe themselves as "environmentally aware, hip," and "very liberal." Overall, people at PSU are "invested in their education and are friendly." There's a large population of non-traditional undergraduates, so students are "either typical college-age...or people in their thirties and forties with kids and full-time job trying to juggle everything." Even within this large, diverse student body, "everyone finds a niche pretty quickly." "It's easy to find people you get along with, but it's also easy to find people who are completely different from you, which makes school a lot more interesting."

FINANCIAL AID: 800-547-8887 • E-MAIL: ADMISSIONS@PDX.EDU • WEBSITE: WWW.PDX.EDU

THE PRINCETON REVIEW SAYS

Admissions

Very important factors considered include: rigor of secondary school record, academic GPA. *Other factors considered include:* standardized test scores, application essay. SAT or ACT required for some. ACT with or without writing accepted. SAT with or without Essay component accepted. TOEFL required of all international applicants. High school diploma is required and GED is accepted. *Academic units required:* 4 English, 3 math, 2 science, 2 foreign language, 2 social studies, 1 history. *Academic units recommended:* 1 science lab.

Financial Aid

Students should submit: FAFSA. Priority filing deadline is 2/28. The Princeton Review suggests that all financial aid forms be submitted as soon as possible after October 1. *Need-based scholarships/grants offered:* Federal Pell, FSEOG, State scholarships/grants, Private scholarships, College/university scholarship or grant aid from institutional funds, United Negro College Fund. *Loan aid offered:* Direct Subsidized Stafford Loans, Direct Unsubsidized Stafford Loans, Direct PLUS loans, Federal Perkins Loans. Applicants will be notified of awards on a rolling basis beginning 3/15. Federal Work-Study Program available. Institutional employment available.

The Inside Word

PSU offers a range of admission options for new freshmen, transfers, students enrolled at local community colleges, continuing students, and those with nontraditional high school backgrounds. Regardless of an applicant's status, admissions officers look for a secondary school GPA of at least 3.0, though high test scores can make up for a lower average.

THE SCHOOL SAYS "..."

From the Admissions Office

"Portland State University is Oregon's most diverse public university located in the heart of one of America's most progressive cities. It offers more than sixty undergraduate and forty graduate programs in fine and performing arts, liberal arts and sciences, business administration, education, urban and public affairs, social work, engineering, and computer science. PSU offers more than 120 bachelor's, master's, and doctoral degrees.

"The forty-nine-acre downtown campus—whose motto is 'Let Knowledge Serve the City'—places students in a vibrant center of culture, business, and technology. Portland State's urban mission offers opportunities for every student to participate in internships and community-based projects in business, education, social services, government, technology, and the arts and sciences.

"The award-winning University Studies curriculum provides small class sizes and mentoring for undergraduates and culminates in Senior Capstone, which takes students out of the classroom and into the field, where they utilize their knowledge and skills to develop community projects.

"Portland State has taken aggressive steps to enhance the student experience and campus life, with new student housing and a comprehensive recreation complex and remodeled science and performing arts facilities. The university also has hired more academic and career advisers and created new programs to support students. Sustainability—initiatives that balance environmental, economic, and social concerns—is incorporated throughout the curriculum and across the campus."

SELECTIVITY

Admissions Rating	74
# of applicants	6,299
% of applicants accepted	86
% of acceptees attending	32

FRESHMAN PROFILE

Range SAT Critical Reading	470–590
Range SAT Math	460–570
Range SAT Writing	440–560
Range ACT Composite	19–25
Minimum paper TOEFL	527
Minimum internet-based TOEFL	60
Average HS GPA	3.4
% graduated top 10% of class	11
% graduated top 25% of class	36
% graduated top 50% of class	79

DEADLINES

Regular	
Priority	6/1
Nonfall registration?	Yes

FINANCIAL FACTS

Financial Aid Rating	78
Annual in-state tuition	$6,750
Annual out-of-state tuition	$22,725
Room and board	$10,260
Required fees	$1,284
Books and supplies	$1,263
Average frosh need-based scholarship	$6,367
Average UG need-based scholarship	$6,008
% needy frosh rec. need-based scholarship or grant aid	73
% needy UG rec. need-based scholarship or grant aid	78
% needy frosh rec. non-need-based scholarship or grant aid	2
% needy UG rec. non-need-based scholarship or grant aid	1
% needy frosh rec. need-based self-help aid	71
% needy UG rec. need-based self-help aid	77
% frosh rec. any financial aid	75
% UG rec. any financial aid	56
% UG borrow to pay for school	65
Average cumulative indebtedness	$32,018
% frosh need fully met	9
% ugrads need fully met	5
Average % of frosh need met	75
Average % of ugrad need met	57

PRESCOTT COLLEGE

220 GROVE AVENUE, PRESCOTT, AZ 86301 • ADMISSIONS: 877-350-2100 • FAX: 928-776-5242

STUDENTS SAY "..."

Academics

Prescott College, a small, progressive school, "encourages critical and forward thinking around issues of social justice and sustainability." The school shines in interdisciplinary fields, such as environmental studies, human development and psychology, outdoor adventure education, and arts-based fields such as photography and creative writing. Prescott "is about taking learning out of the classroom," and true to its word, classes, according to the university, "take place in field sites throughout the Southwest, in art galleries, wilderness areas, along the U.S./Mexico border and in local schools, to name a few." Students see their education as "experiential, hands-on, real-world, and self-directed," and consider it to be a "journey, not a destination." Prescott's academic calendar is a unique "block and quarter system," which is "very effective at immersing students in their studies." Students take only one course for three four-week blocks before entering a ten-week semester. The quality of teaching "really varies. Some teachers are excellent and experienced and work well with the majority of the student body," and are "engaging and committed to their students." However, many students feel that "visiting" and "adjunct" professors "tend to be not so good." All the freedom at Prescott means that "academics are what you make them," and while some students find Prescott to be "academically stimulating but not very challenging," others think "there are plenty of opportunities for a rigorous academic experience."

Life

Prescott's emphasis on outdoor education and its ideal location near 1.4 million acres of National Forest mean that most students "live and play outside." One student says, "The majority of students rock climb, mountain bike, ski, snowboard, surf, raft, kayak, skydive, or ice climb." "If you want to go on an adventure, have no fear, you'll have an accomplice in less than an hour." The laid-back, artsy town of Prescott has a few bars that host "some good live music," which lots of students see whenever possible, though "sometimes you have to go to a larger city for that." Most students at Prescott are community-minded individuals, so it makes sense that one of the most popular social activities is to go to, or host, a potluck. As one student enthuses, "students also love potlucks; cooking is huge here." Others confirm that "potlucks are a huge part of student life," and that "much revolves around food." These gatherings can be "really fun and sometimes is crazy and sometimes really low-key." At potlucks and other gatherings, students "really enjoy each other's company." Generally, students do "not drink to get drunk, but drink as a part of a great evening out with friends," and most students seem to think people at Prescott "have good heads on their shoulders" and don't indulge in out-of-control partying.

Student Body

Prescott's emphasis on individual education, the environment, and sustainability means students are "environmentally and politically conscious" and "committed to their learning and creating a better community." Students are there because "they want to better themselves and have a positive impact on the world at large," and they're "motivated, empowered, and feisty." Additionally, students are very invested in social activism. Prescott's location means it attracts "athletic nerds" and "typical students love spending time outdoors." Yes, you'll probably see a lot of "hippies, hippies, hippies," but many students "wouldn't identify themselves that way." Though the school is predominantly white, students feel the community is "from a wide variety of cultural backgrounds" and that there's "a colorful array of people." As one student put it, the school "is made up of hundreds of different individuals who all bring their unique aspects to classes and social settings." Though students at Prescott tend to lean left, they say "any student fits in here. Everyone talks to everyone."

FINANCIAL AID: 928-350-1112 • E-MAIL: ADMISSIONS@PRESCOTT.EDU • WEBSITE: WWW.PRESCOTT.EDU

THE PRINCETON REVIEW SAYS

Admissions

Very important factors considered include: rigor of secondary school record, application essay, recommendation(s). *Important factors considered include:* academic GPA, standardized test scores, interview, extracurricular activities, talent/ability, volunteer work, work experience, level of applicant's interest. *Other factors considered include:* character/personal qualities. SAT or ACT required; SAT Subject Tests considered if submitted. ACT with or without writing accepted. TOEFL required of all international applicants. High school diploma is required and GED is accepted. *Academic units recommended:* 4 English, 3 math, 2 science, 1 foreign language, 3 social studies, 1 visual/performing arts.

Financial Aid

Students should submit: FAFSA. Priority filing deadline is 3/1. The Princeton Review suggests that all financial aid forms be submitted as soon as possible after October 1. *Need-based scholarships/grants offered:* Federal Pell, FSEOG, State scholarships/grants, Private scholarships, College/university scholarship or grant aid from institutional funds. *Loan aid offered:* Direct Subsidized Stafford Loans, Direct Unsubsidized Stafford Loans, Direct PLUS loans. Federal Work-Study Program available. Institutional employment available.

The Inside Word

The acceptance rate at Prescott is high, but the applicant pool is very self-selecting, and Prescott is the kind of place where you have to want to be. For example, while many colleges have fun-filled, low-pressure orientation programs for incoming students, Prescott students spend their first four weeks engaged in an immersion orientation experience in the Arizona wilderness that builds student's experiential education skills and integrates them into the Prescott academic community.

THE SCHOOL SAYS "..."

From the Admissions Office

"Prescott College highlights the dramatic educational return on investment when experience is at the center of learning. Tucked into a corner of the town in central Arizona of the same name, Prescott College is based in collaboration and teamwork as the cornerstone of learning. This is an educational institution that puts students at the center in everything it does and is. Narrative Evaluations are an essential part of grading. No barriers. Limited bureaucracy. No summa or magna or 'best in show' ribbons. Just a peripatetic community of lively intellects and fearless explorers whose connecting threads are a passion for social responsibility, practical application of theory and the environment, and a keen sense of adventure.

"At Prescott College, our goal is to fuel your passion and give you a deeper understanding of the world around you through collaborative learning and personal experience. We don't settle for the mundane college experience. Instead, we take learning outside the classroom and into the real world through experiential and field-based learning. From field studies, internships, and independent studies to community service and study abroad opportunities (about 50 percent of PC students study abroad!), our students are challenged to think critically, explore the world up close, and form solutions through collaborative efforts.

"If you're looking for a college experience unlike any other—the kind that enables you to take control of your education , have practical impact and truly make a positive impact in your community and in the world—then Prescott College is the ideal college for you."

SELECTIVITY

Admissions Rating	79
# of applicants	573
% of applicants accepted	68
% of acceptees attending	12
# of early decision applicants	12
% accepted early decision	58

FRESHMAN PROFILE

Range SAT Critical Reading	455–635
Range SAT Math	435–570
Range SAT Writing	430–575
Range ACT Composite	20–28
Minimum paper TOEFL	550
Minimum internet-based TOEFL	61
Average HS GPA	3.2
% graduated top 10% of class	0
% graduated top 50% of class	0

DEADLINES

Early decision	
Deadline	12/1
Notification	12/15
Regular	
Nonfall registration?	Yes

APPLICANTS ALSO LOOK AT
AND OFTEN PREFER
College of the Atlantic; Earlham College; Mills College

AND SOMETIMES PREFER
Whitman College

AND RARELY PREFER
Sarah Lawrence College; The Evergreen State College; University of Arizona; Reed College

FINANCIAL FACTS

Financial Aid Rating	81
Annual tuition	$26,088
Room and board	$8,374
Required fees	$1,415
Books and supplies	$2,842
Average frosh need-based scholarship	$16,564
Average UG need-based scholarship	$14,231
% needy frosh rec. need-based scholarship or grant aid	100
% needy UG rec. need-based scholarship or grant aid	99
% needy frosh rec. non-need-based scholarship or grant aid	3
% needy UG rec. non-need-based scholarship or grant aid	3
% needy frosh rec. need-based self-help aid	97
% needy UG rec. need-based self-help aid	97
% frosh rec. any financial aid	93
% UG rec. any financial aid	88
% frosh need fully met	3
% ugrads need fully met	6
Average % of frosh need met	65
Average % of ugrad need met	59

PRINCETON UNIVERSITY

PO BOX 430, ADMISSION OFFICE, PRINCETON, NJ 08544-0430 • ADMISSIONS: 609-258-3060 • FAX: 609-258-6743

STUDENTS SAY ". . ."

Academics
As a member of the grand old Ivy League, Princeton University has long maintained a "sterling reputation" for quality academics; however, students say Princeton's "unique focus on the undergraduate experience" is what makes their school stand out among institutions. It attracts "really experienced and big-name professors, who actually want to teach undergraduates." Introductory lecture classes can be rather large, but "once you take upper-level courses, you'll have a lot of chances to work closely with professors and study what you are most interested in." A current undergrad enthuses, "The discussions I have in seminar are the reason I get out of bed in the morning; after a great class, I feel incredibly invigorated." Though all Princeton professors are "leading scholars in their field," students admit that some classes can be "dry." Fortunately, "the overwhelming majority of professors are wonderful, captivating lecturers" who are "dedicated to their students." While you may be taking a class from a Nobel laureate, "the humility and accessibility of world-famous researchers and public figures is always remarkable." At Princeton, "there are so many chances to meet writers, performers, and professionals you admire." A student details, "The two years I've been here, I've been in discussions with Frank Gehry, David Sedaris, Peter Hessler, John McPhee, Jeff Koons, Chang-rae Lee, Joyce Carol Oates, W.S. Merwin, and on and on." No matter what you study, Princeton is an "intellectually challenging place," and the student experience is "intense in almost every way." Hard work pays off, though "the academic caliber of the school is unparalleled," and a Princeton education is "magnificently rewarding."

Life
Princeton students "tend to participate in a lot of different activities, from varsity sports (recruits), intramural sports (high school athletes), and more academically restricted activities like autonomous vehicle design club, Engineers Without Borders, and the literary magazine." In and out of the classroom, there are a "billion opportunities to do what you know you love" on the Princeton campus, from performance to sports to research. "Princeton offers a lot of different opportunities to relax and de-stress," including "sporting events, concerts, recreational facilities," "a movie theater that frequently screens current films for free," and "arts and crafts at the student center." For some, social life is centered along Prospect Avenue, where "Princeton's eating clubs are lined up like ten booze-soaked ducklings in a row." These eating clubs—private houses that serve as social clubs and cafeterias for upperclassmen—"play a large role in the social scene at the university." On the weekends, "the eating clubs are extremely popular for partying, chatting, drinking, and dancing"—not to mention, "free beer." "The campus is gorgeous year-round;" however, when students need a break from the college atmosphere, "there's NJ Transit if you want to go to New York, Philly, or even just the local mall."

Student Body
It's not surprising that most undergraduates are "driven, competitive, and obsessed with perfection." "Academics come first," and Princeton students are typified by dedication to their studies and "a tendency to overwork." "Almost everyone at Princeton is involved with something other than school about which they are extremely passionate," and most have "at least one distinct, remarkable talent." "It's fairly easy for most people to find a good group of friends with whom they have something in common," and many students get involved in one of the "infinite number of clubs" on campus. Superficially, "the preppy Ivy League stereotype" is reflected in the student population, and many students are "well-spoken," "dress nicely," and stay in shape. A student jokes, "Going to Princeton is like being in a contest to see who can be the biggest nerd while simultaneously appearing least nerdy."

FINANCIAL AID: 609-258-3330 • E-MAIL: UAOFFICE@PRINCETON.EDU • WEBSITE: WWW.PRINCETON.EDU

THE PRINCETON REVIEW SAYS

Admissions

Very important factors considered include: rigor of secondary school record, class rank, academic GPA, standardized test scores, application essay, recommendation(s), talent/ability, character/personal qualities. *Important factors considered include:* extracurricular activities. *Other factors considered include:* interview, first generation, alumni/ae relation, geographical residence, racial/ethnic status, volunteer work, work experience, level of applicant's interest. SAT with writing or ACT with writing required. TOEFL, IELTS, or Pearson required of all international applicants whose native language is not English. High school diploma or equivalent is not required. *Academic units recommended:* 4 English, 4 math, 4 science, 2 science labs, 4 foreign language, 2 social studies, 2 history, 1 visual/performing arts.

Financial Aid

Students should submit: FAFSA, Institution's own financial aid form. Priority filing deadline is 11/1. The Princeton Review suggests that all financial aid forms be submitted as soon as possible after October 1. *Need-based scholarships/grants offered:* Federal Pell, FSEOG, State scholarships/grants, Private scholarships, College/university scholarship or grant aid from institutional funds. *Loan aid offered:* Direct Subsidized Stafford Loans, Direct Unsubsidized Stafford Loans, Direct PLUS loans, College/university loans from institutional funds. Applicants will be notified of awards on or about 4/1. Federal Work-Study Program available. Institutional employment available.

The Inside Word

Not surprisingly, admission to Princeton is highly selective. Only about 7 percent of applicants are accepted, and these students usually rank at the top of their high school class. Prospective students should prepare for Princeton by excelling in honors, AP, and upper-level course work during high school. The application materials and personal essays are carefully read and evaluated, so students should also allocate time to prepare their applications. Admission to Princeton comes with a great deal of prestige, and to make the deal even sweeter, Princeton's remarkable no-loan financial aid program means that every student has 100 percent of their financial need met, without student loans.

THE SCHOOL SAYS ". . ."

From the Admissions Office

"Methods of instruction at Princeton vary widely, but common to all areas is a strong emphasis on individual responsibility and the free interchange of ideas. This is displayed most notably in the wide use of preceptorials and seminars, in the provision of independent study for all upperclass students and qualified underclass students, and in the availability of a series of special programs to meet a range of individual interests. The undergraduate college encourages the student to be an independent seeker of information and to assume responsibility for gaining both knowledge and judgment that will strengthen later contributions to society. Two hallmarks of the academic experience are the junior paper and senior thesis, which allow students the opportunity to pursue original research and scholarship in a field of their choosing.

"Princeton offers a distinctive financial aid program that provides grants, which do not have to be repaid, rather than loans. Princeton meets the full demonstrated financial need of all students—domestic and international—offered admission. About 60 percent of Princeton's undergraduates receive financial aid.

"All applicants must submit results for both the SAT as well as SAT Subject Tests in two different subject areas."

SELECTIVITY

Admissions Rating	99
# of applicants	27,290
% of applicants accepted	7
% of acceptees attending	68
# offered a place on the wait list	1,206
% accepting a place on wait list	71
% admitted from wait list	5

FRESHMAN PROFILE

Range SAT Critical Reading	690–790
Range SAT Math	700–800
Range SAT Writing	710–790
Range ACT Composite	32–35
Minimum paper TOEFL	600
Average HS GPA	3.9
% graduated top 10% of class	94
% graduated top 25% of class	98
% graduated top 50% of class	100

DEADLINES

Early action	
Deadline	11/1
Notification	12/15
Regular	
Deadline	1/1
Notification	4/1
Nonfall registration?	No

APPLICANTS ALSO LOOK AT AND SOMETIMES PREFER

Massachusetts Institute of Technology; Yale University; Stanford University; Harvard College

AND RARELY PREFER

University of Pennsylvania; Brown University

FINANCIAL FACTS

Financial Aid Rating	99
Annual tuition	$43,450
Room and board	$14,160
Books and supplies	$1,050
Average frosh need-based scholarship	$46,208
Average UG need-based scholarship	$44,890
% needy frosh rec. need-based scholarship or grant aid	100
% needy UG rec. need-based scholarship or grant aid	100
% needy frosh rec. non-need-based scholarship or grant aid	0
% needy UG rec. non-need-based scholarship or grant aid	0
% needy frosh rec. need-based self-help aid	100
% needy UG rec. need-based self-help aid	100
% frosh rec. any financial aid	59
% UG rec. any financial aid	60
% UG borrow to pay for school	16
Average cumulative indebtedness	$8,577
% frosh need fully met	100
% ugrads need fully met	100
Average % of frosh need met	100
Average % of ugrad need met	100

PROVIDENCE COLLEGE

HARKINS 222, PROVIDENCE, RI 02918 • ADMISSIONS: 401-865-2535 • FAX: 401-865-2826

CAMPUS LIFE

Quality of Life Rating	88
Fire Safety Rating	93
Green Rating	60*
Type of school	Private
Affiliation	Roman Catholic
Environment	City

STUDENTS

Total undergrad enrollment	4,201
% male/female	44/56
% from out of state	85
% frosh from public high school	58
% frosh live on campus	98
% ugrads live on campus	76
% African American	4
% Asian	1
% Caucasian	77
% Hispanic	8
% Native American	<1
% Pacific Islander	<1
% Two or more races	2
% Race and/or ethnicity unknown	5
% international	2
# of countries represented	24

SURVEY SAYS...

Students are happy
Career services are great
School is well run
Students are very religious
Easy to get around campus
Recreation facilities are great
Lots of beer drinking
Hard liquor is popular
Intramural sports are popular
Campus newspaper is popular
Alumni active on campus

ACADEMICS

Academic Rating	81
% students returning for sophomore year	90
% students graduating within 4 years	81
% students graduating within 6 years	85
Calendar	Semester
Profs interesting rating	76
Profs accessible rating	82

Most classes have 20–29 students.
Most lab/discussion sessions have
10–19 students.

MOST POPULAR MAJORS
Marketing/Marketing Management; Finance;
Biology

STUDENTS SAY "..."

Academics

Providence College is committed to maintaining small class sizes and facilities in order to provide its students with a strong liberal arts education and traditional campus life. With fewer than 5,000 undergrads, it is "uncommon for a student to not know or have interacted with the school president, dean of student affairs, dean of undergraduate studies, etc."

The universally small classes lead to "more discussion and less lecture," and professors "encourage student participation to not only learn concepts but apply them as well." They are "truly invested in student understanding/success," making themselves available through multiple channels, and "their passion for teaching can be felt within the classroom." Most teachers "provide plenty of opportunities to meet outside of class for help with school, talk about of life, or possibilities for careers after graduation." The classes "are no cake walk, but will give you the knowledge and experience for the real world," and "even the toughest graders have been reasonable with their explanations," says a junior English major.

The "strong liberal core curriculum" (using the Development of Western Civilization program as its centerpiece) and Catholic values of the school helps to prepare students "to serve as responsible and engaged world citizens." PC is "fantastic" at setting up students with internships that lead to future jobs, and professors place "a high value in experiential learning: getting involved with the community and taking advantage of opportunities to work and serve in the greater Providence Community." PC also has an incredible alumni base; alumni "are dedicated to the school, and dedicated to PC graduates."

Life

The school's location and the city of Providence offers the perfect balance for living: with "a beautiful, friendly campus as well as a vibrant city life just three minutes away from campus, students get the best of both worlds." It's the smallest 'big' school and the biggest small school," sums up a student. With Division I athletics (there are also "many opportunities to play through intramurals") but a small class size, students "can easily say that there is so much to do and so many opportunities that it's easy to get involved and not be bored." "Club involvement is huge," and just about everyone is on some type of club or in a student leadership position.

The "welcoming, upbeat, friendly environment" created on campus is due in part to the fact that "all the students live in one giant community." For fun, students like to explore the city of Providence, which "has a lot to offer", or go to on-campus events, such as "movie showings, bingo nights," and hockey and basketball games. There is "a large drinking culture" at PC, and though "students love to party and go out...come Sunday night, the library is packed and everyone has their nose in the books." The city and campus are quite secure: "I have never felt unsafe on campus, even if I am walking across it by myself at 3:00 A.M.," says a student. "Diversity and dining" are the two Ds that many students agree could use improvement; others also complain about the parietal rules, which impose curfews for the opposite sex to be in one another's dorms.

Student Body

"The Catholic Dominican tradition has a strong presence here," and the majority of the student body "is from New England and proud of it." Most students "look like they stepped out of a J. Crew advertisement," though there is a hipster contingent; everyone "is friendly and generally hangs out together," possibly because "the homogeneity and common experience creates strong bonds among the student body." Social groups "do not revolve around your class background at all," and students fit in through joining clubs or attending a lot of the big social events on campus. "We all bond over our Western Civ experience in our freshmen and sophomore years, so if you have gone through that then you fit in here," adds one junior.

FINANCIAL AID: 401-865-2286 • E-MAIL: PCADMISS@PROVIDENCE.EDU • WEBSITE: WWW.PROVIDENCE.E

THE PRINCETON REVIEW SAYS

Admissions

Very important factors considered include: rigor of secondary school record, academic GPA, application essay. *Important factors considered include:* recommendation(s), extracurricular activities, character/personal qualities. *Other factors considered include:* class rank, standardized test scores, talent/ability, first generation, alumni/ae relation, geographical residence, racial/ethnic status, volunteer work, work experience, level of applicant's interest. SAT or ACT considered if submitted. ACT with Writing required. SAT with Essay component required. TOEFL required of all international applicants. High school diploma is required and GED is not accepted. *Academic units required:* 4 English, 4 math, 3 science, 2 science labs, 3 foreign language, 2 social studies, 2 history. *Academic units recommended:* 4 English, 4 math, 4 science, 2 science labs, 4 foreign language, 2 social studies, 2 history.

Financial Aid

Students should submit: FAFSA, CSS/Financial Aid PROFILE. Regular filing deadline is 2/1. The Princeton Review suggests that all financial aid forms be submitted as soon as possible after October 1. *Need-based scholarships/grants offered:* Federal Pell, FSEOG, State scholarships/grants, Private scholarships, College/university scholarship or grant aid from institutional funds. *Loan aid offered:* Direct Subsidized Stafford Loans, Direct Unsubsidized Stafford Loans, Direct PLUS loans, Federal Perkins Loans, State Loans. Applicants will be notified of awards on or about 3/16. Federal Work-Study Program available. Institutional employment available.

The Inside Word

Few schools can claim a more transparent admissions process than Providence College. The admissions section of the school's website includes a voluminous blog authored by the associate dean of admissions. Providence has a test-optional policy, meaning applicants aren't required to submit standardized test scores.

THE SCHOOL SAYS "..."

From the Admissions Office

"A Providence College education challenges students to find commonality among topics that seem, on the surface, to be opposites. 'Or' often becomes 'and.' There are shared academic experiences such as the Core Curriculum and the distinctive Development of Western Civilization sequence, but the college also encourages students to explore differences of opinion and unfamiliar lines of thought. PC's Catholic and Dominican identity fuels intellectual, spiritual, and emotional growth by encouraging students to view subjects through the complementary lenses of faith and reason. It also fosters a respectful, supportive community that feels like home.

"Submission of standardized test scores is optional for students applying for admission. This policy change allows each student to decide whether they wish to have their standardized test results considered as part of their application for admission. Students who choose not to submit SAT or ACT test scores will not be penalized in the review for admission. Additional details about the test-optional policy can be found on our website at www.providence.edu/admission/Pages/test-optional-policy.aspx."

SELECTIVITY
Admissions Rating	
# of applicants	
% of applicants accepted	
% of acceptees attending	
# offered a place on the wait list	
% accepting a place on wait list	
% admitted from wait list	26
# of early decision applicants	196
% accepted early decision	87

FRESHMAN PROFILE
Range SAT Critical Reading	520–620
Range SAT Math	530–630
Range SAT Writing	520–630
Range ACT Composite	23–28
Minimum internet-based TOEFL	90
Average HS GPA	3.4
% graduated top 10% of class	9
% graduated top 25% of class	69
% graduated top 50% of class	94

DEADLINES
Early decision	
Deadline	12/1
Notification	1/1
Early action	
Deadline	11/15
Notification	1/1
Regular	
Priority	1/15
Deadline	1/15
Notification	4/1
Nonfall registration?	Yes

APPLICANTS ALSO LOOK AT AND OFTEN PREFER
Boston College; College of the Holy Cross

AND SOMETIMES PREFER
Villanova University

FINANCIAL FACTS
Financial Aid Rating	83
Annual tuition	$44,520
Room and board	$13,390
Required fees	$880
Books and supplies	$940
Average frosh need-based scholarship	$26,300
Average UG need-based scholarship	$23,825
% needy frosh rec. need-based scholarship or grant aid	94
% needy UG rec. need-based scholarship or grant aid	87
% needy frosh rec. non-need-based scholarship or grant aid	27
% needy UG rec. non-need-based scholarship or grant aid	17
% needy frosh rec. need-based self-help aid	92
% needy UG rec. need-based self-help aid	81
% frosh rec. any financial aid	84
% UG rec. any financial aid	81
% UG borrow to pay for school	64
Average cumulative indebtedness	$37,740
% frosh need fully met	28
% ugrads need fully met	22
Average % of frosh need met	84
Average % of ugrad need met	82

CAMPUS LIFE

Quality of Life Rating	92
Fire Safety Rating	95
Green Rating	94
Type of school	Public
Affiliation	No Affiliation
Environment	Town

STUDENTS

Total undergrad enrollment	29,497
% male/female	57/43
% from out of state	34
% frosh live on campus	94
% ugrads live on campus	38
# of fraternities (% ugrad men join)	50 (19)
# of sororities (% ugrad women join)	31 (21)
% African American	3
% Asian	6
% Caucasian	64
% Hispanic	4
% Native American	<1
% Pacific Islander	<1
% Two or more races	2
% Race and/or ethnicity unknown	2
% international	18
# of countries represented	123

SURVEY SAYS...

Students are happy
Great library
Career services are great
Internships are widely available
School is well run
Great food on campus
Recreation facilities are great
Everyone loves the Boilermakers
Intramural sports are popular
Campus newspaper is popular
Alumni active on campus

ACADEMICS

Academic Rating	79
% students graduating within 4 years	52
% students graduating within 6 years	75
Calendar	Semester
Student/faculty ratio	12:1
Profs interesting rating	70
Profs accessible rating	83

Most classes have 10–19 students.
Most lab/discussion sessions have 20–29 students.

MOST POPULAR MAJORS

Mechanical Engineering; Biology; Business Administration and Management

STUDENTS SAY "..."

Academics

Purdue is a Big Ten school that provides "a world class education" with a name "that is known all over the world and not just the state of Indiana." The university is especially "known for being a great engineering school," but has a bevy of amazing programs including "a great nursing program," "a great Pharmacy program" and a "speech pathology program [that] is one of the best." "I knew that I would receive an unparalleled education here," an Aeronautical and Astronautical Engineering major says. Purdue, "cradle of engineers and quarterbacks alike," is known for its athletics as well as its academics. There is "great school spirit exhibited in student organizations and athletic events." Yet despite the "big campus atmosphere," the school still maintains "small-school feel within its individual colleges." The "knowledgeable and helpful" professors are "very excited about their topic of teaching" and "the classes are excellent and stimulating." "Many of my professors have at least ten years under their belts with PhD's," one student boasts. Students are not going to find easy classes here. Purdue has teachers that "expect the most out of you." However, "the difficult and rigorous curriculum" is a bonding experience that "increases out of the classroom skills such as communication and collaboration." Some students did worry that "many things (such as Industrial Roundtable) are focused almost exclusively on engineers, which leaves some other majors out in the cold." "The dining services are immaculate" at Purdue, and students love how the school "promotes green technology." One Biology major explains the Purdue appeal: "It has everything a college kid could want: sports, academics, clubs, and delicious food." Purdue provides an educational experience that students will remember the rest of their lives. As one student puts it: "Once a Boilermaker, always a Boilermaker."

Life

Life at Purdue involves a lot of "time management" and "a typical student has a hard time completing all three S's (sleep, study, socialize) but has fun trying." As a Big Ten university, athletics make up a large part of campus life. "We have Ross-Ade Brigade and Paint Crew, student clubs for cheering on the athletic teams, and they're fairly large," one Biology major explains. "Partying and hard alcohol [are] common," but seem to divide the student body. Some wish the administration put "more control on partying and drinking" while others wish it was "less strict on alcohol/drug policies." "Sometimes there isn't a lot to do in West Lafayette besides drink," and "students typically spend their time partying hard on Thursday nights at the Cactus and cramming on Sunday nights." "Greek life is huge at Purdue" although "not essential." West Lafayette is "close to Chicago and Indy" for weekend trips, and "students stay on campus most of the time, so it's not a huge deal that the town around us sucks." There is "always something fun to do on campus" too, such as "a club meeting, a social event/recreational event, or just plain studying." "Most people unwind and have fun by joining a club or organization" and everyone seems to find a place to fit in. Even quiet students blossom at Purdue as "the atmosphere on campus coaxes most out of their shell sooner or later."

Student Body

Located in Indiana, Purdue has a student body that is largely "white and from the Midwest" with "conservative political views." That said, one student points out that "West Lafayette is a pretty progressive town and usually ends up going Democratic if you check election records." A fair number of students say the school needs to work to bring "better diversity." "Most students are really down to earth" and "students can all find their niche here and get along well." Students tend to bond "within their majors" which "helps create a small-school feel within a huge university," although "it is not unheard of for people involved in different things to be with different people." There is a fair amount of animosity between majors since "science and engineering majors DO look down on other majors" and tend to think that non-technical majors "are a 'joke' to the point that people are arrogant, obnoxious, and rude." Still, most students "fit in well" and at the end of the day "we take all kinds here and turn everyone into Boilermakers."

FINANCIAL AID: 765-494-0998 • E-MAIL: ADMISSIONS@PURDUE.EDU • WEBSITE: WWW.PURDUE.EDU

THE PRINCETON REVIEW SAYS

Admissions

Very important factors considered include: rigor of secondary school record, academic GPA, standardized test scores. *Important factors considered include:* application essay, recommendation(s), extracurricular activities, character/personal qualities, first generation. *Other factors considered include:* class rank, talent/ability, geographical residence, state residency, racial/ethnic status, volunteer work, work experience, level of applicant's interest. SAT or ACT required. High school diploma is required and GED is accepted. *Academic units required:* 4 English, 3 math, 3 science, 2 science labs, 3 foreign language. *Academic units recommended:* AP, IB, or honors courses.

Financial Aid

Students should submit: FAFSA. Priority filing deadline is 3/1. The Princeton Review suggests that all financial aid forms be submitted as soon as possible after October 1. *Need-based scholarships/grants offered:* Federal Pell, FSEOG, State scholarships/grants, Private scholarships, College/university scholarship or grant aid from institutional funds. *Loan aid offered:* Direct Subsidized Stafford Loans, Direct Unsubsidized Stafford Loans, Direct PLUS loans, Federal Perkins Loans, College/university loans from institutional funds. Applicants will be notified of awards on or about 3/15. Federal Work-Study Program available. Institutional employment available.

The Inside Word

Purdue looks at student applications holistically. Having said that, Purdue does have minimum high school course requirements, so make sure you have met or exceeded all of those requirements before applying.

THE SCHOOL SAYS "..."

From the Admissions Office

"Although it is one of America's largest universities, Purdue does not 'feel' big to its students. The campus is very compact when compared to universities with similar enrollment. Purdue is a comprehensive university with an international reputation in a wide range of academic fields. A strong work ethic prevails at Purdue. As a member of the Big Ten, Purdue has a strong and diverse athletic program. Purdue offers more than 1,000 clubs and organizations. The residence halls and Greek community offer many participatory activities for students. Numerous convocations and lectures are presented each year. Purdue is all about people, and allowing students to grow academically as well as socially, preparing them for the real world.

"Applicants seeking admission are required to have their SAT or ACT test score sent from the testing agency. Purdue accepts either test, and will use the best available score, for admission and scholarship decisions.

"To be considered for the full range of merit-based scholarships, students must complete their admission application by November 1.

"Purdue is a member of the Common Application and the Coalition Application."

SELECTIVITY

Admissions Rating	89
# of applicants	45,023
% of applicants accepted	59
% of acceptees attending	26

FRESHMAN PROFILE

Range SAT Critical Reading	520–630
Range SAT Math	560–700
Range SAT Writing	520–640
Range ACT Composite	25–31
Minimum paper TOEFL	550
Minimum internet-based TOEFL	79
Average HS GPA	3.7
% graduated top 10% of class	43
% graduated top 25% of class	79
% graduated top 50% of class	97

DEADLINES

Early action	
Deadline	11/1
Notification	Rolling
Regular	
Priority	1/1
Notification	Rolling
Nonfall registration?	Yes

AND SOMETIMES PREFER

Indiana University—Bloomington; University of Illinois at Urbana-Champaign

FINANCIAL FACTS

Financial Aid Rating	88
Annual in-state tuition	$9,208
Annual out-of-state tuition	$28,010
Room and board	$10,030
Required fees	$794
Books and supplies	$1,220
Average frosh need-based scholarship	$13,865
Average UG need-based scholarship	$12,834
% needy frosh rec. need-based scholarship or grant aid	62
% needy UG rec. need-based scholarship or grant aid	66
% needy frosh rec. non-need-based scholarship or grant aid	45
% needy UG rec. non-need-based scholarship or grant aid	39
% needy frosh rec. need-based self-help aid	76
% needy UG rec. need-based self-help aid	83
% frosh rec. any financial aid	74
% UG rec. any financial aid	77
% UG borrow to pay for school	48
Average cumulative indebtedness	$27,711
% frosh need fully met	48
% ugrads need fully met	42
Average % of frosh need met	83
Average % of ugrad need met	86

QUINNIPIAC UNIVERSITY

275 MOUNT CARMEL AVENUE, HAMDEN, CT 06518 • ADMISSIONS: 203-582-8600 • FAX: 203-582-8906

CAMPUS LIFE
Quality of Life Rating	87
Fire Safety Rating	98
Green Rating	79
Type of school	Private
Affiliation	No Affiliation
Environment	Town

STUDENTS
Total undergrad enrollment	6,982
% male/female	39/61
% from out of state	70
% frosh from public high school	70
% frosh live on campus	95
% ugrads live on campus	77
# of fraternities (% ugrad men join)	8 (24)
# of sororities (% ugrad women join)	10 (25)
% African American	5
% Asian	3
% Caucasian	77
% Hispanic	9
% Native American	<1
% Pacific Islander	<1
% Two or more races	2
% Race and/or ethnicity unknown	3
% international	2
# of countries represented	43

SURVEY SAYS...
Students are happy
Classroom facilities are great
Great library
Dorms are like palaces
Lots of beer drinking
Hard liquor is popular
Campus newspaper is popular

ACADEMICS
Academic Rating	81
% students returning for sophomore year	87
% students graduating within 4 years	71
% students graduating within 6 years	76
Calendar	Semester
Student/faculty ratio	12:1
Profs interesting rating	78
Profs accessible rating	81

Most classes have 20–29 students.
Most lab/discussion sessions have 10–19 students.

MOST POPULAR MAJORS
Psychology; Business/Commerce; Registered Nursing/Registered Nurse

STUDENTS SAY "..."

Academics
Located on a "beautiful" campus near New Haven, Connecticut, Quinnipiac University is a liberal arts school that "wants every student to graduate with a well-rounded education." The school "is about educating students in both their major and in general knowledge so they are prepared for life after college." Though health science, business, and communications are the school's most notable programs, the entire university "takes pride in its academics" and is "invested in preparing students for their potential career in the best way possible." No matter your major, the school stresses that "the most important aspect is the student's undergraduate experience on the journey of finding themselves."

Since class sizes are so small, teachers "are able to engage with each student individually." The professors at Quinnipiac "really look out for the students and want them to achieve." Like at any college, "there are amazing professors and terrible professors," but "looking up the reviews and trusting students' opinions" will help you know which ones to pick. Professors all "encourage discussion and bring in real-life stories," and "they are always enthusiastic to share their knowledge. They implement hands-on learning, too." Students cite "the accessibility to meet with professors during their office hours" as a huge plus. "It is very easy to get in contact with them when needed," says a student. "I have close bonds with several, and my academic experience has been nothing but enjoyable," says another. As one student sums up, "Quinnipiac University is extremely dedicated to helping students make their college experience not only beneficial, but enjoyable as well."

Life
Students at the school "value the closeness of our community and bringing everyone together," according to a student. The campus is "just plain gorgeous" ("When I came to this school I got the 'wedding dress feeling,'" says a student.), and there's a lot going on there, too. "Campus life is awesome!" There are "so many ways" of getting involved: "numerous clubs and activities, supporting the athletic teams, intramural sports, and much more." The student body is "heavily devoted" to the subjects they are involved in, and everywhere you look "friendly faces" are taking advantage of the "very programmed schedule" of events. A "good majority of the students here like to party hard Thursday through Saturday night," but if you don't like to drink or go out, the programming board "does an excellent job providing events on campus such as casino night, drive-in movies, stand-up comics, games, etc."

Despite the Quinnipiac love, there are some gripes. The living facilities "could stand to be updated," "more onsite parking" is definitely needed, and everyone pretty much universally agrees that the "food could always be better." However, people do love the duality of a "college-town feel with a city nearby," and the shuttles that run into nearby New Haven are extremely popular. The "great sports teams" also help bring together the student body, and "on Friday nights, hockey and basketball are big."

Student Body
The typical student here is a "middle- to upper-class Caucasian from the tristate area" and "a little preppy, but casual at the same time." "Students are easy to make friends with," so "it's easy to find a niche here." "Students all seem to have a place, there are so many different groups that it's hard not to find someplace for everyone," says one. "I feel like it's a good place to go if you want a balance between social life and school work," says a student. This "studious" and "well-motivated" group is usually "involved in at least one program outside of academics," but also "likes to enjoy themselves on weekends." Though Quinnipiac "is not very diverse," it "is becoming more diverse." Many students are "very interested in fashion and culture."

FINANCIAL AID: 203-582-8750 • E-MAIL: ADMISSIONS@QUINNIPIAC.EDU • WEBSITE: WWW.QUINNIPIAC.EDU

THE PRINCETON REVIEW SAYS

Admissions

Very important factors considered include: rigor of secondary school record, academic GPA. *Important factors considered include:* class rank, standardized test scores, application essay, recommendation(s). *Other factors considered include:* interview, extracurricular activities, talent/ability, character/personal qualities, first generation, alumni/ae relation, racial/ethnic status, volunteer work, work experience, level of applicant's interest. SAT or ACT required. ACT with or without writing accepted. SAT with or without Essay component accepted. TOEFL required of all international applicants. High school diploma is required and GED is accepted. *Academic units required:* 4 English, 3 math, 3 science, 2 science labs, 2 foreign language, 2 social studies, and 4 units from above areas or other academic areas. *Academic units recommended:* 4 English, 4 math, 4 science, 3 science labs, 2 foreign language, 3 social studies.

Financial Aid

Students should submit: FAFSA, CSS/Financial Aid PROFILE, Noncustodial PROFILE. Priority filing deadline is 3/1. The Princeton Review suggests that all financial aid forms be submitted as soon as possible after October 1. *Need-based scholarships/grants offered:* Federal Pell, FSEOG, State scholarships/grants, Private scholarships, College/university scholarship or grant aid from institutional funds. *Loan aid offered:* Direct Subsidized Stafford Loans, Direct Unsubsidized Stafford Loans, Direct PLUS loans, Federal Perkins Loans. Applicants will be notified of awards on a rolling basis beginning 2/15. Federal Work-Study Program available. Institutional employment available.

The Inside Word

Quinnipiac offers early decision (deadline November 1) and also admits students on a rolling basis, a process that favors those who get their applications in early. Programs in physical therapy, nursing, and physician assistant are quite competitive. The school strongly recommends that those seeking spots in these programs apply no later than November 15.

THE SCHOOL SAYS "..."

From the Admissions Office

"Quinnipiac today is 'three settings, one university,' with an undergraduate population growing to 6,500, many of whom remain at QU for the ever expanding graduate programs, and a continuing focus on our core values: academic excellence, a student oriented environment and a strong sense of community.

"The Mount Carmel campus, the academic home to all undergraduates with traditional, suite and apartment housing for freshmen and sophomores, is 250-acres in a stunning setting adjacent to Sleeping Giant state park. The nearby 250-acre York Hill campus is home to juniors and seniors in apartments with breathtaking views, a lodge style student center, covered parking, and the TD Bank sports center with twin arenas for hockey and basketball. The 100-acre North Haven campus, just four miles distant, is the home to graduate programs in Health Sciences, and Education, and the Frank H. Netter, MD School of Medicine.

"Academic initiatives such as the honors program, 'writing across the curriculum', QU seminar series, extensive internship experiences, study abroad opportunities and a highly regarded emerging leaders student-life program form the foundation for excellence in business, communication, health sciences, nursing, engineering, education, liberal arts, and law.

"State of the art facilities include the Financial Technology Center, HD fully digital production studio, extensive health science labs, recreation and sports fields and arenas. More than 100 student organizations, twenty-one Division I teams, community service, student publications, and a strong student government offer a variety of outside-of-class experiences. "

SELECTIVITY

Admissions Rating	83
# of applicants	22,745
% of applicants accepted	74
% of acceptees attending	11
# offered a place on the wait list	1,570
% accepting a place on wait list	55
% admitted from wait list	9
# of early decision applicants	433
% accepted early decision	62

FRESHMAN PROFILE

Range SAT Critical Reading	490–590
Range SAT Math	500–620
Range SAT Writing	490–590
Range ACT Composite	22–27
Minimum paper TOEFL	550
Minimum internet-based TOEFL	80
Average HS GPA	3.4
% graduated top 10% of class	27
% graduated top 25% of class	69
% graduated top 50% of class	94

DEADLINES

Early decision	
Deadline	11/1
Notification	12/1
Regular	
Priority	2/1
Nonfall registration?	Yes

APPLICANTS ALSO LOOK AT AND OFTEN PREFER
Boston University; Villanova University

AND SOMETIMES PREFER
Northeastern University; University of Delaware

AND RARELY PREFER
Sacred Heart University; Ithaca College

FINANCIAL FACTS

Financial Aid Rating	79
Annual tuition	$41,990
Room and board	$14,200
Required fees	$1,650
Books and supplies	$800
Average frosh need-based scholarship	$21,166
Average UG need-based scholarship	$20,683
% needy frosh rec. need-based scholarship or grant aid	98
% needy UG rec. need-based scholarship or grant aid	97
% needy frosh rec. non-need-based scholarship or grant aid	78
% needy UG rec. non-need-based scholarship or grant aid	63
% needy frosh rec. need-based self-help aid	75
% needy UG rec. need-based self-help aid	81
% frosh rec. any financial aid	88
% UG rec. any financial aid	83
% UG borrow to pay for school	67
Average cumulative indebtedness	$47,873
% frosh need fully met	18
% ugrads need fully met	15
Average % of frosh need met	67
Average % of ugrad need met	65

RANDOLPH COLLEGE

2500 RIVERMONT AVENUE, LYNCHBURG, VA 24503-1555 • ADMISSIONS: 434-947-8100 • FAX: 434-947-8996

STUDENTS SAY "..."

Academics

Rest assured, at Randolph College, "You're not just a number; you matter as an individual." Indeed, this "small, tight-knit community" instantly "makes you feel welcome." Additionally, students at Randolph are grateful they attend a college that "promotes self discovery, personal growth, and individuality." Further, "small class sizes" allow for an "emphasis on student-professor relationships," a hallmark of a Randolph education. One undergrad happily confirms, "My academic experience has been challenging, there's no doubt, but the professor support has made that challenge enjoyable and exciting." A fellow student agrees, sharing, "My professors are excellent. Everyone I have had here has been supremely knowledgeable, understanding and helpful to students. The number one goal is always to make students better thinkers." Finally, as this student gushes, "My professors are amazing! Their passion for the subject matter and course content is infectious. I look forward to each class each day and feel confident in my education. Learning is interesting and fun here, and professors are eager to answer questions and provide resources to supplement lectures and experiments. Often professors list their home phone numbers on syllabi to allow students to contact them outside of office hours. Every professor replies to e-mail quickly, and professors are all very easy to communicate with in the classroom and one-on-one."

Life

According to many undergrads, "life at Randolph is always busy and exciting." As one ecstatic student quickly asserts, "I don't think I have [been] bored [since] the day I stepped foot on this campus." And why would you be? Indeed, there are "a wide variety of clubs and organizations [in which] to become involved." Moreover, there are "many sports teams and exciting competitions to watch" as well as intramurals, which "offer a chance for non-athletes to" participate. In addition, there are a myriad of "parties and dances...sponsored by various organizations." These events are typically well-attended by students, as "they never disappoint." And for those undergrads looking for an activity a little more out of the box, there's "even a game called Humans vs Zombies where students dress up and try to 'turn people into zombies' with Nerf guns. It's a lot of fun." Randolph is also home to many proud traditions and students love to partake. An insider reveals, "The even-odd class rivalry is definitely one popular school tradition. Skeller Sings are one of the events where the even spirit society (ETAs) and odd spirit society (Gammas) will sing (read: shout) songs at each other and try to create distractions while the other group sings." Finally, when students want to look beyond the campus for fun, they can "go hiking, swimming, and boating at all the lakes, rivers, and trails. [Indeed] there is a lot of nature and history surrounding the Lynchburg area."

Student Body

Undergrads at Randolph emphatically state that there's no typical student to be found wandering around campus. As one knowing undergrad shares, "Students vary widely in background and personality, preferences, [and] habits." Additionally, a "considerable percentage of the student body is comprised of international students," which certainly adds to the diversity of the school. Of course, if pressed to throw out some adjectives, Randolph undergrads will likely say that their peers are "hardworking, artistic, and caring." They are also "intelligent," "unafraid to speak their minds," and "committed to doing excellent work." Fortunately, "being such a small campus, it is hard not [to] develop lots of friends from several different social groups," and certainly, "campus traditions help form a very strong sense of community here." Or, as one content undergrad simply states, "Everyone gets along fairly well and it's not too hard to fit in when there aren't really any labels for people."

FINANCIAL AID: 434-947-8128 • E-MAIL: ADMISSIONS@RANDOLPHCOLLEGE.EDU • WEBSITE: WWW.RANDOLPHCOLLEGE.EDU

THE PRINCETON REVIEW SAYS

Admissions

Very important factors considered include: academic GPA, standardized test scores, recommendation(s). *Important factors considered include:* rigor of secondary school record, application essay, extracurricular activities, alumni/ae relation, level of applicant's interest. *Other factors considered include:* class rank, interview, talent/ability, character/personal qualities, first generation, volunteer work, work experience. SAT or ACT required; SAT Subject Tests considered if submitted. ACT with or without writing accepted. SAT with or without Essay component accepted. High school diploma is required and GED is accepted. *Academic units required:* 4 English, 3 math, 3 science, 2 science labs, 2 history, 1 academic elective. *Academic units recommended:* 4 math, 3 foreign language, 3 academic electives.

Financial Aid

Students should submit: The Princeton Review suggests that all financial aid forms be submitted as soon as possible after October 1. *Need-based scholarships/grants offered:* Federal Pell, FSEOG, State scholarships/grants, Private scholarships, College/university scholarship or grant aid from institutional funds. *Loan aid offered:* Direct Subsidized Stafford Loans, Direct Unsubsidized Stafford Loans, Direct PLUS loans, College/university loans from institutional funds. Applicants will be notified of awards on a rolling basis beginning 10/1. Federal Work-Study Program available. Institutional employment available.

The Inside Word

Officers at Randolph College take a fairly traditional approach to their admissions decisions. Certainly your transcript and test scores hold the most weight. However, recommendations, personal essays, and extracurricular activities are also taken into consideration, so it's best not to slack off any facet of your application.

THE SCHOOL SAYS "..."

From the Admissions Office

"Students who thrive in a close-knit community that values original thinking and research will enjoy the educational and cultural environment at Randolph College where they may earn a BA, BS, or BFA degree.

"Nationally ranked for both its academic programs and affordability, Randolph College offers students the best features of an honors education with a wide range of majors and an emphasis on developing intercultural competence. Embedded within the strong, liberal arts foundation are ample opportunities for study abroad, leadership roles, working closely with faculty on research, and real-world experience through internships and service learning. All students are encouraged to pursue and achieve goals with personal meaning.

"A graduate of Randolph College understands the intellectual foundations of the arts, sciences, and humanities and has developed critical skills to learn, adapt, and succeed in a rapidly changing global environment. The college's strong emphasis on writing enables students to communicate clearly and persuasively, and the diverse student population and study abroad programs enable students to see and live through the eyes of another culture. The long-standing and distinctive honor system is a central part of daily life at Randolph and adds to the already close-knit community feel.

"A member of the Old Dominion Athletic Conference and IHSA (Randolph has a 100-acre riding center), Randolph enables scholar-athletes to excel and participate in a variety of sports while focusing on academics. Located in the heart of Virginia near the Blue Ridge Mountains, Randolph College's campus is part of the growing college town of Lynchburg with its abundant cultural, entertainment, and recreational opportunities."

SELECTIVITY

Admissions Rating	75
# of applicants	1,207
% of applicants accepted	81
% of acceptees attending	19

FRESHMAN PROFILE

Range SAT Critical Reading	460–570
Range SAT Math	450–550
Range SAT Writing	440–550
Range ACT Composite	19–24
Average HS GPA	3.5
% graduated top 10% of class	13
% graduated top 25% of class	35
% graduated top 50% of class	80

DEADLINES

Early action	
Deadline	11/15
Notification	1/1
Regular	
Deadline	3/1
Notification	Rolling
Nonfall registration?	Yes

APPLICANTS ALSO LOOK AT AND OFTEN PREFER
Lynchburg College; University of Mary Washington

AND SOMETIMES PREFER
Virginia Tech; James Madison University

AND RARELY PREFER
Randolph-Macon College

FINANCIAL FACTS

Financial Aid Rating	84
Annual tuition	$34,800
Room and board	$12,106
Required fees	$610
Books and supplies	$1,000
Average frosh need-based scholarship	$25,373
Average UG need-based scholarship	$24,925
% needy frosh rec. need-based scholarship or grant aid	100
% needy UG rec. need-based scholarship or grant aid	99
% needy frosh rec. non-need-based scholarship or grant aid	18
% needy UG rec. non-need-based scholarship or grant aid	15
% needy frosh rec. need-based self-help aid	98
% needy UG rec. need-based self-help aid	83
% frosh rec. any financial aid	99
% UG rec. any financial aid	99
% UG borrow to pay for school	80
Average cumulative indebtedness	$35,441
% frosh need fully met	25
% ugrads need fully met	23
Average % of frosh need met	76
Average % of ugrad need met	77

RANDOLPH-MACON COLLEGE

P. O. Box 5005, Ashland, VA 23005-5505 • Admissions: 804-752-7305 • Fax: 804-752-4707

STUDENTS SAY ". . ."

Academics

Randolph-Macon College in Virginia is a small liberal arts school that "puts the needs of the student first, creates equal opportunity," and "provides as much as the student wishes to garner from the experience." The school places a focus on student development both inside and outside of the classroom, and offers "a lot of free resources and support for every student" who wishes to take advantage, including generous financial aid and study abroad included in tuition.

The majority of students here cite the possibility of "personal connections" as the main reason for coming to Randolph-Macon, which "is all about the one-on-one interactions between the entire community." Lectures are relatively infrequent and most of the academic classes are interactive and discussion-based so as to "maximize learning," and students also "get a lot of opportunities to write throughout your classes." "I love the small class sizes here; my largest class has eighteen students in it which makes it easy to get extra help and ask questions," says a freshman. To top it off, the "very personable" professors are "extremely helpful and are willing to meet with you if you want to go over material." They "bring their dogs to class, have class outside, invite students over for dinner and supply us with the resources to succeed."

There are "many different opportunities to get involved and strengthen your leadership skills" outside of the classroom, such as study abroad, "the J-Term, working on campus, and career services/internship offices." The "challenging but rewarding academic environment" also allows for undergrads to conduct and publish research quite easily. The "accessible" alumni network and staff are also "wonderful." They are "truly interested in your success and are more than helpful when it comes to resumes, cover letters, internships, and anything related to the business professional world."

Life

Students at Randolph-Macon fit in by being a part of something bigger than themselves, whether it's "greek life, athletics, intramurals, choir, orientation leaders, or Resident Assistants," and "virtually EVERYONE is involved." In addition, "many of the clubs are given a grant, so all of the events and trips you go on are free." "It is impossible to not be involved in something here," says a student. "If you are bored here, it is your own fault." There is a college-sponsored activity going on every weekend, such as "ice cream socials, crafting, performances, comedians, etc."; occasionally students travel off-campus for parties or other activities (Richmond is nearby for students who want a little urban action), but "life is generally centered on campus." Some students do wish they could be kept a little more abreast of happenings around campus: "There isn't a lot of advertisement for campus events, even though most of them are pretty fun."

Dining options are universally panned by students, who frequently grab bites to eat elsewhere, and though "there is a party scene" it's not the only option by a long shot. "There are so many subgroups that you might have to try to NOT find someone with similar interests," assures a junior.

Student Body

Though most students here are "white," "preppy," and "southern," the common thread is that this is "a small community of intelligent minded students that enjoy their weekends." There is "fantastic student involvement and diversity of interests" at R-MC, and the typical student "knows that academics are the most important, but never forgets that extracurriculars are a must!" People here are "driven and passionate about their success here while at college and in their futures." By "going to parties on the weekend and saying 'hi' to people you have classes with" students have no problem making friends, as "the campus is too small to not find a group to fit in with."

RANDOLPH-MACON COLLEGE

FINANCIAL AID: (804) 752-7259 • E-MAIL: ADMISSIONS@RMC.EDU • WEBSITE: WWW.RMC.EDU

THE PRINCETON REVIEW SAYS

Admissions

Very important factors considered include: rigor of secondary school record, academic GPA. *Important factors considered include:* class rank, standardized test scores, application essay, recommendation(s). *Other factors considered include:* interview, extracurricular activities, talent/ability, character/personal qualities, first generation, alumni/ae relation, racial/ethnic status, volunteer work, work experience, level of applicant's interest. SAT or ACT required; SAT Subject Tests considered if submitted. ACT with Writing recommended. TOEFL required of all international applicants. High school diploma is required and GED is accepted. *Academic units required:* 4 English, 3 math, 3 science, 2 science labs, 2 social studies, 1 history, 1 academic elective. *Academic units recommended:* 4 English, 4 math, 4 science, 4 science labs, 4 foreign language, 3 social studies, 3 history, 2 academic electives.

Financial Aid

Students should submit: FAFSA, State aid form. Regular filing deadline is 3/1. The Princeton Review suggests that all financial aid forms be submitted as soon as possible after October 1. *Need-based scholarships/grants offered:* Federal Pell, FSEOG, State scholarships/grants, Private scholarships, College/university scholarship or grant aid from institutional funds. *Loan aid offered:* Direct Subsidized Stafford Loans, Direct Unsubsidized Stafford Loans, Direct PLUS loans, Federal Perkins Loans. Applicants will be notified of awards on or about 3/1. Federal Work-Study Program available. Institutional employment available.

The Inside Word

Randolph-Macon is a solid liberal arts college, but it must contend with a wealth of Virginia schools for applicants. Students who are academically competitive should easily gain acceptance. Admissions officers ascribe the most weight to objective data, primarily grades and test scores. Recommendations, special skills and talents, and personal attributes also figure into the decision.

THE SCHOOL SAYS "..."

From the Admissions Office

"A Randolph-Macon College education begins with your future in mind the moment you arrive on campus. R-MC's unique approach integrates an extraordinary education with a personalized, four-year career preparation program, The Edge, to give students a distinct, competitive advantage after graduation in reaching their career or graduate school goals. Self-assessment programs, workshops to develop strong communication and life skills, and opportunities to network and be mentored by business leaders and well-connected alumni culminate in confident students developing their own 'brand.' Randolph-Macon's dedicated, collaborative team of faculty, staff, coaches and alumni provides a campus-wide support system to help you make the most of your R-MC experience. Campus life offers dozens of organizations, a dynamic event schedule, and exceptional leadership opportunities that prepare tomorrow's leaders. Randolph-Macon ranks sixteenth in the nation in alumni giving, a testament to alumni loyalty, engagement and gratitude. R-MC's challenging curriculum and national and global opportunities through internships and study-abroad adventures, including its unique January Term, make students competitive for any career or academic pursuit. The college's accessibility and ideal location just outside of Richmond, Virginia, and its proximity to Washington, D.C., offer a wide range of educational and career possibilities. Partnerships with prestigious medical institutions guarantee admission to qualified students to medical or nursing school. Our Four-Year-Degree Guarantee program promises in writing that freshmen who meet the necessary requirements will graduate within four calendar years. Ninety-five percent of Randolph-Macon graduates earn their degree in four years or fewer. Randolph-Macon helps you build an extraordinary future."

SELECTIVITY

Admissions Rating	84
# of applicants	2,968
% of applicants accepted	60
% of acceptees attending	23
# offered a place on the wait list	219
% accepting a place on wait list	26
% admitted from wait list	22

FRESHMAN PROFILE

Range SAT Critical Reading	500–600
Range SAT Math	500–580
Range SAT Writing	480–580
Range ACT Composite	22–27
Minimum paper TOEFL	550
Minimum internet-based TOEFL	80
Average HS GPA	3.7
% graduated top 10% of class	21
% graduated top 25% of class	56
% graduated top 50% of class	86

DEADLINES

Early action	
Deadline	11/15
Notification	1/1
Regular	
Priority	2/1
Deadline	3/1
Notification	4/1
Nonfall registration?	Yes

APPLICANTS ALSO LOOK AT AND SOMETIMES PREFER

Christopher Newport University; Hampden-Sydney College; Roanoke College; University of Mary Washington; Virginia Tech; University of Virginia; James Madison University

FINANCIAL FACTS

Financial Aid Rating	86
Annual tuition	$36,600
Room and board	$10,880
Required fees	$1,000
Books and supplies	$1,100
Average frosh need-based scholarship	$24,571
Average UG need-based scholarship	$23,494
% needy frosh rec. need-based scholarship or grant aid	100
% needy UG rec. need-based scholarship or grant aid	100
% needy frosh rec. non-need-based scholarship or grant aid	28
% needy UG rec. non-need-based scholarship or grant aid	23
% needy frosh rec. need-based self-help aid	72
% needy UG rec. need-based self-help aid	76
% frosh rec. any financial aid	99
% UG rec. any financial aid	99
% UG borrow to pay for school	77
Average cumulative indebtedness	$35,937
% frosh need fully met	32
% ugrads need fully met	30
Average % of frosh need met	83
Average % of ugrad need met	80

REED COLLEGE

3203 SOUTHEAST WOODSTOCK BOULEVARD, PORTLAND, OR 97202-8199 • ADMISSIONS: 503-777-7511 • FAX: 503-777-7553

STUDENTS SAY "..."

Academics

Reed is a college synonymous with academic rigor and a "passion for learning" certainly permeates this campus. A political science major steadfastly agrees stating, "Reed's commitment to academic excellence blew me away. The students here work like demons and love it!" In fact, "Reedies are proud that the most popular location on campus is the library, regardless of the night of the week." Fortunately, "there is a collective humor on campus and no one takes themselves too seriously." Undergrads also closely adhere to an "Honor Principle" which ensures that "cheating, peer-pressure or antagonism of any kind [is] extremely rare." This also helps to foster a culture where "people would rather help each other learn than be the best." Additionally, small classes are integral to the academic experience here. The "10:1 student to faculty ratio assures that the professors have the time to devote to their students, and students have plenty of opportunities to use that time, be it in thesis meetings, regular office hours, or just to bug the professor about a question they had about that day's conference or lab." And these undergrads are eager to lap up conversation with their "brilliant" professors who "love teaching" and "will not allow you to settle for mediocrity." All in all, the college "breeds free thought, pushes students to their intellectual limits, and strengthens each student's character all in the context of the liberal, free-spirited, and welcoming environment that is the Reed campus and the surrounding city of Portland, Oregon."

Life

Intellectual discussions and debates are most definitely woven into the fabric of life here. As a physics major reveals, "One of my favorite things about Reed is how often people will strike up engaged discussions about anything. Be it conversations about the axiom of choice, the existence of free will, or the various merits of 1990s television shows, every conversation is fascinating. Best, you'll hear these conversations everywhere you go: dining hall, dorms, academic buildings, even just people walking around campus." Of course, this isn't wholly surprising given that life at Reed "revolves around academics." But fear not; even Reedies cannot survive by books alone. And, "while work and fun are, in many cases, synonymous, the need to break free from the library manifests on the weekends by campus dances and other forms of spontaneous creativity." A psychology major quickly adds, "I'm never bored because there's always something going on and it's never the same. Glittery dance parties in the Student Union? Check. Movie night in one of the Language Houses? Check. Debate-watching in Vollum? Check. Visiting lecturers? Check. Pool hall tournament? Check. RPG gaming night? Check." We are also told that "a lot of students partake in various substances." However, an understanding junior qualifies this statement, "If you are straightedge or the like, like me, your boundaries will be pushed, but almost always by people who are respectful and who genuinely desire to keep the dorms a safe space for you." Finally, despite grumblings that public transport "can be annoying," undergrads may take advantage of anything downtown Portland has to offer.

Student Body

As you probably already gleaned, the typical Reedie has "an overwhelming curiosity and desire to question everything." "Socially liberal" and a tad "socially awkward," these undergrads also define their peers as "smart," "quirky," "witty and talented." A content sophomore explains, "Everyone brings their own unique spin to everything—everyone has a hidden talent or skill that they would love to teach you about, or a wealth of knowledge in some obscure subject you've probably never heard of. Everyone is passionate about something, and it creates a dynamic and wonderful atmosphere." Additionally, "fitting in isn't hard, because student interests are so diverse that there's almost always a number of other people who like the same things you like and want to do the same things you want to do." Finally, a succinct sophomore sums up, "At Reed I found the kind of student body I craved in high school."

FINANCIAL AID: 503-777-7223 • E-MAIL: ADMISSION@REED.EDU • WEBSITE: WWW.REED.EDU

THE PRINCETON REVIEW SAYS

Admissions

Very important factors considered include: rigor of secondary school record, academic GPA, application essay. *Important factors considered include:* class rank, standardized test scores, recommendation(s), interview, level of applicant's interest. *Other factors considered include:* extracurricular activities, talent/ability, character/personal qualities, first generation, alumni/ae relation, geographical residence, racial/ethnic status, volunteer work, work experience. SAT or ACT required; SAT Subject Tests recommended. ACT with or without writing accepted. TOEFL required of all international applicants. High school diploma is required and GED is accepted. *Academic units recommended:* 4 English, 3 science, 3 foreign language.

Financial Aid

Students should submit: FAFSA, CSS/Financial Aid PROFILE, Noncustodial PROFILE, Business/Farm Supplement. Regular filing deadline is 2/1. The Princeton Review suggests that all financial aid forms be submitted as soon as possible after October 1. *Need-based scholarships/grants offered:* Federal Pell, FSEOG, State scholarships/grants, Private scholarships, College/university scholarship or grant aid from institutional funds. *Loan aid offered:* Direct Subsidized Stafford Loans, Direct Unsubsidized Stafford Loans, Direct PLUS loans, Federal Perkins Loans, College/university loans from institutional funds. Federal Work-Study Program available. Institutional employment available.

The Inside Word

While there are no fixed requirements or "cut-off" points for applicants, Reed College is definitely on the lookout for students who maintain a thirst for knowledge and take their academics seriously. A rigorous curriculum is a must, so if possible load up on honors and advanced placement classes. Candidates who demonstrate social consciousness, a desire to join an intellectual community and who appear to be independent thinkers might have a leg up.

THE SCHOOL SAYS "..."

From the Admissions Office

"Intellectual. Intense. Inspiring. Transformative. For over 100 years, Reed has sought to provide the finest educational program in the country, offering students an extraordinary environment in which to discover their passions and pursue them with depth and determination.

"Reed provides a singular example of the liberal arts experience: a structured curriculum with an emphasis on independent inquiry; extensive feedback from professors emphasized instead of letter grades on assignments; and a deeply collaborative academic environment. You will learn how to learn—how to dedicate yourself to studying and how to work toward the production of new knowledge.

"The Reed community is self directed and guided by the Honor Principle. This dual commitment to independence of thought and mutual trust and respect helps to create an environment in which students feel inspired, challenged, and fulfilled.

"Students at Reed dedicate themselves to the life of the mind."

SELECTIVITY

Admissions Rating	94
# of applicants	5,396
% of applicants accepted	35
% of acceptees attending	22
# offered a place on the wait list	1,468
% accepting a place on wait list	30
% admitted from wait list	1

FRESHMAN PROFILE

Range SAT Critical Reading	670–760
Range SAT Math	620–720
Range SAT Writing	640–730
Range ACT Composite	29–33
Minimum paper TOEFL	600
Minimum internet-based TOEFL	100
Average HS GPA	3.9
% graduated top 10% of class	53
% graduated top 25% of class	87
% graduated top 50% of class	98

DEADLINES

Early decision	
Deadline	11/15
Notification	12/15
Regular	
Deadline	1/1
Notification	2/1
Nonfall registration?	No

APPLICANTS ALSO LOOK AT AND OFTEN PREFER

University of California–Berkeley; University of Chicago

AND SOMETIMES PREFER

Oberlin College; Swarthmore College

AND RARELY PREFER

Lewis & Clark College

FINANCIAL FACTS

Financial Aid Rating	99
Annual tuition	$49,640
Room and board	$12,590
Required fees	$300
Books and supplies	$1,050
Average frosh need-based scholarship	$43,617
Average UG need-based scholarship	$39,329
% needy frosh rec. need-based scholarship or grant aid	98
% needy UG rec. need-based scholarship or grant aid	99
% needy frosh rec. non-need-based scholarship or grant aid	0
% needy UG rec. non-need-based scholarship or grant aid	0
% needy frosh rec. need-based self-help aid	94
% needy UG rec. need-based self-help aid	93
% frosh rec. any financial aid	53
% UG rec. any financial aid	54
% frosh need fully met	99
% ugrads need fully met	100
Average % of frosh need met	100
Average % of ugrad need met	100

RENSSELAER POLYTECHNIC INSTITUTE

110 EIGHTH STREET, TROY, NY 12180-3590 • ADMISSIONS: 518-276-6216 • FAX: 518-276-4072

STUDENTS SAY "..."

Academics

As the nation's oldest technological university, Rensselaer Polytechnic Institute in upstate New York has a rightfully deserved reputation in the science and engineering world, having led tens of thousands of bright minds to look at "innovation and the future." "Research opportunities" and facilities are everywhere, and students are encouraged to work in interdisciplinary programs that allow them to combine scholarly work from several departments or schools. When their four years are complete, students are encouraged to take what they learn and use it for the greater good. "Why not change the world?" asks a student.

The professors at RPI are "passionate about teaching," "very accessible, and really there for the students." Though there are certainly some "dull" professors ("I've seen the good, the bad, and the ugly!" says one student), most find that the faculty is praiseworthy and "serve as great mentors for students." "My professors in my direct major are extremely hands-on and discussion-based," says a student. Thanks to the "focus on problem-solving," professors are always looking to get students involved in projects, and one of "the greatest strengths of [the] school is the resources that they offer." On top of that, the "welcoming overall community" fosters success, as "students are not extremely competitive and everyone tends to help each other out."

The school is "rigorous," but the students "do find time to enjoy the downtime when we get it." RPI "is a place where nerds can get both an excellent education and an enjoyable four years," according to one student. The student union is entirely student-run, giving students "a lot of freedom to control our educational experience." Many of the student clubs both "suit your interests and work toward your professional career after college." All in all, "community and knowledge drive this school to push students to excel in school and after graduation."

Life

Everyone agrees that RPI is just the right size: "The kind of size where you don't know everybody but you see ten people you know as you walk across campus (and it only takes ten minutes to walk across campus)." People at RPI "don't care how weird or different you are, they let you be." "You can be anyone you want—the kid sword-fighting with his friends in quad or an avid musician who has a 4.0," says a student. Most students do have a "nerdy" side to them, and they inherently love math/science—"even the humanities at RPI are laced with the sweet smell of science," and "physics equation graffiti" can be found on some walls.

Academics are definitely an important priority here, but "extracurricular activities are balanced alongside the classes, labs, homework, and studying." There are hundreds of clubs on campus (such as Engineers for a Sustainable World and the Model Railroad Society, which does model railroading of upstate New York and Vermont all circa the early- to mid-1950s), and "most people are involved in several." There are always campus events that students can attend, which range from "athletic events and cultural programs to student ensemble concerts and open mic shows." Downtown Troy has some "quaint cafes and places to explore," Albany has shopping malls, parks, and movie theaters, and a ski trip to Lake Placid is easily accomplished. "There is so much to do around here—you'll never be bored if you take the time to explore." Men's hockey games are a large part of student life here, and "Greek life accounts for about one-fourth of the undergraduate student body and is a great leadership experience and a large contributor to the social scene."

Student Body

Everyone here is pretty much without a doubt "a little bit nerdy, but friendly and helpful." This tinge of nerdiness in everyone "brings the students together and makes it a fun environment with little to no discrimination." "The typical student at my school is studious, but also social in their own way," explains a student. There is a whole spectrum of social students, which ranges "from socializing with a select few to the person that is a social butterfly," but no matter which path you choose, "people don't judge at RPI."

RENSSELAER POLYTECHNIC INSTITUTE

FINANCIAL AID: 518-276-6813 • E-MAIL: ADMISSIONS@RPI.EDU • WEBSITE: WWW.RPI.EDU

THE PRINCETON REVIEW SAYS

Admissions

Very important factors considered include: rigor of secondary school record, class rank, academic GPA, standardized test scores. *Important factors considered include:* application essay, recommendation(s), extracurricular activities, character/personal qualities, level of applicant's interest. *Other factors considered include:* talent/ability, first generation, alumni/ae relation, racial/ethnic status, volunteer work, work experience. SAT or ACT required; SAT Subject Tests considered if submitted. ACT with or without writing accepted. SAT with or without Essay component accepted. TOEFL required of all international applicants. High school diploma is required and GED is accepted. *Academic units required:* 4 English, 4 math, 3 science, 3 social studies. *Academic units recommended:* 4 science, 3 social studies.

Financial Aid

Students should submit: FAFSA, CSS/Financial Aid PROFILE. Priority filing deadline is 2/1. The Princeton Review suggests that all financial aid forms be submitted as soon as possible after October 1. *Need-based scholarships/grants offered:* Federal Pell, FSEOG, State scholarships/grants, Private scholarships, College/university scholarship or grant aid from institutional funds. *Loan aid offered:* Direct Subsidized Stafford Loans, Direct Unsubsidized Stafford Loans, Direct PLUS loans, Federal Perkins Loans, State Loans. Applicants will be notified of awards on or about 3/15. Federal Work-Study Program available. Institutional employment available.

The Inside Word

Outstanding test scores and grades are pretty much a must for any applicant hopeful of impressing the RPI admissions committee. Underrepresented minorities and women—two demographics the school would like to augment—will get a little more leeway than others, but in all cases, the school is unlikely to admit anyone who lacks the skills and background to survive here.

THE SCHOOL SAYS "..."

From the Admissions Office

"The oldest degree-granting technological research university in the U.S., Rensselaer was founded in 1824 to instruct students to apply 'science to the common purposes of life.' Students immerse themselves in course work that combines theory with learning by experience in unparalleled facilities, using advanced technology. Rensselaer offers more than 100 programs and 1,000 courses leading to bachelor's, master's, and doctoral degrees. Undergraduates pursue studies in architecture; engineering; humanities, arts, and social sciences; management; science; and information technology (web science). A pioneer in interactive learning, Rensselaer provides real-world, hands-on educational opportunities that cut across academic disciplines. The Rensselaer student experience, or CLASS (Clustered Learning Advocacy and Support for Students) provides programs and support for students that begins even before they arrive on campus. Students have ready access to laboratories and classes involving lively discussion, problem solving, and faculty mentoring. Students are able to take full advantage of Rensselaer's unique research platforms: the Center for Biotechnology and Interdisciplinary Studies; one of the world's most powerful academic supercomputers, the Center for Computational Innovations; and the Experimental Media and Performing Arts Center, which encourages students to explore the intersection of science, technology, and the arts. Newly renovated residence halls, wireless computing network, and studio classrooms create a fertile environment for study and learning. Rensselaer offers recreational and fitness facilities plus numerous student-run organizations and activities, including fraternities and sororities, newspaper, television and radio station, drama and musical groups, and more than 200 clubs. In addition to intra¬mural sports, NCAA varsity sports include Division I men's and women's ice hockey teams and twenty-one Division III men's and women's teams in thirteen sports. The East Campus Athletic Village raises the bar for student athletic facilities for varsity and non-varsity athletes alike, and includes a football arena, basketball stadium, and sports medicine and training complex."

SELECTIVITY

Admissions Rating	95
# of applicants	17,752
% of applicants accepted	42
% of acceptees attending	19
# offered a place on the wait list	4,087
% accepting a place on wait list	54
% admitted from wait list	3
# of early decision applicants	554
% accepted early decision	65

FRESHMAN PROFILE

Range SAT Critical Reading	610–720
Range SAT Math	670–770
Range ACT Composite	28–32
Minimum paper TOEFL	570
Minimum internet-based TOEFL	88
Average HS GPA	3.9
% graduated top 10% of class	72
% graduated top 25% of class	94
% graduated top 50% of class	99

DEADLINES

Early decision	
Deadline	11/1
Notification	12/12
Regular	
Deadline	1/15
Notification	3/14
Nonfall registration?	Yes

APPLICANTS ALSO LOOK AT AND OFTEN PREFER

Massachusetts Institute of Technology; Cornell University

AND SOMETIMES PREFER

University of Rochester; Boston University; Carnegie Mellon University

AND RARELY PREFER

State University of New York at Binghamton

FINANCIAL FACTS

Financial Aid Rating	83
Annual tuition	$49,520
Room and board	$14,630
Required fees	$270
Average frosh need-based scholarship	$35,340
Average UG need-based scholarship	$30,943
% needy frosh rec. need-based scholarship or grant aid	100
% needy UG rec. need-based scholarship or grant aid	100
% needy frosh rec. non-need-based scholarship or grant aid	21
% needy UG rec. non-need-based scholarship or grant aid	14
% needy frosh rec. need-based self-help aid	99
% needy UG rec. need-based self-help aid	97
% frosh rec. any financial aid	89
% UG rec. any financial aid	89
% frosh need fully met	27
% ugrads need fully met	21
Average % of frosh need met	87
Average % of ugrad need met	79

RHODES COLLEGE

2000 NORTH PARKWAY, MEMPHIS, TN 38112 • ADMISSIONS: 901-843-3700 • FAX: 901-843-3631

CAMPUS LIFE

Quality of Life Rating	97
Fire Safety Rating	87
Green Rating	72
Type of school	Private
Affiliation	Presbyterian
Environment	Metropolis

STUDENTS

Total undergrad enrollment	2,046
% male/female	43/57
% from out of state	74
% frosh from public high school	46
% frosh live on campus	97
% ugrads live on campus	71
# of fraternities (% ugrad men join)	8 (40)
# of sororities (% ugrad women join)	7 (62)
% African American	6
% Asian	6
% Caucasian	74
% Hispanic	5
% Native American	<1
% Pacific Islander	<1
% Two or more races	4
% Race and/or ethnicity unknown	2
% international	3
# of countries represented	18

SURVEY SAYS...

Students always studying
Students are happy
Classroom facilities are great
Great library
Career services are great
Internships are widely available
Class discussions encouraged
School is well run
Great financial aid
No one cheats
Students are friendly
Diverse student types interact on campus
Students get along with local community
Students involved in community service
Students love Memphis, TN
Great off-campus food
Easy to get around campus
Lots of beer drinking
Hard liquor is popular

ACADEMICS

Academic Rating	97
% students returning for sophomore year	91
% students graduating within 4 years	76
% students graduating within 6 years	83
Calendar	Semester
Student/faculty ratio	10:1
Profs interesting rating	97
Profs accessible rating	98

Most classes have 10–19 students.
Most lab/discussion sessions have 20–29 students.

MOST POPULAR MAJORS

Biology; Business Administration and Management; Psychology

STUDENTS SAY "..."

Academics

A "beautiful" campus located in the heart of Memphis, Tennessee, the "tight-knit community" of Rhodes College offers "individual study in a liberal arts mold," which involves exposing students to "as many different disciplines as possible in order to gain a broader understanding of the world." Academics here are extremely challenging, "but nothing that hard work and study time can't handle." "I have been pushed (in a good way) to the outer limits of my academic capabilities," says a sophomore. Professors are undoubtedly "one of Rhodes' best assets"—invitations to faculty members' houses for dinner are par for the course—and "truly care about our achievement, grasping the right concepts, and progressing in our education." "Professors don't just care about passing the tests, they want students to be able to take what they have learned and apply it to real life," beams a student. The "small classes" and "comprehensive honor code" only help to further students' love of the Rhodes' classroom experience. The concerned individuals making up the Rhodes administration are "not just doing a job," they are "dedicated to the mission of this college and committed to the students they serve." Though some students have had some bad experiences with administrators, most are content, and it doesn't hurt that the school "took all of the different offices that were spread throughout campus and consolidated them into one newly-renovated building that makes any form or process/meeting much simpler."

Life

With "gothic architecture [that] will make you feel like you live in a fantasy world," the Rhodes campus is "easy on the eyes," while the food used to be "tough on the gut," Rhodes opened a new best-in-class dining facility in the fall of 2012. There is a huge Greek contingent here—"frat parties on campus are always fun and wild"—and all students are sure to find their niche since "each fraternity is different." Generally speaking, the typical student schedule breaks down like this: "weekdays and nights in the library (which is beautiful, so it's not as bad as it could be), and starting Thursdays, partying." Don't be fooled, though: "Most people here work hard and see it academically pay off." "Students focus on getting their school work done before going out and hold their friends accountable so not many get behind," says another student. The school itself offers tons of service activities, cultural events, speakers, and intramurals, and people like to get off campus and have fun in Memphis, which is "surrounded by fun sports teams" to which the school provides cheap tickets. The library can also be a social place, especially during exams, "because so many people spend their time there."

Student Body

Rhodes has its fair share of "white, upper-middle-class" students, but "no one is elitist," and the overall student body itself is diverse on many fronts. Many students here are from the South and "preppy," and you can spot many "polos and khakis around campus." "Everyone is well accepted regardless of socio-economic status," and the few atypical student groups "mix freely" and "interact with few problems." The school is full of hard workers ("academic but not full of nerds") and the school's honor code is taken very seriously. "People rarely ever cheat or steal"—most students live on campus and "a large percentage don't ever lock their doom rooms." One thing is for certain, though—students here are "busy" in all areas of their life: studying, taking advantage of the "countless service opportunities," arts/athletics, and Greek life. The typical student is generally an "overachiever" while still "[liking] to have fun and enjoy him or herself." "Rhodes is filled with the types of students that are any high school counselor's...dream," sums up a student.

FINANCIAL AID: 901-843-3810 • E-MAIL: ADMINFO@RHODES.EDU • WEBSITE: WWW.RHODES.EDU

THE PRINCETON REVIEW SAYS

Admissions

Very important factors considered include: rigor of secondary school record, class rank, academic GPA. *Important factors considered include:* standardized test scores, application essay, recommendation(s), character/personal qualities, alumni/ae relation, racial/ethnic status. *Other factors considered include:* interview, extracurricular activities, talent/ability, first generation, geographical residence, state residency, volunteer work, work experience, level of applicant's interest. SAT or ACT required. ACT with or without writing accepted. SAT with or without Essay component accepted. TOEFL required of all international applicants. High school diploma is required and GED is accepted. *Academic units required:* 4 English, 3 math, 2 science, 2 science labs, 2 foreign language, 2 social studies, 3 academic electives.

Financial Aid

Students should submit: FAFSA, CSS/Financial Aid PROFILE, Noncustodial PROFILE. Regular filing deadline is 3/1. The Princeton Review suggests that all financial aid forms be submitted as soon as possible after October 1. *Need-based scholarships/grants offered:* Federal Pell, FSEOG, State scholarships/grants, Private scholarships, College/university scholarship or grant aid from institutional funds. *Loan aid offered:* Direct Subsidized Stafford Loans, Direct Unsubsidized Stafford Loans, Direct PLUS loans, Federal Perkins Loans. Federal Work-Study Program available. Institutional employment available.

The Inside Word

Rhodes' national profile is growing. Even though the majority of students come from Tennessee and nearby states, students from farther-flung points of origin will enjoy a leg up because they add to the geographic diversity. As with all small, selective schools, applicants are advised to schedule a campus visit and to interview to demonstrate their interest in attending.

THE SCHOOL SAYS "..."

From the Admissions Office

"Rhodes is a residential college committed to liberal arts and sciences. Our highest priorities are intellectual engagement, service to others, and honor among ourselves. We live this life on one of the country's most beautiful campuses in the heart of Memphis, Tennessee, an economic, political, and cultural center, making Rhodes one of a handful of top-tier, liberal arts colleges in a major metropolitan area.

"Rhodes has the soul of a liberal arts college coupled with a real-world mindset. Our students put their liberal arts knowledge to work in the world starting their first year. You'll be encouraged to engage in research, leadership and service opportunities—and to take responsibility for shaping your educational experience to meet your personal interests and goals. Memphis is a thriving city right on Rhodes' doorstep, with spectacular resources for students, and the college has pioneered the establishment of programs with world-class institutions and companies, including St. Jude Children's Research Hospital, FedEx and the Memphis Zoo, which take advantage of the college's metropolitan location and provide students with real-world opportunities for academic and personal growth."

SELECTIVITY

Admissions Rating	93
# of applicants	4,666
% of applicants accepted	47
% of acceptees attending	26
# offered a place on the wait list	1,290
% accepting a place on wait list	21
% admitted from wait list	16
# of early decision applicants	188
% accepted early decision	76

FRESHMAN PROFILE

Range SAT Critical Reading	600–700
Range SAT Math	580–680
Range ACT Composite	27–32
Minimum paper TOEFL	550
Average HS GPA	3.9
% graduated top 10% of class	54
% graduated top 25% of class	83
% graduated top 50% of class	98

DEADLINES

Early decision	
Deadline	11/1
Notification	12/1
Early action	
Deadline	11/15
Notification	1/15
Regular	
Priority	1/15
Notification	4/1
Nonfall registration?	Yes

APPLICANTS ALSO LOOK AT AND OFTEN PREFER
Washington University in St. Louis

AND SOMETIMES PREFER
Furman UniversitySewanee; The University of the South; Tulane University

FINANCIAL FACTS

Financial Aid Rating	88
Annual tuition	$42,914
Room and board	$10,746
Required fees	$310
Books and supplies	$1,125
Average frosh need-based scholarship	$26,954
Average UG need-based scholarship	$27,938
% needy frosh rec. need-based scholarship or grant aid	99
% needy UG rec. need-based scholarship or grant aid	99
% needy frosh rec. non-need-based scholarship or grant aid	52
% needy UG rec. non-need-based scholarship or grant aid	34
% needy frosh rec. need-based self-help aid	42
% needy UG rec. need-based self-help aid	60
% frosh rec. any financial aid	95
% UG rec. any financial aid	94
% UG borrow to pay for school	51
Average cumulative indebtedness	$28,008
% frosh need fully met	56
% ugrads need fully met	40
Average % of frosh need met	93
Average % of ugrad need met	88

RICE UNIVERSITY

MS 17, PO BOX 1892, HOUSTON, TX 77251-1892 • ADMISSIONS: 713-348-7423 • FAX: 713-348-5952

CAMPUS LIFE

Quality of Life Rating	97
Fire Safety Rating	95
Green Rating	90
Type of school	Private
Affiliation	No Affiliation
Environment	Metropolis

STUDENTS

Total undergrad enrollment	3,910
% male/female	53/47
% from out of state	50
% frosh live on campus	99
% ugrads live on campus	72
% African American	7
% Asian	24
% Caucasian	37
% Hispanic	14
% Native American	<1
% Pacific Islander	<1
% Two or more races	4
% Race and/or ethnicity unknown	1
% international	12
# of countries represented	46

SURVEY SAYS...

Students always studying
Students are happy
Classroom facilities are great
Lab facilities are great
Great library
Internships are widely available
School is well run
Great financial aid
Students are friendly
Diverse student types interact on campus
Students get along with local community
Students love Houston, TX
Great off-campus food
Dorms are like palaces
Easy to get around campus
Recreation facilities are great
Lots of beer drinking
Active minority support groups

ACADEMICS

Academic Rating	93
% students returning for sophomore year	97
% students graduating within 4 years	80
% students graduating within 6 years	91
Calendar	Semester
Student/faculty ratio	6:1
Profs interesting rating	84
Profs accessible rating	86

Most classes have 10–19 students.

MOST POPULAR MAJORS

Biology; Psychology; Economics

STUDENTS SAY "..."

Academics

Students at Rice are generous with their praise for professors, who "are very accessible and happy to talk about the material and give help outside of class," and make "their course material relevant, being sure to include modern-day and industry applications." Students caution that some faculty members are "more focused on their research," but others "learn every student's name in their 200-person lecture" and "everyone certainly knows their stuff very well." While "a lot is expected of you, so be prepared to have to do a lot of work on your own," professors "are there if you are struggling," the academic "emphasis is more on collaboration than competition," and that work will contribute to "meaningful discussion during class." Professors serve as "masters" within the residential colleges, "which provides a wonderful opportunity [for students] to get to know the faculty and staff on a more personal level." Students are assigned to one of eleven colleges for all four years and about 75 percent of undergrads live at their colleges, which creates smaller, close-knit communities within the university. All of this crossover between personal and academic areas helps make life at Rice well-balanced: "Overall the academic experience is rigorous, but not particularly stressful."

Life

Continuing with the theme of balance, "students at Rice work hard and accomplish great things in academics and extracurriculars. But this is complemented and supported by a thriving social life." Students report a wide range of activities and interests outside the classroom. What they all have in common is their satisfaction with life at Rice. "The environment is very inclusive. People are free to do whatever they want with whoever they want." "On any given Friday night you might find various religious organizations meeting, a group of friends playing board games in the commons space, a crowd of people heading to a party, and a carload of students heading off-campus to see a movie." School-sponsored activities often include "lecture series, recruiting sessions, movie nights, sporting events, parties, board game nights, etc, usually...with free food."

Intramural sports and campus traditions are popular, and "the typical student seems to be involved in at least three or four activities." Rice undergrads also seem to have a healthy perspective on partying: "This is a wet campus, after all...that said, Rice's alcohol policy fosters a culture of care in which students... help each other stay safe and make good decisions." "You can be a drinker or not a drinker and you will find others who choose the same as you." Finally, some students report that they don't get off campus much, but others praise Houston's music and restaurant scenes, and everyone loves the warm, sunny weather!

Student Body

Most students are quick to claim they can't be typified, and many use the term "quirky" to describe themselves and each other. Rather than quirky in the hipster sense, they seem to mean that "everyone is...interesting in some way" and "people have such a far-reaching range of interests." One student shares their "impression that Rice admits people who excel in [a] particular area or who have specialized interests rather than...a cookie-cutter class of people." "There is no racial majority here on campus, and I've met students of varied political affiliations, religions, socio-economic status, and sexual orientations." Commonalities across this "wide array of people" include dedication to rigorous academic courses and "a leadership position in one or two campus clubs or organizations." "The student body is extremely collaborative, friendly, accepting, and social—it's not cliquey," though "there are some rifts...but these are not very pronounced." "Most students respect others students and enjoy learning more about people who have different backgrounds and beliefs than their own...there is most likely someone with whom to share a common interest, be it something like LARPing, rock-climbing, or fashion."

FINANCIAL AID: 713-348-4958 • E-MAIL: ADMI@RICE.EDU • WEBSITE: WWW.RICE.EDU

THE PRINCETON REVIEW SAYS

Admissions

Very important factors considered include: rigor of secondary school record, class rank, academic GPA, standardized test scores, application essay, recommendation(s), extracurricular activities, talent/ability, character/personal qualities. *Other factors considered include:* interview, first generation, alumni/ae relation, geographical residence, state residency, racial/ethnic status, volunteer work, work experience, level of applicant's interest. SAT or ACT required. ACT with Writing required. TOEFL required of all international applicants. High school diploma or equivalent is not required. *Academic units required:* 4 English, 3 math, 2 science, 2 science labs, 2 foreign language, 2 social studies, 3 academic electives. *Academic units recommended:* 4 English, 4 math, 4 science, 3 science labs, 4 foreign language, 3 social studies, 3 academic electives.

Financial Aid

Students should submit: FAFSA, CSS/Financial Aid PROFILE, Noncustodial PROFILE, Business/Farm Supplement. Priority filing deadline is 2/15. The Princeton Review suggests that all financial aid forms be submitted as soon as possible after October 1. *Need-based scholarships/grants offered:* Federal Pell, FSEOG, State scholarships/grants, Private scholarships, College/university scholarship or grant aid from institutional funds. *Loan aid offered:* Direct Subsidized Stafford Loans, Direct Unsubsidized Stafford Loans, Direct PLUS loans, Federal Perkins Loans, State Loans. Applicants will be notified of awards on or about 4/1. Federal Work-Study Program available. Institutional employment available.

The Inside Word

With students who are so vocal about their happiness, it's no surprise that Rice has a large applicant pool and a low acceptance rate. In addition to strong transcripts and test scores, prospective students should demonstrate their unique passions through electives and extracurricular activities: admissions officers look for applicants who are motivated and creative. Interviews are optional, but recommended.

THE SCHOOL SAYS "..."

From the Admissions Office

"We seek students of keen intellect and diverse backgrounds who show potential to succeed at Rice and will also contribute to the educational environment of those around them.

"Student applications are reviewed within the context of the division to which they apply. Admission committee decisions are based not only on high school grades and test scores but also on such qualities as leadership, participation in extracurricular activities, and personal creativity. Admission is extremely competitive. Rice attempts to seek out and identify those students who have demonstrated exceptional ability and the potential for personal and intellectual growth.

"Our individualized, holistic evaluation process employs many different means to identify these qualities in applicants.

"Required admission testing includes the SAT and two Subject Tests, or ACT with writing. All test scores must be sent to Rice directly from the official testing agency."

SELECTIVITY

Admissions Rating	97
# of applicants	17,951
% of applicants accepted	16
% of acceptees attending	34
# offered a place on the wait list	2,237
% accepting a place on wait list	74
% admitted from wait list	8
# of early decision applicants	1,389
% accepted early decision	20

FRESHMAN PROFILE

Range SAT Critical Reading	680–760
Range SAT Math	710–800
Range SAT Writing	680–770
Range ACT Composite	32–35
Minimum paper TOEFL	600
Minimum internet-based TOEFL	100
% graduated top 10% of class	89
% graduated top 25% of class	96
% graduated top 50% of class	100

DEADLINES

Early decision	
Deadline	11/1
Notification	12/15
Regular	
Deadline	1/1
Notification	4/1
Nonfall registration?	No

APPLICANTS ALSO LOOK AT AND OFTEN PREFER

Yale University; Stanford University; Harvard College

AND SOMETIMES PREFER

University of Pennsylvania; Cornell University; Duke University

AND RARELY PREFER

The University of Texas at Austin

FINANCIAL FACTS

Financial Aid Rating	96
Annual tuition	$41,560
Room and board	$13,650
Required fees	$693
Books and supplies	$800
Average frosh need-based scholarship	$36,568
Average UG need-based scholarship	$36,025
% needy frosh rec. need-based scholarship or grant aid	97
% needy UG rec. need-based scholarship or grant aid	97
% needy frosh rec. non-need-based scholarship or grant aid	5
% needy UG rec. non-need-based scholarship or grant aid	3
% needy frosh rec. need-based self-help aid	65
% needy UG rec. need-based self-help aid	75
% frosh rec. any financial aid	41
% UG rec. any financial aid	39
% frosh need fully met	99
% ugrads need fully met	99
Average % of frosh need met	100
Average % of ugrad need met	100

RIDER UNIVERSITY

2083 Lawrenceville Road, Lawrenceville, NJ 08648-3099 • Admissions: 609-896-5042 • Fax: 609-895-6645

STUDENTS SAY "..."

Academics

A private coed institution in Lawrenceville, New Jersey, Rider University offers a friendly and intimate college experience to a largely local crowd. In addition to dozens of majors in the liberal arts and sciences, Rider operates a "highly respected business school" and an accounting program that's "the best in the state of New Jersey." Rider "prepares you for all facets of life after college," fostering "interpersonal relationships between successful alumni and undergraduates" and offering great services like "tutoring for every class, writing labs, career services, internships, and co-ops." A current student attests, "The science professors have been really helpful with helping me achieve my goals by introducing me to opportunities for grants, internships, and other experiential learning." While course work can be challenging, "the professors present the material in a way in which you can do well if you work hard." Teaching is emphasized, and there are "some phenomenal professors at Rider University who go out of their way to give their students a great education." At the same time, students admit, "While many professors are highly accessible, there are surely a few—mostly adjunct-professors—who are inadequate," both as mentors and as teachers. On the whole, Rider is "very student-oriented," and the administration "goes the extra mile in making sure all students are treated equally." Even so, things don't always run smoothly, and "dealing with financial aid, administrative offices such as residence life, and career services is the hardest part about going to Rider University." While Rider is a private college, it helps students finance their education through "generous financial aid package," loans, and "lots of opportunities for work study."

Life

Whether they live on campus or commute to school, students enjoy a friendly and social atmosphere at Rider. On campus, "basketball games are always a big draw," and the university hosts "major comedians, musicians, [and] film nights" in the evenings. Even though the university's alcohol rules are rather strict, "most students drink for fun, either on campus or off." For mellower times, the "residence advisors set up a lot events in their respective dorm," or students get together to "play video games, go to Zumba classes, hold hallway-parties (no alcohol), or movie nights." In addition, the "Student Rec Center is a great place to hang out because it's got basketball courts, a pool table, ping pong table, all the video game systems, a gym, a track, and a pool." When they want to pop off campus, "there are coffee shops, frozen yogurt places, [and] a house of cupcakes" in the nearby town of Princeton, and "New York City and Philly are only a train ride away." "On the weekends, the school empties out pretty quickly," as most students go home. While some complain that Rider is a "suitcase school," others insist, "the lifestyle on campus is what people make of it." For those who want a more traditional college experience, "Greek life is a great way to meet new people and get involved in campus."

Student Body

Many Rider students come from a "middle-class background," and most are East Coasters "from the Lawrenceville area" or greater New Jersey. However, "the student body is very diverse politically, socially, and academically," reflecting the "vastly varied demographics of the state of New Jersey: all races, all religions, and all levels of mental and physical abilities." "There is a good mix of jocks, brainy people who are committed to studying, and artsy hipster types," so most "students can usually find at least one group to fit in with." While some students "love to party," others "really care about how well they do in school and are involved in so many different organizations on campus." Rider also operates an evening program, which attracts "older, working, returning students," who are often very serious about their studies.

FINANCIAL AID: 609-896-5360 • E-MAIL: ADMISSIONS@RIDER.EDU • WEBSITE: WWW.RIDER.EDU

THE PRINCETON REVIEW SAYS

Admissions

Very important factors considered include: rigor of secondary school record, academic GPA, standardized test scores, application essay, recommendation(s). *Important factors considered include:* level of applicant's interest. *Other factors considered include:* interview, extracurricular activities, talent/ability, character/personal qualities, alumni/ae relation, geographical residence, state residency, volunteer work, work experience. SAT or ACT required. TOEFL required of all international applicants. High school diploma is required and GED is accepted. *Academic units required:* 4 English, 3 math. *Academic units recommended:* 4 math, 4 science, 2 science labs, 2 foreign language, 2 social studies, 2 history.

Financial Aid

Students should submit: FAFSA. Priority filing deadline is 2/1. The Princeton Review suggests that all financial aid forms be submitted as soon as possible after October 1. *Need-based scholarships/grants offered:* Federal Pell, FSEOG, State scholarships/grants, Private scholarships, College/university scholarship or grant aid from institutional funds. *Loan aid offered:* Direct Subsidized Stafford Loans, Direct Unsubsidized Stafford Loans, Direct PLUS loans, Federal Perkins Loans. Applicants will be notified of awards on a rolling basis beginning 11/1. Federal Work-Study Program available. Institutional employment available.

The Inside Word

To prepare for college, Rider University suggests that high school students follow a rigorous curriculum of college prep courses, including AP and honors classes. Students need at least four years of high school English and three years of math to be considered for admission to Rider. The most recent incoming class had an average high school GPA of 3.35 and a SAT score of 1610. Although most students major in the liberal arts and sciences, more than a quarter of undergraduates are enrolled in the business school.

THE SCHOOL SAYS "..."

From the Admissions Office

"Rider students are driven by their dreams of a fulfilling career and a desire to have an impact on the world around them. Rider is a place to apply your imagination, talents and aspirations in ways that will make a difference. A Rider education will prepare you as a leader and as a member of a team. When you graduate from Rider, you'll be a different person, confidently ready for your life's challenges and opportunities.

"We invite you to visit and experience Rider firsthand. Open houses are offered in the fall. Tours are available daily and most weekends throughout the academic year and weekdays in the summer.

"Freshmen applicants are required to submit the results of either the SAT or ACT exam. The highest scores from either test will be considered for admission."

SELECTIVITY
Admissions Rating	77
# of applicants	9,851
% of applicants accepted	69
% of acceptees attending	13
# offered a place on the wait list	58
% accepting a place on wait list	14

FRESHMAN PROFILE
Range SAT Critical Reading	450–550
Range SAT Math	460–560
Range SAT Writing	450–540
Range ACT Composite	19–25
Minimum paper TOEFL	550
Minimum internet-based TOEFL	80
Average HS GPA	3.3
% graduated top 10% of class	14
% graduated top 25% of class	37
% graduated top 50% of class	75

DEADLINES
Early action	
Deadline	11/15
Notification	12/20
Regular	
Notification	Rolling
Nonfall registration?	Yes

FINANCIAL FACTS
Financial Aid Rating	82
Annual tuition	$37,650
Room and board	$13,770
Required fees	$710
Books and supplies	$1,500
Average frosh need-based scholarship	$24,203
Average UG need-based scholarship	$23,433
% needy frosh rec. need-based scholarship or grant aid	99
% needy UG rec. need-based scholarship or grant aid	99
% needy frosh rec. non-need-based scholarship or grant aid	16
% needy UG rec. non-need-based scholarship or grant aid	19
% needy frosh rec. need-based self-help aid	83
% needy UG rec. need-based self-help aid	82
% frosh need fully met	16
% ugrads need fully met	15
Average % of frosh need met	73
Average % of ugrad need met	73

RIPON COLLEGE

PO Box 248, Ripon, WI 54971 • Admissions: 920-748-8337 • Fax: 920-748-8335

STUDENTS SAY "..."

Academics

Described as a "close-knit community," "Ripon is a place where a student's best interest matters; all other agendas are secondary." One student chose Ripon because, "I was looking for a liberal arts school that allowed me to do the things I like, namely, be involved in multiple student groups, study abroad, and take classes in different fields, all of which I have been able to do at Ripon." The "quiet beauty," "welcoming nature of the campus," along with "small class sizes and a lot of personal attention from professors" create a "friendly, home-away-from-home atmosphere." Students appreciate the education they are receiving and how it prepares them for a productive life after college. The school's motto, "more together" "is exactly what our school is all about; becoming something more with the help of those here to guide us." "Ripon College prepares students to be productive, service-minded leaders who are ready and willing to influence the direction of our nation's future." "Ripon College is not all about sitting in a classroom listening to lectures and taking notes; it's about teaching us to become more educated in the world around us and helping us to develop the skills needed to succeed." "The hands-on, experiential, service-learning projects have been particularly valuable for my own personal growth and for preparing me for life after college." Another student agrees, saying, "Ripon is a prime example of a college with a positive and supportive living and learning community." "Ripon professors provide an interesting and intellectually challenging environment for students to discuss and to learn." Students say, Ripon is an "amazing community of learners and educators who support one another" and a "unique institution that helps ordinary people uncover their extraordinary potential to do great things." Professors "are not just teachers, but mentors!" Scholarships make a Ripon College education possible for some that otherwise could not attend. One student says, "They offered me a great scholarship and were really willing to work with me to make my college education affordable."

Life

With its "tight-knit and welcoming community," Ripon conveys "a friendly environment conducive to learning, fun, and overall personal growth." It is "not uncommon to sit down to lunch with a professor, or even go over to their house for tea." Life at Ripon has proven blissful for one student who now says, "I cannot remember a time when I wanted to be anywhere else." Besides a "strong academic core," Ripon College has "many successful sports teams," and Greek life "is abundant." Greeks host events and are a big part of many students' life. Partying "is evident but not huge by any respect." "Since Ripon College is in a small town, the college sets up a lot of events on weekends for us to take part in!" "The small-town feel of Ripon forces you sometimes to create your own fun, which usually makes for the best memories." "Being close to several metropolitan areas (Chicago, Milwaukee, Madison, and the Twin Cities), there is rarely a weekend when people are not getting off campus to go explore." But if you are looking for snow days to figure into your schedule, then Ripon may not be for you "because most professors will keep classes going even in negative temperatures with two feet of snow."

Student Body

A typical Ripon student is described as "laid-back and friendly." One student cautions, "You have to plan extra time in between classes because you're guaranteed to be stopped by someone you know along the way to talk for a few minutes." Students are "outgoing, personable, and motivated," "involved in multiple clubs," and may "hold more than one internship at a time. From Student Senate to Ultimate Frisbee to volunteering in the community, there is never a lack of activities in which one can participate." Students are "always looking for something new and exciting to do, and [are] ready to volunteer their time and energy to someone in need."

FINANCIAL AID: 920-748-8301 • E-MAIL: ADMINFO@RIPON.EDU • WEBSITE: WWW.RIPON.EDU

THE PRINCETON REVIEW SAYS
Admissions
Very important factors considered include: rigor of secondary school record, interview. *Important factors considered include:* class rank, academic GPA, standardized test scores, recommendation(s), extracurricular activities, character/personal qualities. *Other factors considered include:* application essay, talent/ability, volunteer work. SAT or ACT required; SAT Subject Tests considered if submitted. ACT with or without writing accepted. SAT with or without Essay component accepted. TOEFL required of all international applicants. High school diploma is required and GED is accepted. *Academic units required:* 4 English, 2 math, 2 science, 2 social studies. *Academic units recommended:* 4 math, 4 science, 2 foreign language, 4 social studies.

Financial Aid
Students should submit: FAFSA. Priority filing deadline is 3/1. The Princeton Review suggests that all financial aid forms be submitted as soon as possible after October 1. *Need-based scholarships/grants offered:* Federal Pell, FSEOG, State scholarships/grants, Private scholarships, College/university scholarship or grant aid from institutional funds. *Loan aid offered:* Direct Subsidized Stafford Loans, Direct Unsubsidized Stafford Loans, Direct PLUS loans, Federal Perkins Loans. Applicants will be notified of awards on a rolling basis beginning 3/1. Federal Work-Study Program available. Institutional employment available.

The Inside Word
Ripon seeks accomplished high school students who have challenged themselves in and out of the classroom. Solid performers—those earning a B-plus average in a college-prep curriculum and exceeding 1100 SAT/22 ACT—should find a clear path awaiting them, although the school does also consider such peripherals as potential contribution to extracurricular life and the likelihood a candidate will flourish in a small-school environment.

THE SCHOOL SAYS "..."
From the Admissions Office
"Since its founding in 1851, Ripon College has adhered to the philosophy that the liberal arts offer the richest foundation for intellectual, cultural, social, and spiritual growth. Academic strength is a 150-year tradition at Ripon. We attract excellent professors who are dedicated to their disciplines; they in turn attract bright, committed students. Together with the other members of our tightly knit learning community, students at Ripon learn more deeply, live more fully, and achieve more success. Students are surprised to discover that here there are more opportunities—to be involved, to lead, to speak out, to make a difference, to explore new interests—than at a college ten times our size. Through collaborative learning, group living, teamwork, and networking, students tap into the power of a community where we all work together to ensure success—at Ripon and beyond.

"All of the best residential liberal arts colleges strive to be true learning communities like Ripon. We succeed better than most because our enrollment of about 1,000 students is perfect for fostering connections inside and outside the classroom. Our students flourish in this environment of mutual respect, where shared values are elevated and diverse ideas are valued. If you are seeking academic challenge and want to benefit from an environment of personal attention and support—then you should take a closer look at Ripon.

"Applicants to Ripon College must submit scores from either the ACT (writing section not required) or the SAT."

SELECTIVITY
Admissions Rating	81
# of applicants	1,874
% of applicants accepted	66
% of acceptees attending	17

FRESHMAN PROFILE
Range SAT Critical Reading	450–640
Range SAT Math	500–620
Range ACT Composite	21–27
Minimum paper TOEFL	550
Minimum internet-based TOEFL	79
Average HS GPA	3.4
% graduated top 10% of class	21
% graduated top 25% of class	51
% graduated top 50% of class	80

DEADLINES
Regular	
Priority	3/15
Nonfall registration?	Yes

APPLICANTS ALSO LOOK AT AND SOMETIMES PREFER
University of Wisconsin–Madison

AND RARELY PREFER
Lawrence University; Beloit College

FINANCIAL FACTS
Financial Aid Rating	86
Annual tuition	$36,214
Room and board	$8,177
Required fees	$300
Books and supplies	$750
Average frosh need-based scholarship	$27,230
Average UG need-based scholarship	$24,941
% needy frosh rec. need-based scholarship or grant aid	100
% needy UG rec. need-based scholarship or grant aid	100
% needy frosh rec. non-need-based scholarship or grant aid	18
% needy UG rec. non-need-based scholarship or grant aid	15
% needy frosh rec. need-based self-help aid	78
% needy UG rec. need-based self-help aid	82
% frosh rec. any financial aid	95
% UG rec. any financial aid	96
% UG borrow to pay for school	73
Average cumulative indebtedness	$39,571
% frosh need fully met	26
% ugrads need fully met	25
Average % of frosh need met	87
Average % of ugrad need met	86

ROANOKE COLLEGE

221 COLLEGE LANE, SALEM, VA 24153-3794 • ADMISSIONS: 540-375-2270 • FAX: 540-375-2267

CAMPUS LIFE

Quality of Life Rating	89
Fire Safety Rating	89
Green Rating	76
Type of school	Private
Affiliation	Lutheran
Environment	City

STUDENTS

Total undergrad enrollment	2,005
% male/female	41/59
% from out of state	47
% frosh from public high school	78
% frosh live on campus	92
% ugrads live on campus	76
# of fraternities (% ugrad men join)	5 (18)
# of sororities (% ugrad women join)	4 (16)
% African American	6
% Asian	1
% Caucasian	82
% Hispanic	4
% Native American	<1
% Pacific Islander	<1
% Two or more races	4
% Race and/or ethnicity unknown	0
% international	2
# of countries represented	32

SURVEY SAYS...

Students are happy
School is well run
Easy to get around campus
Lots of beer drinking

ACADEMICS

Academic Rating	80
% students returning for sophomore year	80
students graduating within 4 years	58
students graduating within 6 years	66
Calendar	Semester
Student/faculty ratio	11:1
Profs interesting rating	85
Profs accessible rating	89

Most classes have 20–29 students.
Most lab/discussion sessions have 10–19 students.

MOST POPULAR MAJORS
Business Administration and Management; Psychology; Biology

STUDENTS SAY "..."

Academics

Located in the mountains in the heart of historic Salem, Virginia, Roanoke College is a small Lutheran-affiliated liberal arts college that is dedicated to making sure all students have the opportunities and resources necessary to succeed after graduation. This school of about 2,000 "guides students in exploring relevant studies and teaches them how to carefully evaluate important issues in society"; excellent scholarships, good work-study opportunities, and "a high commitment to achieving academically" among students round out the package.

The "always available" professors are "very engaging and invite a warm personal relationship" and desire "to not only act as a teacher, but as a mentor to their students." They are "excited about what they are teaching" and "really convey a sense of wonder about their respective subjects." Roanoke "does not just hand A's out like candy"; the course load is "challenging, with an abundant amount of work inside and outside of the classroom" but "getting an A is... worth all the more for the effort." The required core classes are set up "in a unique and exciting way" and incredibly small classes mean "there is a lot of opportunity to make relationships with professors, counselors, and even dining service [staff.]"

This "community-based school with southern values" is most definitely "student-centered," and "the ability to conduct meaningful research as an undergraduate is a major benefit." The curriculum places an emphasis on "broad exposure to the liberal arts," and the tutoring and writing centers are "fabulous and free" for those who need help. "Both my professors and my peers have given me opportunities to succeed in ways I never dreamed I would want, let alone have," says a junior.

Life

Life at Roanoke is filled with "the perfect balance of comfort and challenge." The Roanoke campus "thrives on students that want to get involved" and therefore provides plenty of chances to do so. Clubs and organizations "are always being advertised all across campus" and the Campus Activities Board is always creating "wonderful events for the students, such as Bingo and concerts." "Social interaction is a must": Greek life "takes over the social scene," and "Greek-like" off-campus organizations and athletics help fill in the void. "On the weekends, there are always lots of parties, but it isn't a big deal to not participate," says a student. The mountains near the "gorgeous campus" also provide plenty of relaxation options (the Blue Ridge Parkway and the Appalachian Trail are close), and "kayaking, hiking, mountain biking, and geocaching are all easy things to do nearby." However, students know that working hard "is a good thing" at Roanoke and "the library is always full of students on Sundays."

"Hanging out in the cafeteria is really popular" for the social aspect (you are required to buy a meal plan if you live on campus), but the food options are limited. Older individuals can go to downtown Roanoke or the Main street of Salem "to have drinks with friends," while underage students "go there for a great dinner." Many say that "it is very difficult to live off-campus, which results in chaos during housing selection," and that "dorm maintenance" should be made a priority.

Student Body

Almost everyone here is "studious" but "knows how to have fun." Typically, you'll find a Roanoke student to be "an overachiever who has at least one minor or concentration, is involved in at least one organization, and [has] a social life." People come from all over the country, and "it's impossible to not notice the 'Ivy League' feel of Roanoke (incorporating both 'southern-Preppy' and 'northern-preppy')." Greek life is quite popular on campus, and the stereotype of "Lacoste, Lilly Pulitzer," and lacrosse is pervasive. There "is not a lot of diversity, but it is celebrated when it is present." "It would be surprising to me for someone to struggle to fit in," says a freshman.

FINANCIAL AID: 540-375-2235 • E-MAIL: ADMISSIONS@ROANOKE.EDU • WEBSITE: WWW.ROANOKE.EDU

THE PRINCETON REVIEW SAYS

Admissions

Very important factors considered include: rigor of secondary school record, academic GPA, character/personal qualities. *Important factors considered include:* class rank, standardized test scores, interview, extracurricular activities, level of applicant's interest. *Other factors considered include:* application essay, recommendation(s), talent/ability, alumni/ae relation, racial/ethnic status, volunteer work, work experience. SAT or ACT required; SAT Subject Tests considered if submitted. ACT with or without writing accepted. SAT with or without Essay component accepted. TOEFL required of all international applicants. High school diploma is required and GED is accepted. *Academic units required:* 4 English, 3 math, 2 science, 2 science labs, 2 social studies, 5 academic electives. *Academic units recommended:* 4 foreign language.

Financial Aid

Students should submit: FAFSA, State aid form. Priority filing deadline is 3/1. The Princeton Review suggests that all financial aid forms be submitted as soon as possible after October 1. *Need-based scholarships/grants offered:* Federal Pell, FSEOG, State scholarships/grants, College/university scholarship or grant aid from institutional funds. *Loan aid offered:* Direct Subsidized Stafford Loans, Direct Unsubsidized Stafford Loans, Direct PLUS loans, Federal Perkins Loans, College/university loans from institutional funds. Applicants will be notified of awards on a rolling basis beginning 10/15. Federal Work-Study Program available. Institutional employment available.

The Inside Word

Roanoke takes a holistic approach to the admissions process, so the story your whole application tells is important. While the average grades and test scores of accepted students are high, there are no formulas here, and applicants should show they're well-rounded, emphasizing their passions and extracurriculars. The optional personal statement is highly recommended; use it as an opportunity to both show off your achievements and speak to the specific reasons Roanoke appeals to you.

THE SCHOOL SAYS "..."

From the Admissions Office

"Roanoke is one of only 10 percent of colleges in the United States that qualify academically to house a chapter of the prestigious Phi Beta Kappa honor society. Over 93 percent of surveyed alumni received job offers or continued to graduate school within six months of graduation, and approximately 40 to 50 percent of Roanoke graduates attend or complete graduate school within six years.

"Roanoke is nationally recognized for its core curriculum. Unlike most colleges that require a series of introductory courses in various disciplines, all of Roanoke's core courses are topic based, and students see firsthand how fundamental concepts are applied to important issues. For example, instead of taking a generic Introduction to Chemistry course, students might choose Chemistry and Crime, where they use forensic chemistry to solve crimes. Or, instead of Statistics 101, students might choose Statistics and the Weather and discover how statistical analysis is used in weather forecasting.

"Roanoke provides a residential experience with most students living on campus, making it easy to engage in the life of the college through extracurricular and out-of-classroom activities. With more than 100 clubs, it's easy for students to meet others with common interests and build friendships. Residence halls include a mix of traditional double rooms, singles, suites and apartment-style living. All halls have air conditioning, free laundry and Wi-Fi access. Nine residence halls either have been constructed or renovated in the past ten years."

SELECTIVITY

Admissions Rating	80
# of applicants	4,325
% of applicants accepted	72
% of acceptees attending	16
# offered a place on the wait list	152
# of early decision applicants	51
% accepted early decision	88

FRESHMAN PROFILE

Range SAT Critical Reading	490–610
Range SAT Math	480–590
Range SAT Writing	480–598
Range ACT Composite	21–27
Minimum internet-based TOEFL	80
Average HS GPA	3.5
% graduated top 10% of class	15
% graduated top 25% of class	45
% graduated top 50% of class	78

DEADLINES

Early decision	
Deadline	11/10
Notification	11/26
Regular	
Deadline	3/15
Nonfall registration?	Yes

APPLICANTS ALSO LOOK AT AND OFTEN PREFER

James Madison University; University of Virginia; The College of William & Mary

AND SOMETIMES PREFER

Elon University; Lynchburg College; Virginia Tech

AND RARELY PREFER

Christopher Newport University

FINANCIAL FACTS

Financial Aid Rating	85
Annual tuition	$39,720
Room and board	$12,810
Required fees	$1,584
Books and supplies	$1,000
Average frosh need-based scholarship	$27,462
Average UG need-based scholarship	$25,547
% needy frosh rec. need-based scholarship or grant aid	99
% needy UG rec. need-based scholarship or grant aid	98
% needy frosh rec. non-need-based scholarship or grant aid	98
% needy UG rec. non-need-based scholarship or grant aid	96
% needy frosh rec. need-based self-help aid	77
% needy UG rec. need-based self-help aid	79
% frosh rec. any financial aid	100
% UG rec. any financial aid	99
% UG borrow to pay for school	75
Average cumulative indebtedness	$35,974
% frosh need fully met	25
% ugrads need fully met	22
Average % of frosh need met	81
Average % of ugrad need met	81

ROCHESTER INSTITUTE OF TECHNOLOGY

60 LOMB MEMORIAL DRIVE, ROCHESTER, NY 14623-5604 • ADMISSIONS: 585-475-5502 • FAX: 585-475-7424

CAMPUS LIFE

Quality of Life Rating	89
Fire Safety Rating	89
Green Rating	96
Type of school	Private
Affiliation	No Affiliation
Environment	City

STUDENTS

Total undergrad enrollment	13,543
% male/female	68/32
% from out of state	46
% frosh from public high school	85
% frosh live on campus	96
% ugrads live on campus	55
# of fraternities (% ugrad men join)	19 (5)
# of sororities (% ugrad women join)	10 (6)
% African American	5
% Asian	8
% Caucasian	66
% Hispanic	7
% Native American	<1
% Pacific Islander	<1
% Two or more races	3
% Race and/or ethnicity unknown	5
% international	6
# of countries represented	68

SURVEY SAYS...

Students are happy
Internships are widely available
Recreation facilities are great
Everyone loves the Tigers

ACADEMICS

Academic Rating	80
% students returning for sophomore year	89
% students graduating within 4 years	34
% students graduating within 6 years	70
Calendar	Semester
Student/faculty ratio	13:1
Profs interesting rating	76
Profs accessible rating	74

Most classes have 10–19 students.
Most lab/discussion sessions have
10–19 students.

MOST POPULAR MAJORS

Mechanical Engineering; Mechanical
Engineering Technology; Game Design and
Development

STUDENTS SAY "..."

Academics

This western New York academic stalwart boasts one of the country's oldest (and largest) co-op programs and regularly turns out job-ready students from its arts, business, and engineering programs alike. Rochester Institute of Technology is laser-focused on "creating students that are more than prepared to enter the job force," and faculty "bring the material to life" by keeping lectures work-related and placing emphasis on "how you would use what we are learning on the job site." "Professors work with the students and see them as equals," says one mechanical engineering major. "When I'm in the classroom I feel like I'm learning and that I have a voice."

The workload is legendarily daunting and "you will have to reach out and form study groups and pull all-nighters," but professors are "more than happy to help their students" and "truly take pride in helping their students become successful." While the material may be difficult, faculty "are willing to stay after hours, meet with the student, and hold group study/review sessions to help their students understand the material." The easy A is "not very common, especially in engineering classes," but "if you work hard, you will be recognized and grades will reflect that."

The opportunity for students to dip their toes into real world experience abounds throughout the college, and the paid co-op program (mandatory for most majors) is considered by many to be "the best thing anyone could ever choose to go through if you are a career-driven individual." Additionally, there are "plenty of materials and machines students can use for free where in other schools you still have to pay."

Life

While schoolwork takes up the majority of students' time, outside the classroom they "are constantly doing something to keep busy," whether that's joining one of the 300-plus clubs or chilling at the lab. "RIT has a culture for everybody," so if you are interested in a broad topic like computing, "there are a dozen different clubs/societies that you can join to learn more about whatever niche topic interests you."

Students cop to their being "a large gamer population" at RIT, and both electronic and tabletop gaming clubs and tournaments are wildly popular, as is anime. Hockey is a huge part of RIT and "it is very common to see a large number of students at the games." People also "go to the free on-campus movies, see guest speakers, listen to comedians, and attend events hosted by the College Activities Board."

The atmosphere and layout of the campus are beautifully balanced in that "it is not very spread out but not very small at the same time." More than half of the growing population of students live in on-campus, meaning housing "is not always available for everyone who applies" and dorms can be crowded. As one student notes: "The existing infrastructure is okay at best."

Student Body

RIT is a place "where diversity is highlighted [and] academics are prominent," and the population is "as unique and diverse as they come." This environment "allows for a good [facsimile] of the real world." The school's internationally recognized National Technical Institute for the Deaf means there are "amazing accommodations for deaf and hard of hearing students that attend the university," including "notetaking, interpreters, [and C Print® technology]," and a vibrant LGBT+ community also exists on campus. "Video games are a way of life" and students tend to have a nerdy streak ("We are geeky and we love it"). Large groups and clubs for "anime, World of Warcraft, [and] chain mail" happily thrive among students that are all "very accepting of each other's interests." "This is where students are able to create what their minds generate. It's like teenager's dream," says one.

ROCHESTER INSTITUTE OF TECHNOLOGY

FINANCIAL AID: 585-475-5502 • E-MAIL: ADMISSIONS@RIT.EDU • WEBSITE: WWW.RIT.EDU

THE PRINCETON REVIEW SAYS

Admissions

Very important factors considered include: rigor of secondary school record, academic GPA. *Important factors considered include:* class rank, standardized test scores. *Other factors considered include:* application essay, recommendation(s), interview, extracurricular activities, talent/ability, character/personal qualities, first generation, alumni/ae relation, geographical residence, volunteer work, work experience, level of applicant's interest. SAT or ACT required. ACT with or without writing accepted. TOEFL required of all international applicants. High school diploma is required and GED is accepted. *Academic units required:* 4 English, 2 math, 2 science, 1 science lab, 4 social studies, 10 academic electives. *Academic units recommended:* 4 English, 3 math, 3 science, 2 science labs, 3 foreign language, 4 social studies, 5 academic electives.

Financial Aid

Students should submit: FAFSA, Institution's own financial aid form, State aid form. Priority filing deadline is 3/1. The Princeton Review suggests that all financial aid forms be submitted as soon as possible after October 1. *Need-based scholarships/grants offered:* Federal Pell, FSEOG, State scholarships/grants, Private scholarships, College/university scholarship or grant aid from institutional funds. *Loan aid offered:* Direct Subsidized Stafford Loans, Direct Unsubsidized Stafford Loans, Direct PLUS loans, Federal Perkins Loans. Applicants will be notified of awards on a rolling basis beginning 3/15. Federal Work-Study Program available. Institutional employment available.

The Inside Word

Competition to gain admission into Rochester Institute of Technology is tough. The admissions committee is on the lookout for bright, highly motivated students who will make the most out of the university's experiential learning opportunities, and the majority of students must choose their intended course of study during the admissions process. In addition to a sense of direction, you'll need a transcript that reflects a rigorous high school curriculum (including APs and honors classes) to have a shot at admission here.

THE SCHOOL SAYS "..."

From the Admissions Office

"RIT is a place where brilliant minds pool together their individual talents across disciplines in service of big projects and big ideas. It is a vibrant community of students collaborating with experts and specialists: a hub of innovation and creativity. As one of the world's leading technological universities, RIT offers undergraduate and graduate programs in areas such as engineering, computing, engineering technology, business, hospitality, science, visual arts, biomedical sciences, game design and development, psychology, advertising, public relations, and public policy. Students may choose from more than eighty different minors to develop personal and professional interests. RIT attracts students from every state and over 2,600 international students from more than 100 countries. Embodying our commitment to diversity, more than 3,100 students of color have elected to study at RIT. Adding a social and educational dynamic not found at any other university are more than 1,200 deaf and hard-of-hearing students supported by RIT's National Technical Institute for the Deaf. Experiential learning has been a hallmark of an RIT education since 1912. Every academic program offers some form of experiential education opportunity, which may include cooperative education, internships, study abroad, and undergraduate research. Students work hard, but learning is complemented with plenty of organized and spontaneous events and activities. RIT is a unique blend of rigor and fun, creativity and specialization, intellect and practice. It is a launching pad for a brilliant career, and a highly unique state of mind. It is a perfect environment in which to pursue your passion."

SELECTIVITY

Admissions Rating	88
# of applicants	18,598
% of applicants accepted	57
% of acceptees attending	27
# offered a place on the wait list	376
% accepting a place on wait list	98
% admitted from wait list	22
# of early decision applicants	1,329
% accepted early decision	64

FRESHMAN PROFILE

Range SAT Critical Reading	550–660
Range SAT Math	580–690
Range SAT Writing	520–630
Range ACT Composite	26–31
Minimum paper TOEFL	550
Minimum internet-based TOEFL	79
Average HS GPA	3.6
% graduated top 10% of class	34
% graduated top 25% of class	69
% graduated top 50% of class	96

DEADLINES

Early decision	
Deadline	12/1
Notification	1/15
Regular	
Priority	2/1
Deadline	2/1
Nonfall registration?	Yes

APPLICANTS ALSO LOOK AT AND OFTEN PREFER
Cornell University; Carnegie Mellon University

AND SOMETIMES PREFER
Worcester Polytechnic Institute; University of Rochester; Rensselaer Polytechnic Institute

AND RARELY PREFER
State University of New York–University at Buffalo; Drexel University

FINANCIAL FACTS

Financial Aid Rating	92
Annual tuition	$36,596
Room and board	$11,918
Required fees	$528
Books and supplies	$1,050
Average frosh need-based scholarship	$19,500
Average UG need-based scholarship	$18,500
% needy frosh rec. need-based scholarship or grant aid	95
% needy UG rec. need-based scholarship or grant aid	90
% needy frosh rec. non-need-based scholarship or grant aid	29
% needy UG rec. non-need-based scholarship or grant aid	29
% needy frosh rec. need-based self-help aid	88
% needy UG rec. need-based self-help aid	82
% frosh rec. any financial aid	87
% UG rec. any financial aid	77
% frosh need fully met	81
% ugrads need fully met	82
Average % of frosh need met	87
Average % of ugrad need met	87

ROLLINS COLLEGE

1000 HOLT AVENUE, WINTER PARK, FL 32789-4499 • ADMISSIONS: 407-646-2161 • FAX: 407-646-1502

CAMPUS LIFE

Quality of Life Rating	90
Fire Safety Rating	97
Green Rating	82
Type of school	Private
Affiliation	No Affiliation
Environment	Town

STUDENTS

Total undergrad enrollment	1,948
% male/female	41/59
% from out of state	47
% frosh from public high school	51
% frosh live on campus	88
% ugrads live on campus	60
# of fraternities (% ugrad men join)	6 (38)
# of sororities (% ugrad women join)	7 (42)
% African American	3
% Asian	3
% Caucasian	66
% Hispanic	14
% Native American	<1
% Pacific Islander	0
% Two or more races	3
% Race and/or ethnicity unknown	3
% international	9
# of countries represented	59

SURVEY SAYS...

Students are happy
Career services are great
Internships are widely available
Class discussions encouraged
Great financial aid
Students aren't religious
Students love Winter Park, FL
Great off-campus food
Easy to get around campus
Recreation facilities are great
Lots of beer drinking

ACADEMICS

Academic Rating	89
% students returning for sophomore year	89
% students graduating within 4 years	64
% students graduating within 6 years	71
Calendar	Semester
Student/faculty ratio	10:1
Profs interesting rating	85
Profs accessible rating	91

Most classes have 10–19 students.

MOST POPULAR MAJORS

International Business; Communication
Studies; Economics

STUDENTS SAY "..."

Academics

Located in sunny central Florida, Rollins College is "small enough to help the individual but is fortunate enough to have a large endowment capable of providing each student with necessary academic means." The generous academic merit scholarships bring in a smart crowd, and the small class sizes, dedicated faculty, and numerous "student leadership opportunities, internships, academic presentations, [and] conference opportunities" sweeten the pot.

Rollins is "all about individual growth personally and educationally," but it also stresses "responsible community leadership both on and off campus." Students have a great deal of freedom to study what they choose, and many large projects are individualized toward the student, meaning a student "can tailor my topic to my interests." In addition to the autonomy this approach grants students, it "reinforces the idea of a holistic education," which helps to "make [students] competitive in an ever-changing job market." Working at this speed, students are able to "discover purpose and identify goals." Many services are also available to students, such as free tutoring and counseling.

Professors "perform very well" and create an "open and invigorating classroom environment" that is "open to diverse ideas and perspectives." Teachers "know every student's name, and they will remember you throughout your college experience." "My first year, one called my cell phone when I missed class," says a student. "The interactions that I have with the professors are second to none," says another. The small class sizes (even introductory courses are tiny) make it "very easy to learn and share your opinion," and since professors are "very engaging and willing to hear all points of view," "no one is left feeling like they don't matter."

Life

The "very beautiful and relaxing" campus can often feel sort of like a "country club" in both appearance and attitude. With "so many attractions in the Orlando area, the accessibility of the lake and the beach it is hard not to bring your books outside." Some people like "to go out to nearby downtown Orlando" (which is fifteen minutes away from school), some "live for Disney World," and some just stay in and hang out. A favorite activity among students is "walking up Park Avenue and exploring the delicious culinary endeavors there," and Lake Virginia is a great spot for perching, wakeboarding, or sailing. Students here tend "to travel a lot and explore other towns in Florida during the school year."

There are "always events on campus that are fun," like "a student who is a DJ [who] had a concert on the lawn one night," and almost one-third of the school is involved in Greek life. Community service is also "a pretty big part of the campus," and there is "always something service-related going on either from student groups or from the community engagement office."

Student Body

Rollins is such a small school that "everyone knows everyone." It's a true split at Rollins between in-staters and out-of-staters (and the international contingent) and among socioeconomic classes. "There are extremely wealthy spoiled kids driving Mercedes and smoking, [and] then there are true nerds who busted their butts to get in," says a student. Since the two groups mix constantly, "it is often hard to differentiate between the students who are set to inherit their parent's company after they graduate and those here on scholarship." Luckily, the "family environment and the closeness of all of the campus bring all the students together as scholars." Everyone may have small groups to which they belong, but "there is intermingling going on all the time."

FINANCIAL AID: 407-646-2395 • E-MAIL: ADMISSION@ROLLINS.EDU • WEBSITE: WWW.ROLLINS.EDU

THE PRINCETON REVIEW SAYS

Admissions

Very important factors considered include: rigor of secondary school record, academic GPA. *Important factors considered include:* standardized test scores, application essay, recommendation(s), extracurricular activities, talent/ability. *Other factors considered include:* class rank, character/personal qualities, first generation, alumni/ae relation, volunteer work, work experience, level of applicant's interest. SAT or ACT required for some. TOEFL required of all international applicants. High school diploma is required and GED is accepted. *Academic units required:* 4 English, 3 math, 2 science, 2 foreign language, 2 social studies, 2 history, 2 academic electives. *Academic units recommended:* 4 English, 4 math, 4 science.

Financial Aid

Students should submit: FAFSA. Priority filing deadline is 3/1. The Princeton Review suggests that all financial aid forms be submitted as soon as possible after October 1. *Need-based scholarships/grants offered:* Federal Pell, FSEOG, State scholarships/grants, Private scholarships, College/university scholarship or grant aid from institutional funds. *Loan aid offered:* Direct Subsidized Stafford Loans, Direct Unsubsidized Stafford Loans, Direct PLUS loans, Federal Perkins Loans. Applicants will be notified of awards on a rolling basis beginning 3/1. Federal Work-Study Program available. Institutional employment available.

The Inside Word

Applicants to Rollins who don't seek academic merit scholarships have the Rollins is a test optional school, and both academic and need-based scholarships are available to students who choose to not submit standardized test scores. It's the school's way of creating another opportunity for students whose test results do not match their overall academic performance, and it's characteristic of the individualized approach taken here (about 10 percent of applicants opt for this method). Each applicant is assigned an admissions officer who acts as his or her liaison, ensuring a personalized admissions experience. Early decision applicants are given priority in admissions as well as in considerations for merit-based scholarships and need-based financial aid.

THE SCHOOL SAYS " . . ."

From the Admissions Office

"Rollins' mission is to nurture global citizenship and responsible leadership within its students so they are prepared to lead meaningful lives and productive careers. As you begin the college selection process, remember that you are in control of your destiny. Your academic record—course load, grades earned, test scores—are the most important part of your application credentials. But Rollins also pays close attention to your personal dimension—interests, strengths, values, and potential to contribute to college life. Don't sell yourself short in the application process. Be proud of what you've accomplished and who you are, and be honest when you describe yourself. Finally, the admission committee always likes to see candidates who express interest in the college. If we're your first choice, apply early decision. Each year we admit approximately one-third of the entering class through the early decision process. Are you unsure about your choice? If you can, schedule some visits, meet with an admission counselor, tour campus, and spend time in a class so you can see for yourself what Rollins and other colleges are all about. Take control of your destiny, and enjoy the process along the way."

SELECTIVITY

Admissions Rating	87
# of applicants	4,922
% of applicants accepted	60
% of acceptees attending	17
# offered a place on the wait list	102
% accepting a place on wait list	32
% admitted from wait list	30

FRESHMAN PROFILE

Range SAT Critical Reading	550–650
Range SAT Math	555–660
Range SAT Writing	550–650
Range ACT Composite	24–29
Minimum paper TOEFL	550
Minimum internet-based TOEFL	80
Average HS GPA	3.3
% graduated top 10% of class	34
% graduated top 25% of class	66
% graduated top 50% of class	88

DEADLINES

Early decision	
Deadline	11/15
Notification	12/15
Regular	
Deadline	2/15
Notification	4/1
Nonfall registration?	Yes

APPLICANTS ALSO LOOK AT AND OFTEN PREFER
Florida State University; University of Florida

AND SOMETIMES PREFER
University of Miami; College of Charleston; Stetson University; Furman University

AND RARELY PREFER
University of Tampa

FINANCIAL FACTS

Financial Aid Rating	84
Annual tuition	$44,760
Room and board	$13,910
Books and supplies	$1,244
Average frosh need-based scholarship	$30,035
Average UG need-based scholarship	$28,861
% needy frosh rec. need-based scholarship or grant aid	99
% needy UG rec. need-based scholarship or grant aid	99
% needy frosh rec. non-need-based scholarship or grant aid	17
% needy UG rec. non-need-based scholarship or grant aid	17
% needy frosh rec. need-based self-help aid	71
% needy UG rec. need-based self-help aid	74
% frosh rec. any financial aid	88
% UG rec. any financial aid	86
% UG borrow to pay for school	50
Average cumulative indebtedness	$29,455
% frosh need fully met	18
% ugrads need fully met	18
Average % of frosh need met	71
Average % of ugrad need met	71

ROSE-HULMAN INSTITUTE OF TECHNOLOGY

5500 WABASH AVENUE, TERRE HAUTE, IN 47803-3999 • ADMISSIONS: 812-877-8213 • FAX: 812-877-8941

CAMPUS LIFE
Quality of Life Rating	93
Fire Safety Rating	96
Green Rating	75
Type of school	Private
Affiliation	No Affiliation
Environment	Town

STUDENTS
Total undergrad enrollment	2,270
% male/female	77/23
% from out of state	64
% frosh from public high school	66
% frosh live on campus	99
% ugrads live on campus	57
# of fraternities (% ugrad men join)	8 (35)
# of sororities (% ugrad women join)	3 (36)
% African American	2
% Asian	4
% Caucasian	74
% Hispanic	3
% Native American	<1
% Pacific Islander	<1
% Two or more races	4
% Race and/or ethnicity unknown	<1
% international	12
# of countries represented	15

SURVEY SAYS...
Students always studying
Students are happy
Classroom facilities are great
Lab facilities are great
Career services are great
Internships are widely available
School is well run
No one cheats
Students are friendly
Diverse student types interact on campus
Students get along with local community
Dorms are like palaces
Easy to get around campus
Recreation facilities are great
Very little drug use
Intramural sports are popular
Active minority support groups

ACADEMICS
Academic Rating	90
% students returning for sophomore year	93
% students graduating within 4 years	68
% students graduating within 6 years	77
Calendar	Quarter
Student/faculty ratio	13:1
Profs interesting rating	94
Profs accessible rating	99

Most classes have 20–29 students.
Most lab/discussion sessions have 10–19 students.

MOST POPULAR MAJORS
Chemical Engineering; Mechanical Engineering; Electrical Engineering

STUDENTS SAY "..."

Academics
Rose-Hulman Institute of Technology, in Terre Haute, Indiana, earns its "reputation as an excellent undergraduate engineering school" with a combination of strong academics and "personal attention, small class sizes, and a family atmosphere," a rarity among tech schools. More succinctly, "Rose-Hulman is where nerds go to finally feel like they belong." Sure, "the workload is fairly heavy, especially sophomore year with the engineering curriculum." One mechanical engineering student describes the course work: "The material is difficult . . . but the culture is supportive, so you make it work." Rose-Hulman features an unusually robust support system, and that mitigates the strain. "The transition is made as smooth as possible from high school to college for freshmen" with "on-campus tutoring in the learning center (an excellent resource for students to get homework help)" and "professors who are always available outside of class." One student elaborates, "If you are walking down the hall, [professors] will say hello and usually ask how you are doing." Not only are those professors "happy to be teaching," but they have "real-world industry experience" to back it up. One student sums up the teaching philosophy as "theory is important, but application is everything." All of this hard work pays dividends in the form "a great alumni base" and a near 99 percent job placement rate six months after graduation.

Life
"Life at Rose is academically demanding," but "the community here is so supportive and safe that you get through it," and while "students do a lot of homework and study a lot," they do occasionally find time to close the books and relax. "It's all work and little play Sunday through Thursday," but come Friday "we play hard.'" Students inform us "there's always something to do on campus, whether it's going to a fraternity party or attending a concert or going to a dance or just watching a movie with friends." Greek life is big, "but it's not your typical Animal House," and both intramural and Division III intercollegiate athletics have their supporters. There are also "tons of different groups to get involved in" on campus. Hometown Terre Haute, on the other hand, isn't so lively. "There isn't much to do" in town other than "go to the shadiest bars and check out the locals." As one student points out, "We are located in the middle of nowhere . . . not much they can do about it, but it is not so great."

Student Body
"The kids who attend Rose-Hulman are smart, dedicated, and consequently, nerds," but "this is not a negative thing. Within the students here, there are no outcasts, and even our athletes are most likely also mathletes." "Everyone definitely marches to the beat of his own drum," students assure us. Personality types run the gamut from "geniuses, average students, student-athletes, outspoken, quiet, etc." Demographically, undergrads are "mostly white male engineers from the Midwest" (partly a function of Rose-Hulman's location), but "we are slowly expanding the Rose-Hulman name and getting people from all over the United States and globe." The population "is mostly boys, although the females are catching up," albeit slowly. About half of the incoming freshman class played varsity sports in high school, which is about as many had been involved in the performing arts.

ROSE-HULMAN INSTITUTE OF TECHNOLOGY

FINANCIAL AID: 812-877-8259 • E-MAIL: ADMISSIONS@ROSE-HULMAN.EDU • WEBSITE: WWW.ROSE-HULMAN.EDU

THE PRINCETON REVIEW SAYS

Admissions

Very important factors considered include: rigor of secondary school record, class rank, academic GPA, standardized test scores, recommendation(s), extracurricular activities, character/personal qualities, volunteer work, work experience. SAT or ACT required. TOEFL or IELTS required of all international applicants. High school diploma is required and GED is not accepted. *Academic units required:* 4 English, 4 math, 2 social studies, 1 chemsitry, 1 physics, academic electives.

Financial Aid

Students should submit: FAFSA. Priority filing deadline is 3/1. The Princeton Review suggests that all financial aid forms be submitted as soon as possible after October 1. *Need-based scholarships/grants offered:* Federal Pell, FSEOG, State scholarships/grants, College/university scholarship or grant aid from institutional funds. *Loan aid offered:* Direct Subsidized Stafford Loans, Direct Unsubsidized Stafford Loans, Direct PLUS loans, Federal Perkins Loans. Applicants will be notified of awards on or about 3/10. Federal Work-Study Program available. Institutional employment available.

The Inside Word

Admission to Rose-Hulman is selective, and the admissions committee isn't shy about the fact that they are looking for the best and the brightest. They expect students to be in the top 25 percent of their graduating class (but will look at other factors like the rigor of your classes if your high school doesn't rank). It's a fantastic idea to apply sooner rather than later: Rose-Hulman's Early Action is non-binding, so you can find out if you were admitted sooner in the process without having to commit to attending.

SELECTIVITY

Admissions Rating	93
# of applicants	4,331
% of applicants accepted	58
% of acceptees attending	22
# offered a place on the wait list	326
% accepting a place on wait list	46
% admitted from wait list	25

FRESHMAN PROFILE

Range SAT Critical Reading	550–670
Range SAT Math	630–750
Range SAT Writing	550–660
Range ACT Composite	28–32
Minimum paper TOEFL	550
Minimum internet-based TOEFL	80
Average HS GPA	4.0
% graduated top 10% of class	69
% graduated top 25% of class	90
% graduated top 50% of class	99

DEADLINES

Early action	
Deadline	11/1
Notification	12/15
Regular	
Priority	11/1
Deadline	2/1
Notification	12/15
Nonfall registration?	No

FINANCIAL FACTS

Financial Aid Rating	83
Annual tuition	$41,865
Room and board	$12,660
Required fees	$876
Books and supplies	$1,500
Average frosh need-based scholarship	$25,954
Average UG need-based scholarship	$24,373
% needy frosh rec. need-based scholarship or grant aid	83
% needy UG rec. need-based scholarship or grant aid	84
% needy frosh rec. non-need-based scholarship or grant aid	100
% needy UG rec. non-need-based scholarship or grant aid	99
% needy frosh rec. need-based self-help aid	88
% needy UG rec. need-based self-help aid	87
% frosh rec. any financial aid	99
% UG rec. any financial aid	97
% UG borrow to pay for school	64
Average cumulative indebtedness	$41,804
% frosh need fully met	25
% ugrads need fully met	20
Average % of frosh need met	77
Average % of ugrad need met	73

RUTGERS UNIVERSITY—NEW BRUNSWICK

65 DAVIDSON ROAD, PISCATAWAY, NJ 08854-8097 • ADMISSIONS: 732-445-4636 • FAX: 732-445-0237

STUDENTS SAY "..."

Academics

Rutgers is "a big school with many different types of people," a "diverse university in all aspects of the word—academically, culturally, politically, ethnically, linguistically, and socially," which offers "opportunities around every corner." No matter what students seek from their educations, they're likely to find it here, from engineering to business to pharmacy programs and more. That kind of all-encompassing diversity means the school "offers everyone the opportunity to pursue anything they're interested in." It also means, however, that your instructors will run the gamut "from vivacious to narcoleptic"; students will have their "fair share of great professors, average professors, and bad professors." However, for every professor who is "rude when dealing with students," there are ten who are "intelligent people who have a lot of information to share and a lot of experience that allows them to elaborate on many topics." The best of these professors are "experienced, intelligent, and helpful," as well as "diverse, accessible, proactive, involved in research, and interested in students who take initiative." These educators know how to make learning "enjoyable and informative." Most classes employ a traditional lecture format, but many elective classes "are much smaller and thus much more open to discussion and student presentation." Even more attractive for many, Rutgers' status as a research university means there are ample opportunities for undergraduates "to conduct research and work with professors in any number of fields."

Life

A big campus, "awesome" public transportation, and activities of every type mean staying active at Rutgers is easy. There is certainly no lack of things to do. "There is always something going on," students boast, with sports, "movie screenings, arcade games at the RutgersZone, performing arts, local theaters, university-sponsored concerts, free food events, community service days, Greek life," and more filling whatever down time students might have. Local restaurants abound. School clubs and organizations exist by the hundreds, including those dedicated to theater, music, dance, and community service. "The party scene is definitely present, more so in the warmer months," and there are plenty of bars popular with students. The on-campus party scene tends to be safe, since the school "sends out (campus) police to patrol around the campus twenty-four hours to ensure student safety." Maybe most popular of all is rooting for the scarlet. "During football season...everyone can be found cheering in the student section at the games." For those who need to get off campus, New York City and Philadelphia are both a modest train or bus drive away. With so many opportunities, "Rutgers allows students to do well in school, be a part of an organization, have relationships with friends, and even have a job." Here, "there's rarely a dull moment."

Student Body

Typical student? Not here. The universal refrain from Rutgers students is there is no such thing. "The one common thread most students have is that they are from New Jersey, since it is a state school." Other than that, "Rutgers is truly a melting pot of people from all over the world of all different backgrounds with different interests." Rather than making it more difficult to fit in, students say this melting pot makes it easier because "no matter what you're interested in, there is a group of students here who share the same exact interests. It's really easy to find your own niche." Most students are "dedicated to academics and community service and also to having fun," students who, no matter which group they fall in with, are "very friendly, funny, and nice." Notice the combination of strong academics and a dedication to fun? That, too, is a frequently cited trait common at Rutgers. Even though "there is not one typical student," at the very least most are "serious about their work and studying but know how to party and have fun." With a large, diverse campus of 32,000, it doesn't matter the kind of person you are. "It is not uncommon to meet someone new weekly... With so many students here, everyone is able to find someone to befriend and interact with."

FINANCIAL AID: 848-932-7305 • E-MAIL: ADMISSIONS@UGADM.RUTGERS.EDU • WEBSITE: HTTP://NEWBRUNSWICK.RUTGERS.EDU

THE PRINCETON REVIEW SAYS
Admissions

Very important factors considered include: rigor of secondary school record, class rank, academic GPA, standardized test scores, interview, talent/ability. *Important factors considered include:* application essay, extracurricular activities, first generation, geographical residence, state residency, racial/ethnic status, volunteer work, work experience. SAT or ACT required. ACT with Writing required. TOEFL required of all international applicants. High school diploma is required and GED is accepted. *Academic units required:* 4 English, 3 math (4 math for engineeirng applicants), 2 science, 2 foreign language, 5 academic electives. *Academic units recommended:* 4 math, 2 foreign language.

Financial Aid

Students should submit: FAFSA. Priority filing deadline is 3/15. The Princeton Review suggests that all financial aid forms be submitted as soon as possible after October 1. *Need-based scholarships/grants offered:* Federal Pell, FSEOG, State scholarships/grants, College/university scholarship or grant aid from institutional funds, Federal Nursing Scholarships. *Loan aid offered:* Direct Subsidized Stafford Loans, Direct Unsubsidized Stafford Loans, Direct PLUS loans, Federal Perkins Loans, Federal Nursing Loans, State Loans, College/university loans from institutional funds. Applicants will be notified of awards on a rolling basis beginning 3/1. Federal Work-Study Program available. Institutional employment available.

The Inside Word

One does not need to jump through hoops to get into Rutgers. Because of the vast number of applications the university gets each year, applicants will be reviewed based on the standard criteria—grades, the quality of your high school curriculum, standardized test scores, and your student essay—without much beyond that. Solid students should find acceptance into Rutgers a relatively painless process.

THE SCHOOL SAYS "..."
From the Admissions Office

"Rutgers University—New Brunswick, one of only sixty-two members of the Association of American Universities, is a research university that attracts students from across the nation and around the world. What does it take to be accepted for admission to Rutgers University? Our primary emphasis is on your past academic performance as indicated by your high school grades (particularly in required academic subjects), your class rank or cumulative average, the strength of your academic program, your standardized test scores on the SAT or ACT, any special talents you may have, and your participation in school and community activities. We seek students with a broad diversity of talents, interests, and backgrounds. Above all else, we're looking for students who will get the most out of a Rutgers education—students with the intellect, initiative, and motivation to make full use of the opportunities we have to offer. First-year applicants should take the SAT or the ACT. Test scores are not required for students who graduated high school more than two years ago or have completed more than twelve college credits since graduating.

"Rutgers' absorption of the University of Medicine and Dentistry of New Jersey (UMDNJ) in July 2013 has added two medical schools, a dental school, and a host of health professions programs that have dramatically enhanced already robust undergraduate academic and research opportunities.

"The new highly selective Honors College that includes a new residential facility in the heart of Rutgers University—New Brunswick's College Avenue campus attracts the most exceptional students to a scholarly community where they can explore, learn, and create together with Rutgers' internationally acclaimed faculty."

SELECTIVITY

Admissions Rating	87
# of applicants	35,340
% of applicants accepted	60
% of acceptees attending	33
# offered a place on the wait list	0

FRESHMAN PROFILE

Range SAT Critical Reading	520–640
Range SAT Math	570–700
Range SAT Writing	540–660
Minimum paper TOEFL	550
% graduated top 10% of class	39
% graduated top 25% of class	74
% graduated top 50% of class	96

DEADLINES

Early Action	
Deadline	11/1
Notification	2/28
Regular	
Deadline	12/1
Nonfall registration?	Yes

APPLICANTS ALSO LOOK AT AND OFTEN PREFER

University of Pennsylvania; Cornell University; University of Virginia

AND SOMETIMES PREFER

Penn State—University Park; Boston CollegeNew Jersey Institute of Technology

AND RARELY PREFER

The George Washington University

FINANCIAL FACTS

Financial Aid Rating	79
Annual in-state tuition	$11,217
Annual out-of-state tuition	$26,607
Room and board	$12,054
Required fees	$2,914
Books and supplies	$1,350
Average frosh need-based scholarship	$12,575
Average UG need-based scholarship	$10,698
% needy frosh rec. need-based scholarship or grant aid	69
% needy UG rec. need-based scholarship or grant aid	72
% needy frosh rec. non-need-based scholarship or grant aid	28
% needy UG rec. non-need-based scholarship or grant aid	17
% needy frosh rec. need-based self-help aid	83
% needy UG rec. need-based self-help aid	84
% frosh rec. any financial aid	79
% UG rec. any financial aid	85
Average cumulative indebtedness	$25,334
% frosh need fully met	5
% ugrads need fully met	4
Average % of frosh need met	57
Average % of ugrad need met	52

SACRED HEART UNIVERSITY

5151 PARK AVENUE, FAIRFIELD, CT 06825 • ADMISSIONS: 203-371-7880 • FAX: 203-365-7607

CAMPUS LIFE

Quality of Life Rating	85
Fire Safety Rating	94
Green Rating	66
Type of school	Private
Affiliation	Roman Catholic
Environment	Town

STUDENTS

Total undergrad enrollment	5,205
% male/female	36/64
% from out of state	61
% frosh live on campus	90
% ugrads live on campus	50
# of fraternities (% ugrad men join)	5 (18)
# of sororities (% ugrad women join)	7 (33)
% African American	4
% Asian	2
% Caucasian	71
% Hispanic	8
% Native American	<1
% Pacific Islander	<1
% Two or more races	2
% Race and/or ethnicity unknown	12
% international	1
# of countries represented	24

SURVEY SAYS...

Students are happy
Classroom facilities are great
Internships are widely available
School is well run
Everyone loves the Pioneers
Frats and sororities are popular

ACADEMICS

Academic Rating	77
% students returning for sophomore year	83
% students graduating within 4 years	58
% students graduating within 6 years	67
Calendar	Semester
Student/faculty ratio	15:1
Profs interesting rating	78
Profs accessible rating	78
Most classes have 20–29 students.	

MOST POPULAR MAJORS

Nursing Science; Psychology; Marketing/
Marketing Management

STUDENTS SAY ". . ."

Academics

A fantastic institution, Sacred Heart University brilliantly combines the "community" feel of a small school with the "first class" facilities often associated with larger universities. Moreover, as a Catholic college, Sacred Heart deftly balances "service [with] learning." Academically, while SHU has many "amazing" departments, students rush to highlight the business, health science and dance programs. Undergrads here also appreciate the fact that the university does "a great job of opening up study abroad experiences regardless of major." As one grateful student explains, "Nursing can do a full semester in Ireland which is unheard of in most nursing schools."

Inside the classroom, undergrads are privy to "excellent" professors who "really know how to bring the subjects to life and bring relevancy to the topics being learned." They also tend to be "very passionate about what they do" and excel at making "students feel important." One thrilled student further explains, "The professors here really try to get to know you. They learn about your goals and work hard to help you to achieve them." Perhaps even more impressive, they "remember you even after you have finished their class. They will always stop and say hi to you in the hallway." Finally, a psychology major adds, "Professors go above and beyond when you need it...They genuinely care about your success and happiness, and are always willing to meet...sometimes even mak[ing] special arrangements to [see] you [outside of] office hours."

Life

Undergrads at Sacred Heart lead active, hectic lives. As a marketing major immediately shares, "If people need a break from school work, or just want to have some fun on campus, there is always an opportunity to do so!" More specifically, we're told that "many students are involved in either a sport or a performing arts program which means there are rehearsals and practices throughout the day or multiple times a week." Additionally, "there are a lot of community service opportunities." And we'd be remiss if we neglected to mention that the student activities office brings some great entertainment options to campus including "mind readers and magicians and hypnotists." There's also plenty to take advantage of off-campus as well. For starters, "when the weather is warm, a lot of students visit the beach in Fairfield." Sacred Heart also sponsors a number of trips "to NYC and Boston that include tickets to shows or museums." And, of course, many Sacred Heart undergrads simply love that "the mall is in close proximity to the school." All in all, you have to work pretty hard at being bored at SHU.

Student Body

Sacred Heart students have the utmost respect for their peers. Indeed, when asked to describe their classmates, many undergrads quickly note that they're "kind and considerate." This might stem from the fact that SHU is known as a "door holding school." An English major helpfully clarifies, "Each door I go through, someone holds it for me and each door I leave, I hold it open for them." In other words, you can rest assured that this is a "friendly" community. Sacred Heart students can also be described as "genuine" and "motivated." The majority are bursting "with school spirit" and boundless enthusiasm. And though many students "tend to be wealthier and preppy," thankfully "the university as a whole encompasses all types of people." As another English major beautifully concludes, "Whether you are in theatre or the captain of the [Division I] football team, we are a family here at SHU."

FINANCIAL AID: 203-371-7980 • E-MAIL: ENROLL@SACREDHEART.EDU • WEBSITE: WWW.SACREDHEART.EDU

THE PRINCETON REVIEW SAYS

Admissions

Very important factors considered include: rigor of secondary school record, academic GPA, volunteer work, work experience. *Important factors considered include:* class rank, application essay, recommendation(s), interview, extracurricular activities, talent/ability, character/personal qualities, level of applicant's interest. *Other factors considered include:* standardized test scores, first generation, alumni/ae relation, geographical residence, state residency, religious affiliation/commitment, racial/ethnic status. SAT or ACT considered if submitted. ACT with or without writing accepted. TOEFL required of all international applicants. High school diploma is required and GED is accepted. *Academic units required:* 4 English, 3 math, 3 science, 1 science lab, 2 foreign language, 3 social studies, 3 history, 3 academic electives. *Academic units recommended:* 4 English, 4 math, 4 science, 2 science labs, 4 foreign language, 4 social studies, 4 history, 4 academic electives.

Financial Aid

Students should submit: FAFSA, CSS/Financial Aid PROFILE, Noncustodial PROFILE. Priority filing deadline is 2/15. The Princeton Review suggests that all financial aid forms be submitted as soon as possible after October 1. *Need-based scholarships/grants offered:* Federal Pell, FSEOG, State scholarships/grants, Private scholarships, College/university scholarship or grant aid from institutional funds. *Loan aid offered:* Direct Subsidized Stafford Loans, Direct Unsubsidized Stafford Loans, Direct PLUS loans, Federal Perkins Loans, State Loans. Applicants will be notified of awards on a rolling basis beginning 3/1. Federal Work-Study Program available. Institutional employment available.

The Inside Word

Admissions officers at Sacred Heart really strive to take a well-rounded approach to their decisions. Therefore, they look closely at a variety of factors including GPA, high school curriculum and letters of recommendation. Beyond academics, officers consider each applicant's extracurricular activities. After all, they're also seeking students who will actively contribute to Sacred Heart. Importantly, standardized test scores are optional. Interviews, however, are required for all applicants applying early decision. They are strongly encouraged for individuals applying regular decision.

THE SCHOOL SAYS " . . ."

From the Admissions Office

"Sacred Heart University, recognized for blending excellence in the Liberal Arts with career-focused academic and student development programs, is the second-largest Catholic university in New England. Sacred Heart continues its exceptional growth in enrollment; academic programs including a variety of accelerated Bachelor's-Master's degree programs; and the physical campus where a new Welch College of Business and Department of Communication & Media Studies are currently under construction and will be followed by a new College of Health Professions building and a new freshman residence hall. With an ideal New England location 55 miles from New York City in Fairfield County, Connecticut, plentiful undergraduate research or internship experiences are in place for all majors, and the Career Center works with students as soon as they arrive as freshmen. Students also gain real-world experience taking a wide variety of courses at SHU's two international campuses in Europe, including pre-fall programs for incoming freshmen as well as short-term winter break and late May programs. These experiential learning opportunities are complemented by a rich student life program offering more than eighty student organizations including strong performing arts programs, media clubs, Greek life and an array of community service organizations, as well as thirty-one Division I varsity sports and twenty-four club sports teams."

SELECTIVITY

Admissions Rating	82
# of applicants	9,257
% of applicants accepted	59
% of acceptees attending	24
# of early decision applicants	181
% accepted early decision	87

FRESHMAN PROFILE

Range SAT Critical Reading	478–611
Range SAT Math	483–634
Range SAT Writing	470–626
Range ACT Composite	21–33
Minimum paper TOEFL	550
Minimum internet-based TOEFL	80
Average HS GPA	3.4
% graduated top 10% of class	10
% graduated top 25% of class	35
% graduated top 50% of class	77

DEADLINES

Early decision	
Deadline	12/1
Notification	12/15
Early action	
Deadline	12/15
Notification	1/31
Regular	
Priority	2/5
Nonfall registration?	Yes

APPLICANTS ALSO LOOK AT AND OFTEN PREFER

Quinnipiac University; Fairfield University

AND SOMETIMES PREFER

Fordham University; Providence College; Marist College

FINANCIAL FACTS

Financial Aid Rating	80
Annual tuition	$36,920
Room and board	$14,140
Required fees	$250
Books and supplies	$1,200
Average frosh need-based scholarship	$15,547
Average UG need-based scholarship	$15,991
% needy frosh rec. need-based scholarship or grant aid	100
% needy UG rec. need-based scholarship or grant aid	99
% needy frosh rec. non-need-based scholarship or grant aid	16
% needy UG rec. non-need-based scholarship or grant aid	15
% needy frosh rec. need-based self-help aid	79
% needy UG rec. need-based self-help aid	79
% frosh rec. any financial aid	70
% UG rec. any financial aid	63
% UG borrow to pay for school	72
Average cumulative indebtedness	$47,715
% frosh need fully met	17
% ugrads need fully met	17
Average % of frosh need met	57
Average % of ugrad need met	58

SAINT ANSELM COLLEGE

100 SAINT ANSELM DRIVE, MANCHESTER, NH 03102-1310 • ADMISSIONS: 603-641-7500 • FAX: 603-641-7550

STUDENTS SAY "..."

Academics

Nestled in New Hampshire near the White Mountains, Saint Anselm College is a small, Catholic Benedictine liberal arts college founded in 1889. Its prime location provides not only a beautiful environment in which to learn, but also makes it "the Benedictine college with a box seat on America's most riveting political theater" according to the Washington Post, and adds indelible "real-world experience" for those pursuing an education in politics. The small size of the college—in 2014 there were only 2,000 students—allows Saint Anselm College to provide "a welcoming community" and a "personalized experience" for all students. It encourages "Catholic ideals" of "service and community" and offers "a challenging, quality education" with "in depth learning both inside and outside of the classroom." Students call Saint Anselm a "close knit yet academically motivating environment, with countless opportunities to gain internship and other leadership experiences." "Each individual can thrive in some way," notes an English major, and "be involved, serve others, and have a life-long second home." "The education here is incredible," says a Forensic Science major, and "the teachers are more than happy to help you succeed." Students feel "challenged and enthused" by their professors and note that "discussions inside and outside of class are fantastic," "the lectures and labs prepare" them well for exams, "homework is almost always extremely relevant and beneficial," and professors "rarely lecture [or] read off power points." Professors "seem to love their job" and "come to class ready to stimulate your creative thinking." Students say that there is an "accessible, friendly, and inviting atmosphere in the classroom" and that "the teachers are always accessible." Community service is encouraged, making Saint Anselm a good fit for students who want to "become a better person as a whole and create an intelligent and kind community of students." As one student notes: "Saint Anselm College prepared me for life, and a wonderful, happy, and successful one at that."

Life

Saint Anselm College "is a school with rigorous academics on the weekdays," notes a Communication major, "and tons of different things to be involved in on the weekends." Greek life is not "big on campus," and though there is drinking, some say it is "frowned upon." Students note that they like that "there aren't too many parties." On campus, students hang out and "watch movies," play "pool in their dorms," and attend "sports events." The Campus Activities Board "brings magicians, comedians, and musicians" to campus that students can "see for free." Students can also enjoy the "Abbey Players or various theater performances at the Dana Center," and "many students grab a bite to eat at the Coffee Shop" afterward. "There are plenty of options to keep busy!" says an International Relations major. Including community service work, which is a "big part of Saint Anselm's mission."

Student Body

Saint Anselm students describe their classmates as "smart," "kind," "hard-working" and "friendly." They can be "very preppy" and are "committed to the community and family." A typical student at Saint Anselm College is "very well rounded," communicates well, and "can multi-task." Most students engage in a variety of on-campus opportunities, and "have a lot of experience in their field of study," by engaging in "research studies, literature reviews, and advanced studying." They are inspired by "the generosity of the monks that serve the campus," and are community service oriented. "Never in my life can I recall seeing such a diverse community of people so well integrated and committed to its success as a whole," notes one student. "Students fit in by being Anselmian."

FINANCIAL AID: 603-641-7110 • E-MAIL: ADMISSION@ANSELM.EDU • WEBSITE: WWW.ANSELM.EDU

THE PRINCETON REVIEW SAYS

Admissions

Very important factors considered include: rigor of secondary school record, academic GPA. *Important factors considered include:* application essay, recommendation(s), extracurricular activities, character/personal qualities. *Other factors considered include:* class rank, standardized test scores, talent/ability, first generation, alumni/ae relation, geographical residence, racial/ethnic status, volunteer work, work experience. SAT or ACT required for some; SAT Subject Tests considered if submitted. ACT with Writing recommended. SAT with Essay component recommended. TOEFL required of all international applicants. High school diploma is required and GED is accepted. *Academic units required:* 4 English, 3 math, 3 science, 2 science labs, 2 foreign language, 2 social studies. *Academic units recommended:* 4 English, 4 math, 4 science, 2 science labs, 4 foreign language, 4 social studies.

Financial Aid

Students should submit: FAFSA, CSS/Financial Aid PROFILE, Noncustodial PROFILE. Regular filing deadline is 3/15. The Princeton Review suggests that all financial aid forms be submitted as soon as possible after October 1. *Need-based scholarships/grants offered:* Federal Pell, FSEOG, State scholarships/grants, Private scholarships, College/university scholarship or grant aid from institutional funds. *Loan aid offered:* Direct Subsidized Stafford Loans, Direct Unsubsidized Stafford Loans, Direct PLUS loans, Federal Perkins Loans. Applicants will be notified of awards on a rolling basis beginning 3/1. Federal Work-Study Program available. Institutional employment available.

The Inside Word

Saint Anselm College uses the Common Application and ACT and SAT scores (although test scores are optional for all academic majors except nursing), but places an added focus on personal character and community service extracurriculars in their admissions process. Applicants who feel their grades and test scores are not as high as they'd like should make sure to emphasize their out-of-class skills and experiences in their application. Note that nursing applicants must apply early action or early decision.

THE SCHOOL SAYS "..."

From the Admissions Office

"Saint Anselm is New England's only Benedictine College, a place where a 1,500 year tradition that values a love of learning and a balanced life is coupled with a very contemporary liberal arts education with strong professional preparation on a beautiful 400-acre campus. The college offers over eighty academic programs, but is particularly well-known for nursing, criminal justice, business, politics and psychology. Located in the first in the nation primary state, Saint Anselm is the home of the New Hampshire Institute of Politics which hosts national debates and provides countless opportunities for students of any major to engage with candidates, journalists, elected officials and scholars. A student who wants to meet the next President of the United States has a reasonably good chance of doing so here. Saint Anselm has been named a 'college with a conscience' by the Princeton Review, hailed by the Carnegie Foundation with Classification in both Curricular Engagement and Outreach and Partnerships, and has won federal grants to support its work in public advocacy and engagement with social problems. Faculty from many departments teach in the seminar-based program where students contemplate the fundamental question of what it means to be great. The college's Dana Center for the Humanities, used by both students and the public, hosts a broad and eclectic range of theater programming including contemporary dance and music. Saint Anselm's Alva De Mars Megan Chapel Art Center provides an extraordinary array of art exhibitions from classic to contemporary with recent acquisitions focused on the human form in art. Eighty-five percent of the college's students participates in athletics, intramurals and club sports. New academic majors have been added over the past two years."

SELECTIVITY

Admissions Rating	84
# of applicants	3,955
% of applicants accepted	73
% of acceptees attending	18
# offered a place on the wait list	472
% accepting a place on wait list	37
% admitted from wait list	16

FRESHMAN PROFILE

Range SAT Critical Reading	530–620
Range SAT Math	540–630
Range SAT Writing	530–640
Range ACT Composite	24–28
Minimum paper TOEFL	550
Minimum internet-based TOEFL	80
Average HS GPA	3.3
% graduated top 10% of class	31
% graduated top 25% of class	62
% graduated top 50% of class	89

DEADLINES

Early decision	
Deadline	12/1
Notification	1/1
Early action	
Deadline	11/15
Notification	1/15
Regular	
Deadline	2/1
Notification	3/15
Nonfall registration?	Yes

APPLICANTS ALSO LOOK AT AND OFTEN PREFER
Stonehill College; Providence College

AND SOMETIMES PREFER
University of Massachusetts Amherst

FINANCIAL FACTS

Financial Aid Rating	85
Annual tuition	$37,826
Room and board	$13,734
Required fees	$1,000
Books and supplies	$1,000
Average frosh need-based scholarship	$22,396
Average UG need-based scholarship	$21,681
% needy frosh rec. need-based scholarship or grant aid	99
% needy UG rec. need-based scholarship or grant aid	99
% needy frosh rec. non-need-based scholarship or grant aid	24
% needy UG rec. non-need-based scholarship or grant aid	19
% needy frosh rec. need-based self-help aid	81
% needy UG rec. need-based self-help aid	84
% frosh rec. any financial aid	98
% UG rec. any financial aid	98
% UG borrow to pay for school	83
Average cumulative indebtedness	$38,583
% frosh need fully met	30
% ugrads need fully met	28
Average % of frosh need met	81
Average % of ugrad need met	80

SAINT LOUIS UNIVERSITY

ONE NORTH GRAND BOULEVARD, SAINT LOUIS, MO 63103 • ADMISSIONS: 314-977-2500 • FAX: 314-977-7136

CAMPUS LIFE

Quality of Life Rating	73
Fire Safety Rating	91
Green Rating	82
Type of school	Private
Affiliation	Roman Catholic
Environment	Metropolis

STUDENTS

Total undergrad enrollment	8,248
% male/female	41/59
% from out of state	63
% frosh live on campus	92
% ugrads live on campus	51
# of fraternities (% ugrad men join)	8 (18)
# of sororities (% ugrad women join)	6 (27)
% African American	6
% Asian	9
% Caucasian	66
% Hispanic	6
% Native American	<1
% Pacific Islander	0
% Two or more races	4
% Race and/or ethnicity unknown	2
% international	6
# of countries represented	52

SURVEY SAYS...

Students involved in community service
Students are friendly
Lots of beer drinking
Very little drug use
Hard liquor is popular

ACADEMICS

Academic Rating	80
% students returning for sophomore year	90
% students graduating within 4 years	64
% students graduating within 6 years	74
Calendar	Semester
Student/faculty ratio	11:1
Profs interesting rating	70
Profs accessible rating	69

Most classes have 10–19 students.
Most lab/discussion sessions have
10–19 students.

MOST POPULAR MAJORS

Registered Nursing/Registered Nurse; Biology;
Business Administration and Management

STUDENTS SAY "..."

Academics

"The Jesuit tradition really resonates in everything that happens at SLU," a place where "service, social justice, and political awareness are stressed at every level of your education." This "medium-sized Jesuit school with solid academic programs and a campus that feels close-knit" is best known for its "great premedical programs," which include "a great direct-entry physical therapy program" and "a well-respected accelerated nursing program" as well as the school's premed tracks. Students also speak highly of SLU's offerings in business and pre-law, as well as its unique programs in aviation and "the one-of-a-kind nutrition program with a culinary emphasis." Students praise the way this curriculum "forces you to examine your worldview from the moment you step on campus and helps you discover what your beliefs really are." Academics, especially in the high-profile departments, can be rigorous. In this regard, SLU is "perfect for high achievers and scholars who strive for the best. The professors are nice and professional but are very stern about assignments being turned in on time." One student says, "When it comes to natural sciences, particularly chemistry, biology, etc., I think SLU can be very hard. I guess it works, though. A nursing degree or physical therapy degree from SLU is very highly respected in the health care profession."

Life

"SLU manages to provide everything your parents wish for your college experience and still everything you wouldn't want them to know about," undergrads here confide. Campus life includes "a lot of fun activities the student government puts on…such as outdoor movies, balls, and dances." "Dorm life is very strict and not much fun." The party scene "is decent," because "there are a lot of off-campus living opportunities that are close by and great places to live. The Lofts and Coronado are two great off-campus apartments that are extremely close by." College sports are in the mix. "With the new arena, basketball games are becoming the thing to do." Greek life "is great at SLU." The fraternities and sororities "provide many parties and events for the students and activities such as laser tag and barbecue" to help the students "become involved" and "get to know each other." Being in St. Louis means "great city life around, but most of it is for students that are twenty-one and above," and "off-campus eateries that are close by and range from Drunken Fish Sushi to Rally's Burgers." Students tell us "safety is a huge importance in SLU since we are so close to the city, [and fortunately] there is usually a DPS officer that is always close by to help students in need." "SLU's Jesuit influence encourages the student body to become active in the community. SLU's efforts to encourage community service give many students their first taste of the real world and better prepare them to venture out into it after graduation."

Student Body

SLU "has a pretty homogeneous student population of white, upper-middle-class students coming from a private high school (usually Jesuit, and single-sex) or from the suburbs of bigger Midwestern cities. The girls wear Uggs and North Face fleeces and dye their hair, while the boys live in their…American Eagle jeans." Many "have been in the Catholic school system their entire lives," although there are also "quite a few kids who went to public school." Students are generally committed to the concept of service, and they "put forth a lot of community service hours into the surrounding area, from Habitat for Humanity to the Big Brothers/Big Sisters programs. There are plenty of clubs students use to help raise money for their organizations."

FINANCIAL AID: 314-977-2350 • E-MAIL: ADMISSION@SLU.EDU • WEBSITE: WWW.SLU.EDU

THE PRINCETON REVIEW SAYS

Admissions

Very important factors considered include: academic GPA, standardized test scores, application essay. *Important factors considered include:* rigor of secondary school record, interview, extracurricular activities, talent/ability, character/personal qualities. *Other factors considered include:* recommendation(s), first generation, alumni/ae relation, volunteer work, work experience, level of applicant's interest. SAT or ACT required. ACT with or without writing accepted. SAT with or without Essay component accepted. TOEFL required of all international applicants. High school diploma is required and GED is accepted. *Academic units required:* 4 English, 4 math, 3 science, 3 foreign language, 3 social studies, 3 academic electives. *Academic units recommended:* 4 English, 4 math, 3 science, 3 foreign language, 3 social studies, 3 academic electives.

Financial Aid

Students should submit: FAFSA. Priority filing deadline is 3/1. The Princeton Review suggests that all financial aid forms be submitted as soon as possible after October 1. *Need-based scholarships/grants offered:* Federal Pell, FSEOG, State scholarships/grants, Private scholarships, College/university scholarship or grant aid from institutional funds, Federal Nursing Scholarships. *Loan aid offered:* Direct Subsidized Stafford Loans, Direct Unsubsidized Stafford Loans, Direct PLUS loans, Federal Perkins Loans, Federal Nursing Loans, State Loans, College/university loans from institutional funds. Applicants will be notified of awards on a rolling basis beginning 3/15. Federal Work-Study Program available. Institutional employment available.

The Inside Word

Saint Louis University's student body is primarily regional, but it continually expands its draw so that today nearly 61 percent of all undergrads arrive from out of state. This increase in geographic diversity has brought with it elevated admissions standards. The grades and test scores that got your older brother or sister in here may not be good enough for you (although family ties to the school are a plus). Admissions officers look for students who display a commitment to both scholarship and Jesuit principles. Applicants must demonstrate success in college preparatory classes and a desire to be active participants in the community.

THE SCHOOL SAYS "..."

From the Admissions Office

"A hot Midwestern university with a growing national and international reputation, Saint Louis University gives students the knowledge, skills, and values to build a successful career and make a difference in the lives of those around them. Students live and learn in a safe and attractive campus environment. The beautiful urban, residential campus offers loads of internship, outreach, and recreational opportunities. Ranked as one of the best educational values in the country, the university welcomes students from all fifty states and seventy-five foreign countries who pursue rigorous majors that invite individualization. Accessible faculty, study abroad opportunities, and many small, interactive classes make SLU a great place to learn.

"A leading Jesuit, Catholic university, SLU's goal is to graduate men and women of competence and conscience—individuals who are not only capable of making wise decisions but who also understand why they made them. Since 1818, Saint Louis University has been dedicated to academic excellence, service to others, and preparing students to be leaders in society. Saint Louis University truly is the place where knowledge touches lives.

"For admission, Saint Louis University will accept either the SAT or the ACT with or without the writing component."

SELECTIVITY

Admissions Rating	89
# of applicants	13,216
% of applicants accepted	63
% of acceptees attending	20
# offered a place on the wait list	164
% accepting a place on wait list	100
% admitted from wait list	65

FRESHMAN PROFILE

Range SAT Critical Reading	540–670
Range SAT Math	560–680
Range ACT Composite	25–31
Minimum paper TOEFL	550
Minimum internet-based TOEFL	80
Average HS GPA	3.9
% graduated top 10% of class	42
% graduated top 25% of class	70
% graduated top 50% of class	91

DEADLINES

Regular	
Priority	12/1
Deadline	8/20
Notification	8/20
Nonfall registration?	Yes

APPLICANTS ALSO LOOK AT AND OFTEN PREFER

Fordham University; Washington University in St. Louis

AND SOMETIMES PREFER

Loyola University of Chicago; Marquette University; Xavier University of Louisiana; University of Missouri; University of Illinois at Urbana-Champaign

AND RARELY PREFER

Creighton University; Truman State University; University of Dayton

FINANCIAL FACTS

Financial Aid Rating	81
Annual tuition	$38,700
Room and board	$10,640
Required fees	$526
Books and supplies	$1,200
Average frosh need-based scholarship	$23,362
Average UG need-based scholarship	$21,415
% needy frosh rec. need-based scholarship or grant aid	98
% needy UG rec. need-based scholarship or grant aid	95
% needy frosh rec. non-need-based scholarship or grant aid	14
% needy UG rec. non-need-based scholarship or grant aid	11
% needy frosh rec. need-based self-help aid	69
% needy UG rec. need-based self-help aid	73
% frosh rec. any financial aid	97
% UG rec. any financial aid	89
% UG borrow to pay for school	61
Average cumulative indebtedness	$33,487
% frosh need fully met	26
% ugrads need fully met	21
Average % of frosh need met	76
Average % of ugrad need met	71

SAINT MARY'S COLLEGE OF CALIFORNIA

PO Box 4800, Moraga, CA 94575-4800 • Admissions: 925-631-4224 • Fax: 925-376-7193

STUDENTS SAY ". . ."

Academics

Intimacy rules the day at Saint Mary's, a Catholic college where "small class sizes" and professors who you "get to know personally" are the rule rather than the exception. "They make time for me outside of class," one student boasts, "I even have some of their phone numbers." This intimacy offers "unlimited opportunities for students and very direct interaction with staff and faculty," and makes it feel as if "the professors are learning at the same time from the students." These teachers are "are very optimistic and love what they teach, so it's great to be taught by them because they're so passionate about their subject. It helps make learning about the subject fun and interesting." Indeed, as one student points out, "It's usually very difficult for a math or physics professor to inject their personality into their classes, but the faculty that Saint Mary's employs somehow manage to do it." Some do complain that "when they teach they go really fast and it makes it hard to keep up with them," but that may be a result of the attitude that "lectures are overrated." Instead, "professors help students learn by engaging one another in meaningful dialogue and debate." The idea is to help you to "learn how to talk more in public settings and [give] you life skills that you can rely on and use the rest of your life." The bottom line is, "Saint Mary's offers students an unparalleled education with small class sizes, seminars, high accessibility to professors, and a strong alumni and network association."

Life

Don't expect non-stop parties at Saint Mary's. This is a "distinguished, calm campus" with students focused on their studies. When it comes time to wind down, sports, clubs, and mellow socializing are far more prevalent than rowdy keggers. Saint Mary's "is what you make it, it takes time to adjust," but "there are vast opportunities provided by the school to get involved with others inside and outside of the community." There is "a grove that is a secluded area where everyone goes to just leave the urban world for a bit and just relax," while others "go on great hiking and outdoor adventure trips the rec sports provides the students with." The school is six miles off the freeway, so access to other communities isn't as easy as at other schools, but nearby Orinda has beautiful theaters and restaurants, and all that San Francisco has to offer is accessible to students willing to make the journey. The biggest draw is sports and athletic recreation. Students here are "very active. Everyone wears some sort of active clothes because everyone is basically a regularly active individual. Sports are a big focus at my school, whether it be intercollegiate or just for fun."

Student Body

The "smart, humble, dedicated, and compassionate" students of Saint Mary's make up a group with a "wide range of students from a large spectrum of life and socioeconomic status. Students mix easily and the college climate promotes equality and understanding." At this "very welcoming" school you'll find "few cliques among students," only "normal people who are looking to go on and succeed at life." The "hard-working" students of Saint Mary's have a reputation for being friendly. "You walk through the halls and say hi to almost everyone even if you have never seen them before." Indeed, "students always smile and say have a good day. Students fit in by taking the time to meet others. A simple smile can make a day for a lot of people." Typical students are "involved in sports or some type of club on campus. They are a big part of the community, and are avid NCAA college basketball fans." That, or they are engaged in their studies. Saint Mary's is filled with people serious about their educations—but not at the expense of social interaction. "Students can engage in complex discussion and easily switch to witty banter at any given moment."

SAINT MARY'S COLLEGE OF CALIFORNIA

FINANCIAL AID: 925-631-4522 • E-MAIL: SMCADMIT@STMARYS-CA.EDU • WEBSITE: WWW.STMARYS-CA.EDU

THE PRINCETON REVIEW SAYS

Admissions

Very important factors considered include: rigor of secondary school record, academic GPA. *Important factors considered include:* standardized test scores, application essay, recommendation(s), first generation, racial/ethnic status. *Other factors considered include:* interview, extracurricular activities, talent/ability, character/personal qualities, alumni/ae relation, geographical residence, religious affiliation/commitment, volunteer work, work experience, level of applicant's interest. SAT or ACT required. ACT with or without writing accepted. TOEFL required of all international applicants. High school diploma is required and GED is accepted. *Academic units required:* 4 English, 3 math, 2 science, 1 science lab, 2 foreign language, 1 social studies, 1 history, 2 academic electives. *Academic units recommended:* 4 English, 4 math, 3 science, 1 science lab, 3 foreign language, 1 social studies, 1 history, 2 academic electives.

Financial Aid

Students should submit: FAFSA. Priority filing deadline is 2/15. The Princeton Review suggests that all financial aid forms be submitted as soon as possible after October 1. *Need-based scholarships/grants offered:* Federal Pell, FSEOG, State scholarships/grants, Private scholarships, College/university scholarship or grant aid from institutional funds. *Loan aid offered:* Direct Subsidized Stafford Loans, Direct Unsubsidized Stafford Loans, Direct PLUS loans, Federal Perkins Loans. Applicants will be notified of awards on a rolling basis beginning 2/1. Federal Work-Study Program available. Institutional employment available.

The Inside Word

Saint Mary's has a deep commitment to serving underprivileged students and offering opportunities for low-income students with strong academic potential, which is why the school sets aside 25 percent of its undergraduate population for low economic status students. That core philosophy of the school won't be changing anytime soon, so students with economic difficulties should not hesitate to apply if their academics are strong.

THE SCHOOL SAYS "..."

From the Admissions Office

"Today, Saint Mary's College continues to offer a value-oriented education by providing a classical liberal arts background second to none. The emphasis is on teaching an individual how to think independently and responsibly, how to analyze information in all situations, and how to make choices based on logical thinking and rational examination. Such a program develops students' ability to ask the right questions and to formulate meaningful answers, not only within their professional careers but also for the rest of their lives. Saint Mary's College is committed to preparing young men and women for the challenge of an ever-changing world, while remaining faithful to an enduring academic and spiritual heritage. We believe the purpose of a college experience is to prepare men and women for an unlimited number of opportunities, and that this is best accomplished by educating the whole person, both intellectually and ethically. We strive to recruit, admit, enroll, and graduate students who are generous, faithfilled, and human, and we believe this is reaffirmed in our community of brothers, in our faculty, and in our personal concern for each student.

"For freshman applicants, we will accept the SAT, and the ACT is also accepted. The ACT writing assessment is optional. The highest critical reading and the highest math scores attained on the SAT will be used. SAT Subject Tests are not required."

SELECTIVITY

Admissions Rating	81
# of applicants	4,864
% of applicants accepted	69
% of acceptees attending	18
# offered a place on the wait list	680
% accepting a place on wait list	33
% admitted from wait list	19

FRESHMAN PROFILE

Range SAT Critical Reading	490–600
Range SAT Math	490–600
Range ACT Composite	22–27
Minimum paper TOEFL	550
Minimum internet-based TOEFL	79
Average HS GPA	3.6

DEADLINES

Early action	
Deadline	11/15
Notification	1/15
Regular	
Priority	11/15
Deadline	2/1
Notification	3/15
Nonfall registration?	Yes

APPLICANTS ALSO LOOK AT AND OFTEN PREFER

Santa Clara University; University of California–Davis; Gonzaga University; Loyola Marymount University

AND SOMETIMES PREFER

University of San Francisco

AND RARELY PREFER

Sonoma State University; University of the Pacific; University of California–Santa Cruz

FINANCIAL FACTS

Financial Aid Rating	72
Annual tuition	$42,780
Required fees	$150
Books and supplies	$1,107
Average frosh need-based scholarship	$27,125
Average UG need-based scholarship	$23,443
% needy frosh rec. need-based scholarship or grant aid	100
% needy UG rec. need-based scholarship or grant aid	96
% needy frosh rec. non-need-based scholarship or grant aid	59
% needy UG rec. non-need-based scholarship or grant aid	0
% needy frosh rec. need-based self-help aid	99
% needy UG rec. need-based self-help aid	97
% frosh rec. any financial aid	77
% UG rec. any financial aid	74
% frosh need fully met	8
% ugrads need fully met	8
Average % of frosh need met	85
Average % of ugrad need met	78

SAINT MICHAEL'S COLLEGE

ONE WINOOSKI PARK, BOX 7, COLCHESTER, VT 05439 • ADMISSIONS: 802-654-3000 • FAX: 802-654-2906

CAMPUS LIFE

Quality of Life Rating	94
Fire Safety Rating	85
Green Rating	89
Type of school	Private
Affiliation	Roman Catholic
Environment	City

STUDENTS

Total undergrad enrollment	1,997
% male/female	46/54
% from out of state	82
% frosh from public high school	69
% frosh live on campus	98
% ugrads live on campus	95
% African American	3
% Asian	2
% Caucasian	85
% Hispanic	4
% Native American	<1
% Pacific Islander	<1
% Two or more races	2
% Race and/or ethnicity unknown	1
% international	3
# of countries represented	36

SURVEY SAYS...

Students are happy
Career services are great
Internships are widely available
School is well run
Great financial aid
Students are friendly
Students get along with local community
Students environmentally aware
Students love Colchester, VT
Great off-campus food
Easy to get around campus
College radio is popular

ACADEMICS

Academic Rating	83
% students returning for sophomore year	87
% students graduating within 4 years	69
% students graduating within 6 years	76
Calendar	Semester
Student/faculty ratio	11:1
Profs interesting rating	89
Profs accessible rating	87

Most classes have 10–19 students.
Most lab/discussion sessions have 10–19 students.

MOST POPULAR MAJORS

Business/Commerce; Biology; Psychology

STUDENTS SAY "..."

Academics

"Small classes" help to ensure that "you are not just another number in a lecture hall." Indeed, the college "really wants to help its students realize their full potential." Many tout the "strong academics" and highlight the education, biology, and religion departments in particular. Classes are often "discussion-based" and "require a conscientious student who will actively participate in discussion." Moreover, undergrads here speak effusively about their professors. As one Biology major shares, "Regardless of which class you're in, you can tell that each professor's #1 priority is that the students succeed." A history major succinctly adds, "Whether you like it or not, your professor will know your name," while a Media Studies major notes that their "professors aren't just professors. They're lifelong teachers," with a Business Administration major stating, "I've had professors set up weekend study sessions before exams, bring in donuts for 8:00 A.M. classes, and invite students over for dinner or out for coffee. My professors have also really helped me in beginning my career—setting up research studies in my field of interest, writing incredible letters of recommendation for grad school, or networking to get me internships." It's been said that St. Mike's "could improve the Media Studies, Journalism, and Digital Arts Facility," and that "there are not enough seats in popular or required classes for the amount of students that need to take them."

Life

Burlington Vermont (less than ten minutes from campus minutes by bus) is "one of the greatest places to be in this part of the country. There is so much to do in such a small, convenient area." Of Burlington, students say that "Church Street is crowded with unique shops, fantastic restaurants, and interesting people." Many also love to take advantage of Vermont's outdoor recreational options and the school counts many avid skiers, snowboarders, and hikers among it ranks. In fact, "Saint Michael's provides amazing ski pass deals and transportation to amazing ski resorts in the area." St. Mike's campus is "tiny, but in the cold months of winter, five minute walks to class are a godsend." Life at St. Mike's is "pretty chill." "If a student is one that likes to party, they are able to find it on campus. If a person is more reserved, there are thousands of other things that that person can do." "Saint Mike's students have their heads on straight when it comes to making decisions." Students feel that the food "lacks flavor," although it should be noted that this is the way of most undergraduate dining experiences.

Student Body

In their own words: "the typical student is upper-middle class, environmentally and politically aware, and always says 'Hi,'" and who quickly dons "North Faces and UGGs during the cold Vermont winters," and, although St. Mike's is a Catholic school, students "are all different in regards to religions, races, sexual orientations and genders." The most frequent comment made by first-years "is that they were shocked when a student held the door open for them." Giving back to the community is a main theme in terms of the typical student here at St. Mike's, as exemplified by the statement that "nearly all students participate in at least on service project during their four years here. Most students are concerned about the environment and social justice." Students are "very relaxed for the most part" and enjoy "the outdoors that this great state provides for us." "If you're genuine and true to who you are you're bound to do well at Saint Mike's."

FINANCIAL AID: 802-654-3243 • E-MAIL: ADMISSION@SMCVT.EDU • WEBSITE: WWW.SMCVT.EDU

THE PRINCETON REVIEW SAYS

Admissions

Very important factors considered include: rigor of secondary school record, class rank, academic GPA. *Important factors considered include:* standardized test scores, application essay, recommendation(s), talent/ability, character/personal qualities. *Other factors considered include:* interview, extracurricular activities, first generation, alumni/ae relation, geographical residence, state residency, racial/ethnic status, volunteer work, work experience, level of applicant's interest. SAT or ACT considered if submitted. ACT with Writing recommended. SAT with Essay component recommended. TOEFL required of all international applicants. High school diploma is required and GED is accepted. *Academic units required:* 4 English, 4 math, 3 science, 2 science labs, 2 foreign language, 3 social studies, 3 history. *Academic units recommended:* 4 English, 4 math, 4 science, 3 science labs, 4 foreign language, 4 social studies, 4 history.

Financial Aid

Students should submit: FAFSA, State aid form. Regular filing deadline is 2/1. The Princeton Review suggests that all financial aid forms be submitted as soon as possible after October 1. *Need-based scholarships/grants offered:* Federal Pell, FSEOG, State scholarships/grants, Private scholarships, College/university scholarship or grant aid from institutional funds. *Loan aid offered:* Direct Subsidized Stafford Loans, Direct Unsubsidized Stafford Loans, Direct PLUS Loans. Applicants will be notified of awards on a rolling basis beginning 3/21. Federal Work-Study Program available. Institutional employment available.

Inside Word

Applicants to St. Mike's are more than just a number, and admissions officers do their utmost to consider candidates in their entirety. Officers consider everything from essays to extracurricular activities, though most weight is given to academic record. The college has recently made standardized tests optional, and applicants won't be penalized if they choose not to submit their scores.

THE SCHOOL SAYS "..."

From the Admissions Office

"A residential Catholic college, Saint Michael's is steeped in the social justice spirit of its founding priests, the Edmundites. Students are challenged to do their best, find their niche, take on opportunities to grow, and immerse themselves in academic pursuits. Intellectual rigor, compassion, teamwork, caring—these characterize a Saint Michael's experience. The Saint Michael's academic world is collaborative. Students join scholars on a learning continuum as interested rookies apprenticed to expert guides. Professors model engagement in the academic life, informed by the heart, as the path to make a difference in the world. Students are individually nurtured, and collectively applauded. Professors care. Students care about each other. The supportive ethos at Saint Michael's empowers success, and leads to leadership.

"Leadership opportunities abound, and underscore the transformation of Saint Michael's students. Academically, students are guided to engage in research projects, present results at conferences, study abroad, do service-learning activities. High-impact experiential practices are embedded throughout the Saint Michael's curriculum. Real-world experiences and deeper academic know-how are the result. Outside the classroom, Saint Michael's students grow into impressive leaders through their engagement with the challenging Wilderness Leadership Program, the skilled Fire & Rescue Squads, the intensity of MOVE service work, varsity and club athletics, a uniquely active student government, radio DJ gigs, editorial positions in student media, and numerous other opportunities.

"Located three minutes from Burlington, Vermont, Saint Michael's enjoys the energy and fun of that top-ten college town, as well as the best skiing in the East and the beauty of Lake Champlain."

SELECTIVITY
Admissions Rating	83
# of applicants	2,570
% of applicants accepted	79
% of acceptees attending	23
# offered a place on the wait list	243
% accepting a place on wait list	24
% admitted from wait list	12

FRESHMAN PROFILE
Range SAT Critical Reading	540–630
Range SAT Math	530–630
Range SAT Writing	530–630
Range ACT Composite	24–28
Minimum paper TOEFL	550
Average HS GPA	3.5
% graduated top 10% of class	26
% graduated top 25% of class	56
% graduated top 50% of class	82

DEADLINES
Regular	
Priority	11/1
Deadline	2/1
Notification	4/1
Nonfall registration?	Yes

APPLICANTS ALSO LOOK AT AND OFTEN PREFER
Boston College; College of the Holy Cross

AND SOMETIMES PREFER
Stonehill College; University of Vermont; Providence College; University of Massachusetts Amherst

AND RARELY PREFER
Saint Anselm College

FINANCIAL FACTS
Financial Aid Rating	86
Annual tuition	$40,425
Room and board	$10,975
Required fees	$325
Books and supplies	$1,280
Average frosh need-based scholarship	$22,338
Average UG need-based scholarship	$23,031
% needy frosh rec. need-based scholarship or grant aid	100
% needy UG rec. need-based scholarship or grant aid	100
% needy frosh rec. non-need-based scholarship or grant aid	31
% needy UG rec. non-need-based scholarship or grant aid	21
% needy frosh rec. need-based self-help aid	71
% needy UG rec. need-based self-help aid	78
% frosh rec. any financial aid	99
% UG rec. any financial aid	98
% UG borrow to pay for school	73
Average cumulative indebtedness	$36,625
% frosh need fully met	39
% ugrads need fully met	30
Average % of frosh need met	81
Average % of ugrad need met	79

SALISBURY UNIVERSITY

ADMISSIONS OFFICE, SALISBURY, MD 21801 • ADMISSIONS: 410-543-6161 • FAX: 410-546-6016

CAMPUS LIFE

Quality of Life Rating	88
Fire Safety Rating	96
Green Rating	88
Type of school	Public
Affiliation	No Affiliation
Environment	Town

STUDENTS

Total undergrad enrollment	7,849
% male/female	43/57
% from out of state	14
% frosh from public high school	80
% frosh live on campus	99
% ugrads live on campus	42
# of fraternities (% ugrad men join)	11 (10)
# of sororities (% ugrad women join)	6 (10)
% African American	13
% Asian	3
% Caucasian	70
% Hispanic	4
% Native American	1
% Pacific Islander	<1
% Two or more races	4
% Race and/or ethnicity unknown	3
% international	2
# of countries represented	61

SURVEY SAYS...

Students are happy
School is well run
Lots of beer drinking
Lab facilities are great
Great food on campus
Intramural sports are popular
Hard liquor is popular

ACADEMICS

Academic Rating	76
% students returning for sophomore year	82
% students graduating within 4 years	45
% students graduating within 6 years	67
Calendar	4/1/4
Student/faculty ratio	16:1
Profs interesting rating	78
Profs accessible rating	75
Most classes have 20–29 students.	
Most lab/discussion sessions have 20–29 students.	

MOST POPULAR MAJORS

Registered Nursing/Registered Nurse; Biology; Kinesiology and Exercise Science

STUDENTS SAY "..."

Academics

As part of Maryland's public university system, Salisbury University "provid[es] a diverse, inclusive, and successful learning environment." "A main priority of campus life is to give back to the community." A "Maryland university of national distinction," Salisbury is "a diverse and unique place to be where everyone around you is friendly and willing to help." Students appreciate the "small university feel with big university resources" and the "challenging but rewarding programs in all fields." For the most part, Salisbury professors "love what they do and prepare [students] for the world" and "are knowledgeable and use [hands-on] techniques to involve students in their learning." As one student raves, "going to class is a joy," and "I never go too long without doing something creative or [hands-on] in class." When it comes to the balance between academics and a social life, "it is as difficult and as fun as you make it" and "the academic experience can be a rich and as fulfilling as you make it." Salisbury professors are "generally helpful, knowledgeable, and interesting." As is the case with most universities when it comes to professors, "there [have] been a few bumps in the road, but the great teachers make up for it."

Life

Salisbury encourages "active participation in things that are bigger than yourself" and students praise a school that "is small enough to know a familiar face, but big enough to meet someone new!" The campus "is a beautiful place to sit, study or grab coffee and chat. There are a lot of restaurants within walking distance and there's often a movie playing somewhere on campus." With the "many student clubs and organizations to get involved in," it's easy to see why there's "always something going on on campus." Students rave about the school's proximity—"only 30 minutes"—to the beach at Ocean City, a popular destination in nice weather, and there's "lots to do outdoors." Besides cheering on the Salisbury Sea Gulls, "Fitness in general is very popular," with many students hitting the gym after or between classes. "The party scene has grown rapidly over the last few years," and "on the weekends most students go to parties or the bars at night." But parties don't overshadow academics, as one student stresses: "People usually fill their day with class and studying. The library is always very crowded." Greek life is popular with roughly 10 percent of the student body, though some gripe that fraternities and sororities are "constantly getting in trouble so they could use stricter rules."

Student Body

At Salisbury, "the student body is diverse and accepting" and "there are so many people with different interests that it is not hard to find a place where you fit in." Students says that despite "its location in a very conservative, rural, and secluded area of Maryland, Salisbury has a diverse student body made up of a variety of races, religions, orientations, and ethnicity, and this is reflected in the participation of students in on-campus groups." It's "an eclectic hodgepodge of athletes, art enthusiasts, [and] medical students," underscoring the notion that Salisbury is "about community, education, and stability." As one student puts it, "We've got your academics, but we also have your sporty jocks. We've got a bit of everything." Despite different backgrounds, "everyone is engaged and involved in the campus community" and there are "always on-campus events, activities, community outreach, and [the] smaller class sizes that all allow you to closely interact with the student body."

FINANCIAL AID: 410-543-6165 • E-MAIL: ADMISSIONS@SALISBURY.EDU • WEBSITE: WWW.SALISBURY.EDU

THE PRINCETON REVIEW SAYS

Admissions

Very important factors considered include: rigor of secondary school record, academic GPA. *Important factors considered include:* class rank, standardized test scores. *Other factors considered include:* application essay, recommendation(s), extracurricular activities, talent/ability, character/personal qualities, first generation, alumni/ae relation, geographical residence, state residency, racial/ethnic status, volunteer work, work experience, level of applicant's interest. SAT or ACT required for some. ACT with or without writing accepted. TOEFL or equivalent required of all international applicants. High school diploma is required and GED is accepted. *Academic units required:* 4 English, 4 math, 3 science, 2 science labs, 2 foreign language, 3 social studies. *Academic units recommended:* 4 English, 4 math, 4 science, 3 science labs, 3 foreign language, 3 social studies, 3 academic electives.

Financial Aid

Students should submit: FAFSA. Priority filing deadline is 3/1. The Princeton Review suggests that all financial aid forms be submitted as soon as possible after October 1. *Need-based scholarships/grants offered:* Federal Pell, FSEOG, State scholarships/grants, Private scholarships, College/university scholarship or grant aid from institutional funds. *Loan aid offered:* Direct Subsidized Stafford Loans, Direct Unsubsidized Stafford Loans, Direct PLUS loans, Federal Perkins Loans. Applicants will be notified of awards on a rolling basis beginning 3/15. Federal Work-Study Program available. Institutional employment available.

The Inside Word

As admission to this increasingly popular Maryland university becomes more competitive, prospective students must prove that they'll be able to thrive as a Sea Gull in and out of the classroom. Salisbury encourages a college preparatory curriculum in high school. Standardized test scores optional for applicants with a weighted high school GPA of 3.5 or higher. Applicants who opt not to send scores must submit other evidence of achievement in areas like leadership, creative endeavors, and community service. Test scores are required of all applicants for scholarship consideration.

THE SCHOOL SAYS "..."

From the Admissions Office

"Friendly, convenient, safe, and beautiful are just a few of the words used to describe the campus of Salisbury University. The campus is a compact, self-contained community that offers the full range of student services. New facilities, traditional-style architecture and landscaped grounds combine to create an atmosphere that inspires learning and fosters student pride. Located just thirty minutes from the beaches of Assateague and Ocean City, Maryland, SU students enjoy year-round recreational areas as well as an inside track on summer jobs. Situated some two hours from the urban excitement of Baltimore and Washington, D.C., greater Salisbury makes up for its small size by being strategically located. Within easy driving distance of a number of other major cities, including New York City, Philadelphia, and Norfolk, Salisbury is the hub of the Delmarva Peninsula, a mostly rural region flavored by the salty air of the Chesapeake Bay and Atlantic Ocean. Submission of SAT and/or ACT scores when applying are optional to freshman applicants who present a weighted high school grade point average (GPA) of 3.5 or higher on a 4.0 scale. Students whose applications may benefit from consideration under the test optional policy, or who apply test optional but whose scores may make them more competitive for admission and scholarship may be considered accordingly. For students submitting both ACT and SAT, SU will utilize the highest score from either test that will give the applicant the greatest opportunity for admission. An applicant may wish to submit a standardized test score subsequent to admission for full scholarship consideration as the majority of the university's scholarships include test scores as a requirement."

SELECTIVITY

Admissions Rating	86
# of applicants	8,360
% of applicants accepted	61
% of acceptees attending	23
# of early decision applicants	297
% accepted early decision	61

FRESHMAN PROFILE

Range SAT Critical Reading	540–620
Range SAT Math	540–620
Range SAT Writing	530–605
Range ACT Composite	21–26
Minimum paper TOEFL	79
Minimum internet-based TOEFL	550
Average HS GPA	3.7
% graduated top 10% of class	20
% graduated top 25% of class	54
% graduated top 50% of class	89

DEADLINES

Early decision	
Deadline	11/15
Notification	12/15
Early action	
Deadline	12/1
Notification	1/15
Regular	
Deadline	1/15
Notification	3/15
Nonfall registration?	Yes

FINANCIAL FACTS

Financial Aid Rating	78
Annual in-state tuition	$6,712
Annual out-of-state tuition	$15,058
Room and board	$11,010
Required fees	$2,374
Books and supplies	$1,300
Average frosh need-based scholarship	$6,323
Average UG need-based scholarship	$5,876
% needy frosh rec. need-based scholarship or grant aid	83
% needy UG rec. need-based scholarship or grant aid	78
% needy frosh rec. non-need-based scholarship or grant aid	0
% needy UG rec. non-need-based scholarship or grant aid	0
% needy frosh rec. need-based self-help aid	75
% needy UG rec. need-based self-help aid	81
% frosh rec. any financial aid	87
% UG rec. any financial aid	76
% UG borrow to pay for school	57
Average cumulative indebtedness	$25,376
% frosh need fully met	16
% ugrads need fully met	13
Average % of frosh need met	51
Average % of ugrad need met	50

SAN DIEGO STATE UNIVERSITY

5500 CAMPANILE DRIVE, SAN DIEGO, CA 92182-7455 • ADMISSIONS: 619-594-6336 •

CAMPUS LIFE

Quality of Life Rating	90
Fire Safety Rating	89
Green Rating	81
Type of school	Public
Affiliation	No Affiliation
Environment	City

STUDENTS

Total undergrad enrollment	29,234
% male/female	46/54
% from out of state	8
% frosh from public high school	92
% frosh live on campus	71
% ugrads live on campus	15
# of fraternities (% ugrad men join)	22 (8)
# of sororities (% ugrad women join)	22 (10)
% African American	4
% Asian	14
% Caucasian	34
% Hispanic	31
% Native American	<1
% Pacific Islander	<1
% Two or more races	6
% Race and/or ethnicity unknown	5
% international	6
# of countries represented	125

SURVEY SAYS...

Students are happy
Students love San Diego, CA
Recreation facilities are great
Everyone loves the Aztecs
Frats and sororities are popular

ACADEMICS

Academic Rating	74
% students returning for sophomore year	90
% students graduating within 4 years	30
% students graduating within 6 years	69
Calendar	Semester
Student/faculty ratio	28:1
Profs interesting rating	74
Profs accessible rating	70

Most classes have 20–29 students.
Most lab/discussion sessions have
20–29 students.

MOST POPULAR MAJORS

Psychology; Criminal Justice/Safety Studies;
Business Administration and Management

STUDENTS SAY "..."

Academics

Students lucky enough to attend San Diego State University receive a "quality, affordable education," all while they soak up that brilliant "San Diego sun!" And with a "wide array [of] majors and minors" along with a good deal of "flexibility in course choices," it's understandable why individuals are drawn to this institution. Speaking of majors (and minors), undergrads at SDSU rush to underscore a handful of really stellar academic departments. For starters, the "science programs have vigorous requirements that [truly] prepare you for grad school or medical school." Additionally, the "music program strives to create the best educators and performers." The nursing school is also "amazing" and really works to "accommodate…each individual." And the international business program is considered "one of the top…in the nation."

When it comes to professors, while there's the occasional bad or "boring" apple, the vast majority at SDSU are "dedicated and eager to teach." Moreover, they typically approach their time in the classroom with "enthusiasm" and manage to "bring life to every lecture." Indeed, they "make learning the material easy and fun." It's also quite apparent that they "care about their students" taking the time to "check in with them" and making themselves "accessible outside of the classroom." And, as a grateful religious studies major explains, they often "inspire [you] to become a more intellectual person and involved student."

Life

Simply put, life at San Diego State is "wonderful." And, no matter whether you opt to participate in "Greek life, a student organization or a sport, everyone [finds] something to do." Additionally, the SDSU's Associated Students is great about sponsoring a number of "fun" events such as "Distress Fest, Haunted Montezuma and the Polar Plunge." A thrilled speech pathology major rushes to brag, "Every Thursday, there is a farmer's market on campus where students can enjoy a wide array of international cuisines prepared by local restaurants. SDSU also has "amazing athletics" and undergrads love "attending football [games], basketball [games] and other sporting events." Of course, given that San Diego has "[beautiful] weather year round," you won't catch SDSU students…spend[ing] much time indoors." It's quite common to see students riding "bikes or skateboards across campus." And a business administration major pipes in, "The beach is a huge draw for people whether you like surfing, paddle boarding, or just swimming." Additionally, the "campus is located 10 minutes from Fashion Valley or Balboa Park and there are tons of good restaurants around. It is also very close to the Mexican border for easy day trips."

Student Body

San Diego State is comprised of a "diverse community of students who are as laid-back as they are hard-working." Indeed, the university does a great job of attracting undergrads "from all over the world and all walks of life." Students happily report that their peers are both "social" and "academically driven." As one mechanical engineering major explains, "They are people that know how to party Friday and Saturday but know to stay in when they need to write a paper." Even better, "they are supportive and seem to always be open to help others who are struggling." Undergrads also appreciate that there are "endless opportunities to meet new people because the campus is swarming with students." And, for the most part, San Diego undergrads are "very accepting of one another and open minded." Of course, all of this goodwill can partially be attributed to the lovely surroundings. As one business students sums up, "It's hard not to be happy when living in beautiful San Diego."

FINANCIAL AID: 619-594-6323 • E-MAIL: • WEBSITE: WWW.SDSU.EDU

THE PRINCETON REVIEW SAYS

Admissions

Very important factors considered include: rigor of secondary school record, academic GPA, standardized test scores. *Important factors considered include:* geographical residence, state residency. *Other factors considered include:* SAT or ACT required. ACT with or without writing accepted. SAT with or without Essay component accepted. TOEFL required of all international applicants. High school diploma is required and GED is accepted. *Academic units required:* 4 English, 3 math, 2 science, 2 science labs, 2 foreign language, 1 social studies, 1 history, 1 academic elective, 1 visual/performing arts. *Academic units recommended:* 4 math.

Financial Aid

Students should submit: FAFSA, State aid form. Regular filing deadline is 3/2. The Princeton Review suggests that all financial aid forms be submitted as soon as possible after October 1. *Need-based scholarships/grants offered:* Federal Pell, FSEOG, State scholarships/grants, Private scholarships, College/university scholarship or grant aid from institutional funds. *Loan aid offered:* Direct Subsidized Stafford Loans, Direct Unsubsidized Stafford Loans, Direct PLUS loans, College/university loans from institutional funds. Applicants will be notified of awards on a rolling basis beginning 3/15. Federal Work-Study Program available. Institutional employment available.

The Inside Word

The admissions process at San Diego State is very by the book. Similar to other universities within the California State system San Diego relies on the eligibility index as the crux of their decision making. Hence, your GPA and standardized test scores will be critical. Moreover, the application is major specific; candidates will be ranked against all other individuals applying to that particular major. You will not be able to change your major during this process (though, aside from nursing, you will once you arrive on campus). Finally, all music, dance, and/or theater candidates will have to audition as well.

THE SCHOOL SAYS "..."

From the Admissions Office

"San Diego State University is a major public research institution that provides transformative experiences, both inside and outside of the classroom. Students participate in research, international experiences, sustainability and entrepreneurship initiatives, and a broad range of student life and leadership opportunities. The university's rich campus life features opportunities for students to participate in, and engage with, the creative and performing arts, a Division I athletics program, entrepreneurship and the vibrant cultural life of the San Diego region.

"Innovation at SDSU is driven by researchers and students committed to solving real-world problems, globally and locally. SDSU's Areas of Excellence are high-impact research partnerships that bring the university's top minds to bear on globally important issues like climate change, water scarcity, state-of-the-art neuroscience and cutting-edge medical techniques and devices.

"SDSU is also home to a vibrant arts community that hosts nearly 350 events annually. With academic programs ranging from music and dance, film, musical theatre, visual arts, and music entrepreneurship, students at SDSU engage in transformational arts experiences as part of the arts-rich community on campus.

"SDSU is committed to ensuring that students from all backgrounds achieve excellence, graduate and go on to personal and professional success. One of the country's most diverse universities, SDSU has been recognized nationally for increasing graduation rates across all ethnic and racial groups. And high impact practices such as study abroad, undergraduate research, internships and mentoring, entrepreneurship, service learning and leadership training are priorities across the campus."

SELECTIVITY

Admissions Rating	90
# of applicants	58,970
% of applicants accepted	34
% of acceptees attending	26
# offered a place on the wait list	2,474
% accepting a place on wait list	42
% admitted from wait list	3

FRESHMAN PROFILE

Range SAT Critical Reading	500–600
Range SAT Math	510–630
Range SAT Writing	490–590
Range ACT Composite	22–28
Minimum paper TOEFL	550
Minimum internet-based TOEFL	80
Average HS GPA	3.7
% graduated top 10% of class	33
% graduated top 25% of class	73
% graduated top 50% of class	96

DEADLINES

Regular	
Deadline	11/30
Nonfall registration?	No

FINANCIAL FACTS

Financial Aid Rating	83
Annual in-state tuition	$5,472
Annual out-of-state tuition	$16,632
Room and board	$15,826
Required fees	$1,504
Books and supplies	$1,804
Average frosh need-based scholarship	$10,000
Average UG need-based scholarship	$9,900
% needy frosh rec. need-based scholarship or grant aid	62
% needy UG rec. need-based scholarship or grant aid	74
% needy frosh rec. non-need-based scholarship or grant aid	58
% needy UG rec. non-need-based scholarship or grant aid	40
% needy frosh rec. need-based self-help aid	96
% needy UG rec. need-based self-help aid	96
% frosh rec. any financial aid	61
% UG rec. any financial aid	66
% UG borrow to pay for school	48
Average cumulative indebtedness	$20,100
% frosh need fully met	10
% ugrads need fully met	28
Average % of frosh need met	66
Average % of ugrad need met	70

SANTA CLARA UNIVERSITY

500 EL CAMINO REAL, SANTA CLARA, CA 95053 • ADMISSIONS: 408-554-4700 • FAX: 408-554-5255

CAMPUS LIFE

Quality of Life Rating	92
Fire Safety Rating	91
Green Rating	99
Type of school	Private
Affiliation	Roman Catholic
Environment	City

STUDENTS

Total undergrad enrollment	5,385
% male/female	51/49
% from out of state	27
% frosh from public high school	46
% frosh live on campus	94
% ugrads live on campus	52
% African American	3
% Asian	16
% Caucasian	49
% Hispanic	17
% Native American	<1
% Pacific Islander	<1
% Two or more races	7
% Race and/or ethnicity unknown	4
% international	3
# of countries represented	44

SURVEY SAYS...

Students are happy
Classroom facilities are great
Great library
Career services are great
School is well run
Dorms are like palaces
Easy to get around campus
Lots of beer drinking
Intramural sports are popular
Active minority support groups

ACADEMICS

Academic Rating	86
% students returning for sophomore year	95
% students graduating within 4 years	77
% students graduating within 6 years	84
Calendar	Quarter
Student/faculty ratio	12:1
Profs interesting rating	84
Profs accessible rating	89

Most classes have 10–19 students.
Most lab/discussion sessions have
10–19 students.

MOST POPULAR MAJORS

Finance; Marketing/Marketing Management;
Psychology

STUDENTS SAY ". . ."

Academics

Eco-friendly Santa Clara University is definitely a "prestigious" liberal arts school on the rise. With a "great location in the Silicon Valley" and a "beautiful campus" to boot, it's understandable why undergrads here brag about their "all-around great college experience." A mid-sized Jesuit university, Santa Clara places an "emphasis on study abroad and holistic learning" and maintains "strong connections in technology" as well. Additionally, the university is "a leader in on-campus sustainability" and places high importance on social justice. Students here are also privy to an "exceptional alumni network and [numerous] career opportunities after graduation." Academically, "small class sizes" help ensure that "individual attention" is a given. And, importantly, undergrads are quick to heap praise on their "knowledgeable" professors. Students appreciate how hard most of their teachers work to make sure their classes are "engaging." As a contented English major shares, "Every single one of my professors has devoted time and energy into forming relationships and making sure that material is being presented in the best way possible." All in all, "professors are excited about their material, accessible, and willing to go out of their way to help you learn."

Life

There's plenty of fun to be had at Santa Clara University. Indeed, there "are many activities and events put up by [the] program board that are completely free" and that help you "to meet lots of new people." Moreover, the Santa Clara student body is comprised of "really fit" individuals so it's a given that "the gym and sports facilities are always a popular place to spend time." Many undergrads here also tend to "play a lot of sports [either] for fun or more seriously on a team." Additionally, "Greek life is pretty popular" as well. However, we're told that "it's not the end of the world" if you decide not to join. And, thankfully, "no one ever really has a hard time getting into parties [and] usually all are welcome." The area surrounding Santa Clara also invites plenty of exploration. After all, it's quite easy to "take day trips up to San Francisco or down to Santa Cruz." And more ambitious students even head up to Lake Tahoe. As one grateful accounting major sums up, "The weather is also beautiful year round so you'll rarely end up sitting in your room playing video games and doing nothing."

Student Body

When first interacting with Santa Clara undergrads it will likely appear as though "most students on campus are white and Catholic. Indeed, while they might "not [be] super religious . . . many come from private Catholic high schools." And a majority seem to hail from either "the Bay area or the Northwest." SCU undergrads are also quick to point out that their peers are "laid back and friendly." And these "chill" vibes tend to extend to clothing options as "both boys and girls are usually seen in Patagonia's, flip flops, and generally comfy clothes." Additionally, many students "are athletes and if not, they are still in shape." Of course, education is still a top priority for these "smart" undergrads and everyone seems to be "focused on their individual academics." As a marketing major explains, "Students like to go out and have a good time but will also be in the library the next morning." Typical students here "study throughout the week, help out with the community, participate in multiple environmental events, have multiple jobs or internships and have fun on the weekends." Though "the student body at large is not very diverse," we're assured that "there are niches for all kinds of [people at] Santa Clara."

FINANCIAL AID: 408-554-4505 • E-MAIL: ADMISSION@SCU.EDU • WEBSITE: WWW.SCU.EDU

THE PRINCETON REVIEW SAYS

Admissions

Very important factors considered include: rigor of secondary school record, academic GPA, application essay. *Important factors considered include:* class rank, standardized test scores, recommendation(s), extracurricular activities, talent/ability, character/personal qualities, alumni/ae relation, racial/ethnic status, volunteer work. *Other factors considered include:* first generation, geographical residence, state residency, religious affiliation/commitment, work experience, level of applicant's interest. SAT or ACT required. ACT with or without writing accepted. SAT with or without Essay component accepted. TOEFL required of all international applicants. High school diploma is required and GED is accepted. *Academic units required:* 4 English, 3 math, 2 science, 2 science labs, 2 foreign language, 3 social studies, 1 academic elective. *Academic units recommended:* 4 English, 4 math, 3 science labs, 3 social studies, 1 academic elective, 1 visual/performing arts.

Financial Aid

Students should submit: FAFSA, CSS/Financial Aid PROFILE. Priority filing deadline is 2/1. The Princeton Review suggests that all financial aid forms be submitted as soon as possible after October 1. *Need-based scholarships/grants offered:* Federal Pell, FSEOG, State scholarships/grants, Private scholarships, College/university scholarship or grant aid from institutional funds. *Loan aid offered:* Direct Subsidized Stafford Loans, Direct Unsubsidized Stafford Loans, Direct PLUS loans, Federal Perkins Loans. Applicants will be notified of awards on or about 4/1. Federal Work-Study Program available. Institutional employment available.

The Inside Word

Admissions officers at Santa Clara University are on the hunt for intellectually curious students who will forward the university's mission. To find those individuals, they take a well-rounded approach to the application process. Expect everything from the rigor of a high school transcript to leadership experience to be assessed. Applicants also must select a specific school to apply to like the School of Engineering or the College of Arts and Sciences. Selectivity does not vary much between schools but academic preparedness for specific programs will be considered. Finally, we should note that Santa Clara does not conduct admissions interviews.

THE SCHOOL SAYS ". . ."

From the Admissions Office

"Santa Clara University is a comprehensive Jesuit, Catholic university located forty miles south of San Francisco in Silicon Valley. SCU offers its undergraduates an opportunity to be educated within a challenging, dynamic, and caring community, with more than fifty majors, numerous interdisciplinary programs, and some 2,000 courses from which to choose. Undergraduates find many opportunities to conduct important research alongside professors in a way that is usually reserved for graduate students. Study abroad programs are offered in fifty-five countries. The University blends a sense of tradition and history—as the oldest college in California—with a vision that values innovation and a deep commitment to social justice. Santa Clara's faculty members are talented scholars who are demanding, supportive, and accessible. The students are serious about academics, are ethnically diverse, and enjoy a full range of social, community service, religious, and cultural activities—both on campus and through the many options presented by our northern California location. SCU competes in nineteen Division I athletic teams and offers several varsity, club, and intramural sports. Distinguished nationally by one of the highest graduation rates among all U.S. master's universities, SCU provides rigorous undergraduate curricula in the arts and sciences, business, and engineering."

SELECTIVITY

Admissions Rating	91
# of applicants	14,899
% of applicants accepted	49
% of acceptees attending	17
# offered a place on the wait list	2,203
% accepting a place on wait list	50
% admitted from wait list	25
# of early decision applicants	215
% accepted early decision	63

FRESHMAN PROFILE

Range SAT Critical Reading	590–690
Range SAT Math	620–710
Range ACT Composite	27–32
Minimum paper TOEFL	575
Minimum internet-based TOEFL	90
Average HS GPA	3.7
% graduated top 10% of class	50
% graduated top 25% of class	83
% graduated top 50% of class	98

DEADLINES

Early decision	
Deadline	11/1
Early action	
Deadline	11/1
Regular	
Deadline	1/7
Nonfall registration?	No

APPLICANTS ALSO LOOK AT AND OFTEN PREFER
Stanford University; University of Southern California

AND SOMETIMES PREFER
Loyola Marymount University; University of San Diego; University of California–Davis

AND RARELY PREFER
University of San Francisco; Gonzaga University; Saint Mary's College (CA)

FINANCIAL FACTS

Financial Aid Rating	82
Annual Tuition	$47,112
Room and board	$13,965
Average frosh need-based scholarship	$26,964
Average UG need-based scholarship	$24,937
% needy frosh rec. need-based scholarship or grant aid	80
% needy UG rec. need-based scholarship or grant aid	70
% needy frosh rec. non-need-based scholarship or grant aid	43
% needy UG rec. non-need-based scholarship or grant aid	32
% needy frosh rec. need-based self-help aid	47
% needy UG rec. need-based self-help aid	45
% frosh rec. any financial aid	70
% UG rec. any financial aid	77
% UG borrow to pay for school	47
Average cumulative indebtedness	$27,407
% frosh need fully met	42
% ugrads need fully met	32
Average % of frosh need met	81
Average % of ugrad need met	75

SARAH LAWRENCE COLLEGE

ONE MEAD WAY, BRONXVILLE, NY 10708-5999 • ADMISSIONS: 914-395-2510 • FAX: 914-395-2515

STUDENTS SAY "..."

Academics

Simply put, Sarah Lawrence College is "a school that gives you the tools to open the world." Though that may sound like a grand assertion, it can be attributed (at least partially) to the fact that Sarah Lawrence has few requirements. Therefore, a Sarah Lawrence education is "self directed," allowing a new generation of "independent" thinkers to flourish. Additionally, undergrads here truly love the "fact that most of the classes are discussion based rather than just lectures." Ultimately, this "provide[s] students with a deeper understanding and experience of the topics offered." The college places a significant "emphasis on study abroad" as well.

Across the board, Sarah Lawrence students affirm that the "professors are the best thing about this school." It certainly helps that "they are truly enthralled by what they are teaching." An international studies major colorfully explains, "It is like watching a little kid in a candy shop when you watch them talk about [their discipline]." More importantly, if "you show that you're interested and engaged, they will really help you out when you need it." One thrilled undergrad elaborates, "At Sarah Lawrence College, the professors became my mentors. They were there for me since the beginning of the first day of my freshman year. They help me to chart out my future while allowing me to explore the breadth and depth of my intellectual curiosity."

Life

Given that Sarah Lawrence seems to attract academically-minded students, it's none too surprising that most individuals here are "generally very happy and passionate about their classes." Hence, they spend "a lot of time...studying." Of course, even these intellectual undergrads need to kick back every now and again. Thankfully, the school sponsors a number of fun activities such as the "college basketball contest, health fair, winter carnival, writing workshop, and free lectures to name a few." Additionally, the "Activities Council hosts [numerous] movies, and [undergrads] are often hired to DJ at the Blue Room, the [hot] student [spot] for dance[s]." Further, while Sarah Lawrence does have a party scene, we've been told that it's quite "low key and chill." Parties generally comprise of "talking and drinking...no keggers or ragers" here. Finally, students often head into Bronxville "and have a coffee or just walk around on a nice day." Or they'll take advantage of Sarah Lawrence's close proximity to New York City, which is only a 30 minute train ride away. Who could resist?

Student Body

Sarah Lawrence students have "a reputation for being weird, arty types" and many here affirm that that is "to a certain extent true." More importantly, they also tend to be "really smart and genuinely interested in their studies." As one content English lit major explains, "This is the kind of school where you go to a party and end up having an interesting conversation about your conference work with someone you've never met." Most individuals at Sarah Lawrence "have a wide variety of interests" as well. One thrilled student explains, "My roommate studies physics and creative writing and I have other friends who have concentrated on similarly disparate subjects and found ways to weave the two together." Undergrads also describe their peers as being "very liberal," and that the campus community overall is "very friendly to LGBT students." Many also note that Sarah Lawrence has a "particularly large trans population" as well. Hence, it's none too surprising to hear that it's "a very socially conscious campus, and [students] pay a lot of attention to current issues." Another undergrad shares, "We feel very passionate about our world, and participate in a lot of events and rallies for social change." And an experimental psychology student humorously concludes, "We're the island of misfit toys, but we all somehow fit in with each other."

FINANCIAL AID: 914-395-2570 • E-MAIL: SLCADMIT@SLC.EDU • WEBSITE: WWW.SARAHLAWRENCE.EDU

THE PRINCETON REVIEW SAYS

Admissions

Very important factors considered include: rigor of secondary school record, application essay, recommendation(s). *Important factors considered include:* academic GPA, extracurricular activities, talent/ability, character/personal qualities. *Other factors considered include:* class rank, standardized test scores, interview, first generation, alumni relation, geographical residence, racial/ethnic status, volunteer work, work experience, level of applicant's interest. SAT or ACT considered if submitted. ACT with or without writing accepted. SAT with or without Essay component accepted. TOEFL required of all international applicants. High school diploma is required and GED is accepted. *Academic units required:* 4 English, 2 math, 2 science, 2 foreign language, 2 history. *Academic units recommended:* 4 math, 4 science, 4 foreign language, 4 social studies, 4 history.

Financial Aid

Students should submit: FAFSA, CSS/Financial Aid PROFILE, State aid form, Noncustodial PROFILE. Regular filing deadline is 2/1. The Princeton Review suggests that all financial aid forms be submitted as soon as possible after October 1. *Need-based scholarships/grants offered:* Federal Pell, FSEOG, State scholarships/grants, Private scholarships, College/university scholarship or grant aid from institutional funds. *Loan aid offered:* Direct Subsidized Stafford Loans, Direct Unsubsidized Stafford Loans, Direct PLUS loans, Federal Perkins Loans. Applicants will be notified of awards on or about 4/1. Federal Work-Study Program available. Institutional employment available.

The Inside Word

Gaining admission to Sarah Lawrence is certainly competitive. Thankfully, admissions officers take a well-rounded approach. Of course, a strong college prep curriculum and solid GPA are of utmost important, though submitting standardized test scores is optional. Candidates are encouraged to submit scores only if it will enhance their application. Additionally, interviews are optional, but may offer an opportunity to demonstrate what you can bring to this unique community.

THE SCHOOL SAYS "..."

From the Admissions Office

"Students who come to Sarah Lawrence are curious about the world, and they have an ardent desire to satisfy that curiosity. Sarah Lawrence offers such students two innovative academic structures: the seminar/conference system and the arts components. Courses in the humanities, social sciences, natural sciences, and mathematics are taught in the seminar/conference style. The seminars enroll an average of eleven students and consist of lecture, discussion, readings, and assigned papers. For each seminar, students also meet one-on-one in biweekly conferences, for which they conceive of individualized projects and shape them under the direction of professors. Arts components let students combine history and theory with practice. Painters, printmakers, photographers, sculptors, filmmakers, composers, musicians, choreographers, dancers, actors, and directors work in readily available studios, editing facilities, and darkrooms, guided by accomplished professionals. The suburban, wooded campus is thirty minutes from midtown Manhattan, and the diversity of people and ideas at Sarah Lawrence make it an extraordinary educational environment.

"Sarah Lawrence College is 'test optional,' accepting and reviewing standardized test scores if they are submitted; however, they are not required as part of the admission application."

SELECTIVITY

Admissions Rating	90
# of applicants	2,814
% of applicants accepted	53
% of acceptees attending	24
# offered a place on the wait list	1,025
% accepting a place on wait list	62
% admitted from wait list	16
# of early decision applicants	155
% accepted early decision	64

FRESHMAN PROFILE

Range SAT Critical Reading	620–710
Range SAT Math	550–680
Range SAT Writing	600–700
Range ACT Composite	27–31
Minimum paper TOEFL	600
Minimum internet-based TOEFL	100
Average HS GPA	3.6
% graduated top 10% of class	36
% graduated top 25% of class	71
% graduated top 50% of class	90

DEADLINES

Early decision	
Deadline	11/1
Notification	12/15
Regular	
Deadline	1/15
Nonfall registration?	No

FINANCIAL FACTS

Financial Aid Rating	88
Tuition	$51,196
Room and board	$14,440
Required fees	$1,345
Books and supplies	$600
Average frosh need-based scholarship	$37,713
Average UG need-based scholarship	$35,239
% needy frosh rec. need-based scholarship or grant aid	98
% needy UG rec. need-based scholarship or grant aid	97
% needy frosh rec. non-need-based scholarship or grant aid	16
% needy UG rec. non-need-based scholarship or grant aid	13
% needy frosh rec. need-based self-help aid	76
% needy UG rec. need-based self-help aid	75
% frosh rec. any financial aid	79
% UG rec. any financial aid	76
% UG borrow to pay for school	68
Average cumulative indebtedness	$22,334
% frosh need fully met	18
% ugrads need fully met	15
Average % of frosh need met	79
Average % of ugrad need met	76

SCRIPPS COLLEGE

1030 COLUMBIA AVENUE, CLAREMONT, CA 91711 • ADMISSIONS: 909-621-8149 • FAX: 909-607-7508

STUDENTS SAY "..."

Academics

One of the five members of the Claremont College consortium, Scripps College is a small, liberal arts school in California that develops women into critically thinking and socially conscious individuals set to improve their surroundings. With an enrollment of approximately 950 students, Scripps is able to provide many elements of a small school experience within the umbrella of the Consortium, which "allows for access to the resources of a much larger institution" and gives undergrads "space . . . to find their interest while also fostering an incredible sense of community." The benefits of the women's college experience are "undeniable," according to students: "To be surrounded by a group of strong educated women is a very empowering experience." Professors at Scripps are "accomplished in their fields, challenging, and interesting people," who are always willing to take time after class to speak to an individual student or to explain a certain point of a lecture. "I look forward to going to class every day; my professors motivate me to do my best," says a student. Aside from the required core class that all first-semester freshmen must take, almost every class has fewer than twenty students, and there is "lots of dialogue about interesting and important issues." "If you're not angry about the status quo, you're doing it wrong," says a student. There are a fair number of people who double major or minor in very unusual combinations, "which is unique to Scripps," due to the emphasis on interdisciplinary learning and the idea that "no academic field exists in a vacuum." "This is huge when you're trying to apply things to the real world or imagine where your career might take you," says a student.

Life

The social scene is not isolated to a single campus, which is what allows "such a diversity of types of personalities": "We often call the 5Cs, Camp Claremont." For fun, students "go to any of the events thrown by the 5C" (which are open to everyone), or "work out, go to the pool, have picnics outside, and venture into Los Angeles when they're not doing work." On sunny days, you can find the main quad filled with people studying and sunbathing. "Most of the nightlife that Scripps students are involved in takes place on other campuses" that are just a five-minute walk away, but social life at Scripps is balanced with "parties, carnivals, movie nights, trivia nights, off-campus events, and other forms of entertainment." The "quieter, and more feminist" campus is also "one of the most beautiful" many have seen, with "large open spaces that contain gardens and a variety of fruit trees for picking." With "endless orange trees and endless opportunities," some say "Scripps seems like a dream." The gym (known as the Field House) is "impeccable and was designed particularly for women." Going into other parts of Los Angeles is easy with a car, but most students choose to have fun in the village, which has "great restaurants and bars, a movie theater, and decent shopping."

Student Body

Students here are all "engaged, outgoing, and passionate about something." The campus "can be a little cliquey," but everyone maintains a high level of respect and appreciation for the interests of others, and "are really open to meeting new people both within and outside their grade level." A lot of students have on-campus jobs. Most are "politically aware" and "social activist(s)," "use 'they' pronouns" and pepper conversation with terminology "like 'heteropatriarchy' and 'neoliberalism.'" And of course, "every Scripps student is a feminist." For those who are hesitant about the single sex enrollment, never fear: "The cross-registration process, dining halls, and friendships mean there are plenty of males on campus."

FINANCIAL AID: 909-621-8275 • E-MAIL: ADMISSION@SCRIPPSCOLLEGE.EDU • WEBSITE: WWW.SCRIPPSCOLLEGE.EDU

THE PRINCETON REVIEW SAYS

Admissions

Very important factors considered include: rigor of secondary school record, class rank, academic GPA, standardized test scores, application essay, recommendation(s), extracurricular activities, talent/ability, character/personal qualities. *Other factors considered include:* interview, first generation, alumni/ae relation, geographical residence, racial/ethnic status, volunteer work, work experience. SAT or ACT required. ACT with or without writing accepted. SAT with or without Essay component accepted. TOEFL required of all international applicants. High school diploma is required and GED is accepted. *Academic units required:* 4 English, 3 math, 3 science, 3 foreign language, 3 social studies.

Financial Aid

Students should submit: FAFSA, CSS/Financial Aid PROFILE, State aid form, Noncustodial PROFILE, Business/Farm Supplement. Regular filing deadline is 2/1. The Princeton Review suggests that all financial aid forms be submitted as soon as possible after October 1. *Need-based scholarships/grants offered:* Federal Pell, FSEOG, State scholarships/grants, Private scholarships, College/university scholarship or grant aid from institutional funds. *Loan aid offered:* Direct Subsidized Stafford Loans, Direct Unsubsidized Stafford Loans, Direct PLUS loans, Federal Perkins Loans, College/university loans from institutional funds. Applicants will be notified of awards on or about 4/1. Federal Work-Study Program available. Institutional employment available.

The Inside Word

Strong academics are important, yes, but women hoping to be accepted to Scripps should be ready to showcase more than academic excellence. A strong and unique personal statement, powerful writing skills, and intellectual curiosity are all vital to being accepted here. Successful applicants will show the admissions committee how they envision themselves contributing to the Scripps community with a focus on what sets them apart from the average college student.

THE SCHOOL SAYS "..."

From the Admissions Office

"Scripps College, a top liberal arts college in the country, offers students a life-changing experience that combines demanding academic rigor with the powerful support of a collaborative women's college community. At Scripps, students thrive in an intellectually challenging yet supportive community where undergraduate research and critical-thinking skills are top priorities. Scripps' faculty are distinguished teachers and leaders who are experts in their field, and classes are purposefully small (an average of sixteen students or fewer) to promote discussion and debate. More than sixty-five majors are available to Scripps students, which include a number of joint and intercollegiate programs. The College's Core Curriculum in Interdisciplinary Studies is a three-semester interdisciplinary program that provides a common academic experience for all students. As they explore provocative and relevant topics, students gain a foundation for the critical thinking, writing, and dialogue that distinguish the Scripps curriculum and graduate with new perspectives on the most complex issues facing the world today. Sixty percent of students study abroad, more than 86 percent hold at least one internship, and students can participate in eleven NCAA Division III sports. Scripps is a member of The Claremont Colleges, a consortium of five prestigious undergraduate institutions all located within walking distance, and two distinguished graduate institutions. Scripps College meets 100 percent of demonstrated financial need for admitted students, and all first-year applicants to the College are automatically considered for merit-based scholarships."

SELECTIVITY

Admissions Rating	97
# of applicants	2,613
% of applicants accepted	28
% of acceptees attending	38
# offered a place on the wait list	641
% accepting a place on wait list	44
% admitted from wait list	0
# of early decision applicants	219
% accepted early decision	47

FRESHMAN PROFILE

Range SAT Critical Reading	650–730
Range SAT Math	630–718
Range SAT Writing	653–730
Range ACT Composite	29–32
Minimum paper TOEFL	600
Minimum internet-based TOEFL	100
Average HS GPA	4.1
% graduated top 10% of class	72
% graduated top 25% of class	95
% graduated top 50% of class	98

DEADLINES

Early decision	
Deadline	11/15
Regular	
Deadline	1/1
Notification	4/1
Nonfall registration?	Yes

FINANCIAL FACTS

Financial Aid Rating	94
Annual tuition	$48,938
Room and board	$15,108
Required fees	$214
Books and supplies	$800
Average frosh need-based scholarship	$37,042
Average UG need-based scholarship	$36,444
% needy frosh rec. need-based scholarship or grant aid	100
% needy UG rec. need-based scholarship or grant aid	98
% needy frosh rec. non-need-based scholarship or grant aid	3
% needy UG rec. non-need-based scholarship or grant aid	3
% needy frosh rec. need-based self-help aid	86
% needy UG rec. need-based self-help aid	91
% UG borrow to pay for school	44
Average cumulative indebtedness	$18,692
% frosh need fully met	100
% ugrads need fully met	91
Average % of frosh need met	100
Average % of ugrad need met	100

SEATTLE UNIVERSITY

ADMISSIONS OFFICE, SEATTLE, WA 98122-1090 • ADMISSIONS: 206-296-2000 • FAX: 206-296-5656

CAMPUS LIFE

Quality of Life Rating	90
Fire Safety Rating	97
Green Rating	88
Type of school	Private
Affiliation	Roman Catholic-Jesuit
Environment	Metropolis

STUDENTS

Total undergrad enrollment	4,711
% male/female	40/60
% from out of state	57
% frosh from public high school	64
% frosh live on campus	93
% ugrads live on campus	46
% African American	3
% Asian	16
% Caucasian	44
% Hispanic	9
% Native American	<1
% Pacific Islander	1
% Two or more races	7
% Race and/or ethnicity unknown	9
% international	11
# of countries represented	80

SURVEY SAYS...
Students are happy
Students love Seattle, WA
Great food on campus

ACADEMICS

Academic Rating	80
% students returning for sophomore year	85
% students graduating within 4 years	64
% students graduating within 6 years	79
Calendar	Semester
Student/faculty ratio	12:1
Profs interesting rating	80
Profs accessible rating	79

Most classes have 10–19 students.
Most lab/discussion sessions have 10–19 students.

MOST POPULAR MAJORS
Liberal Arts and Sciences; Registered Nursing/Registered Nurse; Business/Commerce

STUDENTS SAY "..."

Academics
Though Seattle University is renowned for its excellent academics, particularly its nursing program, it is its Jesuit philosophy of holistic education that is Seattle U's main claim to fame. The university requires its 4,500 undergraduates to take a collection of core classes that are more than "just a random collection of math, writing, and social science classes. There's a lot more philosophy, theology, psychology, ethics, and actual service-learning" involved, and students say that "often times the core classes that [they are] required to take ended up being the most memorable classes." The dynamic professors "ensure that the students have a chance not only to digest and memorize the information but also a chance to critically think about it and discuss different viewpoints." The university's commitment to social justice issues is "more than just rhetoric—there are classes structured around specific kinds of service learning." There is a growing sentiment "that SU is increasingly being known for the Albers School of Business." Overall, students feel that Seattle U "is about finding community in a large city, and being able to discuss and have deep meaningful conversations about the issues we encounter in our everyday lives."

Life
It's "very much a city lifestyle" at Seattle U; "however, the mountains are not too far away." Here "you have the best of both worlds you can go to happy hours, brunch, clubs, bars and restaurants, hiking, skiing, canoeing, and swimming in the summer. There is a lot to do in the area." In fact, "as soon as you step off campus, you are in the hustle and bustle of Capitol Hill, a booming, youthful neighborhood that is LGBT friendly. There are coffee shops . . . concert venues, and parks within a two-block radius." It's "a quick bus ride to downtown and Pike Place Market or a nice half-hour walk. Chinatown is nearby, too." And it's fine if you don't feel like walking because "the university loans out bus passes free of charge." Living in the heart of Seattle means that you can never run out of fun things to do on weekends. You could "see plays, go to the Seattle Art Museum, eat all sorts of different types of food, hang out in the international district, [or] attend film festivals. You name it, Seattle has it!" The campus is "super green," providing students with "composting and recycling options in every location possible." The food is not only "delicious," but is also "locally grown, organic, and well-prepared."

Student Body
As "one of the most liberal Catholic schools," Seattle University is a place where "all faiths are not only accepted, but they are welcomed and encouraged." The "majority of students are liberal," and "everyone is aware of social issues." There is a "very large LGBTQ community" on campus, as well as "lots of international students." At Seattle U, students "frequently discuss gender norms, privilege, and how race influences identity. Identity is a popular topic of discussion—how we all use who we are to impact how we interact in the world." Here, "students are creative, insightful, and dedicated to making their educational experience unique and personal. Community is strongly felt amongst students and staff."

FINANCIAL AID: 206-220-8020 • E-MAIL: ADMISSIONS@SEATTLEU.EDU • WEBSITE: WWW.SEATTLEU.EDU

THE PRINCETON REVIEW SAYS

Admissions

Very important factors considered include: rigor of secondary school record, academic GPA, standardized test scores, character/personal qualities. *Important factors considered include:* application essay, recommendation(s), extracurricular activities, level of applicant's interest. *Other factors considered include:* class rank, interview, talent/ability, first generation, alumni/ae relation, geographical residence, state residency, religious affiliation/commitment, racial/ethnic status, volunteer work, work experience. SAT or ACT required. ACT with or without writing accepted. TOEFL required of all international applicants. High school diploma is required and GED is accepted. *Academic units required:* 4 English, 3 math, 2 science, 2 science labs, 2 foreign language, 3 social studies, 1 history, 2 academic electives. *Academic units recommended:* 4 English, 3 math, 2 science, 2 science labs, 2 foreign language, 3 social studies, 1 history, 2 academic electives.

Financial Aid

Students should submit: FAFSA. Priority filing deadline is 2/1. The Princeton Review suggests that all financial aid forms be submitted as soon as possible after October 1. *Need-based scholarships/grants offered:* Federal Pell, FSEOG, State scholarships/grants, Private scholarships, College/university scholarship or grant aid from institutional funds, Federal Nursing Scholarships. *Loan aid offered:* Direct Subsidized Stafford Loans, Direct Unsubsidized Stafford Loans, Direct PLUS loans, Federal Perkins Loans, Federal Nursing Loans. Applicants will be notified of awards on a rolling basis beginning 3/1. Federal Work-Study Program available. Institutional employment available.

The Inside Word

At this Jesuit school, admissions officers tend to value community service as well as overall "life experience." Those who demonstrate a significant commitment to volunteering will find themselves at an advantage, as will those who convey a clear sense of their academic and career goals. Applicants should keep in mind that Seattle University has more stringent test score and course work requirements for certain majors.

THE SCHOOL SAYS "..."

From the Admissions Office

"Students who are adventurous, forward-thinking, creative and have an interest in social justice are drawn to Seattle University, located in the heart of a city with unparalleled access to innovation and culture. Personalized learning provides opportunities for research alongside accomplished faculty. Internships and community involvement give students relevant experience for their resumes and the chance to be noticed by some of the world's most influential nonprofits and companies that call the Seattle area home, such as Microsoft, the Gates Foundation, Starbucks, Amazon and Costco. Seattle U is a school of action with an ever-growing impact on the city, the region and throughout the world. In Washington state, where dozens of different languages are spoken and every race, religion and perspective is represented, Seattle U's 4,700 undergraduate students from fifty-three states and territories and eighty-nine nations fit right in. Service is a cornerstone of the Seattle U experience. That spirit is especially visible in the Seattle University Youth Initiative—recognized by the White House in 2012 with its highest recognition for community service. As the university's largest-ever community engagement project, the Youth Initiative is transforming lives of Seattle's underserved children while becoming a model of service. An increasing number of new students say the Youth Initiative is a key reason they selected SU.

"Discover Seattle University's sustainable campus, which is pesticide-free and wins top awards for its environmental leadership and energy conservation. The urban campus is woven into Seattle's thriving Capitol Hill neighborhood, which pulsates with culture and entertainment options."

SELECTIVITY

Admissions Rating	82
# of applicants	7,806
% of applicants accepted	73
% of acceptees attending	18
# offered a place on the wait list	691
% accepting a place on wait list	42
% admitted from wait list	21

FRESHMAN PROFILE

Range SAT Critical Reading	530–650
Range SAT Math	530–630
Range SAT Writing	530–630
Range ACT Composite	24–27
Minimum paper TOEFL	520
Minimum internet-based TOEFL	68
Average HS GPA	3.6

DEADLINES

Early action	
Deadline	11/15
Notification	12/23
Regular	
Priority	1/15
Nonfall registration?	Yes

APPLICANTS ALSO LOOK AT AND OFTEN PREFER

University of Washington; Gonzaga University

AND SOMETIMES PREFER

Santa Clara University; Washington State University

FINANCIAL FACTS

Financial Aid Rating	81
Annual tuition	$38,970
Room and board	$11,121
Required fees	$720
Books and supplies	$1,500
Average frosh need-based scholarship	$22,736
Average UG need-based scholarship	$21,855
% needy frosh rec. need-based scholarship or grant aid	84
% needy UG rec. need-based scholarship or grant aid	90
% needy frosh rec. non-need-based scholarship or grant aid	59
% needy UG rec. non-need-based scholarship or grant aid	45
% needy frosh rec. need-based self-help aid	70
% needy UG rec. need-based self-help aid	76
% frosh rec. any financial aid	95
% UG rec. any financial aid	83
% UG borrow to pay for school	68
Average cumulative indebtedness	$28,284
% frosh need fully met	12
% ugrads need fully met	12
Average % of frosh need met	69
Average % of ugrad need met	68

SETON HALL UNIVERSITY

ENROLLMENT SERVICES, SOUTH ORANGE, NJ 07079 • ADMISSIONS: 973-761-9332 • FAX: 973-275-2040

CAMPUS LIFE

Quality of Life Rating	74
Fire Safety Rating	92
Green Rating	60*
Type of school	Private
Affiliation	Roman Catholic
Environment	Village

STUDENTS

Total undergrad enrollment	5,497
% male/female	41/59
% from out of state	22
% frosh from public high school	70
% frosh live on campus	74
% ugrads live on campus	41
# of fraternities (% ugrad men join)	11 (0)
# of sororities (% ugrad women join)	11 (0)
% African American	13
% Asian	8
% Caucasian	51
% Hispanic	16
% Native American	<1
% Pacific Islander	<1
% Two or more races	2
% Race and/or ethnicity unknown	7
% international	2
# of countries represented	71

SURVEY SAYS...

College radio is popular
Students politically aware
Campus newspaper is popular

ACADEMICS

Academic Rating	71
% students returning for sophomore year	85
% students graduating within 4 years	0
Calendar	Semester
Profs interesting rating	73
Profs accessible rating	76

MOST POPULAR MAJORS

Speech Communication and Rhetoric;
Criminal Justice/Safety Studies;
Communication

STUDENTS SAY "..."

Academics

With its South Orange, New Jersey location "fourteen miles from New York City," students at Seton Hall, many of whom are Jersey natives, enjoy prime bridge-and-tunnel access to the world's capital. The university's academic programs are "renowned in many subjects," but the Whitehead School of Diplomacy and International relations is "practically unparalleled," affording students direct "connections to the U.N." Seton Hall's Stillman School of Business, offering concentrations in finance, accounting, sport management, and marketing, among others, also attracts a number of students, who find numerous "internship opportunities" and "connections" in New York and New Jersey. While "professors are for the most part very engaging and work hard to encourage students to learn," students find mixed results when it comes to personal attention, concurring that "the level of involvement really depends on the professor." The "technologically connected" campus "completely dedicates itself to its undergrads," who appreciate the administrative "connectivity of students to staff" and find that Seton Hall achieves "cohesiveness as one unit to give us the best possible education." Financially, even though many students choose Seton Hall because "it's affordable" or because "I got a fantastic scholarship," once they get to campus they're pleased to discover that "the school offers all the great things that come with a private education." Whether students know what they want to study upon their entrance or not, Seton Hall's academic experience offers plenty of choices to "fuel my own desire to educate myself in fields that both pertain and have little to do with my major."

Life

On one hand, because "a lot of students are from the NY or NJ area," it's perceptible that "life at Seton Hall revolves around the hours 9:00 A.M.–5:00 P.M.," and "campus is a ghost town on weekends." On the other hand, "New York City is only twenty minutes away and is frequented by many students during the weekends." Residents who do stick around "develop close bonds, heading to the nearby city or taking a day trip to one of the small towns near by." Students enjoy Hoboken's close proximity, and around campus in South Orange there are "plenty of parties to attend but none of them last very long. South Orange PD is always out to shut them down." South Orange is "not very safe but we are well informed to stay safe." In terms of housing, "quality of facilities" doesn't rank highly on things to love about Seton Hall, and upperclassmen confide that "student life improves dramatically as you move through the years, and you move off campus." However, others say that the school does succeed in "creating a sense of community," that there "are a plethora of clubs and organizations that students can get involved in and those groups are always hosting events," and that spending "free time doing activities with clubs or with friends" is common.

Student Body

According to Seton Hall's undergrads, the "typical student is from New Jersey, goes home on the weekends, and out to off campus parties on Thursday and Friday nights," but "there is still a considerable amount of students who attend SHU from all over the country." As at many schools, "there are certain patterns within students in certain majors." Students in business and diplomacy are known as the most studious: "Diplomacy students focus on academics and are often very intelligent. Business students give 100 percent to their programs." "Students fit in very easily" at the university "by being themselves and getting involved." Seton Hall is a Catholic university with enduring values of "servant leadership," but "diversity is at the heart of the university": "The Seton Hall community consists of good-hearted, friendly people." Overall, students reflect that the university surrounds them with a "strong and loving community that fosters emotional, educational, and social growth."

FINANCIAL AID: 973-761-9332 • E-MAIL: THEHALL@SHU.EDU • WEBSITE: WWW.SHU.EDU

THE PRINCETON REVIEW SAYS

Admissions

Other factors considered include: SAT or ACT required. ACT with or without writing accepted. TOEFL required of all international applicants. *Academic units required:* 4 English, 3 math, 1 science, 1 science lab, 2 foreign language, 2 social studies, 4 academic electives.

Financial Aid

Students should submit: FAFSA. The Princeton Review suggests that all financial aid forms be submitted as soon as possible after October 1. *Loan aid offered:* Federal Work-Study Program available. Institutional employment available.

The Inside Word

Seton Hall accepts both its online application and the Common Application. The university publicizes that its students' median test scores are 1070 for the SAT and 24 for the ACT, and it is generally acknowledged that students with reasonably solid high school transcripts, strong recommendations, and test scores within the median range won't have trouble getting in, and Seton Hall makes an effort to sweeten the deal financially for standout students.

THE SCHOOL SAYS "..."

From the Admissions Office

"For more than 150 years, Seton Hall University has been a catalyst for leadership, developing the whole student—mind, heart and spirit. As a Catholic university that embraces students of all races and religions, Seton Hall combines the resources of a large university with the personal attention of a small liberal arts college. The university's attractive suburban campus is only fourteen miles by train, bus or car to New York City, with the wealth of employment, internship, cultural, and entertainment opportunities the city offers. Outstanding faculty, a technologically advanced campus, and a values-centered curriculum challenge Seton Hall students. Students are exposed to a world of ideas from great scholars, opening their minds to the perspectives, history and achievements of many cultures. Our new core curriculum focuses on the need for our students to have common experiences and encourages them to become thinking, caring, communicative and ethically responsible leaders while emphasizing practical proficiencies and intellectual development. Our commitment to our students goes beyond textbooks and homework assignments, though. At Seton Hall, developing servant leaders who will make a difference in the world is a priority. That's why all students take classes in ethics and learn in a community informed by Catholic ideals and universal values. While Seton Hall certainly enjoys a big reputation, our campus community is close-knit and inclusive. Students, faculty and staff come from around the world, bringing with them a kaleidoscope of experiences and perspectives to create a diverse yet unified campus environment."

SELECTIVITY

Admissions Rating	79
# of applicants	10,180
% of applicants accepted	84
% of acceptees attending	17
# offered a place on the wait list	0

FRESHMAN PROFILE

Range SAT Critical Reading	490–590
Range SAT Math	510–610
Range SAT Writing	490–600
Range ACT Composite	22–27
Minimum paper TOEFL	550
Average HS GPA	3.5
% graduated top 10% of class	37
% graduated top 25% of class	61
% graduated top 50% of class	86

DEADLINES

Early action	
Deadline	12/15
Notification	1/1
Regular	
Priority	3/1
Nonfall registration?	Yes

APPLICANTS ALSO LOOK AT AND OFTEN PREFER

Penn State—University Park; New York University

AND SOMETIMES PREFER

Fordham University; Rider University; University of Connecticut

AND RARELY PREFER

St. Bonaventure University; Monmouth University (NJ); Hofstra University

FINANCIAL FACTS

Financial Aid Rating	62
Annual tuition	$35,940
Room and board	$11,522
Required fees	$1,782
% needy frosh rec. need-based scholarship or grant aid	0
% needy UG rec. need-based scholarship or grant aid	0
% needy frosh rec. non-need-based scholarship or grant aid	0
% needy UG rec. non-need-based scholarship or grant aid	0
% needy frosh rec. need-based self-help aid	0
% needy UG rec. need-based self-help aid	0
% frosh rec. any financial aid	97
% UG rec. any financial aid	97

SEWANEE—THE UNIVERSITY OF THE SOUTH

735 UNIVERSITY AVENUE, SEWANEE, TN 37383-1000 • ADMISSIONS: 931-598-1238 • FAX: 931-538-3248

STUDENTS SAY "..."

Academics

The University of the South is a small, "very demanding" school "in the middle of rural Tennessee." Students describe it as "an oasis of perfection" "dripping with both Southern and academic tradition." "Sewanee embodies what a liberal arts education should," beams a history major. Classes are "small" and there's a "well-rounded curriculum." "The volume of work can make you want to pull your hair out," warns an economics major. "Sewanee does not inflate grades," either. "You must work hard to earn an A." "Occasionally a professor or two takes the absent-minded professor stereotype to a ridiculous level," but "it is hard to find a truly bad teacher among the whole lot." Professors here "care about their students." "Their passion for their fields and students is unparalleled." Profs are also very approachable. "We have incredible access to the faculty," gushes a religion major. "Many professors invite students to their homes for social and educational activities somewhat regularly," adds a music major. Students also love the "extremely reachable" administration. The only complaint we hear about academic life concerns the lack of course availability.

Life

A few dorms at Sewanee "really need some work." "Give me air conditioning," demands a sweaty sophomore. The "secluded" town that surrounds the school is "void of any good restaurants, bars, and general distractions a city provides." The campus is "absolutely gorgeous," though. It's a "serene haven" in "an idyllic setting" atop a mountain. Also, the school owns an "incredible amount of land." "Hiking the beautiful perimeter trail" is a favorite pastime, and students can bike, kayak, and "play in the woods" to their hearts' content. Socially, "Sewanee is unique in its quirks." There's a revered honor code. Faculty members wear academic gowns when they teach, and "most Sewanee students follow the tradition of dressing up for class." You'll see men in bow ties and seersucker suits and women in "pointy heels and pearls." There's also an "ever-present" sense of community. "You can't compartmentalize your life here," and for good or ill, "everyone knows what everyone else did last night." During the week, studying is paramount. "We spend a lot of time in the library," notes a sophomore. However, alcohol policies here are "lenient" and "Sewanee is a pretty big party school." Booze is "by no means forced upon you," but "students here drink often and heavily." The frat scene is absolutely massive. "Almost everyone becomes involved in a fraternity or a sorority." "The administration requires all Greek events to be open to the entire campus," but "there is no other social network except the Greek organizations."

Student Body

Even though the administration here is "pushing the diversity card to the nth degree," Sewanee is "strikingly homogenous." "A lot more students here are liberal than you would guess," and Yankees are "not viewed as aliens," but "Sewanee is a Southern and conservative school in every sense of the word." Students are typically "laid-back," "rich, conservative, and fun" "children of the Southern aristocracy" who like to "get drunk on the weekends." Some are "heavily spoiled and coddled." "We have lots of cookie-cutter, preppy, extreme social drinkers, but then again you can also find people who wear only organic hemp, sleep outside, and have dreadlocks," explains a junior. "There are a lot of outdoorsy styles mixed in as well." While "social arrangements are very cliquish," students tell us they are "relatively peacefully coexisting." "It really is one of the friendliest communities that I have ever seen," declares a sophomore.

FINANCIAL AID: 800-522-2234 • E-MAIL: ADMISS@SEWANEE.EDU • WEBSITE: WWW.SEWANEE.EDU

THE PRINCETON REVIEW SAYS

Admissions

Very important factors considered include: rigor of secondary school record, academic GPA, recommendation(s). *Important factors considered include:* application essay, extracurricular activities, character/personal qualities, volunteer work, work experience. *Other factors considered include:* class rank, standardized test scores, interview, talent/ability, first generation, alumni/ae relation, geographical residence, level of applicant's interest. SAT or ACT required for some; SAT Subject Tests considered if submitted. ACT with or without writing accepted. SAT with or without Essay component accepted. TOEFL required of all international applicants. High school diploma is required and GED is not accepted. *Academic units required:* 4 English, 3 math, 2 science, 2 science labs, 2 foreign language, 1 social studies, 1 history. *Academic units recommended:* 4 English, 4 math, 4 science, 3 science labs, 4 foreign language, 2 social studies, 2 history.

Financial Aid

Students should submit: FAFSA, CSS/Financial Aid PROFILE. Regular filing deadline is 2/1. The Princeton Review suggests that all financial aid forms be submitted as soon as possible after October 1. *Need-based scholarships/grants offered:* Federal Pell, FSEOG, State scholarships/grants, Private scholarships, College/university scholarship or grant aid from institutional funds. *Loan aid offered:* Direct Subsidized Stafford Loans, Direct Unsubsidized Stafford Loans, Direct PLUS loans, Federal Perkins Loans. Applicants will be notified of awards on a rolling basis beginning 3/1. Federal Work-Study Program available. Institutional employment available.

The Inside Word

The admissions office at Sewanee is very personable and accessible to students. Its staff includes some of the most well-respected admissions professionals in the South, and it shows in the way they work with students. Despite a fairly high acceptance rate, candidates who take the admissions process here lightly may find themselves disappointed. Applicant evaluation is too personal for a lackadaisical approach to succeed.

THE SCHOOL SAYS " . . ."

From the Admissions Office

"Sewanee is consistently ranked among the top tier of national liberal arts universities. Sewanee is committed to a rigorous academic curriculum that focuses on the liberal arts as the most enlightening and valuable form of undergraduate education. It offers thirty-six majors, thirty-two minors, and pre-professional programs including business, medicine, and education. Founded by leaders of the Episcopal Church in 1857, Sewanee continues to be owned by twenty-eight Episcopal dioceses in twelve states. The university is located on a 13,000-acre campus atop Tennessee's Cumberland Plateau between Chattanooga and Nashville. Largely forested, rich in biodiversity, this land is a distinctive asset offering an unparalleled outdoor laboratory and boundless recreational opportunities.

"The university has an impressive record of academic achievement—twenty-six Rhodes Scholars and thirty NCAA postgraduate scholarship recipients have graduated from Sewanee. Four of the last ten Tennessee Professors of the Year have been members of Sewanee's faculty. Professors are leading scholars and researchers with a commitment to teaching, and in Sewanee's close community they develop rich and enduring relationships with their students.

"Beginning in 2009, prospective students may choose not to submit standardized test scores. Other critical factors long considered in the Sewanee admission process remain, including strength of the high school curriculum, high school academic performance, extracurricular activities, and evidence of character and talent."

SELECTIVITY

Admissions Rating	91
# of applicants	4,509
% of applicants accepted	41
% of acceptees attending	26
# offered a place on the wait list	1,039
% accepting a place on wait list	19
% admitted from wait list	10
# of early decision applicants	190
% accepted early decision	75

FRESHMAN PROFILE

Range SAT Critical Reading	580–670
Range SAT Math	560–650
Range SAT Writing	560–660
Range ACT Composite	26–30
Minimum paper TOEFL	577
Minimum internet-based TOEFL	90
Average HS GPA	3.7
% graduated top 10% of class	29
% graduated top 25% of class	64
% graduated top 50% of class	91

DEADLINES

Early decision	
Deadline	11/15
Notification	12/15
Early action	
Deadline	12/1
Regular	
Deadline	2/1
Nonfall registration?	No

FINANCIAL FACTS

Financial Aid Rating	87
Annual tuition	$54,500
Room and board	$12,100
Required fees	$272
Books and supplies	$1,200
Average frosh need-based scholarship	$24,549
Average UG need-based scholarship	$25,917
% needy frosh rec. need-based scholarship or grant aid	98
% needy UG rec. need-based scholarship or grant aid	98
% needy frosh rec. non-need-based scholarship or grant aid	26
% needy UG rec. non-need-based scholarship or grant aid	27
% needy frosh rec. need-based self-help aid	74
% needy UG rec. need-based self-help aid	74
% frosh rec. any financial aid	85
% UG rec. any financial aid	80
% UG borrow to pay for school	42
Average cumulative indebtedness	$22,362
% frosh need fully met	30
% ugrads need fully met	41
Average % of frosh need met	91
Average % of ugrad need met	94

SIENA COLLEGE

515 LOUDON ROAD, LOUDONVILLE, NY 12211-1462 • ADMISSIONS: 518-783-2423 • FAX: 518-783-2436

CAMPUS LIFE

Quality of Life Rating	87
Fire Safety Rating	85
Green Rating	60*
Type of school	Private
Affiliation	Roman Catholic
Environment	Town

STUDENTS

Total undergrad enrollment	3,122
% male/female	49/51
% from out of state	19
% frosh live on campus	90
% ugrads live on campus	80
% African American	4
% Asian	4
% Caucasian	80
% Hispanic	7
% Native American	<1
% Pacific Islander	<1
% Two or more races	2
% Race and/or ethnicity unknown	1
% international	1
# of countries represented	13

SURVEY SAYS...

Students are happy
Great financial aid
Students love Loudonville, NY
Easy to get around campus
Everyone loves the Saints
Intramural sports are popular

ACADEMICS

Academic Rating	80
% students returning for sophomore year	90
% students graduating within 4 years	72
Calendar	Semester
Student/faculty ratio	12:1
Profs interesting rating	77
Profs accessible rating	79

Most classes have 20–29 students.
Most lab/discussion sessions have
10–19 students.

MOST POPULAR MAJORS
Accounting; Biology; Psychology

STUDENTS SAY "..."

Academics

A small Roman Catholic college near Albany, New York, Siena is all about "upholding Catholic Franciscan qualities while providing the best education possible," with an emphasis on "critical thinking and preparing students for life after college." Students say that "Siena is a religious school, but many of the students are not religious," and the college's Franciscan values are reflected in the tight-knit community on campus. The professors here are among Siena's "greatest strengths...They push so hard to make us successful." With small class sizes—there are less than 3,100 students at Siena—"You feel like your professor really knows who you are and cares about you and how you do." Science majors are among the most popular but, as one engineering major notes, "I also like that Siena is a liberal arts school, so we are encouraged to take classes outside of our major, which contributes to a well-rounded education." Professors are generally "very approachable and accessible outside of class, unlike a large research-based intuition," and "Siena College places as much emphasis on teaching as research." Not all the professors receive rave reviews, with one student remarking that it's like "a box of chocolates" because you "never know what you will get."

Life

At Siena, "Students are very friendly, and make campus seem more like a community and home than just a college campus." Despite the lack of fraternities and sororities, alcohol is still present on campus, though students are quick to point out that those who aren't into the party scene "are not pressured into it," and the school is known for having a fairly rigid policy on drinking: "Partying...is very strictly monitored by public safety." "There are a lot of [school-]sponsored activities, such as sporting events, guest speakers, recreational activities (laser tag, '90s night, karaoke, etc.) that students attend." In general, students say, "People fill their days with being studious but social" and "like to go off campus and enjoy what [nearby] Albany has to offer." During the week, students attend classes "and then on the weekend they leave campus to do something fun." As a Division I school, sports are popular social events, particularly men's basketball and hockey—"Many students travel with friends or by bus to the Albany County Hockey Facility where students tailgate and have a great night."

Student Body

Students at Siena are "generally friendly." The student body is primarily from "Long Island or Upstate New York" and everyone is hardworking, as "there is no way to not study or do no work at Siena and still pass." Students describe themselves as are "polite and all around generally good people" who are "friendly, willing to help, [and] outgoing." As one chemistry major puts it, "Siena College values itself on its four main ideals, called DORS, which are Diversity, Optimism, Respect, and Service. As Siena students, we uphold each other to these ideals. We are [known] to hold doors for each other all over campus, so in a way, we physically and mentally hold doors for each other." While not particularly cliquey, one student notes that "the school is pretty much divided into the School of Business and the School of Science for majors, and students tend to hang out with those in similar majors."

FINANCIAL AID: 518-783-2423 • E-MAIL: ADMISSIONS@SIENA.EDU • WEBSITE: WWW.SIENA.EDU

THE PRINCETON REVIEW SAYS

Admissions

Very important factors considered include: rigor of secondary school record, academic GPA. *Important factors considered include:* standardized test scores, recommendation(s), interview. *Other factors considered include:* class rank, application essay, extracurricular activities, talent/ability, character/personal qualities, first generation, alumni/ae relation, geographical residence, racial/ethnic status, volunteer work, work experience, level of applicant's interest. SAT or ACT considered if submitted. ACT with or without writing accepted. SAT with or without Essay component accepted. TOEFL required of all international applicants. High school diploma is required and GED is accepted. *Academic units required:* 4 English, 3 math, 3 science, 3 science labs, 2 foreign language, 3 social studies, 3 history. *Academic units recommended:* 4 English, 4 math, 4 science, 4 science labs, 3 foreign language, 4 social studies, 4 history.

Financial Aid

Students should submit: FAFSA, State aid form. Regular filing deadline is 5/1. The Princeton Review suggests that all financial aid forms be submitted as soon as possible after October 1. *Need-based scholarships/grants offered:* Federal Pell, FSEOG, State scholarships/grants, Private scholarships, College/university scholarship or grant aid from institutional funds. *Loan aid offered:* Direct Subsidized Stafford Loans, Direct Unsubsidized Stafford Loans, Direct PLUS loans, Federal Perkins Loans. Applicants will be notified of awards on or about 4/1. Federal Work-Study Program available. Institutional employment available.

The Inside Word

The applicant pool here is primarily regional—81 percent of incoming first year students come from New York—and the acceptance is relatively high. Don't be fooled, though: Siena is home to several first-rate programs and admissions have grown more competitive over the past few years. Standardized test scores are optional, unless you're a student-athlete or hoping to apply to one Siena's tandem pre-med or pre-law programs with Albany Medical College or Albany Law School, respectively.

THE SCHOOL SAYS "..."

From the Admissions Office

"Siena College is a welcoming community that encourages its students to pursue their academic passions, get involved and develop skills and connections that will prepare them for a lifetime of career success and achievement. Siena is a private, Franciscan and Catholic college located in the heart of New York's Capital Region and Tech Valley. Students enjoy life on a park-like suburban campus yet they are minutes away from high-tech companies, city hotspots, entertainment options and historic sites. The College boasts a four-year graduation rate of 74 percent, which is well above the national average. There are no teaching assistants at Siena which means all classes are taught by faculty members. Siena students are able to customize their curriculum to match their career interests through internships, study abroad and travel courses, undergraduate research with faculty and more than 1,200 program combinations. Popular programs include the liberal arts, accounting, marketing, biology, pre-law and the Siena College/Albany Medical College joint acceptance program. The College also offers a master's in accounting program to meet New York State requirements to sit for the CPA exam. Siena is also the only college in New York State to offer the Bonner Service Leaders scholarship program."

SELECTIVITY

Admissions Rating	83
# of applicants	8,919
% of applicants accepted	59
% of acceptees attending	14
# offered a place on the wait list	549
% accepting a place on wait list	29
% admitted from wait list	7
# of early decision applicants	103
% accepted early decision	35

FRESHMAN PROFILE

Range SAT Critical Reading	480–590
Range SAT Math	500–610
Range SAT Writing	470–590
Range ACT Composite	21–27
Minimum paper TOEFL	550
Minimum internet-based TOEFL	79
Average HS GPA	3.5
% graduated top 10% of class	21
% graduated top 25% of class	50
% graduated top 50% of class	84

DEADLINES

Early decision	
Deadline	12/1
Notification	1/1
Early action	
Deadline	12/1
Notification	1/7
Regular	
Priority	2/15
Deadline	2/15
Notification	3/15
Nonfall registration?	Yes

FINANCIAL FACTS

Financial Aid Rating	85
Annual tuition	$34,326
Room and board	$14,105
Required fees	$285
Books and supplies	$1,200
Average frosh need-based scholarship	$23,060
Average UG need-based scholarship	$19,492
% needy frosh rec. need-based scholarship or grant aid	100
% needy UG rec. need-based scholarship or grant aid	100
% needy frosh rec. non-need-based scholarship or grant aid	91
% needy UG rec. non-need-based scholarship or grant aid	92
% needy frosh rec. need-based self-help aid	76
% needy UG rec. need-based self-help aid	80
% frosh rec. any financial aid	98
% UG rec. any financial aid	91
% UG borrow to pay for school	78
Average cumulative indebtedness	$36,738
% frosh need fully met	33
% ugrads need fully met	28
Average % of frosh need met	81
Average % of ugrad need met	77

SIMMONS COLLEGE

300 THE FENWAY, BOSTON, MA 02115 • ADMISSIONS: 617-521-2051 • FAX: 617-521-3190

STUDENTS SAY "..."

Academics

A women's college "rich in history and achievement," Simmons College equips its undergraduates with the tools and confidence they need to succeed in the real-world. With a student population of about "2,000 very driven, smart, active, and hard working women," Simmons offers a surprisingly wide range of undergraduate majors, while also running a "nursing program that is second to none." Across academic programs, there's a "particular focus on experiential learning and leadership," and the curriculum excels at "educating women for positions of powerful and principled leadership." Simmons professors "are very dedicated to the classes they teach as well as their students." A chemistry major remembers, "My college has many research opportunities and connections. I have been able to do scientific research every semester since my first year at Simmons." Small discussion-based classes "really challenge you to do your best and to actually put some thought into your work," and Simmons professors are described as "the greatest strengths of Simmons College." The Simmons School of Management also offers "many other networking opportunities." Students have mixed opinions when it comes to the administrative offices of the college. Some majors "with hard-to-come-by internships have A LOT of red tape" and others "do not communicate well all the time" with both professors and students. The college does "take advantage of its Boston location through class trips, job placement, and internship opportunities." However, when it comes to the all-important problem of paying for school, students admit that the "financial aid counselors make you want to rip out your hair out."

Life

Location, location, location is a sentiment echoed far and wide by Simmons undergraduates. "We are in Boston," raves one sophomore. "We can do anything the city has to offer." Packed with culture and entertainment, "the city offers many great places to hang out like bowling places, karaoke bars, college parties at other colleges, and great scenery." In addition, Simmons is part of the Colleges of the Fenway association, so "students get discounts at art museums and cultural events around the city such as plays or dances." Simmons is a "dry campus so the bar scene is where to go, and where else is better than right in the heart of Boston?" Other students prefer mellower activities, like "sitting in the common room and talking or watching a show together." Since so much social life takes place off campus, "the dorms are quiet and a great place to concentrate on school work." The peacefulness of campus is a plus for many students, who "spend a lot of time studying and preparing for labs and lecture." Housing has become more of an issue as the "dorms are beginning to get overcrowded" as each year brings a "large influx of first-year students" and some "freshman now live in forced triples."

Student Body

Putting aside the fact that they're all female, Simmons students say there's a lot of diversity on their small campus. "Students attempt to be aware of cultural diversity," and "the community here is very accepting, regardless of race, ethnicity, economic status, religion, sexual orientation, gender expression, or disability." Politically, you'll meet students who are "very conservative to very liberal," though "most students are very supportive of the LGBTQ community and women's rights in general." When it comes to academics, "all of the people here have their lives together and have an idea of what they want to do with their lives." Socially, "birds of a feather flock together," and students admit, "There are different cliques within the student body." However, "everyone is generally accepted" on this friendly and community-oriented campus. A general sentiment that "people here work very hard at everything they do," pervades the student responses.

FINANCIAL AID: 617-521-2001 • E-MAIL: UGADM@SIMMONS.EDU • WEBSITE: WWW.SIMMONS.EDU

THE PRINCETON REVIEW SAYS

Admissions

Very important factors considered include: rigor of secondary school record, academic GPA, standardized test scores. *Important factors considered include:* application essay, recommendation(s), extracurricular activities. *Other factors considered include:* class rank, interview, talent/ability, character/personal qualities, first generation, alumni/ae relation, volunteer work, work experience, level of applicant's interest. SAT or ACT required. ACT with Writing recommended. SAT with or without Essay component accepted. TOEFL required of all international applicants. High school diploma is required and GED is accepted. *Academic units required:* 4 English, 3 math, 4 science, 3 science labs, 3 foreign language, 3 social studies, 2 history, 3 academic electives. *Academic units recommended:* 4 math, 4 science, 4 foreign language, 3 social studies, 3 history, 4 academic electives.

Financial Aid

Students should submit: FAFSA, Institution's own financial aid form. Priority filing deadline is 3/1. The Princeton Review suggests that all financial aid forms be submitted as soon as possible after October 1. *Need-based scholarships/grants offered:* Federal Pell, FSEOG, State scholarships/grants, Private scholarships, College/university scholarship or grant aid from institutional funds. *Loan aid offered:* Direct Subsidized Stafford Loans, Direct Unsubsidized Stafford Loans, Direct PLUS loans, Federal Perkins Loans, College/university loans from institutional funds. Applicants will be notified of awards on a rolling basis beginning 3/15. Federal Work-Study Program available.

The Inside Word

Simmons evaluates prospective students for both academic strength and personal qualities, like community involvement or leadership. Applicants to Simmons should use their personal essays, letters of recommendation, and applications to show the admissions committee who they are as a person. Although a personal interview isn't required, it can be a great way to augment your application, as well as a chance to experience Simmons unique environment. A current student tells us, "It felt like a I belonged here when I visited."

THE SCHOOL SAYS "..."

From the Admissions Office

"For more than a century, Simmons College has offered a pioneering liberals arts education integrated with professional work experience. Founded in 1899, Simmons was the first college in the United States to offer women a liberal arts education integrated with career preparation. At Simmons, we ignore arguments about whether leaders are born or made. Because here, leaders make themselves.

"Located in the heart of Boston, Simmons is best known for its small classes, access to faculty, and internship and research opportunities. Students say that Simmons's location offers the best of both worlds—an intimate college experience in the heart of a vibrant city. Simmons's nearly 2,000 undergraduates love the fact that they can easily access the city's rich social and cultural resources but also come home to a safe, friendly campus.

"Simmons offers a learning experience that is highly collaborative and much more personal than that of large universities. Simmons professors include distinguished researchers, published authors, Fulbright scholars, health professionals, and community leaders. Seventy percent of faculty are women, and nearly 100 percent hold a terminal degree. They advise numerous government, nonprofit, and corporate organizations in the United States and in the world.

"To help students succeed, career support starts as soon as students step on campus and continues as an ongoing, lifelong service. Ninety-eight percent of the class of 2013 were employed or in graduate school within one year of graduation. At Simmons, students work, discover and evolve, eventually becoming a leader for themselves, their community and the world."

SELECTIVITY
Admissions Rating	87
# of applicants	4,575
% of applicants accepted	58
% of acceptees attending	18
# offered a place on the wait list	0

FRESHMAN PROFILE
Range SAT Critical Reading	540–630
Range SAT Math	520–610
Range SAT Writing	530–630
Range ACT Composite	24–29
Minimum paper TOEFL	83
Minimum internet-based TOEFL	83
% graduated top 10% of class	35
% graduated top 25% of class	72
% graduated top 50% of class	97

DEADLINES
Early action	
Deadline	12/1
Notification	1/15
Regular	
Priority	11/1
Deadline	2/1
Notification	3/15
Nonfall registration?	Yes

APPLICANTS ALSO LOOK AT AND OFTEN PREFER
Smith College; Mount Holyoke College; Boston University; Northeastern University

AND SOMETIMES PREFER
University of Vermont; University of New Hampshire; University of Connecticut; Boston College

AND RARELY PREFER
University of Massachusetts Amherst; Suffolk University; Quinnipiac University

FINANCIAL FACTS
Financial Aid Rating	80
Annual tuition	$37,500
Room and board	$14,040
Required fees	$1,060
Books and supplies	$1,280
Average frosh need-based scholarship	$27,523
Average UG need-based scholarship	$25,324
% needy frosh rec. need-based scholarship or grant aid	100
% needy UG rec. need-based scholarship or grant aid	100
% needy frosh rec. non-need-based scholarship or grant aid	11
% needy UG rec. non-need-based scholarship or grant aid	6
% needy frosh rec. need-based self-help aid	84
% needy UG rec. need-based self-help aid	89
% frosh rec. any financial aid	99
% UG rec. any financial aid	91
% frosh need fully met	15
% ugrads need fully met	6
Average % of frosh need met	77
Average % of ugrad need met	75

SKIDMORE COLLEGE

815 NORTH BROADWAY, SARATOGA SPRINGS, NY 12866-1632 • ADMISSIONS: 518-580-5570 • FAX: 518-580-5584

STUDENTS SAY "..."

Academics

"Creative Thought Matters": this is the motto of upstate New York's Skidmore College, which can be found all over campus and in every student's mind. The small school looks to turn out "well-rounded, open-minded, [and] interested" students, and to that end stresses "the doing of interesting things outside of, or in complement to, academics." Students, faculty, and staff alike embrace the tenets of Skidmore life, and make sure that the college "represents the meeting point between a phenomenal social atmosphere and an interdisciplinary take on academics."

Professors "actively engage students in friendships, or at the very least, senior colleague to junior colleague camaraderie." This "enriches the experience of learning" and "makes 'doing work' an inspired, meaningful, and highly consequential practice." Faculty expects a lot from their students in regards to papers and class participation: "Reading is almost always a must." "I love that the professors hold me accountable," says a junior. They "present the material in the context of Skidmore's community and general student body's political and social values" and "show a true interest in their field which they attempt to stir within their students." "Even the classes I have taken to fulfill requirements have been some of my favorite classes," says a student.

Some of Skidmore's greatest strengths are the academic support resources available to all students and the variety of majors available; there are also "many opportunities to study abroad or do internships." The school has "a great balance of arts and sciences"; the crossing point between the two areas is a pleasant surprise for those who study here. Within the science departments, Skidmore "melds a small college atmosphere with equipment and resources expected at a large university." Students also "have a good amount of freedom to explore within their academic field of interest beyond the standard curriculum."

Life

Located in "the city in the country" in upstate Saratoga Springs, New York (a "horse town" due to the famed racetracks), Skidmore is "very close to the Adirondacks and beautiful hiking." Downtown is just a 15-minute walk from campus, and people often make a quick trip to nearby Lake George or to the mall. Aside from all the events going on, it's also great "to just sit on the main lawn with a group of friends, pretend to do work or actually do work, chat about nothing in particular, people watch, play Frisbee, enjoy the live music and the beautiful weather."

The excellent first-year experience kicks off the Skidmore love-fest; it helps that the school is "just the right size" so that "you still meet new people, but it's small enough to make you feel comfortable." The "diverse and abundant club opportunities" offer many outlets for creativity, as "we have a capella groups (five), comedy groups (three), writing clubs (two), and dance troupes (two)." During the week people don't typically party, it's "more a time for extracurriculars and school work"; however on the weekends, "the bar scene is very popular as well as apartment parties" and "everyone smokes weed." The arts are also a huge draw if substances aren't your thing, and "there's always plays and shows to go to."

Student Body

Some people stereotype Skidmore as a "hipster" school ("you see a lot of people chain-smoking cigarettes, drinking coffee out of mason jars, and wearing torn-up 'vintage' clothing), though there is also an athlete contingent in the mix. Generally, "everyone gets along pretty well." Students are "very open-minded," and everyone can find a niche here. "We love people who think creatively and critically while accepting any weirdness that comes with those traits," says a student. Many agree that "while there is a lot of intellectual diversity, Skidmore could definitely make more of an effort to include more diverse backgrounds."

FINANCIAL AID: 518-580-5750 • E-MAIL: ADMISSIONS@SKIDMORE.EDU • WEBSITE: WWW.SKIDMORE.EDU

THE PRINCETON REVIEW SAYS

Admissions

Very important factors considered include: rigor of secondary school record. *Important factors considered include:* class rank, academic GPA, application essay, recommendation(s), extracurricular activities, talent/ability, character/personal qualities, volunteer work, work experience, level of applicant's interest. *Other factors considered include:* standardized test scores, interview, first generation, alumni/ae relation, geographical residence, racial/ethnic status. SAT or ACT required for some; SAT Subject Tests considered if submitted. ACT with or without writing accepted. SAT with or without Essay component accepted. High school diploma is required and GED is accepted. *Academic units recommended:* 4 English, 4 math, 4 science, 3 science labs, 4 foreign language, 4 social studies.

Financial Aid

Students should submit: CSS/Financial Aid PROFILE, Noncustodial PROFILE. Regular filing deadline is 2/1. The Princeton Review suggests that all financial aid forms be submitted as soon as possible after October 1. *Need-based scholarships/grants offered:* Federal Pell, FSEOG, State scholarships/grants, Private scholarships, College/university scholarship or grant aid from institutional funds. *Loan aid offered:* Direct Subsidized Stafford Loans, Direct Unsubsidized Stafford Loans, Direct PLUS loans, Federal Perkins Loans, State Loans. Applicants will be notified of awards on or about 4/1. Federal Work-Study Program available. Institutional employment available.

The Inside Word

Admission to Skidmore is highly competitive, and the admissions staff carefully considers each applicant's academic background and standardized test scores. However, consistent with their motto—"Creative Thought Matters"—Skidmore carefully reviews a student's extracurricular talents, achievements, and passions when making an admissions decision. While admissions interviews aren't a requirement for a Skidmore applicant, students may request a personal interview on campus or with an alumnus in their area.

THE SCHOOL SAYS "..."

From the Admissions Office

"At Skidmore, we believe a great education is about putting academic theory and creative expression into practice; hence, our belief that creative thought matters. It's a place where faculty and students work together, then figure out how to use what they've learned to make a difference. This often leads to multidisciplinary approaches, where students carry more than one major, student-faculty research is common, most students study abroad, and internships and community service are standard. Skidmore students develop into independent, creative problem-solvers who aren't restricted to looking at things in traditional ways. This personal journey starts with the First-Year Experience—fifty seminars from which to choose, faculty and peer mentors, and living in close proximity to seminar classmates in residence halls. It's meant to ensure that first-year students hit the ground running on day one, connected and involved. When it comes to your major, you can choose from nearly fifty offerings in the sciences, social sciences, and humanities, as well as pre-professional fields like management and business. Since we have no fraternities or sororities, student life centers on the nearly 100 student clubs and organizations, which range from the Environmental Action Club to a capella groups to snowboarding. Add to this the prominence of the arts, which has long set Skidmore apart. Science classes collaborate on exhibits at the Tang Museum. Hundreds of students perform, often in the new Zankel Music Center. Enroll in dance courses. Do theater performances. Most are not even arts majors. At Skidmore, the arts don't dominate, they permeate. As for location, who wouldn't want to go to college in Saratoga Springs? A downtown brimming with shops, galleries, coffeehouses, and great restaurants. Boston, New York City, and Montreal are a three-hour car ride from campus. The Adirondacks, Berkshires, and Green Mountains provide opportunities for skiing, mountain biking, hiking, rock-climbing, and kayaking."

SELECTIVITY

Admissions Rating	92
# of applicants	8,508
% of applicants accepted	36
% of acceptees attending	22
# offered a place on the wait list	1,742
% accepting a place on wait list	22
% admitted from wait list	3
# of early decision applicants	415
% accepted early decision	67

FRESHMAN PROFILE

Range SAT Critical Reading	550–670
Range SAT Math	560–673
Range SAT Writing	560–670
Range ACT Composite	26–30
Minimum paper TOEFL	590
% graduated top 10% of class	41
% graduated top 25% of class	72
% graduated top 50% of class	96

DEADLINES

Early decision	
Deadline	11/15
Notification	12/15
Regular	
Deadline	1/15
Notification	4/1
Nonfall registration?	No

APPLICANTS ALSO LOOK AT AND OFTEN PREFER

Vassar College; Oberlin College; New York University

AND SOMETIMES PREFER

Sarah Lawrence College; Connecticut College; Bard College

AND RARELY PREFER

University of Vermont; Wheaton College (MA)

FINANCIAL FACTS

Financial Aid Rating	95
Annual tuition	$48,024
Room and board	$13,072
Required fees	$946
Books and supplies	$1,300
Average frosh need-based scholarship	$42,000
Average UG need-based scholarship	$39,300
% needy frosh rec. need-based scholarship or grant aid	100
% needy UG rec. need-based scholarship or grant aid	100
% needy frosh rec. non-need-based scholarship or grant aid	7
% needy UG rec. non-need-based scholarship or grant aid	8
% needy frosh rec. need-based self-help aid	77
% needy UG rec. need-based self-help aid	72
% frosh rec. any financial aid	49
% UG rec. any financial aid	51
% UG borrow to pay for school	42
Average cumulative indebtedness	$22,557
% frosh need fully met	100
% ugrads need fully met	93
Average % of frosh need met	100
Average % of ugrad need met	95

SMITH COLLEGE

SEVEN COLLEGE LANE, NORTHAMPTON, MA 01063 • ADMISSIONS: 413-585-2500 • FAX: 413-585-2527

STUDENTS SAY "..."

Academics

Smith College is "an incredibly prestigious, diverse, academically rigorous, socially liberal, and well-respected institution," located in the consummate college town of Northampton, Massachusetts. A Smith education is all about "finding and pursuing your passions." Offering "academic freedom," "Smith doesn't have course requirements" beyond the major, other than a writing-intensive course for first-years, and "self-scheduled finals" allow students to take exam week at their own pace. "One of the most prominent women's colleges in the country," Smith "builds the self-confidence of smart women," and "most classes, even in math and sciences, are very interdisciplinary and often have a feminist bias." Classes are "engaging and promote critical thought," and professors are "inspiring, dynamic, accessible, and brilliant." Smith professors "care deeply about students" and "take the time to get to know you on a first-name basis." Smith also offers fabulous academic facilities and "countless resources" to augment your education, including a "wonderful study abroad department" and ample opportunities for research. There's "a large number of undergrads doing serious scientific research" in addition to course work. If they can't find what they need amid Smith's ample course selection, students "can take classes at the other four schools nearby (UMass Amherst, Amherst College, Hampshire College, and Mount Holyoke College)" through the Five College Consortium. When graduation approaches, Smith students benefit from the school's "excellent alumnae network." "The Career Development Office will do everything in its power to help you get a job."

Life

Smith attracts hardworking and idealistic students, who are "striving to succeed in our classes, as well as make a difference in the Smith College community and the outside community." There's a decided "focus on academics" at Smith, and most students "study, write papers, rehearse, or practice the majority of the time." Students augment course work with "lectures and symposium on campus," as well as "involvement in community service and activism for global issues, women's rights, LGBTQ rights, the environment, and pretty much anything that fights oppression." When they want to relax, Smithies can attend "free movies and concerts, plays, speakers, sports events, and dances," as well as "school-sponsored house parties almost every weekend." When they want to branch out or rub elbows with the opposite sex, students "go to other college parties at surrounding campuses," or head out in Northampton, which is "always bustling" with "concerts, restaurants, and cute shops." The "quality of life is outstanding" on campus, where "the dorms are not dorms but beautiful houses," and cafeteria food is a cut above the average.

Student Body

"Smithies are passionate about everything they do," especially academics. Throughout the semester, undergraduates are known to "study hard" and get "ridiculously stressed" about course work. "It's the nature of Smithies to be driven, but we all want to see our friends and housemates succeed as well." Smith's unique environment attracts "a great mix of nerdy, edgy, [and] traditional" students, including "hipsters, WASPs, crazy partiers, international students, and the average New Englander." Fortunately, there's a "strong sense of community," and "students fit in easily, even if they have different interests." Despite diversity, "one thing all students have in common here is the will for women's empowerment and acceptance of any gender or sexual preference." On that note, many students "love the queer life on campus," where some students are either gay or have "a fluid perception of sexuality." Though there's some political diversity on campus, most Smithies hold "very liberal views," and many are "very conscious and aware, not only of their community but the world in general."

SMITH COLLEGE

FINANCIAL AID: 413-585-2530 • E-MAIL: ADMISSION@SMITH.EDU • WEBSITE: WWW.SMITH.EDU

THE PRINCETON REVIEW SAYS

Admissions

Very important factors considered include: rigor of secondary school record, academic GPA, application essay, recommendation(s), character/personal qualities. *Important factors considered include:* class rank, interview, extracurricular activities, talent/ability. *Other factors considered include:* standardized test scores, first generation, alumni/ae relation, racial/ethnic status, volunteer work, work experience. SAT or ACT required for some. ACT with or without writing accepted. SAT with or without Essay component accepted. TOEFL required of all international applicants. High school diploma or equivalent is not required. *Academic units recommended:* 4 English, 3 math, 3 science, 3 science labs, 3 foreign language, 2 history, 1 academic elective.

Financial Aid

Students should submit: FAFSA, Institution's own financial aid form, CSS/Financial Aid PROFILE, Noncustodial PROFILE. Regular filing deadline is 2/15. The Princeton Review suggests that all financial aid forms be submitted as soon as possible after October 1. *Need-based scholarships/grants offered:* Federal Pell, FSEOG, State scholarships/grants, Private scholarships, College/university scholarship or grant aid from institutional funds. *Loan aid offered:* Direct Subsidized Stafford Loans, Direct Unsubsidized Stafford Loans, Direct PLUS loans, Federal Perkins Loans, College/university loans from institutional funds. Applicants will be notified of awards on or about 4/1. Federal Work-Study Program available. Institutional employment available.

The Inside Word

Every prospective Smithie is carefully evaluated by at least two members of the admissions staff. No hard numbers guarantee admission: Smith is looking for students who will succeed academically and socially in college, evaluating each applicant for both personal and intellectual qualities. To best prepare for admission, Smith recommends that students follow a rigorous college prep curriculum in high school. If you're feeling particularly enthused about your future at Smith, you can become a fan of the admissions department on Facebook, take the online tour, or read student blogs on the admission page.

THE SCHOOL SAYS "..."

From the Admissions Office

"Smith students choose from 1,000 courses in more than fifty areas of study. There are no specific course requirements outside the major; students meet individually with faculty advisers to plan a balanced curriculum. Smith programs offer unique opportunities, including interdisciplinary concentrations, the chance to study abroad, or at another college in the United States, and a semester in Washington, D.C. The Ada Comstock Scholars Program encourages women beyond the traditional age to return to college and complete their undergraduate studies. Smith is located in the scenic Connecticut River valley of western Massachusetts near a number of other outstanding educational institutions. Through the Five College Consortium, Smith, Amherst, Hampshire, and Mount Holyoke colleges, and the University of Massachusetts enrich their academic, social, and cultural offerings by means of joint faculty appointments, joint courses, student and faculty exchanges, shared facilities, and other cooperative arrangements. Smith is the only women's college to offer an accredited major in engineering; it's also the only college in the country that offers a guaranteed paid internship program ('Praxis')."

SELECTIVITY

Admissions Rating	95
# of applicants	5,006
% of applicants accepted	38
% of acceptees attending	32
# offered a place on the wait list	773
% accepting a place on wait list	51
% admitted from wait list	33
# of early decision applicants	409
% accepted early decision	57

FRESHMAN PROFILE

Range SAT Critical Reading	620–740
Range SAT Math	620–720
Range SAT Writing	630–720
Range ACT Composite	28–32
Minimum paper TOEFL	600
Minimum internet-based TOEFL	90
Average HS GPA	3.9
% graduated top 10% of class	64
% graduated top 25% of class	90
% graduated top 50% of class	100

DEADLINES

Early decision	
Deadline	11/15
Notification	12/15
Regular	
Deadline	1/15
Nonfall registration?	No

APPLICANTS ALSO LOOK AT
AND OFTEN PREFER
Brown University

AND SOMETIMES PREFER
Wellesley College

AND RARELY PREFER
Mount Holyoke College

FINANCIAL FACTS

Financial Aid Rating	96
Tuition	$47,620
Room and board	$16,010
Required fees	$248
Books and supplies	$800
Average frosh need-based scholarship	$41,802
Average UG need-based scholarship	$38,040
% needy frosh rec. need-based scholarship or grant aid	97
% needy UG rec. need-based scholarship or grant aid	97
% needy frosh rec. non-need-based scholarship or grant aid	2
% needy UG rec. non-need-based scholarship or grant aid	1
% needy frosh rec. need-based self-help aid	92
% needy UG rec. need-based self-help aid	93
% frosh rec. any financial aid	68
% UG rec. any financial aid	68
% UG borrow to pay for school	63
Average cumulative indebtedness	$20,514
% frosh need fully met	100
% ugrads need fully met	100
Average % of frosh need met	100
Average % of ugrad need met	100

SONOMA STATE UNIVERSITY

1801 EAST COTATI AVENUE, ROHNERT PARK, CA 94928 • ADMISSIONS: 707-664-2778 • FAX: 707-664-2060

CAMPUS LIFE

Quality of Life Rating	84
Fire Safety Rating	85
Green Rating	73
Type of school	Public
Affiliation	No Affiliation
Environment	Town

STUDENTS

Total undergrad enrollment	8,615
% male/female	38/62
% frosh live on campus	87
% ugrads live on campus	22
# of fraternities	8
# of sororities	10
% African American	2
% Asian	5
% Caucasian	48
% Hispanic	29
% Native American	1
% Pacific Islander	<1
% Two or more races	7
% Race and/or ethnicity unknown	7
% international	2

SURVEY SAYS...

Dorms are like palaces
Frats and sororities are popular
Great library

ACADEMICS

Academic Rating	69
% students returning for sophomore year	81
% students graduating within 4 years	28
% students graduating within 6 years	59
Calendar	Semester
Student/faculty ratio	25:1
Profs interesting rating	73
Profs accessible rating	72

Most classes have 20–29 students.
Most lab/discussion sessions have
20–29 students.

MOST POPULAR MAJORS

Liberal Arts and Sciences; Business/
Commerce

STUDENTS SAY "..."

Academics

A member of the reputable California state university system, Sonoma State University distinguishes itself from similar institutions through its low-key atmosphere and strong "focus on undergraduates." Employing "teachers who are willing to take the time to make a difference in students' lives," SSU limits most classes to fewer than fifty, giving students the opportunity to "develop close and meaningful relationships with professors and classmates that will continue even after graduation." During class time, professors often "allow open discussions and emphasize a comfortable, safe environment to express oneself." After class, they "are always available through e-mail or in person during their office hours." Most SSU instructors are excellent in the classroom, but the school is big enough that you'll find "a wide variety of professors, ranging from spectacular to pretty poor." Fortunately, professors are generally "experts in their field" and "stay up to date on current events that affect our field of study." While students benefit from a very low in-state tuition, SSU has been affected by California budget cuts, and the resulting unit cap "makes it almost impossible to graduate in four years." The school could also improve some of its bureaucratic processes; for example, the class "registration process is notoriously buggy." For those hoping to stay in California after graduation, "Sonoma County and the city of San Francisco are two places very rich in career opportunities for Sonoma State students."

Life

SSU boasts a "gorgeous campus" and "impressive" facilities, including "incredible" dormitories and "a new rec center with [a] climbing wall and indoor courts, as well as outside fields." A current student enthuses, "Just come look at the housing and you realize that Sonoma is trying to make everyone as comfortable as possible." With its "beautiful setting in the heart of wine country," "the pace here seems to be a slower one, which creates a peaceful and calm environment to take classes and study in; the stress level here is relatively low." After class, students might "hang out by the pools" or study in the "many little redwood groves" around campus. "There are hundreds of clubs" on campus, including many popular Greek organizations, and, for those with a little initiative, "the leadership opportunities are endless." Off campus, surrounding Rohnert Park is a "more suburban" environment, so "it is difficult to go anywhere unless you have a car." With a set of wheels, students love to take day trips to San Francisco, or go miniature golfing, hiking, and bowling nearby. "Outdoor activities are abundant year-round" and, for those of legal drinking age, "there are also a lot of wineries and vineyards to go wine tasting!" Come the weekend, "a lot of students like to party," while others "enjoy on-campus activities like midnight improv and free movies."

Students

"Many students pick Sonoma because it is close to home," whether they live on campus or commute. Southern Californians and other in-staters round out the largely "Bay Area" crowd, and there are a number of older students mixed in with traditional undergrads. In broad strokes, "most students here come from middle- to upper-class backgrounds, and they are all fairly down-to-earth and really very nice and socially aware." More superficially, you'll notice "a lot of white girls wearing yoga pants, Nike shocks, and drinking Starbucks coffee." That said, "everyone has their own thing" at SSU. Though the school is "not really racially diverse" there is an "eclectic group of students," making it easy to fit in. A wise junior advises, "The important thing is to find your passions, your niche, and pursue it. In the process, you'll come upon like-minded students who share the same interests." "Most of the students here are part of the Greek life," telling us that fraternities and sororities are the best way to make friends and have fun (though others complain that "Greeks feel like they run the school," to the detriment of non-affiliated students). Even if you don't pledge, "the residential community helps build great friendships" for those who live on campus, and "because everyone is friendly most people find it easy to make friends."

FINANCIAL AID: 707-664-2389 • E-MAIL: STUDENT.OUTREACH@SONOMA.EDU • WEBSITE: WWW.SONOMA.EDU

THE PRINCETON REVIEW SAYS

Admissions

Very important factors considered include: academic GPA, standardized test scores. *Important factors considered include: Other factors considered include:* geographical residence. SAT or ACT required; SAT Subject Tests considered if submitted. ACT with or without writing accepted. TOEFL required of all international applicants. High school diploma is required and GED is accepted. *Academic units required:* 4 English, 3 math, 2 science, 1 science lab, 2 foreign language, 2 history, 1 academic elective, 1 visual/performing arts, and 1 unit from above areas or other academic areas.

Financial Aid

Students should submit: FAFSA. Priority filing deadline is 1/31. The Princeton Review suggests that all financial aid forms be submitted as soon as possible after October 1. *Need-based scholarships/grants offered:* Federal Pell, FSEOG, State scholarships/grants, Private scholarships, College/university scholarship or grant aid from institutional funds. *Loan aid offered:* Direct Subsidized Stafford Loans, Direct Unsubsidized Stafford Loans, Direct PLUS loans, Federal Perkins Loans. Applicants will be notified of awards on a rolling basis beginning 3/25. Federal Work-Study Program available. Institutional employment available.

The Inside Word

SSU makes admissions decisions based on an "eligibility index" number, which is calculated using a student's standardized test scores and GPA; note that honors and advanced placement course work is weighted more heavily than regular courses in calculating a grade point average. Because of the school's budget problems, students applying for admission to impacted majors must meet a higher index number. Currently, impacted majors include communication studies, biology, kinesiology, liberal studies, pre-nursing, and psychology.

THE SCHOOL SAYS "..."

From the Admissions Office

"Sonoma State University occupies 269 acres in the beautiful wine country of Sonoma county, in northern California. Located at the foot of the Sonoma hills, the campus is an hour's drive north of San Francisco and centrally located between the Pacific Ocean to the west and the wine country to the north and east. SSU is deeply committed to the teaching of the liberal arts and sciences with selected professional programs. Within its thirty-four academic departments, SSU awards bachelor's degrees in forty-six areas of specialization and master's degrees in fifteen areas. In addition, the university offers a joint master's degree in mathematics with San Francisco State University and a joint Ed.D. with UC Davis.

"All freshmen applicants are required to provide SAT or ACT scores."

SELECTIVITY

Admissions Rating	73
# of applicants	15,265
% of applicants accepted	77
% of acceptees attending	16

FRESHMAN PROFILE

Range SAT Critical Reading	440–550
Range SAT Math	440–550
Range SAT Writing	440–540
Range ACT Composite	19–24
Minimum paper TOEFL	500
Minimum internet-based TOEFL	61
Average HS GPA	3.2

DEADLINES

Regular	
Priority	3/1
Deadline	11/30
Notification	3/1
Nonfall registration?	Yes

FINANCIAL FACTS

Financial Aid Rating	82
Annual out-of-state tuition	$16,632
Room and board	$11,799
Required fees	$7,276
Books and supplies	$1,764
Average frosh need-based scholarship	$10,184
Average UG need-based scholarship	$9,642
% needy frosh rec. need-based scholarship or grant aid	68
% needy UG rec. need-based scholarship or grant aid	66
% needy frosh rec. non-need-based scholarship or grant aid	42
% needy UG rec. non-need-based scholarship or grant aid	39
% needy frosh rec. need-based self-help aid	69
% needy UG rec. need-based self-help aid	63
% frosh rec. any financial aid	59
% UG rec. any financial aid	51
% frosh need fully met	31
% ugrads need fully met	16
Average % of frosh need met	62
Average % of ugrad need met	79

SOUTHERN METHODIST UNIVERSITY

PO Box 750181, DALLAS, TX 75275-0181 • ADMISSIONS: 214-768-3147 • FAX: 214-768-1083

CAMPUS LIFE

Quality of Life Rating	98
Fire Safety Rating	97
Green Rating	60*
Type of school	Private
Affiliation	Methodist
Environment	Metropolis

STUDENTS

Total undergrad enrollment	6,411
% male/female	50/50
% from out of state	54
% frosh from public high school	43
% frosh live on campus	98
% ugrads live on campus	57
# of fraternities	15
# of sororities	13
% African American	5
% Asian	7
% Caucasian	65
% Hispanic	11
% Native American	<1
% Pacific Islander	<1
% Two or more races	4
% Race and/or ethnicity unknown	<1
% international	8
# of countries represented	65

SURVEY SAYS...

Students are happy
Classroom facilities are great
Great library
Career services are great
Internships are widely available
School is well run
Great financial aid
Students get along with local community
Students love Dallas, TX
Great off-campus food
Dorms are like palaces
Easy to get around campus
Recreation facilities are great
Frats and sororities are popular
Alumni active on campus

ACADEMICS

Academic Rating	87
% students returning for sophomore year	90
% students graduating within 4 years	67
% students graduating within 6 years	79
Calendar	Semester
Student/faculty ratio	11:1
Profs interesting rating	89
Profs accessible rating	90

Most classes have 10–19 students.
Most lab/discussion sessions have 20–29 students.

MOST POPULAR MAJORS
Finance; Economics; Accounting

STUDENTS SAY "..."

Academics

Located on a tree-lined, "beautiful campus" in the heart of Dallas, Southern Methodist University is a mid-size private university with a lot going on. The school has a "unique culture" that relies on "top academics" and a "long-standing history of strong traditions" to build "incredible alumni support," which in turn brings students excellent internship and job opportunities. SMU offers everything "from a great social life and extracurricular activities to fun and interesting classes," including a "phenomenal business school" and "amazing" facilities. The school prides itself on being "a close-knit community of the intellectually elite," and this translates into "a wealth of academic resources [with which] to be successful, a flood of opportunities for those who want them, and thus a community of intellectuals who happen to genuinely care about each other." Professors are "incredibly gifted in their fields and exceptional communicators." They "love interacting with students" and "are willing to put in extra time to convey the material accurately to students." "If their office hours don't match yours, they will change their schedule to accommodate people," says a student. Most have worked in the industry that they teach in, and therefore they "can offer real-life connections to the material we learn." The syllabus is also modeled "to what you'll face in the real world." The legion of SMU alumni provides excellent connections into the business world (among others), and a "dedicated career services center" only sweetens the employment pot. Since many attend SMU for the Cox School of Business, it helps that the school is in the ideal location "to secure great jobs with Fortune 500 companies right here in Dallas." The school's administration also "understands that studying abroad, internships, extracurriculars, etc., also play a crucial role in developing students into the adults and professionals they want to become." "SMU puts the 'classy' back in classical education," says a student.

Life

Despite the fact it is located in the heart of Dallas, "the atmosphere is very calm and relaxing." SMU students frequently head to uptown Dallas "for fine dining and dancing" and often see movies, shop, and attend concerts and sports games. Everyone is always on campus for the football games for "boulevarding" ("basically tailgating but on steroids"), and "we love to have alums come visit us for the tailgate," says a student. Students generally fit in with this "a vibrant social life" best once they have found an extracurricular organization that is right for them, and oftentimes "sororities and fraternities tend to be this venue." However, some wish there was "less emphasis on Greek Life," since "if you're not Greek, you can sometimes feel left out or looked down on." Students devote a large portion of their time to their studies, but "there is always a social event every weekend night to blow off steam." This heavy concentration on future careers means that most here are "definitely wanting to become leaders in their field or profession," so "fraternity parties and formals are popular, but at the same time so are speeches from prominent members of the community and theatrical performances."

Student Body

This student body is "happy and leads a balanced life" at a school that it loves. Most students at SMU "tend to be a bit preppy," "polite," and tend to come from "influential backgrounds." Many "work a lot for pay or do internships," take a lot of class hours, "are involved...and have fun a lot." "They are very busy people, and they prefer it that way," says one student. All of these "motivated, outgoing," people "thrive on leadership" and are "dedicated to academics and involvement, both at SMU and in the greater community." Fashion "is a big part of SMU culture." This group is "very social" and frequently interacts with the Dallas community and "amazing arts and restaurant scene around campus."

SOUTHERN METHODIST UNIVERSITY

FINANCIAL AID: 214-768-3147 • E-MAIL: UGADMISSION@SMU.EDU • WEBSITE: WWW.SMU.EDU

THE PRINCETON REVIEW SAYS

Admissions

Very important factors considered include: rigor of secondary school record, academic GPA, standardized test scores, application essay, recommendation(s). *Important factors considered include:* class rank, extracurricular activities, talent/ability, character/personal qualities. *Other factors considered include:* first generation, alumni/ae relation, racial/ethnic status, volunteer work, work experience, level of applicant's interest. SAT or ACT required. ACT with or without writing accepted. SAT with or without Essay component accepted. TOEFL required of all international applicants. High school diploma is required and GED is not accepted. *Academic units required:* 4 English, 3 math, 3 science, 2 science labs, 2 foreign language, 3 social studies. *Academic units recommended:* 4 English, 4 math, 3 science, 2 science labs, 3 foreign language, 3 history, 3 academic electives.

Financial Aid

Students should submit: FAFSA, CSS/Financial Aid PROFILE, Noncustodial PROFILE. Priority filing deadline is 2/15. The Princeton Review suggests that all financial aid forms be submitted as soon as possible after October 1. *Need-based scholarships/grants offered:* Federal Pell, FSEOG, State scholarships/grants, Private scholarships, College/university scholarship or grant aid from institutional funds. *Loan aid offered:* Direct Subsidized Stafford Loans, Direct Unsubsidized Stafford Loans, Direct PLUS loans, Federal Perkins Loans, State Loans, College/university loans from institutional funds. Applicants will be notified of awards on a rolling basis beginning 4/1. Federal Work-Study Program available. Institutional employment available.

The Inside Word

SMU boasts a potent combination: high-caliber academics, a desirable location, and a beautiful campus. No surprise then that gaining admission is challenging, and growing more so all the time. Solid high school grades and a compelling list of extracurricular activities will usually do the trick. "Special talent" students—aesthetes and athletes in particular—can make up for academic deficiencies; those in the arts must undergo an audition/portfolio review, while promising athletes are scouted. Except for those in the performing arts, all admitted students enter as "pre-majors" in the Dedman College of Humanities and Sciences.

THE SCHOOL SAYS ". . ."

From the Admissions Office

"SMU students are ambitious and motivated, balancing rigorous academics with a vibrant campus experience in the booming city of Dallas. Professors who are as dedicated to teaching as they are to their research give personal attention in small classes. With a diverse student body representing every state and more than 100 countries, students thrive in a community built on a convergence of ideas and backgrounds. Opportunities outside the classroom abound in the form of undergraduate research, internships, community service and study abroad programs. Unique to SMU is the campus in Taos, New Mexico, which offers credit-bearing experiential learning courses on the site of a 13th-century pueblo. On the main campus, the George W. Bush Presidential Center and renowned Tate Lecture Series offer students access to dignitaries ranging from former presidents to Nobel Laureates in a non-partisan context. Students can attend the more than 400 arts and cultural events on campus each year, or take in one of thousands more events in the nation's largest urban arts district, located in downtown Dallas. The more than 180 student organizations and Board of Trustees, which includes a voting student member, gives them the chance to hone their leadership skills. Generous merit scholarship programs enhance the financial aid offered to more than 70 percent of undergraduates. Top-rated career services and close ties with the global city of Dallas ensure students have access to some of the best graduate and professional schools in the nation and careers with firms recognized around the world."

SELECTIVITY

Admissions Rating	91
# of applicants	12,992
% of applicants accepted	49
% of acceptees attending	22
# offered a place on the wait list	1,757
% accepting a place on wait list	33
% admitted from wait list	21
# of early decision applicants	687
% accepted early decision	30

FRESHMAN PROFILE

Range SAT Critical Reading	600–690
Range SAT Math	620–720
Range SAT Writing	600–690
Range ACT Composite	28–32
Minimum paper TOEFL	550
Minimum internet-based TOEFL	80
Average HS GPA	3.6
% graduated top 10% of class	44
% graduated top 25% of class	75
% graduated top 50% of class	93

DEADLINES

Early decision	
Deadline	11/1
Notification	12/31
Early action	
Deadline	11/1
Notification	12/31
Regular	
Priority	1/15
Deadline	1/15
Notification	4/1
Nonfall registration?	Yes

APPLICANTS ALSO LOOK AT AND OFTEN PREFER
University of Southern California

AND SOMETIMES PREFER
Vanderbilt University; Boston University

FINANCIAL FACTS

Financial Aid Rating	86
Annual tuition	$44,694
Room and board	$16,125
Required fees	$5,664
Books and supplies	$800
Average frosh need-based scholarship	$20,909
Average UG need-based scholarship	$20,746
% needy frosh rec. need-based scholarship or grant aid	64
% needy UG rec. need-based scholarship or grant aid	74
% needy frosh rec. non-need-based scholarship or grant aid	75
% needy UG rec. non-need-based scholarship or grant aid	65
% needy frosh rec. need-based self-help aid	72
% needy UG rec. need-based self-help aid	79
% frosh rec. any financial aid	73
% UG rec. any financial aid	70
% UG borrow to pay for school	38
Average cumulative indebtedness	$30,826
% frosh need fully met	38
% ugrads need fully met	27
Average % of frosh need met	88
Average % of ugrad need met	84

SOUTHWESTERN UNIVERSITY

ADMISSIONS OFFICE, GEORGETOWN, TX 78627-0770 • ADMISSIONS: 512-863-1200 • FAX: 512-863-9601

CAMPUS LIFE
Quality of Life Rating	91
Fire Safety Rating	91
Green Rating	91
Type of school	Private
Affiliation	Methodist
Environment	Town

STUDENTS
Total undergrad enrollment	1,538
% male/female	42/58
% from out of state	12
% frosh from public high school	75
% frosh live on campus	100
% ugrads live on campus	77
# of fraternities (% ugrad men join)	4 (22)
# of sororities (% ugrad women join)	4 (21)
% African American	5
% Asian	5
% Caucasian	64
% Hispanic	19
% Native American	<1
% Pacific Islander	<1
% Two or more races	3
% Race and/or ethnicity unknown	1
% international	3
# of countries represented	6

SURVEY SAYS...
Students are happy
Career services are great
Internships are widely available
School is well run
Great financial aid
No one cheats
Students are friendly
Students environmentally aware
Easy to get around campus

ACADEMICS
Academic Rating	85
% students graduating within 4 years	65
Calendar	Semester
Student/faculty ratio	12:1
Profs interesting rating	94
Profs accessible rating	91

Most classes have 10–19 students.
Most lab/discussion sessions have 10–19 students.

MOST POPULAR MAJORS
Business/Commerce; Biology; Psychology

STUDENTS SAY ". . ."

Academics

One of Texas' top-ranked universities, Southwestern offers students a "welcoming environment" and invites them to become part of a "close community" of scholars. "Small and rigorous," undergrads here truly appreciate that Southwestern "focuses heavily on student development and improvement." Though at times they might complain about the "huge work load," many value the fact that they're really learning "to think critically" and gaining "leadership skills." Impressively, a number of students feels that the university really imbues them with "the love for knowledge." Undergrads are quick to praise their professors, noting that they "sincerely care about their students' education" and are always "willing to help students in any way they can." For the most part, they encourage "participation, whether it is a class discussion or in the middle of a lecture, which allows you to get a feel for the real core of whatever topic you're studying." One history major does caution, "Don't expect to just show up and succeed—you're going to have to work." Fortunately, though the academics might be "challenging," professors are always ready to "meet with you whenever you need guidance or clarification on an assignment." Overall, the university provides a "very engaging learning experience" and allows undergrads to reach their "full potential." And as this supremely satisfied student shares, Southwestern is "the best liberal arts school you've never heard of."

Life

Though students at Southwestern are "very focused on their studies," many also try and take advantage of the myriad activities happening around campus. Fraternities and sororities are fairly popular here, and "Greek life provides the main entertainment for students if they're into the partying scene." However, don't fret if you fear that frat life isn't for you; they're not the only game in town. As one math and music double-major tells us, "There are plenty of opportunities to see shows put on by the theater department, concerts of all types, or recitals. The school also brings in music groups like Cake or Spoon or comedians like Eric O'Shea for Friday Night Live every week." Additionally, campus sponsored events like "movie nights" and "casino nights" are usually well-attended. Undergrads also appreciate leisure time outdoors and students can frequently be found "lounging on the academic mall or riding their bikes to the local park." Though some students find that the surrounding Georgetown area offers "little to do," others enjoy taking advantage of the local "movie theater or bowling alley." As when undergrads are anxious for a little more action, they often head to nearby Austin.

Student Body

Southwestern attracts "intelligent," academically inclined students who fortunately don't "obsess over their grades." They manage to be both "studious" and "fun-loving" and are typically "swamped with a million activities." Though it's a small school, undergrads assure us that "everybody finds their niche somewhere." Indeed, people at Southwestern are "warm," "friendly," and "pretty approachable." An English major adds, "Students are willing to make friends with just about anyone." While the majority are "white, middle- or upper-middle-class, [and] Christian" there are students "from every race, religion, and background," and many people are "open-minded." A large number of students are "in sororities/fraternities," and "liberals outnumber conservatives." Further, most "people dress fairly conservatively, but it is not unheard of to see colored hair, Disturbed t-shirts, or a random guy in a skirt." Perhaps this English and business double-major says it best: "It doesn't take long to find some people you fit in with at school, because you find so many types of people here that it is hard to feel like an outcast."

FINANCIAL AID: 512-863-1259 • E-MAIL: ADMISSION@SOUTHWESTERN.EDU • WEBSITE: WWW.SOUTHWESTERN.EDU

THE PRINCETON REVIEW SAYS

Admissions

Very important factors considered include: rigor of secondary school record, class rank, academic GPA, standardized test scores, application essay, recommendation(s). *Important factors considered include:* interview, extracurricular activities, talent/ability, character/personal qualities, first generation, alumni/ae relation, geographical residence, state residency, racial/ethnic status, volunteer work. *Other factors considered include:* religious affiliation/commitment, work experience, level of applicant's interest. SAT or ACT required. ACT with or without writing accepted. TOEFL required of all international applicants. High school diploma is required and GED is accepted. *Academic units required:* 4 English, 4 math, 3 science, 2 science labs, 2 foreign language, 2 social studies, 1 history, 1 academic elective. *Academic units recommended:* 4 English, 4 math, 4 science, 3 science labs, 3 foreign language, 3 social studies, 2 history, 1 academic elective.

Financial Aid

Students should submit: FAFSA. Regular filing deadline is 3/1. The Princeton Review suggests that all financial aid forms be submitted as soon as possible after October 1. *Need-based scholarships/grants offered:* Federal Pell, FSEOG, State scholarships/grants, Private scholarships, College/university scholarship or grant aid from institutional funds. *Loan aid offered:* Direct Subsidized Stafford Loans, Direct Unsubsidized Stafford Loans, Direct PLUS loans, Federal Perkins Loans, State Loans, College/university loans from institutional funds. Applicants will be notified of awards on a rolling basis beginning 3/1. Federal Work-Study Program available. Institutional employment available.

The Inside Word

Successful applicants to Southwestern demonstrate intellectual curiosity and a strong desire to participate in an active collegiate community. Students need to be well-rounded and highly motivated. The vast majority of those who receive that coveted thick envelope are in the top quarter of their class and have above-average SAT scores.

THE SCHOOL SAYS "..."

From the Admissions Office

"Southwestern is the leading liberal arts institution in Texas. As Texas's first institution of higher learning, Southwestern has been providing students with a distinctive, values-centered education since 1840. Our tree-lined residential campus is everything you imagine when you dream about going to college, and then some. Grand, century-old limestone buildings accent the heart of campus, offering spacious sports and recreational facilities, multiple research laboratories, two live-performance theaters, roomy residence halls, and so much more. Our community Pirate Bike program is unlike anything in Texas. These bright yellow bikes scattered across campus are ready to ride anytime, day or night. The Paideia experience introduces students to intentional connections. Through collaboration, participation in civic engagement activities, intercultural learning experiences and undergraduate research, students think across the disciplines to form new solutions, ultimately integrating their knowledge, high-level problem solving skills and deep learning as they apply their scholarship to essential questions of the world around them. The results are impressive, Post Graduate Survey data for 2012 reports that 91 percent of students are either employed, attending medical, law and other professional schools or pursuing advanced studies.Georgetown has much to offer, but if at the end of the day you are in the mood for a quick drive, grab your friends and help 'Keep Austin Weird!' Experience SXSW Music, Film and Interactive, ACL Music Festival, or face your fears at Bat Fest. What's more, with the year-round sunshine and a wealth of recreational activities within your reach, the outdoors becomes a popular playground."

SELECTIVITY

Admissions Rating	88
# of applicants	3,487
% of applicants accepted	49
% of acceptees attending	23
# offered a place on the wait list	92
% accepting a place on wait list	11
% admitted from wait list	50

FRESHMAN PROFILE

Range SAT Critical Reading	520–630
Range SAT Math	530–630
Range ACT Composite	23–28
Minimum paper TOEFL	570
Minimum internet-based TOEFL	88
% graduated top 10% of class	36
% graduated top 25% of class	66
% graduated top 50% of class	95

DEADLINES

Early action	
Deadline	11/14
Notification	2/15
Regular	
Priority	2/1
Notification	4/1
Nonfall registration?	No

APPLICANTS ALSO LOOK AT AND OFTEN PREFER
Trinity University

AND SOMETIMES PREFER
Texas A&M University–College Station; The University of Texas at Austin; Austin College; Rhodes College

AND RARELY PREFER
Baylor University; Texas Christian University; Rice University

FINANCIAL FACTS

Financial Aid Rating	87
Annual tuition	$37,560
Room and board	$12,108
Books and supplies	$1,200
Average frosh need-based scholarship	$27,629
Average UG need-based scholarship	$26,126
% needy frosh rec. need-based scholarship or grant aid	100
% needy UG rec. need-based scholarship or grant aid	99
% needy frosh rec. non-need-based scholarship or grant aid	99
% needy UG rec. non-need-based scholarship or grant aid	96
% needy frosh rec. need-based self-help aid	83
% needy UG rec. need-based self-help aid	85
% frosh rec. any financial aid	99
% UG rec. any financial aid	97
% frosh need fully met	26
% ugrads need fully met	27
Average % of frosh need met	90
Average % of ugrad need met	88

SPELMAN COLLEGE

350 SPELMAN LANE, SOUTHWEST, ATLANTA, GA 30314-4399 • ADMISSIONS: 404-270-5193 • FAX: 404-270-5201

CAMPUS LIFE

Quality of Life Rating	87
Fire Safety Rating	95
Green Rating	88
Type of school	Private
Affiliation	No Affiliation
Environment	Metropolis

STUDENTS

Total undergrad enrollment	2,144
% male/female	0/100
% from out of state	73
% frosh live on campus	99
% ugrads live on campus	68
# of sororities (% ugrad women join)	5 (2)
% African American	96
% Asian	<1
% Caucasian	<1
% Hispanic	<1
% Native American	<1
% Pacific Islander	0
% Two or more races	2
% Race and/or ethnicity unknown	0
% international	1
# of countries represented	10

SURVEY SAYS...

Lots of liberal students
Students are happy
Career services are great
Internships are widely available
Students are very religious
Easy to get around campus

ACADEMICS

Academic Rating	81
% students returning for sophomore year	90
% students graduating within 4 years	69
% students graduating within 6 years	76
Calendar	Semester
Student/faculty ratio	10:1
Profs interesting rating	77
Profs accessible rating	74

Most classes have 10–19 students.
Most lab/discussion sessions have
10–19 students.

MOST POPULAR MAJORS

Political Science and Government;
Psychology; Biology

STUDENTS SAY "..."

Academics

A historically black women's institution, Spelman College has built a strong reputation for "molding intelligent, goal-oriented young ladies into determined, successful, free-thinking women." Many prospective students are attracted to the school's "powerful history," including the "long list of successful, educated, strong, black women who have attended Spelman College" during the century since its founding. Once on campus, students are happy to report that Spelman's "professors are committed to the mission of the school," and they really "bring out the best" in their students. In the classroom, students are "encouraged to state our opinions," and professors "allow room for us to challenge and discuss what they present." You'll definitely work hard to stay afloat in this "challenging academic environment," because professors "do not allow for even a minute amount of slacking when it comes to completing assignments and being on time for class." Fortunately, there are "many academic resources available to help us, such as tutoring services and a writing center." Plus, the majority of Spelman professors "take additional time outside of instructional time to assist their students" with course work. Of particular note, Spelman is "very focused on the sciences and improving the number of African American women in this field, and they offer many facilities, faculty, and opportunities" for advanced study. As graduation approaches, the "Career Counseling Center is extremely strong and has helped numerous students find employment and graduate school placements." While the future looks bright for Spelman grads, many say this private institution could better serve its students by providing "more money for scholarships and financial aid."

Life

There's a "strong sense of tradition and loyalty" on the Spelman campus, and most students are deeply involved in the community. From service groups to sororities, "there are so many organizations and clubs that you're bound to find one that fits you." There are tons of "opportunities to obtain leadership positions" outside the classroom, and many students are "very involved in campus life." A first-year student details, "In my freshman year already, I've walked in a fashion show, I was crowned Miss Glee Club, I write for the campus newspaper, and I play on the softball team." There's a constant buzz of activity on campus, and "informational forums, career fairs, college fairs, performances, and sporting events are at the forefront of everyone's campus life." Socially, "Greek Life is quite important at Spelman College, but isn't a must." Even if you don't join a sorority, "there are a lot of social events on campus," and two other historically black colleges, Clark Atlanta and Morehouse, "are only inches away." Spelman undergrads say, "The camaraderie between the schools is great," and "joint homecoming with Morehouse is the highlight of the entire year." Off campus, students "go skating, bowling, and to Six Flags Over Georgia, as well as to Atlanta Falcons, Hawks, and Braves [games]." Nearby, Atlantic Station is home to "a major movie theater, shopping, restaurants, and a bowling alley."

Student Body

Spelman College is "full of warm, welcoming, sisterly, and highly educated African American women." A unique environment, "Spelman College offers a chance for African American women to be the majority," and students appreciate being "surrounded and empowered by other young, intelligent, and goal-oriented women like myself." At the same time, "the institution promotes diversity within the student body," and Spelman women "come in all shapes and sizes and from all walks of life, though linked by our African descent. Anyone can find their place here." Confidence and individuality are prized at Spelman, and the typical undergraduate "speaks her mind, wears what she wants, [and] is comfortable in her own skin, yet she has empathy and a strong sense of social justice." Many students "love to do service for the community" and are involved in philanthropic projects around Atlanta. Spelman women are "hardworking and focused on academics." However, most are "excellent at balancing a full course load and an active social life."

FINANCIAL AID: 404-270-5222 • E-MAIL: ADMISS@SPELMAN.EDU • WEBSITE: WWW.SPELMAN.EDU

THE PRINCETON REVIEW SAYS

Admissions

Very important factors considered include: rigor of secondary school record, academic GPA, standardized test scores, application essay, recommendation(s), character/personal qualities. *Important factors considered include:* class rank, extracurricular activities, volunteer work. *Other factors considered include:* talent/ability, alumni/ae relation, geographical residence, work experience, level of applicant's interest. SAT or ACT required; SAT Subject Tests considered if submitted. ACT with or without writing accepted. SAT with or without Essay component accepted. TOEFL required of all international applicants. High school diploma is required and GED is accepted. *Academic units required:* 4 English, 2 math, 2 science, 1 science lab, 2 foreign language, 6 academic electives. *Academic units recommended:* 4 English, 4 math, 3 science, 2 science labs, 3 foreign language, 2 social studies, 1 history, 3 academic electives.

Financial Aid

Students should submit: FAFSA, Institution's own financial aid form, State aid form, Noncustodial PROFILE. Priority filing deadline is 2/1. The Princeton Review suggests that all financial aid forms be submitted as soon as possible after October 1. *Need-based scholarships/grants offered:* Federal Pell, FSEOG, State scholarships/grants, Private scholarships, College/university scholarship or grant aid from institutional funds, United Negro College Fund. *Loan aid offered:* Direct Subsidized Stafford Loans, Direct Unsubsidized Stafford Loans, Direct PLUS loans, Federal Perkins Loans, State Loans. Applicants will be notified of awards on a rolling basis beginning 2/15. Federal Work-Study Program available. Institutional employment available.

The Inside Word

The best way to prepare for admission to Spelman is to pursue a strong, precollege academic curriculum during high school. In 2010, admitted students had an average GPA of 3.65. Students who are particularly interested in Spelman have two early application options: early decision, which is binding, and early notification, which is nonbinding, but allows students to receive a response more quickly.

THE SCHOOL SAYS " . . ."

From the Admissions Office

"As an outstanding Historically Black College for women, Spelman strives for academic excellence in liberal arts education. This predominantly residential private college provides students with an academic climate conducive to the full development of their intellectual and leadership potential. The college is a member of the Atlanta University Center consortium, and Spelman students enjoy the benefits of a small college while having access to the resources of the other three participating institutions. The purpose extends beyond intellectual development and professional career preparation of students. It seeks to develop the total person. The college provides an academic and social environment that strengthens those qualities that enable women to be self-confident as well as culturally and spiritually enriched. This environment attempts to instill in students both an appreciation for the multicultural communities of the world and a sense of responsibility for bringing about positive change in those communities.

"Applicants for are required to submit standardized test scores from an appropriate venue (i.e., ACT, TOEFL, SAT). The highest composite score will be used in admissions decisions. Writing scores from either the SAT or ACT will not be taken into consideration in the admission process."

SELECTIVITY

Admissions Rating	88
# of applicants	5,051
% of applicants accepted	48
% of acceptees attending	23
# offered a place on the wait list	333
% accepting a place on wait list	75
% admitted from wait list	8
# of early decision applicants	134
% accepted early decision	53

FRESHMAN PROFILE

Range SAT Critical Reading	470–570
Range SAT Math	450–550
Range SAT Writing	450–550
Range ACT Composite	20–23
Minimum paper TOEFL	550
Minimum internet-based TOEFL	120
Average HS GPA	3.6
% graduated top 10% of class	23
% graduated top 25% of class	62
% graduated top 50% of class	84

DEADLINES

Early decision	
Deadline	11/1
Notification	12/15
Early action	
Deadline	11/15
Notification	12/31
Regular	
Deadline	2/1
Notification	4/1
Nonfall registration?	Yes

APPLICANTS ALSO LOOK AT AND OFTEN PREFER
Georgia Institute of Technology

AND SOMETIMES PREFER
Howard University; Hampton University

FINANCIAL FACTS

Financial Aid Rating	75
Annual tuition	$22,827
Room and board	$12,363
Required fees	$3,561
Books and supplies	$2,000
Average frosh need-based scholarship	$11,056
Average UG need-based scholarship	$12,276
% needy frosh rec. need-based scholarship or grant aid	85
% needy UG rec. need-based scholarship or grant aid	80
% needy frosh rec. non-need-based scholarship or grant aid	2
% needy UG rec. non-need-based scholarship or grant aid	3
% needy frosh rec. need-based self-help aid	93
% needy UG rec. need-based self-help aid	93
% frosh rec. any financial aid	84
% UG rec. any financial aid	90
% UG borrow to pay for school	77
Average cumulative indebtedness	$32,550
% frosh need fully met	8
% ugrads need fully met	10
Average % of frosh need met	35
Average % of ugrad need met	42

ST. BONAVENTURE UNIVERSITY

3261 WEST STATE ROAD, BONAVENTURE, NY 14778 • ADMISSIONS: 716-375-2400 • FAX: 716-375-4005

STUDENTS SAY "..."

Academics

Uniting a liberal arts education with "Franciscan values," St. Bonaventure University is a small Catholic school that succeeds in "shaping its students into well-rounded, intelligent, and good people." Many students choose St. Bonaventure for its "nationally recognized journalism program" or for one of several prestigious "dual-admissions programs with medical, dental, physical therapy, and pharmacy schools" in the region. No matter what their major, undergrads must complete the Clare College curriculum, which provides an "overall liberal arts education" mixed with religion and philosophy. While students are encouraged to "become extraordinary" and ethics are woven into the curriculum, "religion is by no means forced on you," despite the college's Catholic heritage. Within major departments, "classes are no larger than thirty students per classroom" and "professors are always available if you need help." Talented instructors "make class both fun and informative," and most "do a good job at engaging the class and promoting discussion" between students. "The school is very focused on making successful graduates, and not just in the classroom"; therefore, the curriculum "puts a huge emphasis on real-world experience in a student's field, whether it is journalism, business, or education." Students are further benefited by the school's "amazing alumni network" in and around New York State. While engaging and worthwhile, "academics are serious, no matter your major." However, "a steady effort will get you good grades" in most Bonaventure classes, and students appreciate the fact that "the school isn't super-competitive like the Ivy League schools. Students are willing to help each other out, and there's no cutthroat competition for internships or job interviews."

Life

Outgoing and social, students enjoy a classic college lifestyle in the "Bona bubble." "November to March is Bonnies' basketball season," and attending games is a universally popular pastime. There's also an active intramural sports program, and many students "love going to the fitness center on campus" to work out or take classes. "Student involvement in the radio station is huge," and many claim, "WSBU is the best college radio station in the country." Because the school is located in upstate New York, "it is ridiculously snowy" in the winter months and there's little to do in surrounding Olean, a "very, very small town." "People drink, snowboard, or leave for Buffalo." On campus, "nearly everyone parties every Friday and Saturday." A student elaborates, "Occasionally people will go to the movies or order in and have a quiet night in the dorm, but parties are definitely the big plans on the weekend." At the same time, "there are options for people who do not want to party and drink." In particular, "the Campus Activities Board always has something going on." By the time they graduate, most Bonas share "a lifetime bond forged over beer, basketball, and the worst weather ever."

Student Body

St. Bonaventure students describe their classmates as "hardworking, religious, fun-loving, outgoing, involved in many activities, friendly, and accepting." "Everyone loves sports, as evidenced by the huge intramural program," and "nearly all students love to party." Demographically similar, most undergraduates are "white and from the tristate area." However, the "student body is becoming increasingly diverse" and currently includes students "from all different age groups and backgrounds." Despite the school's religious affiliation, "not everyone is Catholic," and politically speaking, "there are some diehard conservatives, but most people are pretty open-minded." When it comes to social groups, you'll meet plenty of East Coast preppies, but also "edgy kids who work at the campus radio station and listen to underground music." With extracurricular activities catering to a wide range of interests, "it's easy to make friends and find a good fit" at St. Bonaventure. There are some cliques; however, most "people tend to branch out of their comfort zone" to make friends.

FINANCIAL AID: 800-462-5050 • E-MAIL: ADMISSIONS@SBU.EDU • WEBSITE: WWW.SBU.EDU

THE PRINCETON REVIEW SAYS

Admissions

Very important factors considered include: rigor of secondary school record, academic GPA, recommendation(s), character/personal qualities. *Important factors considered include:* standardized test scores, application essay, extracurricular activities, talent/ability, volunteer work, work experience, level of applicant's interest. *Other factors considered include:* class rank, interview, first generation, alumni/ae relation, geographical residence, state residency. SAT or ACT required. ACT with or without writing accepted. TOEFL required of all international applicants. High school diploma is required and GED is accepted. *Academic units recommended:* 4 English, 3 math, 3 science, 3 science labs, 2 foreign language, 4 social studies.

Financial Aid

Students should submit: FAFSA, State aid form. Priority filing deadline is 2/15. The Princeton Review suggests that all financial aid forms be submitted as soon as possible after October 1. *Need-based scholarships/grants offered:* Federal Pell, FSEOG, State scholarships/grants, Private scholarships, College/university scholarship or grant aid from institutional funds. *Loan aid offered:* Direct Subsidized Stafford Loans, Direct Unsubsidized Stafford Loans, Direct PLUS loans, Federal Perkins Loans. Applicants will be notified of awards on a rolling basis beginning 3/1. Federal Work-Study Program available. Institutional employment available.

The Inside Word

There's no admissions formula at St. Bonaventure. Here, prospective students are evaluated individually and accepted based on their capacity for success in college. Though St. Bonaventure recommends that applicants submit academic transcripts, standardized test scores, recommendations, and a personal essay, the admissions committee will consider any other supporting materials that prove a student's overall eligibility for admission. St. Bonaventure has a rolling admissions program, so applications are reviewed as soon as they arrive at the admissions office.

THE SCHOOL SAYS ". . ."

From the Admissions Office

"The St. Bonaventure University family has been imparting an extraordinary Franciscan tradition to men and women of a rich diversity of backgrounds for more than 150 years. This tradition encourages all who become a part of it to face the world confidently, respect the earthly environment, and work for productive change in the world. Every student participates in community service, and many make it their primary co-curricular activity. The charm of our campus and the inspirational beauty of the surrounding hills provide a special place where growth in learning and living is abundantly realized. St. Bonaventure establishes pathways to internships, graduate schools and careers through its innovate Career and Professional Readiness Center, which engages students from the time they step onto campus. The Richter Recreation Center provides all students with state-of-the-art facilities for athletics and wellness. As a student at one of the smallest Division I schools in the country, you get the benefits of big-time sports along with those of a small, student-centered university. St. Bonaventure is a member of the Atlantic 10.

"Academics at St. Bonaventure are challenging. Small classes and personalized attention encourage individual growth and development. St. Bonaventure's nationally known schools of Arts and Sciences, Business, Journalism & Mass Communication, and Education offers more than forty-five majors. The School of Graduate Studies also offers several programs leading to the master's degree.

"Applicants can submit SAT or ACT scores. The biology Subject Test is required only for students applying to one of our many dual-degree medical programs."

SELECTIVITY

Admissions Rating	80
# of applicants	2,985
% of applicants accepted	66
% of acceptees attending	20

FRESHMAN PROFILE

Range SAT Critical Reading	460–580
Range SAT Math	470–590
Range SAT Writing	445–550
Range ACT Composite	21–27
Minimum paper TOEFL	550
Average HS GPA	3.4
% graduated top 10% of class	19
% graduated top 25% of class	47
% graduated top 50% of class	74

DEADLINES

Regular	
Priority	2/15
Deadline	7/1
Nonfall registration?	Yes

APPLICANTS ALSO LOOK AT AND RARELY PREFER

Syracuse University

FINANCIAL FACTS

Financial Aid Rating	85
Annual tuition	$30,424
Room and board	$11,128
Required fees	$965
Books and supplies	$800
Average frosh need-based scholarship	$20,524
Average UG need-based scholarship	$18,899
% needy frosh rec. need-based scholarship or grant aid	100
% needy UG rec. need-based scholarship or grant aid	100
% needy frosh rec. non-need-based scholarship or grant aid	94
% needy UG rec. non-need-based scholarship or grant aid	94
% needy frosh rec. need-based self-help aid	75
% needy UG rec. need-based self-help aid	79
% frosh rec. any financial aid	99
% UG rec. any financial aid	97
% frosh need fully met	20
% ugrads need fully met	19
Average % of frosh need met	85
Average % of ugrad need met	86

ST. JOHN'S COLLEGE (MD)

60 COLLEGE AVE., ANNAPOLIS, MD 21401 • ADMISSIONS: 410-626-2522 • FAX: 410-269-7916

STUDENTS SAY "..."

Academics

St. John's College is a "one of a kind" institution, which "teaches its students how to think for themselves" through a series of rigorous, discussion-based seminars. Here, every student follows the same academic curriculum, which consists entirely of "reading and discussing the great books of Western civilization." Students study "math, science, philosophy, language, history, and literature," and then, through in-class discussion, are "encouraged to question everything, develop their own logical conclusions, and understand Western thought starting at the basics." The school's "brilliant" professors (known as tutors in St. John's parlance) gently oversee class discussions, though they're "more like moderators" in that they "do not lecture or 'teach' in the traditional sense." Tutors always "treat the students as equals," and "outside of class, they are available and friendly." A current undergrad relates, "The fact that tutors are always available (for lunch, coffee, or just to chat with a student) is wonderful. I have had many delightful discussions with tutors outside of class on topics ranging from Baudelaire to quantum mechanics." With tons of assigned reading and provoking in-class debates, the curriculum is "difficult and taxing, yet supremely rewarding." Tutors "don't cut you slack if you don't deserve it," and most "have high expectations" for their students throughout the semester, which can be frustrating for those accustomed to receiving top marks. "Work is sometimes stressful, and the material is often difficult," but students reassure us that "there is always someone to work through it with you, and you can always ask for help."

Life

There's no strict division between study and social life at St. John's. "Discussions from in class spill out into the quad." While most Johnnies say their school is sublime, they also warn that, "If you don't like endlessly talking about books, you'll feel oppressed by the social scene at St. John's." While "school is intense and exhausting," students "rarely differentiate between schoolwork and lives outside of class." On this quirky campus, "fun can be translating Greek or it can be taking a nap; it can be playing intramurals or drinking a beer and watching 'les sportifs' run around; it can be making music or researching Appalachian folk songs." For a lighter evening, students attend "school-run dance parties" or get together for "hard liquor, film noir, classical books, cigarettes, and being off on an adventure." "Impromptu trips off campus are frequent," and students head to Annapolis for "sailing, watching tourists, bowling, [or] ice skating." In addition, "many students participate in the excellent intramural sports program," which includes "soccer, football, Ultimate Frisbee, basketball, croquet, crew, fencing, aikido, boxing, and more." Social dance is also remarkably popular, and there are "swing dancing parties on a regular basis."

Student Body

The unusual St. John's curriculum tends to attract students who are "intellectual, very thoughtful, and inclined to discuss Aristotle, Hobbes, or Tolstoy at the dinner table." Talkative and analytical, St. John's students are "always down for a good conversation, whether one-on-one or in a group, whether the topic is personal or impersonal." "Students come from across the country and around the world, from all religious, political, and economic backgrounds," though there's a noticeable "proliferation of East Coast preppies and hipsters." "The diversity of personalities is astounding," and, exclusivity is minimized on this "friendly" campus. "Because the school is so small, and because of the universal curriculum, by your senior year you have a pretty strong bond with your entire class." Activists and pop culture junkies take note: "If you're interested in current events, or pretty much anything that happened after, say, 1925, it can sometimes be hard to find people who know what you're talking about."

FINANCIAL AID: 410-626-2502 • E-MAIL: ANNAPOLIS.ADMISSIONS@SJC.EDU • WEBSITE: WWW.SJC.EDU

THE PRINCETON REVIEW SAYS

Admissions

Very important factors considered include: application essay. *Important factors considered include:* rigor of secondary school record, recommendation(s), character/personal qualities, level of applicant's interest. *Other factors considered include:* class rank, academic GPA, standardized test scores, interview, extracurricular activities, talent/ability, first generation, alumni/ae relation, geographical residence, racial/ethnic status, volunteer work, work experience. SAT or ACT required for some. ACT with or without writing accepted. SAT with or without Essay component accepted. TOEFL required of all international applicants. High school diploma is required and GED is accepted. *Academic units recommended:* 4 English, 3 science, 3 social studies.

Financial Aid

Students should submit: FAFSA, State aid form. Priority filing deadline is 2/15. The Princeton Review suggests that all financial aid forms be submitted as soon as possible after October 1. *Need-based scholarships/grants offered:* Federal Pell, FSEOG, State scholarships/grants, Private scholarships, College/university scholarship or grant aid from institutional funds. *Loan aid offered:* Direct Subsidized Stafford Loans, Direct Unsubsidized Stafford Loans, Direct PLUS loans, Federal Perkins Loans, College/university loans from institutional funds. Applicants will be notified of awards on a rolling basis beginning 12/15. Federal Work-Study Program available. Institutional employment available.

The Inside Word

St. John's is a unique environment, best suited to students of a quirky yet serious intellectual predilection. To test the waters before you jump in, consider taking a campus tour or even sitting in on an active tutorial session with students. You can also send your questions about the school to a current student through the St. John's website. Each applicant is evaluated individually for potential success in the program. Among application materials, SAT/ACT scores are an optional component.

THE SCHOOL SAYS "..."

From the Admissions Office

"St. John's College offers a unique and transformative education for the intellectually adventurous. Across a wide-ranging, interdisciplinary curriculum, students read and discuss foundational works of Western philosophy, literature, history, political science, theology, economics, music, mathematics, and the laboratory sciences. Classes are small (fourteen to twenty students) and conducted as conversational seminars in which students assume a leadership role. The college's coeducational community, without religious affiliation, takes an open-minded approach to ideas of all kinds. St. John's students are asked to reach their own conclusions about questions that have been the subject of human inquiry from prehistory yet still have great relevance to contemporary problems.

"All students at St. John's College earn a B.A. in Liberal Arts. There are no majors and no departments; the four-year curriculum is a unified, all-required whole. Each year's work lays the foundation for the next. The Program's structure, rather than making distinctions between 'sciences' and 'humanities,' encourages students to see the interrelatedness of modes of human thought.

"In 1964, a second campus was opened in historic Santa Fe, a cultural center and the capital of New Mexico. With a shared curriculum, students can alternate their studies between Annapolis and Santa Fe without sacrificing any time toward graduation, quality of instruction, or benefit of the curriculum. More than a third of students spend at least a year on both campuses. The college also offers a Summer Academy for rising high school juniors and seniors, a great way to try this remarkable academic experience on for size."

SELECTIVITY

Admissions Rating	87
# of applicants	332
% of applicants accepted	78
% of acceptees attending	40

FRESHMAN PROFILE

Range SAT Critical Reading	620–740
Range SAT Math	590–700
Range SAT Writing	600–700
Range ACT Composite	24–30
% graduated top 10% of class	37
% graduated top 25% of class	49
% graduated top 50% of class	81

DEADLINES

Early action	
Deadline	11/15
Notification	12/15
Regular	
Priority	11/15
Nonfall registration?	No

APPLICANTS ALSO LOOK AT AND SOMETIMES PREFER

Reed College; University of Chicago; American University; Amherst College; Boston University; The College of William & Mary; Columbia University; Cornell University; Dartmouth College; Georgetown University; Hampshire College; Harvard College; New York University; Oberlin College; Princeton University; Swarthmore College; University of Maryland–College Park; University of Pennsylvania; University of Virginia; Yale University

FINANCIAL FACTS

Financial Aid Rating	84
Annual tuition	$48,544
Room and board	$11,598
Required fees	$450
Books and supplies	$630
Average frosh need-based scholarship	$31,235
Average UG need-based scholarship	$32,347
% needy frosh rec. need-based scholarship or grant aid	99
% needy UG rec. need-based scholarship or grant aid	98
% needy frosh rec. non-need-based scholarship or grant aid	28
% needy UG rec. non-need-based scholarship or grant aid	18
% needy frosh rec. need-based self-help aid	96
% needy UG rec. need-based self-help aid	96
% frosh rec. any financial aid	82
% UG rec. any financial aid	71
% UG borrow to pay for school	74
Average cumulative indebtedness	$34,212
% frosh need fully met	32
% ugrads need fully met	23
Average % of frosh need met	85
Average % of ugrad need met	82

ST. JOHN'S COLLEGE (NM)

1160 CAMINO CRUZ BLANCA, SANTA FE, NM 87505 • ADMISSIONS: 505-984-6060 • FAX: 505-984-6162

STUDENTS SAY "..."

Academics

At St. John's College in Santa Fe, students read and explore a common body of "great books"—including many of the most important books in history—in close partnership with their classmates and teachers. Every professor "must teach (learn) Euclid, Plato, and Darwin, whether he or she has a Ph.D. in mathematics, classics, or biology." This common curriculum and dedication to the liberal arts means that "students are respected for what they can bring, and need never feel self-conscious about whether they're 'smart enough.'" Everywhere you look, there is a "commitment, sincerity, and passion for learning of the community and the faculty." This truly is an academic community that sincerely loves "the journey in its pursuit of knowledge, not simply the destination." The "liberation of the mind" at SJC comes primarily by means of the Socratic Method. SJC does not have professors, but tutors, who are there not to lecture, but to "help lead the class through the curriculum." The tutors are "very different in personality," but also "very knowledgeable and excitable about what we do." As experienced academics, they are "skillful when it comes to managing the classroom discussions and helping students articulate their thoughts" and are "truly open-minded and give everyone a chance to participate." "They really care about their students and treat us as peers in the classroom since they consider themselves also to be constantly learning." "Everyone shares fundamental values of how to treat others in the classroom," says a student. The greatest asset of SJC is the community; with everyone on board this nontraditional learning train, it's hard not to be at your best. "You're thinking nonstop at SJC," says a student. Though the self-selecting student body pretty much ensures success, students can choose how connected they wish to be to the rest of the school. "You can go four years without having an interaction with the president of the college, or you can see him every Tuesday at the Foreign Relations study group," says a student.

Life

At St. John's, "you have to work intensely and relax intensely. Life is more distilled, here." "Is it hard work?" asks a student. "Yes and no. Does staying up until 1:00 A.M. reading Shakespeare or Darwin sound like work?" Santa Fe is "stunning," and the proximity of the mountains (for hiking and skiing) is more than welcome. Though each week is "epic" in its schoolwork, there are dozens of clubs and activities to take part in, from "dance (beginners always welcome) to search and rescue to astronomy to rock-climbing." If you're artsy, there are many galleries in Santa Fe, or "you can stay on campus, join a study group or sports team, or go to the gym." The student government is also responsible for dispersing several thousand dollars to support student clubs annually, so "if you can get signatures to show support, you can probably get funding for snacks or supplies." Many say that food services could have better hours and prices. There are "frequent" field trips to some of the extraordinary places in New Mexico.

Student Body

Most of the 350 undergrads at St. John's are "friendly," "big readers," and "interested in discussions." It's easy to find commonalities, since "you're always able to discuss the program as long as they're the same year or lower." All are here "because we have a genuine interest in the larger questions that are posed in life through academia," and "that's enough for most of us to feel like we're 'fitting in,' however that may be defined." Johnnies are "fascinated with learning in a way different from most schools" and "thrive on epiphanies through the 'great books,' especially ones shared with others."

ST. JOHN'S COLLEGE (NM)

FINANCIAL AID: 505-984-6058 • E-MAIL: ADMISSIONS@MAIL.SJCSF.EDU • WEBSITE: WWW.SJCSF.EDU

THE PRINCETON REVIEW SAYS

Admissions

Very important factors considered include: application essay. *Important factors considered include:* rigor of secondary school record, recommendation(s), character/personal qualities, level of applicant's interest. *Other factors considered include:* class rank, academic GPA, standardized test scores, interview, extracurricular activities, talent/ability, first generation, alumni/ae relation, racial/ethnic status, volunteer work, work experience. SAT or ACT required for some; SAT Subject Tests considered if submitted. ACT with or without writing accepted. SAT with or without Essay component accepted. TOEFL, SAT, or ACT required of all international applicants. High school diploma is required and GED is accepted. *Academic units required:* 3 math, 2 foreign language. *Academic units recommended:* 4 English, 4 math, 3 science, 3 science labs, 4 foreign language, 2 history.

Financial Aid

Students should submit: FAFSA. Priority filing deadline is 3/1. The Princeton Review suggests that all financial aid forms be submitted as soon as possible after October 1. *Need-based scholarships/grants offered:* Federal Pell, FSEOG, State scholarships/grants, Private scholarships, College/university scholarship or grant aid from institutional funds. *Loan aid offered:* Direct Subsidized Stafford Loans, Direct Unsubsidized Stafford Loans, Direct PLUS loans, Federal Perkins Loans, College/university loans from institutional funds. Applicants will be notified of awards on a rolling basis beginning 2/15. Federal Work-Study Program available. Institutional employment available.

The Inside Word

Self-selection drives this admissions process—more than one-half of the entire applicant pool each year indicates that St. John's is their first choice, and half of those admitted send in tuition deposits. Even so, no one in admissions takes things for granted, and neither should any student considering an application. The admissions process is highly personal on both sides of the coin. Only the intellectually curious and highly motivated need apply.

THE SCHOOL SAYS "..."

From the Admissions Office

"Students at St. John's study the Great Books Program, which equally emphasizes literature, language, math, music, science, politics, and philosophy in intimate discussion based classrooms. There is virtually no use of textbooks. Instead of reading about the Theory of Relativity, students read the Theory of Relativity. Grades are not emphasized and quietly reside in the Registrar's Office for the purpose of applying to graduate school. With a robust and well-established internship program, students have infinite options including grad school. Notable alumnus, writer Salvatore Scibona says, 'The gravity of the whole thing would have been laughable if it hadn't been so much fun, and if it hadn't been such a gift to find my tribe.'

"The city of Santa Fe is known internationally for its art and culture, food scene, and endless outdoor activities. Students are also able to transfer to the Annapolis campus to experience both. With small classes that encourage spirited discussions and an equally dynamic student life, students develop their intellect and imagination for which St. John's graduates are known. Indeed, New York Times columnist and bestselling author Frank Bruni has described St. John's as a 'fascinating, fierce, one of a kind institution.'"

SELECTIVITY

Admissions Rating	87
# of applicants	177
% of applicants accepted	81
% of acceptees attending	53
# offered a place on the wait list	0

FRESHMAN PROFILE

Range SAT Critical Reading	600–730
Range SAT Math	560–690
Range SAT Writing	570–680
Range ACT Composite	26–31
Minimum paper TOEFL	550
Minimum internet-based TOEFL	79
% graduated top 10% of class	26
% graduated top 25% of class	57
% graduated top 50% of class	88

DEADLINES

Early action	
Deadline	11/15
Notification	12/15
Regular	
Priority	11/15
Nonfall registration?	Yes

APPLICANTS ALSO LOOK AT AND OFTEN PREFER

Smith College; Agnes Scott College; New College of Florida; Reed College; Kenyon College; Southwestern University

AND SOMETIMES PREFER

Arizona State University; Hampshire College; Macalester College

AND RARELY PREFER

Franklin and Marshall College; Grinnell College; Mills College; The Evergreen State College; University of Colorado Boulder; Wellesley College

FINANCIAL FACTS

Financial Aid Rating	93
Annual tuition	$38,630
Room and board	$8,440
Required fees	$830
Books and supplies	$630
Average frosh need-based scholarship	$31,415
Average UG need-based scholarship	$28,805
% needy frosh rec. need-based scholarship or grant aid	100
% needy UG rec. need-based scholarship or grant aid	99
% needy frosh rec. non-need-based scholarship or grant aid	18
% needy UG rec. non-need-based scholarship or grant aid	9
% needy frosh rec. need-based self-help aid	100
% needy UG rec. need-based self-help aid	99
% frosh rec. any financial aid	100
% UG rec. any financial aid	81
% UG borrow to pay for school	76
Average cumulative indebtedness	$26,195
% frosh need fully met	92
% ugrads need fully met	87
Average % of frosh need met	93
Average % of ugrad need met	92

St. John's University

8000 Utopia Parkway, Queens, NY 11439 • Admissions: 718-990-2000 • Fax: 718-990-2096

STUDENTS SAY ". . ."

Academics

St. John's University upholds the Catholic and Vincentian traditions set forth at its founding in 1870. At the main campus located in a residential area of Queens (as well as at the two additional New York City campuses found in Staten Island and Manhattan), students receive "a well-nurtured education that can help one turn into a specialist in whatever field they desire." A wide range of support systems, such as career services, campus ministry, the writing center, and a clinic ensure that "every student has a safe, healthy and challenging academic career" while at St. John's.

Most professors are generous "when it comes to providing help and any aids for you to succeed" and "are here to help you and prepare you for the rest of your life." "Almost all my experiences with professors have been positive. If you are willing to put in the work they are willing to work with you," says one actuarial science major. They are very helpful "in making sure you actually understand the information rather than memorize it and not use it outside the classroom," and "provide guidance with classwork, finding jobs and internships, and more." On top of faculty help, the career services office is "amazing:" "They help you with your résumé, cover letter, [telling] you when there are career fairs, picking graduate schools, [and] finding internships."

Classes are "easy to follow and there are never any surprises from the professors," and most are discussion-based. Students in all majors find that "the workload is not overwhelming and the assignments are helpful and relevant to the subjects." For commuter and non-commuter students alike, the Monday and Thursday afternoon common hour provides a universal time for most social and academic clubs meet up.

Life

From athletics to coffeehouse shows and cultural events, there are "multiple things to do on campus every day." Many people take advantage of the gym and the classes it offers, or "hang out on the Great Lawn and play frisbee and other similar games." Students "sometimes have to wait a long time for their next class" so the school provides "too many extracurricular activities to count" to help time pass. There are clubs to represent "almost every racial, religious and interest group" and "there's never a day where there isn't anything to do." Basketball season is a huge rally booster (the team plays some games at Madison Square Garden), and St. John's also hosts "many great events on off days such as family day, picnics, barbecues and more." There are a fair number of commuters, and those who live on campus often venture into the city to "enjoy the fast pace and vibrant life of New York City" when all the commuters are away on weekends. Between "the spring carnival, the free commuter breakfasts, reduced prices on movie tickets, [and] Broadway shows, St. John's wants their students' experience to be unforgettable."

Student Body

This "very diverse" group has students from all over the country and world (it "falls perfectly into place with the diversity of the New York City area as a whole"), which "exposes everyone to new ideas and helps us better define where we stand on our own views." "There's an atmosphere of the core staples of the university: Catholic, Vincentian, and metropolitan," says a student. People speak of the sense of unity that comes from everyone being "more than happy to be here, excited to learn, and participate in campus activities." There is a lot of collaboration when it comes to student organizations, and students also "have great initiative when it comes to getting their voice heard."

FINANCIAL AID: 718-990-2000 • E-MAIL: ADMHELP@STJOHNS.EDU • WEBSITE: WWW.STJOHNS.EDU

THE PRINCETON REVIEW SAYS

Admissions

Very important factors considered include: academic GPA, standardized test scores. *Important factors considered include:* rigor of secondary school record. *Other factors considered include:* class rank, application essay, recommendation(s), extracurricular activities, talent/ability, character/personal qualities, first generation, alumni/ae relation, geographical residence, state residency, volunteer work, work experience. SAT or ACT required; SAT Subject Tests considered if submitted. ACT with or without writing accepted. TOEFL required of all international applicants. High school diploma is required and GED is accepted. *Academic units required:* 4 English, 1 science, 1 history. *Academic units recommended:* 4 English, 1 science, 1 history.

Financial Aid

Students should submit: FAFSA. Priority filing deadline is 2/1. The Princeton Review suggests that all financial aid forms be submitted as soon as possible after October 1. *Need-based scholarships/grants offered:* Federal Pell, FSEOG, State scholarships/grants, Private scholarships, College/university scholarship or grant aid from institutional funds. *Loan aid offered:* Direct Subsidized Stafford Loans, Direct Unsubsidized Stafford Loans, Direct PLUS loans, Federal Perkins Loans. Applicants will be notified of awards on a rolling basis beginning 3/1. Federal Work-Study Program available. Institutional employment available.

The Inside Word

The admissions process at St. John's doesn't include many surprises. High school grades and standardized test scores are undoubtedly the most important factors, though volunteer work and extracurricular activities are also highly regarded. The university doesn't consider religious affiliation at all when making admissions decisions; there are students of every religious stripe here.

THE SCHOOL SAYS "..."

From the Admissions Office

"Founded in 1870, St. John's is a Catholic and Vincentian university that emphasizes academic excellence without bounds, providing talented students with an outstanding education that builds upon their abilities and aspirations. Since 2012, twenty-eight students won Fulbright Awards. Undergraduates also received prestigious awards including a Marshall Fellowship to pursue advanced study at the University of London. On the playing courts and fields, St. John's is New York City's team—with seventeen men's and women's athletic teams.

"Faith, service, and success are central to a St. John's education. This year, students nearly 100,000 service hours in 125 city agencies and at eleven sites on four continents. St. John's is among the few universities admitted with distinction to the President's Higher Education Community Service Honor Roll.

"St. John's offers more than 100 associate, bachelor's, master's, and doctoral degrees in the arts, business, education, law, pharmacy, and the natural and applied sciences. More than 90 percent of our professors hold a Ph.D. or comparable terminal degree in their field. Our seventeen-to-one student/faculty ratio ensures personal attention.

"Our students enjoy a global experience that starts at our three residential New York City campuses—in Queens, Staten Island, and Manhattan; an international campus in Rome, Italy; and study abroad locations in Paris, France, and Seville, Spain, and around the world. Enhancing the University's cosmopolitan character, students come from nearly fifty states and close to 120 foreign countries—all of them benefiting from the University's network of 170,000 alumni."

SELECTIVITY

Admissions Rating	82
# of applicants	36,105
% of applicants accepted	65
% of acceptees attending	14
# offered a place on the wait list	1,624

FRESHMAN PROFILE

Range SAT Critical Reading	480–580
Range SAT Math	480–600
Range ACT Composite	22–27
Minimum paper TOEFL	550
Minimum internet-based TOEFL	80
Average HS GPA	3.5
% graduated top 10% of class	21
% graduated top 25% of class	48
% graduated top 50% of class	81

DEADLINES

Regular	
Nonfall registration?	Yes

APPLICANTS ALSO LOOK AT AND OFTEN PREFER

State University of New York–Stony Brook University; City University of New York—Baruch College

AND SOMETIMES PREFER

Rutgers, The State University of New Jersey–New Brunswick; Fordham University

AND RARELY PREFER

St. Bonaventure University; Siena College

FINANCIAL FACTS

Financial Aid Rating	81
Annual tuition	$37,870
Room and board	$16,390
Required fees	$810
Books and supplies	$610
Average frosh need-based scholarship	$9,231
Average UG need-based scholarship	$10,683
% needy frosh rec. need-based scholarship or grant aid	80
% needy UG rec. need-based scholarship or grant aid	83
% needy frosh rec. non-need-based scholarship or grant aid	0
% needy UG rec. non-need-based scholarship or grant aid	97
% needy frosh rec. need-based self-help aid	80
% needy UG rec. need-based self-help aid	84
% frosh rec. any financial aid	98
% UG rec. any financial aid	96
% UG borrow to pay for school	75
Average cumulative indebtedness	$33,179
% frosh need fully met	13
% ugrads need fully met	12
Average % of frosh need met	86
Average % of ugrad need met	74

ST. LAWRENCE UNIVERSITY

PAYSON HALL, CANTON, NY 13617 • ADMISSIONS: 315-229-5261 • FAX: 315-229-5818

CAMPUS LIFE

Quality of Life Rating	91
Fire Safety Rating	81
Green Rating	91
Type of school	Private
Affiliation	No Affiliation
Environment	Village

STUDENTS

Total undergrad enrollment	2,435
% male/female	45/55
% from out of state	59
% frosh from public high school	69
% frosh live on campus	100
% ugrads live on campus	99
# of fraternities (% ugrad men join)	2 (10)
# of sororities (% ugrad women join)	4 (15)
% African American	3
% Asian	2
% Caucasian	79
% Hispanic	4
% Native American	<1
% Pacific Islander	<1
% Two or more races	2
% Race and/or ethnicity unknown	<1
% international	9
# of countries represented	62

SURVEY SAYS...

Students are happy
Lab facilities are great
Great library
Career services are great
Internships are widely available
School is well run
Great financial aid
Students environmentally aware
Great food on campus
Easy to get around campus
Recreation facilities are great
Lots of beer drinking
Hard liquor is popular
Everyone loves the Saints
Campus newspaper is popular
Alumni active on campus

ACADEMICS

Academic Rating	92
% students returning for sophomore year	89
% students graduating within 4 years	82
% students graduating within 6 years	87
Calendar	Semester
Student/faculty ratio	11:1
Profs interesting rating	93
Profs accessible rating	90

Most classes have 10–19 students.
Most lab/discussion sessions have 10–19 students.

MOST POPULAR MAJORS

Economics; Political Science and Government; Psychology

STUDENTS SAY "..."

Academics

Located in tiny Canton, New York, near the Canadian border, St. Lawrence University is a "warm and welcoming" little school with myriad merit scholarships, great study abroad programs, and a reputation as "the snowiest place where you will have the time of your life and meet amazing people." A low student-faculty ratio and strong alumni network really ice the cake on this "extremely tight-knit community" that carries on a "long lasting tradition of Laurentian pride, academic rigor and sustainability efforts."

The "very intelligent professors" are always available to give insight and help, and "aim to engage students in every way, even if the students seem uninterested." "They never cease to impress!" Faculty does a good job of tying in a lot of different themes, so "eventually all of your classes intersect." "They would rather we internalize the information and material of the class well than get through the syllabus on time, leading to more in depth learning," says a student.

St. Lawrence encourages students to participate in all aspects of their education, and there is great ability "for students to make an impact and have meaningful change on the way operations occur on campus." The "projects/research being done surround you" and St. Lawrence "emphasizes students taking initiative and holding leadership positions for various clubs," providing "everything one can need in their four years of college on a camp in the middle of nowhere." "The alumni still love it even fifty years after they graduate, so there must be a certain charm to it (and there is)!" surmises up a student.

Life

St. Lawrence is a school that "manages to find fun in everything despite being in 'the middle of nowhere.'" The athletic facilities are "top notch," work opportunities abound, and there is plenty of "accessibility to funds for student activities." "Free laundry" is a surprisingly big draw, as are free weekend movies, as well as the community building aspect of the [living-learning] First-Year Program, which "will make you friends for life." Being in such a small town means there are lots of activities that take place at school, so "if you are bored you are not paying attention to what is happening on campus."

Theme houses allow students to live with others that share a common interest or goal, which can be an academic area, specific issue, or hobby or skill. The security on this "gorgeous" campus is "amazing" and "does safe walks for anyone who feels unsafe on campus alone." This is a very outdoorsy bunch, and most people love to ski, rock climb, canoe, and hike (all of which is easily accessible through the Adirondacks). People "will always drink for fun on the weekends," but can also be found "at sports games, watching movies at the student center, or hanging out on our quad." Hockey games are largely attended, and there are "comedians, bands, movies, [and] petting zoos brought to campus every weekend."

Student Body

Preppy is the done thing here, with "basically anything in khakis and a button down for guys and Ralph Lauren and Hunter boots or summer dresses for girls," and the majority of people hail from "just outside of Boston, New York, Connecticut, or Vermont." The positive atmosphere of the student body is "palpable," from "the smiles to the school spirit, to the passion for everything that students do." It's quickly apparent "how happy everyone is to be here," and there's "a sense of love and respect for our school" all around.

ST. LAWRENCE UNIVERSITY

FINANCIAL AID: 315-229-5265 • E-MAIL: ADMISSIONS@STLAWU.EDU • WEBSITE: WWW.STLAWU.EDU

THE PRINCETON REVIEW SAYS

Admissions

Very important factors considered include: rigor of secondary school record, academic GPA, application essay, recommendation(s), character/personal qualities. *Important factors considered include:* class rank, interview, extracurricular activities, racial/ethnic status. *Other factors considered include:* standardized test scores, talent/ability, first generation, alumni/ae relation, geographical residence, volunteer work, work experience, level of applicant's interest. SAT or ACT considered if submitted; SAT Subject Tests considered if submitted. ACT with or without writing accepted. SAT with or without Essay component accepted. TOEFL required of all international applicants. High school diploma is required and GED is accepted. *Academic units recommended:* 4 English, 4 math, 4 science, 4 foreign language, 2 social studies, 2 history.

Financial Aid

Students should submit: FAFSA, Noncustodial PROFILE. Regular filing deadline is 2/1. The Princeton Review suggests that all financial aid forms be submitted as soon as possible after October 1. *Need-based scholarships/grants offered:* Federal Pell, FSEOG, State scholarships/grants, Private scholarships, College/university scholarship or grant aid from institutional funds. *Loan aid offered:* Direct Subsidized Stafford Loans, Direct Unsubsidized Stafford Loans, Direct PLUS loans, Federal Perkins Loans, College/university loans from institutional funds. Applicants will be notified of awards on or about 3/30. Federal Work-Study Program available. Institutional employment available.

The Inside Word

At St. Lawrence, you're not required to submit scores from the SAT or the ACT, but that means your high school transcript and teacher recommendations better be stellar. If you're a homeschooled student or an international student seeking financial aid, it's probably a good idea to submit some standardized test scores. Good scores help since scholarship selection is based on overall academic profile.

THE SCHOOL SAYS "..."

From the Admissions Office

"Situated in an ideal location, St. Lawrence University is a diverse liberal arts learning community of talented students and inspiring faculty, guided by tradition and focused on the future. We are a vibrant, collaborative community of learners who value thought and action. Students tap into their full potential, as they embrace the nature environment, engage with global challenges, and experience the relevance and adventure of a liberal arts education in a complex and changing world.

"Our faculty has chosen St. Lawrence intentionally because they know there is institutional commitment to support great teaching. They are dedicated to making each student's experience challenging and rewarding. Our graduates make up one of the strongest networks of support among any alumni body and are ready, willing, and able to connect with students and help them succeed.

"Every student has diverse opportunities to connect classroom theory to hands-on, real-world experience through internships, international study, and community projects. Faculty know their students and act as their mentors, guides, and colleagues on their journeys. Creative degree paths allow students to discover new dimensions of themselves and prepare for lives of personal fulfillment and career success.

"Our location on the edge of the Adirondack Mountains gives us easy access to enviable outdoor spaces to learn and to practice environmental sustainability and to participate year-round in all things outdoors. You must visit and meet our students to get a sense of the energy on campus to begin to understand just what makes St. Lawrence University a place our students, faculty, staff, and alumni call home."

SELECTIVITY
Admissions Rating	92
# of applicants	5,876
% of applicants accepted	46
% of acceptees attending	50
# offered a place on the wait list	73
% accepting a place on wait list	18
% admitted from wait list	0
# of early decision applicants	251
% accepted early decision	90

FRESHMAN PROFILE
Range SAT Critical Reading	550–650
Range SAT Math	550–660
Range SAT Writing	540–640
Range ACT Composite	26–30
Minimum paper TOEFL	600
Minimum internet-based TOEFL	82
Average HS GPA	3.6
% graduated top 10% of class	45
% graduated top 25% of class	77
% graduated top 50% of class	95

DEADLINES
Early decision Deadline	11/1
Regular Deadline	2/1
Nonfall registration?	Yes

APPLICANTS ALSO LOOK AT AND OFTEN PREFER
Middlebury College; Williams College; Dartmouth College

AND SOMETIMES PREFER
Bowdoin College; Colby College; Colgate University

AND RARELY PREFER
Ithaca College

FINANCIAL FACTS
Financial Aid Rating	87
Annual tuition	$49,060
Room and board	$12,730
Required fees	$350
Books and supplies	$750
Average frosh need-based scholarship	$37,312
Average UG need-based scholarship	$34,228
% needy frosh rec. need-based scholarship or grant aid	100
% needy UG rec. need-based scholarship or grant aid	100
% needy frosh rec. non-need-based scholarship or grant aid	76
% needy UG rec. non-need-based scholarship or grant aid	72
% needy frosh rec. need-based self-help aid	75
% needy UG rec. need-based self-help aid	79
% frosh rec. any financial aid	100
% UG rec. any financial aid	96
% UG borrow to pay for school	60
Average cumulative indebtedness	$26,756
% frosh need fully met	28
% ugrads need fully met	26
Average % of frosh need met	87
Average % of ugrad need met	85

ST. MARY'S COLLEGE OF MARYLAND

ADMISSIONS OFFICE, 47645 COLLEGE DRIVE, ST. MARY'S CITY, MD 20686-3001 • ADMISSIONS: 240-895-5000 • FAX: 240-895-5001

CAMPUS LIFE

Quality of Life Rating	89
Fire Safety Rating	88
Green Rating	92
Type of school	Public
Affiliation	No Affiliation
Environment	Rural

STUDENTS

Total undergrad enrollment	1,746
% male/female	43/57
% from out of state	8
% frosh from public high school	75
% frosh live on campus	94
% ugrads live on campus	82
% African American	8
% Asian	3
% Caucasian	73
% Hispanic	8
% Native American	<1
% Pacific Islander	0
% Two or more races	5
% Race and/or ethnicity unknown	3
% international	1
# of countries represented	11

SURVEY SAYS...

Students politically aware
Students are happy
Students are friendly
Students aren't religious
Students environmentally aware
Active minority support groups

ACADEMICS

Academic Rating	84
% students returning for sophomore year	86
% students graduating within 4 years	70
% students graduating within 6 years	78
Calendar	Semester
Student/faculty ratio	11:1
Profs interesting rating	94
Profs accessible rating	90

Most classes have 10–19 students.
Most lab/discussion sessions have 10–19 students.

MOST POPULAR MAJORS
English; Biology

STUDENTS SAY ". . ."

Academics

St. Mary's College of Maryland, in cozy St. Mary's City, is itself "like a small town in that everyone knows everyone" and "the minute you step on this campus, you're a part of the family." Students boast that the school is "a place to grow as a person and become part of a life long family." Students enjoy classes that are always "challenging but never impossible" taught by professors who "get to know you personally" and "take an interest in your future." One student a describes a favorite professor, saying, "I only took a single class with him, and yet he helped me get a paper for his class published, I talk with him weekly, and he has mentored my sister through difficult academic situations." SMCM professors "are an interesting bunch, not afraid to speak their minds and push students to become involved." Students find that "many professors are extremely good at making classes interesting and at engaging students" through "discussion based" approaches. While SMCM "professors are demanding" and "expect a great deal from students," "they are always willing to help." Professors help students look towards the future with "internships and research opportunities" and "post-graduate plans." Many students cite the relationships they built with faculty as "largest benefit to attending SMCM." They "provided an extensive network" of professional and academic connections, but they also "let students babysit their kids." "When the professors know you by name and care about your personal life and your general well-being," it "fosters an atmosphere of accountability and responsibility" among the student body. "I would feel guilty," one student explains, "if I didn't go to class, didn't read, or didn't compete my work."

Life

Students say "there is a sense of community" at SMCM "and people are extremely friendly" because it is part of "the St. Mary's way." These academically minded "students mostly go to class, study or work during the week," but some may relax from time to time at a "local bar called the Green Door where they are weekday specials." But "without much of a town nearby," students "are kept entertained through the vast selection of clubs available as well as the student organized events." Students stage "cook-offs between houses" on campus and support one another by attending the attending "orchestra, dance club, theater, [and] burlesque" performances, as well as "scientific presentations/lectures." In spring, when the weather is warm, "people enjoy the waterfront and natural landscape around campus." Whether they are admiring "the beauty of the St. Mary's River" from a kayak, "[tanning] on the docs," "taking walks in the woods," or keeping warm next to a bonfire, outdoor activities are popular and "only short walk from the campus center." For others there is nothing better "on a warm day" than "to sit outside at the campus center or on the patio of an academic building with a cup of coffee and a few friends."

Student Body

At SMCM "there are plenty of students who are super involved, and almost everyone is very intelligent and well spoken." Students "value difference" and try to "foster relationships based on mutual respect," so it is no wonder that many describe themselves as having an eclectic group of friends. "It's hard not to have a diverse friend group here," one religious studies major tells us, "and that is greatly comforting." Students feel free to be themselves, without pretence, because, as another student explains, "This is a place that is full of people who just want to be accepted, and therefore accept others." As a result, SMCM students are "kind, and even a little goofy! We like to keep St. Mary's weird." "There is no one group someone belongs to" at St. Mary's "because it seems like everyone belongs together." One biology major sums up the student body, saying, "I am so happy that I am able to walk about this campus knowing that every person I walk past could be a conversation away from being a friend of mine."

ST. MARY'S COLLEGE OF MARYLAND

FINANCIAL AID: 240-895-3000 • E-MAIL: ADMISSIONS@SMCM.EDU • WEBSITE: WWW.SMCM.EDU

THE PRINCETON REVIEW SAYS

Admissions

Very important factors considered include: rigor of secondary school record, academic GPA, standardized test scores, application essay, recommendation(s). *Important factors considered include:* class rank, extracurricular activities, talent/ability, character/personal qualities, volunteer work. *Other factors considered include:* interview, first generation, alumni/ae relation, geographical residence, state residency, racial/ethnic status, work experience, level of applicant's interest. SAT or ACT required; SAT Subject Tests considered if submitted. ACT with or without writing accepted. TOEFL required of all international applicants. High school diploma is required and GED is accepted. *Academic units required:* 4 English, 3 math, 3 science, 2 science labs, 2 social studies, 1 history. *Academic units recommended:* 4 math, 4 foreign language, 3 social studies.

Financial Aid

Students should submit: FAFSA. Regular filing deadline is 2/28. The Princeton Review suggests that all financial aid forms be submitted as soon as possible after October 1. *Need-based scholarships/grants offered:* Federal Pell, FSEOG, State scholarships/grants, Private scholarships, College/university scholarship or grant aid from institutional funds. *Loan aid offered:* Direct Subsidized Stafford Loans, Direct Unsubsidized Stafford Loans, Direct PLUS Loans. Applicants will be notified of awards on or about 3/15. Federal Work-Study Program available. Institutional employment available.

The Inside Word

As Maryland's public honors college, gaining admissions to St. Mary's is competitive. Admissions officers here really strive to get to know the applicant as an individual, not just a set of numbers on a paper. St. Mary's accepts the Common App, but make sure to take note of the unique essay on the Questions page. While academic rigor definitely holds the most weight, admissions officers thoroughly evaluate your essays, recommendations, and extracurricular activities as well.

THE SCHOOL SAYS "..."

From the Admissions Office

"St. Mary's College of Maryland occupies a distinctive niche and represents a real value in American higher education. It is a public college, dedicated to the ideal of affordable, accessible education and committed to quality teaching and excellent programs for undergraduate students. St. Mary's is designated by law the state of Maryland's 'public honors college,' one of only two public colleges in the nation to hold that distinction. It is this mix of honors and affordability that makes St. Mary's an education for the twenty-first century."

SELECTIVITY

Admissions Rating	79
# of applicants	1,675
% of applicants accepted	79
% of acceptees attending	30

FRESHMAN PROFILE

Range SAT Critical Reading	530–640
Range SAT Math	500–620
Range SAT Writing	510–630
Range ACT Composite	22–28
Minimum paper TOEFL	550
Minimum internet-based TOEFL	90
Average HS GPA	3.36

DEADLINES

Early action	
Deadline	11/15
Notification	12/20
Regular	
Priority	11/1
Deadline	2/15
Notification	4/1
Nonfall registration?	Yes

FINANCIAL FACTS

Financial Aid Rating	79
Annual in-state tuition	$11,195
Annual out-of-state tuition	$26,045
Room and board	$12,080
Required fees	$2,700
Books and supplies	$1,200
Average frosh need-based scholarship	$10,337
Average UG need-based scholarship	$9,771
% needy frosh rec. need-based scholarship or grant aid	89
% needy UG rec. need-based scholarship or grant aid	72
% needy frosh rec. non-need-based scholarship or grant aid	69
% needy UG rec. non-need-based scholarship or grant aid	59
% needy frosh rec. need-based self-help aid	66
% needy UG rec. need-based self-help aid	69
% frosh rec. any financial aid	72
% UG rec. any financial aid	74
% frosh need fully met	12
% ugrads need fully met	8
Average % of frosh need met	73
Average % of ugrad need met	69

ST. OLAF COLLEGE

1520 St. Olaf Avenue, Northfield, MN 55057 • Admissions: 507-786-3025 • Fax: 507-786-3832

STUDENTS SAY "..."

Academics

With roots in a "Norwegian heritage," St. Olaf College in Northfield, Minnesota, provides students "a wonderful liberal arts education" with a strong focus on "classical music appreciation," while still offering "academic opportunities for everyone." St. Olaf emphasizes the need for "globally conscious citizens." To help them "[build] a global perspective," St. Olaf encourages students "to ask questions and explore their beliefs." Students agree that "the professors here are simply phenomenal in every respect, and their approachability is absolutely a hallmark of this campus." Nearly everyone we heard from praised their professors as "readily available to help," offering "late night review sessions," encouraging "academic conversations outside of the classroom," and "[extending] office hours to all five days a week the week before" major projects are due. St. Olaf students feel their professors "care about their students as whole people." But "this does not mean that they are lax and let students walk all over them." St. Olaf faculty maintain "high expectations" for their students, "but [they] want to see students succeed" as well. "Being a professor isn't just a 9-to-5 job for them," one student explains, "but a life they truly enjoy." While the school is affiliated with the Lutheran church, students assure us that "even if you aren't religious, you won't feel out of place at St. Olaf," explaining how "the religious aspect of the school" is rooted in its history "and allows those that are religious to find a community of people who are religious as well."

Life

Oles enjoy an active and engaging campus life where "most students are busy on school days and nights either studying or attending school functions." Olaf students take their community and club involvement seriously. With "250 student clubs and organizations" that "[provide] opportunities for students to explore and nourish their passions," students find that "it is really easy to get involved in multiple activities." While this can make it so their "days are pretty full, sometimes hectic," "being an Ole means you are fully devoted to your school or your community." Even so, Oles say they have "a pretty good work/life balance since there are so many opportunities to de-stress and spend time with friends (even if you are just working the the same room)." Among the "million extra activities" that Oles love, "choir and music are hugely popular—[about 25 percent] of students are in a music ensemble and [many] students participate in the nationally renowned St. Olaf Christmas Festival." During the Christmas Festival, "alumni from all over [flock] back to the Hill to relive their Ole days. The campus is decorated everywhere, and the cafeteria even serves Norwegian food for the big weekend.' And for Oles this "close knit, inquisitive student body" is "literally home." "I leave for break, excited to see my family" one environmental science major explains, "But to be honest? I find myself longing for the day when I come back to campus. Back to my home."

Student Body

Students express concern about the "lack of diversity on campus," but they hold one another in high esteem. "It's an accepting and trusting community" where students are comfortable "leaving laptops and backpacks around" without worry, and "if you lose your ID or wallet, you can expect it to appear in your PO box within a few hours." Students tend to be "a little preppy, type A personalities" who are "trustworthy" and considerate: "a local florist sells 'Friday flowers'—which people buy for their friends and leave in their POs with notes." These "sincere" students "wear Norwegian sweater non-ironically" and exude a "very mid-western. . .niceness." Olaf is an alcohol-free school, and "although it definitely has a presence on campus," students "agree that there is no pressure to drink" from fellow Oles. "I would say if you're not into socializing at parties and are into good clean fun," one student explains, "then there are options for you." With such strong music programs, it is no wonder that "music is very important to the average St. Olaf student, especially choir."

ST. OLAF COLLEGE

FINANCIAL AID: 507-786-3019 • E-MAIL: ADMISSIONS@STOLAF.EDU • WEBSITE: WWW.STOLAF.EDU

THE PRINCETON REVIEW SAYS

Admissions

Very important factors considered include: rigor of secondary school record, academic GPA, application essay. *Important factors considered include:* class rank, standardized test scores, recommendation(s), interview, extracurricular activities, talent/ability, character/personal qualities. *Other factors considered include:* first generation, alumni/ae relation, geographical residence, state residency, religious affiliation/commitment, racial/ethnic status, volunteer work, work experience, level of applicant's interest. SAT or ACT required; SAT Subject Tests considered if submitted. ACT with or without writing accepted. SAT with or without Essay component accepted. TOEFL required of all international applicants. High school diploma is required and GED is accepted. *Academic units recommended:* 4 English, 4 math, 4 science, 2 science labs, 4 foreign language, 4 social studies.

Financial Aid

Students should submit: FAFSA, CSS/Financial Aid PROFILE, Noncustodial PROFILE. Regular filing deadline is 3/1. The Princeton Review suggests that all financial aid forms be submitted as soon as possible after October 1. *Need-based scholarships/grants offered:* Federal Pell, FSEOG, State scholarships/grants, Private scholarships, College/university scholarship or grant aid from institutional funds. *Loan aid offered:* Direct Subsidized Stafford Loans, Direct Unsubsidized Stafford Loans, Direct PLUS loans, Federal Nursing Loans, State Loans, College/university loans from institutional funds. Applicants will be notified of awards on or about 4/1. Federal Work-Study Program available. Institutional employment available.

The Inside Word

As St. Olaf's academic reputation steadily rises, so too does competition to gain admission. First and foremost, admissions officers here assess the rigor of each applicant's course load (and subsequent success in the classroom). Of course, as a tight-knit community, the college also looks to admit students who will complement St. Olaf's ethos. To that end, admissions officers also closely analyze personal essays, recommendations and participation in extracurricular activities.

THE SCHOOL SAYS "..."

From the Admissions Office

"One of the nation's leading liberal arts colleges, St. Olaf College offers a distinctive education grounded in academic rigor, residential learning, global engagement, and a vibrant Lutheran faith tradition.

"Many excellent colleges provide one, two, or even three elements of the St. Olaf experience. What makes St. Olaf unique is the combination of so many distinguishing features working together at the highest level: an intense academic program that sharpens minds and an emphasis on a global perspective that broadens them; the vitality of a residential community that engages thoughtful people across the full range of human experiences; and a faith tradition that encourages reflection and honors different perspectives.

"By cultivating the habits of mind and heart that enable graduates to lead lives of financial independence, professional accomplishment, personal fulfillment, and community engagement, St. Olaf College provides an uncommon educational experience that fully prepares students to make a meaningful difference in a changing world."

SELECTIVITY

Admissions Rating	92
# of applicants	7,571
% of applicants accepted	36
% of acceptees attending	28
# offered a place on the wait list	729
% accepting a place on wait list	21
% admitted from wait list	75
# of early decision applicants	245
% accepted early decision	73

FRESHMAN PROFILE

Range SAT Critical Reading	560–710
Range SAT Math	580–700
Range ACT Composite	26–31
Minimum internet-based TOEFL	90
Average HS GPA	3.6
% graduated top 10% of class	43
% graduated top 25% of class	77
% graduated top 50% of class	96

DEADLINES

Early decision	
Deadline	11/15
Notification	12/15
Regular	
Deadline	1/15
Notification	3/20
Nonfall registration?	Yes

APPLICANTS ALSO LOOK AT AND OFTEN PREFER

Carleton College; Northwestern University

AND SOMETIMES PREFER

Grinnell College; Macalester College; University of Minnesota–Twin Cities Campus; University of Wisconsin–Madison

AND RARELY PREFER

Lawrence University

FINANCIAL FACTS

Financial Aid Rating	97
Annual tuition	$44,180
Room and board	$10,080
Books and supplies	$100
Average frosh need-based scholarship	$32,224
Average UG need-based scholarship	$30,182
% needy frosh rec. need-based scholarship or grant aid	100
% needy UG rec. need-based scholarship or grant aid	99
% needy frosh rec. non-need-based scholarship or grant aid	24
% needy UG rec. non-need-based scholarship or grant aid	23
% needy frosh rec. need-based self-help aid	100
% needy UG rec. need-based self-help aid	100
% frosh rec. any financial aid	92
% UG rec. any financial aid	93
% UG borrow to pay for school	57
Average cumulative indebtedness	$29,617
% frosh need fully met	91
% ugrads need fully met	90
Average % of frosh need met	99
Average % of ugrad need met	98

STANFORD UNIVERSITY

UNDERGRADUATE ADMISSION, STANFORD, CA 94305-6106 • ADMISSIONS: 650-723-2091 • FAX: 650-725-2846

STUDENTS SAY ". . ."

Academics

There are few universities that can match the prestige and caliber of Stanford University. At "the forefront of [nearly] every field of study," it's easy to understand why so many students are attracted to the school. Of course, far more than simply offering access to highly rated departments, Stanford strives to "expand your creativity, challenge and deepen your world view, and make you a passionate and informed citizen of the world." Moreover, the opportunities for research "are incredible" and "the support for students (residential, emotional, academic) is unrivaled." And while the university is certainly "academically rigorous," it is "without the competitive edge that many top-tier institutions are known for." Inside the classroom, undergrads are privy to "dynamic" professors who easily "draw [students] into the material because they are so excited to share their passion for the subject." Though instructors are "at the top of their respective fields," most are also "engaging and approachable." A mechanical engineering major supports this sentiment sharing, "I play basketball on Friday mornings with my major adviser and will often bring my homework with me in order to talk to him about problems I'm stuck on afterward." Ultimately, as this senior boasts, "At Stanford, anything is possible; I've lived on a schooner with faculty studying sharks, snorkeled on the Great Barrier Reef, hiked in the Australian rainforest, studied Antarctic phytoplankton with world-class scientists, and spent countless nights discussing philosophy, politics, film, and art until sunrise."

Life

Undergrads agree that "it's pretty much impossible to be bored" at Stanford. Though students "work insanely hard during the week," they "also make it a priority to have a great time." And with so much to take advantage of, having fun is pretty easy. For example, the university sponsors "Cardinal Nights," a non-alcoholic program that hosts a number of events including "trips to Great America, a local amusement park, *The Great Gatsby* movie pre-screening, and Stanford's Got Talent. All of the events are either free or extremely cheap for students." Undergrads also look forward to "special dinners...a common event in upper class housing." These are "nice on-campus dinners that are catered by house chefs. The meals usually have themes, such as Saturday Night Live or Moulin Rouge." Moreover, while there is certainly a drinking scene, it's pretty laid back. A sophomore explains, "You can find as much or as little of a party culture here as you're looking for. There's always a frat party to attend on the weekends, and there's always people to just hang out with at the dorm." Finally, students love the fact that hometown Palo Alto leaves them in close proximity to San Francisco. "A trip to the city is a short train-ride or car-ride away, so going to concerts and events in the city is always a fun option. Same goes for the nearby beaches." However, "there's always so much going on on campus that sometimes it's hard to leave!"

Student Body

Stanford undergrads speak glowingly of their peers: "Everyone here is smart and has some story that will blow you out of the water if you ask, but are very humble and really just looking to have a good time." They also steadfastly assert, "There really is no typical Stanford student." And, thankfully, that "makes it easy to be an integrated and diverse student body." That being said, most Stanford undergrads are "very driven, independently motivated and willing to seek out opportunities." One senior elaborates by sharing, "Everyone fits in because we're united by a fire that drives us all to be excited about what we do. The trends you'll see will be along the lines of leadership and crazy intellect." Ultimately, students at Stanford are "ridiculously friendly and you can meet new people all over campus at almost every type of event."

FINANCIAL AID: 650-723-3058 • E-MAIL: ADMISSION@STANFORD.EDU • WEBSITE: WWW.STANFORD.EDU

THE PRINCETON REVIEW SAYS

Admissions

Very important factors considered include: rigor of secondary school record, class rank, academic GPA, standardized test scores, application essay, recommendation(s), extracurricular activities, talent/ability, character/personal qualities. *Important factors considered include: Other factors considered include:* interview, first generation, alumni/ae relation, geographical residence, racial/ethnic status, volunteer work, work experience. SAT or ACT required; SAT Subject Tests recommend. ACT with Writing required. SAT with or without Essay component accepted. High school diploma is required and GED is accepted. *Academic units recommended:* 4 English, 4 math, 3 science, 3 science labs, 3 foreign language, 3 social studies, 3 history.

Financial Aid

Students should submit: FAFSA, CSS/Financial Aid PROFILE, Noncustodial PROFILE. Priority filing deadline is 2/15. The Princeton Review suggests that all financial aid forms be submitted as soon as possible after October 1. *Need-based scholarships/grants offered:* Federal Pell, FSEOG, State scholarships/grants, Private scholarships, College/university scholarship or grant aid from institutional funds. *Loan aid offered:* Direct Subsidized Stafford Loans, Direct Unsubsidized Stafford Loans, Direct PLUS loans, Federal Perkins Loans. Applicants will be notified of awards on a rolling basis beginning 4/1. Federal Work-Study Program available. Institutional employment available.

The Inside Word

Receiving a highly coveted acceptance letter from Stanford is no easy feat! Indeed, competition to gain admission is fierce. And, unfortunately, there is no magic formula. Clearly, a stellar academic record is a must. Beyond strong transcripts and test scores, successful applicants readily display intellectual curiosity and vigor, commitment to the topics and activities they are passionate about and initiative in seeking out opportunity.

THE SCHOOL SAYS "..."

From the Admissions Office

"Stanford looks for distinctive students who exhibit energy, personality, a sense of intellectual vitality and extraordinary impact outside the classroom. While there is no minimum grade point average, class rank, or test score one needs to be admitted to Stanford, the vast majority of successful applicants will be among the strongest students (academically) in their secondary schools. The most compelling applicants for admission will be those who have thus far achieved state, regional, national, and international recognition in their academic and extracurricular areas of interest.

"The Common Application and Stanford Writing Supplement are both required and must be submitted online. In the Stanford Writing Supplement, accessed at www.commonapp.org, candidates write about an idea or experience important to their intellectual development, as well as a note to their future roommate. In the final essay, candidates are asked to write about what matters to them and why.

"While the SAT or ACT is required for admission, SAT subject tests are not required (and only recommended). AP scores are also not required but can be used for placement/credit purposes if an admitted student decides to enroll."

SELECTIVITY

Admissions Rating	99
# of applicants	42,167
% of applicants accepted	5
% of acceptees attending	78
# offered a place on the wait list	1,256
% accepting a place on wait list	74
% admitted from wait list	0

FRESHMAN PROFILE

Range SAT Critical Reading	690–780
Range SAT Math	700–800
Range SAT Writing	690–780
Range ACT Composite	31–35
Average HS GPA	4.0
% graduated top 10% of class	96
% graduated top 25% of class	99
% graduated top 50% of class	100

DEADLINES

Early action	
Deadline	11/1
Notification	12/15
Regular	
Deadline	1/3
Notification	4/1
Nonfall registration?	No

APPLICANTS ALSO LOOK AT AND OFTEN PREFER
Harvard College

AND SOMETIMES PREFER
Massachusetts Institute of Technology; Yale University; Princeton University

AND RARELY PREFER
Columbia University

FINANCIAL FACTS

Financial Aid Rating	97
Annual tuition	$45,729
Room and board	$14,107
Required fees	$591
Books and supplies	$1,425
Average frosh need-based scholarship	$43,291
Average UG need-based scholarship	$43,167
% needy frosh rec. need-based scholarship or grant aid	95
% needy UG rec. need-based scholarship or grant aid	100
% needy frosh rec. non-need-based scholarship or grant aid	3
% needy UG rec. non-need-based scholarship or grant aid	3
% needy frosh rec. need-based self-help aid	58
% needy UG rec. need-based self-help aid	77
% frosh rec. any financial aid	86
% UG rec. any financial aid	85
% UG borrow to pay for school	22
Average cumulative indebtedness	$21,238
% frosh need fully met	91
% ugrads need fully met	91
Average % of frosh need met	100
Average % of ugrad need met	100

STATE UNIVERSITY OF NEW YORK AT BINGHAMTON

PO Box 6001, Binghamton, NY 13902-6001 • Admissions: 607-777-2171 • Fax: 607-777-4445

CAMPUS LIFE

Quality of Life Rating	82
Fire Safety Rating	92
Green Rating	97
Type of school	Public
Affiliation	No Affiliation
Environment	City

STUDENTS

Total undergrad enrollment	13,491
% male/female	52/48
% from out of state	8
% frosh from public high school	88
% frosh live on campus	98
% ugrads live on campus	51
# of fraternities (% ugrad men join)	34 (14)
# of sororities (% ugrad women join)	17 (10)
% African American	5
% Asian	14
% Caucasian	56
% Hispanic	10
% Native American	<1
% Pacific Islander	<1
% Two or more races	2
% Race and/or ethnicity unknown	2
% international	10
# of countries represented	115

SURVEY SAYS...

Campus newspaper is popular
Diverse student types interact on campus
Lots of beer drinking
Great library

ACADEMICS

Academic Rating	73
% students returning for sophomore year	91
% students graduating within 4 years	69
% students graduating within 6 years	81
Calendar	Semester
Student/faculty ratio	20:1
Profs interesting rating	67
Profs accessible rating	69

Most classes have 10–19 students.
Most lab/discussion sessions have 20–29 students.

MOST POPULAR MAJORS

Business Administration and Management;
Engineering; Psychology

STUDENTS SAY " . . ."

Academics

SUNY Binghamton provides "the best bang for your buck" to "hard-working, high-achieving kids" who want an "Ivy League workload at a SUNY school price." The school provides "students the ability to receive a top notch education at an affordable price" while maintaining "high standards" and a "commitment to excellence." Like many SUNY schools, Binghamton has "a diverse and active student body" that "take responsibility and pursue what is interesting" to them. Its "great reputation," "value" and "positive, respectful environment" make for "the archetype of an overall college experience." A key part of a great college experience is challenging professors, and Binghamton boasts "approachable, understanding," "very knowledgeable and experienced professors who care about their students." While some students say "professors are very hit or miss," they agree that the faculty is generally "available outside of class" and "eager to help students." "My academic experience is truly amazing, I can honestly say I'm learning from the best of the bests," a Political Science major proclaims. One student wished the school would "improve on getting more diverse faculty/staff," while another says "there is diversity in the student body, faculty, and courses taught." "There is a wide range of majors to choose from and a lot of interesting course options" making for "a great value for the quality of the education." The school's location is "close enough to a number of really fun and interesting cities" to be a selling point. Some of "the buildings and classrooms" need improvement, but "the school has been under constant construction for years and seems to be addressing this issue." One undecided student says SUNY Binghamton "is about finding the right path for you with challenging academics and a lot of fun along the way."

Life

"The motto" at Binghamton is "work hard, play hard." Students here "have a pretty rigorous workload but we also have fun on the weekends whether it be at a party or hanging out with friends." Since SUNY Binghamton does "not have a lot going on in the immediate towns surrounding it," student life revolves around campus. "Binghamton offers a wide array of student-run organizations and school-run activities to participate in during the year," a bio-engineering major explains. "There are a number of different clubs and groups for people to join" and many students participate in them. Still, "school spirit could be improved." "The bus system runs efficiently overall and gives transportation around the city" although students are divided on the value of venturing off campus. Some say the city of Binghamton is "very rundown and somewhat terrifying," but others caution that "the surrounding town, although not fantastic, does have things to do" such as "shopping centers, restaurants, cafes, bars, galleries and museums." Things are improving off campus as "the town of Binghamton is growing because of the University's influence and it has so much potential." Other students use the weekends "to travel because the relative distance to large cities isn't too far." The heavy workload means that a casual air pervades campus, and students "don't care how they look. Sweatpants or pajama pants and a sweatshirt are a must!" That said, there is a sizable contingent who "take[s] the time to look nice here." When the weekend rolls around, it is "button downs, polos, cocktail dresses, tights, heels, leather jackets."

Student Body

"Diversity" is a real plus at Binghamton. As a SUNY state school, "there's about every type of person you can imagine making it easy to make friends and expand what you're used to." If you have to generalize, "most students are from New York City" and often "Jewish and from Long Island or Asian and from NYC." Most people "were serious student in high school with many AP classes" and now are "really driven," "really smart," "liberal" and "willing to be friends with everyone." The typical student is active on campus, being "involved with [a] school organization, committed to their studies, but also goes out on the weekends." The school's "rich, diverse atmosphere...challenges its students while providing an enjoyable experience." Overall, students at SUNY Binghamton "seem to have a very optimistic and happy attitude of just about everything."

FINANCIAL AID: 607-777-2428 • E-MAIL: ADMIT@BINGHAMTON.EDU • WEBSITE: WWW.BINGHAMTON.EDU

THE PRINCETON REVIEW SAYS

Admissions

Very important factors considered include: rigor of secondary school record, academic GPA, standardized test scores. *Important factors considered include:* class rank, application essay, recommendation(s), extracurricular activities. *Other factors considered include:* talent/ability, character/personal qualities, first generation, alumni/ae relation, geographical residence, state residency, racial/ethnic status, volunteer work, work experience, level of applicant's interest. SAT or ACT required. ACT with Writing required. TOEFL required of all international applicants. High school diploma is required and GED is accepted. *Academic units required:* 4 English, 3 math, 2 science, 3 foreign language, 2 social studies. *Academic units recommended:* 4 math, 4 science, 4 social studies, 4 history.

Financial Aid

Students should submit: FAFSA, State aid form. Priority filing deadline is 2/1. The Princeton Review suggests that all financial aid forms be submitted as soon as possible after October 1. *Need-based scholarships/grants offered:* Federal Pell, FSEOG, State scholarships/grants, Private scholarships, College/university scholarship or grant aid from institutional funds. *Loan aid offered:* Direct Subsidized Stafford Loans, Direct Unsubsidized Stafford Loans, Direct PLUS loans, Federal Perkins Loans, Federal Nursing Loans, College/university loans from institutional funds. Applicants will be notified of awards on a rolling basis beginning 3/4. Federal Work-Study Program available. Institutional employment available.

The Inside Word

Like the vast majority of New York state schools, Binghamton accepts the single apply SUNY application. Binghamton also accepts the Common Application, making it easy to apply to SUNY Binghamton and other schools at the same time. Binghamton is one of the top public universities in the country, so expect competition to be stiff.

THE SCHOOL SAYS "..."

From the Admissions Office

"Binghamton has established itself as the premier public university in the Northeast, because of our outstanding undergraduate programs, vibrant campus culture, and committed faculty. Students are academically motivated, but there is a great deal of mutual help as they compete against the standard of a class rather than each other. Faculty and students work side by side in research labs or on artistic pursuits. Achievement, exploration, and leadership are hallmarks of a Binghamton education. Add to that a campus wide commitment to internationalization that includes a robust study abroad program, cultural offerings, languages and international studies, and you have a place where graduates leave prepared for success. Binghamton University graduates lead the nation in top starting salaries among public universities, demonstrating that our students are recognized by employers and recruiters for having strong abilities to be leaders, critical thinkers, decision makers, analysts, and researchers in many fields and industries."

SELECTIVITY

Admissions Rating	90
# of applicants	30,616
% of applicants accepted	42
% of acceptees attending	20
# offered a place on the wait list	3,961

FRESHMAN PROFILE

Range SAT Critical Reading	600–680
Range SAT Math	630–703
Range SAT Writing	580–670
Range ACT Composite	27–31
Minimum paper TOEFL	560
Minimum internet-based TOEFL	83
Average HS GPA	3.7

DEADLINES

Early action	
Deadline	11/1
Notification	1/15
Regular	
Priority	1/15
Nonfall registration?	Yes

APPLICANTS ALSO LOOK AT AND OFTEN PREFER

University of Pennsylvania; Cornell University

AND SOMETIMES PREFER

Boston University; New York University

AND RARELY PREFER

State University of New York–Stony Brook University; Rutgers; The State University of New Jersey–New Brunswick

FINANCIAL FACTS

Financial Aid Rating	80
Annual in-state tuition	$6,470
Annual out-of-state tuition	$19,590
Room and board	$13,198
Required fees	$2,583
Books and supplies	$1,000
Average frosh need-based scholarship	$9,032
Average UG need-based scholarship	$8,551
% needy frosh rec. need-based scholarship or grant aid	80
% needy UG rec. need-based scholarship or grant aid	84
% needy frosh rec. non-need-based scholarship or grant aid	13
% needy UG rec. non-need-based scholarship or grant aid	6
% needy frosh rec. need-based self-help aid	97
% needy UG rec. need-based self-help aid	97
% frosh rec. any financial aid	81
% UG rec. any financial aid	70
% UG borrow to pay for school	53
Average cumulative indebtedness	$25,844
% frosh need fully met	16
% ugrads need fully met	16
Average % of frosh need met	66
Average % of ugrad need met	73

STATE UNIVERSITY OF NEW YORK AT GENESEO

ONE COLLEGE CIRCLE, GENESEO, NY 14454-1401 • ADMISSIONS: 585-245-5571 • FAX: 585-245-5550

STUDENTS SAY "..."

Academics
Students are attracted to SUNY Geneseo because it offers "a quality education and support at an affordable price;" when they arrive they fall in love with the "views of the valley and the famous sunsets," "the old architecture of the buildings and the iconic ivy that grows" over them. "When I first walked onto this campus it felt like home." Students praise "the small class sizes and liberal arts education" and the school's "great reputation, especially when it comes to looking for jobs or applying for graduate schools." "Geneseo is known and well respected for having challenging academic programs," one student tells us, "which makes it a great deal in terms of price." Students are generally happy with their professors. With "few exceptions, the professors are mostly really great and [are] always available and willing to help and answer questions." Students say they get to experience a range of different teaching styles and strengths, "I have had amazing, intelligent, influential professors, and I have had supportive, entertaining professors. However, there have been some professors who might be better at research than teaching." But even among the more research focused faculty members, "many provide research or TA experiences for students." Students appreciate classes where " engage the students and encourage discussion" and generally praise the faculty as "accessible and. . .fair." Overall students say that "Geneseo is a community that values kindness, academic discussion, [and] hard work," where students build "lifelong connections with professors."

Life
Geneseo offers plenty of "opportunities to get involved in extracurricular organizations," and luckily Genesco students "are great at time management and being a part of a lot of things." "Greek Life is very popular on campus" with about "a solid quarter of the students" taking part in some way. While "students spend a great deal of time working on academics during the day," on weekends "and sometimes in the middle of the week" students have fun at parties "either in dorms, at frat houses, or at the local bar/club." While opinions are sometimes mixed, most would agree that "parties are a large part of the culture" "but it's by no means a party school." Everyone at Geneseo "genuinely [cares] about succeeding in something, whether classes, research, sports, theater" or another extracurricular activity. However, the academics can be rigorous, and even if students don't always feel like they are in "a pressure cooker," "during finals week many students do feel plenty of stress." But "the college offers many opportunities for them to relax when they can" and "here is plenty of nature around here and walking through it can be very relaxing." The rural setting also offers outdoor attractions, like "hiking in Letchworth State Park."

Student Body
Students agree that "everyone is extremely friendly and kind." Students are "always looking out for each other" and "willing to help you if you just ask." Many Geneseo students are diligent students, enjoy sports and hold "diverse interests," so it is great for anyone who is "interested in trying something new." While the majority of the student body hails from the state of New York, students report that campus feels "very diverse." The student body is mostly liberal but "is full of people with different experiences." Students say "they are generally like-minded individuals with goals and aspirations" who "take their work seriously." Geneseo is full of "down to earth people" who are "interesting and friendly," so "making friends is easy."

STATE UNIVERSITY OF NEW YORK AT GENESEO

FINANCIAL AID: 585-245-5731 • E-MAIL: ADMISSIONS@GENESEO.EDU • WEBSITE: WWW.GENESEO.EDU

THE PRINCETON REVIEW SAYS

Admissions

Very important factors considered include: rigor of secondary school record, standardized test scores. *Important factors considered include:* class rank, academic GPA, application essay, recommendation(s), extracurricular activities, talent/ability, racial/ethnic status. *Other factors considered include:* character/personal qualities, first generation, alumni/ae relation, state residency, volunteer work, work experience, level of applicant's interest. SAT or ACT required; SAT Subject Tests considered if submitted. ACT with or without writing accepted. SAT with or without Essay component accepted. TOEFL required of all international applicants. High school diploma is required and GED is accepted. *Academic units recommended:* 4 English, 4 math, 4 science, 4 foreign language, 4 social studies.

Financial Aid

Students should submit: FAFSA, State aid form. Regular filing deadline is 2/15. The Princeton Review suggests that all financial aid forms be submitted as soon as possible after October 1. *Need-based scholarships/grants offered:* Federal Pell, FSEOG, State scholarships/grants *Loan aid offered:* Direct Subsidized Stafford Loans, Direct Unsubsidized Stafford Loans, Direct PLUS loans, Federal Perkins Loans. Applicants will be notified of awards on a rolling basis beginning 3/15. Federal Work-Study Program available. Institutional employment available.

The Inside Word

While the current acceptance rate is high, the applicant pool for SUNY Geneseo grows increasingly competitive each year. Grades and test scores carry the most weight with the admission committee here, followed by the rigor of an applicant's high school classes. The essay, extracurricular activities, and recommendations round out the holistic application review.

THE SCHOOL SAYS "..."

From the Admissions Office

"Geneseo has carved a distinctive niche among the nation's premier public liberal arts colleges. With its highly regarded program of scholarly, cultural, social, and recreational activities as well as numerous volunteer service opportunities, Geneseo students attest that 'there is no place like here.' Within the SUNY System, Geneseo is the only undergraduate college to be granted a chapter of Phi Beta Kappa, the world's most prestigious academic honor society. While the college competes for students with the nation's most selective private colleges, it is increasingly viewed as a first-choice selection for academic rigor and learning outcomes among financially-savvy students who recognize Geneseo's value and the financial advantage it affords. Founded in 1871, the college occupies a beautiful 220-acre campus in the historic Village of Geneseo, overlooking the scenic Genesee Valley. More than two-thirds of the students live in residence halls. Geneseo is noted for its distinctive core curriculum and the extraordinary opportunities it offers undergraduates to pursue independent study and research with faculty who value close working relationships with talented students. Geneseo graduates lead lives of purpose around the world, and 33 percent pursue graduate study immediately following graduation. The College is in the top five among all the country's Master's colleges in the number of alumni who earn doctorates in STEM fields and in the top ten in the number who earn doctorates in all disciplines. With 81 percent of courses offered taught by full-time faculty and 0 percent by teaching assistants, Geneseo enjoys a national reputation for excellence in undergraduate teaching."

SELECTIVITY

Admissions Rating	86
# of applicants	9,118
% of applicants accepted	73
% of acceptees attending	20
# offered a place on the wait list	542
% accepting a place on wait list	33
% admitted from wait list	27
# of early decision applicants	238
% accepted early decision	90

FRESHMAN PROFILE

Range SAT Critical Reading	550–640
Range SAT Math	550–650
Range ACT Composite	25–29
Minimum paper TOEFL	525
Minimum internet-based TOEFL	71
Average HS GPA	3.7
% graduated top 10% of class	36
% graduated top 25% of class	74
% graduated top 50% of class	95

DEADLINES

Early decision	
Deadline	11/15
Notification	12/15
Regular	
Deadline	1/1
Notification	3/1
Nonfall registration?	Yes

APPLICANTS ALSO LOOK AT AND OFTEN PREFER
Colgate University; Cornell University

AND SOMETIMES PREFER
Skidmore College

FINANCIAL FACTS

Financial Aid Rating	88
Annual in-state tuition	$6,470
Annual out-of-state tuition	$16,320
Room and board	$11,980
Required fees	$1,643
Books and supplies	$1,000
Average frosh need-based scholarship	$6,556
Average UG need-based scholarship	$6,116
% needy frosh rec. need-based scholarship or grant aid	51
% needy UG rec. need-based scholarship or grant aid	78
% needy frosh rec. non-need-based scholarship or grant aid	18
% needy UG rec. non-need-based scholarship or grant aid	26
% needy frosh rec. need-based self-help aid	48
% needy UG rec. need-based self-help aid	78
% UG borrow to pay for school	49
Average cumulative indebtedness	$22,300
% frosh need fully met	60
% ugrads need fully met	60
Average % of frosh need met	60
Average % of ugrad need met	60

CAMPUS LIFE

Quality of Life Rating	90
Fire Safety Rating	98
Green Rating	99
Type of school	Public
Affiliation	No Affiliation
Environment	City

STUDENTS

Total undergrad enrollment	1,727
% male/female	55/45
% from out of state	18
% frosh from public high school	90
% frosh live on campus	95
% ugrads live on campus	30
# of fraternities (% ugrad men join)	26 (5)
# of sororities (% ugrad women join)	21 (5)
% African American	1
% Asian	3
% Caucasian	84
% Hispanic	4
% Native American	<1
% Pacific Islander	0
% Two or more races	3
% Race and/or ethnicity unknown	3
% international	2
# of countries represented	11

SURVEY SAYS...

Students are happy
School is well run
Students aren't religious
Students get along with local community
Students environmentally aware
Dorms are like palaces

ACADEMICS

Academic Rating	79
% students returning for sophomore year	85
% students graduating within 4 years	47
% students graduating within 6 years	68
Calendar	Semester
Student/faculty ratio	13:1
Profs interesting rating	87
Profs accessible rating	78

Most classes have 10–19 students.
Most lab/discussion sessions have 10–19 students.

MOST POPULAR MAJORS

Environmental Science; Environmental Biology; Landscape Architecture

STUDENTS SAY "..."

Academics

SUNY's College of Environmental Science and Forestry is "dedicated to its mission of sustainability." It is "a great school for those interested in research and theory." The school's "unique class offerings" include using its "thousands of acres of forest" for "education, research, and forestry." Students are "out in the field learning how to do what they want to do in life." With Syracuse University right next-door, SUNY ESF "has a great small school atmosphere," with "all of the perks of a big university." This "great partnership" between the two schools gives SUNY ESF students "the option to take their classes" and "enjoy the amenities and even the social life of a larger, private school." For in-state students, SUNY ESF is "very affordable." One transfer student says, "ESF is definitely the best 'bang for your buck.' I attended a private university prior, and I have paid for four years what one year costs there. And the courses are just as well taught." Professors "have diverse teaching styles, and different students prefer different teachers. Some seem over-committed between their research and teaching duties, and this can make them difficult to reach or rely on." "Professors are committed to their beliefs and are mostly all in active research." Don't expect to breeze through classes at ESF. "If you plan on coasting through college, ESF is not for you!" Professors "set the bar high for expectations and keep it there. I'm consistently challenged and encouraged." There are "well maintained chemistry and computing lab facilities," and the "newer lab buildings are first class." "SUNY ESF is a great school whether you love plants, animals, or the environment, and offers great opportunities for real world experience related to your field of study."

Life

Students at SUNY ESF have access to Syracuse University's "food services, gyms, and health center." ESF "doesn't have many sports (but we can play club sports over at SU)" which are "formed with students of both colleges." "The dorms are fantastic; the building was built in 2011 and all the rooms have private baths." "ESF offers lots of activities including monthly free movies, breakfasts, presentations, ski trips, ice-skating, craft fairs, etc. We get weekly emails letting us know about all the events, and there's always something to do." In nice weather, students make good use of the quad. "It's fairly large, so people hang out there between classes with friends." Because of the "outdoorsy" nature of many students also enjoy, "running, biking, hiking, scuba, rock climbing, travel, you name it!" "Armory Square is a short bus ride away and offers some great off campus lunch and dinner options." There are "fun house parties and the downtown scene is great in my opinion. There are also several ski resorts and lakes nearby for fun in every season." According to one student, "drug use is more prevalent than it should be," but there is a sober crowd, like this student who says, "I spend my Friday nights at Insomniac Events, which is for people who don't want to go out and party. Each event is themed and they are really fun."

Student Body

"There's extremes here at ESF... It's likely that you'll see someone with bare feet, dreadlocks and a tie-dye t-shirt walking around campus, and there's people who dress in slacks everyday. The typical student is usually happily between the two extremes, and spends a lot of time in the library and/or the computer labs!" "Attending SUNY ESF means being surrounded by people who are passionate about the earth and science in general, while all having unique perspectives and interests to share."

STATE UNIVERSITY OF NEW YORK—COLLEGE OF ENVIRONMENTAL SCIENCE AND FORESTRY

FINANCIAL AID: 315-470-6706 • E-MAIL: ESFINFO@ESF.EDU • WEBSITE: WWW.ESF.EDU

THE PRINCETON REVIEW SAYS

Admissions

Very important factors considered include: rigor of secondary school record, academic GPA, standardized test scores, application essay, level of applicant's interest. *Important factors considered include:* class rank, recommendation(s), interview, extracurricular activities, talent/ability, character/personal qualities, volunteer work, work experience. *Other factors considered include:* first generation, alumni/ae relation, geographical residence, state residency, racial/ethnic status. SAT or ACT required; SAT Subject Tests considered if submitted. ACT with or without writing accepted. TOEFL required of all international applicants. High school diploma is required and GED is accepted. *Academic units required:* 4 English, 3 math, 3 science, 3 science labs, 3 social studies. *Academic units recommended:* 4 math, 4 science, 2 foreign language, 3 social studies, 1 history.

Financial Aid

Students should submit: FAFSA, State aid form. Priority filing deadline is 3/1. The Princeton Review suggests that all financial aid forms be submitted as soon as possible after October 1. *Need-based scholarships/grants offered:* Federal Pell, FSEOG, State scholarships/grants, Private scholarships, College/university scholarship or grant aid from institutional funds. *Loan aid offered:* Direct Subsidized Stafford Loans, Direct Unsubsidized Stafford Loans, Direct PLUS loans, Federal Perkins Loans. Applicants will be notified of awards on a rolling basis beginning 3/15. Federal Work-Study Program available. Institutional employment available.

The Inside Word

SUNY ESF is an excellent value even for those students hailing from outside the Empire State. While there are many specialized Bachelor of Science degrees, there are also coordinated programs between the college and the Upstate Medical University as well as a host of pre-professional programs. Stats are an important aspect in the calculus of admission but level of demonstrated interest is considered equal to SAT scores. Aspiring Mighty Oaks should make their interest known early and often.

SELECTIVITY

Admissions Rating	89
# of applicants	1,538
% of applicants accepted	51
% of acceptees attending	37
# offered a place on the wait list	151
% accepting a place on wait list	28
% admitted from wait list	40
# of early decision applicants	128
% accepted early decision	66

FRESHMAN PROFILE

Range SAT Critical Reading	530–630
Range SAT Math	550–630
Range ACT Composite	22–26
Minimum paper TOEFL	550
Minimum internet-based TOEFL	79
Average HS GPA	3.7
% graduated top 10% of class	30
% graduated top 25% of class	66
% graduated top 50% of class	95

DEADLINES

Early decision	
Deadline	12/1
Notification	1/15
Regular	
Priority	2/1
Nonfall registration?	Yes

APPLICANTS ALSO LOOK AT AND OFTEN PREFER
State University of New York–Stony Brook University; Cornell University

AND SOMETIMES PREFER
Penn State University Park; Rochester Institute of Technology

AND RARELY PREFER
Clarkson University; State University of New York at Geneseo

FINANCIAL FACTS

Financial Aid Rating	90
Annual in-state tuition	$6,470
Annual out-of-state tuition	$16,320
Room and board	$14,490
Required fees	$1,300
Books and supplies	$1,200
Average frosh need-based scholarship	$6,200
Average UG need-based scholarship	$4,720
% needy frosh rec. need-based scholarship or grant aid	89
% needy UG rec. need-based scholarship or grant aid	93
% needy frosh rec. non-need-based scholarship or grant aid	53
% needy UG rec. non-need-based scholarship or grant aid	46
% needy frosh rec. need-based self-help aid	88
% needy UG rec. need-based self-help aid	87
% frosh rec. any financial aid	91
% UG rec. any financial aid	93
% frosh need fully met	45
% ugrads need fully met	69
Average % of frosh need met	83
Average % of ugrad need met	86

STATE UNIVERSITY OF NEW YORK—PURCHASE COLLEGE

735 ANDERSON HILL ROAD, PURCHASE, NY 10577 • ADMISSIONS: 914-251-6300 • FAX: 914-251-6314

STUDENTS SAY "..."

Academics

Its motto "Think Wide Open" perfectly sums up SUNY Purchase, long the artsy lodestone in the SUNY system: the conservatory here "deserves and receives the highest respect." Beyond the School of the Arts, the School of Liberal Arts & Sciences offers twenty-three major options, as well as the chance to design an individualized, interdisciplinary major through the Liberal Arts program. Nearly all bachelor's students must complete a senior project in which they devote two semesters to in-depth, original, and creative study, and students welcome the chance to explore. "We're all about finding new ways to think about things, from science to art to management," says one.

Classes tend to be about "learning through discussion" rather than lecture, and professors "go out of their way to make sure that everyone is on the same page, and don't leave anyone behind." They often actively work in the field in which they teach, and therefore "bring the material life and take learning outside the classroom." Classes in both the creative arts and general education are "rich and exciting," such as the professor who "teaches classes about Jack Kerouac on a train and walks the path of *On the Road*." Students benefit from the school's proximity to New York City (less than an hour away), where auditions, showcases, and a fertile alumni network thrive, and "some of the best artists in the NY area become adjunct faculty at this school at some point."

Life

For fun, there's "a TON of things going on": weekly dance parties and concerts, lectures, an on-campus museum, free yoga classes, zumba, and tons of festivals. People "pay a lot of money to see bands and they support music and musicians here," and theatre is also "very, very big and popular." Athletics get less emphasis, and Greek life is non-existant. Students recieve email digests of all the events on campus, and for those who want to get off campus, it's easy to take a bus into White Plains or take the train into Manhattan. "The question isn't 'What to do for fun?' but rather 'Where do you even start?'" Professors usually "know a lot about what's going on" and will often get free tickets to performances for students. While the Student Center (Stood) and library facilities are admittedly great ("there are different levels, so students never have to be isolated in one spot"), many say that Purchase could improve the dorms, as "a lot of the on-campus living needs to be updated badly."

Student Body

Overwhelmingly accepting of "the weird and strange," the school is known as a beacon for those that didn't fit in in high school. This "artsy, unique, passionate, intelligent" group of students has "a definite sense of unity and acceptance," meaning that everyone is free to be themselves. "People walk around confident in who they are and they aren't afraid to show their unique styles and personalities," says one student. There are a lot of "free spirits" and the atmosphere is "filled with liberal ideologies," and the high concentration of visual/multi-media artists, musicians, and dancers means that "creativity and the arts flourish." The decent number of commuters don't have any real problem integrating with the resident population, and "you can always incorporate your craft into whatever you create at Purchase."

STATE UNIVERSITY OF NEW YORK—PURCHASE COLLEGE

FINANCIAL AID: 914-251-6350 • E-MAIL: ADMISSIONS@PURCHASE.EDU • WEBSITE: WWW.PURCHASE.EDU

THE PRINCETON REVIEW SAYS

Admissions

Very important factors considered include: academic GPA, application essay, talent/ability. *Important factors considered include:* standardized test scores. *Other factors considered include:* rigor of secondary school record, class rank, recommendation(s), interview, extracurricular activities, character/personal qualities. SAT or ACT required. ACT with or without writing accepted. TOEFL required of all international applicants. High school diploma is required and GED is accepted. *Academic units recommended:* 4 English, 4 math, 3 science, 3 foreign language, 4 social studies, 2 academic electives.

Financial Aid

Students should submit: FAFSA, State aid form. Priority filing deadline is 2/1. The Princeton Review suggests that all financial aid forms be submitted as soon as possible after October 1. *Need-based scholarships/grants offered:* Federal Pell, FSEOG, State scholarships/grants, Private scholarships, College/university scholarship or grant aid from institutional funds. *Loan aid offered:* Direct Subsidized Stafford Loans, Direct Unsubsidized Stafford Loans, Direct PLUS loans, Federal Perkins Loans. Applicants will be notified of awards on a rolling basis beginning 3/1. Federal Work-Study Program available. Institutional employment available.

The Inside Word

Almost 40 percent of Purchase students are enrolled in the highly selective School of the Arts. Arts applicants should know that to apply to the programs in dance, theatre arts, music, School of Art+Design, or School of Film and Media Studies—the audition, portfolio, or other applicable work samples are of paramount importance, and criteria such as standardized test scores and high school transcripts are weighted less than demonstrated artistic excellence. However, to apply to Purchase's liberal arts and sciences programs, traditional academic criteria are the primary considerations for admission.

THE SCHOOL SAYS "..."

From the Admissions Office

"Whether for our top-ranked and innovative liberal arts majors or our world-class arts programs, Purchase attracts students from around the globe seeking to cultivate their intellectual identity, develop their talents, expand their minds and transform their passions into action. By choosing Purchase, students make a conscious decision to join an intense community with a deep respect for individuality and diversity and an unparalleled environment of creativity and innovation.

"Our dynamic faculty are not only among the most accomplished in their fields but also partner with students on research projects and work tirelessly to ensure students succeed in their chosen fields of study or career. The intimate classroom setting and engaged faculty inspire lively classroom discussion and debate, critical thinking, originality and discovery and invention.

"Purchase students represent a broad spectrum of familial, social, ethnic, economic, and geographical backgrounds. Highly talented, motivated, and entrepreneurial, they strive to impact our society through civic and cultural engagement.

"Still a relatively young college, Purchase offers students an opportunity to build upon established campus traditions as well as create new ones. Our proximity to New York City provides students access to outstanding cultural and career-related opportunities. On campus, students can see world-class performances at the PAC and notable exhibitions at the Neuberger Museum.

"We seek to enroll highly motivated, hard-working and academically strong students with a consistent record of achievement in a challenging high school curriculum. Admission criteria vary amongst programs."

SELECTIVITY

Admissions Rating	83
# of applicants	7,928
% of applicants accepted	41
% of acceptees attending	24

FRESHMAN PROFILE

Range SAT Critical Reading	490–510
Range SAT Math	470–570
Range ACT Composite	22–27
Minimum paper TOEFL	550
Average HS GPA	3.1

DEADLINES

Early action	
Deadline	11/15
Notification	12/15
Regular	
Priority	3/1
Deadline	7/15
Nonfall registration?	Yes

APPLICANTS ALSO LOOK AT AND OFTEN PREFER
New York University

FINANCIAL FACTS

Financial Aid Rating	71
Annual in-state tuition	$6,470
Annual out-of-state tuition	$16,320
Room and board	$12,574
Required fees	$1,797
Books and supplies	$1,225
Average frosh need-based scholarship	$5,886
Average UG need-based scholarship	$9,469
% needy frosh rec. need-based scholarship or grant aid	98
% needy UG rec. need-based scholarship or grant aid	98
% needy frosh rec. non-need-based scholarship or grant aid	15
% needy UG rec. non-need-based scholarship or grant aid	19
% needy frosh rec. need-based self-help aid	90
% needy UG rec. need-based self-help aid	92
% UG borrow to pay for school	67
Average cumulative indebtedness	$28,638
% frosh need fully met	1
% ugrads need fully met	1
Average % of frosh need met	44
Average % of ugrad need met	49

STATE UNIVERSITY OF NEW YORK—STONY BROOK UNIVERSITY

OFFICE OF ADMISSIONS, STONY BROOK, NY 11794-1901 • ADMISSIONS: 631-632-6868 • FAX: 631-632-9898

CAMPUS LIFE

Quality of Life Rating	84
Fire Safety Rating	81
Green Rating	97
Type of school	Public
Affiliation	No Affiliation
Environment	Town

STUDENTS

Total undergrad enrollment	16,831
% male/female	54/46
% from out of state	8
% frosh from public high school	90
% frosh live on campus	85
% ugrads live on campus	51
# of fraternities (% ugrad men join)	18 (3)
# of sororities (% ugrad women join)	14 (3)
% African American	7
% Asian	24
% Caucasian	36
% Hispanic	11
% Native American	<1
% Pacific Islander	<1
% Two or more races	2
% Race and/or ethnicity unknown	7
% international	13
# of countries represented	90

SURVEY SAYS...

Students are happy
Recreation facilities are great
Lots of beer drinking
Great library
Students environmentally aware

ACADEMICS

Academic Rating	73
% students returning for sophomore year	90
% students graduating within 4 years	47
% students graduating within 6 years	68
Calendar	Semester
Student/faculty ratio	17:1
Profs interesting rating	68
Profs accessible rating	66

Most classes have 10–19 students.
Most lab/discussion sessions have 20–29 students.

MOST POPULAR MAJORS

Biology; Business Administration and Management; Health Services

STUDENTS SAY "..."

Academics

Students at Stony Brook University get all the advantages of a "premiere science and research university," while also benefiting from the diverse atmosphere and low tuition costs of a large public institution. The school has a "great reputation in science and engineering," as well as strong pre-med and pre-health programs; however, it's the "access to hands-on, real-world experiences" that truly distinguishes a Stony Brook education. Motivated undergrads find "the opportunities to do research are phenomenal"; in addition to the school's proximity to the myriad opportunities in New York City, "there is a hospital right across the street, shuttles to Brookhaven National Lab, and hundreds of professors that look for undergrads to work in the lab." That said, "you must be proactive in order to succeed" at Stony Brook. "The professors are challenging and expect a lot from you," and the "vast, sometimes overwhelming size" means classes are sometimes "packed to the brim with 500-some students." Fortunately, Stony Brook has found ways to make the experience more personal. For one thing, first-year students are all "broken down into smaller colleges," learning communities of "like minded individuals" who live in the same dorms and take freshman seminars together. On top of that, "all classes in large lecture styles attempt to make the learning experience more personal through section meetings with TAs, online interactive discussion boards and/or professors that are very willing to discuss the material with you." Once you get through the first few years, "Upperclassmen have excellent classes," which are often smaller and lead by "very entertaining, interactive and challenging" professors.

Life

Academics at Stony Brook University are no walk in the park, and many students say their life consists of little more than "studying all the time and staying up very late and just stressing" to stay on top of course work. Others have an easier time finding the "balance between getting work done and socializing with friends," and the majority of students are "involved in at least one or two clubs on campus." When they want to blow off steam, students "hang out and drink and listen to music," or partake of the "brand new, state-of-the-art recreational facility, indoor swimming pool, and bike trails all around campus through woods." Come Friday, a lot of students leave campus for home, so "social life dies down on weekends." In response, the school is working hard to make student life at Stony Brook more exciting. Currently, "the Weekend Life council has partnered up with organizations to make weekend events commonplace, and larger groups like the Undergraduate Student Government have done amazing things, like reviving the Stony Brook Concert Series." A testament to the changing culture, a student points out that, "This past year we set an attendance record at our stadium for homecoming (which is a Saturday!)." Even if life on campus can be a bit subdued, students reassure us, "As long as you make a solid group of friends you'll always have something to do."

Students

"Students from around the world and all different socio-economic backgrounds" come to Stony Brook, and the school excels at "bringing a large population of diverse backgrounds, identities and cultures together for the common purpose of learning." In addition to the "many international students," there are "a lot of commuters" from the Stony Brook area, as well as "Long Island locals" who live on campus but spend weekends at home. In terms of personality, you'll meet people of every ilk, including "gamers that never leave their rooms and social butterflies that are very involved and generally know what's going on everywhere on campus." No matter what your style, "there are so many different social circles that it would be more impossible to not find somewhere to fit in." While social life is important to many Stony Brook undergrads, academics come first for the majority of this "very bright" and "studious" student body. Always keeping an eye on their future, "students are committed to their academics so that they can get a solid job soon after they graduate."

STATE UNIVERSITY OF NEW YORK—STONY BROOK UNIVERSITY

FINANCIAL AID: 631-632-6840 • E-MAIL: ENROLL@STONYBROOK.EDU • WEBSITE: WWW.STONYBROOK.EDU

THE PRINCETON REVIEW SAYS

Admissions

Very important factors considered include: rigor of secondary school record, academic GPA, standardized test scores. *Important factors considered include:* application essay, recommendation(s). *Other factors considered include:* class rank, interview, extracurricular activities, talent/ability, character/personal qualities, first generation, alumni/ae relation, geographical residence, state residency, volunteer work, work experience, level of applicant's interest. SAT or ACT required; SAT Subject Tests considered if submitted. ACT with Writing recommended. SAT with Essay component recommended. TOEFL required of all international applicants. High school diploma is required and GED is accepted. *Academic units required:* 4 English, 3 math, 3 science, 2 foreign language, 4 social studies. *Academic units recommended:* 4 math, 4 science, 3 foreign language.

Financial Aid

Students should submit: FAFSA, State aid form. Priority filing deadline is 3/1. The Princeton Review suggests that all financial aid forms be submitted as soon as possible after October 1. *Need-based scholarships/grants offered:* Federal Pell, FSEOG, State scholarships/grants, Private scholarships, College/university scholarship or grant aid from institutional funds. *Loan aid offered:* Direct Subsidized Stafford Loans, Direct Unsubsidized Stafford Loans, Direct PLUS loans, Federal Perkins Loans. Applicants will be notified of awards on a rolling basis beginning 4/1. Federal Work-Study Program available. Institutional employment available.

The Inside Word

Admission to Stony Brook University is competitive. Successful applicants for the freshman class will have typically followed a rigorous college-prep curriculum in high school and have strong standardized test scores, though the university will also give special consideration to students with leadership experience or talents demonstrated through extracurricular activities or volunteer work. Students with a particularly strong academic record may be considered for the university's special programs, including the Honors Program, the University Scholars program, Women in Science and Engineering, and the Scholars in Medicine program.

THE SCHOOL SAYS " . . ."

From the Admissions Office

"A degree from Stony Brook University—an institution with award-winning faculty, accomplished students, innovative academic programs, and a thriving research environment—opens doors to countless career possibilities. Situated on 1,040 wooded acres on the North Shore of Long Island, Stony Brook offers more than 200 majors, minors, and combined-degree programs, including our Fast Track MBA program; unique research opportunities at nearby Brookhaven National Laboratory, which Stony Brook has a role in running; and a dynamic first-year experience in one of six small undergraduate communities. We offer a variety of honors programs—such as University Scholars, Honors College, Women in Science and Engineering, and Scholars for Medicine, as well as honors tracks in Computer Science and Business—to challenge, inspire and sustain our most gifted students. Faculty include Nobel laureates, Guggenheim fellows, MacArthur grant recipients, and Pulitzer Prize-winning investigative journalist Carl Bernstein. Students enjoy comfortable campus housing and outstanding recreational facilities, including an 8,300-seat stadium, a modern student activities center, a sports complex housing our newly renovated 4,000-seat arena, and a state-of-the-art 85,000-square-foot campus recreation center devoted entirely to the health and well-being of the campus community. In addition, the Staller Center for the Arts offers spectacular theatrical and musical performances throughout the year. Stony Brook goes far beyond the expectations of today's public universities. We invite students who possess both intellectual curiosity and academic ability to explore the many exciting opportunities available at Stony Brook."

SELECTIVITY

Admissions Rating	90
# of applicants	34,146
% of applicants accepted	41
% of acceptees attending	20
# offered a place on the wait list	3,512
% accepting a place on wait list	41
% admitted from wait list	22

FRESHMAN PROFILE

Range SAT Critical Reading	550–660
Range SAT Math	600–720
Range SAT Writing	540–660
Range ACT Composite	26–31
Minimum paper TOEFL	550
Minimum internet-based TOEFL	80
Average HS GPA	3.8
% graduated top 10% of class	46
% graduated top 25% of class	79
% graduated top 50% of class	96

DEADLINES

Regular	
Priority	1/15
Notification	4/1
Nonfall registration?	Yes

APPLICANTS ALSO LOOK AT AND OFTEN PREFER

State University of New York at Binghamton (Binghamton University); Rensselaer Polytechnic Institute; Rensselaer Polytechnic Institute; Cornell University

AND SOMETIMES PREFER

Penn State University Park; Rutgers; The State University of New Jersey–New Brunswick

AND RARELY PREFER

Hofstra University

FINANCIAL FACTS

Financial Aid Rating	81
Annual in-state tuition	$6,470
Annual out-of-state tuition	$21,550
Room and board	$12,032
Required fees	$2,385
Books and supplies	$900
Average frosh need-based scholarship	$9,316
Average UG need-based scholarship	$7,765
% needy frosh rec. need-based scholarship or grant aid	89
% needy UG rec. need-based scholarship or grant aid	83
% needy frosh rec. non-need-based scholarship or grant aid	12
% needy UG rec. non-need-based scholarship or grant aid	6
% needy frosh rec. need-based self-help aid	89
% needy UG rec. need-based self-help aid	90
% frosh rec. any financial aid	76
% UG rec. any financial aid	69
% UG borrow to pay for school	58
Average cumulative indebtedness	$23,592
% frosh need fully met	19
% ugrads need fully met	17
Average % of frosh need met	71
Average % of ugrad need met	66

CAMPUS LIFE

Quality of Life Rating	72
Fire Safety Rating	89
Green Rating	94
Type of school	Public
Affiliation	No Affiliation
Environment	City

STUDENTS

Total undergrad enrollment	12,929
% male/female	52/48
% from out of state	6
% frosh live on campus	92
% ugrads live on campus	58
# of fraternities (% ugrad men join)	19 (1)
# of sororities (% ugrad women join)	17 (2)
% African American	15
% Asian	8
% Caucasian	51
% Hispanic	14
% Native American	<1
% Pacific Islander	<1
% Two or more races	3
% Race and/or ethnicity unknown	3
% international	6
# of countries represented	84

SURVEY SAYS...

Students politically aware
Diverse student types on campus
Lots of beer drinking
Hard liquor is popular

ACADEMICS

Academic Rating	65
% students returning for sophomore year	80
% students graduating within 4 years	53
Calendar	Semester
Student/faculty ratio	18:1
Profs interesting rating	67
Profs accessible rating	66

Most classes have 20–29 students.
Most lab/discussion sessions have
  10–19 students.

MOST POPULAR MAJORS

English; Psychology; Business Administration
and Management

STUDENTS SAY "..."

Academics

Is SUNY Albany (UAlbany to those in the know) the perfect-sized school? Many here think so. Students describe it as "a big school numbers-wise that feels small." Notes one student, "It has a very broad range of quality academic programs, which is very important for an undecided senior in high school." Another adds, "If you know what you want and are motivated, the sky is the limit." The school exploits its location in the state capital to bolster programs in political science, criminal justice, and business, and it "offers internship opportunities to college students that very few schools can." Other standout departments include psychology, Japanese studies, mathematics, and many of the hard sciences. Professors here vary widely in quality, but a surprising number "are receptive, active, and engaging"—in other words, "a lot more accessible than I would have thought for a school this big." Teachers are especially willing to "go out of their way to help students who are interested in learning, come to class regularly, and care about their academic work." The administration, as at most state-run schools, "is basically an over-bloated bureaucracy. Students are sent from department to department in each of their endeavors. It is advisable to avoid [the] administration if at all possible."

Life

There are three distinct social orbits on the Albany campus. Some students take the initiative "by joining one of the many clubs or groups or getting involved with the student government." Others "party for a good time," telling us that "any night of the week you can find people to go out to the bars and clubs with you" and that "the average night ends between 2:30 A.M. and 4:00 A.M." Both of these groups are likely to tell you that "there is a lot to do in Albany and the surrounding area," including "a great arts district, tons of awesome restaurants, museums, [and] a state park." A third, sizable group primarily complains about the cold weather and asserts that "there's nothing to do in Albany." The school works to excite these students with "fun programs and entertainers who come to the campus. We have had a series of comedians, rappers/singers, guests from MTV and VH1, authors, political figures, musical performances, sporting events, spirit events, and many other things around campus." School spirit is on the rise among all groups, we're told. The reason? "A few years ago, the basketball team began winning, and everyone came out of the woodwork to support them—it was really a great thing to see."

Student Body

Undergrads here believe that the student body is very diverse in terms of ethnicity and also in terms of personality type; one student observes, "You have your motivated students [who] get good grades, are involved, and get amazing jobs in NYC after college. Then you have your unmotivated kids [who] complain, don't go to class, and blame a bad grade on the professor (when really it is because they crammed the night before and didn't go to class)." Geographically, the school is less diverse. Nearly everyone is a New York State resident, with many coming from "downstate New York"—Long Island, New York City, and Westchester County. There's a fair amount of upstate kids as well, and "a lot of people have certain stereotypes in their heads when they first come to Albany. The Long Islander has his idea about the upstater and vice versa. After a few weeks, though, people see that these aren't always true. I think people from anywhere get along pretty well." The international students, who form a small but noticeable contingent, "tend to keep to themselves," perhaps "due to a culture or language barrier." About one-quarter of the campus population is Jewish.

STATE UNIVERSITY OF NEW YORK—UNIVERSITY AT ALBANY

FINANCIAL AID: 518-442-3202 • E-MAIL: UGADMISSIONS@ALBANY.EDU • WEBSITE: WWW.ALBANY.EDU

THE PRINCETON REVIEW SAYS

Admissions

Very important factors considered include: rigor of secondary school record, class rank, academic GPA, standardized test scores, recommendation(s), character/personal qualities. *Important factors considered include:* application essay. *Other factors considered include:* extracurricular activities, talent/ability, first generation, alumni/ae relation, geographical residence, volunteer work, work experience. SAT or ACT required; SAT Subject Tests considered if submitted. ACT with Writing required. TOEFL required of all international applicants. High school diploma is required and GED is accepted. *Academic units required:* 4 English, 2 math, 2 science, 2 science labs, 1 foreign language, 3 social studies, 2 history, 4 academic electives. *Academic units recommended:* 4 math, 3 science, 3 science labs, 3 foreign language.

Financial Aid

Students should submit: FAFSA. Priority filing deadline is 3/15. The Princeton Review suggests that all financial aid forms be submitted as soon as possible after October 1. *Need-based scholarships/grants offered:* Federal Pell, FSEOG, State scholarships/grants, Private scholarships, College/university scholarship or grant aid from institutional funds. *Loan aid offered:* Direct Subsidized Stafford Loans, Direct Unsubsidized Stafford Loans, Direct PLUS loans, Federal Perkins Loans. Applicants will be notified of awards on a rolling basis beginning 3/20. Federal Work-Study Program available. Institutional employment available.

The Inside Word

The Wall Street Journal has noted a growing trend among students who, in the past, had limited their postsecondary options to high-end private schools: More such students, the paper reported, have broadened their vision to include prestigious state schools such as SUNY Albany. The driving force, unsurprisingly, is economic. Unless there is an unlikely decline in the cost of private education, expect admissions at schools like UAlbany to grow more competitive in coming years.

THE SCHOOL SAYS "..."

From the Admissions Office

"Increasing numbers of well-prepared students are discovering the benefits of study in UAlbany's nationally ranked programs and are taking advantage of outstanding internship and employment opportunities in upstate New York's 'Tech Valley.' The already strong undergraduate program is further enhanced by The Honors College, a university-wide program for ambitious students, offering enhanced honors courses and co-curricular options including honors housing. Living-Learning Communities provide additional opportunities for incoming freshmen to live and take classes with others who share their interests. Study Abroad programs offer global access to over 600 programs worldwide.

"Eight schools and colleges offer bachelor's, master's, and doctoral programs to nearly 13,000 undergraduates and 4,500 graduate students. An award-winning advisement program helps students take advantage of all these options by customizing the undergraduate experiences. More than two-thirds of UAlbany graduates go on for advanced degrees, and acceptance to law and medical school is above the national average.

"Student life on campus includes 200 clubs, honor societies, and other groups, and nineteen Division I varsity teams. Nearly 8,000 UAlbany students engage in community service activities. With twenty other colleges in the region, Albany is a great college town, adjacent to the spectacular natural and recreational centers of New York and New England.

"Freshmen are awarded more than $2.1 million in merit scholarships each year and nearly two-thirds of our students receive financial aid."

SELECTIVITY
Admissions Rating	83
# of applicants	21,755
% of applicants accepted	56
% of acceptees attending	10

FRESHMAN PROFILE
Range SAT Critical Reading	490–580
Range SAT Math	520–600
Range ACT Composite	22–26
Minimum paper TOEFL	550
Minimum internet-based TOEFL	79
Average HS GPA	3.5
% graduated top 10% of class	18
% graduated top 25% of class	49
% graduated top 50% of class	86

DEADLINES
Early action	
Deadline	11/15
Notification	1/15
Regular	
Priority	3/1
Deadline	3/1
Nonfall registration?	Yes

FINANCIAL FACTS
Financial Aid Rating	77
Annual in-state tuition	$6,470
Annual out-of-state tuition	$19,590
Room and board	$12,426
Required fees	$2,526
Books and supplies	$1,200
Average frosh need-based scholarship	$8,194
Average UG need-based scholarship	$7,358
% needy frosh rec. need-based scholarship or grant aid	84
% needy UG rec. need-based scholarship or grant aid	84
% needy frosh rec. non-need-based scholarship or grant aid	3
% needy UG rec. non-need-based scholarship or grant aid	2
% needy frosh rec. need-based self-help aid	75
% needy UG rec. need-based self-help aid	78
% frosh rec. any financial aid	64
% UG rec. any financial aid	57
% frosh need fully met	70
% ugrads need fully met	7
Average % of frosh need met	59
Average % of ugrad need met	61

STEPHENS COLLEGE

1200 EAST BROADWAY, COLUMBIA, MO 65215 • ADMISSIONS: 573-876-7207 • FAX: 573-876-7237

STUDENTS SAY "..."

Academics
Stephens College is one of the oldest all women's educational institutions in the country, having spent more than 180 years "empowering women to be independent and show that we can change the world." Class sizes are very small, so it makes for "a very intensive learning experience," but luckily the programs here are "so awesome and creative, no Stephens woman is ever bored." The fashion program is wildly popular and an annual fashion show is one of the school's most anticipated events, and a strong theatre program "consistently produces great performers." "Although we are small, we are mighty," says a student. "It feels like a warm hug everyday on campus."

Stephens is "blessed" to have an incredible teaching staff. "By creating an amazing and comfortable environment to learn in and ask questions we are set up to succeed in our futures," says a student. "They also make class time meaningful and always worth going." "You hit up your favorite professors... during their office hours and catch up with them the same way you caught up with your friends in the morning over coffee," says a student. All professors "make time to work with you on a personal level" both inside and outside of the classroom and "include lesson plans for every type of learner," taking time for the experts and the newbies no matter their skill level. Each student gets an adviser in their department who "attentive to their needs and goals," and the student body and staff "have amazing communication amongst each other" as well.

Life
Stephens 'Susies' "enjoy having a great time, but realize when it is time to study." School-sponsored events can be as frequent as two to four in a day with big events (such as "Half the Sky Day, Citizen Jane, and Diversity Week") happening once or twice a week. When students "aren't throwing little parties or fighting the good fight, we just chill." People enjoy "making meals together in the community kitchens" or at an on-campus apartment, and the lobbies have TVs so "self-organized movie nights are popular," as well. Some dorm halls "could use a bit of an update," but all speak lovingly of the "cozy" hallway parties and ensuing friendships. Also of note: the school allows pets on campus.

Most girls are committed to multiple clubs or sports, as "you'd have to go out of your way to not participate in something." Columbia itself is a great three-college town filled with everything from "awesome food joints like Gumby's Pizza and Strange Donuts to art galleries, clubs/bars, Saturday college football games, arcades, geek/novelty stores, and much more." Students like to go out and shop, hit the bars (if they're of age), or just go hiking or exploring the local caves and trails surrounding the city.

Student Body
This community of "inspiring, supportive and motivating women" is "a melting pot of women" where everyone "appreciates the outcasts and black sheep." There are no cookie-cutter college groups here, and a quick survey of the campus will reveal a group of "genuine" women who embody what they love, and whether that means "wearing riding boots, stage makeup, or toting a way too heavy light kit, students are always working on something and looking to achieve their dreams." "We come from literally all over the world. It's such a welcoming, diverse atmosphere," says one girl. Unsurprisingly, feminism "runs strong" here and Stephens is also a "very liberal LGBT+ friendly" place. "Imagine if Katniss from *The Hunger Games*, Rey from *Star Wars*, Anna and Elsa from *Frozen*, Hermione from *Harry Potter*, and Tris from *The Hunger Games* all went to school together," says a student. "Yeah, it's that."

FINANCIAL AID: 573-876-7106 • E-MAIL: APPLY@STEPHENS.EDU • WEBSITE: WWW.STEPHENS.EDU/

THE PRINCETON REVIEW SAYS

Admissions

Very important factors considered include: rigor of secondary school record, academic GPA, standardized test scores, application essay. *Important factors considered include:* recommendation(s), extracurricular activities. *Other factors considered include:* class rank, interview, talent/ability, character/personal qualities, volunteer work, work experience, level of applicant's interest. SAT or ACT required. ACT with or without writing accepted. TOEFL required of all international applicants. High school diploma is required and GED is accepted. *Academic units recommended:* 4 English, 3 math, 2 science, 2 foreign language, 1 social studies.

Financial Aid

Students should submit: FAFSA. Priority filing deadline is 3/15. The Princeton Review suggests that all financial aid forms be submitted as soon as possible after October 1. *Need-based scholarships/grants offered:* Federal Pell, FSEOG, State scholarships/grants, Private scholarships, College/university scholarship or grant aid from institutional funds. *Loan aid offered:* Federal Perkins Loans. Applicants will be notified of awards on a rolling basis beginning 3/1. Federal Work-Study Program available. Institutional employment available.

The Inside Word

Even with only half the population eligible for admission, the applicant pool at Stephens is still quite small, so anyone bearing less than a solid B average had better have the test scores and activities to make up space. A little over half of all applicants get in, and early decision is recommended for students who know this distinctive college is where they want to be.

THE SCHOOL SAYS ". . ."

From the Admissions Office

"Stephens College prepares students to become leaders and innovators in a rapidly changing world, and engages lifelong learners in an educational experience characterized by intellectual rigor, creative expression and professional practice. Since its founding in 1833, the College has been offering innovative, career-focused programs sound in the liberal arts with a focus on creative arts and sciences. Stephens takes a hands-on, experiential approach to education, making sure students get both quality classroom instruction and external work experiences.

"The second-oldest women's college in the U.S., Stephens is committed to educating and empowering women at all stages in life. At Stephens, women learn to think critically, communicate powerfully, lead responsibly and engage for change. The curriculum is thoughtful and respects those values.

"Stephens is a pet-friendly campus proudly located in Columbia, Missouri, home to more than 36,000 college students, and the campus is located just minutes from Columbia's thriving downtown district."

SELECTIVITY

Admissions Rating	89
# of applicants	1,153
% of applicants accepted	54
% of acceptees attending	30

FRESHMAN PROFILE

Range ACT Composite	26–29
Minimum paper TOEFL	550
Average HS GPA	3.3
% graduated top 10% of class	16
% graduated top 25% of class	41
% graduated top 50% of class	77

DEADLINES

Early decision	
Deadline	11/15
Notification	12/1
Early action	
Deadline	1/1
Notification	1/15
Regular	
Priority	1/1
Nonfall registration?	Yes

APPLICANTS ALSO LOOK AT AND OFTEN PREFER
University of Missouri

AND RARELY PREFER
Butler University

FINANCIAL FACTS

Financial Aid Rating	79
Annual tuition	$28,976
Room and board	$9,818
Books and supplies	$1,000
Average frosh need-based scholarship	$12,945
Average UG need-based scholarship	$11,618
% needy frosh rec. need-based scholarship or grant aid	100
% needy UG rec. need-based scholarship or grant aid	100
% needy frosh rec. non-need-based scholarship or grant aid	65
% needy UG rec. non-need-based scholarship or grant aid	75
% needy frosh rec. need-based self-help aid	91
% needy UG rec. need-based self-help aid	93
% frosh rec. any financial aid	100
% UG rec. any financial aid	99
% frosh need fully met	1
% ugrads need fully met	1
Average % of frosh need met	45
Average % of ugrad need met	48

STETSON UNIVERSITY

421 N. WOODLAND BLVD, DELAND, FL 32723 • ADMISSIONS: 386-822-7100 • FAX: 386-822-7112

STUDENTS SAY "..."

Academics

The moment they arrive at Central Florida's Stetson University, students sense the "welcoming" atmosphere that permeates the campus. Indeed, this small school of 3,000 undergrads excels at fostering a "tight knit community," "personal growth" and "intellectual development." It also doesn't hurt that the campus is simply "stunning." Moreover, Stetson students value that the university really sees students as "individual[s], not number[s]." Certainly, that can be partially attributed to "small class sizes" which allow for "individualized attention." Academically, among the many top-notch majors offered at Stetson are the "great political science department" and "great education program." Inside the classroom, undergrads are greeted by professors that "care more about how much you learn rather than individual exam grades." As one marketing major boasts, "Professors have allowed me to tailor assignments after my own personal interests." Teachers here are also "extremely supportive and push you harder than you've been pushed before." Professors here, a student explains, "really take the time to get to know their students and want to develop personal connections. This creates a more robust learning environment in which everyone can learn from each other." And a fellow environmental studies student eloquently sums up her experience stating, "The level of care and community that this place holds still astounds me, and it is what makes Stetson special."

Life

You have to work extremely hard to be bored at Stetson. To begin with, undergrads love to take advantage of the university's beautiful campus: "We often spend time on the university's green space playing football, relaxing, studying or flying kites." Additionally, "there are a lot of gatherings around campus, and something is always going on, either organized by the school itself or by student-run clubs. More specifically, "there are tons of campus events like the farmer's market, movie nights, guest speakers, and sports games that nearly everyone goes to and loves." Greek life is also fairly prevalent at Stetson and "frats usually have parties every Thursday, Friday, and Saturday." Thankfully, "Greek life is very accepting at this school and most of the Greek organizations are very service oriented." Though hometown Deland is "small," a marketing student insists "it offers a lot if you explore it." Certainly, "between the Springs, historic downtown, and the relative closeness of New Smyrna Beach, Daytona, and Orlando, there's a lot to do outside of the campus."

Student Body

Undergrads at Stetson are an active lot and we're told that a "large portion of the student body is either involved in Greek life or plays a sport." However, there's no need to worry if you don't fall into either demographic. A marketing major assures us that "Stetson is very diverse. You have people dedicated to academics, athletics, global issues, politics, social constraints, etc. I haven't known many students who felt like they didn't fit in." Of course, it's also easy for these "hard working" undergrads to find common ground. After all, most of them are quite "dedicated to their studies." Additionally, since "most students live on campus" it is "easy to make friends and find a group to hang out with." Many undergrads also emphasize that their peers are "nice and sociable." And we're told that "no matter where you go there's someone new to meet and that is willing to meet you."

FINANCIAL AID: 800-688-7120 • E-MAIL: ADMISSIONS@STETSON.EDU • WEBSITE: STETSON.EDU

THE PRINCETON REVIEW SAYS

Admissions

Very important factors considered include: rigor of secondary school record, academic GPA. *Important factors considered include:* class rank, standardized test scores, application essay, recommendation(s), interview, extracurricular activities, talent/ability, character/personal qualities, volunteer work, work experience. *Other factors considered include:* alumni/ae relation, geographical residence, state residency, racial/ethnic status. SAT or ACT required for some. ACT with or without writing accepted. SAT with or without Essay component accepted. TOEFL required of all international applicants. High school diploma is required and GED is accepted. *Academic units required:* 4 English, 3 math, 3 science, 2 foreign language, 2 social studies.

Financial Aid

Students should submit: FAFSA. Priority filing deadline is 12/1. The Princeton Review suggests that all financial aid forms be submitted as soon as possible after October 1. *Need-based scholarships/grants offered:* Federal Pell, FSEOG, State scholarships/grants, Private scholarships, College/university scholarship or grant aid from institutional funds. *Loan aid offered:* Direct Subsidized Stafford Loans, Direct Unsubsidized Stafford Loans, Direct PLUS loans, Federal Perkins Loans. Applicants will be notified of awards on a rolling basis beginning 12/1. Federal Work-Study Program available. Institutional employment available.

The Inside Word

"Creative problem solving and innovation are traditional hallmarks of a Stetson education. In fact, Stetson University is home to many Florida firsts—the first private university in the state, the first collegiate newspaper, the first schools of business administration and music, the first college of law, and the first private university to integrate.

"Stetson University students are daring, hardworking, open-minded, and caring. Our mission is providing a challenging education in a creative community where learning, leadership, and values meet. We mentor students; cultivating in them the qualities of mind and heart and preparing them to gain confidence as informed citizens of local communities and the world. Undergraduate leadership, research, internships, and community-engaged learning flourish here.

"Stetson University is home to eighteen Division I athletics teams, over 100 clubs, and seventy-three academic programs with both undergraduate and graduate studies in many areas. Accredited by numerous accrediting agencies, including the Southern Association of College and Schools Commission on Colleges, Stetson is among only a handful of schools worldwide where both Business and Accounting programs are accredited by AACSB International at the undergraduate and graduate levels.

"Academic and campus life programs are centered on a rigorous examination of values with leadership potential, records of personal growth, and community service. Here, graduation isn't just the end goal. It's one stop along the way, as students pursue something greater for themselves and the world around them.

"At Stetson University, we dare students to be significant."

SELECTIVITY

Admissions Rating	85
# of applicants	11,216
% of applicants accepted	63
% of acceptees attending	14
# offered a place on the wait list	522
% accepting a place on wait list	95
% admitted from wait list	39

FRESHMAN PROFILE

Range SAT Critical Reading	530–640
Range SAT Math	520–620
Range SAT Writing	500–620
Range ACT Composite	24–28
Minimum paper TOEFL	550
Minimum internet-based TOEFL	79
Average HS GPA	3.9
% graduated top 10% of class	28
% graduated top 25% of class	60
% graduated top 50% of class	88

DEADLINES

Regular	
Priority	12/1
Nonfall registration?	Yes

APPLICANTS ALSO LOOK AT AND OFTEN PREFER
Florida State University; University of Florida; University of Central Florida

AND SOMETIMES PREFER
Rollins College; University of Tampa

AND RARELY PREFER
Elon University; University of Miami; Florida Southern College

FINANCIAL FACTS

Financial Aid Rating	83
Annual tuition	$42,890
Room and board	$12,326
Required fees	$350
Books and supplies	$1,200
Average frosh need-based scholarship	$28,926
Average UG need-based scholarship	$26,952
% needy frosh rec. need-based scholarship or grant aid	100
% needy UG rec. need-based scholarship or grant aid	99
% needy frosh rec. non-need-based scholarship or grant aid	21
% needy UG rec. non-need-based scholarship or grant aid	18
% needy frosh rec. need-based self-help aid	72
% needy UG rec. need-based self-help aid	73
% frosh rec. any financial aid	100
% UG rec. any financial aid	99
% UG borrow to pay for school	69
Average cumulative indebtedness	$32,443
% frosh need fully met	23
% ugrads need fully met	21
Average % of frosh need met	78
Average % of ugrad need met	76

STEVENS INSTITUTE OF TECHNOLOGY

CASTLE POINT ON HUDSON, HOBOKEN, NJ 07030 • ADMISSIONS: 201-216-5194 • FAX: 201-216-8348

STUDENTS SAY "..."

Academics

Located in New Jersey (just a pizza's throw away from New York City), Stevens Institute of Technology gives students a practical engineering education with top-tier access to employers, accelerated programs, free summer classes, and co-op opportunities. The career development services are by far one of the school's greatest strengths, and the associated offices "work hard to help students obtain internships and also full time positions" in which to apply the knowledge they've picked up from the "very rigorous and challenging" curriculum.

Professors are for the most part "very knowledgeable and always finding new ways to communicate that knowledge," and are "engaging but can be a little dry." They "are masters in their field and very available," and "watch out for you and make sure you are on track and understand the material." There are certainly some professors that have detractors (particularly the ones more focused on their research), but "upperclassmen are very good at letting younger generations know which professors they can expect to work with...and which ones are not as understanding."

Above all, Stevens students are "focused on making a difference on campus and being innovative in the workforce following the completion of their program." A multitude of research and entrepreneurship programs help channel students in the right direction, and "the ability to graduate with five semesters of full-time work experience is incredible." "The opportunities at this school are meaningful and unique," says a student. "The school makes me want to push myself to be the best that I can be."

Life

Even though the school is just a PATH train ride away from Manhattan, Hoboken itself is "amazing with lots of fun events and activities." While students "do spend most of their time studying," there is plenty of fun to be had on campus and people here "love all the activities that are provided to us by the entertainment committee." The committee "gets tickets at reduced admission to various shows and concerts in the surrounding area," and there are larger traditional events throughout the school year such as Techfest (a huge concert with DJs and artists), or Boken, which is a weekend long event that follows a theme and lets students "participate in activities, eat good food and obtain giveaways." The school is "great at giving back to the community and providing a wealth of services to Hoboken."

Still, "being able to be in New York at the drop of the hat is pretty unparalleled," and a lot of students take advantage of various free activities that go on in NYC. If you're more of a homebody, then "you could host card games or play video games with pretty much anybody you're familiar with; everyone is pretty eager to make friends and be social." On-campus housing is "more crowded and more expensive compared to what is available off-campus," which is quite plentiful. There is a good deal of greek activity on campus, and "fraternity parties and apartment parties are common."

Student Body

This "technologically minded, friendly" group of "predominantly white males" tends to be "somewhat nerdy," and "there are clubs for just about every interest." A large international population brings in people from all over the world, but since this is a specialized school "there are a lot of baseline ways of thinking that run across the majority of campus" that make it easy for people to fit in. Though the experience can vary greatly depending on whether one is "a foreigner or native, undergrad or grad, athlete or non-athlete, male or female," this is a group that "will help anyone who needs it." "I have never met a group of people who are so friendly and kind," says a student.

FINANCIAL AID: 201-216-5555 • E-MAIL: ADMISSIONS@STEVENS.EDU • WEBSITE: WWW.STEVENS.EDU

THE PRINCETON REVIEW SAYS

Admissions

Very important factors considered include: rigor of secondary school record, academic GPA, standardized test scores. *Important factors considered include:* talent/ability, character/personal qualities. *Other factors considered include:* class rank, application essay, recommendation(s), interview, extracurricular activities, first generation, alumni/ae relation, geographical residence, state residency, racial/ethnic status, volunteer work, work experience, level of applicant's interest. SAT or ACT required for some. ACT with or without writing accepted. SAT with or without Essay component accepted. TOEFL required of all international applicants. High school diploma is required and GED is not accepted. *Academic units required:* 4 English, 4 math, 3 science, 3 science labs. *Academic units recommended:* 4 science, 4 science labs, 2 foreign language, 2 social studies, 2 history, 4 academic electives.

Financial Aid

Students should submit: FAFSA, CSS/Financial Aid PROFILE. Priority filing deadline is 2/15. The Princeton Review suggests that all financial aid forms be submitted as soon as possible after October 1. *Need-based scholarships/grants offered:* Federal Pell, FSEOG, State scholarships/grants, Private scholarships, College/university scholarship or grant aid from institutional funds, United Negro College Fund. *Loan aid offered:* Direct Subsidized Stafford Loans, Direct Unsubsidized Stafford Loans, Direct PLUS loans, Federal Perkins Loans, State Loans. Federal Work-Study Program available. Institutional employment available.

The Inside Word

Often preferred by students who can't (or don't want to) get into MIT or Caltech, Stevens is among the best of the second-tier programs in engineering, math, science, and technology, and its visibility to employers in New York and New Jersey makes it a great choice for students who dream of jobs in the tri-state area. As well as grades, test scores, and recommendations, the school encourages all applicants to interview with them.

THE SCHOOL SAYS "..."

From the Admissions Office

"A strong commitment to discovery, collaboration and mentorship drive the Stevens academic culture, which has been built on a legacy of technological innovation since 1870. Students and faculty collaborate in an interdisciplinary, student-centric, entrepreneurial environment to leverage technology to confront global challenges. From Habitat to Humanity projects to the Solar Decathlon team advancing energy efficient housing, Stevens continues to contribute to the community on our campus, in our hometown of Hoboken, NJ, and to the global community at large. Stevens is known as The Innovation University® and is consistently ranked among the nation's elite for ROI for students, career services, and mid-career salaries of alumni. Stevens' proximity to New York City and the surrounding metro area cultivates unmatchable internships, cooperative education placements, and other project-based learning opportunities for Stevens students.

"Choose from more than thirty undergraduate majors in business, humanities, arts, computer science, engineering and sciences; double major or pursue both a bachelor's and a master's degrees. Students participate in a capstone project often undertaken in collaboration with students from other disciplines, mentored by faculty, and sponsored by industry partners. Graduates are highly skilled in creating solutions at the intersections of disciplines and can lead in today's complex, cross-functional and highly technical environments. A strong career development program and excellent preparation pay off: graduates fare exceptionally well in career and graduate school placement. A robust student life, an exciting college town, and more than 100 student organizations and twenty-six NCAA Division III athletics teams add to an enriching student experience."

SELECTIVITY

Admissions Rating	94
# of applicants	6,540
% of applicants accepted	44
% of acceptees attending	24
# offered a place on the wait list	1,047
% accepting a place on wait list	34
% admitted from wait list	52
# of early decision applicants	798
% accepted early decision	56

FRESHMAN PROFILE

Range SAT Critical Reading	590–680
Range SAT Math	650–745
Range ACT Composite	29–32
Minimum paper TOEFL	550
Minimum internet-based TOEFL	82
Average HS GPA	3.9
% graduated top 10% of class	62
% graduated top 25% of class	92
% graduated top 50% of class	99

DEADLINES

Early decision	
Deadline	11/15
Notification	12/15
Regular	
Deadline	2/1
Notification	4/1
Nonfall registration?	No

APPLICANTS ALSO LOOK AT AND OFTEN PREFER

Princeton University; Massachusetts Institute of Technology; Carnegie Mellon University

AND SOMETIMES PREFER

Lehigh University; New York University

AND RARELY PREFER

Rensselaer Polytechnic Institute

FINANCIAL FACTS

Financial Aid Rating	82
Annual tuition	$47,134
Room & board	$14,350
Required fees	$1,704
Books and supplies	$1,000
Average frosh need-based scholarship	$13,691
Average UG need-based scholarship	$13,299
% needy frosh rec. need-based scholarship or grant aid	43
% needy UG rec. need-based scholarship or grant aid	61
% needy frosh rec. non-need-based scholarship or grant aid	97
% needy UG rec. non-need-based scholarship or grant aid	94
% needy frosh rec. need-based self-help aid	62
% needy UG rec. need-based self-help aid	72
% frosh rec. any financial aid	99
% UG rec. any financial aid	91
% UG borrow to pay for school	75
Average cumulative indebtedness	$48,244
% frosh need fully met	28
% ugrads need fully met	20
Average % of frosh need met	74
Average % of ugrad need met	67

STONEHILL COLLEGE

320 WASHINGTON STREET, EASTON, MA 02357-5610 • ADMISSION: 508-565-1373 • FAX: 508-565-1545

STUDENTS SAY "..."

Academics

This small liberal arts college located between Boston and Providence "creates an inclusive environment and presents its students with countless opportunities for internships and other pre-grad networking opportunities," opportunities pushed by educators who are "very engaging and passionate about their material." The professors here "have all worked in the field they teach," meaning "the academics are incredibly relevant to the real world." The school's modest size carries over to the classroom, where "class sizes are small enough to engage in meaningful discussions" with professors who "provide plenty of opportunities to meet with them outside of class and form lasting relationships with students." These discussion-based classes "involve the students and engage them in the learning process," while the "extremely helpful" educators "make students aware that they consider students real people and are always available both to discuss class material or personal matters if they can help." The idea is to help students "work toward nurturing the whole person through a comprehensive education." Some see the lack of graduate students as a plus, too, since "no graduate students means more opportunities for undergraduates, especially research positions." With "small classes so students get to know their professors more intimately than at a larger university" and opportunities to study abroad and for internships, students say Stonehill is "worth the money."

Life

For many at Stonehill, life is "mainly centered around academics." Even downtime is spent doing things other than partying. Students are "provided with opportunities that abound, especially in the form of internships and community service," so most "get pretty involved in clubs, sports, and community service." These organizations allow students to "form very strong, long lasting relationships." The "great atmosphere" includes a strong focus on sports—"even if someone isn't involved in varsity sports, the campus is very active in Rec sports, intramurals, and just general fitness and use of the athletic facility"—along with the expected "watching movies, taking hikes around campus, playing video games with friends and taking the school shuttle to the mall." Trivia, bingo, campus coffeehouse gatherings, and going out to "sweat all over each other on a dance floor" provide other distractions. If this sounds far removed from keggers and drunken binges, it is. The idea that partying is not the be-all and end-all of weekend life "is present among a strong population of Stonehill College students." One student sums it up: "I never thought my weekends would be full of volunteering until I came here and now I truly wouldn't have it any other way."

Student Body

"Stonehill is always described as a place where people hold the door open for you," a campus full of "relatively normal and sociable" "middle class white kids." Expect a student body that is "very New England—lots of plaid, jeans, Stonehill sweatshirts." There may be "some diversity," but not much in the way of ethnic minorities. Instead, "students stand out like they would in high school; there's the jocks, nerds, school activists, party animals, and so on." For the most part, "everyone is pretty laid back." The "friendly and helpful" students here are "academically driven and community focused," making it "feel like family even after being here for only a couple months." There are cliques, but they "tend to be predicated on what type of activities you do or your major" rather than who you are, because no matter what, "everyone is still friendly to everyone else." Though "there is a place for everyone at Stonehill," those "who are less community-focused have a harder time clicking with the student body but will undoubtedly find friends if they try." This openness and willingness to embrace one another "is what has led us to become such a strong community."

FINANCIAL AID: 508-565-1088 • E-MAIL: ADMISSION@STONEHILL.EDU • WEBSITE: WWW.STONEHILL.EDU

THE PRINCETON REVIEW SAYS

Admissions

Very important factors considered include: rigor of secondary school record, class rank, academic GPA, talent/ability. *Important factors considered include:* application essay, recommendation(s), extracurricular activities. *Other factors considered include:* standardized test scores, interview, character/personal qualities, first generation, alumni/ae relation, geographical residence, religious affiliation/commitment, racial/ethnic status, volunteer work, work experience, level of applicant's interest. SAT Subject Tests considered if submitted. ACT with Writing required. TOEFL required of all international applicants. High school diploma is required and GED is accepted. *Academic units required:* 4 English, 3 math, 3 science, 3 science labs, 3 foreign language, 3 history. *Academic units recommended:* 4 English, 4 math, 4 science, 3 science labs, 4 foreign language, 4 history.

Financial Aid

Students should submit: FAFSA, CSS/Financial Aid PROFILE, Noncustodial PROFILE. Regular filing deadline is 2/1. The Princeton Review suggests that all financial aid forms be submitted as soon as possible after October 1. *Need-based scholarships/grants offered:* Federal Pell, FSEOG, State scholarships/grants, Private scholarships, College/university scholarship or grant aid from institutional funds. *Loan aid offered:* Direct Subsidized Stafford Loans, Direct Unsubsidized Stafford Loans, Direct PLUS loans, Federal Perkins Loans, State Loans. Applicants will be notified of awards on or about 4/1. Federal Work-Study Program available. Institutional employment available.

The Inside Word

Stonehill may not be as selective as the elite colleges of the Boston area, but students here are still expected to be top students. Half were in the top 10 percent of their high school classes, so if you want to compete, ensure your grades and are strong. Test scores are optional.

THE SCHOOL SAYS "..."

From the Admissions Office

"Founded by the Congregation of Holy Cross, Stonehill is a Catholic college that values integrity, tradition and the rewards that come when you pair rigorous academics with world-class faculty committed to student success. Our approach to liberal arts education is distinctive because it melds challenging courses, nationally recognized experiential learning and life-changing service opportunities to shape graduates into compassionate leaders and global thinkers.

"Stonehill is on a beautiful 384-acre campus with architecture ranging from traditional brick-and-ivy academic buildings to a state-of-the-art science center. With its ideal location between Boston and Providence, two of New England's most vibrant cities, Stonehill is perfectly situated for internships, professional networking, cultural experiences, pro sports and countless entertainment and dining options.

"More than 90 percent of our students study abroad, complete an internship or perform field research before graduation. Such experiences along with thirty-nine majors and fifty-one minors in the liberal arts, sciences and business prepare them for productive careers or lives of service. Our students are also active outside of class. Whether its Ultimate Disc, dance or one of our Division II varsity teams, most participate in some form of athletics. With a student/faculty ratio of 12:1 and an average class size of nineteen, individual attention is a Stonehill hallmark. Whether collaborating on research or mentoring students on careers and graduate school, our faculty puts students first. The result shows in our students' successes: 98 percent of Stonehill graduates over the last five years were employed, volunteering or in graduate school within one year of graduation."

SELECTIVITY
Admissions Rating	80
# of applicants	5,892
% of applicants accepted	75
% of acceptees attending	15
# offered a place on the wait list	390
% accepting a place on wait list	25
% admitted from wait list	24
# of early decision applicants	64
% accepted early decision	89

FRESHMAN PROFILE
Range SAT Critical Reading	510–600
Range SAT Math	510–620
Range SAT Writing	500–610
Range ACT Composite	22–27
Minimum paper TOEFL	575
Minimum internet-based TOEFL	90
Average HS GPA	3.3
% graduated top 10% of class	27
% graduated top 25% of class	59
% graduated top 50% of class	89

DEADLINES
Early decision	
Deadline	12/1
Notification	12/31
Early action	
Deadline	11/1
Notification	12/31
Regular	
Deadline	1/15
Notification	3/15
Nonfall registration?	Yes

APPLICANTS ALSO LOOK AT AND OFTEN PREFER
Providence College; College of the Holy Cross; University of Massachusetts Amherst

AND SOMETIMES PREFER
Assumption College; Quinnipiac University

FINANCIAL FACTS
Financial Aid Rating	87
Annual tuition	$38,550
Room and board	$14,720
Books and supplies	$893
Average frosh need-based scholarship	$25,498
Average UG need-based scholarship	$24,544
% needy frosh rec. need-based scholarship or grant aid	99
% needy UG rec. need-based scholarship or grant aid	96
% needy frosh rec. non-need-based scholarship or grant aid	25
% needy UG rec. non-need-based scholarship or grant aid	20
% needy frosh rec. need-based self-help aid	75
% needy UG rec. need-based self-help aid	80
% frosh rec. any financial aid	99
% UG rec. any financial aid	95
% UG borrow to pay for school	76
Average cumulative indebtedness	$33,942
% frosh need fully met	50
% ugrads need fully met	49
Average % of frosh need met	92
Average % of ugrad need met	92

SUFFOLK UNIVERSITY

EIGHT ASHBURTON PLACE, BOSTON, MA 02108 • ADMISSIONS: 617-573-8460 • FAX: 617-573-1574

STUDENTS SAY "..."

Academics

Located in "the heart of downtown Boston," Suffolk University offers a "happy environment" for "anyone who wants to be at a school and still be directly in the city." The university offers "a wide selection of interesting majors" and small class sizes throughout its College of Arts and Sciences and Sawyer Business School, giving this "united, diverse mass of students" a "global perspective in a real-world, urban setting." Students observe that depending on "[which] professor you have...you will like the class or not." Across the board, the teachers come across as being "very friendly" and genuine, and they "speak to you like an adult with respect." Some professors are "a bit dry;" however, "when you find [a great professor], they will be there for you through anything." Some students "wish the classes were more challenging," saying, though others report that course work "is not easy." The school "offers students the resources they need should they want to put more effort into classes, job searching, and anything else, really;" including a newly-launched Student Success Division. "Class participation comes naturally because class size is so small and the professor knows your name," says a freshman. "The administration is a little ridiculous sometimes with [its] rules," but overall it has "good relationships with the students."

Life

With the city as its "campus and playground," there is an "endless array of things to do" at Suffolk University, including shopping, museums, restaurants, and culture. "The students become part of the city," says a sophomore. "Suffolk doesn't really have a campus," though no one really seems to mind, as most students knew what they had signed on for when they enrolled. Due to space constraints, not all upperclassmen can live on campus, and many happily choose to live in Boston apartments. "My classes require me to walk through the Common everyday," says one student. For those who do live on campus, the university offers freshman orientation activities that "students can participate [in] to ease the tensions of moving into a dorm and being on your own." Most students take their social lives off campus, choosing to hang out at other colleges and in the city itself. Suffolk's campus is dry, so "students have to find other places in which to party" on the weekends (weeknights are typically dedicated to homework). As for the commuters, most "don't interact directly with [resident] students as much." Unsurprisingly, "there's a lot of Boston pride among Suffolk students." "Everyone loves the Red Sox, the Celtics, and the Bruins."

Student Body

While more than half of the student body hails from Massachusetts, Suffolk is also home to a lot of international students. "It is very easy for a student to blend in due to Suffolk being a very diverse campus." Cultures and beliefs do indeed vary greatly—"that is definitely a part of what makes Suffolk so unique"—but "most students are friendly and interact with one another regardless of where they are from." However, there is a slight—though not tense—divide between two other classifications of Suffolk students: the large commuter populations and those who live in on-campus housing. "Suffolk is not very successful at integrating the two, but everyone seems to get along okay," says a student. Luckily, classes also require several group projects, "forcing students to work together." Preppy seems to be what the Suffolk student body preaches, and button downs, polo shirts, and Uggs abound—"most would *never* wear pajamas or sweatpants to class."

SUFFOLK UNIVERSITY

FINANCIAL AID: 617-573-8470 • E-MAIL: ADMISSION@SUFFOLK.EDU • WEBSITE: WWW.SUFFOLK.EDU

THE PRINCETON REVIEW SAYS

Admissions

Very important factors considered include: rigor of secondary school record, academic GPA. *Important factors considered include:* class rank. *Other factors considered include:* standardized test scores, application essay, recommendation(s), interview, extracurricular activities, talent/ability, character/personal qualities, first generation, volunteer work, work experience, level of applicant's interest. SAT or ACT considered if submitted; SAT Subject Tests considered if submitted. ACT with or without writing accepted. SAT with or without Essay component accepted. TOEFL required of all international applicants. High school diploma is required and GED is accepted. *Academic units required:* 4 English, 3 math, 2 science, 1 science lab, 2 foreign language, 1 social studies, 1 history, 3 computer science. *Academic units recommended:* 4 English, 4 math, 4 science, 4 foreign language, 2 social studies, 3 history, 3 computer science.

Financial Aid

Students should submit: FAFSA. Regular filing deadline is 3/1. The Princeton Review suggests that all financial aid forms be submitted as soon as possible after October 1. *Need-based scholarships/grants offered:* Federal Pell, FSEOG, State scholarships/grants, Private scholarships, College/university scholarship or grant aid from institutional funds. *Loan aid offered:* Direct Subsidized Stafford Loans, Direct Unsubsidized Stafford Loans, Direct PLUS loans, Federal Perkins Loans, State Loans, College/university loans from institutional funds. Applicants will be notified of awards on a rolling basis beginning 2/5. Federal Work-Study Program available. Institutional employment available.

The Inside Word

Suffolk is unapologetic about its mission to provide access and opportunity to college-bound students. That said, test scores and high school GPA requirements are average. Applicants whose numbers are above-average have a good chance of gaining admission.

THE SCHOOL SAYS "..."

From the Admissions Office

"Suffolk University is a comprehensive private university located on Boston's historic Beacon Hill. This global university offers a wide range of undergraduate and graduate degrees in over seventy areas of study. Distinguished by its teaching, the university utilizes the intellectual contributions of its faculty to provide a diverse, challenging and uniquely supportive environment in which motivated and capable students flourish. Students and faculty work together on our Beacon Hill campus, in the heart of historic Boston. They also come together at satellite campuses elsewhere in Massachusetts and in China, Europe and Africa. Suffolk students also meet virtually in our Suffolk MBA online program. The University's three schools—the College of Arts and Sciences, Sawyer School of Management and the Law School—provide a challenging, yet supportive educational environment for motivated students. Through the Student Success Division, classroom experiences flow seamlessly into internship opportunities that are just steps away from campus."

SELECTIVITY
Admissions Rating	74
# of applicants	8,650
% of applicants accepted	82
% of acceptees attending	19
# offered a place on the wait list	427
% accepting a place on wait list	100
% admitted from wait list	0

FRESHMAN PROFILE
Range SAT Critical Reading	450–560
Range SAT Math	460–560
Range SAT Writing	450–560
Range ACT Composite	20–25
Minimum paper TOEFL	550
Minimum internet-based TOEFL	77
Average HS GPA	3.2
% graduated top 10% of class	11
% graduated top 25% of class	40
% graduated top 50% of class	73

DEADLINES
Early action	
Deadline	11/15
Notification	12/15
Nonfall registration?	Yes

FINANCIAL FACTS
Financial Aid Rating	81
Annual tuition	$33,800
Room and board	$14,648
Required fees	$134
Books and supplies	$1,200
Average frosh need-based scholarship	$9,604
Average UG need-based scholarship	$14,356
% needy frosh rec. need-based scholarship or grant aid	81
% needy UG rec. need-based scholarship or grant aid	83
% needy frosh rec. non-need-based scholarship or grant aid	99
% needy UG rec. non-need-based scholarship or grant aid	72
% needy frosh rec. need-based self-help aid	83
% needy UG rec. need-based self-help aid	85
% frosh rec. any financial aid	94
% UG rec. any financial aid	73
% UG borrow to pay for school	75
Average cumulative indebtedness	$42,584
% frosh need fully met	12
% ugrads need fully met	13
Average % of frosh need met	69
Average % of ugrad need met	69

SUSQUEHANNA UNIVERSITY

514 UNIVERSITY AVENUE, SELINSGROVE, PA 17870 • ADMISSIONS: 570-372-4260 • FAX: 570-372-2760

CAMPUS LIFE

Quality of Life Rating	87
Fire Safety Rating	98
Green Rating	71
Type of school	Private
Affiliation	Lutheran
Environment	Town

STUDENTS

Total undergrad enrollment	2,196
% male/female	45/55
% from out of state	50
% frosh from public high school	84
% frosh live on campus	97
% ugrads live on campus	92
# of fraternities (% ugrad men join)	6 (18)
# of sororities (% ugrad women join)	5 (14)
% African American	6
% Asian	2
% Caucasian	81
% Hispanic	6
% Native American	<1
% Pacific Islander	<1
% Two or more races	3
% Race and/or ethnicity unknown	<1
% international	2
# of countries represented	20

SURVEY SAYS...

Students are happy
Lab facilities are great
Career services are great
Easy to get around campus
Lots of beer drinking

ACADEMICS

Academic Rating	77
% students returning for sophomore year	86
% students graduating within 4 years	68
% students graduating within 6 years	71
Calendar	Semester
Student/faculty ratio	12:1
Profs interesting rating	77
Profs accessible rating	85

Most classes have 10–19 students.
Most lab/discussion sessions have
10–19 students.

MOST POPULAR MAJORS

Business Administration and Management;
Speech Communication and Rhetoric; Biology

STUDENTS SAY "..."

Academics

Susquehanna University is an institution that "thrives on building strong leaders and independent thinkers." The school's "small" size means undergrads are joining a "close-knit community" replete with a "strong alumni network." Perhaps more importantly, it's evident that the school "is invested...in the success of their students." While Susquehanna offers a variety of great majors, students are prone to highlight the "top-notch creative writing program," "outstanding music education program" and "strong" science departments. Undergrads also praise a more unique aspect of a Susquehanna education— mandatory study off campus in a culture different from one's own (90 percent of students choose to go abroad). One senior elated about this requirement shares, "I believe that every young adult should have access to a cross-cultural experience and I value Susquehanna for making such an experience a priority for its students." Thankfully, for the most part, undergrads enjoy their on-campus education as well. By and large, this can be attributed to "fantastic" professors who "take a personal interest in their students." Indeed, the "friendly" teachers here really strive to make themselves "accessible." And, as one impressed creative writing major adds, a handful "often invite [students] up to their houses for dinner and discussion." However, one neuroscience major does caution that "you usually have to fight to get into a class with a 'good' professor and the registration process is always a hassle."

Life

There is always something exciting to seek out at Susquehanna! To begin with, "there are over [145] clubs and organizations (academic, cultural, religious, arts, service, special interest, etc.)" in which students can participate. Additionally, "the Student Activities Committee [sponsors] a lot of free events—including the occasional trapeze and gyroscope!" Many undergrads also enjoy the "on-campus nightclub [which] hosts free dances on the weekends." Moreover, Susquehanna is a fairly athletic school. Indeed, "varsity sports are huge on campus; we have a large number of athletic teams for such a small school. Students love "tailgating [at] sporting events" as well. Undergrads also flock to "Charlie's coffee house to watch movies or hang out with friends during the week." And, for students looking to unwind, "every Wednesday, Friday and Saturday night there is usually off campus partying happening." If students are itching to escape for a bit, they can take advantage of several "recreational places off campus (Bounce Plex, bowling alley, racetrack, rock climbing, hiking, etc.)" And though Selinsgrove "is a small town, it's got everything you need." A senior confidently proclaims that "there are plenty of places to eat and shop!"

Student Body

It can easily feel as though most Susquehanna students hail from "upper-middle class" homes located in either the "Mid-Atlantic [region or] New England." Fortunately, to the delight of many students, the "campus has been steadily diversifying over the years." And besides, these "outgoing" undergrads are able to forge bonds that go well beyond geography. After all, this is the type of student body that "will hold the door for you, even if you are 100 feet away." However, there are a handful of students who feel that, to fully fit in, you have to be "part of either Greek life or a sport." Naturally, other undergrads vehemently disagree, emphatically stating that "students find their niche quickly and make friends easily." A history major helps clarify by relaying that "roughly 25 percent of students are athletes and 17 percent are involved in Greek life. However for the most part students from every range of the spectrum interact and support each other." And one immensely proud and satisfied speech communication major triumphantly sums up, "We are all awesome. There's no other way to describe it besides awesomeness."

FINANCIAL AID: 570-372-4450 • E-MAIL: SUADMISS@SUSQU.EDU • WEBSITE: WWW.SUSQU.EDU

THE PRINCETON REVIEW SAYS
Admissions
Very important factors considered include: rigor of secondary school record, academic GPA. *Important factors considered include:* class rank, standardized test scores, application essay, recommendation(s), interview, extracurricular activities, talent/ability, character/personal qualities, alumni/ae relation, racial/ethnic status, volunteer work, work experience, level of applicant's interest. *Other factors considered include:* first generation, geographical residence, state residency. SAT or ACT considered if submitted. ACT with or without writing accepted. SAT with or without Essay component accepted. TOEFL required of all international applicants. High school diploma is required and GED is accepted. *Academic units required:* 4 English, 3 math, 2 science, 2 science labs, 2 foreign language, 2 social studies, 2 history, 2 academic electives. *Academic units recommended:* 4 English, 4 math, 3 science, 3 science labs, 4 foreign language, 4 social studies, 2 history, 3 academic electives.

Financial Aid
Students should submit: FAFSA, CSS/Financial Aid PROFILE, Business/Farm Supplement. Regular filing deadline is 5/1. The Princeton Review suggests that all financial aid forms be submitted as soon as possible after October 1. *Need-based scholarships/grants offered:* Federal Pell, FSEOG, State scholarships/grants, Private scholarships, College/university scholarship or grant aid from institutional funds. *Loan aid offered:* Direct Subsidized Stafford Loans, Direct Unsubsidized Stafford Loans, Direct PLUS loans, Federal Perkins Loans, College/university loans from institutional funds. Applicants will be notified of awards on a rolling basis beginning 3/15. Federal Work-Study Program available. Institutional employment available.

The Inside Word
Admissions officers at Susquehanna aim to understand the candidate behind the numbers. They want students who demonstrate intellect, creativity and leadership. The university also realizes that standardized test scores aren't always representative of a student's abilities. Therefore, applicants who believe their test scores do not reflect their abilities may apply Test Score Optional. Finally, Susquehanna operates on a rolling admissions policy.

THE SCHOOL SAYS "..."
From the Admissions Office
"No matter your major or career plans, you will graduate from Susquehanna with the broad-based academic foundation and 21st-century job skills—critical thinking, writing, teamwork and communication skills—that employers and graduate schools seek. Our challenging and relevant academic programs—plus internships, practica and research completed by 90 percent of students—result in 96 percent of new graduates employed or in graduate school within six months.

"Choose from over sixty majors and minors in liberal arts and science or preprofessional programs. Our business school is AACSB-accredited, placing it among the top 5 percent of business schools worldwide.

"Susquehanna faculty members are exceptional teachers and scholars, and many involve students in their research. They also mentor students about career choices or strategies for getting into graduate school, and support you with letters of recommendation. Many professors stay connected and follow their students' careers after graduation.

"You and 100 percent of your classmates will study off campus through our nationally-recognized Global Opportunities (GO) program. By completing a cross-cultural experience for at least two weeks in the U.S. or abroad, you'll broaden your perspective and options through your ability to connect with people from other backgrounds, be they coworkers or clients.

"You will enjoy first-rate learning and living facilities on our beautiful 325-acre residential campus. Make friends through 145 student-run clubs and organizations, twenty-three NCAA Division III intercollegiate sports, fraternities, sororities and service groups. With easy access to major East Coast cities, you'll network with alumni, pursue internships, explore professional opportunities and have fun!"

SELECTIVITY
Admissions Rating	80
# of applicants	5,304
% of applicants accepted	76
% of acceptees attending	17
# offered a place on the wait list	0
# of early decision applicants	96
% accepted early decision	80

FRESHMAN PROFILE
Range SAT Critical Reading	500–610
Range SAT Math	510–610
Range SAT Writing	480–600
Range ACT Composite	23–27
Minimum paper TOEFL	550
Minimum internet-based TOEFL	81
Average HS GPA	3.5
% graduated top 10% of class	26
% graduated top 25% of class	57
% graduated top 50% of class	87

DEADLINES
Early decision	
Deadline	11/15
Notification	12/1
Early action	
Deadline	11/1
Notification	12/1
Nonfall registration?	Yes

APPLICANTS ALSO LOOK AT AND OFTEN PREFER
Bucknell University; Villanova University; Gettysburg College; Muhlenberg College; Franklin and Marshall College

AND SOMETIMES PREFER
Quinnipiac University; Ithaca College

AND RARELY PREFER
Ursinus College; Juniata College

FINANCIAL FACTS
Financial Aid Rating	84
Annual tuition	$43,160
Room and board	$11,620
Required fees	$560
Books and supplies	$900
Average frosh need-based scholarship	$30,505
Average UG need-based scholarship	$28,023
% needy frosh rec. need-based scholarship or grant aid	100
% needy UG rec. need-based scholarship or grant aid	100
% needy frosh rec. non-need-based scholarship or grant aid	17
% needy UG rec. non-need-based scholarship or grant aid	15
% needy frosh rec. need-based self-help aid	81
% needy UG rec. need-based self-help aid	83
% frosh rec. any financial aid	99
% UG rec. any financial aid	99
% UG borrow to pay for school	83
Average cumulative indebtedness	$32,918
% frosh need fully met	21
% ugrads need fully met	19
Average % of frosh need met	85
Average % of ugrad need met	82

SWARTHMORE COLLEGE

500 COLLEGE AVENUE, SWARTHMORE, PA 19081 • ADMISSIONS: 610-328-8300 • FAX: 610-328-8580

STUDENTS SAY "..."

Academics

Swarthmore College "has a lovely campus, the people are almost unbelievably friendly, it's a safe environment, and it's really, really challenging academically," and "although it's not one of the most well-known schools, those who do know of it also know of its wonderful reputation. It's where to go for a real education—for learning for the sake of truly learning, rather than just for grades." Students warn that "academics here are definitely stressful, especially when you sign up for extracurricular activities that take up some more time—and almost everyone here is involved in something outside of classes, because you don't want to just go to class, study, and sleep every day." As a result, "Swarthmore is truly challenging. It teaches its students tough lessons not only about classes but about life, and though it may be extremely, almost unbearably difficult sometimes, it's totally worth it." Undergrads also note that "there are tons of resources to help you—professors, academic mentors, writing associates (who are really helpful to talk to when you have major papers), residential assistants, psychological counseling, multicultural support groups, queer/trans support groups—basically, whenever you need help with something, there's someone you can talk to." Swatties also love how "Swarthmore is amazingly flexible. The requirements are very limited, allowing you to explore whatever you are interested in and change your mind millions of times about your major and career path. If they don't offer a major you want, you can design your own with ease."

Life

The Swarthmore community is "a family of students who are engaged in academics, learning, politics, activism, and civic responsibility, with a work hard, play hard, intense mentality, who don't get enough sleep because they're too busy doing all they want to do in their time here, and who (this is kind of cheesy, but true) when you really think about it are really just smart students who care about the world and want to make it better." There "is a misconception that Swarthmore students do nothing but study, [but] while we certainly do a lot of it, we still find many ways to have fun." Not so much in hometown Swarthmore—"there isn't a lot to do right in the area"—but "with a train station on campus, Philly is very accessible." Additionally, "there are so many organizations and clubs on campus that you'd be pressed to find none of the activities interesting. Even then, you can start your own club, so that takes care of it." The small size of the school means that "opportunities to participate in many different programs" are usually available. On-campus activities "are varied, and there is almost always something to do on the weekend. There are student musical performances, drama performances, movies, speakers, and comedy shows," as well as "several parties every weekend, with and without alcohol, and a lot of pre-partying with friends." One student sums up, "While it is tough to generalize on the life of a Swarthmore student, one word definitely applies to us all: busy. All of us are either working on extracurriculars, studying, or fighting sleep to do more work."

Student Body

Students are "not sure if there is a typical Swattie" but suspect that "the defining feature among us is that each person is brilliant at something: maybe dance, maybe quantum physics, maybe philosophy. Each person here has at least one thing that [he or she does] extraordinarily well." A Swattie "is [typically] liberal, involved in some kind of activism group or multicultural group, talks about classes all the time, was labeled a nerd by people in high school, and is really smart—one of those people where you just have to wonder, how do they get all their homework done and manage their extracurriculars and still have time for parties?" The campus "is very diverse racially but not in terms of thought—in other words, pretty much everyone's liberal, you don't get many different points of view. Multicultural and queer issues are big here, but you don't have to be involved in that to enjoy Swarthmore. You just have to accept it."

FINANCIAL AID: 610-328-8358 • E-MAIL: ADMISSIONS@SWARTHMORE.EDU • WEBSITE: WWW.SWARTHMORE.EDU

THE PRINCETON REVIEW SAYS

Admissions

Very important factors considered include: rigor of secondary school record, class rank, academic GPA, application essay, recommendation(s), character/personal qualities. *Important factors considered include:* standardized test scores, extracurricular activities. *Other factors considered include:* interview, talent/ability, first generation, alumni/ae relation, geographical residence, state residency, religious affiliation/commitment, racial/ethnic status, volunteer work, work experience, level of applicant's interest. SAT or ACT required. High school diploma or equivalent is not required. *Academic units recommended:* 4 English, 3 math, 3 science, 3 foreign language, 3 social studies, 3 history.

Financial Aid

Students should submit: FAFSA, CSS/Financial Aid PROFILE, State aid form, Noncustodial PROFILE, Business/Farm Supplement. Priority filing deadline is 2/18. The Princeton Review suggests that all financial aid forms be submitted as soon as possible after October 1. *Need-based scholarships/grants offered:* Federal Pell, FSEOG, State scholarships/grants, Private scholarships, College/university scholarship or grant aid from institutional funds. *Loan aid offered:* Direct Subsidized Stafford Loans, Direct Unsubsidized Stafford Loans, Direct PLUS loans, Federal Perkins Loans, State Loans, College/university loans from institutional funds. Applicants will be notified of awards on or about 4/1. Federal Work-Study Program available. Institutional employment available.

The Inside Word

Competition for admission to Swarthmore remains fierce, as the school consistently receives applications from top students across the country. Applicants should understand that Swarthmore receives more than enough applications from well-qualified students to fill its classrooms. The optional Writing compotents are not required for either the SAT or ACT. Admissions officers comb applications carefully for evidence of intellectually curious, highly motivated, and creative-minded candidates.

THE SCHOOL SAYS "..."

From the Admissions Office

"Swarthmore College, a highly selective college of liberal arts and engineering, has empowered students to pursue their academic curiosity with purpose for over 150 years. Swarthmore's world-class faculty collaborates with students on joint research projects, which helps students call on their diverse backgrounds to envision themselves as scholars and leaders and doers. The Honors Program brims with intellectual exploration, celebrating the free and critical exchange of ideas through small-group interactions. Swatties are just as passionate about life outside the classroom as they are about academic pursuits. Free time at Swarthmore means throwing a surprise birthday party for a friend, dancing at the Hogwarts-themed Yule Ball, taking the train from campus into Philadelphia to see a concert, or tossing a Frisbee with friends on Parrish Beach. Almost half of the student body enjoys playing sports, whether it's at the competitive Division III level, or in more casual club and intramural sport teams. The College's Quaker roots emphasize the concept of access regardless of income, and manifest themselves in a cash-free campus; the annual activity fee covers everything from digital printing and sporting events to campus movie screenings and dance performances. Swarthmore's financial aid program ensures affordability—without loans. More than half of its students received aid in 2015-16, with an average award of $47,564. Swarthmore makes admissions decisions for U.S. citizens and permanent residents without considering a family's ability to pay. International applicants are admitted on a need-aware basis, and are eligible for financial aid."

SELECTIVITY

Admissions Rating	98
# of applicants	5,540
% of applicants accepted	17
% of acceptees attending	43
# of early decision applicants	555
% accepted early decision	36

FRESHMAN PROFILE

Range SAT Critical Reading	680–770
Range SAT Math	680–770
Range SAT Writing	675–770
Range ACT Composite	29–34
% graduated top 10% of class	88
% graduated top 25% of class	98
% graduated top 50% of class	100

DEADLINES

Early decision	
Deadline	11/15
Notification	12/15
Regular	
Deadline	1/1
Notification	4/1
Nonfall registration?	No

FINANCIAL FACTS

Financial Aid Rating	95
Annual tuition	$47,070
Room and board	$13,958
Required fees	$372
Books and supplies	$1,290
Average frosh need-based scholarship	$42,195
Average UG need-based scholarship	$40,134
% needy frosh rec. need-based scholarship or grant aid	100
% needy UG rec. need-based scholarship or grant aid	100
% needy frosh rec. non-need-based scholarship or grant aid	0
% needy UG rec. non-need-based scholarship or grant aid	0
% needy frosh rec. need-based self-help aid	97
% needy UG rec. need-based self-help aid	98
% frosh rec. any financial aid	52
% UG rec. any financial aid	50
% frosh need fully met	100
% ugrads need fully met	100
Average % of frosh need met	100
Average % of ugrad need met	100

SYRACUSE UNIVERSITY

100 CROUSE-HINDS HALL, SYRACUSE, NY 13244-2130 • ADMISSIONS: 315-443-3611 • FAX: 315-443-4226

STUDENTS SAY "..."

Academics

The school spirit is definitely palpable the minute you set foot onto Syracuse's campus. Indeed, it's highly evident that "everyone here bleeds orange." Frankly, it's no surprise that 'Cuse undergrads truly love their school. The university provides students with the triple threat of "a great reputation," "incredible academic programs" and a "great social scene." Many also highlight the "excellent study abroad program" and boast about "the quality of career services." Additionally, known for its fabulous arts and media departments, undergrads especially tout the S. I. Newhouse School of Public Communications. At Newhouse, students benefit from "prestige and connections" as well as "hands-on, interactive learning environments." Of course, not to be outdone, undergrads also praise (among others) the "reputable business school," "great architecture school" and "top ranked sports management program." Further, students value that professors have a lot of real world experience. As one pleased senior shares, "Our professors are all accomplished in their respective industries and bring that to life in classes." Importantly, for the most part, they "truly care about their students and have your best interests at heart." However, a sophomore does caution, "Classes can be hard if you don't stay on top of things." Finally, as an impressed nutrition major brags, "The opportunities are endless and when I say endless I mean endless! This school has so many connections and great opportunities for every single student on campus."

Life

Life at Syracuse moves at a frenzied pace and the busy undergrads here wouldn't have it any other way. To begin with, the university nets a fairly athletic student body and participation in club sports is quite high. A bioengineering major chimes in adding, "All of the sports here are huge events, especially basketball. Every team is worth going to see at least once." Many undergrads are also civic minded. Indeed, "volunteering is also a big part of life at Syracuse—there is a large effort to get students off 'the hill' that is our campus and into the larger Syracuse community." Students do cop to the fact that they maintain a lively party culture. For starters, "fraternities and sororities are huge." As a freshman reveals, "We're a pretty big party school...On the weekends, most people go to house parties, frat parties or apartment parties on South Campus. Many people also go to the bars that are short walks from all the dorms." However, she also assures that "not everyone parties like you would think . . . and there are plenty of things to do for all social groups." When students are itching to get off campus, downtown Syracuse offers "great shops and food." A pleased senior elaborates, "The newly expanded shopping and entertainment center—Destiny USA—is also a huge draw. You can literally see a movie, ride Go-Karts, and shop all in one place. It makes for a pretty great Saturday."

Student Body

At first glance, it can seem as though the typical Syracuse student is "wealthy," "from the Northeast," and "[involved with] Greek life." However, others insist that the campus "is a melting pot of different cultures and ethnicities" and that "there is something to fit everyone." As a proud junior exclaims, "Our international student population is huge and we attract students not only from across the country but across the world." By and large, undergrads at Syracuse are the types who excel at maintaining a work/life balance. Certainly, they "care deeply...about academic pursuits" but also realize that there is more to college than studying. Indeed, a public relations major tells us that "many students spend just as much time in extracurricular activities and internships, as well as managing a fruitful social life." Perhaps this content junior best explains his peers by stating, "It's a mix of people out to have a great time and people focused on learning. As well as everything in between. It's easy to find a spot to fit in."

FINANCIAL AID: 315-443-1513 • E-MAIL: ORANGE@SYR.EDU • WEBSITE: WWW.SYR.EDU

THE PRINCETON REVIEW SAYS

Admissions

Very important factors considered include: rigor of secondary school record, class rank, academic GPA, standardized test scores, application essay, recommendation(s), interview, extracurricular activities, talent/ability, character/personal qualities, volunteer work, level of applicant's interest. *Other factors considered include:* first generation, alumni/ae relation, geographical residence, state residency, racial/ethnic status, work experience. SAT or ACT required. ACT with Writing required. SAT with Essay component required. TOEFL required of all international applicants. High school diploma is required and GED is accepted. *Academic units recommended:* 4 English, 4 math, 4 science, 3 foreign language, 4 social studies, 4 history.

Financial Aid

Students should submit: FAFSA, CSS/Financial Aid PROFILE, Noncustodial PROFILE. Regular filing deadline is 2/1. The Princeton Review suggests that all financial aid forms be submitted as soon as possible after October 1. *Need-based scholarships/grants offered:* Federal Pell, FSEOG, State scholarships/grants, Private scholarships, College/university scholarship or grant aid from institutional funds. *Loan aid offered:* Direct Subsidized Stafford Loans, Direct Unsubsidized Stafford Loans, Direct PLUS loans, Federal Perkins Loans. Applicants will be notified of awards on or about 3/15. Federal Work-Study Program available. Institutional employment available.

The Inside Word

Syracuse's admissions process is certainly competitive. Successful candidates often have strong GPAs and solid test scores. It's also important to note that students interested in applying to any fine or performing arts or architecture programs will need to audition and/or submit a portfolio. Finally, applicants who strongly feel that Syracuse is their first choice are highly encouraged to apply early decision.

THE SCHOOL SAYS "..."

From the Admissions Office

"Syracuse University students blend rigorous classroom scholarship with real-world experiences that prepare them for personal and professional success in a rapidly changing world. You'll customize your education through interdisciplinary study across a collection of prominent schools and colleges; and connect classroom learning and hands-on experience through internships, research, start-up ventures, and professional immersion experiences in the City of Syracuse and via University centers in New York City, Washington, D.C., and Los Angeles. SU experiential learning also spans the globe, and nearly half of undergraduates study abroad. The university operates centers in Beijing, Florence, Hong Kong, Istanbul, London, Madrid, Santiago, and Strasbourg, and offers short-term, summer, and semester options in these and many other cities.

"An SU education is also defined by breadth of opportunity combined with individualized attention. You'll choose from more than 200 majors and 100 minors, and work closely with top scholars who are professionals in their fields that share their research/writing to further the classroom experience. You can pursue multiple majors and/or minors, and round out your experience with participation in one or more of 300 extracurricular groups. Upon graduation, you'll join one of the proudest, most supportive alumni networks in the world with alum that include founding principal of Fox & Fowle Architects Bruce Fowle (1960), Joe Biden, Law (1968), space shuttle commander Eileen Collins (1978), screenwriter Aaron Sorkin (1983), actor Taye Diggs (1993), Arielle Tepper Madover (1994), and Foursquare cofounder Dennis Crowley (1998)."

SELECTIVITY

Admissions Rating	89
# of applicants	33,254
% of applicants accepted	48
% of acceptees attending	22
# offered a place on the wait list	5,592
% accepting a place on wait list	28
% admitted from wait list	42
# of early decision applicants	1,839
% accepted early decision	65

FRESHMAN PROFILE

Range SAT Critical Reading	530–630
Range SAT Math	560–660
Range SAT Writing	530–640
Range ACT Composite	24–29
Minimum paper TOEFL	550
Minimum internet-based TOEFL	85
Average HS GPA	3.6
% graduated top 10% of class	35
% graduated top 25% of class	70
% graduated top 50% of class	95

DEADLINES

Early decision	
Deadline	11/15
Regular	
Priority	1/1
Deadline	1/1
Nonfall registration?	Yes

FINANCIAL FACTS

Financial Aid Rating	87
Tuition	$43,440
Room and board	$15,217
Required fees	$1,582
Books and supplies	$1,440
Average frosh need-based scholarship	$29,715
Average UG need-based scholarship	$28,435
% needy frosh rec. need-based scholarship or grant aid	93
% needy UG rec. need-based scholarship or grant aid	92
% needy frosh rec. non-need-based scholarship or grant aid	10
% needy UG rec. non-need-based scholarship or grant aid	7
% needy frosh rec. need-based self-help aid	91
% needy UG rec. need-based self-help aid	92
% frosh rec. any financial aid	71
% UG rec. any financial aid	73
% UG borrow to pay for school	64
Average cumulative indebtedness	$36,500
% frosh need fully met	44
% ugrads need fully met	37
Average % of frosh need met	96
Average % of ugrad need met	91

TEMPLE UNIVERSITY

1801 NORTH BROAD STREET (041-09), PHILADELPHIA, PA 19122-6096 • ADMISSIONS: 215-204-7200 • FAX: 215-204-5694

CAMPUS LIFE

Quality of Life Rating	90
Fire Safety Rating	98
Green Rating	93
Type of school	Public
Affiliation	No Affiliation
Environment	Metropolis

STUDENTS

Total undergrad enrollment	28,609
% male/female	49/51
% from out of state	18
% frosh from public high school	82
% frosh live on campus	76
% ugrads live on campus	21
# of fraternities (% ugrad men join)	17 (4)
# of sororities (% ugrad women join)	13 (7)
% African American	13
% Asian	11
% Caucasian	56
% Hispanic	6
% Native American	<1
% Pacific Islander	<1
% Two or more races	3
% Race and/or ethnicity unknown	5
% international	6
# of countries represented	118

SURVEY SAYS...

Students are happy
Internships are widely available
Students love Philadelphia, PA
Easy to get around campus
Recreation facilities are great
Everyone loves the Owls

ACADEMICS

Academic Rating	77
% students returning for sophomore year	90
% students graduating within 4 years	43
% students graduating within 6 years	71
Calendar	Semester
Student/faculty ratio	14:1
Profs interesting rating	78
Profs accessible rating	78

Most classes have 10–19 students.
Most lab/discussion sessions have
20–29 students.

MOST POPULAR MAJORS

Biology; Psychology; Kinesiology and Exercise
Science

STUDENTS SAY "..."

Academics

Pennsylvania's Temple University offers undergraduates an education replete with "opportunities" yet one that "won't break the bank." As if that wasn't enough, the school's location is pretty enviable—"a subway ride from downtown Philadelphia and a train ride to DC, NYC, or Boston!" And students definitely seem to appreciate the "diverse, exciting urban atmosphere" that permeates the campus at this public research university. They also love Temple's robust study abroad program as well as the school's myriad internship options. Academically speaking, Temple has "a renowned media program" and "one of the best art schools" around. Additionally, the engineering school is "[highly] reputable," and the university at large is considered a "great research facility." Students at Temple also seem to be quite content with their classroom experience. Undergrads happily report that their professors are both engaged and "very engaging." They "encourage students to do well, they embrace discussions and [are] very open to debates." Fortunately, they "ALWAYS, ALWAYS encourage questions and comments." A film student happily sums up, "One could talk to a professor about their field of study for hours on end outside of class."

Life

Life at Temple moves at a pretty hectic pace. After all, students here "are very engaged in academics, their social lives, political/social causes and extracurricular activities and community service." Though school work generally takes precedent, these undergrads also leave plenty of time to kick back. As a media studies major shares, "When people are not studying on Thursday to Saturday, everybody wants to know where the parties are happening. There are no shortages of house parties at Temple and they are a great time." Fortunately, it's not a problem if parties aren't your scene. We're told that "numerous intramural sports teams and . . . clubs offer students an alternative to partying on the weekends." Of course, perhaps Temple's most winning attribute is its prime location. An American history major brags, "There is NOTHING that a person can't do in Philadelphia. It's a world class city with some of the best history around." And a mechanical engineering major excitedly adds, "I've been to a few football games and tailgates, I've seen an art show and heard the Philadelphia orchestra, I've also been to a rave and other festivals. I've taken the duck tour . . . and have done a scavenger hunt around Philly. [And I've even] visited the Art museum." In other words, "there is a lot to do."

Student Body

Though a decent number of students come from "middle or upper class families" and tend to hail from the surrounding "tristate area," most undergrads are still quick to praise Temple's "very diverse student body." Many appreciate that their peers are "smart and hard-working, but not arrogant about their abilities or background." And, just as important, we're told that "it's very easy to fit in at Temple" since "everyone is open and welcoming." A history major quickly adds, "The typical student is friendly, outgoing and [will] freely . . . start a discussion with you." Temple undergrads also "tend to be well-rounded [and] involved in several types of activities." Lastly, an engineering student sums up his peers by stating, "Many people at Temple do their own thing, believe what they want to believe, wear what they want to wear, etc. but are open to other people's opinions and ideas. There isn't one type of person that attends Temple; it is a literal melting pot of cultures."

FINANCIAL AID: 215-204-8760 • E-MAIL: ASKANOWL@TEMPLE.EDU • WEBSITE: WWW.TEMPLE.EDU

THE PRINCETON REVIEW SAYS

Admissions

Very important factors considered include: rigor of secondary school record, academic GPA. *Important factors considered include:* class rank, standardized test scores. *Other factors considered include:* application essay, recommendation(s), extracurricular activities, talent/ability, character/personal qualities, alumni/ae relation, geographical residence, state residency, volunteer work, work experience, level of applicant's interest. SAT or ACT considered if submitted. ACT with or without writing accepted. SAT with or without Essay component accepted. TOEFL required of all international applicants. High school diploma is required and GED is accepted. *Academic units required:* 4 English, 3 math, 2 science, 1 science lab, 2 foreign language, 2 social studies, 1 history, 1 academic elective. *Academic units recommended:* 4 English, 4 math, 3 science, 2 science labs, 2 foreign language, 2 social studies, 1 history, 3 academic electives.

Financial Aid

Students should submit: FAFSA. Priority filing deadline is 3/1. The Princeton Review suggests that all financial aid forms be submitted as soon as possible after October 1. *Need-based scholarships/grants offered:* Federal Pell, FSEOG, State scholarships/grants, Private scholarships, College/university scholarship or grant aid from institutional funds, Federal Nursing Scholarships. *Loan aid offered:* Direct Subsidized Stafford Loans, Direct Unsubsidized Stafford Loans, Direct PLUS loans, Federal Perkins Loans, Federal Nursing Loans, State Loans, College/university loans from institutional funds. Applicants will be notified of awards on a rolling basis beginning 2/15. Federal Work-Study Program available. Institutional employment available.

The Inside Word

Gaining admission to Temple is competitive and a solid academic record is a must. Students need to have earned at least a minimum of a B-minus average or a 3.0 GPA in college prep courses to be considered serious contenders. Submitting SAT or ACT results is optional. However, those applicants who choose not to send their scores will have to answer a series of open-ended questions instead.

THE SCHOOL SAYS "..."

From the Admissions Office

"Temple University has a long tradition of self-made success and enjoys a reputation for providing an affordable, high-quality education that prepares students for the real world. At Temple, students turn opportunities into achievements: World-class labs are the proving grounds for world-changing ideas. A classroom doubles as the boardroom of a tech startup. Professors become mentors through graduate school and beyond. All because Temple students are driven to make a difference, and at Temple they find everything they need to reach their goals. More than 3,500 distinguished faculty; top art, business, dental, law and medical schools; five professional schools; and dozens of renowned programs make Temple an academic powerhouse. Students enjoy the advantages of a large urban, public research university with the individualized attention of a 14:1 student-to-faculty ratio. Home to nearly 40,000 students, Temple is the fifth-largest provider of professional education in the U.S., and offers more than 450 academic programs in seventeen schools and colleges, on nine campuses, including locations in Japan and Italy. The majority of freshmen students live on campus, where they are steps away from class, the TECH Center and the library; fitness and recreation facilities; dining options from cafés and dining halls to food trucks; and the many arts, cultural, sports and scholarly events that happen daily university wide and throughout the vibrant city of Philadelphia. Temple is experiencing incredible momentum powered by innovative approaches in admissions and affordability; a campus transformation; plentiful creative and research opportunities; rigorous academic programs; an indelible bond with the city of Philadelphia; and groundbreaking work in science, research and technology."

SELECTIVITY

Admissions Rating	88
# of applicants	28,886
% of applicants accepted	56
% of acceptees attending	31
# offered a place on the wait list	1,852
% accepting a place on wait list	31
% admitted from wait list	28

FRESHMAN PROFILE

Range SAT Critical Reading	520–620
Range SAT Math	530–630
Range SAT Writing	500–620
Range ACT Composite	23–29
Minimum paper TOEFL	550
Minimum internet-based TOEFL	79
Average HS GPA	3.5
% graduated top 10% of class	22
% graduated top 25% of class	54
% graduated top 50% of class	90

DEADLINES

Early action	
Deadline	11/1
Notification	1/10
Regular	
Deadline	3/1
Nonfall registration?	Yes

APPLICANTS ALSO LOOK AT AND OFTEN PREFER

Penn State University Park; Drexel University; Rutgers, The State University of New Jersey–New Brunswick; University of Delaware; University of Pittsburgh–Pittsburgh Campus

AND SOMETIMES PREFER

University of Maryland–College Park; West Chester University

FINANCIAL FACTS

Financial Aid Rating	81
Annual in-state tuition	$14,898
Annual out-of-state tuition	$25,204
Room and board	$11,146
Required fees	$790
Books and supplies	$1,000
Average frosh need-based scholarship	$7,029
Average UG need-based scholarship	$6,390
% needy frosh rec. need-based scholarship or grant aid	85
% needy UG rec. need-based scholarship or grant aid	82
% needy frosh rec. non-need-based scholarship or grant aid	61
% needy UG rec. non-need-based scholarship or grant aid	42
% needy frosh rec. need-based self-help aid	79
% needy UG rec. need-based self-help aid	84
% frosh rec. any financial aid	90
% UG rec. any financial aid	83
% UG borrow to pay for school	77
Average cumulative indebtedness	$37,372
% frosh need fully met	29
% ugrads need fully met	24
Average % of frosh need met	70
Average % of ugrad need met	65

TEXAS A&M UNIVERSITY—COLLEGE STATION

PO BOX 30014, COLLEGE STATION, TX 77843-3014 • ADMISSIONS: 979-845-3741 • FAX: 979-847-8737

STUDENTS SAY "..."

Academics

The "untold spirit at Texas A&M" lies in its tradition, which is "the underlying pulse of Aggieland." This large research school has "deep-rooted values" and "runs as a tight-knit family despite the numerous population." This strong family dynamic makes the school an "open, friendly place to learn and grow," and the incredibly strong engineering and life science programs certainly don't hurt. The academics can be "difficult," but "the goal is to set [students] apart from the rest, so [they] can excel." The "wonderful" professors "do their best to bring the topics from pages to the real world." They "all have life experiences working with the topics that they teach making them the perfect resource for information." These "top-notch" professors (well, aside from a very few who are "extremely dry") come back to A&M after working in powerful industry positions "because they love the atmosphere and the students." "I have never skipped a class because I thoroughly enjoy going," says one student. Particularly with the sciences, professors offer students the opportunity to participate in "world-changing research," and all such experiences "have had something useful to add to the material," which helps students when they go out into the real world. The "Aggie network" is something to behold; it reaches far across the nation ("Aggie alumni are loyal to their school forever") and "is good for getting jobs after graduation." The sense of pride here motivates students to do well "because they're part of something bigger than themselves." There is "great support" from both the faculty and staff together. "The mindset they have is to effectively prepare students for world-class challenges," says one student. "At Texas A&M, you learn to be a well-rounded, moral, and ethical person."

Life

Student organizations positively abound at Texas A&M (there are more than 1,000), and they are a huge social outlet for students looking to find those with similar interests. "Get involved in something you're passionate about; there is a club for just about *everything*," says a student. Off-campus, there are "four-dollar movies, many dancehalls, endless restaurants to eat at, and a large mall," as well as "an ice-skating rink, bowling alley, and miniature golf place." Students at Texas A&M are "loyal to one another and are always willing to support their fellow Aggies." "Tradition and chivalry run the school," and students all "work hard during the week so we can party hard on the weekends," usually at Northgate, the "bar street." "Texas A&M is kind of like a cult—a really happy cult," explains a student. The "immense school spirit" is derived from the many "time-honored traditions," including the Big Event, which is the largest one-day, student-run service project in the nation. That's not even to mention the football: "Saturdays in the fall are owned by football." "Although the school is very large, whenever the...Aggies at Kyle Field are belting the war hymn and linking arms, I feel like I am part of a huge family." As one student cryptically sums up his school's mythology, "From the outside looking in, you can't understand it. From the inside looking out you can't explain it."

Student Body

A typical student is "white," "conservative," "involved in at least one club, spends a fair amount of time studying, and learns to two-step for Thursday nights." This being Texas, "some wear cowboy boots, a flannel shirt, a cowboy hat/baseball cap, and jeans." There is also a strong faction of members of the Corps of Cadets, as well as religious folk (the school has "the largest Bible study in the world"). Though lacking cultural diversity, interests and hobbies run the gamut, and "students from other races and classes fit in just fine and are able to make friends just like anybody else." While it's a big school, "a lot of classes are pretty small, so it's easy to make friends in class." There are "no pretenses" among Aggies, and "everyone shows who they are." "Most of the people I have met here are truly genuine individuals," says a student.

TEXAS A&M UNIVERSITY—COLLEGE STATION

FINANCIAL AID: 979-845-3236 • E-MAIL: ADMISSIONS@TAMU.EDU • WEBSITE: WWW.TAMU.EDU

THE PRINCETON REVIEW SAYS

Admissions

Very important factors considered include: rigor of secondary school record, class rank, academic GPA, standardized test scores, extracurricular activities, talent/ability. *Important factors considered include:* application essay, first generation, geographical residence, state residency, volunteer work, work experience. *Other factors considered include:* recommendation(s), character/personal qualities, level of applicant's interest. SAT or ACT required. ACT with Writing required. SAT with Essay component required. TOEFL required of all international applicants. High school diploma is required and GED is accepted. *Academic units required:* 4 English, 3 math, 3 science, 1 science lab, 2 foreign language, 3 social studies, 5 academic electives, 1 visual/performing arts, and 1 unit from above areas or other academic areas. *Academic units recommended:* 4 English, 4 math, 4 science, 2 science labs, 2 foreign language, 4 social studies, 7 academic electives, 1 visual/performing arts, and 1 unit from above areas or other academic areas.

Financial Aid

Students should submit: FAFSA. Priority filing deadline is 3/15. The Princeton Review suggests that all financial aid forms be submitted as soon as possible after October 1. *Need-based scholarships/grants offered:* Federal Pell, FSEOG, State scholarships/grants, Private scholarships, College/university scholarship or grant aid from institutional funds. *Loan aid offered:* Direct Subsidized Stafford Loans, Direct Unsubsidized Stafford Loans, Direct PLUS loans, Federal Perkins Loans, State Loans, College/university loans from institutional funds. Applicants will be notified of awards on a rolling basis beginning 4/1. Federal Work-Study Program available. Institutional employment available.

The Inside Word

Texas A&M uses some cut-and-dried admissions criteria: Students graduating in the top 10 percent of a recognized public or private high school in the state of Texas are automatically in; all they have to do is get their applications in on time. Applicants in the top quarter of their graduating class who have a combined SAT math/critical reading score of 1300 (minimum score of 600 in each component) are also automatically in, as are such students who earn a composite ACT score of 30 (minimum 27 on the math and English sections). Students must also take the writing component of the SAT and/or ACT for the test score to be considered. All other applications are deemed "Review Admits" to be sorted through by the admissions committee.

THE SCHOOL SAYS "..."

From the Admissions Office

"Established in 1876 as the first public college in the state, Texas A&M University has become a world leader in teaching, research, and public service. Located in College Station in the heart of Texas, it is centrally situated among three of the country's ten largest cities: Dallas, Houston, and San Antonio. Texas A&M is ranked nationally in these four areas: enrollment, enrollment of top students, value of research, and endowment.

"Freshman applicants are required to take the SAT or the ACT. We will use the applicant's best single testing date score in decision making."

SELECTIVITY
Admissions Rating	89
# of applicants	33,970
% of applicants accepted	66
% of acceptees attending	46
# offered a place on the wait list	0

FRESHMAN PROFILE
Range SAT Critical Reading	520–640
Range SAT Math	550–670
Range SAT Writing	490–610
Range ACT Composite	25–30
Minimum paper TOEFL	550
Minimum internet-based TOEFL	80
% graduated top 10% of class	66
% graduated top 25% of class	91
% graduated top 50% of class	99

DEADLINES
Regular	
Deadline	12/1
Nonfall registration?	Yes

APPLICANTS ALSO LOOK AT AND OFTEN PREFER
Rice University

AND SOMETIMES PREFER
The University of Texas at Austin; Baylor University; Louisiana State University

AND RARELY PREFER
Southern Methodist University

FINANCIAL FACTS
Financial Aid Rating	81
Annual in-state tuition	$6,149
Annual out-of-state tuition	$24,742
Room and board	$10,338
Required fees	$3,279
Books and supplies	$1,194
Average frosh need-based scholarship	$11,610
Average UG need-based scholarship	$9,818
% needy frosh rec. need-based scholarship or grant aid	94
% needy UG rec. need-based scholarship or grant aid	86
% needy frosh rec. non-need-based scholarship or grant aid	13
% needy UG rec. non-need-based scholarship or grant aid	8
% needy frosh rec. need-based self-help aid	48
% needy UG rec. need-based self-help aid	59
% frosh rec. any financial aid	75
% UG rec. any financial aid	70
% UG borrow to pay for school	43
Average cumulative indebtedness	$24,276
% frosh need fully met	37
% ugrads need fully met	28
Average % of frosh need met	73
Average % of ugrad need met	66

TEXAS CHRISTIAN UNIVERSITY

OFFICE OF ADMISSIONS, TCU BOX 297013, FORT WORTH, TX 76129 • ADMISSIONS: 817-257-7490 • FAX: 817-257-7268

CAMPUS LIFE

Quality of Life Rating	89
Fire Safety Rating	92
Green Rating	80
Type of school	Private
Affiliation	Disciples of Christ
Environment	Metropolis

STUDENTS

Total undergrad enrollment	8,894
% male/female	40/60
% from out of state	45
% frosh from public high school	58
% frosh live on campus	97
% ugrads live on campus	49
# of fraternities (% ugrad men join)	20 (41)
# of sororities (% ugrad women join)	20 (55)
% African American	5
% Asian	3
% Caucasian	73
% Hispanic	11
% Native American	1
% Pacific Islander	<1
% Two or more races	<1
% Race and/or ethnicity unknown	2
% international	5
# of countries represented	70

SURVEY SAYS...

Students are happy
Classroom facilities are great
Lab facilities are great
Great library
Career services are great
School is well run
No one cheats
Students love Fort Worth, TX
Dorms are like palaces
Easy to get around campus
Recreation facilities are great
Lots of beer drinking
Everyone loves the Horned Frogs
Frats and sororities are popular
Alumni active on campus

ACADEMICS

Academic Rating	83
% students returning for sophomore year	90
% students graduating within 4 years	59
% students graduating within 6 years	76
Calendar	Semester
Student/faculty ratio	13:1
Profs interesting rating	89
Profs accessible rating	87

Most classes have 10–19 students.
Most lab/discussion sessions have
20–29 students.

MOST POPULAR MAJORS

Registered Nursing/Registered Nurse;
Finance; Speech Communication and Rhetoric

STUDENTS SAY "..."

Academics

The popular conception of Texas is that everything there is big, big, big, but Texas Christian University is one Lone Star institution that bucks this trend, insisting on "smaller classroom sizes" that allows professors to be "very interested in [students] personally." One undergrad explains: "If I have a problem and need to talk with the profs, they go out of their way to meet with me, especially when it comes to career options and what my best options are in terms of what I want to do. They are very helpful." While "there are some programs with more students than others, overall the academic experience at TCU is very personal and rewarding. Many students are easily able to latch onto a professor's lab research...Getting involved in the academic programs at TCU will really pay off." Students enjoy a strong support network; the school "offers many resources such as the library, writing center, career center, student support services, and other educational and personal resources," and alumni "are really involved and give a lot back to the school." Business, education, and physical therapy are among the standout offerings here. Access to the Dallas-Fort Worth business community means plenty of good internship and networking opportunities.

Life

"Greek life is one of the most popular activities" at TCU; some say "the Greeks rule the social scene at the school," while others see slightly more diverse options. The school "puts a lot of its money to good use, such as new residence halls, a nice recreational facility, funding for numerous clubs and organizations, and great activities to bring the campus community together," creating "a focus on the student community" that extends beyond the Greek houses. TCU football is another pillar of campus life, and students "have a lot of pride" in both the program and the school itself. Beyond these choices, life at TCU "is what you make it. If you want to make grades your top priority, it's very easy to do so. If you want to go out and party a lot, it's very easy to do [that] as well. Lots of people drink on campus, but not everyone makes that their life. It's all about what your priorities are because it is easy to go either way." Off-campus opportunities are plentiful thanks to access to Dallas-Fort Worth, a major metropolis.

Student Body

Undergrads tend to be "middle- to upper-class...in good physical shape, and like to have a good time." Many, "but not all, dress extremely well...First impressions mean a lot here, so do not mess up." "The student body is very Greek" at TCU. Students differ on how this impacts social dynamics; some insist that "if you aren't in a fraternity or sorority, it is very hard to fit in," while others point out that "there are other types of people on campus," and "if you are open-minded and have a good personality overall you won't find it hard to make friends inside and outside of Greek life and find yourself belonging at TCU." While "the student population is mostly made up of Caucasian students," there is "a growing minority student population," the largest segment of which is Latina. Some complain about the pervasive materialism, but others think the issue is overblown; one tells us, "Some may find the money an issue, but that's only because they make it an issue. I've never been ashamed that I can't buy the latest Prada handbag, and no one has ever looked down on me because of that. If you don't bring it up, nobody cares. A lack of character may make these people feel left out."

FINANCIAL AID: 817-257-7858 • E-MAIL: FROGMAIL@TCU.EDU • WEBSITE: WWW.TCU.EDU

THE PRINCETON REVIEW SAYS

Admissions

Very important factors considered include: rigor of secondary school record, class rank, academic GPA. *Important factors considered include:* standardized test scores, application essay, recommendation(s), extracurricular activities, character/personal qualities, first generation, alumni/ae relation, racial/ethnic status. *Other factors considered include:* interview, talent/ability, geographical residence, state residency, religious affiliation/commitment, volunteer work, work experience, level of applicant's interest. SAT or ACT required. ACT with or without writing accepted. SAT with or without Essay component accepted. TOEFL required of all international applicants. High school diploma is required and GED is not accepted. *Academic units required:* 4 English, 3 math, 3 science, 1 science lab, 2 foreign language, 3 social studies, 2 academic electives. *Academic units recommended:* 4 English, 4 math, 4 science, 1 science lab, 4 foreign language, 4 social studies.

Financial Aid

Students should submit: FAFSA, CSS/Financial Aid PROFILE, Noncustodial PROFILE. Regular filing deadline is 5/1. The Princeton Review suggests that all financial aid forms be submitted as soon as possible after October 1. *Need-based scholarships/grants offered:* Federal Pell, FSEOG, State scholarships/grants, Private scholarships, College/university scholarship or grant aid from institutional funds. *Loan aid offered:* Direct Subsidized Stafford Loans, Direct Unsubsidized Stafford Loans, Direct PLUS loans, Federal Perkins Loans, Federal Nursing Loans, State Loans. Applicants will be notified of awards on a rolling basis beginning 3/15. Federal Work-Study Program available. Institutional employment available.

The Inside Word

The sheer volume of applications sent to TCU—the school receives more than 18,000 each year—requires the school to apply some baseline criteria for winnowing out unlikely candidates. TCU accepts the Common App, ApplyTexas, and their own application. No preference is given for one over the other.

THE SCHOOL SAYS "..."

From the Admissions Office

"TCU is a major teaching and research university with the feel of a small college. The TCU academic experience includes small classes with top faculty; cutting-edge technology; a liberal arts and sciences core curriculum; and real-life application though faculty-directed research, group projects, and internships. While TCU faculty members are recognized for research, their main focus is on teaching and mentoring students. The friendly campus community welcomes new students at Frog Camp before classes begin, where students find three days of fun meeting new friends, learning campus traditions, and serving the community. Campus life includes 200 clubs and organizations, a spirited NCAA Division I athletics program in the Big 12 Conference, and numerous professional-scale productions from the TCU College of Fine Arts. More than half of the students participate in a wide array of intramural sports, and about 40 percent are involved in Greek organizations, including ones emphasizing ethnic diversity as well as the Christian faith. The historic relationship to the Christian Church (Disciples of Christ) means that instead of teaching a particular viewpoint, TCU encourages students to consider and follow their own beliefs. The university's mission—to educate individuals to think and act as ethical leaders and responsible citizens in a global community—influences everything from course work to study abroad to the way Horned Frogs act and interact. From National Merit Scholars to those just now realizing their academic potential, TCU attracts and serves students who are learning to change the world.

"TCU will accept either the SAT or the ACT (with or without the writing component) in admission and scholarship processes. The writing sections will be considered alongside the TCU application essay."

SELECTIVITY

Admissions Rating	90
# of applicants	18,423
% of applicants accepted	43
% of acceptees attending	26
# offered a place on the wait list	1,644
% accepting a place on wait list	34
% admitted from wait list	5
# of early decision applicants	807
% accepted early decision	29

FRESHMAN PROFILE

Range SAT Critical Reading	530–630
Range SAT Math	550–650
Range SAT Writing	530–640
Range ACT Composite	25–30
Minimum paper TOEFL	550
Minimum internet-based TOEFL	80
% graduated top 10% of class	44
% graduated top 25% of class	76
% graduated top 50% of class	96

DEADLINES

Early decision	
Deadline	11/1
Notification	12/5
Early action	
Deadline	11/1
Notification	12/15
Regular	
Deadline	2/15
Notification	4/1
Nonfall registration?	Yes

FINANCIAL FACTS

Financial Aid Rating	82
Annual tuition	$42,580
Room and board	$12,000
Required fees	$90
Books and supplies	$1,050
Average frosh need-based scholarship	$25,971
Average UG need-based scholarship	$24,694
% needy frosh rec. need-based scholarship or grant aid	94
% needy UG rec. need-based scholarship or grant aid	94
% needy frosh rec. non-need-based scholarship or grant aid	67
% needy UG rec. non-need-based scholarship or grant aid	61
% needy frosh rec. need-based self-help aid	71
% needy UG rec. need-based self-help aid	74
% frosh rec. any financial aid	77
% UG rec. any financial aid	76
% UG borrow to pay for school	39
Average cumulative indebtedness	$34,152
% frosh need fully met	37
% ugrads need fully met	27
Average % of frosh need met	70
Average % of ugrad need met	65

THOMAS AQUINAS COLLEGE

10000 OJAI ROAD, SANTA PAULA, CA 93060 • ADMISSION: 805-525-4417 • FAX: 805-421-5905

STUDENTS SAY "..."

Academics

Students at Thomas Aquinas College relish attending a school that "takes learning seriously for its own sake, not just as preparation for a job." With a "strong Catholic identity" and "rigorous curriculum," TAC offers a "holistic education" that's "demanding on every level." The college promotes a "Great Books education," which really forces its undergrads to "read and think critically." All classes are seminar-based, a method many students here feel "better facilitates learning." Importantly, the "Catholic/small-college setting creates an atmosphere of trust and faith that makes it easier to study, to live, and to grow at school." Unlike other colleges, "there aren't any majors at Thomas Aquinas." Students simply graduate with a bachelor's degree in liberal arts. Class time is solely "devoted to discussion of the [reading] material assigned" with professors (or tutors as they are known) facilitating said discussion. Undergrads happily report that professors are "more than happy to continue the discussion outside class and are always ready to help their students." Moreover, they're "welcoming" and "easy to talk to," and all seem to "have a passion for intellectual formation." As one content senior succinctly states, "The professors are great and lead you to truth without forcing it on you."

Life

TAC inspires and encourages a contemplative life, and students spend a large portion of their time in "an intellectual discussion." That being said, even TAC undergrads need to kick back every now and again. On this active campus, intramural sports are quite popular, and "running, hiking, basketball, soccer, and football are major pastimes on campus." Further, "four times a year there is a formal dance hosted by one of the classes." As one enthusiastic sophomore explains, "I waltz, swing, lindy hop, tango, salsa, rumba, contra dance, polka, Virginia reel, and do other dances. People on this campus actually learn and know how to dance well." Students here also know how to make their own fun. As one freshman shares, there are "spontaneous student pranks, such as the day the freshmen men all wore blue while the freshmen women wore pink (officially titled 'Trip Out the Tutors Tuesday')." Additionally, "once or twice a semester, the school arranges field trips to the Getty Center, Villa, operas, art galleries, science museums, and other points of interest in the wider LA area." It's also quite common for students to "leave campus for the weekend for fun activities either to Ventura Beach (thirty minutes), Santa Barbara (one hour), or Ojai (twenty minutes)."

Student Body

Undergrads at TAC might, in some respects, appear "homogenous." Indeed, the vast majority of students "are Catholic," "devoted to learning and their faith," and politically "conservative." That being said, a senior assures us, "Any student with any interest can usually find a group that shares his or her passion." Importantly, many agree that their peers are "very kind and inclusive" as well as "joyful and inviting." One junior elaborates saying, "You walk down the hallways and sidewalks and are personally greeted by freshmen and seniors alike." An overwhelming number of undergrads here declare their fellow students "intellectually curious" and "somewhat obsessed with philosophy." Indeed, the typical student "is a thinker [who] will never hesitate to get in[to] a philosophical argument." Naturally, people here are "committed to the academic life," and most students study "very hard." They're "focused [and] mature" and make a point of "coming prepared to class." As one honest and insightful senior admits, "Most [students] would probably be considered a bit geeky elsewhere." But perhaps this student sums up his TAC peers the best, "You get all different kinds of people here—but one thing they have in common is a desire to search for the truth."

FINANCIAL AID: 800-634-9797 • E-MAIL: ADMISSIONS@THOMASAQUINAS.EDU • WEBSITE: WWW.THOMASAQUINAS.EDU

THE PRINCETON REVIEW SAYS

Admissions

Very important factors considered include: rigor of secondary school record, standardized test scores, application essay, recommendation(s), character/personal qualities, level of applicant's interest. *Important factors considered include:* academic GPA. *Other factors considered include:* class rank, interview, extracurricular activities, talent/ability, religious affiliation/commitment, volunteer work, work experience. SAT or ACT required. ACT with or without writing accepted. SAT with or without Essay component accepted. TOEFL required of all international applicants. High school diploma is required and GED is accepted. *Academic units required:* 4 English, 3 math, 2 science, 2 foreign language, 2 history. *Academic units recommended:* 4 English, 4 math, 3 science, 2 science labs, 2 history, 3 academic electives.

Financial Aid

Students should submit: FAFSA, Institution's own financial aid form, State aid form. Regular filing deadline is 3/2. The Princeton Review suggests that all financial aid forms be submitted as soon as possible after October 1. *Need-based scholarships/grants offered:* Federal Pell, State scholarships/grants, Private scholarships, College/university scholarship or grant aid from institutional funds. *Loan aid offered:* Direct Subsidized Stafford Loans, Direct Unsubsidized Stafford Loans, Direct PLUS loans, College/university loans from institutional funds. Applicants will be notified of awards on a rolling basis beginning 2/1. Institutional employment available.

The Inside Word

A unique academic institution, TAC thoroughly analyzes their applicants to ensure their accepted students will be a good fit. Academic prowess is a must, and candidates should also demonstrate intellectual curiosity. Because of their holistic approach, admissions officers pay close attention to the application essays. The college operates on a rolling admissions schedule and, if interested, you should apply as early as possible.

THE SCHOOL SAYS "..."

From the Admissions Office

"Thomas Aquinas College holds with confidence that the human mind is capable of knowing the truth about reality, that living according to the truth is necessary for human happiness, and that truth is best comprehended through the harmonious work of faith and reason. The intellectual virtues are understood to be essential, and the college considers the cultivation of those virtues the primary work of Catholic liberal education.

"The academic program designed to achieve this goal is comprehensive and unified—and it includes no textbooks or lecture classes. In every subject—from philosophy, theology, mathematics, and science to language, music, literature, and history—students read the greatest written works in those disciplines, both ancient and modern: Homer, Plato, Aristotle, Augustine, Aquinas, Newton, Maxwell, Einstein, the Founding Fathers of the American Republic, Shakespeare, and T. S. Eliot, to name just a few. Instead of attending lecture classes, students gather in small tutorials, seminars, and laboratories for Socratic-style discussions.

"One mark of the program's success is the variety of professions and careers that graduates enter. Many attend graduate and professional schools in a wide array of disciplines; among them, philosophy, theology, law, literature, and the sciences are most often chosen.

"SAT or ACT scores are required, and the writing component on each test is encouraged. However, scores in critical reading and math (SAT), or English and mathematics (ACT) are more central in the consideration of that aspect of a student's application."

SELECTIVITY

Admissions Rating	88
# of applicants	189
% of applicants accepted	63
% of acceptees attending	66
# offered a place on the wait list	37
% accepting a place on wait list	100
% admitted from wait list	57

FRESHMAN PROFILE

Range SAT Critical Reading	610–730
Range SAT Math	552–650
Range SAT Writing	590–700
Range ACT Composite	26–30
Minimum paper TOEFL	570
Average HS GPA	3.8
% graduated top 10% of class	44
% graduated top 25% of class	50
% graduated top 50% of class	75

DEADLINES

Regular	
Nonfall registration?	No

APPLICANTS ALSO LOOK AT AND OFTEN PREFER
University of Notre Dame

AND SOMETIMES PREFER
The Catholic University of America; University of Dallas

FINANCIAL FACTS

Financial Aid Rating	99
Annual tuition	$24,500
Room and board	$7,950
Books and supplies	$50
Average frosh need-based scholarship	$14,711
Average UG need-based scholarship	$14,977
% needy frosh rec. need-based scholarship or grant aid	94
% needy UG rec. need-based scholarship or grant aid	89
% needy frosh rec. non-need-based scholarship or grant aid	2
% needy UG rec. non-need-based scholarship or grant aid	0
% needy frosh rec. need-based self-help aid	98
% needy UG rec. need-based self-help aid	99
% frosh rec. any financial aid	82
% UG rec. any financial aid	81
% UG borrow to pay for school	78
Average cumulative indebtedness	$17,101
% frosh need fully met	100
% ugrads need fully met	100
Average % of frosh need met	100
Average % of ugrad need met	100

TRANSYLVANIA UNIVERSITY

300 NORTH BROADWAY, LEXINGTON, KY 40508-1797 • ADMISSIONS: 859-233-8242 • FAX: 859-281-3649

CAMPUS LIFE

Quality of Life Rating	90
Fire Safety Rating	90
Green Rating	68
Type of school	Private
Affiliation	Disciples of Christ
Environment	City

STUDENTS

Total undergrad enrollment	1,056
% male/female	42/58
% from out of state	23
% frosh from public high school	78
% frosh live on campus	91
% ugrads live on campus	65
# of fraternities (% ugrad men join)	4 (51)
# of sororities (% ugrad women join)	4 (54)
% African American	3
% Asian	2
% Caucasian	79
% Hispanic	6
% Native American	<1
% Pacific Islander	0
% Two or more races	3
% Race and/or ethnicity unknown	3
% international	4
# of countries represented	7

SURVEY SAYS...

Students are happy
Class discussions encouraged
Students love Lexington, KY
Easy to get around campus
Recreation facilities are great
Frats and sororities are popular
Campus newspaper is popular

ACADEMICS

Academic Rating	85
% students returning for sophomore year	85
% students graduating within 4 years	70
% students graduating within 6 years	73
Calendar	Semester
Student/faculty ratio	11:1
Profs interesting rating	93
Profs accessible rating	91

Most classes have 10–19 students.
Most lab/discussion sessions have 10–19 students.

MOST POPULAR MAJORS

Business/Commerce; Accounting; Psychology

STUDENTS SAY "..."

Academics

Individual attention is paramount at Transylvania University, a small school in Lexington in the heart of Kentucky's Bluegrass region. Students who enroll here can expect a "rigorous," "high quality" education and an experience enriched by a "strong sense of community." As a liberal arts school that "emphasizes interdisciplinary work," Transylvania excels at "prepar[ing] students to think and question critically." It also provides "great scholarships" and fantastic "study abroad options." At an enrollment of about 1,000 undergrads, Transylvania's small size allows for an "intimate" classroom setting populated by "extremely engaging" and "very insightful" professors. As one sociology major brags, " They are extremely devoted to teaching and you can see their passion shine through." It's also quite evident that they strive to make themselves "very accessible" and that "they care about their students on a personal level." Transy professors also manage to foster "lively" discussions. And while "there is a strong desire to teach and convey information" instructors take great care in "letting students form their own opinions" as well. Finally, as one content physics and computer science double major happily up, "Transylvania University transform students into good communicators, leaders, and pioneers in their field of study."

Life

Undergrads happily tell us that "there is always something to do or get involved in" at Transylvania because the university "makes it very possible to get involved in all kinds of things on and off campus." A typically busy student's schedule: "I am on the soccer team, track and field team, Transylvania Environmental Action League, Gaming Club, RPG Adventure Club, Quidditch, Beta Beta Beta, Alpha Lambda Delta, I work in the Language Lab as a German tutor, and volunteer off campus at a comic book shop." Additionally, Greek life is "huge" at Transylvania and "a number of [social] opportunities are presented . . . through Greek organizations." Thankfully, "independent students are also invited to most if not all events" and we've been assured that "no one is left out of the fun here on campus." Moreover, there's also a good deal of "support for athletics so people go to most of the games." Lastly students love to take advantage of their home city of Lexington, which offers "a rich culture of art, locally-grown food served in restaurants, and a decent nightlife." And, as an added bonus, "downtown Lexington is very close to campus" so it's quite easy to head out for some fun!

Student Body

When asked to categorize their peers, many Transylvania undergrads say that the average student here "comes from an upper-middle class background and went to high school in KY." Additionally, he or she is likely to be involved "either [with] a sports team [or] part of Greek life." Unfortunately, a handful of individuals do bemoan the fact that fraternities and sororities "can sometimes create a very exclusive atmosphere that permeates the rest of the campus." Others, however, argue that friendliness abounds. As one undergrad shares, "I can't walk across campus without saying hello to at least a handful of people." Many people at Transylvania are also "very politically and socially active." Of course, even more important, the typical Transy undergrad can be characterized as "passionate, involved, kind and intelligent." And, as a psychology and philosophy double major concludes, "Everyone can find others with similar interests to them and no one is without friends. We all care about each other and are ready to stand together to support a cause or a friend in need."

TRANSYLVANIA UNIVERSITY

FINANCIAL AID: 859-233-8239 • E-MAIL: ADMISSIONS@TRANSY.EDU • WEBSITE: WWW.TRANSY.EDU

THE PRINCETON REVIEW SAYS

Admissions

Very important factors considered include: rigor of secondary school record, academic GPA, standardized test scores, application essay. *Important factors considered include:* recommendation(s), extracurricular activities, talent/ability, character/personal qualities. *Other factors considered include:* class rank, interview, first generation, alumni/ae relation, geographical residence, racial/ethnic status, volunteer work, work experience. SAT or ACT considered if submitted. ACT with or without writing accepted. SAT with or without Essay component accepted. TOEFL required of all international applicants. High school diploma is required and GED is accepted. *Academic units required:* 4 English, 3 math, 3 science, 2 science labs, 2 foreign language, 2 social studies, 2 academic electives. *Academic units recommended:* 4 English, 4 math, 4 science, 3 science labs, 2 foreign language, 2 social studies, 1 history, 2 academic electives.

Financial Aid

Students should submit: FAFSA. Priority filing deadline is 1/1. The Princeton Review suggests that all financial aid forms be submitted as soon as possible after October 1. *Need-based scholarships/grants offered:* Federal Pell, FSEOG, State scholarships/grants, Private scholarships, College/university scholarship or grant aid from institutional funds. *Loan aid offered:* Direct Subsidized Stafford Loans, Direct Unsubsidized Stafford Loans, Direct PLUS loans, Federal Perkins Loans. Applicants will be notified of awards on or about 3/15. Federal Work-Study Program available. Institutional employment available.

Inside Word

As a small liberal arts school, Transylvania aims to take an all-inclusive approach to the admissions process. High school transcripts, standardized test scores, recommendation letters and application essays will all be thoroughly vetted. Students who would like to receive priority consideration for both admissions and scholarships are highly encouraged to apply by Transylvania's early action deadline. Don't worry; admission is not binding. Lastly, though the university does maintain a regular admission deadline, Transylvania will accept applications after that date and continue to consider candidates depending on the availability of spaces.

THE SCHOOL SAYS "..."

From the Admissions Office

"Bright, highly motivated students choose Transylvania for our personal approach to learning and our record of success in preparing them for rewarding careers and fulfilling lives. They attend small classes (many have fewer than ten students) with highly qualified professors (no teaching assistants) and tackle faculty-directed student research projects in intriguing subjects like neurotransmitters and receptors, computer animation, and local Hispanic culture. Transylvania graduates have won prestigious scholarships and distinguished themselves at highly selective graduate and professional schools. Transylvania students consider the world their classroom. They enjoy May term travel courses studying the ancient polis in Greece, language and culture in France, and tropical ecology in Hawaii. Study abroad takes them to Germany, England, Japan, Mexico, and other destinations for a summer, a semester, or a year. You'll find Transylvania, a small college, nestled in a big city. Transylvania students soak up the advantages of Lexington, Kentucky, with its population of 300,000, numerous internships and job opportunities, and lots of entertainment. On campus, we have more than sixty co-curricular activities, and twenty-three varsity teams competing in NCAA Division III. While Transylvania is the nation's sixteenth oldest college and proud of its rich history, its commitments to the exploration of a variety of disciplines, to intellectual inquiry, and to critical thinking have never been more relevant than in today's rapidly changing twenty-first-century world.

"Transylvania University is a Test Optional school and does not require that students submit standardized test scores as part of the admission process. Read more at www.transy.edu/optional."

SELECTIVITY

Admissions Rating	83
# of applicants	1,538
% of applicants accepted	93
% of acceptees attending	22

FRESHMAN PROFILE

Range SAT Critical Reading	520–640
Range SAT Math	500–660
Range ACT Composite	24–30
Minimum paper TOEFL	550
Minimum internet-based TOEFL	80
Average HS GPA	3.7
% graduated top 10% of class	39
% graduated top 25% of class	76
% graduated top 50% of class	91

DEADLINES

Early action	
Deadline	12/1
Notification	12/20
Regular	
Priority	12/1
Nonfall registration?	Yes

APPLICANTS ALSO LOOK AT AND SOMETIMES PREFER

Centre College; University of Kentucky

FINANCIAL FACTS

Financial Aid Rating	85
Annual tuition	$32,970
Room and board	$9,310
Required fees	$1,400
Books and supplies	$1,000
Average frosh need-based scholarship	$23,656
Average UG need-based scholarship	$23,663
% needy frosh rec. need-based scholarship or grant aid	100
% needy UG rec. need-based scholarship or grant aid	100
% needy frosh rec. non-need-based scholarship or grant aid	21
% needy UG rec. non-need-based scholarship or grant aid	16
% needy frosh rec. need-based self-help aid	71
% needy UG rec. need-based self-help aid	74
% frosh rec. any financial aid	99
% UG rec. any financial aid	98
% UG borrow to pay for school	64
Average cumulative indebtedness	$26,937
% frosh need fully met	32
% ugrads need fully met	27
Average % of frosh need met	84
Average % of ugrad need met	83

TRINITY COLLEGE (CT)

300 SUMMIT STREET, HARTFORD, CT 06106 • ADMISSIONS: 860-297-2180 • FAX: 860-297-2287

STUDENTS SAY ". . ."

Academics
"[It's all] about getting a top-notch education in small classes with professors who know you and being able to also have a good time outside of class" at Trinity College, a small and prestigious liberal arts school located in Connecticut's state capital. A "great political science department" exploits TC's location "about two blocks away from the state capitol, which is great for internships." Other social sciences, including economics and history, earn students' praises, as do offerings in engineering and education. Strength across the liberal arts bolsters the school's Humanities Gateway Program, in which students undertake a fixed curriculum of interdisciplinary study to survey the entirety of European cultures from the classical age to the present. In all disciplines, "small classes, very involved professors, and a very conscious student body" combine to provide "an excellent liberal arts education that will provide [students] with the skills to be thoughtful, independent adults." Professors "are always available to talk and offer help to students. They often invite students out to lunch." Likewise, administrators are easy to access. Students also appreciate that "the career services office is amazing" here.

Life
"The fraternity scene is the draw for the majority of campus" at Trinity College, where "on a typical weekend night, people go out to dinner, go back to their room and nap, get ready for the evening, and go meet up with a friend or two where they chill out and then go to someone's room for pregaming...Then when it's about 1:00 A.M. they go out and do some frat hopping. It's great for people who like their life to be predictable." The frats are hardly the only option, though; in fact, "there are a ton of underappreciated options on or near campus. Hartford has amazing restaurants, there are movie theaters and bowling alleys nearby, the Cinestudio is a ninety-second walk from the main dining hall." There is also a Health and Wellness Residence Hall. "Plus, plenty of student groups hold events" in such places as "the arts and cultural houses." Trinity's theater and dance department offer regular performances. Hometown Hartford "may be [an economically] depressed city, but it is still a city, and it affords benefits that tiny college towns just can't match."

Student Body
The stereotype about Trinity undergrads is that "most...are from the tristate area and appear to have just stepped off a yacht or out of a country club," and students confirm that while "there are a lot of students who are not" in this crowd, the preppy contingent is "the main group" and "socially dominant" here. "There are definitely some very preppy girls and boys—blond hair, sunglasses, Chanel flats, a polo," one student concedes before adding that "sometimes people identify these students as typical Trinity students; however there are many students who are not like that at all." All students tend to be "well-rounded" and "very passionate," "intelligent but also social," with "good verbal skills." They "care deeply about their work and really like to have fun when they can," and while many gravitate to the Greek community for their fun, "there are [also] communities here for those who do not enjoy the frat scene, for people who are passionate about music and acting, and [for] those who want to spend their weekends giving back to the community."

FINANCIAL AID: 860-297-2047 • E-MAIL: ADMISSIONS.OFFICE@TRINCOLL.EDU • WEBSITE: WWW.TRINCOLL.EDU

THE PRINCETON REVIEW SAYS

Admissions

Very important factors considered include: rigor of secondary school record. *Important factors considered include:* class rank, academic GPA, application essay, recommendation(s), interview, extracurricular activities, talent/ability, character/personal qualities, racial/ethnic status. *Other factors considered include:* first generation, alumni/ae relation, geographical residence, volunteer work, work experience, level of applicant's interest. SAT or ACT not used. ACT with Writing recommended. TOEFL or IELTS required of all international applicants. High school diploma is required and GED is accepted. *Academic units required:* 4 English, 3 math, 2 science, 2 science labs, 3 foreign language, 2 history.

Financial Aid

Students should submit: FAFSA, CSS/Financial Aid PROFILE, Noncustodial PROFILE, Business/Farm Supplement. Regular filing deadline is 3/1. The Princeton Review suggests that all financial aid forms be submitted as soon as possible after October 1. *Need-based scholarships/grants offered:* Federal Pell, FSEOG, State scholarships/grants, Private scholarships, College/university scholarship or grant aid from institutional funds. *Loan aid offered:* Direct Subsidized Stafford Loans, Direct Unsubsidized Stafford Loans, Direct PLUS loans, Federal Perkins Loans, College/university loans from institutional funds. Applicants will be notified of awards on or about 4/1. Federal Work-Study Program available. Institutional employment available.

The Inside Word

Students describe Trinity as "the home of Yale rejects," an appraisal that accurately, if somewhat hyperbolically, characterizes the school's reputation as an Ivy safety. The hefty tuition and fees here ensure that a large percentage of the student body is made up of wealthy, preppy types, but the school does offer generous financial aid packages to top candidates who can't afford the considerable price of attending. The school would love to broaden its demographic, so competitive minority students should receive a very welcome reception here.

THE SCHOOL SAYS "..."

From the Admissions Office

"An array of distinctive curricular options—including an interdisciplinary neuroscience major and a professionally accredited engineering degree program, a unique Human Rights Program, a Health Fellows Program, and interdisciplinary programs such as the Cities Program, Interdisciplinary Science Program, and InterArts—is one reason record numbers of students are applying to Trinity. In fact, applications are up 80 percent over the past five years. In addition, the college has been recognized for its commitment to diversity; students of color have represented approximately 20 percent of the freshman class for the past four years, setting Trinity apart from many of its peers. Trinity's capital city location offers students unparalleled 'real-world' learning experiences to complement classroom learning. Students take advantage of extensive opportunities for internships for academic credit and community service, and these opportunities extend to Trinity's global learning sites in cities around the world. Trinity's faculty is a devoted and accomplished group of exceptional teacher-scholars; our 100-acre campus is beautiful; Hartford is an educational asset that differentiates Trinity from other liberal arts colleges; our global connections and foreign study opportunities prepare students to be good citizens of the world; and our graduates go on to excel in virtually every field. We invite you to learn more about why Trinity might be the best choice for you.

"Students applying for admission may submit the following testing options: SAT or ACT with writing."

SELECTIVITY

Admissions Rating	93
# of applicants	7,570
% of applicants accepted	33
% of acceptees attending	22
# offered a place on the wait list	1,796
% accepting a place on wait list	32
% admitted from wait list	1
# of early decision applicants	506
% accepted early decision	59

FRESHMAN PROFILE

Range SAT Critical Reading	540–670
Range SAT Math	570–700
Range SAT Writing	550–680
Range ACT Composite	26–31
Minimum paper TOEFL	550
Minimum internet-based TOEFL	95
% graduated top 10% of class	64
% graduated top 25% of class	84
% graduated top 50% of class	98

DEADLINES

Early decision	
Deadline	11/15
Notification	12/15
Regular	
Deadline	1/1
Notification	4/1
Nonfall registration?	No

AND SOMETIMES PREFER
Middlebury College; Wesleyan University; Boston College; Fordham University

AND RARELY PREFER
Boston University; Villanova University

FINANCIAL FACTS

Financial Aid Rating	97
Annual tuition	$48,446
Room and board	$13,144
Required fees	$2,330
Books and supplies	$1,000
Average frosh need-based scholarship	$42,325
Average UG need-based scholarship	$42,969
% needy frosh rec. need-based scholarship or grant aid	95
% needy UG rec. need-based scholarship or grant aid	96
% needy frosh rec. non-need-based scholarship or grant aid	3
% needy UG rec. non-need-based scholarship or grant aid	6
% needy frosh rec. need-based self-help aid	74
% needy UG rec. need-based self-help aid	74
% frosh rec. any financial aid	48
% UG rec. any financial aid	45
% frosh need fully met	100
% ugrads need fully met	100
Average % of frosh need met	98
Average % of ugrad need met	100

TRINITY COLLEGE DUBLIN

ACADEMIC REGISTRY, WATTS BUILDING, TRINITY COLLEGE, DUBLIN 2, IRELAND • INTERNATIONAL ADMISSIONS: +353-1-896-4500

CAMPUS LIFE

Quality of Life Rating	90
Fire Safety Rating	90
Green Rating	71
Type of school	Public
Affiliation	No Affiliation

STUDENTS

Total undergrad enrollment	11,839
% male/female	0/0
% from out of state	15
% frosh live on campus	31
% ugrads live on campus	16
% African American	0
% Asian	0
% Caucasian	0
% Hispanic	0
% Native American	0
% Pacific Islander	0
% Two or more races	0
% Race and/or ethnicity unknown	0
% international	0
# of countries represented	122

SURVEY SAYS...

Students are happy
Great library
Students aren't religious
Students love Dublin, Ireland
Great off-campus food
Lots of beer drinking
Campus newspaper is popular

ACADEMICS

Academic Rating	65
% students returning for sophomore year	91
Calendar	Semester
Student/faculty ratio	17:1
Profs interesting rating	72
Profs accessible rating	66

STUDENTS SAY "..."

Academics

Perhaps Ireland's most famous university, Trinity College Dublin is an idyllic, world famous institution that has carried on a 400-year-old tradition of scholarship on the Emerald Isle. This "beautiful and prestigious university" boasts a lot on offer, both academically and socially, and the degree graduates receive is highly respected internationally. "Personal development is available for those who pursue it," says a student. "You grow up to be an adult here, one that has diverse life experience and a broad exposure to classical and modern study."

Professors in general are "pleasant and fluid," "bring their passion and enthusiasm for their subject to every lecture." "A professor of mine has cried during a lecture when explaining why Kant's attempt at revising metaphysics was so important," says a sophomore. The school "really holds you to a higher standard" so self-motivation is key, and "the teachers don't baby [students]. You are expected to be responsible for your own study." "Your job is to be a university student and to do it well," says another student. However, if help is needed then teachers are "extremely good at helping you outside class hours. Just email them and they will arrange a time to meet." The scene here is "more like a master's program in the states, but with [student] societies that are given millions of euros to make sure you have fun and opportunities." There is always room for discussion in lectures, and "classes tend to be really interactive so students aren't just sitting there passively learning." Many do feel that there could "be a slicker process administratively," particularly with regard to registration and exams. The libraries "own an incredibly broad selection of works between them," and are "absolutely incredible both in selection of books, and space to study." On top of the very active clubs and societies, a great strength is the "small tutorials that correspond with lectures," as well the "great speakers giving talks on a weekly basis."

Life

It's "a self-contained university world, bang-smack in Dublin's city centre," acting as "an island all to itself." The legendary front entrance "looks damn good" to all ye who enter here, and passing through the gothic arches "[is] like [entering] a calm academic hub within a busy city." In fact, those who live on campus "practically have their own world if they so desire, as it is so self-contained." In general, people are "fairly studious and interested in their course, [but] they make room in their schedule for partying though as well." Students have great choice for meeting people and fitting in with a large number of societies, which "are inclusive and social, [and] all are catered for in the vast smorgasbord of college life." The annual Trinity ball is "an amazing event, Europe's largest private party." Alcohol forms part of college life (there is even a college bar, the Pav, "overlooking the cricket pitch"), and "outside of society events it is by far the most common social activity." However, by the time exams roll around in May, everyone is "all about cramming into the library and getting to work."

Student Body

This "self-motivated, tightly knit intellectual community of a huge variety of students" is composed of "bright inquisitive minds" who tend to be "trendy and intelligent and well-travelled and somewhat well-off." The vast majority come from Ireland, and since "there's literally a niche or society for everyone to fit in, all varieties of personality interact agreeably." "There are a lot of sociable societies which are easy to join and they generally welcome you with open arms," says a biochemistry major. Ireland is a small country, so "often students know each other from school before coming to Trinity."

FINANCIAL AID: • E-MAIL: ACADEMIC.REGISTRY@TCD.IE / INTERNATIONAL@TCD.IE • WEBSITE: WWW.TCD.IE

THE PRINCETON REVIEW SAYS

Admissions

Very important factors considered include: rigor of secondary school record, academic GPA, standardized test scores. *Important factors considered include:* application essay, recommendation(s). *Other factors considered include:* extracurricular activities, character/personal qualities, volunteer work, work experience, level of applicant's interest. SAT or ACT required; SAT Subject Tests considered if submitted. ACT with or without writing accepted. TOEFL required of all international applicants.

Financial Aid

Students should submit: FAFSA. Priority filing deadline is 6/1. The Princeton Review suggests that all financial aid forms be submitted as soon as possible after October 1. *Need-based scholarships/grants offered:* State scholarships/grants, Private Scholarships. *Loan aid offered:* Direct Subsidized Stafford Loans, Direct Unsubsidized Stafford Loans, Direct PLUS loans, Federal Perkins Loans, Federal Nursing Loans, State Loans. Federal Work-Study Program available.

The Inside Word

The cost of attendance at Trinity is still less for most Irish students than the cost of a private university in the United States, so the school tends to draw Ireland's best students; only around 4 percent of students come from North or Central America, and only around 11 percent from the EU. Non-EU students from the United States must have completed all of the necessary high school curriculum (with a GPA of at least 3.3) and have minimum SAT score of 1300 on any two of the Critical Reading, Math and Writing sections (and no score less than 500); or, an ACT composite score of 29.

THE SCHOOL SAYS "..."

From the Admissions Office

"Situated in the centre of Ireland's vibrant capital city, Trinity's stunning campus is home to a community of scholars at the cutting-edge of research and teaching. Combining historic traditions with world-renowned centres of research excellence, Trinity offers a unique opportunity to blend a rigorous academic programme with an unparalleled array of cultural, social and professional experiences. Trinity's President, Dr Patrick Prendergast says: 'Our inspiring professors are global leaders in their fields, and they work alongside students in a common enterprise of discovery. The Trinity curriculum isn't just about imparting knowledge; it's aimed at developing the critical faculties of the mind, through freedom of expression, willingness to engage in debate, and original research'. Trinity's diverse, intellectual and curious community is the perfect setting for students who wish to pursue their intellectual interests while also passionately engaging in creative, entrepreneurial, innovative and charitable pursuits. At Trinity, students are equipped with the skills and knowledge they need to build the lives they want and succeed in their chosen careers. A Trinity degree is one of the most respected in the world. Over 94 percent of graduates are employed or in further study within six months of completing their degrees. With Trinity alumni working in the highest offices of corporations and governments around the world, global employers are eager to hire Trinity graduates.

"In order to be considered for admission all applicants are required to satisfy minimum entry requirements of 1300 on any two of the Critical Reading, Math and Writing sections in the SAT, or achieve a minimum composite score of 29 in the ACT. More information is online at www.tcd.ie/Study."

SELECTIVITY	
Admissions Rating	80
# of applicants	18,995
% of applicants accepted	16
% of acceptees attending	93
# offered a place on the wait list	388
% accepting a place on wait list	52
% admitted from wait list	100

DEADLINES	
Regular Priority	2/1
Deadline	6/1
Nonfall registration?	No

FINANCIAL FACTS	
Financial Aid Rating	60*
Room and board	$9,300
% needy frosh rec. need-based scholarship or grant aid	0
% needy UG rec. need-based scholarship or grant aid	0
% needy frosh rec. non-need-based scholarship or grant aid	0
% needy UG rec. non-need-based scholarship or grant aid	0
% needy frosh rec. need-based self-help aid	0
% needy UG rec. need-based self-help aid	0

TRINITY UNIVERSITY (TX)

ONE TRINITY PLACE, SAN ANTONIO, TX 78212-7200 • ADMISSIONS: 210-999-7207 • FAX: 210-999-8164

STUDENTS SAY "..."

Academics

Located in San Antonio, Trinity University is a small liberal arts college that offers substantial financial aid and encourages the exploration of academic interests and personal goals. Strong science programs and research opportunities abound, and students are interested in many different branches of academia and extracurricular life: "It's rare to find a student with one major and no minor." The Dean and President "have steady communication with the student body," and "they're open to criticism and willing to change the school's policy in order to advocate for the students' needs." The "highly intelligent" faculty "know their stuff and love what they do"; they are "very self-aware and are constantly trying to improve themselves and their students." The most distinguishable trait about Trinity professors is "the deeply-ingrained willingness to connect with and help their students," which is possible due to Trinity's small class sizes. Academics here are rigorous, and professors "expect their students to treat the class . . . as if it was the only class students have." Luckily, they will "bend over backwards to help you understand and complete material," and some professors even hold extra study sessions on Sundays (one-on-one attention from professors is common, as the university does not have TAs).

Above all else, Trinity University encourages students to take a wide range of classes and pursue a wide variety of interests, and a fair number of students choose to study abroad their junior year. The school "focuses on building a community based on the individual" and "fosters a space for the easy transfer of knowledge between faculty and students as well as the creation of new knowledge in research."

Life

Most students at Trinity live on campus (and it's "hard to get off campus and do things if you don't have a car"), so there are always campus-wide events happening. Most people here are "happily overcommitted" and the "lovely campus" is big enough for all sorts of people to find their niche, but small enough "that you can connect with others who share similar interests as you within and without your major." Intramural sports and Greek life are popular, and "there's no tension between Greeks and non-Greeks." A healthy mix of activities complements the healthy mix of academic areas, and some people go out to parties on weekends, other people get ahead on studies, other people sleep." For those looking for some city culture, downtown San Antonio is ten minutes away, Austin is just a 90-minute drive, and "there are tons of restaurants and historical monuments and museums" nearby. Cowboys, the local country dance club ("only in Texas") gets a lot of Trinity students visiting on weekends, and many people here "enjoy outdoor pursuits." Laid back, casual fun is the name of the game at Trinity, and students are perfectly happy to "catch a movie at the nearby theater, go to the local farmers' market, go to Spurs' games . . . or just hang out on campus."

Student Body

There is an "open-minded open-to-all mindset" that is readily seen on campus: "At Trinity, you're cool if you competitively roller skate, are an amateur baker, play a competitive sport, are freaky good at laser tag (ninja status), or anything else you can do well and makes you happy," says a student. Though most are "pretty middle- to upper middle-class," the school "encourages interactions with others from all walks of life." For the most part, everyone is "smart, committed, and involved," and an "overarching friendliness" pervades the entire student population.

FINANCIAL AID: 210-999-8315 • E-MAIL: ADMISSIONS@TRINITY.EDU • WEBSITE: WWW.TRINITY.EDU

THE PRINCETON REVIEW SAYS

Admissions

Very important factors considered include: rigor of secondary school record, class rank, academic GPA, standardized test scores. *Important factors considered include:* application essay, recommendation(s), interview, extracurricular activities, talent/ability, character/personal qualities. *Other factors considered include:* first generation, alumni/ae relation, geographical residence, volunteer work, work experience, level of applicant's interest. SAT or ACT required. ACT with or without writing accepted. SAT with or without Essay component accepted. High school diploma is required and GED is accepted. *Academic units recommended:* 4 English, 3 math, 3 science, 2 science labs, 2 foreign language, 3 social studies.

Financial Aid

Students should submit: FAFSA, CSS/Financial Aid PROFILE. Priority filing deadline is 2/15. The Princeton Review suggests that all financial aid forms be submitted as soon as possible after October 1. *Need-based scholarships/grants offered:* Federal Pell, FSEOG, State scholarships/grants, Private scholarships, College/university scholarship or grant aid from institutional funds. *Loan aid offered:* Direct Subsidized Stafford Loans, Direct Unsubsidized Stafford Loans, Direct PLUS loans, Federal Perkins Loans, State Loans, College/university loans from institutional funds. Applicants will be notified of awards on or about 3/15. Federal Work-Study Program available. Institutional employment available.

The Inside Word

As Trinity embraces a small, close-knit community of students, admissions officers are looking for the complete package: bright, capable, motivated students who are ready to take advantage of all the school has to offer. While academic performance is the factor considered most heavily on each application, recommendations, extracurricular activities, and standardized test scores should all be very strong as well.

THE SCHOOL SAYS "..."

From the Admissions Office

"Three qualities separate Trinity University from other selective, academically challenging institutions around the country. First, Trinity is unusual in the quality and quantity of resources devoted almost exclusively to its undergraduate students. Those resources give rise to a second distinctive aspect of Trinity—its emphasis on undergraduate research. Our students prefer being involved over observing. With superior laboratory facilities and strong, dedicated faculty, our undergraduates fill many of the roles formerly reserved for graduate students, and our professors often go to their undergraduates for help with their research. Other experiential learning opportunities including internships, study abroad, and service projects are also available to students. Finally, Trinity stands apart for the attitude of its students. In an atmosphere of academic camaraderie, our students work together to stretch their minds and broaden their horizons across academic disciplines. For quality of resources, for dedication to undergraduate research, and for the disposition of its student body, Trinity University holds a unique position in American higher education.

"Students applying for admission must submit either the SAT or the ACT. The highest composite test scores from one or multiple dates are evaluated. The SAT writing section and ACT writing component are not required."

SELECTIVITY

Admissions Rating	90
# of applicants	5,563
% of applicants accepted	48
% of acceptees attending	23
# offered a place on the wait list	257
% accepting a place on wait list	43
% admitted from wait list	34
# of early decision applicants	71
% accepted early decision	76

FRESHMAN PROFILE

Range SAT Critical Reading	580–690
Range SAT Math	580–680
Range SAT Writing	560–660
Range ACT Composite	27–32
Average HS GPA	3.5
% graduated top 10% of class	47
% graduated top 25% of class	75
% graduated top 50% of class	96

DEADLINES

Early decision	
Deadline	11/1
Notification	12/15
Early action	
Deadline	11/1
Notification	12/15
Regular	
Deadline	2/1
Notification	4/1
Nonfall registration?	Yes

APPLICANTS ALSO LOOK AT AND RARELY PREFER
Rhodes College

FINANCIAL FACTS

Financial Aid Rating	90
Annual tuition	$39,560
Room and board	$12,754
Average frosh need-based scholarship	$29,089
Average UG need-based scholarship	$27,899
% needy frosh rec. need-based scholarship or grant aid	100
% needy UG rec. need-based scholarship or grant aid	99
% needy frosh rec. non-need-based scholarship or grant aid	36
% needy UG rec. non-need-based scholarship or grant aid	23
% needy frosh rec. need-based self-help aid	63
% needy UG rec. need-based self-help aid	67
% frosh rec. any financial aid	98
% UG rec. any financial aid	93
% UG borrow to pay for school	51
Average cumulative indebtedness	$36,626
% frosh need fully met	83
% ugrads need fully met	58
Average % of frosh need met	98
Average % of ugrad need met	94

TRUMAN STATE UNIVERSITY

100 EAST NORMAL AVENUE, KIRKSVILLE, MO 63501 • ADMISSIONS: 660-785-4114 • FAX: 660-785-7456

STUDENTS SAY "..."

Academics

If you are looking for "value," check out Truman State University. "Few schools can provide a similar undergraduate experience at a comparable price." Most current students were hard-pressed to find a better deal than they got at this "highly regarded," "very affordable" school located in Kirksville, Missouri. A high percentage of students receive financial aid and/or scholarships making Truman "far more affordable than other institutions." One out-of-state student who experienced this firsthand says, "It was far cheaper for me to go to Truman than to any of the schools in my own state or to any private school to which I applied. Between Truman scholarships and private scholarships, I'm basically being paid to go here. My friends from high school are already panicking about how they're going to pay off their loans, and knowing I'm graduating debt-free is the best feeling in the world." Students do not appear to be sacrificing quality for a cheaper education. They say professors "really push you to work hard." They are all "very qualified," and students say, "Grades actually reflect the student's qualifications." Small class sizes enable "fantastic one-on-one experience between professors and students." "The faculty care way more about teaching than about their own research or interests." Classes are "small and engaging," and "Nearly all [professors] are available beyond their scheduled office hours and do their best to make sure we understand material." Students did also mention that there seems to be a lack of funding recently and that "some majors seem short-staffed." "Truman could improve by offering more classes and hiring more professors in order to decrease the congestion in classrooms for the more popular courses." One student sums up why this school was a good choice: "I wanted a college where I could be academically challenged as well as actively involved in [extracurricular] activities. I wanted to be surrounded by intellectually stimulating peers and professors in order to gain a comprehensive liberal arts education. I found all of this at Truman and saved a significant amount of money in the process." Another student is concerned that "Truman is a small school and is not easily recognized on a national scale. In the post-graduation job search, this fact could become very frustrating."

Life

"College life is hectic and amazing all at the same time." "Truman is an academically challenging school, so separating your school time and social life is an important task that we need to learn." The school's "very pretty" campus might be "in the middle of nowhere," but Truman brings "tons of really great activities, shows, bands, etc., to campus to keep us entertained." "Kirksville is not a big town," and homework consumes much of a student's day. Still, "there is always time to have a social life though. Hanging out with friends and just watching a movie or going out to [see] a comedian or performance on campus are viable options on any given weekend. A social life is just something that you have to plan for rather than something that is just given to you." "On the weekends, students usually go out to parties. The students who do not party will go to events on campus or hang out with friends in the dorms." Students are pleased with facilities, including "newly renovated" dorms, and the "library is excellent." "Also, the atmosphere on campus is very safe and welcoming." However, administrative services sometimes make life difficult. "A lot of the offices (financial aid, study abroad, registrar, etc.) are extremely disorganized."

Student Body

Students coined the "term T.T.S. (Typical Truman Student)...to describe academically focused, very studious students." This is reflected in classrooms where "teachers barely ever take attendance because people go to class." That term seems to fit most, but definitely not everyone on campus. Students point out, "People definitely party, somewhat during the week, and a lot on the weekends, especially if they're involved in a sorority/fraternity." Truman is not an overly diverse campus, but classmates are "accepting of others." A student says, "It is not hard to fit in at this school. Every single person I have met brings something unique to this institution."

TRUMAN STATE UNIVERSITY

FINANCIAL AID: 660-785-4130 • E-MAIL: ADMISSIONS@TRUMAN.EDU • WEBSITE: WWW.TRUMAN.EDU

THE PRINCETON REVIEW SAYS

Admissions

Very important factors considered include: rigor of secondary school record, class rank, academic GPA, standardized test scores. *Important factors considered include:* application essay. *Other factors considered include:* recommendation(s), extracurricular activities, talent/ability, character/personal qualities, first generation, alumni/ae relation, geographical residence, state residency, racial/ethnic status, volunteer work, work experience, level of applicant's interest. SAT or ACT required. ACT with or without writing accepted. TOEFL required of all international applicants. High school diploma is required and GED is accepted. *Academic units required:* 4 English, 3 math, 3 science, 2 science labs, 2 foreign language, 2 social studies, 1 history, 5 academic electives, 1 visual/performing arts, and 3 units from above areas or other academic areas. *Academic units recommended:* 4 math.

Financial Aid

Students should submit: FAFSA. Priority filing deadline is 4/1. The Princeton Review suggests that all financial aid forms be submitted as soon as possible after October 1. *Need-based scholarships/grants offered:* Federal Pell, FSEOG, State scholarships/grants, Private scholarships, College/university scholarship or grant aid from institutional funds. *Loan aid offered:* Direct Subsidized Stafford Loans, Direct Unsubsidized Stafford Loans, Direct PLUS loans, Federal Perkins Loans, Federal Nursing Loans, College/university loans from institutional funds. Applicants will be notified of awards on a rolling basis beginning 3/1. Federal Work-Study Program available. Institutional employment available.

The Inside Word

Those interested in studying at Truman had better get to work; the school places a large emphasis on GPA, class rank, and academic rigor. The selectivity and quality of education numbers are high, but annual tuition is low for all students. Although early application has no bearing on admission, greatest scholarship consideration is given to those who apply before December 1st.

THE SCHOOL SAYS "..."

From the Admissions Office

"Truman's talented student body enjoys small classes where undergraduate research and personal interaction with professors are the norm. Our outstanding internship and study abroad opportunities allow students to attend top graduate schools and have great job prospects.

"Truman is recognized consistently as one of the nation's 'Best Values' in higher education. The university offers a variety of competitive scholarships, and there is no separate scholarship application. Students wishing to be considered for all scholarship programs are strongly encouraged to apply for admission by December 1st.

"Students applying to Truman State University can submit scores from both the ACT and the SAT. The best composite score from either test will be considered in admission and scholarship selection. The writing section is not required. Admission requirements are selective and there is no application fee.

"At Truman, we believe a quality college experience does not stop at the classroom door. It should permeate the entire campus, offering opportunities that entertain, pique students' interest, and invite them to fully embrace this extraordinary journey. It is about making great friends, getting involved in one of over 200 student organizations, exploring the amazing world that surrounds them and creating memories that will last a lifetime. This is a university that transforms lives. Truman's success as one of the nation's premier public liberal arts and sciences institutions can be traced to one guiding principle: an unwavering devotion to the pursuit of knowledge, wherever your journey leads you."

SELECTIVITY	
Admissions Rating	88
# of applicants	3,900
% of applicants accepted	79
% of acceptees attending	41

FRESHMAN PROFILE	
Range SAT Critical Reading	580–730
Range SAT Math	560–680
Range ACT Composite	25–30
Minimum paper TOEFL	550
Minimum internet-based TOEFL	79
Average HS GPA	3.8
% graduated top 10% of class	47
% graduated top 25% of class	79
% graduated top 50% of class	97

DEADLINES	
Regular	
Priority	12/1
Nonfall registration?	Yes

APPLICANTS ALSO LOOK AT AND OFTEN PREFER
University of Missouri; Saint Louis University

AND SOMETIMES PREFER
Washington University in St. Louis

AND RARELY PREFER
Illinois Wesleyan University; University of Iowa

FINANCIAL FACTS	
Financial Aid Rating	87
Annual in-state tuition	$7,152
Annual out-of-state tuition	$13,376
Room and board	$8,480
Required fees	$304
Books and supplies	$1,000
Average frosh need-based scholarship	$8,180
Average UG need-based scholarship	$7,171
% needy frosh rec. need-based scholarship or grant aid	99
% needy UG rec. need-based scholarship or grant aid	94
% needy frosh rec. non-need-based scholarship or grant aid	96
% needy UG rec. non-need-based scholarship or grant aid	79
% needy frosh rec. need-based self-help aid	70
% needy UG rec. need-based self-help aid	78
% frosh rec. any financial aid	99
% UG rec. any financial aid	86
% UG borrow to pay for school	56
Average cumulative indebtedness	$24,220
% frosh need fully met	43
% ugrads need fully met	36
Average % of frosh need met	88
Average % of ugrad need met	83

TUFTS UNIVERSITY

BENDETSON HALL, MEDFORD, MA 02155 • ADMISSIONS: 617-627-3170 • FAX: 617-627-3860

STUDENTS SAY "..."

Academics

The campus culture at Tufts University in Massachusetts is "thriving and alive," and as such it really encourages students to merge their academic and social interests and "pursue both in a passionate way." This is a place where, through active discussion and a student body with a zest for life, "passion meets reality." The academic experience here is marked by "small classes with knowledgeable and interesting professors." "I have had the opportunity to explore a huge amount of academic subjects and really challenge myself," says a student. If students actively seek out their "highly accessible and prompt" professors, they will be rewarded with "a better learning experience and with incomparable relationships with brilliant (yet down to earth) professors." "Whenever I ask them a question that they might not know the answer to, they do research on it immediately and return quickly with a detailed response." The academic curriculum is a "perfect mix of liberal arts and university," and the professors are actively concerned with making sure that students leave with a true understanding of the course material, "not just a book list under their arms." These "global minded, ambitious" students rise to the challenge and beyond, as "most every student focuses on life beyond their education" and seeks out a well-rounded life. "It is far easier to succeed here than to fail, as long as you are committed to getting as strong an education as possible," advises a student. "I've literally been offered a research position by asking questions multiple times," says another. The international relations program at this globally-aware school is particularly strong (as are study abroad options), but activism spills over into the entirety of the student body. "Change is easily made here," and "if you have a problem with something, you can easily address it." A lot of effort is put into ensuring that every student transitions well into college and success. A strong alumni network and excellent internship opportunities also "open up a world of opportunities after graduation."

Life

Though the campus itself is gorgeous, "the true beauty of the school is in the unique and quirky nature of its student body." Generally, there are "always a lot of events going on around campus that attract students every weekend" and the variety of clubs and activities available is "amazing." "Almost everything here is run by clubs and student organizations," and the Tufts Dance Collective and Quidditch clubs are some of the most popular and fun options, as is a capella. Public transportation "makes everything accessible," and on the weekends, students often go into Boston or Davis Square and spend the day shopping and "eating non-dining hall food," and at night "there are usually good parties to go to." "There is more to do in this city than anyone can possibly do in four years," says a student.

People here are "always thinking about politics" and all have a lot of spirit for Tufts and "it's really nice to walk around campus knowing that you're in a place where almost everyone is excited to be there." "This is a great place to share knowledge you have, because everyone wants to hear it and share their own experiences and thoughts," says a student.

Student Body

This is a group of go-getters, so here "everyone has the same passion for excellence" and "is engaged in so many activities on campus." Tufts is "a quirky (yet normal) compilation of a bunch of young adults with not only big dreams for the world, but with dedication and motivation to complete them." "It's like a competition to be the "most interesting man/woman in the world," says a senior. Even better, "being nerdy is cool!" "We here embrace weirdness. If talking to new people in daily life is awkward, we know it and we revel in it," says a sophomore. There is "no discrimination whatsoever," though "it can actually get frustrating how politically correct everyone is." From "dancing and singing to teaching and tutoring to international community service," students here are "stunningly busy, and happy to be so."

FINANCIAL AID: 617-627-2000 • E-MAIL: UNDERGRADUATE.ADMISSIONS@TUFTS.EDU • WEBSITE: WWW.TUFTS.EDU

THE PRINCETON REVIEW SAYS

Admissions

Very important factors considered include: rigor of secondary school record, class rank, academic GPA, standardized test scores, application essay, recommendation(s), character/personal qualities. *Important factors considered include:* extracurricular activities, talent/ability, volunteer work, work experience. *Other factors considered include:* interview, first generation, alumni/ae relation, geographical residence, racial/ethnic status, level of applicant's interest. ACT with or without writing accepted. SAT with or without Essay component accepted. TOEFL required of all international applicants. High school diploma is required and GED is accepted. *Academic units required:* 4 English, 4 math, 4 science, 3 foreign language, 4 social studies. *Academic units recommended:* 4 foreign language.

Financial Aid

Students should submit: FAFSA, CSS/Financial Aid PROFILE, Noncustodial PROFILE. Regular filing deadline is 2/15. The Princeton Review suggests that all financial aid forms be submitted as soon as possible after October 1. *Need-based scholarships/grants offered:* Federal Pell, FSEOG, State scholarships/grants, Private scholarships, College/university scholarship or grant aid from institutional funds. *Loan aid offered:* Direct Subsidized Stafford Loans, Direct Unsubsidized Stafford Loans, Direct PLUS loans, Federal Perkins Loans, College/university loans from institutional funds. Applicants will be notified of awards on or about 4/1. Federal Work-Study Program available. Institutional employment available.

The Inside Word

Admission at Tufts is competitive. You'll need a stellar transcript and high test scores to get accepted here, rounded out with strong recommendations and extracurriculars that reflect substantive engagement with your school or community. The Common App with Tufts' own writing supplement is required, along with scores from the ACT or from the SAT plus two SAT subject tests (the essay component is not required on the ACT or SAT).

THE SCHOOL SAYS "..."

From the Admissions Office

"The world we live in is not easily segmented by academic disciplines. Problems in the world will not fit into neatly labeled categories and solutions will not come from a single point of view. Global challenges like the European debt crisis or climate change are intertwined across economic, political, technological, linguistic, and cultural lines. Tufts' educational philosophy recognizes this and adapts to it with requirements that push students towards interdisciplinary thought. Students are asked to understand world culture and languages, and to see the importance of context beyond any singular discipline. Tufts believes in using intellect to impact the world and in understanding how the world impacts our intellectual pursuits. It is not uncommon to find a computer scientist partnering with faculty in mechanical engineering and drama to program robots that can tell a good story or a religion major studying to become a doctor who understands of how faith, ethics, and health are linked. Tufts' cross-disciplinary strength is possible because of its intimate size contrasted against a world-class research focus. Tufts' mission to impact the world benefits from Boston, the premier higher education destination in the United States as well as the constellation of schools that defines the university: the School of Arts & Sciences, the School of Engineering, the Fletcher School of Law and Diplomacy, the Graduate School of Arts & Sciences, the Cummings School of Veterinary Medicine, the Friedman School of Nutrition Science and Policy, the Sackler School of Graduate Biomedical Sciences, and the School of Medicine."

SELECTIVITY

Admissions Rating	97
# of applicants	19,063
% of applicants accepted	16
% of acceptees attending	44
# of early decision applicants	1,839
% accepted early decision	39

FRESHMAN PROFILE

Range SAT Critical Reading	680–750
Range SAT Math	690–770
Range SAT Writing	680–750
Range ACT Composite	30–33
Minimum paper TOEFL	600
Minimum internet-based TOEFL	100

DEADLINES

Early decision	
Deadline	11/1
Notification	12/15
Regular	
Deadline	1/1
Notification	4/1
Nonfall registration?	No

APPLICANTS ALSO LOOK AT AND OFTEN PREFER

Brown University; Cornell University; Georgetown University; Harvard College; University of Pennsylvania

AND SOMETIMES PREFER

Dartmouth College; Johns Hopkins University; Northwestern University; University of Chicago; Washington University in St. Louis

AND RARELY PREFER

Boston College; Boston University; Carnegie Mellon University; New York University

FINANCIAL FACTS

Financial Aid Rating	95
Tuition	$49,520
Room and board	$13,904
Required fees	$1,048
Books and supplies	$800
Average frosh need-based scholarship	$40,048
Average UG need-based scholarship	$39,908
% needy frosh rec. need-based scholarship or grant aid	92
% needy UG rec. need-based scholarship or grant aid	93
% needy frosh rec. non-need-based scholarship or grant aid	6
% needy UG rec. non-need-based scholarship or grant aid	4
% needy frosh rec. need-based self-help aid	83
% needy UG rec. need-based self-help aid	89
% frosh rec. any financial aid	37
% UG rec. any financial aid	38
% UG borrow to pay for school	38
Average cumulative indebtedness	$26,185
% frosh need fully met	100
% ugrads need fully met	100
Average % of frosh need met	100
Average % of ugrad need met	100

TULANE UNIVERSITY

6823 St. Charles Avenue, New Orleans, LA 70118 • Admissions: 504-865-5731

STUDENTS SAY "..."

Academics

"Nobody comes to Tulane and dislikes it," argues one of its undergraduates. "The city of New Orleans, and Tulane, have a way of grabbing you and never letting you go." Tulane's home city looms large in its students' reason for choosing it, as do its competitive "scholarship packages," distinct among schools of Tulane's reputation. Moreover, "Tulane encourages students not only to learn in the classroom but also through involvement in the New Orleans community," especially through its "unique public service requirement" for undergraduates to give back to the city. Indeed, it's "the only university to require public service for graduation," and students value that its location "in New Orleans gives so many opportunities for internships outside the classroom as well as a whole lot of fun." Students are both serious about their academics and committed to enjoying their education: "Tulane is about learning to apply the skills you were born with and having fun while doing it." Well-rounded students find that balance is key and that "I feel challenged in most of my courses, but I rarely feel overwhelmed by the work." In accordance with these values, the "professors care about and enjoy what they do. The majority of my classes are engaging regardless of if I'm personally interested in the subject." "Tulane's professors encourage you to think outside the box. They want you to succeed, and will make you fall in love with course/materials that you never thought you could love." Upperclassmen appreciate the way that "classes get better and better as you move from [core courses] into to major-related courses, and that "more classes are discussion-based and have twenty or fewer students as you get older." This commitment extends beyond traditional coursework: "the professors are all willing to help and meet outside of the classroom," and "bring real life experiences into the classroom." The rigor of Tulane's course requirements might leave some students "surprised by how many classes you still have to take come senior year," but that said, "Tulane offers a wide variety of academic courses so I have been able to explore my interests."

Life

A vast majority of Tulane students report that "work hard, play hard" is the school's "unofficial motto and it couldn't be more accurate!" They adore New Orleans, saying "it's impossible not to fall in love with the place," and "it has the best of everything—academics, social life, culture, beautiful weather. Tulane truly has it all." "I visit a lot of the festivals and everyone obviously loves Mardi Gras. There is a ton of great food and it's always warm enough to have a beer on the porch." Without a doubt, "every day at Tulane is a new experience," and "there is always something for Tulane students to do on and off campus." For those interested, "Greek life is popular as well, with roughly 45 percent of the student population participating in it." "People are definitely partiers. If you're not going out at least twice a week you're in the minority." But don't mistake a love for fun for lack of seriousness: "Intelligence is respected. What do we do for fun? We party. But we don't just get drunk. We party with a purpose." On the whole, Tulane undergrads seek a "balance of school and social" and find it in "a beautiful place filled with driven and fun students."

Student Body

"Overall, a Tulane student is very well rounded." They're "liberal, open minded, and opinionated," often "from the Northeast," and typically "overly involved on campus and ready to gush about New Orleans to whoever is willing to listen." "Having students from all fifty states and over sixty nations allows the student body to be diverse, and exciting," and Tulane is "the perfect size where you always see someone you know walking to class and at the same time see a bunch of unrecognizable faces." As previously mentioned, Tulane students highly value balance: "The students here are driven and ambitious, but balance the social and academic worlds flawlessly." And most of all, they're happy with their choice: "I have met amazing people here at Tulane and absolutely love this school."

FINANCIAL AID: 504-865-5723 • E-MAIL: UNDERGRAD.ADMISSION@TULANE.EDU • WEBSITE: WWW.TULANE.EDU

THE PRINCETON REVIEW SAYS

Admissions

Very important factors considered include: rigor of secondary school record, class rank, academic GPA, standardized test scores. *Important factors considered include:* application essay, recommendation(s), character/personal qualities. *Other factors considered include:* interview, extracurricular activities, talent/ability, first generation, alumni/ae relation, volunteer work, work experience, level of applicant's interest. SAT or ACT required. ACT with Writing recommended. SAT with Essay component recommended. TOEFL required of all international applicants. High school diploma is required and GED is accepted. *Academic units recommended:* 4 English, 4 math, 4 science, 4 science labs, 3 foreign language, 3 social studies, 3 academic electives.

Financial Aid

Students should submit: FAFSA, CSS/Financial Aid PROFILE, Noncustodial PROFILE, Business/Farm Supplement. Priority filing deadline is 2/15. The Princeton Review suggests that all financial aid forms be submitted as soon as possible after October 1. *Need-based scholarships/grants offered:* Federal Pell, FSEOG, State scholarships/grants, Private scholarships, College/university scholarship or grant aid from institutional funds. *Loan aid offered:* Direct Subsidized Loans, Direct Unsubsidized Loans, Direct PLUS loans, Federal Perkins Loans. Applicants will be notified of awards on a rolling basis beginning 3/15. Federal Work-Study Program available. Institutional employment available.

The Inside Word

Tulane is geographically diverse, historically competitive (its admissions rate tends to hover around 25 percent), and ever more desirable as it and New Orleans revitalize after 2005's Hurricane Katrina, so well-rounded excellence is key for applicants. It offers better merit-based financial aid opportunities than many schools equal to it in prestige, making it a great option for students who can't or don't want to afford Ivy-level tuition.

THE SCHOOL SAYS "..."

From the Admissions Office

"With more than 6,600 full-time undergraduate students in five schools, Tulane University offers the personal attention and teaching excellence traditionally associated with small colleges together with the facilities and interdisciplinary resources found only at major research universities. As the only major research University in America with a Public Service requirement for graduation, Tulane students are wholly committed to giving back to their communities. The opportunities for students to be involved in the rebirth of New Orleans offer an experience unavailable at any other place, at any other time.

"Tulane is committed to undergraduate education. Senior faculty members teach most introductory and lower-level courses, and most classes have twenty-five or fewer students. The close student-teacher relationship pays off. Tulane graduates are among the most likely to be selected for several prestigious fellowships that support graduate study abroad. Founded in 1834 and reorganized as Tulane University in 1884, Tulane is one of the major private research universities in the South.

"The Tulane campus offers a traditional collegiate setting in an attractive residential neighborhood, four miles from downtown New Orleans."

SELECTIVITY
Admissions Rating	94
# of applicants	31,988
% of applicants accepted	25
% of acceptees attending	21
# offered a place on the wait list	3,834
% accepting a place on wait list	30
% admitted from wait list	0

FRESHMAN PROFILE
Range SAT Critical Reading	620–710
Range SAT Math	620–700
Range SAT Writing	640–720
Range ACT Composite	30–33
Minimum paper TOEFL	550
Average HS GPA	3.6
% graduated top 10% of class	55
% graduated top 25% of class	85
% graduated top 50% of class	96

DEADLINES
Early decision	
Deadline	11/1
Early action	
Deadline	11/15
Notification	12/20
Regular	
Deadline	1/15
Notification	4/1
Nonfall registration?	Yes

APPLICANTS ALSO LOOK AT AND RARELY PREFER
Skidmore College; Rollins College; Southern Methodist University; University of Richmond

FINANCIAL FACTS
Financial Aid Rating	89
Annual tuition	$51,010
Room and board	$13,844
Required fees	$3,880
Books and supplies	$1,200
Average frosh need-based scholarship	$30,318
Average UG need-based scholarship	$30,297
% needy frosh rec. need-based scholarship or grant aid	97
% needy UG rec. need-based scholarship or grant aid	97
% needy frosh rec. non-need-based scholarship or grant aid	35
% needy UG rec. non-need-based scholarship or grant aid	25
% needy frosh rec. need-based self-help aid	71
% needy UG rec. need-based self-help aid	78
% UG borrow to pay for school	42
Average cumulative indebtedness	$32,040
% frosh need fully met	57
% ugrads need fully met	48
Average % of frosh need met	96
Average % of ugrad need met	94

TUSKEGEE UNIVERSITY

OLD ADMINISTRATION BUILDING, TUSKEGEE, AL 36088 • ADMISSIONS: 334-727-8500 • FAX: 334-727-5750

STUDENTS SAY "..."

Academics

For the past 132 years, Tuskegee University has strived to continue the legacy of higher learning created by Booker T. Washington and upheld by its other notable presidents and benefactors. The "rich history" of the school has always been about "achieving the...highest level of performance" in all areas of service, leadership, and academics, and everyone in the community works to ensure that "the Tuskegee Experience is like none other." The veterinary and engineering schools are standouts here, but the school can transform any individual into a leader. "Tuskegee, figuratively speaking, is often given coal, and it *always* produces diamonds," says one student. Academics are "a top priority" for Tuskegee, and the classes and structure are designed to "effectively nurture students' academic, social, and professional potentials and produce great leaders in society." "School is about gaining independence and responsibility so that you will be able to grow and compete in the real world." Small classes and personal interaction with professors help further this process along, and the school aims for "excellence within every aspect of education offered at the institution." "My professors don't teach because it's their job, they do it because they care and want you to learn and succeed. It's very obvious," says one student. Though the alumni network is positively rock solid, and fundraising isn't a problem, some students question the allocation of funds. Many agree that "the development of new facilities/buildings around the campus" is a sore spot, and though the administration is in the process of updating some, "there is a lot of work to be done," particularly in the student housing arena.

Life

The heritage of Tuskegee is felt in every step; "We literally walk on historic grounds," says a student of going to school on the only college or university campus in the nation to be designated a National Historic Site by Congress. The traditional festivities the school usually hosts are "quite enjoyable," and the school is in a "very quaint" town, which "allows for constant interaction among students on campus to occur." When there is nothing to do in Tuskegee, students usually go to Auburn, Montgomery, or even Atlanta. TU is for "academically inclined individuals," but when the books do shut, most people "go to the local clubs (The Soul Inn or Club Extreme)," or hangout at houses off campus. "Home football and basketball games are usually really fun," as well. "Even though people are serious about their work and classes, we all know how to have fun," says one student. "We're a school of weekend warriors." "It can be raining cats and dogs...and you will still see people going to class, or if it's the weekend you will see students going to a party."

Student Body

At this go-getter university, the typical student here is "someone who is driven to becoming successful in the future through studious methods." Though this HBCU is naturally predominantly black, there is much diversity in that "people from all across the country come to school in this small city in Alabama." Most students here are "very outspoken and easy to work with" and "open to meeting and interacting with new people"; with students from all over the world, "the diverse environment helps keep the campus from getting too dull."

FINANCIAL AID: 334-727-8500 • E-MAIL: ADMISSIONS@TUSKEGEE.EDU • WEBSITE: WWW.TUSKEGEE.EDU

THE PRINCETON REVIEW SAYS

Admissions

Very important factors considered include: rigor of secondary school record, class rank, academic GPA, standardized test scores, recommendation(s), talent/ability. *Important factors considered include:* character/personal qualities, alumni/ae relation. *Other factors considered include:* application essay, interview, extracurricular activities, first generation, geographical residence, state residency, volunteer work, work experience. SAT or ACT required. ACT with or without writing accepted. TOEFL required of all international applicants. High school diploma is required and GED is accepted. *Academic units required:* 4 English, 3 math, 2 science, 3 social studies, 4 academic electives.

Financial Aid

Students should submit: FAFSA, Institution's own financial aid form, CSS/Financial Aid PROFILE. Priority filing deadline is 3/31. The Princeton Review suggests that all financial aid forms be submitted as soon as possible after October 1. *Need-based scholarships/grants offered:* Federal Pell, FSEOG, State scholarships/grants, Private scholarships, College/university scholarship or grant aid from institutional funds, United Negro College Fund, Federal Nursing Scholarships. *Loan aid offered:* Direct Subsidized Stafford Loans, Direct Unsubsidized Stafford Loans, Direct PLUS loans, Federal Perkins Loans, Federal Nursing Loans, State Loans, College/university loans from institutional funds. Federal Work-Study Program available. Institutional employment available.

The Inside Word

Tuskegee presents its students with a myriad of opportunities for discovery and research. Therefore, Tuskegee seeks applicants who have proven themselves successful in the classroom. Admissions counselors consider each application holistically and individually. What they really like to see, though, is a GPA of at least 3.0 and a composite ACT score of 21 or better. Note also that requirements for the nursing and engineering programs are more stringent. For example, you'll probably need four years of high school math if you want to major in engineering here. Prospective students interested in either field should investigate the specific criteria.

THE SCHOOL SAYS "..."

From the Admissions Office

"Tuskegee University, located in south central Alabama, was founded in 1881 under the dynamic and creative leadership of Booker T. Washington. As a state-related, independent institution, Tuskegee offers undergraduate and graduate degrees through five colleges and two schools: the College of Agriculture, Environment and Nutrition Sciences; the Brimmer College of Business and Information Sciences; the College of Engineering; the College of Veterinary Medicine, Nursing and Allied Health; the Taylor School of Architecture and Construction Science; and the School of Education. Substantial research and service programs make Tuskegee University an effective comprehensive institution geared toward preparing tomorrow's leaders today.

"First-year applicants must take the SAT or ACT; the SAT is preferred. International applicants must complete the TOEFL. Nursing applicants must complete the National Nursing exam."

SELECTIVITY

Admissions Rating	89
# of applicants	9,582
% of applicants accepted	36
% of acceptees attending	17
# offered a place on the wait list	0

FRESHMAN PROFILE

Range SAT Critical Reading	440–510
Range SAT Math	420–520
Range ACT Composite	18–23
Minimum paper TOEFL	500
Minimum internet-based TOEFL	62
Average HS GPA	3.2
% graduated top 10% of class	20
% graduated top 25% of class	60
% graduated top 50% of class	100

DEADLINES

Early action	
Deadline	8/31
Notification	10/1
Regular	
Priority	3/31
Deadline	7/15
Notification	3/15
Nonfall registration?	Yes

APPLICANTS ALSO LOOK AT AND RARELY PREFER

The University of Alabama–Tuscaloosa;
Auburn University

FINANCIAL FACTS

Financial Aid Rating	79
Annual tuition	$18,100
Room and board	$8,510
Required fees	$3,525
Books and supplies	$1,282
Average frosh need-based scholarship	$1,500
Average UG need-based scholarship	$1,500
% needy frosh rec. need-based scholarship or grant aid	100
% needy UG rec. need-based scholarship or grant aid	100
% needy frosh rec. non-need-based scholarship or grant aid	17
% needy UG rec. non-need-based scholarship or grant aid	22
% needy frosh rec. need-based self-help aid	100
% needy UG rec. need-based self-help aid	68
% frosh rec. any financial aid	90
% UG rec. any financial aid	92
% UG borrow to pay for school	49
Average cumulative indebtedness	$18,100
% frosh need fully met	0
% ugrads need fully met	0
Average % of frosh need met	70
Average % of ugrad need met	70

UNION COLLEGE (NY)

807 UNION STREET, SCHENECTADY, NY 12308 • ADMISSIONS: 518-388-6112 • FAX: 518-388-6986

CAMPUS LIFE

Quality of Life Rating	87
Fire Safety Rating	95
Green Rating	94
Type of school	Private
Affiliation	No Affiliation
Environment	Town

STUDENTS

Total undergrad enrollment	2,269
% male/female	54/46
% from out of state	66
% frosh from public high school	65
% frosh live on campus	99
% ugrads live on campus	89
# of fraternities (% ugrad men join)	11 (37)
# of sororities (% ugrad women join)	6 (42)
% African American	4
% Asian	6
% Caucasian	73
% Hispanic	7
% Native American	<1
% Pacific Islander	0
% Two or more races	2
% Race and/or ethnicity unknown	0
% international	7
# of countries represented	33

SURVEY SAYS...
Students always studying
Students are happy
Classroom facilities are great
Career services are great
Easy to get around campus
Recreation facilities are great
Lots of beer drinking
Hard liquor is popular
Frats and sororities are popular

ACADEMICS

Academic Rating	93
% students returning for sophomore year	93
% students graduating within 4 years	82
% students graduating within 6 years	88
Calendar	Trimester
Student/faculty ratio	10:1
Profs interesting rating	96
Profs accessible rating	95

Most classes have 10–19 students.
Most lab/discussion sessions have
10–19 students.

MOST POPULAR MAJORS
Economics; Psychology; Political Science and
Government

STUDENTS SAY "..."

Academics
Founded in 1795, Union College in upstate New York is a small, independent liberal arts college that provides a wide "breadth of education" that allows students to learn across the curriculum and graduate with a respected degree and a true liberal arts education. The "great historical roots" are apparent all around the "beautiful campus full of school-spirited students," but the school keeps a firm eye on the future as well, and "encourages students to develop and be prepared for graduation."

The professors are "interested in the lives of their students" and "work to make sure the student gets the academic support needed to succeed," and best of all, "you will never EVER have a teaching assistant instead of a professor at Union." Professors have an open door policy to always allow students right on in—"students are their main priority." Research opportunities are plentiful—"any professor with a lab is always looking for new recruits"—and a small but strong engineering department ensures that the sciences get a fair shake at a traditionally liberal arts school. The school also strives "to create interesting interdisciplinary classes that combine science and humanities in innovative ways."

Union is small, so "the sense of community is very important to the overall experience." The administration "wants you to enjoy your four years of college not just by studying but get to know other people and do things you never did before." A senior neuroscience major agrees: "Union is all about finding the best mix of the challenging courses and millions of activities happening each night." The trimester schedule is "fantastic," and the school "melds academic, social, and cultural life together seamlessly." "Union is also a prestigious institution that is small enough to allow every student a presence on campus," says one.

Life
The unique Minerva House system blends academic, social and residential interests. All students and faculty are assigned to one of the seven houses, which host hundreds of events each year (some professors even teach preceptorials there). There are also "Theme Houses," which are on-campus housing where people who have similar interests can live, such as the Ozone House for environmentally-oriented people.

Between Greek and Minerva life, there is "a vibrant social life" for all students, though quite a few admit that the emphasis on the "huge" Greek life "could certainly be reduced." "Most of the campus attends parties on weekends," which is "a great way to relieve the stress caused by being at such an academically rigorous school and also meet new people." In class, however, "we're all nerds at heart, and we can talk books and numbers all day long." Everyone also goes to free campus movies and other events like "concerts, magicians, comedians, roller skating, and others."

The Capital Region is "all around us, so if you're bored you're just not trying hard enough," says a student. There is a bounty of events and organizations, so "one has to try to NOT be involved." "I never feel like the campus runs out of things for me to do," says a senior. Dating is "thin" at Union: "it is not a couples' school," however it IS a hockey school.

Student Body
Most come to Union from "some part of the northeast," are "from middle/upper-middle class families," and are "very active, career-oriented, [and] serious about academics." One student tells us, "I'm not going to lie, it's a pretty white campus." "Everyone fits in because everyone seems to love Union." These "intellectuals" tend to dress "very preppy" ("wearing Patagonia jackets, Lilly Pulitzer handbags, and Ugg boots is basically the uniform") and are "a great group of people"; "there don't seem to be any barriers between them."

UNION COLLEGE (NY)

FINANCIAL AID: 518-388-6123 • E-MAIL: ADMISSIONS@UNION.EDU • WEBSITE: WWW.UNION.EDU

THE PRINCETON REVIEW SAYS

Admissions

Very important factors considered include: rigor of secondary school record, class rank, academic GPA, standardized test scores (for those who submit). *Important factors considered include:* application essay, recommendation(s), extracurricular activities, talent/ability, character/personal qualities, volunteer work, work experience. *Other factors considered include:* interview, first generation, alumni/ae relation, geographical residence, state residency, racial/ethnic status, level of applicant's interest. SAT or ACT required for some; SAT Subject Tests considered if submitted. ACT with or without writing accepted. SAT with or without Essay component accepted. TOEFL required of all international applicants. High school diploma is required and GED is not accepted. *Academic units required:* 4 English, 3 math, 2 science, 2 science labs, 2 foreign language, 1 social studies, 1 history. *Academic units recommended:* 4 English, 4 math, 4 science, 4 science labs, 4 foreign language, 2 social studies, 2 history.

Financial Aid

Students should submit: FAFSA, CSS/Financial Aid PROFILE, State aid form, Noncustodial PROFILE. Regular filing deadline is 2/1. The Princeton Review suggests that all financial aid forms be submitted as soon as possible after October 1. *Need-based scholarships/grants offered:* Federal Pell, FSEOG, State scholarships/grants, Private scholarships, College/university scholarship or grant aid from institutional funds. *Loan aid offered:* Direct Subsidized Stafford Loans, Direct Unsubsidized Stafford Loans, Direct PLUS loans, Federal Perkins Loans, College/university loans from institutional funds. Applicants will be notified of awards on or about 3/25. Federal Work-Study Program available. Institutional employment available.

The Inside Word

Union College is an SAT-optional college. Students may simply indicate on their application if they would like the admissions committee to consider their test scores or not. However, applicants to the Leadership in Medicine Program (an eight-year MD/MBA program with Albany Medical College and Clarkson University Capital Region Campus) and to the Law and Public Policy program (a combined BA and JD with Albany Law School) must submit test scores for consideration. For students who know that Union is their first choice, the school offers two early decision deadlines.

THE SCHOOL SAYS ". . ."

From the Admissions Office

"The Union academic program is characterized by breadth and flexibility across a range of disciplines and interdisciplinary programs in the liberal arts, sciences, and engineering. With nearly 1,000 courses to choose from, Union students may major in a single field, combine work in two or more departments or create their own organizing-theme major. Opportunities for undergraduate research are robust and give students a chance to work closely with professors year-round, take part in professional-level conferences and use sophisticated scientific equipment. More than half of Union's students take advantage of the college's extensive international study program, with new opportunities created regularly. A rich array of service learning programs and strong athletic, cultural, and social activities also enhance the overall Union experience. Union's seven student-run Minerva Houses are lively hubs for intellectual and social activities. They bring together students, faculty and staff for hundreds of events, from dinners with invited speakers, lectures, and live bands, to trips to local attractions.

"The Union community welcomes talented and diverse students, and we work closely with each one to help identify and cultivate their passions. Admission to the college is based on excellent academic credentials as reflected in the high school transcript, quality of courses selected, teacher and counselor recommendations, and personal essays. Personal interviews are strongly recommended. All candidates who apply to Union receive a thorough and thoughtful review of their application. Submission of SAT and ACT scores is optional except for the law and medicine programs."

SELECTIVITY

Admissions Rating	94
# of applicants	5,996
% of applicants accepted	38
% of acceptees attending	25
# offered a place on the wait list	1,167
% accepting a place on wait list	54
% admitted from wait list	10
# of early decision applicants	399
% accepted early decision	60

FRESHMAN PROFILE

Range SAT Critical Reading	610–680
Range SAT Math	630–720
Range SAT Writing	600–680
Range ACT Composite	29–32
Minimum paper TOEFL	600
Minimum internet-based TOEFL	90
Average HS GPA	3.4
% graduated top 10% of class	71
% graduated top 25% of class	87
% graduated top 50% of class	97

DEADLINES

Early decision	
Deadline	11/15
Notification	12/15
Regular	
Deadline	1/15
Notification	4/1
Nonfall registration?	Yes

APPLICANTS ALSO LOOK AT AND OFTEN PREFER

Colgate University; Cornell University; Tufts University

AND SOMETIMES PREFER

Hamilton College; Lafayette College; University of Rochester

FINANCIAL FACTS

Financial Aid Rating	96
Annual tuition	$49,542
Room and board	$12,261
Required fees	$471
Books and supplies	$1,500
Average frosh need-based scholarship	$35,750
Average UG need-based scholarship	$35,500
% needy frosh rec. need-based scholarship or grant aid	98
% needy UG rec. need-based scholarship or grant aid	98
% needy frosh rec. non-need-based scholarship or grant aid	23
% needy UG rec. non-need-based scholarship or grant aid	9
% needy frosh rec. need-based self-help aid	93
% needy UG rec. need-based self-help aid	95
% frosh rec. any financial aid	84
% UG rec. any financial aid	80
% UG borrow to pay for school	67
Average cumulative indebtedness	$31,820
% frosh need fully met	100
% ugrads need fully met	100
Average % of frosh need met	100
Average % of ugrad need met	100

UNITED STATES AIR FORCE ACADEMY

HQ USAFA/RRS, USAF ACADEMY, CO 80840-5025 • ADMISSIONS: 719-333-2520 • FAX: 719-333-3012

STUDENTS SAY "..."

Academics

"Honor, Discipline, and hard work" are three characteristics that summarize what the U.S. Air Force Academy in Colorado is about. The chosen few that make it through the gauntlet of getting admitted to USAFA are rewarded with a free education, "tremendous opportunities after graduation," as the "rigorous" institution is designed to "[create] officers of good character, ready to lead in the Air Force."

The academy has "a very difficult academic environment with a high focus on engineering classes," and the core curriculum includes basic engineering, engineering mechanics, electrical engineering, aeronautical engineering, and astronautical engineering. Fortunately, professors are "very accessible," "present a challenging classroom experience that promotes critical thought," and "make class a discussion." There is "also extra instruction from teachers and the resources available for research," and students help each other out when another is struggling, as well. Faculty is a mix of civilian and military professors, which "gives a great insight into the jobs we can expect in the military after graduation as well as potential civilian career fields after service," according to one cadet.

Students can expect "absolutely no lecture hall classes," as every section is held in a classroom with anywhere from five to thirty students. Given the future careers of the cadets, plenty of learning takes place experientially, and airmanship programs (such as "powered flight, soaring (flying gliders), the aerobatic demonstration team, and our skydiving teams") are a huge part of the school and are "an extremely fun and unique part of our lives." If there is one downside to such thorough training, it is that cadets universally clamor for more freedom and free time.

Life

"Everyone here is pretty accepting to other cultures and backgrounds and it is easy to make friends," says a cadet of the many organizations to fit into, including "your squad, your team, your club, your academic major, and failing all that your friends." Regardless of what social group you find yourself in, "you end up knowing everyone eventually." There are plenty of USAFA-specific traditions; most interaction occurs within the squadron, and "most cadets really enjoy the squadron activities and leadership opportunities."

Life is "very controlled" here, and as it is a military academy students "have to follow military laws in addition to civilian laws." Therefore, most students "do not drink underage and would not ever do any sort of drug." In order to leave, one must sign out on a "pass" which is limited for each class (freshman have six passes per semester), and in the "likely" event that students are restricted to campus for a random weekend, they can always "find creative ways to have fun, such as tying bedsheets to chairs and sailing across the terrazzo (main campus area) at high speed." For fun, cadets do "normal things," such as "[skiing] in the winter, pickup basketball, video games, go watch a movie, [and] go to Denver and walk around the city."

Student Body

Unsurprisingly, cadets here are all "highly motivated, A-type personalities that give 100 percent in everything they do." This group of "super smart," "driven" individuals are also "respectable" and "athletic," which explains what one junior refers to as "the smartest offensive line in the NCAA." Everyone is in a uniform from 7 A.M. to 4 P.M. so there is a commonality from the start. Basic Cadet Training (BCT) "makes people work together," and "with going through the same experience, allows lifetime bonds to start growing." This experience is unique, and "each class year has a specific sense of pride and unity as a team." "We are all going into the same Air Force after we graduate so we need to learn to work together," says a junior.

E-MAIL: RR_WEBMAIL@USAFA.EDU • WEBSITE: WWW.ACADEMYADMISSIONS.COM

THE PRINCETON REVIEW SAYS

Admissions

Very important factors considered include: rigor of secondary school record, class rank, academic GPA, standardized test scores, application essay, recommendation(s), interview, extracurricular activities, character/personal qualities, level of applicant's interest. *Important factors considered include:* talent/ability, volunteer work, work experience. *Other factors considered include:* first generation, alumni/ae relation, geographical residence, racial/ethnic status. SAT or ACT required. ACT with or without writing accepted. High school diploma is required and GED is accepted. *Academic units recommended:* 4 English, 4 math, 4 science, 4 science labs, 2 foreign language, 3 social studies, 3 history, 1 computer science.

Financial Aid

Students should submit: The Princeton Review suggests that all financial aid forms be submitted as soon as possible after October 1. *Loan aid offered:* Federal Work-Study Program available. Institutional employment available.

The Inside Word

The Air Force Academy promises a demanding four years, and the fainthearted need not apply. Due to the rigorous nature of the school, it's no wonder that applicants face stringent requirements right at the outset. Aside from an excellent academic record, successful candidates need to be physically fit. All applicants must secure a nomination from their congressperson or one of the affiliated military academies. Honor is a valued quality at the academy, and admissions officers will accept only those with the strength of character and determination necessary to succeed at one of the country's most elite institutions.

THE SCHOOL SAYS " . . ."

From the Admissions Office

"The United States Air Force Academy offers one of the most prestigious and respected undergraduate programs available. With twenty-seven majors and three minors offered at the Academy, there are programs of study for every interest. The academic challenges and expectations are high—but so are the rewards. You will emerge from the Academy with a well-rounded knowledge in many fields, an intimate knowledge in your major area of study, and the ability to serve our nation as a Second Lieutenant in the world's greatest air, space, and cyberspace force.

"At the United States Air Force Academy, every cadet is an athlete. Our extensive athletic program includes twenty-nine men's and women's NCAA Division I intercollegiate teams, intramural sports, physical education courses, and physical fitness tests tailored to prepare you for Air Force leadership by building confidence, physical courage, and the ability to perform under pressure.

"The Academy experience requires cadets to become active participants in leadership roles and opportunities that give a sense of honor and duty. The Air Force Academy's mission is to educate, train, and inspire men and women to become officers of character motivated to lead the United States Air Force in service to our nation. If you choose to accept the challenges, you will be rewarded with unique experiences and opportunities incomparable to any other college experience and the honor of serving your country in the United States Air Force."

SELECTIVITY

Admissions Rating	98
# of applicants	9,122
% of applicants accepted	17
% of acceptees attending	80

FRESHMAN PROFILE

Range SAT Critical Reading	600–690
Range SAT Math	630–710
Range ACT Composite	29–32
Average HS GPA	3.8
% graduated top 10% of class	52
% graduated top 25% of class	81
% graduated top 50% of class	97

DEADLINES

Early action	
Deadline	11/1
Notification	1/15
Regular	
Deadline	12/31
Nonfall registration?	No

APPLICANTS ALSO LOOK AT AND SOMETIMES PREFER

United States Military Academy; United States Naval Academy; United States Coast Guard Academy; United States Merchant Marine Academy

FINANCIAL FACTS

Financial Aid Rating	60*
Annual in-state tuition	$0
Annual out-of-state tuition	$0
Average frosh need-based scholarship	$0
% needy frosh rec. need-based scholarship or grant aid	0
% needy UG rec. need-based scholarship or grant aid	0
% needy frosh rec. non-need-based scholarship or grant aid	0
% needy UG rec. non-need-based scholarship or grant aid	0
% needy frosh rec. need-based self-help aid	0
% needy UG rec. need-based self-help aid	0
Average % of frosh need met	0
Average % of ugrad need met	0

UNITED STATES COAST GUARD ACADEMY

31 MOHEGAN AVENUE, NEW LONDON, CT 06320-8103 • ADMISSIONS: 860-444-8503 • FAX: 860-701-6700

CAMPUS LIFE

Quality of Life Rating	85
Fire Safety Rating	91
Green Rating	63
Type of school	Public
Affiliation	No Affiliation
Environment	City

STUDENTS

Total undergrad enrollment	898
% male/female	65/35
% from out of state	95
% frosh from public high school	76
% frosh live on campus	100
% ugrads live on campus	100
% African American	4
% Asian	7
% Caucasian	67
% Hispanic	10
% Native American	<1
% Pacific Islander	<1
% Two or more races	8
% Race and/or ethnicity unknown	2
% international	2
# of countries represented	12

SURVEY SAYS...

Students always studying
Career services are great
School is well run
No one cheats
Diverse student types interact on campus
Students involved in community service
Very little drug use
Everyone loves the Bears
Intramural sports are popular
Alumni active on campus

ACADEMICS

Academic Rating	89
% students returning for sophomore year	90
% students graduating within 4 years	84
Calendar	Semester
Student/faculty ratio	8:1
Profs interesting rating	78
Profs accessible rating	99

Most classes have 10–19 students.
Most lab/discussion sessions have
10–19 students.

MOST POPULAR MAJORS

Oceanography; Political Science and
Government; Business Administration and
Management

STUDENTS SAY ". . ."

Academics

Students at the United States Coast Guard Academy recommend their school as "highly demanding, immensely rewarding, professionally oriented and the best choice to make the best friends you are ever going to have." Many appreciate the "regimented environment," which, according to one management major, "Gives me a standard to live up to and hold myself to, even when I am away from here." Cadets are "pushed to [the] limits" "academically, emotionally, and physically," and they wouldn't have it any other way. Importantly, "the academy fosters camaraderie amongst the Corps of Cadets that can't be found anywhere else. With a student body numbering a little less than 1,000, the Coast Guard Academy is truly unique in its ability to provide an environment where classmates become shipmates, friends, and eventually family." Though there are a number of excellent programs, cadets call the most attention to the strong engineering department. The academics are "challenging but rewarding." Professors challenge cadets "to reach farther, expand their horizons, and to develop outside the classroom as much as inside of it." An electrical engineering major expounds, "The most surprising and excellent trait that all teachers have is that they are always willing to help outside of the class rooms. Always." Some students contend "the best part about my school is the summer training programs." Students have traveled "across the Atlantic Ocean" stopping "in London, Iceland, and Nova Scotia." Others have been to "Bermuda, St. Pierre France, Guantanamo Bay, and St. Petersburg Florida since coming to the Academy which is absolutely amazing."

Life

"Life at USCGA is unique. Only way to put it," says one junior. Day-to-day life at the Coast Guard Academy is "orderly and predictable." During the week, it's difficult for people to do anything "outside of their military, athletic, and academic obligations." As one honest marine and environmental science major reveals, "Every moment of every day is planned out." Required sports credits "keep people active and involved either intercollegiate or intramurals." Of course, life at the Academy isn't 100 percent work and stress. Free time is at a premium on weekdays but "weekends are the time to explore New England, New York City, and the downtown New London area." A senior shares, cadets "go to the beach, head up to Vermont for some hiking or skiing... there is a lot to do if you look for it." While "students aren't allowed off campus during the week," unless participating in an academy sanctioned activity, "most try and get away for the weekend." Another senior elaborates, "Underage students tend to go to the movies or the local mall. Of-age students usually spend their time off drinking at the bars downtown." Life at USCGA can be "very challenging and demanding at times, but the goal of becoming an officer makes it worth it." A "guaranteed job upon graduation" is pretty persuasive as well.

Student Body

While in past, USGCA has been described as homogeneous; "the academy has been stressing diversity in its admissions and has had a good deal of success." Luckily, a civil engineering major assures us, "Those students of different backgrounds easily fit in with everyone else." In fact, one cadet goes so far to say "sometimes, I don't think that cadets recognize diversity because we all wear the same uniforms, take the same classes, and are going through the same experiences." Not surprisingly, the academy seems to attract "highly motivated [people] with a strong desire to serve in the Coast Guard." Certainly, another hallmark of Coast Guard cadets is that they're "hard working, smart, motivated, and in great shape." A naval architecture and marine engineering major adds, "Type-A personalities are most common among the Corps." A senior describes student as "very close with each other and for the most part, everyone has a group of friends that they fit in quite well with." This sophomore cheekily sums up his peers, "A typical student here is just like a typical student anywhere else but works harder, follows stricter rules, is in better shape, and is owned by the federal government."

UNITED STATES COAST GUARD ACADEMY

FINANCIAL AID: 860-444-8309 • E-MAIL: ADMISSIONS@USCGA.EDU • WEBSITE: WWW.USCGA.EDU

THE PRINCETON REVIEW SAYS

Admissions

Very important factors considered include: rigor of secondary school record, class rank, academic GPA, standardized test scores, extracurricular activities, character/personal qualities. *Important factors considered include:* application essay, recommendation(s), talent/ability. *Other factors considered include:* interview, first generation, alumni/ae relation, geographical residence, state residency, religious affiliation/commitment, racial/ethnic status, volunteer work, work experience, level of applicant's interest. SAT or ACT required. ACT with Writing required. TOEFL required of all international applicants. High school diploma is required and GED is accepted. *Academic units required:* 4 English, 4 math, 3 science, 3 science labs. *Academic units recommended:* 4 English, 4 math, 4 science, 3 science labs.

Financial Aid

Students should submit: The Princeton Review suggests that all financial aid forms be submitted as soon as possible after October 1.

The Inside Word

Gaining acceptance into the Coast Guard Academy is a highly competitive process. The admissions committee is looking not only for outstanding academic achievement but also for applicants who demonstrate leadership ability and strong moral character. In addition, unlike other colleges, you'll also need a physical fitness examination and evaluation.

THE SCHOOL SAYS "..."

From the Admissions Office

"Established in 1876, the Coast Guard Academy educates, trains, and inspires Cadets to serve their country and humanity. Leadership and character development are emphasized in academic life, athletic pursuits, and military training. Commitment to helping those in need is a personal quality shared by every student selected to attend the Coast Guard Academy. High levels of personal accountability are expected of Cadets and graduates.

"Fourth Class (freshmen) arrive in June to begin a strenuous seven week training program (Swab Summer) that prepares them to join the Corps of Cadets in August. Swab Summer culminates with a week at sea aboard America's only active tall ship, the EAGLE.

"The Corps of Cadets is comprised of talented Cadets from all fifty states and about twenty other nations. The Academy is diverse: Women and students of color, as groups, each comprise over 30 percent of the student body. Most Cadets are athletes—over 60 percent play on at least one NCAA Division III team. The opportunity to play is nearly unmatched in college athletics.

"The Academy's value proposition is also tough to beat. This is the only small, highly selective four year college in the U.S. that is free of charge to attend. This is possible because Academy grads go straight to a position of responsibility as a commissioned officer in the Coast Guard. All are obligated to serve for five years, and most make it a career. Aside from the satisfaction of saving lives and protecting others, the opportunity to fly is exceptional. And, about 85 percent of officers also earn a graduate degree at Coast Guard expense.

"If you are smart, adventuresome, physically fit, and want to achieve a higher purpose in your life, the U.S. Coast Guard Academy may be for you!"

SELECTIVITY

Admissions Rating	97
# of applicants	2,214
% of applicants accepted	18
% of acceptees attending	75
# offered a place on the wait list	148
% accepting a place on wait list	100
% admitted from wait list	24
# of early decision applicants	648
% accepted early decision	24

FRESHMAN PROFILE

Range SAT Critical Reading	570–660
Range SAT Math	610–690
Range SAT Writing	560–650
Range ACT Composite	26–31
Minimum paper TOEFL	560
Minimum internet-based TOEFL	90
Average HS GPA	3.8
% graduated top 10% of class	45
% graduated top 25% of class	79
% graduated top 50% of class	96

DEADLINES

Early action	
Deadline	11/15
Notification	2/1
Regular	
Priority	11/15
Deadline	2/1
Notification	4/15
Nonfall registration?	No

FINANCIAL FACTS

Financial Aid Rating	60*
Annual in-state tuition	$0
Annual out-of-state tuition	$0
Required fees	$978
Books and supplies	$2,199
% needy frosh rec. need-based scholarship or grant aid	0
% needy UG rec. need-based scholarship or grant aid	0
% needy frosh rec. non-need-based scholarship or grant aid	0
% needy UG rec. non-need-based scholarship or grant aid	0
% needy frosh rec. need-based self-help aid	0
% needy UG rec. need-based self-help aid	0
% frosh rec. any financial aid	0
% UG rec. any financial aid	0

UNITED STATES MERCHANT MARINE ACADEMY

OFFICE OF ADMISSIONS, KINGS POINT, NY 11024-1699 • ADMISSIONS: 516-773-5391 • FAX: 516-773-5390

CAMPUS LIFE

Quality of Life Rating	68
Fire Safety Rating	98
Green Rating	64
Type of school	Public
Affiliation	No Affiliation
Environment	Village

STUDENTS

Total undergrad enrollment	904
% male/female	83/17
% from out of state	90
% frosh from public high school	75
% frosh live on campus	100
% ugrads live on campus	100
% African American	3
% Asian	7
% Caucasian	74
% Hispanic	10
% Native American	2
% Pacific Islander	0
% Two or more races	0
% Race and/or ethnicity unknown	4
% international	1
# of countries represented	4

SURVEY SAYS...

Lots of conservative students
Great financial aid
Very little drug use
Alumni active on campus

ACADEMICS

Academic Rating	67
% students returning for sophomore year	94
% students graduating within 4 years	74
% students graduating within 6 years	83
Calendar	Trimester
Student/faculty ratio	13:1
Profs interesting rating	65
Profs accessible rating	64

Most classes have 10–19 students.

MOST POPULAR MAJORS

Logistics; Engineering; Systems;
Transportation and Management

STUDENTS SAY "..."

Academics

Tucked away on Long Island, the United States Merchant Marine Academy offers students the chance to pursue a prestigious though rigorous and regimented education. Further, it allows undergrads to join "a group of elite students who work hard and [are] honest and patriotic." Students here caution that the academics are "extremely difficult," especially given the "fast-paced classroom environment." Additionally, when asked about their professors, students dole out mixed reviews. Though most assert that their teachers are "very intelligent," some bemoan a "lack of enthusiasm." While some professors are described as "fair, approachable, and extremely helpful," other professors come across as "heartless and condescending." Regardless of which classes you enroll in, the Merchant Marine Academy is "a school that requires plenty of effort on behalf of the student." As one midshipman proudly sums up, "The opportunities afforded by this Academy are unparalleled by any other college I have come across. Despite the immense sacrifices and hardships of this school, it is completely worth it for the right person."

Life

Undergrads at the Merchant Marine Academy don't mince words about life at their school. Indeed, the majority seem to be in agreement that because "it is a military academy, fun is generally limited." As one straightforward student explains, "We are restricted to the campus grounds during the week until senior year. Life is pretty drab, dull, and boring [with] most time spent either in class, studying, or working out." Moreover, undergrads are "restricted by the regiment and disciplinary system." Of course, even these hardworking midshipmen get to kick back every now and again. Another undergrad cheerfully shares, "When the spring comes, everyone gets out to play rec sports (Ultimate Frisbee, tag football, soccer, swim, or bike ride) and goes to the park to BBQ." A fellow student chimes in, "We have a good time, and usually, it is the little things that make us happy. We enjoy hanging out on weekends and doing things that normal college students would do. Recently a few friends and I had a Nerf gun battle, which was pretty fun." When they are allowed, midshipmen rush to get off campus. Indeed, students here love to take advantage of the fact that they are "only twenty minutes from downtown NYC." As this wise midshipman concludes, "New York City in uniform boils down to cheap food, movies, plays, concerts, easy way to meet girls, you name it...we work hard all week, but when it comes time, we get to play hard as well."

Student Body

At first glance, the average Merchant Marine Academy midshipman could be described as "a white, conservative male." Of course, there's definitely more to these students than race, gender, and political views. Certainly, undergrads can also be depicted as "respectful," "athletic," and "outgoing." They can also be categorized as "those that want to work in the maritime industry and those that want to join the military." Moreover, many are "hardworking and serious." As one undergrad explains, "If you aren't willing to work, you won't be here long." Another student continues, "The typical student has tons on his plate, whether it's regimental duties or academic ones. [However], no matter what, if you need help with something, somebody will be there for you." A fellow midshipman concurs, summing up, "The students here are all a family. Each one of us here at the Merchant Marine Academy [has] experienced the same rigorous training and tough treatment plebe year. We all work together in everything we do, and without one another it is almost impossible to succeed at the Academy." Actually, the U.S. Merchant Marine Academy is increasing the diversity of its student body every year.

UNITED STATES MERCHANT MARINE ACADEMY

FINANCIAL AID: 516-773-5295 • E-MAIL: ADMISSIONS@USMMA.EDU • WEBSITE: WWW.USMMA.EDU

THE PRINCETON REVIEW SAYS

Admissions

Very important factors considered include: rigor of secondary school record, standardized test scores, character/personal qualities. *Important factors considered include:* class rank, academic GPA, application essay, recommendation(s), extracurricular activities, talent/ability, level of applicant's interest. *Other factors considered include:* interview, first generation, geographical residence, state residency, racial/ethnic status, volunteer work, work experience. SAT or ACT required. ACT with or without writing accepted. TOEFL required of all international applicants. High school diploma is required and GED is accepted. *Academic units required:* 4 English, 3 math, 3 science, 1 science lab, 8 academic electives. *Academic units recommended:* 4 math, 4 science, 2 science labs, 2 foreign language, 4 social studies.

Financial Aid

Students should submit: FAFSA. The Princeton Review suggests that all financial aid forms be submitted as soon as possible after October 1. *Need-based scholarships/grants offered:* Federal Pell, State scholarships/grants, Private Scholarships. *Loan aid offered:* Direct Subsidized Stafford Loans, Direct Unsubsidized Stafford Loans, Direct PLUS Loans. Applicants will be notified of awards on a rolling basis beginning 5/1.

The Inside Word

Securing admittance to the Merchant Marine Academy is no easy feat. The admissions committee is looking for stellar candidates who have the intelligence, fortitude, and leadership capabilities to survive (and thrive) at this institution. In addition to your transcripts and test scores, the admissions crew will closely assess your letters of recommendation. Moreover, unlike traditional colleges, you'll also have to pass a fitness requirement and secure a nomination from a U.S. representative or senator.

THE SCHOOL SAYS "..."

From the Admissions Office

"The U. S. Merchant Marine Academy (USMMA) at Kings Point, New York, is a federal service academy with the mission to educate and graduate licensed Merchant Marine Officers of exemplary character who serve America's marine transportation and defense needs in peace and war. The Academy's four-year program is a demanding academic schedule that includes hands on experience. In addition, each cadet participates in Sea Year, during which cadets acquire more hands-on experience working aboard commercial and military vessels sailing around the world. Due to the Academy's unique mission, its graduates have civilian and military career choices that are unmatched by any other federal or maritime academy.

"Kings Point graduates earn (1) a Bachelor of Science degree, (2) an unlimited U.S. Coast Guard license (Deck or Engine), as well as (3) an officer's commission in one of the U.S. Armed Forces. Graduates are obligated to serve as a licensed officer in the U.S. Merchant Marine for five years, and as a commissioned officer in one of the U.S. Armed Forces reserves for eight years following graduation. Alternatively, graduating midshipmen can apply for an active duty commission in any branch of the U.S Armed Forces or the National Oceanic and Atmospheric Administration (NOAA) Corps.

"USMMA graduates are highly sought after as officers in the military and the U.S. Merchant Marine. Further, according to recent reports from the Department of Education and others, Kings Point graduates earn some of the highest salaries of college graduates in the United States."

SELECTIVITY

Admissions Rating	97
# of applicants	1,662
% of applicants accepted	22
% of acceptees attending	71
# offered a place on the wait list	197
% accepting a place on wait list	100

FRESHMAN PROFILE

Range SAT Critical Reading	570–660
Range SAT Math	620–690
Range ACT Composite	26–30
Minimum paper TOEFL	540
Minimum internet-based TOEFL	83
Average HS GPA	3.6
% graduated top 10% of class	33
% graduated top 25% of class	57
% graduated top 50% of class	92

DEADLINES

Regular	
Deadline	3/1
Nonfall registration?	No

APPLICANTS ALSO LOOK AT AND OFTEN PREFER

United States Naval Academy; United States Coast Guard Academy

AND SOMETIMES PREFER

United States Air Force Academy; United States Military Academy

FINANCIAL FACTS

Financial Aid Rating	60*
Annual in-state tuition	$0
Annual out-of-state tuition	$0
Required fees	$1,107
Books and supplies	$2,887
Average frosh need-based scholarship	$0
% needy frosh rec. need-based scholarship or grant aid	100
% needy UG rec. need-based scholarship or grant aid	100
% needy frosh rec. non-need-based scholarship or grant aid	100
% needy UG rec. non-need-based scholarship or grant aid	100
% needy frosh rec. need-based self-help aid	100
% needy UG rec. need-based self-help aid	100
% frosh rec. any financial aid	33
% UG rec. any financial aid	30
% UG borrow to pay for school	34
Average cumulative indebtedness	$7,500
% frosh need fully met	100
% ugrads need fully met	100
Average % of frosh need met	100
Average % of ugrad need met	100

UNITED STATES MILITARY ACADEMY (WEST POINT)

646 SWIFT ROAD, WEST POINT, NY 10996-1905 • ADMISSIONS: 845-938-4041 • FAX: 845-938-3021

CAMPUS LIFE

Quality of Life Rating	86
Fire Safety Rating	91
Green Rating	60*
Type of school	Public
Affiliation	No Affiliation
Environment	Village

STUDENTS

Total undergrad enrollment	4,348
% male/female	0/0
% from out of state	93
% frosh from public high school	79
% frosh live on campus	100
% ugrads live on campus	100
% African American	10
% Asian	6
% Caucasian	65
% Hispanic	12
% Native American	1
% Pacific Islander	1
% Two or more races	3
% Race and/or ethnicity unknown	1
% international	1
# of countries represented	33

SURVEY SAYS...

Students politically aware
Students always studying
Students are happy
Classroom facilities are great
Lab facilities are great
Great library
Career services are great
Internships are widely available
Class discussions encouraged
School is well run
No one cheats
Diverse student types interact on campus
Students get along with local community
Recreation facilities are great
Very little drug use
Everyone loves the Black Knights
Intramural sports are popular
Alumni active on campus

ACADEMICS

Academic Rating	99
% students returning for sophomore year	93
% students graduating within 4 years	80
% students graduating within 6 years	83
Calendar	Semester
Student/faculty ratio	7:1
Profs interesting rating	97
Profs accessible rating	99

Most classes have 10–19 students.
Most lab/discussion sessions have 10–19 students.

MOST POPULAR MAJORS

Economics; Business Administration and Management; Engineering/Industrial Management

STUDENTS SAY "..."

Academics

Throughout its more than 200 year history, the United States Military Academy in West Point, New York has produced United States presidents, NASA astronauts, notable generals, business leaders and many medal of honor recipients. So it is no wonder that cadets say the academy's "leadership training is second to none." Cadets praise the school for "helping the students succeed not only in the classroom, but also outside in our daily lives as people and as leaders" by pairing "academic vigor" with "[experiences] which enrich your character and ultimately make you a better person." The academy extends its holistic education "with countless academic enrichment activities," like "trips all over the world during spring break with the history department," "scuba diving with NASA" or parachuting lessons. The United States Military Academy also "sends cadets all over the world for study abroad" and gives students practical experience to apply what they learn in the classroom through programs like Advanced Individual Academic Development where students say they can work at "government research facilities during the summer doing relevant and cutting edge research." Professors are universally admired as "amazing," "very accessible and devoted" to their students. Students say this contributes an environment where "everyone goes to all classes and cares about academics." "Academics are hard," but because professors "[teach] only a few sections," "aren't sidetracked by research while they are teaching" and are willing to "bend over backwards to accommodate" the busy schedules of West Point cadets, any student can "succeed if you're willing to ask" for help.

Life

To put it mildly, "life is extremely busy" at West Point. "Time management is one the biggest things that you [will] learn" one cadet advises. Most days start with "formation in the morning before 7:30 A.M. classes" and cadets "are either working, in class, or exercising for most of the day. After classes are over at 4:00 P.M.," time is divided between activities and studies. "Every cadet is required to play a sport," but that doesn't necessarily mean that everyone is an athlete. While most admit that they "live a regimented lifestyle," cadets still nonetheless find ways to relax and socialize: "upper class [cadets] often go to one of the bars on post and drink till TAPS, when everyone must be in their rooms. We play video games, go to clubs, play instruments, and go to NYC on the weekends for fun." The academic schedules of first and second year students are pre-selected "but junior and senior classes are chosen on your own depending on your major." Students praise the system because "you don't have to worry about a class filling up," and cadets "can study ANY major they want because we are all guaranteed a great job after graduation." And like any old institution there are "a lot of silly traditions that we hold on to long after we're gone."

Student Body

The academy's unique application process requires students be nominated by their congressional representative, so cadets assure us that they "never cease to be impressed with [their] peers," who are some "of the smartest sons and daughters of America." Cadets provide a litany of praise for their peers: "People are courteous, respectful, honest, honorable, and simply amazing at West Point USMA." Cadets say that their "shared hardships foster an environment of camaraderie unparalleled anywhere else in the world." Many stress the importance of teamwork, cooperation and leadership, explaining that "by the time you become a senior, you may be responsible for 120 other people." Cadets say the student body is geographically diverse with "students from every state in the US." represented as well as "some students from other countries like, Nigeria, Qatar, and France."

UNITED STATES MILITARY ACADEMY (WEST POINT)

FINANCIAL AID: 845-938-4041 • E-MAIL: ADMISSIONS@USMA.EDU • WEBSITE: WWW.WESTPOINT.EDU

THE PRINCETON REVIEW SAYS

Admissions

Very important factors considered include: rigor of secondary school record, class rank, academic GPA, standardized test scores, extracurricular activities, character/personal qualities. *Important factors considered include:* application essay, recommendation(s), talent/ability, level of applicant's interest. *Other factors considered include:* interview, first generation, racial/ethnic status, volunteer work, work experience. SAT or ACT required. ACT with Writing required. SAT with Essay component required. TOEFL required of all international applicants. High school diploma is required and GED is accepted. *Academic units recommended:* 4 English, 4 math, 4 science, 2 science labs, 2 foreign language, 3 social studies, 1 history, 3 academic electives.

Financial Aid

Students should submit: The Princeton Review suggests that all financial aid forms be submitted as soon as possible after October 1.

The Inside Word

The fact that you must be nominated by your Congressional representative in order to apply to West Point tells you all you need to know about the school's selectivity. Contact your district's Congressional representative to learn the deadline for nomination requests; typically these are made in the spring of your junior year. Successful candidates must demonstrate excellence in academics, physical conditioning, extracurricular involvement, and leadership. They must also be willing to commit to five years of active duty and three years of reserve duty upon graduation. The rigorous requirements and demanding commitments of a West Point education hardly dissuade applicants. More than 15,000 applied for the 1,150 available slots.

THE SCHOOL SAYS "..."

From the Admissions Office

"West Point is searching for applicants who possess the leadership skills, cultural sensibilities, and the moral fiber to handle the volatile, uncertain, complex, and ambiguous contemporary operating environment of today's world as a future U.S. Army Officer. As a crucible for leadership, we are looking for critical thinkers that have who have the judgment and experience to become a leader of character upon graduation.

"To assess your ability and preparation, admissions looks at more than your GPA or standardized test scores. The applications of almost 15,000 students are evaluated based on academic, physical, and leadership potential to find approximately 1,150 candidates who are ready to be offered the challenge of admission into the Corps of Cadets. With an amazingly high offer-acceptance rate, only the most dedicated, enthusiastic applicants make it to the finish line for the report date each June.

"If you accept the challenge, you will be immersed in a military training program that ranges from marksmanship to orienteering, an academic program that offers over forty majors ranging from electrical engineering to philosophy, and a physical program that finds every cadet participating in an intercollegiate, club, or intramural-level sport. The fully funded, four-year college education includes tuition, room, board, and full medical and dental care. In return, you will graduate with a Bachelor of Science degree and be commissioned as a U.S. Army Officer with an active duty service obligation of five years active and three years reserve. Complete admissions guidance found online."

SELECTIVITY

Admissions Rating	98
# of applicants	14,635
% of applicants accepted	10
% of acceptees attending	83

FRESHMAN PROFILE

Range SAT Critical Reading	580–680
Range SAT Math	610–710
Range SAT Writing	560–670
Range ACT Composite	26–31
Minimum paper TOEFL	500
Minimum internet-based TOEFL	75
% graduated top 10% of class	52
% graduated top 25% of class	76
% graduated top 50% of class	94

DEADLINES

Regular	
Deadline	2/28
Nonfall registration?	No

APPLICANTS ALSO LOOK AT AND SOMETIMES PREFER

United States Naval Academy; United States Air Force Academy

FINANCIAL FACTS

Financial Aid Rating	60*
Annual in-state tuition	$0
Annual out-of-state tuition	$0
Average frosh need-based scholarship	$0
% needy frosh rec. need-based scholarship or grant aid	0
% needy UG rec. need-based scholarship or grant aid	0
% needy frosh rec. non-need-based scholarship or grant aid	0
% needy UG rec. non-need-based scholarship or grant aid	0
% needy frosh rec. need-based self-help aid	0
% needy UG rec. need-based self-help aid	0
% frosh rec. any financial aid	0
% UG rec. any financial aid	0
Average % of frosh need met	0
Average % of ugrad need met	0

UNITED STATES NAVAL ACADEMY

117 Decatur Road, Annapolis, MD 21402 • Admissions: 410-293-4361 • Fax: 410-295-1815

CAMPUS LIFE

Quality of Life Rating	90
Fire Safety Rating	77
Green Rating	60*
Type of school	Public
Affiliation	No Affiliation
Environment	Town

STUDENTS

Total undergrad enrollment	4,525
% male/female	75/25
% from out of state	93
% frosh from public high school	60
% frosh live on campus	100
% ugrads live on campus	100
% African American	7
% Asian	7
% Caucasian	64
% Hispanic	11
% Native American	<1
% Pacific Islander	1
% Two or more races	8
% Race and/or ethnicity unknown	1
% international	1
# of countries represented	28

SURVEY SAYS...
Students always studying
Classroom facilities are great
Lab facilities are great
Great library
Career services are great
Internships are widely available
School is well run
No one cheats
Students are very religious
Students get along with local community
Students involved in community service
Students love Annapolis, MD
Great off-campus food
Easy to get around campus
Recreation facilities are great
Very little drug use
Everyone loves the Navy
Intramural sports are popular
Alumni active on campus

ACADEMICS

Academic Rating	91
% students returning for sophomore year	98
% students graduating within 4 years	86
% students graduating within 6 years	86
Calendar	Semester
Student/faculty ratio	8:1
Profs interesting rating	76
Profs accessible rating	97
Most classes have 10–19 students.	

MOST POPULAR MAJORS
Economics; Political Science and Government; Systems Engineering

STUDENTS SAY "..."

Academics

One of the nation's most prestigious institutions, the United States Naval Academy provides undergraduates with the opportunity "to be among America's next generation of leaders, and to represent the best this country has to offer." Certainly, these midshipmen are drawn to the promise of serving their country and "receiving an Ivy League-equivalent education" all while "push[ing themselves] further than [they] ever thought possible." Indeed, students greatly value the fact that "[t]he curriculum is designed around training and developing leaders, and takes a whole-person aspect into view." As one senior explains, "character is a must, and ethical-leadership is the standard. We are encouraged and enabled to perform academically, physically, and morally." Additionally, undergrads speak highly of their overall classroom experience as well as their "excellent" professors. Many students are pleased to discover that their teachers focus on "how course material can be applied in the real world." They also feel that, by and large, professors here are "extremely knowledgeable in their field." Perhaps even more importantly, these midshipmen brag that instructors "are willing to devote a lot of extra time to help students outside of class." And a grateful sophomore emphasizes, "Professors will go out of their way to help students at practically every hour of the day." Surely, there's no doubt that the Naval Academy provides students "with the tools to succeed."

Life

"I call the Naval Academy the world's most beautiful prison...we work to defend freedom, not enjoy it." Yes, as this midshipman colorfully alludes, life at the Naval Academy is quite regimented and rules here are "strictly enforced." Students are quick to note that, with the exception of a few seniors, "no one is allowed to leave campus during the week." Nevertheless, the "lifestyle is very busy" despite the ban. An aerospace engineering major explains, "There is constantly something to be done between formations, room inspections, mandatory parades and evening lectures." Thankfully, even with these highly regulated schedules, students can participate in "a wide variety of extracurricular activities." Indeed, "from salsa dancing to marathon club to combat arms team, there is something for everyone to get involved with." When precious free time is available, many students enjoy engaging in outdoor activities such as "rock climbing, sailing, fishing, hiking, and camping." Additionally, a lot of midshipmen can be found "running and biking when the weather is good." The Academy itself has virtually no party scene since "it's a completely dry campus." And a sophomore warns that "if you are found with alcohol you are kicked out." However, during the weekends, midshipmen who are of age love sampling the bars around Annapolis. And all undergrads appreciate the school's proximity to both Baltimore and Washington, D.C. Finally, many midshipmen conclude by stressing that life at the Academy "gets better as you progress."

Student Body

Without a doubt, many midshipmen would define their peers as "hard charging," "motivated," "type A personalities." They could also easily be seen as "goal-oriented, physically fit" and occasionally "cynical about academy life." Of course, wandering around campus, it might appear as though the typical student is "a Caucasian male...very conservative, religious [and] very morally upright." However, a junior happily points out, "Our school is required to have students from all over the country, and people from very different backgrounds all meld together." And one sophomore explains that ultimately, "Because we all go through such rigorous evolutions every week, we have this unspoken understanding/respect for each other that acts as a great ice breaker when making friends."

E-MAIL: WEBMAIL@USNA.EDU • WEBSITE: WWW.USNA.EDU

THE PRINCETON REVIEW SAYS
Admissions
Very important factors considered include: rigor of secondary school record, class rank, academic GPA, application essay, recommendation(s), interview, extracurricular activities, character/personal qualities, level of applicant's interest. *Important factors considered include:* standardized test scores, talent/ability. *Other factors considered include:* first generation, alumni/ae relation, geographical residence, state residency, racial/ethnic status, volunteer work, work experience. SAT or ACT required. TOEFL required of all international applicants. High school diploma or equivalent is not required. *Academic units recommended:* 4 English, 4 math, 2 science, 1 science lab, 2 foreign language, 2 history, and 1 unit from above areas or other academic areas.

Financial Aid
Students should submit: The Princeton Review suggests that all financial aid forms be submitted as soon as possible after October 1.

The Inside Word
Securing admission to the Naval Academy is no easy feat. To begin with, a top-notch academic record is a must. In addition to strong GPA and test scores, applicants also have to secure an official nomination (typically granted by a U.S. representative, U.S. senator, or the Vice President). Further, candidates need to prove physical fitness, be an unmarried U.S. citizen between the ages of seventeen and twenty-three and have no dependents. And, perhaps most importantly, applicants should also demonstrate strong moral character. Finally, the earlier you apply the better.

THE SCHOOL SAYS "..."
From the Admissions Office
"The finest young men and women in the country come to the Naval Academy to develop into leaders to serve the nation; USNA is the school of admirals, presidents, Nobel Prize winners, astronauts, jet pilots and CEOs. At USNA, you will have the opportunity to pursue a four-year degree program that develops you mentally, morally, and physically as no civilian college can. As you might expect, this program is demanding, but the opportunities are limitless and more than worth the effort.

"Upon throwing the iconic Midshipmen hat into the air at graduation, you will serve your country in one of dozens of professional fields—primarily aviation, submarines, ships, or the Marine Corps, but with additional limited options for the SEALs, medical, and other communities."

SELECTIVITY
Admissions Rating	98
# of applicants	16,101
% of applicants accepted	9
% of acceptees attending	87
# offered a place on the wait list	187
% accepting a place on wait list	76
% admitted from wait list	3

FRESHMAN PROFILE
Range SAT Critical Reading	570–680
Range SAT Math	610–700
% graduated top 10% of class	58
% graduated top 25% of class	81
% graduated top 50% of class	94

DEADLINES
Regular	
Deadline	1/31
Notification	4/15
Nonfall registration?	No

APPLICANTS ALSO LOOK AT AND OFTEN PREFER
Duke University; Harvard College; University of Virginia; United States Air Force Academy

AND SOMETIMES PREFER
Penn State University Park; Massachusetts Institute of Technology; Georgia Institute of Technology; United States Military Academy

AND RARELY PREFER
Boston University; St. John's College (MD); Purdue University–West Lafayette

FINANCIAL FACTS
Financial Aid Rating	60*
Annual in-state tuition	$0
Annual out-of-state tuition	$0
Average frosh need-based scholarship	$0
% needy frosh rec. need-based scholarship or grant aid	0
% needy UG rec. need-based scholarship or grant aid	0
% needy frosh rec. non-need-based scholarship or grant aid	0
% needy UG rec. non-need-based scholarship or grant aid	0
% needy frosh rec. need-based self-help aid	0
% needy UG rec. need-based self-help aid	0
% frosh rec. any financial aid	0
% UG rec. any financial aid	0
Average % of frosh need met	0
Average % of ugrad need met	0

THE UNIVERSITY OF ALABAMA AT BIRMINGHAM

OFFICE OF UNDERGRADUATE ADMISSIONS, BIRMINGHAM, AL 35294-1150 • ADMISSIONS: 205-934-8221 • FAX: 205-975-7114

CAMPUS LIFE

Quality of Life Rating	93
Fire Safety Rating	92
Green Rating	71
Type of school	Public
Affiliation	No Affiliation
Environment	Metropolis

STUDENTS

Total undergrad enrollment	11,679
% male/female	42/58
% from out of state	9
% frosh live on campus	68
% ugrads live on campus	21
# of fraternities (% ugrad men join)	12 (4)
# of sororities (% ugrad women join)	11 (4)
% African American	26
% Asian	5
% Caucasian	59
% Hispanic	3
% Native American	<1
% Pacific Islander	<1
% Two or more races	4
% Race and/or ethnicity unknown	1
% international	2
# of countries represented	53

SURVEY SAYS...

Students are happy
Lab facilities are great
Great library
Career services are great
Internships are widely available
School is well run
Diverse student types interact on campus
Students get along with local community
Students involved in community service
Recreation facilities are great
Alumni active on campus

ACADEMICS

Academic Rating	71
% students returning for sophomore year	83
% students graduating within 4 years	33
% students graduating within 6 years	56
Calendar	Semester
Student/faculty ratio	18:1
Profs interesting rating	80
Profs accessible rating	81

Most classes have 10–19 students.
Most lab/discussion sessions have 20–29 students.

MOST POPULAR MAJORS
Biology; Psychology; Speech Communication and Rhetoric

STUDENTS SAY "..."

Academics
At the University of Alabama at Birmingham, professors and administrators "care about you." "For many of the professors, it's not just about a grade in a class that you are taking. Rather it's an experience and preparation for any of our further endeavors." The professors here are "experts in their fields," they're "accessible and exciting," and "they're down-to-earth enough to give students a real view of what it's like to enter the world of academia." Despite the fact that this is a large university, there are "small class sizes in even the 100-level classes," and "many professors are available for help outside the classroom and care about teaching their subjects to the students." Of particular note, students say professors in the science departments "are great. They do a great job with interactive learning, and they really put forth every effort to make sure that those who want help get it." Academically, students feel that the workload is rigorous, but "certainly worth the challenge." As one student notes, a graduate tends to feel like "a better person for having experienced the challenge of UAB as well as the diversity." With a biannual student forum, "the faculty and administration are very close with students and actively look to pursuing perfection and improving the collegiate experience."

Life
"Campus life is vibrant and exciting," boasts the student body. With UAB being "in the city of Birmingham, right outside of the school is something for everyone. There are malls, many restaurants, museums, and live music." UAB "strongly encourages their students to get involved on campus in some shape or form," presenting the student body with such opportunities as "the widely used Campus Recreation Center where students can take free U-Fit Classes (kickboxing, krunk/hip-hop class, yoga, spin, etc.), swim in the wave pool, climb the rock wall, or play intramurals (flag football, dodgeball, soccer, volleyball, slow pitch softball, etc.)." In addition, the surrounding city of Birmingham offers many venues for arts and entertainment; "students can dine or shop at the many malls located throughout the city. There are also many museums, art shows, concerts, dance clubs, [and] movie theaters to choose from." Students say that the list of attractions in Birmingham "goes on and on." "Students have the problem of having to narrow down their opportunities, rather than having to find something to do." Students "love the size of the school," finding it "like a small town in a big city." The impression is that "the campus is large enough that [you] meet and see new faces daily, but small enough to where [you] have personal relationships with teachers and the administration." Additionally, "there is a genuine interest among students in learning about the other cultures and religions represented on campus and in other cultures around the world."

Student Body
"Everyone is so diverse that there is...something for everyone to get involved in." With more than 250 campus organizations, students say you'd "have to choose to not become involved." Many students love "how no one looks down on anyone," and how "everyone is so down-to-earth!" Most feel that they all come "from modest households." Regarding potential changes that could be made, "the meal plan situation could use some serious help." At UAB students feel, "it is easy to find a place where you fit in." Although the student body will insist that "there is no typical student!" In general, students are "hardworking and serious," while doing their best to always "enjoy weekend fun with friends."

FINANCIAL AID: 205-934-8223 • E-MAIL: UNDERGRADADMIT@UAB.EDU • WEBSITE: WWW.UAB.EDU

THE PRINCETON REVIEW SAYS

Admissions

Very important factors considered include: rigor of secondary school record, academic GPA, standardized test scores. *Important factors considered include: Other factors considered include:* SAT or ACT required. ACT with or without writing accepted. TOEFL required of all international applicants. High school diploma is required and GED is accepted. *Academic units required:* 4 English, 3 math, 3 science, 2 science labs, 1 foreign language, 3 social studies, 3 academic electives.

Financial Aid

Students should submit: FAFSA. Priority filing deadline is 3/1. The Princeton Review suggests that all financial aid forms be submitted as soon as possible after October 1. *Need-based scholarships/grants offered:* Federal Pell, FSEOG, State scholarships/grants, Private scholarships, College/university scholarship or grant aid from institutional funds, United Negro College Fund. *Loan aid offered:* Direct Subsidized Stafford Loans, Direct Unsubsidized Stafford Loans, Direct PLUS loans, Federal Perkins Loans, State Loans, College/university loans from institutional funds. Applicants will be notified of awards on a rolling basis beginning 3/15. Federal Work-Study Program available. Institutional employment available.

The Inside Word

UAB's incoming class tends to have an average GPA of 3.5. The most important factors for admission are GPA and test scores. At the minimum, students need a GPA of 2.25 and a 950 SAT score. Administrators here are looking to admit a student body that's friendly, diverse, and intelligent with students who strive to be active in the community.

THE SCHOOL SAYS " . . . "

From the Admissions Office

"The University of Alabama at Birmingham (UAB) is a young, dynamic teaching and research university that has—in just four decades—won international renown for our collaborative and interdisciplinary culture. Our academic programs afford students unrivaled, hands-on experience in research and scholarship as UAB is first in the nation among public universities of federal research dollars per freshman. With over 120 areas of study, UAB attracts the best and brightest students from Alabama, the nation, and 109 countries around the globe.

"UAB students learn from—and work alongside—some of the world's top researchers, scholars, performers, and experts. Programs from the sciences and engineering to the arts and humanities give students the benefit of globally recognized faculty, exciting academic challenges, and experiences that will prepare them for a future in the job market.

"At UAB, we understand that having a fulfilling student life experience is as important as having a fulfilling academic experience. UAB has a rich mix of academic organizations, honor clubs, social fraternities and sororities, volunteer groups, and activities ranging from intramural sports and SGA to program-related clubs and supporting Blazer athletics. With 250 campus organizations to keep students involved, UAB offers the chance to make lifelong friendships while assisting in the development of skills essential to leadership and teamwork."

SELECTIVITY

Admissions Rating	76
# of applicants	5,710
% of applicants accepted	86
% of acceptees attending	36

FRESHMAN PROFILE

Range ACT Composite	21–27
Minimum internet-based TOEFL	77
Average HS GPA	3.6
% graduated top 10% of class	28
% graduated top 25% of class	55
% graduated top 50% of class	83

DEADLINES

Regular	
Priority	6/1
Nonfall registration?	Yes

FINANCIAL FACTS

Financial Aid Rating	79
Annual in-state tuition	$9,596
Annual out-of-state tuition	$21,956
Room and board	$10,266
Books and supplies	$1,200
Average frosh need-based scholarship	$5,197
Average UG need-based scholarship	$4,658
% needy frosh rec. need-based scholarship or grant aid	61
% needy UG rec. need-based scholarship or grant aid	64
% needy frosh rec. non-need-based scholarship or grant aid	71
% needy UG rec. non-need-based scholarship or grant aid	40
% needy frosh rec. need-based self-help aid	68
% needy UG rec. need-based self-help aid	76
% frosh need fully met	9
% ugrads need fully met	4
Average % of frosh need met	54
Average % of ugrad need met	47

THE UNIVERSITY OF ALABAMA AT TUSCALOOSA

Box 870132, Tuscaloosa, AL 35487-0132 • Admissions: 205-348-5666 • Fax: 205-348-9046

CAMPUS LIFE

Quality of Life Rating	76
Fire Safety Rating	80
Green Rating	60*
Type of school	Public
Affiliation	No Affiliation
Environment	City

STUDENTS

Total undergrad enrollment	31,958
% male/female	45/55
% from out of state	54
% frosh live on campus	94
% ugrads live on campus	26
# of fraternities (% ugrad men join)	37 (26)
# of sororities (% ugrad women join)	23 (39)
% African American	11
% Asian	1
% Caucasian	78
% Hispanic	4
% Native American	<1
% Pacific Islander	<1
% Two or more races	3
% Race and/or ethnicity unknown	<1
% international	2
# of countries represented	57

SURVEY SAYS...

Recreation facilities are great
Everyone loves the Crimson Tide
Frats and sororities are popular

ACADEMICS

Academic Rating	70
% students returning for sophomore year	86
% students graduating within 4 years	41
% students graduating within 6 years	67
Calendar	Semester
Student/faculty ratio	24:1
Profs interesting rating	66
Profs accessible rating	65

Most classes have 10–19 students.
Most lab/discussion sessions have
20–29 students.

MOST POPULAR MAJORS

Business Administration; Mechanical
Engineering; Nursing

STUDENTS SAY "..."

Academics

The University of Alabama is a ridiculously affordable, "technologically advanced," "student-centered" institution that enjoys an outrageous degree of alumni support. "Course offerings are pretty diverse," and there are "tons of majors." Highlights include a "great" engineering college and three honors programs. Other standout programs include business, communication studies, and nursing. Some students say that the "bold and visionary" top brass runs the school "fairly well." Others gripe that the administration is "very bogged down in red tape." "Working with the administration is really terrible sometimes," undergrads say. Professors here are "top researchers or writers in their fields," and some are "very enthusiastic about having undergraduate students helping them with research." The faculty as a whole is also "approachable" and "generally very easy to get in touch with for outside assistance." Teaching ability is "hit-or-miss," though. While many professors are "very animated and interesting to listen to," "others do not have the same talent." "Being a great researcher does not necessarily make a person a good teacher," notes one student.

Life

"An atmosphere of almost antebellum charm" permeates this "pretty" campus. "On sunny days in the fall and spring, students enjoy studying and playing on the quad." Recreational facilities are "excellent." "Life during football season revolves around football." So does morale. Win or lose, though, UA boasts "one of the best college football atmospheres in the country. On Saturdays when the Crimson Tide plays at home, the campus is "a sea of tents for tailgating," "and Alabama fans are singing the fight song." Otherwise, "the Greek organizations rule this campus." They wield "an inordinate amount of power" in student government as well. Whether you pledge or not, though, students promise "an outstanding social atmosphere." "While not everyone participates in the party scene on campus, it is very popular." In addition to the house parties and the festivities at the frat houses, "people enjoying going to the bars on the strip." "Comfort" abounds in surrounding Tuscaloosa, and it is "definitely a college town." People are "very open and courteous" to the students, and virtually everything you need is within "walking distance." When students at UA hanker for more urban environs, "Birmingham is only an hour away, and there is plenty to do there."

Student Body

Students here are "extremely friendly" and "usually well-dressed and well-mannered." "People tend to be a bit conservative," and "a lot are religious." "The typical student is active in a few organizations, makes decent grades, and finds time to relax, too." African American students are the largest minority group. They represent more than 10 percent of the student body. Some students maintain that UA is "not diverse socially, ideologically, and culturally." "The different ethnic groups stick together," they say. They look around campus and see "frat boys or sorority girls for the most part"—"same hair, same sunglasses with a string on the back, and stupid visors." Other students vigorously disagree. "We truly aren't a university filled with cookie-cutter people," asserts one student. "There are many diverse groups of students who all have their own roles on campus." "It is easy for someone to come from up north and say this campus is full of close-minded Southern Baptist Republicans, just like it is easy for someone to come from a small town...and think this campus is full of liberal heathens," points out another student. "Few people are really atypical, because no matter where you fall in any category, there are people around you who you can connect with."

FINANCIAL AID: 205-348-6756 • E-MAIL: ADMISSIONS@UA.EDU • WEBSITE: WWW.UA.EDU

THE PRINCETON REVIEW SAYS

Admissions

Very important factors considered include: rigor of secondary school record, academic GPA, standardized test scores. *Important factors considered include:* class rank. *Other factors considered include:* application essay, recommendation(s), interview, extracurricular activities, talent/ability, character/personal qualities, first generation, alumni/ae relation, volunteer work, work experience. SAT or ACT required. ACT with or without writing accepted. SAT with or without Essay component accepted. TOEFL required of all international applicants. High school diploma is required and GED is accepted. *Academic units required:* 4 English, 3 math, 3 science, 2 science labs, 1 foreign language, 4 social studies, 5 academic electives. *Academic units recommended:* 4 English, 3 math, 3 science, 2 science labs, 2 foreign language, 4 social studies, 5 academic electives.

Financial Aid

Students should submit: FAFSA, Institution's own financial aid form, CSS/Financial Aid PROFILE, State aid form, Noncustodial PROFILE, Business/Farm Supplement. Priority filing deadline is 3/1. The Princeton Review suggests that all financial aid forms be submitted as soon as possible after October 1. *Need-based scholarships/grants offered:* Federal Pell, FSEOG, State scholarships/grants, Private scholarships, College/university scholarship or grant aid from institutional funds, Federal Nursing Scholarships. *Loan aid offered:* Direct Subsidized Stafford Loans, Direct Unsubsidized Stafford Loans, Direct PLUS loans, Federal Perkins Loans, College/university loans from institutional funds. Applicants will be notified of awards on a rolling basis beginning 4/1. Federal Work-Study Program available. Institutional employment available.

The Inside Word

The University of Alabama relies heavily on objective data in the application process. Admission is not highly competitive, and applicants with satisfactory grades and modest test scores are likely to be accepted.

THE SCHOOL SAYS "..."

From the Admissions Office

"Since its founding in 1831 as the first public university in the state, the University of Alabama has been committed to providing the best, most complete education possible for its students. Our commitment to that goal means that as times change, we sharpen our focus and methods to keep our graduates competitive in their fields. By offering outstanding teaching in a solid core curriculum enhanced by multimedia classrooms and campus-wide computer labs, the University of Alabama keeps its focus on the future while maintaining a traditional college atmosphere. Extensive international study opportunities, internship programs, and cooperative education placements help our students prepare for successful futures. Consisting of eleven colleges and schools offering 193 degrees in more than 100 fields of study, the university gives its students a wide range of choices and offers courses of study at the bachelor's, master's, specialist, and doctoral levels. The university emphasizes quality and breadth of academic opportunities and challenging programs for well-prepared students through its Honors College, including the University Honors Program, International Honors Program, and Computer-Based Honors Programs and Blount Undergraduate Initiative (liberal arts program). Thirty-one percent of undergraduates are from out of state, providing an enriching social and cultural environment.

"Applicants may submit either the SAT or the ACT. The writing component is required for admission."

SELECTIVITY

Admissions Rating	89
# of applicants	36,203
% of applicants accepted	54
% of acceptees attending	37

FRESHMAN PROFILE

Range SAT Critical Reading	490–600
Range SAT Math	490–610
Range SAT Writing	480–600
Range ACT Composite	22–31
Minimum paper TOEFL	550
Minimum internet-based TOEFL	79
Average HS GPA	3.7
% graduated top 10% of class	37
% graduated top 25% of class	57
% graduated top 50% of class	82

DEADLINES

Regular	
Priority	2/1
Nonfall registration?	Yes

APPLICANTS ALSO LOOK AT AND OFTEN PREFER

Florida State University; University of Georgia; Duke University; University of Tennessee–Knoxville; Vanderbilt University

AND SOMETIMES PREFER

Auburn University; Tulane University; Louisiana State University

FINANCIAL FACTS

Financial Aid Rating	64
Annual in-state tuition	$10,170
Annual out-of-state tuition	$25,950
Room and board	$9,030
Books and supplies	$1,200
Average frosh need-based scholarship	$13,123
Average UG need-based scholarship	$10,745
% needy frosh rec. need-based scholarship or grant aid	79
% needy UG rec. need-based scholarship or grant aid	74
% needy frosh rec. non-need-based scholarship or grant aid	63
% needy UG rec. non-need-based scholarship or grant aid	48
% needy frosh rec. need-based self-help aid	67
% needy UG rec. need-based self-help aid	77
% frosh rec. any financial aid	81
% UG rec. any financial aid	73
% UG borrow to pay for school	46
Average cumulative indebtedness	$31,697
% frosh need fully met	27
% ugrads need fully met	19
Average % of frosh need met	58
Average % of ugrad need met	53

UNIVERSITY OF ARIZONA

PO Box 210073, Tucson, AZ 85721-0073 • Admissions: 520-621-3237 • Fax: 520-621-9799

STUDENTS SAY "..."

Academics

In the simplest terms, the University of Arizona is all about providing its students with "endless opportunities." Located on a "gorgeous" campus in vibrant Tucson, the UA offers a "great education" in a "relaxed community." Students here truly appreciate the university's "strong commitment to undergraduate research." Moreover, Arizona really "helps make the cost of education manageable," even "offering many scholarships to out-of-state students who qualify." While undergrads are impressed by a myriad of disciplines, they call special attention to the "excellent" agriculture department and the "great" engineering program. Students also highlight the physiology program and note that the UA is "the only university that offers an undergraduate major through its medical school." Undergrads do admit that professors can range from "very boring" to "extremely fun and interesting." One sophomore does assure us that, by and large, "Professors are enthusiastic and genuinely care about students." A knowledgeable junior adds, "As I get into the higher level classes or the classes that are more focused on my major, I find that the teachers are more enthusiastic and dedicated to their students to see that they succeed." Fortunately, "one thing that is consistent about all of them (and the TAs as well) is their availability through office hours for one-on-one instruction." As this public health major concludes, "The University of Arizona is an institution that provides a well-rounded education and numerous opportunities that prepare students for their future ambitions, whatever they may be."

Life

Students at the UA are "motivated academically" and devote a decent percentage of their weekdays to hitting the books. Of course, undergrads here are also "very social," and as a sophomore enthusiastically shares, "There is always something to do on campus, and there are a variety of clubs to get involved in." Indeed, there are a number of activities available, ranging "from swing dance to intramural volleyball," which "help alleviate stress." Additionally, "people are really into the athletics. It builds school spirit for everyone involved, [and] tailgates are common on the weekends." Greek life is also extremely popular, and "on the weekends, frats have huge [theme] parties including... AEPirates, Heaven and Hell, Swampwater, Pajama Jam, and many more." Undergrads also enjoy hometown Tucson, which has "great live music, art, and cinema." The city also "generally has a lot of community activities like Day of the Dead, which is extremely popular." Lastly, students also like to take advantage of the numerous outdoor recreation options available, and many often go "hiking or biking at the nearby mountain ranges."

Student Body

Undergrads at the UA report that the "relaxed" nature of their peers contributes to a "laid-back" atmosphere, which permeates the campus. While some students are most assuredly "in school to learn," others seem "to party their way through." However, an optical engineering major confidently states, "There is a place for you to fit in no matter what you want to get out of your college education." A fellow engineering student adds, "Most students are very friendly and will greet each other around campus." The UA is quite "diverse," and you can easily find students of/from all different "socio-economic statuses, states, countries, races, ethnicities, ages, etc." A junior tells us that people often make friends by simply getting "involved with something they are interested in and meeting like-minded individuals." One thing that unites these undergrads? Nearly all these "Wildcats" are "full of pride for their school." Perhaps this content freshman says it best, "In a school of 30,000, there is really no typical student, but with such a great number of students, people find their niche."

FINANCIAL AID: 520-621-1858 • E-MAIL: ADMISSIONS@ARIZONA.EDU • WEBSITE: WWW.ARIZONA.EDU

THE PRINCETON REVIEW SAYS

Admissions

Very important factors considered include: rigor of secondary school record, academic GPA, standardized test scores, application essay. *Important factors considered include:* extracurricular activities, talent/ability, character/personal qualities, level of applicant's interest. *Other factors considered include:* recommendation(s), first generation, volunteer work, work experience. SAT or ACT recommend; SAT Subject Tests considered if submitted. ACT with or without writing accepted. TOEFL required of all international applicants. High school diploma is required and GED is accepted. *Academic units required:* 4 English, 4 math, 3 science, 3 science labs, 2 foreign language, 2 social studies, 1 visual/performing arts. *Academic units recommended:* 4 English, 4 math, 3 science labs, 2 second languages, 2 social studies, 1 visual/performing arts or career/technical course.

Financial Aid

Students should submit: FAFSA. The Princeton Review suggests that all financial aid forms be submitted as soon as possible after October 1. *Need-based scholarships/grants offered:* Federal Pell, FSEOG, State scholarships/grants, Private scholarships, College/university scholarship or grant aid from institutional funds, Federal Nursing Scholarships. *Loan aid offered:* Direct Subsidized Stafford Loans, Direct Unsubsidized Stafford Loans, Direct PLUS loans, Federal Perkins Loans, Federal Nursing Loans, College/university loans from institutional funds. Federal Work-Study Program available. Institutional employment available.

The Inside Word

Admission to the UA is competitive, and you'll need to demonstrate achievement in college prep courses. Arizona residents should take note: Candidates applying from within the state who graduate in the top 25 percent of their class and meet all course requirements gain automatic acceptance through the assured admission program. Applicants should also recognize that some programs, such as the College of Engineering, College of Nursing, and College of Fine Arts, mandate additional materials and requirements.

THE SCHOOL SAYS "..."

From the Admissions Office

"The University of Arizona offers endless opportunities for its students to make an impact on campus and beyond. From day one, students are part of Arizona's mission to provide every undergrad with real-world experience in the form of internships, research, study abroad, or community service by the time they graduate. Arizona boasts many of the nation's best programs in fields as diverse as astronomy, business, nursing, management information systems, computer and aerospace engineering, anthropology, sociology, and creative writing. The UA fills its world-class research curriculum with a faculty that includes Nobel and Pulitzer Prize winners and offers more than 100 majors, as well as minors and many concentration options. Our students also enjoy an active, cheerful, and inviting campus atmosphere that includes more than 600 student clubs and organizations, conference-winning and national title–winning basketball, baseball, swimming, softball, and football teams; and countless recreational opportunities."

SELECTIVITY

Admissions Rating	80
# of applicants	35,408
% of applicants accepted	76
% of acceptees attending	30

FRESHMAN PROFILE

Range SAT Critical Reading	480–600
Range SAT Math	480–620
Range SAT Writing	470–590
Range ACT Composite	21–27
Minimum internet-based TOEFL	70
Average HS GPA	3.4
% graduated top 10% of class	28
% graduated top 25% of class	54
% graduated top 50% of class	84

DEADLINES

Regular	
Priority	5/1
Deadline	5/1
Nonfall registration?	Yes

APPLICANTS ALSO LOOK AT AND OFTEN PREFER

University of California–Irvine

AND RARELY PREFER

Baylor University; Arizona State University

FINANCIAL FACTS

Financial Aid Rating	81
Annual in-state tuition	$9,864
Annual out-of-state tuition	$29,017
Room and board	$9,840
Required fees	$1,013
Books and supplies	$1,200
Average frosh need-based scholarship	$11,041
Average UG need-based scholarship	$10,726
% needy frosh rec. need-based scholarship or grant aid	94
% needy UG rec. need-based scholarship or grant aid	90
% needy frosh rec. non-need-based scholarship or grant aid	11
% needy UG rec. non-need-based scholarship or grant aid	7
% needy frosh rec. need-based self-help aid	56
% needy UG rec. need-based self-help aid	63
% frosh need fully met	12
% ugrads need fully met	9
Average % of frosh need met	62
Average % of ugrad need met	60

UNIVERSITY OF ARKANSAS—FAYETTEVILLE

232 Silas Hunt Hall, Fayetteville, AR 72701 • Admissions: 479-575-5346 • Fax: 479-575-7515

CAMPUS LIFE

Quality of Life Rating	90
Fire Safety Rating	91
Green Rating	88
Type of school	Public
Affiliation	No Affiliation
Environment	City

STUDENTS

Total undergrad enrollment	22,159
% male/female	48/52
% from out of state	40
% frosh from public high school	83
% frosh live on campus	89
% ugrads live on campus	26
# of fraternities (% ugrad men join)	19 (22)
# of sororities (% ugrad women join)	14 (37)
% African American	5
% Asian	2
% Caucasian	77
% Hispanic	8
% Native American	1
% Pacific Islander	<1
% Two or more races	3
% Race and/or ethnicity unknown	<1
% international	3
# of countries represented	85

SURVEY SAYS...

Students are happy
Students are very religious
Students love Fayetteville, AR
Everyone loves the Razorbacks
Frats and sororities are popular

ACADEMICS

Academic Rating	73
% students returning for sophomore year	82
% students graduating within 4 years	39
% students graduating within 6 years	62
Calendar	Semester
Student/faculty ratio	19:1
Profs interesting rating	71
Profs accessible rating	71

Most classes have 10–19 students.
Most lab/discussion sessions have 20–29 students.

MOST POPULAR MAJORS

Finance; Registered Nursing/Registered Nurse; Biology

STUDENTS SAY "..."

Academics

The University of Arkansas is affordable, "student-centered," and large without being intimidating. Though many of the professors "are incredibly experienced and passionate about their field," "there are also lots of graduate students teaching lower level and introductory courses, and they have a huge range of quality." "The facilities are exceptional" and otherwise "state-of-the-art." More than 100 undergraduate majors and programs are available. The Sam Walton College of Business is awash in cash and "one of the strongest assets;" students feel that the university has the "best engineering college in Arkansas," and its Agricultural programs are strong and diverse. The Honors College is "wonderful," with an English/creative writing major saying "I think if I hadn't joined the Honors College right away, my experience would not have been as good as I've had. I love the professors and small class size that you get at the honors level." Also, some 13 percent of all Arkansas students study abroad, with summer programs available in China and Egypt, just to a name two examples.

Life

The University of Arkansas "is a great place for people looking for a middle-sized college town." It is "nestled in the beautiful Ozark Mountains and provides easy access to outdoor activities such as hiking, rock climbing, and canoeing. There is also a nice downtown area with a variety of bars and restaurants, shopping access, and places to see concerts and theatre performances." Students "especially enjoy seeking out new coffee shops, visiting the Buffalo River, and going to Crystal Bridges (a museum of American art)." It has the characteristics of "both a small town and a city," "creating a unique atmosphere that is simultaneously Southern and hipster. Be prepared for eating BBQ . . . cheering for the Hogs, exploring the Dickson Street Book Shop, and attending concerts at George's Majestic Lounge." Sports, and especially Razorbacks football, are things the campus takes very seriously. Students here reportedly enjoy a "vibrant extracurricular and social scene," and report that "there are lots of things to do that don't involve booze." With more than 380 clubs and groups to choose from "the vast majority of students participate in at least a few campus organizations." For outdoorsy types, wilderness activities abound throughout northwestern Arkansas. "The nearby mountains" provide numerous opportunities for climbing, biking, and hiking.

Student Body

Students come for the "good business school" and "low tuition" and stay for the Razorbacks football. A political science and Middle Eastern studies major says, "The typical student is Caucasian, southern, and moderately conservative in political and religious views; however, students who differ from this 'type' find that they do have a place to belong on campus. There is little discrimination amongst students, except possibly with the LGBT students, although much has changed for the better on this front in my three years at this campus. In five years, I imagine that this situation will be entirely different." "Party-frat kids abound," as do "southern sorority girls who walk to class in pearls and heels." However, you'll also find "hicks," "artists, musicians, nerds," and "NPR listening, sandal-wearing, health-food-shopping people," as well as the occasional "middle-aged boomer returning to school to start a whole new career."

UNIVERSITY OF ARKANSAS—FAYETTEVILLE

FINANCIAL AID: 479-575-3806 • E-MAIL: UOFA@UARK.EDU • WEBSITE: WWW.UARK.EDU

THE PRINCETON REVIEW SAYS

Admissions

Very important factors considered include: academic GPA, standardized test scores. *Other factors considered include:* rigor of secondary school record, class rank, application essay, recommendation(s), extracurricular activities, talent/ability, character/personal qualities, first generation, alumni/ae relation, geographical residence, state residency, volunteer work, work experience. SAT or ACT required. ACT with or without writing accepted. SAT with or without Essay component accepted. TOEFL required of all international applicants. High school diploma is required and GED is accepted. *Academic units required:* 4 English, 4 math, 3 science, 1 science lab, 1 social studies, 2 history, 2 academic electives. *Academic units recommended:* 2 foreign language.

Financial Aid

Students should submit: FAFSA. The Princeton Review suggests that all financial aid forms be submitted as soon as possible after October 1. *Need-based scholarships/grants offered:* Federal Pell, FSEOG, State scholarships/grants, Private scholarships, College/university scholarship or grant aid from institutional funds. *Loan aid offered:* Direct Subsidized Stafford Loans, Direct Unsubsidized Stafford Loans, Direct PLUS loans, Federal Perkins Loans. Applicants will be notified of awards on or about 4/1. Federal Work-Study Program available. Institutional employment available.

The Inside Word

The admissions policy at the University of Arkansas is very straightforward. In-state students need a 3.0 grade-point average (on a 4.0 scale) in their serious academic course work and at least a 20 on the ACT; out-of-state admission requirements depend on demand. The SAT is fine, too, as long as get a comparable minimum score. If you fail to meet these requirements, you still may gain admission based on a case-by-case review process. Also, UA has a rolling admissions policy. As such, candidates will find it in their best interest to apply early.

THE SCHOOL SAYS "..."

From the Admissions Office

"The University of Arkansas, the flagship campus of the University of Arkansas System, is located in Fayetteville and overlooks the beautiful Ozark Mountains. The university is both the major land-grant university for Arkansas and the state university, encompassing more than 130 buildings on 718 acres and providing more than 200 graduate and undergraduate academic programs—more than some universities twice its size. At the same time, the University of Arkansas maintains a low student-to-faculty ratio—currently 19:1—that makes personal attention possible. The university aggressively promotes undergraduate research in virtually every discipline and makes higher education affordable with competitively priced tuition and generous financial aid. In the last decade, university undergraduates have earned many honors; fifty-two received Goldwater Scholarships. There have been 122 National Science Foundation graduate fellows; sixty-eight Fulbright scholars; seven British Marshall scholars and nineteen Truman scholars. Nine undergraduates have received Udall scholarships; seven earned Madison scholarships; and ten received Rhodes scholarships. Quality programs, affordable tuition and the level of student achievement all contribute to the University of Arkansas consistently being ranked in the top tier of national universities. The city of Fayetteville is home to more than 80,000 people and is growing every day. Northwest Arkansas is the headquarters to several major international corporations that have close ties to the university: Tyson Foods, the world's largest protein producer; J.B. Hunt Transport Services Inc., a major transportation and logistics company; and Wal-Mart Stores Inc., the world's largest corporation. Fayetteville has been named no. 3 in 'Best Places to Live,' 'One of America's 'Hottest' Cities,' one of the nation's 'least stressful' metro areas, by publications such as *U.S. News & World Reports, Forbes, Frommer's Guide,* and *Money* magazine. The university enjoys academic partnerships with the world-class Crystal Bridges Museum of American Art, located in nearby Bentonville, Ark."

SELECTIVITY

Admissions Rating	87
# of applicants	20,542
% of applicants accepted	60
% of acceptees attending	40
# offered a place on the wait list	160
% accepting a place on wait list	92
% admitted from wait list	85

FRESHMAN PROFILE

Range SAT Critical Reading	500–600
Range SAT Math	510–620
Range ACT Composite	23–28
Minimum paper TOEFL	550
Minimum internet-based TOEFL	79
Average HS GPA	3.6
% graduated top 10% of class	26
% graduated top 25% of class	54
% graduated top 50% of class	85

DEADLINES

Early action	
Deadline	11/1
Notification	12/15
Regular	
Priority	11/1
Deadline	8/1
Nonfall registration?	Yes

FINANCIAL FACTS

Financial Aid Rating	81
Annual in-state tuition	$7,028
Annual out-of-state tuition	$20,332
Room and board	$9,880
Required fees	$1,494
Books and supplies	$1,000
Average frosh need-based scholarship	$6,662
Average UG need-based scholarship	$6,706
% needy frosh rec. need-based scholarship or grant aid	82
% needy UG rec. need-based scholarship or grant aid	77
% needy frosh rec. non-need-based scholarship or grant aid	12
% needy UG rec. non-need-based scholarship or grant aid	8
% needy frosh rec. need-based self-help aid	64
% needy UG rec. need-based self-help aid	70
% frosh rec. any financial aid	79
% UG rec. any financial aid	72
% frosh need fully met	17
% ugrads need fully met	13
Average % of frosh need met	59
Average % of ugrad need met	57

UNIVERSITY OF CALIFORNIA—BERKELEY

110 SPROUL HALL, BERKELEY, CA 94720-5800 • ADMISSIONS: 510-642-3175 • FAX: 510-642-7333

STUDENTS SAY "..."

Academics

The flagship campus of the University of California school system with a "highly respectable name," UC Berkeley "has great faculty, great research, great classes, and everyone knows it." The school "really encourages us to go out and learn, both inside and outside the classroom," and there is a real commitment to "a well- rounded, diverse education" that permeates the curriculum. "Berkeley is defined by its open, liberal education and culture for independent and collaborative thinking across all fields," sums up a senior molecular toxicology major.

Professors here are "fantastic," "the best in their fields," and each "offers a diverse perspective" toward the academic experience. There are some complaints that larger freshman courses can be "somewhat terrible" and "experience from professors can range widely" (though graduate student instructors "are very accessible and helpful"), but it is universally agreed that "after getting through lower division prerequisite classes, [the] academic experience has significantly improved." All faculty "have full command of their subjects and are determined to find an answer to anything they don't know, within their discipline."

UC Berkeley is known for having "some of the best engineering programs across the board among colleges," and it doesn't hurt that the school's Silicon Valley home is the "best location in the country for entrepreneurship and innovation." "Top-notch" research abounds, and there are "plenty of opportunities for undergrads to engage in it." "Berkeley will offer you all the opportunity you can handle, it's up to you to take hold of it," says a student.

Life

There's "a constant buzz of student activity that drives everyday life" at Cal, where "academics are a priority" and "every single person has something that they are very passionate about and talking to them for five minutes about it makes you wonder if you should change your major." Students also really appreciate all of the tradition present at Cal. "It's a great choice for students who want the feeling of a big state school but want to also be pushed to their limits," says one. Berkeley is "very hard so free time isn't like it is at other places," but an "amazing community" of student-run organizations and "clubs, sports, student-run classes, seminars, [and] research opportunities" are among the "many different venues for people to find their passion." There's a lot to do off-campus in the downtown Berkeley area, and using the BART is "really convenient and time-saving to go to San Francisco." On campus, there is everything "from frat houses to coffee shop discussions, hiking the fire trails to studying for finals." In those moments that studying abates (a particular rarity for engineers), a lot of students enjoy going to football games, restaurant hopping, or (especially during welcome week) party hopping. Many people here do like to party and drink, but "if that's not your style there are plenty of others to spend time with."

Student Body

Berkeley is a large school, so clusters naturally form along lines such as major or dorm, but all "mix among each other easily." "From clubs to DeCal courses, there is no way a student will not make a group of friends while here at Cal," says a junior. Most Berkeley students are generally "politically liberal, nonreligious, and pretty independent," and there is a large Asian student contingent here. One of the defining characteristics of a Cal student is "the ability to hold high-level conversation about basically anything." Everyone is accepted in here, "regardless of their sexual orientation, religion or political beliefs."

FINANCIAL AID: 510-642-6442 • WEBSITE: WWW.BERKELEY.EDU

THE PRINCETON REVIEW SAYS

Admissions

Very important factors considered include: rigor of secondary school record, academic GPA, standardized test scores, application essay. *Important factors considered include:* extracurricular activities, character/personal qualities, volunteer work, work experience. *Other factors considered include:* first generation, state residency. SAT or ACT required; SAT Subject Tests recommend. ACT with Writing required. TOEFL required of all international applicants. High school diploma is required and GED is accepted. *Academic units required:* 4 English, 3 math, 2 science, 2 science labs, 2 foreign language, 2 history, 1 academic elective, 1 visual/performing arts. *Academic units recommended:* 4 English, 4 math, 3 science, 3 science labs, 3 foreign language, 2 history, 1 academic elective, 1 visual/performing arts.

Financial Aid

Students should submit: FAFSA, State aid form. Regular filing deadline is 3/2. The Princeton Review suggests that all financial aid forms be submitted as soon as possible after October 1. *Need-based scholarships/grants offered:* Federal Pell, FSEOG, State scholarships/grants, Private scholarships, College/university scholarship or grant aid from institutional funds. *Loan aid offered:* Direct Subsidized Stafford Loans, Direct Unsubsidized Stafford Loans, Direct PLUS loans, Federal Perkins Loans. Applicants will be notified of awards on or about 3/31. Federal Work-Study Program available. Institutional employment available.

The Inside Word

UC Berkeley is a top-notch public university with a well-regarded English and Literature department. Importance is placed on the totality of a student's application with a joint focus on the personal statement and academic excellence as noted by a student's GPA. Class rank isn't considered. The school is home to an incredible amount of students with as wide a range of interests. Successful applicants here are generally stellar both academically and personally. Applications, especially the personal statement, should create a picture of a unique candidate with a diversity of skills to offer this active community.

THE SCHOOL SAYS " . . ."

From the Admissions Office

"One of the top public universities in the nation and the world, the University of California—Berkeley offers a vast range of courses and a full menu of extracurricular activities. Berkeley's academic programs are internationally recognized for their excellence. Undergraduates can choose one of 100 majors. Thirty-five departments are top ranked, more than any other college or university in the country. Access to one of the foremost university libraries enriches studies. There are twenty-three specialized libraries on campus and distinguished museums of anthropology, paleontology, and science.

"All applicants must take the ACT plus writing or the SAT Reasoning Test. UC admissions requirements are found at http://www.universityofcalifornia. edu/admissions/freshman/requirements/index.html."

SELECTIVITY

Admissions Rating	98
# of applicants	78,924
% of applicants accepted	15
% of acceptees attending	46
# offered a place on the wait list	3,760
% accepting a place on wait list	65
% admitted from wait list	36

FRESHMAN PROFILE

Range SAT Critical Reading	610–730
Range SAT Math	640–770
Range SAT Writing	620–750
Range ACT Composite	29–34
Minimum paper TOEFL	550
Minimum internet-based TOEFL	80
Average HS GPA	3.87
% graduated top 10% of class	98
% graduated top 25% of class	100
% graduated top 50% of class	100

DEADLINES

Regular	
Deadline	11/30
Notification	3/31
Nonfall registration?	Yes

APPLICANTS ALSO LOOK AT AND OFTEN PREFER
Stanford University

AND SOMETIMES PREFER
University of California–Los Angeles

AND RARELY PREFER
University of California–Santa Barbara; University of California–Davis; University of California–Santa Cruz; University of California–San Diego

FINANCIAL FACTS

Financial Aid Rating	90
Annual in-state tuition	$11,220
Annual out-of-state tuition	$37,902
Room and board	$16,042
Required fees	$2,298
Books and supplies	$1,262
Average frosh need-based scholarship	$20,864
Average UG need-based scholarship	$19,087
% needy frosh rec. need-based scholarship or grant aid	97
% needy UG rec. need-based scholarship or grant aid	98
% needy frosh rec. non-need-based scholarship or grant aid	5
% needy UG rec. non-need-based scholarship or grant aid	3
% needy frosh rec. need-based self-help aid	80
% needy UG rec. need-based self-help aid	55
% frosh need fully met	19
% ugrads need fully met	26
Average % of frosh need met	78
Average % of ugrad need met	81

UNIVERSITY OF CALIFORNIA—DAVIS

UC Davis Welcome Center 550 Alumni Lane Davis, CA 95616 • Admissions: 530-752-2971 • Fax: 530-752-1280

CAMPUS LIFE

Quality of Life Rating	91
Fire Safety Rating	95
Green Rating	98
Type of school	Public
Affiliation	No Affiliation
Environment	Town

STUDENTS

Total undergrad enrollment	28,384
% male/female	41/59
% from out of state	3
% frosh from public high school	84
% frosh live on campus	92
% ugrads live on campus	25
# of fraternities (% ugrad men join)	40 (7)
# of sororities (% ugrad women join)	28 (10)
% African American	2
% Asian	32
% Caucasian	28
% Hispanic	19
% Native American	<1
% Pacific Islander	<1
% Two or more races	5
% Race and/or ethnicity unknown	2
% international	11
# of countries represented	121

SURVEY SAYS...

Students are happy
Students environmentally aware
Students love Davis, CA
Dorms are like palaces
Recreation facilities are great

ACADEMICS

Academic Rating	75
% students returning for sophomore year	92
% students graduating within 4 years	58
% students graduating within 6 years	85
Calendar	Quarter
Student/faculty ratio	18:1
Profs interesting rating	74
Profs accessible rating	70

Most classes have 20–29 students.
Most lab/discussion sessions have
20–29 students.

MOST POPULAR MAJORS

Biology; Psychology; Economics

STUDENTS SAY "..."

Academics

Situated on a "large campus [with] lots of land" in northern California, the University of California, Davis is "a prestigious research university with great professors and brilliant students." With a longtime "focus on the agriculture and biological science," Davis has cultivated a "strong science-based education." Students also praise its "other great programs...such as engineering and political science," as well as the "large variety of majors and [programs] offered" by the university. "Davis does have a fast-paced quarter system," but the "resources available to assist students" help them "feel at ease with their quarters." Beyond the "abundant research, internship, and job opportunities," Davis students rave about the support they receive from "tutoring and advising resources, opportunities to have a focus within each major, study abroad opportunities," and "all the counselors who can answer every question." "Professors here are true experts," and they have generated "a great research legacy in the animal, ag, environmental, health, and food sciences." "Top researchers are clearly going to get a place at UC Davis," which means that "classes are full of challenging, hands-on experiences." Students benefit from "passionate and devoted" scholars who "have their own research projects going on, and apply what they are teaching to their work." Students point out that "research skills do not translate into teaching skills," so some professors who "are pioneers," "superb at research," "and enthusiastic about their field of study" "might not be too good at teaching." But even when professors "seem to be more focused on research," "teaching assistants who want to help students" and "are also really great and amazing people" provide support. These stellar "TAs have a HUGE impact on classes" and contribute to the "very supportive campus community." Overall, UC Davis students agree that "the majority of my professors [care] very deeply about teaching" and provide a "challenging, but rewarding and successful academic experience."

Life

UC Davis students boast about belonging to "green school" that "promotes sustainability." Many students gravitate towards "outdoor activities to fill their time," like "pick-up soccer, slack lining," visiting the local farmers market or "reading at the arboretum." Students tell us that "even if you don't have a car," the "bike paths make it really easy to get around the city and campus" and the "free convenient bus systems" ensure there are "plenty of transportation options" available to students. Many say that Davis owes its "relaxed vibe" to the " close-knit" campus community where "everyone is very supportive of each other" and to the surrounding town that "supports the school." But many students point out that "despite the friendly community, we can still be educationally competitive." The "fast paced quarter system" keeps students busy, but students still say they maintain a good "balance between school life and their social life because of all the opportunities and activities to do on campus." With "700+ clubs on campus including seventy-one Greek organizations," many students spend their weeknights at club events. The downtown Davis nightlife is "mostly low-key," but students can enjoy "good food, open mic night, trivia night," " local shows, line dancing, and just about everything in between." And because it is near "Tahoe, San Francisco, [and] Napa" Davis is "a great location for day trips or weekend trips."

Student Body

Davis is a "pretty diverse community" where most students are "very friendly and thoughtful" and "few are quick to judge." "Most students spend their days biking furiously from class to class," but "everyone is very nice and welcoming." "Anyone can ask any student for directions and the student will gladly stop biking to help out." While Davis "is a top university, you don't feel like everyone is competing against you" and "help from your peers" is easy to find. And while Davis students "are academically rigorous" they are "quirky and [creative]" too, creating "the perfect mixture of serious about studying and down to earth and fun." They like to take advantage of the "beautiful campus," and "on sunny days, the quad is always filled with students lying down or sleeping in the hammocks." "Most people get involved in one of the clubs or athletics" groups, and "most are also very open to making new friends or trying something new."

UNIVERSITY OF CALIFORNIA—DAVIS

FINANCIAL AID: 530-752-2390 • E-MAIL: ADMISSIONS.UCDAVIS.EDU/CONTACT • WEBSITE: WWW.UCDAVIS.EDU

THE PRINCETON REVIEW SAYS

Admissions

Very important factors considered include: rigor of secondary school record, academic GPA, standardized test scores, application essay. *Important factors considered include:* extracurricular activities, leadership/contributions, talent/ability, character/personal qualifications, volunteerism/work experience. *Other factors considered include:* response to life challenges, socio-economic and educational experiences, state residency. SAT and Writing or ACT and Writing required; SAT Subject Tests considered if submitted. TOEFL required of all international applicants. High School diploma is required and GED is accepted. *Academic units required:* 4 English, 3 math, 2 science, 2 science labs, 2 foreign language, 1 social studies, 1 history, 1 academic elective, 1 visual/performing arts.

Financial Aid

Students should submit: FAFSA, State aid form. Priority filing deadline is 3/2. The Princeton Review suggests that all financial aid forms be submitted as soon as possible after October 1. *Need-based scholarships/grants offered:* Federal Pell, FSEOG, State scholarships/grants, Private scholarships, College/university scholarship or grant aid from institutional funds. *Loan aid offered:* Direct Subsidized Stafford Loans, Direct Unsubsidized Stafford Loans, Direct PLUS loans, Federal Perkins Loans, College/university loans from institutional funds. Applicants will be notified of awards beginning 3/16.

The Inside Word

Admission to UC Davis is not as competitive as, say, admission to Berkeley. Nevertheless, every school in the UC system is world-class, and the UC system in general is geared toward the best and brightest of not only California's high school students but the nation and the globe.

THE SCHOOL SAYS "..."

From the Admissions Office

"One of the world's top-tier public research universities, UC Davis offers undergraduates a challenging education and unmatched research opportunities in more than 100 majors. Our community encourages students to ask questions and work alongside faculty members, who are engaged in research and solving today's critical issues. UC Davis supports student involvement in leadership and honors programs, career exploration through internships, learning by studying abroad and volunteering through programs like our student-run community clinics.

"UC Davis students are part of an active, diverse student community on a beautiful campus immersed in the arts and sciences. Aggies enjoy world-class cultural programs at the Robert and Margrit Mondavi Center for the Performing Arts, cheer on our NCAA Division I sports teams, learn how to ride at the Equestrian Center and stay fit at the Activities and Recreation Center. The friendly, supportive nature of our campus and surrounding community welcomes exploration of all kinds: learning about new cultures at a cultural celebration or in a themed residence hall, meeting new friends through our more than 750 student-run organizations, or building a career network before graduation.

"Apply and discover why the value of a UC Davis education and the income potential of our graduates placed UC Davis on The Princeton Review's elite list of *Colleges That Pay You Back*. The UC application is available in August. Freshman applicants are required to take the ACT Assessment plus Writing or the SAT Reasoning Test no later than December. SAT subject tests are not required."

SELECTIVITY

Admissions Rating	90
# of applicants	64,510
% of applicants accepted	38
% of acceptees attending	22
# offered a place on the wait list	9,033
% accepting a place on wait list	30
% admitted from wait list	74

FRESHMAN PROFILE

Range SAT Critical Reading	510–630
Range SAT Math	560–710
Range SAT Writing	530–660
Range ACT Composite	24–30
Minimum paper TOEFL	550
Minimum internet-based TOEFL	60
Average HS GPA	4.0

DEADLINES

Regular	
Deadline	11/30
Notification	3/31
Nonfall registration?	No

APPLICANTS ALSO LOOK AT AND OFTEN PREFER

University of California–Berkeley; University of California–San Diego; University of California–Los Angeles

AND SOMETIMES PREFER

University of California–Santa Barbara

AND RARELY PREFER

University of California–Riverside

FINANCIAL FACTS

Financial Aid Rating	80
Annual in-state tuition	$11,220
Annual out-of-state tuition	$37,902
Room and board	$14,838
Required fees	$2,826
Books and supplies	$1,601
Average frosh need-based scholarship	$20,111
Average UG need-based scholarship	$17,591
% needy frosh rec. need-based scholarship or grant aid	96
% needy UG rec. need-based scholarship or grant aid	96
% needy frosh rec. non-need-based scholarship or grant aid	2
% needy UG rec. non-need-based scholarship or grant aid	1
% needy frosh rec. need-based self-help aid	60
% needy UG rec. need-based self-help aid	56
% UG rec. any financial aid	61
% frosh need fully met	16
% ugrads need fully met	15
Average % of frosh need met	80
Average % of ugrad need met	78

UNIVERSITY OF CALIFORNIA—LOS ANGELES

1147 MURPHY HALL, LOS ANGELES, CA 90095-1436 • ADMISSIONS: 310-825-3101 • FAX: 310-206-1206

STUDENTS SAY "..."

Academics

Undergrads at this esteemed university don't mince words when boasting about all that UCLA has to offer. As a geography and environmental science double-major proudly declares, "There's nothing that can't be accomplished at UCLA. The possibilities are endless, and the resources are unparalleled." Moreover, students appreciate the "ideal" location as well as the "pride of going to a Division I school with more NCAA championships than any other college/university." Perhaps more notable, "UCLA is the kind of school that pushes you to work hard academically but reminds you that interaction with people outside of the classroom is just as important." Students are continually impressed by their professors who are "leaders in their field." Indeed, most consider it "a privilege to study under them." While some undergrads caution that you might encounter some teachers simply "in it for the research," others insist, "Most professors care about their students." A political science major interjects, saying that professors "are willing to work extra hours with students and help us with anything we need." An English major concurs, sharing, "I have never had a professor that I did not feel comfortable approaching, which has made my academic experience incredibly more beneficial." As this grateful junior succinctly explains, "UCLA is the campus. The people, the weather, the academics, the sports; it has absolutely everything I could ever want."

Life

There's so much "hustle and bustle" at UCLA that it would be virtually "impossible to [be] bored." While nearly everyone's "main focus is on school," most students also know how to "play hard." Indeed, "whether it be in Greek life, a club or organization, everybody has somewhere they can go to relax and have some fun. The apartments are close to campus, so nearly everybody lives in a small area with close proximity." Sports "are extremely popular here, and conversations about the Bruins are common." There are also "tons of movie showings on campus, recreation centers, pools, activities, [and] events." Additionally, students love being located in Los Angeles. A happy senior reveals, "You can take a five-minute drive and you'll be soaking in the Pacific Ocean, or take an hour drive where you can be hitting the slopes in Big Bear. You can walk down to the theater and run into Jennifer Lopez or head to the UCLA gym and watch...Kobe Bryant practicing. The possibilities are endless here, with or without money."

Student Body

UCLA "is the mold that fits you." Indeed, more than "26,000 students and more than 950 student groups," virtually assures that "there is no 'typical' student" to be found at UCLA. This wide range of individuals and activities guarantees that "everyone has their niche." Certainly, the Bruin community is a "vibrant" one, and "the unmatched diversity broadens students' horizons culturally and socially." Of course, undergrads here do tread some common ground. Many define their peers as "very hardworking and ambitious," and they typically "strive for success and to do their absolute best." They "know how to have a good time, but they also know when it is time to study." Further, it's an active student body, and it often "seems like everyone is in at least one club or organization." Friendliness is another trademark of UCLA undergrads as a physiology major assures us, "It is very easy to talk to and meet new people and make new friends." Fortunately, most people are "laid-back" and while "academically invested...[they're] not outright competitive with other students." This bio major sums up his peers easily by saying, "Everyone comes from different backgrounds with varied interests. The only common denominator is truly an appetite for excellence."

FINANCIAL AID: 310-206-0400 • E-MAIL: UGADM@SAONET.UCLA.EDU • WEBSITE: WWW.UCLA.EDU

THE PRINCETON REVIEW SAYS

Admissions

Very important factors considered include: rigor of secondary school record, academic GPA, standardized test scores, application essay. *Important factors considered include:* extracurricular activities, talent/ability, character/personal qualities, volunteer work, work experience. *Other factors considered include:* first generation, geographical residence. SAT or ACT with Writing required; SAT Subject Tests considered if submitted. TOEFL required of all international applicants. High school diploma is required and GED is accepted. *Academic units required:* 4 English, 3 math, 2 science, 2 science labs, 2 foreign language, 2 history, 1 academic elective, 1 visual/performing arts. *Academic units recommended:* 4 English, 4 math, 3 science, 3 science labs, 3 foreign language, 2 history, 1 academic elective, 1 visual/performing arts.

Financial Aid

Students should submit: FAFSA. Priority filing deadline is 3/2. The Princeton Review suggests that all financial aid forms be submitted as soon as possible after October 1. *Need-based scholarships/grants offered:* Federal Pell, FSEOG, State scholarships/grants, Private scholarships, College/university scholarship or grant aid from institutional funds, United Negro College Fund. *Loan aid offered:* Direct Subsidized Stafford Loans, Direct Unsubsidized Stafford Loans, Direct PLUS loans, Federal Perkins Loans, Federal Nursing Loans, College/university loans from institutional funds. Applicants will be notified of awards on a rolling basis beginning 3/15. Federal Work-Study Program available. Institutional employment available.

The Inside Word

Competition is fierce to secure admittance to one of the nation's top public universities. Academic success is paramount, and your GPA and standardized test scores factor heavily into admissions decisions. You'll want to load up on challenging courses in high school. Indeed, taking advanced placement, IB, or honors classes is a must. Of course, UCLA also wants students who will actively contribute to their community, and it's also important to demonstrate commitment to extracurricular activities.

THE SCHOOL SAYS "..."

From the Admissions Office

"Undergraduates arrive at UCLA from throughout California and around the world with exceptional levels of academic preparation. They are attracted by our acclaimed degree programs, distinguished faculty, and the beauty of a park-like campus set amid the dynamism of the nation's second-largest city. UCLA's highly ranked undergraduate programs incorporate cutting-edge technology and teaching techniques that hone the critical-thinking skills and the global perspectives necessary for success in our rapidly changing world. The diversity of these programs draws strength from a student body that mirrors the cultural and ethnic vibrancy of Los Angeles. Generally ranked among the nation's top half-dozen universities, UCLA is at once distinguished and dynamic, academically rigorous and responsive.

"All applicants must take the ACT plus writing or the SAT Reasoning Test. Be sure to complete these tests by December. Engineering applicants are strongly urged to take the SAT Subject Test in math level 2, to demonstrate the proficiency in mathematics needed for success in Engineering courses."

SELECTIVITY	
Admissions Rating	97
# of applicants	92,728
% of applicants accepted	17
% of acceptees attending	21

FRESHMAN PROFILE	
Range SAT Critical Reading	570–700
Range SAT Math	600–750
Range SAT Writing	580–720
Range ACT Composite	25–33
Minimum paper TOEFL	550
Minimum internet-based TOEFL	83
Average HS GPA	4.3
% graduated top 10% of class	97
% graduated top 25% of class	100
% graduated top 50% of class	100

DEADLINES	
Regular	
Deadline	11/30
Nonfall registration?	No

FINANCIAL FACTS	
Financial Aid Rating	84
Annual in-state tuition	$11,220
Annual out-of-state tuition	$35,928
Room and board	$13,452
Required fees	$1,743
Books and supplies	$1,383
Average frosh need-based scholarship	$20,255
Average UG need-based scholarship	$18,806
% needy frosh rec. need-based scholarship or grant aid	97
% needy UG rec. need-based scholarship or grant aid	97
% needy frosh rec. non-need-based scholarship or grant aid	2
% needy UG rec. non-need-based scholarship or grant aid	1
% needy frosh rec. need-based self-help aid	59
% needy UG rec. need-based self-help aid	62
% frosh rec. any financial aid	53
% UG rec. any financial aid	55
% frosh need fully met	25
% ugrads need fully met	25
Average % of frosh need met	83
Average % of ugrad need met	83

UNIVERSITY OF CALIFORNIA—RIVERSIDE

3106 Student Services Building, Riverside, CA 92521 • Admissions: 951-827-3411 • Fax: 951-827-6344

CAMPUS LIFE

Quality of Life Rating	83
Fire Safety Rating	94
Green Rating	88
Type of school	Public
Affiliation	No Affiliation
Environment	City

STUDENTS

Total undergrad enrollment	18,608
% male/female	48/52
% from out of state	1
% frosh from public high school	90
% frosh live on campus	73
% ugrads live on campus	35
# of fraternities (% ugrad men join)	20 (6)
# of sororities (% ugrad women join)	20 (10)
% African American	4
% Asian	36
% Caucasian	13
% Hispanic	38
% Native American	<1
% Pacific Islander	<1
% Two or more races	5
% Race and/or ethnicity unknown	1
% international	3
# of countries represented	100

SURVEY SAYS...

Great library
Recreation facilities are great
Diverse student types interact on campus
Frats and sororities are popular
Campus newspaper is popular

ACADEMICS

Academic Rating	75
% students returning for sophomore year	91
% students graduating within 4 years	48
% students graduating within 6 years	73
Calendar	Quarter
Student/faculty ratio	22:1
Profs interesting rating	70
Profs accessible rating	71

Most classes have 20–29 students.
Most lab/discussion sessions have
20–29 students.

MOST POPULAR MAJORS

Psychology; Business Administration and
Management; Biological and Biomedical
Sciences

STUDENTS SAY "..."

Academics

Students at the University of California—Riverside are in love with many things—the "small class size" and "beautiful campus" come up often—but the educators here receive the lion's share of the praise. Professors here are "very skilled in teaching" and "have passion to teach and help their students." Teachers "don't just read from a book and teach you the stuff, they also bring the material to life and make class really enjoyable." This is because they "really know the material they are teaching and are very passionate about it," resulting in "lively discussions" and an "open and diverse campus." This is a school that is devoted to "helping students achieve their academic goals while at the same time connecting them to their community." Some students admit their "overall academic experience has had its ups and downs," saying, "Some classes were interesting and structured well, while others were not," but by and large, educators are "willing to dedicate an enormous amount of time to interact with and help students in order for us to succeed." Career-minded students will find that counselors here are "more than willing to help you with your career path," and the school also "has great connections and support, which is vital for creating a network that helps with internships and future jobs in your major." Graduates of UCR "have integrity, accountability, excellence, and respect."

Life

It's not hard to make friends at UCR, "but I know it would've been easier if I tried joining a club or organization," one student comments, which comes as no surprise, since "many students are involved in campus clubs and organizations." It's easy to find activities for the student who looks, since "there is always an event going on such as athletic games, plays, and musical shows." Students here "aren't under extreme pressure," so they manage to "find the time to explore our own interests and ideas with others." School-based clubs and organizations may be the option of choice, however, since "Riverside city isn't the prettiest, and it gets ridiculously hot during the summer." That said, some students think that "downtown Riverside is beautiful," and UCR students like going there to "go ice skating or shopping at the various malls." Outdoorsy types will be glad to know that the "weather is awesome," and "the beaches are an hour away, and so are the mountains and desert in opposite directions." Active students say, "It's always nice to travel, hike, camp, and just have fun with friends."

Student Body

The active, community-focused students of UCR are "usually part of at least one extracurricular group," the result of "a diverse student body anxious to learn about the world and what they can do to make the world a better place." Though UCR's campus can't be called cozy, it is small enough that "everyone knows everyone through at least one connection." The typical student is "friendly, engaging, outgoing, and eager to learn." Those attending almost universally report that making friends here is easy "because the acceptance level at UCR [among students] is 100 percent." The school "is like a giant melting pot; every student is different but we all fit together perfectly." Getting involved in social causes is not unusual among the student body, though "a typical student is always more worried about their outfits than politics and social issues," which isn't to say many aren't driven by such causes. One student reports, "I like to organize forums and participate in social justice rallies on and off campus." Overall, though, laid-back and inviting is the rule of the day. "Students fit in by being who they are because everyone is friendly," and they "always attend classes, go to org meetings, and campus events, and make it home in time to do four to five hours of studying."

FINANCIAL AID: 951-827-3878 • E-MAIL: ADMIT@UCR.EDU • WEBSITE: WWW.UCR.EDU

THE PRINCETON REVIEW SAYS

Admissions

Very important factors considered include: rigor of secondary school record, academic GPA, standardized test scores, application essay. *Important factors considered include: Other factors considered include:* extracurricular activities, talent/ability, character/personal qualities, first generation, state residency, volunteer work, work experience. SAT or ACT required; SAT Subject Tests considered if submitted. ACT with Writing required. TOEFL required of all international applicants. High school diploma is required and GED is accepted. *Academic units required:* 4 English, 3 math, 2 science, 2 science labs, 2 foreign language, 2 history, 1 academic elective, 1 visual/performing arts. *Academic units recommended:* 4 math, 3 science, 3 science labs, 3 foreign language.

Financial Aid

Students should submit: FAFSA, State aid form. Regular filing deadline is 6/15. The Princeton Review suggests that all financial aid forms be submitted as soon as possible after October 1. *Need-based scholarships/grants offered:* Federal Pell, FSEOG, State scholarships/grants, Private scholarships, College/university scholarship or grant aid from institutional funds. *Loan aid offered:* Direct Subsidized Stafford Loans, Direct Unsubsidized Stafford Loans, Direct PLUS loans, Federal Perkins Loans, College/university loans from institutional funds. Applicants will be notified of awards on a rolling basis beginning 3/1. Federal Work-Study Program available. Institutional employment available.

The Inside Word

The UC—Riverside admissions process is based heavily on quantitative factors. Applicants who have strong GPAs and standardized test scores should have no problem gaining acceptance. There is a priority filing period, so students should apply as early as possible.

THE SCHOOL SAYS "..."

From the Admissions Office

"The University of California—Riverside offers the quality, rigor, and facilities of a major research institution, while assuring its undergraduates personal attention and a sense of community. Academic programs, teaching, advising, and student services all reflect the supportive attitudes that characterize the campus. Among the exceptional opportunities are the Thomas Haider Program in Biomedical Sciences, which provides an exclusive path to medical school: the University Honors Program, an extensive undergraduate research program, UC's largest undergraduate program is psychology, and UC's only bachelor's degree in creative writing. More than 300 student clubs and organizations and a variety of athletic and arts events give students a myriad of ways to get involved and have fun.

"All applicants must take the ACT plus writing or the SAT Reasoning Test. SAT Subject Tests are not required for admission; however, students interested in admission to any major in the College of Natural and Agricultural Sciences or the Bourns College of Engineering are strongly recommended to take the SAT Subject Test math level 2 and the SAT Subject Test in chemistry or physics."

SELECTIVITY

Admissions Rating	92
# of applicants	38,505
% of applicants accepted	56
% of acceptees attending	19
# offered a place on the wait list	6,231
% accepting a place on wait list	60
% admitted from wait list	74

FRESHMAN PROFILE

Range SAT Critical Reading	500–600
Range SAT Math	520–650
Range SAT Writing	500–610
Range ACT Composite	22–28
Minimum paper TOEFL	550
Minimum internet-based TOEFL	80
Average HS GPA	3.7
% graduated top 10% of class	94
% graduated top 25% of class	100
% graduated top 50% of class	100

DEADLINES

Regular	
Deadline	11/30
Notification	3/31
Nonfall registration?	No

APPLICANTS ALSO LOOK AT AND OFTEN PREFER

University of California–Los Angeles; University of California–Berkeley; University of California–San Diego

AND SOMETIMES PREFER

University of California–Irvine; University of California–Santa Barbara; University of California–Davis

AND RARELY PREFER

University of California–Santa Cruz

FINANCIAL FACTS

Financial Aid Rating	83
Annual in-state tuition	$11,220
Annual out-of-state tuition	$35,928
Room and board	$15,700
Required fees	$2,307
Books and supplies	$1,700
Average frosh need-based scholarship	$20,872
Average UG need-based scholarship	$17,712
% needy frosh rec. need-based scholarship or grant aid	97
% needy UG rec. need-based scholarship or grant aid	96
% needy frosh rec. non-need-based scholarship or grant aid	1
% needy UG rec. non-need-based scholarship or grant aid	2
% needy frosh rec. need-based self-help aid	78
% needy UG rec. need-based self-help aid	69
% frosh rec. any financial aid	89
% UG rec. any financial aid	85
% UG borrow to pay for school	69
Average cumulative indebtedness	$21,464
% frosh need fully met	24
% ugrads need fully met	20
Average % of frosh need met	85
Average % of ugrad need met	81

UNIVERSITY OF CALIFORNIA—SAN DIEGO

9500 GILMAN DRIVE, LA JOLLA, CA 92093-0021 • ADMISSIONS: 858-534-4831 • FAX: 858-534-5723

CAMPUS LIFE

Quality of Life Rating	84
Fire Safety Rating	92
Green Rating	96
Type of school	Public
Affiliation	No Affiliation
Environment	Metropolis

STUDENTS

Total undergrad enrollment	26,590
% male/female	52/48
% from out of state	6
% frosh live on campus	95
% ugrads live on campus	43
# of fraternities (% ugrad men join)	24
# of sororities (% ugrad women join)	19
% African American	2
% Asian	46
% Caucasian	21
% Hispanic	16
% Native American	<1
% Other	9
% international	18
# of countries represented	110

SURVEY SAYS...

Students are happy
Great library
Recreation facilities are great
Very little drug use

ACADEMICS

Academic Rating	75
% students returning for sophomore year	95
% students graduating within 4 years	59
% students graduating within 6 years	86
Calendar	Quarter
Student/faculty ratio	19:1
Profs interesting rating	67
Profs accessible rating	66

Most classes have 10–19 students.
Most lab/discussion sessions have
 10–19 students.

MOST POPULAR MAJORS

Economics; Biology

STUDENTS SAY ". . ."

Academics

UC San Diego is widely regarded by students as "one of the top science universities in the United States." As a result, the school attracts bright students who benefit from "access to cutting edge technology and theories" and "great opportunities for undergraduates to do research." Professors "are incredibly knowledgeable about their material, and many of them are actively doing research in their field." Research opportunities are widely available to undergraduate science majors. However, sciences are not the only attraction here. The university is home to six colleges, a system that students say is "a great way to not feel like a small fish in a huge ocean." Whereas it might seem like some science professors "are more interested in research than teaching," students say, "Humanities professors tend to be more accessible and more interested in their students as well as what they are teaching." Overall, however, "professors are very helpful and willing to take extra time to help students understand material." Given the fact that this is a large public university, students say, "Professors are extremely willing to help and mentor students if you seek them out." Another major benefit to attending a large university is that "there are a lot of resources, and there is always a faculty member or organization that will help you achieve what you want." Students say, "This university will undoubtedly set the new standard of what it means to be an elite public university in the years to come."

Life

Students love to take advantage of UC San Diego's "unbeatable location," ten minutes from the beach and a quick ride away from downtown San Diego. It is easy to enjoy "all the nature around the campus by hiking, biking, [and] camping," or taking surf lessons, which "are offered on campus for a modest fee." It is also "super easy to get to San Diego proper for a fun night out." There is a perception that social life is somewhat lacking on the campus itself, which may be the result of UC San Diego being such a large, academically intensive school. While some students have trouble fitting a social life into their busy study schedules, others say that, in fact, there are "tons of resources and ways to get involved" on campus; students "just have to actively seek them." Plenty of people "play sports or participate in clubs." "Lots of people enjoy...small parties but the party scene isn't too big here." In the spring, the Sun God Festival is "always a popular event" that brings the entire campus together. There "is not really a huge emphasis on the athletics department," much to the annoyance of some students. However, students who make the most of their experience here maintain, "There is always an event going on and so many clubs to be involved in. From the Greek life, to the intramural sports, to the variety of clubs, there is literally a place for everyone."

Student Body

The typical student at UC San Diego "is a little nerdy and studies a lot." "Doing well academically at UC San Diego is an extreme priority, even to students who are not good students. Most of the students are geared toward extended education or professional school." However, "there are plenty of students who balance academics with other things, like sports or clubs." The student body "has such a diverse range of personalities" that most anyone "can fit in here because it's such a big school, and there are so many different organizations and places where you can find people that enjoy the same things as you." Students say that the population of students in the humanities has been growing "rapidly" in recent years, but some still see room for improvement among the diversity of the student body. There are those who would love "to see more students become socially conscious" to enhance the overall student body experience on campus.

UNIVERSITY OF CALIFORNIA—SAN DIEGO

FINANCIAL AID: 858-534-4480 • E-MAIL: ADMISSIONSINFO@UCSD.EDU • WEBSITE: WWW.UCSD.EDU

THE PRINCETON REVIEW SAYS

Admissions

Important factors considered include: rigor of secondary school record, academic GPA, standardized test scores, application essay, extracurricular activities, talent/ability, character/personal qualities, state residency, volunteer work, first generation, geographical residence, work experience. SAT or ACT with Writing required; SAT Subject Tests recommended. TOEFL required of all international applicants. High school diploma is required and GED is accepted. *Academic units required:* 4 English, 3 math, 2 science, 2 science labs, 2 foreign language, 2 history, 1 visual/performing arts. *Academic units recommended:* 4 English, 4 math, 3 science, 3 science labs, 3 foreign language, 2 history, 1 academic elective, 1 visual/performing arts.

Financial Aid

Students should submit: FAFSA, State aid form. Priority filing deadline is 3/2. The Princeton Review suggests that all financial aid forms be submitted as soon as possible after October 1. *Need-based scholarships/grants offered:* Federal Pell, FSEOG, State scholarships/grants, Private scholarships, College/university scholarship or grant aid from institutional funds. *Loan aid offered:* Direct Subsidized Stafford Loans, Direct Unsubsidized Stafford Loans, Direct PLUS loans, Federal Perkins Loans, College/university loans from institutional funds. Applicants will be notified of awards on a rolling basis beginning 3/15. Federal Work-Study Program available. Institutional employment available.

The Inside Word

UC San Diego is rapidly earning its place as one of the gems of the UC system, and admission is competitive. Applications are reviewed thoroughly by at least two readers. Applicants will need excellent grades and test scores, and to demonstrate personal qualities like leadership, tenacity, compassion, and independence.

THE SCHOOL SAYS "..."

From the Admissions Office

"UC San Diego is recognized for the exceptional quality of its academic programs. UC San Diego ranks fifth in the nation and first in the University of California system for the amount of federal research dollars spent on research and development; and the university ranks tenth in the nation in the excellence of its graduate programs and the quality of its faculty, according to the most recent National Research Council college rankings.

"About 40 percent of UC San Diego's undergraduates participate in research, developing critical thinking and effective communication skills as well as greater cultural understanding. Their faculty mentors are in the divisions and schools of arts and humanities, biology, engineering, medicine, pharmacy, physical sciences, social sciences, and UC San Diego's Scripps Institution of Oceanography, California Institute for Telecommunications and Information Technology and the San Diego Supercomputer Center. Undergraduates also participate in research at the Salk Institute for Biological Studies and other nearby research institutes and biotechnology companies."

SELECTIVITY

Admissions Rating	97
# of applicants	84,198
% of applicants accepted	34

FRESHMAN PROFILE

Range SAT Critical Reading	560–670
Range SAT Math	620–750
Range SAT Writing	580–690
Range ACT Composite	27–32
Minimum paper TOEFL	550
Average HS GPA	4.14
% graduated top 10% of class	100
% graduated top 25% of class	100
% graduated top 50% of class	100

DEADLINES

Regular	
Deadline	11/30
Notification	3/31
Nonfall registration?	Yes

APPLICANTS ALSO LOOK AT AND OFTEN PREFER

University of Southern California; University of California–Los Angeles; University of California–Berkeley; Stanford University

AND SOMETIMES PREFER

Stanford University; University of California–Davis; University of California–Santa Barbara

AND RARELY PREFER

San Diego State University

FINANCIAL FACTS

Financial Aid Rating	85
Annual in-state tuition	$13,631
Annual out-of-state tuition	$26,682
Room and board	$12,447
Required fees	$1,337
Books and supplies	$1,542
Average frosh need-based scholarship	$13,799
Average UG need-based scholarship	$17,624
% needy frosh rec. need-based scholarship or grant aid	92
% needy UG rec. need-based scholarship or grant aid	94
% needy frosh rec. non-need-based scholarship or grant aid	1
% needy UG rec. non-need-based scholarship or grant aid	1
% needy frosh rec. need-based self-help aid	82
% needy UG rec. need-based self-help aid	83
% frosh rec. any financial aid	77
% UG rec. any financial aid	63
% frosh need fully met	39
% ugrads need fully met	35
Average % of frosh need met	87
Average % of ugrad need met	87

UNIVERSITY OF CALIFORNIA—SANTA BARBARA

OFFICE OF ADMISSIONS, SANTA BARBARA, CA 93106-2014 • ADMISSIONS: 805-893-2881 • FAX: 805-893-2676

CAMPUS LIFE

Quality of Life Rating	93
Fire Safety Rating	95
Green Rating	98
Type of school	Public
Affiliation	No Affiliation
Environment	City

STUDENTS

Total undergrad enrollment	20,607
% male/female	47/53
% from out of state	5
% frosh from public high school	84
% frosh live on campus	95
% ugrads live on campus	39
# of fraternities (% ugrad men join)	17 (8)
# of sororities (% ugrad women join)	18 (13)
% African American	2
% Asian	19
% Caucasian	35
% Hispanic	26
% Native American	<1
% Pacific Islander	<1
% Two or more races	8
% Race and/or ethnicity unknown	1
% international	7
# of countries represented	82

SURVEY SAYS...

Students are happy
School is well run
Students are friendly
Students aren't religious
Students love Santa Barbara, CA
Easy to get around campus
Recreation facilities are great
Lots of beer drinking
Hard liquor is popular

ACADEMICS

Academic Rating	82
% students returning for sophomore year	93
% students graduating within 4 years	68
% students graduating within 6 years	81
Calendar	Quarter
Student/faculty ratio	18:1
Profs interesting rating	81
Profs accessible rating	81

Most classes have fewer than 10 students.
Most lab/discussion sessions have 20–29 students.

MOST POPULAR MAJORS
Biology; Economics; Psychology

STUDENTS SAY "..."

Academics

It's easy to be dazzled by this University of California's "incredible location" in stunning Santa Barbara, but UCSB is much more than a "safe and beautiful campus." "It has one of the top chemical engineering departments in the country," a "highly ranked" mechanical engineering program, and is generally "strong in the sciences." Outstanding students can enroll in the College of Creative Studies, which acts as the university's Honors program and requires a supplemental application: CCS students report that it "allows me to pursue my academic interests with maximum freedom." While they love the "laid-back" atmosphere, students regard their course work in any school as both "academically challenging" and "down to earth": "Every other college on my list seemed locked in an ivory tower. UCSB was the exception with both the warm, sun-kissed charm of a beach town and excellent academics." "I would challenge any Ivy school to match" the quality of professors at UCSB, asserts one student, and another says the "outstanding professors" "are definitely an important source of inspiration for me." Some students comment on the "wide range of professors," and point out that "many of [the] professors are Nobel Prize winners or well-known in their field; however, these individuals are not necessarily the best teachers." Overall, though, UBSB undergrads name the "accessibility and knowledge of the professors" as one of the university's strengths. If you're seeking a dynamic college experience with choices within and outside the classroom, UCSB could be for you: "UCSB is the perfect blend of academics and social life. I get to study at a renowned research university and work closely with professors, while living on the beach and making lifelong friendships."

Life

No matter the activity, UCSB students love to be involved: "85 percent of our student body is in at least one extracurricular activity—and I've met the smartest people of my life here." Outdoor pastimes like "rock climbing, beach volleyball," "surfing and hiking," "bik[ing], skateboard[ing]," figure prominently in students' favorite ways to spend free time wholesomely. After the sun goes down, "a lot of people party at UCSB. What do you expect, we live on a beach? But don't be fooled. I've met some of the smartest, most hard-working people at UCSB." Social life at UCSB is as "varied" as you want it to be: "People think of UCSB exclusively as a party school but it's what you make of it." The party scene "is totally avoidable if you want," but "UCSB is famous for its party life" for a reason. Students looking to avoid drinking and drug culture entirely might be best advised to look elsewhere, and insiders say that "substance abuse is somewhat common off campus and not as much on campus; campus alcohol and drug policies are typically enforced strictly." At the end of the day, "everything is give and take here. You spend your week busting your butt in your internship and churning out research papers, and finish everything up in time to go indulge in some of the debauchery that is DP on a Friday night."

Student Body

To find your place at a big school, get ready to get out and do something: "The typical student is active and involved. Whether it be with sports, or in a community service or environmental club, rock climbing, politics, the list goes on. Students fit in by finding a good group of friends in the dorms and by getting involved in extracurricular activities." Because the university is accessible to so many different types of students, "there is a great sense of community among the students, and those with all sorts of socio-economic backgrounds feel at home here." UCSB undergrads care about more than partying, and are "intelligent, sociable, engaging" as well as "very motivated and driven to succeed academically." People are "laid-back but hard-working," at least partially because "the sunny weather keeps people happy." UCSB is "extremely diverse personality wise": "We've got the hippies, the sorority girls, the surfer dudes, the Jesus-lovers, the anarchists, the school-oriented folk and everything in between. Everyone finds their niche here."

UNIVERSITY OF CALIFORNIA—SANTA BARBARA

FINANCIAL AID: 805-893-2118 • E-MAIL: ADMISSIONS@SA.UCSB.EDU • WEBSITE: WWW.UCSB.EDU

THE PRINCETON REVIEW SAYS

Admissions

Very important factors considered include: rigor of secondary school record, academic GPA, standardized test scores, application essay. *Important factors considered include: Other factors considered include:* class rank, extracurricular activities, talent/ability, character/personal qualities, first generation, state residency, volunteer work, work experience, level of applicant's interest. SAT or ACT required; SAT Subject Tests recommend. ACT with Writing required. SAT with Essay component required. TOEFL required of all international applicants. High school diploma is required and GED is accepted. *Academic units required:* 4 English, 3 math, 2 science labs, 2 foreign language, 2 history, 1 academic elective, 1 visual/performing arts. *Academic units recommended:* 4 math, 3 science labs, 3 foreign language.

Financial Aid

Students should submit: FAFSA. Regular filing deadline is 5/31. The Princeton Review suggests that all financial aid forms be submitted as soon as possible after October 1. *Need-based scholarships/grants offered:* Federal Pell, FSEOG, State scholarships/grants, College/university scholarship or grant aid from institutional funds. *Loan aid offered:* Direct Subsidized Stafford Loans, Direct Unsubsidized Stafford Loans, Direct PLUS loans, Federal Perkins Loans. Federal Work-Study Program available. Institutional employment available.

The Inside Word

UCSB uses a "minimum eligibility" index as a formula to calculate a student's viability for admission; other standards in high school courseload and standardized tests are synthesized with a 3.0 minimum GPA for California students and a 3.4 for out-of-state applicants. Weakness in one area may be balanced out by strength in another, but don't be fooled by the fact that it's a state school: UCSB is competitive.

The School Says "..."
From the Admissions Office

"The University of California—Santa Barbara is a major research institution offering undergraduate and graduate education in the arts, humanities, sciences and technology, and social sciences. Large enough to have excellent facilities for study, research, and other creative activities, the campus is also small enough to foster close relationships among faculty and students. The faculty numbers more than 1,000. A member of the most distinguished system of public higher education in the nation, UC—Santa Barbara is committed equally to excellence in scholarship and instruction. Through the general education program, students acquire good grounding in the skills, perceptions, and methods of a variety of disciplines. In addition, because they study with a research faculty, they not only acquire basic skills and broad knowledge but also are exposed to the imagination, inventiveness, and intense concentration that scholars bring to their work. UCSB is one of sixty-two members of the prestigous Association of American Universities.

"All applicants must take the ACT plus writing or the SAT Reasoning Test. SAT Subject Tests are no longer required by the University of California. Students applying to engineering majors are encouraged to take SAT Subject Tests in math (level 2) and a science exam of their choice."

SELECTIVITY

Admissions Rating	96
# of applicants	70,444
% of applicants accepted	33
% of acceptees attending	19
# offered a place on the wait list	5,006
% accepting a place on wait list	58
% admitted from wait list	10

FRESHMAN PROFILE

Range SAT Critical Reading	550–670
Range SAT Math	580–700
Range SAT Writing	560–680
Range ACT Composite	24–30
Minimum paper TOEFL	550
Minimum internet-based TOEFL	80
Average HS GPA	4.0
% graduated top 10% of class	100
% graduated top 25% of class	100
% graduated top 50% of class	100

DEADLINES

Regular	
Deadline	11/30
Notification	3/1
Nonfall registration?	No

APPLICANTS ALSO LOOK AT AND OFTEN PREFER

University of California–Berkeley; University of California–Los Angeles

AND SOMETIMES PREFER

University of California–Davis; University of California–Irvine

AND RARELY PREFER

University of California–Santa Cruz

FINANCIAL FACTS

Financial Aid Rating	83
Annual in-state tuition	$12,240
Annual out-of-state tuition	$36,948
Room and board	$14,192
Required fees	$1,716
Books and supplies	$1,403
Average frosh need-based scholarship	$20,515
Average UG need-based scholarship	$17,948
% needy frosh rec. need-based scholarship or grant aid	95
% needy UG rec. need-based scholarship or grant aid	96
% needy frosh rec. non-need-based scholarship or grant aid	1
% needy UG rec. non-need-based scholarship or grant aid	1
% needy frosh rec. need-based self-help aid	80
% needy UG rec. need-based self-help aid	79
% UG rec. any financial aid	60
% frosh need fully met	28
% ugrads need fully met	25
Average % of frosh need met	83
Average % of ugrad need met	82

UNIVERSITY OF CALIFORNIA—SANTA CRUZ

OFFICE OF ADMISSIONS, COOK HOUSE, SANTA CRUZ, CA 95064 • ADMISSIONS: 831-459-4008 • FAX: 831-459-4452

CAMPUS LIFE

Quality of Life Rating	74
Fire Safety Rating	80
Green Rating	99
Type of school	Public
Affiliation	No Affiliation
Environment	City

STUDENTS

Total undergrad enrollment	16,231
% male/female	47/53
% from out of state	3
% frosh from public high school	87
% frosh live on campus	98
% ugrads live on campus	53
# of fraternities (% ugrad men join)	6 (5)
# of sororities (% ugrad women join)	11 (7)
% African American	2
% Asian	21
% Caucasian	33
% Hispanic	31
% Native American	<1
% Pacific Islander	<1
% Two or more races	7
% Race and/or ethnicity unknown	2
% international	4
# of countries represented	50

SURVEY SAYS...

Students politically aware
Students environmentally aware
Students are happy
Students are friendly

ACADEMICS

Academic Rating	75
% students returning for sophomore year	87
% students graduating within 4 years	56
% students graduating within 6 years	78
Calendar	Quarter
Student/faculty ratio	19:1
Profs interesting rating	67
Profs accessible rating	65

Most classes have 20–29 students.
Most lab/discussion sessions have
20–29 students.

MOST POPULAR MAJORS
Psychology; Business/Managerial Economics;
Biology

STUDENTS SAY "..."

Academics

The University of California—Santa Cruz offers one of the nation's best combinations of "focus on scholastic endeavors in a beautiful forest setting" and is, by all accounts "a great place to live and study!" Students attribute their enthusiasm to "intelligent, eloquent, and easily accessible professors," academics that are "impressive and challenging," and fellow students who are "happy, open-minded, and a little bit crazy." This school is best suited to those who can motivate themselves in a "chill" environment and the sort of student whose motto might be, "There's no point in learning if you're too stressed to enjoy it." The sciences are "world-class" at UCSC, and the school also boasts "one of the finest engineering programs in the UCs" as well as "a great marine biology program." While the "professors all do research," what sets them apart from those at the typical research-driven university is that "they are very passionate about their subject even when teaching undergrads," and they "also tend to be quite approachable despite having large class sizes and allow students to attend their office hours for extra help." The school also offers undergrads "a lot of opportunities in terms of internships, research opportunities, job opportunities, and networking." "There's a focus on undergraduate study" here, one student contentedly reports.

Life

Undergrads rave about the "take-your-breath-away beauty" of the heavily wooded UCSC campus; one says it's like "taking paths through the forest that resemble Endor only to find a lecture hall at the end." Another adds, "Almost every time my friends and I walk around outside, someone comments on how lucky we are to be surrounded by such beauty. Whether the silvery ocean, the fog in the trees, the wind in the fields of green, the wildlife such as deer, raccoons, squirrels, newts, etc., it all comes together like a painting." The school's setting means "there is much to do recreationally, such as hiking, biking, swimming, trail running, tree climbing, or rock-climbing. You can walk in any direction and find some hiking trail that leads to some other part of the forest." Students note that, "It is also nice to get off campus from time to time and enjoy the city of Santa Cruz. Downtown is lively and usually has something fun going on such as local farmer's markets and cultural festivals." Ambitious students "may head to San Jose or San Francisco on the weekend for a more rowdy bar or club scene." Both cities are "readily accessible via public transportation." The party scene on and off campus consists of "mostly decentralized, smaller parties, due to the near-absence of fraternities and sororities."

Student Body

"The 'stereotypical' Santa Cruz student is a hippie," and the school certainly has its fair share of those, but "there are many different types who attend UCSC." "The typical student is very hardworking," and "it seems that almost every student here has a personal passion, whether it be an activism or cause of some sort, etc.," one student writes. "Everyone is so...alive." "Most are liberal," and there's a definite propensity for earnestness; it's the sort of place where students declare without irony that they "not only possess a great respect for one another but the world and life in general. The world to an average UCSC student is a sacred and beautiful place to be shared and enjoyed by all its inhabitants."

FINANCIAL AID: 831-459-2963 • E-MAIL: ADMISSIONS@UCSC.EDU • WEBSITE: WWW.UCSC.EDU

THE PRINCETON REVIEW SAYS

Admissions

Very important factors considered include: rigor of secondary school record, academic GPA, standardized test scores, application essay, state residency. *Important factors considered include:* extracurricular activities, talent/ability, character/personal qualities, first generation, geographical residence. *Other factors considered include:* volunteer work, work experience. SAT or ACT required. ACT with Writing required. SAT with or without Essay component accepted. TOEFL required of all international applicants. High school diploma is required and GED is accepted. *Academic units required:* 4 English, 3 math, 2 science, 2 science labs, 2 foreign language, 1 social studies, 1 history, 1 academic elective, 1 visual/performing arts. *Academic units recommended:* 4 English, 4 math, 3 science, 3 science labs, 3 foreign language, 1 social studies, 1 history, 1 academic elective, 1 visual/performing arts.

Financial Aid

Students should submit: FAFSA, State aid form. Regular filing deadline is 3/2. The Princeton Review suggests that all financial aid forms be submitted as soon as possible after October 1. *Need-based scholarships/grants offered:* Federal Pell, FSEOG, State scholarships/grants, Private scholarships, College/university scholarship or grant aid from institutional funds. *Loan aid offered:* Direct Subsidized Stafford Loans, Direct Unsubsidized Stafford Loans, Direct PLUS loans, Federal Perkins Loans. Applicants will be notified of awards on a rolling basis beginning 4/1. Federal Work-Study Program available. Institutional employment available.

The Inside Word

Professionally-trained Admissions readers conduct an in-depth review of your academic and personal achievements in light of the opportunities available to you and your demonstrated capacity to contribute to the intellectual and cultural life at UCSC. UCSC's acceptance rate belies the high caliber of applicants it regularly receives.

THE SCHOOL SAYS "..."

From the Admissions Office

"UC—Santa Cruz students, faculty, and researchers are working together to make a world of difference. Within our extraordinary educational community, students participate in the creation of new knowledge, new technologies, and new forms of expressing and understanding cultures. From helping teachers improve their skills to building more efficient solar cells and working to save endangered sea turtles, our focus is on improving our planet and the lives of all its inhabitants. The academic programs at UCSC are challenging and rigorous, and many of them are in newer fields that focus on interdisciplinary thinking. At UCSC, undergraduates conduct and publish research, working closely with faculty on leading-edge projects. Taking advantage of the campus' proximity to centers of industry and innovation such as the Monterey Bay National Marine Sanctuary and Silicon Valley, many students at UC—Santa Cruz take part in fieldwork and internships that complement their studies and provide practical experience in their fields.

"All frosh applicants must take the ACT assessment plus the ACT writing test or the SAT Reasoning Test."

SELECTIVITY

Admissions Rating	94
# of applicants	44,871
% of applicants accepted	51
% of acceptees attending	16
# offered a place on the wait list	0

FRESHMAN PROFILE

Range SAT Critical Reading	520–640
Range SAT Math	550–670
Range SAT Writing	520–640
Range ACT Composite	23–29
Minimum paper TOEFL	550
Minimum internet-based TOEFL	83
Average HS GPA	3.8
% graduated top 10% of class	96
% graduated top 25% of class	100
% graduated top 50% of class	100

DEADLINES

Regular	
Deadline	11/30
Notification	3/31
Nonfall registration?	No

APPLICANTS ALSO LOOK AT AND OFTEN PREFER

Stanford University; University of California–Berkeley; University of California–Los Angeles

AND SOMETIMES PREFER

University of California–Santa Barbara; University of California–Davis; University of California–San Diego

AND RARELY PREFER

University of California–Riverside

FINANCIAL FACTS

Financial Aid Rating	81
Annual in-state tuition	$12,240
Annual out-of-state tuition	$36,948
Room and board	$15,123
Required fees	$1,241
Books and supplies	$1,449
Average frosh need-based scholarship	$19,339
Average UG need-based scholarship	$18,125
% needy frosh rec. need-based scholarship or grant aid	95
% needy UG rec. need-based scholarship or grant aid	95
% needy frosh rec. non-need-based scholarship or grant aid	1
% needy UG rec. non-need-based scholarship or grant aid	1
% needy frosh rec. need-based self-help aid	77
% needy UG rec. need-based self-help aid	77
% frosh rec. any financial aid	67
% UG rec. any financial aid	68
% frosh need fully met	18
% ugrads need fully met	21
Average % of frosh need met	81
Average % of ugrad need met	82

UNIVERSITY OF CENTRAL FLORIDA

PO Box 160111, ORLANDO, FL 32816-0111 • ADMISSIONS: 407-823-3000 • FAX: 407-823-5625

STUDENTS SAY ". . ."

Academics

While it's one of the largest universities in the United States, University of Central Florida manages to maintain a campus with "an extremely welcoming, safe, and comfortable atmosphere." Undergrads also value UCF's prime Orlando location. Indeed, it's "great for finding internships and jobs." As one thrilled architecture major explains, "I can get hands-on experience and connect what I'm learning to actual situations." Overall, the school has a number of fantastic academic programs. However, UCF is an absolute stalwart when it comes to the health sciences. Indeed, the university has "a great reputation [when it comes to] placing their students in good medical schools." Further, the nursing school boasts an "NCLEX pass rate [that] is consistently 95 percent or higher." Fortunately, no matter their chosen course of study, UCF undergrads are fairly happy with their classroom experience. Though a few complain that some professors are more "interested in research [rather than] teaching," most assert that their instructors are "enthusiastic and engaging." Moreover, it's evident that they "care about student success." An electrical engineering student brags, "My professors have helped me become a better student and have personally prepared me for job interviews." And a thrilled biology major concurs, adding, "All of my professors so far have been more than helpful both inside and outside of the classroom and are always willing and available during office hours and [appointments] to talk."

Life

If there's one thing that University of Central Florida undergrads agree on it's that "life is never boring here." After all, given that UCF "is such a large school, there are so many ways...to get involved." Working out is also a popular pastime for students and we've been warned that "the gym is always packed." Undergrads can also frequently be found "us[ing] the pool or play[ing] volleyball at the sand volleyball courts." Additionally, "Lake Claire...is very popular among the student body...[and] provides free canoeing, paddle boating, and kayaking." And while the actual football team isn't especially popular, students do still love to tailgate. For individuals anxious to get off campus, the immediate area surrounding UCF offers "places to shop, bowl, play mini-golf, see movies [and has a selection of] bars if you're into that kind of thing." And, of course, the city of Orlando offers a wealth of attractions including Universal Studios and Disney World, for which students can purchase annual passes.

Student Body

With a student body that's more than 60,000 strong, it's understandable that many UCF undergrads describe their school as a proverbial "melting pot." As an environmental studies major explains, "the student population is a mix of races, a balance of genders, all with a variety of interests and ambitions." Indeed, "UCF is not a cookie-cutter place, where there is a set style." Regardless, there is definitely common ground to be found. For example, the majority of undergrads are "full of [school] spirit no matter the occasion and...bleed black and gold at all time[s]." Undergrads are also quick to describe their peers as "friendly" and "welcoming." A statistics student supports this sentiment adding, "I don't feel like I need to join a certain club or Greek life in order to have friends or feel welcome. Everyone in my classes are polite and kind and always there to work together on assignments or study." All in all, "UCF provides the perfect environment for students to be themselves and fulfill their education at the same time."

FINANCIAL AID: 407-823-2827 • E-MAIL: ADMISSION@UCF.EDU • WEBSITE: WWW.UCF.EDU

THE PRINCETON REVIEW SAYS

Admissions

Very important factors considered include: rigor of secondary school record, academic GPA, standardized test scores. *Important factors considered include:* application essay, recommendation(s). *Other factors considered include:* class rank, extracurricular activities, talent/ability, character/personal qualities, first generation, alumni/ae relation, geographical residence, state residency, volunteer work, work experience, level of applicant's interest. SAT or ACT required. ACT with Writing required. TOEFL or IELTS may be required of international applicants. High school diploma is required and GED is accepted. *Academic units required:* 4 English, 4 math, 3 science, 2 science labs, 2 foreign language, 3 social studies, 2 academic electives.

Financial Aid

Students should submit: FAFSA. Regular filing deadline is 6/30. The Princeton Review suggests that all financial aid forms be submitted as soon as possible after October 1. *Need-based scholarships/grants offered:* Federal Pell, FSEOG, State scholarships/grants, Private scholarships, College/university scholarship or grant aid from institutional funds. *Loan aid offered:* Direct Subsidized Stafford Loans, Direct Unsubsidized Stafford Loans, Direct PLUS loans, Federal Perkins Loans. Applicants will be notified of awards on a rolling basis beginning 3/15. Federal Work-Study Program available. Institutional employment available.

Inside Word

The admissions process at University of Central Florida is fairly straightforward. Expect admissions officers to pay close attention to your high school transcript. Therefore, to be a competitive applicant, you'll need a solid cumulative GPA. Your standardized test scores will also be heavily weighed. Please note that for the 2016–2017 admissions cycle, UCF will accept scores from either the redesigned SAT (out of 1600) or the previous SAT (out of 2400). Finally, though the application essay is not required, UCF strongly encourages serious candidates to submit one.

THE SCHOOL SAYS ". . ."

From the Admissions Office

"The University of Central Florida offers competitive advantages to its student body. We're committed to teaching, providing advisement, and academic support services for all students. Our undergraduates have access to state-of-the-art wireless buildings, high-tech classrooms, research labs, web-based classes, and an undergraduate research and mentoring program.

"Our Career Services professionals help students gain practical experiences at NASA, schools, hospitals, high-tech companies, local municipalities, and the entertainment industry. With an international focus to our curricula and research programs, we enroll international students from 140 nations. Our study abroad programs and other study and research opportunities include agreements with ninety-eight institutions and thirty-six countries.

"UCF's 1,415-acre campus provides a safe and serene setting for learning, with natural lakes and woodlands. The bustle of Orlando lies a short distance away: the pro sport teams, the Kennedy Space Center, film studios, Walt Disney World, Universal Orlando, Sea World, and sandy beaches are all nearby.

"Applicants are required to take the SAT or the ACT. We will use a student's best scores from either test."

SELECTIVITY

Admissions Rating	89
# of applicants	35,572
% of applicants accepted	49
% of acceptees attending	38
# offered a place on the wait list	3,928
% accepting a place on wait list	58
% admitted from wait list	13

FRESHMAN PROFILE

Range SAT Critical Reading	540–630
Range SAT Math	540–640
Range SAT Writing	510–610
Range ACT Composite	24–28
Minimum paper TOEFL	550
Minimum internet-based TOEFL	80
Average HS GPA	3.9
% graduated top 10% of class	33
% graduated top 25% of class	74
% graduated top 50% of class	98

DEADLINES

Regular	
Deadline	5/1
Nonfall registration?	Yes

FINANCIAL FACTS

Financial Aid Rating	80
Annual in-state tuition	$6,368
Annual out-of-state tuition	$22,467
Room and board	$9,300
Books and supplies	$1,146
Average frosh need-based scholarship	$5,382
Average UG need-based scholarship	$5,257
% needy frosh rec. need-based scholarship or grant aid	66
% needy UG rec. need-based scholarship or grant aid	72
% needy frosh rec. non-need-based scholarship or grant aid	65
% needy UG rec. non-need-based scholarship or grant aid	49
% needy frosh rec. need-based self-help aid	54
% needy UG rec. need-based self-help aid	60
% frosh rec. any financial aid	86
% UG rec. any financial aid	78
% UG borrow to pay for school	52
Average cumulative indebtedness	$21,824
% frosh need fully met	8
% ugrads need fully met	7
Average % of frosh need met	55
Average % of ugrad need met	57

THE UNIVERSITY OF CHICAGO

1101 East Fifty-eighth Street, Chicago, IL 60637 • Admissions: 773-702-8650 • Fax: 773-702-4199

CAMPUS LIFE

Quality of Life Rating	92
Fire Safety Rating	95
Green Rating	86
Type of school	Private
Affiliation	No Affiliation
Environment	Metropolis

STUDENTS

Total undergrad enrollment	5,844
% male/female	53/47
% from out of state	85
% frosh from public high school	59
% frosh live on campus	100
% ugrads live on campus	52
# of fraternities (% ugrad men join)	13 (8)
# of sororities (% ugrad women join)	8 (12)
% African American	5
% Asian	17
% Caucasian	44
% Hispanic	9
% Native American	<1
% Pacific Islander	<1
% Two or more races	3
% Race and/or ethnicity unknown	10
% international	11
# of countries represented	70

SURVEY SAYS...

Students always studying
Students are happy
Classroom facilities are great
Great library
Career services are great
Internships are widely available
School is well run
Students aren't religious
Students love Chicago, IL
Dorms are like palaces
Easy to get around campus
Recreation facilities are great

ACADEMICS

Academic Rating	96
% students returning for sophomore year	99
% students graduating within 4 years	86
% students graduating within 6 years	92
Calendar	Semester
Student/faculty ratio	5:1
Profs interesting rating	83
Profs accessible rating	80

Most classes have 10–19 students.
Most lab/discussion sessions have
10–19 students.

MOST POPULAR MAJORS

Economics; Biology; Political Science and
Government

STUDENTS SAY "..."

Academics

Described as "an academic paradise near an awesome city," The University of Chicago is a research institution dedicated to "cultivating a rigorous mentality that enables students to think through and solve any problem they might confront." Students say, UChicago "is a rigorous institution," but they celebrate the fact that "you can't just stick up your hand and not expect to be challenged by your professors and your peers," and note that the professors "are really good at asking students 'Why?' instead of the usual 'What?'" Classrooms are small and foster a "collaborative learning environment." It's a place that "pushes smart people to make new discoveries, challenge their limits, and find new ways of understanding the world." Students say of the faculty that "there's really nothing that compares to working with people on the cutting edge of research and discussing books with their authors," and that they are "very focused on inspiring conversation between students." The "wide array of strong academic programs" offered at UChicago are set on the quarter system, which can be "a bit intensive." "The sheer amount of material one covers in any given quarter is simply massive." If you are up for it, you can "learn a ton" in this fast-paced system.

Life

The College Houses are a very important aspect of student life and gets rave reviews for being a "supportive, fun, community environment" with a "family atmosphere." "Your house becomes your family and the center of your social life on campus. You go to parties with your house, your best friends come from the house, and you will likely move off campus with members of your house. The house system is truly one of the great aspects of the University of Chicago." Although the "harsh Chicago winter" may not appeal to everyone, the city of Chicago clearly does. Students report that "there are a lot of really cool lectures and events for undergrads on campus that enable us to take advantage of the whole university." Students feel that "the nice thing is that everyone here is so unique; you can go from talking about a TV show to religion to career plans—really anything is fair game. And the common Core gives every student some grounds of connection." In terms of social life, one student reports that "I like to have the option of going downtown for fun, or just staying in with friends, or going out. You really do get the best of all of these worlds and have choices, but never are you pressured into doing anything. There is always a group of people willing to do any of those things, so you never have to go through it alone!"

Student Body

Students find it difficult to describe a typical student except as someone "you wouldn't expect. Football players are computer programmers, sorority girls are poets, nerds are hip-hop dance prodigies," and "the lead role in the play is going into investment banking." "It runs the gamut from complete nerd to complete jock. It even includes people who are both!" What students do "have in common is a genuine interest in ideas and a profound investment in the life of the mind." While "students almost always looked stressed . . . they also look like they are loving their stress." Students "fit in by finding other like-minded individuals—either through the house system (the easiest method), by joining clubs, or through classes." Continuing the theme of having dedicated and intelligent students, one notes that "everyone here is so intelligent that sometimes people think they're unintelligent for being surrounded by so many smart people. Everyone is dedicated to something and most everyone has been through significant struggles of some kind." "A typical student loves to learn, does a lot of homework, enjoys their time here, but also loves to complain about it, is probably not religious, has probably considered majoring in econ at one point," driving home the point that economics is, in fact, popular.

FINANCIAL AID: 773-702-8655 • E-MAIL: COLLEGEADMISSIONS@UCHICAGO.EDU • WEBSITE: WWW.UCHICAGO.EDU

THE PRINCETON REVIEW SAYS

Admissions

Very important factors considered include: rigor of secondary school record, class rank, academic GPA, standardized test scores, application essay, recommendation(s), talent/ability, character/personal qualities. *Important factors considered include:* extracurricular activities, volunteer work. *Other factors considered include:* interview, first generation, alumni/ae relation, racial/ethnic status, work experience, level of applicant's interest. SAT or ACT required. ACT with or without writing accepted. SAT with or without Essay component accepted. TOEFL required of all international applicants. High school diploma or equivalent is not required. *Academic units recommended:* 4 English, 4 math, 4 science, 3 foreign language, 2 social studies, 2 history.

Financial Aid

Students should submit: FAFSA, Institution's own financial aid form, CSS/Financial Aid PROFILE. Priority filing deadline is 2/15. The Princeton Review suggests that all financial aid forms be submitted as soon as possible after October 1. *Need-based scholarships/grants offered:* Federal Pell, FSEOG, State scholarships/grants, Private scholarships, College/university scholarship or grant aid from institutional funds. *Loan aid offered:* Direct Subsidized Stafford Loans, Direct Unsubsidized Stafford Loans, Direct PLUS loans, Federal Perkins Loans. Applicants will be notified of awards on or about 4/1. Federal Work-Study Program available. Institutional employment available.

The Inside Word

Students at the University of Chicago dwell on deep thoughts and big ideas. In your application, you'll need to demonstrate outstanding grades in tough courses and that you will fit in with a bunch of big thinkers. Although the University of Chicago uses the Common Application, essay topics remain "uncommon" and thought-provoking. Interviews are optional.

THE SCHOOL SAYS "..."

From the Admissions Office

"The University of Chicago is universally recognized for its devotion to open and rigorous inquiry. The strength of our intellectual traditions—intense critical analysis, lively debate, and creative solutions to complex problems—rests on the scholars who continue to engage them. Graduates of the college have made discoveries in every field of academic study; they are ambitious thinkers who are unafraid to take on the most pressing questions of our time. Their accomplishments have helped establish the university's legacy as one of the world's finest academic institutions. The University of Chicago has been home to eighty-nine Nobel Prize winners, thirty-two MacArthur "Genius" Fellows, and twenty Pulitzer Prize winners. With over 150 research centers and institutes, numerous cultural opportunities, and three of the nation's top professional schools in law, business, and medicine—all within blocks of one another on our campus—UChicago is known for the unparalleled resources it provides its undergraduate students.

"UChicago maintains a student-faculty ratio of six to one, ensuring that every classroom experience exemplifies our commitment to a student's ability to interact closely with our faculty. Our Core curriculum provides students with a common vocabulary and a well-balanced academic experience, while allowing the flexibility to explore their own particular interests in small discussion-style seminars. Students also enjoy a successful Division III sports program, small but active Greek life, over thirty student theatrical productions a year, a rich music scene, celebrations of culture and community—and the extraordinary opportunities in politics, music, theater, commerce, architecture, and neighborhood life in the city of Chicago."

SELECTIVITY

Admissions Rating	99
# of applicants	30,069
% of applicants accepted	8
% of acceptees attending	61

FRESHMAN PROFILE

Range SAT Critical Reading	720–800
Range SAT Math	720–800
Range SAT Writing	700–780
Range ACT Composite	32–35
Minimum paper TOEFL	600
Minimum internet-based TOEFL	104
Average HS GPA	4.3
% graduated top 10% of class	98
% graduated top 25% of class	99
% graduated top 50% of class	100

DEADLINES

Early action	
Deadline	11/1
Notification	12/17
Regular	
Deadline	1/1
Notification	4/1
Nonfall registration?	No

APPLICANTS ALSO LOOK AT AND OFTEN PREFER

Harvard College; Yale University; Massachusetts Institute of Technology

AND SOMETIMES PREFER

Cornell University; Columbia University; Stanford University

AND RARELY PREFER

Washington University in St. Louis; University of California–Berkeley; Northwestern University; University of Pennsylvania; Georgetown University

FINANCIAL FACTS

Financial Aid Rating	96
Annual tuition	$49,026
Room and board	$14,772
Required fees	$1,167
Books and supplies	$1,800
Average frosh need-based scholarship	$46,854
Average UG need-based scholarship	$42,467
% needy frosh rec. need-based scholarship or grant aid	98
% needy UG rec. need-based scholarship or grant aid	100
% needy frosh rec. non-need-based scholarship or grant aid	0
% needy UG rec. non-need-based scholarship or grant aid	0
% needy frosh rec. need-based self-help aid	13
% needy UG rec. need-based self-help aid	47
% frosh rec. any financial aid	64
% UG rec. any financial aid	62
% UG borrow to pay for school	34
Average cumulative indebtedness	$21,291
% frosh need fully met	100
% ugrads need fully met	100
Average % of frosh need met	100
Average % of ugrad need met	100

UNIVERSITY OF CINCINNATI

PO Box 210091, Cincinnati, OH 45221-0091 • Admissions: 513-556-1100 • Fax: 513-556-1105

CAMPUS LIFE

Quality of Life Rating	87
Fire Safety Rating	96
Green Rating	88
Type of school	Public
Affiliation	No Affiliation
Environment	Metropolis

STUDENTS

Total undergrad enrollment	25,054
% male/female	50/50
% from out of state	16
% frosh live on campus	79
% ugrads live on campus	20
# of fraternities (% ugrad men join)	24
# of sororities (% ugrad women join)	15
% African American	7
% Asian	3
% Caucasian	75
% Hispanic	3
% Native American	<1
% Pacific Islander	<1
% Two or more races	3
% Race and/or ethnicity unknown	4
% international	4
# of countries represented	109

SURVEY SAYS...

Students are happy
Great library
Great off-campus food
Recreation facilities are great
Everyone loves the Bearcats

ACADEMICS

Academic Rating	71
% students returning for sophomore year	88
% students graduating within 4 years	30
% students graduating within 6 years	66
Calendar	Semester
Student/faculty ratio	18:1
Profs interesting rating	72
Profs accessible rating	72
Most classes have 20–29 students.	

MOST POPULAR MAJORS

Marketing/Marketing Management;
Psychology; Criminal Justice/Safety Studies

STUDENTS SAY "...

Academics

The University of Cincinnati "offers students a balance of educational excellence and real-world experience" on an expansive campus comprised of eleven separate colleges and two regional campuses. Students agree it's "a large school with many great programs and infinite opportunities that still retains the feeling of a small university." Many have praise for the "cooperative education program that gives students a real edge in the job market" by allowing them the opportunity to pursue competitive internships while enrolled. Students also feel confident that "UC provides excellent opportunities outside of the classroom to make me successful post-graduation." As one student puts it, "The University of Cincinnati is not only known for its great academics, but for all of the incredible opportunities students have including cooperative education, on-campus activities and clubs, along with athletics and one of the most beautiful campuses in the world." The university's size assures that there are "a wide variety of majors to choose from," and students name the College-Conservatory of Music, the School of Architecture and Interior Design, and the engineering programs as stand outs. Nevertheless, many carp, "the school could be a little bit better at communicating" and say the "registration process is terrible." Overall, students feel that "the professors here have so much life experience in what they are teaching. It makes me trust and respect them more," and "Advisors have been helpful." However, they note, "The professors are as diverse as the classes offered here," which means that, "like anything else, there is variation. Some are horrible, and some are fantastic."

Life

It's common for students to remark on the "ample green spaces, [and] innovative architectural designs" that make up the "beautiful campus" at UC. One student explains, "The University of Cincinnati has rewarding educational programs and a beautiful urban campus with many opportunities to stay involved. What more can I ask for?" Although most feel that "campus is very safe," some note, "As soon as you step off of campus, it's a different story." However, many acknowledge, "The school does work hard on maintaining a safe environment for us to live and work in." The majority of students describe campus as having a "fun atmosphere" that makes "UC great" but are divided on the topic of university-sponsored activities. Some think the administration should provide "more afterschool activities," while others believe "UC offers a million and one activities for students to partake in during school and on the weekend. Friday Night Live is an extremely popular program offering awesome activities that don't involve alcohol or drugs." A significant portion of undergraduates are from Cincinnati and point out that UC "is a huge commuter school, so many of the students do things all over the city." However, all agree, "People are very passionate about sports here and have great school spirit." A common campus exclamation is "go Bearcats!!"

Student Body

The most common sentiment from UC students is that "there really isn't a typical student." Although "many students are from Cincinnati," most agree, "UC has students from all walks of life, which makes it extremely diverse and very interesting." While many say, "Students can find their niche, be it in LGBTQ groups, ethnic groups, or academic intercollegiate groups," some reveal that although "students fit in well...racial cliques are obvious around campus." However, all concur that the student body is "outgoing and expressive" and proclaim that "students come together to work on issues they care about such as sustainability." Most UC students can be found in a "sweatshirt, [and] jeans...[with a] coffee in hand," and students like to point out that "many students work as well so they seem to be more 'grounded' and well-rounded." Speaking about the student body, one UC student declares, "The majority are young sports fans that like to party, but being a research school there are some academic heavyweights as well." The consensus seems to be that "students at UC are open-minded, and everyone can find a place to fit in."

FINANCIAL AID: 513-556-6982 • E-MAIL: ADMISSIONS@UC.EDU • WEBSITE: WWW.UC.EDU

THE PRINCETON REVIEW SAYS

Admissions

Very important factors considered include: rigor of secondary school record, academic GPA, standardized test scores. *Important factors considered include:* class rank, application essay, recommendation(s), talent/ability. *Other factors considered include:* extracurricular activities, character/personal qualities, volunteer work, work experience. SAT or ACT required. TOEFL required of all international applicants. High school diploma is required and GED is accepted. *Academic units required:* 4 English, 4 math, 3 science, 3 social studies, and 3 units from above areas or other academic areas. *Academic units recommended:* 2 foreign language.

Financial Aid

Students should submit: FAFSA. The Princeton Review suggests that all financial aid forms be submitted as soon as possible after October 1. *Need-based scholarships/grants offered:* Federal Pell, FSEOG, State scholarships/grants, Private scholarships, College/university scholarship or grant aid from institutional funds, United Negro College Fund, Federal Nursing Scholarships. *Loan aid offered:* Direct Subsidized Stafford Loans, Direct Unsubsidized Stafford Loans, Direct PLUS loans, Federal Perkins Loans, Federal Nursing Loans, State Loans, College/university loans from institutional funds. Applicants will be notified of awards on a rolling basis beginning 3/15. Federal Work-Study Program available. Institutional employment available.

The Inside Word

UC offers hundreds of undergraduate majors and stresses the importance of exploring the specific admission criteria for your program of choice. Prospective students are reminded to work hard while still in high school, with admissions representative saying to hone your GPA from ninth grade on because "it counts!" UC seeks a student who shows evidence of self-reflection. Ideal candidates will exhibit this self-awareness through participation in extracurricular activities that speak to who they are, not to what they think an admissions board wants. Campus visits are strongly suggested.

THE SCHOOL SAYS "..."

From the Admissions Office

"Remarkable architecture, park-like open spaces, engaging student tour guides, and a welcoming admissions staff make the University of Cincinnati a must-visit destination. UC's campus has been transformed over the past ten years and is drawing national and international attention for blending student life, learning, research, and recreation in a unique urban environment.

"UC is a member of The Common Application. Freshman application materials include high school transcripts, test scores, a personal statement, and a list of co-curricular activities. Some academic programs require additional materials.

"Sign up for a visit and request more information via our website. Apply online via The Common Application. Information about all UC majors is linked from the website. Nothing beats a visit for assessing how well you'll fit in here.

"Either the SAT or ACT is required for students applying to bachelor's degree programs. SAT Subject Tests are not required."

SELECTIVITY

Admissions Rating	81
# of applicants	15,286
% of applicants accepted	86
% of acceptees attending	34

FRESHMAN PROFILE

Range SAT Critical Reading	510–630
Range SAT Math	530–660
Range SAT Writing	490–620
Range ACT Composite	23–28
Minimum paper TOEFL	517
Minimum internet-based TOEFL	66
Average HS GPA	3.5
% graduated top 10% of class	21
% graduated top 25% of class	47
% graduated top 50% of class	83

DEADLINES

Early action	
Deadline	12/1
Regular	
Priority	12/1
Deadline	3/1
Nonfall registration?	Yes

FINANCIAL FACTS

Financial Aid Rating	77
Annual in-state tuition	$9,322
Annual out-of-state tuition	$24,656
Room and board	$10,750
Required fees	$1,678
Books and supplies	$1,500
Average frosh need-based scholarship	$6,894
Average UG need-based scholarship	$6,039
% needy frosh rec. need-based scholarship or grant aid	39
% needy UG rec. need-based scholarship or grant aid	44
% needy frosh rec. non-need-based scholarship or grant aid	55
% needy UG rec. non-need-based scholarship or grant aid	39
% needy frosh rec. need-based self-help aid	73
% needy UG rec. need-based self-help aid	76
% frosh rec. any financial aid	84
% UG rec. any financial aid	77
% UG borrow to pay for school	67
Average cumulative indebtedness	$27,938
% frosh need fully met	8
% ugrads need fully met	5
Average % of frosh need met	48
Average % of ugrad need met	46

University of Colorado Boulder

552 UCB, BOULDER, CO 80309-0552 • ADMISSIONS: 303-492-6301 • FAX: 303-492-6301

CAMPUS LIFE

Quality of Life Rating	93
Fire Safety Rating	91
Green Rating	96
Type of school	Public
Affiliation	No Affiliation
Environment	City

STUDENTS

Total undergrad enrollment	27,010
% male/female	55/45
% from out of state	40
% frosh live on campus	95
% ugrads live on campus	29
# of fraternities (% ugrad men join)	18 (10)
# of sororities (% ugrad women join)	14 (19)
% African American	2
% Asian	5
% Caucasian	71
% Hispanic	11
% Native American	<1
% Pacific Islander	<1
% Two or more races	5
% Race and/or ethnicity unknown	1
% international	6
# of countries represented	113

SURVEY SAYS...

Students are happy
Students environmentally aware
Students love Boulder, CO
Great food on campus
Great off-campus food
Easy to get around campus
Recreation facilities are great
Lots of beer drinking
Everyone loves the Buffaloes
Intramural sports are popular

ACADEMICS

Academic Rating	76
% students returning for sophomore year	86
% students graduating within 4 years	47
% students graduating within 6 years	71
Calendar	Semester
Student/faculty ratio	18:1
Profs interesting rating	78
Profs accessible rating	78

Most classes have 10–19 students.
Most lab/discussion sessions have
20–29 students.

MOST POPULAR MAJORS
Physiology; Psychology; Communication

STUDENTS SAY "..."

Academics

Located in the Rocky Mountain region, the University of Colorado Boulder is a "comprehensive public research university" boasting "five Nobel laureates and more than fifty members of prestigious academic academies." It "provides a modern, research-based education that focuses on creating aware citizens to go on to change the world (while having fun)." Students call it a "strong school academically with all the perks of a big state university" including "excellent diversity in subjects and courses, school spirit, packed sports games, and a fun, beautiful college town." Students get to enjoy a "beautiful campus with outdoor-oriented people" in addition to "a great research university," notes an international affairs major. Boulder offers a wide variety of degree programs, but students praise the "top-notch leadership program," "great business program," and "strong physics reputation" in particular. CU-Boulder also offers a "strong environmental program" with opportunities for "both on- and off-campus" study. Students say the professors are "amazing," "approachable," "interested in students personally," and "will treat you as an adult." Professors are "consistently excellent across the wide variety of subjects I have taken courses in, from geography to astronomy and economics to literature," notes one student. "In my four years as an undergrad," says an environmental studies major, "I have traveled places and learned things that I never imagined I would or could experience." In addition, "the price for an education of this caliber is phenomenal," a creative writing major notes. "I was going to a private college for two years and can safely say that this education is significantly better, while the cost is relatively minimal." CU-Boulder is a perfect fit for students who want to be in a "college town surrounded by other young intellectuals."

Life

"Boulder is the best college town in the U.S.," raves one student. With the foothills of the Rockies as their home, "being active and outdoors is a staple for students." "Regardless of the time of day, students can be seen outside relaxing, exercising, or just hanging out with friends," according to one marketing major. Students "go hiking when the weather is nice" and many "go skiing in the mountains on days that [they] don't have classes." Snowboarding is also "extremely popular." And there is also a "prominent night life at the bars," including a music scene that is "diverse and active." Students "go shopping and eat out on Pearl Street" in "downtown Boulder" and "Farrand Field is always busy on nice days with students playing Frisbee, football, soccer, and tanning." It's a "fun college town," and "everyone likes to go out and party on the weekends."

Student Body

CU-Boulder students consider themselves a diverse bunch from "diverse backgrounds" with "diverse passions." "There isn't really a typical student, which is awesome," notes a marketing major. But an international affairs major says, "Students are mostly upper-middle class white kids from Colorado, California, Texas, or Illinois." Typical CU-Boulder students are "kind," "genuine," "smart," and "athletic." They are "outdoorsy, outgoing, and always up for anything." They "love to be outside and often will spend their weekends in the mountains." And though "partying is big," "most take school very seriously and are irritated by [its] depiction as a 'party school'" in the "media." "The school is so large that everyone fits into a group, no matter what your interests are," says an environmental studies major. In addition to those attracted to Greek life, there are "hippy concert going types and everything in between." An architecture major says, those "who make an effort to meet new people and try new things, will be very happy, and have a great time at CU-Boulder." As one student notes: "When I stepped foot on CU's campus, I immediately felt at home." She adds: "Everyone is so friendly and welcoming. It's such a community atmosphere. Everyone watches out for each other and has each other's backs, even strangers."

FINANCIAL AID: 303-492-5091 • E-MAIL: APPLY@COLORADO.EDU • WEBSITE: WWW.COLORADO.EDU

THE PRINCETON REVIEW SAYS

Admissions

Very important factors considered include: rigor of secondary school record, class rank, academic GPA, standardized test scores. *Important factors considered include:* application essay, recommendation(s), extracurricular activities, talent/ability, character/personal qualities, first generation. *Other factors considered include:* alumni/ae relation, geographical residence, state residency, racial/ethnic status, volunteer work, work experience, level of applicant's interest. SAT or ACT required. ACT with or without writing accepted. SAT with or without Essay component accepted. High school diploma is required and GED is accepted. *Academic units required:* 4 English, 4 math, 3 science (2 labs), 3 foreign language, 3 social studies (incl 1 history, 1 geography).

Financial Aid

Students should submit: FAFSA. Priority filing deadline is 3/1. The Princeton Review suggests that all financial aid forms be submitted as soon as possible after October 1. *Need-based scholarships/grants offered:* Federal Pell, FSEOG, State scholarships/grants, Private scholarships, College/university scholarship or grant aid from institutional funds. *Loan aid offered:* Direct Subsidized Stafford Loans, Direct Unsubsidized Stafford Loans, Direct PLUS loans, Federal Perkins Loans, College/university loans from institutional funds. Applicants will be notified of awards on a rolling basis beginning 3/15. Federal Work-Study Program available. Institutional employment available.

The Inside Word

Applicants must apply to a specific school within CU-Boulder. Some programs are more competitive than others. Engineering and Applied Science and the Leeds School of Business are the most competitive. Those who apply to a competitive school within CU-Boulder and are not selected will be automatically entered into consideration for admission to the College of Arts and Sciences.

THE SCHOOL SAYS ". . ."

From the Admissions Office

"Located at the foot of the Rocky Mountains, the University of Colorado Boulder has a breathtaking view from campus. But don't just come for the view. CU-Boulder and its nationally and internationally ranked faculty have built a global reputation for outstanding teaching, research and creative work across more than 150 academic fields. Our innovative academic programs, hands-on opportunities, and rigorous coursework will prepare you for a complex global society. While working with faculty, you'll develop a broad understanding of the world, strong leadership skills and an enhanced ability to think critically.

"Within CU-Boulder's inclusive community, you'll find many ways to get involved and make lifelong friends. We have one of the most active college campuses in the nation, where recreation, sports and student groups play a key role in the unique CU-Boulder experience. We don't claim that we can change the world. Instead, we teach, inspire and encourage our students, faculty and researchers. So they can change the world. Live in spectacular surroundings and learn in a campus environment of extraordinary opportunities.

"Come to CU-Boulder and discover what you can be.

"To find out if CU-Boulder is the place for you, we encourage you to learn more. Check out our website, visit campus or take a virtual tour online.

"Be inspired. Be unique. Be driven.

"Be Boulder."

SELECTIVITY

Admissions Rating	82
# of applicants	31,326
% of applicants accepted	80
% of acceptees attending	25
# offered a place on the wait list	2,110
% accepting a place on wait list	17
% admitted from wait list	0

FRESHMAN PROFILE

Range SAT Critical Reading	530–640
Range SAT Math	540–660
Range ACT Composite	24–30
Average HS GPA	3.6
% graduated top 10% of class	28
% graduated top 25% of class	57
% graduated top 50% of class	89

DEADLINES

Early action	
Deadline	11/15
Notification	2/1
Regular	
Priority	11/15
Deadline	1/15
Notification	4/1
Nonfall registration?	Yes

FINANCIAL FACTS

Financial Aid Rating	85
Annual in-state tuition	$9,312
Annual out-of-state tuition	$32,346
Room and board	$13,194
Required fees	$1,779
Books and supplies	$1,800
Average frosh need-based scholarship	$10,283
Average UG need-based scholarship	$10,248
% needy frosh rec. need-based scholarship or grant aid	76
% needy UG rec. need-based scholarship or grant aid	77
% needy frosh rec. non-need-based scholarship or grant aid	5
% needy UG rec. non-need-based scholarship or grant aid	3
% needy frosh rec. need-based self-help aid	83
% needy UG rec. need-based self-help aid	85
% UG borrow to pay for school	44
Average cumulative indebtedness	$25,605
% frosh need fully met	42
% ugrads need fully met	36
Average % of frosh need met	81
Average % of ugrad need met	79

UNIVERSITY OF CONNECTICUT

2131 HILLSIDE ROAD, STORRS, CT 06268-3088 • ADMISSIONS: 860-486-3137 • FAX: 860-486-1476

CAMPUS LIFE

Quality of Life Rating	85
Fire Safety Rating	91
Green Rating	98
Type of school	Public
Affiliation	No Affiliation
Environment	Town

STUDENTS

Total undergrad enrollment	18,395
% male/female	50/50
% from out of state	22
% frosh from public high school	88
% frosh live on campus	97
% ugrads live on campus	71
# of fraternities (% ugrad men join)	18 (8)
# of sororities (% ugrad women join)	15 (12)
% African American	5
% Asian	10
% Caucasian	62
% Hispanic	8
% Native American	<1
% Pacific Islander	<1
% Two or more races	3
% Race and/or ethnicity unknown	8
% international	4
# of countries represented	113

SURVEY SAYS...

Students are happy
Lots of beer drinking
Everyone loves the Huskies

ACADEMICS

Academic Rating	75
% students returning for sophomore year	93
% students graduating within 4 years	67
% students graduating within 6 years	81
Calendar	Semester
Student/faculty ratio	16:1
Profs interesting rating	68
Profs accessible rating	67

Most classes have 10–19 students.
Most lab/discussion sessions have
10–19 students.

MOST POPULAR MAJORS
Psychology; Biology; Economics

STUDENTS SAY "..."

Academics

The University of Connecticut may be "known for our amazing athletics," but it's also "one of the top research universities and state schools," a "university truly cares about their students." As one political science major puts it, UConn is "unique because it is comprised of all different types of students both in backgrounds and ethnicities. What makes us different than other universities is our cohesiveness despite these differences. We all go to one school, we all cheer on the same team, and we all bleed blue." While "basketball games are like religion," students say that, "UConn is focused on academic achievement." For one student, the school's main appeal is that it is a "large, public university [with] a variety of programs and diversity on campus." As the "flagship state school," UConn provides "research opportunities for undergrads" and "every student is supported in order to be the most successful student possible; UConn cares." When it comes to professors, the "performance level [varies], more so during the first couple years when the students are required to take general education requirements." Students say that in more advanced, major-specific courses, "the professors tend to be more interested in the topics of the course and thus more engaging." Those professors are "truly amazing, inspiring, and add so much to my academics" but the general consensus is that "UConn is a really big university, so professors can be hit or miss."

Life

"Since it's a big school, there is always something going on on campus, whether it's free movies, lectures, concerts, food, or more." For students who want to experience nature, "There's always the opportunity to go outdoors and walk to Horsebarn Hill, go on runs around campus or go on hikes in the UConn forest." Even though the campus a little off the beaten path—one transfer student laments "the nickname for Storrs is Snores"—students say "the downtown area has developed into its own mini city" with restaurants and cafés. As one student puts it, "I am never bored on the weekend between the many shows and concerts, movies and other activities offered by the university." Greek life plays a significant role on campus—some say that "Greek life dominates many aspects of social scene" while others say only that there are "frat parties if you're into that kind of scene." The school's reputation for top notch athletics is legendary; as one student puts it, "the celebrations after victories are unlike anything I've ever experienced elsewhere." Some students are frustrated that "athletics sometimes overshadows academic achievements in funding" but others underscore the rigorousness of UConn's academics, saying "UConn is a research school so classes are difficult and professors will not go out of their way to ensure you get a good grade." When it comes to kicking back after a long week, one student succinctly sums up the alcohol culture at the school: "UConn doesn't seem to be a party school, it is a drinking school—there is a difference."

Student Body

UConn students are typically "very diverse due to the large student body"—you can find "students who love to go out every weekend at the bar [and] you can find students whose hobby is knitting or [to] go to ComiCONN...there really is a peer group for everyone." The students, "the majority of which are from Connecticut," are "uniquely passionate and spirited." As one student puts it, the school is comprised of "many small communities based on academics, sports, clubs, and interests, that come together to form a large community connected by a mutual love of UConn." Some pinpoint the average student as "white, upper middle class and wears L.L. Bean boots, North Face coats" but others stress that "it's a big school, so there is no one word to describe my peers." With "more happening on campus than you expect," there are "athletic teams and Greek life" but also "human rights organizations, activists and volunteers."

FINANCIAL AID: 860-486-2819 • E-MAIL: BEAHUSKY@UCONN.EDU • WEBSITE: WWW.UCONN.EDU

THE PRINCETON REVIEW SAYS

Admissions

Very important factors considered include: rigor of secondary school record, class rank, academic GPA, standardized test scores. *Important factors considered include:* application essay, recommendation(s), extracurricular activities, talent/ability, character/personal qualities, first generation, racial/ethnic status, volunteer work. *Other factors considered include:* alumni/ae relation, geographical residence, state residency, work experience, level of applicant's interest. SAT or ACT required. ACT with Writing required. TOEFL required of all international applicants. High school diploma is required and GED is accepted. *Academic units required:* 4 English, 3 math, 2 science, 2 science labs, 2 foreign language, 2 social studies, 3 academic electives. *Academic units recommended:* 3 foreign language.

Financial Aid

Students should submit: FAFSA. Priority filing deadline is 3/1. The Princeton Review suggests that all financial aid forms be submitted as soon as possible after October 1. *Need-based scholarships/grants offered:* Federal Pell, FSEOG, State scholarships/grants, Private scholarships, College/university scholarship or grant aid from institutional funds. *Loan aid offered:* Direct Subsidized Stafford Loans, Direct Unsubsidized Stafford Loans, Direct PLUS loans, Federal Perkins Loans, Federal Nursing Loans. Applicants will be notified of awards on a rolling basis beginning 3/1. Federal Work-Study Program available. Institutional employment available.

The Inside Word

The UConn admissions committee looks at every aspect of a prospective first year's application, taking everything from GPA, class rank, extracurricular activities, standardized test scores, a required essay, and two letters of recommendation into consideration. The university is a very selective school—college preparatory coursework in high school is required, with additional requirements for School of Engineering and School of Nursing applicants—and students should be sure that all aspects of their application pass muster.

THE SCHOOL SAYS "..."

From the Admissions Office

"Founded in 1881, the University of Connecticut is ranked as one of the best public universities in the United States. With a combination of dynamic faculty, strong athletic pride and an extraordinary sense of community, UConn is a university like no other. Offering over 100 majors and the ability to create a major of your own, a broad range of academic choices is provided. Faculty members are top experts in their fields, and serve as mentors and advisors to students. Distinctive research opportunities pair undergraduate students with faculty in every academic discipline offered. The main campus in Storrs is located in a safe New England town midway between New York City and Boston. With one of the highest percentages of students living on campus of any public university in the United States, UConn is its own community within a thriving rural town. With on-campus museums and performances, and newly-released movies right inside the Student Union's theater, UConn students work hard and play hard. Over 600 student clubs and organizations allow students to pursue their passions outside the classroom. Face paint, chants, and school spirit permeate throughout the campus. Students can cheer on one of our twenty-four Division I teams, or join one of our intramural or club sports teams. No matter how students are involved, they exemplify the Husky Spirit.

"Interested in learning more about what UConn can offer you? For details on the admissions process or to schedule a campus tour, visit admissions.uconn.edu."

SELECTIVITY

Admissions Rating	89
# of applicants	31,280
% of applicants accepted	50
% of acceptees attending	23
# offered a place on the wait list	4,259
% accepting a place on wait list	45
% admitted from wait list	81

FRESHMAN PROFILE

Range SAT Critical Reading	560–660
Range SAT Math	590–690
Range SAT Writing	550–660
Range ACT Composite	26–30
Minimum paper TOEFL	550
Minimum internet-based TOEFL	79
% graduated top 10% of class	50
% graduated top 25% of class	85
% graduated top 50% of class	98

DEADLINES

Regular	
Deadline	1/15
Nonfall registration?	Yes

APPLICANTS ALSO LOOK AT AND OFTEN PREFER

University of Maryland–College Park; University of Delaware; Boston College

AND SOMETIMES PREFER

Boston University; Northeastern University; Penn State University Park

AND RARELY PREFER

University of Massachusetts Amherst; University of New Hampshire; University of Rhode Island; Rutgers, The State University of New Jersey–New Brunswick; University of Vermont

FINANCIAL FACTS

Financial Aid Rating	79
Annual in-state tuition	$10,522
Annual out-of-state tuition	$32,066
Room and board	$12,174
Required fees	$2,842
Books and supplies	$850
Average frosh need-based scholarship	$9,827
Average UG need-based scholarship	$8,754
% needy frosh rec. need-based scholarship or grant aid	68
% needy UG rec. need-based scholarship or grant aid	72
% needy frosh rec. non-need-based scholarship or grant aid	51
% needy UG rec. non-need-based scholarship or grant aid	36
% needy frosh rec. need-based self-help aid	72
% needy UG rec. need-based self-help aid	73
% frosh rec. any financial aid	49
% UG rec. any financial aid	48
% frosh need fully met	14
% ugrads need fully met	13
Average % of frosh need met	60
Average % of ugrad need met	61

UNIVERSITY OF DALLAS

1845 EAST NORTHGATE DRIVE, IRVING, TX 75062 • ADMISSIONS: 972-721-5266 • FAX: 972-721-5017

CAMPUS LIFE

Quality of Life Rating	90
Fire Safety Rating	87
Green Rating	60*
Type of school	Private
Affiliation	Roman Catholic
Environment	City

STUDENTS

Total undergrad enrollment	1,342
% male/female	44/56
% from out of state	54
% frosh from public high school	50
% frosh live on campus	90
% ugrads live on campus	68
% African American	2
% Asian	5
% Caucasian	65
% Hispanic	21
% Native American	<1
% Pacific Islander	<1
% Two or more races	3
% Race and/or ethnicity unknown	1
% international	2
# of countries represented	19

SURVEY SAYS...

Lots of conservative students
Students are happy
Great financial aid
Students are friendly
Students are very religious
Intramural sports are popular
Theater is popular
Campus newspaper is popular

ACADEMICS

Academic Rating	82
% students returning for sophomore year	81
% students graduating within 4 years	66
% students graduating within 6 years	70
Calendar	Semester
Student/faculty ratio	10:1
Profs interesting rating	92
Profs accessible rating	91

Most classes have 10–19 students.
Most lab/discussion sessions have 10–19 students.

MOST POPULAR MAJORS
English; Biology; History

STUDENTS SAY "..."

Academics

Students overwhelmingly choose the University of Dallas for its "liberal arts core and strong Catholic identity," saying that "what the University of Dallas offers is education as formation." UD's "core curriculum forces you to learn an extensive amount of information and broadens your horizons in classical education," and some of its 1,300 undergrads feel it makes UD "the best academically rigorous Catholic liberal arts university in the country." As on student puts it, "UD has an incredibly strong Core program, and I wanted to make sure I left college with a comprehensive education. As a senior, I feel prepared for a job in any field." Through "liberal education in the western intellectual tradition, grounded on a firm fidelity to the Catholic Church," "The University of Dallas strives for the attainment of the truth, by the practicing virtue, in the light of wisdom." Undergraduates report that "our professors' dedication to our student body is truly inspiring. They are always available. They participate in school events. Their passion and expertise is tangible in class." One student argues that because "the professors expect a lot out of students, they actually help students achieve new intellectual heights," and another feels "like most professors are not satisfied with students just "getting by" and not truly learning, which makes for a rigorous and fruitful academic experience." Students see themselves as united in UD's "common sense of purpose" among "students, alumni, faculty, and the administration" to produce "independent and critically-thinking Catholics, able to communicate effectively with a keen understanding of what it means to be a socially aware and responsible person." UD's "study abroad program in Rome" is also hugely popular. "The success of our alumni is a testament to the quality of the education offered by the University of Dallas," and "only at UD could the liberal arts meet the hard sciences in . . . a cohesive manner that produces truly well-rounded, well-spoken, independent intellectuals."

Life

Of University of Dallas's social culture, one student says, "The sport here is engaging in intellectual debates." It's widely agreed upon that "you can always find a good intellectual discussion at UD," which "often gravitate towards your favorite books, a paper/project you're working on or what your thesis is about. The whole world becomes your classroom, effectively." "There is a wide variety of social milieus" and "quite a few people party hard, but there are plenty of musical, literary, or sporting opportunities for students." UD has its "own train station as part of the Dallas Transit system, making excursions to downtown, Uptown, Deep Ellum, the Dallas House of Blues, and the Bishop Arts District very easy." Also, the Dallas Museum of Art is free for UD students, and the university "does an outstanding job of making cheap tickets available for students to a variety of events—everything from Cowboys/Rangers/Mavericks games to the Dallas Opera and indoor skydiving." "Two-stepping and swing dancing are popular favorites here" and "theological and academic lectures are also given some evenings." Overall, "the University of Dallas is not all about academics, it's about living a balanced life (spiritually, intellectually, and physically). So students bring all of these things together in practically everything they do."

Student Body

The typical UD student often, but not always, is "conservative and Catholic, regularly attends church, devotes a great deal of time to schoolwork, and drinks a significant amount from Thursday to Saturday." Undergrads "all accept each other here no matter how different we are," share "a desire to learn more about the world," and are "friendly and intelligent enough to carry on a good conversation on nearly any subject." Many grew up in "stable, middle-class, Christian homes," and they pride themselves on being "very kind and Catholic." "All students are warm and welcoming. Friendliness and agreeableness is an overwhelming feeling. Students need only be nice and approachable to fit in." UD students call themselves "open" and "passionate," and say that "students fit in really well here regardless of whether they come from different cultures or backgrounds."

FINANCIAL AID: 972-721-5266 • E-MAIL: UGADMIS@UDALLAS.EDU • WEBSITE: WWW.UDALLAS.EDU

THE PRINCETON REVIEW SAYS

Admissions

Very important factors considered include: rigor of secondary school record, academic GPA, standardized test scores, application essay, recommendation(s), character/personal qualities. *Important factors considered include:* talent/ability. *Other factors considered include:* class rank, interview, extracurricular activities, first generation, alumni/ae relation, volunteer work, work experience, level of applicant's interest. SAT or ACT required. ACT with Writing recommended. SAT with Essay component recommended. TOEFL required of all international applicants. High school diploma is required and GED is accepted. *Academic units required:* 4 English, 3 math, 3 science, 2 foreign language, 3 social studies, 3 history, 4 academic electives, 2 visual/performing arts. *Academic units recommended:* 4 English, 4 math, 3 science, 3 science labs, 3 foreign language, 4 social studies, 4 history, 4 academic electives, 2 visual/performing arts.

Financial Aid

Students should submit: FAFSA. Priority filing deadline is 3/1. The Princeton Review suggests that all financial aid forms be submitted as soon as possible after October 1. *Need-based scholarships/grants offered:* Federal Pell, FSEOG, State scholarships/grants, Private scholarships, College/university scholarship or grant aid from institutional funds. *Loan aid offered:* Direct Subsidized Stafford Loans, Direct Unsubsidized Stafford Loans, Direct PLUS loans, Federal Perkins Loans, State Loans. Applicants will be notified of awards on a rolling basis beginning 3/1. Federal Work-Study Program available. Institutional employment available.

The Inside Word

Because of University of Dallas's distinction as a Catholic liberal arts school, its applicant pool is frequently small but self-selective. As such, don't be fooled by its relatively high acceptance rate—strong academic performance and test scores are closely considered, as are students who demonstrate moral and ethical commitment in addition to intellectual curiosity.

THE SCHOOL SAYS "..."

From the Admissions Office

"Quite unabashedly, the curriculum at the University of Dallas is based on the supposition that truth and virtue exist and are the proper objects of search in an education. The curriculum further supposes that this search is best pursued through an acquisition of philosophical and theological principles on the part of a student and has for its analogical field a vast body of great literature—perhaps more extensive than is likely to be encountered elsewhere—supplemented by a survey of the sweep of history and an introduction to the political and economic principles of society. An understanding of these subjects, along with an introduction to the quantitative and scientific worldview and a mastery of a language, is expected to form a comprehensive and coherent experience, which, in effect, governs the intellect of a student in a manner that develops independence of thought in its most effective mode."

SELECTIVITY

Admissions Rating	86
# of applicants	2,001
% of applicants accepted	83
% of acceptees attending	24

FRESHMAN PROFILE

Range SAT Critical Reading	540–690
Range SAT Math	540–650
Range SAT Writing	530–650
Range ACT Composite	24–30
Minimum internet-based TOEFL	79
Average HS GPA	3.8
% graduated top 10% of class	39
% graduated top 25% of class	67
% graduated top 50% of class	88

DEADLINES

Early action	
Deadline	11/1
Notification	12/1
Regular	
Priority	1/15
Deadline	8/1
Nonfall registration?	Yes

APPLICANTS ALSO LOOK AT AND OFTEN PREFER

University of Notre Dame; Texas A&M University–College Station

AND SOMETIMES PREFER

Austin College; Trinity University; The Catholic University of America

AND RARELY PREFER

The University of Texas at Austin; Texas Christian University

FINANCIAL FACTS

Financial Aid Rating	85
Annual tuition	$34,650
Room and board	$11,540
Required fees	$2,580
Books and supplies	$1,200
Average frosh need-based scholarship	$28,287
Average UG need-based scholarship	$25,113
% needy frosh rec. need-based scholarship or grant aid	99
% needy UG rec. need-based scholarship or grant aid	98
% needy frosh rec. non-need-based scholarship or grant aid	0
% needy UG rec. non-need-based scholarship or grant aid	0
% needy frosh rec. need-based self-help aid	65
% needy UG rec. need-based self-help aid	71
% frosh rec. any financial aid	96
% UG rec. any financial aid	94
% UG borrow to pay for school	58
Average cumulative indebtedness	$33,511
% frosh need fully met	21
% ugrads need fully met	24
Average % of frosh need met	83
Average % of ugrad need met	80

UNIVERSITY OF DAYTON

300 COLLEGE PARK, DAYTON, OH 45469-1669 • ADMISSIONS: 1-800-837-7433 • FAX: 937-229-4729

STUDENTS SAY "..."

Academics

The University of Dayton is a Roman Catholic research university, founded in 1850 by the Society of Mary, and the largest private university in Ohio. It has grown to 8,600 undergraduate students and honors its roots by continuing to encourage "Marianist values including faith, service, and community." An "inclusive and diverse school with programs and activities for everyone," students regularly praise the "importance of community" and "making a difference in the world." UD "strives to represent community through its dedicated professors, friendly students," and "welcoming atmosphere." Students say this "togetherness and community" at Dayton "is something most people don't get at other schools." "It's about making connections that will last a lifetime," notes a Biology major, "whether it is friends or relationships with professors." UD professors are "helpful" and "friendly" and thanks to "UD's unique small class sizes, are always willing to meet out of class and help you to understand the material." Even when teaching difficult material, they "provide an environment in which you are comfortable enough to ask for help." The professors go out of their way to "help those students who are struggling in classes, social, and religious life." "A medium-size school" with "the perks of a large university," students here are "committed to the pursuit of knowledge, the betterment of the community, and the quest for an education of the whole person." For students, UD becomes a "second home and family," providing them "with a strong faith community, education, and support from faculty and staff."

Life

"Life at school is awesome," says a Marketing major. UD "provides a perfect home away from home in the sense that there is a place for everyone." And though students at UD "take school work very seriously," "there is also a fun and care-free atmosphere and vibe." "It's the perfect balance!" Students can join a "multitude of organizations," "fraternities, and sororities." There are regular "campus wide events," as well as "nearby bars," and "house parties," for those so inclined. There are also lots of "non drinking activities," including "bowling, basketball, swimming, soccer, volleyball, movies, game nights, and much more." Students frequent "nearby malls," hang out on "ArtStreet and see student bands," visit "the Oregon District [in] downtown Dayton" and Brown Street "where all the restaurants are." On campus, there is a "bowling alley and billiard hall." "You never find yourself bored or out of options," says an Early Education major. "Almost every student is involved with intramural sports," and the student body "cares deeply about our basketball team." The Flyers, as they are called, reached the NCAA Division I Elite Eight in 2014 (men) and 2015 (women), and the basketball team is "extremely popular and is watched and celebrated by all." In fact, the team regularly ranks in the top thirty for basketball attendance. For students interested in getting off campus, there are "study abroad programs" and "immersion retreats."

Student Body

UD students consider their classmates "open," "happy," "ready to share" and "very welcoming." They are "intelligent" and "outgoing." UD students are "highly involved in not only their studies but also extracurriculars" and "they are passionate about their major." Most students are "very conscious about community service and are very friendly." This sense of community encourages students to be "very respectful of beliefs/values," as well as to be helpful community members who "hold doors/elevators open," and "ask if you are okay if you look sad." The typical student is "white," "Catholic," and "upper-middle class." But even though the "majority of students are white," there is "a diverse range of other races."

FINANCIAL AID: 1-800-837-7433 • E-MAIL: ADMISSION@UDAYTON.EDU • WEBSITE: WWW.UDAYTON.EDU

THE PRINCETON REVIEW SAYS

Admissions

Very important factors considered include: rigor of secondary school record, academic GPA, standardized test scores, application essay. *Important factors considered include:* recommendation(s), extracurricular activities, character/personal qualities, alumni/ae relation, level of applicant's interest. *Other factors considered include:* class rank, talent/ability, first generation, racial/ethnic status, volunteer work, work experience. SAT or ACT required. TOEFL required of all international applicants. High school diploma is required and GED is accepted. *Academic units recommended:* 4 English, 4 math, 4 science, 1 science lab, 2 foreign language, 4 social studies, 4 history, 4 computer science, 4 visual/performing arts.

Financial Aid

Students should submit: FAFSA. Priority filing deadline is 2/1. The Princeton Review suggests that all financial aid forms be submitted as soon as possible after October 1. *Need-based scholarships/grants offered:* Federal Pell, FSEOG, State scholarships/grants, Private scholarships, College/university scholarship or grant aid from institutional funds. *Loan aid offered:* Direct Subsidized Stafford Loans, Direct Unsubsidized Stafford Loans, Direct PLUS loans, Federal Perkins Loans. Applicants will be notified of awards on a rolling basis beginning 2/15. Federal Work-Study Program available. Institutional employment available.

The Inside Word

Though a top-tier research university, University of Dayton has less stringent acceptance criteria than Georgetown or Notre Dame, and gives "balanced consideration" to all academic factors on the application. Students with a strong commitment to community service, extracurricular activities, and decent grades will most likely be accepted. Students apply to UD on the general admission application (or Common Application). Their application is then reviewed for admission to the academic major or program they selected, and different majors may have slightly different admission criteria.

THE SCHOOL SAYS "..."

From the Admissions Office

"The University of Dayton founded in 1850 by the Society of Mary, is a top ten Catholic research university. The university seeks outstanding diverse faculty, staff, and students who value its mission and share its commitment to academic excellence in teaching, study, research and creativity, the development of the whole person, and leadership and service in the local and global community. More than eighty challenging academic programs are offered in the College of Arts and Sciences and the Schools of Business Administration, Education and Health Sciences, Engineering, and Law. Classes are small— twenty-seven students on average. Our faculty are committed to teaching undergraduate students and involving them in their research projects. The University of Dayton Research Institute ranks second in the nation in the amount of materials research performed annually. Technology-enhanced learning ensures students gain expertise in the tools that will prepare them for the future. Students can spend a full semester at the China Institute in Suzhou, China, for the same cost as a semester on campus. Recent campus construction provides a modern home for the university's cutting-edge academic programs. A fitness and recreation complex, the RecPlex, provides 130,000 square feet of space for classrooms, courts, a natatorium, and other recreational facilities. A strong sense of community is a hallmark feature of the university; an emphasis on leadership and service contributes to students' participation in more than 180 clubs and organizations. Division I intercollegiate athletics and club and intramural sports are also popular."

SELECTIVITY

Admissions Rating	86
# of applicants	16,968
% of applicants accepted	58
% of acceptees attending	22

FRESHMAN PROFILE

Range SAT Critical Reading	510–620
Range SAT Math	520–630
Range SAT Writing	520–610
Range ACT Composite	24–29
Minimum paper TOEFL	550
Minimum internet-based TOEFL	80
Average HS GPA	3.6
% graduated top 10% of class	25
% graduated top 25% of class	58
% graduated top 50% of class	88

DEADLINES

Early action	
Deadline	11/1
Notification	12/15
Regular	
Priority	11/1
Deadline	2/1
Notification	2/15
Nonfall registration?	Yes

APPLICANTS ALSO LOOK AT AND OFTEN PREFER

The Ohio State University–Columbus; Miami University

AND SOMETIMES PREFER

Indiana University Bloomington; Xavier University (OH); University of Cincinnati; Saint Louis University; Purdue University–West Lafayette

AND RARELY PREFER

Ohio University–Athens; Marquette University; Loyola University of Chicago

FINANCIAL FACTS

Financial Aid Rating	86
Annual tuition	$39,090
Room and board	$12,190
Books and supplies	$1,000
Average frosh need-based scholarship	$23,610
Average UG need-based scholarship	$20,508
% needy frosh rec. need-based scholarship or grant aid	100
% needy UG rec. need-based scholarship or grant aid	99
% needy frosh rec. non-need-based scholarship or grant aid	19
% needy UG rec. non-need-based scholarship or grant aid	20
% needy frosh rec. need-based self-help aid	85
% needy UG rec. need-based self-help aid	83
% frosh rec. any financial aid	98
% UG rec. any financial aid	94
% frosh need fully met	31
% ugrads need fully met	35
Average % of frosh need met	86
Average % of ugrad need met	84

UNIVERSITY OF DELAWARE

210 SOUTH COLLEGE AVENUE, NEWARK, DE 19716-6210 • ADMISSIONS: 302-831-8123 • FAX: 302-831-6905

CAMPUS LIFE

Quality of Life Rating	88
Fire Safety Rating	98
Green Rating	71
Affiliation	No Affiliation
Environment	Town

STUDENTS

Total undergrad enrollment	17,575
% male/female	42/58
% from out of state	62
% frosh from public high school	80
% frosh live on campus	94
% ugrads live on campus	43
# of fraternities (% ugrad men join)	24 (19)
# of sororities (% ugrad women join)	19 (23)
% African American	5
% Asian	5
% Caucasian	75
% Hispanic	7
% Native American	<1
% Pacific Islander	<1
% Two or more races	3
% Race and/or ethnicity unknown	1
% international	4
# of countries represented	82

SURVEY SAYS...

Students are happy
Students love Newark, DE
Lots of beer drinking
Frats and sororities are popular

ACADEMICS

Academic Rating	77
% students returning for sophomore year	92
% students graduating within 4 years	65
% students graduating within 6 years	81
Calendar	4/1/4
Student/faculty ratio	13:1
Profs interesting rating	70
Profs accessible rating	77

Most classes have 20–29 students.
Most lab/discussion sessions have 10–19 students.

MOST POPULAR MAJORS
Finance; Nursing

STUDENTS SAY "..."

Academics

As the largest university in the state, the University of Delaware is a medium-sized interdisciplinary school with "a wide range of opportunities [and] full of students with pride, ambition and eagerness to make impact during the college years and beyond." This research university offers over 135 majors and plenty of chances to get into the lab, classroom, or a real world setting for your major (particularly for the school's notable STEM and health-related programs). One strong aspect of UD is their range of 4+1 programs, which allow a student to receive a master's degree in the year immediately following the completion of their bachelor's, and "the unusual schedule (winter session)" allows for students to take advantage of the "variety of study abroad programs" through a short-term study abroad program.

Professors here are "helpful and available outside of the classroom," "invested in their classes," and "truly want students to succeed." The school's "many support systems and safety nets" ensure that students never get lost in the crowd. "Those who are falling behind have many resources they can refer to," says an early childhood education major. Students admit that teaching here can be "hit or miss" in terms of the quality of lectures, so "It is usually good to get in touch with other students and find out what professors are good or bad." Many professors conduct research or are involved with organizations around campus, and "they're always willing to let students join them or get more involved," as well.

Life

The beautiful campus is "so pleasing" that students immediately fall in love with the campus and offers "many places to study or just hang out and enjoy the company of fellow Blue Hens." Hanging out on Main Street is also "a big thing here," and its proximity means that "you don't feel confined to a campus because you can enjoy different restaurants and shopping." School work is "a large part of the day," however, "everyone gets their work done to be able to be social during the night." Small mixers and socials are held during the week, while weekends find a large chunk of students going to bars or house parties. Greek life is "definitely prominent" and tends to be popular on campus, and some say "you can't go a single day without seeing a fraternity or sorority event or fundraiser." For students who aren't on the hunt for a party, "there are more and more alternatives to parties for the students who are not big into partying," such the weekly events at the student center on Friday and Saturday nights.

Student Body

Students have "a plethora of opportunities to get involved with any number of clubs and activities all over campus" and the majority are involved with "Greek life, club sports, interest clubs, or working for the university." The Delaware student body "has a lot of school spirit" and is a welcoming bunch: "Everyone is so friendly and nice it seems impossible to think you would ever meet someone otherwise." Though UD is "not very diverse in a sense of... ethnicity," it is "very diverse...regarding personality" so "everyone should be able to find the right group for them." There is a strong interest in the many registered student organizations on campus grounds to help students find communities, but no matter what your interests are at UD, "whenever you go anywhere you see many smiling faces."

FINANCIAL AID: 302-831-8761 • E-MAIL: ADMISSIONS@UDEL.EDU • WEBSITE: WWW.UDEL.EDU

THE PRINCETON REVIEW SAYS

Admissions

Very important factors considered include: rigor of secondary school record, academic GPA, state residency. *Important factors considered include:* standardized test scores, application essay, recommendation(s), extracurricular activities, talent/ability, character/personal qualities, volunteer work, work experience. *Other factors considered include:* class rank, interview, first generation, alumni/ae relation, geographical residence, racial/ethnic status, level of applicant's interest. SAT or ACT required; SAT Subject Tests recommend. ACT with Writing required. TOEFL required of all international applicants. High school diploma is required and GED is accepted. *Academic units required:* 4 English, 3 math, 3 science, 2 science labs, 2 foreign language, 2 social studies, 2 history, 2 academic electives. *Academic units recommended:* 4 English, 4 math, 4 science, 3 science labs, 4 foreign language, 2 social studies, 2 history.

Financial Aid

Students should submit: FAFSA. Regular filing deadline is 3/15. The Princeton Review suggests that all financial aid forms be submitted as soon as possible after October 1. *Need-based scholarships/grants offered:* Federal Pell, FSEOG, State scholarships/grants, Private scholarships, College/university scholarship or grant aid from institutional funds. *Loan aid offered:* Direct Subsidized Stafford Loans, Direct Unsubsidized Stafford Loans, Direct PLUS loans, Federal Perkins Loans, Federal Nursing Loans. Applicants will be notified of awards on a rolling basis beginning 3/15. Federal Work-Study Program available. Institutional employment available.

Inside Word

Although UD is run by the state of Delaware, out-of-state students also benefit from the school's academic and social offerings at a reasonable tuition. Even so, the school is expressly committed to supporting Delawarean students, who compose about 30 percent of each incoming class (close to 90 percent of Delawareans who apply are admitted to UD). More details and samples of qualifying high school curricula are available on the admissions department website. In all admissions decisions, UD considers the entirety of a student's application; there are no minimum test scores or GPAs.

THE SCHOOL SAYS "..."

From the Admissions Office

"An East Coast classic, the University of Delaware is a rich, historic campus in Newark, Delaware, midway between New York City and Washington, D.C. UD is known for its problem-based, hands-on learning in every college and a relatively small enrollment that engages students with interested, accessible faculty. Over 90 percent of our students land jobs within six months of graduation and continue their educations at the top graduate and professional schools in the world. Three signers of the Declaration of Independence were among our first class and recent alumni include the vice president of the United States, the governor of New Jersey, and the top campaign strategist for the president of the United States. UD is also a talent magnet, attracting top scholars and innovators, including a recent Nobel Prize winner and a Rhodes Scholar. The University of Delaware is working on the most compelling social, civic, artistic, and scientific challenges of our age. As the flagship university in the first state of the union, we dare to be first in ways that matter—first in new energy technologies, first in global study, first in political leadership, first in interdisciplinary engineering, first in educating teachers, first in design innovation, first in championship athletics, first in translational medicine. We challenge our students to be first in what matters most to them."

SELECTIVITY

Admissions Rating	88
# of applicants	24,881
% of applicants accepted	63
% of acceptees attending	26
# offered a place on the wait list	2,138
% accepting a place on wait list	40
% admitted from wait list	0

FRESHMAN PROFILE

Range SAT Critical Reading	550–650
Range SAT Math	560–660
Range SAT Writing	550–650
Range ACT Composite	25–29
Minimum paper TOEFL	570
Minimum internet-based TOEFL	90
Average HS GPA	3.7
% graduated top 10% of class	33
% graduated top 25% of class	68
% graduated top 50% of class	94

DEADLINES

Regular	
Deadline	1/15
Nonfall registration?	Yes

APPLICANTS ALSO LOOK AT AND OFTEN PREFER

University of Pennsylvania; Princeton University; College of William and Mary

AND SOMETIMES PREFER

Cornell University; University of Virginia; New York University; Brandeis University; University of Michigan–Ann Arbor

AND RARELY PREFER

Northeastern University; Rutgers; The State University of New Jersey–New Brunswick; State University of New York at Binghamton (Binghamton University)

FINANCIAL FACTS

Financial Aid Rating	88
Annual in-state tuition	$11,230
Annual out-of-state tuition	$30,130
Room and board	$11,830
Required fees	$1,290
Books and supplies	$800
Average frosh need-based scholarship	$9,756
Average UG need-based scholarship	$8,991
% needy frosh rec. need-based scholarship or grant aid	92
% needy UG rec. need-based scholarship or grant aid	82
% needy frosh rec. non-need-based scholarship or grant aid	62
% needy UG rec. non-need-based scholarship or grant aid	55
% needy frosh rec. need-based self-help aid	73
% needy UG rec. need-based self-help aid	79
% frosh rec. any financial aid	54
% UG rec. any financial aid	49
% frosh need fully met	51
% ugrads need fully met	47
Average % of frosh need met	76
Average % of ugrad need met	75

UNIVERSITY OF DENVER

2197 S. UNIVERSITY BLVD., DENVER, CO 80208 • ADMISSIONS: 303-871-2036 • FAX: 303-871-3301

STUDENTS SAY "..."

Academics

At the University of Denver—the oldest private university in the Rocky Mountain region—the faculty and staff are "extremely dedicated to ensuring that the students receive a high-quality, worthwhile education." The business and accountancy programs are the standouts of the "plethora of classes to choose from," but the school is all about "a global view and interdisciplinary courses" and so has one of the best study abroad programs in the nation, giving students the option to do so without straying from their majors or incurring additional expense, and offering international travel Winter Interterm courses to students.

The "lively, passionate" professors teach with hands-on, real life examples that "prompt students to critically think and apply what is learned in the classroom to our future careers and life." Teachers usually allow students to dictate speed and amount of discussion on a class as topic allows, and take a vested interest in each student's success: They "care more about how you do in the long run than how you may perform in individual classes." "If you try hard, they will engage with you and truly become your friends." "The face-to-face time you get with them is a big reason why I feel so connected to my school," says another student.

Networking here "happens almost without effort; it is ingrained in every aspect of most classes and activities" and there is a "good connection with Denver business community." DU has "basically every resource on campus for advising, counseling, health, and assistance with school work," an "awesome" library, and "there are a lot of 'green' initiatives ... and it feels quite progressive." Though the common curriculum isn't universally beloved, students appreciate that DU runs on a quarterly system, so people "can take more credits than other semester schools...if you don't like a particular class... you are done within ten weeks and you can move on with classes you enjoy."

Life

DU is close enough to the city of Denver that it is possible for students to head downtown whenever they feel like it (the light rail stops on campus and is free for students), but "far enough away that I still get the 'campus' feel." "The nightlife is great around the DU area (for students of age) and downtown has amazing bars and restaurants." The residential living communities and programs get high marks, and "there is never a dull moment on campus." "Everyone is so active and there is so much going on that you almost feel bad if you're not doing anything," says a student. "Microbrews! Pub Quizzes! Poetry Slams! Sleep! Reading! Concerts!" sums up another.

If there's one trait that DU students share, it's "outdoorsy." Many students spend their weekends being active, active, active and enjoy meeting people through the Alpine Club, which "sponsors trips to nearby mountains, deserts, and parks for outdoor activities like skiing, hiking, biking, and backpacking." "Find a friend who comes from one of the ski towns, and see if you can bum a ride from them for a weekend on the slopes," suggests a student. About a quarter of the student population goes Greek, and intramurals and hockey are huge. Denver also has an amazing music scene; "Red Rocks Amphitheatre is—no exaggeration—the best music venue on the globe."

Student Body

DU has a wide variety of people (the majority being "white and middle to upper class") who are "pretty driven," while still "[knowing] how to make time to do something outdoorsy on the weekends." Everybody "respects themselves and the people around them, especially in the learning environment." Obviously, everyone here "loves to ski" and social lives are a huge part of the DU campus culture, so "many join club sports, student orgs, or student alliances" through which they "are able to easily find people to relate to."

FINANCIAL AID: 303-871-4020 • E-MAIL: ADMISSION@DU.EDU • WEBSITE: WWW.DU.EDU

THE PRINCETON REVIEW SAYS

Admissions

Very important factors considered include: rigor of secondary school record, academic GPA, standardized test scores. *Important factors considered include:* application essay, recommendation(s), extracurricular activities, talent/ability, character/personal qualities. *Other factors considered include:* first generation, alumni/ae relation, geographical residence, racial/ethnic status, volunteer work, work experience, level of applicant's interest. SAT or ACT required. ACT with or without writing accepted. TOEFL required of all international applicants. High school diploma is required and GED is accepted.

Financial Aid

Students should submit: FAFSA, CSS/Financial Aid PROFILE, Noncustodial PROFILE. Regular filing deadline is 1/15. The Princeton Review suggests that all financial aid forms be submitted as soon as possible after October 1. *Need-based scholarships/grants offered:* Federal Pell, FSEOG, State scholarships/grants, Private scholarships, College/university scholarship or grant aid from institutional funds. *Loan aid offered:* Direct Subsidized Stafford Loans, Direct Unsubsidized Stafford Loans, Direct PLUS loans. Applicants will be notified of awards on or about 3/20. Federal Work-Study Program available. Institutional employment available.

The Inside Word

Admissions officers at University of Denver take a holistic approach to the application process. Therefore, they strive to look beyond quantitative factors and will also review your essay, recommendations, and extracurricular activities. The average high school GPA for fall 2015 accepted students was 3.72.

THE SCHOOL SAYS " . . . "

From the Admissions Office

"At the University of Denver—in our setting of great natural beauty, cultural richness, and intellectual energy—you'll experience meaningful interaction with professors who set you on paths toward personal discovery, paths that can change the course of your future. Our diverse student body, engaged faculty, and prime location provide a culture of opportunity that is unique and unrivaled. DU is continually developing educational initiatives that help students prepare for an ever-changing world. Our Living and Learning Communities and Pioneer Leadership Program provide extracurricular and co-curricular programming in specialized areas; the Partners in Scholarship (PinS) program funds undergraduate research for students wishing to pursue a topic of personal interest in greater depth; and 65 to 70 percent of our students are taking advantage of invaluable internship opportunities in laboratories, corporate offices, government agencies, and cultural settings. One of the university's signature offerings is the Cherrington Global Scholars program, which allows students to study abroad at the same cost of a quarter spent on campus at DU. Nearly 70 percent of our students study abroad, which ranks DU fourth in the nation among doctoral and research institutions for percentage of students participating. Outside the classroom, DU students put ideas and ideals into action. They are active members of our community and they take advantage of the numerous recreational opportunities available to them, including club, intramural, and seventeen Division I sports. Whatever their majors and interests, DU students are inspired by Denver's Rocky Mountain spirit of exploration and openness, and are encouraged to engage in and personalize their educational journey."

SELECTIVITY

Admissions Rating	87
# of applicants	15,036
% of applicants accepted	73
% of acceptees attending	13
# offered a place on the wait list	2,442
% accepting a place on wait list	19
% admitted from wait list	8

FRESHMAN PROFILE

Range SAT Critical Reading	550–660
Range SAT Math	560–660
Range SAT Writing	530–630
Range ACT Composite	23–30
Minimum paper TOEFL	550
Minimum internet-based TOEFL	80
Average HS GPA	3.7
% graduated top 10% of class	45
% graduated top 25% of class	80
% graduated top 50% of class	97

DEADLINES

Early action	
Deadline	11/1
Notification	12/31
Regular	
Deadline	1/15
Notification	3/15
Nonfall registration?	Yes

FINANCIAL FACTS

Financial Aid Rating	87
Annual tuition	$45,288
Room and board	$12,021
Required fees	$1,134
Books and supplies	$1,200
Average frosh need-based scholarship	$29,496
Average UG need-based scholarship	$29,644
% needy frosh rec. need-based scholarship or grant aid	46
% needy UG rec. need-based scholarship or grant aid	42
% needy frosh rec. non-need-based scholarship or grant aid	46
% needy UG rec. non-need-based scholarship or grant aid	41
% needy frosh rec. need-based self-help aid	46
% needy UG rec. need-based self-help aid	42
% frosh rec. any financial aid	85
% UG rec. any financial aid	83
% frosh need fully met	30
% ugrads need fully met	28
Average % of frosh need met	82
Average % of ugrad need met	83

UNIVERSITY OF FLORIDA

201 CRISER HALL, GAINESVILLE, FL 32611-4000 • ADMISSIONS: 352-392-1365 • FAX: 352-392-3987

STUDENTS SAY ". . ."

Academics

Located in the heart of the "Gator Nation," Gainesville, Florida, the University of Florida offers "a hell of a deal" on "one of the best educations in the nation." Students are proud that UF is "the best state school in Florida" and "one of the top public universities in the nation"; they also love that it's "a great school with a large alumni network," that there's plenty of "intellectual stimulation" to be found there, and that UF's "research opportunities are abundant." Though the school has "strong academic standards" across the board, programs in Business and Journalism are particularly "highly ranked." "Access to alumni" pays off when students seek "opportunities for networking and research," and they find that "as a large school, [UF] has a lot of funding and a large number of opportunities for student involvement." Students say that the university's size doesn't sacrifice individuals' ability to focus on their course of study: "Classes for your major are hard, but they prepare you for more than easier classes would. They better prepare you for your career." Moreover, "as a research university with nearly every graduate program imaginable, the opportunities are endless." Students praise the "truly incredible faculty and staff" and appreciate that "one of the greatest strengths of UF is the fact there is always someone to turn to for help." Class structure is still impacted by the school's size in that "lectures are 80–90 percent of class activities," but conversely, students love "having experts in my field teaching all of my classes for my major." If "breadth of opportunities" for a value price is a priority for you, "The Gator Nation is one where anyone can build a future for themselves."

Life

"The University of Florida is in Gainesville. The Gator Nation is everywhere." In terms of town-gown relations, "Gainesville revolves around UF, most everything is catered to the students and student life." "Bars are the big scene," and students "love going out with friends on the weekends to Midtown. It is a UF staple to party at Grog, Balls, and Salty Dog once you turn twenty-one." "Tons of school spirit" ranks high on the list of things students love about UF, as "A lot of UF culture is based around sports." "Greek life...is a big deal in both the social and extracurricular scene" and "When you are in the Greek community, there are many things to do." For other students, "I find myself working or studying in a computer lab most of the time" and "there is a really intense nightlife but when it comes to exams, papers and finals week it is pretty quiet everywhere." Extracurricular life can also be as forward-looking as you want it to be: "In addition to classes, I research in a lab with the College of Medicine and volunteer at the hospital located on campus." Students "play sports," and "For fun, there are several places to go such as Paynes Prairie, Devil's Millhopper, or other outdoor activities." If you want to get involved, join one of the "961 clubs": "There is literally a club for everyone at UF" and "you make it what you want. You can party every day or you can study every day. I keep it pretty balanced."

Student Body

While "everyone is different," "fraternity and sorority participation....dominates the student culture." Students are "hard working and interested in getting ahead," and "even though UF is considered a party school, it is full of people who put their future careers first." "Students fit in by taking part in and participating in the various things our campus offers" and are often "busy and focused usually on one subject matter or area of interest to be involved in through extracurricular activities." Even though it's a large campus, one student remarks on the sense of community: "We're students? I thought we were all part of one big family!" They find each other "mostly accepting and friendly," but as a whole "hard to define. Gators are religious and non-religious, Greek and non-Greek, obsessed with athletics and some couldn't care less." Overall, the typical UF student "knows how to balance their school work and still have a good time."

FINANCIAL AID: 352-392-6684 • WEBSITE: WWW.UFL.EDU

THE PRINCETON REVIEW SAYS

Admissions

Very important factors considered include: rigor of secondary school record, academic GPA, application essay, extracurricular activities, talent/ability, character/personal qualities, volunteer work. *Important factors considered include:* standardized test scores, first generation, geographical residence, work experience. *Other factors considered include:* class rank, alumni/ae relation, state residency, level of applicant's interest. SAT or ACT required. ACT with Writing required. SAT with or without Essay component accepted. High school diploma is required and GED is accepted. *Academic units required:* 4 English, 4 math, 3 science, 2 science labs, 2 foreign language, 3 social studies.

Financial Aid

Students should submit: FAFSA. Priority filing deadline is 3/15. The Princeton Review suggests that all financial aid forms be submitted as soon as possible after October 1. *Need-based scholarships/grants offered:* Federal Pell, FSEOG, State scholarships/grants, Private scholarships, College/university scholarship or grant aid from institutional funds. *Loan aid offered:* Direct Subsidized Stafford Loans, Direct Unsubsidized Stafford Loans, Direct PLUS loans, Federal Perkins Loans, College/university loans from institutional funds. Applicants will be notified of awards on a rolling basis beginning 4/15. Federal Work-Study Program available. Institutional employment available.

The Inside Word

Unlike many state universities, UF doesn't publish an admissions formula, saying rather that they use a "holistic review" process to determine candidates' eligibility. Their application's short-answer and essay questions are emphasized in factors considered, and first-generation college students from low-income backgrounds should take note of the Florida Opportunity Scholars program, which covers four years of tuition in full.

THE SCHOOL SAYS "..."

From the Admissions Office

"University of Florida students come from more than 100 countries, all fifty states, and every one of the sixty-seven counties in Florida. Twenty-three percent of the student body is composed of graduate students. Approximately 3,230 African-American students, 8,268 Hispanic students, and 3,530 Asian American students attend UF. Ninety percent of the entering freshmen rank above the national mean of scores on standard entrance exams. UF consistently ranks near the top among public universities in the number of new National Merit and Achievement scholars in attendance."

"Students must submit the SAT or ACT with the writing section. UF considers your highest section scores across all SAT test dates."

SELECTIVITY

Admissions Rating	94
# of applicants	29,837
% of applicants accepted	51
% of acceptees attending	51

FRESHMAN PROFILE

Range SAT Critical Reading	580–670
Range SAT Math	590–680
Range SAT Writing	570–670
Range ACT Composite	27–31
% graduated top 10% of class	72
% graduated top 25% of class	96
% graduated top 50% of class	100

DEADLINES

Regular	
Deadline	11/1
Nonfall registration?	Yes

FINANCIAL FACTS

Financial Aid Rating	85
Annual in-state tuition + fees	$6,381
Annual out-of-state tuition + fees	$28,658
Room and board	$9,650
Books and supplies	$1,300
Average frosh need-based scholarship	$7,346
Average UG need-based scholarship	$6,778
% needy frosh rec. need-based scholarship or grant aid	62
% needy UG rec. need-based scholarship or grant aid	63
% needy frosh rec. non-need-based scholarship or grant aid	94
% needy UG rec. non-need-based scholarship or grant aid	81
% needy frosh rec. need-based self-help aid	39
% needy UG rec. need-based self-help aid	46
% frosh rec. any financial aid	94
% UG rec. any financial aid	91
% frosh need fully met	23
% ugrads need fully met	20
Average % of frosh need met	99
Average % of ugrad need met	96

UNIVERSITY OF GEORGIA

TERRELL HALL, ATHENS, GA 30602 • ADMISSIONS: 706-542-8776 • FAX: 706-542-1466

CAMPUS LIFE

Quality of Life Rating	93
Fire Safety Rating	85
Green Rating	94
Type of school	Public
Affiliation	No Affiliation
Environment	City

STUDENTS

Total undergrad enrollment	27,547
% male/female	43/57
% from out of state	8
% frosh from public high school	71
% frosh live on campus	98
% ugrads live on campus	36
# of fraternities (% ugrad men join)	35 (22)
# of sororities (% ugrad women join)	27 (29)
% African American	7
% Asian	10
% Caucasian	71
% Hispanic	5
% Native American	<1
% Pacific Islander	<1
% Two or more races	4
% Race and/or ethnicity unknown	1
% international	2
# of countries represented	125

SURVEY SAYS...

Students are happy
Great library
School is well run
Students love Athens, GA
Great food on campus
Great off-campus food
Recreation facilities are great
Lots of beer drinking
Hard liquor is popular
Everyone loves the Bulldogs
Intramural sports are popular
Frats and sororities are popular
Alumni active on campus

ACADEMICS

Academic Rating	78
% students returning for sophomore year	95
% students graduating within 4 years	62
% students graduating within 6 years	84
Calendar	Semester
Profs interesting rating	77
Profs accessible rating	72

MOST POPULAR MAJORS

Biology; Psychology; Finance

STUDENTS SAY "..."

Academics

As at many large universities, UGA has a "mixed bag of professors," but there are "more good teachers" than bad. Though students don't love the core curriculum classes due to their large size and the prevalence of TAs, "once [you're] in your particular program, the teachers are outstanding and easy to reach." "The professors really do want to see you at office hours if you have questions," and they "want to share their love of learning with you." "My major-related classes are very small, and each student receives individual attention." The honors program also receives raves: "Many of my best classes and favorite teachers have come from the honors program, but non-honors classes are generally good as well." "The study spaces are well-equipped and quiet," but "the school of social work is still housed in an old dorm." "Administration is a pain (not the people, only the requirements), but I think that describes academia in general." In general students "feel that the administration can be very accommodating at times, but at other times it can seem like it is full of red tape." Registration technology "needs to be brought out of the 1980s and into the twenty-first century." "The administration [can] seem like a bunch of penny-pinchers, but they must be to run a major research facility."

Life

Life at UGA seems to be a good mix of the two different worlds of sports and arts: football, frats, and tailgating on campus come together nicely with the coffee shops and music scene in downtown Athens. "On Saturday afternoons in the fall, nearly everyone on campus is at the football game. It's a way of life here." "Everybody really gets behind the team, and Saturdays in Athens feel like mini vacations." Fraternities and sororities dominate the party scene, but "there is definitely plenty to do, even if you don't go Greek." Students love to brag about the high number of bars per capita in Athens, but there's plenty more to boast about. "The Athens music and art scene is very inspiring, and there are tons of opportunities for creativity here." "Downtown Athens is fabulous! Whether you drink or don't drink, all are welcome and all congregate there." Campus life offers plenty of activity, too. "Fun is a part of daily life...with a dozen intramural sports each semester...and many community activities (multiple movie theaters, bowling allies, golf course)." "Ultimate Frisbee, walks around the multiple parks, days lounging on North Campus, and spending *lots* of time downtown are a couple ways I like to have fun at school." "There are so many organizations that everyone can find a place that will feel like home or find a place to meet new people." "It's no secret that UGA knows how to party. However, most of the students know how to manage social and academic time."

Student Body

"Students are generally white, upper-middle-class, smart, [and] involved, and [they] have a good time," "seem to be predominantly conservative," and "are usually involved in at least one organization whether it be Greek, a club, or sports." "The typical student at UGA is one who knows how and when to study but allows himself or herself to have a very active social life." The majority are Southerners, with many students from within Georgia. "The stereotype is Southern, Republican, football-loving, and beer-drinking. While many, many of UGA's students do not fit this description, there is no lack of the above," and "there is a social scene for everyone in Athens." "There are a great number of atypical students in the liberal arts," which "creates a unique and exciting student body with greatly contrasting opinions."

FINANCIAL AID: 706-542-6147 • E-MAIL: ADMPROC@UGA.EDU • WEBSITE: WWW.UGA.EDU

THE PRINCETON REVIEW SAYS

Admissions

Very important factors considered include: rigor of secondary school record, academic GPA. *Important factors considered include:* standardized test scores. *Other factors considered include:* application essay, recommendation(s), extracurricular activities, talent/ability, character/personal qualities, first generation, volunteer work, work experience. SAT or ACT required; SAT Subject Tests considered if submitted. ACT with or without writing accepted. SAT with or without Essay component accepted. TOEFL required of all international applicants. High school diploma is required and GED is accepted. *Academic units required:* 4 English, 4 math, 4 science, 2 science labs, 2 foreign language, 3 social studies. *Academic units recommended:* 4 English, 4 math, 4 science, 2 science labs, 3 foreign language, 1 social studies, 2 history, 1 academic elective.

Financial Aid

Students should submit: FAFSA. Priority filing deadline is 3/1. The Princeton Review suggests that all financial aid forms be submitted as soon as possible after October 1. *Need-based scholarships/grants offered:* Federal Pell, FSEOG, State scholarships/grants, Private scholarships, College/university scholarship or grant aid from institutional funds. *Loan aid offered:* Direct Subsidized Stafford Loans, Direct Unsubsidized Stafford Loans, Direct PLUS loans, Federal Perkins Loans, State Loans, College/university loans from institutional funds. Applicants will be notified of awards on a rolling basis beginning 5/1. Federal Work-Study Program available. Institutional employment available.

The Inside Word

A school as large as UGA must start winnowing applicants by the numbers. If you fail to meet certain baseline curricular, GPA, and standardized-test-score floors, only exceptional talent elsewhere (a gift for the arts or, better still, throwing a football) will get you past the first cut. Some students here are Georgia residents reaping the benefits of the state's HOPE/Zell Miller scholarship programs, which pays tuition and most school-related fees for state residents who earn at least a 3.7 GPA in high school, a 1200 SAT or 26 ACT score, and maintain a 3.3 in college. Georgia state residents who earn at least a 3.0 in high school will also have a large portion of their tuition paid.

THE SCHOOL SAYS ". . ."

From the Admissions Office

"The University of Georgia offers students the advantages and resources of a top public research university, including a wide range of majors and exceptional academic facilities such as the 260,000 square-foot Miller Learning Center. At the same time, UGA provides opportunities more common to smaller, private schools, such as first-year seminars led by distinguished faculty and learning communities that connect students with similar academic interests. The university is committed to challenging its academically superior students in the classroom and beyond, with increased emphasis on undergraduate research, service-learning, and study abroad. UGA students taking advantage of such offerings find themselves well positioned to compete with the best undergraduates in the country, as evidenced by their recent string of successes in winning Rhodes, Marshall, Truman, and other major scholarships. The UGA campus, considered one of the most beautiful in the nation, adjoins vibrant downtown Athens. While Athens is renowned for its local music scene, UGA also houses the Performing Arts Center, the Hugh Hodgson School of Music, the Lamar Dodd School of Art, and the Georgia Museum of Art. Sports—from football to gymnastics—are also a major attraction, with UGA teams perennially ranked among the best in the country. To experience the excitement of UGA, most prospective students visit campus, a ninety-minute drive northeast of the Atlanta airport. See the admissions website to sign up for a tour with the Visitors Center, view the weekday schedule of admissions information sessions, and find application details. Applicants for first-year admission will be required to submit either the SAT or ACT. Students submitting only the ACT must also submit the optional ACT writing test."

SELECTIVITY

Admissions Rating	91
# of applicants	21,945
% of applicants accepted	53
% of acceptees attending	45
# offered a place on the wait list	954
% accepting a place on wait list	61
% admitted from wait list	6

FRESHMAN PROFILE

Range SAT Critical Reading	570–660
Range SAT Math	580–670
Range SAT Writing	560–660
Range ACT Composite	26–30
Minimum paper TOEFL	550
Minimum internet-based TOEFL	80
Average HS GPA	3.9
% graduated top 10% of class	53
% graduated top 25% of class	88
% graduated top 50% of class	99

DEADLINES

Early action	
Deadline	10/15
Notification	12/1
Regular	
Priority	10/15
Deadline	1/15
Nonfall registration?	Yes

FINANCIAL FACTS

Financial Aid Rating	83
Annual out-of-state tuition	$27,574
Room and board	$9,450
Required fees	$2,258
Books and supplies	$840
Average frosh need-based scholarship	$10,210
Average UG need-based scholarship	$8,923
% needy frosh rec. need-based scholarship or grant aid	98
% needy UG rec. need-based scholarship or grant aid	92
% needy frosh rec. non-need-based scholarship or grant aid	24
% needy UG rec. non-need-based scholarship or grant aid	16
% needy frosh rec. need-based self-help aid	47
% needy UG rec. need-based self-help aid	54
% frosh rec. any financial aid	47
% UG rec. any financial aid	48
% UG borrow to pay for school	48
Average cumulative indebtedness	$22,087
% frosh need fully met	29
% ugrads need fully met	22
Average % of frosh need met	78
Average % of ugrad need met	72

UNIVERSITY OF HAWAII—MANOA

2600 CAMPUS ROAD, HONOLULU, HI 96822 • ADMISSIONS: 808-956-8975 • FAX: 808-956-4148

STUDENTS SAY "..."

Academics

This flagship school of the University of Hawaii system offers nearly one hundred bachelor's programs to the 15,000 or so students who call the Oahu campus home during the school year. A lot of the school's vibe is "very laid back, just like the Hawaiian lifestyle," and students often show up to class with bikinis and swim trunks under their clothes from that morning's beach trip. More than 200 degree programs across eighteen schools are available to students but no matter the course of study, Hawaii plays TA. "When someone goes to UH Manoa, they aren't expecting to receive a Hawaiian education but that is exactly what they get. Whether they are learning the Hawaiian language, Hawaiian culture, or about the Hawaiian ecosystem, there is a lot for everyone that goes along with their major," says a student. "UH really incorporates how important Hawaii really is."

Sciences are particularly strong here, and the language offerings are incredibly diverse (think Ilocano and Tagalog). Teachers are "always willing to go the extra mile to help students by offering office hours" and many professors challenge students while simultaneously "letting us know what content will be useful in our future careers and/or graduate level exams." However, the real gold here is in the added resources for extra help in classes. There is "free one-on-one tutoring" and review sessions through the learning center, a writing center, a learning emporium for certain subjects, and "[you] can even walk into the library and librarian will help to find sources for papers and guide students in a great direction."

Life

UH Manoa is on an island that offers a bit of everything. Here you can find "the city, the country, the surf, the mountains, the malls, and so on and so on. Oahu has something to fit my every mood and need," says a student. There are always cultural festivals and activities, and Hawaii is made for active people who "like to get lost in nature's beauty." Whether you're "running up Koko Head, swimming with dolphins on the west side, catching some rays between classes on the Waikiki strip, or jumping off rocks on the north shore, there's no way to escape the beauty that is Hawaii." On the weekend many local students travel home so the campus can get very quiet, but students do use their IDs for free bus transportation to explore the relatively small island and student services and student affairs are "excellent." As is common with college students, "many of us do not have enough money enjoy the nightlife, therefore we enjoy our free time at the beach." Still, students "have work that we can't just blow off for a swim or something." People like to use the grill that the school has set up, and there are "always people walking from place to place until late at night, hanging out with friends in the courtyards, skateboarding, or cooking out."

Student Body

This group—mainly from the Asia-Pacific region and mainland USA, with the occasional European or South American throw in—is a "huge melting pot" that is just "filled with Aloha." An "incredible amount of culture is exhibited here," most of all the Hawaiian cool: "I have never been on another college campus where it is completely normal to ride your skateboard barefoot or walk around with your surfboard." This is good news for the plenty of exchange students from Asia are here "trying to have an American campus experience;" ROTC also has a "very large" presence. On the whole, this is a "very relaxed and cool" bunch of students with whom "you can strike up friendly conversations with strangers in the cafeteria, or while waiting to cross the street, or while ordering food."

UNIVERSITY OF HAWAII—MANOA

FINANCIAL AID: 808-956-7251 • E-MAIL: UHMANOA.ADMISSIONS@HAWAII.EDU • WEBSITE: MANOA.HAWAII.EDU

THE PRINCETON REVIEW SAYS

Admissions

Very important factors considered include: rigor of secondary school record, academic GPA, standardized test scores. *Important factors considered include:* class rank, state residency. *Other factors considered include:* application essay, recommendation(s), interview, extracurricular activities, talent/ability, geographical residence. SAT or ACT required. ACT with Writing required. SAT with or without Essay component accepted. TOEFL required of all international applicants. High school diploma is required and GED is accepted. *Academic units required:* 4 English, 3 math, 3 science, 3 social studies, 5 academic electives.

Financial Aid

Students should submit: FAFSA. Priority filing deadline is 3/1. The Princeton Review suggests that all financial aid forms be submitted as soon as possible after October 1. *Need-based scholarships/grants offered:* Federal Pell, FSEOG, State scholarships/grants, Private scholarships, College/university scholarship or grant aid from institutional funds. *Loan aid offered:* Direct Subsidized Stafford Loans, Direct Unsubsidized Stafford Loans, Direct PLUS loans, Federal Perkins Loans, State Loans. Applicants will be notified of awards on a rolling basis beginning 4/1. Federal Work-Study Program available. Institutional employment available.

The Inside Word

All students must have a minimum GPA of 2.8, be in the top 40 percent of their high school class, and must take either the SAT or the ACT. All applicants are encouraged to apply by the priority consideration deadline of January 5, as this deadline increases your chance of receiving financial aid and student housing. Certain programs (nursing, social work, education, and others) may have earlier admission deadlines.

THE SCHOOL SAYS "..."

From the Admissions Office

"Aloha and welcome to UH Manoa, the largest campus in the University of Hawaii System. We are located on the island of O'ahu, in Honolulu's lush Manoa valley. With almost 90 undergraduate majors, over 200 student organizations, and a variety of Division I and intramural sports to choose from, we think you'll agree that UH Manoa is a great place for you to realize your academic, professional, and personal dreams.

"UH Manoa is one of only a handful of institutions to hold the distinction of being a land-, sea-, and space-grant research institution. Classified by the Carnegie Foundation as having 'very high research activity,' UH Manoa is known for its pioneering research in such fields as oceanography, astronomy, Pacific Islands and Asian area studies, linguistics, cancer research, and genetics.

"Applicants to UH Manoa are expected to have a minimum score of 510 on all three sections of the SAT (or a 22 on all four sections of the ACT), and have completed a college preparatory high school curriculum. All applicants are encouraged to apply for priority consideration. Applying by this deadline (January 5 for fall admission, September 1 for spring) increases your chance of receiving financial aid and student housing."

SELECTIVITY

Admissions Rating	78
# of applicants	7,658
% of applicants accepted	81
% of acceptees attending	31

FRESHMAN PROFILE

Range SAT Critical Reading	480–580
Range SAT Math	500–610
Range SAT Writing	470–570
Range ACT Composite	21–26
Minimum paper TOEFL	500
Minimum internet-based TOEFL	61
Average HS GPA	3.5
% graduated top 10% of class	25
% graduated top 25% of class	56
% graduated top 50% of class	90

DEADLINES

Regular	
Priority	1/5
Deadline	3/1
Nonfall registration?	Yes

FINANCIAL FACTS

Financial Aid Rating	82
Annual in-state tuition	$10,872
Annual out-of-state tuition	$32,904
Room and board	$11,529
Required fees	$820
Books and supplies	$952
Average frosh need-based scholarship	$9,904
Average UG need-based scholarship	$9,099
% needy frosh rec. need-based scholarship or grant aid	98
% needy UG rec. need-based scholarship or grant aid	92
% needy frosh rec. non-need-based scholarship or grant aid	27
% needy UG rec. non-need-based scholarship or grant aid	22
% needy frosh rec. need-based self-help aid	54
% needy UG rec. need-based self-help aid	63
% frosh rec. any financial aid	62
% UG rec. any financial aid	59
% UG borrow to pay for school	47
Average cumulative indebtedness	$24,324
% frosh need fully met	35
% ugrads need fully met	29
Average % of frosh need met	76
Average % of ugrad need met	70

UNIVERSITY OF HOUSTON

OFFICE OF ADMISSIONS, HOUSTON, TX 77204-2023 • ADMISSIONS: 713-743-1010

STUDENTS SAY "..."

Academics

With more than 120 undergraduate majors and minors, a 594-acre campus, and 42,700 students, the University of Houston is a world-class research institution and fixture in Texas education. The school "provides some of the greatest opportunities in the world" at an affordable price and urges its students to achieve as much as they can "while living in a real-world environment." The school has been on the rise in recent years and "is attracting many more bright students to the university" as it begins to toughen up admission standards.

Professors here are "always prepared and make lecture interesting" through "effective teaching strategies" that "provide eye opening real-life information" to what can be "a motley group of students coming together to pursue higher education." Though there are a few who receive low marks, most "take into consideration the needs of students and many post lectures and notes online." Even in the larger classes, professors make and keep their office hours, so "if you are willing to work hard, you do have the tools available to learn the material." TAs are especially helpful, and "the tutoring services are very accessible and widely used."

Careers are a main focus of Cougars, and there is a wide range of majors and many interdisciplinary systems for students looking to specify their education, and there are also "many ties to local business and industry," including the chemical and space industries, and the medical center. "The flexibility of my degree plan cannot be found in any other school," says a student. Red tape is the main grumble for UH students, with the financial aid office drawing the most ire, and many students also "have difficulty fixing problems regarding registration and enrollment for classes."

Life

A very large percentage of the student body lives off campus, so "the campus grows much more quiet in the evenings and on weekends," and stores and restaurants close earlier than normal. However, UH "is in the middle of a transition from being a commuter campus to a residential campus" and has announced plans to build two more dorms in the next few years and to require freshmen to live on campus. Even for those who travel home at night, "the recreational facility and other organizations are a way to meet friendly people." Flyers for events "can be found everywhere on campus," which is "great for networking purposes or if you just need a break from studying."

Football is understandably huge, but be warned: "If you don't come early enough to the football game, forget about it." Basically, "unless you are supremely shy, there are countless opportunities to make friends and fit in." "We also can't leave out the tiny fact that we are in Houston," says a proud local. There are plenty of fun places "to eat, party, hang out, and exercise, and it's all within a fifteen-minute radius." As one student sums up, "If you feel there's nothing you could do here...you, my friend, are wrong."

Student Body

University of Houston "is the epitome of the grand melting pot." This remarkably "ethnically and culturally diverse" student body loves the variety that the university offers and the ensuing "acceptance on all levels." "One can come and grow socially, politically, and intellectually," says a student. One commonality is the "dedicated spirit" of all Cougars, helped in part by their devotion to UH sports, and "a typical student supports our athletic teams by wearing our red." Many take part in some sort of extracurricular club, but mostly, "everyone is trying to pass their classes and set themselves on the best track to get a job after school."

FINANCIAL AID: 713-743-1010 • E-MAIL: ADMISSIONS@UH.EDU • WEBSITE: WWW.UH.EDU

THE PRINCETON REVIEW SAYS

Admissions

Very important factors considered include: rigor of secondary school record, class rank, standardized test scores. *Important factors considered include:* academic GPA. *Other factors considered include:* application essay, recommendation(s), extracurricular activities, talent/ability, first generation, volunteer work, work experience, level of applicant's interest. SAT or ACT required. ACT with or without writing accepted. TOEFL required of all international applicants. High school diploma is required and GED is accepted. *Academic units required:* 4 English, 4 math, 4 science, 4 social studies. *Academic units recommended:* 2 science labs, 2 foreign language, 1 computer science, 1 visual/performing arts.

Financial Aid

Students should submit: FAFSA. Priority filing deadline is 3/15. The Princeton Review suggests that all financial aid forms be submitted as soon as possible after October 1. *Need-based scholarships/grants offered:* Federal Pell, FSEOG, State scholarships/grants, Private scholarships, College/university scholarship or grant aid from institutional funds. *Loan aid offered:* Direct Subsidized Stafford Loans, Direct Unsubsidized Stafford Loans, Direct PLUS loans, Federal Perkins Loans, State Loans. Applicants will be notified of awards on a rolling basis beginning 4/1. Federal Work-Study Program available. Institutional employment available.

Inside Word

The school's large size means that acceptance is easier to achieve than at some smaller schools. Students who meet the State of Texas Uniform Admissions Policy and satisfy a certain scale of requirements for class ranking and/or SAT or ACT scores are assured admission. But even if your grades aren't seemingly up to par, the admissions committee will consider students individually based on a holistic review of certain aspects, such as first-generation, socioeconomic background, rigor of high school curriculum, family responsibilities, special talents, public service, and strong letters of recommendation or a persuasive statement explaining your special circumstances.

THE SCHOOL SAYS "..."

From the Admissions Office

"The University of Houston is a Carnegie-designated Tier One public research university that is recognized throughout the world as a leader in energy research, which is centered in a visionary Energy Research Park, law, business, and environmental education. Located in America's fourth-largest city, the University of Houston is one of the most ethnically diverse metropolitan research universities in the United States. Its 42,700 students hail from 117 countries.

"In addition to preparing its students to succeed in today's global economy, the University of Houston also is a catalyst within its own community—changing lives through health, education, and outreach projects that help build a future for children in Houston, in Texas, and in the world.

"Other distinctive merits of the University of Houston include a limitless student experience, a historic Division I athletic program, energetic arts programs, and an internationally recognized faculty including a Nobel Laureate; winners of the National Medal of Science, Pulitzer, and Tony awards; and members of prestigious National Academies. The Princeton Review has chosen the University of Houston for inclusion in its guidebook of the nation's best colleges.

"Discover the greatness of the University of Houston's dynamic tree-lined campus of more than 594 acres—nestled just minutes from Houston's bustling theater and museum districts—where innovative teaching, revolutionary research, and nationally recognized and motivated students work together to create a globally competitive educational environment."

SELECTIVITY	
Admissions Rating	86
# of applicants	17,971
% of applicants accepted	60
% of acceptees attending	39

FRESHMAN PROFILE	
Range SAT Critical Reading	510–610
Range SAT Math	540–640
Range ACT Composite	23–28
Minimum paper TOEFL	550
Minimum internet-based TOEFL	79
% graduated top 10% of class	30
% graduated top 25% of class	64
% graduated top 50% of class	89

DEADLINES	
Regular	
Priority	12/1
Deadline	7/1
Notification	4/15
Nonfall registration?	Yes

FINANCIAL FACTS	
Financial Aid Rating	80
Annual in-state tuition	$9,756
Annual out-of-state tuition	$24,456
Room and board	$9,849
Required fees	$954
Books and supplies	$1,300
Average frosh need-based scholarship	$9,671
Average UG need-based scholarship	$8,127
% needy frosh rec. need-based scholarship or grant aid	90
% needy UG rec. need-based scholarship or grant aid	82
% needy frosh rec. non-need-based scholarship or grant aid	9
% needy UG rec. non-need-based scholarship or grant aid	5
% needy frosh rec. need-based self-help aid	50
% needy UG rec. need-based self-help aid	63
% frosh rec. any financial aid	87
% UG rec. any financial aid	77
% UG borrow to pay for school	53
Average cumulative indebtedness	$22,763
% frosh need fully met	18
% ugrads need fully met	16
Average % of frosh need met	66
Average % of ugrad need met	63

UNIVERSITY OF IDAHO

UI ADMISSIONS OFFICE, MOSCOW, ID 83844-4264 • ADMISSIONS: 208-885-6326 • FAX: 208-885-9119

STUDENTS SAY "..."

Academics

With its annual tuition for Idaho residents hovering around just $6,000, numerous students name "in-state tuition" and "bang for the buck" among their top reasons for attending the University of Idaho. There's much more to love about the university, though, whether it's "one of the best agricultural programs in the northwest," "a great college of engineering," "an excellent natural resources program" or "a great art program." U of I takes a "progressive and modern attitude towards education" and fosters "tight-knit connections between the faculty [and] students." Undergraduates are rewarded when they reach out: "UI has a lot to offer to those who seek help, resources, or advice." While professors are "experts in their field," and often "some of the most interesting and enlightening people I've ever met," students offered them mixed reviews, saying their quality "varies substantially; some professors are dedicated to giving their students a engaging and hands-on experience while other professors seem to be stuck in the world of academia and care very little for the input of students in discussions." Despite this, students feel loyal to U of I's "holistic approach to education," where "academics are only part of the focus." They appreciate the university's emphasis on "giving you experiences to prepare you for the real world with a balance of classroom instruction and hands on learning." One student offers the ultimate endorsement: "If knowledge was a drug, we would be high all the time."

Life

"There isn't a lot to do in little Moscow," and "life is pretty slow during the weekdays," but on the weekends, students find "activities in the town and people blowing off steam at the bars or eighteen-and-up clubs" off campus. Because "there are a lot of Greek students"—indeed, "nearly half of campus is or has been affiliated to a fraternity or sorority"—"partying is undeniably one of the most widespread activities" and "Greek life is at the center of the campus social scene." Whether you decide to rush or not may determine your social life entirely: "Unfortunately, non-Greeks and Greeks don't always interact a whole lot." Drinking and partying are hardly the only things to do, though: "There's really strong volunteer programs all over campus and a ton of involvement opportunities through a host of clubs and organizations...student government provides weekly entertainment in the form of movies, concerts, speakers, and comedians." Students also "enjoy the outdoors," and "Hunting, fishing, and skiing are especially popular," as well as "biking, hiking, running, mountain biking, ice skating and rock climbing." They recommend ways to find your tribe: "Living in the dorms was a great way to meet new people that you could later move off campus with." As with anywhere, the quality of your social life depends on who you spend it with: "Students usually find their group of friends early and keep them."

Student Body

In order to find their place, the typical U of I student "is very involved in campus life." Students' interests run the gamut, from "a lot of Greek students and outdoorsy students" to "a math oriented student looking for a technical degree." Many students "are laid back and enjoy the outdoors," and "party but know where to draw the line and get to work." Students don't take their education for granted: "The typical student is someone who knows they are paying for their education, and takes pride" in that fact. They bring hometown values to the campus, and are often "religious and from some type of country background, [as] not very many students [come] from bigger cities like Portland or Seattle." "They are down-to-earth, friendly, kind, motivated, and many view family, friends, and social awareness [as] important." For these reasons, U of I students are "really into community and the small town atmosphere."

FINANCIAL AID: 208-885-6312 • E-MAIL: ADMISSIONS@UIDAHO.EDU • WEBSITE: WWW.UIDAHO.EDU

THE PRINCETON REVIEW SAYS

Admissions

Very important factors considered include: academic GPA, standardized test scores. *Other factors considered include:* SAT or ACT required. ACT with or without writing accepted. TOEFL required of all international applicants. High school diploma is required and GED is accepted. *Academic units required:* 4 English, 3 math, 3 science, 1 science lab, and 1 unit from above areas or other academic areas.

Financial Aid

Students should submit: FAFSA. Priority filing deadline is 2/15. The Princeton Review suggests that all financial aid forms be submitted as soon as possible after October 1. *Need-based scholarships/grants offered:* Federal Pell, FSEOG, State scholarships/grants, Private scholarships, College/university scholarship or grant aid from institutional funds. *Loan aid offered:* Direct Subsidized Stafford Loans, Direct Unsubsidized Stafford Loans, Direct PLUS loans, Federal Perkins Loans, College/university loans from institutional funds. Applicants will be notified of awards on a rolling basis beginning 3/30. Federal Work-Study Program available. Institutional employment available.

The Inside Word

The U of I doesn't put a whole lot of bells and whistles on the application process: If you meet their requirements for high school GPA and standardized test scores, which they publish on their website, you'll probably get in. As with many schools' formulas, a weaker test score can be balanced out by a stronger GPA, and vice versa.

THE SCHOOL SAYS "..."

From the Admissions Office

"A leading public research university in the West, the University of Idaho offers a traditional residential campus experience in a spectacular natural setting. It provides more than 130 undergraduate degree options and graduate degrees in forty-seven discipline areas, which helps provide unprecedented undergraduate research opportunities. Idaho has become known for its academic excellence, student-centered, experiential learning, and an exceptional student living environment that coupled with dedicated faculty, world-class facilities, and renowned research has produced a proven track record of high-achieving graduates. The student population of 12,000 includes first-generation college students and ethnically diverse scholars, who select from hands-on learning experiences in the colleges of Agricultural and Life Sciences; Art and Architecture; Business and Economics; Education; Engineering; Law; Letters, Arts, and Social Sciences; Natural Resources; and Science. The university also provides medical education for the state through the WWAMI program. Increasingly its interdisciplinary teams involved in environmental, sustainability, engagement, and resource management have gained national recognition. Idaho combines the strength of a large, land grant university with the intimacy of a small learning community to help students succeed and become leaders. It is home to the Vandals and competes in the Western Athletic Conference.

"Students applying for admission are required to take either the SAT or the ACT. The writing component is not required from the ACT. SAT Subject Test scores are not used for admission purposes."

SELECTIVITY

Admissions Rating	81
# of applicants	8,515
% of applicants accepted	67
% of acceptees attending	28

FRESHMAN PROFILE

Range SAT Critical Reading	450–580
Range SAT Math	460–590
Range SAT Writing	450–560
Range ACT Composite	20–27
Minimum paper TOEFL	525
Minimum internet-based TOEFL	70
Average HS GPA	3.4
% graduated top 10% of class	20
% graduated top 25% of class	45
% graduated top 50% of class	73

DEADLINES

Regular	
Priority	2/15
Deadline	8/1
Nonfall registration?	Yes

APPLICANTS ALSO LOOK AT AND SOMETIMES PREFER

Boise State University; Utah State University

AND RARELY PREFER

Idaho State University

FINANCIAL FACTS

Financial Aid Rating	84
Annual in-state tuition	$4,784
Annual out-of-state tuition	$18,314
Room and board	$8,022
Required fees	$2,000
Books and supplies	$1,232
Average frosh need-based scholarship	$4,681
Average UG need-based scholarship	$4,753
% needy frosh rec. need-based scholarship or grant aid	73
% needy UG rec. need-based scholarship or grant aid	76
% needy frosh rec. non-need-based scholarship or grant aid	90
% needy UG rec. non-need-based scholarship or grant aid	60
% needy frosh rec. need-based self-help aid	72
% needy UG rec. need-based self-help aid	77
% frosh rec. any financial aid	90
% UG rec. any financial aid	80
% frosh need fully met	39
% ugrads need fully met	30
Average % of frosh need met	80
Average % of ugrad need met	75

University of Illinois at Urbana-Champaign

901 West Illinois Street, Urbana, IL 61801 • Admissions: 217-333-0302 • Fax: 217-244-0903

CAMPUS LIFE

Quality of Life Rating	87
Fire Safety Rating	60*
Green Rating	96
Type of school	Public
Affiliation	No Affiliation
Environment	City

STUDENTS

Total undergrad enrollment	32,959
% male/female	56/44
% from out of state	9
% frosh live on campus	99
% ugrads live on campus	50
# of fraternities (% ugrad men join)	(23)
# of sororities (% ugrad women join)	(23)
% African American	5
% Asian	16
% Caucasian	51
% Hispanic	9
% Native American	<1
% Pacific Islander	<1
% Two or more races	3
% Race and/or ethnicity unknown	1
% international	15
# of countries represented	114

SURVEY SAYS...

Students are happy
Great library
Career services are great
Recreation facilities are great
Lots of beer drinking
Hard liquor is popular
Everyone loves the Fighting Illini
Frats and sororities are popular

ACADEMICS

Academic Rating	76
% students returning for sophomore year	93
% students graduating within 4 years	69
Calendar	Semester
Student/faculty ratio	18:1
Profs interesting rating	71
Profs accessible rating	73

Most classes have 10–19 students.
Most lab/discussion sessions have
20–29 students.

STUDENTS SAY "..."

Academics

The University of Illinois' massive size means "opportunities, lots of classes, lots of student groups," and "an incredibly lively campus." "The research support is phenomenal on campus" and "there are a lot of resources to supplement your studies." Students find the university's "fantastic library system" and "phenomenal advisors" to be "such a benefit for research projects," and "countless on-campus resources such as the Career Center, Writers Workshop, Office of Minority Student Affairs, free tutoring services, and the Study Abroad Office" also support students' academic experiences. They praise their professors as "wonderful," "not just good at research but also instructing and mentoring," and "very approachable," and students thrive on the emphasis on experiences outside the classroom: "The field work (tons of field work) that they make us do really helped in getting used to the field." "Most professors here are devoted to teaching, not researching." Classes can be big—"As an underclassman, many classes I've taken have been with very large classes"—but "the professors are engaging and know how to keep a class of 700-plus entertained." U of I's programs in business and engineering have long been recognized as among the best, and one student says, "I liked the breadth of the engineering program and the opportunities associated with it." Even if you're not sure what you want to study yet, its undergrads feel that the university has "an amazing reputation and strong programs in many different majors, and that if I needed to change majors (which I ended up doing) I would still be getting a great degree."

Life

In terms of location, "campus is located perfectly between Chicago, Indianapolis, and St. Louis, providing a unique atmosphere in town but close access to other urban areas for a change of pace." Students call social life "very exciting," and say, "The bars in downtown Champaign are great and super relaxed, plus there is an awesome music scene that most people don't expect from a college town." "People here like to party, but there are a lot of other fun things to do," whether it's "going to the Krannert Center to see plays or concerts" or the "movie theater and mall…on Saturday afternoons. Champaign-Urbana seems small to city kids, but to me it's the land of opportunity." Students relish the "nineteen-year-old bar age," and U of I also has "one of the largest Greek communities in the country." The combination of these facts does mean that "drinking culture is huge here" but "there's also tons to do beyond the bars." The range of social opportunities is nearly limitless: "There are 40,000 students, thousands of clubs, two gyms and several sport facilities, and array of establishments to explore on Green Street." As a whole, students report happily that "life is busy, but rewarding."

Student Body

"The diversity of the students here is astounding. Race, religion, major, you've got it all." Because in-state tuition is a major draw, "a majority of the students that you meet here will be from the Chicago suburbs," but the school also attracts "a wide variety of students from all across the world." "University of Illinois houses so many different types of students that the only way we are alike is our dedication to getting an education and our loyalty to UIUC." Undergrads feel that their peers "really know how to be academically successful," and shed state-school stereotypes like so many dirty socks: "It obviously takes a lot to get into this school so students aren't ready to throw it all away to sleep in every day." Social life changes as you find your "niche": "The typical student starts out going to a school of 40,000 students and are lucky if they know a handful of people. Within one week, life as that freshman student grows. There are so many opportunities to get involved on the floor of your residence hall, in organizations, in your classes, that it's hard not to make friends and close relationships."

UNIVERSITY OF ILLINOIS AT URBANA-CHAMPAIGN

FINANCIAL AID: 217-333-0100 • E-MAIL: UGRADADMISSIONS@ILLINOIS.EDU • WEBSITE: WWW.ILLINOIS.EDU

THE PRINCETON REVIEW SAYS

Admissions

Very important factors considered include: rigor of secondary school record, academic GPA. *Important factors considered include:* standardized test scores, application essay, extracurricular activities, talent/ability. *Other factors considered include:* class rank, character/personal qualities, first generation, geographical residence, state residency, racial/ethnic status, volunteer work, work experience. SAT or ACT required. ACT with or without writing accepted. TOEFL required of all international applicants. High school diploma is required and GED is accepted. *Academic units required:* 4 English, 2 science labs, 2 foreign language, 2 social studies, 2 academic electives. *Academic units recommended:* 4 English, 4 math, 4 science labs, 4 foreign language, 4 social studies, 4 academic electives.

Financial Aid

Students should submit: FAFSA. Priority filing deadline is 3/15. The Princeton Review suggests that all financial aid forms be submitted as soon as possible after October 1. *Need-based scholarships/grants offered:* Federal Pell, FSEOG, State scholarships/grants, Private scholarships, College/university scholarship or grant aid from institutional funds, United Negro College Fund. *Loan aid offered:* Direct Subsidized Stafford Loans, Direct Unsubsidized Stafford Loans, Direct PLUS loans, Federal Perkins Loans, College/university loans from institutional funds. Applicants will be notified of awards on a rolling basis beginning 3/15. Federal Work-Study Program available. Institutional employment available.

The Inside Word

The University of Illinois' application review process distinguishes itself from that of many state schools in that every application is considered individually—no small feat for a campus of about 30,000 students. Don't be fooled by the university's high acceptance rate: U of I's applicant pool tends to be self-selective, and those without sufficient qualifications won't make the cut.

THE SCHOOL SAYS "..."

From the Admissions Office

"The campus has been aptly described as a collection of neighborhoods constituting a diverse and vibrant city. The neighborhoods are of many types: students and faculty within a department; people sharing a room or house; the members of a professional organization, a service club, or an intramural team; or simply people who, starting out as strangers sharing a class or a study lounge or a fondness for a weekly film series, have become friends. The city of this description is the university itself—a rich cosmopolitan environment constructed by students and faculty to meet their educational and personal goals. The quality of intellectual life parallels that of other great universities, and many faculty and students who have their choice of top institutions select Illinois over its peers. While such choices are based often on the quality of individual programs of study, another crucial factor is the 'tone' of the campus life that is linked with the virtues of Midwestern culture. There is an informality and a near-absence of pretension, which, coupled with a tradition of commitment to excellence, creates an atmosphere that is unique among the finest institutions.

"Applicants are required to take the SAT or the ACT with the writing section."

SELECTIVITY

Admissions Rating	90
# of applicants	35,819
% of applicants accepted	59
% of acceptees attending	33
# offered a place on the wait list	3,008
% accepting a place on wait list	62
% admitted from wait list	54

FRESHMAN PROFILE

Range SAT Critical Reading	590–690
Range SAT Math	700–790
Range SAT Writing	600–690
Range ACT Composite	26–32
Minimum internet-based TOEFL	80
% graduated top 10% of class	59
% graduated top 25% of class	90
% graduated top 50% of class	99

DEADLINES

Regular	
Priority	11/1
Deadline	12/1
Notification	2/13
Nonfall registration?	No

APPLICANTS ALSO LOOK AT AND OFTEN PREFER
University of Michigan–Ann Arbor; Northwestern University

AND SOMETIMES PREFER
Indiana University Bloomington; University of Wisconsin–Madison; Washington University in St. Louis; University of Iowa

AND RARELY PREFER
Purdue University–West Lafayette

FINANCIAL FACTS

Financial Aid Rating	78
Annual in-state tuition	$12,036
Annual out-of-state tuition	$26,662
Room and board	$10,848
Required fees	$3,590
Books and supplies	$1,200
Average frosh need-based scholarship	$14,418
Average UG need-based scholarship	$13,591
% needy frosh rec. need-based scholarship or grant aid	80
% needy UG rec. need-based scholarship or grant aid	79
% needy frosh rec. non-need-based scholarship or grant aid	20
% needy UG rec. non-need-based scholarship or grant aid	11
% needy frosh rec. need-based self-help aid	78
% needy UG rec. need-based self-help aid	81
% frosh need fully met	14
% ugrads need fully met	11
Average % of frosh need met	69
Average % of ugrad need met	64

THE UNIVERSITY OF IOWA

107 CALVIN HALL, IOWA CITY, IA 52242 • ADMISSIONS: 319-335-3847 • FAX: 319-333-1535

CAMPUS LIFE

Quality of Life Rating	89
Fire Safety Rating	92
Green Rating	98
Type of school	Public
Affiliation	No Affiliation
Environment	City

STUDENTS

Total undergrad enrollment	23,357
% male/female	48/52
% from out of state	34
% frosh from public high school	90
% frosh live on campus	96
% ugrads live on campus	26
# of fraternities (% ugrad men join)	27 (13)
# of sororities (% ugrad women join)	23 (18)
% African American	3
% Asian	4
% Caucasian	67
% Hispanic	7
% Native American	<1
% Pacific Islander	<1
% Two or more races	3
% Race and/or ethnicity unknown	4
% international	12
# of countries represented	63

SURVEY SAYS...
Students are happy
School is well run
Students love Iowa City, IA
Great off-campus food
Recreation facilities are great
Lots of beer drinking
Hard liquor is popular
Everyone loves the Hawkeyes
Campus newspaper is popular

ACADEMICS

Academic Rating	73
% students returning for sophomore year	85
% students graduating within 4 years	51
% students graduating within 6 years	72
Calendar	Semester
Student/faculty ratio	15:1
Profs interesting rating	72
Profs accessible rating	75

Most classes have 10–19 students.
Most lab/discussion sessions have 20–29 students.

MOST POPULAR MAJORS
Business/Commerce; Pre-Medicine/Pre-Medical Studies; Engineering

STUDENTS SAY "..."

Academics

The University of Iowa manages to pull off an amazing feat: It's a "Big Ten university full of exciting opportunities," yet it's still able to maintain "a small-college feel." Moreover, as the state's flagship school, Iowa provides a "great education" at a "reasonable price." Additionally, students here welcome the fact that "requirements are minimal." In turn, this truly encourages undergrads to "make [their] education [their] own." While there are certainly a "[wide] range of degree programs" from which to choose, students here are especially impressed with Iowa's journalism, premed, writing, nursing, and engineering departments. Though professors certainly run the gamut from "amazing" to "boring," the majority of them are "very engaged with students and are always helpful to any student looking to push their learning beyond the classroom." A fellow student concurs adding that her professors are "passionate, encouraging, and invested in the success of their students both inside and outside of academia." Undergrads at Iowa also appreciate that their teachers really "do a nice job of balancing lectures with real-world applications of the material." Finally, as this pleased undergrad summarizes her school, "The University of Iowa is a platform to launch yourself to the top of your field at an affordable price."

Life

If there's one thing that undergrads tend to agree on, it's that "life is pretty fun at The University of Iowa." To begin with, sports culture is definitely big here. As one student relays, "During football season, Saturdays get crazy. There is just a sea of black and gold swarming toward the stadium. Nothing can really compare to 70,000 Hawkeye fans in one place." Additionally, students love the new rec center, which frequently runs trips "to go rock-climbing, camping, hiking, or kayaking." Of course, the university also sponsors a number of other events outside of athletics. For example, "there are always concerts and comedians on campus, [and] many [of these shows] are even free to students. There are also free movies shown at the Iowa Memorial Union." Students also stress that the university has a lively drinking scene. Indeed, "there is always a party going on here at Iowa." Lastly, undergrads also love hometown Iowa City, which offers a "vibrant downtown" that's "literally across the street from campus." Students happily take advantage of the city's "unique places to eat, shop, or go out." As this undergrad poetically concludes, "When a man is tired of Iowa City, he is tired of life."

Student Body

With such a large student body, undergrads here all posit that there is no "typical" student. One pleased undergrad elaborates, "Everyone is unique and has a different story, but that's one thing that makes life here so great. You have the ability to meet people from around the country and around the world, and we all get to share the experience of college together." Indeed, students feel very fortunate to be surrounded by such diversity. "We have a strong LGBTQA presence on campus, [along with] different religious places near campus. [In addition,] there are many different organizations for minorities, religions, and everything else here on campus. I couldn't imagine someone coming here and not being able to find a student organization that is for them." Of course, if pressed to generalize, students will describe their fellow Hawkeyes as "friendly, hardworking, and studious" but also "laid-back" and "very social." However, what ultimately unites this student body is the fact that most undergrads have "their season football tickets by June."

FINANCIAL AID: 319-335-1450 • E-MAIL: ADMISSIONS@UIOWA.EDU • WEBSITE: WWW.UIOWA.EDU

THE PRINCETON REVIEW SAYS

Admissions

Very important factors considered include: rigor of secondary school record, class rank, academic GPA, standardized test scores. *Important factors considered include: Other factors considered include:* recommendation(s), talent/ability, character/personal qualities, state residency. SAT or ACT required. ACT with Writing recommended. TOEFL required of all international applicants. High school diploma is required and GED is accepted. *Academic units required:* 4 English, 3 math, 3 science, 2 foreign language, 3 social studies. *Academic units recommended:* 4 math, 4 foreign language.

Financial Aid

Students should submit: FAFSA, Institution's own financial aid form. Priority filing deadline is 3/1. The Princeton Review suggests that all financial aid forms be submitted as soon as possible after October 1. *Need-based scholarships/ grants offered:* Federal Pell, FSEOG, State scholarships/grants, Private scholarships, College/university scholarship or grant aid from institutional funds. *Loan aid offered:* Direct Subsidized Stafford Loans, Direct Unsubsidized Stafford Loans, Direct PLUS loans, Federal Perkins Loans, Federal Nursing Loans, College/university loans from institutional funds. Applicants will be notified of awards on a rolling basis beginning 3/15. Federal Work-Study Program available. Institutional employment available.

The Inside Word

Like many large public universities, admissions officers at the University of Iowa rely heavily on quantitative factors when determining an applicant's status. Therefore, GPA and standardized test scores will likely hold the most weight. It should also be noted that the majority of applicants are admitted to the College of Liberal Arts & Sciences or the College of Engineering. Students interested in other programs (say within the College of Business or Nursing) often apply after they have enrolled in the university.

THE SCHOOL SAYS "..."

From the Admissions Office

"The University of Iowa offers all of the opportunities and resources of a large, research university, while putting a strong emphasis on the undergraduate student experience. As the first public university to enroll men and women on an equal basis, Iowa is proud of its history in providing a world-class education to students from all backgrounds. Today, the University of Iowa offers nationally ranked academic programs, strong pre-professional programs in the health sciences and law, and access to world-renowned faculty. With an emphasis on small class sizes, students interact with faculty both inside and outside the classroom. Located in one of the top college towns in American, Iowa's campus is undergoing a historic physical makeover with construction underway on a new residence hall, school of music, school of art and art history, and Hancher Auditorium, the UI's world-renowned performing arts venue."

SELECTIVITY

Admissions Rating	80
# of applicants	26,222
% of applicants accepted	81
% of acceptees attending	25
# offered a place on the wait list	0

FRESHMAN PROFILE

Range SAT Critical Reading	460–630
Range SAT Math	540–690
Range ACT Composite	23–28
Minimum paper TOEFL	530
Minimum internet-based TOEFL	80
Average HS GPA	3.7

DEADLINES

Regular	
Deadline	4/1
Nonfall registration?	Yes

APPLICANTS ALSO LOOK AT AND OFTEN PREFER

University of Illinois at Urbana-Champaign;
Northwestern University

AND SOMETIMES PREFER

Indiana University Bloomington; Iowa State
University; University of Missouri

AND RARELY PREFER

Missouri University of Science and
Technology; Cornell College

FINANCIAL FACTS

Financial Aid Rating	82
Annual in-state tuition	$6,878
Annual out-of-state tuition	$26,966
Room and board	$10,108
Required fees	$1,447
Books and supplies	$950
Average frosh need-based scholarship	$8,695
Average UG need-based scholarship	$7,952
% needy frosh rec. need-based scholarship or grant aid	77
% needy UG rec. need-based scholarship or grant aid	71
% needy frosh rec. non-need-based scholarship or grant aid	71
% needy UG rec. non-need-based scholarship or grant aid	47
% needy frosh rec. need-based self-help aid	83
% needy UG rec. need-based self-help aid	87
% frosh rec. any financial aid	79
% UG rec. any financial aid	72
% UG borrow to pay for school	51
Average cumulative indebtedness	$28,771
% frosh need fully met	35
% ugrads need fully met	26
Average % of frosh need met	70
Average % of ugrad need met	67

UNIVERSITY OF KANSAS

OFFICE OF ADMISSIONS, LAWRENCE, KS 66045-7576 • ADMISSIONS: 785-864-3911 • FAX: 785-864-5017

CAMPUS LIFE

Quality of Life Rating	94
Fire Safety Rating	97
Green Rating	84
Type of school	Public
Affiliation	No Affiliation
Environment	City

STUDENTS

Total undergrad enrollment	19,245
% male/female	50/50
% from out of state	27
% frosh live on campus	63
% ugrads live on campus	25
# of fraternities (% ugrad men join)	29 (18)
# of sororities (% ugrad women join)	17 (25)
% African American	4
% Asian	4
% Caucasian	71
% Hispanic	7
% Native American	<1
% Pacific Islander	<1
% Two or more races	5
% Race and/or ethnicity unknown	1
% international	7
# of countries represented	75

SURVEY SAYS...

Students are happy
Great library
Career services are great
School is well run
Students get along with local community
Students love Lawrence, KS
Great off-campus food
Recreation facilities are great
Lots of beer drinking
Hard liquor is popular
Everyone loves the Jayhawks
Campus newspaper is popular
Alumni active on campus

ACADEMICS

Academic Rating	72
% students returning for sophomore year	80
% students graduating within 4 years	37
% students graduating within 6 years	61
Calendar	Semester
Student/faculty ratio	17:1
Profs interesting rating	73
Profs accessible rating	80

Most classes have 10–19 students.
Most lab/discussion sessions have
10–19 students.

MOST POPULAR MAJORS
Biology; Business/Commerce; Psychology

STUDENTS SAY "..."

Academics

Located in the heartland's quintessential college town, University of Kansas's flagship campus is a "place of tradition" as well as opportunity, combining "stimulating academics with a community that is passionate about the school." Most of KU's 2,800 faculty members are "actively engaged in research in their particular field," but there is nonetheless a real emphasis on undergraduate teaching. Here, "the faculty is obviously willing to do what it takes to help," and "teachers are always urging students to contact them with questions or visit their office hours." An undergrad details, "The personalities and teaching styles of KU's professors vary widely, but all of the instructors I have had are fully engaged in teaching and truly enjoy helping students learn." That said, "there are a lot of giant lecture halls your freshmen and sophomore year," which some students find "overwhelming." On the flip side, the big-school setting proffers "abundant resources," including "research opportunities" for undergraduates and "one of the best study abroad programs in the nation." In fact, many say, "The experience outside of the classroom is what sets you up for success after college." Speaking of life after graduation, KU's "career center is committed to getting students hired," and "there are many job opportunities" in nearby Topeka and Kansas City. To make the deal sweeter, KU graduates aren't strapped with insurmountable debt: "In-state tuition is very affordable."

Life

In the pursuit of an "incredible college experience," KU undergrads definitely keep busy: "The typical student probably volunteers in the community, has a part time job, [and] has some special hobby (from rock climbing to tightrope walking)." Incoming freshman will find "over 600 student groups to participate in," ranging from "Quidditch to chess club to the arts," and "there is never a dull night" on campus, where "Student Union Activities brings in comedians, authors, and movies on a regular basis." During the winter months, "KU basketball is our religion, and Allen Fieldhouse is our church." An undergrad admits, "I schedule everything in my life around the KU men's basketball schedule, as does much of the student population." Described as "the perfect college town," "Lawrence has a great live music scene, cool coffee shops, and eclectic stores," as well as bars and nightclubs popular with students. "People in Lawrence are also very outdoorsy," and, when the weather is nice, "you can rent camping equipment from the rec for a weekend out at the lake" or "go rock climbing" nearby. For a more cosmopolitan outing, "being close to Kansas City provides a lot of entertainment from museums and art shows to music and dining."

Students

Students say you'd be surprised by the diversity on this friendly Midwestern campus, lauding the KU's "ability to unite 30,000 people of different values and backgrounds." There are "students from every county in Kansas, every state, and over 100 countries," with noticeable representations from out-of-state cities like St. Louis and Denver mixing into the large in-state crowd. "KU students find a great balance in work and play," with some undergrads tipping the scales in one direction or the other: "You have your 'here for a good time' types, absolutely rock-star scholars, and dedicated students who balance their GPA and their social calendar." In terms of making friends and fitting in, getting involved is the best way to mitigate the campus's size: "There are so many opportunities at KU that it can seem a bit overwhelming, but students really find their niche and run with it." Of particular note, "there is definitely a big Greek life presence" on campus, which some say causes a "schism" in the undergraduate community. In counterpoint, a student reassures us, "The Greek community does intermingle frequently with non-Greeks. I'm not Greek, but I see it a lot and have a lot of Greek friends."

UNIVERSITY OF KANSAS

FINANCIAL AID: 785-864-4700 • E-MAIL: ADM@KU.EDU • WEBSITE: WWW.KU.EDU

THE PRINCETON REVIEW SAYS

Admissions

Very important factors considered include: academic GPA, standardized test scores. *Other factors considered include:* SAT or ACT required. ACT with or without writing accepted. SAT with or without Essay component accepted. TOEFL required of all international applicants. High school diploma is required and GED is accepted. *Academic units required:* 4 English, 3 math, 3 science (1 lab), 3 social studies, 3 academic electives. *Academic units recommended:* 4 English, 4 math, 3 science, 3 social studies, 3 academic electives.

Financial Aid

Students should submit: FAFSA. Priority filing deadline is 3/1. The Princeton Review suggests that all financial aid forms be submitted as soon as possible after October 1. *Need-based scholarships/grants offered:* Federal Pell, FSEOG, State scholarships/grants, Private scholarships, College/university scholarship or grant aid from institutional funds. *Loan aid offered:* Direct Subsidized Stafford Loans, Direct Unsubsidized Stafford Loans, Direct PLUS loans, Federal Perkins Loans, Federal Nursing Loans, College/university loans from institutional funds. Applicants will be notified of awards on a rolling basis beginning 4/1. Federal Work-Study Program available. Institutional employment available.

The Inside Word

KU has a great program for assured admission! The standards for 2016 are: 2.0 GPA (resident) or 2.5 GPA (nonresident) in the Kansas Qualified high school core curriculum and 21 ACT/980 SAT and 3.25 cumulative GPA or 24 ACT/1090 SAT and 3.0 cumulative GPA. Professional schools have different standards. SAT only includes math and critical reading.

THE SCHOOL SAYS "..."

From the Admissions Office

"The University of Kansas has a tradition of academic excellence. The mission of KU is to lift students and society by educating leaders, building healthy communities, and making discoveries that will change the world. Outstanding students from around the world attend KU for its outstanding academics, challenging opportunities, the Jayhawk community, and incredible value including four-year renewable scholarships. KU provides students exceptional opportunities in the University Honors Program, experiential learning, undergraduate research, internships, study abroad, and more than 600 clubs and organizations. The university is located in Lawrence (forty minutes from Kansas City), a vibrant community of 93,000 consistently recognized as one of the nation's top ten college towns.

"All students are encouraged to apply. KU does an individual review of each application. We consider many factors that are provided on the application such as cumulative high school GPA, ACT or SAT scores, GPA in the core curriculum, and strength of courses. We may also ask you to respond to shortessay questions that will provide additional information to support your application."

SELECTIVITY

Admissions Rating	77
# of applicants	15,155
% of applicants accepted	93
% of acceptees attending	30

FRESHMAN PROFILE

Range ACT Composite	22–28
Average HS GPA	3.5
% graduated top 10% of class	26
% graduated top 25% of class	56
% graduated top 50% of class	87

DEADLINES

Regular	
Priority	11/1
Nonfall registration?	Yes

FINANCIAL FACTS

Financial Aid Rating	84
Annual in-state tuition	$9,123
Annual out-of-state tuition	$23,774
Room and board	$9,324
Required fees	$934
Books and supplies	$1,040
Average frosh need-based scholarship	$7,001
Average UG need-based scholarship	$6,383
% needy frosh rec. need-based scholarship or grant aid	84
% needy UG rec. need-based scholarship or grant aid	75
% needy frosh rec. non-need-based scholarship or grant aid	9
% needy UG rec. non-need-based scholarship or grant aid	6
% needy frosh rec. need-based self-help aid	69
% needy UG rec. need-based self-help aid	76
% frosh rec. any financial aid	77
% UG rec. any financial aid	65
% UG borrow to pay for school	52
Average cumulative indebtedness	$27,492
% frosh need fully met	36
% ugrads need fully met	33
Average % of frosh need met	73
Average % of ugrad need met	73

UNIVERSITY OF KENTUCKY

100 FUNKHOUSER BUILDING, LEXINGTON, KY 40506 • ADMISSIONS: 859-257-2000 • FAX: 859-257-3823

STUDENTS SAY "..."

Academics

The University of Kentucky in Lexington is "all about making a name for yourself by preparing for and getting involved in future career goals while having fun and enjoying what college is all about." "Making a name for yourself" here requires distinguishing yourself in a crowd of almost 19,000 undergraduates; daunting as that sounds, students tell us it can be done. "Getting involved in future career goals" is easy enough, given the "great selection of courses and majors" available. Kentucky offers undergraduate degrees in twelve of its nineteen divisions. Choices include the College of Agriculture (with popular majors in animal science, agricultural economics, and hospitality management), the College of Business and Management, the College of Education, the College of Engineering, the College of Communications and Information Studies (advertising, journalism, and library science), and the College of Arts and Sciences (biology, history, and political science). Students here laud the "impressive teaching staff, dedicated to enhancing student knowledge and teaching students about the future." UK's brand-new library "is also quite amazing. It is the perfect place to go study because usually the dorms can be a bit too distracting." All told, go-getters willing to take initiative will find UK offers "a safe and fun atmosphere where you have unlimited opportunities to get involved at a reasonable price."

Life

"Everyone is a Wildcat" at UK, because "UK has tremendous sports programs and big fans all around the United States." Men's basketball fans "are among the craziest in the nation," and students "would be football fanatics if our team would win a game every now and then." "Because UK is dry, most parties are held off campus." Social life for many revolves around the off-campus Greek houses where "there is always a party going on, but you have to be a part of a fraternity or sorority to really know about it and attend." Some students report, "There are a lot of nonalcoholic parties in the dorms that might be crazier than the alcoholic parties," although others advise, "It's better to live off campus because the residence halls are pretty bad (except for the new ones), the meal plan is awful, and everything off campus is a lot cheaper." Hometown Lexington "is a great city with much to do and lots of opportunities. It offers many different clubs, bars, and restaurants that college students can go to as well as horse racing. All of these venues have a 'College Day' where students get discounts." One sophomore warns, however, "Small-town students can become distracted by the lights of the city."

Student Body

"The typical UK student has a Southern accent, likes to party, and often shops at J. Crew," but, "as the undergraduate population is about 19,000, there are a lot of people who do not fit that description." True, one of the most common "types"—or at least the most conspicuous one—are the "beautiful people, the hot girls and guys who roam the campus and dress up to go to class." But for every "collar-popping, stuck-up frat boy" there's also "your typical country Kentucky boy, boots and all." What you won't find many of at UK are "liberals—they are few and far between—and the type of atypical student with wild hair colors or other style extremes." Most "lean right politically, but generally the student body is apathetic." School spirit is rampant, so much so that "on an average day, one in three students will have some sort of UK clothing on."

FINANCIAL AID: 859-257-3172 • E-MAIL: ADMISSION@UKY.EDU • WEBSITE: WWW.UKY.EDU

THE PRINCETON REVIEW SAYS

Admissions

Very important factors considered include: rigor of secondary school record, academic GPA, standardized test scores. *Other factors considered include:* class rank, application essay, recommendation(s), interview, extracurricular activities, talent/ability, character/personal qualities, alumni/ae relation, geographical residence, racial/ethnic status, volunteer work. SAT or ACT required. ACT with or without writing accepted. TOEFL required of all international applicants. High school diploma is required and GED is accepted. *Academic units required:* 4 English, 3 math, 3 science, 1 science lab, 2 foreign language, 3 social studies, 7 academic electives, 1 visual/performing arts, and 1 unit from above areas or other academic areas.

Financial Aid

Students should submit: FAFSA. Regular filing deadline is 2/15. The Princeton Review suggests that all financial aid forms be submitted as soon as possible after October 1. *Need-based scholarships/grants offered:* Federal Pell, FSEOG, State scholarships/grants, Private scholarships, College/university scholarship or grant aid from institutional funds. *Loan aid offered:* Direct Subsidized Stafford Loans, Direct Unsubsidized Stafford Loans, Direct PLUS loans, Federal Perkins Loans, State Loans, College/university loans from institutional funds. Applicants will be notified of awards on a rolling basis beginning 4/1. Federal Work-Study Program available. Institutional employment available.

The Inside Word

The University of Kentucky's admissions team is about as objective as they come. If you have the GPA, class rank, and test scores, you'll in all likelihood be welcomed into the Wildcat community. The university is continually looking to improve its selectivity, so hitting the books is a must if you want to be a serious contender.

THE SCHOOL SAYS "..."

From the Admissions Office

"The University of Kentucky offers you an outstanding learning environment and quality instruction through its excellent faculty. Of the 1,892 full-time faculty, 98 percent hold the doctorate degree or the highest degree in their field of study. Many are nationally and internationally known for their research, distinguished teaching, and scholarly service to Kentucky, the nation, and the world. UK's scholars (students, faculty, and alumni) have been honored by Nobel, Pulitzer, Rhodes, Fulbright, Guggenheim, and Grammy awards, and most recently the Metropolitan Opera and the Marshall Foundation. Yet, with a student to teacher ratio of only seventeen to one, UK faculty are accessible and willing to answer your questions and discuss your interests.

"UK will accept the SAT. The writing sections of the ACT and SAT will not be used in the admission process."

SELECTIVITY

Admissions Rating	83
# of applicants	20,677
% of applicants accepted	72
% of acceptees attending	35
# offered a place on the wait list	1,032

FRESHMAN PROFILE

Range SAT Critical Reading	490–620
Range SAT Math	510–640
Range SAT Writing	480–610
Range ACT Composite	22–28
Minimum paper TOEFL	527
Average HS GPA	3.6
% graduated top 10% of class	30
% graduated top 25% of class	57
% graduated top 50% of class	85

DEADLINES

Early action	
Deadline	12/1
Regular	
Priority	2/15
Deadline	2/15
Notification	8/15
Nonfall registration?	Yes

APPLICANTS ALSO LOOK AT AND OFTEN PREFER

Indiana University Bloomington; Miami University; Centre College; Transylvania University

AND SOMETIMES PREFER

University of Louisville; Bellarmine University; University of Tennessee–Knoxville

AND RARELY PREFER

Florida State University; University of Florida; University of Illinois at Urbana-Champaign; Purdue University–West Lafayette

FINANCIAL FACTS

Financial Aid Rating	79
Annual in-state tuition	$8,610
Annual out-of-state tuition	$18,798
Room and board	$10,192
Required fees	$1,066
Books and supplies	$800
Average frosh need-based scholarship	$5,969
Average UG need-based scholarship	$5,306
% needy frosh rec. need-based scholarship or grant aid	46
% needy UG rec. need-based scholarship or grant aid	49
% needy frosh rec. non-need-based scholarship or grant aid	90
% needy UG rec. non-need-based scholarship or grant aid	73
% needy frosh rec. need-based self-help aid	59
% needy UG rec. need-based self-help aid	68
% frosh rec. any financial aid	40
% UG rec. any financial aid	38
% frosh need fully met	22
% ugrads need fully met	18
Average % of frosh need met	67
Average % of ugrad need met	63

UNIVERSITY OF LOUISIANA AT LAFAYETTE

PO DRAWER 41210, LAFAYETTE, LA 70504 • ADMISSIONS: 337-482-6553 • FAX: 337-482-1112

STUDENTS SAY " . . . "

Academics

With a "beautiful campus" and "friendly atmosphere," it's quite easy to understand how students could be drawn to University of Louisiana at Lafayette. This public research university strives to provide undergrads with an affordable education and offers an "abundance [of] scholarship opportunities." Undergrads also appreciate the breadth of fantastic academic departments, from the "wonderful" nursing program and the "exceptional biology program" to the "good architecture program" and "phenomenal art [department]." And, since it's "smaller than most state schools," undergrads here are really able to interact with their professors and receive "quality in-class instruction." Indeed, students seem to thoroughly enjoy their courses. This can definitely be attributed to "amazing faculty." As an English major explains, "Most of the professors I've had have been very passionate about their subjects, which in turn makes the student interested in the class. They're all very open to questions and discussions." A fellow English student agrees, "My professors have been helpful and knowledgeable, and they are always willing to help their students succeed." Perhaps this pre-med student best sums up the experience here: "UL is all about melding creativity, spicy Cajun culture, and academia into a gumbo-pot of successful scholars!"

Life

Students who attend University of Louisiana at Lafayette will likely never be bored. There's always something of which to take advantage. To begin with, we're told that "a lot of the buzz around campus [surrounds] sports." An English major confirms, "Football is a major thing in South Louisiana. I think we're the second biggest 'sports fan base' behind LSU, of course." Come game day, many people "tailgate and there is a big community of RV's and tents from [both] out-of-towners and [those who reside] on campus." Students also report that "the Ragin Cajun Catholics and Christian community is awesome and dynamic!" Many undergrads can also be found "working out in the gym." And a large number participate in Greek life as well. Lastly, students love the area surrounding UL. A biology major happily shares, "Throughout the year, there are tons of festivals unique to Lafayette, all of which are free to attend, such as Festivale Acadiens, which celebrates Cajun culture, as well as Festivale Internationale, which is the largest free world-music festival in the world."

Student Body

Undergrads at UL steadfastly insist that "there is no typical . . . student." Those who enroll here will discover all types, "from quiet students [and] outgoing students [to] sporty students [and] artsy students." A biology major explains, "We have students of all ethnicities, races, religions, and styles. There are very few social boundaries and mostly everyone is accepting of our diverse student body." Of course, when pressed, one journalism major admits that there is a typical UL Lafayette undergrad, one that "reflects Lafayette's culture: creative, friendly, and food-loving." Many are also "involved in Greek life, and therefore [frequently participate] in community service and [embody] school spirit." By and large, undergrads also report that their peers are "dedicated and determined to succeed." Finally, an art education major encapsulates her fellow students by simply stating, "Everyone accepts one another for who they are. There are friends for everyone." And "as long as you make it a point to get out of your dorm once in a while, you will have close knit circle of friends in no time."

FINANCIAL AID: 337-482-6506 • E-MAIL: ENROLL@LOUISIANA.EDU • WEBSITE: WWW.LOUISIANA.EDU

THE PRINCETON REVIEW SAYS

Admissions

Very important factors considered include: rigor of secondary school record, class rank, academic GPA, standardized test scores. *Other factors considered include:* state residency. SAT or ACT required. ACT with or without writing accepted. TOEFL required of all international applicants. High school diploma is required and GED is accepted. *Academic units required:* 4 English, 4 math, 3 science, 2 foreign language, 1 social studies, 2 history, 1 visual/performing arts, and 1 unit from above areas or other academic areas.

Financial Aid

Students should submit: FAFSA. Priority filing deadline is 5/1. The Princeton Review suggests that all financial aid forms be submitted as soon as possible after October 1. *Need-based scholarships/grants offered:* Federal Pell, FSEOG, State scholarships/grants, Private scholarships, College/university scholarship or grant aid from institutional funds, Federal Nursing Scholarships. *Loan aid offered:* Federal Perkins Loans, Federal Nursing Loans. Applicants will be notified of awards on a rolling basis beginning 4/1. Federal Work-Study Program available. Institutional employment available.

The Inside Word

Students hoping to attend the University of Louisiana at Lafayette must make sure they take a solid college prep curriculum in high school. Applicants need to complete 4 units of English, 4 units of math, 4 units of social studies, 4 units of science, 2 units of foreign language and 1 unit within the arts in order to qualify. Students must have a minimum overall GPA of 2.0 (on a 4 point scale), a composite ACT score of 23 and/or SAT score of 1050 (critical reading & math) to gain admission. Finally, any candidate requiring remedial classes should complete that coursework prior to enrolling at UL.

THE SCHOOL SAYS "..."

From the Admissions Office

"The University of Louisiana at Lafayette offers students from throughout the United States and more than ninety countries strong academic training and personal enrichment opportunities in a friendly, comfortable, student-centered environment. UL Lafayette students are taught, mentored, and advised by some of the brightest and most accomplished faculty members in the United States. Although UL Lafayette offers more than 100 programs of study and the research opportunities, internship possibilities, and facilities of a major research-intensive university, average class size is approximately the same as that at many high schools and smaller higher education institutions. UL students receive a good deal of individual attention and support—both personal and academic—from faculty and staff.

"A wide range of cultural, recreational, and social activities are available on and off campus, including more than 150 campus organizations and clubs, NCAA Division I and intramural athletics, a state-of-the-art recreation and aquatic center, a thriving arts scene, a wide range of live music venues, shopping, a great variety of excellent restaurants, theaters, the second largest Mardi Gras in the nation, and an international music festival. In fact, *Utne Reader* magazine selected the city of Lafayette as Louisiana's 'Most Enlightened Town.' Recently, Lafayette was also listed as one of America's most optimistic cities.

"Our generous financial aid and scholarship programs, including an out-of-state tuition waiver for qualified students, make UL Lafayette one of the most affordable universities in the nation. Students who have completed the required college preparatory core curriculum in high school may qualify for admission on the basis of a combination of their high school cumulative grade point average and ACT or SAT scores."

SELECTIVITY
Admissions Rating	88
# of applicants	9,386
% of applicants accepted	56
% of acceptees attending	56

FRESHMAN PROFILE
Range SAT Critical Reading	470–590
Range SAT Math	490–590
Range ACT Composite	21–25
Minimum paper TOEFL	525
Average HS GPA	3.3
% graduated top 10% of class	19
% graduated top 25% of class	43
% graduated top 50% of class	74

DEADLINES
Regular	
Priority	7/20
Nonfall registration?	Yes

FINANCIAL FACTS
Financial Aid Rating	79
Annual in-state tuition	$4,916
Annual out-of-state tuition	$17,316
Room and board	$8,566
Required fees	$2,033
Books and supplies	$1,200
Average frosh need-based scholarship	$7,180
Average UG need-based scholarship	$6,558
% needy frosh rec. need-based scholarship or grant aid	96
% needy UG rec. need-based scholarship or grant aid	88
% needy frosh rec. non-need-based scholarship or grant aid	15
% needy UG rec. non-need-based scholarship or grant aid	9
% needy frosh rec. need-based self-help aid	48
% needy UG rec. need-based self-help aid	59
% frosh rec. any financial aid	87
% UG rec. any financial aid	72
% frosh need fully met	15
% ugrads need fully met	9
Average % of frosh need met	61
Average % of ugrad need met	52

UNIVERSITY OF LOUISVILLE

2301 SOUTH THIRD STREET, LOUISVILLE, KY 40292-0001 • ADMISSIONS: 502-852-6531 • FAX: 502-852-4776

STUDENTS SAY "..."

Academics

University of Louisville is an institution that affords undergraduates "endless opportunities." Certainly, as one of Kentucky's premiere public universities, a Louisville education means students are getting a "great value" and an affordable price tag. And when you combine those attributes with a "beautiful" campus that's "easy to navigate," well it's understandable why students eagerly exclaim that Louisville "feels...like home." With regards to academics, undergrads truly appreciate the university's "[emphasis on] critical thinking" as well as the "personalized" attention they receive. Therefore, it's no surprise to hear that Louisville professors "generally [seem to] care about student success [both] in[side] and outside the classroom." As one satisfied biology student further explains, "They are willing to go above and beyond to help you gain a better understanding of course material and obtain supplementary experience outside of the classroom using their own collaborations and affiliations in the field." However, some students do find cause to mention that professors in "higher up courses...are better than professors who teach gen-ed courses." Fortunately, students are pleased to discover that, for the most part, "U of L is about immersing yourself in a diverse community where you have the chance to grow academically, socially, spiritually, and in whatever other ways you choose."

Life

As one excited junior quickly exclaims, life at University of Louisville is "always lively." Indeed, "there is always something going on both on and off campus and numerous ways to get involved and have a great time." To begin with, Greek life is "fairly prominent." And, naturally, there's a small party scene to go with it. Fortunately, we're assured that "things never get out of hand; it's just students trying to wind down and have a good time." Sporting events are extremely popular as well and these undergrads generate a lot of Cardinal pride. As one music education major boasts, "We have several conference championships already this year and our basketball team looks to repeat as national champions." Additionally, Louisville students like to give back and community service is a common activity here. An impressed junior reveals, "People are pretty conscientious. They volunteer a lot and there are a million and one volunteer groups throughout the city. Same goes for environmental groups." Of course Louisville itself is a vibrant city and one which undergrads love to take advantage. For example, students flock to "4th Street Live!, a popular hangout." And they also "enjoy Churchill Downs and going to horse races as well as the eclectic Highlands area of Bardstown Road."

Student Body

Undergrads at University of Louisville really value the amount of diversity found among their student body. As a highly content nursing student immediately chimes in, "We have so many people with different backgrounds, religions, and interests that no matter where you come from or what you are interested in you will fit in." This sentiment is bolstered by a peer who states, "We have a little bit of everyone, from sorority girls to hippies to those who study all the time. You will not have trouble finding friends here." Certainly, there are also plenty of similarities to be found across the student body as well. After all, many undergrads hail from "the Louisville area" and hold "moderate political views." Students also say that "the majority of [individuals] are extremely nice and easy to get along with." And they are more than "willing to help" their peers whenever they're in need. Then again that's not terribly surprising given that, as this music education major eloquently states, "We are all Cardinals."

FINANCIAL AID: 502-852-5511 • E-MAIL: ADMITME@LOUISVILLE.EDU • WEBSITE: WWW.LOUISVILLE.EDU

THE PRINCETON REVIEW SAYS

Admissions

Very important factors considered include: rigor of secondary school record, academic GPA, standardized test scores. *Other factors considered include:* class rank, recommendation(s), extracurricular activities, talent/ability, state residency, racial/ethnic status, volunteer work, work experience. SAT or ACT required. ACT with or without writing accepted. TOEFL required of all international applicants. High school diploma is required and GED is accepted. *Academic units required:* 4 English, 3 math, 3 science, 1 science lab, 2 foreign language, 3 social studies, 5 academic electives, 1 visual/performing arts, and 5 units from above areas or other academic areas. *Academic units recommended:* 4 math, 4 science, 3 foreign language.

Financial Aid

Students should submit: FAFSA. Priority filing deadline is 2/15. The Princeton Review suggests that all financial aid forms be submitted as soon as possible after October 1. *Need-based scholarships/grants offered:* Federal Pell, FSEOG, State scholarships/grants, Private scholarships, College/university scholarship or grant aid from institutional funds. *Loan aid offered:* Direct Subsidized Stafford Loans, Direct Unsubsidized Stafford Loans, Direct PLUS loans, Federal Perkins Loans, Federal Nursing Loans. Applicants will be notified of awards on a rolling basis beginning 4/1. Federal Work-Study Program available. Institutional employment available.

The Inside Word

By and large, admissions decisions at University of Louisville are highly dependent on quantitative data. This means that each applicant's class rank, GPA and standardized test scores will be of utmost importance. Attention will also be paid to course selection; a strong college prep curriculum should be a given. Requirements will vary depending on the specific school to which a candidate is applying. For example, applicants interested in the School of Music must also pass an audition. And nursing students face a two-part process; applying for the lower-level division in freshman year and then applying for the upper-level division in junior year.

THE SCHOOL SAYS "..."

From the Admissions Office

"The University of Louisville (UofL) has transformed into a premier metropolitan university—and it keeps getting better. It is a tight knit community with the feel of a small college where you can walk anywhere on campus in only ten minutes. Over the past ten years it has dramatically improved its on-campus environment with the addition of new residence halls, new apartments near campus, a new state-of-the-art student recreation center and restaurants and shopping near campus with the right mix of local flavor. Located in a vibrant city that is known worldwide for the Kentucky Derby, students quickly learn to navigate its great parks, discover local restaurants and explore a revitalized downtown and neighborhoods with an eclectic environment.

"With over 50 percent of our entering freshmen beginning their studies with college credit, U of L is a strong academic environment with opportunities inside and outside the classroom to prepare you for professional school or your first job. The city and UofL are closely linked, providing opportunities for internships, coops, part-time jobs and service learning experiences. Our commitment to diversity has created a culture with support for LGBT students and students of all socioeconomic and ethnic backgrounds.

"Although widely known for our engineering, business and medical programs, we offer over 200 academic programs and in recent years have added undergraduate programs in Public Health, Social Work, Asian Studies and Latin American and Latino Studies, demonstrating a desire to prepare students for the 21st Century needs of our city, region and beyond."

SELECTIVITY

Admissions Rating	83
# of applicants	9,430
% of applicants accepted	72
% of acceptees attending	41

FRESHMAN PROFILE

Range SAT Critical Reading	490–620
Range SAT Math	510–620
Range ACT Composite	22–29
Minimum paper TOEFL	550
Average HS GPA	3.6

DEADLINES

Regular	
Priority	2/15
Nonfall registration?	Yes

FINANCIAL FACTS

Financial Aid Rating	81
Annual out-of-state tuition	$24,848
Room and board	$7,942
Books and supplies	$1,000
Average frosh need-based scholarship	$9,568
Average UG need-based scholarship	$9,023
% needy frosh rec. need-based scholarship or grant aid	97
% needy UG rec. need-based scholarship or grant aid	90
% needy frosh rec. non-need-based scholarship or grant aid	19
% needy UG rec. non-need-based scholarship or grant aid	13
% needy frosh rec. need-based self-help aid	54
% needy UG rec. need-based self-help aid	60
% frosh rec. any financial aid	97
% UG rec. any financial aid	79
% UG borrow to pay for school	52
Average cumulative indebtedness	$23,488
% frosh need fully met	26
% ugrads need fully met	23
Average % of frosh need met	64
Average % of ugrad need met	63

UNIVERSITY OF MAINE

5713 Chadbourne Hall, Orono, ME 04469-5713 • Admissions: 207-581-1561 • Fax: 207-581-1213

STUDENTS SAY "..."

Academics

The University of Maine is, put simply, "a fantastic state school." Many students, particularly those for whom the Orono campus is "close to home," love that the school's "tuition is affordable" and "financial aid was fantastic." But UMaine's value doesn't compromise academic quality: the university offers "a great Engineering program," a "wonderful music program," "highly respected forestry and natural resource programs," a great "marine science program and semester by the sea program," and a host of other academic concentration opportunities. UMaine makes sustainability learning and practice a priority: it's a very "green" school that both cares about its students and the environment." Indeed, one students lists UMaine's unique strengths as "providing students with a quality education, preparing us for the working world, and helping to promote a environmentally friendly future." The university's "difficult professors" will "ensure you learn the material," and provide students with a connection to "to highly recognized people in [their] field." "The majority of the faculty members are brilliant and genuinely care about the progress of their students." "There is quite a bit of discussion in most classes," and another student extols, "I've had three of the greatest teachers I've ever had here already." "The professors are brilliant and expect a lot from their students," so dedicated undergrads appreciate UMaine's "late library hours." From the undergrads' perspective, "The majority of my professors really enjoy what they teach, and I think that really has an impact on whether their students do well or not." Faculty and staff are "supportive and helpful people that make me proud to be a Black Bear" who facilitate valuable "undergrad research opportunities" "in any field." "The resources on campus are top-notch, especially the career services, library, and counseling center," helping to ensure that "UMaine students are prepared to handle college life, as well as post-grad." Top-notch students also appreciate the school's "honors program, which is a fantastic group of thinkers from all majors." In all aspects of UMaine's education, "I am encouraged to think for myself, and work on projects that I want to be a part of, in a wide range of subjects." True to its motto, UMaine's students call it the "College of our hearts, always."

Life

If you "love the outdoors," it can't be disputed that "Maine is very beautiful." UMaine students love to join "clubs that take advantage of natural beauty that Maine has to offer" or hike "beautiful trails around Orono." "Outdoor activities" like "skiing and walking" abound, and "Frisbee is a pretty big thing at UMaine." "The campus is very active and the people are very open and friendly." People display some "health awareness," appreciate the "tobacco free campus" and "great transportation services," and find that "the dorms are great to live in." "Generally, everyone is really nice and neighborly," there's "always something to do either on campus or off," and there's "a sense of community." Off campus, which is "about fifteen minutes from the mall" and "restaurants," students enjoy "going into Old Town on the weekends and getting coffee with friends," "concerts," or "going to hockey games (the school spirit demonstrated at these games is amazing)." From one student's perspective, "there's a lot of drinking that goes on because it's such a rural area," but another reports, "I like to climb at the indoor rock wall for fun; there are a lot of alternate activities for students that don't 'party' on the weekends."

Student Body

As at most places, at UMaine, "you fit in by finding a group, organization, major, that you enjoy and through that you meet people with common interests." "Most kids are Maine locals," but there's still a "myriad of ethnic backgrounds," and a "wide range of personalities" "including fraternity and sorority members, hippy-types, redneck-types, the super-studious and athletes." "In general, the students here are pretty open-minded and kind," there's "a lot of school spirit" and "no one is overly assertive about their personalities." "The typical student is pretty laid back, they accomplish the work assigned, they attend class most of the time, and they are pretty friendly." "Everyone has their own groups of close friends, but it's likely for you to meet a new person every day."

FINANCIAL AID: 207-581-1324 • E-MAIL: UM-ADMIT@MAINE.EDU • WEBSITE: WWW.UMAINE.EDU

THE PRINCETON REVIEW SAYS

Admissions

Very important factors considered include: rigor of secondary school record, class rank, academic GPA, standardized test scores. *Important factors considered include:* application essay, recommendation(s). *Other factors considered include:* interview, extracurricular activities, talent/ability, character/personal qualities, volunteer work, work experience. SAT or ACT required. ACT with or without writing accepted. SAT with or without Essay component accepted. TOEFL required of all international applicants. High school diploma is required and GED is accepted. *Academic units required:* 4 English, 3 math, 2 science, 2 science labs, 2 foreign language, 2 social studies, 4 academic electives, and 1 unit from above areas or other academic areas. *Academic units recommended:* 4 English, 4 math, 4 science, 3 science labs, 2 foreign language, 2 social studies, 1 history, 4 academic electives, and 1 unit from above areas or other academic areas.

Financial Aid

Students should submit: FAFSA. Regular filing deadline is 5/15. The Princeton Review suggests that all financial aid forms be submitted as soon as possible after October 1. *Need-based scholarships/grants offered:* Federal Pell, FSEOG, State scholarships/grants, Private scholarships, College/university scholarship or grant aid from institutional funds, Federal Nursing Scholarships. *Loan aid offered:* Direct Subsidized Stafford Loans, Direct Unsubsidized Stafford Loans, Direct PLUS loans, Federal Perkins Loans, State Loans, College/university loans from institutional funds. Applicants will be notified of awards on a rolling basis beginning 3/15. Federal Work-Study Program available. Institutional employment available.

The Inside Word

Because many UMaine applicants are likely to be local, interviews, campus visits, and tours (run through the Buchanan Alumni House) are particularly encouraged when possible, though not required. Regular admissions are rolling, but February 1 is the recommended deadline to optimize financial aid and housing prospects, and Early Action applications do have a December 15 deadline.

THE SCHOOL SAYS " . . . "

From the Admissions Office

"The University of Maine offers the lauded academics, major research and close-knit community that go beyond your expectations. As Maine's flagship university, UMaine offers more than ninety undergraduate majors and academic programs, seventy-five master's programs and thirty doctoral programs. Top students are invited to join UMaine's Honors College, one of the country's oldest and most prestigious. Ranked 105 in the National Science Foundation's top research universities, UMaine is also included in the top 8 percent of colleges and universities nationwide to be classified by the Carnegie Foundation for the Advancement of Teaching as a 'Research University-High Research Activity' institution. The Laboratory for Surface Science and Technology is a hub for cutting-edge sensor and nanotechnology research, and our Advanced Structures and Composites Center is a global leader in deepwater offshore wind energy development.

"At UMaine, undergraduate classes are taught by professors—and here, faculty members are known for having an open-door policy. Our students work alongside some of the most renowned scholars and scientists in the world—whether they're talking civil engineering over lunch in the Bear's Den or traversing an Antarctic ice sheet with climate researchers.

"UMaine students garner real-world experience that exceeds their expectations. SPIFFY, our student investment club, manages a $2 million real-money portfolio. Wildlife ecology majors learn about bear behavior by going out and tagging cubs. Engineering majors take advantage of co-ops and internships that often lead to employment after graduation. Marine science undergrads spend a semester by the sea at our internationally renowned Darling Marine Center."

SELECTIVITY

Admissions Rating	75
# of applicants	11,044
% of applicants accepted	91
% of acceptees attending	20

FRESHMAN PROFILE

Range SAT Critical Reading	480–600
Range SAT Math	480–610
Range SAT Writing	460–578
Range ACT Composite	21–28
Minimum paper TOEFL	550
Minimum internet-based TOEFL	79
Average HS GPA	3.3
% graduated top 10% of class	19
% graduated top 25% of class	46
% graduated top 50% of class	80

DEADLINES

Early action	
Deadline	12/15
Notification	1/31
Regular	
Priority	2/1
Nonfall registration?	Yes

APPLICANTS ALSO LOOK AT AND OFTEN PREFER
University of New Hampshire

AND SOMETIMES PREFER
University of Connecticut; University of New England; University of Vermont; University of Massachusetts Amherst; University of Rhode Island

FINANCIAL FACTS

Financial Aid Rating	82
Annual in-state tuition	$8,370
Annual out-of-state tuition	$26,640
Room and board	$9,576
Required fees	$2,240
Books and supplies	$1,000
Average frosh need-based scholarship	$10,561
Average UG need-based scholarship	$8,916
% needy frosh rec. need-based scholarship or grant aid	94
% needy UG rec. need-based scholarship or grant aid	85
% needy frosh rec. non-need-based scholarship or grant aid	10
% needy UG rec. non-need-based scholarship or grant aid	6
% needy frosh rec. need-based self-help aid	81
% needy UG rec. need-based self-help aid	84
% frosh rec. any financial aid	93
% UG rec. any financial aid	83
% UG borrow to pay for school	77
Average cumulative indebtedness	$32,921
% frosh need fully met	18
% ugrads need fully met	16
Average % of frosh need met	82
Average % of ugrad need met	79

UNIVERSITY OF MARY WASHINGTON

1301 COLLEGE AVENUE, FREDERICKSBURG, VA 22401 • ADMISSIONS: 540-654-2000 • FAX: 540-654-1857

STUDENTS SAY ". . ."

Academics

University of Mary Washington "lives up to its reputation" while providing "rigorous education in a fun and engaging atmosphere." As an art history major explains, "it is one of (possibly the only) public choice in Virginia for someone who wants to attend a small liberal arts college." Students rave about the "small, beautiful campus" and "strong sense of community." This is a school where "everyone is so friendly" and you are "able to walk somewhere and always see someone" that you know. This "small and quaint school" is filled with "amazing" professors who "are committed to providing outside of the classroom help." "All of my professors know me by name and make classes interesting," one student says. The professors are "passionate about the material they teach" and UMW "does not have TA's so the professors are always the ones teaching the classes." Like the faculty at any school, "some are good; some are bad." However, the "small class sizes" mean "you can get one-on-one attention if you need it." UMW is about "finding what you're passionate about and studying it through multiple disciplines & perspectives while building strong relationships with faculty and peers." There is a "strongly supported honor code" and in general UMW "puts the responsibility in the hands of the students to act respectful and to prove themselves as students who are committed to their education." Some students feel the school "has a bit of a Napoleon complex" and think it should accept that it is "AMAZING at being" a "small liberal arts school." All in all, the school has "an amazing sense of community" that unlike many schools is "not so much featured around sports as it's about the students." "I've never felt so loved, accepted, and academically challenged in my life," one student says. Another sums up UMW as simply the "best school that no one has ever heard of."

Life

UMW is "fun but not [a] crazy party school." There is no "football team or Greek life," which is either a benefit or a drawback depending on your temperament. Some students "think it would be beneficial to have one or the other" to help "improve on social events" on campus. "A lot of people who transfer do so because they crave the excitement of big parties and social drama of Greek life," one student says, but explains that the remaining students "are serious about their studies which makes classes more fun." "Students fit in by finding a club on campus that suits their interests" and "sporting events are popular." Without a football team, students watch "rugby, soccer, lacrosse, or baseball." The campus has "a very inviting atmosphere" and there is "a huge amount of school spirit, but it is not the 'in your face' type of school spirit that plagues most large universities." Events on campus include "bingo Tuesday, trivia Thursday, one dollar movies on the weekend, acoustic night Wednesdays, club carnival, be a kid night, etc." On weekends, "there are parties but you have to know the right people to go to them." The town of Fredericksburg itself is "not a fantastic town due to the lack of entertainment" outside of some "not too shabby" bars. However, many students are "very active and outdoorsy" and find fun off campus in nature. The school is "five minutes away from the river which has awesome kayaking opportunities" and close to "mountains where a lot of students go hiking on the weekends."

Student Body

Most students are "laid back, fun, yet also studious." Several students noted there is "very little diversity" and "the school is not racially balanced AT ALL." With a student population that is over 60 percent female, the student body is "mostly girls but everyone is treated equally" as students are "pretty non-judgmental and open to differences." Others say the school is "very clique like" with "very little intermingling of different student groups." Still, "everyone has a place to fit in" among their "friendly, down to earth" peers. While many students fit "the liberal arts stereotype" of "liberal-leaning or moderate, environmentally conscious, supports social progress…there's a large number of conservative Catholic students as well." Without the giant Greek life other universities have, students "don't get 'distracted' as easily" leading to a student body that is "goal-driven and ready to succeed."

FINANCIAL AID: 800-468-5614 • E-MAIL: ADMIT@UMW.EDU • WEBSITE: WWW.UMW.EDU

THE PRINCETON REVIEW SAYS

Admissions

Very important factors considered include: rigor of secondary school record, academic GPA. *Important factors considered include:* class rank, standardized test scores, application essay, recommendation(s), extracurricular activities. *Other factors considered include:* talent/ability, character/personal qualities, first generation, alumni/ae relation, geographical residence, state residency, racial/ethnic status, volunteer work, work experience. SAT or ACT required; SAT Subject Tests considered if submitted. ACT with or without writing accepted. SAT with or without Essay component accepted. TOEFL required of all international applicants. High school diploma is required and GED is accepted. *Academic units required:* 4 English, 3 math, 3 science, 3 science labs, 2 foreign language, 2 social studies, 1 history. *Academic units recommended:* 4 English, 4 math, 4 science, 4 science labs, 4 foreign language, 2 social studies, 2 history.

Financial Aid

Students should submit: FAFSA. Priority filing deadline is 3/1. The Princeton Review suggests that all financial aid forms be submitted as soon as possible after October 1. *Need-based scholarships/grants offered:* Federal Pell, FSEOG, State scholarships/grants, Private scholarships, College/university scholarship or grant aid from institutional funds. *Loan aid offered:* Direct Subsidized Stafford Loans, Direct Unsubsidized Stafford Loans, Direct PLUS loans, Federal Perkins Loans. Applicants will be notified of awards on a rolling basis beginning 3/2. Federal Work-Study Program available. Institutional employment available.

The Inside Word

There is no special secret to getting into the University of Mary Washington. The school is selective and looks only for quality students. Great SAT/ACT scores and honors and AP class credits are a definite plus. The school uses the Common Application exclusively, and applying online is easy. There is also an online application process for Foundation scholarships with a deadline of 5/1.

THE SCHOOL SAYS "..."

From the Admissions Office

"The University of Mary Washington is one of the nation's premier public, liberal arts and sciences institutions. Highly respected for its commitment to academic excellence, the University boasts three colleges—business, education and arts and sciences and three campuses, conveniently located between Richmond, VA, and Washington, D.C. These two capitals provide a rich resource for undergraduate student internships, as well as a promising job market for graduates. Mary Washington's talented and intellectually curious students work collaboratively in small, interactive classes with innovative and accessible master teachers, including a Fulbright scholars, who motivate them to think critically, engage meaningfully and communicate effectively.

"In addition to rigorous academics, the UMW experience is based on a culture of honor as well as community and global service, exemplified in the 2016 Peace Corps ranking of Mary Washington as one of the nation's top volunteer producers among small colleges. With multiple opportunities for student research and service learning, UMW graduates thrive in our fast-changing society.

"Distinctive to UMW is one of the nation's leading historic preservation programs, as well as strong creative writing and debate programs. Other top majors include political science and international affairs, English, biology, psychology, earth and environmental science, history, visual and performing arts, economics and business. With its classic Jeffersonian architecture, and beautifully manicured grounds, UMW offers an unparallelled American college experience. More than 100 student organizations and clubs provide opportunities for leadership. UMW Eagles varsity teams compete at the championship level in NCAA Division III."

SELECTIVITY

Admissions Rating	76
# of applicants	5,549
% of applicants accepted	83
% of acceptees attending	21
# offered a place on the wait list	341
% accepting a place on wait list	18
% admitted from wait list	17

FRESHMAN PROFILE

Range SAT Critical Reading	510–620
Range SAT Math	490–590
Range SAT Writing	490–600
Range ACT Composite	22–27
Minimum paper TOEFL	570
Minimum internet-based TOEFL	88
Average HS GPA	3.6
% graduated top 10% of class	14
% graduated top 25% of class	41
% graduated top 50% of class	84

DEADLINES

Early decision	
Deadline	11/1
Notification	12/7
Early action	
Deadline	11/15
Notification	1/31
Regular	
Priority	2/1
Notification	4/1
Nonfall registration?	Yes

APPLICANTS ALSO LOOK AT AND OFTEN PREFER

University of Virginia; The College of William & Mary

AND SOMETIMES PREFER

James Madison University; Virginia Tech

FINANCIAL FACTS

Financial Aid Rating	77
Annual in-state tuition	$5,604
Annual out-of-state tuition	$19,768
Room and board	$9,856
Required fees	$5,466
Books and supplies	$1,100
Average frosh need-based scholarship	$2,851
Average UG need-based scholarship	$3,269
% needy frosh rec. need-based scholarship or grant aid	66
% needy UG rec. need-based scholarship or grant aid	54
% needy frosh rec. non-need-based scholarship or grant aid	41
% needy UG rec. non-need-based scholarship or grant aid	23
% needy frosh rec. need-based self-help aid	75
% needy UG rec. need-based self-help aid	80
% frosh rec. any financial aid	67
% UG rec. any financial aid	63
% UG borrow to pay for school	50
Average cumulative indebtedness	$18,029
% frosh need fully met	14
% ugrads need fully met	12
Average % of frosh need met	50
Average % of ugrad need met	49

UNIVERSITY OF MARYLAND—BALTIMORE COUNTY

1000 HILLTOP CIRCLE, BALTIMORE, MD 21250 • ADMISSIONS: 410-455-2291 • FAX: 410-455-1094

CAMPUS LIFE

Quality of Life Rating	88
Fire Safety Rating	98
Green Rating	74
Type of school	Public
Affiliation	No Affiliation
Environment	Metropolis

STUDENTS

Total undergrad enrollment	11,243
% male/female	55/45
% from out of state	6
% frosh live on campus	75
% ugrads live on campus	34
# of fraternities (% ugrad men join)	11 (4)
# of sororities (% ugrad women join)	12 (5)
% African American	17
% Asian	20
% Caucasian	44
% Hispanic	6
% Native American	<1
% Pacific Islander	<1
% Two or more races	4
% Race and/or ethnicity unknown	4
% international	4
# of countries represented	96

SURVEY SAYS...

Students are happy
Career services are great
School is well run

ACADEMICS

Academic Rating	75
% students returning for sophomore year	86
% students graduating within 4 years	0
Calendar	Semester
Student/faculty ratio	20:1
Profs interesting rating	78
Profs accessible rating	73

Most classes have 20–29 students.
Most lab/discussion sessions have 20–29 students.

MOST POPULAR MAJORS

Computer and Information Sciences; Biology; Psychology

STUDENTS SAY " . . ."

Academics

The University of Maryland, Baltimore County has a "great regional reputation" as a "quiet academic school" where "students take education seriously." Undergraduates are enthusiastic about the "academic opportunities and scholarship programs available," and say, "UMBC wants to see every student succeed—they provide you with the tools, people, and resources to make sure you get where you want to go in life." The university is particularly known for its "strong" science and mathematics programs and a commitment to the performing arts. Some students grumble, "The school needs to serve those with different majors apart from the sciences," but others are quick to point out that "UMBC is changing a bit to offer more to the fine arts students," including construction of a new technologically advanced fine arts building. Most agree the university has "extremely intelligent professors that have a knack for inspiring the students," and say, "UMBC is a place where professors aren't just talking heads." Although some complain about dull lectures, a common consensus is that "this is a university where teaching comes first, followed by research, and it shows," and that "most of the professors are so helpful, you can find most of them sitting in their office and they don't mind if you come and ask them questions."

Life

UMBC has a large contingent of commuters and one ancient studies major says, "There are a lot of activities held by student organizations on campus during the week and on the weekends, but many students live close to campus and choose to go home for the weekend." While some may see this as a downside others say, "The location of UMBC is true brilliance—so close to Baltimore. We hop over there on the weekdays even to go shopping or go out to eat." Most lament the absence of a football team and say, "The only real issue with UMBC is the lack of visible school spirit…People have made efforts to try and pump up the school, but nothing's come to fruition yet." In fact, students give the administration poor marks, saying, "Students are not given adequate attention on the matters of housing, financial aid, and advising," and there are complaints about the parking facilities, as well as a desire for "better buildings and food options." Despite these criticisms, a sociology major says, "Everyone on campus is nice and helpful to other students. People will always hold a door for you, help you pick up a dropped folder, or offer to share their notes with a student who missed class."

Student Body

More than one student says, "UMBC is a place where it is cool to be smart, and everything about the campus, including the students, exudes 'nerd-chic.'" In fact, an English major says that even "our president likes to say that it's cool to be smart at UMBC." This mentality is captured by a student who remarks, "Life at UMBC, aside from special events, revolves around classes and learning," and most undergrads agree: "The typical student at UMBC is interested in doing well academically and not just here to party until graduation." However, despite their dedication to hard work, UMBC students call themselves "enthusiastic and bright" and say "that almost every student at UMBC is involved with at least a couple of extracurricular activities, which connect them to the campus." The school has a strong reputation for diversity and students feel "it enriches our school and everyone gets to know everyone despite culture or ethnicity." A mechanical engineering student says, "This is even reflected in the high number of interracial couples I see on campus." Overall, it seems, "People fit in by being intellectually creative and finding a community with which to discuss important issues."

UNIVERSITY OF MARYLAND—BALTIMORE COUNTY

FINANCIAL AID: 410-455-2387 • E-MAIL: ADMISSIONS@UMBC.EDU • WEBSITE: WWW.UMBC.EDU

THE PRINCETON REVIEW SAYS

Admissions

Very important factors considered include: rigor of secondary school record, academic GPA, standardized test scores, application essay, recommendation(s). *Important factors considered include:* class rank, talent/ability. *Other factors considered include:* extracurricular activities, character/personal qualities, volunteer work, work experience. SAT or ACT required. ACT with or without writing accepted. SAT with Essay component required. TOEFL required of all international applicants. High school diploma is required and GED is accepted. *Academic units required:* 4 English, 4 math, 3 science, 2 foreign language, and 3 units from above areas or other academic areas. *Academic units recommended:* 4 English, 4 math, 3 science, 2 foreign language, and 3 units from above areas or other academic areas.

Financial Aid

Students should submit: FAFSA. Priority filing deadline is 2/14. The Princeton Review suggests that all financial aid forms be submitted as soon as possible after October 1. *Need-based scholarships/grants offered:* Federal Pell, FSEOG, State scholarships/grants, Private scholarships, College/university scholarship or grant aid from institutional funds, United Negro College Fund. *Loan aid offered:* Direct Subsidized Stafford Loans, Direct Unsubsidized Stafford Loans, Direct PLUS loans, Federal Perkins Loans. Applicants will be notified of awards on a rolling basis beginning 3/25. Federal Work-Study Program available. Institutional employment available.

The Inside Word

UMBC maintains an Admissions Counselor Blog where prospective students can connect with current members of the admissions team to questions during the application process. The admissions committee considers the strength of your secondary school curriculum and class rank in combination with traditional factors, such as GPA, test scores, and essay when making an acceptance decision. Additionally, it's suggested that at least one letter of recommendation be written by a teacher.

THE SCHOOL SAYS "..."

From the Admissions Office

"When it comes to universities, a mid-sized school can be just right. Some students want the resources of a large community. Others are looking for the attention found at a smaller one. With an undergraduate population of over 10,000, UMBC can offer the best of both. There are always new people to meet and things to do—from Division I sports to more than 200 student clubs. As a research university, we offer an abundance of programs, technology, and opportunities for hands-on experiences. Yet we are small enough that students don't get lost in the shuffle. More than 80 percent of our classes have fewer than forty students. Among public research universities, UMBC is recognized for its success in placing students in the most competitive graduate programs and careers. Of course, much of the success of UMBC has to do with the students themselves—highly motivated students who get involved in their education.

"Freshman applicants are required to take the SAT or ACT."

SELECTIVITY

Admissions Rating	89
# of applicants	60,629
% of applicants accepted	10
% of acceptees attending	25
# offered a place on the wait list	404
% accepting a place on wait list	100
% admitted from wait list	69

FRESHMAN PROFILE

Range SAT Critical Reading	540–640
Range SAT Math	570–670
Range SAT Writing	530–640
Range ACT Composite	24–30
Minimum paper TOEFL	460
Minimum internet-based TOEFL	48
Average HS GPA	3.8
% graduated top 10% of class	25
% graduated top 25% of class	54
% graduated top 50% of class	84

DEADLINES

Early action	
Deadline	11/1
Notification	12/15
Regular	
Priority	11/1
Deadline	2/1
Nonfall registration?	Yes

APPLICANTS ALSO LOOK AT AND OFTEN PREFER
Johns Hopkins University; Virginia Tech

AND SOMETIMES PREFER
Penn State University Park; University of Maryland–College Park

AND RARELY PREFER
Salisbury University

FINANCIAL FACTS

Financial Aid Rating	80
Annual in-state tuition	$11,006
Annual out-of-state tuition	$24,316
Room and board	$13,310
Required fees	$1,200
Books and supplies	$1,200
Average frosh need-based scholarship	$9,055
Average UG need-based scholarship	$7,957
% needy frosh rec. need-based scholarship or grant aid	76
% needy UG rec. need-based scholarship or grant aid	77
% needy frosh rec. non-need-based scholarship or grant aid	32
% needy UG rec. non-need-based scholarship or grant aid	12
% needy frosh rec. need-based self-help aid	53
% needy UG rec. need-based self-help aid	67
% frosh rec. any financial aid	74
% UG rec. any financial aid	70
% UG borrow to pay for school	51
Average cumulative indebtedness	$26,391
% frosh need fully met	20
% ugrads need fully met	12
Average % of frosh need met	63
Average % of ugrad need met	54

University of Maryland—College Park

Mitchell Building, College Park, MD 20742-5235 • Admissions: 301-314-8385 • Fax: 301-314-9693

CAMPUS LIFE

Quality of Life Rating	72
Fire Safety Rating	89
Green Rating	99
Type of school	Public
Affiliation	No Affiliation
Environment	Metropolis

STUDENTS

Total undergrad enrollment	27,443
% male/female	53/47
% from out of state	21
% frosh live on campus	93
% ugrads live on campus	42
# of fraternities (% ugrad men join)	36 (15)
# of sororities (% ugrad women join)	28 (19)
% African American	13
% Asian	16
% Caucasian	52
% Hispanic	9
% Native American	<1
% Pacific Islander	<1
% Two or more races	4
% Race and/or ethnicity unknown	2
% international	4
# of countries represented	65

SURVEY SAYS...
Students politically aware
Recreation facilities are great
Diverse student types interact on campus
Everyone loves the Terrapins
Campus newspaper is popular
Lots of beer drinking

ACADEMICS

Academic Rating	73
% students returning for sophomore year	95
% students graduating within 4 years	69
% students graduating within 6 years	86
Calendar	Semester
Student/faculty ratio	16:1
Profs interesting rating	70
Profs accessible rating	66

Most classes have 10–19 students.
Most lab/discussion sessions have 20–29 students.

MOST POPULAR MAJORS
Biology; Criminology; Economics

STUDENTS SAY "..."

Academics
The University of Maryland—College Park is a grand mix of "twenty-minute walks to class across one of the country's most beautiful campuses, [an introduction] to high-level courses taught by the nation's top researchers, [and] a motivated 'green' campus" as well as "crowded, smelly frat parties, [and] living-learning communities that can make the gigantic campus much smaller." Students are quick to boast about sports, too, especially the men's and women's basketball teams. In short: It's a quintessential large university, offering "a great experience with a variety of opportunities that are what you make of them." Students crow about Maryland's "nationally recognized business program," a "top-ranked criminology program," a solid engineering school, a great political science department that capitalizes on the school's proximity to Washington, D.C., and the "top-notch honors program." Most of all, they love the "great price. This school gives you a great education for a really cheap price." Low cost doesn't translate to budget accommodations. On the contrary, "the administration shows a desire to always upgrade facilities, as can be witnessed by the tremendous business school and the brand new engineering building." In conclusion, students applaud "the widely diverse opportunities available at UMD. You can never get bored because there is always something to do."

Life
"Life at UMD is awesome," with "a good mix of fun activities" including "school-sponsored parties, games," a "campus recreation center that has virtually everything you could wish for, including pools, an extensive gym, a rock wall, squash courts, an indoor track," and a student union "loaded with fun places like the arcade area, bowling alley," and "tons of places to eat as well." In addition, "there are always open games of soccer, football, or ultimate Frisbee being played on the mall and elsewhere." There are bars close to campus, and "students are always having parties," especially along College Park's raucous Frat Row. Terrapin sports are a passion for many. If all that isn't enough, "the proximity to D.C. makes clubbing, nights out on the town, and general visits to D.C. frequent." With all this going on, no wonder students say that "the social life at UMD is unsurpassed." Some warn the surrounding area is dicey; "It's pretty annoying and scary to get crime alerts from the police informing us of incidents close to campus," one student explains. Undergrads also warn that parking regulations are brutal. "Bus transportation around campus provided by the university is great, but for students and visitors with cars, it's a huge hassle. Permits are expensive, and free parking for visitors is impossible to find. School officials are strict with violations, and tickets are seventy-five dollars. They are hard to refute and very costly."

Student Body
"The University of Maryland is a very large school," so "there is no 'typical' student here. Everyone will find that they can fit in somewhere." Better still, "different groups are very accepting of other groups. Students in Greek life are just as accepting of students in non-Greek life. Athletes blend in with non-athletes. UMD provides a great environment for students to meet people they would normally not know and helps to provide great connections with these people." UMD is "an especially diverse school," and this makes people "more tolerant and accepting of people from different backgrounds and cultures." A student from New Jersey explains it this way: "Coming from a very diverse area, I thought it was going to be hard to find a school that had that same representation of minority and atypical students until I found Maryland. I don't think I have ever learned so much about different religions, cultures, orientations, or lifestyles. All of them are accepted and even celebrated" at UMD.

FINANCIAL AID: 301-314-9000 • E-MAIL: UM-ADMIT@UMD.EDU • WEBSITE: WWW.MARYLAND.EDU

THE PRINCETON REVIEW SAYS

Admissions

Very important factors considered include: rigor of secondary school record, academic GPA, standardized test scores. *Important factors considered include:* class rank, application essay, recommendation(s), talent/ability, first generation, state residency. *Other factors considered include:* extracurricular activities, character/personal qualities, alumni/ae relation, geographical residence, racial/ethnic status, volunteer work, work experience. SAT or ACT required. ACT with Writing required. TOEFL required of all international applicants. High school diploma is required and GED is accepted. *Academic units required:* 4 English, 4 math, 3 science, 2 science labs, 2 foreign language, 3 social studies, 3 history. *Academic units recommended:* 4 English, 4 math, 3 science, 2 science labs, 2 foreign language, 3 social studies, 3 history.

Financial Aid

Students should submit: FAFSA. Priority filing deadline is 2/15. The Princeton Review suggests that all financial aid forms be submitted as soon as possible after October 1. *Need-based scholarships/grants offered:* Federal Pell, FSEOG, State scholarships/grants, Private scholarships, College/university scholarship or grant aid from institutional funds. *Loan aid offered:* Direct Subsidized Stafford Loans, Direct Unsubsidized Stafford Loans, Direct PLUS loans, Federal Perkins Loans. Applicants will be notified of awards on a rolling basis beginning 4/1. Federal Work-Study Program available. Institutional employment available.

The Inside Word

Maryland admissions officers don't simply crunch numbers and apply a formula. The school considers no fewer than twenty-five factors when determining who's in and who's out. Essays, recommendations, extracurricular activities, talents and skills, and demographic factors all figure into the mix along with high school transcript and standardized test scores. Give all aspects of your application your utmost attention; admissions is very competitive.

THE SCHOOL SAYS "..."

From the Admissions Office

"The University of Maryland (UMD) is a top-ranked flagship public research university, located within minutes from Washington, D.C. Students have opportunities to learn, explore and succeed through interaction with outstanding faculty that include Nobel Prize, Pulitzer Prize, Emmy and Tony winners. The beautifully landscaped 1,335-acre campus' proximity to major East Coast cities allows students to extend their education beyond the classroom through education abroad programs, and internships at U.S. federal agencies, research labs, global think tanks, major media outlets, world-class museums, and thriving companies. The university strongly encourages innovation, entrepreneurship and creativity by assisting students to launch startups, and serves as a model of cultural excellence through its arts programming. The University of Maryland also thrives on diversity, inclusion and engagement to prepare graduates to become excellent leaders in their communities and careers."

SELECTIVITY

Admissions Rating	91
# of applicants	28,301
% of applicants accepted	45
% of acceptees attending	31

FRESHMAN PROFILE

Range SAT Critical Reading	590–690
Range SAT Math	620–730
Minimum internet-based TOEFL	100
Average HS GPA	4.2

DEADLINES

Early action	
Deadline	11/1
Notification	1/31
Regular	
Priority	11/1
Deadline	1/20
Nonfall registration?	Yes

FINANCIAL FACTS

Financial Aid Rating	81
Annual in-state tuition	$8,152
Annual out-of-state tuition	$29,300
Room and board	$10,972
Required fees	$1,844
Books and supplies	$1,130
Average frosh need-based scholarship	$11,040
Average UG need-based scholarship	$9,288
% needy frosh rec. need-based scholarship or grant aid	85
% needy UG rec. need-based scholarship or grant aid	80
% needy frosh rec. non-need-based scholarship or grant aid	12
% needy UG rec. non-need-based scholarship or grant aid	6
% needy frosh rec. need-based self-help aid	83
% needy UG rec. need-based self-help aid	91
% frosh rec. any financial aid	86
% UG rec. any financial aid	72
% UG borrow to pay for school	43
Average cumulative indebtedness	$26,818
% frosh need fully met	37
% ugrads need fully met	29
Average % of frosh need met	78
Average % of ugrad need met	75

UNIVERSITY OF MASSACHUSETTS AMHERST

UNIVERSITY ADMISSIONS CENTER, AMHERST, MA 01003-9291 • ADMISSIONS: 413-545-0222 • FAX: 413-545-4312

CAMPUS LIFE
Quality of Life Rating	91
Fire Safety Rating	92
Green Rating	98
Type of school	Public
Affiliation	No Affiliation
Environment	Town

STUDENTS
Total undergrad enrollment	22,748
% male/female	51/49
% from out of state	20
% frosh live on campus	99
% ugrads live on campus	58
# of fraternities (% ugrad men join)	19 (8)
# of sororities (% ugrad women join)	12 (6)
% African American	4
% Asian	9
% Caucasian	67
% Hispanic	5
% Native American	<1
% Pacific Islander	<1
% Two or more races	3
% Race and/or ethnicity unknown	8
% international	4
# of countries represented	69

SURVEY SAYS...
Students are happy
Students love Amherst, MA
Great food on campus
Dorms are like palaces
Recreation facilities are great

ACADEMICS
Academic Rating	77
% students returning for sophomore year	91
% students graduating within 4 years	66
% students graduating within 6 years	78
Calendar	Semester
Student/faculty ratio	17:1
Profs interesting rating	72
Profs accessible rating	66

Most classes have 10–19 students.
Most lab/discussion sessions have 20–29 students.

MOST POPULAR MAJORS
Psychology; Biology; Communication

STUDENTS SAY "..."

Academics
The crown jewel in the UMass system, the University of Massachusetts Amherst is a "large [yet] warm and welcoming community." And with its highly "affordable" price tag and strong academic reputation, it is quite easy to see why students are drawn here. The university also excels at providing undergrads with a good deal of "real world experience." Moreover, students love that they're able to tap into an incredibly extensive "alumni network," making the eventual job hunt slightly less daunting. They are also bursting with pride that UMass is home to "a number of highly regarded [departments within the] Isenberg School of Management, the [College of Engineering] and more."

As expected at a school of this size, some instructors can be hit or miss, but for the most part undergrads here are generally full of praise for their "excellent professors." And what's not to love? After all, they tend to be "very approachable." What's more, they "take a sincere interest in [their] students." And they endeavor to be "accessible [both] inside and outside of [the] class[room]." Best of all, UMass Amherst professors continually prove to be "very reasonable [when it comes to] understand[ing student]...stress."

Life
UMass students manage to achieve a good work/life balance. As a computer engineering major explains, "The range of extracurricular activities, club sports, club activities, and volunteer organizations, is incredibly broad. Everyone I know is involved outside of academics in some way, shape, or form." A theater student agrees sharing, "I'm in...the UMASS Theatre Guild and the UMASS Minuteman Marching Band, both of which are amazing experiences." Overall, the student body is fairly active and these undergrads "love intramural sports." They are also quite likely to hit the gym at some point during their busy day. On big game days, "tailgate parties" are quite popular. After all, these students love to support their fellow Minutemen. Finally, when undergrads need a moment away from campus, hometown Amherst and nearby Northampton both offer plenty of dining and entertainment options.

Student Body
UMass Amherst is home to a "very diverse student body," "from all racial and ethnic backgrounds." And, according to one environmental design student, you'll find "a variety of different character types" as well. For example, there are the "athletes and socialites in Southwest, the hipsters in Central, the engineers in Northeast, and the really smart people in the Honors College." We're also told that there's "a prominent LGBTQ community." Thankfully, regardless of what category they might fall into, most UMass students appear to be "super nice" and "respectful." A computer science student wholeheartedly agrees with that statement sharing, "Everyone always greets me with a smile as we all patiently move about our day." In general, UMass Amherst undergrads are also "enthusiastic individuals that love to enjoy life" and strive "to make the world a better place." And as one finance major joyously sums up, "This is probably the greatest group of students that I've ever met...it's unbelievable...[and I] couldn't be happier."

FINANCIAL AID: 413-545-0801 • E-MAIL: MAIL@ADMISSIONS.UMASS.EDU • WEBSITE: WWW.UMASS.EDU

THE PRINCETON REVIEW SAYS

Admissions

Very important factors considered include: rigor of secondary school record, academic GPA, standardized test scores. *Important factors considered include:* class rank, application essay, recommendation(s), extracurricular activities, talent/ability, character/personal qualities, first generation, work experience, level of applicant's interest. *Other factors considered include:* alumni/ae relation, geographical residence, state residency, racial/ethnic status, volunteer work. SAT or ACT required. TOEFL required of all international applicants. High school diploma is required and GED is accepted. *Academic units required:* 4 English, 4 math, 3 science labs, 2 foreign language, 2 social studies, 2 academic electives.

Financial Aid

Students should submit: FAFSA. Priority filing deadline is 3/1. The Princeton Review suggests that all financial aid forms be submitted as soon as possible after October 1. *Need-based scholarships/grants offered:* Federal Pell, FSEOG, State scholarships/grants, Private scholarships, College/university scholarship or grant aid from institutional funds. *Loan aid offered:* Direct Subsidized Stafford Loans, Direct Unsubsidized Stafford Loans, Direct PLUS loans, Federal Perkins Loans, Federal Nursing Loans. Applicants will be notified of awards on a rolling basis beginning 4/1. Federal Work-Study Program available. Institutional employment available.

The Inside Word

UMass Amherst takes a fairly straightforward approach to the admissions game. High school transcripts and standardized test scores will be of primary importance. Candidates who have taken a rigorous course load will have an advantage, and should expect admissions officers also pay close attention to grade trends. Applicants are also encouraged to register for a challenging schedule senior year as this helps to demonstrate a commitment to higher education. Extracurricular activities and work experience will be considered. Applicants for the College of Engineering, Isenberg School of Management or the College of Information and Computer Sciences must satisfy additional math and science requirements. And candidates for architecture, dance, art and/or music must allow for enough time for auditions and portfolio reviews.

THE SCHOOL SAYS "..."

From the Admissions Office

"The University of Massachusetts Amherst is the flagship campus of the Commonwealth and the largest public university in New England, offering its students an almost limitless variety of academic programs and activities. The Commonwealth Honors College Residential Complex is a national model and welcomes students who seek additional academic challenge and meet the requirements for acceptance. The school takes a holistic view of the student's application package and considers test scores (SAT or ACT) as only part of the evaluation criteria. Greater weight in the selection process is placed on the student's performance in a rigorous curriculum. Increased applications in recent years have made admission more selective. Over one-hundred majors are offered, including a unique program called Bachelor's Degree with Individual Concentration (BDIC) in which students create their own program of study. First-year students participate in the Residential First-Year Experience with opportunities to explore every possible interest through residential life. The extensive library system is the largest at any public institution in the Northeast. The campus completes in NCAA Division I sports for men and women, with teams winning national recognition. About 12,000 students a year participate in the intramural sports program. The town of Amherst is consistently ranked one of the top college towns in the country. Through the Five College Interchange, students enroll in classes at nearby Amherst, Hampshire, Mount Holyoke, and Smith Colleges at no extra charge. A free bus system connects these five campuses, allowing students to participate in a wide array of social and cultural events."

SELECTIVITY

Admissions Rating	88
# of applicants	40,010
% of applicants accepted	58
% of acceptees attending	20
# offered a place on the wait list	5,450
% accepting a place on wait list	23
% admitted from wait list	2

FRESHMAN PROFILE

Range SAT Critical Reading	550–640
Range SAT Math	580–670
Range ACT Composite	25–30
Minimum internet-based TOEFL	80
Average HS GPA	3.8
% graduated top 10% of class	32
% graduated top 25% of class	73
% graduated top 50% of class	97

DEADLINES

Early action	
Deadline	11/1
Regular	
Priority	1/15
Nonfall registration?	Yes

APPLICANTS ALSO LOOK AT AND OFTEN PREFER

Boston College; Boston University; Tufts University; Cornell University

AND SOMETIMES PREFER

Northeastern University; University of Connecticut; Syracuse University; Worcester Polytechnic Institute

AND RARELY PREFER

University of New Hampshire; University of Rhode Island; University of Vermont

FINANCIAL FACTS

Financial Aid Rating	81
Annual in-state tuition	$13,790
Annual out-of-state tuition	$30,123
Room and board	$12,028
Required fees	$381
Books and supplies	$1,000
Average frosh need-based scholarship	$10,480
Average UG need-based scholarship	$9,905
% needy frosh rec. need-based scholarship or grant aid	91
% needy UG rec. need-based scholarship or grant aid	85
% needy frosh rec. non-need-based scholarship or grant aid	7
% needy UG rec. non-need-based scholarship or grant aid	54
% needy frosh rec. need-based self-help aid	76
% needy UG rec. need-based self-help aid	80
% frosh rec. any financial aid	90
% UG rec. any financial aid	85
% UG borrow to pay for school	70
Average cumulative indebtedness	$31,958
% frosh need fully met	14
% ugrads need fully met	13
Average % of frosh need met	81
Average % of ugrad need met	81

UNIVERSITY OF MIAMI

PO Box 248025, Coral Gables, FL 33124-4616 • Admissions: 305-284-4323 • Fax: 305-284-6605

STUDENTS SAY "..."

Academics

Located in Coral Gables, the University of Miami offers "the best balance between social life and academics." The school boasts a "beautiful campus, many research opportunities, [and] helpful resources throughout campus available to students," and the curriculum mirrors the diversity of the school's location by "catering to the students with a multitude of student-oriented classes and organizations." Tons of extracurricular activities, events happening "constantly," and the "ability to bring in amazing world-class guests" help flesh out the experience at UM. "Miami is the type of school where you can go to... class in the afternoon, a club meeting in the evening, and then still hit the gym and the library before you ever think about going to bed," says a student.

The "caring and renowned faculty" at UM are "insightful and have years of professional experience in the fields they teach." They are "very willing to meet during office hours and exceptionally helpful during that time," are "engaging and force students to think critically when learning," and "get very involved in helping the students with advising and internships/job opportunities." The networking opportunities also happen to be "second-to-none." "You are more than confident that you are going to get a job in your desired field when you graduate," says a senior broadcast journalism major.

The marine science and pre-med programs are standouts at University of Miami, but a "strong undergraduate focus" means that no matter the major, "career development is great" and has "amazing opportunities that are not available anywhere else."

Life

Students are pretty blunt about their love of the University of Miami: "It quite literally is a paradise." Palm trees surrounding a vast lake at the heart of campus, an amazing wellness center, and a brand new student activities center are just a few of the school's beloved attributes, and "students proudly wear green and orange and participate in many school events." Greek life doesn't run the campus, but "it's apparent," and students can head to the beach during the day and a club (South Beach, Brickell and Coconut Grove) at night. If you're not interested in partying constantly—and there are "quite a few"—relaxing around campus or near campus is "still really enjoyable." Concerts are also very popular, and "involvement in club and intramural sports is significant."

Though the temptations are plentiful, when it comes down to it ("the location is conducive to limitless activities"), "students at University of Miami get their work done." "Going to school in one of Miami's most affluent neighborhoods certainly makes you think about success and your career goals," says a junior electronic media major. Students "are generally happy all the time because the warm weather positively influences their lives."

Student Body

The typical UM student is "relatively wealthy," "takes pride in their appearance," and is "very hardworking but also extremely involved in social activities." While there are a good deal of international students and students on scholarship, the availability of organizations and activities help unite the population into "a big friendly family who always has your back." Miami being Miami, many students are "Greek life types," and there is "a lot of importance placed on dress and material possessions." One student jokes, "The gym is mandatory for full-time students." Thanks to the location in "a tropical paradise with a million things to do," people "are really easy to get along with."

FINANCIAL AID: 305-284-5212 • E-MAIL: ADMISSION@MIAMI.EDU • WEBSITE: WWW.MIAMI.EDU

THE PRINCETON REVIEW SAYS

Admissions

Very important factors considered include: rigor of secondary school record, class rank, academic GPA, standardized test scores, application essay, recommendation(s), extracurricular activities, character/personal qualities. *Important factors considered include:* talent/ability, volunteer work, work experience. *Other factors considered include:* first generation, alumni/ae relation, geographical residence, racial/ethnic status, level of applicant's interest. SAT or ACT required. ACT with Writing required. SAT with Essay component required. TOEFL required of all applicants whose native language is not English. High school diploma is required and GED is accepted. *Academic units recommended:* 4 English, 4 math, 3 science, 2 science labs, 2 foreign language, 3 social studies, 2 history, 1 computer science, 1 visual/performing arts.

Financial Aid

Students should submit: FAFSA, CSS/Financial Aid PROFILE, Noncustodial PROFILE, Business/Farm Supplement. Regular filing deadline is 4/15. The Princeton Review suggests that all financial aid forms be submitted as soon as possible after October 1. *Need-based scholarships/grants offered:* Federal Pell, FSEOG, State scholarships/grants, Private scholarships, College/university scholarship or grant aid from institutional funds. *Loan aid offered:* Direct Subsidized Stafford Loans, Direct Unsubsidized Stafford Loans, Direct PLUS loans, Federal Perkins Loans, Federal Nursing Loans, College/university loans from institutional funds. Applicants will be notified of awards on a rolling basis beginning 1/20. Federal Work-Study Program available. Institutional employment available.

The Inside Word

The University of Miami's campaign to overcome its reputation as a "football school" is an unqualified success. Each recent academic year has seen an increase in applications, and UM's selectivity is on the rise. The school partially attributes this accomplishment to its alumni and gladly repays them by giving legacies a boost during the admissions process. Of course, having a Cane for a parent isn't enough; students must demonstrate achievement in arduous classes, intellectual promise, and strong moral character.

THE SCHOOL SAYS "..."

From the Admissions Office

"At the University of Miami, we educate leaders, problem-solvers, and change-makers. Our students are passionate about learning, driven to contribute to their community, and free to innovate. Whether you seek to make your mark in science, service, or the arts, we will nurture that passion every step of the way. With the flexibility to choose from more than 180 majors and programs across eleven schools and colleges, you're encouraged to design a curriculum that crosses disciplines and is distinctly you. Here, coursework integrates academic rigor and theory with hands-on experience so students are able to convert knowledge and connections into fulfilling achievements. Students collaborate with award-winning faculty on projects ranging from volunteer experiences to cutting-edge research in topics like genomics, the humanities, and climate change. This means you can start making major contributions to your field of study as early as freshman year.

"Our international location, near the bustling metropolis of Miami, provides students and scholars with meaningful opportunities for experiential learning locally and in countries around the world. UM on Location programs bring study abroad experiences within reach. Our sequences are taught by UM faculty and coordinated by staff, so you never have to worry about transferring credits or financial assistance. On campus, our community of scholars is united in its diversity; working to ensure each member of our family has their voice heard.

"The variety of academics, resources, and students at UM make it the perfect place to obtain an extraordinary, global education."

SELECTIVITY

Admissions Rating	94
# of applicants	33,415
% of applicants accepted	38
% of acceptees attending	16
# offered a place on the wait list	5,563
% accepting a place on wait list	23
% admitted from wait list	6
# of early decision applicants	638
% accepted early decision	39

FRESHMAN PROFILE

Range SAT Critical Reading	590–690
Range SAT Math	610–700
Range SAT Writing	580–680
Range ACT Composite	28–32
Minimum paper TOEFL	550
Minimum internet-based TOEFL	80
Average HS GPA	4.0
% graduated top 10% of class	63
% graduated top 25% of class	90
% graduated top 50% of class	96

DEADLINES

Early decision	
Round 1 / 2	
Deadline	11/1 / 1/1
Notification	12/20 / 2/15
Early action	
Deadline	11/1
Notification	1/20
Regular	
Deadline	1/1
Notification	4/15
Nonfall registration?	Yes

FINANCIAL FACTS

Financial Aid Rating	87
Annual tuition	$45,600
Room and board	$12,908
Required fees	$1,324
Books and supplies	$930
Average frosh need-based scholarship	$11,456
Average UG need-based scholarship	$9,585
% needy frosh rec. need-based scholarship or grant aid	30
% needy UG rec. need-based scholarship or grant aid	24
% needy frosh rec. non-need-based scholarship or grant aid	78
% needy UG rec. non-need-based scholarship or grant aid	67
% needy frosh rec. need-based self-help aid	32
% needy UG rec. need-based self-help aid	30
% frosh rec. any financial aid	85
% UG rec. any financial aid	74
% UG borrow to pay for school	40
Average cumulative indebtedness	$19,000
% frosh need fully met	100
% ugrads need fully met	94
Average % of frosh need met	99
Average % of ugrad need met	94

UNIVERSITY OF MICHIGAN—ANN ARBOR

1220 STUDENT ACTIVITIES BUILDING, ANN ARBOR, MI 48109-1316 • ADMISSIONS: 734-764-7433 • FAX: 734-936-0740

CAMPUS LIFE

Quality of Life Rating	93
Fire Safety Rating	88
Green Rating	94
Type of school	Public
Affiliation	No Affiliation
Environment	City

STUDENTS

Total undergrad enrollment	28,312
% male/female	51/49
% from out of state	38
% frosh live on campus	98
% ugrads live on campus	34
# of fraternities (% ugrad men join)	36 (17)
# of sororities (% ugrad women join)	28 (24)
% African American	4
% Asian	13
% Caucasian	62
% Hispanic	5
% Native American	<1
% Pacific Islander	<1
% Two or more races	3
% Race and/or ethnicity unknown	6
% international	7
# of countries represented	89

SURVEY SAYS...

Students politically aware
Students always studying
Students are happy
Classroom facilities are great
Great library
Career services are great
Internships are widely available
School is well run
Students aren't religious
Students environmentally aware
Students love Ann Arbor, MI
Recreation facilities are great
Lots of beer drinking
Hard liquor is popular
Everyone loves the Wolverines
Intramural sports are popular
Campus newspaper is popular
Alumni active on campus
Active minority support groups

ACADEMICS

Academic Rating	89
% students returning for sophomore year	97
% students graduating within 4 years	76
% students graduating within 6 years	91
Calendar	Trimsester
Student/faculty ratio	15:1
Profs interesting rating	72
Profs accessible rating	76

Most classes have 10–19 students.
Most lab/discussion sessions have
20–29 students.

MOST POPULAR MAJORS

Experimental Psychology; Economics;
Business Administration and Management

STUDENTS SAY "..."

Academics

Among the many allures of the University of Michigan—Ann Arbor is that the school offers "a great environment both academically and socially." One student explains, "It has the social, fun atmosphere of any Big Ten university, but most people are still incredibly focused on their studies. It's great to be at a place where there is always something to do, but your friends completely understand when you have to stay in and get work done." With "an amazing honors program," a "wide range of travel-abroad opportunities," and "research strength" all available "at a low cost," it's no wonder students tell us that UM "provides every kind of opportunity at all times to all people." Academically, Michigan "is very competitive, and the professors have high academic standards for all the students." In fact, some here insist that "Michigan is as good as Ivy League schools in many disciplines." Standout offerings include business ("We have access to some of the brightest leaders" in the business world, students report), a "great engineering program," and "a good undergraduate program for medical school preparation." Those seeking add-on academic experiences here will find "a vast amount of resources. Internships, career opportunities, tutoring, community service projects, a plethora of student organizations, and a wealth of other resources" are all available, but "you need to make the first move" because no one "will seek you out."

Life

Michigan is a huge university, meaning that students have endless extracurricular options here. One explains: "If you seek it out, you can find organizations for *any* interest. There are always people out there who share your interests. That's part of the benefit of 40,000-plus students!" There is a robust party scene. Students tell us that "most students go to house parties [or] hit the bars." There's also a vigorous social scene for the non-drinking crowd, with "great programs like UMix...phenomenal cultural opportunities in Ann Arbor especially music and movies," and "the hugely popular football Saturdays. The sense of school spirit here is impressive." Michigan students tend to be both academically serious and socially outgoing, which "is great because you can have a stimulating conversation with someone one day, and, the next day, be watching a silly movie or playing video games with this person."

Student Body

The Michigan student body "is hugely diverse," which "is one of the things Michigan prides itself on." "If you participate in extracurricular activities and make an effort to get to know other students in class and elsewhere, you'll definitely end up with a pretty diverse group of friends," undergrads assure us. Although varied, students tend to be similar in that they "are social but very academically driven." A number of students "are on the cutting edge of both research and progressive thinking," and there is a decided liberal tilt to campus politics. Even so, there's a place for everyone here, because "there are hundreds of mini-communities within the campus, made of everything from service fraternities to political organizations to dance groups. If you have an interest, you can find a group of people who enjoy the same thing."

UNIVERSITY OF MICHIGAN—ANN ARBOR

FINANCIAL AID: 734-763-6600 • WEBSITE: WWW.UMICH.EDU

THE PRINCETON REVIEW SAYS

Admissions

Very important factors considered include: rigor of secondary school record, academic GPA. *Important factors considered include:* standardized test scores, application essay, recommendation(s), character/personal qualities, first generation. *Other factors considered include:* extracurricular activities, talent/ability, alumni/ae relation, geographical residence, state residency, volunteer work, work experience, level of applicant's interest. SAT or ACT required; SAT Subject Tests required for some. ACT with Writing required. SAT with Essay component required. TOEFL required of all international applicants. High school diploma is required and GED is accepted. *Academic units required:* 4 English, 1 science lab. *Academic units recommended:* 4 English, 4 math, 4 science, 1 science lab, 4 foreign language, 1 social studies, 3 history, 1 computer science, 2 visual/performing arts.

Financial Aid

Students should submit: FAFSA, CSS/Financial Aid PROFILE. Regular filing deadline is 4/30. The Princeton Review suggests that all financial aid forms be submitted as soon as possible after October 1. *Need-based scholarships/grants offered:* Federal Pell, FSEOG, State scholarships/grants, Private scholarships, College/university scholarship or grant aid from institutional funds. *Loan aid offered:* Direct Subsidized Stafford Loans, Direct Unsubsidized Stafford Loans, Direct PLUS loans, Federal Perkins Loans, Federal Nursing Loans, College/university loans from institutional funds. Applicants will be notified of awards on a rolling basis beginning 3/15. Federal Work-Study Program available. Institutional employment available.

The Inside Word

Michigan admissions are extremely competitive, so you will need high test scores, exemplary grades in challenging courses, and strong teacher recommendations to make the cut here. Though Michigan receives over 50,000 applications, each one is read three times. Use your extracurricular activities to demonstrate leadership and originality to stand out from the crowd.

THE SCHOOL SAYS "..."

From the Admissions Office

"The University of Michigan is one of the great public research universities of the U.S. and the world, located in vibrant Ann Arbor. Since 1817, U-M has been a global model of a diverse, comprehensive academic institution committed to the public good. Nineteen schools and colleges offer 260 degree programs, featuring tremendous academic breadth and opportunity for discovery. Our thriving innovation ecosystem cultivates the ingenuity and entrepreneurial spirit of students across campus. Students study the liberal arts and the sciences in a spirited, cross-disciplinary environment that encourages inquiry in the classroom and in undergraduate research, with a 15:1 student/faculty ratio and 1,400 students participating in undergraduate research partnerships with faculty. More than 150 first-year seminars have twenty or fewer students taught by senior faculty. Numerous service learning programs link academics with volunteerism, such as Semester in Detroit. Global learning is achieved through more than 100 study-abroad programs on six continents; overseas internships and work; more than sixty-five global languages taught on campus; and various global intercultural experiences for students. Twelve Learning Communities allow undergraduates with similar interests or goals to live and study together, making a large campus small. With access to top-ranked programs and distinguished faculty, students have the resources and support they need to reach their full potential, to find their true voice, and to make a positive impact on the world. Upon graduation, more than 564,000 living alumni around the globe enable graduates to make personal and professional connections almost anywhere."

SELECTIVITY

Admissions Rating	96
# of applicants	51,761
% of applicants accepted	26
% of acceptees attending	45
# offered a place on the wait list	4,512
% admitted from wait list	2

FRESHMAN PROFILE

Range SAT Critical Reading	630–730
Range SAT Math	660–770
Range SAT Writing	640–730
Range ACT Composite	29–33
Minimum paper TOEFL	600
Minimum internet-based TOEFL	100
Average HS GPA	3.8

DEADLINES

Early action	
Deadline	11/1
Notification	12/24
Regular	
Priority	11/1
Deadline	2/1
Nonfall registration?	Yes

APPLICANTS ALSO LOOK AT AND OFTEN PREFER

Northwestern University; University of California–Berkeley; Cornell University; Washington University in St. Louis

AND SOMETIMES PREFER

University of California–Los Angeles; Purdue University–West Lafayette

AND RARELY PREFER

Boston University; Grand Valley State University; Indiana University

FINANCIAL FACTS

Financial Aid Rating	88
Annual in-state tuition	$14,401
Annual out-of-state tuition	$44,674
Room and board	$10,554
Required fees	$328
Books and supplies	$1,048
Average frosh need-based scholarship	$15,006
Average UG need-based scholarship	$15,400
% needy frosh rec. need-based scholarship or grant aid	83
% needy UG rec. need-based scholarship or grant aid	85
% needy frosh rec. non-need-based scholarship or grant aid	73
% needy UG rec. non-need-based scholarship or grant aid	65
% needy frosh rec. need-based self-help aid	75
% needy UG rec. need-based self-help aid	83
% frosh rec. any financial aid	68
% UG rec. any financial aid	61
% UG borrow to pay for school	44
Average cumulative indebtedness	$26,034
% frosh need fully met	77
% ugrads need fully met	81
Average % of frosh need met	86
Average % of ugrad need met	86

UNIVERSITY OF MINNESOTA—TWIN CITIES

240 WILLIAMSON HALL, MINNEAPOLIS, MN 55455-0213 • ADMISSIONS: 612-625-2008

CAMPUS LIFE

Quality of Life Rating	90
Fire Safety Rating	88
Green Rating	95
Type of school	Public
Affiliation	No Affiliation
Environment	Metropolis

STUDENTS

Total undergrad enrollment	34,071
% male/female	48/52
% from out of state	27
% frosh live on campus	89
% ugrads live on campus	23
# of fraternities	31
# of sororities	12
% African American	4
% Asian	9
% Caucasian	70
% Hispanic	4
% Native American	<1
% Pacific Islander	<1
% Two or more races	4
% Race and/or ethnicity unknown	1
% international	9
# of countries represented	134

SURVEY SAYS...

Students are happy
School is well run
Students love Minneapolis, MN
Recreation facilities are great
Everyone loves the Golden Gophers
Intramural sports are popular

ACADEMICS

Academic Rating	76
% students returning for sophomore year	93
% students graduating within 4 years	59
% students graduating within 6 years	77
Calendar	Semester
Student/faculty ratio	17:1
Profs interesting rating	73
Profs accessible rating	70

Most classes have 20–29 students.
Most lab/discussion sessions have 20–29 students.

MOST POPULAR MAJORS
Psychology; Rhetoric and Composition; Journalism

STUDENTS SAY "..."

Academics

"Great research opportunities," and "phenomenal" engineering programs" among other fantastic department, attract students to the University of Minnesota, Twin Cities. "A top-ranked university in a beautiful city that has a lot of great job opportunities"—how could you resist? And, given its "large" size, it's a virtual guarantee that "anyone can find what they want to do." Even better, they university really makes an effort to "help students discover themselves." An impressed psych major explains, "Our school pushes us to expand our horizons, to go outside of our comfort zones, and to try things that we never would have considered trying before." And Minnesota deftly maintains "a small school feeing" amidst "an urban setting," something many undergrads here value. By and large, Minnesota professors tend to be "approachable and are more than willing to take time out of their day to ensure you understand the material." They are also "very knowledgeable" and "strive to make [the subject matter] exciting." In short, "the University of Minnesota is a place with endless opportunity for those willing to discover their passions."

Life

Attending the University of Minnesota means that your life is likely be "full of variety." Indeed, from "biking [and] outdoor games [to] reading in the park, going to the farmers market, attending events at Coffman or TCF Bank Stadium, or taking the green line down town to explore" undergrads here "can get involved in almost anything." UMN also "hosts a lot of lectures and discussions with prominent figures" like Sandra Day O'Connor and the Dalai Lama. Further, as a member of the Big 10 conference, it's no surprise that "sporting events are widely popular, even if we aren't doing very well." As if that wasn't enough, "the Coffman building always has something going on—movies, book signings—and there are a ton of student groups to join, no experience necessary." There is also a "thriving" Greek population on campus, and a social scene that also involves a handful of "house parties," which typically feature "alcohol and lots of dancing." And, of course, the Twin Cities themselves have "a lot going on!" As a political science student succinctly puts it, "If you're bored on a weekend then you're not looking hard enough."

Student Body

Given the university's large undergraduate population, it's rather difficult to put "[students] into one category." Indeed, Minnesota truly manages to net "a wide variety of people." A dental hygiene student confirms this stating, "We have so much diversity here, that it is hard to pinpoint a general student type." And a mechanical engineering major quickly follows up, "Due to its size, everyone can find their niche and be free to express who they are." That being said, undergrads report that most of their peers are "generally quite friendly and outgoing." And everyone is "pretty willing to go out of their way for others, we are Minnesota nice after all." Further, many "students are driven to succeed and to make the most of the vast opportunities offered by the UMN." And a political science matter-of-factly asserts that a large number of students are "white, middle to upper middle-class Midwesterner[s], most likely hailing from Minnesota, Wisconsin, or the Dakotas." Of course, at the very least, nearly all Minnesota undergrads can "fit in by bonding over how much [they] hate winter."

Fax: 612-626-1693 • Financial Aid: 612-624-1111 • Website: www.umn.edu

THE PRINCETON REVIEW SAYS

Admissions

Very important factors considered include: rigor of secondary school record, class rank, academic GPA, standardized test scores. *Other factors considered include:* extracurricular activities, talent/ability, character/personal qualities, first generation, alumni/ae relation, geographical residence, racial/ethnic status, volunteer work, work experience. SAT or ACT required. ACT with Writing required. SAT with Essay component required. High school diploma is required and GED is accepted. *Academic units required:* 4 English, 4 math, 3 science, 1 science lab, 2 foreign language, 3 social studies, 1 visual/performing arts. *Academic units recommended:* 4 English, 4 math, 4 science, 1 science lab, 2 foreign language, 3 social studies, 1 visual/performing arts.

Financial Aid

Students should submit: FAFSA. Priority filing deadline is 2/1. The Princeton Review suggests that all financial aid forms be submitted as soon as possible after October 1. *Need-based scholarships/grants offered:* Federal Pell, FSEOG, State scholarships/grants, Private scholarships, College/university scholarship or grant aid from institutional funds, Federal Nursing Scholarships. *Loan aid offered:* Direct Subsidized Stafford Loans, Direct Unsubsidized Stafford Loans, Direct PLUS loans, Federal Perkins Loans, Federal Nursing Loans, State Loans, College/university loans from institutional funds. Applicants will be notified of awards on a rolling basis beginning in February. Federal Work-Study Program available. Institutional employment available.

The Inside Word

University of Minnesota, Twin Cities is a well-regarded institution and gaining admission is no easy feat. Academic preparation and performance are of primary concern. Therefore, course selection, GPA, class rank and standardized test scores will hold the most weight. However, plenty of consideration is also given to secondary factors such as outstanding talent and achievement in a particular area, military service, strong leadership experience, and extenuating circumstances.

THE SCHOOL SAYS ". . ."

From the Admissions Office

"The University of Minnesota is one of the nation's top public research universities. That means your college experience will be enhanced by world- renowned faculty, state-of-the-art learning facilities, and an unprecedented variety of options (such as 135 majors). Eighty-one percent of our classes have fewer than fifty students, and our caring advisers will help you find opportunities that are right for you. Hands-on courses, volunteer opportunities, internships, study abroad, and undergraduate research are part of the U of M experience. Students benefit from programs and traditions designed to support their success, like Welcome Week, where freshmen explore campus, meet their classmates, and connect with faculty and staff before the school year begins. Our classic Big Ten campus is located in the heart of the vibrant Twin Cities. Just minutes away, intern at a Fortune 500 company, volunteer at a major hospital, or relax at the beautiful Chain of Lakes. With a wealth of cultural, career, and recreational opportunities, there's no better place to earn your degree. Last year, we awarded over $12 million in four-year scholarship packages. Residents of Minnesota benefit from in-state tuition. Minnesota residents may also qualify for the University of Minnesota Promise Scholarship, which guarantees tuition aid to eligible students with a family income up to $100,000. Residents of North Dakota, South Dakota, Wisconsin, or Manitoba qualify for special reciprocity tuition rates.

"The University of Minnesota has been named a 'Best Value in Public Colleges' by multiple ranking organizations. As a U of M student, you will experience this value first-hand: you will step into a thriving academic community with some of the world's most renowned researchers. In fact, you'll often find that your professors are leading discoveries in their fields and developing curricula used across the country. With direct access to these incredible resources, you will get a great education and a prestigious degree that helps you achieve your dreams."

SELECTIVITY

Admissions Rating	90
# of applicants	46,165
% of applicants accepted	45
% of acceptees attending	28

FRESHMAN PROFILE

Range SAT Critical Reading	560–700
Range SAT Math	620–740
Range SAT Writing	570–690
Range ACT Composite	26–31
Minimum paper TOEFL	550
% graduated top 10% of class	49
% graduated top 25% of class	85
% graduated top 50% of class	99

DEADLINES

Regular	
Priority	11/1
Deadline	12/15
Notification	3/31
Nonfall registration?	Yes

APPLICANTS ALSO LOOK AT AND OFTEN PREFER

University of Michigan–Ann Arbor;
Northwestern University

FINANCIAL FACTS

Financial Aid Rating	81
Annual in-state tuition	$14,168
Room and Board	$8,962
Books and supplies	$1,000
Average frosh need-based scholarship	$10,320
Average UG need-based scholarship	$9,919
% needy frosh rec. need-based scholarship or grant aid	84
% needy UG rec. need-based scholarship or grant aid	83
% needy frosh rec. non-need-based scholarship or grant aid	10
% needy UG rec. non-need-based scholarship or grant aid	7
% needy frosh rec. need-based self-help aid	80
% needy UG rec. need-based self-help aid	81
% UG borrow to pay for school	59
Average cumulative indebtedness	$26,006
% frosh need fully met	29
% ugrads need fully met	24
Average % of frosh need met	78
Average % of ugrad need met	73

UNIVERSITY OF MISSISSIPPI

145 MARTINDALE, UNIVERSITY, MS 38677 • ADMISSIONS: 662-915-7226 • FAX: 662-915-5869

STUDENTS SAY "..."

Academics Ole Miss is a prime example of Southern hospitality combined with the opportunity for greatness. Founded in 1848, the legendary university offers "'big-time' SEC athletics in the safe, quaint, and picturesque town of Oxford." Many of the school's services "are cheap if not free," and the school "puts on many programs that bring together lots of different people of different backgrounds." "It has a togetherness about it...there is something for a person with any interest here," says a student. There is also "a highly academic side to Ole Miss that many outsiders do not see." Business and international studies are programs of note, and the Honors College is a particular standout here, as it provides "unparalleled academic opportunities, such as beginning research as a freshman."

Most of the professors "hit the ball out of the park" when it comes to teaching, being available, and helping students acquire internships. Professors constantly organize discussion groups, dinner events, and other gatherings in order to "develop our ability to speak academically in a non-academic setting." Going to class is "critical"; professors "add much more than the textbook has to offer." Classes are designed to be "informative but also engaging and dynamic," and there is a deep understanding that individuals have an effect on the whole. "The teachers care, the university cares, [and] the students all care about the school and what it stands for."

It can be said again and again, but even beyond the "world-class programs and faculty," the thing that students at Ole Miss value the most is the traditions and legacy of this school. People "are proud to have graduated from Ole Miss," and the tremendous amount of alumni support "gives Ole Miss a lot of confidence."

Life

An Ole Miss existence is "always super busy." There is "a lot of work to be done" as "school and grades are a very important aspect of life," but there are also "a lot of opportunities for fun." "During football season, the Grove consumes our weekends. It's an amazing experience!" says a student. As a school that most admit is "known for its Greek life, beautiful women, and great parties," it's a common misconception that "most people's minds revolve around drinking, college football, and church on Sunday." If you take a closer look, you'll find that there is a huge literary scene "with Thacker Mountain Radio on Thursdays and poetry readings monthly at Proud Larry's," and students here also "really want to be active in making changes in the world."

The closeness of the community makes it easy to feel part of the University. "You'll hear the term the 'Ole Miss family,' and it won't seem forced or strange," explains a student. Oxford is also very appealing due to its "small, hometown feel," and the rich history you see everywhere you go (the Square is the center of town life, and most students can be found there at some point in a week). Basically, "there is never a dull moment, especially on the weekends."

Student Body

Ole Miss is a fairly diverse campus, with most students possessing "decent grades and an extravagant social life." One third of the student body "belongs to either a fraternity or sorority, fancying the appropriate attire of a Polo shirt and loafers or baggy t-shirts and Nike shorts." The divide between Greek and non-Greek is stark here, though the two groups are not necessarily always adverse towards each other; this is a group of "open minds" in "a small-town" setting, with "a blend of Southern charm and laid-back manners" thrown in, after all. "Studying for your next exam over a glass of sweet tea is a common practice." As there are a lot of different groups on campus, "you can find a group of friends without much effort."

FINANCIAL AID: 800-891-4596 • E-MAIL: ADMISSIONS@OLEMISS.EDU • WEBSITE: WWW.OLEMISS.EDU

THE PRINCETON REVIEW SAYS

Admissions

Important factors considered include: academic GPA, standardized test scores. *Other factors considered include:* rigor of secondary school record, class rank. SAT or ACT required for some. ACT with or without writing accepted. TOEFL required of all international applicants. High school diploma is required and GED is accepted. *Academic units required:* 4 English, 3 math, 3 science, 2 science labs, 3 social studies, 1 visual/performing arts. *Academic units recommended:* 4 English, 4 math, 4 science, 2 science labs, 2 foreign language, 4 social studies, and 2 units from above areas or other academic areas.

Financial Aid

Students should submit: FAFSA. Priority filing deadline is 1/5. The Princeton Review suggests that all financial aid forms be submitted as soon as possible after October 1. *Need-based scholarships/grants offered:* Federal Pell, FSEOG, State scholarships/grants, Private scholarships, College/university scholarship or grant aid from institutional funds. *Loan aid offered:* Direct Subsidized Stafford Loans, Direct Unsubsidized Stafford Loans, Direct PLUS loans, Federal Perkins Loans, College/university loans from institutional funds. Applicants will be notified of awards on a rolling basis beginning 4/1. Federal Work-Study Program available. Institutional employment available.

The Inside Word

Ole Miss offers students tremendous educational opportunities and its admissions policies are designed to help in-state students attain a college degree. In-state applicants must have a 3.2 GPA or greater, or a 2.5 GPA and a 16 on the ACT or 760 on the SAT). Non-residents will need a 2.75 GPA and score 22 on the ACT or 980 on the SAT.

THE SCHOOL SAYS "..."

From the Admissions Office

"The state's flagship university, affectionately known as Ole Miss, offers extraordinary opportunities through more than 100 areas of study from medicine and law to creative writing and accountancy. Its acclaimed offerings include the Sally McDonnell Barksdale Honors College, the Croft Institute for International Studies and the Center for Manufacturing Excellence, which incorporates coursework from schools of engineering, accountancy and business into its curriculum. Its Patterson School of Accountancy is nationally ranked for undergraduate and graduate education, the School of Law is a national leader in the fields of air and space law and sports law, and nearly 100 percent of School of Pharmacy graduates pass the national licensure exam on their first try. It is the state's only public university to shelter a chapter of the nation's oldest and most prestigious honor society, Phi Beta Kappa. Strong academic programs and a rich and varied campus life have helped Ole Miss graduate twenty-five Rhodes Scholars and twelve Truman Scholars. Since 1998 alone, UM has produced ten Goldwater Scholars, eighteen Fulbright Scholars, and seventeen Boren Scholars.

"The campuses are diverse; 40 percent come from out of state, with forty-eight states and ninety foreign countries represented, and 13 percent are black Americans. Recent significant campus improvements include several new residence halls and a totally renovated and expanded dining facility. Ole Miss is home to twenty research centers, including the National Center for Justice and the Rule of Law, which provides training on investigating and prosecuting cybercrime; the National Center for Physical Acoustics, which is helping to quiet jet engines and use infrasound to detect tornadoes; and the National Center for Natural Products Research, where scientists are working to find new drugs to treat cancer, AIDS, fungal infections, and more. Students applying will be allowed to take the SAT or the ACT but are not required to take the ACT writing section. The university will not consider the writing section of either exam when evaluating students for admission, but certain specialty programs may request these scores."

SELECTIVITY

Admissions Rating	77
# of applicants	18,059
% of applicants accepted	79
% of acceptees attending	28

FRESHMAN PROFILE

Range SAT Critical Reading	490–600
Range SAT Math	500–600
Range ACT Composite	21–28
Minimum paper TOEFL	550
% graduated top 10% of class	24
% graduated top 25% of class	49
% graduated top 50% of class	78

DEADLINES

Regular	
Priority	4/1
Deadline	9/1
Nonfall registration?	Yes

FINANCIAL FACTS

Financial Aid Rating	83
Annual in-state tuition	$7,344
Annual out-of-state tuition	$20,574
Room and board	$10,128
Required fees	$100
Books and supplies	$1,000
Average frosh need-based scholarship	$8,532
Average UG need-based scholarship	$7,978
% needy frosh rec. need-based scholarship or grant aid	88
% needy UG rec. need-based scholarship or grant aid	84
% needy frosh rec. non-need-based scholarship or grant aid	16
% needy UG rec. non-need-based scholarship or grant aid	10
% needy frosh rec. need-based self-help aid	68
% needy UG rec. need-based self-help aid	73
% frosh rec. any financial aid	86
% UG rec. any financial aid	81
% UG borrow to pay for school	50
Average cumulative indebtedness	$27,535
% frosh need fully met	16
% ugrads need fully met	12
Average % of frosh need met	75
Average % of ugrad need met	72

UNIVERSITY OF MISSOURI

230 JESSE HALL, COLUMBIA, MO 65211 • ADMISSIONS: 573-882-7786 • FAX: 573-882-7887

CAMPUS LIFE

Quality of Life Rating	88
Fire Safety Rating	95
Green Rating	92
Type of school	Public
Affiliation	No Affiliation
Environment	City

STUDENTS

Total undergrad enrollment	27,812
% male/female	48/52
% from out of state	28
% frosh live on campus	90
% ugrads live on campus	25
# of fraternities (% ugrad men join)	31 (24)
# of sororities (% ugrad women join)	23 (31)
% African American	8
% Asian	2
% Caucasian	78
% Hispanic	4
% Native American	<1
% Pacific Islander	<1
% Two or more races	3
% Race and/or ethnicity unknown	1
% international	4
# of countries represented	122

SURVEY SAYS...

Students are happy
School is well run
Students love Columbia, MO
Recreation facilities are great
Lots of beer drinking
Hard liquor is popular
Everyone loves the Tigers
Alumni active on campus

ACADEMICS

Academic Rating	69
% students returning for sophomore year	87
% students graduating within 4 years	44
% students graduating within 6 years	89
Calendar	Semester
Student/faculty ratio	20:1
Profs interesting rating	70
Profs accessible rating	71

Most classes have 10–19 students.
Most lab/discussion sessions have
20–29 students.

MOST POPULAR MAJORS

Business/Commerce; Biological and
Biomedical Sciences; Journalism

STUDENTS SAY ". . ."

Academics

The "gorgeous campus" at the University of Missouri is filled with "a diverse group of students who are eager to learn and a staff that is eager to teach them." The school is all about "learning while networking," and the administration always has an ear to the students. "When we say there is a problem, it gets fixed," one student says. Mizzou takes pride in tradition, which is to be found "in all aspects that involve the University name," which makes for "a campus full of pride and spirit." There is a "constant focus on beautification, which makes for a great campus," and "top-of-the-line facilities" are available to all. One of the university's greatest strengths is its dependability: "From mass e-mails to mass texts, if there is an issue anywhere on campus you will know about it."

Professors teach "comprehensive courses" and "are always available to answer a question"; "even with large classes they are very attentive to individuals." "I've always had professors who have had a million ways to explain any given theory, problem, or question," says a student. The school boasts one of the country's best and most "intense" journalism schools (nursing is also a strong suit), and there are tons of "participation opportunities" for whatever area you choose to study. Classes may be hard, but "good grades are attainable." In addition to the "quality" academics, the advising system is "great," and Mizzou sets itself as a real model for its students: "It is always striving to achieve better, and not in just one specific category or area, but all around." "I came into college undecided and wanted to have plenty of options and opportunities to decide on a major," says a student of her reasoning for choosing Mizzou.

Life

"There is never a dull moment to be had" at the University of Missouri. All athletic events are "heavily attended," especially football and basketball. Everyone walks or bikes everywhere in Columbia "because it's such a pedestrian friendly place," and "there are plenty of opportunities to chill out downtown." It is "the perfect mixture of small town and big city," and local attractions include a mall, small shops, micro-breweries, and tons of parks and hiking trails. If you're used to bigger cities, then it also happens to be located between Kansas City and St. Louis. "Best of both worlds!" says a student. The school has "a huge Greek Life," and "it's a pretty close community." "Students enjoy going to off-campus parties or the bars downtown." "A lot of students spend their time in class, but every night of the week there is a party to go to," explains a student. Many agree that both the residential life system and the dorms "could use some work," and "having a car is the key to living off campus."

Student Body

The school has a giant spectrum of diversity, meaning "everyone is different. Anyone could fit in and find a group here." If a typical student has to be defined, most here are "friendly, outgoing, social, [and] very involved." Most of all, they are "proud to be Tiger[s]." "We all fit in because we have this in common," says a student. "It's pretty great company." "Classes have always felt like big families," and the majority of students find friends "by joining one of our million organizations," which is a common pastime among this "on-the-go" group. As everyone is "pretty easygoing and easy to get along with," "fitting in is easy; you just act like yourself!"

FINANCIAL AID: 573-882-7506 • E-MAIL: MU4U@MISSOURI.EDU • WEBSITE: WWW.MISSOURI.EDU

THE PRINCETON REVIEW SAYS

Admissions

Very important factors considered include: class rank, academic GPA, standardized test scores. *Important factors considered include:* rigor of secondary school record. *Other factors considered include:* application essay, recommendation(s), talent/ability, first generation, racial/ethnic status, volunteer work, work experience, level of applicant's interest. SAT or ACT required. ACT with or without writing accepted. TOEFL required of all international applicants. High school diploma is required and GED is accepted. *Academic units required:* 4 English, 4 math, 3 science, 1 science lab, 2 foreign language, 3 social studies, and 1 unit from above areas or other academic areas.

Financial Aid

Students should submit: FAFSA. Priority filing deadline is 3/1. The Princeton Review suggests that all financial aid forms be submitted as soon as possible after October 1. *Need-based scholarships/grants offered:* Federal Pell, FSEOG, State scholarships/grants, Private scholarships, College/university scholarship or grant aid from institutional funds, Federal Nursing Scholarships. *Loan aid offered:* Direct Subsidized Stafford Loans, Direct Unsubsidized Stafford Loans, Direct PLUS loans, Federal Perkins Loans, Federal Nursing Loans, State Loans, College/university loans from institutional funds. Applicants will be notified of awards on a rolling basis beginning 4/1. Federal Work-Study Program available. Institutional employment available.

The Inside Word

If your application suggests that you can handle the workload here, the school will find a place for you. Average test scores in conjunction with a college-prep high school curriculum should be all it takes. Even those who don't meet these criteria have a chance; admissions officers consider essays, recommendations, and special talents in the cases of borderline candidates.

THE SCHOOL SAYS "..."

From the Admissions Office

"Founded in 1839 as the first public university west of the Mississippi River, MU is a member of the nation's most prestigious group of sixty-two public and private teaching/research institutions: the Association of American Universities. The National Science Foundation has recognized MU as one of the top ten universities in the country for integrating research into undergraduate education; Missou offers twelve major undergraduate research programs, some with freshmen participants.

"Service learning is important at Mizzou. The Service Learning Office at MU formally integrates community service into 250 courses. Last year 4,500 undergraduates earned academic credit while volunteering 209,000 hours for 290 community and government partners.

"More than 39 percent of the fall 2015 freshman class came from another state or another country, and a strong international community thrives in Columbia. At the same time, MU's Study Abroad program is Missouri's largest with 300 programs in fifty countries.

"Mizzou offers many strong, unique programs. Some in the sciences are taught in collaboration with MU's medical school, and humanities classes include such areas as music composition and creative writing where students frequently win national awards.

"Students can find admissions requirements at missouri.edu. As students apply online, it is clear whether they are admissible or not. That may partially explain Missouri's high acceptance rate."

SELECTIVITY
Admissions Rating	79
# of applicants	21,988
% of applicants accepted	78
% of acceptees attending	40

FRESHMAN PROFILE
Range SAT Critical Reading	530–650
Range SAT Math	530–650
Range ACT Composite	24–29
Minimum paper TOEFL	500
Minimum internet-based TOEFL	61
% graduated top 10% of class	28
% graduated top 50% of class	87

DEADLINES
Regular	
Priority	5/1
Nonfall registration?	Yes

FINANCIAL FACTS
Financial Aid Rating	81
Annual in-state tuition	$8,286
Annual out-of-state tuition	$23,943
Room and board	$9,808
Required fees	$1,223
Books and supplies	$1,124
Average frosh need-based scholarship	$9,877
Average UG need-based scholarship	$8,783
% needy frosh rec. need-based scholarship or grant aid	84
% needy UG rec. need-based scholarship or grant aid	80
% needy frosh rec. non-need-based scholarship or grant aid	8
% needy UG rec. non-need-based scholarship or grant aid	5
% needy frosh rec. need-based self-help aid	69
% needy UG rec. need-based self-help aid	74
% frosh need fully met	16
% ugrads need fully met	13
Average % of frosh need met	79
Average % of ugrad need met	76

THE UNIVERSITY OF MONTANA—MISSOULA

LOMMASSON CENTER 103, MISSOULA, MT 59812 • ADMISSIONS: 406-243-6266 • FAX: 406-243-5711

CAMPUS LIFE

Quality of Life Rating	88
Fire Safety Rating	90
Green Rating	95
Type of school	Public
Affiliation	No Affiliation
Environment	City

STUDENTS

Total undergrad enrollment	10,778
% male/female	46/54
% from out of state	26
# of fraternities (% ugrad men join)	6 (6)
# of sororities (% ugrad women join)	4 (6)
% African American	1
% Asian	1
% Caucasian	77
% Hispanic	4
% Native American	3
% Pacific Islander	<1
% Two or more races	4
% Race and/or ethnicity unknown	8
% international	2
# of countries represented	68

SURVEY SAYS...

Students are happy
Students love Missoula, MT
Recreation facilities are great
Everyone loves the Grizzlies

ACADEMICS

Academic Rating	71
% students returning for sophomore year	73
% students graduating within 4 years	24
% students graduating within 6 years	46
Calendar	Semester
Student/faculty ratio	18:1
Profs interesting rating	76
Profs accessible rating	69

Most classes have 10–19 students.
Most lab/discussion sessions have
20–29 students.

MOST POPULAR MAJORS
Business Administration and Management;
Psychology; Forest Management/Forest
Resources Management

STUDENTS SAY "..."

Academics

Nestled in beautiful Missoula, The University of Montana is "a great place to live, work, and study." Indeed, Montana's awesome location and solid reputation coupled with low in-state tuition make it "hard to beat." Moreover, while it has a substantial number of students, we're assured that you're never "just a number" here. Undergrads also appreciate the university's focus on "environmental sustainability...and social justice" along with the fact that the University of Montana strives to develop "creative thinkers and engaged citizens." While the university maintains a fantastic liberal arts program, students especially laud the wildlife biology, forestry, physical therapy, and forensic anthropology departments. Moreover, undergrads at Montana are highly complementary of their teachers who are generally "helpful, engaging, and accessible." One thrilled student claims that the professors are "amazing! Math and science has never come easy for me, and my professors have taught in a way I completely understand the material." Another enthusiastic student summarizes her experience by stating, "The professors here are very knowledgeable and passionate about what they are teaching, because of this, the learning experience is always interesting and inviting. I truly appreciate all the effort that is put forward to help students succeed and prepare for the next steps in their life."

Life

Undergrads seem to truly enjoy life at U of M. Indeed, the campus is often buzzing with activity. As one student happily shares, "When it's not snowing in the fall or spring you can find people playing Frisbee, walking their dogs, catching footballs, and even playing with lightsabers." Additionally, there are "many music concerts and dance parties" one can attend. "Football is [also] really big here," and games are often packed with students. Beyond the campus, Montana offers a myriad of options for the outdoor enthusiast. As one ecstatic undergrad tells us, "Western Montana is a divine place for hiking, hunting, fishing, camping, snowshoeing, swimming, huckleberry picking, going to hot springs, mushroom picking, antler collecting, and just being immersed in nature. Near where I live there is access to the Rattlesnake Wilderness, mountains surround the valley, and the Clark Fork River runs right through town." Those with a more adventurous spirit can delight in "skiing and skydiving, hand gliding and parasailing, mountain climbing and repelling, caving and biking." As this pleased undergrad summarizes, "There is always something to do no matter what your interest are and great people to do them with."

Student Body

The University of Montana attracts a student body that's "pretty laid-back and easygoing." Many are "outdoorsy" and self-described as "hippies." Indeed, there are "quite a few granola kids" and "Carhartt-sporting, plaid-proud, future biologists" types. Though many students hail from within the state, one undergrad assures us that "increasing diversity efforts have begun to show in the past three years." Fortunately, for the most part, everyone is "accepting, friendly, and very involved in college and community life." Another student expands on this idea, stating, "People here do not seem to judge others or hold stereotypes against each other. If you're lost or need to ask a question you can ask anyone, and they're willing to give you the best answer they know in order to help you out even if they don't know you." A fellow undergrad agrees softly, sharing, "I feel like I've stepped into a melting pot of all beliefs and ideals. You can be yourself, and never be looked down on for that at this school."

THE UNIVERSITY OF MONTANA—MISSOULA

FINANCIAL AID: 406-243-5373 • E-MAIL: ADMISS@UMONTANA.EDU • WEBSITE: WWW.UMONTANA.EDU

THE PRINCETON REVIEW SAYS

Admissions

Very important factors considered include: rigor of secondary school record, class rank, academic GPA, standardized test scores. *Important factors considered include:* extracurricular activities, talent/ability. *Other factors considered include:* application essay, recommendation(s). SAT or ACT required. ACT with Writing recommended. SAT with Essay component recommended. TOEFL required of all international applicants. High school diploma is required and GED is accepted. *Academic units required:* 4 English, 3 math, 2 science, 2 science labs, 3 social studies, 2 history. *Academic units recommended:* 2 foreign language, 2 computer science, 2 visual/performing arts, and 2 units from above areas or other academic areas.

Financial Aid

Students should submit: FAFSA. Priority filing deadline is 2/15. The Princeton Review suggests that all financial aid forms be submitted as soon as possible after October 1. *Need-based scholarships/grants offered:* Federal Pell, FSEOG, State scholarships/grants, Private scholarships, College/university scholarship or grant aid from institutional funds. *Loan aid offered:* Federal Perkins Loans. Applicants will be notified of awards on a rolling basis beginning 4/1. Federal Work-Study Program available. Institutional employment available.

The Inside Word

The admissions game at the University of Montana is fairly straightforward. Officers here rely heavily on quantitative data. Applicants who meet standardized test and GPA minimums and are in the top half of their graduating class generally receive an acceptance letter. Those who did not meet the minimum requirements can often enroll on a conditional basis.

THE SCHOOL SAYS "..."

From the Admissions Office

"There's something special about this place. It's something different for each person. For some, it's the blend of academic quality and outdoor recreation. The University of Montana ranks fifth in the nation among public institutions for producing Rhodes scholars, and Outside Magazine lists Missoula in its 'Top Ten Amazing Places for Outdoor Recreation.' For others, it's size—not too big, not too small. The University of Montana is a midsized university in the heart of the Rocky Mountains—accessible in both admission and tuition bills— that produces graduates considered among the best and brightest in the world. It is located in a community that could pass for a cozy college town or a bustling big city, depending on your point of view. There's a lot happening, but you won't get lost. People are friendly and diverse. They come from all over the world to study and learn and to live a good life. They come to a place to be inspired, a place where they feel comfortable yet challenged. Some never leave. Most never want to."

SELECTIVITY

Admissions Rating	74
# of applicants	5,600
% of applicants accepted	91
% of acceptees attending	34

FRESHMAN PROFILE

Range SAT Critical Reading	490–620
Range SAT Math	490–600
Range SAT Writing	480–600
Range ACT Composite	20–27
Minimum paper TOEFL	525
Minimum internet-based TOEFL	70
Average HS GPA	3.3
% graduated top 10% of class	18
% graduated top 25% of class	39
% graduated top 50% of class	72

DEADLINES

Regular	
Priority	3/1
Nonfall registration?	Yes

FINANCIAL FACTS

Financial Aid Rating	80
Annual in-state tuition	$4,604
Annual out-of-state tuition	$22,720
Room and board	$8,826
Required fees	$1,842
Books and supplies	$1,400
Average frosh need-based scholarship	$4,789
Average UG need-based scholarship	$4,914
% needy frosh rec. need-based scholarship or grant aid	68
% needy UG rec. need-based scholarship or grant aid	69
% needy frosh rec. non-need-based scholarship or grant aid	58
% needy UG rec. non-need-based scholarship or grant aid	40
% needy frosh rec. need-based self-help aid	100
% needy UG rec. need-based self-help aid	99
% frosh rec. any financial aid	62
% UG rec. any financial aid	56
% frosh need fully met	12
% ugrads need fully met	8
Average % of frosh need met	71
Average % of ugrad need met	65

UNIVERSITY OF NEBRASKA—LINCOLN

1410 Q STREET, LINCOLN, NE 68588-0417 • ADMISSIONS: 402-472-2023

CAMPUS LIFE

Quality of Life Rating	91
Fire Safety Rating	83
Green Rating	90
Type of school	Public
Affiliation	No Affiliation
Environment	City

STUDENTS

Total undergrad enrollment	21,182
% male/female	53/47
% from out of state	22
% frosh live on campus	94
% ugrads live on campus	43
# of fraternities (% ugrad men join)	28 (19)
# of sororities (% ugrad women join)	19 (22)
% African American	3
% Asian	2
% Caucasian	77
% Hispanic	5
% Native American	<1
% Pacific Islander	<1
% Two or more races	3
% Race and/or ethnicity unknown	2
% international	8
# of countries represented	107

SURVEY SAYS...

Students are happy
School is well run
Students love Lincoln, NE
Recreation facilities are great
Everyone loves the Cornhuskers
Intramural sports are popular
Frats and sororities are popular

ACADEMICS

Academic Rating	72
% students returning for sophomore year	83
% students graduating within 4 years	33
% students graduating within 6 years	67
Calendar	Semester
Student/faculty ratio	22:1
Profs interesting rating	73
Profs accessible rating	71

Most classes have 20–29 students.
Most lab/discussion sessions have
20–29 students.

MOST POPULAR MAJORS

Business Administration and Management;
Psychology; Foods, Nutrition, and Wellness
Studies

STUDENTS SAY "..."

Academics

At the University of Nebraska—Lincoln, students feel that their professors are "very knowledgeable" and "engage the class in discussion rather than a lot of lecture," and that "overall the professors genuinely care and want the students to succeed," although they feel that "UNL could definitely improve on the communication between the students, particularly first year, and the advisors or deans of colleges," with some students sticking up for the Business school saying "the advisors in the business school are great." Students feel that, at UNL, they "have so many resources such as the Career Center, Student Involvement, Writing Resource Center, etc." Students are "particularly pleased with the honors program at the University of Nebraska–Lincoln...The opportunities for unique academic projects are endless and strongly supported by the faculty." Because of the university's location "right next to downtown Lincoln... there are infinite opportunities for socializing or jobs and internships within walking distance." A Microbiology major sums it up by saying, "Nebraska is an excellent school academically yet athletics are very prominent."

Life

Students love UNL's "location," "affordability," and the fact that it's in the Big Ten, along with Husker football. The sense of community on our campus is second to none," according to students. They are proud to be members of the University of Nebraska–Lincoln and think that the sense of "tradition here is amazing, and the support from the alumni and the community is awesome." "There is a real sense of unity around the athletics here," as students rally around Husker football games with staggering amounts of "school spirit and pride." Many of the parties on campus revolve around the Greek scene. UNL provides students with access to all that Lincoln has to offer via their program called "Arts-For-All, which allows students to go to shows at the Lied Performing Arts Center for free." "Life in Lincoln is fantastic. Campus is a five minute walk away from downtown, where there are a variety of restaurants, bars, shops, and anything else you could want. For fun, people go to the bars downtown, go to the movie theaters, go shopping, or hang out at one of the many cool little places around town." Alternately, if you were to simply walk around campus, "you're bound to run into people doing something fun, and they're usually welcoming and will let you join." For fun, many students "play sports at the outdoor sporting areas or at the rec."

Student Body

"The typical student is from Nebraska somewhere, but they are starting to diversify the campus more recently." "Typical Midwesterner, nice and friendly." "The typical student at University of Nebraska-Lincoln is friendly, often from within the state, and moderately studious. A large part of the student body is socially and politically conservative." "A lot of people drink," but students don't think that that is something which is "exclusive to UNL." Greek life is "a big part of this school." Some older students "feel very alienated at times by my classmates and professors." Students love to get involved in extracurricular activities and campus-wide events, which is usually how "everyone can find a niche that suits them." "Even though it's a big school," says one student, "I never feel lost in the crowd," and a Biology major says, "Every person I have met has had the courage to talk with me, listen to my story, and share with me their story. I have not met a single person that I couldn't find something in common with."

UNIVERSITY OF NEBRASKA—LINCOLN

Fax: 402-472-0670 • Financial Aid: 402-472-2030 • E-mail: ADMISSIONS@UNL.EDU • Website: WWW.UNL.EDU

THE PRINCETON REVIEW SAYS

Admissions

Very important factors considered include: class rank, standardized test scores. *Important factors considered include:* rigor of secondary school record. *Other factors considered include:* academic GPA. SAT or ACT required. ACT with or without writing accepted. High school diploma is required and GED is accepted. *Academic units required:* 4 English, 4 math, 3 science, 1 science lab, 2 foreign language, 2 social studies, 1 history.

Financial Aid

Students should submit: FAFSA. The Princeton Review suggests that all financial aid forms be submitted as soon as possible after October 1. *Need-based scholarships/grants offered:* Federal Pell, FSEOG, State scholarships/grants, Private scholarships, College/university scholarship or grant aid from institutional funds. *Loan aid offered:* Direct Subsidized Stafford Loans, Direct Unsubsidized Stafford Loans, Direct PLUS loans, Federal Perkins Loans. Applicants will be notified of awards on a rolling basis beginning 4/1. Federal Work-Study Program available. Institutional employment available.

The Inside Word

UNL offers more than 150 majors. All applications will be weighed on the combined strength of course work, GPAs, and test scores. Applicants interested in applying to a specific school at UNL should take into account those school's specialized requirements as they may include additional high school course work than what is required by UNL's general studies program.

THE SCHOOL SAYS "..."

From the Admissions Office

"If you make it to Lincoln, you can go anywhere. UNL graduates have a world of opportunity ahead of them because not only is NEBRASKA a world-class institution recognized as one of the best values in higher education, our faculty is directly invested in and involved with our students' success. Students are equipped with the tools they need to succeed thanks to our robust student support system, low student-to-faculty ratio, substantial out-of-state scholarship program, and one of the nation's leading undergraduate research programs.

"In recent years, people across the nation have started to realize what we've known for a while: something great is happening in Lincoln. As the heart of the Silicon Prairie, startups are flocking to Lincoln to recruit talent from UNL and get involved with our cutting-edge Innovation Campus. Combine this with a bustling downtown steps away from campus, recent renovations to the Union and Rec Centers, and a true Big Ten campus culture, life as a student in Lincoln just feels right.

"Since 1869, UNL has had a rich history as one of the nation's leading public universities with more than 200,000 alumni who've gone on to truly make a difference in the world. As a UNL alum, you'll join a history of excellence and a red "N" on your resume will open doors wherever you go."

SELECTIVITY

Admissions Rating	86
# of applicants	9,724
% of applicants accepted	76
% of acceptees attending	47

FRESHMAN PROFILE

Range SAT Critical Reading	500–630
Range SAT Math	500–660
Range ACT Composite	22–28
Minimum internet-based TOEFL	70
% graduated top 10% of class	26
% graduated top 25% of class	52
% graduated top 50% of class	83

DEADLINES

Regular	
Priority	1/15
Deadline	5/1
Nonfall registration?	Yes

APPLICANTS ALSO LOOK AT AND OFTEN PREFER

University of Nebraska at Omaha

AND SOMETIMES PREFER

Creighton University; Iowa State University; Nebraska Wesleyan University; University of Iowa; University of Kansas; University of Minnesota–Twin Cities Campus

AND RARELY PREFER

Arizona State University; Doane College; Kansas State University; Michigan State University

FINANCIAL FACTS

Financial Aid Rating	83
Annual out-of-state tuition	$20,760
Room and board	$10,310
Required fees	$1,686
Books and supplies	$1,070
Average frosh need-based scholarship	$7,871
Average UG need-based scholarship	$7,325
% needy frosh rec. need-based scholarship or grant aid	80
% needy UG rec. need-based scholarship or grant aid	75
% needy frosh rec. non-need-based scholarship or grant aid	8
% needy UG rec. non-need-based scholarship or grant aid	7
% needy frosh rec. need-based self-help aid	71
% needy UG rec. need-based self-help aid	70
% frosh rec. any financial aid	90
% UG rec. any financial aid	78
% frosh need fully met	22
% ugrads need fully met	19
Average % of frosh need met	82
Average % of ugrad need met	78

UNIVERSITY OF NEW ENGLAND

11 HILLS BEACH ROAD, BIDDEFORD, ME 04005-9599 • ADMISSIONS: 207-602-2297 • FAX: 207-602-5900

STUDENTS SAY ". . ."

Academics
With its stellar track record in the health sciences and liberal arts, "small classes," and "fantastic location" on the waterfront of southern Maine, it's easy to see the allure of the University of New England. Undergrads here certainly value the school's "small" size, which helps to create a "welcoming community." And they also appreciate that UNE frequently awards "great financial aid package[s]." Academically, the university is hailed for its "strong" science programs which focus on "clinical experiences" and offer "very good research opportunities." Indeed, UNE really places an emphasis on "individualized, hands-on experience." Students here are pleased to discover that the majority of their professors are "really passionate about their subjects" and bring "innovative and inspiring" teaching methods to the classroom. It's also quite evident that "professors at UNE are here for the students." As a grateful athletic training major shares, "[Teachers are often] willing to meet outside of the classroom not only during office hours but hours that work with your schedule." All in all, as an elementary education major simply sums up, "it's a really amazing educational environment."

Life
At the University of New England "life on campus is [still] very active." To begin with, the college hosts a number of activities such as "bingo nights, dances and comedians." And there are plenty of "open mics" and "karaoke [events]" to attend as well. Hockey and ice skating are quite popular, and, given that the university is in Maine, you're guaranteed to find students "play[ing] in the snow" during the winter months. Of course, UNE's coastal location in Biddleford is an outdoor enthusiast's paradise. Indeed, from "kayaking on the Saco River [to] taking the bus to skiing with friends on the mountain, learning how to scuba dive in the pool, or going to free skate in the Forum," it's quite easy for undergrads to "take advantage of Maine's natural surroundings." Moreover, the school's close proximity to the water allows students to quickly head "down to the beach and hang out." And for those undergrads who love getting off campus, the student activity board offers a lot of free trips "including apple picking, dog-sledding and cupcake tours," Lastly, the citiy of Portland with it's lively Old Port area are roughly thirty minutes away and offer a wide variety of great dining and entertainment options.

Student Body
University of New England tends to attract "hard working" and "driven" students, many of whom seem to have an eye towards pursuing graduate school. In addition to a studious nature, you'll also discover a "friendly" student body that's "always willing to lend a hand." As a pre-occupational therapy major explains, "Everyone is comfortable with being who they are and the students here accept each person as an individual. It's not cliquey like high school sometimes is." And a marine biology major quickly concurs stating, "I will walk by a stranger and we will say hi and ask how each other is doing. Random people will sit with you at lunch or dinner and you will be able to have a nice conversation." Of course, some students do complain about the "disproportionate male-to-female ratio;" females at University of New England far outnumber the males. Many of these undergrads also tend to be "Caucasian," and come from "middle class families" and "small Maine towns." A lot of UNE students strive to be "eco-friendly." Although there is "little racial diversity" here, undergrads stress that there's "no discrimination." Additionally, "there is a major LGBT community on campus that create events that welcome everyone." In the end, an elementary education major promises that "everyone finds their friends and many people seem very happy with it all."

FINANCIAL AID: 207-602-2342 • E-MAIL: ADMISSIONS@UNE.EDU • WEBSITE: WWW.UNE.EDU

THE PRINCETON REVIEW SAYS

Admissions

Very important factors considered include: rigor of secondary school record, academic GPA. *Important factors considered include:* class rank. *Other factors considered include:* standardized test scores, application essay, recommendation(s), extracurricular activities, talent/ability, character/personal qualities, alumni/ae relation, geographical residence, volunteer work, work experience, level of applicant's interest. SAT or ACT required; SAT Subject Tests considered if submitted. ACT with or without writing accepted. TOEFL required of all international applicants. High school diploma is required and GED is accepted. *Academic units required:* 4 English, 3 math, 3 science, 2 science labs, 2 social studies, 2 history. *Academic units recommended:* 4 math, 4 science, 3 science labs, 2 foreign language, 4 social studies, 4 history, 4 academic electives.

Financial Aid

Students should submit: FAFSA. Regular filing deadline is 5/1. The Princeton Review suggests that all financial aid forms be submitted as soon as possible after October 1. *Loan aid offered:* Applicants will be notified of awards on a rolling basis beginning 3/15. Federal Work-Study Program available. Institutional employment available.

The Inside Word

Applicants to the University of New England should expect the school to thoroughly vet their high school transcript and strongly consider their standardized test scores. Admissions officers will also be on the lookout for candidates who'll thoroughly invest in the school and make the most of their time on campus. Since UNE has a strong focus in the health sciences, a rigorous science and math curriculum will certainly strengthen your candidacy. Finally, students eager to attend UNE should consider applying early action. After all, admission is non-binding.

THE SCHOOL SAYS "..."

From the Admissions Office

"The University of New England is an innovative health sciences university grounded in the liberal arts with two campuses located in picturesque southern Maine communities and a third campus in Tangier, Morocco. With over forty undergraduate degree programs UNE ensures that students have plenty of opportunities for extensive fieldwork, clinical experiences, research, internships and global experiences. All undergraduate programs have a core curriculum as a common thread. Qualified UNE students can pursue a UNE graduate or professional degree through Early Assurance in dental medicine, occupational therapy, osteopathic medicine, pharmacy, physical therapy, physician assistant, and social work.

"UNE's Student Academic Success Center provides a range of academic support services to help students attain their personal educational goals. The Career Services Office provides academic and career exploration assistance, guidance in applying to graduate schools, self-assessment, personal interest exploration, resume help, and information and access to job listings and job fairs.

"UNE's campuses offer a variety of cultural and social events and students are encouraged to become involved in activities, clubs and sports. Popular interests include scuba diving, skiing, hiking, biking, swimming, surfing, music, theater, photography, community service, and student leadership development programs.

"UNE's Department of Athletics operates an NCAA Division III varsity athletics program. Varsity sports for men are basketball, cross country, football (2018), golf, ice hockey, lacrosse and soccer. Varsity sports for women are basketball, cross country, field hockey, ice hockey, lacrosse, rugby (2016), soccer, softball, swimming and volleyball."

SELECTIVITY	
Admissions Rating	75
# of applicants	4,416
% of applicants accepted	85
% of acceptees attending	17

FRESHMAN PROFILE	
Range SAT Critical Reading	480–580
Range SAT Math	480–590
Minimum paper TOEFL	550
Average HS GPA	3.3

DEADLINES	
Early action	
Deadline	12/1
Notification	12/31
Regular	
Priority	12/1
Nonfall registration?	Yes

FINANCIAL FACTS	
Financial Aid Rating	63
Annual tuition	$33,540
Room and board	$12,920
Required fees	$1,220
Books and supplies	$1,400
% needy frosh rec. need-based scholarship or grant aid	0
% needy UG rec. need-based scholarship or grant aid	0
% needy frosh rec. non-need-based scholarship or grant aid	0
% needy UG rec. non-need-based scholarship or grant aid	0
% needy frosh rec. need-based self-help aid	0
% needy UG rec. need-based self-help aid	0
% frosh rec. any financial aid	98
% UG rec. any financial aid	98

UNIVERSITY OF NEW HAMPSHIRE

UNH OFFICE OF ADMISSIONS, DURHAM, NH 03824 • ADMISSIONS: 603-862-1360 • FAX: 603-862-0077

STUDENTS SAY "..."

Academics

The benefits of going to a large, well-established state school, such as the University of New Hampshire, are exactly what one expects—its low in-state tuition, firmly established reputation, and place in the system allow it to offer "many resources to help students out in life." Located in tiny, beautiful Durham, the school "emphasizes research in every field, including non-science fields," and a lot of importance is placed "on the outdoors and the environment." The small town really fosters "lots of school spirit," and the laid-back denizens of UNH make it known that "having a good time" is a priority in their lives: "Weekends are for the Warriors." Most professors "truly care" about the students' learning so that "you never feel like a number at the school but rather a respected student," and professors "will get down and dirty when it comes to experiencing what they're teaching firsthand." Though there are definitely complaints that some can be "sub-par," a student "just needs to posses the initiative to go to their office hours" and they will get all the help they need. Some of the general education classes "are *huge*," and TAs can be difficult to understand, but for the most part, students report that they've had a "good experience" and that their academic career has been "very successful." The Honors program is particularly challenging (in a very positive way) and offers "great seminar/inquiry classes that have about fifteen students." Students universally pan the administration, claiming it "is a massive bureaucracy that gets little done," partially due to poor communication, or one student puts it that "the left hand has no idea what the right hand is doing." "The school is way more challenging than I thought it would be because the administration makes things harder than they need to be," says a sophomore.

Life

The school is just "fifteen minutes to the beach, one hour to the mountains, and one hour to Boston," making the world a Wildcat's oyster. Partying is big here, and the weekends are crazy; "Everyone goes out pretty much every Thursday, Friday, and Saturday night." The small number of bars in town "makes the age limit pretty well enforced." After a hard night out, "there are many late night convenience stores and food places to go to." In fact, it can be "difficult to find activities to do on the weekend that don't involve drinking," though UNH does a good job of bringing in "popular comedians, musicians, bands, political figures, etc.," and the school has tons of "amazing" a capella groups, so there is "almost always something to go see." Sports are also big here: "We love our hockey and football," says a student. Though there's a pretty big housing crunch, the oft-used athletic and recreational facilities here are both convenient and excellent, and since everything on this "beautiful" campus is only about ten minutes away, "you walk pretty much everywhere," though public transportation and school-provided buses run often. Students do a lot of socializing over meals at the "eight cafés or in any of the three dining halls."

Student Body

This being New Hampshire, people are "very politically and socially aware." Students here are mostly middle-class and hail from New England (especially from New Hampshire, naturally), and a main point of contention among students is that there "is not a lot of ethnic/racial diversity," though the school is working on it. The size of UNH means that "even the most unique individual will find a group of friends," and even the most atypical students "fit in perfectly well." Most of these "laid-back" and "easy-to-get-along-with" Wildcats party, and it can be "hard to find one that doesn't." "*Everyone* skis or snowboards," and in the cold weather "Uggs and North Face fleece jackets abound."

FINANCIAL AID: 603-862-3600 • E-MAIL: ADMISSIONS@UNH.EDU • WEBSITE: WWW.UNH.EDU

THE PRINCETON REVIEW SAYS

Admissions

Very important factors considered include: rigor of secondary school record, class rank, academic GPA. *Important factors considered include:* recommendation(s). *Other factors considered include:* standardized test scores, application essay, extracurricular activities, talent/ability, character/personal qualities, first generation, alumni/ae relation, geographical residence, state residency, racial/ethnic status, volunteer work, work experience. SAT or ACT required. ACT with Writing required. SAT with or without Essay component accepted. TOEFL required of all international applicants. High school diploma is required and GED is accepted. *Academic units required:* 4 English, 3 math, 3 science, 2 science labs, 2 foreign language, 3 social studies. *Academic units recommended:* 4 English, 4 math, 4 science, 3 science labs, 3 foreign language, 3 social studies, 1 visual/performing arts.

Financial Aid

Students should submit: FAFSA. Regular filing deadline is 3/1. The Princeton Review suggests that all financial aid forms be submitted as soon as possible after October 1. *Need-based scholarships/grants offered:* Federal Pell, FSEOG, State scholarships/grants, Private scholarships, College/university scholarship or grant aid from institutional funds. *Loan aid offered:* Direct Subsidized Stafford Loans, Direct Unsubsidized Stafford Loans, Direct PLUS loans, Federal Perkins Loans. Applicants will be notified of awards on a rolling basis beginning 3/1. Federal Work-Study Program available. Institutional employment available.

The Inside Word

New Hampshire's emphasis on academic accomplishment in the admissions process makes it clear that the admissions committee is looking for students who have taken high school seriously. Standardized tests take as much of a backseat here as is possible at a large, public university.

THE SCHOOL SAYS "..."

From the Admissions Office

"At UNH, you are always on the edge of a new vista; a new possibility. That's because we are spectacularly located near the Atlantic coast, the White Mountains and Boston. It's because we are a research university where relationships matter. The big opportunities and the small ones, what you learn, the friends you make, the adventures you have and the passions you discover here will be relevant and rewarding for the rest of your life.

"The University of New Hampshire is an institution best defined by the students who take advantage of its opportunities. Enrolled students who are willing to engage in a high-quality academic community in some meaningful way, who have a genuine interest in discovering or developing new ideas, and who believe in each person's obligation to improve the community they live in typify the most successful students at UNH. Undergraduate students practice these three basic values in a variety of ways: by undertaking their own, independent research projects; by collaborating in faculty research; and by participating in study abroad, residential communities, community service, and other cultural programs."

SELECTIVITY

Admissions Rating	78
# of applicants	19,255
% of applicants accepted	79
% of acceptees attending	21

FRESHMAN PROFILE

Range SAT Critical Reading	500–600
Range SAT Math	500–610
Range SAT Writing	490–590
Range ACT Composite	22–27
Minimum paper TOEFL	550
Minimum internet-based TOEFL	80
Average HS GPA	3.4
% graduated top 10% of class	18
% graduated top 25% of class	45
% graduated top 50% of class	86

DEADLINES

Early action	
Deadline	11/15
Notification	12/15
Regular	
Deadline	2/1
Nonfall registration?	Yes

FINANCIAL FACTS

Financial Aid Rating	79
Annual in-state tuition	$14,050
Annual out-of-state tuition	$27,320
Room and board	$10,618
Required fees	$2,936
Books and supplies	$1,200
Average frosh need-based scholarship	$5,412
Average UG need-based scholarship	$4,494
% needy frosh rec. need-based scholarship or grant aid	75
% needy UG rec. need-based scholarship or grant aid	70
% needy frosh rec. non-need-based scholarship or grant aid	8
% needy UG rec. non-need-based scholarship or grant aid	5
% needy frosh rec. need-based self-help aid	95
% needy UG rec. need-based self-help aid	95
% frosh rec. any financial aid	88
% UG rec. any financial aid	80
% UG borrow to pay for school	77
Average cumulative indebtedness	$37,242
% frosh need fully met	17
% ugrads need fully met	16
Average % of frosh need met	78
Average % of ugrad need met	76

UNIVERSITY OF NEW HAVEN

300 BOSTON POST ROAD, WEST HAVEN, CT 06516 • ADMISSIONS: 203-932-7319 • FAX: 203-931-6093

STUDENTS SAY "..."

Academics

The University of New Haven is a small private university that grooms students for future careers through an emphasis on experiential education. The school is all about "providing students with avenues of experience inside and outside the classroom throughout the education process," and the "culturally diverse" city of New Haven provides "massive" opportunities with local organizations for internships and research. The incredibly popular Criminal Justice program (and the concentrations therein) is one of the best in the country, and a huge draw to UNH. The university "goes the extra mile to create well-rounded, successful students," successfully preparing students for the life after college by providing its students with real-life statistics and situations to help better their education.

All of the professors have real world experience, and "are able to bring their research experiences into each lecture and provide pertinent examples for everything." They are "completely supportive and only want the best for their students" and "challenge the students during classes," but will give additional help if requested. Students have many options for tutoring and assistance at the university, and "there is support everywhere for all kinds of different problems," so "it is almost impossible to fail socially or academically."

The school puts a lot of money and "endless resources" into making sure students have all the tools they need to get the most out of their classes. Most importantly, staff members "want students to succeed, take action, and be involved." "The University of New Haven is all about a sense of community and preparing students for the next step in their lives," says a junior.

Life

With more than 150 clubs, sports teams, living learning communities, and on-campus employment opportunities, "it is very hard not to get involved on campus." "An exorbitant amount of activities occur on my campus everyday," says one student, with clubs ranging from "professional and major to scuba diving and snowboarding to paranormal investigations and research." The area that the university is in is gorgeous and "easily accessible to many stores if things for classes are needed," and "there are plenty of beautiful spaces on campus where people can meet up and hang out." However, all say that "parking really needs to improve on campus." Partying and greek life do have their place at UNH (as do the downtown clubs: "There is a bus that runs late from Thursday night to Saturday night, picking up students on campus"), but studies come first. As for non-alcoholic options, SCOPE is a non-greek organization devoted to organizing activities on campus, which include "taking student's photos in a giant snowglobe, to weekly movie showings, to monthly Beanhouse events where music and poetry are shared." Students can also "jump on a train or bus and go into New Haven, New York, or Boston"; downtown New Haven offers plenty of opportunities to "eat out, shop, or walk around in the Yale green." "It is absolutely impossible to be bored because there is always something to do," says a student.

Student Body

Thanks to the variety of majors available, the "friendly and welcoming atmosphere" is composed of "a giant mish-mash of every type of student." Everyone "cares about [their] studies as much as they do about their individual lives," and UNH even has the option of residential Living Learning Communities in which students of like majors live together. Everyone is involved in "many different clubs and/or sports" and so is "extremely busy, but having so much fun doing it!" There is "a large international population," which provides "an excellent way to make friends from various walks of life, and to gain a new perspective." Students usually stay in their own cliques, but "they are not unfriendly towards other people or strangers." "All the students at UNH are amicable; doors are always being held open and smiles are seen around campus a lot," says a student.

FINANCIAL AID: 203-932-7315 • E-MAIL: ADMISSIONS@NEWHAVEN.EDU • WEBSITE: WWW.NEWHAVEN.EDU

THE PRINCETON REVIEW SAYS

Admissions

Very important factors considered include: academic GPA, standardized test scores. *Important factors considered include:* application essay, recommendation(s). *Other factors considered include:* rigor of secondary school record, interview, extracurricular activities, character/personal qualities, volunteer work, work experience, level of applicant's interest. SAT or ACT required. ACT with or without writing accepted. SAT with or without Essay component accepted. TOEFL required of all international applicants. High school diploma is required and GED is accepted. *Academic units recommended:* 4 English, 3 math, 3 science, 2 science labs, 2 foreign language, 3 social studies.

Financial Aid

Students should submit: FAFSA. Priority filing deadline is 3/1. The Princeton Review suggests that all financial aid forms be submitted as soon as possible after October 1. *Need-based scholarships/grants offered:* Federal Pell, FSEOG, State scholarships/grants, Private scholarships, College/university scholarship or grant aid from institutional funds. *Loan aid offered:* Direct Subsidized Stafford Loans, Direct Unsubsidized Stafford Loans, Direct PLUS loans, Federal Perkins Loans. Applicants will be notified of awards on a rolling basis beginning 3/1. Federal Work-Study Program available. Institutional employment available.

THE SCHOOL SAYS "..."

From the Admissions Office

"The University of New Haven is a national leader in experiential education, offering several unique and innovative majors housed in five distinct colleges: the College of Arts & Sciences, AACSB-accredited College of Business, Tagliatela College of Engineering (ABET-accredited), Henry C. Lee College of Criminal Justice and Forensic Sciences, and Lyme Academy College of Fine Arts.

"We offer our students a number of exciting facilities on campus, such as our National Crime Scene Training & Technology Center, Cyber Forensics Research and Education Lab, Digital & Analog Recording Studios, Dental Center, Finance & Technology Center, and soon-to-be-built Marine Sciences Center.

"We pride ourselves on providing students with great experiences and opportunities through Faculty-Mentored Student Research, Internships and Co-Ops, Academic Service Learning & Community Service, and Study Abroad. Our satellite campus in Prato, Italy is popular as well as our two-week intensive study abroad programs where students can earn six credits at a number of different places around the world.

"Some of our newest academic offerings include undergraduate degrees in Genetics & Biotechnology, Cyber Systems, Paramedicine, Marine Affairs, and National Security Studies in addition to graduate programs in Data Science, Forensic Technology, Biomedical Engineering, and Healthcare Administration.

"NCAA Division II athletics, a 275-member marching band, student-run 88.7 FM radio station (WNHU), an amazing theater production company, Model United Nations team, and full-service sixty-seat restaurant managed entirely by our students are just a few more of the great things you can get involved with at the University of New Haven."

SELECTIVITY

Admissions Rating	77
# of applicants	10,748
% of applicants accepted	82
% of acceptees attending	14
# offered a place on the wait list	958
# of early decision applicants	168
% accepted early decision	60

FRESHMAN PROFILE

Range SAT Critical Reading	480–580
Range SAT Math	480–580
Range SAT Writing	470–570
Range ACT Composite	21–26
Minimum internet-based TOEFL	80
Average HS GPA	3.4
% graduated top 10% of class	16
% graduated top 25% of class	40
% graduated top 50% of class	78

DEADLINES

Early decision	
Deadline	12/1
Notification	12/15
Early action	
Deadline	12/15
Notification	1/15
Regular	
Priority	3/1
Nonfall registration?	Yes

APPLICANTS ALSO LOOK AT AND OFTEN PREFER

University of Connecticut; Quinnipiac University

AND SOMETIMES PREFER

Sacred Heart University

FINANCIAL FACTS

Financial Aid Rating	80
Annual tuition	$34,330
Room and board	$14,620
Required fees	$1,320
Average frosh need-based scholarship	$19,888
Average UG need-based scholarship	$18,818
% needy frosh rec. need-based scholarship or grant aid	100
% needy UG rec. need-based scholarship or grant aid	100
% needy frosh rec. non-need-based scholarship or grant aid	13
% needy UG rec. non-need-based scholarship or grant aid	12
% needy frosh rec. need-based self-help aid	81
% needy UG rec. need-based self-help aid	81
% UG borrow to pay for school	81
Average cumulative indebtedness	$45,633
% frosh need fully met	15
% ugrads need fully met	14
Average % of frosh need met	61
Average % of ugrad need met	60

UNIVERSITY OF NEW MEXICO

OFFICE OF ADMISSIONS, ALBUQUERQUE, NM 87196-4895 • ADMISSIONS: 505-277-8900 • FAX: 505-277-6686

CAMPUS LIFE

Quality of Life Rating	72
Fire Safety Rating	80
Green Rating	60*
Type of school	Public
Affiliation	No Affiliation
Environment	Metropolis

STUDENTS

Total undergrad enrollment	20,522
% male/female	45/55
% from out of state	7
% frosh live on campus	23
% ugrads live on campus	8
# of fraternities (% ugrad men join)	10 (5)
# of sororities (% ugrad women join)	10 (6)
% African American	2
% Asian	3
% Caucasian	35
% Hispanic	47
% Native American	6
% Pacific Islander	<1
% Two or more races	3
% Race and/or ethnicity unknown	1
% international	1
# of countries represented	92

SURVEY SAYS...

Diverse student types interact on campus
Students get along with local community
Great off-campus food
Students are happy

ACADEMICS

Academic Rating	69
% students returning for sophomore year	80
% students graduating within 4 years	15
% students graduating within 6 years	47
Calendar	Semester
Student/faculty ratio	17:1
Profs interesting rating	67
Profs accessible rating	64

Most classes have 10–19 students.
Most lab/discussion sessions have 10–19 students.

MOST POPULAR MAJORS

Biology; Psychology; Business Administration and Management

STUDENTS SAY "..."

Academics

Offering a "solid education" in a beautiful setting, the University of New Mexico offers "academic excellence...through some of the best teachers and tough classes." Students also cited affordability and excellent scholarships awarded to both in-state and out-of-state applicants as a decisive factor in attending UNM. The affordability also extends to "amazing opportunities to travel abroad." At UNM, "there is something here for everyone." The education program and variety of science programs—including Earth and planetary sciences, biology, and the premed and nursing programs—also attract students. Some students express frustration with it at times being "difficult to work your way around the student services system," but the "very knowledgeable" teaching faculty are roundly praised as "teachers who care." UNM students also agree that "professors are helpful [and] genuinely interested in your personal success." Professors are approachable both in class and out and "talk to and with you and not just at you." "It's very easy to come to instructors outside of class with questions," and "most professors are willing to meet with you at your convenience." As for UNM's greatest strengths, students cite both the "research-oriented staff" and "the research opportunities available. Oftentimes the research can be done with top-of-the-line equipment" nearby at Sandia National Labs, Los Alamos National Labs, and other well-known research institutes. In UNM's collaborative environment, students also often work together and "are eager to form study groups." Also, students who need additional help can rely on academic support with "tutoring, study groups and, supplemental instruction for most courses."

Life

With "ways for everyone to get involved," UNM offers "hundreds of great student organizations" providing "opportunities for fun events." There is a student group "that will fit everyone," and at UNM, "everyone seems to find their niche." Offering another opportunity to become more involved on campus, the Greek community "makes up a lot of the senate and other extracurricular activities" and "with them, any activity has fun attached." UNM students are divided in their support of the school's athletics program. With some thinking "this school should concentrate less on sports and more on academics," other students feel "attending games is a must." Students enjoy spending time at the Student Union Building (SUB), because "there is always something going on." Even with a dry campus, "a lot of people drink, just like at any college." Students often leave campus for Albuquerque and its "excellent nightlife." UNM students also mention attending concerts and art shows for fun. Students also go to the weekly free movies at The Cellar, and to stay active, students frequent the Johnson Gym. Students say that "hanging out at the duck pond is a great way to pass time between classes in warmer months," and "during the winter season, there are numerous ski resorts and places to go snowboarding that are not far away."

Student Body

Time and time again, students select UNM's "diversity" as its greatest strength, and one student even stated "no one will ever feel ethnically alone since there are so many different kinds of people." This also means at UNM, "people never get boring," and "you meet someone different every day." In addition to the diversity, the prevailing atmosphere is a friendly one where "people get along regardless of origin," but "like any school there are cliques...but that does not mean they do not interact with each other." One student reserved special praise for the university, "UNM is sensitive and very engaged with its diverse population of students...concerned with facilitating in-depth inquiry and learning," and more than one student observed that at UNM, "everyone brings something to the table."

FINANCIAL AID: 505-277-8900 • E-MAIL: APPLY@UNM.EDU • WEBSITE: WWW.UNM.EDU

THE PRINCETON REVIEW SAYS

Admissions

Very important factors considered include: rigor of secondary school record, academic GPA. *Important factors considered include:* standardized test scores. *Other factors considered include:* application essay, extracurricular activities, talent/ability, character/personal qualities, volunteer work, work experience. SAT or ACT required. ACT with or without writing accepted. SAT with or without Essay component accepted. TOEFL required of all international applicants. High school diploma is required and GED is accepted. *Academic units required:* 4 English, 4 math, 3 science, 2 science labs, 2 foreign language, 2 social studies, 1 history.

Financial Aid

Students should submit: FAFSA. Priority filing deadline is 3/1. The Princeton Review suggests that all financial aid forms be submitted as soon as possible after October 1. *Need-based scholarships/grants offered:* Federal Pell, FSEOG, State scholarships/grants, Private scholarships, College/university scholarship or grant aid from institutional funds, United Negro College Fund, Federal Nursing Scholarships. *Loan aid offered:* Direct Subsidized Stafford Loans, Direct Unsubsidized Stafford Loans, Direct PLUS loans, Federal Perkins Loans, Federal Nursing Loans, State Loans, College/university loans from institutional funds. Applicants will be notified of awards on a rolling basis beginning 4/15. Federal Work-Study Program available. Institutional employment available.

The Inside Word

UNM offers online applications through its website, and you will also find specific scholastic standards for traditional and nontraditional students interested in applying to UNM. Traditional applicants should have completed core coursework, taken the ACT or SAT exam and have an average or above-average GPA if they would like to be considered for admission at UNM.

THE SCHOOL SAYS "..."

From the Admissions Office

"The University of New Mexico is a major research institution nestled in the heart of multicultural Albuquerque on one of the nation's most beautiful and unique campuses. Students learn in an environment graced by distinctive Southwestern architecture, beautiful plazas and fountains, spectacular art and a national arboretum...all within view of the 10,000-foot Sandia Mountains. At UNM, diversity is a way of learning with education enriched by a lively mix of students being taught by a world-class research faculty that includes a Nobel laureate, a MacArthur Fellow, and members of several national academies. UNM offers more than 200 degree programs and majors and has earned national recognition in dozens of disciplines, ranging from primary care medicine and clinical law to engineering, photography, Latin American history, and intercultural communications. Research and the quest for new knowledge fuels the university's commitment to an undergraduate education where students work side-by-side with many of the finest scholars in their fields.

"The university will continue to accept SAT or ACT scores, but the University of New Mexico does not require the writing component at this time. The SAT critical reading portion will be used with the SAT math to be considered in any admission decision based on formula. The use of ACT composite remains unchanged. These requirements are subject to change."

SELECTIVITY	
Admissions Rating	83
# of applicants	13,517
% of applicants accepted	50
% of acceptees attending	49

FRESHMAN PROFILE	
Range SAT Critical Reading	480–610
Range SAT Math	470–600
Range SAT Writing	460–590
Range ACT Composite	19–25
Minimum paper TOEFL	520
Minimum internet-based TOEFL	68
Average HS GPA	3.4

DEADLINES	
Regular	
Priority	5/1
Nonfall registration?	Yes

FINANCIAL FACTS	
Financial Aid Rating	60*
Annual in-state tuition	$5,157
Annual out-of-state tuition	$20,048
Room and board	$8,690
Required fees	$1,507
Books and supplies	$1,064
% needy frosh rec. need-based scholarship or grant aid	0
% needy UG rec. need-based scholarship or grant aid	0
% needy frosh rec. non-need-based scholarship or grant aid	0
% needy UG rec. non-need-based scholarship or grant aid	0
% needy frosh rec. need-based self-help aid	0
% needy UG rec. need-based self-help aid	0

UNIVERSITY OF NEW ORLEANS

UNIVERSITY OF NEW ORLEANS ADMISSIONS, NEW ORLEANS, LA 70148 • ADMISSIONS: 504-280-6595 • FAX: 504-280-5522

CAMPUS LIFE

Quality of Life Rating	86
Fire Safety Rating	83
Green Rating	60*
Type of school	Public
Affiliation	No Affiliation
Environment	Metropolis

STUDENTS

Total undergrad enrollment	6,601
% male/female	50/50
% from out of state	6
% frosh live on campus	29
% ugrads live on campus	10
# of fraternities (% ugrad men join)	6 (2)
# of sororities (% ugrad women join)	5 (2)
% African American	16
% Asian	8
% Caucasian	34
% Hispanic	11
% Native American	<1
% Pacific Islander	<1
% Two or more races	4
% Race and/or ethnicity unknown	2
% international	5
# of countries represented	65

SURVEY SAYS...

Students get along with local community
Students love New Orleans, LA
Great off-campus food

ACADEMICS

Academic Rating	71
% students returning for sophomore year	62
% students graduating within 4 years	15
% students graduating within 6 years	35
Calendar	Semester
Student/faculty ratio	21:1
Profs interesting rating	73
Profs accessible rating	74
Most classes have 20–29 students.	

MOST POPULAR MAJORS

Business Administration and Management;
Multi-/Interdisciplinary Studies; Biology

STUDENTS SAY "..."

Academics

The University of New Orleans is a public research university in one of the world's most fascinating and unique cities. This "not too big, not too small" school is a "diverse environment that makes it a welcoming area to be" and provides "lots of opportunities to develop our personality, leadership skills, and career skills." The diversity is a huge draw to students from all over the world (international students can even receive financial aid), and UNO "opens doors to students who come from different social and economic backgrounds," giving them "the opportunity to get an education that helps students to get a better future."

Professors at this "inclusive" school "push students to do excellence." You "can always find them in their office during office hours," and they "really connect with students." The engineering, film, and accounting programs are all popular programs at UNO (accounting is one of the few accredited by AACSB International), and classes stress real-world applicability. "There has never been a moment at UNO that I wasn't able to leave the classroom and go apply what I learned to my job immediately," says one part-time student. "My professors are generous with their time and knowledge," says another. Class sizes are small, and many classes focus on discussion, which "allows for increased learning and understanding." The school is "blessed" with having a large traditional student body matched with an equal percentage of nontraditional students (adult education), which "allows great mentorship between students and also pushed both sides to be aware of how they can positively affect the other generation's education."

Life

Obviously, the fact that the school is located in New Orleans "is a big plus," and "there is never a dull moment." "Eating and nightlife in New Orleans is a big part of our lives," says a student. "There is so much to do on campus and around the city, students often have to make efforts to keep their social calendars in check so that they have time to study," says a student. The campus is large enough to offer "many diverse academic, extracurricular, and social activities," yet small enough to easily access all classes. However, "upgrading facilities" (and cleaning them) is on the wish list of pretty much everyone here.

UNO offers "plenty of on campus activities" for students "to meet and work with other students of all backgrounds," including sports, movies, and "a lot of free entertainment." There are also "always political discussions happening on campus, as well as debates." "You can feel at home here but not get bored," says a student. The older students feel similarly comfortable in their environment. "I am unusual in that I am a much older student living on campus. Yet, the younger students have accepted me warmly and I have many friends," says one.

Student Body

More so than most schools, there really is no typical at this "very eclectic university," other than "determined, hardworking, and considerate." The school's large number of international students, adult learners, commuters, and locals "tend to get along rather well," with "those who live right on or near campus probably being more close-knit." Many students live off campus and work full time, which "creates in an environment where the people in your classes are there for a purpose." People here are "very colorful and outgoing" and "have no problem expressing themselves whether it's through clothing, lifestyles, or speech." "It is very easy to make friends here," says a student.

FINANCIAL AID: 504-280-6603 • E-MAIL: ADMISSIONS@UNO.EDU • WEBSITE: WWW.UNO.EDU

THE PRINCETON REVIEW SAYS

Admissions

Very important factors considered include: rigor of secondary school record, academic GPA, standardized test scores. *Important factors considered include: Other factors considered include:* geographical residence, state residency. SAT or ACT required. ACT with or without writing accepted. TOEFL required of all international applicants. High school diploma is required and GED is accepted. *Academic units required:* 4 English, 4 math, 4 science, 2 foreign language, 4 social studies, 1 visual/performing arts.

Financial Aid

Students should submit: FAFSA. Priority filing deadline is 1/15. The Princeton Review suggests that all financial aid forms be submitted as soon as possible after October 1. *Need-based scholarships/grants offered:* Federal Pell, FSEOG, State scholarships/grants, Private scholarships, College/university scholarship or grant aid from institutional funds. *Loan aid offered:* Direct Subsidized Stafford Loans, Direct Unsubsidized Stafford Loans, Direct PLUS loans, Federal Perkins Loans. Applicants will be notified of awards on a rolling basis beginning 3/15. Federal Work-Study Program available. Institutional employment available.

The Inside Word

Admission is straightforward here. Complete a basic college-bound high school curriculum with a GPA of at least 2.5 (with no remedial course work) and get at least an 23 on your ACT (SAT 1060), including a minimum score at or above 19 Math (460 SAT), 18 English (450 SAT). Nontraditional students who don't want to pay the exorbitant prices of the more well-known private universities in New Orleans can find their niche at UNO; if you're twenty-five or older, the only requirement for admission is a legitimate high school diploma or a GED.

THE SCHOOL SAYS ". . ."

From the Admissions Office

"The University of New Orleans has a wide array of academic programs. Quality student life programs include a campus bar, first-run movies, and a host of exciting student activities.

"UNO embraces its mission by providing the best educational opportunities for undergraduate and graduate students, conducting world-class research, and serving a diverse and cultured community in critical areas. UNO's most outstanding offerings include planning and urban studies; hotel, restaurant and tourism administration; computer science; educational leadership; earth and environmental studies; one of the nation's few programs in naval architecture and marine engineering; a leading jazz studies program; one of the top film programs in the region; and the only graduate arts administration program in the Gulf South.

"UNO will use the total score from the critical reading/verbal and math sub sections of the SAT or the composite score for the ACT. The writing components of the ACT and SAT will be used for placement purposes, but not for admission purposes, at the time."

SELECTIVITY

Admissions Rating	90
# of applicants	3,932
% of applicants accepted	38
% of acceptees attending	41

FRESHMAN PROFILE

Range SAT Critical Reading	460–600
Range SAT Math	480–630
Range ACT Composite	20–24
Minimum paper TOEFL	550
Minimum internet-based TOEFL	213
Average HS GPA	3.14
% graduated top 10% of class	14
% graduated top 25% of class	32
% graduated top 50% of class	61

FINANCIAL FACTS

Financial Aid Rating	79
Annual in-state tuition	$6,090
Annual out-of-state tuition	$19,907
Room and board	$9,515
Required fees	$2,004
Books and supplies	$1,220
Average frosh need-based scholarship	$5,873
Average UG need-based scholarship	$5,621
% needy frosh rec. need-based scholarship or grant aid	63
% needy UG rec. need-based scholarship or grant aid	61
% needy frosh rec. non-need-based scholarship or grant aid	69
% needy UG rec. non-need-based scholarship or grant aid	45
% needy frosh rec. need-based self-help aid	41
% needy UG rec. need-based self-help aid	42
% frosh rec. any financial aid	67
% UG rec. any financial aid	63
% frosh need fully met	8
% ugrads need fully met	6
Average % of frosh need met	66
Average % of ugrad need met	60

THE UNIVERSITY OF NORTH CAROLINA AT ASHEVILLE

CPO #1320, ASHEVILLE, NC 28804-8502 • ADMISSIONS: 828-251-6481 • FAX: 828-251-6482

CAMPUS LIFE

Quality of Life Rating	94
Fire Safety Rating	97
Green Rating	84
Type of school	Public
Affiliation	No Affiliation
Environment	Town

STUDENTS

Total undergrad enrollment	3,858
% male/female	44/56
% from out of state	11
% frosh from public high school	88
% frosh live on campus	96
% ugrads live on campus	39
# of fraternities (% ugrad men join)	2 (3)
# of sororities (% ugrad women join)	2 (3)
% African American	4
% Asian	2
% Caucasian	80
% Hispanic	5
% Native American	1
% Pacific Islander	<1
% Two or more races	4
% Race and/or ethnicity unknown	4
% international	1
# of countries represented	28

SURVEY SAYS...

Students are happy
Students aren't religious
Students get along with local community
Students environmentally aware
Students love Asheville, NC
Great off-campus food
Easy to get around campus
Recreation facilities are great

ACADEMICS

Academic Rating	79
% students returning for sophomore year	79
% students graduating within 4 years	36
% students graduating within 6 years	60
Calendar	Semester
Student/faculty ratio	14:1
Profs interesting rating	91
Profs accessible rating	84

Most classes have 20–29 students.
Most lab/discussion sessions have 10–19 students.

MOST POPULAR MAJORS
Psychology; Environmental Studies; Biology

STUDENTS SAY "..."

Academics

Located in Asheville in North Carolina's Blue Ridge Mountains, the University of North Carolina at Asheville is "a liberal arts university, and the only public one in North Carolina, with a focus on undergraduate students," with a goal of giving "students a very diverse education and experience while still emphasizing a focus on [their] areas of interest." Students say their school is "all about creating a positive, creative, and open learning community to prepare students to be socially aware, productive members of society" and describe their peers as "fun, quirky, open-minded, adventurous, nature and peace-loving, and cognizant." Popular majors include psychology, English literature, and environmental studies, and one student admits, "We are kind of a nerd school, and that's pretty great." Students praise the "small class sizes," the "undergraduate research opportunities" and say that the "small liberal arts atmosphere ensures that every student who wants to has the opportunity to create relationships with professors and get research and internship opportunities that would be more exclusive at other schools, and it also allows students to take classes in a wide variety of disciplines." Professors on the whole are "incredibly smart, kind, and compassionate" and their "passion for their subject is rivaled [only] by their love for teaching." Overall, "The work load is substantial, but not unmanageable" and "Although studying is very important here, everyone makes an effort to make time for their hobbies."

Life

Though most first years live on campus, after that, many students live off campus, leading one student to lament the "lack of school spirit." But others counter that "Because of [the] ease of access to national parks and nature, along with great bars, the city and surrounding area are great to also go to during week if free time is available," if students aren't participating in "club activities" or studying. Being in Asheville, which one student describes as "the blue dot in a sea of red," the "majority of the students are liberal or at least centrist Democrats. There are still Republicans and conservatives but [they] make up the minority of the campus." Outdoor activities abound in "western North Carolina such as hiking on the Appalachian Trail, mountain biking in the Pisgah National Forest, kayaking and rafting on first class whitewater rivers and creeks and skiing in the winter." Students rave that the small but bustling city of Asheville "has so much to offer downtown and the food, especially, is amazing." When it comes to finding your niche on campus, as one student puts it, "There are so many diverse clubs I couldn't list them all. There isn't really one big thing that everyone is interested in." In keeping with UNCA's dedication to social justice, "Protests and political activism is popular." Says one student, "We aren't known to be a huge party school and we tend to take part in more constructive social activities."

Student Body

While social diversity is acknowledged and appreciated on campus— "Conformity is not a word that will come to mind at UNCA" and "very LGBT-friendly"—the school is admittedly "not racially diverse," though students say, "The school is actively trying to create a more racially diverse environment." "Everyone is overall very accepting and very friendly." The typical UNCA student is "hard-working and dedicated but also [knows] how to have fun." For the most part, "The students are quite liberal, open minded, socially and environmentally aware here, so community service is a huge deal." As one student puts it, "Music and art and the outdoors are probably the three main loves of every UNCA student." For the most part, students are "fairly laid back during the day to day, but can become very passionate about subjects they care for."

THE UNIVERSITY OF NORTH CAROLINA AT ASHEVILLE

FINANCIAL AID: 828-251-6535 • E-MAIL: ADMISSIONS@UNCA.EDU • WEBSITE: WWW.UNCA.EDU

THE PRINCETON REVIEW SAYS

Admissions

Very important factors considered include: rigor of secondary school record, academic GPA. *Important factors considered include:* class rank, standardized test scores, application essay, recommendation(s). SAT or ACT required; SAT Subject Tests considered if submitted. ACT with Writing required. SAT with Essay component required. TOEFL required of all international applicants. High school diploma is required and GED is not accepted. *Academic units required:* 4 English, 4 math, 3 science, 1 science lab, 2 foreign language, 1 social studies, 1 history. *Academic units recommended:* 4 academic electives.

Financial Aid

Students should submit: FAFSA. Priority filing deadline is 3/1. The Princeton Review suggests that all financial aid forms be submitted as soon as possible after October 1. *Need-based scholarships/grants offered:* Federal Pell, FSEOG, State scholarships/grants, Private scholarships, College/university scholarship or grant aid from institutional funds. *Loan aid offered:* Direct Subsidized Stafford Loans, Direct Unsubsidized Stafford Loans, Direct PLUS loans, Federal Perkins Loans, State Loans, College/university loans from institutional funds. Applicants will be notified of awards on a rolling basis beginning 3/1. Federal Work-Study Program available. Institutional employment available.

The Inside Word

Applicants to UNCA can apply via either the Common Application or The College Foundation of NC online application. In addition to your standardized test scores and high school GPA (the average accepted student's is 3.42), UNCA admissions officers are looking for critical and creative thinkers. A heads up for students interested in being considered for the (merit-based) Laurels Scholarship: application material is due by November 15, the same date as early action applications. UNCA's regular admissions deadline is rolling for incoming first years and April 15 for transfers.

THE SCHOOL SAYS "..."

From the Admissions Office

"If you want to learn how to think, how to analyze and solve problems on your own, and how to become your own best teacher, then a broad-based liberal arts education is the key. UNC Asheville focuses on undergraduates, with a core curriculum covering natural science, math, social sciences, humanities, language and culture, arts and ideas, and health and fitness. Students thrive in small classes, with a faculty dedicated first of all to teaching. The liberal arts emphasis develops discriminating thinkers, expert and creative communicators with a passion for learning. These are qualities you need for today's challenges and the changes of tomorrow.

"The University of North Carolina at Asheville requires the SAT or for students submitting an ACT score, the ACT with the writing component."

SELECTIVITY

Admissions Rating	81
# of applicants	3,324
% of applicants accepted	79
% of acceptees attending	28

FRESHMAN PROFILE

Range SAT Critical Reading	530–640
Range SAT Math	520–610
Range SAT Writing	510–610
Range ACT Composite	23–28
Minimum paper TOEFL	550
Minimum internet-based TOEFL	79
Average HS GPA	3.4
% graduated top 10% of class	21
% graduated top 25% of class	52
% graduated top 50% of class	91

DEADLINES

Early action	
Deadline	11/15
Notification	12/15
Regular	
Priority	11/15
Deadline	2/15
Notification	12/15
Nonfall registration?	Yes

FINANCIAL FACTS

Financial Aid Rating	82
Annual in-state tuition	$4,041
Annual out-of-state tuition	$20,436
Room and board	$8,746
Required fees	$2,936
Books and supplies	$1,200
Average frosh need-based scholarship	$5,995
Average UG need-based scholarship	$6,650
% needy frosh rec. need-based scholarship or grant aid	92
% needy UG rec. need-based scholarship or grant aid	90
% needy frosh rec. non-need-based scholarship or grant aid	12
% needy UG rec. non-need-based scholarship or grant aid	12
% needy frosh rec. need-based self-help aid	70
% needy UG rec. need-based self-help aid	72
% frosh rec. any financial aid	71
% UG rec. any financial aid	71
% UG borrow to pay for school	57
Average cumulative indebtedness	$23,483
% frosh need fully met	20
% ugrads need fully met	20
Average % of frosh need met	70
Average % of ugrad need met	70

THE UNIVERSITY OF NORTH CAROLINA AT CHAPEL HILL

CAMPUS BOX #2200, CHAPEL HILL, NC 27599-2200 • ADMISSIONS: 919-966-3621 • FAX: 919-962-3045

CAMPUS LIFE

Quality of Life Rating	90
Fire Safety Rating	96
Green Rating	94
Type of school	Public
Affiliation	No Affiliation
Environment	Town

STUDENTS

Total undergrad enrollment	18,415
% male/female	42/58
% from out of state	17
% frosh from public high school	82
% frosh live on campus	100
% ugrads live on campus	52
# of fraternities (% ugrad men join)	34 (18)
# of sororities (% ugrad women join)	24 (18)
% African American	8
% Asian	10
% Caucasian	63
% Hispanic	8
% Native American	1
% Pacific Islander	<1
% Two or more races	4
% Race and/or ethnicity unknown	3
% international	3
# of countries represented	94

SURVEY SAYS...

Students politically aware
Students are happy
School is well run
Students love Chapel Hill, NC
Recreation facilities are great
Everyone loves the Tar Heels
Intramural sports are popular
Alumni active on campus

ACADEMICS

Academic Rating	80
% students returning for sophomore year	97
% students graduating within 4 years	82
% students graduating within 6 years	90
Calendar	Semester
Student/faculty ratio	14:1
Profs interesting rating	71
Profs accessible rating	68

Most classes have 10–19 students.
Most lab/discussion sessions have
10–19 students.

MOST POPULAR MAJORS
Biology; Psychology; Economics

STUDENTS SAY "..."

Academics

It's quite an understatement to say students at UNC—Chapel Hill are proud of their school. One calls it his "dream school," while another calls it the "perfect mixture of academics, sports, and social life." Although its relative low cost makes UNC a great bargain in higher education, academic rigor doesn't take a back seat, and the vast majority of students say it's one of the main reasons they chose the school. The media and journalism, business, pharmacy, public health, and nursing programs are ranked among the best in the country, but the students hail the overall arts and sciences curriculum because it creates well-rounded adults who "can handle any intellectual obstacle." In describing the instructors, students use words like "world-class," "brilliant," and "incredible," while also noting that they're "warm," "welcoming," and "passionate" about their work and their students. "Most of my professors have been great, and some have been phenomenal." Faculty members are generous with their time outside of class, patiently explaining "even the most difficult material" and using e-mail to announce changes. Some complain about large classes and warn incoming students that they will have to take the initiative and "speak up," because they won't be "coddled."

Life

With more than 18,000 undergrads, UNC is large enough that students rarely are lacking for something to do. Tar Heel men's basketball probably is at the top of the list; indeed, for many rabid fans, the Dean Smith Center is the center of the universe, especially when Duke is the opponent. One student sums up the school's essence this way: "It's the feeling of running through the beautiful old quad by Davie Poplar on the way to Franklin Street after a big win." The consensus is maintaining grades requires such an effort, letting off steam on weekends is a reward. "Life at UNC is full throttle. People work hard and play hard." Many flock to the bars, restaurants and coffee shops of Franklin Street, but others prefer the music scene in nearby Carrboro or staying on campus to participate in a function sponsored by one of the hundreds of student groups. The campus itself is gorgeous and filled with history. Although only 18 percent of students belong to a fraternity or sorority, the Greek organizations are a big part of the social scene. "When you're writing thirty-page papers on twentieth-century German philosophy and working two jobs, a night where you get to dress up as a biker chick and listen to AC/DC all night at the bar is a welcome reprieve," one sorority member says.

Student Body

One student after another comments about the feeling of generosity that pervades UNC—"the epitome of Southern hospitality"—and how it extends beyond mere school spirit and the wearing of Carolina blue and white on game days. "Carolina is family," one student says. "Most of us here are crazy about sports, but most will do anything at all to help a fellow UNC student." "Although the student body is very diverse, a commonality among students is the desire to serve others and work for humanitarian efforts." One reason for the closeness is that the vast majority of students hail from the Tar Heel state. So there are "lots of down-home, North Carolina types who excelled in their rural high schools." Students and faculty are viewed as leaning liberal politically, which makes for some interesting exchanges. "Political activism is huge here," a student says. But even though it's a vast school, "it has a place for everyone." "There are really only two common denominators: commitment to some kind of excellence (academic, extracurricular, etc.) and rooting against Duke."

THE UNIVERSITY OF NORTH CAROLINA AT CHAPEL HILL

FINANCIAL AID: 919-962-8396 • E-MAIL: UNCHELP@ADMISSIONS.UNC.EDU • WEBSITE: WWW.UNC.EDU

THE PRINCETON REVIEW SAYS

Admissions

Very important factors considered include: rigor of secondary school record, standardized test scores, application essay, recommendation(s), extracurricular activities, talent/ability, character/personal qualities, state residency. *Important factors considered include:* class rank, academic GPA, volunteer work, work experience. *Other factors considered include:* first generation, alumni/ae relation, racial/ethnic status. SAT or ACT required; SAT Subject Tests considered if submitted. ACT with or without writing accepted. SAT with or without Essay component accepted. TOEFL required of all international applicants. High school diploma is required and GED is not accepted. *Academic units required:* 4 English, 4 math, 3 science, 1 science lab, 2 foreign language, 1 social studies, 1 history, 1 academic elective.

Financial Aid

Students should submit: FAFSA, CSS/Financial Aid PROFILE. Priority filing deadline is 3/1. The Princeton Review suggests that all financial aid forms be submitted as soon as possible after October 1. *Need-based scholarships/grants offered:* Federal Pell, FSEOG, State scholarships/grants, Private scholarships, College/university scholarship or grant aid from institutional funds. *Loan aid offered:* Direct Subsidized Stafford Loans, Direct Unsubsidized Stafford Loans, Direct PLUS loans, Federal Perkins Loans, State Loans, College/university loans from institutional funds. Applicants will be notified of awards on a rolling basis beginning 3/15. Federal Work-Study Program available. Institutional employment available.

The Inside Word

UNC's admissions process is highly selective. North Carolina students compete against other students from across the state for 82 percent of all spaces available in the freshman class; out-of-state students compete for the remaining 18 percent of the spaces. State residents will find the admissions standards high, and out-of-state applicants will find that it's one of the hardest offers of admission to come by in the country.

THE SCHOOL SAYS "..."

From the Admissions Office

"One of the leading research and teaching institutions in the world, UNC Chapel Hill offers first-rate faculty, innovative academic programs, and students who are smart, friendly, and committed to public service. Students take full advantage of extensive undergraduate research opportunities, a study abroad program with programs on every continent except Antarctica, and 700-plus clubs and organizations. We offer all this in Chapel Hill, one of the greatest and most welcoming college towns anywhere.

"Carolina's commitment to excellence, access, and affordability is reflected in premier scholarships, such as the prestigious Morehead-Cain and Robertson Scholarships, as well the Carolina Covenant, a national model that enables students from low-income families to graduate from Carolina debt-free. We invite you to visit—talk with our professors, attend a class, spend time with our students, and stroll across our beautiful residential campus, where friendly people and exciting events are within easy walking distance.

"All first-year applicants are required to submit results from the SAT or an ACT. While test scores are important, our holistic review includes other important factors such course work, grades, and extracurricular activities.

"Just by applying for admission, applicants are considered for a variety of special programs open only to first-year students including assured admission into business, education and journalism or summer study abroad immersion and research programs. We offer two admission deadlines, neither of which are binding."

SELECTIVITY

Admissions Rating	96
# of applicants	31,953
% of applicants accepted	30
% of acceptees attending	43
# offered a place on the wait list	3,144
% accepting a place on wait list	48
% admitted from wait list	5

FRESHMAN PROFILE

Range SAT Critical Reading	590–690
Range SAT Math	610–700
Range SAT Writing	590–700
Range ACT Composite	27–32
Minimum paper TOEFL	600
Minimum internet-based TOEFL	100
Average HS GPA	4.6
% graduated top 10% of class	77
% graduated top 25% of class	96
% graduated top 50% of class	99

DEADLINES

Early action	
Deadline	10/15
Notification	1/31
Regular	
Priority	10/15
Deadline	1/15
Nonfall registration?	No

APPLICANTS ALSO LOOK AT AND SOMETIMES PREFER
Duke University; Harvard College; Princeton University; University of Virginia

AND RARELY PREFER
North Carolina State University

FINANCIAL FACTS

Financial Aid Rating	92
Annual in-state tuition	$6,648
Annual out-of-state tuition	$31,730
Room and board	$10,902
Required fees	$1,943
Books and supplies	$1,442
Average frosh need-based scholarship	$16,972
Average UG need-based scholarship	$17,244
% needy frosh rec. need-based scholarship or grant aid	93
% needy UG rec. need-based scholarship or grant aid	91
% needy frosh rec. non-need-based scholarship or grant aid	6
% needy UG rec. non-need-based scholarship or grant aid	4
% needy frosh rec. need-based self-help aid	66
% needy UG rec. need-based self-help aid	73
% frosh rec. any financial aid	67
% UG rec. any financial aid	63
% UG borrow to pay for school	41
Average cumulative indebtedness	$20,127
% frosh need fully met	87
% ugrads need fully met	82
Average % of frosh need met	100
Average % of ugrad need met	100

THE UNIVERSITY OF NORTH CAROLINA AT GREENSBORO

1400 SPRING GARDEN STREET, GREENSBORO, NC 27402-6170 • ADMISSIONS: 336-334-5243 • FAX: 336-334-4180

CAMPUS LIFE

Quality of Life Rating	89
Fire Safety Rating	65
Green Rating	93
Type of school	Public
Affiliation	No Affiliation
Environment	City

STUDENTS

Total undergrad enrollment	15,951
% male/female	34/66
% from out of state	5
% frosh from public high school	95
% frosh live on campus	81
% ugrads live on campus	34
# of fraternities	11
# of sororities	11
% African American	28
% Asian	5
% Caucasian	52
% Hispanic	8
% Native American	<1
% Pacific Islander	<1
% Two or more races	4
% Race and/or ethnicity unknown	<1
% international	2
# of countries represented	47

SURVEY SAYS...

Students are happy
School is well run
Students love Greensboro, NC

ACADEMICS

Academic Rating	78
% students returning for sophomore year	77
% students graduating within 4 years	32
Calendar	Semester
Student/faculty ratio	15:1
Profs interesting rating	75
Profs accessible rating	69

Most classes have 20–29 students.
Most lab/discussion sessions have 20–29 students.

MOST POPULAR MAJORS

Business Administration and Management;
Biology

STUDENTS SAY ". . ."

Academics

"Well known for its nursing, arts, apparel, business schools," students at the University of North Carolina at Greensboro find much to praise about their school, from its "breathtaking" campus vistas and "strong academic programs" to the "low cost of attendance" and the many "many on campus resources." Students appreciate "the level of professionalism and knowledge" among the faculty, who they describe as "exemplary" teachers who "truly seemed to care about education." Students emphasize the personalized service they receive, and say they feel like they are treated fairly. Professors "teach without reading off a PowerPoint" and work hard to "make class fun and interesting." "The ones who are good," one buisness administration and management major explains, "really care about students' success and will explain things in a different way to help you understand." Students say they are able to establish "decent relationships with professors, in smaller classes in particular," but "many professors emphasize small group discussion even in large lecture halls." Students say that they appreciate how this academic environment "[emphasizes] our personal development over testing" and provides them with an "incredible" number of internship opportunities. UNCG students offer equal praise for the school's tutoring services and other campus resources, like the "high tech library, online library, writing and speaking services" and media technology. Students also say that their academic experience is enriched by the school's diversity, both in the student body and in the academic majors and variety of classes. While some praise the free bus system, most students grumble that "parking can be a hassle."

Life

One student described the "quality and quantity of relationships the institution has within the community" as one of UNCG's greatest strengths. The school provides students with "great campus activities" and "many clubs and opportunity for off-campus engagement," which help create a "sense of community." Students agree that "there is a greater emphasis on academics than athletics, which is a rarity these days"—and many like it that way. "Most students do not go to athletic events" because they "don't come [to UNCG] for athletics, they come for arts or business." Instead, students pursue more leisurely outdoor activities. "One super popular thing to do when the weather is good is to hang an eno somewhere on campus because UNCG has a good amount of hammocking spots," one student explains. Additionally, "there are also many good hiking trails a short drive away from campus, and many people enjoy doing that." "Downtown Greensboro is just a few blocks away" where the "nightlife...is great" and students can find "several clubs, fraternity/sorority parties," "movie theaters, ice skating rinks, Four Seasons Mall, and the trampoline park." But students can stay entertained on campus as well. "There are a lot of campus events that I go to, whether it is grocery bingo, athletic events, movie nights, etc. There is always something fun to do on and around campus."

Student Body

Students boast that UNCG "is one of the most tolerant and diverse schools in the UNC College system" and "admire the efforts the school [takes] in order to cater to its international students." These collaboratively minded students "root for the successes of others as well as their own" and "would never view academics as a competition." "Although there are social groups on campus," their boundaries seem fluid and some students argue that "cliques are nonexistent" on campus. Students say that most people on campus are "open minded, involved, and creative thinkers. People are kind and genuinely care for your wellbeing." Many told us that UNCG isn't really a party school. Instead "the majority of people who attend this school are serious about their academics" and "party to blow off steam after they're done working."

THE UNIVERSITY OF NORTH CAROLINA AT GREENSBORO

FINANCIAL AID: 336-334-5702 • E-MAIL: ADMISSIONS@UNCG.EDU • WEBSITE: WWW.UNCG.EDU

THE PRINCETON REVIEW SAYS

Admissions

Very important factors considered include: rigor of secondary school record, academic GPA. *Important factors considered include:* standardized test scores. *Other factors considered include:* application essay, recommendation(s). SAT or ACT required. ACT with Writing required. SAT with Essay component required. TOEFL required of all international applicants. High school diploma is required and GED is not accepted. *Academic units required:* 4 English, 4 math, 3 science, 1 science lab, 2 foreign language, 2 social studies.

Financial Aid

Students should submit: FAFSA. Priority filing deadline is 3/1. The Princeton Review suggests that all financial aid forms be submitted as soon as possible after October 1. *Need-based scholarships/grants offered:* Federal Pell, FSEOG, State scholarships/grants, Private scholarships, College/university scholarship or grant aid from institutional funds. *Loan aid offered:* Direct Subsidized Stafford Loans, Direct Unsubsidized Stafford Loans, Direct PLUS loans, Federal Perkins Loans, State Loans, College/university loans from institutional funds. Applicants will be notified of awards on a rolling basis beginning 3/15. Federal Work-Study Program available. Institutional employment available.

The Inside Word

UNCG has yet to gain much attention outside of regional circles so, at least for the moment, gaining admission is not particularly difficult. The usual public university considerations apply; expect the admissions office to focus primarily on grades and test scores, but other items submitted by the student are considered as well. UNCG is looking for students with a proven track record in demanding academic endeavors. Out-of-staters will find a much smoother path to admission here than at Chapel Hill and will still be within reasonable reach of internship and career possibilities in the Research Triangle.

THE SCHOOL SAYS "..."

From the Admissions Office

"UNCG is committed to student success. In addition to excellent academics, the university offers active, hands-on learning experiences through internships, undergraduate research guided by faculty mentors, study abroad, and service learning. A welcoming, supportive environment characterizes the UNCG campus. The student population, known for its diversity, stands at approximately 19,000, a size that allows students to excel as individuals while also connecting with others to engage in the campus community and the vibrant local community beyond.

"UNCG takes pride in its global focus. The affordable study abroad program has exchange partners in more than thirty countries, and many majors encourage participation. The Lloyd International Honors College offers a unique opportunity for high-achieving students in any major to benefit from scholarship with a global perspective.

"UNCG seeks students with strong academic backgrounds who will benefit from a challenging learning environment. We assess a student's entire academic record, beginning with a combination of overall cumulative GPA and standardized test scores. Freshman applicants must submit at least one SAT or ACT score. We also review other factors, such as the comprehensive high school record (including course selection and senior class schedule), awards, leadership potential, participation in activities, and the optional application essay.

"Greensboro (pop. 277,000) is the third-largest city in North Carolina. Greensboro's dynamic downtown, lively arts and culture scene, mix of shops and restaurants, and miles of green space add up for a city that is fun to explore and feels like home."

SELECTIVITY

Admissions Rating	85
# of applicants	10,566
% of applicants accepted	59
% of acceptees attending	45

FRESHMAN PROFILE

Range SAT Critical Reading	470–560
Range SAT Math	470–550
Range SAT Writing	440–540
Range ACT Composite	20–25
Minimum paper TOEFL	550
Minimum internet-based TOEFL	79
Average HS GPA	3.6
% graduated top 10% of class	13
% graduated top 25% of class	41
% graduated top 50% of class	79

DEADLINES

Regular	
Priority	11/1
Deadline	3/1
Nonfall registration?	Yes

FINANCIAL FACTS

Financial Aid Rating	78
Annual in-state tuition	$4,129
Annual out-of-state tuition	$18,991
Room and board	$7,774
Required fees	$2,616
Books and supplies	$1,300
Average frosh need-based scholarship	$6,194
Average UG need-based scholarship	$5,955
% needy frosh rec. need-based scholarship or grant aid	75
% needy UG rec. need-based scholarship or grant aid	69
% needy frosh rec. non-need-based scholarship or grant aid	78
% needy UG rec. non-need-based scholarship or grant aid	72
% needy frosh rec. need-based self-help aid	68
% needy UG rec. need-based self-help aid	68
% frosh rec. any financial aid	87
% UG rec. any financial aid	81
% UG borrow to pay for school	72
Average cumulative indebtedness	$26,123
% frosh need fully met	21
% ugrads need fully met	17
Average % of frosh need met	57
Average % of ugrad need met	57

UNIVERSITY OF NORTH DAKOTA

Gorecki Center, 3501 University Ave., Grand Forks, ND 58202-8357 • Admissions: 701-777-3000 • Fax: 701-777-2721

CAMPUS LIFE

Quality of Life Rating	86
Fire Safety Rating	86
Green Rating	78
Type of school	Public
Affiliation	No Affiliation
Environment	Town

STUDENTS

Total undergrad enrollment	11,577
% male/female	57/43
% from out of state	60
% frosh from public high school	92
% frosh live on campus	92
% ugrads live on campus	29
# of fraternities (% ugrad men join)	12 (10)
# of sororities (% ugrad women join)	7 (11)
% African American	2
% Asian	2
% Caucasian	83
% Hispanic	3
% Native American	1
% Pacific Islander	<1
% Two or more races	3
% Race and/or ethnicity unknown	2
% international	4
# of countries represented	72

SURVEY SAYS...

Students are happy
Recreation facilities are great
Everyone loves the North Dakota
Intramural sports are popular

ACADEMICS

Academic Rating	68
% students returning for sophomore year	81
% students graduating within 4 years	24
% students graduating within 6 years	53
Calendar	Semester
Student/faculty ratio	22:1
Profs interesting rating	69
Profs accessible rating	67

Most classes have 20–29 students.
Most lab/discussion sessions have 10–19 students.

MOST POPULAR MAJORS

Registered Nursing/Registered Nurse; Psychology; Mechanical Engineering

STUDENTS SAY "..."

Academics

Established before North Dakota was even a state, the University of North Dakota in Grand Forks is the largest university in the state. It is home to nearly 12,000 undergraduates, more than 3,300 graduate and professional students, and twenty-one Division I NCAA athletic teams. This "affordable and attainable" college option offers "a hearty education and freezing cold weather," and the medical and aviation programs are among the strongest in the nation. Beyond classwork, undergrads say it is "easy to get involved and develop leadership skills." Student care for academic, personal, mental, spiritual, and physical wellness needs is "incredible." The school is all about "preparing the student with not only the education, but also the critical and creative thinking skills to succeed in a global market." For the most part, the faculty is excellent and "friendly in a true 'North Dakota Nice' way," though "others have clearly been teaching too long and should have moved on years ago." They are "helpful and kind and accommodating," and they make the college experience "a positive one." More than 225 majors means that a lot of students get the "small school classroom experience" even at a large research university. Some of the classrooms are "outdated in appearance" but still functional, and many find that the old buildings "actually add to the collegiate look." "They add beauty, culture, and charm to an otherwise very bleak area of the country," says a student.

Life

Grand Forks is most definitely a college town, and "there is not a whole lot" to it, though there are a number of restaurants and "big concerts a few times a year." Unsurprisingly, "North Dakota is cold," and "hockey and drinking are the main weekend activities." "We drink to stay warm and not go crazy," says a student. It can be "a struggle to get good turnouts" at weekend events, but the university is constantly trying to improve campus life for minors who may not have a car on campus or don't drink. The aforementioned hockey is everyone's favorite distraction, and "the games cause great excitement for the students" who "have so much pride for our team." "Hockey is the number one activity at this campus, odds are if you ask a random student what they're doing that weekend, they'll respond with 'going to hockey game.'" The tenacious students keep going and going "even though the weather may not be so permitting," and the Greeks are the "most active" organization on campus.

Student Body

As you might expect, a lot of North Dakotans end up at UND, with a sizeable contingency from the Twin Cities joining in; many students have friend groups from high school already in place the first time they set foot on campus. An international population is drawn to the university's petroleum engineering program, and many students hail from South Korea and China thanks to the aviation program. This is a friendly bunch, and the typical student is "usually willing to talk to someone who is lost, or needs help, and will frequently go out of their way to help someone." The majority of students are "outdoorsy" and enjoy "hunting, fishing and sports," and also hold down one or two part-time jobs.

FINANCIAL AID: 701-777-3121 • E-MAIL: ADMISSIONS@UND.EDU • WEBSITE: UND.EDU

THE PRINCETON REVIEW SAYS

Admissions

Very important factors considered include: rigor of secondary school record, academic GPA, standardized test scores. *Other factors considered include:* recommendation(s). SAT or ACT required for students under 25. ACT with or without writing accepted. SAT with or without Essay component accepted. TOEFL required of all international applicants. High school diploma is required and GED is accepted. *Academic units required:* 4 English, 3 math, 3 science labs, 3 social studies, and 1 world language or an additional unit from any of the other categories.

Financial Aid

Students should submit: The Princeton Review suggests that all financial aid forms be submitted as soon as possible after October 1. Federal Work-Study Program available. Institutional employment available.

The Inside Word

As a potential incoming student, the University of North Dakota is ready and willing to help you apply; the website has applications broken down by student type, and for those unable to schedule a visit in person, there is also a virtual tour of campus. You'll also find admissions guidelines to help you see if you would be accepted for admission: The higher your GPA, the lower your SAT and ACT scores can be and vice-versa. However, the school says that everyone should apply for admission, even if you don't meet these standards, since your application will be reviewed by a committee that may make the decision based on other factors.

THE SCHOOL SAYS "..."

From the Admissions Office

"More than 11,000 undergraduate students come to the University of North Dakota each year, from every state in the nation and more than eighty-five countries. They're impressed by our academic excellence, more than 225 programs, our dedication to the liberal arts mission, and alumni success record. More than 75 percent of the University's new students rank in the top half of their high school classes, with more 41 percent in the top quarter. As the oldest and most diversified institution of higher education in the Dakotas, Montana, Wyoming, and western Minnesota, UND is a comprehensive teaching and research university. Yet the University provides individual attention that may be missing at very large universities. UND graduates are highly regarded among prospective employers. Representatives from more than 200 regional and national companies recruit UND students every year. Our campus is approximately 98 percent accessible."

SELECTIVITY

Admissions Rating	80
# of applicants	4,920
% of applicants accepted	82
% of acceptees attending	47

FRESHMAN PROFILE

Range ACT Composite	21–26
Minimum paper TOEFL	550
Minimum internet-based TOEFL	76
Average HS GPA	3.4
% graduated top 10% of class	17
% graduated top 25% of class	41
% graduated top 50% of class	77

DEADLINES

Regular	
Priority	3/1
Nonfall registration?	Yes

APPLICANTS ALSO LOOK AT AND OFTEN PREFER

University of Minnesota–Twin Cities Campus; University of Wisconsin–Madison

FINANCIAL FACTS

Financial Aid Rating	67
Annual in-state tuition	$6,548
Annual out-of-state tuition	$17,482
Room and board	$7,236
Required fees	$1,417
Books and supplies	$1,000
% needy frosh rec. need-based scholarship or grant aid	42
% needy UG rec. need-based scholarship or grant aid	37
% UG rec any financial aid	74
% UG borrow to pay for school	62
Average cumulative indebtedness	$19,311

UNIVERSITY OF NOTRE DAME

220 MAIN BUILDING, NOTRE DAME, IN 46556 • ADMISSIONS: 574-631-7505 • FAX: 574-631-8865

STUDENTS SAY "..."

Academics

Notre Dame has many traditions, including a "devotion to undergraduate education" you might not expect from a school with such an athletic reputation. Professors here are, by all accounts, "wonderful": "Not only are they invested in their students," they're "genuinely passionate about their fields of study," "enthusiastic and animated in lectures," and "always willing to meet outside of class to give extra help." Wary that distance might breed academic disengagement, professors ensure "large lectures are broken down into smaller discussion groups once a week to help with class material and...give the class a personal touch." For its part, "the administration tries its best to stay on top of the students' wants and needs." They make it "extremely easy to get in touch with anyone." Like the professors, administrators try to make personal connections with students. For example, "our president (a priest), as well as both of our presidents emeritus, make it a point to interact with the students in a variety of ways—teaching a class, saying mass in the dorms, etc." Overall, "while classes are difficult," "students are competitive against one another," and "it's necessary to study hard and often, [but] there's also time to do other things."

Life

Life at Notre Dame is centered around two things—"residential life" and "sports." The "dorms on campus provide the social structure" and supply undergrads with tons of opportunities to get involved and have fun. "During the school week" students "study a lot, but on the weekends everyone seems to make up for the lack of partying during the week." The school "does not have any fraternities or sororities, but campus is not dry, and drinking/partying is permitted within the residence halls." The administration reportedly tries "to keep the parties on campus due to the fact that campus is such a safe place and they truly do care about our safety." In addition to parties the dorms are really competitive in the Interhall Sport System, and "virtually every student plays some kind of sport [in] his/her residence hall." Intercollegiate sports, to put it mildly, "are huge." "If someone is not interested in sports upon arrival, he or she will be by the time he or she leaves." "Everybody goes to the football games, and it's common to see 1,000 students at a home soccer game." Beyond residential life and sports, "religious activities," volunteering, "campus publications, student government, and academic clubs round out the rest of ND life."

Student Body

Undergrads at Notre Dame report "the vast majority" of their peers are "very smart" "white kids from upper- to middle-class backgrounds from all over the country, especially the Midwest and Northeast." The typical student "is a type-A personality that studies a lot, yet is athletic and involved in the community. They are usually the outstanding seniors in their high schools," the "sort of people who can talk about the BCS rankings and Derrida in the same breath." Additionally, something like "85 percent of Notre Dame students earned a varsity letter in high school." "Not all are Catholic" here, though most are, and it seems that most undergrads "have some sort of spirituality present in their daily lives." "ND is slowly improving in diversity concerning economic backgrounds, with the university's policy to meet all demonstrated financial need." As things stand now, those who "don't tend to fit in with everyone else hang out in their own groups made up by others like them (based on ethnicity, sexual orientation, etc.)."

FINANCIAL AID: 574-631-6436 • E-MAIL: ADMISSIONS@ND.EDU • WEBSITE: WWW.ND.EDU

THE PRINCETON REVIEW SAYS

Admissions

Very important factors considered include: rigor of secondary school record. *Important factors considered include:* class rank, academic GPA, standardized test scores, application essay, recommendation(s), extracurricular activities, talent/ability, character/personal qualities, alumni/ae relation, volunteer work. *Other factors considered include:* first generation, religious affiliation/commitment, racial/ethnic status, work experience, level of applicant's interest. SAT or ACT required; SAT Subject Tests considered if submitted. ACT with or without writing accepted. TOEFL required of all international applicants. High school diploma is required and GED is not accepted. *Academic units required:* 4 English, 3 math, 2 science, 2 science labs, 2 foreign language, 2 history, 3 academic electives. *Academic units recommended:* 4 English, 4 math, 4 science, 2 science labs, 4 foreign language, 4 history.

Financial Aid

Students should submit: FAFSA, CSS/Financial Aid PROFILE, Noncustodial PROFILE, Business/Farm Supplement. Priority filing deadline is 2/15. The Princeton Review suggests that all financial aid forms be submitted as soon as possible after October 1. *Need-based scholarships/grants offered:* Federal Pell, FSEOG, State scholarships/grants, Private scholarships, College/university scholarship or grant aid from institutional funds. *Loan aid offered:* Direct Subsidized Stafford Loans, Direct Unsubsidized Stafford Loans, Direct PLUS loans, Federal Perkins Loans. Applicants will be notified of awards on a rolling basis beginning 3/28. Federal Work-Study Program available. Institutional employment available.

The Inside Word

Notre Dame is one of the most selective colleges in the country. Almost everyone who enrolls is in the top 10 percent of their graduating class and possesses test scores in the highest percentiles. But, as the student respondents suggest, strong academic ability isn't enough to get you in here. The school looks for students with other talents, and seems to have a predilection for athletic achievement. Legacy students get a leg up but are by no means assured of admission.

THE SCHOOL SAYS "..."

From the Admissions Office

"Notre Dame is a Catholic university, which means it offers unique opportunities for academic, ethical, spiritual, and social service development. The First Year of Studies program provides special assistance to our students as they make the adjustment from high school to college. The first-year curriculum includes many core requirements, while allowing students to explore several areas of possible future study. Each residence hall is home to students from all classes; most will live in the same hall for all their years on campus. An average of 93 percent of entering students will graduate within five years.

"The highest critical reading score and the highest math score from either test will be accepted; the writing component score is not required. The ACT is also accepted (with or without writing component) in lieu of the SAT."

SELECTIVITY

Admissions Rating	98
# of applicants	18,157
% of applicants accepted	20
% of acceptees attending	56
# offered a place on the wait list	1,602
% accepting a place on wait list	54
% admitted from wait list	0

FRESHMAN PROFILE

Range SAT Critical Reading	670–760
Range SAT Math	680–770
Range SAT Writing	650–750
Range ACT Composite	32–34
Minimum paper TOEFL	560
Minimum internet-based TOEFL	100
% graduated top 10% of class	91
% graduated top 25% of class	98
% graduated top 50% of class	100

DEADLINES

Early action	
Deadline	11/1
Notification	12/21
Regular	
Deadline	1/1
Notification	4/10
Nonfall registration?	Yes

FINANCIAL FACTS

Financial Aid Rating	94
Annual tuition	$49,178
Room and board	$14,358
Required fees	$507
Books and supplies	$1,050
Average frosh need-based scholarship	$38,335
Average UG need-based scholarship	$35,807
% needy frosh rec. need-based scholarship or grant aid	93
% needy UG rec. need-based scholarship or grant aid	94
% needy frosh rec. non-need-based scholarship or grant aid	56
% needy UG rec. non-need-based scholarship or grant aid	55
% needy frosh rec. need-based self-help aid	70
% needy UG rec. need-based self-help aid	76
% frosh rec. any financial aid	66
% UG rec. any financial aid	77
% UG borrow to pay for school	50
Average cumulative indebtedness	$27,237
% frosh need fully met	100
% ugrads need fully met	100
Average % of frosh need met	100
Average % of ugrad need met	100

UNIVERSITY OF OKLAHOMA

1000 ASP AVENUE, NORMAN, OK 73019-4076 • ADMISSIONS: 405-325-2252 • FAX: 405-325-7124

STUDENTS SAY "..."

Academics The University of Oklahoma (OU), located in Norman, OK, outranks all other public universities in National Merit Scholars, and boasts 171 undergraduate degree programs. It is an "intellectually fertile, opportunity-laden public research institution" with a "rich tradition of community" that offers "an Ivy League quality education within a public university." OU has over 30,000 students, but still manages to have a "small town feel" that is "very comfortable and welcoming." Students call OU "not just a school," but "a place to meet others in the OU family, be a part of long-standing traditions," and "receive a quality education from challenging courses." Home of the Sooners football team, which won seven national championships, it's no wonder OU's school spirit is strong. The University also boasts twenty-nine overall NCAA National Championships, and a host of other athletic championships and accolades. Though OU "might be known for its athletic program," student say "academics don't suffer from it." OU has "fantastic," "engaging," "encouraging" "professors that truly care for the well-being of the students." "The professors here don't feel like your average teachers," notes a Psychology and Economics major, "but exceptional instructors who relate on a personal basis and actually help you comprehend the material." OU gives "tons of opportunities to its students," including "jobs, networking, study abroad" programs and more. The university combines "tradition with advancement to encourage you to become the best version of yourself possible" says an Elementary Education major. Student after student noted the sense of "family" everyone has at OU, as well as the importance of "tradition, unity, and togetherness."

Life

OU is home to a host of strong athletic teams and students frequent "football games and other athletic events for fun." During the fall, "most students attend at least one football game." "Greek life" is also "very important." Some complain that "if you're not in a fraternity or sorority, there's not a lot to do on campus on the weekends." Others, though, say "there are many opportunities to be involved on campus," including "free movie nights and pool." There is always "something going on, and whether it be a sports event or a fine arts event, the quality is always excellent." Students can visit the world-renowned art in the Fred Jones Jr. Museum of Art or the twenty-six-foot tall dinosaur (an Apatosaurus!) at OU's Sam Noble Museum of Natural History. There is also "Campus Corner," which has "restaurants, bars and boutiques." And it's also "an easy drive to the movies, a nice restaurant, or night life." Students note that the "social atmosphere is very alive most of the time." But it's not all about football and parties. "People are very considerate of one another and make efforts to support each other during rough times," notes a Psychology and Mathematics major. That extends beyond campus as well, and students take advantage of "all kinds of volunteering opportunities." In fact, "every year everyone on campus drops what they're doing for one weekend to spend all day volunteering in the local Norman and Oklahoma City communities." Students value their commitment to community service. "We genuinely care for one another and are very passionate about the university," says one student. "I cannot imagine there being a happier campus than OU anywhere in the country." Or, as another says: "Life is great."

Student Body

A typical OU student is "friendly," "down to earth," "aware," and "motivated." They have a "nice balance" between their "academic and social lives" and are committed to "volunteering," "sports" and "Greek life." Many students join a fraternity or sorority. Incoming students are most likely to "fit in" by "being involved on campus" and joining "lot of organizations." Students describe their classmates as primarily "white, upper-middle class, and Christian," but "with a "with a broad mix of international and minority students."

FINANCIAL AID: 405-325-5505 • E-MAIL: ADMREC@OU.EDU • WEBSITE: WWW.OU.EDU

THE PRINCETON REVIEW SAYS

Admissions

Very important factors considered include: rigor of secondary school record, class rank, academic GPA, standardized test scores. *Important factors considered include:* application essay, recommendation(s). *Other factors considered include:* interview, extracurricular activities, talent/ability, character/personal qualities, alumni/ae relation, volunteer work, work experience, level of applicant's interest. SAT or ACT required. ACT with or without writing accepted. SAT with or without Essay component accepted. TOEFL required of all international applicants. High school diploma is required and GED is accepted. *Academic units required:* 4 English, 3 math, 3 science, 3 science labs, 1 social studies, 2 history, 2 academic electives. *Academic units recommended:* 4 math, 4 science, 2 foreign language, 1 computer science.

Financial Aid

Students should submit: FAFSA. Priority filing deadline is 3/1. The Princeton Review suggests that all financial aid forms be submitted as soon as possible after October 1. *Need-based scholarships/grants offered:* Federal Pell, FSEOG, State scholarships/grants, Private scholarships, College/university scholarship or grant aid from institutional funds, United Negro College Fund. *Loan aid offered:* Direct Subsidized Stafford Loans, Direct Unsubsidized Stafford Loans, Direct PLUS loans, Federal Perkins Loans, College/university loans from institutional funds. Applicants will be notified of awards on a rolling basis beginning 3/15. Federal Work-Study Program available. Institutional employment available.

The Inside Word

Accepted students at OU graduated from high school with an average GPA of 3.6. But while academic grades and standardized test scores (ACT/SAT) are very important to the admissions process at OU, they also place importance on community service, leadership, and extracurricular activities. In fact, the applicant's "engagement" accounts for a quarter of their decision.

THE SCHOOL SAYS "..."

From the Admissions Office

"Ask yourself some significant questions. What are your ambitions, goals, and dreams? Do you desire opportunity, and are you ready to accept challenge? What do you hope to gain from your educational experience? Are you looking for a university that will provide you with the tools, resources, and motivation to convert ambitions, opportunities, and challenges into meaningful achievement? To effectively answer these questions you must carefully seek out your options, look for direction, and make the right choice. The University of Oklahoma combines a unique mixture of academic excellence, varied social cultures, and a variety of campus activities to make your educational experience complete. At OU, comprehensive learning is our goal for your life. Not only do you receive a valuable classroom learning experience, but OU is also one of the finest research institutions in the United States. This allows OU students the opportunity to be a part of technology in progress. It's not just learning, it's discovery, invention, and dynamic creativity, a hands-on experience that allows you to be on the cutting edge of knowledge. Make the right choice and consider the University of Oklahoma!

"The SAT (or ACT) will be used when considering freshman applicants for admission. The writing component of either test is not required of students and is not used in determining admission to the university. The student's best composite score from any one test will be used."

SELECTIVITY

Admissions Rating	86
# of applicants	12,002
% of applicants accepted	78
% of acceptees attending	45
# offered a place on the wait list	1,322
% accepting a place on wait list	100
% admitted from wait list	16

FRESHMAN PROFILE

Range SAT Critical Reading	520–670
Range SAT Math	540–670
Range ACT Composite	24–29
Minimum paper TOEFL	550
Minimum internet-based TOEFL	79
Average HS GPA	3.6
% graduated top 10% of class	37
% graduated top 25% of class	68
% graduated top 50% of class	93

DEADLINES

Regular	
Deadline	2/1
Nonfall registration?	Yes

FINANCIAL FACTS

Financial Aid Rating	90
Annual in-state tuition	$4,296
Annual out-of-state tuition	$17,682
Room and board	$9,742
Required fees	$3,769
Books and supplies	$714
Average frosh need-based scholarship	$6,662
Average UG need-based scholarship	$5,713
% needy frosh rec. need-based scholarship or grant aid	48
% needy UG rec. need-based scholarship or grant aid	58
% needy frosh rec. non-need-based scholarship or grant aid	65
% needy UG rec. non-need-based scholarship or grant aid	52
% needy frosh rec. need-based self-help aid	61
% needy UG rec. need-based self-help aid	69
% frosh rec. any financial aid	88
% UG rec. any financial aid	86
% UG borrow to pay for school	44
Average cumulative indebtedness	$27,255
% frosh need fully met	74
% ugrads need fully met	76
Average % of frosh need met	76
Average % of ugrad need met	79

UNIVERSITY OF OREGON

1217 UNIVERSITY OF OREGON, EUGENE, OR 97403-1217 • ADMISSIONS: 541-346-3201 • FAX: 541-346-5815

CAMPUS LIFE

Quality of Life Rating	87
Fire Safety Rating	85
Green Rating	97
Type of school	Public
Affiliation	No Affiliation
Environment	City

STUDENTS

Total undergrad enrollment	20,538
% male/female	47/53
% from out of state	41
% frosh live on campus	80
% ugrads live on campus	20
# of fraternities (% ugrad men join)	19 (15)
# of sororities (% ugrad women join)	12 (20)
% African American	2
% Asian	6
% Caucasian	60
% Hispanic	10
% Native American	<1
% Pacific Islander	<1
% Two or more races	7
% Race and/or ethnicity unknown	1
% international	14
# of countries represented	80

SURVEY SAYS...

Students are happy
Students aren't religious
Students environmentally aware
Recreation facilities are great
Lots of beer drinking
Everyone loves the Ducks

ACADEMICS

Academic Rating	74
% students returning for sophomore year	88
% students graduating within 4 years	50
% students graduating within 6 years	72
Calendar	Semester
Student/faculty ratio	18:1
Profs interesting rating	75
Profs accessible rating	73

Most classes have 10–19 students.
Most lab/discussion sessions have 20–29 students.

MOST POPULAR MAJORS

Business/Commerce; Psychology; Social Sciences

STUDENTS SAY "..."

Academics

If the University of Oregon excels at anything, it is in providing students with a wealth of academic opportunities. Indeed, students feel it is "a perfect place for someone seeking a well-rounded liberal arts secondary education," a school that has "all of the creative perks of a small learning environment with all of the excitement of a big school." Sports are a big deal here, "but there is also an emphasis on rigorous academics." Business, architecture, ecology, journalism, international studies, and political science all win accolades. If there is a chink in UO's armor, it is the "inability for some students to get the classes they need." With such a wide array of fields of study available, some students find that essential classes are only available at difficult hours. Students also give mixed grades to the professors, who range from "remarkable" and "really passionate" educators who "are invested in their students" to a few "quite terrible" teachers who "are not dedicated to the students." Those attending UO should be self-motivating, since "the weight falls on the students to create relationships with professors." It is worth the effort, though, as "doing so can open many doors." When it all clicks—and many students report that once that once they were focused on their major things began to fall into place—students have enjoyed an education that "deeply altered the way I see things."

Life

Eugene, Oregon, is not going to give the nation's big cities a run for their money, but students here like it that way. When the weather is nice, students can be found outside "playing Frisbee, football, soccer, or just lounging in the grass," and when the rainy weather of the Pacific Northwest forces people indoors, "you find students in coffee shops on campus and off, studying, visiting, or relaxing." Music, hiking, and other outdoor activities are also popular pastimes. Indeed, the scenery proves a draw for many. "The coast is an hour away, hiking trails and mountains are everywhere, and you can even drive or take a bus up to Portland to get some city life." Greek life is growing on campus but does not dominate the school, and despite prohibitions on drinking in the dorms, students manage it anyway. "We are a dry campus," one attendee notes, "but that doesn't stop students." With the gorgeous scenery and wealth of things to do, it's no wonder students think that "life at school is pretty great."

Student Body

What kind of student attends the University of Oregon? The typical answer is that there is no typical answer. "You have your hipsters, hippies, jocks, athletes, drunks, nerds, and every other cliché you can think of"—students from "dreadlocked hippies to straight-laced conservatives, and everything else in between." That diversity in the student body means, "if you're willing to put forth any sort of effort into meeting people, you'll find a group" who will click with you. "No matter who you are," another student agrees, "there are programs and clubs on campus to take part in." Greek or non-Greek does make a difference. Students say there is a "huge divide between Greek-life and the rest of the student body." But overall, University of Oregon students are "friendly, open-minded, and generally environmentally/socially conscious." In other words, "there are all sorts of students at Oregon, and it is pretty diverse."

FINANCIAL AID: 800-760-6953 • E-MAIL: UOADMIT@UOREGON.EDU • WEBSITE: WWW.UOREGON.EDU

THE PRINCETON REVIEW SAYS

Admissions

Very important factors considered include: rigor of secondary school record, academic GPA. *Important factors considered include:* standardized test scores, application essay. *Other factors considered include:* class rank, extracurricular activities, talent/ability, character/personal qualities, first generation, geographical residence, state residency, racial/ethnic status, volunteer work, work experience. SAT or ACT required. ACT with or without writing accepted. SAT with or without Essay component accepted. TOEFL required of all international applicants. High school diploma is required and GED is accepted. *Academic units required:* 4 English, 3 math, 3 science, 2 foreign language, 3 social studies. *Academic units recommended:* 1 science lab.

Financial Aid

Students should submit: FAFSA. Priority filing deadline is 3/1. The Princeton Review suggests that all financial aid forms be submitted as soon as possible after October 1. *Need-based scholarships/grants offered:* Federal Pell, FSEOG, State scholarships/grants, Private scholarships, College/university scholarship or grant aid from institutional funds. *Loan aid offered:* Direct Subsidized Stafford Loans, Direct Unsubsidized Stafford Loans, Direct PLUS loans, Federal Perkins Loans, College/university loans from institutional funds. Applicants will be notified of awards on a rolling basis beginning 4/1. Federal Work-Study Program available. Institutional employment available.

The Inside Word

No need to worry about elaborate written statements and mile-long academic résumés. Maintain a 3.0 or better GPA in a college prep curriculum and your ticket to UO is all but written. Even substandard test scores can be overlooked for applicants who meet that requirement. There is further leniency for less than stellar grades if personal circumstances got in the way of academic achievement; applicants for whom this applies should make the school aware when applying.

THE SCHOOL SAYS "..."

From the Admissions Office

"At the UO, you'll be part of a community dedicated to making a difference in the world and you'll find the inspiration and resources you'll need to succeed. You'll attend classes alongside students from all fifty states and more than 100 countries, and learn from people whose cultural, ethnic, political, and religious perspectives differ from your own. You'll have opportunities to participate in cutting-edge research and study with renowned faculty. You'll graduate with the critical thinking skills and professional preparation necessary to succeed in an increasingly global job market. Set in a 295-acre arboretum, the UO is literally green. Academic and outdoor programs will bring you into forests, mountains, rivers, and lakes. The state-of-the-art Lewis Integrative Science Building earned a 'platinum' certification from the U.S. Green Building Council's Leadership in Energy and Environmental Design program; the new student union and recreation center are both on track for the same distinction. You'll have access to nationally recognized programs in sustainable architecture, psychology, geography, economics, education, and business. With a student/teacher ratio of eighteen to one and median class size of nineteen students, you'll find a campus that meets your individual needs. You'll also have the benefits of a premier research university: 316 academic programs, excellent academic facilities, and more than 250 student organizations. To be eligible for freshman admission, submit your official high school transcript and SAT or ACT scores, graduate from an accredited high school, and write an essay."

SELECTIVITY
Admissions Rating	83
# of applicants	22,000
% of applicants accepted	74
% of acceptees attending	25
# offered a place on the wait list	1,186
% accepting a place on wait list	41
% admitted from wait list	6

FRESHMAN PROFILE
Range SAT Critical Reading	500–620
Range SAT Math	500–610
Range SAT Writing	490–600
Range ACT Composite	22–27
Minimum paper TOEFL	500
Minimum internet-based TOEFL	61
Average HS GPA	3.6
% graduated top 10% of class	29
% graduated top 25% of class	64
% graduated top 50% of class	93

DEADLINES
Early action	
Deadline	11/1
Notification	12/15
Regular	
Deadline	1/15
Nonfall registration?	Yes

FINANCIAL FACTS
Financial Aid Rating	78
Annual in-state tuition	$8,505
Annual out-of-state tuition	$30,240
Room and board	$11,785
Required fees	$1,784
Books and supplies	$1,068
Average frosh need-based scholarship	$8,692
Average UG need-based scholarship	$7,770
% needy frosh rec. need-based scholarship or grant aid	72
% needy UG rec. need-based scholarship or grant aid	72
% needy frosh rec. non-need-based scholarship or grant aid	6
% needy UG rec. non-need-based scholarship or grant aid	3
% needy frosh rec. need-based self-help aid	72
% needy UG rec. need-based self-help aid	77
% frosh rec. any financial aid	85
% UG rec. any financial aid	91
% UG borrow to pay for school	51
Average cumulative indebtedness	$25,049
% frosh need fully met	8
% ugrads need fully met	6
Average % of frosh need met	60
Average % of ugrad need met	60

UNIVERSITY OF THE PACIFIC

3601 PACIFIC AVENUE, STOCKTON, CA 95211 • ADMISSIONS: 209-946-2211 • FAX: 209-946-2413

STUDENTS SAY ". . ."

Academics

Educational diversity and strong academic programs bring many students to the University of the Pacific in Stockton, California. The school "provides an array of opportunities to suit anyone." "The accelerated programs in dentistry, law, and pharmacy" are a big hit, as well as the "amazing co-op program for engineers" and the "prestigious speech and language pathology program." The "four year guarantee" for some majors and the time and money saved by finishing earlier than other schools' programs is the deciding factor for many. "The Elementary Education program appealed to me because I would get my teaching credential and degree in four years, rather than five or six." Another reason people choose Pacific is the appeal of "very small" and "intimate" classes. One student says this allows for "the proper and necessary attention that I need in order to succeed academically." "Professors know you by name, and they are very involved and helpful." This "emphasis on close relationships between staff and students" shows that Pacific is "a school that truly cares about each student's education." A good deal of students describe professors as "extremely challenging," but also "extremely motivating." "They encourage me and push me to put 110 percent effort in everything inside and outside the classroom." Another student confirms that each class is "manageable but requires effort." If needed, assistance is readily available. "There is always someone around who can help you and plenty of tutors." "There are so many resources in place to help students succeed, that it's practically impossible not to do well." Although the cost may seem high, several students did benefit from "a lot of financial aid."

Life

Students love the "gorgeous and well-maintained" campus, but the surrounding city of Stockton does not get rave reviews. One student describes the University of the Pacific as a "nice school in an unlikely neighborhood." One student does not recommend "walking around certain parts of campus late at night," but adds, "We have great campus police and a STRIPE program that can transport you wherever you want on golf carts if you call them and let you know where you are." Students say the campus is fairly self-contained, with "a movie theater that shows free movies on the weekends for all Pacific students. We also have an on-campus grocery store and a cafeteria that is open until 1:00 A.M." Since there is no strong pull to leave campus, "students tend to resort to joining fraternities to give them something to do. It isn't always partying though. Pacific is not usually considered a party school since the campus "drug and alcohol policy is extremely strict." A lot of frats on campus are professional ones (i.e. pharmacy fraternities) that are committed to giving back to the community and hosting health fairs." Students say, "Student life varies widely by major." "Some majors are a lot more difficult than others, so not everyone studies." Keeping active and fit are also popular. "Our gym is very nice and hygienic. We also have a swimming pool with open hours and several soccer fields for recreational use."

Student Body

Some students agree that there is "a wide gap between the 'serious' students and the 'not serious' students." This may explain the seemingly contradictory observations that "people seem to party a lot" and that there is "not much time for anything but studying." Student comments suggest that the typical student "is involved in multiple organizations on campus, gets good grades, finds time for fun on the weekends, [and] stays late in the library even if they are just socializing." Pacific's size lends itself to a "friendly atmosphere." The "small campus contributes to a small town ambiance where you know everyone." One downside to this is that "student life becomes very cliquey, almost like high school."

FINANCIAL AID: 209-946-2421 • E-MAIL: ADMISSIONS@PACIFIC.EDU • WEBSITE: WWW.PACIFIC.EDU

THE PRINCETON REVIEW SAYS

Admissions

Very important factors considered include: rigor of secondary school record. *Important factors considered include:* academic GPA, standardized test scores, application essay, recommendation(s), extracurricular activities, first generation. *Other factors considered include:* class rank, talent/ability, character/personal qualities, alumni/ae relation, geographical residence, volunteer work, work experience. SAT or ACT required. ACT with or without writing accepted. TOEFL required of all international applicants. High school diploma is required and GED is accepted. *Academic units recommended:* 4 English, 2 foreign language, 2 social studies, 1 history, 1 academic elective, 1 visual/performing arts.

Financial Aid

Students should submit: FAFSA. Priority filing deadline is 2/15. The Princeton Review suggests that all financial aid forms be submitted as soon as possible after October 1. *Need-based scholarships/grants offered:* Federal Pell, FSEOG, State scholarships/grants, Private scholarships, College/university scholarship or grant aid from institutional funds. *Loan aid offered:* Direct Subsidized Stafford Loans, Direct Unsubsidized Stafford Loans, Direct PLUS loans, Federal Perkins Loans. Applicants will be notified of awards on a rolling basis beginning 3/1. Federal Work-Study Program available. Institutional employment available.

The Inside Word

While many factors are considered on applications, competition throughout California is intense. Exceptional performance in honors and advanced placement courses will help you stand out in the crowd.

THE SCHOOL SAYS "..."

From the Admissions Office

"One of the most concise ways of describing the University of the Pacific is that it is 'a major university in a small college package.' Our 3,877 undergraduates get the personal attention that you would expect at a small, residential college. But they also have the kinds of opportunities offered at much larger institutions, including more than ninety majors and programs; hundreds of student organizations; drama, dance, and musical productions; sixteen NCAA Division I athletic teams; and two dozen club and intramural sports. We offer undergraduate major programs in the arts, sciences and humanities, business, education, engineering, international studies, music, pharmacy, and health sciences. Some of the unique aspects of our academic programs include the following: We have the only independent, coed, nonsectarian liberal arts and sciences college located between Los Angeles and central Oregon; we have the only undergraduate professional school of international studies in California—and it's the only one in the nation that actually requires you to study abroad; we have the only engineering program in the West that requires students to complete a year's worth of paid work experience as part of their degree; our Conservatory of Music focuses on performance but also offers majors in music management, music therapy, music education, and music industry studies; and we offer several accelerated programs in business, dentistry, dental hygiene, education, law, engineering, and pharmacy. Our beautiful New England–style main campus is located in Stockton (population: about 300 thousand) and is within two hours or less of San Francisco, Santa Cruz, Yosemite National Park, and Lake Tahoe. SAT Subject Tests recommended: mathematics, chemistry (natural science majors only)."

SELECTIVITY
Admissions Rating	83
# of applicants	14,449
% of applicants accepted	65
% of acceptees attending	10
# offered a place on the wait list	367
% accepting a place on wait list	39
% admitted from wait list	31

FRESHMAN PROFILE
Range SAT Critical Reading	490–620
Range SAT Math	520–660
Range SAT Writing	490–630
Range ACT Composite	22–29
Minimum paper TOEFL	475
Minimum internet-based TOEFL	52
Average HS GPA	3.5
% graduated top 10% of class	33
% graduated top 25% of class	66
% graduated top 50% of class	90

DEADLINES
Regular	
Priority	11/15
Deadline	1/15
Nonfall registration?	Yes

APPLICANTS ALSO LOOK AT AND OFTEN PREFER
University of California–Davis; University of California–Berkeley

AND SOMETIMES PREFER
University of California–Davis; University of California–Berkeley; University of California–Los Angeles; University of Southern California

FINANCIAL FACTS
Financial Aid Rating	72
Annual tuition	$42,414
Room and board	$12,858
Required fees	$520
Books and supplies	$1,764
Average frosh need-based scholarship	$24,608
Average UG need-based scholarship	$23,653
% needy frosh rec. need-based scholarship or grant aid	99
% needy UG rec. need-based scholarship or grant aid	97
% needy frosh rec. non-need-based scholarship or grant aid	0
% needy UG rec. non-need-based scholarship or grant aid	0
% needy frosh rec. need-based self-help aid	89
% needy UG rec. need-based self-help aid	94
% frosh rec. any financial aid	91
% UG rec. any financial aid	83
% frosh need fully met	13
% ugrads need fully met	10

UNIVERSITY OF PENNSYLVANIA

34TH & SPRUCE STREETS, PHILADELPHIA, PA 19104 • ADMISSIONS: 215-898-7507 • FAX: 215-898-9670

STUDENTS SAY ". . ."

Academics

At the University of Pennsylvania, students share an intellectual curiosity and top-notch resources but don't "buy into the stigma of being an Ivy League school." Students here are "very passionate about what they do outside the classroom" and the "flexible core requirements." The university is composed of four undergraduate schools (and "a library for pretty much any topic"). "You can take courses in any of the schools, including graduate-level courses." Luckily, there's a vast variety of disciplines available to students: "I can take a course in old Icelandic and even another one about the politics of food," says a student. Wharton, Penn's highly regarded, "highly competitive undergraduate business school" attracts "career-oriented" students who don't mind a "strenuous course load." There are "more than enough" resources, funding, and opportunity here for any student to take advantage of, and "Penn encourages students to truly take advantage of it all!" Professors can "sometimes seem to be caught up more in their research than their classes," but all "are incredibly well-versed in their subject (as well as their audience)." If you're willing to put in the time and effort, your professors "will be happy to reciprocate." In general, the instructors here are "very challenging academically" and are "always willing to offer their more than relevant life experience in class discussion."

Life

Penn students don't mind getting into intellectual conversations during dinner—"Politics and religion come up often, but so does baseball, types of wine, and restaurants"—but some "partying is a much higher priority here than it is at other Ivy League schools." "Campus is split between the downtown club scene and the frat/bar scene, depending on your preference." However, when it comes down to midterms and finals, "people get really serious and...buckle down and study." There's easy access to downtown Philadelphia, yet "still the comfortable feeling of having our own campus," giving students plenty of access to restaurants (BYO restaurants in Philly are "a huge hit"), shopping, concerts, and sports games, as well as plain old "hanging out with hallmates playing Mario Kart." "It's the perfect mix between an urban setting a traditional college campus." The school provides plenty of guest speakers, cultural events, clubs, and organizations for students to channel their energies (all of which "makes the campus feel smaller"), and seniors can even attend "Feb Club" in the month of February, which is essentially an event every night. The weekend buses to/from New York and D.C. "are always packed." It's a busy life at Penn, and "people are constantly trying to think about how they can balance getting good grades academically and their weekend plans."

Student Body

This "determined" bunch "is either focused on one specific interest, or very well-rounded." Pretty much everyone "was an overachiever ('that kid') in high school," and some students "are off-the-charts brilliant," making everyone here "sort of fascinated by everyone else." Everyone has "a strong sense of personal style and his or her own credo," but no group deviates too far from the more mainstream stereotypes. There's a definite lack of "emos" and hippies. There's "the career-driven Wharton kid who will stab you in the back to get your interview slot" and "the nursing kid who's practically nonexistent," but on the whole, there's tremendous school diversity, with "people from all over the world of all kinds of experiences of all perspectives."

FINANCIAL AID: 215-898-1988 • E-MAIL: INFO@ADMISSIONS.UPENN.EDU • WEBSITE: WWW.UPENN.EDU

THE PRINCETON REVIEW SAYS

Admissions

Very important factors considered include: rigor of secondary school record, academic GPA, standardized test scores, application essay, recommendation(s), character/ personal qualities. *Important factors considered include:* class rank, extracurricular activities, talent/ability. *Other factors considered include:* interview, first generation, alumni/ae relation, geographical residence, state residency, racial/ethnic status, volunteer work, work experience, level of applicant's interest. SAT or ACT required. Two SAT Subject Tests recommended. TOEFL required of all international applicants. High school diploma or equivalent is not required. *Academic units recommended:* 4 English, 4 math, 3 science, 3 science labs, 4 foreign language, 2 social studies, 3 history.

Financial Aid

Students should submit: FAFSA, Institution's own financial aid form, CSS/ Financial Aid PROFILE, Noncustodial PROFILE, Business/Farm Supplement. Priority filing deadline is 2/15. The Princeton Review suggests that all financial aid forms be submitted as soon as possible after October 1. *Need-based scholarships/grants offered:* Federal Pell, FSEOG, State scholarships/grants, Private scholarships, College/university scholarship or grant aid from institutional funds. *Loan aid offered:* Direct Subsidized Stafford Loans, Direct Unsubsidized Stafford Loans, Direct PLUS loans, Federal Perkins Loans, Federal Nursing Loans, College/university loans from institutional funds. Applicants will be notified of awards on or about 4/1. Federal Work-Study Program available. Institutional employment available.

The Inside Word

After a small decline four cycles ago, applications are once again climbing at Penn—the fifth increase in six years. The competition in the applicant pool is formidable. Applicants can safely assume that they need to be one of the strongest students in their graduating class in order to be successful.

THE SCHOOL SAYS ". . ."

From the Admissions Office

"Founded by Benjamin Franklin in 1740 to push the frontiers of knowledge and to benefit society, Penn continues to nurture a sense of public mindedness in its students, inspiring them to make vital contributions as they become engaged citizens in an evolving world. Penn's students and faculty work toward the shared goal of enacting change by questioning, thinking, and doing—often across traditional academic disciplines. The integration of knowledge and learning spans four undergraduate schools: the College of Arts & Sciences, the School of Engineering & Applied Science, the Wharton School of Business, and the School of Nursing. Penn offers more than ninety majors, eighty minors, and the ability to earn more than one degree in four years.

"The Penn community thrives on the open exchange of ideas and shared learning experiences, made possible by the faculty and students of all four undergraduate and twelve graduate schools who coexist and collaborate on one beautiful 300 acre campus in Philadelphia. Students regularly conduct research with faculty and actively participate in over 500 clubs and organizations. Education through engagement is made possible by Penn's extensive partnerships around the world and close to our Philadelphia campus, ranging from over 150 Academically-Based Community Service courses to internships in twenty-two foreign countries.

"Penn understands that the best minds should have access to the finest education, regardless of their families' ability to pay. To achieve this, Penn practices need-blind admissions for applicants who are citizens and permanent residents of the United States, Canada, and Mexico, meets 100 percent of demonstrated financial need, and provides an all-grant aid package for all undergraduates receiving financial aid. Our goal is to allow students to pursue their aspirations without assuming a burden of debt."

SELECTIVITY

Admissions Rating	99
# of applicants	35,866
% of applicants accepted	10
% of acceptees attending	65
# offered a place on the wait list	2,651
% accepting a place on wait list	60
% admitted from wait list	9
# of early decision applicants	5,141
% accepted early decision	25

FRESHMAN PROFILE

Range SAT Critical Reading	670–770
Range SAT Math	690–780
Range SAT Writing	690–780
Range ACT Composite	31–34
Average HS GPA	3.9
% graduated top 10% of class	93
% graduated top 25% of class	98
% graduated top 50% of class	100

DEADLINES

Early decision	
Deadline	11/1
Notification	12/15
Regular	
Deadline	1/1
Notification	4/1
Nonfall registration?	No

APPLICANTS ALSO LOOK AT AND OFTEN PREFER

Harvard College; Princeton University; Yale University

AND SOMETIMES PREFER

Stanford University; Columbia University; Massachusetts Institute of Technology; Brown University

AND RARELY PREFER

Cornell University; Georgetown University

FINANCIAL FACTS

Financial Aid Rating	94
Annual tuition	$43,838
Room and board	$13,990
Required fees	$5,698
Books and supplies	$1,250
Average frosh need-based scholarship	$48,605
Average UG need-based scholarship	$41,194
% needy frosh rec. need-based scholarship or grant aid	99
% needy UG rec. need-based scholarship or grant aid	99
% needy frosh rec. non-need-based scholarship or grant aid	0
% needy UG rec. non-need-based scholarship or grant aid	0
% needy frosh rec. need-based self-help aid	100
% needy UG rec. need-based self-help aid	100
% frosh rec. any financial aid	45
% UG rec. any financial aid	47
% frosh need fully met	100
% ugrads need fully met	100
Average % of frosh need met	100
Average % of ugrad need met	100

UNIVERSITY OF PITTSBURGH—PITTSBURGH CAMPUS

4227 FIFTH AVENUE, PITTSBURGH, PA 15260 • ADMISSIONS: 412-624-7488 • FAX: 412-648-8815

STUDENTS SAY "..."

Academics

At the University of Pittsburgh (or Pitt," to its undergraduates), students enjoy "a large, urban campus that is very involved in its city." One undergrad comments, "I love its location, and it has a great reputation." At this public research university, students feel encouraged that "everyone can succeed academically and feel like part of a community." Partly due to its large size (and approximately 19,000 undergrads), "Pitt is a school that provides students with a plethora of opportunities, both inside and outside the classroom." Many students name "financial aid" as a key part of their decision to attend Pitt, and some even report receiving a "full tuition scholarship." In terms of academic offerings, a wide range of programs stand out, many within STEM fields: Pitt "has an amazing engineering school," its "nursing program is well known and respected," it has "one of the best physical therapy programs" in the Northeast, a "great pharmacy program," "strong Neuroscience department, and a "guaranteed medical program." One student notes jokingly, "Pitt is all about the pre-meds." Across the board, students feel that at Pitt they're receiving "a strong education with a down-to-earth mindset." Often, Pitt undergrads report that "professors are amazing within my major and my overall academic experience has been amazing because of them," and that faculty "are willing to write letters of recommendation, give extra help, and go beyond what is required." "Most of them are really interested in their lectures as well as their research and do a great job of incorporating that into lessons." Other students observe that some professors can be "hit or miss, so it's important to do your homework [in researching instructors] before registering." "Freshman advisors and career counselors are very helpful," and undergrads "really enjoy the way . . . students must be independent, but have plenty of resources for help available."

Life

Using their university-issued "free bus pass," Pitt undergrads love to "take advantage of the free entertainment and cultural experiences around campus, such as museums" and "many bars and restaurants," meaning that at a vibrant urban university, "there is never a lack of things to do." On campus, "there are definitely always parties going on, but there is absolutely no pressure for people who are not interested in that type of thing . . . The program council is constantly planning events that are interesting and fun for any undergrad to attend." "On the weekdays, everyone is focused on their work and classes, but when weekend comes, it's all parties and going out." "There is a big drinking culture at Pitt, but not more than any other average university," and sports are also popular: "Hockey is a major pastime here," and "basketball games are definitely a big component to having fun." "Life can be kind of hectic," since "students are busy with extracurricular activities and school," but "life here is great for those who want to live in a city."

Student Body

University of Pittsburgh undergrads repeatedly assert that "there is no typical student" at Pitt: "The population is too diverse, and I honestly believe that any student can fit in and find their niche." "Students fit in by valuing differences" and because they all want the same thing: "academic success with a little fun." They view themselves as "studious and friendly," "very down to earth," and "kind, driven in their own way, curious, and respectful." They're "hard workers" who are "proud to call Pitt home." Pitt is all about "educating the whole student," and "offers more opportunities than any one student could experience—so as a student you should seize as many of these opportunities as you can!"

UNIVERSITY OF PITTSBURGH—PITTSBURGH CAMPUS

FINANCIAL AID: 412-624-7488 • E-MAIL: OAFA@PITT.EDU • WEBSITE: WWW.PITT.EDU

THE PRINCETON REVIEW SAYS

Admissions

Very important factors considered include: rigor of secondary school record, academic GPA, standardized test scores. *Important factors considered include:* application essay. *Other factors considered include:* class rank, recommendation(s), extracurricular activities, talent/ability, character/personal qualities, first generation, alumni/ae relation, geographical residence, state residency, racial/ethnic status, volunteer work, work experience, level of applicant's interest. SAT or ACT required. ACT with Writing accepted. SAT with or without Essay component accepted. TOEFL required of all international applicants. High school diploma is required and GED is not accepted. *Academic units required:* 4 English, 3 math, 3 science, 3 science labs, 2 foreign language, 2 social studies, 3 academic electives. *Academic units recommended:* 4 English, 4 math, 4 science, 4 science labs, 3 foreign language, 3 social studies, 5 academic electives.

Financial Aid

Students should submit: FAFSA. Priority filing deadline is 3/1. The Princeton Review suggests that all financial aid forms be submitted as soon as possible after October 1. *Need-based scholarships/grants offered:* Federal Pell, FSEOG, State scholarships/grants, Private scholarships, College/university scholarship or grant aid from institutional funds, Federal Nursing Scholarships. *Loan aid offered:* Direct Subsidized Stafford Loans, Direct Unsubsidized Stafford Loans, Direct PLUS loans, Federal Perkins Loans, Federal Nursing Loans, State Loans, College/university loans from institutional funds. Applicants will be notified of awards on a rolling basis beginning 3/1. Federal Work-Study Program available. Institutional employment available.

The Inside Word

The University of Pittsburgh offers admissions on a rolling basis, but don't wait too long—Pitt admits students until the Dean of Admissions closes applications, so you're chancers are better if you apply on the earlier side of "rolling." Pitt offers extensive need- and merit-based financial aid, including the prestigious University Academic Scholarship, for which applications are due Jan. 15.

THE SCHOOL SAYS "..."

From the Admissions Office

"The University of Pittsburgh, a public research university, is a member of the Association of American Universities. Home to sixteen undergraduate, graduate, and professional schools, including an internationally renowned health sciences educational and research complex, Pitt is also affiliated with the University of Pittsburgh Medical Center. Its five-campus system offers more than 470 degree programs, and awards academic merit scholarships and guaranteed admission to graduate and professional programs. Pitt faculty have pioneered major medical advances including the Salk polio vaccine, multiple-organ transplantation, and CPR. Putt alumni have won the Nobel Peace prize, the Nobel Prize in Medicine, the Pulitzer Prize, the National Medal of Science, Olympic gold medals, Academy Awards, and Super Bowl championships. University Honors College students have a proven track record of earning prestigious honors including Rhodes, Marshall, Goldwater, and Churchill scholarships, Pitt educates the whole student through a unique Outside the Classroom Curriculum program that helps students develop holistically; University Center for International Studies certificate programs; and Engineering Co-Op program; study abroad just about anywhere in the world; and more. There are 490 student organizations and student-athletes participate in Division I college athletics, supported by one of the most recognizable student-led fan bases in the nation. Encouraging students to take advantage of the city as their campus, Pitt grants fare-free access to city buses and discounted tickets to cultural events, opening them to the full experiences of a city that has been cited as the most livable in the U.S."

SELECTIVITY

Admissions Rating	90
# of applicants	30,626
% of applicants accepted	54
% of acceptees attending	24
# offered a place on the wait list	2,382
% accepting a place on wait list	23
% admitted from wait list	30

FRESHMAN PROFILE

Range SAT Critical Reading	580–660
Range SAT Math	600–690
Range SAT Writing	570–670
Range ACT Composite	26–31
Minimum paper TOEFL	600
Minimum internet-based TOEFL	100
Average HS GPA	4.0
% graduated top 10% of class	50
% graduated top 25% of class	83
% graduated top 50% of class	99

DEADLINES

Nonfall registration?	Yes

APPLICANTS ALSO LOOK AT AND OFTEN PREFER

Penn State University Park; The Ohio State University–Columbus; University of Maryland–College Park

AND SOMETIMES PREFER

Boston University; Case Western Reserve University; University of Virginia; Carnegie Mellon University; New York University; Rochester Institute of Technology; Virginia Tech; University of Delaware

AND RARELY PREFER

Duquesne University; Drexel University

FINANCIAL FACTS

Financial Aid Rating	79
Annual in-state tuition	$17,292
Annual out-of-state tuition	$28,058
Room and board	$10,900
Required fees	$900
Books and supplies	$762
Average frosh need-based scholarship	$9,239
Average UG need-based scholarship	$8,334
% needy frosh rec. need-based scholarship or grant aid	80
% needy UG rec. need-based scholarship or grant aid	70
% needy frosh rec. non-need-based scholarship or grant aid	8
% needy UG rec. non-need-based scholarship or grant aid	5
% needy frosh rec. need-based self-help aid	81
% needy UG rec. need-based self-help aid	86
% frosh rec. any financial aid	63
% UG rec. any financial aid	58
% UG borrow to pay for school	63
Average cumulative indebtedness	$38,045
% frosh need fully met	15
% ugrads need fully met	12
Average % of frosh need met	61
Average % of ugrad need met	55

UNIVERSITY OF PUGET SOUND

1500 NORTH WARNER STREET CMB 1062, TACOMA, WA 98416-1062 • ADMISSIONS: 253-879-3211 • FAX: 253-879-3993

CAMPUS LIFE
Quality of Life Rating	91
Fire Safety Rating	85
Green Rating	93
Type of school	Private
Affiliation	No Affiliation
Environment	City

STUDENTS
Total undergrad enrollment	2,553
% male/female	43/57
% from out of state	76
% frosh from public high school	73
% frosh live on campus	100
% ugrads live on campus	65
# of fraternities (% ugrad men join)	3 (27)
# of sororities (% ugrad women join)	4 (31)
% African American	1
% Asian	7
% Caucasian	75
% Hispanic	7
% Native American	<1
% Pacific Islander	0
% Two or more races	9
% Race and/or ethnicity unknown	1
% international	<1
# of countries represented	9

SURVEY SAYS...
Lots of liberal students
Students are happy
Classroom facilities are great
Lab facilities are great
School is well run
Great financial aid
Students aren't religious
Easy to get around campus

ACADEMICS
Academic Rating	85
% students returning for sophomore year	87
% students graduating within 4 years	68
Calendar	Semester
Student/faculty ratio	11:1
Profs interesting rating	96
Profs accessible rating	96

Most classes have 10–19 students.
Most lab/discussion sessions have 10–19 students.

MOST POPULAR MAJORS
Psychology; Business/Commerce; Biology

STUDENTS SAY "..."

Academics
The University of Puget Sound is "the ideal learning environment with plenty of opportunity for both academic and personal growth." Students are encouraged to "branch out and go beyond their comfort zone in class and outside of class," and the school is "all about having involving intellectual exchanges of ideas...in the relaxed but conscientious cultural setting of the Pacific Northwest." "The academic culture requires a lot of hard work without being competitive," and the "laid-back culture" belies an "excellent and engaging science program," "nationally acclaimed" orientation program, good financial aid, and small, discussion-based classes. "Come as you are, work hard, do what you love, and expect the support of the entire student body and staff," says a student.

The professors at UPS are "fantastic, "passionate, engaging, and completely devoted to helping students learn, improve, and achieve." Most of the professors "are very focused on ensuring that the students are not only able to understand the topics discussed in class, but can also apply them practically in broader and interdisciplinary discussions." "Going to a small school means that you can learn things about professors from other students ahead of time," says a student of avoiding the few bad apple teachers. There is "a wide variety of classes" available in a large amount of subject areas, though the smaller ones tend to fill up quickly and it can be a struggle to get into some classes.

In this "open, intellectually critical, and socially engaging environment," academics come first and "it really shows." "The University of Puget Sound is a place to work hard without being miserable," says a biochemistry major. "It is almost impossible to lose interest when every professor brings their own area of expertise into the classroom and endorses an understanding of real world application," says another student.

Life
The "stunning" campus is located "in a unique part of the country" and is in a "nice neighborhood" that is both close to the waterfront and major metropolitan areas. "Classes take up a lot of time" but students make time for pleasure on the weekends, and like "to hang out at the cellar, the student-run pizza restaurant" or tale frequent backpacking and hiking trips ("Puget Sound Outdoors, a student-run organization, organizes trips every weekend"). A lot of people tend to relax with friends at off-campus houses, and "most parties are house parties, or the occasional frat party/Greek function." Most of the students are "in some way involved with a sports team, either varsity rec or intramural," and "there are always a lot of things going on on campus, like concerts or lectures or student-run events like a market."

People here "ponder life and things they are passionate" about quite often, and "everyone is very socially/politically active and active in different clubs on campus that promote community service." "Students here hold deep conversations and climb mountains daily (both figuratively and literally)," sums up one witty student. Many also find their way to downtown Tacoma with a group of friends and eat at some of the great restaurants, go to the art museums, or "go swing dancing."

Student Body
Puget Sound is "a place of fantastic tolerance" where students "accept, embrace, and applaud each other's differences." However, students admit that since many students are "middle-class white kids from semi-privileged to privileged backgrounds," a bit more diversity is needed. The "liberal student body" is "friendly and socially-minded" and made up of "talented people who are trying to change the world" (and "there are a lot of hipsters, as well"). Studies are a priority, but everyone at Puget Sound "knows how to balance work, study, and relaxation very well." The "Pacific Northwest Lifestyle" is prevalent, meaning the typical student is "into the outdoors, wears very casual clothing, [and] has a relaxed demeanor."

FINANCIAL AID: 253-879-3214 • E-MAIL: ADMISSION@PUGETSOUND.EDU • WEBSITE: WWW.PUGETSOUND.EDU

THE PRINCETON REVIEW SAYS

Admissions

Very important factors considered include: rigor of secondary school record, academic GPA, application essay, character/personal qualities. *Important factors considered include:* recommendation(s), extracurricular activities, talent/ability, alumni/ae relation, volunteer work, work experience. *Other factors considered include:* class rank, standardized test scores, interview, first generation, racial/ethnic status, level of applicant's interest. SAT or ACT required. ACT with Writing recommended. TOEFL required of all international applicants. High school diploma is required and GED is accepted. *Academic units recommended:* 4 English, 3 social studies, 3 history, 1 visual/performing arts.

Financial Aid

Students should submit: FAFSA. Priority filing deadline is 2/1. The Princeton Review suggests that all financial aid forms be submitted as soon as possible after October 1. *Need-based scholarships/grants offered:* Federal Pell, FSEOG, State scholarships/grants, Private scholarships, College/university scholarship or grant aid from institutional funds. *Loan aid offered:* Direct Subsidized Stafford Loans, Direct Unsubsidized Stafford Loans, Direct PLUS loans, Federal Perkins Loans. Applicants will be notified of awards on a rolling basis beginning 3/15. Federal Work-Study Program available. Institutional employment available.

The Inside Word

Puget Sound supplies students with detailed information about the selection process, which can help alleviate some of that college application angst. While academic background is the primary consideration of every admissions committee (and that includes both grades and the rigor of the classes in which those grades were obtained), Puget Sound considers the whole candidate, and demonstrated interest in a particular issue or extracurricular activity will strengthen any application. Applicants can count on a considerate and caring attitude before, during, and after the review process.

THE SCHOOL SAYS "..."

From the Admissions Office

"We're a classic, forward-thinking and entrepreneurial liberal arts college with a renowned School of Music and an innovative business and leadership program. Our 2,600 students are proudly unclassifiable and universally kind. Our professors win a metric ton of teaching awards and do research with students that pushes the figurative envelope. We're ambitious and modest. We're collaborative and independent minded. We're rooted in the pioneering Pacific Northwest and in love with the world. None of these things are contradictions. All of them make sense. They add up to an education that is perfectly suited to this vast, brave, unclassifiable world."

SELECTIVITY

Admissions Rating	84
# of applicants	5,583
% of applicants accepted	79
% of acceptees attending	15
# offered a place on the wait list	477
% accepting a place on wait list	36
% admitted from wait list	6
# of early decision applicants	136
% accepted early decision	93

FRESHMAN PROFILE

Range SAT Critical Reading	560–680
Range SAT Math	550–650
Range SAT Writing	550–660
Range ACT Composite	25–30
Minimum paper TOEFL	550
Minimum internet-based TOEFL	79
Average HS GPA	3.5
% graduated top 10% of class	35
% graduated top 25% of class	64
% graduated top 50% of class	94

DEADLINES

Early decision	
Deadline	11/15
Notification	12/15
Regular	
Priority	1/15
Deadline	1/15
Notification	4/1
Nonfall registration?	Yes

APPLICANTS ALSO LOOK AT AND OFTEN PREFER
Oberlin College; Stanford University; University of California–Berkeley

AND SOMETIMES PREFER
Pitzer College; Boston University

AND RARELY PREFER
Willamette University

FINANCIAL FACTS

Financial Aid Rating	84
Annual tuition	$43,200
Room and board	$11,180
Required fees	$228
Books and supplies	$1,000
Average frosh need-based scholarship	$24,168
Average UG need-based scholarship	$23,410
% needy frosh rec. need-based scholarship or grant aid	98
% needy UG rec. need-based scholarship or grant aid	99
% needy frosh rec. non-need-based scholarship or grant aid	19
% needy UG rec. non-need-based scholarship or grant aid	12
% needy frosh rec. need-based self-help aid	76
% needy UG rec. need-based self-help aid	77
% frosh rec. any financial aid	96
% UG rec. any financial aid	94
% frosh need fully met	19
% ugrads need fully met	15
Average % of frosh need met	75
Average % of ugrad need met	73

UNIVERSITY OF REDLANDS

1200 EAST COLTON AVENUE, REDLANDS, CA 92373 • ADMISSIONS: 909-748-8074 • FAX: 909-335-4089

CAMPUS LIFE
Quality of Life Rating	93
Fire Safety Rating	86
Green Rating	60*
Type of school	Private
Affiliation	No Affiliation
Environment	Town

STUDENTS
Total undergrad enrollment	3,493
% male/female	44/56
% from out of state	24
% frosh live on campus	92
% ugrads live on campus	59
# of fraternities (% ugrad men join)	5 (13)
# of sororities (% ugrad women join)	5 (20)
% African American	5
% Asian	6
% Caucasian	48
% Hispanic	27
% Native American	1
% Pacific Islander	1
% Two or more races	5
% Race and/or ethnicity unknown	8
% international	1
# of countries represented	17

SURVEY SAYS...
Students are happy
Classroom facilities are great
Career services are great
Class discussions encouraged
School is well run
Great financial aid
Students are friendly
Diverse student types interact on campus
Students environmentally aware
Easy to get around campus
Recreation facilities are great
Active minority support groups

ACADEMICS
Academic Rating	83
% students returning for sophomore year	88
% students graduating within 4 years	63
% students graduating within 6 years	69
Calendar	Semester
Student/faculty ratio	14:1
Profs interesting rating	91
Profs accessible rating	93
Most classes have 10–19 students.	

MOST POPULAR MAJORS
Business/Commerce; Psychology; Liberal Arts and Sciences

STUDENTS SAY "..."

Academics
The University of Redlands is a smallish liberal arts college in Southern California that offers "great financial aid" and "emphasizes a balanced, broad education." "Small class sizes provide a more hands-on learning experience" and "personal attention." Class discussions are "often spicy and provoking." Professors are "friendly," "always prepared," and "willing to help you with anything." Some students call the coursework here "demanding." Whatever the case, there are "endless academic opportunities," and Redlands has the "resources for just about anything" you can conjure up to study. Through the College of Arts and Sciences (CAS), the majority of students follow a conventional undergraduate curriculum, declaring majors and minors. About 200 students choose the innovative approach of the Johnston Center for Integrative Studies. They design their own majors, work with professors to create contracts for their courses, and receive narrative evaluations of their work (instead of letter grades). Other academic highlights at Redlands include an impressive school of music, an uncommon major in communicative disorders, and excellence across the hard sciences. The study abroad program is also awesome. Some 40 percent of these undergrads take coursework in places far-flung, either for a traditional semester or during the fairly unique May Term, an intensive four-week period when students focus on one class. As far as complaints, red tape is pretty annoying—especially for a school this size. "Any bureaucratic task takes a million years to accomplish." Also, "a lot of courses aren't offered every year," and the ones that are available tend to "fill up fast."

Life
No one could deny that the Redlands campus "has incredible aesthetic appeal" and eye-popping scenery. It's also "bustling with fun people and tons of activities." "The whole campus is full of creativity." "There are programs and things to do every night, usually so much that you end up overbooking yourself and having to run from one thing to another in order to be everywhere you want to be." Though some note, "Some of the facilities are really old and outdated." This doesn't flag students' enthusiasm. "There is a lot of school spirit," and intercollegiate sports are popular. The Greek system, which consists of a handful of sororities and fraternities that are "not nationally affiliated," is pretty popular. However, "the party scene is only one part of life on campus and does not take over social life by any means." "There's a real spectrum of hard partiers and stone-cold sober people." The town of Redlands is "quirky" but "a bit isolated." Critics gripe that "there is not a lot to do" off campus. Devotees of the surrounding area tell us that there's "an excellent downtown" "with coffee shops, restaurants, and bars." "If you give the town half a chance," they maintain, "it actually has some cool features." In addition, the school sponsors a wealth of outdoor adventures and "rents out equipment such as snowboards, backpacks, sleeping bags, and anything else you would need in the wilderness." Students also take "trips up to Joshua Tree and Big Bear" or, for more urban fare, trek to Los Angeles.

Student Body
Students at Redlands are "passionate." They have a "sense of wonder and enthusiasm" and "a huge variety of interests." As a whole, students are "quite liberal" politically. Most students are "fairly involved in many aspects of school," and they promise that "everyone can find a niche somewhere on campus." The undergraduate population melds pretty well. There's "no separation of athletes, geeks, Greeks, etc." To the extent that there's any division, it's between Johnston students and students in the CAS. Johnston students—the ones who make their own majors and get evaluations instead of grades—definitely "pride themselves on their uniqueness," and they can be "eccentric." "There are colorful characters on both sides of the spectrum," though, and students assure us that any segregation is self-imposed. "I really don't see a line between the CAS and Johnston," observes one student. "It is only there for those who want it to be."

FINANCIAL AID: 909-748-8047 • E-MAIL: ADMISSIONS@REDLANDS.EDU • WEBSITE: WWW.REDLANDS.EDU

THE PRINCETON REVIEW SAYS

Admissions

Very important factors considered include: rigor of secondary school record, academic GPA, recommendation(s), talent/ability, character/personal qualities. *Important factors considered include:* standardized test scores, application essay. *Other factors considered include:* interview, extracurricular activities, first generation, alumni/ae relation, geographical residence, state residency, racial/ethnic status, volunteer work, work experience. SAT or ACT required. ACT with Writing recommended. TOEFL required of all international applicants. High school diploma is required and GED is accepted. *Academic units required:* 4 English, 3 math, 2 science, 1 science lab, 2 foreign language, 2 social studies. *Academic units recommended:* 4 English, 4 math, 3 science, 1 science lab, 3 foreign language, 2 social studies, 1 history.

Financial Aid

Students should submit: FAFSA, State aid form. Priority filing deadline is 2/15. The Princeton Review suggests that all financial aid forms be submitted as soon as possible after October 1. *Need-based scholarships/grants offered:* Federal Pell, FSEOG, State scholarships/grants, Private scholarships, College/university scholarship or grant aid from institutional funds. *Loan aid offered:* Federal Perkins Loans, College/university loans from institutional funds. Applicants will be notified of awards on a rolling basis beginning 2/28. Federal Work-Study Program available.

The Inside Word

The admit rate here is reasonably high and students with above-average high school records and respectable standardized test scores should consider the school a target. Candidates who are interested in pursuing the self-designed programs available through the Johnston Center will find the admissions process to be distinctly more personal. Note, though, that you have to be admitted as a regular student in the CAS first.

THE SCHOOL SAYS "..."

From the Admissions Office

"We've created an unusually blended curriculum of the liberal arts and pre-professional study because we think education is about learning how to think and learning how to do. For example, our environmental studies students have synthesized their study of sociology, biology, and economics to develop an actual resource management plan for the local mountain communities. Our creative writing program encourages internships with publishing or television production companies. We educate managers, poets, environmental scientists, teachers, musicians, and speech therapists to be reflective about culture and society so that they can better understand and improve the world they'll enter upon graduation.

"First-year students applying for admission are required to submit the results of either the SAT or the ACT. We do not require the writing section of either test."

SELECTIVITY

Admissions Rating	85
# of applicants	4,790
% of applicants accepted	68
% of acceptees attending	16
# offered a place on the wait list	131
% accepting a place on wait list	40
% admitted from wait list	89

FRESHMAN PROFILE

Range SAT Critical Reading	510–610
Range SAT Math	510–610
Range ACT Composite	22–28
Minimum paper TOEFL	550
Average HS GPA	3.6
% graduated top 10% of class	38
% graduated top 25% of class	68
% graduated top 50% of class	90

DEADLINES

Early action	
Deadline	11/15
Notification	1/15
Regular	
Priority	1/15
Nonfall registration?	Yes

APPLICANTS ALSO LOOK AT AND OFTEN PREFER

Occidental College; Chapman University

AND SOMETIMES PREFER

University of San Diego; Loyola Marymount University; University of California–Santa Barbara

AND RARELY PREFER

University of California–Riverside; Whittier College

FINANCIAL FACTS

Financial Aid Rating	87
Annual tuition	$42,836
Room and board	$12,710
Required fees	$350
Books and supplies	$1,746
Average frosh need-based scholarship	$30,331
Average UG need-based scholarship	$28,780
% needy frosh rec. need-based scholarship or grant aid	100
% needy UG rec. need-based scholarship or grant aid	99
% needy frosh rec. non-need-based scholarship or grant aid	74
% needy UG rec. non-need-based scholarship or grant aid	57
% needy frosh rec. need-based self-help aid	84
% needy UG rec. need-based self-help aid	91
% frosh rec. any financial aid	94
% UG rec. any financial aid	94
% frosh need fully met	31
% ugrads need fully met	25
Average % of frosh need met	87
Average % of ugrad need met	85

UNIVERSITY OF RHODE ISLAND

NEWMAN HALL, KINGSTON, RI 02881 • ADMISSIONS: 401-874-7100 • FAX: 401-874-5523

CAMPUS LIFE

Quality of Life Rating	89
Fire Safety Rating	89
Green Rating	86
Type of school	Public
Affiliation	No Affiliation
Environment	Village

STUDENTS

Total undergrad enrollment	13,641
% male/female	46/54
% from out of state	45
% frosh live on campus	74
% ugrads live on campus	44
# of fraternities (% ugrad men join)	11 (17)
# of sororities (% ugrad women join)	9 (22)
% African American	5
% Asian	3
% Caucasian	71
% Hispanic	9
% Native American	<1
% Pacific Islander	<1
% Two or more races	3
% Race and/or ethnicity unknown	7
% international	1
# of countries represented	49

SURVEY SAYS...

Students are happy
Recreation facilities are great
Frats and sororities are popular
Alumni active on campus

ACADEMICS

Academic Rating	71
% students returning for sophomore year	84
% students graduating within 4 years	44
% students graduating within 6 years	63
Calendar	Semester
Student/faculty ratio	16:1
Profs interesting rating	70
Profs accessible rating	69

Most classes have 20–29 students.
Most lab/discussion sessions have 10–19 students.

MOST POPULAR MAJORS

Speech Communication and Rhetoric; Psychology

STUDENTS SAY "..."

Academics

Located in the village of Kingston in the southern part of the state, The University of Rhode Island is a public research institution known for having "excellent science programs," including a "marine biology program [that] is one of the best in the Northeast." URI is a school that challenges me to think big and outside the box," says one student. Other stand-out majors include "nursing, pharmacy," which students feel is "excellent—one of the top in the country," and engineering." Students feel that "all professors have a unique style of teaching. Most are very willing to adapt their style to fit students' needs though" and many "are able to share stories from their experiences that make the material more accessible and interesting." Another student observes that the staff is also "great at helping freshmen transferring from home to college, and there are lots of different programs offered to help students excel academically." Overall, URI is known to have a solid liberal ideology with "openness to creative and critical exploration." This engineering major finds the environment to be rather "forward-thinking [with an] emphasis on today's global workforce."

Life

The school's proximity to the beach and to other major cities like Providence and Boston make it appealing to students from all over the Northeast. One student reports that "driving to one of the nearby beaches to just clear your mind and relax is one of the many benefits of URI's location." Students are said to have a "two brain track" in terms of serious attention to study followed by equal attention to "relaxing and having a good time." If fine dining is meaningful to your quality of life, it's worth noting that URI's dining hall has "won a national award the past two years in a row." And, while there are complaints about the dry campus, one senior notes that this is a surmountable obstacle, in that "people usually live in the surrounding neighborhoods, so you can travel to your friends' houses and party." Others say that students who live nearby still choose to stay on campus during weekends, since this is where their social life is centered. Life isn't all about "getting wasted," chides one sophomore. "Sometimes we get together [to] make dinner and just have a movie night inside our apartment."

Student Body

URI, as an affordable state school, naturally attracts a large percentage of Rhode Islanders. Rumor has it that this group "sticks to their friends from high school," yet one undergrad observes, "Rhody-borns are so afraid of college turning into another four years of high school that we go searching for new people to meet." The typical URI student "is involved in at least one student organization, but many are involved in more than one. They usually go out about once a week on average and study about an hour a day." There are "many students . . . involved in at least one type of extracurricular activity" "then there are students who are not involved at all." Campus diversity is strong, and most groups intermingle without issue.

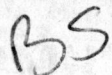

FINANCIAL AID: 401-874-7530 • E-MAIL: ADMISSION@URI.EDU • WEBSITE: WWW.URI.EDU

THE PRINCETON REVIEW SAYS

Admissions

Very important factors considered include: rigor of secondary school record, academic GPA. *Important factors considered include:* class rank, standardized test scores, application essay. *Other factors considered include:* recommendation(s), extracurricular activities, talent/ability, character/personal qualities, first generation, alumni/ae relation, geographical residence, state residency, racial/ethnic status, volunteer work, work experience, level of applicant's interest. SAT or ACT required. ACT with or without writing accepted. SAT with or without Essay component accepted. TOEFL required of all international applicants. High school diploma is required and GED is accepted. *Academic units required:* 4 English, 3 math, 2 science, 1 science lab, 2 foreign language, 2 social studies, 5 academic electives.

Financial Aid

Students should submit: FAFSA. Priority filing deadline is 3/1. The Princeton Review suggests that all financial aid forms be submitted as soon as possible after October 1. *Need-based scholarships/grants offered:* Federal Pell, FSEOG, State scholarships/grants, Private scholarships, College/university scholarship or grant aid from institutional funds. *Loan aid offered:* Direct Subsidized Stafford Loans, Direct Unsubsidized Stafford Loans, Direct PLUS loans, Federal Perkins Loans, Federal Nursing Loans, College/university loans from institutional funds. Applicants will be notified of awards on a rolling basis beginning 3/15. Federal Work-Study Program available. Institutional employment available.

The Inside Word

Applications here are evaluated on the basis of course selection, academic performance, standardized test scores, and unique talents. Don't forget to apply to URI's merit-based scholarships, which are open to international students as well. Remember if you're a resident of another New England state (besides Rhode Island) you may be eligible, depending on your major, for discounted tuition.

THE SCHOOL SAYS "..."

From the Admissions Office

"The University of Rhode Island offers a wide range of merit scholarships to students who have demonstrated academic success in a challenging college preparatory curriculum. You may be eligible for these awards if you have earned a GPA of 3.2/4.0, as well as SATs of 1050+ (critical reading and math) or ACT of 23+, and have demonstrated leadership and involvement in your school and/or community. To be considered for our highest scholarships, we recommend that you apply by our December 1 Early Action deadline.

"We also strongly recommend that students interested in engineering, nursing, and the doctorate in pharmacy apply by December 1 as spaces are limited in these programs.

1. The latest test scores we will consider for scholarship review are the November SATs and the October ACT.

2. We consider the single highest score on each section of the SAT (and ACT) across test dates, so there is no need to use "Score Choice."

3. The SAT critical reading, writing and math scores are used for admission evaluation. Currently, only the critical reading and math scores are used for scholarship consideration in addition to the other criteria lised above.

4. Merit Scholarships are four-year awards, renewable each semester as long as you maintain continuous full-time enrollment (twelve credits per semester) and a minimum GPA of 2.8.

5. Unlike 'Early Decision,' Early Action is non-binding. You will not have to commit to URI until May 1."

SELECTIVITY

Admissions Rating	80
# of applicants	21,261
% of applicants accepted	71
% of acceptees attending	21
# offered a place on the wait list	1,262
% accepting a place on wait list	31
% admitted from wait list	5

FRESHMAN PROFILE

Range SAT Critical Reading	500–590
Range SAT Math	510–600
Range SAT Writing	490–580
Range ACT Composite	22–26
Minimum internet-based TOEFL	79
Average HS GPA	3.5
% graduated top 10% of class	19
% graduated top 25% of class	50
% graduated top 50% of class	86

DEADLINES

Early action	
Deadline	12/1
Notification	1/31
Regular	
Deadline	2/1
Notification	3/31
Nonfall registration?	Yes

APPLICANTS ALSO LOOK AT AND RARELY PREFER

Carnegie Mellon University; Occidental College; University of Maryland; Baltimore County

FINANCIAL FACTS

Financial Aid Rating	83
Annual in-state tuition	$11,128
Annual out-of-state tuition	$27,118
Room and board	$11,700
Required fees	$1,734
Books and supplies	$1,200
Average frosh need-based scholarship	$10,254
Average UG need-based scholarship	$10,000
% needy frosh rec. need-based scholarship or grant aid	83
% needy UG rec. need-based scholarship or grant aid	76
% needy frosh rec. non-need-based scholarship or grant aid	15
% needy UG rec. non-need-based scholarship or grant aid	10
% needy frosh rec. need-based self-help aid	80
% needy UG rec. need-based self-help aid	72
% frosh rec. any financial aid	89
% UG rec. any financial aid	85
% UG borrow to pay for school	71
Average cumulative indebtedness	$32,587
% frosh need fully met	3
% ugrads need fully met	3
Average % of frosh need met	64
Average % of ugrad need met	57

UNIVERSITY OF RICHMOND

Sarah Brunet Hall, 28 Westhampton Way, Richmond, VA 23173 • Admission: 804-289-8640 • Fax: 804-287-6003

CAMPUS LIFE

Quality of Life Rating	96
Fire Safety Rating	93
Green Rating	93
Type of school	Private
Affiliation	No Affiliation
Environment	City

STUDENTS

Total undergrad enrollment	2,889
% male/female	48/52
% from out of state	81
% frosh from public high school	56
% frosh live on campus	99
% ugrads live on campus	90
# of fraternities (% ugrad men join)	6 (17)
# of sororities (% ugrad women join)	8 (29)
% African American	6
% Asian	7
% Caucasian	59
% Hispanic	8
% Native American	<1
% Pacific Islander	<1
% Two or more races	4
% Race and/or ethnicity unknown	6
% international	9
# of countries represented	61

SURVEY SAYS...

Students politically aware
Students always studying
Students are happy
Classroom facilities are great
Lab facilities are great
Great library
Career services are great
Internships are widely available
Class discussions encouraged
School is well run
Students love University of Richmond, VA
Great food on campus
Great off-campus food
Dorms are like palaces
Recreation facilities are great
Lots of beer drinking
Frats and sororities are popular

ACADEMICS

Academic Rating	97
% students returning for sophomore year	93
% students graduating within 4 years	83
% students graduating within 6 years	88
Calendar	Semester
Student/faculty ratio	8:1
Profs interesting rating	96
Profs accessible rating	96

Most classes have 10–19 students.
Most lab/discussion sessions have
10–19 students.

MOST POPULAR MAJORS

Business Administration and Management;
Leadership; Biology

STUDENTS SAY "..."

Academics

At the University of Richmond, students "like to enjoy themselves but most have their priorities straight" and they know that "school comes first." As one student puts it, "There is a good balance of work and play here, and students are competitive, but to a healthy extent. The expectations for students here really push you to be involved, get at least two internships or research opportunities, and secure a good job by graduation." Students praise the University of Richmond's "unparalleled resources," particularly the "high number of research, internship, and study abroad opportunities available." As one business administration major gushes, at the University of Richmond "we combine the resources of a major research institution, the breadth of development of a liberal arts education, and amplifying effect of out of classroom opportunities (speakers, programs, student activities) to deliver an undergraduate experience that is both unique to every student and universally top notch." One key resource available to all students that "the university is willing to pay $4,000 for all students to participate in an [otherwise unpaid] internship, research opportunity, or project." This allows all students "an opportunity to have meaningful, career-oriented experiences." Professors at the University of Richmond earn generally high marks, with one student admitting, "My professors showed me how to love to learn again." Another echoes that "the entire University of Richmond staff treats everyone like an individual and not just another student circling through the system." "The schoolwork is difficult, but manageable" and "Richmond is incredibly generous with not only need-based but merit-based aid, which is unusual for liberal arts colleges of a similar caliber."

Life

"The student body is academic but also enjoys having a social life," and which tends to be centered on the Greek system. Though there are no dedicated fraternity or sorority houses on campus (lodges are "our equivalent of Greek houses" where Greek events are thrown), "the social scene is generally dominated by events thrown by Greek life; however, these events are open to all students no matter your affiliation." Most students are involved in more than one extracurricular activity: "There's also plenty to get involved with, so you would have a hard time finding a student who is not involved with some sport, artistic group, club, or organization." As one student puts it, "Everyone is doing some sort of juggling act" but "students are also academically driven, and because classes are difficult and demanding, people will find themselves doing a lot of academic work throughout the week." Weekends are a time to kick back and enjoy what Richmond has to offer in the way of "clubs downtown," "the Virginia Museum of Fine Arts, over 900 restaurants, Carytown (a hipster area with boutiques and unique restaurants), various festivals and events and athletic competitions."

Student Body

"In general, the typical Richmond student cares not only about performing extremely well in class and extracurriculars, but knows it is important to look the part, as well." Some students say that the University of Richmond is getting more diverse, branching out from "New England prepsters and Old South heirs/heiresses" to a more inclusive view that sees the university's students as "diverse, from their backgrounds, races, religions, and ethnicity to their interests, beliefs, goals, and hobbies." One student estimates that "fraternity brothers [and] sorority girls are a large group." But there "is no cut throat competition to do better than your peers when it comes to grades—students are laid back in the sense that they are happy to see their peers do well." Students stress the friendliness of their fellow Spiders, saying, "Everyone that I have met has been super helpful and kind—even as a first year."

FINANCIAL AID: 804-289-8438 • E-MAIL: ADMISSION@RICHMOND.EDU • WEBSITE: WWW.RICHMOND.EDU

THE PRINCETON REVIEW SAYS

Admissions

Very important factors considered include: rigor of secondary school record, academic GPA. *Important factors considered include:* class rank, standardized test scores, application essay, recommendation(s), extracurricular activities, talent/ability, character/personal qualities. *Other factors considered include:* first generation, alumni/ae relation, geographical residence, state residency, racial/ethnic status, volunteer work, work experience, level of applicant's interest. SAT or ACT required. ACT with or without writing accepted. SAT with or without Essay component accepted. TOEFL required of international applicants. High school diploma is required and GED is accepted. *Academic units required:* 4 English, 3 math, 2 science, 2 science labs, 2 foreign language, 2 history. *Academic units recommended:* 4 English, 4 math, 4 science, 4 science labs, 4 foreign language, 4 history.

Financial Aid

Students should submit: FAFSA, CSS/Financial Aid PROFILE, Noncustodial PROFILE. Regular filing deadline is 2/15. The Princeton Review suggests that all financial aid forms be submitted as soon as possible after October 1. *Need-based scholarships/grants offered:* Federal Pell, FSEOG, State scholarships/grants, Private scholarships, College/university scholarship or grant aid from institutional funds. *Loan aid offered:* Direct Subsidized Stafford Loans, Direct Unsubsidized Stafford Loans, Direct PLUS loans, Federal Perkins Loans. Applicants will be notified of awards on or about 4/1. Federal Work-Study Program available. Institutional employment available.

The Inside Word

University of Richmond office of admission takes a holistic view towards applications, and demonstration of character, leadership, and independence is evaluated alongside academic record. That said, applicants will need strong transcripts and high test scores to compete in this applicant pool. The school offers generous merit-based scholarships to those who demonstrate exemplary academic achievement.

THE SCHOOL SAYS "..."

From the Admissions Office

"University of Richmond is one of less than one percent of colleges that is need blind and meets 100 percent of demonstrated financial need. University of Richmond combines the characteristics of a small college with the dynamics and resources of a large university. Our unique size, beautiful suburban campus and outstanding facilities offer students an extraordinary range of opportunities for intellectual achievement and personal growth. While faculty-student interaction and dialogue are at the forefront of the academic experience, research, internships and international experiences are important components of students' lives. Richmond is committed to providing students with rigorous academics and experiential learning. The university offers funding for undergraduate research, summer fellowships and internships. Our global approach to education shines through our many study-abroad and language immersion programs. We are committed to diversity and believe in leveraging its benefits in all aspects of college life. The student body is composed of scholars from a variety of backgrounds. One in four undergraduates is a domestic student of color; one in seven is the first in his or her family to attend college; one in eleven is an international student; and more than 80 percent hail from outside of Virginia."

SELECTIVITY

Admissions Rating	94
# of applicants	9,977
% of applicants accepted	31
% of acceptees attending	26
# offered a place on the wait list	4,070
% accepting a place on wait list	38
% admitted from wait list	10
# of early decision applicants	791
% accepted early decision	42

FRESHMAN PROFILE

Range SAT Critical Reading	600–700
Range SAT Math	620–720
Range SAT Writing	610–700
Range ACT Composite	29–32
Minimum paper TOEFL	550
Minimum internet-based TOEFL	80
% graduated top 10% of class	61
% graduated top 25% of class	89
% graduated top 50% of class	97

DEADLINES

Early decision	
Deadline	11/15
Notification	12/15
Regular	
Deadline	1/15
Notification	4/1
Nonfall registration?	No

APPLICANTS ALSO LOOK AT AND OFTEN PREFER

Brown University; Cornell University; Duke University; Georgetown University

AND SOMETIMES PREFER

Boston College; College of William and Mary

AND RARELY PREFER

Davidson College; Northeastern University

FINANCIAL FACTS

Financial Aid Rating	96
Annual tuition	$49,420
Room and board	$11,460
Books and supplies	$1,100
Average frosh need-based scholarship	$39,666
Average UG need-based scholarship	$38,985
% needy frosh rec. need-based scholarship or grant aid	99
% needy UG rec. need-based scholarship or grant aid	98
% needy frosh rec. non-need-based scholarship or grant aid	23
% needy UG rec. non-need-based scholarship or grant aid	18
% needy frosh rec. need-based self-help aid	75
% needy UG rec. need-based self-help aid	80
% frosh rec. any financial aid	59
% UG rec. any financial aid	67
% UG borrow to pay for school	43
Average cumulative indebtedness	$26,250
% frosh need fully met	86
% ugrads need fully met	83
Average % of frosh need met	100
Average % of ugrad need met	100

UNIVERSITY OF ROCHESTER

300 WILSON BOULEVARD, ROCHESTER, NY 14627 • ADMISSIONS: 585-275-3221 • FAX: 585-461-4595

STUDENTS SAY "..."

Academics

The University of Rochester is a top tier research university comprising more than two hundred majors, two thousand faculty, and instructional staff, and "a wealth and myriad of opportunity." "If you want to be successful, you have the chance to do it here," says a student. The flexibility with majors and the ability to pick and choose classes "without being forced to complete gen eds in subjects that you're not interested in" is a huge boon in "shaping everyone to be a Renaissance man." It allows the student "to personalize their experience while mandating that they receive exposure to the different ways of thinking present in the natural sciences, social sciences, and humanities."

The courses at U of R are "hard but rewarding," and each professor has his or her own teaching style, bringing all the material being taught to life. The "passionate and compassionate alike" teachers "are there to help and want you to succeed, but you still have to work hard to get a good grade"; luckily, the "enormous" administrator to student ratio means plenty of accessibility for students. Still, many students are no stranger to lectures and agree that "small classes are always better than large."

One of the greatest benefits of U of R is that it "offers world class research opportunities to passionate students at any level." Everyone is very serious about their major—"taking difficult course loads is extremely common"—and "Rochester is populated with students who would turn the library into a social spot."

Life

Rochester is budding with "a vibrant community of passionate, creative people and it's really easy to be involved in it." The school's size gives it a "homey and close-knit feeling": "enough people that you feel a part of it, and enough people so that there is always an opportunity to meet new people." While Rochester does get a lot of snow, that just means "the school knows how to handle it (the sidewalks are plowed before it even finishes snowing)." The area surrounding the university itself (called the Ward) is not the most pleasant, but since more and more students are moving into the area of the Ward directly off the footbridge to campus, "the area is getting mildly safer." There's near-complete agreement among students that the "food is terrible."

There are hundreds of student groups on campus, including "multiple a capella groups that perform on the weekends," and students at U of R tend to be more "music-oriented kids as opposed to sports oriented" due in part to the school's beloved Eastman School of Music. Greek life is a popular social channel, as are cheap weekend movies at Hoyt auditorium and your standard hallway and mall hangs.

Rochester is "really great about bringing entertainment to campus, so students never really need to leave if they don't want to."

Student Body

This "close community of highly driven individuals" is "nerdy yet social" and "very friendly." "We are here because we want to be here, not because anyone is making us study here," says a student. Or, as another student describes the population: "Frat boys, science nerds, grad students and musicians all complaining about the snow." While all students are pretty "motivated and naturally hard-working," they also "know how to be laid back and relaxed when socializing." A percentage of students "party pretty hard," while others "spend more time pursuing their interests, watching movies together, [and] going to Lake Ontario." Students "are not cliquey" and it's quite easy to make friends involved in different organizations and across different areas of academics.

FINANCIAL AID: 585-275-3226 • E-MAIL: ADMIT@ADMISSIONS.ROCHESTER.EDU • WEBSITE: WWW.ROCHESTER.EDU

THE PRINCETON REVIEW SAYS

Admissions

Very important factors considered include: rigor of secondary school record, recommendation(s), character/personal qualities. *Important factors considered include:* academic GPA, standardized test scores, application essay, interview, extracurricular activities, talent/ability. *Other factors considered include:* class rank, first generation, alumni/ae relation, geographical residence, racial/ethnic status, volunteer work, work experience, level of applicant's interest. SAT or ACT recommend; SAT Subject Tests required for some. ACT with or without writing accepted. SAT with or without Essay component accepted. TOEFL required of all international applicants. High school diploma is required and GED is accepted.

Financial Aid

Students should submit: FAFSA, CSS/Financial Aid PROFILE, State aid form, Noncustodial PROFILE. Priority filing deadline is 2/15. The Princeton Review suggests that all financial aid forms be submitted as soon as possible after October 1. *Need-based scholarships/grants offered:* Federal Pell, FSEOG, State scholarships/grants, Private scholarships, College/university scholarship or grant aid from institutional funds. *Loan aid offered:* Direct Subsidized Stafford Loans, Direct Unsubsidized Stafford Loans, Direct PLUS loans, Federal Perkins Loans. Applicants will be notified of awards on or about 4/1. Federal Work-Study Program available. Institutional employment available.

The Inside Word

With nearly 5,300 undergrads, applicants to Rochester can expect a highly individualized academic experience—something that makes this school not only a great place to learn, but also an increasingly competitive institution when it comes to admissions. The most important consideration for admission is rigor of class work and recommendations, followed closely by grades and standardized test scores. Keep in mind that Rochester is looking for students who will fit well within the school's academic environment and demonstrate a true interest in attending—that is, scheduling an interview could go a long way in increasing your odds.

THE SCHOOL SAYS "..."

From the Admissions Office

"Rochester believes that excellence requires freedom. In the Rochester Curriculum, students are free to select the courses that appeal to them most. There are no required subjects; students' interests drive their education. Students major in either sciences and engineering, humanities, or social sciences and complete a 'cluster' of at least three related courses in each of the other two areas. Because Rochester is among America's smallest research universities, its students can pursue advanced studies and research in graduate courses, in arts and science or in any one of Rochester's nationally ranked schools of engineering, medicine, nursing, music, education, and business.

"Learning here takes place on a personal scale. Rochester remains one of the most collegiate among top research universities, with smaller classes and a ten to one student-faculty ratio—all within a university setting that attracts more than $400 million in research funding each year. Rochester faculty publish articles across the globe, win awards for their work, and collaborate with undergraduate students on a level that is rare in higher education.

"The expectation is that each student will live up to Rochester's motto, 'Meliora' (ever better), recognizing that they are future leaders in industry, education, and culture. Navigating through world-renowned facilities and resources, a day in the life of two Rochester students or any two days in the life of a single student s never the same."

SELECTIVITY

Admissions Rating	94
# of applicants	17,932
% of applicants accepted	34
% of acceptees attending	23
# offered a place on the wait list	2,507
% accepting a place on wait list	48
% admitted from wait list	0
# of early decision applicants	801
% accepted early decision	41

FRESHMAN PROFILE

Range SAT Critical Reading	600–710
Range SAT Math	640–760
Range SAT Writing	610–710
Range ACT Composite	29–33
Minimum paper TOEFL	600
Minimum internet-based TOEFL	100
Average HS GPA	3.8
% graduated top 10% of class	66
% graduated top 25% of class	92
% graduated top 50% of class	100

DEADLINES

Early decision	
Deadline	11/1
Notification	12/15
Regular	
Deadline	1/5
Notification	4/1
Nonfall registration?	Yes

APPLICANTS ALSO LOOK AT AND RARELY PREFER

Franklin and Marshall College

FINANCIAL FACTS

Financial Aid Rating	93
Annual tuition	$47,450
Room and board	$14,366
Required fees	$840
Books and supplies	$1,310
Average frosh need-based scholarship	$40,556
Average UG need-based scholarship	$37,467
% needy frosh rec. need-based scholarship or grant aid	100
% needy UG rec. need-based scholarship or grant aid	99
% needy frosh rec. non-need-based scholarship or grant aid	15
% needy UG rec. non-need-based scholarship or grant aid	14
% needy frosh rec. need-based self-help aid	81
% needy UG rec. need-based self-help aid	83
% frosh rec. any financial aid	85
% UG borrow to pay for school	58
Average cumulative indebtedness	$30,873
% frosh need fully met	91
% ugrads need fully met	90
Average % of frosh need met	97
Average % of ugrad need met	95

UNIVERSITY OF SAN DIEGO

5998 ALCALA PARK, SAN DIEGO, CA 92110-2492 • ADMISSIONS: 619-260-4506 • FAX: 619-260-6836

STUDENTS SAY "..."

Academics
A moderately sized Catholic school, University of San Diego "strives to provide a quality liberal arts education that expands students' worldviews and underscores the importance of service to others." Indeed, the university offers undergrads "amazing opportunities for educational, social and spiritual growth." Of course, USD's "proximity to the beach" and "friendly SoCal culture" also make the university a highly attractive option as well. Academically, students have their pick of great departments and disciplines, from the "outstanding business school" to a "strong marine science program." And undergrads appreciate that they are taught "to think critically and apply [their] education to real world problems." Many also find their professors to be fair, engaging, well-prepared, and open-minded when conducting their classes; it's clearly evident that they "love what they do." Additionally, professors here make a concerted effort to both ensure they are "accessible" and to get to know "students on a personal level." As an ecstatic biology major sums up her experience, "USD is all about manicured lawns and gardens, the tastiest cafeteria food you will ever have, classes that are so small that you and your professor can be BFFs, and a view of the ocean off in the distance awaiting you for a sunset surf."

Life
Undergrads at USD happily report that life here "is pretty laid back" with students focused on both school and the beach in equal measure. In fact, it's quite common for "upperclassmen to live right on Mission Beach and . . . underclassmen often head [there] after class." But fear not; there's plenty of action on campus as well. As a delighted international relations major shares, "The school has a great entertainment board who schedules free on campus concerts and carnivals (Young the Giant, Magic!, and Imagine Dragons [have played here within the] last 3 years) as well as winter festivals, movies on the lawn, distinguished guest speakers, magicians, comedians, and more." And a philosophy major interjects to tell us that there "are many opportunities to get involved in community service and volunteer work [as well]." Students also love living in Southern California "which lends itself very easily to spending time outdoors and being active." For example, there's a "canyon with a nice running/hiking path . . . right next to campus." And many students can be found "surfing," playing "beach volleyball," and other outdoor pursuits. Additionally, "Outdoor Adventures organizes trips anywhere between paddle boarding in Mission Bay to hiking through Havasu Falls in Arizona or Zion National Park." It's no wonder this content student said, "I almost never have a weekend devoid of anything where I'm stuck in my room bored."

Student Body
Not surprisingly, many an undergrad at University of San Diego could be described as a "friendly, beach loving SoCal kid." Additionally, walking around campus, one gets the sense that USD is "glitzy and . . . comprised of many beautiful people." And it frequently feels as though a lot of students come from "upperclass" families that are "pretty well off financially." Thankfully, a bio major explains that "although this is the impression that USD gives off, there is a place for everyone. You can be a member of the Rock Climbing team or a guide for Outdoor Adventures program and be the opposite of the typical USD student while still absolutely loving the university." Perhaps most importantly, undergrads report that their peers are "welcoming." An accounting major pipes in, "A lot of people will hold the door open for you and 'please' or 'thank you' are commonly heard throughout the campus." Overall, the typical USD student is "smart, hard-working, fun, friendly, dedicated, and passionate." And a behavioral neuroscience major sums up, "Students that put in the initiative to work hard in class, join clubs/organizations, etc. fit in very well. There are lots of opportunities for all different types of people."

FINANCIAL AID: 619-260-4514 • E-MAIL: ADMISSIONS@SANDIEGO.EDU • WEBSITE: WWW.SANDIEGO.EDU

THE PRINCETON REVIEW SAYS

Admissions

Very important factors considered include: rigor of secondary school record, academic GPA, standardized test scores. *Important factors considered include:* class rank, application essay, recommendation(s), extracurricular activities, talent/ability, character/personal qualities, alumni/ae relation, religious affiliation/commitment, volunteer work. *Other factors considered include:* interview, first generation, geographical residence, racial/ethnic status, work experience, level of applicant's interest. SAT or ACT required; SAT Subject Tests considered if submitted. ACT with Writing required. SAT with Essay component required. TOEFL required of all international applicants. High school diploma is required and GED is accepted. *Academic units required:* 4 English, 3 math, 3 science, 2 science labs, 3 foreign language, 2 social studies. *Academic units recommended:* 4 English, 4 math, 4 science, 3 science labs, 4 foreign language, 3 social studies.

Financial Aid

Students should submit: FAFSA. Regular filing deadline is 3/2. The Princeton Review suggests that all financial aid forms be submitted as soon as possible after October 1. *Need-based scholarships/grants offered:* Federal Pell, FSEOG, State scholarships/grants, Private scholarships, College/university scholarship or grant aid from institutional funds, Federal Nursing Scholarships. *Loan aid offered:* Direct Subsidized Stafford Loans, Direct Unsubsidized Stafford Loans, Direct PLUS loans, Federal Perkins Loans, College/university loans from institutional funds. Applicants will be notified of awards on a rolling basis beginning 3/1. Federal Work-Study Program available. Institutional employment available.

The Inside Word

Admissions officers at University of San Diego really aim to take a well-rounded approach to the application process. Hence, they thoroughly evaluate all aspects of a candidate's application, from test scores to personal statements and recommendations. Of course, since gaining admission to the university is competitive (each year USD admits less than half of those who apply), a strong academic showing is a must. And admissions officers really keep an eye out for students who demonstrate talent and leadership or who show genuine interest in participating in community service.

THE SCHOOL SAYS "..."

From the Admissions Office

"The University of San Diego has received many local, regional, and national honors in its short, sixty-year history. We are known around the world for our beautiful campus, our outstanding faculty, our sustainability efforts, study abroad programs and the community service work done by our students. Recently, USD was selected as a 'change maker' campus, one of only fourteen schools in the world so designated by the Ashoka Foundation. It is this honor that captures the spirit of USD and ties together all the others.

"We believe that the world's problems can be solved. We believe that the solution to these problems will not be found through a single discipline or focus. Instead, we know that the world's problems will be solved through innovation, collaboration, and compassion. USD was founded six decades ago with the principles of Catholic social teaching, a living tradition to work for socially just and peaceful societies and a mission to prepare generations of people changing the world for the better.

"We seek students who also believe in social innovation and change. Students at USD are bright, as our rapidly-growing student profile attests. But they also bring a passion for learning and making a difference. Through our strong liberal arts curriculum, international experiences, faculty and programs, we take that passion and turn it into a lifetime of making the world a better place."

SELECTIVITY
Admissions Rating	89
# of applicants	13,675
% of applicants accepted	52
% of acceptees attending	16
# offered a place on the wait list	1,133
% accepting a place on wait list	47
% admitted from wait list	64

FRESHMAN PROFILE
Range SAT Critical Reading	550–640
Range SAT Math	560–670
Range SAT Writing	540–650
Range ACT Composite	26–30
Minimum paper TOEFL	550
Minimum internet-based TOEFL	80
Average HS GPA	3.8
% graduated top 10% of class	36
% graduated top 25% of class	71
% graduated top 50% of class	91

DEADLINES
Regular	
Deadline	12/15
Nonfall registration?	Yes

APPLICANTS ALSO LOOK AT AND OFTEN PREFER
San Diego State University; University of California–Los Angeles; University of California–Santa Barbara; Loyola Marymount University; Santa Clara University; University of California–San Diego

AND SOMETIMES PREFER
University of California–Davis; University of California–Irvine; University of Arizona

AND RARELY PREFER
University of San Francisco

FINANCIAL FACTS
Financial Aid Rating	81
Annual tuition	$44,000
Room and board	$12,042
Required fees	$586
Books and supplies	$1,764
Average frosh need-based scholarship	$25,383
Average UG need-based scholarship	$25,010
% needy frosh rec. need-based scholarship or grant aid	96
% needy UG rec. need-based scholarship or grant aid	95
% needy frosh rec. non-need-based scholarship or grant aid	72
% needy UG rec. non-need-based scholarship or grant aid	50
% needy frosh rec. need-based self-help aid	72
% needy UG rec. need-based self-help aid	78
% frosh rec. any financial aid	84
% UG rec. any financial aid	73
% UG borrow to pay for school	51
Average cumulative indebtedness	$28,598
% frosh need fully met	15
% ugrads need fully met	13
Average % of frosh need met	73
Average % of ugrad need met	70

UNIVERSITY OF SAN FRANCISCO

2130 FULTON STREET, SAN FRANCISCO, CA 94117 • ADMISSIONS: 415-422-6563 • FAX: 415-422-2217

CAMPUS LIFE
Quality of Life Rating	91
Fire Safety Rating	60*
Green Rating	63
Type of school	Private
Affiliation	Roman Catholic
Environment	Metropolis

STUDENTS
Total undergrad enrollment	6,782
% male/female	38/62
% from out of state	20
% frosh from public high school	26
% frosh live on campus	94
% ugrads live on campus	32
# of fraternities (% ugrad men join)	3 (3)
# of sororities (% ugrad women join)	4 (4)
% African American	3
% Asian	21
% Caucasian	27
% Hispanic	20
% Native American	<1
% Pacific Islander	1
% Two or more races	7
% Race and/or ethnicity unknown	2
% international	19
# of countries represented	63

SURVEY SAYS...
Students are happy
Students love San Francisco, CA
Great off-campus food
Recreation facilities are great

ACADEMICS
Academic Rating	79
% students returning for sophomore year	83
% students graduating within 4 years	60
% students graduating within 6 years	71
Calendar	Semester
Student/faculty ratio	14:1
Profs interesting rating	85
Profs accessible rating	82

Most classes have 10–19 students.
Most lab/discussion sessions have 10–19 students.

MOST POPULAR MAJORS
Psychology; Business/Commerce

STUDENTS SAY "..."

Academics

Students find the quality of University of San Francisco's "location" to be inseparable from the school's "small-ish private liberal arts college" appeal: "San Francisco is a global city with a wealth of opportunity." However, USF is more than a "diverse education in an even more diverse setting" in its "dedication to social justice." "USF is known for its Jesuit pursuit of social justice, and does so through philanthropy and a relatively left and liberal style of teaching." Undergrads love USF's "small class sizes, good work opportunities in the city," and "comprehensive core curriculum." "USF is interested in developing the individual into a strong leader with a particular emphasis on the forces of self reflective and self awareness," and the school's "Jesuit education…is outstanding for students who care about their community and the world beyond themselves." Holding true to its command to students to "change the world from here," a USF education empowers students to make "an impact in the world in an area that you are passionate about." The "extremely talented, well-educated, hard-working, and passionate professors" are "well qualified and deeply care for my education," facilitating "fun and learning combined" in "interesting, engaging classes that are small." In class, students find "the opportunity to discuss, to ask questions, and to give feedback. It was not the professor's classroom, where the professor was controlling the classroom, it was our classroom, all of us together." Students are encouraged to think for themselves in an intellectual atmosphere that "emphasizes acceptance, diversity, and critical thinking." That said, the university offers plenty of support: "We have academic success advisers who help make sure we are on track with graduation, help with major changes, and choosing class schedules." USF's "very prestigious nursing program" and a "five-year program for obtaining a Masters in Education" stand out as major attractions, as do its "financial aid" resources.

Life

To many students, USF is all about "getting to know each other academically, socially and morally while allowing ourselves to get distracted by the city of San Francisco." One can't help but note that the campus is "in a beautiful location" that's "the ultimate city to be in as a young person," and "USF is located near the Haight, which means that there's always something to do even near the campus." "The Muni bus pass that USF gives you" makes it easy to get around the city (and also means that "public transportation becomes your best friend"), and "students very very often go off-campus on weekends to visit tourist attractions, go hiking, explore new food places, go shopping," "hit the nightclubs and bars around the city," and enjoy "concerts and trips to various museums, shows, and performances." "The city is full of activities and free, fun things to do," and "whether you enjoy hiking and nature (Golden Gate Park) or enjoy small coffee shops for a nice read, you'll always be able to find something." USF tends not to "care for Greek life/ sports," and on "weekends campus is barren because everyone is out exploring," but campus is still a "welcoming, second home for all of its students."

Student Body

At USF, students combine in "in one of the best cities in the world" to form what they perceive as "a culturally diverse community that teaches, respect, dignity, and honor for all individuals." They describe themselves and their peers as "artistic, smart, morally sound," "quirky and interesting." True to San Francisco's long history as a haven for all kinds of refugees and trailblazers, at USF, students will find a "very LGBT friendly environment" where it may even be "more normal to be diverse and weird or queer." Students "care about the community and believe in taking action to demonstrate their beliefs," and "the average student may be working for an NGO or volunteering regularly at one of the many nonprofits in San Francisco." They "come from all over the world," as well as from many "different cultural backgrounds and hobbies and interests," but hold a common interest of being "committed to their education" and, for the most part, "everyone gets along very well."

FINANCIAL AID: 415-422-6303 • E-MAIL: ADMISSION@USFCA.EDU • WEBSITE: WWW.USFCA.EDU

THE PRINCETON REVIEW SAYS

Admissions

Very important factors considered include: rigor of secondary school record, academic GPA, standardized test scores, application essay. *Important factors considered include:* class rank, recommendation(s), extracurricular activities, character/personal qualities, volunteer work. *Other factors considered include:* interview, talent/ability, first generation, alumni/ae relation, racial/ethnic status, work experience. SAT or ACT required. ACT with Writing required. SAT with Essay component required. TOEFL required of all international applicants. High school diploma is required and GED is accepted. *Academic units required:* 4 English, 3 math, 2 science, 2 foreign language, 3 social studies, 6 academic electives, and 2 units from above areas or other academic areas.

Financial Aid

Students should submit: FAFSA, CSS/Financial Aid PROFILE. Priority filing deadline is 2/1. The Princeton Review suggests that all financial aid forms be submitted as soon as possible after October 1. *Need-based scholarships/grants offered:* Federal Pell, FSEOG, State scholarships/grants, Private scholarships, College/university scholarship or grant aid from institutional funds, Federal Nursing Scholarships. *Loan aid offered:* Direct Subsidized Stafford Loans, Direct Unsubsidized Stafford Loans, Direct PLUS loans, Federal Perkins Loans, Federal Nursing Loans, College/university loans from institutional funds. Applicants will be notified of awards on a rolling basis beginning 4/1. Federal Work-Study Program available. Institutional employment available.

The Inside Word

Though it offers attractive financial aid packages in a gorgeous city, getting into USF isn't purely a competitive numbers game: successful applications show genuine intellectual and moral curiosity. Make sure there's real heart in your essay and recommendations. Also, interested students are encouraged to check out USF's early action and decision options, and their multicultural recruitment.

THE SCHOOL SAYS "..."

From the Admissions Office

"The University of San Francisco has experienced a significant increase in applications for admission over the past five years. We select applicants with strong academic credentials who will make the most of the university's academic opportunities, location in San Francisco, and its mission to educate minds and hearts to challenge the world. Community outreach and service to others, along with academic excellence, are characteristics that help distinguish those offered admission.

"The university has just completed a major upgrade to all administrative computer systems, including software that will help with student compatibility matching in residence halls.

"Applicants are required to take the SAT reasoning test (or the ACT with the writing section). The writing sections will be used for advising and placement purposes. SAT Subject Test scores will also be accepted."

SELECTIVITY

Admissions Rating	85
# of applicants	15,462
% of applicants accepted	64
% of acceptees attending	25
# offered a place on the wait list	1
% accepting a place on wait list	0
# of early decision applicants	62
% accepted early decision	58

FRESHMAN PROFILE

Range SAT Critical Reading	530–620
Range SAT Math	540–640
Range SAT Writing	520–620
Range ACT Composite	24–28
Minimum internet-based TOEFL	79
Average HS GPA	3.6
% graduated top 10% of class	25
% graduated top 25% of class	67
% graduated top 50% of class	94

DEADLINES

Early decision	
Deadline	11/15
Early action	
Deadline	11/15
Notification	12/31
Regular	
Priority	11/15
Deadline	1/15
Nonfall registration?	Yes

APPLICANTS ALSO LOOK AT AND OFTEN PREFER

University of California–Santa Barbara; Santa Clara University; Seattle University; University of California–Berkeley

AND SOMETIMES PREFER

University of Oregon

AND RARELY PREFER

Fordham University

FINANCIAL FACTS

Financial Aid Rating	73
Annual tuition	$44,040
Room and board	$13,990
Required fees	$454
Books and supplies	$1,600
Average frosh need-based scholarship	$23,776
Average UG need-based scholarship	$20,119
% needy frosh rec. need-based scholarship or grant aid	76
% needy UG rec. need-based scholarship or grant aid	84
% needy frosh rec. non-need-based scholarship or grant aid	82
% needy UG rec. non-need-based scholarship or grant aid	58
% needy frosh rec. need-based self-help aid	76
% needy UG rec. need-based self-help aid	81
% frosh rec. any financial aid	87
% UG rec. any financial aid	81
% UG borrow to pay for school	58
Average cumulative indebtedness	$33,851
% frosh need fully met	8
% ugrads need fully met	5

UNIVERSITY OF SCRANTON

800 LINDEN STREET, SCRANTON, PA 18510-4699 • ADMISSIONS: 570-941-7540 FAX: 570-941-5928

STUDENTS SAY ". . ."

Academics

The professors at the University of Scranton "really care about the students and always make themselves available to help students" and students feel that "they are a great asset to" the learning experience. With "an outstanding record for admission to graduate programs, not only in law and medicine but also in several other fields." The University of Scranton is a good fit for ambitious students seeking "a Jesuit school in every sense of the word. If you come here, expect to be challenged to become a better person, to develop a strong concern for the poor and marginalized, and to grow spiritually and intellectually." The school manages to accomplish this without "forcing religion upon you, which is nice." Undergraduates also approve of the mandatory liberal-arts-based curriculum that "forces you to learn about broader things than your own major." The professors "make class fun and interactive regardless of the difficulty of the class. There are a few odd-balls that are dry during lecture but this does not deter from the contents of their lectures." Students do feel that "there could be more communication between the three colleges to offer combined opportunities."

Life

The University of Scranton "offers many trips through various clubs and organizations as well as the University of Scranton Programming Board to offer students alternative plans on weekends. I have been on trips to NYC, the Bronx Zoo, and Philadelphia. I like to do community service, go out to eat, and shop for fun but many of the places I like to go to require busing or cars to get there," notes an Occupational Therapy major. Furthermore, "being a Jesuit school, social justice issues are huge. They are taught in the classroom, and students spend a lot of time volunteering." Hometown Scranton is big enough to provide "movie theaters, two malls, parks, a bowling alley, and a skiing/snowboarding mountain." There are, in short, plenty of choices for the non-partier at Scranton. Many we heard from in our survey reported busy extracurricular schedules. But those seeking a party won't be disappointed here, either. Scranton undergrads "party a lot, but they balance it with studying. Parties are chances to go out, see people, dance, and drink if you want." You "can find a party any time of day, seven days a week" here, usually with a keg tapped and pouring. Few here feel the party scene is out of hand, however a typical student writes, "It's very different than at schools with Greek systems. It is a lot more laid-back, and all about everyone having a good time."

Student Body

"There are a lot of different clubs and organizations for each individual to be a part of," and, while "the typical Scranton student is white, Catholic,...from the suburbs," and "preppy," students hasten to point out "within this sameness... there are people who couldn't care at all about religion, and there are people who are deeply religious. Even in the Catholic atmosphere of the school, the school only requires that you learn about Catholicism as it stands. Theology classes...are prefaced with the idea that 'You do not have to believe this!'" Students feel that the University of Scranton "is not very diverse." They point out that it's "just like every college, but better because there is no "in your face" Greek life, and no football team."

FINANCIAL AID: 570-941-7700 • E-MAIL: ADMISSIONS@SCRANTON.EDU • WEBSITE: WWW.SCRANTON.EDU

THE PRINCETON REVIEW SAYS

Admissions

Very important factors considered include: rigor of secondary school record, class rank, academic GPA, standardized test scores. *Important factors considered include:* extracurricular activities. *Other factors considered include:* application essay, recommendation(s), interview, talent/ability, character/personal qualities, alumni/ae relation, volunteer work, work experience, level of applicant's interest. SAT or ACT required. ACT with or without writing accepted. SAT with or without Essay component accepted. TOEFL required of all international applicants. High school diploma is required and GED is accepted. *Academic units required:* 4 English, 3 math, 1 science, 2 foreign language, 2 history, and 4 units from above areas or other academic areas. *Academic units recommended:* 4 English, 4 math, 2 science, 2 foreign language, 3 history, and 4 units from above areas or other academic areas.

Financial Aid

Students should submit: FAFSA. Priority filing deadline is 2/15. The Princeton Review suggests that all financial aid forms be submitted as soon as possible after October 1. *Need-based scholarships/grants offered:* Federal Pell, FSEOG, State scholarships/grants, Private scholarships, College/university scholarship or grant aid from institutional funds. *Loan aid offered:* Direct Subsidized Stafford Loans, Direct Unsubsidized Stafford Loans, Direct PLUS loans, Federal Perkins Loans. Applicants will be notified of awards on a rolling basis beginning 3/15. Federal Work-Study Program available. Institutional employment available.

The Inside Word

Admission to Scranton gets harder each year. A steady stream of smart kids from the tri-state area keeps classes full and the admit rate low. Successful applicants will need solid grades and test scores. As with many religiously affiliated schools, students should be a good match philosophically as well.

THE SCHOOL SAYS "..."

From the Admissions Office

"The University of Scranton is a Catholic and Jesuit institution known for the quality of its academic programs, campus life and commitment to service. Our fifty-eight-acre campus offers the best of both worlds—the city and the mountains. We are in the heart of the city of Scranton, in Pennsylvania's Pocono Northeast, just two hours from New York City and Philadelphia. In recent years, we have invested more than $204 million in campus improvements, including new residence halls, a science center and the state-of-the-art Leahy Hall, which houses our physical therapy, occupational therapy and exercise science departments.

"This university is more than a respected institution; it's also a caring, nurturing community whose graduates are known for their devotion to the welfare of other human beings and by their special commitment to the pursuit of social justice.

"We offer more than sixty majors, eighty clubs and organizations, and eighteen Division III athletic teams to the nearly 4,000 undergraduate students in attendance.

"Scranton develops leaders in every sense through rigorous preparation in students' chosen fields coupled with a commitment to educating the whole person in the liberal arts tradition. Students extend their academic experience through participation in honors programs, internships, faculty-student research and study abroad, and the university provides excellent preparation for medical and other health professions doctoral programs, law school, graduate school, and post-graduate fellowships and scholarships.

"Students can apply online for free at scranton.edu/apply, or schedule a visit online at scranton.edu/visit, or by calling us at 1-888-SCRANTON."

SELECTIVITY

Admissions Rating	84
# of applicants	10,049
% of applicants accepted	72
% of acceptees attending	13
# offered a place on the wait list	1,525
% accepting a place on wait list	35
% admitted from wait list	38

FRESHMAN PROFILE

Range SAT Critical Reading	510–610
Range SAT Math	520–620
Range ACT Composite	22–28
Minimum internet-based TOEFL	80
Average HS GPA	3.4
% graduated top 10% of class	34
% graduated top 25% of class	62
% graduated top 50% of class	88

DEADLINES

Early action	
Deadline	11/15
Notification	12/15
Regular	
Deadline	3/1
Nonfall registration?	Yes

APPLICANTS ALSO LOOK AT AND OFTEN PREFER

Penn State University Park; University of Delaware; Quinnipiac University

AND SOMETIMES PREFER

Loyola University Maryland; Marist

FINANCIAL FACTS

Financial Aid Rating	81
Annual tuition	$41,762
Room and board	$14,744
Required fees	$450
Books and supplies	$1,300
Average frosh need-based scholarship	$23,875
Average UG need-based scholarship	$21,367
% needy frosh rec. need-based scholarship or grant aid	96
% needy UG rec. need-based scholarship or grant aid	95
% needy frosh rec. non-need-based scholarship or grant aid	12
% needy UG rec. non-need-based scholarship or grant aid	8
% needy frosh rec. need-based self-help aid	79
% needy UG rec. need-based self-help aid	84
% frosh rec. any financial aid	96
% UG rec. any financial aid	96
% UG borrow to pay for school	78
Average cumulative indebtedness	$40,640
% frosh need fully met	13
% ugrads need fully met	12
Average % of frosh need met	71
Average % of ugrad need met	68

UNIVERSITY OF SOUTH CAROLINA—COLUMBIA

OFFICE OF UNDERGRADUATE ADMISSIONS, COLUMBIA, SC 29208 • ADMISSIONS: 803-777-7700 • FAX: 803-777-0101

CAMPUS LIFE

Quality of Life Rating	90
Fire Safety Rating	96
Green Rating	94
Type of school	Public
Affiliation	No Affiliation
Environment	City

STUDENTS

Total undergrad enrollment	25,237
% male/female	46/54
% from out of state	39
% frosh live on campus	92
% ugrads live on campus	29
# of fraternities (% ugrad men join)	22 (17)
# of sororities (% ugrad women join)	16 (35)
% African American	9
% Asian	3
% Caucasian	76
% Hispanic	4
% Native American	<1
% Pacific Islander	<1
% Two or more races	4
% Race and/or ethnicity unknown	1
% international	2
# of countries represented	115

SURVEY SAYS...

Students are happy
Students love Columbia, SC
Recreation facilities are great
Everyone loves the Fighting Gamecocks
Frats and sororities are popular

ACADEMICS

Academic Rating	75
% students returning for sophomore year	88
% students graduating within 4 years	55
% students graduating within 6 years	72
Calendar	Semester
Student/faculty ratio	19:1
Profs interesting rating	75
Profs accessible rating	73

Most classes have 20–29 students.
Most lab/discussion sessions have
20–29 students.

MOST POPULAR MAJORS

Experimental Psychology; Registered Nursing/
Registered Nurse; Criminal Justice/Law
Enforcement Administration

STUDENTS SAY ". . ."

Academics

More than 200 years of southern traditions and academic leadership provide the foundation for the University of South Carolina—Columbia, a historic institution that is "constantly working on being the absolute best university it can be for its students" and "open to any suggestions." The school provides "a wealth of opportunities for undergraduate research, study abroad, service learning, and unique organizations," and advisors and the Student Success Center are "always looking to help" students find post-graduation plans. "The University of South Carolina is about what you make it, as the university provides opportunities for everyone to make the absolute most of their time here," says one student.

Those who teach here are "intent on getting their students involved outside of the classroom," and "able to relate their in-class lectures to the real world." "I've had a ton of professors present me with opportunities for research, internship, or part-time employment on campus which has all developed me into being a very employable prospect upon graduation," says one student. While classes "can sometimes be very difficult," there are tutors and supplemental instructors through the university ("for free!") who "will always fill in the gaps that you are missing." USC's size "lends itself to interdisciplinary degree programs and individual projects," and faculty fosters academic exploration in asking for student opinions and "[encouraging] us to argue and consider other students' opinions."

Life

The students at the University of South Carolina are "extraordinarily social:" "From tailgates to intramural sports to Greek life, there is always something to do." Saturday football games are such a tradition that "traffic patterns are altered because it is such a huge deal." Traditions are "highly important" to the school, and events such as Tiger Burn and Homecoming are dotted throughout the year. Greene Street (the main street on campus) is closed off to traffic 24/7, which allows students to walk freely between classes and also allows organizations and activities such as Hip Hop Wednesdays and a farmer's market to take place. The weather is usually beautiful, and many students can be found "sitting on the horseshoe between classes or grabbing a bite to eat" or availing themselves of the "ton of outdoor recreation activities run through the university."

On the weekends, many upperclassmen spend time in Five Points, a "very student-friendly bar district beside campus," and Columbia's central location "grants shorter distances to the beach as well as the mountains"; the town itself is very easy to get around on foot and "very artsy." There is "literally a club for everything," from "skydiving to latin dance to language," and service opportunities are also very popular. Additionally, the amenities that USC provides are "phenomenal," and include everything from "free athletic tickets to twelve free counseling sessions a year." USC really cares about the well-being and safety of its students, and "offers so many things to help the students here to succeed."

Student Body

This medium-sized, genteel Southern institution is "all about being a family and feeling like the University of South Carolina is your home away from home." There is a "good mix" of people of different ethnicity, genders, and personalities, and a lot of the student body is "relatively laid-back in dress and attitude." There is "certainly that southern charm, especially because of the large greek population" on campus, and this is "a unified student body in relation to each other and between students and faculty and staff." "The university welcomes everyone with open arms to make everyone feel included in the Gamecock experience," says a student.

UNIVERSITY OF SOUTH CAROLINA—COLUMBIA

FINANCIAL AID: 803-777-8134 • E-MAIL: ADMISSIONS-UGRAD@SC.EDU • WEBSITE: WWW.SC.EDU

THE PRINCETON REVIEW SAYS

Admissions

Very important factors considered include: academic GPA, application essay. *Important factors considered include:* rigor of secondary school record. *Other factors considered include:* class rank, standardized test scores, recommendation(s), extracurricular activities, talent/ability, character/personal qualities, first generation, state residency, volunteer work, work experience. SAT or ACT required. TOEFL required of all international applicants. High school diploma is required and GED is accepted. *Academic units required:* 4 English, 4 math, 3 science, 3 science labs, 2 foreign language, 2 social studies, 1 history, 1 academic elective, 1 visual/performing arts, and 1 unit from above areas or other academic areas.

Financial Aid

Students should submit: FAFSA. Priority filing deadline is 4/1. The Princeton Review suggests that all financial aid forms be submitted as soon as possible after October 1. *Need-based scholarships/grants offered:* Federal Pell, FSEOG, State scholarships/grants, Private scholarships, College/university scholarship or grant aid from institutional funds, United Negro College Fund, Federal Nursing Scholarships. *Loan aid offered:* Direct Subsidized Stafford Loans, Direct Unsubsidized Stafford Loans, Direct PLUS loans, Federal Perkins Loans, Federal Nursing Loans. Applicants will be notified of awards on a rolling basis beginning 4/1. Federal Work-Study Program available. Institutional employment available.

The Inside Word

At University of South Carolina, as at most large schools, admissions decisions are based almost entirely on a prospective student's grades, test scores, and high school curriculum. A personal statement is required. Applicants with an A-minus average and SAT scores (Critical Reading plus Math) in the 1150–1280 range (or an ACT composite of 25–30) often get in. Higher standardized scores can offset a lower GPA, and vice versa.

THE SCHOOL SAYS "..."

From the Admissions Office

"In just six years, the number of annual undergraduate applicants to USC has doubled, making it more critical than ever for students to meet the university's regular application deadline. The University of South Carolina is a destination of choice for students from all fifty states and more than 100 countries. USC is one of only forty public research institutions to earn both the top-tier research classification and the community service classification from the Carnegie Foundation. As early as their freshman year, undergraduates are encouraged to compete for research grants. As South Carolina's flagship institution, USC offers more than 350 degree programs. More than 30,000 students seek baccalaureate, masters, or doctoral degrees. USC is known for its top-ranked academic programs, including its international business and exercise science programs—both rated number one nationally. Other notable programs include chemical and nuclear engineering; health education; hotel, restaurant, and tourism; marine science; law; medicine; nursing; and psychology, among others. USC is recognized for its pioneering efforts in freshman outreach, and the South Carolina Honors College is ranked number one in the country compared to all other honors colleges in public university settings. USC offers student support in such areas as career development, leadership training, research grants, pre-professional planning, and study abroad. On campus, students enjoy a state-of-the-art fitness center, an 18,000-seat arena, an 80,000-seat stadium, and more than 400 student organizations. Off campus, South Carolina's world-famous beaches and the Blue Ridge Mountains are each less than a three-hour drive away. The University of South Carolina is located in the state's capital city, making it a great place for internships and job opportunities."

SELECTIVITY

Admissions Rating	87
# of applicants	25,738
% of applicants accepted	65
% of acceptees attending	31
# offered a place on the wait list	1,032

FRESHMAN PROFILE

Range SAT Critical Reading	550–640
Range SAT Math	560–650
Range ACT Composite	25–30
Minimum paper TOEFL	550
Minimum internet-based TOEFL	77
Average HS GPA	4.2
% graduated top 10% of class	30
% graduated top 25% of class	65
% graduated top 50% of class	94

DEADLINES

Early action	
Deadline	10/15
Notification	12/15
Regular	
Deadline	12/1
Notification	3/15
Nonfall registration?	Yes

APPLICANTS ALSO LOOK AT AND OFTEN PREFER
The University of North Carolina at Chapel Hill

AND SOMETIMES PREFER
Clemson University

AND RARELY PREFER
Wake Forest University

FINANCIAL FACTS

Financial Aid Rating	83
Annual in-state tuition	$11,082
Annual out-of-state tuition	$29,898
Room and board	$9,872
Required fees	$400
Books and supplies	$1,008
Average frosh need-based scholarship	$5,174
Average UG need-based scholarship	$4,973
% needy frosh rec. need-based scholarship or grant aid	36
% needy UG rec. need-based scholarship or grant aid	55
% needy frosh rec. non-need-based scholarship or grant aid	88
% needy UG rec. non-need-based scholarship or grant aid	73
% needy frosh rec. need-based self-help aid	69
% needy UG rec. need-based self-help aid	93
% frosh rec. any financial aid	96
% UG rec. any financial aid	87
% frosh need fully met	30
% ugrads need fully met	27
Average % of frosh need met	68
Average % of ugrad need met	78

THE UNIVERSITY OF SOUTH DAKOTA

414 EAST CLARK, VERMILLION, SD 57069 • ADMISSIONS: 605-677-5434 • FAX: 605-677-6323

CAMPUS LIFE

Quality of Life Rating	83
Fire Safety Rating	98
Green Rating	67
Type of school	Public
Affiliation	No Affiliation
Environment	Village

STUDENTS

Total undergrad enrollment	7,541
% male/female	37/63
% from out of state	33
% frosh from public high school	75
% frosh live on campus	90
% ugrads live on campus	33
# of fraternities (% ugrad men join)	7 (20)
# of sororities (% ugrad women join)	3 (12)
% African American	2
% Asian	1
% Caucasian	87
% Hispanic	3
% Native American	2
% Pacific Islander	<1
% Two or more races	3
% Race and/or ethnicity unknown	<1
% international	2
# of countries represented	46

SURVEY SAYS...

Lots of beer drinking
Campus newspaper is popular
Great library

ACADEMICS

Academic Rating	70
% students returning for sophomore year	75
% students graduating within 4 years	33
% students graduating within 6 years	57
Calendar	4/1/4
Student/faculty ratio	17:1
Profs interesting rating	72
Profs accessible rating	68

Most classes have 10–19 students.
Most lab/discussion sessions have 20–29 students.

MOST POPULAR MAJORS

Psychology; Business/Commerce; Education

STUDENTS SAY "..."

Academics

With an honors program that is "the best-kept secret in the country" and professors who are "nearly always willing to go the extra mile for students," the University of South Dakota offers a "great student to faculty communicative experience at a reasonable price." Numerous departments garner praise from students, and the University boasts winners "almost every year for big scholarships like the Goldwater and Truman, competing with big, Ivy League, private colleges that charge quadruple the amount for the same education." While the nursing school is the most frequently praised, the "business, biology, premed, law, and psychology classes are very solid," and the "dental hygiene, music, and journalism schools" also stand out, with the most copious laurels heaped on the music department's professors who are "some of the best." All told, the wide selection of quality academics "gives students many options as far as majors go," and for students willing to throw themselves into their studies "the odds of getting into a professional or graduate program are good."

Life

"We work hard, so we can play hard," sums up the undergraduate philosophy at USD. "Although there is a lot of partying that happens, the students keep themselves occupied with school work, intramural sports, and hanging out with their friends." Vermillion's small size seems to be a double-edged sword; some insist that "the size of the town means no one is more than a 10-minute walk/bike ride away!" and that "since it is a smaller campus students have more opportunities to be involved in internships and various other activities." But the fact remains that "many of the upperclassmen live in the larger cities to the north and south." In general, "students have to make their own fun, which often involves partying or taking small road trips to other cities in the area." For those planning to roam further afield, "Vermillion is located very close to Yankton, Sioux City (IA), and Sioux Falls (all within an hour). They are bigger cities and offer everything a person would want to do (shopping, movies, entertainment)."

Student Body

A typical USD student "would be a conservative Midwesterner. He or she would be Caucasian" and would most likely have originated in "small towns in South Dakota, Iowa, and Nebraska." "Many people join a Greek system or are athletes or musicians. Those who do not fit into these three main groups seem to focus on their academics" and "[fit] in fine with the majority because of the open mindedness of most students." For example, "gay students are able to get along with the rest of student population." There's no denying that "partying is a definite part of the culture, though many of the 'smart' kids both party and work hard." Student organizations call out to many, and "it seems like every person on campus is part of at least one of them. It is a great way to meet new people and [to participate in] activities."

FINANCIAL AID: 605-677-5446 • E-MAIL: ADMISSIONS@USD.EDU • WEBSITE: WWW.USD.EDU

THE PRINCETON REVIEW SAYS

Admissions

Very important factors considered include: rigor of secondary school record, class rank, academic GPA, standardized test scores. *Important factors considered include:* alumni/ae relation. *Other factors considered include:* application essay, recommendation(s), extracurricular activities, talent/ability, character/personal qualities, geographical residence, state residency, racial/ethnic status, volunteer work, work experience. SAT or ACT required. ACT with or without writing accepted. TOEFL required of all international applicants. High school diploma is required and GED is accepted. *Academic units required:* 4 English, 3 math, 3 science labs, 3 social studies. *Academic units recommended:* 4 math, 4 science, 2 foreign language, and 1 unit from above areas or other academic areas.

Financial Aid

Students should submit: FAFSA. Priority filing deadline is 3/15. The Princeton Review suggests that all financial aid forms be submitted as soon as possible after October 1. *Need-based scholarships/grants offered:* Federal Pell, FSEOG, Private scholarships, College/university scholarship or grant aid from institutional funds, Federal Nursing Scholarships. *Loan aid offered:* Federal Perkins Loans, Federal Nursing Loans, College/university loans from institutional funds. Applicants will be notified of awards on a rolling basis beginning 3/1. Federal Work-Study Program available. Institutional employment available.

The Inside Word

To be a candidate for general admission to USD, you must meet one of three general requirements: rank in the top 50 percent of your graduating class or obtain an ACT/SAT composite score of 21/990 or higher or have a minimum grade point average of at least 2.6 on a 4.0 scale in all high school courses. An applicant's high school curricula must also meet certain minimum requirements.

THE SCHOOL SAYS "..."

From the Admissions Office

"The University of South Dakota is the perfect fit for students looking for a smart educational investment. USD is South Dakota's only designated liberal arts university and is consistently rated among the top doctoral institutions in the country. Annually, USD awards scholarships to more than 800 first-year students, and more than 80 percent of USD students receive some form of financial aid through grants, loans, and work-study jobs.

"USD students earn the nation's most prestigious scholarships. Our quality of teaching and research prepares students to pursue their passions all over the world, at institutions such as Columbia, Johns Hopkins, The University of Chicago, and beyond. Fifty-nine students have been awarded prestigious Fulbright, Rhodes, National Science Foundation, Boren, Truman, Udall, Gilman, and Goldwater scholarships and grants for graduate study. Personal attention from our award-winning faculty and our welcoming environment makes students feel right at home.

"As the flagship liberal arts institution in South Dakota, USD—founded in 1862—has long been regarded as a leader in the state and the region. Notable undergraduate and postgraduate alumni include journalist Ken Bode, author and former news anchor Tom Brokaw, writer and Emmy Award–winner Dorothy Cooper Foote, U.S. Senator Tim Johnson, USA Today founder Al Neuharth, and U.S. Senator John Thune.

"Applicants are not required to take the writing test for either SAT or ACT. USD recommends taking the ACT over the SAT. Students who wish to send their SAT scores will have their scores converted to ACT scores for placement and scholarship consideration."

SELECTIVITY
Admissions Rating	74
# of applicants	3,542
% of applicants accepted	89
% of acceptees attending	40

FRESHMAN PROFILE
Range SAT Critical Reading	400–440
Range SAT Math	470–610
Range SAT Writing	410–510
Range ACT Composite	20–25
Minimum paper TOEFL	550
Minimum internet-based TOEFL	81
Average HS GPA	3.4
% graduated top 10% of class	15
% graduated top 25% of class	37
% graduated top 50% of class	72

DEADLINES
Nonfall registration?	Yes

APPLICANTS ALSO LOOK AT AND OFTEN PREFER
University of Nebraska–Lincoln

FINANCIAL FACTS
Financial Aid Rating	87
Annual in-state tuition	$4,164
Annual out-of-state tuition	$6,246
Room and board	$7,089
Required fees	$3,858
Books and supplies	$1,100
Average frosh need-based scholarship	$4,444
Average UG need-based scholarship	$4,192
% needy frosh rec. need-based scholarship or grant aid	47
% needy UG rec. need-based scholarship or grant aid	50
% needy frosh rec. non-need-based scholarship or grant aid	90
% needy UG rec. non-need-based scholarship or grant aid	59
% needy frosh rec. need-based self-help aid	80
% needy UG rec. need-based self-help aid	86
% frosh rec. any financial aid	94
% UG rec. any financial aid	81
% frosh need fully met	58
% ugrads need fully met	59
Average % of frosh need met	78
Average % of ugrad need met	77

UNIVERSITY OF SOUTH FLORIDA

4202 EAST FOWLER AVENUE, TAMPA, FL 33620-9951 • ADMISSIONS: 813-974-3350 • FAX: 813-974-9689

STUDENTS SAY "..."

Academics

Conveniently located in Tampa, Florida, this top-tier state university attracts students for whom "price, diversity, and opportunities" are as important as a location that's "close to home." The University of South Florida "is all about community." One student says, "It was close to home, offered the degree that I wanted, offered me the most financial aid, and had many ties to the community and surrounding areas culturally and academically." USF may be huge, but this "does not affect the level of personal attention that students receive." Many here laud the honors program: "Classes are almost always discussion-based." In general, professors here "really want you to succeed." Students universally cheer, "The campus is beautiful!" Most of the professors "have worked twenty plus years in the field and are not strictly academia experienced, which results in more content-related discussions." Another adds, "Most professors, especially the business and philosophy related people, know their material and provide an open forum for learning." The College of Education has a sterling reputation for building "a caring community that expects excellence." With a large commuter population, there's a great diversity in the student body, "not just ethnically or culturally, but older students that bring experience and students from all socioeconomic levels." In addition, USF "is a top school for medical-related studies." USF offers the total package: "Fair tuition prices, a great city/location, excellent professors and [an excellent] learning atmosphere." USF is "doing everything within its capacity to provide the best education it can to every student, regardless of major, background, or ethnicity." This is an institution "dedicated to enriching their students and communities lives through eclectic methods."

Life

Life at USF "strongly promotes building a cohesive, comfortable community." The university enjoys "a diverse student population on a beautiful urban campus surrounded by a bustling city." Tampa "has a lot to offer for students. USF has so many clubs that each have various events, there is always something going on." Popular recreations include the "flea markets, poster sales, Patio Tuesdays (social event in the student center), clubs and organizations, free speech areas, residence hall parties, coffee houses, performances put on by the orchestras, bands, and theater, sports (Go Bulls!), guest speakers, etc." Many students enjoy the bustling club scene in Ybor City, a historic-district-turned-night-clubbing-district in Tampa's Latin Quarter where "there are a plethora of local bars and clubs to hang out at for fun."

Student Body

The USF student body is "a diverse mix socioeconomically, culturally, religiously, and racially." As one returning student testifies, "I am a non-traditional student in my fifties, and [I] feel completely comfortable in classes with students half my age. It's a very friendly school. All walks of life. I could not describe a typical student." USF "is a huge university." Every student "is completely different, so it's impossible to describe a 'typical' one." This makes for a welcome mix of professional and extracurricular interests; "So far, in every class it's been incredibly easy to get along with other classmates and everyone is really accepting of each other, no matter your background." As is often noted at many large universities with an active nightlife, "most people here have two personalities. One is extremely studious persona and the other is a party animal. Basically when it's time to let loose we let loose." On-campus students "are involved in campus and community activities, friendly, busy, and often have active social lives." There's "a strong sense of community fostered by club and organization involvement." USF "offers plenty of places to gather on campus." Despite the size of the school, social life is filled by "all sorts of activities and organizations that make it very easy to interact with people who share your views and interests."

FINANCIAL AID: 813-974-4700 • E-MAIL: ADMISSIONS@USF.EDU • WEBSITE: WWW.USF.EDU

THE PRINCETON REVIEW SAYS

Admissions

Very important factors considered include: rigor of secondary school record, academic GPA. *Important factors considered include:* standardized test scores, first generation. *Other factors considered include:* application essay, recommendation(s), extracurricular activities, talent/ability, character/personal qualities, geographical residence, state residency, volunteer work, work experience. SAT or ACT required. ACT with Writing required. TOEFL required of all international applicants. High school diploma is required and GED is accepted. *Academic units required:* 4 English, 4 math, 3 science, 2 science labs, 2 foreign language, 3 social studies, 3 academic electives. *Academic units recommended:* 4 English, 4 math, 4 science, 3 science labs, 4 foreign language, 3 social studies, 3 academic electives.

Financial Aid

Students should submit: FAFSA. Priority filing deadline is 3/1. The Princeton Review suggests that all financial aid forms be submitted as soon as possible after October 1. *Need-based scholarships/grants offered:* Federal Pell, FSEOG, State scholarships/grants, Private scholarships, College/university scholarship or grant aid from institutional funds. *Loan aid offered:* Direct Subsidized Stafford Loans, Direct Unsubsidized Stafford Loans, Direct PLUS loans, Federal Perkins Loans, College/university loans from institutional funds. Applicants will be notified of awards on a rolling basis beginning 3/1. Federal Work-Study Program available. Institutional employment available.

The Inside Word

A traditional college-prep high school course load is required for admission to USF. Beyond making sure that you complete all prerequisite classes, however, keep two other things in mind when applying to USF. First, admissions decisions are made on a rolling basis, so the earlier one applies, the better his or her chance of acceptance since there are more unfilled seats early in the admissions cycle. Second, AP and international baccalaureate classes are looked on favorably in the admissions office, so if your school offers them, load up on them and do well.

THE SCHOOL SAYS "..."

From the Admissions Office

"Located in the Tampa Bay metropolitan area, USF is recognized as a top-fifty public research university. USF takes great pride in its global faculty. Professors in all academic areas are responsible for discovering new solutions to existing and emerging problems. As an undergraduate at USF, you can participate actively in the creation of the knowledge that will be taught on other college campuses for decades to come. The faculty at USF is diverse as well.

"As students begin the application process, they should become familiar with USF's admission requirements. USF used extensive institutional research to validate that the high school GPA coupled with grade trends and the rigor of student's curriculum in high school are the most critical factors in student academic success at USF. Preference in admission, therefore, is given to students who complete at least three AP or IB courses, at least two college-level courses through dual enrollment, and additional coursework in math, science or foreign language beyond minimum requirements. SAT and ACT scores, while important, are less critical in USF's admission decisions when the high school GPA and rigor of curriculum are both strong. USF does use the SAT writing and the ACT English/writing components to make decisions, as scores of 550 and 24 respectively are additional indicators of potential for academic success. USF also takes into account special talents in and outside of the classroom as well as whether a student would be in the first generation of the family to attend college. With some of the best weather in the country, it's always a great time to visit USF. Campus tours, information sessions and tours of the residence halls are offered on weekdays throughout the year and on most Saturday mornings from September through April. Reservations are strongly encouraged."

SELECTIVITY

Admissions Rating	88
# of applicants	30,386
% of applicants accepted	45
% of acceptees attending	30

FRESHMAN PROFILE

Range SAT Critical Reading	530–630
Range SAT Math	540–640
Range SAT Writing	510–600
Range ACT Composite	24–28
Minimum paper TOEFL	550
Minimum internet-based TOEFL	79
Average HS GPA	3.9
% graduated top 10% of class	34
% graduated top 25% of class	59
% graduated top 50% of class	69

DEADLINES

Regular	
Priority	3/1
Deadline	3/1
Notification	4/15
Nonfall registration?	Yes

APPLICANTS ALSO LOOK AT AND OFTEN PREFER
University of Florida

AND SOMETIMES PREFER
Florida State University; University of Central Florida

FINANCIAL FACTS

Financial Aid Rating	80
Annual in-state tuition	$4,559
Annual out-of-state tuition	$15,474
Room and board	$9,400
Required fees	$1,851
Books and supplies	$1,200
Average frosh need-based scholarship	$9,173
Average UG need-based scholarship	$7,169
% needy frosh rec. need-based scholarship or grant aid	88
% needy UG rec. need-based scholarship or grant aid	87
% needy frosh rec. non-need-based scholarship or grant aid	7
% needy UG rec. non-need-based scholarship or grant aid	4
% needy frosh rec. need-based self-help aid	55
% needy UG rec. need-based self-help aid	63
% frosh rec. any financial aid	70
% UG rec. any financial aid	66
% UG borrow to pay for school	60
Average cumulative indebtedness	$22,899
% frosh need fully met	15
% ugrads need fully met	11
Average % of frosh need met	66
Average % of ugrad need met	60

UNIVERSITY OF SOUTHERN CALIFORNIA

OFFICE OF ADMISSION/JOHN HUBBARD HALL, LOS ANGELES, CA 90089-0911 • ADMISSIONS: 213-740-1111 • FAX: 213-821-0200

CAMPUS LIFE

Quality of Life Rating	84
Fire Safety Rating	97
Green Rating	83
Type of school	Private
Affiliation	No Affiliation
Environment	Metropolis

STUDENTS

Total undergrad enrollment	18,810
% male/female	49/51
% from out of state	32
% frosh from public high school	54
% frosh live on campus	98
% ugrads live on campus	30
# of fraternities (% ugrad men join)	32 (26)
# of sororities (% ugrad women join)	26 (27)
% African American	4
% Asian	22
% Caucasian	40
% Hispanic	14
% Native American	<1
% Pacific Islander	<1
% Two or more races	5
% Race and/or ethnicity unknown	1
% international	13
# of countries represented	114

SURVEY SAYS...
Students are happy
Everyone loves the Trojans
Campus newspaper is popular
Alumni active on campus

ACADEMICS

Academic Rating	81
% students returning for sophomore year	96
% students graduating within 4 years	77
% students graduating within 6 years	92
Calendar	Semester
Student/faculty ratio	9:1
Profs interesting rating	70
Profs accessible rating	67

Most classes have 10–19 students.
Most lab/discussion sessions have
20–29 students.

MOST POPULAR MAJORS
Social Sciences; Visual and Performing Arts;
Business Administration and Management

STUDENTS SAY "..."

Academics
The University of Southern California boasts "a dynamic and culturally diverse campus located in a world-class city which is equally dynamic and culturally diverse." Everything related to cinema is "top notch." Among the other 150 or so majors here, programs in journalism, business, engineering, and architecture are particularly notable. The honors programs are "very good," too. One of the best perks about USC is its "large and enthusiastic alumni network." Becoming "part of the Trojan Family" is a great way to jump-start your career because USC graduates love to hire other USC graduates. "Almost everyone talks about getting job offers based solely on going to USC." "The school seems to run very smoothly, with few administrative issues ever being problematic enough to reach the awareness of the USC student community," says an international relations major. The top brass "is a bit mysterious and heavy handed," though. Also, "they milk every dime they can get from you." Academically, some students call the general education courses "a complete waste of time." There are a few "real narcissists" on the faculty as well as some professors "who seem to just be there because they want to do research." Overall, though, students report professors "make the subject matter come alive" and make themselves "very available" outside the classroom. "My academic experience at USC is fabulous," gushes an aerospace engineering major. "I would not choose any other school."

Life
On campus, life is "vibrant." There are more than 850 student organizations. Theatrical and musical productions are "excellent." School spirit is "extreme" and "infectious." "Football games are huge." "There is absolutely nothing that can top watching our unbelievable football team throttle the competition," says a merciless sophomore. "Drinking is a big part of the social scene" as well. "We definitely have some of the sickest parties ever," claims an impressed freshman. "Greek life is very big" and, on the weekends, a strong contingent of students "religiously" visits "The Row, the street lined with all the fraternity and sorority houses." Students also have "the sprawling city of Los Angeles as their playground." It's an "eclectic place with both high and low culture and some of the best shopping in the world." "Hollywood clubs and downtown bars" are popular destinations. Art exhibits, concerts, and "hip restaurants" are everywhere. However, "you need a car." Los Angeles traffic may be "a buzz kill" but students report that it's considerably preferable to the "absolutely terrible" public transportation system.

Student Body
The one thing that unites everyone here is "tons of Trojan pride." USC students are also "intensely ambitious" and, while there are some "complete slackers," many students hit the books "harder than they let on." Otherwise, students insist that, "contrary to popular belief, USC has immense diversity." "The stereotypical USC student is a surfer fraternity bro or a tan, trendy sorority girl from the O.C." You'll find plenty of those. Many students are also "extremely good looking." "No one cares what your orientation is," says a first-year student. There are "prissy Los Angeles types" and "spoiled" kids. In some circles, "family income and the brands of clothes you wear definitely matter." However, "though there are quite a few who come from mega wealth, there are also many who are here on a great deal of financial aid." There are "lots of nerds," too, and a smattering of "band geeks and film freaks."

UNIVERSITY OF SOUTHERN CALIFORNIA

FINANCIAL AID: 213-740-1111 • E-MAIL: ADMITUSC@USC.EDU • WEBSITE: WWW.USC.EDU

THE PRINCETON REVIEW SAYS

Admissions

Very important factors considered include: rigor of secondary school record, academic GPA, standardized test scores, application essay, recommendation(s). *Important factors considered include:* extracurricular activities, talent/ability. *Other factors considered include:* class rank, interview, character/personal qualities, first generation, alumni/ae relation, racial/ethnic status, volunteer work, work experience. SAT or ACT required; SAT Subject Tests considered if submitted. ACT with or without writing accepted. SAT with or without Essay component accepted. TOEFL required of all international applicants. High school diploma is required and GED is not accepted. *Academic units required:* 4 English, 3 math, 2 science, 2 science labs, 2 foreign language, 2 social studies, 3 academic electives. *Academic units recommended:* 4 English, 4 math, 3 science, 3 science labs, 3 foreign language, 3 social studies, 3 academic electives.

Financial Aid

Students should submit: FAFSA, CSS/Financial Aid PROFILE, Noncustodial PROFILE, Business/Farm Supplement. Priority filing deadline is 2/16. The Princeton Review suggests that all financial aid forms be submitted as soon as possible after October 1. *Need-based scholarships/grants offered:* Federal Pell, FSEOG, State scholarships/grants, Private scholarships, College/university scholarship or grant aid from institutional funds. *Loan aid offered:* Direct Subsidized Stafford Loans, Direct Unsubsidized Stafford Loans, Direct PLUS loans, Federal Perkins Loans, College/university loans from institutional funds. Applicants will be notified of awards on or about 4/1. Federal Work-Study Program available. Institutional employment available.

The Inside Word

USC doesn't have the toughest admissions standards in California but it's up there. Your grades and test scores need to be outstanding to compete. Even if you are a borderline candidate, though, USC is certainly worth a shot. Few schools on the planet have a better alumni network and the "Trojan Family" really does create all kinds of opportunities for its members upon graduation.

THE SCHOOL SAYS "..."

From the Admissions Office

"One of the best ways to discover if USC is right for you is to walk around campus, talk to students, and get a feel for the area both as a place to study and a place to live. If you can't visit, we hold admission information programs around the country. Watch your mailbox for an invitation, or send us an e-mail if you're interested.

"Freshman applicants are required to submit a standardized writing exam. We will accept either the SAT or the ACT with its optional writing section."

SELECTIVITY

Admissions Rating	98
# of applicants	51,924
% of applicants accepted	18
% of acceptees attending	32

FRESHMAN PROFILE

Range SAT Critical Reading	620–730
Range SAT Math	650–770
Range SAT Writing	650–750
Range ACT Composite	30–33
Average HS GPA	3.7
% graduated top 10% of class	88
% graduated top 25% of class	97
% graduated top 50% of class	100

DEADLINES

Regular	
Priority	12/1
Deadline	1/15
Notification	4/1
Nonfall registration?	Yes

APPLICANTS ALSO LOOK AT AND OFTEN PREFER

Columbia University; Duke University; Harvard College; Stanford University; Yale University; University of Pennsylvania

AND SOMETIMES PREFER

Cornell University; Northwestern University; University of California–Berkeley; Washington University in St. Louis; Brown University; University of California–Los Angeles

AND RARELY PREFER

New York University; University of California–San Diego; University of Michigan–Ann Arbor; Boston University; University of Washington; University of California–Santa Barbara

FINANCIAL FACTS

Financial Aid Rating	93
Annual tuition	$49,464
Room and board	$13,855
Required fees	$746
Books and supplies	$1,500
Average frosh need-based scholarship	$34,948
Average UG need-based scholarship	$32,291
% needy frosh rec. need-based scholarship or grant aid	86
% needy UG rec. need-based scholarship or grant aid	91
% needy frosh rec. non-need-based scholarship or grant aid	62
% needy UG rec. non-need-based scholarship or grant aid	46
% needy frosh rec. need-based self-help aid	89
% needy UG rec. need-based self-help aid	94
% frosh rec. any financial aid	68
% UG rec. any financial aid	65
% UG borrow to pay for school	44
Average cumulative indebtedness	$27,925
% frosh need fully met	98
% ugrads need fully met	93
Average % of frosh need met	100
Average % of ugrad need met	100

THE UNIVERSITY OF TAMPA

401 WEST KENNEDY BOULEVARD, TAMPA, FL 33606-1490 • ADMISSIONS: 813-253-6211 • FAX: 813-258-7398

STUDENTS SAY "..."

Academics

The University of Tampa is a "comprehensive, independent university" that "delivers challenging and high quality educational experiences to a diverse group of learners." "It's in an awesome climate" that offers "a good education" at a "reasonable price" and "the area is absolutely beautiful." Students enjoy the "small," "beautiful campus" on the riverfront. "I go to school in paradise!" one student exclaims. This combination of location and academics are a big draw for students who want to be "outdoors more" while also being able to "get a real college experience" and "be a part of a beautiful campus and city." UT offers nearly 200 academic programs of study, the most popular of which are communication, biology, international business, management, criminology, and nursing. The nursing program in particular is "vigorous," and "has had a 100 percent NCLEX pass rate for the past six years." UT is also "one of the only schools in Florida that actually offers" a degree in marine biology, and is a "top program" in that field. Students say it has "one of the BEST education departments!" "Professors are enthusiastic about what they teach" and make sure students "are learning it." They "care about their students and are willing to help anyone that puts in effort." Students praise the "small class sizes" which are "often better for class-wide discussion." "Interactions with professors are great," says a student majoring in psychology. "Small class sizes allow for help on an individual basis as well as with an entire class." Professors try to "involve all students present" and are "open to their opinions." They don't just "make the class all about them standing up and lecturing," notes a criminology major. The faculty really care about the students here and make sure you "are not just a number." For athletics, UT's baseball team is "top five in the country for NCAA" and the "soccer and volleyball teams are top ten," boasts one student. Overall, UT is a "relaxed, but academic focused community" that offers a "fun, friendly, and great education."

Life

Students at UT have the best of both worlds: the bustling excitement of downtown Tampa and the beauty of nearby beaches and waterfront. "There is always something to do around town," and students "can go to the beach, go shopping, discover new restaurants or go out to the clubs and bars," as well as "NFL games, NHL games, music festivals, and so much more." On campus, there are "fun events like [Casino] Night" and the "glow arcade" as well as "comedians and shows." UT students are active on campus and "a lot of students get involved in clubs or Greek life." Sixty-five percent of full-time students live in campus housing in "luxurious dorm rooms." Even when studying, many students hang out by the campus "pool or lay in the park" as a "result of the beautiful weather in Florida."

Student Body

The typical UT student is described as "hard working," "well-rounded," "fun" and "friendly." Students are "very focused on succeeding and networking" and quick to make friends. Many students hail from "the New England area and the North," while the bulk of the student body, approximately 50 percent of students in 2014-2015, is from Florida. One student notes that the "student body overall is very good looking" and "they are also very accepting of other opinions." Even though 92 percent of students in 2014-2015 received some form of financial aid, students often describe their classmates as "affluent." "A typical student is wealthy," notes one student, "and loves the outdoors." "A lot of the students here come from upper class families," says a Nursing major, "but for the most part there is a good mix of different kinds of students." In addition, "The University of Tampa prides itself on having students from all over the world." In 2014, students hailed from fifty states and 137 countries.

FINANCIAL AID: 813-253-6219 • E-MAIL: ADMISSIONS@UT.EDU • WEBSITE: WWW.UT.EDU

THE PRINCETON REVIEW SAYS

Admissions

Very important factors considered include: rigor of secondary school record, academic GPA, standardized test scores. *Important factors considered include:* application essay, recommendation(s), talent/ability. *Other factors considered include:* class rank, interview, extracurricular activities, character/personal qualities, first generation, alumni/ae relation, volunteer work, work experience, level of applicant's interest. SAT or ACT required. TOEFL required of all international applicants. High school diploma is required and GED is accepted. *Academic units required:* 4 English, 3 math, 3 science, 2 science labs, 2 foreign language, 3 social studies, 3 academic electives.

Financial Aid

Students should submit: FAFSA. The Princeton Review suggests that all financial aid forms be submitted as soon as possible after October 1. *Need-based scholarships/grants offered:* Federal Pell, FSEOG, State scholarships/grants, Private scholarships, College/university scholarship or grant aid from institutional funds, Federal Nursing Scholarships. *Loan aid offered:* Direct Subsidized Stafford Loans, Direct Unsubsidized Stafford Loans, Direct PLUS loans, Federal Perkins Loans, College/university loans from institutional funds. Applicants will be notified of awards on a rolling basis beginning 3/1. Federal Work-Study Program available. Institutional employment available (not awarded through financial aid).

The Inside Word

UT accepts either its own application or the Common Applications. Along with the usual high scores and grades, UT looks favorably on extracurricular activities, such as internships, leadership activities, or participation in sports.

THE SCHOOL SAYS "..."

From the Admissions Office

"High school students may apply for admission after their junior year. Applicants are evaluated holistically using many criteria; guidance counselor or teacher recommendations and an essay are not required if you have graduated high school and completed seventeen or more college credit hours.

"A college preparatory curriculum is required, including a minimum of eighteen academic units: four English courses, three sciences (two must be laboratory sciences), three mathematics, three social studies, two foreign languages and three academic electives. The 2015-2016 class had an average (unweighted) GPA of 3.3 on the 4.0 scale, 1110 SAT (math and critical reading sections only) or a score of 24 on the ACT. Certain majors require separate departmental applications and/or requirements.

"The interdisciplinary Honors Program allows students to go beyond the classroom and regular coursework to study one-on-one with faculty through enrichment tutorials, Honors Abroad, internships, research and classroom-to-community outreach. One of the program's salient benefits is the Oxford Semester Abroad, awarded to UT's most qualified undergraduates each semester. Students are automatically considered for the Honors Program when they apply and are admitted to the University.

"While the University's facilities are state-of-the-art, our greatest features and benefits include our diverse student body (students from fifty states and 140 countries) and internships within walking distance of campus. UT's historic campus, coupled with our downtown, riverfront location, provides the perfect environment for academic enrichment and career preparation."

SELECTIVITY

Admissions Rating	88
# of applicants	18,721
% of applicants accepted	51
% of acceptees attending	19
# offered a place on the wait list	1,556
% accepting a place on wait list	8

FRESHMAN PROFILE

Range SAT Critical Reading	490–580
Range SAT Math	500–590
Range SAT Writing	480–570
Range ACT Composite	22–26
Minimum paper TOEFL	550
Minimum internet-based TOEFL	79
Average HS GPA	3.4
% graduated top 10% of class	18
% graduated top 25% of class	45
% graduated top 50% of class	81

DEADLINES

Early action	
Deadline	11/15
Notification	12/15
Regular	
Priority	11/15
Nonfall registration?	Yes

FINANCIAL FACTS

Financial Aid Rating	80
Annual tuition	$25,202
Room and board	$9,900
Required fees	$1,842
Books and supplies	$1,200
Average frosh need-based scholarship	$13,276
Average UG need-based scholarship	$12,740
% needy frosh rec. need-based scholarship or grant aid	100
% needy UG rec. need-based scholarship or grant aid	99
% needy frosh rec. non-need-based scholarship or grant aid	100
% needy UG rec. non-need-based scholarship or grant aid	98
% needy frosh rec. need-based self-help aid	79
% needy UG rec. need-based self-help aid	80
% frosh rec. any financial aid	93
% UG rec. any financial aid	89
% UG borrow to pay for school	62
Average cumulative indebtedness	$33,304
% frosh need fully met	100
% ugrads need fully met	9
Average % of frosh need met	62
Average % of ugrad need met	61

THE UNIVERSITY OF TENNESSEE AT KNOXVILLE

320 STUDENT SERVICE BUILDING, KNOXVILLE, TN 37996-0230 • ADMISSIONS: 865-974-2184

CAMPUS LIFE

Quality of Life Rating	88
Fire Safety Rating	95
Green Rating	92
Type of school	Public
Affiliation	No Affiliation
Environment	City

STUDENTS

Total undergrad enrollment	21,863
% male/female	51/49
% from out of state	11
% frosh live on campus	90
% ugrads live on campus	33
# of fraternities (% ugrad men join)	23 (16)
# of sororities (% ugrad women join)	18 (24)
% African American	7
% Asian	3
% Caucasian	79
% Hispanic	3
% Native American	<1
% Pacific Islander	0
% Two or more races	3
% Race and/or ethnicity unknown	3
% international	2
# of countries represented	63

SURVEY SAYS...
Students are happy
Great library
Career services are great
Recreation facilities are great
Lots of beer drinking
Everyone loves the Volunteers

ACADEMICS

Academic Rating	74
% students returning for sophomore year	85
% students graduating within 4 years	43
% students graduating within 6 years	46
Calendar	Semester
Student/faculty ratio	17:1
Profs interesting rating	69
Profs accessible rating	71
Most classes have 20–29 students.	

MOST POPULAR MAJORS
Biology; Psychology; Kinesiology and Exercise Science

STUDENTS SAY "..."

Academics

The University of Tennessee "provides a family-like atmosphere full of opportunity and support!" Life at UT is all about "atmosphere, affordability, and school spirit." Many here tout "the school spirit and sense of community." In addition, the "in-state tuition and scholarship money" make "Tennessee a good deal for the amount you pay. I have fabulous teachers, great friends, fun activities to participate in, nice housing, a decent meal plan, and I pay $2,000 for all of it." "Although [UT is] a large school, you're not just a number; you're a face, a person, and a name." In general, "professors greatly appreciate an appetite to learn, and they welcome challenges that help us learn and grow as students." Most are "very intelligent, open to debate, well-versed on their topics, and willing to meet with students outside of class for any reason." One student says, "the majority of my experience with academia and professors has been diverse and excellent." UT embraces a classic liberal arts core dedicated to "helping students find their passions by providing a friendly and intellectually enriching environment to learn, lead, and grow." UT offers "many opportunities for involvement" and "sets a high standard for success." Attending UT "is about pursuing excellence in all areas of your life and using the knowledge you gain to prepare you for your future." It also "has a well-known medical program" and—for many—is "close to home."

Life

The typical UT student "loves all aspects of the university's life from its sports to its long-standing traditions." Students flock here for "family history, athletics, and to sing 'Rocky Top.'" "We love football just about as much as academics." However, academics here are just as intense as athletics. "Being a larger university, I have had many more opportunities than people I know at smaller schools in education as well as extracurriculars." "The University of Tennessee combines the best of all worlds: great education for a great price, sports, social life, and a ton of extracurriculars to choose from." In fact, many say, "there are so many clubs and groups that on a social level UT doesn't feel large at all." "There's also a great selection of food and a wonderful gym." Life at UT is all "about education, community, and becoming a true Tennessee volunteer." "There's a great sense of unity." The university "tries extremely hard to encourage acceptance of several kinds of diversity." A "LGBTQ Resource Center...opened on campus" in 2010. "There is also a large 'Stop Bias' program that is promoted." In general, there are "tons of clubs and organizations to get involved with if you are passionate about something." If pressed to note a campus flaw, students say UT is "stuck between a river and downtown Knoxville, so it now has no room to expand and way too many hills. So they've crammed all these buildings into too small of a space."

Student Body

"There is not one 'popular' group of students. We have athletes, artists, musicians, dancers, religious students, scientists, Greeks, volunteers, etc." In general a live-and-let-live atmosphere pervades this "friendly" "energetic," "personable" campus; "All students fit in extremely well." The Greek community here "is especially prevalent." Some wonder "how non-Greeks fit in." "The conservative, upper-class attitude is definitely the one with the strongest voice." However, others counter this stalwart image. "The best thing about being an average student here? If you don't want to conform, you don't have to." "Once you go beyond the surface and away from the jocks and sorority girls, there are all types of students at UT." Others enthusiastically concede, "The literary snob crowd is small, but it's here, they do cool stuff, and they welcome new folks all the time with open arms." A typical student "studies hard, but parties even harder at the appropriate times." Classical entrees to social life include "to become part of the Greek system here or be an athlete." Most students exhibit the hallmark "Southern hospitality" and are "industrious, honest, charitable, and compassionate."

FINANCIAL AID: 865-974-3131 • E-MAIL: ADMISSIONS@UTK.EDU • WEBSITE: WWW.UTK.EDU

THE PRINCETON REVIEW SAYS

Admissions

Very important factors considered include: rigor of secondary school record, academic GPA, standardized test scores, application essay. *Important factors considered include:* extracurricular activities, talent/ability, volunteer work, work experience, level of applicant's interest. *Other factors considered include:* class rank, recommendation(s), first generation, alumni/ae relation, geographical residence, state residency, racial/ethnic status. SAT or ACT required. ACT with or without writing accepted. SAT with or without Essay component accepted. TOEFL required of all international applicants. High school diploma is required and GED is accepted. *Academic units required:* 4 English, 4 math, 3 science, 3 science labs, 2 foreign language, 1 social studies, 1 history, 1 visual/performing arts.

Financial Aid

Students should submit: FAFSA. Priority filing deadline is 2/15. The Princeton Review suggests that all financial aid forms be submitted as soon as possible after October 1. *Need-based scholarships/grants offered:* Federal Pell, FSEOG, State scholarships/grants, Private scholarships, College/university scholarship or grant aid from institutional funds. *Loan aid offered:* Direct Subsidized Stafford Loans, Direct Unsubsidized Stafford Loans, Direct PLUS loans, Federal Perkins Loans, State Loans, College/university loans from institutional funds. Applicants will be notified of awards on a rolling basis beginning 3/15. Federal Work-Study Program available.

The Inside Word

UT must winnow through more than 15,000 freshman applications each year. That sort of volume doesn't allow for nuance. Students with above-average high school GPAs (achieved in a reasonable college prep curriculum) and above-average standardized test scores pretty much all make the cut. The school will consider additional evidence of an applicant's potential (school and community involvement, awards, essays, special talents, and recommendations) in making admissions decisions, particularly for marginal candidates.

THE SCHOOL SAYS "..."

From the Admissions Office

"The University of Tennessee, Knoxville, offers students the great program diversity of a major university, opportunities for research or original creative work in every degree program, and a welcoming campus environment. Nine colleges offer more than 170 undergraduate majors and concentrations to students from all fifty states and 100 foreign countries, and UT students can make the world their campus through study abroad programs. More than 400 clubs and organizations on campus allow students to further individualize their college experience in service, recreation, academics, and professional development. UT blends more than 200 years of history, tradition, and 'Volunteer Spirit' with the latest technology and innovation."

SELECTIVITY

Admissions Rating	88
# of applicants	17,081
% of applicants accepted	76
% of acceptees attending	36

FRESHMAN PROFILE

Range SAT Critical Reading	520–630
Range SAT Math	530–630
Range ACT Composite	24–30
Minimum paper TOEFL	523
Minimum internet-based TOEFL	70
Average HS GPA	3.9
% graduated top 10% of class	54
% graduated top 25% of class	90
% graduated top 50% of class	100

DEADLINES

Regular	
Priority	11/1
Deadline	12/1
Nonfall registration?	Yes

APPLICANTS ALSO LOOK AT AND SOMETIMES PREFER

Clemson University; Vanderbilt University; University of South Carolina–Columbia

AND RARELY PREFER

The University of Alabama at Tuscaloosa; University of Mississippi; Virginia Tech

FINANCIAL FACTS

Financial Aid Rating	81
Annual in-state tuition	$10,190
Annual out-of-state tuition	$28,380
Room and board	$9,926
Required fees	$1,758
Books and supplies	$1,598
Average frosh need-based scholarship	$11,049
Average UG need-based scholarship	$9,318
% needy frosh rec. need-based scholarship or grant aid	95
% needy UG rec. need-based scholarship or grant aid	89
% needy frosh rec. non-need-based scholarship or grant aid	0
% needy UG rec. non-need-based scholarship or grant aid	0
% needy frosh rec. need-based self-help aid	99
% needy UG rec. need-based self-help aid	99
% frosh rec. any financial aid	89
% UG rec. any financial aid	93
% UG borrow to pay for school	52
Average cumulative indebtedness	$24,272
% frosh need fully met	25
% ugrads need fully met	22
Average % of frosh need met	62
Average % of ugrad need met	57

THE UNIVERSITY OF TEXAS AT AUSTIN

PO Box 8058, Austin, TX 78713-8058 • Admissions: 512-475-7440 • Fax: 512-475-7478

STUDENTS SAY ". . ."

Academics

Students insist that the University of Texas at Austin has "everything you want in a college: academics, athletics, social life, location," and it's hard to argue with them. UT is "a huge school and has a lot to offer," meaning students have "an infinite number of possibilities open to them and can use them in their own way to figure out what they want for their lives." As one student tells us about arriving on campus, "I did not realize how much was available to me just as an enrolled student. There is free tutoring, gym membership, professional counseling, doctors visits, legal help, career advising, and many distinguished outside speakers. The campus is crawling with experts in every field you can imagine." Standout academic departments are numerous: from the sciences to the humanities to creative arts, UT makes a strong bid for the much-sought-after mantle of "Harvard of the south." Also, the school does a surprisingly good job of avoiding the factory-like feel of many large schools. One student observes: "Coming to a large university, there was a prejudgment that the huge classes will make it impossible to know your professor and vice versa. The university has dispelled that myth with professors who want to know you and [who] provide opportunities to get to know them." While professors "can vary greatly across a spectrum from 'I'm smarter than him' to 'I want to follow in his footsteps,'" "the class offerings at UT are generally vast and diverse, and students can often avoid taking the less-qualified professors with a little research."

Life

Life at UT Austin is "very relaxed...Students usually wear shorts and a t-shirt to class. When the weather gets cold, you might find students wearing the same shorts and t-shirt with a sweatshirt. Students and faculty frequently picnic all over campus. There are plenty of outdoor tables and grassy areas to sit." Undergrads "are often found throwing a Frisbee outside the tower or taking a nap under a tree. It's truly what you see in one of those cheesy brochures with everyone studying and smiling. Of course, the smiles aren't so bright during finals. We switch to an over-caffeinated, glazed-eye look instead." Hometown Austin "provides a social education that a college student newly out on his own would not find anywhere else," with "festivals or fairs of some kind going on downtown all the time" and "the infamous 6th Street with nightlife that dies down only after the bars close." Campus and the surrounding area offer "many hike-and-bike trails and fitness organizations. It's possible for students to train for marathons, half marathons, and triathlons while in school. Barton Springs pool is a natural spring that is very popular year-round. On any given Saturday you will find students throwing a football, going for a run, biking through the hills, kayaking in the river, having a late lunch at one of Austin's great restaurants, or just sleeping in."

Student Body

"Because of the huge Greek life at UT, a 'typical student' would be a sorority girl or fraternity boy," but—and it's a big but—such students "are hardly the majority, since UT is actually made of more 'atypical' people than most other schools. Everyone here has his own niche, and I could not think of any type of individual who would not be able to find one of his own." Indeed, "everyone at Texas is different! When you walk across campus, you see every type of ethnicity. There are a lot of minorities at Texas. Also, I see many disabled people, whom the school accommodates well. Everyone seems to get along. The different types of students just blend in together." Especially by Texas standards, "Austin is known for being 'weird.' If you see someone dressed in a way you've never seen before, you just shrug it off and say 'That's Austin!'"

FINANCIAL AID: 512-475-6203 • WEBSITE: WWW.UTEXAS.EDU

THE PRINCETON REVIEW SAYS

Admissions

Very important factors considered include: rigor of secondary school record, class rank. *Important factors considered include:* standardized test scores, application essay, extracurricular activities, talent/ability, volunteer work, work experience. *Other factors considered include:* recommendation(s), character/personal qualities, first generation, state residency, racial/ethnic status, level of applicant's interest. SAT or ACT required. ACT with Writing required. SAT with Essay component required. TOEFL required of all international applicants. High school diploma is required and GED is accepted. *Academic units required:* 4 English, 4 math, 4 science, 2 foreign language, 4 social studies, 6 academic electives, and 2 units from above areas or other academic areas.

Financial Aid

Students should submit: FAFSA, Institution's own financial aid form. Priority filing deadline is 3/15. The Princeton Review suggests that all financial aid forms be submitted as soon as possible after October 1. *Need-based scholarships/ grants offered:* Federal Pell, FSEOG, State scholarships/grants, Private scholarships, College/university scholarship or grant aid from institutional funds. *Loan aid offered:* Direct Subsidized Stafford Loans, Direct Unsubsidized Stafford Loans, Direct PLUS loans, Federal Perkins Loans, State Loans. Applicants will be notified of awards on a rolling basis in the fall. Federal Work-Study Program available. Institutional employment available.

The Inside Word

The university is required to automatically admit enough Texas applicants to fill 75 percent of available spaces set aside for students from Texas. The university will admit applicants from Texas who are in the top 7 percent of their high school class for the summer/fall 2017 and the spring 2018 entering freshman class. The rank needed for automatic admission for future classes will be announced each September. All students, including those eligible for automatic admission, should submit the strongest possible application to increase the likelihood of admission to the university and to their requested major. Admissions are quite competitive. Space for out-of-state students is limited, meaning they'll have even higher hurdles to clear.

THE SCHOOL SAYS "..."

From the Admissions Office

"For more than 125 years, students from all over the world have come to The University of Texas at Austin to obtain a first-class education. Recognized for research, teaching, and public service, the university boasts more than 130 undergraduate academic programs, hundreds of study abroad programs, outstanding student services, cultural centers, and volunteer and leadership opportunities designed to prepare students to make a difference in the world. Along with its nationally ranked athletic programs, the university's spirit is enhanced by cultural, artistic, and scientific opportunities that help to make Austin one of the most inviting destinations in the country. The Performing Arts Center hosts plays, Austin's opera and symphony, and visiting musical and dance groups. Students access more than eight million volumes in the university's seventeen libraries and study prehistoric fossils at the Texas Memorial Museum, Renaissance and Baroque paintings in the Blanton Museum, original manuscripts at the Ransom Center, and life in the 1960s at the Lyndon B. Johnson Library and Museum. Each year the university enrolls about 50,000 students from richly varied ethnic and geographic backgrounds. Every day graduates contribute to the world community as volunteers, teachers, journalists, artists, engineers, business leaders, scientists, and lawyers. With world-renowned faculty, top-rated academic programs, successful alumni, and such an enticing location, it's no surprise that The University of Texas at Austin ranks among the best universities in the world."

SELECTIVITY

Admissions Rating	92
# of applicants	43,592
% of applicants accepted	39
% of acceptees attending	46
# offered a place on the wait list	1,634
% accepting a place on wait list	71
% admitted from wait list	31

FRESHMAN PROFILE

Range SAT Critical Reading	570–680
Range SAT Math	600–710
Range SAT Writing	560–680
Range ACT Composite	26–31
Minimum paper TOEFL	550
Minimum internet-based TOEFL	79
% graduated top 10% of class	72
% graduated top 25% of class	92
% graduated top 50% of class	98

DEADLINES

Regular	
Deadline	12/1
Nonfall registration?	Yes

FINANCIAL FACTS

Financial Aid Rating	79
Annual in-state tuition	$9,806
Annual out-of-state tuition	$34,676
Room and board	$11,456
Books and supplies	$750
Average frosh need-based scholarship	$9,229
Average UG need-based scholarship	$9,088
% needy frosh rec. need-based scholarship or grant aid	75
% needy UG rec. need-based scholarship or grant aid	78
% needy frosh rec. non-need-based scholarship or grant aid	51
% needy UG rec. non-need-based scholarship or grant aid	29
% needy frosh rec. need-based self-help aid	67
% needy UG rec. need-based self-help aid	69
% UG rec. any financial aid	42
% UG borrow to pay for school	46
Average cumulative indebtedness	$25,349
% frosh need fully met	23
% ugrads need fully met	21
Average % of frosh need met	68
Average % of ugrad need met	69

THE UNIVERSITY OF TEXAS AT DALLAS

800 WEST CAMPBELL ROAD, RICHARDSON, TX 75080 • ADMISSIONS: 972-883-2270 • FAX: 972-883-2599

CAMPUS LIFE

Quality of Life Rating	87
Fire Safety Rating	95
Green Rating	81
Type of school	Public
Affiliation	No Affiliation
Environment	Metropolis

STUDENTS

Total undergrad enrollment	15,575
% male/female	57/43
% from out of state	3
% frosh from public high school	90
% frosh live on campus	60
% ugrads live on campus	27
# of fraternities (% ugrad men join)	11 (2)
# of sororities (% ugrad women join)	11 (3)
% African American	6
% Asian	29
% Caucasian	37
% Hispanic	18
% Native American	<1
% Pacific Islander	<1
% Two or more races	4
% Race and/or ethnicity unknown	2
% international	3
# of countries represented	70

SURVEY SAYS...

Classroom facilities are great
Career services are great
School is well run
Great financial aid
Dorms are like palaces

ACADEMICS

Academic Rating	72
% students returning for sophomore year	84
% students graduating within 4 years	48
% students graduating within 6 years	67
Calendar	Semester
Student/faculty ratio	21:1
Profs interesting rating	71
Profs accessible rating	71

Most classes have 10–19 students.
Most lab/discussion sessions have
  20–29 students.

MOST POPULAR MAJORS

Biology; Computer and Information Sciences;
Game and Interactive Media Design

STUDENTS SAY "..."

Academics

Though nowhere near the size of some of its fellow state schools, UT Dallas provides its more than 15,000 undergraduates with a wealth of resources, financial aid, and opportunities, striving for "a future of talented and smart individuals." UTD has "one of the best tech schools around" and draws a good deal of students to its STEM programs (one student lovingly calls it "the nerd capital of the UT system"), causing a senior computer engineer to remark: "Engineering and the sciences for the win." The school is without many sports programs (notably football), but instead "emphasizes academics, which is what we are all here for."

Administration is responsive and invested in UTD's growing reputation, and the school "grows and changes year by year, continually getting better and better," with students acting as "a big part of that process." Someone is "always willing to help you with any problem you encounter," and the tutoring available also "really helps in understanding the material." They are dedicated to their students, this being apparent in "their open office hours and timely replies to e-mails."

Most of the professors "are very enthused about what they are teaching and genuinely want us to learn," and bring new topics to light through "very informative" discussion. "Their passion for their subject make it easy to love your classes!" says a student. "I get pushed academically, but I love it," says another. One of the shining benefits of UTD is the chance to get "actively involved with the faculty in research," which provides "several opportunities for honors, and ultimately allows you to prepare for a continued education after undergrad."

Life

The "well-kept campus" is "not too large," though "parking is a bit of an issue sometimes." There is a lot of studying going on, so "you can always find a group or just a lot of people hanging around on a specific area studying." "Some people practically build shrines to their GPA's and worship them on weekends," says one sophomore.

A lot of students commute (which makes life "pretty quiet") and there is no football team to rally around, so "it's hard to have a lot of school spirit"; however, "the social scene is definitely growing," and the Student Union acts as the "hub" for the entire school where "students can mingle and find friends." Computer labs also give many the chance to game and have fun (the video game culture is "strong"), and "there are usually always at least five to ten gamers in the room at once." The school provides "many things to do," with campus events like movies happening every week, and people often leave campus to seek more options, such as "movies, bowling, shopping, skating, concert, etc."

Student Body

There is "no clear majority of one race, creed, or background" at UT Dallas. Since most of the "exceptionally nice" and "very diverse" people are here for the sciences, there are "lots of smart people everywhere" and "everyone here is so open about the geeky side in everyone." Most agree that there could stand to be a bit more of a creative voice on campus and the school would do well to attract "more students to fine arts." Most students are "serious about their academics, but not too serious" and remember to take the time to relax; "video games/card games and...anime" are popular here, as are clubs and organizations.

THE UNIVERSITY OF TEXAS AT DALLAS

FINANCIAL AID: 972-883-2941 • E-MAIL: INTEREST@UTDALLAS.EDU • WEBSITE: WWW.UTDALLAS.EDU

THE PRINCETON REVIEW SAYS

Admissions

Very important factors considered include: rigor of secondary school record, class rank, academic GPA, standardized test scores. *Important factors considered include:* application essay. *Other factors considered include:* recommendation(s), extracurricular activities, state residency, volunteer work, work experience, level of applicant's interest. SAT or ACT required; SAT Subject Tests required for some. ACT with Writing required. SAT with Essay component required. TOEFL required of all international applicants. High school diploma is required and GED is accepted. *Academic units required:* 4 English, 4 math, 3 science, 3 science labs, 2 foreign language, 3 social studies. *Academic units recommended:* 4 English, 4 math, 3 science, 3 science labs, 3 foreign language, 4 social studies, 1 computer science, 1 visual/performing arts, and 2 units from above areas or other academic areas.

Financial Aid

Students should submit: FAFSA. Priority filing deadline is 3/31. The Princeton Review suggests that all financial aid forms be submitted as soon as possible after October 1. *Need-based scholarships/grants offered:* Federal Pell, FSEOG, State scholarships/grants, Private scholarships, College/university scholarship or grant aid from institutional funds. *Loan aid offered:* Direct Subsidized Stafford Loans, Direct Unsubsidized Stafford Loans, Direct PLUS loans, Federal Perkins Loans, State Loans, College/university loans from institutional funds. Applicants will be notified of awards on a rolling basis beginning 3/1. Federal Work-Study Program available. Institutional employment available.

The Inside Word

UT Dallas is one of those by-the-numbers schools for the majority of its admitted students. Texas law requires that prospective students are automatically admitted to the university as first-time freshmen if they graduated from an accredited Texas high school among the top 10 percent of their class, and then there is a separate set of numbers for students of good standing, including an SAT score of 1200 (math and reading) or an ACT score of 26. Students outside of these ranges are subject to a more traditional review based on individual strengths.

THE SCHOOL SAYS "..."

From the Admissions Office

"Founded in 1969, The University of Texas at Dallas has evolved into one of the top research institutions in Texas. UT Dallas provides some of the state's most-lauded business, engineering and science programs, and has also gained prominence for a breadth of educational paths, from arts and technology to audiology to biomedical engineering.

"The University's faculty consists of more than 500 tenured and tenure-track members hailing from the world's best colleges and includes a Nobel laureate and members of the National Academy of Sciences and the National Academy of Engineering. In addition, UT Dallas is home to more than fifty centers, labs and institutes that facilitate undergraduate research, internships and collaborations with local industry.

"UT Dallas students graduate with less debt than most college students in the country and are highly marketable upon graduation. UT Dallas graduates are recruited by eighteen of the top twenty *Fortune* 500 companies and accepted into the top law and medical schools in the country."

SELECTIVITY

Admissions Rating	88
# of applicants	11,237
% of applicants accepted	61
% of acceptees attending	40

FRESHMAN PROFILE

Range SAT Critical Reading	560–670
Range SAT Math	600–700
Range SAT Writing	520–650
Range ACT Composite	25–31
Minimum paper TOEFL	550
Minimum internet-based TOEFL	80
% graduated top 10% of class	33
% graduated top 25% of class	64
% graduated top 50% of class	88

DEADLINES

Regular	
Deadline	7/1
Nonfall registration?	Yes

FINANCIAL FACTS

Financial Aid Rating	83
Annual in-state tuition	$11,806
Annual out-of-state tuition	$32,168
Room and board	$9,944
Books and supplies	$1,200
Average frosh need-based scholarship	$11,085
Average UG need-based scholarship	$8,726
% needy frosh rec. need-based scholarship or grant aid	91
% needy UG rec. need-based scholarship or grant aid	87
% needy frosh rec. non-need-based scholarship or grant aid	17
% needy UG rec. non-need-based scholarship or grant aid	8
% needy frosh rec. need-based self-help aid	78
% needy UG rec. need-based self-help aid	86
% frosh rec. any financial aid	78
% UG rec. any financial aid	71
% UG borrow to pay for school	36
Average cumulative indebtedness	$21,174
% frosh need fully met	30
% ugrads need fully met	17
Average % of frosh need met	76
Average % of ugrad need met	65

UNIVERSITY OF TORONTO

172 St. George Street, Toronto, ON M5R 0A3 • Admissions: 416-978-2190 • Fax: 416-978-7022

STUDENTS SAY "..."

Academics

With "an excellent reputation and a huge selection of courses" as well as "a world-class city" to call home, the University of Toronto "provides expert knowledge in every field" to its 60,000-plus undergraduates and nearly 16,000 graduate students. True, it can be "hard to relate to the instructors given that the class sizes are so huge," and those looking for an intimate and supportive academic environment might not find a good fit at U of T. "The general attitude is one of professionalism and very little mercy [here]." Still, self-starters will find the limitless opportunities outweigh the drawbacks. As one student puts it, "Most of the professors are premier representatives of their respective industries." Another adds, "The fact that you are learning from Nobel Prize winners in a city full of adventures is unbeatable." "Excellent research facilities" are among the other assets here. The school also capitalizes on its location in the center of Toronto: "The city and the university draw on each other in a variety of ways—clinical opportunities and research flow in both directions." On top of that, industrious undergrads tell us, "The libraries and other research facilities here are excellent and contribute much to the overall academic experience."

Life

When they aren't hitting the books, University of Toronto students enjoy life in "one of the coolest cities in North America" where "there's always something new happening: the Toronto International Film Festival, skating in Nathan Phillips Square, etc." Students benefit from the fact that "the Royal Ontario Museum is on campus, a ton of pubs and art galleries are within walking distance, and a nightlife to suit just about any type of person" can be found in Toronto. When it comes to campus life, many students feel the school's spirit and unity is negatively affected by the large number of commuter students. "Off-campus students, of whom there are many, rarely participate in extracurricular activities," one student complains, "Interest in varsity sports is just pathetic" among all undergraduates. Others focus on the positives, pointing out the social and recreational opportunities available to those willing to look. A junior says, "Getting involved here takes some research in terms of navigating the 300 clubs and endless academic/research opportunities, but once I did some searching, I found several places where I fit in well and have fun." For those who live on campus, sororities and fraternities help nurture social bonds, and "most of the residential colleges have tons of events, from campus-wide capture the flag [games] to movie nights" or "intramural sports."

Student Body

At this large public school, the demographics on campus reflect those of surrounding Toronto, "one of the most diverse cities around." As one junior puts it, "It can be said that all students here have in common an excellent academic record prior to university. Beyond that, anything goes: There are huge variances in race, religion, sexual orientation, academic focus, postgraduate aspirations, socioeconomic background, disability, nationality, athleticism, and community involvement." A freshman chimes in, "On my floor alone there are kids from at least ten different countries and, even with the different cultures, we have blended together to make a big family." Most students say it's relatively easy to find a social group among like-minded individuals, despite the school's impressive size and diversity. According to one senior, "Most students will find a niche where they feel comfortable; there's a place for everyone."

FINANCIAL AID: 416-978-2190 • E-MAIL: ADMISSIONS.HELP@UTORONTO.CA • WEBSITE: WWW.UTORONTO.CA

THE PRINCETON REVIEW SAYS

Admissions

Very important factors considered include: academic GPA, standardized test scores. *Other factors considered include:* SAT or ACT required. ACT with Writing required. TOEFL required of all international applicants. High school diploma is required and GED is accepted.

Financial Aid

Students should submit: The Princeton Review suggests that all financial aid forms be submitted as soon as possible after October 1. *Loan aid offered:* Federal Work-Study Program available. Institutional employment available.

The Inside Word

University of Toronto takes a numbers-based approach to admissions. American students must submit not only high school transcripts and SAT/ACT scores but also results for three SAT Subject Tests/APs/IBs. Only those who perform well by all these metrics are likely to gain admission. Candidates should be aware that qualifications vary from program to program, and as an international student you'll have more paperwork to file. The University of Toronto is a recognized postsecondary institution for Federal Stafford Loans. All applicants are automatically considered for admission scholarships.

THE SCHOOL SAYS ". . ."

From the Admissions Office

"The University of Toronto is committed to being an internationally significant research university with undergraduate, graduate, and professional programs of study.

"Admission requirements for Arts, Science, Commerce/Management, Kinesiology & Physical Education, and Music:

U.S. Grade 12 in an accredited high school with a high grade point average and high scores on SAT Reasoning/Redesigned SAT/ACT exams and a minimum of two appropriate SAT Subject Tests/APs/IBs (or a combination of SAT Subject Tests/APs/IBs covering different subjects). English Grade 12/AP is required for all programs.

"Those seeking admission to science or commerce programs are strongly advised to complete AP Calculus.

"Minimum Admission Requirements: Excellent CGPA and Grade 12 GPA; scores of at least 1800 on SAT Reasoning/Redesigned SAT or 26 on the ACT. SAT scores below 500 in any part of the SAT Reasoning/Redesigned SAT or Subject Tests are not acceptable.

"Admission requirements for Engineering: Grade 12 at an accredited high school, including senior level courses in Math, Chemistry and Physics, and SAT Reasoning/ Redesigned SAT/ACT scores. It is also recommended, but not required, that students submit either AP or SAT subject test results in Math, Chemistry and Physics. English Grade 12 is required for all programs.

"Minimum Admission Requirements: Excellent CGPA, Grade 12 GPA and SAT Reasoning/Redesigned SAT/ACT scores.

"Refer to discover.engineering.utoronto.ca for complete information."

SELECTIVITY

Admissions Rating	64
# of applicants	75,773
% of applicants accepted	66
% of acceptees attending	26

FRESHMAN PROFILE

Minimum paper TOEFL	600

DEADLINES

Early decision	
Deadline	11/1
Regular	
Deadline	2/1
Nonfall registration?	No

FINANCIAL FACTS

Financial Aid Rating	60*
Room and board	$8,105–$11,515
Required fees	$24,285–$35,330
Books and supplies	$1,200
% needy frosh rec. need-based scholarship or grant aid	0
% needy UG rec. need-based scholarship or grant aid	0
% needy frosh rec. non-need-based scholarship or grant aid	0
% needy UG rec. non-need-based scholarship or grant aid	0
% needy frosh rec. need-based self-help aid	0
% needy UG rec. need-based self-help aid	0

THE UNIVERSITY OF TULSA

800 SOUTH TUCKER DRIVE, TULSA, OK 74104 • ADMISSIONS: 918-631-2307 • FAX: 918-631-5003

CAMPUS LIFE
Quality of Life Rating	90
Fire Safety Rating	95
Green Rating	77
Type of school	Private
Affiliation	Presbyterian
Environment	Metropolis

STUDENTS
Total undergrad enrollment	3,478
% male/female	58/42
% from out of state	43
% frosh from public high school	71
% frosh live on campus	83
% ugrads live on campus	71
# of fraternities (% ugrad men join)	7 (20)
# of sororities (% ugrad women join)	9 (22)
% African American	5
% Asian	4
% Caucasian	56
% Hispanic	5
% Native American	3
% Pacific Islander	<1
% Two or more races	1
% Race and/or ethnicity unknown	1
% international	26
# of countries represented	59

SURVEY SAYS...
Students are happy
Great financial aid
Students are very religious
Students love Tulsa, OK
Recreation facilities are great
Intramural sports are popular

ACADEMICS
Academic Rating	86
% students returning for sophomore year	88
% students graduating within 4 years	52
% students graduating within 6 years	69
Calendar	Semester
Student/faculty ratio	11:1
Profs interesting rating	80
Profs accessible rating	80

Most classes have 10–19 students.
Most lab/discussion sessions have 20–29 students.

MOST POPULAR MAJORS
Petroleum Engineering; Psychology; Finance

STUDENTS SAY "..."

Academics

According to its happy undergrads, the University of Tulsa provides the "best aspects of a large state school and a small private school, in addition to great scholarships." Students name "a combination of excellent scholarship money, transferable credits from my high school," and "great programs across the board," as factors that attracted them to the Oklahoman campus of about 4,500. TU "offers full-ride scholarships for National Merit Finalists," and students enjoy "interesting classes that are actually relevant to our fields of study." They feel well-rounded, saying their "school is truly dedicated to providing the premier college experience academically, athletically, and socially." Students rave about the "great student-to-faculty ratio" and love that TU has a "small school feel while still being big enough to be Division I" in college athletics. They call their professors "smart, entertaining, caring individuals," who "have reached peak success in their fields" and are "very dedicated to their classes and course material. They all seem to love what they do and want us to love it too." One student comments, "All my professors know me by my first name." Students appreciate "all the hands-on, extra opportunities" they are offered along with classes, as well as having "plenty of opportunities for undergraduate research." TU's "exceptional engineering degree" and "nursing program" stand out, among other programs. Undergrads say, "Major-specific 'Special Topics' courses . . . are limited to a very small number of students and taught by an expert in that field," and these "tend to be the best classes." "I feel better prepared than many of my friends who have attended other universities because of the challenging workload and the professors."

Life

TU students feel that "Tulsa is a great city to live in" with "a great downtown bar scene." The "campus is not too lively for wild parties, but downtown has a great nightlife and the frats will have a decent party every now and then." "For the most part, people generally study or work on weeknights. Greek life is big here, but there are other social options besides Greek life, such as sport teams, campus ministries, and music." "All students are very involved and extremely friendly," and they value TU's "beautiful, well-kept campus," as well as the "personal attention and general hospitality of the school." "Life at TU is contemplative in the sense that students are always trying to explore issues and find new solutions," one being "perfect balance between work and play," and they feel their peers are "supportive of my success academically and socially." Students say "keeping our campus safe for women is important to both men and women," and they appreciate how TU brings them into "contact with a wide variety of people every day," allowing them to "be a part of different people's passions."

Student Body

TU students describe their campus community as a "small student population in a growing city" and feel that "the size is perfect." While "the typical student goes to class and takes his or her studies seriously," that student is also likely to be both "very studious and fun." "There are various groups on campus and pretty much everyone finds something for them," meaning that collectively, "our quirky attitudes mesh together and the student culture is fleshed out well." "There is an interesting mix at TU because one fourth of the students are international," and "this diversity is well appreciated and allows students to find areas where they will fit in and excel." Indeed, one student sums TU up by calling it "a diverse community striving together to better ourselves and the world around us." TU students are "often religious, "smart, ambitious and pretty friendly," and perhaps "conservative."

FINANCIAL AID: 918-631-2526 • E-MAIL: ADMISSION@UTULSA.EDU • WEBSITE: WWW.UTULSA.EDU

THE PRINCETON REVIEW SAYS

Admissions

Very important factors considered include: rigor of secondary school record, academic GPA, standardized test scores. *Important factors considered include:* class rank, application essay, recommendation(s), interview, level of applicant's interest. *Other factors considered include:* extracurricular activities, talent/ability, character/personal qualities, first generation, alumni/ae relation, racial/ethnic status, volunteer work, work experience. SAT or ACT required. ACT with or without writing accepted. SAT with or without Essay component accepted. TOEFL required of all international applicants. High school diploma is required and GED is accepted. *Academic units recommended:* 4 English, 4 math, 3 science, 3 science labs, 2 foreign language, 3 social studies, 1 computer science, 1 visual/performing arts.

Financial Aid

Students should submit: FAFSA. Priority filing deadline is 3/1. The Princeton Review suggests that all financial aid forms be submitted as soon as possible after October 1. *Need-based scholarships/grants offered:* Federal Pell, FSEOG, State scholarships/grants, Private scholarships, College/university scholarship or grant aid from institutional funds. *Loan aid offered:* Direct Subsidized Stafford Loans, Direct Unsubsidized Stafford Loans, Direct PLUS loans, Federal Perkins Loans. Applicants will be notified of awards on a rolling basis beginning 3/15. Federal Work-Study Program available. Institutional employment available.

The Inside Word

The University of Tulsa offers flexible, accessible application options: the Common Application, Early Action (due Nov. 1), and rolling admissions. For students seeking scholarship consideration, TU strongly recommends submitting applications by Feb. 1. A personal interview with an admissions counselor is also highly recommended.

THE SCHOOL SAYS "..."

From the Admissions Office

"The University of Tulsa is a private university with a comprehensive scope. Students choose from more than sixty majors offered through four undergraduate colleges—Kendall College of Arts and Sciences, Collins College of Business, Oxley College of Health Sciences, and the College of Engineering and Natural Sciences. Curricula can be customized with collaborative and interdisciplinary research, joint undergraduate and graduate programs, the Global Scholars Program and an honors program. Professors are equally committed to teaching undergraduates and to scholarly research. This results in extraordinary individual achievement, resulting in the nationally competitive scholarships students have won since 1995: sixty-two Goldwaters, sixty-six National Science Foundation scholars, nine Trumans, nine Department of Defense scholars, eighteen Fulbrights, eleven Phi Kappa Phi, nine Udalls, and five British Marshalls. In the past decade, over 1,000,000 square feet of facilities have been added. These include athletic venues, 400 additional apartments, fitness center, Legal Information Center, library expansion and renovation, two new engineering buildings and a new performing arts center. Over 160 registered clubs, and interest groups, including intramural and recreational sports teams exist along with seven fraternities and nine sororities. The 8,300 seat Reynolds Center is home to the men's and women's basketball teams, campus events, and concerts. A forty-acre sports complex includes the fitness center and indoor tennis center. An outdoor freshman orientation program launches an entire first-year experience dedicated to developing students' full potential.

"Applicants are required to submit the SAT or ACT. The writing component is not required. For admission and scholarship review, the best subscores of submitted tests will be used."

SELECTIVITY

Admissions Rating	94
# of applicants	6,762
% of applicants accepted	44
% of acceptees attending	24

FRESHMAN PROFILE

Range SAT Critical Reading	560–700
Range SAT Math	570–700
Range ACT Composite	26–32
Minimum paper TOEFL	550
Minimum internet-based TOEFL	80
Average HS GPA	3.9
% graduated top 10% of class	73
% graduated top 25% of class	91
% graduated top 50% of class	99

DEADLINES

Early action	
Deadline	11/1
Notification	12/15
Regular	
Priority	2/1
Nonfall registration?	Yes

APPLICANTS ALSO LOOK AT AND OFTEN PREFER

Texas Christian University; University of Oklahoma; Southern Methodist University; Saint Louis University

AND SOMETIMES PREFER

Trinity University; Baylor University; Tulane University; Washington University in St. Louis

AND RARELY PREFER

Texas A&M University–College Station; University of Kansas; University of Missouri

FINANCIAL FACTS

Financial Aid Rating	88
Annual tuition	$37,580
Room and board	$11,116
Required fees	$540
Books and supplies	$1,200
Average frosh need-based scholarship	$6,508
Average UG need-based scholarship	$5,648
% needy frosh rec. need-based scholarship or grant aid	33
% needy UG rec. need-based scholarship or grant aid	36
% needy frosh rec. non-need-based scholarship or grant aid	96
% needy UG rec. non-need-based scholarship or grant aid	93
% needy frosh rec. need-based self-help aid	50
% needy UG rec. need-based self-help aid	55
% frosh rec. any financial aid	91
% UG rec. any financial aid	86
% UG borrow to pay for school	49
Average cumulative indebtedness	$37,008
% frosh need fully met	55
% ugrads need fully met	48
Average % of frosh need met	86
Average % of ugrad need met	82

UNIVERSITY OF UTAH

201 SOUTH 1460 EAST, ROOM 250 S, SALT LAKE CITY, UT 84112 • ADMISSIONS: 801-581-7281 • FAX: 801-585-7864

STUDENTS SAY "..."

Academics

Nestled amid Salt Lake City's snowcapped mountains, the University of Utah is a large public school that offers extensive academic programs, ample research opportunities, and a surprisingly student-friendly atmosphere. No matter what your interests, you'll find like minds at The U. "I have studied everything from Tai Chi/Yoga movement and stage combat to differential equations and linear algebra," says a junior. "The one thing that has remained consistent throughout is the appreciation and dedication the people have for the topic they are involved in." The U is a research university that actually takes teaching seriously, and "every teacher that I've had shows incredible knowledge in their area, as well as personality and wit." "Classes are informative, challenging, and genuinely enjoyable." As is the case in many larger universities, "most general education courses are taught by grad students," whose teaching abilities can range from great to below average. "Ninety percent of my professors are fantastic; the ones that aren't are usually grad students," explains a junior. On this large campus, students have little contact with the school's administration and "there's definitely no hand-holding at the The U. If you're unsure of your major or career plans, it's easy to slip through the cracks." However, students assure us, "The administration puts student interests first whenever possible with a focus on keeping tuition low, creating a diverse environment, and providing opportunities and experience in order to prepare students to be productive citizens."

Life

While a large percentage of the undergraduate community at the University of Utah commutes to campus, there are still plenty of activities for the school's 4,000 resident students. There are many people "active in politics, environmental issues, and international issues," and, after hours, "the school holds different events throughout the year, such as Crimson Nights that feature activities such as bowling, crafts, games, food, and music." Socially, "Greek life is not as large as at other schools but is definitely a lot of fun and the best way to get to know more people your age." In addition, "during football season there are great tailgate parties with friends, drinks, and food." Right off campus, there are a range of great restaurants, and "the nightlife is hard to keep up with." There's always something good going on—whether it's at the bars and clubs downtown, or at small music venues." For outdoorsy types, The U is a paradise. "We have all four seasons and some of the best outdoors in the nation," explains one student. "Killer snow, amazing hills, mountains, lakes, and streams." In this natural wonderland, "hiking, biking, boating, snow-skiing, and snowboarding are just a few of the hundreds of activities available to students."

Student Body

Located in Salt Lake City, hometown to the Church of Jesus Christ of Latter Day Saints, The U has "plenty of social niches to fall into, and none of them are rigidly exclusive." A current student adds, "About half the student body is the typical Utah Mormon, and the other half is a mix of everything. The two halves usually stay separate but they get along." University of Utah students agree that "there is more diversity here than in any other part of the state." However, out-of-state students are uncommon, and "those of us not from Utah are definitely in the minority." While there are a number of residential students, a very large percentage of students also choose to commute to school while living with their parents or family. In addition, "there are a lot of older students and a lot of married students." Academically, however, U undergraduates are "independent, smart, and come to class ready to discuss ideas."

FINANCIAL AID: 801-581-6211 • E-MAIL: ADMISSIONS@SA.UTAH.EDU • WEBSITE: WWW.UTAH.EDU

THE PRINCETON REVIEW SAYS

Admissions

Very important factors considered include: rigor of secondary school record. *Important factors considered include:* academic GPA, standardized test scores, extracurricular activities, talent/ability, character/personal qualities. *Other factors considered include:* class rank, first generation, alumni/ae relation, geographical residence, state residency, racial/ethnic status, volunteer work, work experience, level of applicant's interest. SAT or ACT required for some. ACT with or without writing accepted. SAT with or without Essay component accepted. TOEFL required of all international applicants. High school diploma is required and GED is accepted. *Academic units required:* 4 English, 2 math, 3 science, 1 science lab, 2 foreign language, 1 history, 4 academic electives. *Academic units recommended:* 4 English, 4 math, 3 science, 2 science labs, 3 foreign language, 1 social studies, 2 history, 4 academic electives.

Financial Aid

Students should submit: FAFSA. Priority filing deadline is 3/15. The Princeton Review suggests that all financial aid forms be submitted as soon as possible after October 1. *Need-based scholarships/grants offered:* Federal Pell, FSEOG, State scholarships/grants, Private scholarships, College/university scholarship or grant aid from institutional funds, Federal Nursing Scholarships. *Loan aid offered:* Direct Subsidized Stafford Loans, Direct Unsubsidized Stafford Loans, Direct PLUS loans, Federal Perkins Loans, Federal Nursing Loans, State Loans, College/university loans from institutional funds. Applicants will be notified of awards on a rolling basis beginning 4/1. Federal Work-Study Program available. Institutional employment available.

The Inside Word

Admission is based primarily on the big three: Course selection, grades, and test scores. If you have a 3.0 GPA or better and average test scores, you're close to a sure bet for admission.

THE SCHOOL SAYS "..."

From the Admissions Office

"The University of Utah is a distinctive community of learning in the American West. Today's 31,515 students are from every state and 129 foreign countries. The university has research ties worldwide, with national standing among the top comprehensive research institutions. The university offers 100 undergraduate and more than ninety graduate degree programs. Nationally recognized honors and undergraduate research programs stimulate intellectual inquiry. Undergraduates collaborate with faculty on important investigations. In 2011-2012, the university's intercollegiate athletes began competing in the NCAA PAC-12 Conference. The football team has been nationally ranked for several years, as have our women's gymnastics and skiing teams. The university's location in Salt Lake City provides easy access to the arts, theater, Utah Jazz basketball, and hockey. Utah's great outdoors—skiing, hiking, and five national parks—are nearby. The university was the site for the opening and closing ceremonies and the Athletes Village for the 2002 Olympic Winter Games.

"Housing and residential education has greatly expanded the opportunity for students to live on campus with a new and wide variety of housing. Heritage Commons, constructed during the 2002 Olympics, is located in historic Fort Douglas on campus, and consists of twenty-one buildings, which accommodate more than 2,500 students. The university also has apartment housing available for students located minutes from campus in downtown Salt Lake City. In addition, a new housing complex recently opened for a 'living/learning community' that houses approximately 300 honors students.

"Applicants are required to submit ACT or SAT scores which must be received directly from the appropriate testing agency. Students are encouraged to take the ACT or SAT their junior year of high school."

SELECTIVITY

Admissions Rating	79
# of applicants	12,174
% of applicants accepted	81
% of acceptees attending	34
# offered a place on the wait list	0

FRESHMAN PROFILE

Range SAT Critical Reading	500–640
Range SAT Math	510–660
Range SAT Writing	490–620
Range ACT Composite	21–28
Minimum paper TOEFL	550
Minimum internet-based TOEFL	80
Average HS GPA	3.6
% graduated top 10% of class	25
% graduated top 25% of class	53
% graduated top 50% of class	86

DEADLINES

Early action	
Deadline	12/1
Notification	1/15
Regular	
Priority	12/1
Deadline	4/1
Nonfall registration?	Yes

FINANCIAL FACTS

Financial Aid Rating	80
Annual in-state tuition	$7,130
Annual out-of-state tuition	$24,955
Room and board	$9,000
Required fees	$1,067
Books and supplies	$1,006
Average frosh need-based scholarship	$7,988
Average UG need-based scholarship	$6,910
% needy frosh rec. need-based scholarship or grant aid	88
% needy UG rec. need-based scholarship or grant aid	82
% needy frosh rec. non-need-based scholarship or grant aid	13
% needy UG rec. non-need-based scholarship or grant aid	6
% needy frosh rec. need-based self-help aid	82
% needy UG rec. need-based self-help aid	90
% frosh rec. any financial aid	75
% UG rec. any financial aid	64
% UG borrow to pay for school	39
Average cumulative indebtedness	$19,056
% frosh need fully met	15
% ugrads need fully met	12
Average % of frosh need met	67
Average % of ugrad need met	63

THE UNIVERSITY OF VERMONT

UNIVERSITY OF VERMONT ADMISSIONS, BURLINGTON, VT 05401-3596 • ADMISSIONS: 802-656-3370 • FAX: 802-656-8611

CAMPUS LIFE

Quality of Life Rating	90
Fire Safety Rating	97
Green Rating	98
Type of school	Public
Affiliation	No Affiliation
Environment	Town

STUDENTS

Total undergrad enrollment	10,973
% male/female	44/56
% from out of state	71
% frosh from public high school	70
% frosh live on campus	98
% ugrads live on campus	49
# of fraternities (% ugrad men join)	9 (7)
# of sororities (% ugrad women join)	6 (8)
% African American	1
% Asian	3
% Caucasian	82
% Hispanic	4
% Native American	<1
% Pacific Islander	<1
% Two or more races	3
% Race and/or ethnicity unknown	3
% international	4
# of countries represented	46

SURVEY SAYS...

Lots of liberal students
Students are happy
Students aren't religious
Students environmentally aware
Students love Burlington, VT
Great off-campus food
Lots of beer drinking
Campus newspaper is popular

ACADEMICS

Academic Rating	77
% students returning for sophomore year	86
% students graduating within 4 years	68
% students graduating within 6 years	77
Calendar	Semester
Student/faculty ratio	17:1
Profs interesting rating	77
Profs accessible rating	77

Most classes have 10–19 students.
Most lab/discussion sessions have 10–19 students.

MOST POPULAR MAJORS
Business Administration and Management;
Environmental Studies; Mechanical Engineering

STUDENTS SAY ". . ."

Academics

At The University of Vermont—"a mid-sized university in a cute town that offers a quality education"—you'll get that quintessential college experience: a relaxed but academically-focused atmosphere amid big stone buildings and beautiful foliage. The school is "earthy with a touch of prep, strong outdoor ties, [and] a solid academic program," particularly in the sciences; the "ability to speak freely" is relished, and "UVM is about openness, acceptance, and sustainability while having fun." "The University of Vermont is focused on building a community from within its classrooms, rather than its Division I sports program." says a student. UVM is "not only aware of social-justice issues, it's a school that is actively involved in making change." The Rubenstein School (within UVM) is "an excellent environmental program known around the country" and is a huge draw; it's also "very easy" to switch schools (there is a "wide variety of majors") if you discover a new passion while you're here—which you very well might. Tuition increases have been small of late (less than 3 percent in 2013-14), which is one thing that the green students agree is essential to "sustainability." (True for all institutions of higher education.)

Faculty are overall much-lauded, but most agree that there can be some bad teachers: "You may get an amazing professor, or a professor that will lead you to your death." Small class sizes "allow for a more intimate learning experience," as do the resources available (such as a learning co-op, writing center, and career offices)."I am on a first-name basis with all of my professors and I feel comfortable talking to them at any time," says one senior environmental science major. The professors "can be tough on you, but it is reasonable." "As long as you try your hardest and put in the time, you can usually pass," says a student.

Life

As one might guess, the "landscape, scenery, and outdoor activities are plentiful" at UVM, and "it seems like at least half the school is involved in either the Ski & Snowboard Club, the Outing Club, or both." The Outing Club offers numerous outdoor trips every weekend, and people are pretty into "hiking, going down to Lake Champlain, or just hanging out on Church Street." "We are certainly academically based, yet you might not think it because people here are so independent, involved, and always have something fun going on or somewhere to be," says a junior.

The school has a huge campus, but "it is very easy to travel" and the school's "CATS buses help a huge amount, especially in bad weather!" There exists "a really good relationship with the Burlington community," and the music scene is really big: "lots of great bands come to Burlington, both on and off campus." Though not raging, students at UVM "know how to have a good time" in bars and at parties, and as far as pot use goes, one student summarizes: "It's Burlington, VT. You don't have to smoke, but you had better understand that 4/20 is a holiday." "There's something for everyone here, and it's just a lovely place to be!" says a happy student. However, some think that the meal plans "could really improve to be more flexible and better quality,"

Student Body

Students refer to the "Vermonter-ness", which encompasses a big focus on sustainability ("We compost and recycle as much as possible!"), a "liberal/left minded culture," and being "being green, healthy and happy." The "laid-back atmosphere" has "every kind of individual," all of whom are "passionate about their interests, supportive, and excited to do hands-on work to create positive changes within communities." "Racially, UVM is not diverse; but socially, it is heterogenous." Admittedly, there are a lot of hippies here, "but anyone can fit in." Everyone here is "dedicated to their studies, but in a non-competitive manner": instead of comparing exam grades, "students work together to study so that each student can do their best."

FINANCIAL AID: 802-656-5700 • E-MAIL: ADMISSIONS@UVM.EDU • WEBSITE: WWW.UVM.EDU

THE PRINCETON REVIEW SAYS

Admissions

Very important factors considered include: rigor of secondary school record. *Important factors considered include:* class rank, academic GPA, standardized test scores, application essay, character/personal qualities, state residency. *Other factors considered include:* extracurricular activities, talent/ability, first generation, alumni/ae relation, geographical residence, racial/ethnic status, volunteer work, work experience, level of applicant's interest. SAT or ACT required. ACT with or without writing accepted. SAT with or without Essay component accepted. TOEFL required of all international applicants. High school diploma is required and GED is accepted. *Academic units required:* 4 English, 3 math, 3 science, 1 science lab, 2 foreign language, 3 social studies.

Financial Aid

Students should submit: FAFSA. Priority filing deadline is 2/1. The Princeton Review suggests that all financial aid forms be submitted as soon as possible after October 1. *Need-based scholarships/grants offered:* Federal Pell, FSEOG, State scholarships/grants, Private scholarships, College/university scholarship or grant aid from institutional funds, Federal Nursing Scholarships. *Loan aid offered:* Direct Subsidized Stafford Loans, Direct Unsubsidized Stafford Loans, Direct PLUS loans, Federal Perkins Loans, Federal Nursing Loans, College/university loans from institutional funds. Applicants will be notified of awards on a rolling basis beginning 3/31. Federal Work-Study Program available. Institutional employment available.

The Inside Word

UVM is a very popular choice among out-of-state students, whom the school welcomes; more than half the student body originates from outside of Vermont. While admissions standards are significantly more rigorous for out-of-staters, solid candidates (B-plus/A-minus average, about a 600 on each section of the SAT) should do fine here. The school assesses applications holistically, meaning students who are weak in one area may be able to make up for it with strengths or distinguishing skills and characteristics in other areas.

THE SCHOOL SAYS "..."

From the Admissions Office

"Founded in 1791, the University of Vermont is among the oldest universities in the United States and one of the nation's premier small research universities. During much of its first century, the university was a private liberal college dedicated to undergraduate teaching. In 1868, it became Vermont's public land grant university and expanded its mission to include research and service. Today, UVM combines both elements of its heritage. Undergraduates work in small classes with faculty who are both mentors and world-class researchers. UVM's location in Vermont, known for its civic-mindedness, commitment to the environment, and essential values, strengthens the overall spirit of the university as a tolerant, enlightened, and unusually welcoming community. Not surprisingly, students are drawn to UVM from nearly every state (one third are from Vermont) and fifty countries.

"Academics at UVM are supplemented and deepened by a world of hands-on learning opportunities, from travel-study to service learning, and a wide array of internships in locations ranging from Vermont to China. Many students also assist faculty with their groundbreaking research in state-of-the-art facilities across campus, including UVM's highly-ranked medical school. The university is widely recognized for its environmental conscience, commitment to social justice, and global perspective. In recognition of this achievement outside the classroom, more than 114 UVM students have been selected as winners or finalists in the country's most competitive scholarships, such as the Truman, Fulbright, Udall and Goldwater. The University of Vermont is located in Burlington, one of America's liveliest small cities surrounded by idyllic countryside, the Green Mountains, and Lake Champlain. As the state's educational, medical, financial and cultural epicenter, Burlington is ranked one of the most desirable place to live and a top college town. In addition, Vermont's 'human scale' is often cited as offering UVM students unique opportunities to get involved and gain essential experience."

SELECTIVITY

Admissions Rating	87
# of applicants	25,274
% of applicants accepted	71
% of acceptees attending	13
# offered a place on the wait list	3,759
% accepting a place on wait list	23
% admitted from wait list	0

FRESHMAN PROFILE

Range SAT Critical Reading	550–650
Range SAT Math	550–640
Range SAT Writing	540–650
Range ACT Composite	25–30
Minimum paper TOEFL	577
Minimum internet-based TOEFL	90
Average HS GPA	3.5
% graduated top 10% of class	32
% graduated top 25% of class	74
% graduated top 50% of class	96

DEADLINES

Early action	
Deadline	11/1
Notification	12/15
Regular	
Deadline	1/15
Notification	3/15
Nonfall registration?	Yes

FINANCIAL FACTS

Financial Aid Rating	79
Annual in-state tuition	$14,664
Annual out-of-state tuition	$37,056
Room and board	$11,150
Required fees	$2,104
Books and supplies	$1,200
Average frosh need-based scholarship	$16,660
Average UG need-based scholarship	$15,014
% needy frosh rec. need-based scholarship or grant aid	99
% needy UG rec. need-based scholarship or grant aid	97
% needy frosh rec. non-need-based scholarship or grant aid	12
% needy UG rec. non-need-based scholarship or grant aid	8
% needy frosh rec. need-based self-help aid	69
% needy UG rec. need-based self-help aid	73
% frosh rec. any financial aid	93
% UG rec. any financial aid	83
% UG borrow to pay for school	61
Average cumulative indebtedness	$27,006
% frosh need fully met	17
% ugrads need fully met	12
Average % of frosh need met	70
Average % of ugrad need met	65

UNIVERSITY OF VIRGINIA

OFFICE OF ADMISSION, CHARLOTTESVILLE, VA 22906 • ADMISSIONS: 434-982-3200 • FAX: 434-924-3587

CAMPUS LIFE

Quality of Life Rating	39
Fire Safety Rating	88
Green Rating	94
Type of school	Public
Affiliation	No Affiliation
Environment	City

STUDENTS

Total undergrad enrollment	16,736
% male/female	44/56
% from out of state	28
% frosh from public high school	71
% frosh live on campus	100
% ugrads live on campus	40
# of fraternities (% ugrad men join)	31 (23)
# of sororities (% ugrad women join)	15 (25)
% African American	6
% Asian	13
% Caucasian	60
% Hispanic	6
% Native American	<1
% Pacific Islander	<1
% Two or more races	5
% Race and/or ethnicity unknown	6
% international	5
# of countries represented	118

SURVEY SAYS...

Students are happy
Great library
Students love Charlottesville, VA
Recreation facilities are great
Lots of beer drinking
Everyone loves the Cavaliers
Frats and sororities are popular
Campus newspaper is popular
Alumni active on campus
Active minority support groups

ACADEMICS

Academic Rating	85
% students returning for sophomore year	97
% students graduating within 4 years	87
% students graduating within 6 years	93
Calendar	Semester
Student/faculty ratio	15:1
Profs interesting rating	77
Profs accessible rating	77

Most classes have 10–19 students.
Most lab/discussion sessions have
20–29 students.

MOST POPULAR MAJORS
Business/Commerce; Biology; Economics

STUDENTS SAY "..."

Academics

Along with the low in-state tuition, academic rigor is the reason many students choose UVA. "All our schools are pretty strong and we have beautiful facilities, numerous options to choose from in regards to liberal arts education, and most professors are so excited to be here and be teaching," a sophomore reports. The school's greatest strengths, according to one senior, "include its location in Charlottesville, the wide variety of courses and their high level of academic rigor, and the many ways to work or volunteer outside the classroom." "Each class caters to the smartest kids and elevates everyone. " On the whole, students are very happy with their professors, who are "extremely knowledgeable, passionate, excellent teachers, with a few exceptions. The teachers are generally very accessible and responsive to emails, and are genuinely interested in helping students succeed and encouraging exploration of interesting topic material outside of class." While students note that in large lecture classes it can be a challenge to engage, "professors are very accessible if you seek them out," and "are genuinely interested in helping students succeed and encouraging exploration of interesting topic material outside of class." Academics here are almost universally described as rigorous and challenging, with a particularly tough grading curve in the sciences, but students praise the available resources and academic advising. "Having a personal relationship with faculty members outside of the classroom helps with the academic experience."

Life

Between the gorgeous campus (called "Grounds" within the community) and "the bucolic college town of Charlottesville," students are very happy with life outside the classroom here. Studying occupies much of the week, in the many libraries and study spaces available. There's a lot of school spirit and varsity sporting events are well-attended. On weekends, "there is a significant party culture here...but not necessarily more than at other public universities." "Frat parties dominate the social scene" for first and second year students, with juniors and seniors migrating off-campus to bars and apartment parties. Roughly a quarter of the student body goes Greek. That said, "if students don't like the party scene, Charlottesville's adorable downtown mall is easily accessible by bus and has lots of fun activities!" "There's an ice skating rink downtown, as well as various restaurants and shopping. ""There is always a lot going on on Grounds," as well. "Head to the lawn and you'll never be bored!" "During the warmer months you can always find people outside tossing a Frisbee, or maybe setting up an impromptu volleyball game. There are plenty of great hiking trails in the area and the athletics facilities are great." Students report "lots of student involvement and wide-range of opportunities of activities offered outside the classroom from research to internships to clubs," and "community service is very popular." Some students are eager to see the school make changes in policies pertaining to student safety and sexual misconduct; the administration is responding and has shared a lengthy, proposed new policy with the UVA community for review and comment.

Student Body

"The typical UVA student is reasonably wealthy, white, and very preppy. Other groups can be found within the student body, but you have to actively seek them out." This sums up how students describe themselves, though they're quick to acknowledge that there are other types beyond the typical. Roughly two-thirds of the student body is from Virginia. Some praise the diversity of the school while others would like to see even more. "Preppy" and "involved" are also common adjectives. "The typical student is very involved outside of academics and usually has a million things to do," including socialize. "Student are highly involved in academics, extracurriculars, and socially. Your average UVA student is very well-rounded and extremely busy, but enjoys that lifestyle." This involvement makes it easy for students to find niches within the larger community that suit their interests, and there's no question that everyone here is very driven in the direction of their choosing.

FINANCIAL AID: 434-982-6000 • E-MAIL: UNDERGRADADMISSION@VIRGINIA.EDU • WEBSITE: WWW.VIRGINIA.EDU

THE PRINCETON REVIEW SAYS

Admissions

Very important factors considered include: rigor of secondary school record, class rank, academic GPA, recommendation(s), first generation, alumni/ae relation, state residency, racial/ethnic status. *Important factors considered include:* standardized test scores, application essay, extracurricular activities, talent/ability, character/personal qualities. *Other factors considered include:* geographical residence, volunteer work, work experience. SAT or ACT required; SAT Subject Tests recommend. ACT with Writing required. TOEFL required of all international applicants. High school diploma is required and GED is accepted. *Academic units required:* 4 English, 4 math, 2 science, 2 foreign language, 1 social studies. *Academic units recommended:* 5 math, 4 science, 5 foreign language, 4 social studies.

Financial Aid

Students should submit: FAFSA, CSS/Financial Aid PROFILE. Priority filing deadline is 3/1. The Princeton Review suggests that all financial aid forms be submitted as soon as possible after October 1. *Need-based scholarships/grants offered:* Federal Pell, FSEOG, State scholarships/grants, Private scholarships, College/university scholarship or grant aid from institutional funds, Federal Nursing Scholarships. *Loan aid offered:* Direct Subsidized Stafford Loans, Direct Unsubsidized Stafford Loans, Direct PLUS loans, Federal Perkins Loans, Federal Nursing Loans, College/university loans from institutional funds. Applicants will be notified of awards on or about 4/5. Federal Work-Study Program available. Institutional employment available.

The Inside Word

Unlike many public universities, UVA does not use a formula or minimum scores in its admission process, but applicants must have stellar academic records and demonstrate willingness to rise to the school's academic challenges. The most important parts of the application are GPA, rigor of high school curriculum, test scores (the SAT or ACT is required), and recommendations. Admission here is competitive, particularly for students from out of state.

THE SCHOOL SAYS ". . ."

From the Admissions Office

"Admission to the University of Virginia is competitive. Students who stretch themselves and take rigorous courses in high school (honors-level, AP, A-level, IB, and DE courses, when offered) are more qualified for admission than those who do not. Many students applying to the University present solid academic credentials, but we are also looking beyond the numbers and are interested in a student's life and contributions outside of the classroom. Non-cognitive factors play a significant role in our review, and we are especially interested in students who exhibit strong leadership and personal qualities. Love of learning, the ability to think critically, analytically, and globally, strong writing skills, and the desire to make a difference in the world are also attributes of UVA students.

"SAT or ACT is required but neither is preferred. The writing section on either test is not required, and SAT Subject Tests are optional."

SELECTIVITY

Admissions Rating	97
# of applicants	30,840
% of applicants accepted	30
% of acceptees attending	40
# offered a place on the wait list	3,547
% accepting a place on wait list	59
% admitted from wait list	19

FRESHMAN PROFILE

Range SAT Critical Reading	620–720
Range SAT Math	630–740
Range SAT Writing	620–720
Range ACT Composite	29–33
Average HS GPA	4.2
% graduated top 10% of class	89
% graduated top 25% of class	97
% graduated top 50% of class	99

DEADLINES

Early action	
Deadline	11/1
Notification	1/31
Regular	
Deadline	1/1
Notification	4/1
Nonfall registration?	No

APPLICANTS ALSO LOOK AT AND OFTEN PREFER
College of William and Mary; Virginia Tech

AND SOMETIMES PREFER
Duke University; The University of North Carolina at Chapel Hill

AND RARELY PREFER
James Madison University

FINANCIAL FACTS

Financial Aid Rating	93
Annual in-state tuition	$10,892
Annual out-of-state tuition	$40,506
Room and board	$10,400
Required fees	$2,576
Books and supplies	$1,270
Average frosh need-based scholarship	$19,470
Average UG need-based scholarship	$20,137
% needy frosh rec. need-based scholarship or grant aid	85
% needy UG rec. need-based scholarship or grant aid	84
% needy frosh rec. non-need-based scholarship or grant aid	9
% needy UG rec. non-need-based scholarship or grant aid	8
% needy frosh rec. need-based self-help aid	62
% needy UG rec. need-based self-help aid	64
% frosh rec. any financial aid	55
% UG rec. any financial aid	50
% UG borrow to pay for school	35
Average cumulative indebtedness	$24,905
% frosh need fully met	100
% ugrads need fully met	100
Average % of frosh need met	100
Average % of ugrad need met	100

UNIVERSITY OF WASHINGTON

1410 NORTHEAST CAMPUS PARKWAY, SEATTLE, WA 98195-5852 • ADMISSIONS: 206-543-9686

STUDENTS SAY ". . ."

Academics

Students find "a great combination of high-powered academics, an excellent social life, and a wide variety of courses, all in the midst of the exciting Seattle life" at the University of Washington, the state's flagship institution of higher learning. UW offers "a lot of really stellar programs and the best bang for the buck, especially for in-state students or those in the sciences." Indeed, science programs "are incredible. The research going on here is cutting-edge and the leaders of biomedical sciences, stem cell research, etc. are accessible to students." Undergrads warn, however, that science programs are extremely competitive, "high pressure," and "challenging," with "core classes taught in lectures that seat more than 500 people," creating the sense that "professors don't seem to care too much whether you succeed." Pre-professional programs in business, law, nursing, medicine and engineering all earn high marks, although again with the caveat that the workload is tough and the hand-holding nominal. As one student puts it, "The University of Washington provides every resource and opportunity for its students to succeed. You just have to take advantage of them. No one will do it for you." For those fortunate enough to get in, the Honors Program "creates a smaller community of highly motivated students...It puts this school on top."

Life

UW students typically "have a good balance in their lives of education and fun." They "generally study hard and work in the libraries, but once the nighttime hits, they look forward to enjoying the night with their friends." Between the large university community and the surrounding city of Seattle, undergrads have a near-limitless selection of extracurricular choices. As one student explains, "There are tons of options for fun in Seattle. Going down to Pike's Market on a Saturday and eating your way through is always popular. There are tons of places to eat on 'The Ave,'" the shopping district that abuts campus, "and the UVillage shopping mall is a five minute walk from campus with chain-store comfort available. Intramural sports are big for activities, and going to undergraduate theater productions is never a disappointing experience. During autumn or spring renting a canoe and paddling around lake Washington down by the stadium is fun." Husky football games "are amazing," and the Greek community "is very big" without dominating campus social life. In short, "the UW has anything you could want to do in your free time."

Student Body

"At such a large university, there is no 'typical' student," undergrads tell us, observing "one can find just about any demographic here and there is a huge variety in personalities." There "are quite a lot of yuppies, but then again, it's Seattle," and by and large "the campus is ultraliberal. Most students care about the environment, are not religious, and are generally accepting of other diverse individuals." Otherwise, "you've got your stereotypes: the Greeks, the street fashion pioneers, the various ethnic communities, the Oxford-looking grad students, etc." In terms of demographics, "the typical student at UW is white, middle-class, and is from the Seattle area," but "there are a lot of African American students and a very large number of Asian students." All groups "seem to socialize with each other."

FAX: 206-685-3655 • FINANCIAL AID: 206-543-6101 • WEBSITE: WWW.WASHINGTON.EDU

THE PRINCETON REVIEW SAYS

Admissions

Very important factors considered include: rigor of secondary school record, academic GPA, application essay. *Important factors considered include:* standardized test scores, extracurricular activities, talent/ability, first generation, volunteer work, work experience. *Other factors considered include:* character/personal qualities, state residency. SAT or ACT required. ACT with Writing required. TOEFL required of all international applicants. High school diploma or equivalent is not required.

Financial Aid

Students should submit: FAFSA. Priority filing deadline is 2/28. The Princeton Review suggests that all financial aid forms be submitted as soon as possible after October 1. *Need-based scholarships/grants offered:* Federal Pell, FSEOG, State scholarships/grants, Private scholarships, College/university scholarship or grant aid from institutional funds. *Loan aid offered:* Direct Subsidized Stafford Loans, Direct Unsubsidized Stafford Loans, Direct PLUS loans, Federal Perkins Loans, Federal Nursing Loans. Applicants will be notified of awards on or about 4/1. Federal Work-Study Program available. Institutional employment available.

The Inside Word

In recent years, UW committed to a thorough review of all freshman applications, abandoning the previous process by which a formula was used to rank applicants according to high school GPA and standardized test scores. The new, holistic approach allows admissions officers to take into account a student's background, the degree to which he or she has overcome personal adversity, and such intangibles as leadership quality and special skills. The move has so far resulted in increased racial and socioeconomic diversity, a result praised by some and criticized by others, who regard the new system as a poorly disguised affirmative action program.

THE SCHOOL SAYS "..."

From the Admissions Office

"Are you curious about everything, from comet dust to computer game design, salmon to Salman Rushdie, ancient Rome to the atmospherics of Mars? Do you seek the freedom to chart your own course—and work on breakthrough research? Are you ready to cheer on the Division I Huskies and spend your weekends sea kayaking? Would you like to walk to class on a 700-acre stunning, ivy-covered campus, yet be only fifteen minutes from downtown Seattle? If the answers are yes, then the University of Washington may be the place for you. Offering more than 140 majors and 450 student organizations, the UW is looking for students who are both excited about the vast academic and social possibilities available to them and eager to contribute to the campus' cultural and intellectual life.

"We encourage you to take advantage of every opportunity in the application, especially the personal statement and activities summary, to tell us why Washington would be good fit for you and how you will contribute to the freshman class.

"Freshman applicants to the University of Washington are required to submit scores from either the SAT or ACT (with the writing component)."

SELECTIVITY

Admissions Rating	89
# of applicants	36,840
% of applicants accepted	53
% of acceptees attending	35

FRESHMAN PROFILE

Range SAT Critical Reading	540–660
Range SAT Math	580–710
Range SAT Writing	530–650
Range ACT Composite	26–31
Minimum paper TOEFL	540
Minimum internet-based TOEFL	76
Average HS GPA	3.8

DEADLINES

Nonfall registration?	Yes

APPLICANTS ALSO LOOK AT AND OFTEN PREFER
University of Southern California

AND SOMETIMES PREFER
Gonzaga University

AND RARELY PREFER
Washington State University; University of Puget Sound; University of Colorado Boulder

FINANCIAL FACTS

Financial Aid Rating	81
Annual out-of-state tuition	$33,072
Room and board	$11,310
Required fees	$1,071
Books and supplies	$1,206
Average frosh need-based scholarship	$15,000
Average UG need-based scholarship	$15,000
% needy frosh rec. need-based scholarship or grant aid	74
% needy UG rec. need-based scholarship or grant aid	84
% needy frosh rec. non-need-based scholarship or grant aid	12
% needy UG rec. non-need-based scholarship or grant aid	6
% needy frosh rec. need-based self-help aid	71
% needy UG rec. need-based self-help aid	82
% frosh rec. any financial aid	60
% UG rec. any financial aid	60
% UG borrow to pay for school	40
Average cumulative indebtedness	$21,180
% frosh need fully met	40
% ugrads need fully met	23
Average % of frosh need met	82
Average % of ugrad need met	82

UNIVERSITY OF WISCONSIN—MADISON

702 WEST JOHNSON STREET, SUITE 101, MADISON, WI 53715-1007 • ADMISSIONS: 608-262-3961 • FAX: 608-262-7706

CAMPUS LIFE
Quality of Life Rating	94
Fire Safety Rating	82
Green Rating	60*
Type of school	Public
Affiliation	No Affiliation
Environment	City

STUDENTS
Total undergrad enrollment	31,662
% male/female	49/51
% from out of state	33
% frosh live on campus	92
% ugrads live on campus	26
# of fraternities (% ugrad men join)	26 (9)
# of sororities (% ugrad women join)	11 (8)
% African American	2
% Asian	6
% Caucasian	76
% Hispanic	5
% Native American	<1
% Pacific Islander	<1
% Two or more races	3
% Race and/or ethnicity unknown	<1
% international	8
# of countries represented	108

SURVEY SAYS...
Students are happy
Great library
School is well run
Great financial aid
Students love Madison, WI
Great off-campus food
Lots of beer drinking
Hard liquor is popular
Everyone loves the Badgers
Alumni active on campus

ACADEMICS
Academic Rating	82
% students returning for sophomore year	96
% students graduating within 4 years	57
% students graduating within 6 years	85
Calendar	Semester
Student/faculty ratio	17:1
Profs interesting rating	79
Profs accessible rating	76

Most classes have 10–19 students.
Most lab/discussion sessions have 20–29 students.

MOST POPULAR MAJORS
Political Science and Government; Biology; Economics

STUDENTS SAY "..."

Academics

When it comes right down to it, University of Wisconsin—Madison is the total collegiate package. After all, it offers "unparalleled academics, world renowned research, amazing athletics, [a] beautiful campus [and] friendly student body and staff." All of which help explain why UW—Madison is rife with "school spirit." More importantly, the university develops its undergrads into "forward thinkers and well-rounded individuals who [aim to] make a difference." It also places a strong emphasis on "real-world experience," a facet many students find quite valuable. Of course, the breadth of academic departments at Madison is extraordinary. And these Badgers make a point of noting how "strong" the business and engineering programs are in particular. Undergrads do caution that lectures tend to be "huge." Hence, a number of students advise that you should "really...sit up front and interact with the lesson being taught" if you want most to make the most out of the class. By and large, undergrads give their professors relatively high marks. Though many warn that "they aren't going to hold your hand," it's also quite evident that they "want to see students succeed." One grateful creative writing major agrees adding that "they are all willing to meet, email or chat after class if students have questions." Importantly, the majority of Wisconsin professors are "passionate about the subject matter they teach." And they strive to create "curriculum[s that are] meaningful." Finally, one extremely content psychology succinctly states, "All of my classes have been fascinating and invigorating, as well as challenging."

Life

Many Wisconsin undergrads warn that "academics here are really competitive so Sunday through Friday afternoon[s] are usually spent studying and/or working." Fortunately, these Badgers also know how to "let loose," and we're assured that "there is always something fun to do on-campus or off-campus." Indeed, no matter if they're "eating Babcock Dairy ice cream, partying at clubs, sledding on Bascom Hill, going to concerts [or] visiting the free zoo," students "make time for fun." Certainly, they "love to be active" and it's quite common to see undergrads "going for runs or bikes rides when it's nice out." Athletics are quite popular in general and students especially love to support Badger football. One undergrad boasts, "We have one of the best game experiences in the country...You won't find a more friendly place to be as attendees share brats, offer up beers, and join in singing some of our most memorable chants—all before the game even begins." And, certainly, the city of Madison itself "has no shortage of fun." As a marketing major explains, "State Street which connects the campus to the Capitol, is filled with interesting shops, ethnic foods, and plenty of bars. If students are done with class, this is often a great place to walk around and explore."

Student Body

Undergrads at UW—Madison are very eager to sing the praises of their peers. They quickly describe their fellow Badgers as "as passionate and driven" as well as "open minded" and "smart." Moreover, friendliness is definitely a hallmark of the Wisconsin student body. A neurobiology major bolsters this claim chiming in, "Everyone that goes to this school is really [affable]. When you walk down the street to class people smile at you...I've gone into most discussions not knowing anyone and always end the semester with a couple new friends." Fortunately, the "student body is also diverse, so you are bound to find people who have the same interests as you, whether it be sports, music, science or food!" Lastly, as one thrilled student sums up, "There's a sense of pride instilled in every UW—Madison student. I don't know of one person who regrets choosing to go to school here."

FINANCIAL AID: 608-262-3060 • E-MAIL: ONWISCONSIN@ADMISSIONS.WISC.EDU • WEBSITE: WWW.WISC.EDU

THE PRINCETON REVIEW SAYS

Admissions .

Very important factors considered include: rigor of secondary school record, class rank, academic GPA. *Important factors considered include:* standardized test scores, application essay, state residency. *Other factors considered include:* recommendation(s), extracurricular activities, talent/ability, character/personal qualities, first generation, alumni/ae relation, racial/ethnic status, volunteer work, work experience, level of applicant's interest. SAT or ACT required. ACT with or without writing accepted. SAT with or without Essay component accepted. TOEFL required of all international applicants. High school diploma is required and GED is accepted. *Academic units required:* 4 English, 4 math, 3 science, 3 foreign language, 3 social studies, 2 academic electives. *Academic units recommended:* 4 English, 4 math, 4 science, 4 foreign language, 4 social studies, 3 academic electives.

Financial Aid

Students should submit: FAFSA. The Princeton Review suggests that all financial aid forms be submitted as soon as possible after October 1. *Need-based scholarships/grants offered:* Federal Pell, FSEOG, State scholarships/grants, Private scholarships, College/university scholarship or grant aid from institutional funds. *Loan aid offered:* Direct Subsidized Stafford Loans, Direct Unsubsidized Stafford Loans, Direct PLUS loans, Federal Perkins Loans, Federal Nursing Loans. Applicants will be notified of awards on a rolling basis beginning 4/1. Federal Work-Study Program available. Institutional employment available.

The Inside Word

Though UW—Madison is a large state school, it still manages to take a holistic approach to the admissions game. Indeed, there are no minimum GPAs, class ranks, or test scores required. That said, a strong academic record is paramount. Looking beyond your transcript, Wisconsin wants candidates who will actively contribute to campus life. And it also seeks diversity in both background and personal experience. Finally, students who intend to major in either dance or music must schedule an audition in addition to submitting a regular application.

THE SCHOOL SAYS ". . ."

From the Admissions Office

"UW-Madison is the university of choice for some of the best students from around the world. The middle 50 percent of our Fall 2015 freshman class had an ACT score range of 27-32, an SAT score range of 1910-2130, a GPA range of 3.8-4.0, and ranked in the 86-97 percentile of their class.

"These factors combine to make admission to UW-Madison both competitive and selective. We consider academic record, strength of curriculum (honors, AP, IB, etc.), grade trend, class rank, results of the ACT/SAT, and non-academic factors. There is no prescribed minimum test score, GPA, or class rank criteria. Rather, we admit the best and most well-prepared students—students who have challenged themselves and who will contribute to Wisconsin's strength and diversity—for the limited space available. "Each application is personally reviewed by our admission counselors. All freshman applications completed by February 1 receive full and equal consideration. We offer two decision plans for freshman applicants. To receive a decision during the Early Action period, you must complete the application by November 1 and submit all required materials (application fee, official transcript(s), official test scores, personal essays, and one required academic letter of recommendation) by our materials deadline. Early Action period applicants will receive a decision by the end of January. All students who complete their application during the Regular Decision period (after November 1 but before the February 1 deadline) will receive a decision by the end of March. UW-Madison has a commitment to a holistic, competitive, and selective admission process for all applicants."

SELECTIVITY
Admissions Rating	92
# of applicants	32,780
% of applicants accepted	49
% of acceptees attending	39

FRESHMAN PROFILE
Range SAT Critical Reading	560–660
Range SAT Math	630–760
Range SAT Writing	600–690
Range ACT Composite	27–31
Average HS GPA	3.9
% graduated top 10% of class	54
% graduated top 25% of class	91
% graduated top 50% of class	100

DEADLINES
Regular	
Deadline	2/1
Nonfall registration?	Yes

APPLICANTS ALSO LOOK AT AND OFTEN PREFER
University of Illinois at Urbana-Champaign; University of Minnesota–Twin Cities Campus; University of Michigan–Ann Arbor; Marquette University

AND SOMETIMES PREFER
Northwestern University; University of Colorado Boulder

FINANCIAL FACTS
Financial Aid Rating	88
Annual in-state tuition	$9,273
Annual out-of-state tuition	$28,523
Room and board	$8,804
Required fees	$1,142
Books and supplies	$1,200
Average frosh need-based scholarship	$10,259
Average UG need-based scholarship	$10,169
% needy frosh rec. need-based scholarship or grant aid	94
% needy UG rec. need-based scholarship or grant aid	96
% needy frosh rec. non-need-based scholarship or grant aid	9
% needy UG rec. non-need-based scholarship or grant aid	8
% needy frosh rec. need-based self-help aid	74
% needy UG rec. need-based self-help aid	79
% UG borrow to pay for school	49
Average cumulative indebtedness	$26,994
% frosh need fully met	35
% ugrads need fully met	37
Average % of frosh need met	76
Average % of ugrad need met	78

UNIVERSITY OF WYOMING

DEPARTMENT 3435, LARAMIE, WY 82071 • ADMISSIONS: 307-766-5160 • FAX: 307-766-4042

CAMPUS LIFE

Quality of Life Rating	86
Fire Safety Rating	91
Green Rating	73
Type of school	Public
Affiliation	No Affiliation
Environment	Town

STUDENTS

Total undergrad enrollment	10,045
% male/female	48/52
% from out of state	32
% frosh live on campus	88
% ugrads live on campus	24
# of fraternities (% ugrad men join)	9 (6)
# of sororities (% ugrad women join)	6 (6)
% African American	1
% Asian	1
% Caucasian	76
% Hispanic	7
% Native American	1
% Pacific Islander	<1
% Two or more races	3
% Race and/or ethnicity unknown	7
% international	4
# of countries represented	91

SURVEY SAYS...

Students are happy
Classroom facilities are great
Great library
Great financial aid

ACADEMICS

Academic Rating	72
% students returning for sophomore year	76
% students graduating within 4 years	26
% students graduating within 6 years	55
Calendar	Semester
Student/faculty ratio	14:1
Profs interesting rating	73
Profs accessible rating	76

Most classes have 20–29 students.
Most lab/discussion sessions have
20–29 students.

MOST POPULAR MAJORS
Psychology; Elementary Education and
Teaching; Mechanical Engineering

STUDENTS SAY "..."

Academics

Why choose University of Wyoming? "Wyoming scholarships rock!" Hathaway Scholarships allow state residents to graduate virtually debt free, and financial aid for out-of-state students isn't too shabby, either. This allows students to get "an outstanding education for pennies on the dollar." This is a large university, though, which means "you have to make the commitment to do well." In other words, those grades aren't going to earn themselves! The business school, engineering school, and English departments all receive high marks from students, and the school's agricultural programs also have an excellent reputation. "They are on top of developing degree programs and courses focused on sustainability, green design, and climate change." There's "a 50/50 [split between] professors who love what they do and those who are just going with the flow," but "nine times out of ten they will go well out of their way to help you." Many faculty members "have real-world job experience that helps bring their lectures to life." Many students complain about the registration process, which favors athletes and members of the honors program, but others suggest that kicking up a fuss will get you into the classes you want, or they suggest applying for the honors program: "They pull in the best professors across campus, and the requirements are a piece of cake. Plus, you get free printing," semester-long book checkout at the library, and priority registration. (Conservatives take note: Some students describe the honors classes as "very biased and liberal.") "The new library is great and full of awesome resources," and study abroad resources are "absolutely amazing" as well.

Life

"Cowboy football is a blast! We may not have the best team or biggest crowd, but we make up for it in dedicated fans!" Supporting UW's Division I football team is a bit pastime in the fall. Winter in Laramie, Wyoming, may be freezing (student wish lists include reopening underground tunnels for travel between buildings, and/or "fire pits for staying warm on your way to your next class!"), but it's "a great town if you enjoy the outdoors," and "skiing, mountain biking, hiking, camping, fishing, mountain climbing, hunting are all popular activities." "People often say that there is nothing to do in Laramie but drink," and UW has its fair share of partying, though members of the large religious and nontraditional student populations are quick to point out that not everyone is searching for a house party every weekend. "The school offers a wide breadth of other activities from free ice skating to free movies, fly-fishing classes to a capella concerts, and many of these are run by students and are widely attended." Fort Collins and Denver, Colorado, are both about two and a half hours away by car, though if you're bringing a vehicle to campus, four-wheel drive is strongly recommended.

Student Body

"The majority of the students are Wyoming residents with a large portion of the rest coming from Colorado." Students tend to be "good-natured kids [who have] grown up on ranches or farms where a strong work ethic has been established," "usually nice with strong family values and a conservative upbringing." Politically, there seems to be a bit of a divide among students, which reflects the geography of the university: Laramie is considered a more liberal enclave in a traditionally conservative state. "The school creates an open-minded atmosphere within one of the most conservative states in the union," but on the other hand, "many of the Christian campus ministries are very outspoken." Students say, "We are not incredibly diverse ethnically, but we are diverse in so many other ways," and "every semester brings more and more minority and foreign students." There's "a huge amount of nontraditional students as well."

FINANCIAL AID: 307-766-2116 • E-MAIL: ADMISSIONS@UWYO.EDU • WEBSITE: WWW.UWYO.EDU

THE PRINCETON REVIEW SAYS

Admissions

Very important factors considered include: rigor of secondary school record, academic GPA, standardized test scores. *Important factors considered include: Other factors considered include:* application essay. SAT or ACT required. ACT with or without writing accepted. TOEFL required of all international applicants. High school diploma is required and GED is accepted. *Academic units required:* 4 English, 4 math, 4 science, 3 science labs, 2 foreign language, 3 social studies, 2 academic electives, and 2 units from above areas or other academic areas. *Academic units recommended:* 4 English, 4 math, 4 science, 3 science labs, 2 foreign language, 3 social studies, 2 academic electives, and 2 units from above areas or other academic areas.

Financial Aid

Students should submit: FAFSA. Priority filing deadline is 3/1. The Princeton Review suggests that all financial aid forms be submitted as soon as possible after October 1. *Need-based scholarships/grants offered:* Federal Pell, FSEOG, State scholarships/grants, Private scholarships, College/university scholarship or grant aid from institutional funds. *Loan aid offered:* Direct Subsidized Stafford Loans, Direct Unsubsidized Stafford Loans, Direct PLUS loans, Federal Perkins Loans. Applicants will be notified of awards on a rolling basis beginning 3/28. Federal Work-Study Program available. Institutional employment available.

The Inside Word

The admissions process at UW is formula-driven. An unweighted high school GPA of 3.0 in a traditional college prep curriculum combined with some solid test scores (21 ACT or CR+M 980 SAT) will open the door to this university.

THE SCHOOL SAYS "..."

From the Admissions Office

"The University of Wyoming offers a personalized education for a fraction of the cost of other public universities. Located in Laramie, UW is regularly recognized as one of the nation's best college values. This comes as no surprise, as UW is a national research university offering countless academic opportunities.

"Explore 200+ programs of study through seven colleges and three specialized schools. From Engineering to Business, Performing Arts to Geology and Agricultural Economics to Nursing, we are sure you will find your program at UW.

"Over the past seven years, the UW campus has experienced incredible growth. 750 million dollars have been invested in new facilities including a new Business building, Creative Arts facility, UW Library and most recently the introduction of the NCAR supercomputer. The NCAR computer is a joint partnership between UW and the National Center for Atmospheric Research. Undergraduate students have access to all these facilities for instruction, internships and research.

"Set at 7,200 feet above sea level, UW and Laramie are in a pristine location to attend school and enjoy the outdoors. UW was recently recognized by Outside magazine as the fifteenth best college campus in the country for outdoor adventure. Just thirty miles from campus is over two million acres of national forest with peaks climbing over 12,000 feet. Campus life is exciting with 200+ student clubs and organizations as well as NCAA Division 1-A sports in the Mountain West conference."

SELECTIVITY

Admissions Rating	74
# of applicants	4,657
% of applicants accepted	96
% of acceptees attending	38

FRESHMAN PROFILE

Range SAT Critical Reading	480–615
Range SAT Math	490–620
Range ACT Composite	22–27
Minimum paper TOEFL	540
Minimum internet-based TOEFL	76
Average HS GPA	3.5
% graduated top 10% of class	22
% graduated top 25% of class	50
% graduated top 50% of class	81

DEADLINES

Regular	
Priority	3/1
Deadline	8/10
Nonfall registration?	Yes

FINANCIAL FACTS

Financial Aid Rating	81
Annual in-state tuition	$3,570
Annual out-of-state tuition	$14,310
Room and board	$10,037
Required fees	$1,322
Books and supplies	$1,200
Average frosh need-based scholarship	$4,734
Average UG need-based scholarship	$4,918
% needy frosh rec. need-based scholarship or grant aid	60
% needy UG rec. need-based scholarship or grant aid	68
% needy frosh rec. non-need-based scholarship or grant aid	86
% needy UG rec. non-need-based scholarship or grant aid	69
% needy frosh rec. need-based self-help aid	55
% needy UG rec. need-based self-help aid	61
% UG borrow to pay for school	46
% frosh need fully met	25
% ugrads need fully met	14
Average % of frosh need met	65
Average % of ugrad need met	60

URSINUS COLLEGE

URSINUS COLLEGE, COLLEGEVILLE, PA 19426 • ADMISSIONS: 610-409-3200 • FAX: 610-409-3662

STUDENTS SAY "..."

Academics

Set in Collegeville, Pennsylvania, this "small, close-knit college community" offers "an exceptional academic record" and "small-school atmosphere," which "provides accessibility to professors and successful students, enabling a better learning experience." This is "a campus filled with motivated students and professors who worked toward every student's success." "Academic integrity" is "high," "yet fostering leadership, community and personal growth [is] also extremely prided." The "greatest strengths" of Ursinus's program "are probably the focus on community service, the strength of the academic programs, and programs such as CIE (Common Intellectual Experience, an entire class [where the focus is on] the whole campus reading and discussing the same books or movies." Ursinus is also known for its "strong biology and science program," which "allow students to maintain strong connections in other fields, from art to education." Classes "are small," and professors "are accessible and have extensive knowledge in their fields." The academic bar here is high. Professors expect "students to be engaged." They "tend to be very attentive to your performance in class and are available to help if you need it." While "[professors] expect a lot from you, and it is challenging," the workload is "very doable because of the relationships with professors and students." Overall, this small, rigorous program is "about creating free-thinking, intelligent, [and] contributing members of society" and "letting people be who they are without fear and while accomplishing learning beyond the classroom."

Life

During the week, "mostly everyone goes to class and then to the library or another study room to finish homework and study." "There is always something happening on campus, which is contrary to the big misconception about smaller schools." "Because the student population is low, everyone receives e-mails about everything going on." In addition, there "is a large athletic population, and games are highly attended." "Almost every night there is some party going on, and on weekends it can get crazy, but the drinking scene is easily avoidable." Others agree, "The school offers a lot of weekend activities for those of us who do not partake in drinking. They have movie nights, casino nights, game show nights, special dinners, [and] a lot of off campus events." While "the town [of Collegeville] is small, they are expanding and building upon it. Philadelphia is close as is King of Prussia, Phoenixville, Skippack, and Limerick so students have places to go off campus and have fun." "Most students stay on weekends and either attend a campus event or hang out with friends." "Partying does happen; it happens only Thursday through Saturday because most students are extremely serious about their academics."

Student Body

Ursinus students are "well-rounded, mature, and friendly." Everyone at Ursinus "has an interest in their academics as well as their social life." "Because of various requirements, students interact with all sorts of students with different majors, especially our CIE class, which requires a lot of introspection." Most students "can find a group of students they fit in with easily." The typical student "has a core group of friends, friends that they have classes with, many are involved with some kind of sport (intramural or collegiate), and many are involved with community service." While some tout the stereotypical badge of being "upper-middle- or middle-class, involved in a sport in some way"; however, by in large the student body here is "very open to other beliefs and opinions" and "willing to branch out into different areas other than their specified major." Overall, a "supportive and friendly" atmosphere pervades. Ursinus students "are all hard-working and must go above and beyond to compete academically." Students at Ursinus tend to balance their "very studious" academic aspirations "with an active and healthy extracurricular lifestyle." They're "outgoing to others [and] involved in campus and in the society." "Many students are athletes," and "About 20 percent of the campus is affiliated with a Greek organization." In a sentence, "Ursinus students are overachievers."

FINANCIAL AID: 610-409-3600 • E-MAIL: ADMISSIONS@URSINUS.EDU • WEBSITE: WWW.URSINUS.EDU

THE PRINCETON REVIEW SAYS

Admissions

Very important factors considered include: rigor of secondary school record, academic GPA, character/personal qualities. *Important factors considered include:* class rank, application essay, recommendation(s), interview, extracurricular activities, talent/ability. *Other factors considered include:* standardized test scores, first generation, alumni/ae relation, geographical residence, state residency, racial/ethnic status, volunteer work, work experience, level of applicant's interest. SAT or ACT recommend. ACT with Writing required. SAT with Essay component required. TOEFL required of all international applicants. High school diploma is required and GED is accepted. *Academic units required:* 4 English, 3 math, 2 science, 2 science labs, 2 foreign language, 4 social studies. *Academic units recommended:* 4 English, 4 math, 4 science, 3 foreign language, 4 social studies.

Financial Aid

Students should submit: FAFSA, CSS/Financial Aid PROFILE. Regular filing deadline is 2/15. The Princeton Review suggests that all financial aid forms be submitted as soon as possible after October 1. *Need-based scholarships/grants offered:* Federal Pell, FSEOG, State scholarships/grants, Private scholarships, College/university scholarship or grant aid from institutional funds. *Loan aid offered:* Direct Subsidized Stafford Loans, Direct Unsubsidized Stafford Loans, Direct PLUS loans, Federal Perkins Loans. Applicants will be notified of awards on or about 3/15. Federal Work-Study Program available. Institutional employment available.

The Inside Word

Ursinus has been test optional since 2011. But you'll still need a consistently excellent academic record to gain admission. If you're hoping to snag a scholarship, it's essential that you visit campus for an interview, and interviews are strongly encouraged anyway.

THE SCHOOL SAYS " . . ."

From the Admissions Office

"Located in suburban Philadelphia, the college boasts a beautiful 168-acre campus that features a highly individualized academic experience; the nationally recognized Common Intellectual Experience first-year seminar; residential village housing for students; the Floy Lewis Bakes Athletic Center with an indoor track and fieldhouse; the Berman Museum of Art; and the performing arts center. Ursinus is a member of the Centennial Conference along with Dickinson, Franklin & Marshall, Gettysburg, Muhlenberg, and Swarthmore. The academic environment is enhanced by a chapter of Phi Beta Kappa, the Early Assurance Program to medical school with the Drexel University College of Medicine, 3-2 Engineering agreements with Columbia University and Case Western Reserve, Peace Corps preparation, the Center for Science and the Common Good, the U-Imagine! Center for Integrative and Entrepreneurial Studies, Direct Admission Partnership with the Simon Business School at the University of Rochester and worldwide international study abroad. The college offers student research carried out with one-on-one faculty attention and extensive internship opportunities. Financial aid and scholarships are generous with special awards for outstanding academics; distinguished creative writing; music, dance and theater auditions; and Bonner leadership in service. Intercollegiate and intramural sports are very popular on campus. The Ursinus admission application requires strong, consistent performance in a college preparatory curriculum and submission of a graded high school paper. Submission of standardized tests is optional."

SELECTIVITY

Admissions Rating	78
# of applicants	2,634
% of applicants accepted	83
% of acceptees attending	20

FRESHMAN PROFILE

Range SAT Critical Reading	520–620
Range SAT Math	520–630
Range SAT Writing	500–610
Range ACT Composite	23–30
Minimum internet-based TOEFL	80
Average HS GPA	3.2
% graduated top 10% of class	25
% graduated top 25% of class	53
% graduated top 50% of class	89

DEADLINES

Early decision	
Deadline	2/1
Notification	2/15
Early action	
Deadline	1/1
Notification	2/1
Regular	
Priority	2/1
Nonfall registration?	Yes

FINANCIAL FACTS

Financial Aid Rating	84
Annual tuition	$49,370
Room and board	$12,320
Required fees	$0
Books and supplies	$1,000
Average frosh need-based scholarship	$33,250
Average UG need-based scholarship	$30,571
% needy frosh rec. need-based scholarship or grant aid	100
% needy UG rec. need-based scholarship or grant aid	100
% needy frosh rec. non-need-based scholarship or grant aid	20
% needy UG rec. non-need-based scholarship or grant aid	18
% needy frosh rec. need-based self-help aid	79
% needy UG rec. need-based self-help aid	80
% frosh rec. any financial aid	99
% UG rec. any financial aid	97
% UG borrow to pay for school	74
Average cumulative indebtedness	$38,282
% frosh need fully met	21
% ugrads need fully met	19
Average % of frosh need met	88
Average % of ugrad need met	78

VANDERBILT UNIVERSITY

2305 WEST END AVENUE, NASHVILLE, TN 37203 • ADMISSIONS: 615-322-2561 • FAX: 615-343-7765

CAMPUS LIFE
Quality of Life Rating	97
Fire Safety Rating	91
Green Rating	92
Type of school	Private
Affiliation	No Affiliation
Environment	Metropolis

STUDENTS
Total undergrad enrollment	6,883
% male/female	50/50
% from out of state	90
% frosh from public high school	65
% frosh live on campus	100
% ugrads live on campus	92
# of fraternities (% ugrad men join)	17 (35)
# of sororities (% ugrad women join)	16 (53)
% African American	8
% Asian	12
% Caucasian	55
% Hispanic	8
% Native American	<1
% Pacific Islander	<1
% Two or more races	5
% Race and/or ethnicity unknown	5
% international	7
# of countries represented	50

SURVEY SAYS...
Students are happy
Classroom facilities are great
Great library
Career services are great
School is well run
Great financial aid
Students are friendly
Students love Nashville, TN
Great food on campus
Great off-campus food
Easy to get around campus
Lots of beer drinking
Hard liquor is popular
Frats and sororities are popular

ACADEMICS
Academic Rating	93
% students returning for sophomore year	97
% students graduating within 4 years	87
% students graduating within 6 years	92
Calendar	Semester
Student/faculty ratio	8:1
Profs interesting rating	91
Profs accessible rating	89

Most classes have 10–19 students.
Most lab/discussion sessions have
10–19 students.

MOST POPULAR MAJORS
Engineering Science; Social Sciences; Multi-/
Interdisciplinary Studies

STUDENTS SAY "..."

Academics

The word "balance" is much used by students in describing Vanderbilt University, with its "top academics, vibrant social life, student organizations, community service, SEC football, and the city of Nashville" or the "unique balance [that] exists between social life and schoolwork." Students say this "balance" is why at Vanderbilt you'll get "an amazing education while having a good time and exploring all your interests along the way." As one student explains, "Vanderbilt is a place for students who are intelligent, but are more than just book-smart"—"it combines rigorous academics with a great social life." Another student says, "At Vanderbilt, I could [pursue] my interest in music while majoring in engineering, which was not the case in most other schools." The school is heavily influenced by the "diverse," "vibrant" city of Nashville. The "beautiful campus" is "only minutes away from being in the heart of the city," where there's a "crazy fun social scene, all with a Southern twist" and people "like being involved." This correlates well with Vanderbilt students who participate in an "array of extracurriculars" and take advantage of the school's "amazing community service opportunities" on campus and around Nashville. Within the 530 student organizations on campus, a student is hard-pressed not to find a few organizations that they can relate to. "The professors are engaging and the academics [are] challenging but rewarding." Professors are "approachable and helpful" and "are really invested in their students and will go out of their well to help them succeed." Besides the "rigorous but rewarding" academic environment, there are many "opportunities that challenge me beyond the books," says a student. When asked about what improvements might be made to their school, many agreed, "Dining and parking are mediocre at best." "The lines at lunch can be really long, and not as many options are open on the weekends," though some students note that the lunch crunch can be "avoided with some planning."

Life

"Everyone here knows how to be a student when it's time to be a student, and a college kid when outside of the classroom." Students say there's an "academic environment" but Vandy students " take the work hard/play hard mentality to heart when it comes to weekend activities." As one student puts it, "Everyone is outgoing and friendly, that's why we came to the South!" There is "a vibrant Greek [life] community" on campus and students say the social scene is inclusive and interwoven: "It is not unusual for a student to be a tour guide, RA, Fraternity officer, and still kill it in the classroom." The "beautiful" campus provides the "perfect balance between your classic college campus and big city school" and the students are "Passionate, caring, [and] genuine." Even though "academics are usually at the top of everyone's lists," there's "always so much to do on campus or downtown in Nashville," with one student adding that it's also fun to "visit one of the many state parks that are close by, or go to one of the thousands of concerts Nashville has annually." On the whole, the atmosphere is "friendly and welcoming" and students say their peers are "clearly of high intellect, they are not competitive with each other academically and enjoy other things besides school."

Student Body

Vanderbilt has "a very interesting student body that blends traditional Southern students and culture with very distinct Northern influence," and students say that "You can find such a diverse group of people here...not just racially or ethnically or economically, but also in personality." The typical Vandy student is "well-rounded, engaged" and "committed to both learning and to extracurriculars." There's an atmosphere of collaboration rather than competition, students say: "People here don't worry about scoring higher than the person next to them. We're all in this together." While some say that "many fit the stereotype of rich, White, and upper class," most counter that Vanderbilt has "a diverse student body" and "students come from all over and the freshman experience does a good job making us a united class."

FINANCIAL AID: 800-288-0204 • E-MAIL: ADMISSIONS@VANDERBILT.EDU • WEBSITE: WWW.VANDERBILT.EDU

THE PRINCETON REVIEW SAYS

Admissions

Very important factors considered include: rigor of secondary school record, class rank, academic GPA, standardized test scores, application essay, extracurricular activities, character/personal qualities. *Important factors considered include:* recommendation(s), talent/ability. *Other factors considered include:* interview, first generation, alumni/ae relation, geographical residence, state residency, racial/ethnic status, volunteer work, work experience. SAT or ACT required; SAT Subject Tests considered if submitted. ACT with or without writing accepted. SAT with or without Essay component accepted. TOEFL required of all international applicants. High school diploma is required and GED is accepted. *Academic units required:* 4 English, 3 math, 3 science, 2 science labs, 2 foreign language, 2 social studies, 1 history, 3 academic electives. *Academic units recommended:* 4 English, 4 math, 4 science, 3 science labs, 2 foreign language, 3 social studies, 1 history, 3 academic electives.

Financial Aid

Students should submit: FAFSA, CSS/Financial Aid PROFILE. Priority filing deadline is 2/1. The Princeton Review suggests that all financial aid forms be submitted as soon as possible after October 1. *Need-based scholarships/grants offered:* Federal Pell, FSEOG, State scholarships/grants, Private scholarships, College/university scholarship or grant aid from institutional funds. *Loan aid offered:* Direct Subsidized Stafford Loans, Direct Unsubsidized Stafford Loans, Direct PLUS loans, Federal Perkins Loans, Federal Nursing Loans, College/university loans from institutional funds. Applicants will be notified of awards on or about 4/1. Federal Work-Study Program available. Institutional employment available.

The Inside Word

Vanderbilt deliberately keeps its incoming first year class small at roughly 1,600 students and with over 31,000 applicants a year, competition is tough for this very selective Nashville institution. With the admission committee's holistic approach to reviewing candidates, interested students should take stock of more than just their GPAs and standardized test scores. Many students take the early decision route—Vanderbilt has two early decision deadlines.

THE SCHOOL SAYS "..."

From the Admissions Office

"The Vanderbilt undergraduate experience is often described as uniquely balanced. Within the context of an outstanding academic landscape, students are encouraged to participate in a broad spectrum of campus organizations among a highly diverse population. Many students take classes in all four undergraduate schools, stretching their intellectual experience far beyond that of their declared major. Students typically live on campus all four years, beginning with a year at The Martha Rivers Ingram Commons, a living and learning residential community for first-year students. Warren and Moore Colleges, the two newest residential colleges, expanded living-learning opportunities for upperclass students. Students take full advantage of Nashville, often participating in government-, business-, or education-related internships, and enjoying cultural offerings of the city, honored by Business Insider as one of 'The 13 Hottest American Cities for 2016.'

"Through Opportunity Vanderbilt, the university makes three commitments regarding financial aid:

1. Vanderbilt's admissions process is need-blind for all U.S. citizens and eligible non-citizens.

2. Vanderbilt meets 100 percent of a family's demonstrated financial need for all admitted students.

3. Financial aid awards do not include loans. Instead of offering need-based loans, Vanderbilt offers additional grant assistance.

"The admissions process is holistic—Vanderbilt does not employ cutoffs for standardized testing or grade point averages. Students admitted to Vanderbilt typically show exceptional academic accomplishment and are highly engaged in their communities, often serving in leadership roles. The prescreening video and audition are of primary importance for students applying to the Blair School of Music."

SELECTIVITY

Admissions Rating	99
# of applicants	31,464
% of applicants accepted	12
% of acceptees attending	44
# of early decision applicants	3,582
% accepted early decision	23

FRESHMAN PROFILE

Range SAT Critical Reading	710–790
Range SAT Math	720–800
Range SAT Writing	690–770
Range ACT Composite	32–35
Minimum internet-based TOEFL	100
Average HS GPA	3.8
% graduated top 10% of class	91
% graduated top 25% of class	97
% graduated top 50% of class	100

DEADLINES

Early decision	
Deadline	11/1
Notification	12/15
Regular	
Priority	1/1
Deadline	1/1
Notification	4/1
Nonfall registration?	No

APPLICANTS ALSO LOOK AT AND OFTEN PREFER

Harvard College; Massachusetts Institute of Technology; Princeton University

AND SOMETIMES PREFER

Georgetown University; University of Pennsylvania; Cornell University

AND RARELY PREFER

Tulane University; Emory University

FINANCIAL FACTS

Financial Aid Rating	99
Annual tuition	$44,492
Room and board	$14,964
Required fees	$1,114
Books and supplies	$1,294
Average frosh need-based scholarship	$41,718
Average UG need-based scholarship	$40,267
% needy frosh rec. need-based scholarship or grant aid	89
% needy UG rec. need-based scholarship or grant aid	92
% needy frosh rec. non-need-based scholarship or grant aid	56
% needy UG rec. non-need-based scholarship or grant aid	42
% needy frosh rec. need-based self-help aid	39
% needy UG rec. need-based self-help aid	49
% frosh rec. any financial aid	69
% UG rec. any financial aid	65
% UG borrow to pay for school	22
Average cumulative indebtedness	$21,506
% frosh need fully met	98
% ugrads need fully met	99
Average % of frosh need met	100
Average % of ugrad need met	100

VASSAR COLLEGE

124 RAYMOND AVENUE, POUGHKEEPSIE, NY 12604 • ADMISSIONS: 845-437-7300 • FAX: 845-437-7063

STUDENTS SAY "..."

Academics

Vassar College is a small "academically challenging" school that offers a "perfect liberal arts feel" and seeks to broaden students' perspectives. The "strong sense of community" is apparent both in and out of the classroom, where the school drums home the idea that "it's all about being unique and letting your quirky characteristics shine." "We're asked to critically think about the world we live in and how our privilege plays into these systems," says a student. This freedom of character is a main reason why everyone here is "excited to be with each other, which creates this school spirit that isn't necessarily based on sports."

The lack of core requirements is "a great opportunity for students to explore anything they want before settling into a major." "Amazing" professors are "super accessible" and "fully engaged in the total Vassar community." "They are willing to meet you outside their office hours if they don't work for you," says a student. "My professors are...spectacular at illuminating difficult material," says a junior psychology major. Classes are all small and "most are very discussion-based"; students are "not competitive with each other, but with themselves," which creates a more relaxed environment despite the very high academics. Many do admit that there could stand to be "more sections of the most popular classes so that the most amount of people can be happy with their course selections."

Opportunities are there for students' voices to be heard, and "the administration is very willing to work with the student organization to accomplish goals," such as a ban on bottled water from dining services as a result of an initiative by the environmental group on campus. "Vassar students will do things in any way but the traditional way," says a sophomore. "No problem goes undiscussed." "Incredible" study abroad opportunities and a "beautiful campus" don't hurt, either.

Life

"When you get here it starts to feel like home very quickly," says a student of the "stunning" campus. "The vibe of the whole school is so chill," but does not hamper a "vibrant extracurricular scene." Vassar is "bursting at the seams with orgs": there are "a ton of intramural sports teams," nine a cappella groups, plenty of political organizations, a large performing arts contingent, and "basically anything else you can think of." "Close-knit dormitory communities" and an emphasis on being "hyper-socially aware" lead students to be "very politically conscious and deeply involved in volunteerism and activism."

New York City isn't far, so some people take advantage of that, and "there are always parties you can go to if you want to," but "there is nothing wrong with staying in and watching a movie or chatting with friends." There is no Greek life; intellectual conversations abound at all hours, and students spend "significant time thinking about the state of the world, what's going on within the campus community." There are always a decent amount of weekend activities such as "concerts, comedy shows, plays, dances, etc." Be warned: "transportation is limited to get off campus unless you own a car."

Student Body

The "left wing, artsy, intelligent," and "open-minded" individuals that make up the "eclectic" student body "thrive" in the "welcoming" environs of Vassar. The "very generous" amount of need-based financial aid that is awarded "allows for wide socioeconomic diversity," and "Freshman Orientation is a great way for people to make friends here." Many here are philosophically minded and "strive to be as politically correct as possible," and there is "a good amount of hipsters." "You can definitely find at least one other student for every obscure interest you have," assures a student.

FINANCIAL AID: 845-437-5230 • E-MAIL: ADMISSIONS@VASSAR.EDU • WEBSITE: WWW.VASSAR.EDU

THE PRINCETON REVIEW SAYS

Admissions

Very important factors considered include: rigor of secondary school record. *Important factors considered include:* class rank, academic GPA, standardized test scores, application essay, recommendation(s), extracurricular activities, talent/ability, character/personal qualities. *Other factors considered include:* interview, first generation, alumni/ae relation, geographical residence, racial/ethnic status, volunteer work, work experience. ACT with Writing required. SAT with Essay component required. TOEFL required of all international applicants. High school diploma is required and GED is accepted. *Academic units recommended:* 4 English, 4 math, 4 science, 3 science labs, 4 foreign language, 2 social studies, 2 history.

Financial Aid

Students should submit: FAFSA, CSS/Financial Aid PROFILE, Noncustodial PROFILE. Regular filing deadline is 2/15. The Princeton Review suggests that all financial aid forms be submitted as soon as possible after October 1. *Need-based scholarships/grants offered:* Federal Pell, FSEOG, State scholarships/grants, Private scholarships, College/university scholarship or grant aid from institutional funds. *Loan aid offered:* Direct Subsidized Stafford Loans, Direct Unsubsidized Stafford Loans, Direct PLUS loans, Federal Perkins Loans, College/university loans from institutional funds. Applicants will be notified of awards on or about 3/30. Federal Work-Study Program available. Institutional employment available.

The Inside Word

With acceptance rates hitting record lows, stellar academic credentials are a must for any serious Vassar candidate. Standardized test scores are required, but come second to high school transcripts. Once admissions officers see you meet their rigorous scholastic standards, they'll closely assess your personal essay, recommendations, and extracurricular activities. The college prides itself on selecting students who will add to the vitality of the campus. Demonstrating an intellectual curiosity that extends outside the classroom is as important as success within it.

THE SCHOOL SAYS "..."

From the Admissions Office

"Vassar presents a rich variety of social and cultural activities, clubs, sports, living arrangements, and regional attractions. Vassar is a vital, residential college community recognized for its respect for the rights and individuality of others.

"Candidates must submit either the SAT Reasoning Test and two SAT Subject Tests taken in different subject fields, or the ACT exam (the optional ACT writing component is required)."

SELECTIVITY

Admissions Rating	96
# of applicants	7,556
% of applicants accepted	26
% of acceptees attending	34
# offered a place on the wait list	1,017
% accepting a place on wait list	48
% admitted from wait list	2
# of early decision applicants	692
% accepted early decision	39

FRESHMAN PROFILE

Range SAT Critical Reading	670–750
Range SAT Math	660–740
Range SAT Writing	660–750
Range ACT Composite	30–33
Minimum paper TOEFL	600
Minimum internet-based TOEFL	100
% graduated top 10% of class	72
% graduated top 25% of class	96
% graduated top 50% of class	99

DEADLINES

Early decision	
Deadline	11/15
Notification	12/15
Regular	
Deadline	1/1
Notification	4/1
Nonfall registration?	No

APPLICANTS ALSO LOOK AT AND OFTEN PREFER
Williams College; Harvard College

AND SOMETIMES PREFER
Columbia University; Tufts University

AND RARELY PREFER
New York University; Skidmore College

FINANCIAL FACTS

Financial Aid Rating	99
Annual tuition	$50,550
Room and board	$11,980
Required fees	$750
Books and supplies	$900
Average frosh need-based scholarship	$45,358
Average UG need-based scholarship	$45,109
% needy frosh rec. need-based scholarship or grant aid	98
% needy UG rec. need-based scholarship or grant aid	100
% needy frosh rec. non-need-based scholarship or grant aid	0
% needy UG rec. non-need-based scholarship or grant aid	0
% needy frosh rec. need-based self-help aid	100
% needy UG rec. need-based self-help aid	100
% frosh rec. any financial aid	61
% UG rec. any financial aid	58
% UG borrow to pay for school	47
Average cumulative indebtedness	$17,847
% frosh need fully met	100
% ugrads need fully met	100
Average % of frosh need met	100
Average % of ugrad need met	100

VILLANOVA UNIVERSITY

AUSTIN HALL, 800 LANCASTER AVENUE, VILLANOVA, PA 19085 • ADMISSIONS: 610-519-4000 • FAX: 610-519-6450

STUDENTS SAY "..."

Academics

Known for being a basketball powerhouse, Villanova University (located in Pennsylvania) has developed an equally impressive reputation for academics. The school's admissions standards have continued to rise, and there is a "great support system" in place to help students achieve, between professors, advisors, tutors, research librarians, as well as a writing, math, and language learning center. Nova's career center and internship offices focus on getting students into jobs after college, and "the opportunities outside of the classroom really complement your education." "Villanova is full of resources for my success now, as a student, and will continue to be after I graduate as an alum," says a student. There is a real sense of community here, "stemming from service, school spirit around the basketball team, and everyone actively pursuing their own area of academic interest." The "passionate" professors are "true teachers and scholars," and they "go above and beyond their office hours." They are "easily accessible," and though some will seek you out, "it is mostly up to you to take advantage of them as a resource." "If you want to succeed, the community will do everything in its power to make sure you can do so," says a student. In addition to superior classroom quality (the faculty gets "fired up about what they teach"), there are "a lot of projects across majors that have real-world applications and are designed to help students in the long run." Classes are often a mixture of "lecture, discussion, individual/group projects, [and] fieldtrips." Villanova's "emphasis on service" is a point of praise for the student body, and everyone here embraces a sense of duty to make the world a better place. "We are the Nova Nation, built upon an unbreakable foundation of community," says a student.

Life

Many buildings are new or have been recently renovated, and "most residence halls are really impressive and kept up very well." Most of campus "has a focused atmosphere during the week," but come Thursday afternoon, "you can feel campus relax and people are more likely to go out," mainly off campus. During basketball season, "people get their work done early to flock to the [Pavilion] for games." Almost everyone is involved in at least one (but probably more) extracurricular activities and clubs, and "a ton of students get involved with intramurals or club sports teams, as well." The Campus Activity Team puts on different events over the weekend, including "a cinema that is always showing a movie," and the school also offers great service experiences, whether "week-long service break experiences all over the world, cheering on the athletes at Special Olympics Fall Festival, or driving into Philly to play with kids and help them with their studies." Formals are also "a big deal" on campus. For those who want to take a break from college life, the massive King of Prussia Mall is found nearby (with a free weekend shuttle), and it is "an easy short train ride to go to Philadelphia."

Student Body

This "outstanding community" is built on "a lot of mutual respect." People are "well-rounded," "very friendly," and "proud of Villanova," and most everyone here "dresses well" and is "extremely affable, professional, and an achiever." "Sometimes I think of Villanova as a school full of all the high school superstars," says one student. Balance is a skill that all Villanovans possess, and most are involved in some sort of volunteer activity; many also "party on the weekends, and show up ready to all of their classes." One can find a "very attractive student body" here, as well.

FINANCIAL AID: 610-519-4010 • E-MAIL: GOTOVU@VILLANOVA.EDU • WEBSITE: WWW.VILLANOVA.EDU

THE PRINCETON REVIEW SAYS

Admissions

Very important factors considered include: rigor of secondary school record, class rank, academic GPA, standardized test scores. *Important factors considered include:* application essay, recommendation(s), extracurricular activities, talent/ability, character/personal qualities, volunteer work, work experience. *Other factors considered include:* first generation, alumni/ae relation, geographical residence, state residency, racial/ethnic status, level of applicant's interest. SAT or ACT required. ACT with Writing required. SAT with Essay component required. TOEFL required of all international applicants. High school diploma is required and GED is accepted. *Academic units required:* 4 English, 4 math, 4 science, 2 science labs, 2 foreign language, 2 academic electives, and 4 units from above areas or other academic areas. *Academic units recommended:* 4 English, 4 math, 4 science, 3 science labs, 4 foreign language, 2 academic electives, and 4 units from above areas or other academic areas.

Financial Aid

Students should submit: FAFSA, CSS/Financial Aid PROFILE, Noncustodial PROFILE. Priority filing deadline is 2/7. The Princeton Review suggests that all financial aid forms be submitted as soon as possible after October 1. *Need-based scholarships/grants offered:* Federal Pell, FSEOG, State scholarships/grants, Private scholarships, College/university scholarship or grant aid from institutional funds. *Loan aid offered:* Direct Subsidized Stafford Loans, Direct Unsubsidized Stafford Loans, Direct PLUS loans, Federal Perkins Loans, Federal Nursing Loans. Applicants will be notified of awards on or about 4/1. Federal Work-Study Program available. Institutional employment available.

The Inside Word

Villanova's growing academic reputation means its application process is growing more competitive as well: 93 percent of the most recent admitted freshman class ranked in the top 20 percent of their high school graduating class. Although academic achievement is important, the university looks at the whole package when considering applicants and expects candidates to be well rounded. As a private university, Villanova is not exactly cheap, but the school offers a wide variety of scholarships and aid to qualifying students.

THE SCHOOL SAYS "..."

From the Admissions Office

"Villanova is the oldest and largest Catholic university in Pennsylvania, founded in 1842 by the Order of Saint Augustine. Students of all faiths are welcome. The university tends to attract students who are interested in volunteerism. Villanovans provide more than 249,000 hours of service annually and host the largest student-run Special Olympics in the nation. Villanova's scenic campus is located twelve miles west of Philadelphia. The university offers programs through four undergraduate colleges: Liberal Arts and Sciences, Engineering, Nursing, and the Villanova School of Business. There are 265 student organizations and thirty-six National Honor Societies at Villanova. Incoming freshmen can opt to be part of a Learning Community, through which student groups live together in specially-designated residence halls and learn together in courses and co-curricular programs. The university offers Naval and Marine Reserve Officers Training Corps (ROTC) programs and hundreds of options for studying abroad. Nova's alumni body is comprised of more than 118,000 people. Some prominent grads include: John L. Hennessey, President, Stanford University; Kelly Ayotte, U.S. Senator, State of New Hampshire; and Eileen Sullivan, Pulizer Prize-winning journalist, The Associated Press.

"If you're looking to join Nova Nation, be prepared: The competition for admission is getting tougher every year."

SELECTIVITY

Admissions Rating	93
# of applicants	16,206
% of applicants accepted	48
% of acceptees attending	22
# offered a place on the wait list	4,807
% accepting a place on wait list	47
% admitted from wait list	2

FRESHMAN PROFILE

Range SAT Critical Reading	590–690
Range SAT Math	610–710
Range SAT Writing	590–690
Range ACT Composite	29–32
Minimum paper TOEFL	550
Average HS GPA	4.0
% graduated top 10% of class	55
% graduated top 25% of class	87
% graduated top 50% of class	98

DEADLINES

Early action	
Deadline	11/1
Notification	12/20
Regular	
Priority	12/15
Deadline	1/15
Notification	4/1
Nonfall registration?	No

APPLICANTS ALSO LOOK AT AND OFTEN PREFER

Boston College; Georgetown University; University of Notre Dame; University of Virginia

AND SOMETIMES PREFER

Lehigh University; Penn State University Park

AND RARELY PREFER

Fordham University

FINANCIAL FACTS

Financial Aid Rating	82
Annual tuition	$46,966
Room and board	$12,720
Required fees	$650
Books and supplies	$1,100
Average frosh need-based scholarship	$31,640
Average UG need-based scholarship	$30,020
% needy frosh rec. need-based scholarship or grant aid	91
% needy UG rec. need-based scholarship or grant aid	91
% needy frosh rec. non-need-based scholarship or grant aid	24
% needy UG rec. non-need-based scholarship or grant aid	27
% needy frosh rec. need-based self-help aid	84
% needy UG rec. need-based self-help aid	86
% frosh rec. any financial aid	67
% UG rec. any financial aid	68
% UG borrow to pay for school	55
Average cumulative indebtedness	$33,588
% frosh need fully met	20
% ugrads need fully met	17
Average % of frosh need met	80
Average % of ugrad need met	79

CAMPUS LIFE

Quality of Life Rating	99
Fire Safety Rating	86
Green Rating	97
Type of school	Public
Affiliation	No Affiliation
Environment	Town

STUDENTS

Total undergrad enrollment	25,384
% male/female	57/43
% from out of state	24
% frosh live on campus	98
% ugrads live on campus	37
# of fraternities (% ugrad men join)	29 (14)
# of sororities (% ugrad women join)	12 (19)
% African American	4
% Asian	9
% Caucasian	70
% Hispanic	5
% Native American	<1
% Pacific Islander	<1
% Two or more races	4
% Race and/or ethnicity unknown	3
% international	5
# of countries represented	116

SURVEY SAYS...

Students are happy
Great library
Career services are great
School is well run
Students are friendly
Diverse student types interact on campus
Students get along with local community
Students involved in community service
Students love Blacksburg, VA
Great food on campus
Great off-campus food
Recreation facilities are great
Lots of beer drinking
Everyone loves the Hokies
Intramural sports are popular
Alumni active on campus

ACADEMICS

Academic Rating	77
% students returning for sophomore year	94
% students graduating within 4 years	0
% students graduating within 6 years	83
Calendar	Semester
Student/faculty ratio	16:1
Profs interesting rating	77
Profs accessible rating	83

Most classes have 20–29 students.
Most lab/discussion sessions have 20–29 students.

MOST POPULAR MAJORS

Engineering; Biology; Business Administration and Management

STUDENTS SAY "..."

Academics

Virginia Tech is a school with a reputation as big as its campus. Known for its "beautiful campus, amazing community feel, top-notch engineering field," and as a "good value"—not to mention its renowned athletics—Virginia Tech offers "a perfect blend of challenging and fun, encompassed in an unparalleled community feel." That community feel is a big part of the attraction to this top-ranked school, with students saying they feel "more comfortable here than anywhere in the world." Students are here, of course, for an education at a well-respected research university. At Virginia Tech, that education is provided by "passionate professors who bring real-life examples and cases into their teachings." The school's size and correspondingly large teaching staff mean that at times "professors are hit-or-miss," with "a few who just see it as another job." Most, however, "are really there to help you know as much as you can," a group who are "are extremely helpful and devoted to their students." The best of this school's professors "really make students eager to learn." One student enthuses, "My professors here have changed the way I look at the world and have become some of my biggest heroes." But maybe another student sums it up best: "I would definitely say that my academic experience has been outstanding and that it has opened my eyes to even more possibilities.

Life

Living "in the middle of nowhere" may seem like a recipe for boredom, but members of VT's Hokie Nation make the most of this "perfect college town." After all, when "there are 30,000 people around you that are the same age as you, you find stuff to do." When not consumed with Virginia Tech football—you'll see more maroon and orange in a single day here than most people will see in a lifetime—students here do, well, a little bit of everything. "School-related and Greek-life functions are the main sources of weekend activities," students say, but deceptively quiet Blacksburg and the surrounding area offer plenty of other options. On weekends, students "go out to parties or downtown with friends, we go out to eat, we play tennis, lay out on the 'drillfield,' play in the snow when we have some, go on hikes, and go to the river." That's just a start. Students find "there is always something fun going on to do with your friends," including "bowling, movies, club sports, video games," and more. If you can't find it in Blacksburg, it's ten minutes away in Christiansburg. Students enjoy relaxing, getting into discussions, or having outdoor adventures in a pastoral setting. When autumn arrives, "football games dominate the social scene."

Student Body

Better be ready to be part of the Hokie Nation, because the "typical student is someone who has a love for all things Virginia Tech." Those who attend VT "are proud of our school," and "A typical student here wears Virginia Tech clothes practically every day." Indeed, "you will find them at every VT football game." But the student body is about more than cheering for the maroon and orange. These "middle-class, decent-looking" students study hard "but play harder." Education matters here, but maybe not as much as living life. "The typical student is serious about schoolwork," students say, "but also knows how to have a good time." Most of the student body are "white and from Virginia or North Carolina," a group who are "smart, approachable, and kind." "While we may be lacking in racial diversity," one student notes, "we have every personality type and quirk you could ever imagine." If you are "well-rounded, involved, and [have] lots of school spirit," you are likely to fit in at VT.

VIRGINIA POLYTECHNIC INSTITUTE AND STATE UNIVERSITY (VIRGINIA TECH)

FINANCIAL AID: 540-231-5179 • E-MAIL: VTADMISS@VT.EDU • WEBSITE: WWW.VT.EDU

THE PRINCETON REVIEW SAYS

Admissions

Very important factors considered include: rigor of secondary school record, academic GPA, standardized test scores. *Important factors considered include: Other factors considered include:* recommendation(s), extracurricular activities, talent/ability, character/personal qualities, first generation, alumni/ae relation, geographical residence, state residency, racial/ethnic status, volunteer work, work experience, level of applicant's interest. SAT or ACT required; SAT Subject Tests required for some. ACT with Writing required. SAT with or without Essay component accepted. TOEFL required of all international applicants. High school diploma is required and GED is accepted. *Academic units required:* 4 English, 3 math, 2 science, 2 science labs, 1 social studies, 1 history, 4 academic electives. *Academic units recommended:* 4 math, 3 science, 3 foreign language.

Financial Aid

Students should submit: FAFSA. Priority filing deadline is 3/1. The Princeton Review suggests that all financial aid forms be submitted as soon as possible after October 1. *Need-based scholarships/grants offered:* Federal Pell, FSEOG, State scholarships/grants, Private scholarships, College/university scholarship or grant aid from institutional funds. *Loan aid offered:* Direct Subsidized Stafford Loans, Direct Unsubsidized Stafford Loans, Direct PLUS loans, Federal Perkins Loans, College/university loans from institutional funds. Applicants will be notified of awards on a rolling basis beginning 4/1. Federal Work-Study Program available. Institutional employment available.

The Inside Word

With some 20,000 applications pouring into the admissions office each year, it's no wonder that the game here is all about numbers, numbers, numbers. Your high school grades will be top priority, so maintain strong grades. Standardized tests also play a big role. Most solid performers will find that acceptance comes with few problems, though the school's competitive disciplines—engineering and architecture, for example—will demand a higher caliber of student.

THE SCHOOL SAYS "..."

From the Admissions Office

"Virginia Tech offers the opportunities of a large research university in a small-town setting. Undergraduates choose from more than seventy majors in seven colleges, including nationally ranked architecture, business, forestry, and engineering schools, as well as excellent computer science, biology, and communication studies, and architecture programs. Technology is a key focus, both in classes and in general. All first-year students are required to own a personal computer, each residence hall room has Ethernet connections, and every student is provided e-mail and Internet access. Faculty incorporate a wide variety of technology into class, utilizing chat rooms, online lecture notes, and multimedia presentations. The university offers cutting-edge facilities for classes and research, abundant opportunities for advanced study in the honors program, undergraduate research opportunities, study abroad, internships, and cooperative education. Students enjoy nearly 700 organizations which offer something for everyone. Tech offers the best of both worlds—everything a large university can provide and a small-town atmosphere.

"Freshman applicants must take the SAT or ACT with writing section. We will use the highest scores from any SAT or ACT test scores submitted."

SELECTIVITY

Admissions Rating	88
# of applicants	22,280
% of applicants accepted	73
% of acceptees attending	39
# offered a place on the wait list	2,118
% accepting a place on wait list	73
% admitted from wait list	0
# of early decision applicants	2,023
% accepted early decision	52

FRESHMAN PROFILE

Range SAT Critical Reading	540–640
Range SAT Math	570–680
Range SAT Writing	530–640
Minimum paper TOEFL	550
% graduated top 10% of class	41
% graduated top 25% of class	82
% graduated top 50% of class	99

DEADLINES

Early decision	
Deadline	11/1
Notification	12/15
Regular	
Deadline	1/15
Notification	4/1
Nonfall registration?	Yes

APPLICANTS ALSO LOOK AT AND OFTEN PREFER

University of Virginia; College of William and Mary

AND RARELY PREFER

College of William and Mary; The University of North Carolina at Chapel Hill

FINANCIAL FACTS

Financial Aid Rating	81
Annual out-of-state tuition	$25,515
Room and board	$7,924
Required fees	$1,929
Books and supplies	$1,320
Average frosh need-based scholarship	$8,413
Average UG need-based scholarship	$6,736
% needy frosh rec. need-based scholarship or grant aid	65
% needy UG rec. need-based scholarship or grant aid	70
% needy frosh rec. non-need-based scholarship or grant aid	47
% needy UG rec. non-need-based scholarship or grant aid	35
% needy frosh rec. need-based self-help aid	66
% needy UG rec. need-based self-help aid	73
% UG rec. any financial aid	75
% UG borrow to pay for school	53
Average cumulative indebtedness	$28,873
% frosh need fully met	15
% ugrads need fully met	17
Average % of frosh need met	62
Average % of ugrad need met	64

VIRGINIA WESLEYAN COLLEGE

1584 WESLEYAN DRIVE, NORFOLK/VIRGINIA BEACH, VA 23502-5599 • ADMISSIONS: 757-455-3208 • FAX: 757-461-5238

STUDENTS SAY "..."

Academics

Virginia Wesleyan is the quintessential small liberal arts college, providing undergraduates with "a close-knit community" where one "can easily build strong relationship[s]." Indeed, you're guaranteed to be "more than a number" on this Norfolk/Virginia Beach campus of 1,500 undergrads. "Small classes" are a hallmark of a Virginia Wesleyan education with many being "discussion or interaction based." And students love the fact that they are "always taught by . . . professors"—no teaching assistants here! Speaking of professors, VWC undergrads are full of praise for theirs. They seem to "genuinely care about their students and are approachable outside the classroom." A current student agrees, "I have never met a faculty so invested in my own personal success." And an earth and environmental studies student excitedly interjects, "I have never experienced [a] learning environment like this one. Professors not only care about their students, but they go above and beyond to ensure that every student understands the material. Professors make lifelong connections with students." All in all, Virginia Wesleyan offers individuals a college experience that's "all about making every single student feel as though this is their second home and that every person they come into contact with is looking out for the student's best interest."

Life

Despite students reporting that "the food could be better," by and large undergrads seem to enjoy life at Virginia Wesleyan. To begin with, there are plenty of activities with which to get involved, be it "Greek life, music, arts, religion, sciences, business, etc." Indeed, there's truly something for everyone! Students also like taking advantage of various campus amenities such as "the pool, the rock wall, the indoor track, the gymnasium, and the pool table in the student center." Of course, similar to many undergraduate institutions, "social gatherings are huge here." Students "love inviting [their] friends and teammates over to get over a stressful week of studying and homework." However, these get-togethers don't tend to get too raucous. As an English major tells us, "Although fun is encouraged, we are often reminded of how to keep everyone safe. Underage drinking is NOT tolerated, and we take it seriously when rules are broken." Finally, when the weather permits, these undergrads flock to nearby Chick's Beach. And many can be found sampling the "delicious restaurants around Norfolk" and Virginia Beach.

Student Body

Undergrads at Virginia Wesleyan speak very highly of their peers. Granted, this isn't surprising given that the student body is comprised of "friendly and outgoing" individuals who are typically "laid back." A psychology major provides a little more insight by stating, "Students are generally pretty spirited and helpful, and most [people] seem to genuinely care about their academics." By and large, undergrads here are "open to new things." They also tend to be "very busy" since it's quite typical for students to be "involved in several different clubs and community service groups." Of course, though many VWC undergrads "join one of the [eight] Greek organizations available" or become "a member of a sports team" to "fit in," we're also told that it's by no means a necessity. A chemistry major assures us, "Whatever you are interested in, you can easily find a group of people that connect with you. Our school is so inviting that it's hard to not fit in somewhere." Finally, another psychology major boasts, "I feel like my school is extremely accepting, and we have events for all cultures, beliefs, and extracurricular [activities] all the time."

VIRGINIA WESLEYAN COLLEGE

FINANCIAL AID: 757-455-3345 • E-MAIL: ADMISSIONS@VWC.EDU • WEBSITE: WWW.VWC.EDU

THE PRINCETON REVIEW SAYS

Admissions

Very important factors considered include: rigor of secondary school record, academic GPA, level of applicant's interest. *Important factors considered include:* standardized test scores, recommendation(s), extracurricular activities. *Other factors considered include:* interview, talent/ability, character/personal qualities, first generation, alumni/ae relation, volunteer work, work experience. SAT or ACT required; SAT Subject Tests considered if submitted. ACT with or without writing accepted. Proof of English proficiency required of all international applicants. High school diploma is required and GED is accepted. *Academic units required:* 4 English, 3 math, 2 science, 2 science labs, 2 foreign language, 1 history, 1 computer science. *Academic units recommended:* 4 English, 3 math, 2 science, 2 science labs, 2 foreign language, 1 history, 4 academic electives, 1 computer science.

Financial Aid

Students should submit: FAFSA, State aid form. Priority filing deadline is 3/1. The Princeton Review suggests that all financial aid forms be submitted as soon as possible after October 1. *Need-based scholarships/grants offered:* Federal Pell, FSEOG, State scholarships/grants, Private scholarships, College/university scholarship or grant aid from institutional funds. *Loan aid offered:* Direct Subsidized Stafford Loans, Direct Unsubsidized Stafford Loans, Direct PLUS loans, Federal Perkins Loans. Applicants will be notified of awards on a rolling basis beginning 2/15. Federal Work-Study Program available. Institutional employment available.

The Inside Word

As Virginia Wesleyan's profile rises, so too does the number of applications it receives. And each year, competition for admission increases. Therefore, to receive a coveted acceptance letter, applicants need to have earned strong grades in college prep courses. Additionally, given the college's small size, admissions officers are on the lookout for students who will contribute to campus life. Therefore, active and sustained participation in a handful of extracurricular activities help candidates appear more attractive to the admissions committee.

THE SCHOOL SAYS "..."

From the Admissions Office

"Virginia Wesleyan College seeks to enroll qualified students from diverse social, religious, racial, economic, and geographic backgrounds. Admission is based solely on the applicant's academic and personal qualifications. Factors considered include grades, recommendations, standardized test scores, and extracurricular activities. Virginia Wesleyan requires either SAT or ACT scores. Although we do not require more than one SAT or ACT score, we do take the highest individual verbal and math scores from all of the tests taken. A high school diploma is required (GED accepted) and proof of English proficiency is required for all international applicants. Virginia Wesleyan considers applications on a rolling admissions basis. Applicants can typically expect notification within two to three weeks after we receive your completed application and supporting documents. Priority decisions for spring freshman applications is January 1; for fall freshman applications, March 1. Prospective students are encouraged to visit our beautiful 300-acre wooded campus for a tour and to meet with an enrollment counselor. Learn more about admissions at www. vwc.edu."

SELECTIVITY

Admissions Rating	71
# of applicants	2,072
% of applicants accepted	89
% of acceptees attending	22

FRESHMAN PROFILE

Range SAT Critical Reading	440–550
Range SAT Math	430–550
Range SAT Writing	425–530
Range ACT Composite	18–25
Minimum paper TOEFL	550
Average HS GPA	3.3
% graduated top 10% of class	13
% graduated top 25% of class	38
% graduated top 50% of class	74

DEADLINES

Regular	
Priority	3/1
Nonfall registration?	Yes

APPLICANTS ALSO LOOK AT AND SOMETIMES PREFER

Christopher Newport University; James Madison University; Randolph-Macon College; Roanoke College

AND RARELY PREFER

Lynchburg College; George Mason University

FINANCIAL FACTS

Financial Aid Rating	82
Annual tuition	$32,636
Required fees	$650
Books and supplies	$1,500
Average frosh need-based scholarship	$19,469
Average UG need-based scholarship	$18,774
% needy frosh rec. need-based scholarship or grant aid	100
% needy UG rec. need-based scholarship or grant aid	100
% needy frosh rec. non-need-based scholarship or grant aid	19
% needy UG rec. non-need-based scholarship or grant aid	17
% needy frosh rec. need-based self-help aid	78
% needy UG rec. need-based self-help aid	78
% frosh rec. any financial aid	99
% UG rec. any financial aid	98
% frosh need fully met	18
% ugrads need fully met	14
Average % of frosh need met	70
Average % of ugrad need met	66

WABASH COLLEGE

PO Box 352, Crawfordsville, IN 47933 • Admissions: 765-361-6225 • Fax: 765-361-6437

STUDENTS SAY "..."

Academics

Intellectually and individually, Wabash College students live by "The Gentleman's Rule," which challenges "students to become a man who acts responsibly, thinks critically, leads effectively, and lives humanely." One of only three remaining all-male liberal arts colleges in the U.S., Wabash students say that "tradition is in our blood" and "Wabash turns boys into men." "Wabash College is all about building men of character," as well as "dedicated to instilling gentlemanly values into its students." They genuinely appreciate the "personal attention from educators" facilitated by a small (around 900 students) school, meaning "the teacher/student connection is very strong." It provides "a whole experience of education rather than a specialization in a single field," in which the "top-notch" professors "often stress the "why" much more than the "what" of their material." The "course work is rigorous, but the professors usually give you every opportunity to succeed and learn as much as possible." "My professors are all incredibly knowledgeable about not only their subject, but other worldly matters that they bring into the classroom," and students are "continually amazed by" their "encyclopedic knowledge, as well as their remarkable ability to articulate abstract concepts in a concrete and precise way." "I enjoy class so much that I loathe to miss even 5 minutes." "At Wabash there is a strong bond between students, faculty, and alumni, which is rooted in tradition and excellence," and this helps students look toward the future: Wabash attracts many for its "strong alumni network," high "graduate school acceptance rates," and "incredible" "job opportunities." Students believe the college's "academic rigor…will help me succeed later in life" in the way it "focuses on educating men to lead active, influential lives" and on "breeding passion about the school and about life and learning." "The unique environment of the Wabash classroom allows the conversation to flow freely…This educational environment spills over into the everyday conversation." Certainly "Wabash is about hard work in the classroom" and "studying your butt off," but the professors help you get through anything. The school's "very large endowment" from alumni makes a positive impact on student resources like "alumni, the Career Services, the facilities (athletic and academic), registration," as well as the all-important "financial aid."

Life

One student sums up Wabash as a "positive…environment in which students are allowed and encouraged to hold one another accountable." Students care about values as well as work and fun, and "people are constantly thinking about their future lives after college." It's still an all-male college, so "people think about girls. And beer. But mostly girls." That said, many find that their single-sex education "leads to a deeper discussion without any distractions" during the week, and "on the weekends it feels similar to a co-ed campus and other co-ed schools are not far away." "Wabash is not the craziest party school in the state, certainly, but partying is a big part of life here." "This place is seriously beautiful," and "we have some of the greatest school spirit I have ever seen." Wabash's alumni support enriches this: "Our alumni care about this school so much…our athletic center is great, over half of our students play in NCAA sports, we are nearly guaranteed a immersion learning opportunity, and our career services is one of the best in the nation."

Student Body

Wabash's small "tight knit community" feels like a "close brotherhood" to its students, and one "that supports one another through good times and bad times." "The lack of women on campus is a tradition loved and hated by every student, resulting in heated debates with an unfailing conclusion of maintaining the status quo." The "typical" Wabash student might be "a smart jock" who is "outgoing, athletic, and competitive" with a "strong work ethic." On such a small campus, "it is impossible to be invisible," and "students, on average, fit in and treat one another respectfully." "Fraternity life is very popular, with high participation in Intramurals," and "a large amount of students play sports here."

FINANCIAL AID: 765-361-6370 • E-MAIL: ADMISSIONS@WABASH.EDU • WEBSITE: WWW.WABASH.EDU

THE PRINCETON REVIEW SAYS

Admissions

Very important factors considered include: rigor of secondary school record, class rank, academic GPA, level of applicant's interest. *Important factors considered include:* standardized test scores, interview, extracurricular activities, talent/ability. *Other factors considered include:* application essay, recommendation(s), character/personal qualities, first generation, alumni/ae relation, geographical residence, racial/ethnic status, volunteer work, work experience. SAT or ACT required; SAT Subject Tests considered if submitted. ACT with Writing recommended. SAT with Essay component recommended. TOEFL required of all international applicants. High school diploma is required and GED is accepted. *Academic units recommended:* 4 English, 4 math, 2 science, 2 science labs, 2 foreign language, 2 social studies, 2 history, 2 academic electives.

Financial Aid

Students should submit: FAFSA. Regular filing deadline is 2/15. The Princeton Review suggests that all financial aid forms be submitted as soon as possible after October 1. *Need-based scholarships/grants offered:* Federal Pell, FSEOG, State scholarships/grants, Private scholarships, College/university scholarship or grant aid from institutional funds. *Loan aid offered:* Direct Subsidized Stafford Loans, Direct Unsubsidized Stafford Loans, Direct PLUS loans, College/university loans from institutional funds. Applicants will be notified of awards on or about 3/31. Federal Work-Study Program available. Institutional employment available.

The Inside Word

Because Wabash is so specific and unique, it self-selects a small but strong applicant pool. Don't let its relatively high acceptance rate deceive you: admitted students are in for four years of academic rigor, so don't apply if you're not ready to apply serious intellectual muscle and work ethic.

THE SCHOOL SAYS "..."

From the Admissions Office

"Wabash College is different—and distinctive—from other liberal arts colleges. Different in that Wabash is an outstanding college for men only. Distinctive in the quality and character of the faculty, in the demanding nature of the academic program, in the seriousness and maturity of the men who enroll, and in the richness of the traditions that have evolved throughout its 180-year history. Wabash is preeminently a teaching institution, and fundamental to the learning experience is the way faculty and students talk to each other—with mutual respect for the expression of informed opinion. For example, students who collaborate with faculty on research projects are considered their peers in the research—an esteem not usually extended to undergraduates. The college takes pride in the sense of community that such a learning environment fosters. But perhaps the single most striking aspect of student life at Wabash is personal freedom. The college has only one rule: 'The student is expected to conduct himself at all times, both on and off the campus, as a gentleman and a responsible citizen.' Wabash College treats students as adults, and such treatment attracts responsible freshmen and fosters their independence and maturity. "For students seeking admission, Wabash will accept the SAT or the ACT. Wabash will use the student's best scores from either examination and will accept the SAT or ACT writing portions in place of an essay. Wabash does not require SAT Subject Tests."

SELECTIVITY

Admissions Rating	87
# of applicants	1,247
% of applicants accepted	61
% of acceptees attending	31
# offered a place on the wait list	32
% accepting a place on wait list	97
% admitted from wait list	16
# of early decision applicants	48
% accepted early decision	88

FRESHMAN PROFILE

Range SAT Critical Reading	510–610
Range SAT Math	530–640
Range SAT Writing	470–600
Range ACT Composite	22–28
Minimum paper TOEFL	550
Minimum internet-based TOEFL	80
Average HS GPA	3.7
% graduated top 10% of class	35
% graduated top 25% of class	71
% graduated top 50% of class	95

DEADLINES

Early decision	
Deadline	11/15
Notification	11/30
Early action	
Deadline	12/1
Notification	12/19
Regular	
Priority	12/1
Nonfall registration?	Yes

APPLICANTS ALSO LOOK AT AND OFTEN PREFER

Indiana University Bloomington; Purdue University–West Lafayette

AND SOMETIMES PREFER

Butler University; DePauw University

FINANCIAL FACTS

Financial Aid Rating	91
Annual tuition	$40,400
Room and board	$9,600
Required fees	$650
Books and supplies	$1,000
Average frosh need-based scholarship	$28,590
Average UG need-based scholarship	$25,192
% needy frosh rec. need-based scholarship or grant aid	99
% needy UG rec. need-based scholarship or grant aid	98
% needy frosh rec. non-need-based scholarship or grant aid	20
% needy UG rec. non-need-based scholarship or grant aid	15
% needy frosh rec. need-based self-help aid	79
% needy UG rec. need-based self-help aid	82
% frosh rec. any financial aid	99
% UG rec. any financial aid	95
% UG borrow to pay for school	91
Average cumulative indebtedness	$32,916
% frosh need fully met	72
% ugrads need fully met	70
Average % of frosh need met	93
Average % of ugrad need met	91

WAGNER COLLEGE

PAPE ADMISSIONS BUILDING, STATEN ISLAND, NY 10301-4495 • ADMISSIONS: 718-390-3411 • FAX: 718-390-3105

CAMPUS LIFE

Quality of Life Rating	89
Fire Safety Rating	98
Green Rating	62
Type of school	Private
Environment	Metropolis

STUDENTS

Total undergrad enrollment	1,750
% male/female	37/63
% from out of state	54
% frosh from public high school	67
% frosh live on campus	76
% ugrads live on campus	71
# of fraternities (% ugrad men join)	5 (5)
# of sororities (% ugrad women join)	4 (10)
% African American	7
% Asian	3
% Caucasian	66
% Hispanic	11
% Native American	<1
% Pacific Islander	<1
% Two or more races	2
% Race and/or ethnicity unknown	7
% international	3
# of countries represented	36

SURVEY SAYS...

Students are happy
Career services are great
Internships are widely available
Class discussions encouraged
Theater is popular

ACADEMICS

Academic Rating	79
% students returning for sophomore year	86
% students graduating within 4 years	64
% students graduating within 6 years	66
Calendar	Semester
Student/faculty ratio	15:1
Profs interesting rating	79
Profs accessible rating	83

Most classes have 10–19 students.
Most lab/discussion sessions have 10–19 students.

MOST POPULAR MAJORS
Biological Science; Business/Commerce;
Visual and Performing Arts

STUDENTS SAY "..."

Academics

Wagner College, located on Staten Island, is a "tight-knit and fun, yet academically challenging," liberal arts school that operates under the Wagner Plan, combining a solid foundation in the liberal arts with practical and applied experiences like internships, with a commitment to service learning and community. The school is "in the perfect location with a surplus of unique resources" and is composed of "an excellent and vibrant community that supports its students every step of the way." The "commitment of the faculty and staff have for the student body is outstanding." Thanks to the plan, students are encouraged "to explore and reflect upon a myriad of subjects and issues." "Even though I am a biology major, I have the wonderful opportunity to explore interdisciplinary topics in the humanities and social sciences throughout my undergraduate career," says one student. The college's unique first-year program consists of a set of three classes with the same twenty-eight students, which "helps transition us from high school to college by progressively learning how to write college-level pieces as well as by engaging in a mandatory thirty-hour community service requirement." This "small, beautiful learning community" is guided by an "extremely attentive and competent" faculty. The professors "ask you to do your best and to push your limitations away" and are "extremely accessible outside of class." "The first time I was nervous about registration, my advisor sat down had lunch, and we registered together," says a student. "It is comforting that I can go to my professors whenever I need assistance with work." The school's science and physicians' assistant programs are notably strong, as are the "fantastic" theater and musical programs. Students all universally agree that Wagner "lets you experience all different types of subjects by following the concept: learning by doing."

Life

At Wagner, students are "mostly concerned about their careers, whether they want to make it on Broadway or find the cure for cancer." There's plenty of school-run activities "through co-curricular programs and various clubs," so there are "countless things to do." Beyond all doubt, "the best thing to do...is to take advantage of New York City." The campus is just "a ferry ride away from Manhattan," and the majority of people takes the Wagner shuttle to the S.I. ferry ("all for free!") and goes to the city, whether to shop, eat, or go to a Broadway show. On weekends, there are "parties run by organizations from time to time" or in dorm rooms, since "there is no off-campus housing." Every year, the school has an event called Wagner Stock, where a famous musician or group comes to play. Food is a huge pain point here: Students want "more access to the dining hall in the late hours of the night," "more food options," and just better food in general.

Student Body

The student body here celebrates its "diverse" makeup but Division I athletics and the "great theater program" are very visible in this "small close community." But a student not in either of these programs can find their group through clubs and the major that they are in." Many students have "one major and a minor," and "half of them might study abroad for a semester and or have one or two internships before they graduate." Everyone basically goes about their own business, but "is very approachable." No one seems to have any trouble finding their own crowd, but even once that occurs, "different crowds frequently mingle and almost everyone gets along." "People just talk to everyone," says a student.

FINANCIAL AID: 718-390-3183 • E-MAIL: ADM@WAGNER.EDU • WEBSITE: WWW.WAGNER.EDU

THE PRINCETON REVIEW SAYS

Admissions

Very important factors considered include: rigor of secondary school record, class rank, academic GPA. *Important factors considered include:* application essay, recommendation(s), interview, extracurricular activities, talent/ability, character/personal qualities. *Other factors considered include:* standardized test scores, volunteer work, work experience, level of applicant's interest. SAT or ACT required for some; SAT Subject Tests required for some. ACT with or without writing accepted. TOEFL required of all international applicants. High school diploma is required and GED is accepted. *Academic units required:* 4 English, 3 math, 2 science, 1 science lab, 2 foreign language, 3 history, 7 academic electives.

Financial Aid

Students should submit: FAFSA, State aid form. Priority filing deadline is 2/15. The Princeton Review suggests that all financial aid forms be submitted as soon as possible after October 1. *Need-based scholarships/grants offered:* Federal Pell, FSEOG, State scholarships/grants, Private scholarships, College/university scholarship or grant aid from institutional funds. *Loan aid offered:* Direct Subsidized Stafford Loans, Direct Unsubsidized Stafford Loans, Direct PLUS loans, Federal Perkins Loans, Federal Nursing Loans. Applicants will be notified of awards on a rolling basis beginning 3/1. Federal Work-Study Program available. Institutional employment available.

The Inside Word

As far as grades and test scores, the profile of the average freshman class at Wagner is solid. Standardized tests are optional, and there is more value placed on the strength of your course work and your grades in those classes. The admissions staff here is dedicated to finding the right students for their school. Wagner is looking for students who like to be involved in community events, so make sure your application reflects your extracurriculars. An interview bodes well for serious applicants.

THE SCHOOL SAYS "..."

From the Admissions Office

"At Wagner College, we attract and develop active learners and future leaders. Wagner College has received national acclaim (*Time* magazine, American Association of Colleges and Universities) for its innovative curriculum, The Wagner Plan for the Practical Liberal Arts. At Wagner, we capitalize on our unique geography; we are a traditional, scenic, residential campus, which happens to sit atop a hill on an island overlooking lower Manhattan. Our location allows us to offer a program that couples required off-campus experiences (experiential learning), with 'learning community' clusters of courses. This program begins in the first semester and continues through the senior capstone experience in the major. Fieldwork and internships, writing-intensive reflective tutorials, connected learning, 'reading, writing, and doing': At Wagner College our students truly discover 'the practical liberal arts in New York City.'"

SELECTIVITY

Admissions Rating	85
# of applicants	2,803
% of applicants accepted	68
% of acceptees attending	22
# offered a place on the wait list	112
% accepting a place on wait list	85
% admitted from wait list	21

FRESHMAN PROFILE

Range SAT Critical Reading	520–610
Range SAT Math	510–620
Range SAT Writing	510–620
Range ACT Composite	22–27
Minimum paper TOEFL	550
Minimum internet-based TOEFL	79
Average HS GPA	90.5
% graduated top 10% of class	31
% graduated top 25% of class	62
% graduated top 50% of class	89

DEADLINES

Early action	
Deadline	12/1
Notification	11/5
Regular	
Priority	12/1
Deadline	2/15
Nonfall registration?	Yes

APPLICANTS ALSO LOOK AT AND OFTEN PREFER

New York University; Northeastern University

AND SOMETIMES PREFER

Ithaca College; Muhlenberg College; Fordham University

AND RARELY PREFER

Quinnipiac University; Marist; Manhattan College; Drew University

FINANCIAL FACTS

Financial Aid Rating	83
Annual tuition	$42,030
Room and board	$13,000
Required fees	$450
Books and supplies	$822
Average frosh need-based scholarship	$16,866
Average UG need-based scholarship	$22,422
% needy frosh rec. need-based scholarship or grant aid	100
% needy UG rec. need-based scholarship or grant aid	99
% needy frosh rec. non-need-based scholarship or grant aid	0
% needy UG rec. non-need-based scholarship or grant aid	0
% needy frosh rec. need-based self-help aid	73
% needy UG rec. need-based self-help aid	77
% frosh rec. any financial aid	98
% UG rec. any financial aid	93
% frosh need fully met	26
% ugrads need fully met	24
Average % of frosh need met	78
Average % of ugrad need met	73

WAKE FOREST UNIVERSITY

PO BOX 7305, WINSTON SALEM, NC 27109 • ADMISSIONS: 336-758-5201 • FAX: 336-758-4324

STUDENTS SAY ". . ."

Academics

North Carolina's own Wake Forest University prepares students to lead lives that matter and has a reputation for quality that affords its students "excellent placement into jobs and graduate schools." Students come to Wake Forest for an education of the entire person, and the school "practices intentional interactions between professors and students, students with each other, and students and their larger community." This grand scale plan for well-rounded grooming includes "opportunities to serve, to become a leader, and to become part of initiatives that are larger than you." Professors "demand a lot of work but love teaching and students," and classes "are not easy and good grades are tough to come by." "Professors often expect their class to be every student's focus, which is often very difficult," says one student. Fortunately, faculty "are extremely helpful and excited to be teaching or meeting with students one-on-one" and "ensure that students are comfortable with voicing their opinions." Indeed, "from the students to the faculty and staff to the administrators, everyone is open and greets everyone with a smile" here. "Overall I've had a fantastic academic experience with professors that have helped me discover my intellectual passions and have had a vested interest in my success," says a junior. The small school atmosphere matched with the large school resources, and reputation are "some of the greatest aspects of Wake Forest." "I feel that I could ask any professor I've had at Wake for a letter of recommendation, and they would know me personally enough to do so," says a student. There is a similarly "strong vision and support" from the administration and the alumni network, who back "crazy opportunities that meld ideas and people that just don't happen at other colleges." The school is committed to the teacher-scholar model, so not only do professors do cutting edge research, they let undergrads in on it. "Wake Forest is a campus where some of the most academically impressive and competitive students assemble, the community is an encouraging atmosphere evident to anyone who steps on the grounds, and the social life is unbeatable," says a student.

Life

Wake Forest students work extremely hard on weekdays, often spending hours in the library to complete work, but "absolutely let loose on weekends." The school's "vibrant social scene" and a schedule that is "always bustling with extracurricular activities" keeps the candle burning at both ends, and "parties, going to bars downtown, concerts, game nights, and chill hang outs at friends' houses" are other methods of fun. The D1 athletics—perhaps you've heard of them?—lend Wake Forest a "big-school sports feel at a small school"; and many students play intramural sports or exercise fairly regularly as "people are very conscious of their image" at this health-conscious university. While Greek life is highly visible here, there are also organizations like the Student Union that "promote other fun aspects of campus life (i.e. Movie nights, guest speakers, campus carnivals, etc.)" Students take part in "lots of great traditions at Wake Forest, like our annual Shag on the Mag dance in the spring," "rolling the quad after a big athletic win," and dinner at the on-campus restaurant Shorty's. Philanthropy is a "HUGE part of the WFU experience," and there are several extremely large community service events that happen throughout the year, , including the Project Pumpkin Halloween festival, the Hit the Bricks race, and many others.

Student Body

The university is steeped in Southern traditions and hospitality that "most students fit into or learn to adhere to in their tenure as Wake Students," but the school "is also home to students from around the country and the world." In this "tight-knit, supportive community" nearly everybody is "intelligent, ambitious, [and] highly involved," not to mention "beautiful." "It's like a living J.Crew magazine," says one student. Most everyone here is "preppy, involved in greek life, [and] from the east coast (either north or south)." Thanks to a strong foundation of friendliness and acceptance among the student body, "people generally don't have any trouble fitting in here, and can usually easily find groups of people who share their interests."

FINANCIAL AID: 336-758-5154 • E-MAIL: ADMISSIONS@WFU.EDU • WEBSITE: WWW.WFU.EDU

THE PRINCETON REVIEW SAYS

Admissions

Very important factors considered include: rigor of secondary school record, class rank, academic GPA, application essay, character/personal qualities. *Important factors considered include:* recommendation(s), interview, extracurricular activities, talent/ability. *Other factors considered include:* standardized test scores, first generation, alumni/ae relation, geographical residence, state residency, religious affiliation/commitment, racial/ethnic status, volunteer work, level of applicant's interest. SAT or ACT considered if submitted; SAT Subject Tests considered if submitted. ACT with Writing required. SAT with or without Essay component accepted. TOEFL required of all international applicants. High school diploma is required and GED is accepted. *Academic units required:* 4 English, 3 math, 1 science, 2 foreign language, 2 social studies. *Academic units recommended:* 4 English, 4 math, 4 science, 4 foreign language, 4 social studies.

Financial Aid

Students should submit: FAFSA, CSS/Financial Aid PROFILE, State aid form, Noncustodial PROFILE. Regular filing deadline is 3/1. The Princeton Review suggests that all financial aid forms be submitted as soon as possible after October 1. *Need-based scholarships/grants offered:* Federal Pell, FSEOG, State scholarships/grants, Private scholarships, College/university scholarship or grant aid from institutional funds. *Loan aid offered:* Direct Subsidized Stafford Loans, Direct Unsubsidized Stafford Loans, Direct PLUS loans, Federal Perkins Loans, State Loans, College/university loans from institutional funds. Applicants will be notified of awards on a rolling basis beginning 4/1. Federal Work-Study Program available. Institutional employment available.

The Inside Word

Wake Forest's considerable application numbers afford admissions officers the opportunity to be rather selective. In particular, admissions officers remain diligent in their matchmaking efforts—finding students who are good fits for the school—and their hard work is rewarded by a high graduation rate. Candidates will need to be impressive in all areas to gain admission, since all areas of their applications are considered carefully. A relatively large number of qualified students find themselves on Wake Forest's wait list.

THE SCHOOL SAYS "..."

From the Admissions Office

"Wake Forest University has been dedicated to the liberal arts for over a century and a half; this means education in the fundamental fields of human knowledge and achievement. It seeks to encourage habits of mind that ask why, that evaluate evidence, that are open to new ideas, that attempt to understand and appreciate the perspective of others, that accept complexity and grapple with it, that admit error, and that pursue truth. Wake Forest is among a small, elite group of American colleges and universities recognized for their outstanding academic quality. It offers small classes taught by full-time faculty—not graduate assistants—and a commitment to student interaction with those professors. Wake Forest balances the personal attention of a liberal arts college with the academic vitality and broad opportunities of a research university. Students are admitted based on the unique qualities they bring to our community. Wake Forest's generous financial aid program allows deserving students to enroll regardless of their financial circumstances.

"Wake Forest is the first top thirty national university in the United States to make standardized tests such as the SAT and ACT with writing optional in the admissions process. If applicants feel that their SAT or ACT with writing scores are a good indicator of their abilities, they may submit them and they will be considered in the admissions decision. If, however, a prospective student does not feel that their scores accurately represent their academic abilities, they do not need to submit them until after they have been accepted and choose to enroll. Wake Forest takes a holistic look at each applicant."

SELECTIVITY

Admissions Rating	95
# of applicants	13,281
% of applicants accepted	29
% of acceptees attending	33
# of early decision applicants	1,050
% accepted early decision	48

FRESHMAN PROFILE

Range SAT Critical Reading	590–690
Range SAT Math	620–730
Range SAT Writing	610–710
Range ACT Composite	28–32
Minimum paper TOEFL	600
% graduated top 10% of class	77
% graduated top 25% of class	93
% graduated top 50% of class	99

DEADLINES

Early decision	
Deadline	11/15
Regular	
Deadline	1/1
Nonfall registration?	No

APPLICANTS ALSO LOOK AT AND SOMETIMES PREFER

Duke University; Vanderbilt University; University of Virginia; The University of North Carolina at Chapel Hill

FINANCIAL FACTS

Financial Aid Rating	92
Annual tuition	$47,120
Room and board	$12,996
Required fees	$562
Books and supplies	$1,400
Average frosh need-based scholarship	$38,182
Average UG need-based scholarship	$35,551
% needy frosh rec. need-based scholarship or grant aid	93
% needy UG rec. need-based scholarship or grant aid	93
% needy frosh rec. non-need-based scholarship or grant aid	55
% needy UG rec. non-need-based scholarship or grant aid	50
% needy frosh rec. need-based self-help aid	93
% needy UG rec. need-based self-help aid	95
% frosh rec. any financial aid	39
% UG rec. any financial aid	34
% UG borrow to pay for school	39
Average cumulative indebtedness	$36,546
% frosh need fully met	80
% ugrads need fully met	77
Average % of frosh need met	99
Average % of ugrad need met	99

WARREN WILSON COLLEGE

PO Box 9000, Asheville, NC 28815-9000 • Admissions: 800-934-3536 • Fax: 828-298-1440

STUDENTS SAY ". . ."

Academics

Everything at Warren Wilson College, a small liberal arts school outside Asheville, North Carolina, can be attributed to its unique approach to learning, known as the Triad, where academics are combined with "work and service." As one student describes the Triad, it's "work for the hands, service for the heart, learning for the mind." Outside the classroom, "students are also required to work 15 hours a week on one of many work crews" around campus, and "are also required to fulfill a certain amount of community service work in coordination with one of many community partners." The "work program at Warren Wilson is one of the main reasons I chose the school," says one environmental science major, and another student adds that the "work program is [what's] truly interesting about this school. We run our own little country here basically." That doesn't mean academics get short shrift—as one history major points out, "We take as many credits as other college students and we work 15 hours a week." Professors at Warren Wilson earn mostly high praise from students: "They are great at both lectures and discussion, and are able to teach nuanced, complex ideas and concepts in interesting and concise ways." With the small size and strong sense of community, the faculty here is very involved and very accessible.

Life

With class work, community service, and time spent on one of the numerous campus work crews, students say "days are easily filled" and "weekdays tend to be very busy." When it's time to relax, "plenty of students spend as much time outside as possible hiking, swimming, skating, exploring the city of Asheville, and partying." "It's a very outdoorsy campus environment because we are in the middle of Appalachia" and "we have miles and miles of hiking trails that are campus property." Beyond the outdoors, "creative writing and coffee culture are a big part of Warren Wilson's culture," along with live music and "contra dancing on Thursdays." Some students say that the work crews are the closest thing the school has to fraternities and some of the more popular pastimes are "activities related to the crews—like blacksmithing workshops, beekeeping workshops, fabric workshops." With the school's appreciation of music, the "cafe is usually hosting shows that are a huge draw." In one student's estimation, "Everyone at the school loves the outdoors and has a healthy appreciation for taking an afternoon off to explore the river or trails." Warren Wilson is a place where politically-, socially-, and environmentally-focused "discussions are ubiquitous in and out of the classroom."

Student Body

"The student body at [Warren Wilson] is sustainable, eclectic, earthy, hard-working and very community oriented." As one photography major puts it, "If you're looking for someplace different, this is it." The school's former motto was " We're not for everyone, but maybe you're not everyone" and some students find that still holds true, though others note that "limited racial diversity" "does not create a welcoming environment to racial and ethnic minorities on the campus." At the same time, vocal students stress the school's accepting nature, underscoring that Warren Wilson "has a strong LGBTQ community that [faces] a far lesser level of discrimination at this school than at most colleges and universities." As an environmental science major puts it, "The environment and proximity to Asheville attract the typical tree-hugging hippie crowd, but there's really a place for everyone at the college" and nearly everyone is "actively engaged in issues of social justice." In short, Warren Wilson students are "fantastically talented, hardworking, and willing to think outside the box."

FINANCIAL AID: 800-934-3536 • E-MAIL: ADMIT@WARREN-WILSON.EDU • WEBSITE: WWW.WARREN-WILSON.EDU

THE PRINCETON REVIEW SAYS

Admissions

Very important factors considered include: academic GPA. *Important factors considered include:* rigor of secondary school record, application essay, recommendation(s). *Other factors considered include:* class rank, standardized test scores, interview, extracurricular activities, talent/ability, character/personal qualities, first generation, volunteer work, work experience. SAT or ACT considered if submitted; SAT Subject Tests considered if submitted. ACT with or without writing accepted. SAT with or without Essay component accepted. TOEFL required of all international applicants. High school diploma is required and GED is accepted. *Academic units required:* 4 English, 3 math, 2 science, 2 science labs, 3 social studies. *Academic units recommended:* 2 foreign language.

Financial Aid

Students should submit: FAFSA, State aid form. Priority filing deadline is 3/1. The Princeton Review suggests that all financial aid forms be submitted as soon as possible after October 1. *Need-based scholarships/grants offered:* Federal Pell, FSEOG, State scholarships/grants, Private scholarships, College/university scholarship or grant aid from institutional funds. *Loan aid offered:* Direct Subsidized Stafford Loans, Direct Unsubsidized Stafford Loans, Direct PLUS loans, Federal Perkins Loans, College/university loans from institutional funds. Applicants will be notified of awards on a rolling basis beginning 3/1. Federal Work-Study Program available. Institutional employment available.

The Inside Word

In keeping with Warren Wilson College's mission of combining academics, work, and community service, prospective students should be aware that their efforts outside the classroom are as important as their performance in it. The admissions committee looks for signs of maturity, integrity, and a commitment to the mission of the college in each applicant. Warren Wilson accepts the Common Application, with their own writing supplement (not required, but strongly recommended), and standardized test scores are optional.

THE SCHOOL SAYS "..."

From the Admissions Office

"Warren Wilson College students think and act independently, actively participate in their education, and want a college that provides a sense of community. Consider joining us if you're looking for a rigorous liberal arts education that integrates applied learning throughout. Warren Wilson students use work, service, internships and research to round out their core academic program, developing into highly sought-after global citizens."

SELECTIVITY

Admissions Rating	82
# of applicants	809
% of applicants accepted	84
% of acceptees attending	29
# offered a place on the wait list	0
# of early decision applicants	58
% accepted early decision	97

FRESHMAN PROFILE

Range SAT Critical Reading	518–650
Range SAT Math	470–590
Range ACT Composite	21–28
Minimum paper TOEFL	550
Minimum internet-based TOEFL	75
% graduated top 10% of class	17
% graduated top 25% of class	18
% graduated top 50% of class	77

DEADLINES

Early decision	
Deadline	11/1
Notification	12/1
Early action	
Deadline	11/15
Notification	12/15
Regular	
Nonfall registration?	Yes

APPLICANTS ALSO LOOK AT AND OFTEN PREFER
Guilford College

AND SOMETIMES PREFER
The Evergreen State College; Hampshire College; Eckerd College

AND RARELY PREFER
University of North Carolina at Asheville

FINANCIAL FACTS

Financial Aid Rating	86
Annual tuition	$31,980
Room and board	$9,900
Required fees	$580
Books and supplies	$850
Average frosh need-based scholarship	$20,658
Average UG need-based scholarship	$20,860
% needy frosh rec. need-based scholarship or grant aid	100
% needy UG rec. need-based scholarship or grant aid	100
% needy frosh rec. non-need-based scholarship or grant aid	28
% needy UG rec. non-need-based scholarship or grant aid	27
% needy frosh rec. need-based self-help aid	100
% needy UG rec. need-based self-help aid	100
% frosh rec. any financial aid	90
% UG rec. any financial aid	80
% UG borrow to pay for school	71
Average cumulative indebtedness	$20,768
% frosh need fully met	31
% ugrads need fully met	30
Average % of frosh need met	85
Average % of ugrad need met	84

WASHINGTON COLLEGE

300 Washington Avenue, Chestertown, MD 21620 • Admissions: 410-778-7700 • Fax: 410-778-7287

STUDENTS SAY "..."

Academics

Washington College is all about "gaining a distinctive and strong education in the liberal arts through personalized programs and hands-on experience." Located in small-town Chestertown, Maryland, this "small, tight-knit" community fosters a "high level of education" and an "intimate and personalized education experience." Washington College is a place where "students learn to think outside of the box while becoming better people and having the time of their lives." Centrally located between "three major employment markets: Washington, D.C., Philadelphia, and Baltimore," this "beautiful campus" "provides the perfect setting for a learning environment." "There are not as many distractions, but there is enough to keep you busy." Professors here are "highly educated, very personal, and willing to bend over backwards to ensure your education." Unlike at large research universities, faculty at Washington College are "here to teach, and they love to teach." The "attention given to the students by faculty is undeniable." The English and creative writing programs are among "the best in the country," earning Washington College a reputation "as a writing school," with the famous "Rose O'Neill Literary House, and the Sophie Kerr Prize." Students say all in one breath, "The professors are world-class, and the campus is beautiful. Also the Eastern Shore of Maryland is an incredible place to be."

Life

Living at Washington College "is as good as a college experience can get." "No matter what your interests are there is plenty to do." Some note that because of "the small-town environment, we have to make our own fun on weekends, but there's usually something on-campus to make it less of a challenge." "I personally love the environment and being outdoors. I spend a lot of time kayaking at our boat house on the Chester River, fishing on the Eastern Shore of Maryland, and supporting our athletic teams." "The school's rather small, so we know almost all of the athletes, so we're not only supporting a program, we're supporting our best friends." On campus, "there are plenty of student-run activities." When it comes to facilities, "the athletic department is great, and the dining hall is new and wonderful." For fun, students "often go to plays hosted by the drama department, attend interesting guest lectures, play Wii in the dorm rooms, play Frisbee on the campus green, play pool in the student center, go to movies, or stroll around Chestertown and the waterfront." "We drink in the dorms and suites because almost everyone lives on campus." Washington College "is located within a rural town; however, we are not completely isolated. We are about forty minutes away from Annapolis." Students do warn, "Being in a rural town was hard at first."

Student Body

A typical Washington College student "is preppy—from the way they dress to the way that they interact with each other and their professors." It's "an athletic campus, as even non-athletes are generally fit and participate in intramural sports." Most students "come from a somewhat affluent background, and the majority study and work very hard, but they also party very hard on the weekends." Though some note "there is very little diversity on campus," others say while the campus "might lack in racial diversity, people have diverse morals, values, and political views." There seem to be "two major, distinct campus cultures: the athletic/Greek life people and the English/drama people. People generally gravitate to one or the other." "It isn't hard to find your 'place,' though." Most students are "involved in several different types of activities." Students "usually fit in by playing a sport or joining Greek life, but there is always a club for everyone." Others concur, Washington College is a "melting pot of individuals from different backgrounds, but the typical student is open-minded, ambitious, and extremely innovative." Athletes and burgeoning writers alike "have strong pride and love for our school."

FINANCIAL AID: 410-778-7214 • E-MAIL: ADM.OFF@WASHCOLL.EDU • WEBSITE: WWW.WASHCOLL.EDU

THE PRINCETON REVIEW SAYS
Admissions

Very important factors considered include: rigor of secondary school record, academic GPA, interview, level of applicant's interest. *Important factors considered include:* class rank, standardized test scores, application essay. *Other factors considered include:* recommendation(s), extracurricular activities, talent/ability, character/personal qualities, first generation, alumni/ae relation, geographical residence, state residency, racial/ethnic status, volunteer work, work experience. SAT or ACT required. ACT with or without writing accepted. High school diploma is required and GED is accepted. *Academic units required:* 4 English, 3 math, 3 science, 2 science labs, 2 foreign language, 2 social studies, 2 history. *Academic units recommended:* 4 English, 4 math, 4 science, 3 science labs, 4 foreign language, 2 social studies, 2 history.

Financial Aid

Students should submit: FAFSA. Priority filing deadline is 3/1. The Princeton Review suggests that all financial aid forms be submitted as soon as possible after October 1. *Need-based scholarships/grants offered:* Federal Pell, FSEOG, State scholarships/grants, Private scholarships, College/university scholarship or grant aid from institutional funds. *Loan aid offered:* Direct Subsidized Stafford Loans, Direct Unsubsidized Stafford Loans, Direct PLUS Loans. Applicants will be notified of awards on a rolling basis beginning 1/5. Federal Work-Study Program available. Institutional employment available.

THE SCHOOL SAYS "..."
From the Admissions Office

"Founded in 1782 under the patronage of George Washington as the first college of the new nation, Washington College has been dedicated to developing tomorrow's leaders for more than 230 years. We aim to expand your intellect and creativity through independent study and collaborative research with faculty. You'll receive a truly personalized education that stretches your talents and potential. Professors and staff also work hard to link students to real-world experience and networking through professional conferences and internships. No matter what path you choose, we promise to nurture your growth and transformation into an accomplished, curious and independent thinker. Our graduates enter the world challenged and inspired, ready to assume the responsibilities of informed citizenship. We're committed to helping you launch a life filled with purpose and passion.

"All this intellectual and emotional growth happens on a campus that has been through a physical transformation in the past several years: some $80 million in improvements that include a brand new Commons with food court, coffee shop, student center and game room, a totally renovated library and arts center, an expanded fitness center, and two new residence halls with geothermal heating. Our setting on the Chester River in historic Chestertown, close by the Chesapeake Bay, enriches our programs in history and ecology, and we award the largest undergraduate literary prize in the world, the Sophie Kerr Prize.

"Admission to Washington College is selective; decisions are based primarily on a student's record of academic achievement. Campus visits are strongly recommended."

SELECTIVITY

Admissions Rating	88
# of applicants	6,847
% of applicants accepted	54
% of acceptees attending	11
# offered a place on the wait list	384
% accepting a place on wait list	95
% admitted from wait list	1
# of early decision applicants	111
% accepted early decision	58

FRESHMAN PROFILE

Range SAT Critical Reading	530–650
Range SAT Math	540–640
Range SAT Writing	540–650
Range ACT Composite	25–30
Average HS GPA	3.6

DEADLINES

Early decision	
Deadline	11/15
Notification	12/15
Early action	
Deadline	12/1
Notification	1/15
Regular	
Deadline	2/15
Nonfall registration?	Yes

FINANCIAL FACTS

Financial Aid Rating	86
Annual tuition	$42,844
Room and board	$10,612
Required fees	$1,006
Books and supplies	$1,250
Average frosh need-based scholarship	$29,630
Average UG need-based scholarship	$27,166
% needy frosh rec. need-based scholarship or grant aid	100
% needy UG rec. need-based scholarship or grant aid	100
% needy frosh rec. non-need-based scholarship or grant aid	22
% needy UG rec. non-need-based scholarship or grant aid	21
% needy frosh rec. need-based self-help aid	76
% needy UG rec. need-based self-help aid	82
% frosh rec. any financial aid	95
% UG rec. any financial aid	92
% UG borrow to pay for school	64
Average cumulative indebtedness	$36,991
% frosh need fully met	28
% ugrads need fully met	32
Average % of frosh need met	91
Average % of ugrad need met	86

WASHINGTON & JEFFERSON COLLEGE

60 SOUTH LINCOLN STREET, WASHINGTON, PA 15301 • ADMISSIONS: 724-223-6025

CAMPUS LIFE

Quality of Life Rating	81
Fire Safety Rating	93
Green Rating	83
Type of school	Private
Affiliation	No Affiliation
Environment	Village

STUDENTS

Total undergrad enrollment	1,350
% male/female	52/48
% from out of state	22
% frosh from public high school	81
% frosh live on campus	99
% ugrads live on campus	91
# of fraternities (% ugrad men join)	6 (34)
# of sororities (% ugrad women join)	4 (39)
% African American	5
% Asian	2
% Caucasian	81
% Hispanic	4
% Native American	<1
% Pacific Islander	<1
% Two or more races	3
% Race and/or ethnicity unknown	2
% international	3
# of countries represented	29

SURVEY SAYS...

Students are happy
Everyone loves the Presidents
Frats and sororities are popular

ACADEMICS

Academic Rating	84
% students graduating within 4 years	73
Calendar	4/1/4
Student/faculty ratio	11:1
Profs interesting rating	84
Profs accessible rating	85

Most classes have 10–19 students.
Most lab/discussion sessions have 10–19 students.

MOST POPULAR MAJORS

Business/Commerce; Psychology; English

STUDENTS SAY ". . ."

Academics

Washington & Jefferson College is a small, elite school known for its "academic rigor" and "prestigious reputation." In addition to two conventional semesters, the college also features a unique intercession period in January, "which allows for a month of focused learning on a topic that is often much different than something … offered during a semester, including travel and topics of specific interest to professors." Students feel that there is a very "open learning environment," and that "as the class levels increase, so does the amount of open discussion." The professors "want the students to learn" and "are willing to meet with students at any point to discuss how to better their education." "They are very knowledgeable and are very accessible outside of class," and personal connections with professors "oftentimes leads to internships or research projects" for undergraduate students. In general, the college is excellent at providing students with ample opportunities to prepare for their futures. It boasts "a great reputation for graduate school preparation" and has an "impeccable record at placing students in medical, graduate, and law schools." Additionally, there are "so many opportunities with alumni relations." The study abroad office is also excellent, and there are "tons of grants to do a research project abroad or to do internships across the U.S" or overseas with funding from the Magellan Project.

Life

Life at Washington & Jefferson College is a "good balance of schoolwork, athletics, and fun." The "beautiful, small campus" is home to a "friendly, warm," "family-like environment," where the emphasis is placed on the well-being of the students. It is "easy to get involved and be active in campus organizations." Students "study hard during the week, but party hard on the weekends," however, the school also "provides multiple activities over the weekends—especially for students who do not drink." "There are always music, art, speakers, and events" on campus. Some students complain, "There needs to be more to do on campus on the weekends," and the school is trying to respond to this demand by "working hard to produce more student activities, such as bringing in great bands for concerts." A few students also feel that the Greek life on campus is a bit too prevalent. Washington & Jefferson's home city of Washington "isn't ideal" for college students, but student services provides a shuttle to and from nearby Pittsburgh on the weekends, which can be "a great escape from the close-knit campus community."

Student Body

At Washington & Jefferson, "while every student is generally friendly and will help you, interaction between different kinds of people is still limited and at times, the student body can be cliquish," and the average student is a "white upper middle class republican Christian," although there is a "growing number of international students." While many students are "truly good, smart, open-minded people," there are "a few religious bigots who are rich and feel elite." Students tend to be "athletic, sporty, smart," "well-off financially," and "relatively preppy." However, students are also noted for being very social, as well as "extremely friendly and helpful." The typical student at W&J is focused on his or her course work; he or she is "also involved outside of the classroom in clubs, athletics, Greek Life, or one of a variety of other things the school has to offer." The students here "have a common goal to be successful in life," and with this goal in mind, everyone works together to form a tight-knit community and "gets along pretty well."

FAX : 724-223-6534 • FINANCIAL AID: 724-223-6019 • E-MAIL: ADMISSION@WASHJEFF.EDU • WEBSITE: WWW.WASHJEFF.EDU

THE PRINCETON REVIEW SAYS
Admissions

Very important factors considered include: rigor of secondary school record, class rank, academic GPA, application essay, recommendation(s), interview, character/personal qualities. *Important factors considered include:* extracurricular activities. *Other factors considered include:* standardized test scores, talent/ability, alumni/ae relation, geographical residence, state residency, racial/ethnic status, volunteer work, work experience, level of applicant's interest. SAT or ACT considered if submitted. ACT with or without writing accepted. SAT with or without Essay component accepted. TOEFL required of all international applicants. High school diploma is required and GED is accepted. *Academic units required:* 3 English, 3 math, 1 science, 1 science lab, 2 foreign language, 6 academic electives. *Academic units recommended:* 4 English, 4 math, 2 science, 2 science labs, 3 foreign language, 6 academic electives.

Financial Aid

Students should submit: FAFSA. Priority filing deadline is 2/15. The Princeton Review suggests that all financial aid forms be submitted as soon as possible after October 1. *Need-based scholarships/grants offered:* Federal Pell, FSEOG, State scholarships/grants, Private scholarships, College/university scholarship or grant aid from institutional funds. *Loan aid offered:* Direct Subsidized Stafford Loans, Direct Unsubsidized Stafford Loans, Direct PLUS loans, Federal Perkins Loans, College/university loans from institutional funds. Applicants will be notified of awards on a rolling basis beginning 3/1. Federal Work-Study Program available. Institutional employment available.

The Inside Word

Washington & Jefferson College takes a well-rounded approach to admissions, reflecting the type of student the school aims to admit. Academic record, class rank, personal statement, and extracurricular activities are all thoroughly evaluated. Most prospective students are high work diligently to secure a spot at this prestigious institution. The lucky applicants who receive a fat letter in the mail are welcomed into a distinctive community that promises to broaden their horizons and to prepare them for a successful future.

THE SCHOOL SAYS ". . ."
From the Admissions Office

"At Washington & Jefferson College, the entire community is devoted to ensuring student success. In the last three years, 100 percent of W&J graduates taking the Pennsylvania bar exam passed, and we regularly see admission rates of 90 percent for graduates headed to medical and law school. The College has added $100 million in new facilities since 2002, including residence halls, athletic facilities, a state-of-the-art technology center, the Burnett Center (housing accounting, business, economics, education, entrepreneurial studies, and modern languages), and the new Swanson Science Center (dedicated to the physical sciences, including physics, chemistry, biochemistry, and bioinformatics). Unique to W&J is the Magellan Project, providing stipends for innovative internships, research fellowships, and independent study-travel programs, domestic or international. Alumni mentors help students attain valuable internships, and, upon graduation, assist with career placement. You dream it; we make it happen. Our students are balanced, goal-oriented, active, engaged, and involved and we look for applicants who demonstrate these qualities in every stage of the admissions process. If you are a student who thrives on academic rigor, wants a close personal relationship with top-notch faculty, and values being a member of a true college community, we encourage you to consider W&J. Finally, W&J recommends but does not require scores from the SAT (or ACT). If submitted, we will use the best scores from either test. Be sure to check out our new four-year Graduation Guarantee at washjeff.edu."

SELECTIVITY

Admissions Rating	89
# of applicants	6,835
% of applicants accepted	43
% of acceptees attending	13
# offered a place on the wait list	29
% accepting a place on wait list	31
% admitted from wait list	33
# of early decision applicants	21
% accepted early decision	62

FRESHMAN PROFILE

Range SAT Critical Reading	520–620
Range SAT Math	540–630
Range ACT Composite	23–28
Minimum paper TOEFL	563
Minimum internet-based TOEFL	85
Average HS GPA	3.4
% graduated top 10% of class	34
% graduated top 25% of class	64
% graduated top 50% of class	93

DEADLINES

Early decision	
Deadline	12/1
Notification	12/15
Early action	
Deadline	1/15
Notification	2/15
Regular	
Priority	1/15
Deadline	3/1
Nonfall registration?	Yes

FINANCIAL FACTS

Financial Aid Rating	82
Annual tuition	$42,656
Room and board	$11,406
Required fees	$570
Books and supplies	$800
Average frosh need-based scholarship	$14,582
Average UG need-based scholarship	$14,509
% needy frosh rec. need-based scholarship or grant aid	88
% needy UG rec. need-based scholarship or grant aid	86
% needy frosh rec. non-need-based scholarship or grant aid	99
% needy UG rec. non-need-based scholarship or grant aid	90
% needy frosh rec. need-based self-help aid	89
% needy UG rec. need-based self-help aid	87
% frosh rec. any financial aid	100
% UG rec. any financial aid	99
% UG borrow to pay for school	81
% frosh need fully met	16
% ugrads need fully met	17
Average % of frosh need met	78
Average % of ugrad need met	81

WASHINGTON STATE UNIVERSITY

PO Box 641067, Pullman, WA 99164-1067 • ADMISSIONS: 509-335-5586 • FAX: 509-335-4902

CAMPUS LIFE

Quality of Life Rating	94
Fire Safety Rating	92
Green Rating	95
Type of school	Public
Affiliation	No Affiliation
Environment	Town

STUDENTS

Total undergrad enrollment	24,470
% male/female	48/52
% from out of state	10
% frosh from public high school	91
% frosh live on campus	86
% ugrads live on campus	25
# of fraternities (% ugrad men join)	26 (15)
# of sororities (% ugrad women join)	14 (20)
% African American	3
% Asian	5
% Caucasian	63
% Hispanic	13
% Native American	1
% Pacific Islander	<1
% Two or more races	8
% Race and/or ethnicity unknown	2
% international	5
# of countries represented	78

SURVEY SAYS...

Students are happy
Great library
Career services are great
Internships are widely available
School is well run
Students get along with local community
Recreation facilities are great
Lots of beer drinking
Everyone loves the Cougars
Intramural sports are popular
Campus newspaper is popular
Alumni active on campus

ACADEMICS

Academic Rating	73
% students returning for sophomore year	78
% students graduating within 4 years	38
% students graduating within 6 years	64
Calendar	Semester
Student/faculty ratio	15:1
Profs interesting rating	75
Profs accessible rating	80
Most classes have 20–29 students.	

MOST POPULAR MAJORS
Business Administration and Management;
Communication; Education

STUDENTS SAY "..."

Academics

Located in the city of Pullman and home to around 20,000 undergrads, Washington State University is known for its friendly, spirited environment and its motivated student body. The WSU school spirit is evident across the campus "with a wave of a flag or a loud 'Go Cougs!'" "There is no other place that has ever made me feel so invited and generally concerned about my well-being both as a student and as a member of the Coug family," says a student. Faculty members are constantly doing "world changing research projects" and "love getting students involved"; instructors will often bring in "great information they have found while researching something applicable to your learning." This makes classes both "challenging and rewarding, offering many additional opportunities throughout the course." "I've never [come] across a WSU professor who was not extremely knowledgeable and prepared," says a student. Faculty members urge students to ask questions, which lead to "awesome discussions" that take classes "from a one-sided lecture to discussions that have deepened my understanding of material." The school also offers a university-wide Freshman Focus residential learning community program that allows students to take a general education class with other students who live near them in residence halls. There is a top-notch Junior Writing Portfolio program in place to determine if students' writing abilities are up to par, "numerous study-abroad opportunities," and classes that provide "a chance to be innovative while still teaching you the experiences to be a good candidate in prospective fields." This opens the door for students to receive hands-on experiences by "creating connections to job opportunities, life-experiences, and internships." Academic benefits aside, in the end, Wazzu pride trumps all: "Win or lose, we're die hard Cougs."

Life

WSU's location in southeast Washington "makes for a gorgeous campus" and there is a real "college town atmosphere" in Pullman. There are "so many great restaurants" that students frequent. Skiing, hiking, camping, and boating are nearby. Greek life is popular, and students "love giving back to the community": "In Pullman, we don't have hello or goodbye—we have GO COUGS." The campus is "safe to the greatest extent," but the school "provides free rides to those who do not feel safe." The student recreation center is known for its undeniable awesomeness: "We have a pool shaped like the state of Washington and a hot tub that can hold fifty people." The university does an excellent job of providing events, activities and performances to attend, ranging "from movies to restaurants to bowling." Football games are a must for this crimson and grey sporting group, and good old Netflix watching and socializing in the dorms is always in season.

Student Body

Most WSU students are "friendly, and an active member of the community." A lot of WSU students have jobs and are heavily involved in extracurriculars, and "students typically fit in with others in their department." "There is a sort of bond between classmates that can lead to friendships and study partners in other classes," says a student. Most everyone here is "wearing Cougar gear at least three days a week" and "spends some time working out, studying, or hanging out with friends."

WASHINGTON STATE UNIVERSITY

FINANCIAL AID: 509-335-9711 • E-MAIL: ADMISSIONS@WSU.EDU • WEBSITE: WWW.WSU.EDU

THE PRINCETON REVIEW SAYS

Admissions

Very important factors considered include: academic GPA, standardized test scores. *Important factors considered include:* rigor of secondary school record, grade trends. *Other factors considered include:* recommendation(s), extracurricular activities, talent/ability, volunteer work, work experience. SAT or ACT required. ACT with or without writing accepted. English proficiency exam required of all international applicants. High school diploma is required and GED is accepted. *Academic units required:* 4 English, 3 math, 2 lab science, 2 foreign language, 3 social studies, 1 visual/performing arts, and 1 unit from above areas or other academic areas. *Academic units recommended:* 4 English, 4 math, 2 science, 2 foreign language, 3 social studies, 1 visual/performing arts or academic elective.

Financial Aid

Students should submit: FAFSA, General Scholarship Application. Regular filing deadline is 1/31. The Princeton Review suggests that all financial aid forms be submitted as soon as possible after October 1. *Need-based scholarships/grants offered:* Federal Pell, FSEOG, State scholarships/grants, Private scholarships, College/university scholarship or grant aid from institutional funds. *Loan aid offered:* Direct Subsidized Loans, Direct Unsubsidized Loans, Direct PLUS loans, Federal Perkins Loans, Federal Nursing Loans. Applicants will be notified of awards on a rolling basis beginning 10/1. Federal and State Work-Study Program available. Institutional employment available.

The Inside Word

Admission to Washington State University requires successful completion of a college prep curriculum. In addition, the committee will consider standardized test scores. Applicants who are either in the top 10 percent of their high school class or have a minimum cumulative GPA of 3.5 on a 4.0 scale are guaranteed admission. Depending on what your educational purpose is, the requirements and the application may vary.

THE SCHOOL SAYS "..."

From the Admissions Office

"At Washington State University, you work side-by-side with nationally renowned faculty who help you succeed. Many of the 200+ academic programs rank among the nation's best. Programs are designed to give you real-world experience through internships, community service, in-depth labs, and study abroad experiences. Plus, many disciplines encourage you to participate in faculty research or conduct your own. If you have top grades and a passion for learning, the highly acclaimed Honors College challenges you with interdisciplinary studies, rich classroom discussions, and research opportunities.

"The campus forms the heart of a culturally diverse community where faculty and fellow students help you achieve your greatest potential. More than 300 campus organizations connect you with others who share your interests. Each year, employers return to campus seeking WSU graduates. WSU also has three non-residential campuses in Spokane, the Tri-Cities (Richland), and Vancouver. In addition, courses are offered at WSU North Puget Sound at Everett and online through the Global Campus.

"To be considered for admission, you must complete the high school core curriculum and provide official scores from the SAT or ACT. If you apply by the designated date and are among the top 10 percent of your high school class or have at least a 3.5 cumulative GPA on a 4.0 scale, you're assured admission. For current priority dates and deadlines for admission and scholarship applications, check apply.wsu.edu."

SELECTIVITY

Admissions Rating	76
# of applicants	19,766
% of applicants accepted	80
% of acceptees attending	30
# offered a place on the wait list	0

FRESHMAN PROFILE

Range SAT Critical Reading	450–570
Range SAT Math	460–580
Range SAT Writing	440–550
Range ACT Composite	20–26
Minimum paper TOEFL	550
Minimum internet-based TOEFL	79
Average HS GPA	3.3
Nonfall registration?	Yes

APPLICANTS ALSO LOOK AT AND OFTEN PREFER

University of Washington

AND SOMETIMES PREFER

Gonzaga University; University of Oregon; Seattle University; University of Idaho

FINANCIAL FACTS

Financial Aid Rating	81
Annual in-state tuition	$10,916
Annual out-of-state tuition	$24,516
Room and board	$10,874
Required fees	$1,051
Average frosh need-based scholarship	$11,772
Average UG need-based scholarship	$11,659
% needy frosh rec. need-based scholarship or grant aid	87
% needy UG rec. need-based scholarship or grant aid	82
% needy frosh rec. non-need-based scholarship or grant aid	59
% needy UG rec. non-need-based scholarship or grant aid	37
% needy frosh rec. need-based self-help aid	63
% needy UG rec. need-based self-help aid	69
% frosh rec. any financial aid	86
% UG rec. any financial aid	73
% UG borrow to pay for school	61
Average cumulative indebtedness	$25,809
% frosh need fully met	14
% ugrads need fully met	12
Average % of frosh need met	63
Average % of ugrad need met	64

WASHINGTON UNIVERSITY IN ST. LOUIS

CAMPUS BOX 1089, ST. LOUIS, MO 63130-4899 • ADMISSIONS: 314-935-6000 • FAX: 314-935-4290

STUDENTS SAY "..."

Academics

Armed with a "fantastic reputation," Washington University offers undergraduates "unparalleled facilities and resources and a friendly and intellectual atmosphere." Students join a "supportive community" replete with "academic flexibility," a myriad of "research opportunities" and plentiful "merit scholarships." Moreover, Wash U.'s size is "big enough that [you] don't know everyone and...can meet new people often, but it is small enough that [you] recognize a lot of faces and know a considerable percentage of the people there." Academically, students are quick to praise the "strong" pre-med program, which provides excellent MCAT prep. Regardless of major, students warn us that no one should expect to breeze through classes here. Indeed, courses "are difficult." Thankfully, however, "with a good work ethic...they are manageable." Then again, it's also easy to be motivated when you're surrounded and supported by an "amazing" faculty. And these students greatly enjoy learning from professors who "are always engaged and passionate about what they're teaching." Further, many undergrads say it's quite evident that Wash U. professors are invested in the success of their students. A neuroscience major shares, "My professors work hard to make sure both that I fully grasp the material and that I understand its significance in relation to the course and my education as a whole." In the end, as an impressed anthropology major says, "Wash U. pulls out all the stops to make sure you have the best college experience possible, socially and academically."

Life

Boredom is practically nonexistent at Wash U. There's never a day that passes without some form of exciting entertainment. For example, "petting zoos, the carnival on the swamp, and a visiting orchestra are just a few things to look forward to each year." Certainly, extracurricular options abound and "anyone can find organizations on campus that pursue his/her interest." A freshman strongly agrees sharing, "Everyone gets involved with different student groups on campus, from environmental awareness groups to improv groups to butter-churning groups." Additionally, the Greek system is another "major source of entertainment for students." Though one sophomore stresses that "it doesn't [necessarily] dominate campus social life." And a freshman assures us that "there is no large divide between Greek and non-Greek students." Lastly, hometown St. Louis is a "really cool city for the people willing to explore it." Fortunately, the university makes it fairly easy to do so since "every student receives a UPass which covers most of the public transportation in the area." Undergrads can enjoy everything from "art galleries and museums to exquisite restaurants (like the Peruvian 'Mango') and a well-frequented stadium for the Cardinal's baseball games [as well as] other sports (like the Argentina vs. Bosnia soccer game this year!)."

Student Body

Wash U. undergrads agree that their school consistently manages to attract "motivated," "passionate" and "highly engaged" students. They are also quick to categorize their peers as "smart, moderately wealthy, a little bit nerdy, and extremely compassionate." And while most students are "hardworking and focused," a political science student highlights the fact that they are also "collaborative." Indeed, there's no place for cutthroat behavior here and "nobody wants to see their peers fail." Undergrads also tend to be "very socially aware and socially active." And though "people [might] joke about the typical Wash U student being pre-med and Jewish, but in reality...students are diverse in terms of their academic interests, religious inclinations, and cultural affiliations." Additionally, many undergrads boast that "the 'nice factor' advertised by the admissions department really is true: students are quick to smile, greet each other, hold the door, etc. All in all, "the Midwestern feel at Wash U makes it an extremely inclusive school, and a place where everyone is celebrated and welcome."

FINANCIAL AID: 888-547-6670 • E-MAIL: ADMISSIONS@WUSTL.EDU • WEBSITE: WUSTL.EDU

THE PRINCETON REVIEW SAYS

Admissions

Very important factors considered include: rigor of secondary school record, class rank, academic GPA, standardized test scores, application essay, recommendation(s), extracurricular activities, talent/ability, character/personal qualities, volunteer work, work experience. *Important factors considered include: Other factors considered include:* interview, first generation, alumni/ae relation, geographical residence, racial/ethnic status, level of applicant's interest. SAT or ACT required; SAT Subject Tests considered if submitted. ACT with or without writing accepted. SAT with or without Essay component accepted. TOEFL required of all international applicants. High school diploma is required and GED is accepted. *Academic units recommended:* 4 English, 4 math, 4 science, 4 science labs, 2 foreign language, 4 social studies, 4 history.

Financial Aid

Students should submit: FAFSA, Institution's own financial aid form, CSS/Financial Aid PROFILE, Noncustodial PROFILE. Regular filing deadline is 2/1. The Princeton Review suggests that all financial aid forms be submitted as soon as possible after October 1. *Need-based scholarships/grants offered:* Federal Pell, FSEOG, State scholarships/grants, Private scholarships, College/university scholarship or grant aid from institutional funds. *Loan aid offered:* Direct Subsidized Stafford Loans, Direct Unsubsidized Stafford Loans, Direct PLUS loans, Federal Perkins Loans, State Loans, College/university loans from institutional funds. Applicants will be notified of awards on or about 4/1. Federal Work-Study Program available. Institutional employment available.

The Inside Word

Washington University is highly selective and competition for admission is fierce. A strong transcript decorated with high-level classes is recommended. Course selection will also be important, depending on the school/major. For example, it's highly recommended that engineering candidates take the most challenging math program available. Additionally, along with any science/pre-med majors, they should have taken both chemistry and physics. Finally, students applying to the College of Architecture are highly encouraged to submit a portfolio (it is required of applicants to the College of Art).

THE SCHOOL SAYS "..."

From the Admissions Office

"Washington University in St. Louis is a research university that offers a unique environment for undergraduate students to learn and grow. Unparalleled curriculum flexibility and learning opportunities in a friendly and supportive community inspire undergraduates to explore their interests and develop new ones. Working with their advisors, undergraduates may choose a traditional single major, as many do. Others combine majors with minors, second majors, and pre-professional programs—all within their four-year undergraduate experience. We encourage our students to participate in internships, study abroad programs, research and scholarship, and more than 350 clubs and organizations, rounding out Washington University's commitment to help each student identify and pursue his or her passion. Visit campus and ask our students about their experiences at Washington University. As part of this commitment to help our students, Washington University offers a program that eliminates need-based loans as part of its undergraduate financial assistance awards to families of students with incomes of $75,000 or less. At Washington University, we take a personalized approach to financial assistance and encourage families to contact us to discuss any unique circumstances that might exist. This initiative and its goal of helping families with the most need will not lessen our desire, responsibility, or ability to work with all families to ensure they have the financial resources they need. Applicants are required to submit scores from either the SAT or ACT test. Applicants who submit scores from the ACT test may submit with or without the writing component."

SELECTIVITY

Admissions Rating	98
# of applicants	29,259
% of applicants accepted	17
% of acceptees attending	35
# of early decision applicants	1,652
% accepted early decision	37

FRESHMAN PROFILE

Range SAT Critical Reading	690–760
Range SAT Math	710–790
Range SAT Writing	690–770
Range ACT Composite	32–34
% graduated top 10% of class	89
% graduated top 25% of class	100
% graduated top 50% of class	100

DEADLINES

Early decision	
Deadline	11/15
Notification	12/15
Regular	
Deadline	1/15
Notification	4/1
Nonfall registration?	No

APPLICANTS ALSO LOOK AT AND OFTEN PREFER
Harvard College; Stanford University; University of Pennsylvania; Yale University; Princeton University

AND SOMETIMES PREFER
Duke University; Northwestern University; University of Chicago; Cornell University; Rice University

AND RARELY PREFER
University of Michigan–Ann Arbor

FINANCIAL FACTS

Financial Aid Rating	96
Annual tuition	$48,950
Room and board	$15,596
Required fees	$820
Books and supplies	$980
Average frosh need-based scholarship	$40,752
Average UG need-based scholarship	$37,617
% needy frosh rec. need-based scholarship or grant aid	95
% needy UG rec. need-based scholarship or grant aid	97
% needy frosh rec. non-need-based scholarship or grant aid	10
% needy UG rec. non-need-based scholarship or grant aid	6
% needy frosh rec. need-based self-help aid	73
% needy UG rec. need-based self-help aid	63
% frosh rec. any financial aid	50
% UG rec. any financial aid	53
% UG borrow to pay for school	29
Average cumulative indebtedness	$24,243
% frosh need fully met	99
% ugrads need fully met	99
Average % of frosh need met	100
Average % of ugrad need met	100

WEBB INSTITUTE

298 CRESCENT BEACH ROAD, GLEN COVE, NY 11542 • ADMISSIONS: 516-671-8355, • FAX: 516-674-9838

STUDENTS SAY ". . ."

Academics

As Webb Institute proudly boasts: "If you can design a ship, you can design anything." All graduates of this unique Long Island engineering school receive a full tuition scholarship and leave with a dual degree in naval architecture and marine engineering, with paid internships required during every academic year. This eventually lands each student on a pillowy bed made of a 100 percent job placement rate. The curriculum is "intense," but the academics tie in well with the winter work terms: "Work terms give each student a feel for industry sectors and allow them to make improved career decisions when selecting a first job," says a student. "You'll learn something in the classroom and then see it in action." Students find this incredibly valuable; "not only do you know how things work, you understand why they work."

From the second you walk in the door you know that Webb Institute is all about boats. Students "are surrounded by ship models, half hulls on the walls, and people who are all interested in ships, boats, cutters, yachts, and anything else that goes in the water." The professors are "brilliant," and since they all have practical experience they are "able to make our education applicable to what we'll be doing once we graduate." There are only four classrooms at Webb (one for each class); desks are in the back, chairs for class are in the front. Students do their homework at their desk in the classroom, surrounded by classmates, and if help is needed on a problem, "all you have to do is look up and ask the room."

The specialized tools that are made available to students are what "most schools could only dream of buying," and the level of trust from the staff means students can freely take advantage of such resources as the towing tank and student garage. "We are allowed, within reason, to use any shop as we please," says one. The student body at Webb functions based on an honor code, creating a "safe and supportive environment" which "allows our professors to give us take home tests knowing that no one will cheat." "I fully trust any individual at Webb," says a student. You also "cannot beat the alumni network here," which readily helps students find jobs, lodging, and anything else they need.

Life

All students live on campus during their time at Webb, and while "most of the day is devoted to work," there are several comfortable lounges with large television sets that are open 24/7 and a gym "not too far away." The campus has a pub that includes a pool table, darts, and a ping pong table, and sailing, kitesurfing, waterskiing, and other water sports are predictably popular Everyone participates in the student-run government, and extracurriculars are rampant; "if students want to do something, they take it upon themselves to make it happen" (no skill or prior experience is required to join any team at Webb). You "have to really push yourself to get work done to the point where you can leave on a weekend." However, students often tend to mix work and play in smaller increments, which is more doable. Proximity to New York City makes it easy for students to take day trips on weekends if they choose. In addition, "the school offers sponsored trips into the city to see cultural events like Broadway shows or symphony performances several times per semester."

Student Body

Given that there are only about ninety students total, students "become best friends very quickly, giving everyone great support systems both academically and socially." "My classmates are like a family to me," says one. "They are all smart, capable people who work hard and play hard." As another person puts it, "You can tell people apart by the sound of their footsteps." Students come from around the country (and the world in some cases) which "brings different views together and creates a good mix within the student body." Though academic stress can arise, students find easy comfort in each other. "We have all come for the same reasons, and most of us enjoy the same stuff. Therefore, we all have similar quirks and use these to entertain ourselves."

FINANCIAL AID: 516-671-8355 • E-MAIL: ADMISSIONS@WEBB.EDU • WEBSITE: WWW.WEBB.EDU

THE PRINCETON REVIEW SAYS

Admissions

Very important factors considered include: rigor of secondary school record, class rank, academic GPA, standardized test scores, recommendation(s), interview, character/personal qualities, level of applicant's interest. *Important factors considered include:* application essay, extracurricular activities. *Other factors considered include:* talent/ability, volunteer work, work experience. SAT or ACT required; SAT Subject Tests required. ACT with or without writing accepted. SAT with Essay component recommended. High school diploma is required and GED is not accepted. *Academic units required:* 4 English, 4 math, 2 science, 2 science labs, 2 social studies, 4 academic electives.

Financial Aid

Students should submit: FAFSA, Institution's own financial aid form, Business/Farm Supplement. Regular filing deadline is 7/1. The Princeton Review suggests that all financial aid forms be submitted as soon as possible after October 1. *Need-based scholarships/grants offered:* Federal Pell, State scholarships/grants, Private scholarships, College/university scholarship or grant aid from institutional funds. *Loan aid offered:* Direct Subsidized Stafford Loans, Direct Unsubsidized Stafford Loans, Direct PLUS Loans. Applicants will be notified of awards on or about 8/1.

The Inside Word

Although the applicant pool is highly self-selecting, admission to Webb is ultra-tough. The admissions committee is dedicated to finding students who will excel in the school's rigorous program. To apply, prospective students must submit high-school transcripts indicating rank in class, two letters of recommendation, and SAT or ACT scores, plus SAT subject tests in mathematics level I or II and physics or chemistry. Applications and all supporting materials must be filed by October 15 for early decision and February 15 for regular decision.

THE SCHOOL SAYS "..."

From the Admissions Office

"Webb, the only college in the country that specializes in the engineering field of naval architecture and marine engineering, seeks young men and women of all races from all over the country who are interested in receiving an excellent engineering education with a full-tuition scholarship. Students don't have to know anything about ships, they just have to be motivated to study how mechanical, civil, structural, and electrical engineering come together with the design elements that make up a ship and all its systems. Being small and private has its major advantages. Every applicant is special and the President will interview all entering students personally. The student/faculty ratio is eight to one, and since there are no teaching assistants, interaction with the faculty occurs daily in class and labs at a level not found at most other colleges. The entire campus operates under the Student Organization's honor system that allows unsupervised exams and twenty-four-hour access to the library, every classroom and laboratory, and the shop and gymnasium. Despite a total enrollment of between eighty-five and ninety students and a demanding workload, Webb manages to field five intercollegiate teams. Currently more than 60 percent of the members of the student body play on one or more intercollegiate teams. Work hard, play hard and the payoff is a job for every student upon graduation. The placement record of the college is 100 percent every year.

"Freshman applicants must take the SAT or ACT. We also require scores from two SAT Subject Tests in math level 1 or 2 and either physics or chemistry."

SELECTIVITY
Admissions Rating	97
# of applicants	105
% of applicants accepted	36
% of acceptees attending	68
# of early decision applicants	27
% accepted early decision	30

FRESHMAN PROFILE
Range SAT Critical Reading	670–730
Range SAT Math	750–770
Range SAT Writing	680–730
Range ACT Composite	30–33
Average HS GPA	4.2
% graduated top 10% of class	71
% graduated top 25% of class	21
% graduated top 50% of class	8

DEADLINES
Early decision	
Deadline	10/15
Notification	12/15
Regular	
Priority	10/15
Deadline	2/15
Nonfall registration?	No

APPLICANTS ALSO LOOK AT AND OFTEN PREFER
United States Coast Guard Academy; United States Naval Academy; University of Michigan–Ann Arbor

AND SOMETIMES PREFER
The Cooper Union; Virginia Tech

FINANCIAL FACTS
Financial Aid Rating	60*
Annual tuition	$47,000
Room and board	$14,400
Required fees	$400
Books and supplies	$700
Average frosh need-based scholarship	$2,000
Average UG need-based scholarship	$2,000
% needy frosh rec. need-based scholarship or grant aid	100
% needy UG rec. need-based scholarship or grant aid	100
% needy frosh rec. non-need-based scholarship or grant aid	33
% needy UG rec. non-need-based scholarship or grant aid	53
% needy frosh rec. need-based self-help aid	100
% needy UG rec. need-based self-help aid	100
% frosh rec. any financial aid	23
% UG rec. any financial aid	18
% frosh need fully met	0
% ugrads need fully met	0
Average % of frosh need met	80
Average % of ugrad need met	79

WELLESLEY COLLEGE

BOARD OF ADMISSION, WELLESLEY, MA 02481-8203 • ADMISSIONS: 781-283-2270 • FAX: 781-283-3678

STUDENTS SAY "..."

Academics

This "rigorous" all-women's school in Massachusetts is one of the most selective liberal arts schools in the country, boasting notable alumnae such as Madeline Albright, Nora Ephron, and Hillary Rodham Clinton. Since Wellesley is all about "supporting women who will run the world," students are "very well taken care of here," finding themselves part of "a great community that encourages and frees women to find their inner strength." Coupled with "amazing financial aid," and study abroad opportunities, the college "is a supportive, engaging, and downright fun community." The "vibrant," "worldly, interesting" professors here are "top-of-the-line," and "they know so much about their fields [that] an A paper is hard to come by." Students embrace the fact that "they expect a lot from us"; such an atmosphere may not allow for slack classes, but "it does allow for an impressive amount of growth." These "masters of their fields" offer "an immense amount of resources and time" to their students, and "class lectures combine the perfect balance of lecture and discussion to keep them engaging." "If I am not in class, my professors will notice and care to make sure I am doing all right," says one student. Faculty members are also very open to having students help with their research. "My name will be published alongside the professor for whom I worked in her next book!" says one. Alumnae stick together, and Wellesley's support system and alumnae network "guarantee you a top spot in places you are interested in, or at least some guidance on how to get in there." There are plenty of resources available to students from the administration (such as "tons of grants, academic/health advising"), as well as the ability to cross register with MIT, Babson, and Olin, giving students access to a "rich array of courses" and classmates.

Life

The town of Wellesley is "cute, but there's nothing to do after 6:00 P.M." No matter what kind of scene you're into, most students "like to get off the Wellesley campus on the weekend, if not for partying then just for sanity." Many Wellesley women "enjoy going to parties at local coed schools like MIT, Harvard, Babson, and Olin"; going into Boston to "escape the intensity of the campus" (there is a bus that runs, though not as frequently as some would like) is also a great way to relax, see a movie, or grab a bite. If students decide to stay on campus, "organizations are really great about throwing engaging events, bringing off-campus speakers, and creating a fun environment close to home." Wellesley women love to "meet over food and discuss everything under the sun." A typical activity/discussion cycle runs as such: "class work, homework, midterms, politics, the future of the country, the environment, going to MIT to party, going to Harvard to party, music, social construction of gender, you name it." People "actually do a lot of academic things" for fun here, mostly involving extracurricular clubs that explore their interests.

Student Body

Students are "very intense and motivated" at Wellesley, but at the same time remain "passionate, active, and intelligent women." The term used on campus is "Wendy Wellesley," which is someone "who is on top of all their class work plus some extra material, is concerned with the world, has extreme (almost impossible) ambition, and can interact with people in an extremely thoughtful and confident manner." It can be "competitive" here, but "there is a strong belief in women's rights, which comes with women's college territory." "Students are stressed constantly, but mainly because they stress themselves out," says one woman of her "type A, very hardworking, perfectionist" fellow students. Still, "students here really accept each other for all their quirks." The common denominator among all Wellesley students is that "we all strive to do our best and have a greater vision for the world beyond Wellesley."

FINANCIAL AID: 781-283-2360 • E-MAIL: ADMISSION@WELLESLEY.EDU • WEBSITE: WWW.WELLESLEY.EDU

THE PRINCETON REVIEW SAYS

Admissions

Very important factors considered include: rigor of secondary school record, academic GPA, recommendation(s), character/personal qualities. *Important factors considered include:* class rank, standardized test scores, application essay, extracurricular activities, talent/ability. *Other factors considered include:* interview, first generation, alumni/ae relation, geographical residence, state residency, racial/ethnic status, volunteer work, work experience, level of applicant's interest. ACT with Writing required. High school diploma or equivalent is not required. High school diploma is required and GED is not accepted. *Academic units recommended:* 4 English, 4 math, 3 science, 2 science labs, 4 foreign language, 4 social studies, 4 history.

Financial Aid

Students should submit: FAFSA, CSS/Financial Aid PROFILE, Noncustodial PROFILE. Priority filing deadline is 3/1. The Princeton Review suggests that all financial aid forms be submitted as soon as possible after October 1. *Need-based scholarships/grants offered:* Federal Pell, FSEOG, State scholarships/grants, Private scholarships, College/university scholarship or grant aid from institutional funds. *Loan aid offered:* Direct Subsidized Stafford Loans, Direct Unsubsidized Stafford Loans, Direct PLUS loans, Federal Perkins Loans, State Loans, College/university loans from institutional funds. Applicants will be notified of awards on or about 4/1. Federal Work-Study Program available. Institutional employment available.

The Inside Word

When making an admissions decision, Wellesley considers a broad range of factors, including a student's academic record, the difficulty of her high school curriculum, participation in extracurricular activities, class rank, recommendations, personal essay, standardized test scores, leadership, and special talents (students may submit art, music, or theater supplements along with their applications). Personal interviews are highly recommended, but not required, though they can be a useful way to help you stand out in Wellesley's extraordinary applicant pool.

THE SCHOOL SAYS " . . . "

From the Admissions Office

"Widely acknowledged as the nation's best women's college, Wellesley College provides students with numerous opportunities on campus and beyond. With a long-standing commitment to and established reputation for academic excellence, Wellesley offers more than 1,000 courses in fifty-four established majors and supports 180 clubs, organizations, and activities for its students. The College is easily accessible to Boston, a great city in which to meet other college students and to experience theater, art, sports, and entertainment. Considered one of the most diverse colleges in the nation, Wellesley students hail from seventy countries and all fifty states.

"As a community, we are looking for students who possess intellectual curiosity: the ability to think independently, ask challenging questions, and grapple with answers. Strong candidates demonstrate both academic achievement and an excitement for learning. They also display leadership, an appreciation for diverse perspectives, and an understanding of the College's mission to educate women who will make a difference in the world.

"The SAT and two SAT Subject Tests or ACT with writing component are required. We strongly recommend that students planning to apply early decision complete the tests before the end of their junior year and no later than October of their senior year."

SELECTIVITY
Admissions Rating	96
# of applicants	4,667
% of applicants accepted	30
% of acceptees attending	42
# offered a place on the wait list	1,182
% accepting a place on wait list	58
% admitted from wait list	12
# of early decision applicants	354
% accepted early decision	42

FRESHMAN PROFILE
Range SAT Critical Reading	650–740
Range SAT Math	640–740
Range SAT Writing	670–750
Range ACT Composite	30–33
% graduated top 10% of class	78
% graduated top 25% of class	97
% graduated top 50% of class	100

DEADLINES
Early decision	
Deadline	11/1
Notification	12/15
Regular	
Deadline	1/15
Notification	4/1
Nonfall registration?	No

APPLICANTS ALSO LOOK AT AND OFTEN PREFER
Brown University; Princeton University; Harvard College

AND SOMETIMES PREFER
Cornell University; Duke University; Georgetown University; New York University; Washington University in St. Louis; Middlebury College; University of Chicago

AND RARELY PREFER
University of California–Berkeley

FINANCIAL FACTS
Financial Aid Rating	97
Annual tuition	$46,550
Room and board	$14,504
Required fees	$286
Books and supplies	$800
Average frosh need-based scholarship	$39,129
Average UG need-based scholarship	$39,988
% needy frosh rec. need-based scholarship or grant aid	96
% needy UG rec. need-based scholarship or grant aid	97
% needy frosh rec. non-need-based scholarship or grant aid	0
% needy UG rec. non-need-based scholarship or grant aid	0
% needy frosh rec. need-based self-help aid	91
% needy UG rec. need-based self-help aid	90
% frosh rec. any financial aid	61
% UG rec. any financial aid	61
% frosh need fully met	100
Average % of frosh need met	100
Average % of ugrad need met	100

WESLEYAN COLLEGE (GA)

4760 FORSYTH ROAD, MACON, GA 31210-4462 • ADMISSIONS: 478-477-1110 • FAX: 478-757-4030

CAMPUS LIFE

Quality of Life Rating	86
Fire Safety Rating	96
Green Rating	92
Type of school	Private
Affiliation	Methodist
Environment	City

STUDENTS

Total undergrad enrollment	660
% male/female	0/100
% from out of state	9
% frosh from public high school	80
% frosh live on campus	96
% ugrads live on campus	68
% African American	27
% Asian	2
% Caucasian	39
% Hispanic	4
% Native American	0
% Pacific Islander	<1
% Two or more races	3
% Race and/or ethnicity unknown	2
% international	24
# of countries represented	25

SURVEY SAYS...

Classroom facilities are great
Lab facilities are great
Class discussions encouraged
Very little drug use
Alumni active on campus

ACADEMICS

Academic Rating	83
% students returning for sophomore year	79
% students graduating within 4 years	56
% students graduating within 6 years	59
Calendar	Semester
Student/faculty ratio	8:1
Profs interesting rating	87
Profs accessible rating	80

Most classes have 10–19 students.
Most lab/discussion sessions have
 fewer than 10 students.

MOST POPULAR MAJORS

Business Administration and Management;
International Business/Trade/Commerce;
Registered Nursing/Registered Nurse

STUDENTS SAY ". . ."

Academics

To many of its students, the words "sisterhood" and "tradition" are synonymous with Wesleyan College. Founded in 1836, Wesleyan "was the first college [chartered] to offer degrees to women." This private women's college located in Macon, Georgia, is "all about community, academics, and faith." Students say, "Everyone develops into a big family." Although this "diverse college full of brilliant women [is] devoted to sisterhood and tradition," it still manages to "[balance] more modern ideas and practices." Students compliment the "academic rigor, supportive atmosphere, diverse student body, nice facilities, and excellent classroom environment." Professors and academics receive the most praise. "Professors are definitely the best part of Wesleyan. [They are] totally dedicated and engaging." With hardly a negative word against them on student surveys, these "excellent," "open-minded" professors teach "challenging" material, and although they tend to be "strict," they are also "nice" and "encourage critical thinking and looking at things from different perspectives." "The professors here actually care about you, so don't be surprised when you receive an e-mail asking why you were not in class the previous day!" Classes may be "challenging" but "the academic experience is worth the cost of tuition." "The atmosphere is very uplifting and supportive," and students ensure, "There is no failing unless you absolutely, positively strive to fail."

Life

Life at Wesleyan College is not one big party. Students are "very studious and competitive in the classroom." "Everyone came here to get a good education, and that's what drives most of us here." The campus is dry. If you stay on campus, "you have to make your own fun." "It is small and quiet, a good place to study without all the distractions." "Students are usually very busy with classes and most are involved with some kind of school club/organization, so people don't typically spend a lot of time off campus." "If on-campus facilities are closed—the gym, athletic building, barn, science or music building, academic center, etc.—then there are plenty of off-campus facilities, usually within walking distance." "The Macon area has many clubs in it so a lot of girls gather up large groups and hit the town on the weekends. There is a movie theatre five minutes up the road that plays all the latest movies." Although the campus "has lots of trees and good places to take walks," some students would like to see a few improvements. "Upgrades to buildings need to be done," and "the food (has improved drastically) but we need more [vegetarian and healthy] options."

Student Body

Students at Wesleyan "are all very different from places all over the world." "The great international population leads to diverse religious, ethnic, and cultural backgrounds." They are different "in terms of political views, religious affiliation, and sexual orientation," and they are "opinionated." Some are "young and vibrant ready to tackle the world, while some are older ladies with children and jobs but [all] take pride in their education." What ties these students together is academics, sisterhood, and honor code. "The sisterhood program is an amazing tool that helps those who need a support system." "By being assigned a big sister, we have an easier way of adjusting and meeting new people." "There are sisterhood pep rallies every two months, which unite the school as a whole." Unity is important at an all-women school. As noted by one student, "We are all female, so we bump heads occasionally." Due to all the positive comments on student surveys, most would probably echo this comment of a fellow student: "I have had an amazing four years here, and I don't want to leave!"

FINANCIAL AID: 478-757-5205 • E-MAIL: ADMISSION@WESLEYANCOLLEGE.EDU • WEBSITE: WWW.WESLEYANCOLLEGE.EDU

THE PRINCETON REVIEW SAYS

Admissions

Very important factors considered include: rigor of secondary school record. *Important factors considered include:* academic GPA, standardized test scores, recommendation(s), interview, extracurricular activities, talent/ability, alumni/ae relation. *Other factors considered include:* class rank, application essay, character/personal qualities, first generation, volunteer work, work experience, level of applicant's interest. SAT or ACT required. ACT with or without writing accepted. TOEFL required of all international applicants. High school diploma is required and GED is accepted. *Academic units required:* 4 English, 3 math, 3 science, 2 science labs, 2 foreign language, 3 social studies. *Academic units recommended:* 4 English, 4 math, 4 science, 3 science labs, 4 foreign language, 4 social studies, 2 academic electives.

Financial Aid

Students should submit: FAFSA, Institution's own financial aid form, State aid form. Regular filing deadline is 6/15. The Princeton Review suggests that all financial aid forms be submitted as soon as possible after October 1. *Need-based scholarships/grants offered:* Federal Pell, FSEOG, State scholarships/grants, Private scholarships, College/university scholarship or grant aid from institutional funds. *Loan aid offered:* Direct Subsidized Stafford Loans, Direct Unsubsidized Stafford Loans, Direct PLUS loans, Federal Perkins Loans, State Loans, College/university loans from institutional funds. Applicants will be notified of awards on a rolling basis beginning 3/1. Federal Work-Study Program available. Institutional employment available.

The Inside Word

Wesleyan College values diversity. At this small college, you'll find students from more than twenty countries and twenty-one states, with a wide range of interests. To evaluate a student's qualitative characteristics, Wesleyan recommends that applicants submit a teacher recommendation and have a personal interview with the admissions staff (though neither is required). Students are also encouraged to submit samples of their creative work, such as poetry, music, or research projects.

THE SCHOOL SAYS " . . ."

From the Admissions Office

"Wesleyan College in Macon, Georgia was founded in 1836 as the first college in the world chartered to grant degrees to women. Today it is recognized as one of the nation's most diverse and affordable selective four-year liberal arts colleges. Located just ninety minutes south of Atlanta, the beautiful 200-acre wooded campus is listed in the National Register of Historic Places. Students value the College's rigorous academic programs, tradition of service, and reputation for excellence. An exceptional faculty teaches classes in seminar style. A student/faculty ratio of eleven-to-one ensures that students are known by name, not by a grade or a number. The acceptance rate of Wesleyan students into medical, law, business, and other graduate programs is exemplary. Undergraduate degrees are offered in thirty-one majors and twenty-eight minors including self-designed majors and interdisciplinary programs, plus eight pre-professional programs that include engineering, medicine, pharmacy, veterinary medicine, health sciences, dental, law, and theology. Fall semester 2013 the College welcomed its first cohort of students to the new Bachelor of Science in Nursing Program. Both men and women enroll in the Master of Education and accelerated Executive Master of Business Administration programs. Wesleyan has five NCAA Division III sports teams – soccer, basketball, tennis, softball, and volleyball, and an outstanding equestrian program which competes in Intercollegiate Horse Show Association and Affiliated National Riding Commission events. Proud of its longtime affiliation with The United Methodist Church, Wesleyan is excited to open a new environmentally sustainable, $6 million chapel in the spring of 2015."

SELECTIVITY

Admissions Rating	82
# of applicants	848
% of applicants accepted	42
% of acceptees attending	34
# offered a place on the wait list	0

FRESHMAN PROFILE

Range SAT Critical Reading	480–580
Range SAT Math	440–560
Range SAT Writing	450–580
Range ACT Composite	19–25
Minimum paper TOEFL	550
Minimum internet-based TOEFL	80
% graduated top 10% of class	0
% graduated top 25% of class	0
% graduated top 50% of class	0

DEADLINES

Early decision	
Deadline	11/15
Notification	12/15
Early action	
Deadline	2/15
Notification	3/15
Regular Priority	3/1
Deadline	6/1
Nonfall registration?	Yes

APPLICANTS ALSO LOOK AT AND OFTEN PREFER

Mercer University–Macon

AND SOMETIMES PREFER

University of Georgia; Emory University; Agnes Scott College

AND RARELY PREFER

Florida State University; University of Florida; Rhodes College

FINANCIAL FACTS

Financial Aid Rating	83
Annual tuition	$20,140
Room and board	$9,020
Required fees	$150
Books and supplies	$2,000
Average frosh need-based scholarship	$16,450
Average UG need-based scholarship	$14,845
% needy frosh rec. need-based scholarship or grant aid	100
% needy UG rec. need-based scholarship or grant aid	99
% needy frosh rec. non-need-based scholarship or grant aid	17
% needy UG rec. non-need-based scholarship or grant aid	13
% needy frosh rec. need-based self-help aid	78
% needy UG rec. need-based self-help aid	80
% frosh rec. any financial aid	95
% UG rec. any financial aid	85
% UG borrow to pay for school	43
Average cumulative indebtedness	$48,460
% frosh need fully met	19
% ugrads need fully met	16
Average % of frosh need met	77
Average % of ugrad need met	71

WESLEYAN UNIVERSITY (CT)

70 WYLLYS AVENUE, MIDDLETOWN, CT 06459-0265 • ADMISSIONS: 860-685-3000 • FAX: 860-685-3001

STUDENTS SAY "..."

Academics

Simply put, Wesleyan University is "a quirky liberal arts school where people learn to think and be creative." Academic freedom is paramount here and students revel in the fact that general education requirements are "optional." A grateful film student explains, "The flexibility of the academic program has… let me explore a variety of different disciplines and [given me] a holistic education." While the university is an academic powerhouse, it's especially known for its "amazing" arts programs and "really fantastic" science departments. Fortunately, no matter what they choose to study, Wes undergrads all benefit from "small class sizes" which "facilitate discussion and student-teacher relationships." In general, students here tend to find their professors "engaging" and "captivating to listen to." It's also abundantly clear that instructors are "devoted to and enthusiastic about the academic well being of their students." As one amazed psychology major shares, "They want you to interact with them outside of class, and even to invite them to lunch." And, most importantly, Wes professors want to "see that you succeed." All in all, students proudly report that a Wesleyan education "is about discovering your passions, both in and out of the classroom, and finding ways to pursue them."

Life

Undergrads at Wesleyan assure us that "there's never a moment of boredom." Of course, that's to be expected given that "there are a few hundred clubs and student organizations, ranging in subject matter from journalism to environmentalism…to politics…and so on." More specifically, Wesleyan has a very "vibrant" arts scene. To begin with, a number of students are involved in "theatre, dance, film production, and other projects like that." Additionally, "there are 50+ bands on campus, and on every weekend night there are three or more concerts going on, which many students attend." There's also a popular weekly "film series…that plays contemporary and classic films." We've been told that "it's great." Beyond the arts, "there are a lot of social justice groups that are very active [both] at Wesleyan and in the Middletown community [at large]." Many students can also be found attending "speaker events…sports games and teach-ins." Moreover, Wes undergrads are great about making their own fun as well, whether that involves "sledding" down Foss Hill or hosting "wine and cheese nights." And while there "isn't a huge Greek life scene here," an American studies major confirms that "there are still tons of fun parties."

Student Body

Wesleyan students "are nothing if not eclectic." An English major gushes, "As a general rule, Wesleyan is filled with unique, interesting, and passionate students. I have met a wide range of incredible people with very diverse experiences." And you can rest assured that "everybody is interested in something--politics, film, activism, literature, environmentalism, music." Nevertheless, when pressed, many undergrads here admit that "the quintessential Wesleyan student is somewhat bohemian/alternative in their lifestyle choices and artistic sensibilities, appreciative of that which is out-there/different, socially progressive/liberal, ambitious and hard-working yet laid back relative to students at other schools." Or, as a government major succinctly puts it, "If you think of the stereotypical hipster, that's Wesleyan." Moreover, Wes students happily describe their peers as "unbelievably…intelligent." Indeed, "you can have an intellectual and life-changing conversation with almost every person you come across." They also love the fact that the university manages to attract "a high percentage of international students" which allows for a myriad of unique perspectives. And, overall, there is "an extremely social and vibrant atmosphere where everyone wants to learn from each other." One economics major vigorously agrees concluding, "It's truly amazing to me how such a small school can be so engaged, energetic, and exciting."

FINANCIAL AID: 860-685-2800 • E-MAIL: ADMISSIONS@WESLEYAN.EDU • WEBSITE: WWW.WESLEYAN.EDU

THE PRINCETON REVIEW SAYS

Admissions

Very important factors considered include: rigor of secondary school record. *Important factors considered include:* class rank, academic GPA, application essay, recommendation(s), talent/ability, character/personal qualities, first generation, racial/ethnic status. *Other factors considered include:* standardized test scores, interview, extracurricular activities, alumni/ae relation, geographical residence, volunteer work, work experience. ACT with or without writing accepted. SAT with or without Essay component accepted. TOEFL required of all international applicants. High school diploma is required and GED is accepted. *Academic units recommended:* 4 English, 4 math, 4 science, 3 science labs, 4 foreign language, 4 social studies, 4 history.

Financial Aid

Students should submit: FAFSA, CSS/Financial Aid PROFILE, Noncustodial PROFILE. Regular filing deadline is 2/15. The Princeton Review suggests that all financial aid forms be submitted as soon as possible after October 1. *Need-based scholarships/grants offered:* Federal Pell, FSEOG, State scholarships/grants, Private scholarships, College/university scholarship or grant aid from institutional funds. *Loan aid offered:* Direct Subsidized Stafford Loans, Direct Unsubsidized Stafford Loans, Direct PLUS loans, Federal Perkins Loans, College/university loans from institutional funds. Applicants will be notified of awards on or about 4/1. Federal Work-Study Program available. Institutional employment available.

The Inside Word

Gaining acceptance to Wesleyan is no easy feat. A highly regarded institution, the university seeks candidates who demonstrate intellectual curiosity and a real thirst for knowledge. Certainly, a rigorous high school curriculum replete with advanced placement and honors courses is a must. Class rank and teacher recommendations are also heavily considered. However, Wesleyan is a test optional school (with the exception of homeschooled students and applicants who are enrolled in non-traditional secondary school programs). Finally, while interviews are not required they are strongly recommended.

THE SCHOOL SAYS "..."

From the Admissions Office

"Wesleyan faculty believe in an education that is flexible and affords individual freedom and that a strong liberal arts education is the best foundation for success in any endeavor. The broad curriculum provides a rigorous education that values putting ideas into practice. Students have the opportunity to discover what they love to do, work at the highest level, and apply their knowledge in meaningful ways. As a result, Wesleyan students achieve a very personalized but broad education. Wesleyan's Dean of Admission and Financial Aid, Nancy Hargrave Meislahn, describes the qualities Wesleyan seeks in its students: 'Our very holistic process seeks to identify academically accomplished and intellectually curious students who can thrive in Wesleyan's rigorous and vibrant academic environment; we look for personal strengths, accomplishments, and potential for real contribution to our diverse community.'"

SELECTIVITY

Admissions Rating	96
# of applicants	9,822
% of applicants accepted	22
% of acceptees attending	35
# offered a place on the wait list	1,877
% accepting a place on wait list	47
% admitted from wait list	1
# of early decision applicants	960
% accepted early decision	39

FRESHMAN PROFILE

Range SAT Critical Reading	620–730
Range SAT Math	630–740
Range SAT Writing	630–750
Range ACT Composite	29–33
Minimum paper TOEFL	600
Minimum internet-based TOEFL	100
% graduated top 10% of class	72
% graduated top 50% of class	100

DEADLINES

Early decision	
Deadline	11/15
Notification	12/15
Regular	
Deadline	1/1
Notification	4/1
Nonfall registration?	No

APPLICANTS ALSO LOOK AT AND OFTEN PREFER

Yale University; Stanford University

AND SOMETIMES PREFER

Middlebury College; Northwestern University

AND RARELY PREFER

Oberlin College; Vassar College

FINANCIAL FACTS

Financial Aid Rating	96
Annual tuition	$48,704
Room and board	$13,504
Required fees	$270
Books and supplies	$1,300
Average frosh need-based scholarship	$43,059
Average UG need-based scholarship	$41,244
% needy frosh rec. need-based scholarship or grant aid	92
% needy UG rec. need-based scholarship or grant aid	95
% needy frosh rec. non-need-based scholarship or grant aid	1
% needy UG rec. non-need-based scholarship or grant aid	1
% needy frosh rec. need-based self-help aid	92
% needy UG rec. need-based self-help aid	95
% frosh rec. any financial aid	53
% UG rec. any financial aid	48
% UG borrow to pay for school	45
Average cumulative indebtedness	$24,860
% frosh need fully met	100
% ugrads need fully met	100
Average % of frosh need met	100
Average % of ugrad need met	100

WEST VIRGINIA UNIVERSITY

ADMISSIONS OFFICE, MORGANTOWN, WV 26506-6009 • ADMISSIONS: 304-293-2121 • FAX: 304-293-3080

CAMPUS LIFE

Quality of Life Rating	88
Fire Safety Rating	98
Green Rating	76
Type of school	Public
Affiliation	No Affiliation
Environment	Town

STUDENTS

Total undergrad enrollment	22,498
% male/female	54/46
% from out of state	53
% frosh live on campus	85
% ugrads live on campus	15
# of fraternities (% ugrad men join)	15 (7)
# of sororities (% ugrad women join)	10 (6)
% African American	5
% Asian	1
% Caucasian	81
% Hispanic	4
% Native American	<1
% Pacific Islander	<1
% Two or more races	3
% Race and/or ethnicity unknown	<1
% international	6
# of countries represented	71

SURVEY SAYS...

Students are happy
Great library
Recreation facilities are great
Lots of beer drinking
Hard liquor is popular
Everyone loves the Mountaineers
Campus newspaper is popular

ACADEMICS

Academic Rating	69
% students returning for sophomore year	79
% students graduating within 4 years	33
% students graduating within 6 years	57
Calendar	Semester
Student/faculty ratio	21:1
Profs interesting rating	75
Profs accessible rating	77

Most classes have 10–19 students.
Most lab/discussion sessions have
20–29 students.

MOST POPULAR MAJORS

Business Administration and Management;
Engineering; Journalism

STUDENTS SAY ". . ."

Academics

One student reports that West Virginia University boasts "a relaxed, social, and extremely school-spirited environment," and that WVU's academics "challenge students in the classroom" and prepare them "to be successful in the next step of life after college." Another student praises the engineering program, which offers "many opportunities for seniors looking for jobs. I also like the fact that it is a big university, but being in Morgantown gives it a homey feel." Students find a happy medium that combines studying and socializing. "The school is all about connecting academics and leadership with incredible enthusiasm for school activities." "A wonderful experience with a good balance of academics and fun opportunities." "Great academic experience wrapped up in a fun college atmosphere." For in-state undergraduates, affordability is the key to choosing WVU. Many students are drawn to the "diversity of programs" offered at West Virginia University. With this variety of programs comes a "diversified faculty who bring a wide range of knowledge and experiences." Some students would prefer smaller classes because, as one student put it, "The large classes make it difficult to form solid teacher-student relationships." But another student offers a different perspective, "If you put forth any type of effort, you'll get to know your professors at WVU. Of course, with some of the bigger classes, you can sit in the back and go unnoticed, but that's a personal choice."

Life

There is no escaping the "pride" West Virginia University students feel for their school, many of whom say they were "born to be a Mountaineer." Whether it's describing their majors, the marching band, alumni, or the football and basketball teams, it seems unanimous that the "spirit of the university is outstanding." As one student states, "West Virginia University is all about combining such high academic standards with the atmosphere of Mountaineer pride, only something you can feel at a football game singing 'Country Roads' with 50,000 of your closest friends." "Fun" seems to best describe student life at WVU. Whether on campus at the "amazing student recreational center," which is "complete with weight room, indoor swimming pool, hot tubs, indoor track, indoor basketball and racquetball courts, ping-pong tables, and boxing equipment," at the Mountainlair student union watching free movies, or off campus exploring Morgantown, everyone seems to be having a good time. "One of the best things about Morgantown is downtown High Street. People always ask, 'you goin downtown tonight?'" This is referring to the very wide selection of bars, clubs, lounges, and restaurants that are located downtown, most concentrated along High Street. High Street starts at the south end of downtown and travels all the way up through the downtown campus. Some students would like to see an improvement in both parking and transportation, but the beauty of the area and the level of student assistance "outside the classroom with learning centers, free tutors, [and] group work areas" all get high marks.

Student Body

Students describe themselves as "outgoing" as well as "relaxed and social." School spirit is evident. "The typical student always has some piece of WVU apparel on, and that's usually sweatpants." "Students are very involved on campus with academics and various clubs and organizations. It is a very lively campus and there is always something going on. Although one student reports, "A lot of people here drink quite often," students also say that there is plenty to do on campus that doesn't include alcohol.

FINANCIAL AID: 304-293-5242 • E-MAIL: GO2WVU@MAIL.WVU.EDU • WEBSITE: WWW.WVU.EDU

THE PRINCETON REVIEW SAYS

Admissions

Very important factors considered include: academic GPA, standardized test scores. *Important factors considered include:* rigor of secondary school record, state residency. *Other factors considered include:* extracurricular activities, talent/ability. SAT or ACT required. ACT with Writing required. SAT with Essay component required. TOEFL required of all international applicants. High school diploma is required and GED is accepted. *Academic units required:* 4 English, 4 math, 3 science, 3 science labs, 2 foreign language, 3 social studies, 1 visual/performing arts.

Financial Aid

Students should submit: FAFSA, State aid form. Regular filing deadline is 3/1. The Princeton Review suggests that all financial aid forms be submitted as soon as possible after October 1. *Need-based scholarships/grants offered:* Federal Pell, FSEOG, State scholarships/grants, Private scholarships, College/university scholarship or grant aid from institutional funds, Federal Nursing Scholarships. *Loan aid offered:* Direct Subsidized Stafford Loans, Direct Unsubsidized Stafford Loans, Direct PLUS loans, Federal Perkins Loans, Federal Nursing Loans, College/university loans from institutional funds. Applicants will be notified of awards on a rolling basis beginning 3/15. Federal Work-Study Program available. Institutional employment available.

The Inside Word

While standards for general admission to WVU aren't especially rigorous, you'll find admission to its premier programs to be quite competitive. Admission to the College of Business and Economics, for example, requires a high school GPA of at least 3.75 and an SAT math score of at least 610. Programs in computer science, education, engineering, fine arts, forensics, journalism, medicine, and nursing all require fairly impressive credentials. If you're not admitted to the program of your choice, you may be able to transfer to it later if your grades are good enough, but it won't be easy.

THE SCHOOL SAYS ". . ."

From the Admissions Office

"From quality academic programs and outstanding, caring faculty, to incredible new facilities and a campus environment that focuses on students' needs, WVU is a place where dreams can come true. Our tradition of academic excellence attracts some of the region's best high school seniors. WVU has produced twenty-four Rhodes Scholars, thirty-five Goldwater Scholars, twenty-two Truman Scholars, six members of the USA Today's All-USA College Academic First Team, and two Udall Scholarship winners. Whether your goal is to be an aerospace engineer, reporter, physicist, athletic trainer, opera singer, forensic investigator, pharmacist, or CEO, WVU's 191 degree choices can make it happen. Unique student-centered initiatives help students experience true education beyond the classroom. The Mountaineer parents club connects more than 20,000 families, and a parents' helpline (800-WVU-0096) leads to a full-time parent advocate. A Student Recreation Center includes athletic courts, pools, weight/fitness equipment, and a fifty-foot indoor climbing wall. A major building program is creating new classrooms, labs, health-care facilities, an art museum, and a student wellness center. With programs for studying abroad, a Center from Black Culture and Research, and Office of Disability Services, and a student body that comes from every WV county, fifty states, and 100 different countries, WVU encourages diversity. WVU research funding has topped $174 million for the second consecutive year, making WVU a major research institution where undergraduates can participate. All applicants are required to take the ACT writing assessment as part of the ACT exam, or take the SAT to be considered for admission."

SELECTIVITY

Admissions Rating	76
# of applicants	15,353
% of applicants accepted	86
% of acceptees attending	36

FRESHMAN PROFILE

Range SAT Critical Reading	460–560
Range SAT Math	470–580
Range ACT Composite	21–27
Minimum paper TOEFL	550
Minimum internet-based TOEFL	61
Average HS GPA	3.5
% graduated top 10% of class	20
% graduated top 25% of class	46
% graduated top 50% of class	77

DEADLINES

Regular	
Priority	3/1
Deadline	8/1
Nonfall registration?	Yes

APPLICANTS ALSO LOOK AT AND OFTEN PREFER

Virginia Tech; Penn State University Park; University of Maryland–College Park

AND SOMETIMES PREFER

James Madison University; University of Pittsburgh–Pittsburgh Campus

FINANCIAL FACTS

Financial Aid Rating	85
Annual in-state tuition	$7,632
Annual out-of-state tuition	$21,432
Room and board	$9,872
Books and supplies	$900
Average frosh need-based scholarship	$4,814
Average UG need-based scholarship	$4,790
% needy frosh rec. need-based scholarship or grant aid	70
% needy UG rec. need-based scholarship or grant aid	70
% needy frosh rec. non-need-based scholarship or grant aid	94
% needy UG rec. non-need-based scholarship or grant aid	86
% needy frosh rec. need-based self-help aid	90
% needy UG rec. need-based self-help aid	91
% frosh rec. any financial aid	72
% UG rec. any financial aid	75
% UG borrow to pay for school	64
Average cumulative indebtedness	$34,105
% frosh need fully met	21
% ugrads need fully met	36
Average % of frosh need met	72
Average % of ugrad need met	75

WESTMINSTER COLLEGE (UT)

1840 SOUTH 1300 EAST, SALT LAKE CITY, UT 84105 • ADMISSIONS: 801-832-2200 • FAX: 801-832-3101

STUDENTS SAY "..."

Academics

Located in Salt Lake City, Westminster College is "a small private college" with "an urban setting that has easy access to the outdoors." Winter sports are a major part of campus life, but if you are not already proficient on the hills, don't worry, "we have really awesome ski and snowboard classes here." The school is also known for its "outstanding" nursing program, which is perhaps "the best nursing program in the state." Westminster's small size provides students with "intimate classes" and "professors [who] truly care about their students." "I have never felt more comfortable on a college campus," one public health major says. However, "as a small school, Westminster is lacking in some resources," and some students wish the college was "adding more majors to choose from." "Westminster has a very personal culture" and "professors really get to know and care about their students." "I know all of my professors on a first name basis," one student says. "Professors are creative with their teaching methods" and they "focus on helping students to excel and do well in class and otherwise rather than getting published." While the majority of professors "are highly educated in their field, some are better than others at expressing their field." "Westminster gives great financial aid," and "the support staff is amazing! Any question, concern, doubt, general lack of know how, they answered, pacified, and educated." "To me, Westminster was the epitome of that whole 'college package,'" one student says of their decision to attend. "The campus was beautiful and up-to-date, there was a broad range of majors, the location was ideal, and yet it was set within this amazing local and collegiate community." Another puts it more succinctly: "I honestly believe that Westminster is nearly perfect."

Life

Westminster is a place where "everyone looks forward to a good snow day." Skiing and snowboarding are central features of student life, with "six resorts within a half hour drive of campus." Students here are all about "working hard and getting to ski to reward yourself for the hard work." Salt Lake City provides "many opportunities (professional, recreational, and cultural)" and the campus is only "fifteen minutes away from outdoor recreation areas." On campus, "there are awesome student association run events!" Activities range from "spontaneous cupcake wars to international fests to dances to community service projects and everything in between." "I love the small-campus feel and the fact that it has an amazing location in a safe neighborhood," a Communications major reports. "The atmosphere on campus is my favorite part of the school," says a neuroscience major. "It's a really friendly, open, fun place to be." Another student declares that "life is truly elevated at Westminster College."

Student Body

Students at Westminster are either "here to learn, or here to ski; often a combination of the two." The student body is not especially racially diverse, with most students being "white, in shape, environmentally friendly, etc." Still, "all students are unique and are individuals" and can be "anything from snow bro, hipster, intellectual, religious, atheist, or spoiled slacker." In regards to political views, "while it may be fair to call Utah a 'sea of conservatism,' SLC certainly is not. Westminster reflects SLC's more liberal leanings." "The community is close-knit and supportive" and "nearly everyone skis or snowboards" or at least likes to "hike, rock climb, [and] camp." Some students who are not big on outdoor sports can "feel like outsider[s]." As at many colleges, certain students "are more concerned about school while there are many who like to party and rely on their parents to pay their way while they slack off." Overall this "wonderful mix" of students is the "best-kept secret around." Westminster College is a place "where ski bums, overachievers and Mormons collide to make up an awesome, fun residential student body."

FINANCIAL AID: 801-832-2502 • E-MAIL: ADMISSION@WESTMINSTERCOLLEGE.EDU • WEBSITE: WWW.WESTMINSTERCOLLEGE.EDU

THE PRINCETON REVIEW SAYS

Admissions

Very important factors considered include: rigor of secondary school record, academic GPA. *Important factors considered include:* class rank, standardized test scores, application essay, interview, recommendation(s). *Other factors considered include:* extracurricular activities, talent/ability, character/personal qualities, alumni/ae relation, geographical residence, volunteer work, work experience. SAT or ACT required. ACT with Writing recommended. TOEFL required of all international applicants. High school diploma is required and GED is accepted. *Academic units required:* 4 English, 2 math, 3 science, 2 foreign language, 2 social studies, 1 history, 2 academic electives. *Academic units recommended:* 4 English, 3 math, 3 science, 3 foreign language, 2 social studies, 1 history, 3 academic electives.

Financial Aid

Students should submit: FAFSA. Priority filing date is 4/15. The Princeton Review suggests that all financial aid forms be submitted as soon as possible after October 1. *Need-based scholarships/grants offered:* Federal Pell, FSEOG, State scholarships/grants, Private scholarships, College/university scholarship or grant aid from institutional funds. *Loan aid offered:* Direct Subsidized Stafford Loans, Direct Unsubsidized Stafford Loans, Direct PLUS loans, Federal Perkins Loans. Applicants will be notified of awards on a rolling basis beginning in December. Federal Work-Study Program available. Institutional employment available.

The Inside Word

Westminster accepts a solid majority of applicants it receives, so you don't have to have been the valedictorian to apply. Students with good grades and above national average test scores have a very strong chance of being accepted. Students who fall a little short in those categories can still impress the admissions office with extracurricular achievement, powerful essays, or other demonstrable talents.

THE SCHOOL SAYS "..."

From the Admissions Office

"Westminster is a private, independent, and comprehensive university in Salt Lake City, Utah. Students experience the liberal arts blended with professional programs in an atmosphere dedicated to civic engagement. With the goal of enabling its graduates to live vibrant, just, and successful lives, Westminster provides transformational learning experiences for both undergraduate and graduate students in a truly student-centered environment. Faculty focus on teaching, learning, and developing distinctive, innovative programs, while students thrive on Westminster's urban Sugar House campus within minutes of the Rocky Mountains.

"Each application is read and reviewed individually by an admissions committee who takes into account both level of challenge in course work and grades received. Either the SAT or ACT exam is accepted. Writing ability will be assessed through an application essay, and in some cases, other writing samples such as graded papers.

"Westminster College has a rolling application deadline and will accept applications until the class is filled. To be eligible for the widest array of financial aid—and more than 98 percent of freshmen receive scholarship or financial aid—April 15 is the priority consideration deadline for fall semester, and May 15 is the priority deadline for on-campus housing applications."

SELECTIVITY
Admissions Rating	75
# of applicants	2,001
% of applicants accepted	96
% of acceptees attending	24

FRESHMAN PROFILE
Range SAT Critical Reading	500–620
Range SAT Math	503–618
Range ACT Composite	22–27
Minimum paper TOEFL	550
Minimum internet-based TOEFL	79
Average HS GPA	3.6
% graduated top 10% of class	20
% graduated top 25% of class	53
% graduated top 50% of class	84

DEADLINES
Regular	
Priority	2/1
Deadline	8/16
Nonfall registration?	Yes

APPLICANTS ALSO LOOK AT AND OFTEN PREFER
Brigham Young University (UT)

AND SOMETIMES PREFER
University of Utah

FINANCIAL FACTS
Financial Aid Rating	85
Annual tuition	$30,720
Room and board	$9,338
Required fees	$508
Books and supplies	$1,000
Average frosh need-based scholarship	$21,011
Average UG need-based scholarship	$19,482
% needy frosh rec. need-based scholarship or grant aid	100
% needy UG rec. need-based scholarship or grant aid	99
% needy frosh rec. non-need-based scholarship or grant aid	13
% needy UG rec. non-need-based scholarship or grant aid	12
% needy frosh rec. need-based self-help aid	85
% needy UG rec. need-based self-help aid	85
% frosh rec. any financial aid	99
% UG rec. any financial aid	93
% UG borrow to pay for school	63
Average cumulative indebtedness	$29,687
% frosh need fully met	25
% ugrads need fully met	21
Average % of frosh need met	81
Average % of ugrad need met	76

WHEATON COLLEGE (IL)

501 COLLEGE AVENUE, WHEATON, IL 60187 • ADMISSIONS: 630-752-5005 • FAX: 630-752-5285

STUDENTS SAY "..."

Academics

Wheaton College strives to cultivate students' knowledge and to "prepare them to enter the world as strong and capable individuals who serve Christ and His Kingdom." This "academically rigorous" and deeply Christ-centered liberal arts school is equally as interested in the character of each student, with a focus on "developing yourself in ways [that] will affect you long after you've left the school campus." Professors here are "the heart and soul of this campus," and they're "exceptional teachers who genuinely care for the academic and spiritual well-being of their students." They "attempt to connect with students in ways other than the material they are told to teach," and it's "not unusual to meet professors outside of class, whether that be for a meal, coffee, or fun activities." That's not to say that there aren't a few bad apples or that the grading isn't tough; professors "rarely curve," but they do provide "many mentoring and tutoring sessions" to those in need. There's a "serious integration of faith and learning" that "places a high emphasis on opening up our eyes to serious issues going on around the world." "When you see other people using their gifts for God and hear them encouraging you to do the same, it's inspiring," says one student. Class sizes at Wheaton are pleasantly small, and one-on-one interaction is very common through "internships, teaching assistants, research opportunities, and the 'Dine with a Mind' program." This student body that's truly "sincere about learning" goes on to form a "very close-knit network of graduates" that's easily accessible after graduation. Other than that, students laud the "successful career placement, top-notch music conservatory, [and] excellent science facilities."

Life

All Wheaton students adhere to a community covenant, which is a set of rules and regulations governing students that forbids things, such as drinking and smoking. While several students wish that the school was "more lenient in their punishment system," most are happy to comply and even claim that it "forces us to come up with super-creative ways to have fun." "Everyone has at least one costume—bring one if you come here because you will need it," says a mysterious student. Drink-wise, "Wheaton students don't need alcohol to have an awesome time," and food-wise, the school has what some students call the "greatest college food in the country." The train station is a few minutes' walk from campus, which can bring you to nearby Chicago, but most students "just find fun activities to do on campus...like bond with [students who live on their housing] floor or play campus-wide Sardines." The college offers lots of activities during the weekend and has tons of "random traditions," such as a "student 'Iron Chef' competition in the dining hall." Students here are very passionate about social justice issues and "just as likely to be found discussing theology or philosophy as the latest sports game." ESL tutoring, mentoring, and serving on spring break service trips are also popular extracurricular activities for Wheaties.

Student Body

Pretty much the entirety of Wheaton is composed of "academically strong, driven, and Christian students," and the phrase "type A personality" is oft-used. The school draws students from all over the country (including "quite a lot of homeschooled and international students"), and the diversity isn't as strong as some students would like, though "they are making a lot of efforts to change that in the admissions office." Students at Wheaton "take their studies extremely seriously and work very hard to keep high grades," but most still get involved with student activities, ministries, and sports, and enjoy the groups of friends that form when people share a "common identity." In their downtime, people "have a respectful and creative sense of fun and do not waste their time." All in all, "most students find some way to fit in."

WHEATON COLLEGE (IL)

FINANCIAL AID: 630-752-5021 • E-MAIL: ADMISSIONS@WHEATON.EDU • WEBSITE: WWW.WHEATON.EDU

THE PRINCETON REVIEW SAYS

Admissions

Very important factors considered include: rigor of secondary school record, academic GPA, standardized test scores, application essay, recommendation(s), interview, character/personal qualities, religious affiliation/commitment. *Important factors considered include:* extracurricular activities, talent/ability, volunteer work, work experience. *Other factors considered include:* class rank, first generation, alumni/ae relation, geographical residence, state residency, racial/ethnic status, level of applicant's interest. SAT or ACT required. ACT with or without writing accepted. TOEFL required of all international applicants. High school diploma is required and GED is accepted. *Academic units required:* 4 English, 3 math, 3 science, 2 foreign language, 3 social studies. *Academic units recommended:* 4 English, 4 math, 4 science, 3 foreign language, 4 social studies.

Financial Aid

Students should submit: FAFSA, Institution's own financial aid form. Priority filing deadline is 2/15. The Princeton Review suggests that all financial aid forms be submitted as soon as possible after October 1. *Need-based scholarships/grants offered:* Federal Pell, FSEOG, State scholarships/grants, Private scholarships, College/university scholarship or grant aid from institutional funds. *Loan aid offered:* Direct Subsidized Stafford Loans, Direct Unsubsidized Stafford Loans, Direct PLUS loans, Federal Perkins Loans. Applicants will be notified of awards on a rolling basis beginning 2/1. Federal Work-Study Program available. Institutional employment available.

The Inside Word

Although Wheaton College looks for students who are strong academically, the college doesn't have any minimum requirements for GPA, class rank, or standardized test scores. The school does look for evidence of Christian faith when making its decision, and proof of Christian commitment is necessary for admission, but you'll also have to prove the quality of your high school courses.

THE SCHOOL SAYS "..."

From the Admissions Office

"At Wheaton, we're commited to being a community that fearlessly pursues truth, upholds an academically rigorous curriculum, and promotes virtue. The college takes seriously its impact on society. The influence of Wheaton is seen in fields ranging from government (congressmen, senator, U.S. ambassador) to sports (two NBA coaches) to business (the CEO of John Deere) to music (Metropolitan Opera National Competition winners) to education (over forty college presidents) to global ministry (Billy Graham). Wheaton seeks students who want to make a difference and are passionate about their Christian faith and rigorous academic pursuit.

"Applicants are required to submit results from the SAT or the ACT. Wheaton will use the highest of these scores from either test in evaluating a student's application."

SELECTIVITY

Admissions Rating	90
# of applicants	1,971
% of applicants accepted	70
% of acceptees attending	44
# offered a place on the wait list	409
% accepting a place on wait list	29
% admitted from wait list	27

FRESHMAN PROFILE

Range SAT Critical Reading	600–710
Range SAT Math	600–700
Range SAT Writing	590–700
Range ACT Composite	27–32
Minimum paper TOEFL	587
Minimum internet-based TOEFL	95
Average HS GPA	3.7
% graduated top 10% of class	54
% graduated top 25% of class	81
% graduated top 50% of class	96

DEADLINES

Early action	
Deadline	11/1
Notification	12/31
Regular	
Deadline	1/10
Notification	4/1
Nonfall registration?	Yes

APPLICANTS ALSO LOOK AT AND SOMETIMES PREFER
Calvin College

AND RARELY PREFER
Gordon College; Baylor University; Grove City College; University of Michigan–Ann Arbor

FINANCIAL FACTS

Financial Aid Rating	84
Annual tuition	$34,050
Room and board	$9,560
Books and supplies	$800
Average frosh need-based scholarship	$22,035
Average UG need-based scholarship	$21,380
% needy frosh rec. need-based scholarship or grant aid	100
% needy UG rec. need-based scholarship or grant aid	99
% needy frosh rec. non-need-based scholarship or grant aid	35
% needy UG rec. non-need-based scholarship or grant aid	32
% needy frosh rec. need-based self-help aid	75
% needy UG rec. need-based self-help aid	77
% frosh rec. any financial aid	86
% UG rec. any financial aid	79
% UG borrow to pay for school	58
Average cumulative indebtedness	$26,593
% frosh need fully met	26
% ugrads need fully met	26
Average % of frosh need met	88
Average % of ugrad need met	87

WHEATON COLLEGE (MA)

Office of Admission, Norton, MA 02766 • Admissions: 508-286-8251 • Fax: 508-286-8271

CAMPUS LIFE

Quality of Life Rating	83
Fire Safety Rating	83
Green Rating	69
Type of school	Private
Affiliation	No Affiliation
Environment	Village

STUDENTS

Total undergrad enrollment	1,598
% male/female	36/64
% from out of state	63
% frosh from public high school	70
% frosh live on campus	99
% ugrads live on campus	95
% African American	6
% Asian	5
% Caucasian	67
% Hispanic	7
% Native American	<1
% Pacific Islander	<1
% Two or more races	3
% Race and/or ethnicity unknown	1
% international	10
# of countries represented	72

SURVEY SAYS...

Students are happy
Lab facilities are great
Students aren't religious
Easy to get around campus

ACADEMICS

Academic Rating	87
% students returning for sophomore year	86
% students graduating within 4 years	76
% students graduating within 6 years	79
Calendar	Semester
Student/faculty ratio	10:1
Profs interesting rating	90
Profs accessible rating	93

Most classes have 10–19 students.
Most lab/discussion sessions have
10–19 students.

MOST POPULAR MAJORS

Economics; Psychology; Business/Commerce

STUDENTS SAY "..."

Academics

This historic Massachusetts institution, originally founded in 1834 as a female seminary, is now a "small liberal arts college" that provides "a top notch education" for "high performing students." Wheaton is a school that "focuses strongly on creating the well-rounded, aware, worldly and accepting liberal arts graduate." Students love the "small class sizes" that engender a "close connection with faculty." These factors "are incredibly conducive to classroom discussion and cooperative learning in all subjects" and "students are expected to be present and participate in class." Students know that "if you work hard, you will succeed," and if you are struggling people will help you out. "There's an atmosphere of goodwill," a Psychology and Hispanic Studies student explains. "For example, if someone is having trouble in a class or looking for a summer job, help is always available and easily reachable." Another attraction is "the beautiful campus" that is located close to both Providence and Boston. The most common complaint among students is the dining and meal plans, which are "very limited," "could possibly be healthier" and in general are "awful." "It's understandable that it's hard to cater to the tastes of such a diverse community, but it'd be nice if things had a decent flavor to it," one student says. That said, "the food is probably the only issue" at this exciting college. There is a strong "sense of community" on campus, and "professors and students alike are all so friendly, genuine, helpful, motivated, and proactive people." You can tell people are comfortable here as they walk around campus "like any person you would see walking around their own house" and everyone is "very friendly and genuine." "Not only do students here value comfortable clothes, they get to know the campus well and get comfortable being in it," a Psychology major says. At the end of the day, "Wheaton is all about finding your passion and exploring avenues that you might never have thought to explore." One senior raves about their experience, telling potential applicants that Wheaton is "the most diverse, welcoming, accepting, and colorful place you'll ever live in."

Life

As a small school, "the party scene does not compare to a large university" and some suggest "the party scene at Wheaton is practically nonexistent." Instead, students enjoy the "active force" of the college's programming council that ensures "students will always have something to do on weekends." Students are very active in student groups and organizations, including the "over 100 clubs and organizations on campus that do programming in a regular basis." "The typical girl auditions for an a cappella group or a monologue/improv group," one student explains. "The typical male is either involved with a sport or finds a gaming clique." While there is a lot to do on campus, "the surrounding town (if you can call it that) consists of a CVS, Walgreens, two old-man bars, a bad Chinese place and a corner store." Consequentially, students often take trips to "Boston and Providence, which are extremely easy to get to" as "Providence is less than 30 minutes away, and Boston about an hour." Wheaton is a "close-knit community" with a "friendly and accepting campus culture." "People are truly passionate about their academic areas of interest and their hobbies" at Wheaton, and spend late nights debating "everything from politics to Harry Potter."

Student Body

Students at Wheaton "are independent thinkers and take pride in their individuality" while working "well together, no matter what social group you may be a part of." They might be best summed up as "quirky, but in all different ways." "Students usually fall into friend groups very fast," normally finding "a set of friends after first semester." "Students are generally liberal" and often "very New-England" and "smart, social, involved." Many students are "from the northeast, white and middle class," yet "the diversity is mind-bending" and there are plenty of "students of color, international students, queer students, various religious denominations." However, one student points out that "the student body is 60 percent female, and it is not uncommon at all to have a class where most students are women." The main feeling on campus is that of a "tight knit community" where anyone can come "and find a place to fit in or stand out."

FINANCIAL AID: 508-286-8232 • E-MAIL: ADMISSION@WHEATONCOLLEGE.EDU • WEBSITE: WWW.WHEATONCOLLEGE.EDU

THE PRINCETON REVIEW SAYS

Admissions

Very important factors considered include: rigor of secondary school record, academic GPA, application essay, recommendation(s). *Important factors considered include:* character/personal qualities, alumni/ae relation. *Other factors considered include:* class rank, interview, extracurricular activities, talent/ability, geographical residence, state residency, religious affiliation/commitment, volunteer work, work experience, level of applicant's interest. SAT or ACT considered if submitted. ACT with or without writing accepted. SAT with or without Essay component accepted. TOEFL required of all international applicants. High school diploma is required and GED is accepted. *Academic units required:* 4 English. *Academic units recommended:* 4 math, 4 science, 4 foreign language, 4 social studies, 4 history.

Financial Aid

Students should submit: FAFSA, CSS/Financial Aid PROFILE, Noncustodial PROFILE, Business/Farm Supplement. Regular filing deadline is 2/1. The Princeton Review suggests that all financial aid forms be submitted as soon as possible after October 1. *Need-based scholarships/grants offered:* Federal Pell, FSEOG, State scholarships/grants, Private scholarships, College/university scholarship or grant aid from institutional funds. *Loan aid offered:* Direct Subsidized Stafford Loans, Direct Unsubsidized Stafford Loans, Direct PLUS loans, Federal Perkins Loans. Federal Work-Study Program available. Institutional employment available.

The Inside Word

Wheaton tells prospective students, "We want to get to know you, too. Not just your SAT scores, but what do you do for fun?" While the school certainly looks at the traditional measures like GPA and test scores, Wheaton wants to get a sense of you as an individual. The option of submitting a personal portfolio gives you a great opportunity to show Wheaton what makes you tick and what makes you unique.

THE SCHOOL SAYS "..."

From the Admissions Office

"We have been described as a place where world-changing ideas flourish. And we're okay with that. Our students come from all over the country and the world, and they definitely stand out from the crowd. In fact, Wheaton was placed on The Daily Beast/Newsweek's list of America's 25 Brainiac Schools, based on our students' success in winning the most prestigious scholarship awards. Over the past decade, more than 158 Wheaton students have won national and international scholarships, including the Rhodes, Marshall, Fulbright, Truman and Watson awards. Of course, we think our faculty are pretty amazing, too. They are world-class researchers, scholars and artists, who are also outstanding teachers and advisors. Wheaton faculty involve their students in original research and scholarship projects that help to create new knowledge, as well as incredible opportunities. Our Filene Center for Academic Advising and Career Services dedicates nearly $700,000 in stipends and fellowships each year to support internships and research. We also get our students connected to a worldwide alumni network that can help graduates to choose careers, find internships and get started on their first jobs. We are proud of what our graduates do as well as who they become."

SELECTIVITY

Admissions Rating	85
# of applicants	4,322
% of applicants accepted	65
% of acceptees attending	15
# offered a place on the wait list	404
% accepting a place on wait list	26
% admitted from wait list	28
# of early decision applicants	123
% accepted early decision	85

FRESHMAN PROFILE

Range SAT Critical Reading	550–658
Range SAT Math	550–665
Range SAT Writing	540–650
Range ACT Composite	25–30
Minimum internet-based TOEFL	90
Average HS GPA	3.3
% graduated top 10% of class	26
% graduated top 25% of class	60
% graduated top 50% of class	89

DEADLINES

Early decision	
Deadline	11/15
Notification	12/15
Early action	
Deadline	11/15
Notification	1/15
Regular	
Priority	1/1
Deadline	1/15
Notification	4/1
Nonfall registration?	Yes

APPLICANTS ALSO LOOK AT AND OFTEN PREFER

Bates College; Connecticut College

AND SOMETIMES PREFER

Hamilton College; Skidmore College

FINANCIAL FACTS

Financial Aid Rating	87
Annual tuition	$47,390
Room and board	$12,165
Required fees	$310
Books and supplies	$940
Average frosh need-based scholarship	$33,905
Average UG need-based scholarship	$30,394
% needy frosh rec. need-based scholarship or grant aid	100
% needy UG rec. need-based scholarship or grant aid	99
% needy frosh rec. non-need-based scholarship or grant aid	6
% needy UG rec. non-need-based scholarship or grant aid	5
% needy frosh rec. need-based self-help aid	88
% needy UG rec. need-based self-help aid	93
% frosh rec. any financial aid	92
% UG rec. any financial aid	85
% UG borrow to pay for school	66
Average cumulative indebtedness	$32,344
% frosh need fully met	45
% ugrads need fully met	43
Average % of frosh need met	93
Average % of ugrad need met	92

WHITMAN COLLEGE

345 BOYER AVENUE, WALLA WALLA, WA 99362 • ADMISSIONS: 509-527-5176 • FAX: 509-527-4967

STUDENTS SAY "..."

Academics

If learning can be both rigorous and laid-back at the same time, it happens at Whitman College in Walla Walla, WA. The "challenging" academics here are coupled with a "relaxed attitude" in order to give students "the best education possible without sacrificing all the fun one expects of college." Populated mainly by "intelligent, ambitious liberals with far-reaching goals," this somewhat idealistic school seeks to build critical thinking skills through "an earnest discourse about 'life, the universe, and everything.'" So no one starts off with a blank slate, all first-year students are required to take a course referred to as "Encounters" which is a two semester introduction to the liberal arts and the academic construction of knowledge. Distribution requirements ensure that all students get a breadth of courses, and a lack of TAs ensures that they get all the attention they need. Although there's always a dud or two in the mix, professors are "genuinely brilliant and interesting people" and "love to spend time with students outside of class," whether it be for academic help or just conversation. "It is not uncommon to have potlucks, classes, or movie night over at your professor's house with your class," says one student.

On the administrative side of things, bureaucracy and red tape are kept to a minimum in this chill environment through "effortless use of the 'system'" and the administration gets raves all around for its devotion to "maintaining quality student life," which is something of a rarity. "I have never heard of *any* college being as supportive as this place has been to me in just the past two years," says a student. "Whitman's president gave me a ride to campus one semester after I met him at the airport," says another. As one can imagine, all these things come together to form a student body that's "happy, well-balanced, and well-cared-for."

Life

Most people stay on campus for their fun, "especially first-years," and throughout this "bubble" the "sense of closeness and comradeship is very evident through attendance at student-run concerts, art shows, etc." Everything is within ten minutes' walking distance. Academics take precedence for almost everyone, but "most students find time to party on the weekends," due to a "lenient and fair" alcohol policy. Thanks to the campus activities board, "there's almost always something fun going on, whether or not a person chooses to drink," such as Drive-In Movie Night and Casino Night. With "four beautiful seasons," outdoor activities are also very popular, thanks to "a great gear rental program that gets people outside hiking, biking, kayaking, and rock-climbing," and "Frisbees are everywhere when it's warm." In fact, there's so much going on "if someone says they are bored, students laugh and wish they could relate."

Student Body

It's a sociable bunch at Whitman, where most students "are interested in trying new things and meeting new people" and "everyone seems to have a weird interest or talent or passion." The quirky Whitties "usually have a strong opinion about *something*," and one freshman refers to her classmates as "cool nerds." Diversity has risen steadily over the past several years, as the school has made an effort to recruit beyond the typical "mid- to upper-class and white" contingent. Everyone here is pretty outdoorsy and environmentally aware ("to the point where you almost feel guilty for printing an assignment"), and a significant number of students have won fellowships and scholarships such as the Fulbright, Watson, Truman, and Udall.

FINANCIAL AID: 509-527-5178 • E-MAIL: ADMISSION@WHITMAN.EDU • WEBSITE: WWW.WHITMAN.EDU

THE PRINCETON REVIEW SAYS

Admissions

Very important factors considered include: rigor of secondary school record, academic GPA, application essay, character/personal qualities. *Important factors considered include:* standardized test scores, recommendation(s), extracurricular activities, talent/ability. *Other factors considered include:* class rank, interview, first generation, alumni/ae relation, geographical residence, state residency, religious affiliation/commitment, racial/ethnic status, volunteer work, work experience, level of applicant's interest. SAT or ACT required; SAT Subject Tests considered if submitted. ACT with Writing required. SAT with Essay component required. TOEFL required of all international applicants. High school diploma is required and GED is accepted. *Academic units recommended:* 4 English, 4 math, 3 science, 3 science labs, 2 foreign language, 2 social studies, 2 history.

Financial Aid

Students should submit: FAFSA, CSS/Financial Aid PROFILE, Noncustodial PROFILE. Regular filing deadline is 2/1. The Princeton Review suggests that all financial aid forms be submitted as soon as possible after October 1. *Need-based scholarships/grants offered:* Federal Pell, FSEOG, State scholarships/grants, Private scholarships, College/university scholarship or grant aid from institutional funds. *Loan aid offered:* Direct Subsidized Stafford Loans, Direct Unsubsidized Stafford Loans, Direct PLUS loans, Federal Perkins Loans. Applicants will be notified of awards on or about 4/1. Federal Work-Study Program available. Institutional employment available.

The Inside Word

Whitman's admissions committee emphasizes essays and extracurriculars more than SAT scores. The college cares much more about who you are and what you have to offer if you enroll than it does about what your numbers will do for the freshman academic profile. Whitman is a mega-sleeper. Educators all over the country know it as an excellent institution, and the college's alums support it at one of the highest rates of giving at any college in the nation. Students seeking a top-quality liberal arts college owe it to themselves to take a look.

THE SCHOOL SAYS ". . ."

From the Admissions Office

"Whitman College offers a rigorous but collaborative academic environment, a down-to-earth Northwest culture, and a vibrant campus life. Whitman is also distinguished by the following:
- Capstone written and oral assessments in one's major field of study
- Numerous winners of Fulbright, Watson, Goldwater, National Science Foundation, Rhodes, Truman, Beinecke, and Udall fellowships and scholarships
- A Student Engagement Center which oversees internship and community service opportunities as well as graduate school and employment planning
- Science departments that have been recognized by the National Science Foundation as among the top fifty colleges per capita producing graduates who earn Ph.D.'s in science and engineering
- Eighty-eight off-campus study opportunities
- State of the art facilities including a library, computer labs and a health center open 24/7
- The Harper Joy Theatre hosts 8 productions a year open to all students
- An annual undergraduate research conference with over 200 students presenting their original research to the Whitman community
- Strong intramural, club and NCAA Division III sports programs
- A nationally renowned Outdoor Program
- Semester in the West, an experiential, on-the-road study of economic, cultural and environmental issues
- A 94 percent retention rate, 87 percent graduation rate, and a 70 percent graduate school rate.
- Walla Walla is a destination town known for its desirable weather, wine, and arts culture"

SELECTIVITY

Admissions Rating	93
# of applicants	3,790
% of applicants accepted	43
% of acceptees attending	22
# offered a place on the wait list	872
% accepting a place on wait list	42
% admitted from wait list	18
# of early decision applicants	166
% accepted early decision	76

FRESHMAN PROFILE

Range SAT Critical Reading	600–720
Range SAT Math	600–700
Range SAT Writing	600–700
Range ACT Composite	27–32
Minimum paper TOEFL	560
Minimum internet-based TOEFL	85
Average HS GPA	3.7
% graduated top 10% of class	54
% graduated top 25% of class	88
% graduated top 50% of class	98

DEADLINES

Early decision	
Deadline	11/15
Notification	12/20
Regular	
Priority	11/15
Deadline	1/15
Notification	4/1
Nonfall registration?	Yes

APPLICANTS ALSO LOOK AT AND OFTEN PREFER
Pomona College; Stanford University

AND SOMETIMES PREFER
Colorado College; Macalester College

AND RARELY PREFER
University of Washington

FINANCIAL FACTS

Financial Aid Rating	87
Annual tuition	$45,770
Room and board	$11,564
Required fees	$368
Books and supplies	$1,400
Average frosh need-based scholarship	$33,224
Average UG need-based scholarship	$30,721
% needy frosh rec. need-based scholarship or grant aid	100
% needy UG rec. need-based scholarship or grant aid	100
% needy frosh rec. non-need-based scholarship or grant aid	37
% needy UG rec. non-need-based scholarship or grant aid	42
% needy frosh rec. need-based self-help aid	78
% needy UG rec. need-based self-help aid	81
% frosh rec. any financial aid	80
% UG rec. any financial aid	77
% UG borrow to pay for school	47
Average cumulative indebtedness	$21,192
% frosh need fully met	49
% ugrads need fully met	42
Average % of frosh need met	96
Average % of ugrad need met	89

WHITTIER COLLEGE

13406 PHILADELPHIA STREET, WHITTIER, CA 90608 • ADMISSIONS: 562-907-4238 • FAX: 562-907-4870

STUDENTS SAY ". . ."

Academics

This tiny pearl of a liberal arts school is home to around 1,600 undergrads and focuses on an interdisciplinary education for all. Considering the small population, Whittier offers a relatively good breadth in classes and "is a great school for those who are trying to figure out what they want to do or those who want to create their own major." One-on-one interaction is quite prevalent among teachers and students, and everyone here is "passionate about the subject that they teach." It should be unsurprising that a school whose mascot is Johnny Poet provides "a nuanced literary foundation" for all students.

The faculty brings real-world and work experience to their various courses: "they're not just life long academics, most of them have had successful professional careers outside of teaching" and they "really make [Whittier] worthwhile." These professors are "engaged, love what they do," and "truly care about the success of their students, both academically and personally." Discussions are highly encouraged and interesting debates fostered, and assigned papers "always force you to stretch your knowledge." Teachers sometimes challenge the class' knowledge by "presenting a topic that can have pros and cons and by asking to prove where the idea came from." Classes are small, so professors know "know your strengths and weaknesses and try their best to help you out."

Life

The campus is small, so "it's easy to make friends" and there are typically "lots of events (academic or recreational) to go to." Different clubs run the gamut from Anime Club to Fun Night Club to a larping group, but marauders beware: "RAs are required to put on events such as Assassins." "There was once a Beowulf reading at night where you got a free dinner in addition," says a student. Whittier's version of greek life comes in the form of the school's eleven "societies," and a majority of students have some form of involvement in a society or a sport. The school's size naturally leaves enough time to for extracurriculars and outside interests, as "it is difficult not to get involved when everyone is."

Whitter is relatively close to LA and the beach, so the weather is "mostly very nice" and students often "lounge around outside under trees and on the grass to do homework and socialize," "play Frisbee, walk on slack lines, and play soccer for fun in the courtyards." The pool facility is brand new and many "hang out on the decks to tan and cool off in the heat," and there are hills behind the campus that are good for hiking or running. There "is always something going on on-campus and that makes students even more involved."

Student Body

This is a "diverse community" that includes a sizeable number of non-Californians, and most people are "very friendly, respectful of others' different identities, and comfortable with people of different backgrounds." There is "a good meshing" of all the students regardless of what their involvements are, and a real "community-based feeling" abounds. Whittier sees a higher transfer rate than many similar schools, so "it is very easy to know at least ten or more students who transfer after a year or two." The majority of people here are involved in some form of sport, but are not looking to go beyond the collegiate or intramural level.

FINANCIAL AID: 562-907-4285 • E-MAIL: ADMISSION@WHITTIER.EDU • WEBSITE: WWW.WHITTIER.EDU

THE PRINCETON REVIEW SAYS

Admissions

Very important factors considered include: rigor of secondary school record, academic GPA, application essay, recommendation(s), character/personal qualities. *Important factors considered include:* interview, extracurricular activities, talent/ability, volunteer work. *Other factors considered include:* class rank, first generation, alumni/ae relation, geographical residence, state residency, racial/ethnic status, work experience. SAT or ACT recommended. TOEFL required of all international applicants. High school diploma is required and GED is accepted. *Academic units required:* 3 English, 2 math, 1 science, 1 science lab, 2 foreign language, 1 social studies. *Academic units recommended:* 4 English, 3 math, 2 science, 3 foreign language, 2 social studies.

Financial Aid

Students should submit: FAFSA. Regular filing deadline is 6/30. The Princeton Review suggests that all financial aid forms be submitted as soon as possible after October 1. *Need-based scholarships/grants offered:* Federal Pell, FSEOG, State scholarships/grants, Private scholarships, College/university scholarship or grant aid from institutional funds. *Loan aid offered:* Direct Subsidized Stafford Loans, Direct Unsubsidized Stafford Loans, Direct PLUS loans, Federal Perkins Loans. Applicants will be notified of awards on a rolling basis beginning 11/15. Federal Work-Study Program available.

The Inside Word

Whittier is looking for well-rounded students, and so activities and recommendations are just as important as scores and grades—the admissions office hates to focus just on numbers. In fact, test scores are optional for students with a GPA of 3.0 or higher. Though 65 percent of students hail from California, no preference is given to state of origin. Through the Whittier Scholars program, students may construct a personalized major that fits academic and career goals.

THE SCHOOL SAYS "..."

From the Admissions Office

"Faculty and students at Whittier share a love of learning and delight in the life of the mind. They join in understanding the value of the intellectual quest, the use of reason, and a respect for values. They seek knowledge of their own culture and the informed appreciation of other traditions, and they explore the interrelatedness of knowledge and the connections among disciplines. An extraordinary community emerges from teachers and students representing a variety of academic pursuits, individuals who have come together at Whittier in the belief that study within the liberal arts forms the best foundation for rewarding endeavor throughout a lifetime.

"Whittier College is a vibrant, residential, four-year liberal arts institution where intellectual inquiry and experiential learning are fostered in a community that promotes respect for diversity of thought and culture. A Whittier College education produces enthusiastic, independent thinkers who flourish in graduate studies, the evolving global workplace, and life."

SELECTIVITY

Admissions Rating	81
# of applicants	5,192
% of applicants accepted	63
% of acceptees attending	14

FRESHMAN PROFILE

Range SAT Critical Reading	463–580
Range SAT Math	470–590
Range SAT Writing	450–560
Range ACT Composite	20–26
Minimum paper TOEFL	550
Average HS GPA	3.5
% graduated top 10% of class	25
% graduated top 25% of class	1
% graduated top 50% of class	93

DEADLINES

Early action	
Deadline	11/15
Notification	12/30
Regular	
Priority	2/1
Nonfall registration?	Yes

APPLICANTS ALSO LOOK AT AND OFTEN PREFER
University of Redlands; Occidental College

AND SOMETIMES PREFER
Loyola Marymount University; Pitzer College

AND RARELY PREFER
Chapman University; Claremont McKenna College

FINANCIAL FACTS

Financial Aid Rating	83
Annual tuition	$44,184
Room and board	$12,902
Required fees	$590
Books and supplies	$800
Average frosh need-based scholarship	$33,748
Average UG need-based scholarship	$31,278
% needy frosh rec. need-based scholarship or grant aid	83
% needy UG rec. need-based scholarship or grant aid	88
% needy frosh rec. non-need-based scholarship or grant aid	17
% needy UG rec. non-need-based scholarship or grant aid	11
% needy frosh rec. need-based self-help aid	80
% needy UG rec. need-based self-help aid	82
% frosh rec. any financial aid	92
% UG rec. any financial aid	89
% UG borrow to pay for school	79
Average cumulative indebtedness	$33,323
% frosh need fully met	22
% ugrads need fully met	16
Average % of frosh need met	79
Average % of ugrad need met	77

WILLAMETTE UNIVERSITY

900 STATE STREET, SALEM, OR 97301 • ADMISSIONS: 503-370-6303 • FAX: 503-375-5363

CAMPUS LIFE

Quality of Life Rating	91
Fire Safety Rating	98
Green Rating	98
Type of school	Private
Affiliation	Methodist
Environment	City

STUDENTS

Total undergrad enrollment	1,905
% male/female	44/56
% from out of state	78
% frosh from public high school	75
% frosh live on campus	99
% ugrads live on campus	68
# of fraternities (% ugrad men join)	4 (28)
# of sororities (% ugrad women join)	4 (25)
% African American	2
% Asian	9
% Caucasian	62
% Hispanic	12
% Native American	1
% Pacific Islander	<1
% Two or more races	10
% Race and/or ethnicity unknown	2
% international	1
# of countries represented	14

SURVEY SAYS...

Lots of liberal students
Students are happy
Class discussions encouraged
School is well run
Great financial aid
Students are friendly
Students environmentally aware
Easy to get around campus
Campus newspaper is popular

ACADEMICS

Academic Rating	92
% students returning for sophomore year	87
% students graduating within 4 years	71
% students graduating within 6 years	79
Calendar	Semester
Student/faculty ratio	10:1
Profs interesting rating	94
Profs accessible rating	91

Most classes have 10–19 students.
Most lab/discussion sessions have 10–19 students.

MOST POPULAR MAJORS
Biology; Economics; Psychology

STUDENTS SAY " . . ."

Academics

Traditional academics are strong at Willamette, but perhaps what stands out most is that "learning opportunities outside of the classroom are endless." Located right across the street from the Oregon state capitol, there are countless "leadership opportunities and student research opportunities." Professors here are "very willing to help students find internships, jobs and research opportunities." In the classroom, those same professors are "incredible resources" who "are all very dedicated to their classes rather than research or outside obligations," and who provide classes that "are interesting and varied." You will be challenged, but only with the goal of helping you succeed. As one student notes, "I have felt intellectually pushed outside my comfort zone while still being incredibly supported in all of my academic classes." Another noticed that "my professors are not looking to fail me or weed me out of classes; they just believe in me, and want me to excel." These educators "make their material relevant" and tend to be "passionate about their subject." Classes are "often discussion-based, not lecture-based, so students are not just regurgitating information they hear from a professor, but working with the material and exploring their own thoughts and ideas." Overall, the environment here "encourages growth and development, both inside and outside the classroom," which one student says is "unique to a small Liberal Arts school."

Life

"Lots of intellectual discussions," a thriving Greek life, pursuing "social justice" and "social causes," and just plain being busy are the core of life at Willamette. On this campus, "there is a lot of emphasis on how to make an impact on the community and the school as a whole." Indeed, "students are involved in a variety of organizations on campus and off that concern these types of issues," which is not difficult given the school's close proximity to Oregon's seat of government. Students here "often think about politics, civic duties, and volunteering," filling their time with "philanthropic events, house parties, or outdoor trips." This isn't limited to a minority of students, either. "Very few students only attend class; most have three or more activities they are involved in." Less intellectual pursuits are within range, though may be something of a drive. Portland and all its quirky culture (not to mention its thriving craft beer scene) is a close forty minutes away, while the Oregon coast and Mount Hood are about two hours away. But students don't need to venture far. "There is so much to see and do in the Willamette Valley that students have opportunities to do pretty much anything."

Student Body

Given the nature of life on campus, it should come as no surprise that "a typical Willamette student is excited to learn, to explore, and be an active participant within the community." Students here are "interested in helping others through academic tutoring and community service," a group who tend to be "accepting, politically involved, and civic minded." Individuals vary—"students embrace the idea of being unique and proud of it"—but almost all are "academically driven, balanced with social endeavors, and eager to mix in with other students." Most are "from the West Coast," "friendly and open," and, of course, very busy. "Almost all students are involved in multiple things." This common need to be doing things ensures students "share a friendliness that's evident the moment you step onto campus." As one student notes, to get the most out of Willamette, "you have to be willing to challenge yourselves and others, and be accepting of the community you are a part of."

WILLAMETTE UNIVERSITY

FINANCIAL AID: 503-370-6273 • E-MAIL: BEARCAT@WILLAMETTE.EDU • WEBSITE: WWW.WILLAMETTE.EDU

THE PRINCETON REVIEW SAYS

Admissions

Very important factors considered include: rigor of secondary school record, class rank, academic GPA, standardized test scores, application essay. *Important factors considered include:* recommendation(s), interview. *Other factors considered include:* extracurricular activities, talent/ability, character/personal qualities, first generation, alumni/ae relation, geographical residence, racial/ethnic status. SAT or ACT optional. TOEFL required of all international applicants. *Academic units recommended:* 4 English, 4 math, 4 science, 4 foreign language, 4 social studies, 4 academic electives, 4 visual/performing arts.

Financial Aid

Students should submit: FAFSA. Priority filing deadline is 2/1. The Princeton Review suggests that all financial aid forms be submitted as soon as possible after October 1. *Need-based scholarships/grants offered:* Federal Pell, FSEOG, State scholarships/grants, Private scholarships, College/university scholarship or grant aid from institutional funds. *Loan aid offered:* Direct Subsidized Stafford Loans, Direct Unsubsidized Stafford Loans, Direct PLUS loans, Federal Perkins Loans. Applicants will be notified of awards on a rolling basis beginning 4/1. Federal Work-Study Program available. Institutional employment available.

The Inside Word

Your academic record will play the biggest part when being evaluated as a prospective student, especially the rigor of your high school coursework, grade trends, and naturally, your grades themselves. An inconsistent high school performance will be seen unfavorably by admissions officers. Unsurprisingly, a record of community service and strong extracurricular activities will greatly enhance your application in the eyes of Willamette admissions officers, who look to see a habit of participation in something beyond the classroom in their students.

THE SCHOOL SAYS ". . ."

From the Admissions Office

"Willamette University is a place where talented faculty inspire students to examine issues critically, think creatively and act effectively. By leveraging our collaborative community and location in the Pacific Northwest, we challenge students to transform knowledge into action—the foundation of a successful career and a meaningful life.

"With a student-faculty ratio of 10:1, Willamette students can easily find a mentor. Eleven of the twenty-four Oregon Professors of the Year since 1990 are from Willamette—a record unmatched by any other school in the nation.

"With the Oregon State Capitol located across the street, Willamette offers unparalleled access to state government—and numerous chances to explore and implement ideas through research and internships alongside policymakers and the state's top scientists and economists.

"Willamette's 305-acre Zena Forest provides unique outdoor classrooms and laboratories where students can perform scientific research, explore issues of agriculture and ecology, or find inspiration for their music and art. Willamette is also co-located with Tokyo International University of America, creating numerous chances to explore international culture through social, language and living exchanges.

"Our graduates go on to impressive careers and lives of achievement and meaning. Among Willamette's alumni are a Nobel Prize-winning economist, corporate presidents and CEOs, nationally recognized artists, fifteen Oregon Supreme Court justices and numerous Fulbright Grant-winners."

SELECTIVITY

Admissions Rating	87
# of applicants	6,332
% of applicants accepted	78
% of acceptees attending	11
# offered a place on the wait list	433
% accepting a place on wait list	39
% admitted from wait list	32

FRESHMAN PROFILE

Range SAT Critical Reading	550–670
Range SAT Math	550–660
Range SAT Writing	550–650
Range ACT Composite	25–30
Minimum paper TOEFL	550
Minimum internet-based TOEFL	85
Average HS GPA	3.8
% graduated top 10% of class	40
% graduated top 25% of class	73
% graduated top 50% of class	97

DEADLINES

Early decision	
Deadline	11/15
Notification	12/31
Early action	
Deadline	11/15
Notification	12/31
Regular	
Priority	1/15
Notification	3/1
Nonfall registration?	Yes

FINANCIAL FACTS

Financial Aid Rating	86
Annual tuition	$46,900
Room and board	$11,600
Required fees	$317
Books and supplies	$950
Average frosh need-based scholarship	$29,199
Average UG need-based scholarship	$27,843
% needy frosh rec. need-based scholarship or grant aid	99
% needy UG rec. need-based scholarship or grant aid	99
% needy frosh rec. non-need-based scholarship or grant aid	26
% needy UG rec. non-need-based scholarship or grant aid	16
% needy frosh rec. need-based self-help aid	80
% needy UG rec. need-based self-help aid	79
% frosh rec. any financial aid	95
% UG rec. any financial aid	92
Average cumulative indebtedness	$26,643
% frosh need fully met	22
% ugrads need fully met	15
Average % of frosh need met	84
Average % of ugrad need met	84

WILLIAM JEWELL COLLEGE

500 COLLEGE HILL, LIBERTY, MO 64068 • ADMISSIONS: 816-781-7700 • FAX: 816-415-5040

STUDENTS SAY "..."

Academics

The minute students step onto campus at William Jewell, they are welcomed into an "amazing community" replete with "top-notch academics." As one senior gushes, "Everyone on campus makes you feel at home and the faculty and staff are some of the most genuine people you will ever meet." Moreover, as small liberal arts college, William Jewell "provides a superb education" that many undergrads here feel is "unmatched in the Midwest." After all, the college endeavors to transform undergrads into "critical thinkers" who are bound to achieve "success and find [their] passion." This is no doubt due in large part to the fact that "William Jewell provides a well-rounded education for its students and challenges them to step outside of their own perspectives." Though the college has many fantastic majors from which to choose, undergrads are especially quick to highlight "the strong science and pre-med program" along with the "well established" non-profit program. The nursing program also has a "great reputation." On the whole, undergrads speak very highly of their "amazingly dedicated" professors. Impressively, teachers here tend to be "great lecturers...who [also] excel in discussion formatted classes." Another senior adds, "The professors at William Jewell are very personable and willing to go the extra step to build a connection with each and every student. They are always finding the best way to reach out to their students and provide each student with the best chance of success." Overall, William Jewell offers a "rigorous set of programs that push you to the limits of your ability."

Life

Students here agree that "life at Jewell is a busy one." As one knowledgeable senior happily shares, "There are always campus activities going on whether that be sporting events or resident hall gatherings or even the occasional fraternity/sorority party." A junior specifies, "Student organizations often sponsors events like CU-At-the-Movies, Skate Night [and] Bowling Night where we get discounted prices to go out and have fun. We also play 'Gotcha!' (an assassin game), on campus every year and Browning Hall is playing Humans vs. Zombies this year." Additionally, "a number of students...are active in Greek life." Fortunately, we're assured that there's no pressure to join and independent students still feel included. Undergrads here also love to take advantage of the "Harriman-Jewell series [which] offers free tickets to students, and brings world-class arts and culture such as pianists (Emanuel Ax) and dance (Mark Morris Dance Group) to Kansas City." Speaking of KC, William Jewell is only a "twenty-minute drive away" from the heart of the city. As another senior brags, "Once downtown you can do just about anything. There is the Power & Light District with the Sprint Center, the Kaufman Center and just a few miles south you get into Westport where you can find numerous college/young adult students at any given time."

Student Body

Undergrads at William Jewell are a "laid back but focused" lot. Indeed, students are quick to define their peers as "driven" and "intelligent" people who are "committed to their education and community." Of course, some see the typical Jewell student as "a white, Protestant, upper-middle class, girl who loves Pinterest." Although a junior cautions that, "the population isn't as diverse as other schools I have been to," he also counters that, "everyone is pretty open and accepting of just about anyone." Fortunately, many find that "students fit in very easily." Overall, "no one really is ever left out of anything as long as they're putting the effort in to have friends and be a part of an organization as well as the Jewell community as a whole." Another junior adds that, "While most [undergrads] attend college straight out of high school, there is a growing number of non-traditional students especially in the nursing program." Finally, as one satisfied political science student succinctly states, "We have a high retention rate which tells me that students fit in well."

FINANCIAL AID: 816-415-5975 • E-MAIL: ADMISSION@WILLIAM.JEWELL.EDU • WEBSITE: WWW.JEWELL.EDU

THE PRINCETON REVIEW SAYS

Admissions

Very important factors considered include: rigor of secondary school record, academic GPA. *Important factors considered include:* class rank, standardized test scores, recommendation(s), extracurricular activities, talent/ability, character/personal qualities, level of applicant's interest. *Other factors considered include:* application essay, interview, first generation, alumni/ae relation, volunteer work, work experience. SAT or ACT recommend. ACT with Writing recommended. SAT with Essay component recommended. TOEFL required of all international applicants. High school diploma is required and GED is accepted. *Academic units required:* 4 English, 3 math, 3 science, 1 science lab, 2 foreign language, 3 social studies. *Academic units recommended:* 4 math, 3 foreign language, 2 academic electives.

Financial Aid

Students should submit: FAFSA. Priority filing deadline is 3/10. The Princeton Review suggests that all financial aid forms be submitted as soon as possible after October 1. *Need-based scholarships/grants offered:* Federal Pell, FSEOG, State scholarships/grants, College/university scholarship or grant aid from institutional funds. *Loan aid offered:* Federal Perkins Loans, Federal Nursing Loans. Applicants will be notified of awards on a rolling basis beginning 3/1. Federal Work-Study Program available. Institutional employment available.

The Inside Word

Competition for admission is strong and candidates must demonstrate success with a rigorous course load. Of course, similar to most small colleges, Jewell is also looking for applicants who will complement the campus. Therefore, you can be assured that personal statements and recommendations will be closely assessed.

THE SCHOOL SAYS "..."

From the Admissions Office

"William Jewell College is committed to bringing together talented students and gifted faculty mentors within a vibrant community sparked by a rigorous and intentional liberal arts curriculum. A full range of personal and professional development experiences are presented by the selective national liberal arts college's location within the Kansas City metroplex of more than two million. The William Jewell College experience focuses on enhancing the student's ability to apply learning to complex ethical, scientific and cultural problems. The college places a high value on experiential learning and gives students the opportunity to 'live what they learn.' By completing the college's thirty-eight-hour liberal arts core plus three applied learning experiences, Jewell students can receive a second major in Applied Critical Thought and Inquiry. This means that all students can graduate with double majors and some with triple majors. The internationally recognized Oxbridge Honors Program combines British tutorial methods of instruction with opportunities for a year of study in Oxford or Cambridge. It is the only program of its kind in the nation. Jewell's undergraduate Nonprofit Leadership major is one of only thirteen nationwide and ranks among the top three in academic rigor. The Pryor Leadership Studies Program includes course work, community service projects and internships that help students enhance their leadership skills in a variety of settings. William Jewell students graduate equipped with deep content knowledge in their major(s), a host of social and real-world experiences, personal maturity and the intellectual habits of mind for success in a world of change and challenge."

SELECTIVITY

Admissions Rating	89
# of applicants	1,456
% of applicants accepted	49
% of acceptees attending	34

FRESHMAN PROFILE

Range SAT Critical Reading	500–640
Range SAT Math	490–620
Range ACT Composite	23–28
Minimum paper TOEFL	550
Minimum internet-based TOEFL	80
Average HS GPA	3.8
% graduated top 10% of class	30
% graduated top 25% of class	59
% graduated top 50% of class	90

DEADLINES

Priority	12/1
Nonfall registration?	Yes

FINANCIAL FACTS

Financial Aid Rating	85
Annual tuition	$32,210
Room and board	$9,280
Required fees	$720
Books and supplies	$1,200
Average frosh need-based scholarship	$22,452
Average UG need-based scholarship	$23,559
% needy frosh rec. need-based scholarship or grant aid	100
% needy UG rec. need-based scholarship or grant aid	94
% needy frosh rec. non-need-based scholarship or grant aid	100
% needy UG rec. non-need-based scholarship or grant aid	93
% needy frosh rec. need-based self-help aid	72
% needy UG rec. need-based self-help aid	75
% frosh rec. any financial aid	100
% UG rec. any financial aid	99
% UG borrow to pay for school	72
Average cumulative indebtedness	$31,581
% frosh need fully met	56
% ugrads need fully met	27
Average % of frosh need met	80
Average % of ugrad need met	78

WILLIAMS COLLEGE

PO BOX 487, WILLIAMSTOWN, MA 01267 • ADMISSIONS: 413-597-2211 • FAX: 413-597-4052

STUDENTS SAY "..."

Academics

Williams College is a small bastion of the liberal arts "with a fantastic academic reputation." "Williams students tend to spend a lot of time complaining about how much work they have" but they say the academic experience is "absolutely incomparable." Classes are "small" and "intense." "The facilities are absolutely top-notch in almost everything." Research opportunities are plentiful. A one-month January term offers study abroad programs and a host of short pass/fail courses that are "a college student's dream come true." "The hard science departments are incredible." Economics, art history, and English are equally outstanding. Despite the occasional professor "who should not even be teaching at the high school level," the faculty at Williams is one of the best. Most professors "jump at every opportunity to help you love their subject." "They're here because they want to interact with undergrads." "If you complain about a Williams education then you would complain about education anywhere," wagers an economics major.

Life

Students at Williams enjoy a "stunning campus." "The Berkshire mountains are in the background every day as you walk to class" and opportunities for outdoor activity are numerous. The location is in "the boonies," though, and the surrounding "one-horse college town" is "quaint" at best. "There is no nearby place to buy necessities that is not ridiculously overpriced." Student life happens almost exclusively on campus. Dorm rooms are "large" and "well above par." Entertainment options include "lots of" performances, plays, and lectures. Some students are "obsessed with a capella groups." Intramurals are popular, especially Ultimate Frisbee and the Williams Outing Club, which goes hiking, climbing, and camping. Intercollegiate sports are "a huge part of the social scene." For many students, the various varsity teams "are the basic social blocks at Williams." "Everyone for the most part gets along, but the sports teams seem to band together," explains a sophomore. "Booze-laden parties" "and general disorder on weekends" are common. "A lot of people spend their lives between homework and practice and then just get completely smashed on weekends." Nothing gets out of hand, though. "We know how to unwind without being stupid," says a sophomore.

Student Body

The student population at Williams is not the most humble. They describe their peers as "interesting and beautiful" "geniuses of varying interests." They're "quirky, passionate, zany, and fun." They're "athletically awesome." They're "freakishly unique" and at the same time "cookie-cutter amazing." Ethnic diversity is stellar and you'll find all kinds of students including "the goth students," "nerdier students," "a ladle of environmentally conscious pseudo-vegetarians," and a few "west coast hippies." However, "a typical student looks like a rich white kid" who grew up "playing field hockey just outside Boston" and spends summers "vacationing on the Cape." Sporty students abound. "There definitely is segregation between the artsy kids and the athlete types but there is also a significant amount of crossover." "Williams is a place where normal social labels tend not to apply," reports a junior. "Everyone here got in for a reason. So that football player in your theater class has amazing insight on Chekhov and that outspoken environmental activist also specializes in improv comedy."

FINANCIAL AID: 413-597-4181 • E-MAIL: ADMISSION@WILLIAMS.EDU • WEBSITE: WWW.WILLIAMS.EDU

THE PRINCETON REVIEW SAYS

Admissions

Very important factors considered include: rigor of secondary school record, class rank, academic GPA, standardized test scores, recommendation(s), talent/ability. *Important factors considered include:* application essay, extracurricular activities, character/personal qualities, first generation, alumni/ae relation, racial/ethnic status. *Other factors considered include:* geographical residence, volunteer work, work experience. SAT or ACT required. ACT with Writing required. High school diploma or equivalent is not required. *Academic units recommended:* 4 English, 4 math, 4 science, 3 science labs, 4 foreign language, 4 social studies.

Financial Aid

Students should submit: FAFSA, CSS/Financial Aid PROFILE, Noncustodial PROFILE. Priority filing deadline is 2/1. The Princeton Review suggests that all financial aid forms be submitted as soon as possible after October 1. *Need-based scholarships/grants offered:* Federal Pell, FSEOG, State scholarships/grants, Private scholarships, College/university scholarship or grant aid from institutional funds. *Loan aid offered:* Direct Subsidized Stafford Loans, Direct Unsubsidized Stafford Loans, Direct PLUS loans, Federal Perkins Loans, College/university loans from institutional funds. Applicants will be notified of awards on or about 4/1. Federal Work-Study Program available. Institutional employment available.

The Inside Word

As is typical of highly selective colleges, at Williams high grades and test scores work more as qualifiers than to determine admissibility. Beyond a strong record of achievement, evidence of intellectual curiosity, noteworthy non-academic talents, and a non-college family background are some aspects of a candidate's application that might make for an offer of admission. But there are no guarantees—the evaluation process here is rigorous. The admissions committee (the entire admissions staff) discusses each candidate in comparison to the entire applicant pool. The pool is divided alphabetically for individual reading; after weak candidates are eliminated, those who remain undergo additional evaluations by different members of the staff. Admission decisions must be confirmed by the agreement of a plurality of the committee. Such close scrutiny demands a well-prepared candidate and application.

THE SCHOOL SAYS " . . . "

From the Admissions Office

"Special course offerings at Williams include Oxford-style tutorials, where students (in teams of two) research and defend ideas, engaging in weekly debate with a faculty tutor. Half of Williams' students pursue study abroad at some point, with about thirty students annually spending at year at Oxford. Four weeks of winter study each January provide time for individualized projects, research, and novel fields of study. Students compete in thirty-two Division III athletic teams, perform in twenty-five musical groups, stage ten theatrical productions, and volunteer in thirty service organizations. The college receives several million dollars annually for undergraduate science research and equipment. The town offers two distinguished art museums, the Williams College Museum of Art and the Clark Art Institute, and 2,200 forest acres—complete with a treetop canopy walkway—for environmental research and recreation.

"Students are required to submit either the SAT or the ACT including the optional writing section. Applicants should also submit scores from any two SAT Subject Tests. To limit the debt obligations of its graduates, Williams maintains one of the lowest loan expectations of any college or university in the country. Often the aid packages of students whose families demonstrate high financial need are made up entirely of grants and a campus job—and do not include any loans."

SELECTIVITY

Admissions Rating	98
# of applicants	6,883
% of applicants accepted	18
% of acceptees attending	45
# offered a place on the wait list	1,603
% accepting a place on wait list	36
% admitted from wait list	9
# of early decision applicants	593
% accepted early decision	41

FRESHMAN PROFILE

Range SAT Critical Reading	670–780
Range SAT Math	660–770
Range SAT Writing	670–780
Range ACT Composite	31–34
% graduated top 10% of class	93
% graduated top 25% of class	98
% graduated top 50% of class	100

DEADLINES

Early decision	
Deadline	11/15
Notification	12/15
Regular	
Deadline	1/1
Notification	4/1
Nonfall registration?	No

APPLICANTS ALSO LOOK AT AND OFTEN PREFER

Harvard College; Yale University; Princeton University

AND SOMETIMES PREFER

Columbia University, Massachusetts Institute of Technology; University of Pennsylvania

AND RARELY PREFER

Amherst Colege; Middlebury College

FINANCIAL FACTS

Financial Aid Rating	96
Annual tuition	$49,780
Room and board	$13,220
Required fees	$290
Books and supplies	$800
Average frosh need-based scholarship	$48,376
Average UG need-based scholarship	$46,007
% needy frosh rec. need-based scholarship or grant aid	99
% needy UG rec. need-based scholarship or grant aid	100
% needy frosh rec. non-need-based scholarship or grant aid	0
% needy UG rec. non-need-based scholarship or grant aid	0
% needy frosh rec. need-based self-help aid	100
% needy UG rec. need-based self-help aid	100
% frosh rec. any financial aid	50
% UG rec. any financial aid	49
% UG borrow to pay for school	43
Average cumulative indebtedness	$16,593
% frosh need fully met	100
% ugrads need fully met	100
Average % of frosh need met	100
Average % of ugrad need met	100

WITTENBERG UNIVERSITY

PO Box 720, Springfield, OH 45501 • Admissions: 937-327-6314 • Fax: 937-327-6379

STUDENTS SAY "..."

Academics

Located in Springfield, Ohio, Wittenberg combines a "small school atmosphere" with "a wide horizon of learning opportunities." The school offers "high academic standards and a dedication to research" that makes "an environment where students can excel in the classroom and out." This "friendly, athletic campus" "offers a close-knit community where professors and students build professional and personal relationships." The school's motto is "Having Light, We Pass It On To Others." This is taken seriously by the "extremely engaging" professors who are "committed to helping students both in and out of the classroom." The "fabulous" teachers at Wittenberg are "always accessible and willing to help" and really get to know students "on a personal level." "I feel like I am learning from my best friends," one happy student reports. An Environmental Science student agrees, saying, "I have become very close to a few of my professors and have really come to enjoy my classroom experience." Some students say that "communication with the student body" and "upper level administration" "is not always the best." Still, a Communications major lavishes praise on the entire staff, "not only just teachers, but I would go as far to say even down to the maintenance and janitor crew." Part of the reason students love classes at Wittenberg is the small class sizes. This "means excellent attention paid to students." "The class sizes and student-teacher ratio makes it an ideal place to develop professional relationships" and these relationships "really elevates the learning environment and makes classes far more interesting than large schools." The "open-minded and encouraging" faculty really pushes "students to build our own ideas and projects." All in all, "the people, the faculty and students are very happy, connected, and welcoming community." This, combined with the "gorgeous campus" might explain the "high morale among the students." As a Psychology major explains, "Wittenberg is a place where students can develop themselves as a whole person—academically, professionally, and socially."

Life

Students are typically busy and even "often over-involved" at Wittenberg. Your average student might be "involved and overcommitted in at least two clubs and a sport or Greek life." "With over 100 student clubs and organizations, it is easy to find things to get involved in," one student explains. "Witt students generally know how to work hard and play hard" and "party every day." One student says that partying is so pervasive that "if you do not drink then you have no chance of fitting in." "The typical student is one who drinks constantly, and rarely ever gets in trouble for it," since, students say, the University is lax on enforcing drug and alcohol rules. Still, there are plenty of other activities to do on campus from "just hang[ing] out and spend[ing] time with each other" to "Witt Wednesday" in which "comedians or musicians come to entertain." "What don't we do?" one student says. One quirky, or even "downright surreal" part of campus life has to do with the crows. "Our crow-deterrent alarms, which are mounted on the roofs of every building, are triggered by students walking by," one student explains. "It's downright uncanny at night to hear crow death screams played from the rooftops as you walk back to your dorm." Students who love nature will enjoy "a reservoir to swim in, two playground/parks, and three national parks for hiking."

Student Body

This "beautiful school" is filled with "friendly," "outgoing," and "quirky people." "It is hard to describe a typical student because we are very diverse, but with that diversity we all are able to get in," an Environmental Science student says. If you had to generalize, most students are "white, from Ohio, [and] middle class," but "Wittenberg has a wonderful variety of students." Students tend to be "fun personalities, engaged, curious and eager to learn, smart." "All types of students here are welcomed in with ease" and everyone can "find at least one friend group." One student elaborates that these groups "are like amoebas that are constantly shifting, made up of many different people." Overall Wittenberg is a "tight-knit community" where all you have to do to make a friend is "step out and say hello!"

WITTENBERG UNIVERSITY

FINANCIAL AID: 937-327-7321 • E-MAIL: ADMISSION@WITTENBERG.EDU • WEBSITE: WWW.WITTENBERG.EDU

THE PRINCETON REVIEW SAYS

Admissions

Very important factors considered include: rigor of secondary school record, class rank, academic GPA. *Important factors considered include:* application essay, recommendation(s), extracurricular activities, talent/ability, character/personal qualities, volunteer work. *Other factors considered include:* standardized test scores, interview, first generation, alumni/ae relation, work experience. SAT or ACT considered if submitted. ACT with or without writing accepted. SAT with or without Essay component accepted. TOEFL required of all international applicants. High school diploma is required and GED is accepted. *Academic units required:* 4 English, 3 math, 3 science, 2 science labs, 2 foreign language, 2 history. *Academic units recommended:* 4 English, 4 math, 5 science, 2 science labs, 3 foreign language, 3 history.

Financial Aid

Students should submit: FAFSA. Priority filing deadline is 3/1. The Princeton Review suggests that all financial aid forms be submitted as soon as possible after October 1. *Need-based scholarships/grants offered:* Federal Pell, FSEOG, State scholarships/grants, Private scholarships, College/university scholarship or grant aid from institutional funds, United Negro College Fund. *Loan aid offered:* Direct Subsidized Stafford Loans, Direct Unsubsidized Stafford Loans, Direct PLUS loans, Federal Perkins Loans, College/university loans from institutional funds. Applicants will be notified of awards on a rolling basis beginning 3/1. Federal Work-Study Program available. Institutional employment available.

The Inside Word

Wittenberg accepts both its own application and the common application, and the application fee is waived if you apply online. The university only requires a short personal statement instead of the traditional formal essay. Wittenberg has a fairly high acceptance rate, but students will still want to make sure all parts of their application are the best they can be.

THE SCHOOL SAYS "..."

From the Admissions Office

"At Wittenberg, you will experience an active and engaged learning environment, a setting where you can refine your definition of self yet gain exposure to the varied kinds of knowledge, people, views, activities, options, and ideas that add richness to our lives. Wittenberg is a university where students are able to thrive in a small campus environment with many opportunities for intellectual and personal growth in and out of the classroom. Campus life is as diverse as the interests of our students. Wittenberg attracts students from all over the United States and from many other countries. Historically, the university has been committed to geographical, educational, cultural, and religious diversity. With their varied backgrounds and interests, Wittenberg students have helped initiate many of the more than 125 student organizations that are active on campus. The students will be the first to tell you there's never a lack of things to do on or near the campus any day of the week, if you're willing to get involved.

"Wittenberg University is test score optional. Freshman applicants can choose to submit either ACT (with or without writing component) or SAT scores."

SELECTIVITY

Admissions Rating	76
# of applicants	6,487
% of applicants accepted	77
% of acceptees attending	10
# of early decision applicants	552
% accepted early decision	66

FRESHMAN PROFILE

Range SAT Critical Reading	490–610
Range SAT Math	490–610
Range SAT Writing	460–560
Range ACT Composite	22–28
Minimum paper TOEFL	550
Average HS GPA	3.4
% graduated top 10% of class	19
% graduated top 25% of class	45
% graduated top 50% of class	78

DEADLINES

Early decision	
Deadline	11/15
Notification	12/1
Early action	
Deadline	12/1
Notification	1/1
Regular	
Priority	3/15
Nonfall registration?	Yes

APPLICANTS ALSO LOOK AT AND OFTEN PREFER

Denison University; Miami University; Ohio University–Athens; Ohio Wesleyan University; The College of Wooster; The Ohio State University–Columbus

FINANCIAL FACTS

Financial Aid Rating	87
Annual tuition	$37,230
Room and board	$10,126
Required fees	$860
Books and supplies	$1,000
Average frosh need-based scholarship	$27,177
Average UG need-based scholarship	$25,798
% needy frosh rec. need-based scholarship or grant aid	100
% needy UG rec. need-based scholarship or grant aid	100
% needy frosh rec. non-need-based scholarship or grant aid	0
% needy UG rec. non-need-based scholarship or grant aid	0
% needy frosh rec. need-based self-help aid	82
% needy UG rec. need-based self-help aid	80
% frosh rec. any financial aid	100
% UG rec. any financial aid	95
% UG borrow to pay for school	73
Average cumulative indebtedness	$34,178
% frosh need fully met	45
% ugrads need fully met	47
Average % of frosh need met	67
Average % of ugrad need met	68

WOFFORD COLLEGE

429 NORTH CHURCH STREET, SPARTANBURG, SC 29303-3663 • ADMISSIONS: 864-597-4130 • FAX: 864-597-4147

CAMPUS LIFE

Quality of Life Rating	89
Fire Safety Rating	90
Green Rating	60*
Type of school	Private
Affiliation	Methodist
Environment	City

STUDENTS

Total undergrad enrollment	1,613
% male/female	50/50
% from out of state	45
% frosh from public high school	62
% frosh live on campus	96
% ugrads live on campus	92
# of fraternities (% ugrad men join)	6 (45)
# of sororities (% ugrad women join)	4 (54)
% African American	8
% Asian	3
% Caucasian	81
% Hispanic	3
% Native American	<1
% Pacific Islander	<1
% Two or more races	3
% Race and/or ethnicity unknown	1
% international	1
# of countries represented	15

SURVEY SAYS...

Students are happy
Classroom facilities are great
Internships are widely available
School is well run
Easy to get around campus
Lots of beer drinking
Frats and sororities are popular
Alumni active on campus

ACADEMICS

Academic Rating	91
% students returning for sophomore year	88
% students graduating within 4 years	77
% students graduating within 6 years	82
Calendar	4/1/4
Student/faculty ratio	11:1
Profs interesting rating	92
Profs accessible rating	88

Most classes have 20–29 students.
Most lab/discussion sessions have
20–29 students.

MOST POPULAR MAJORS

Biology; Finance; Business/Managerial
Economics

STUDENTS SAY ". . ."

Academics

With its "beautiful" campus, great "sense of community" and "incredible financial aid," Wofford College is a higher education dream! Of course, a strong work ethic is a must for those who end up enrolling here. After all, students warn us that "the classes are hard." Fortunately, the "effort is well worth it," especially when you consider the high "acceptance rates into graduate schools." Wofford students also appreciate that classes tend to be "small" which promotes lots of "discussion...and endless opportunities." Additionally, undergrads love that "Wofford offers an interim course during the month of January where each student takes only one class. The course is unrelated to the student's major and allows them to explore different areas that they are intersected in."

Wofford undergrads also have the benefit of learning from professors who are "so passionate about their [respective] fields and about teaching." Indeed, "their enthusiasm and encouragement helps students to maintain a positive attitude throughout the entire semester." Even better, they "are almost always accessible and are clear about their expectations from day one." As this highly satisfied French major gushes, "If you want to have discussions with your professors outside of class, or if you want to study with professors who legitimately care about their students, Wofford is the place to go."

Life

Wofford undergrads readily admit that since "classes are rigorous," the majority of their week is focused on "studying and [tackling] homework." Thankfully, they still manage to carve out some time for fun. For starters, the student body is fairly athletic and we're told that "basketball and baseball games are very popular in the spring semester." Additionally, "the gym facility is always full of [undergrads] who are taking a break." Of course, once the weekend rolls around, you'll find the majority of the student body "participat[ing] in Greek affiliated social events." An economics student elaborates, "Friday and Saturday nights are spent partying at frat row or the senior apartments on campus." Moreover, from time to time, "Wofford throws band parties and everyone will go and dance and hangout." But don't worry if parties aren't your scene! After all, "there are always student organizations putting on activities [such as]...bonfires with s'mores...and trivia night[s]." Lastly, some students do bemoan the fact that "there's not tons to do" in hometown Spartanburg. However, when they feel like they need a breather from campus life, undergrads can easily head "to Greenville or Asheville (which are 30 minutes and an hour away, respectively)."

Student Body

Wofford does a great job of cultivating a "vibrant and loving community." Indeed, students speak warmly about their "friendly," "outgoing" and "intelligent" peers. As one happy undergrad shares, "There may be unfamiliar faces and unfamiliar names but you never meet a stranger at Wofford." A pre-med student agrees adding, "Everyone is very nice and always smiles or waves when passing by, even if they don't know me." Moreover, the vast majority of students here are "drive[n] to succeed." A chemistry major explains, "We all work incredibly hard and help each other along the way." Of course, some students do point out that the majority of their peers hail from "upper-middle class families with very predisposed views of the world." However, we've been told that Wofford is increasing efforts to attract a more diverse student body." And, more importantly, undergrads assure us that their classmates "are accepting of everyone and willing to take other's values into consideration" no matter where they come from. Finally, as this history major succinctly states, "Wofford is home to the most genuine...and fun humans around!"

WOFFORD COLLEGE

FINANCIAL AID: 864-597-4160 • E-MAIL: ADMISSION@WOFFORD.EDU • WEBSITE: WWW.WOFFORD.EDU

THE PRINCETON REVIEW SAYS

Admissions

Very important factors considered include: rigor of secondary school record, academic GPA. *Important factors considered include:* class rank, standardized test scores, application essay, extracurricular activities, talent/ability, character/personal qualities, volunteer work. *Other factors considered include:* recommendation(s), interview, first generation, alumni/ae relation, geographical residence, racial/ethnic status, work experience. SAT or ACT required. ACT with Writing required. TOEFL required of all international applicants. High school diploma is required and GED is accepted. *Academic units required:* 4 English, 4 math, 3 science, 3 science labs, 3 foreign language, 3 social studies, 2 history. *Academic units recommended:* 4 English, 4 math, 3 science, 3 science labs, 3 foreign language, 3 social studies, 2 history, 1 academic elective, 1 computer science, 1 visual/performing arts.

Financial Aid

Students should submit: FAFSA. Priority filing deadline is 3/1. The Princeton Review suggests that all financial aid forms be submitted as soon as possible after October 1. *Need-based scholarships/grants offered:* Federal Pell, FSEOG, State scholarships/grants, Private scholarships, College/university scholarship or grant aid from institutional funds. *Loan aid offered:* Direct Subsidized Stafford Loans, Direct Unsubsidized Stafford Loans, Direct PLUS loans, Federal Perkins Loans. Applicants will be notified of awards on or about 3/15. Federal Work-Study Program available. Institutional employment available.

The Inside Word

When it comes to making admissions decisions, Wofford College takes a fairly traditional approach. Therefore, your high school transcript will be of utmost importance. And to be competitive, applicants must have a challenging college prep curriculum. Standardized test scores are also significant. Students who have taken the SAT or ACT multiple times take note—the college will only consider your best scores. Finally, those individuals who feel that Wofford is their top choice are highly encouraged to apply early decision.

THE SCHOOL SAYS "..."

From the Admissions Office

"A century ago Wofford College athletics teams chose the Boston Terrier as the mascot. The small but tenacious and fierce dog is full of intelligence and energy making it an ideal mascot for the 1,650 undergraduates who call Wofford home. Nationally known for the strength of its academic program, outstanding faculty, study abroad participation and successful graduates, Wofford scores among the best in the country on the National Survey of Student Engagement, which measures high-impact, transformative learning experiences, and the college was ranked #6 in the nation by Open Doors (2015) for the percentage of students who study abroad for credit. A new strategic vision has Wofford reimagining what it means to be a premier, innovative and distinctive national liberal arts college that includes award-winning housing for seniors in The Village, exciting Division I athletics with student-athletes who excel both on the playing field and in the classroom, and opportunities to prepare for a future of lifelong learning, leadership and citizenship. In the next two years, Wofford students, faculty and staff as well as the upstate South Carolina community will enjoy two new buildings on campus. The Rosalind Sallenger Richardson Center for the Arts and the Jerry Richardson Indoor Stadium, along with a new Greek village, will be game changers, offering exciting and diverse opportunities for academic and social enrichment."

SELECTIVITY

Admissions Rating	88
# of applicants	2,795
% of applicants accepted	72
% of acceptees attending	22
# offered a place on the wait list	147
% accepting a place on wait list	39
% admitted from wait list	24
# of early decision applicants	86
% accepted early decision	85

FRESHMAN PROFILE

Range SAT Critical Reading	520–630
Range SAT Math	530–630
Range SAT Writing	520–620
Range ACT Composite	23–29
Minimum paper TOEFL	550
Minimum internet-based TOEFL	80
Average HS GPA	3.57
% graduated top 10% of class	42
% graduated top 25% of class	72
% graduated top 50% of class	94

DEADLINES

Early decision	
Deadline	11/1
Notification	12/1
Early action	
Deadline	11/15
Notification	2/1
Regular	
Deadline	2/1
Notification	3/15
Nonfall registration?	Yes

**APPLICANTS ALSO LOOK AT
AND SOMETIMES PREFER**
Furman University

AND RARELY PREFER
Clemson University; University of South
Carolina–Columbia

FINANCIAL FACTS

Financial Aid Rating	86
Annual tuition	$38,705
Room and board	$11,180
Books and supplies	$1,200
Average frosh need-based scholarship	$29,962
Average UG need-based scholarship	$30,032
% needy frosh rec. need-based scholarship or grant aid	100
% needy UG rec. need-based scholarship or grant aid	99
% needy frosh rec. non-need-based scholarship or grant aid	38
% needy UG rec. non-need-based scholarship or grant aid	30
% needy frosh rec. need-based self-help aid	50
% needy UG rec. need-based self-help aid	54
% frosh rec. any financial aid	96
% UG rec. any financial aid	94
% frosh need fully met	44
% ugrads need fully met	39
Average % of frosh need met	90
Average % of ugrad need met	91

WORCESTER POLYTECHNIC INSTITUTE

ADMISSIONS OFFICE, BARTLETT CENTER, WORCESTER, MA 01609 • ADMISSIONS: 508-831-5286 • FAX: 508-831-5875

STUDENTS SAY "..."

Academics

The reputation of Worcester Polytechnic Institute amongst engineers around the country is impeccable, and rightfully so: this highly hands-on university in central Massachusetts has a "rigorous academic environment" and is focused on "creative collaboration in a non-competitive environment with a common goal of innovation." The campus "has a real excitement regarding knowledge," and while the majority of students choose to do engineering and math here, "there are opportunities to do humanities and business course as well."

One of the more unique aspects of the WPI curriculum is the project activity, which includes the Major Qualifying Project (MQP) and the Interactive Qualifying Project (IQP) for juniors and seniors, both of which are done with an advisor and often involve off-campus sponsorship. This, along with the grading system (students are awarded a grade of A, B, C, or No Record) "encourages cooperation among students rather than cut-throat competition." Classes run in a quarter system (three classes for each of the four seven-week terms), which means faculty is "forced to only teach us the most important material, without material that may be considered 'filler material.'"

The majority of professors are "very engaging" and "present material in better ways then just showing Powerpoint slides one after the other." As you get into higher level classes the subjects are more focused, and "almost all classes have a lab component." Students are "always helping one another, [and] everyone (including the professors) wants the students to succeed." The project-based learning and reputation of WPI gives students "the ability to work on real engineering projects around the world." As one sophomore puts it: "WPI won't teach you everything you need to know to be a good engineer, but they'll teach you where to find all the information you need to face any obstacle."

Life

WPI "does a great job of making sure we all fit in and have an awesome friend group," says a student. Worcester "isn't the greatest city," but "WPI is in a nice area." There is a great social life on campus as well as off campus, and "there is plenty to do for those eighteen and up as well as twenty-one and up." "It would literally take hours to describe all the amazing things they take place on campus," says a junior.

Students are academically engaged during the week "because it's practically a requirement at WPI," but know how to let go on weekends and occasional weeknights. With around 200 organizations and "a very active Social Committee" there is always something happening on campus, such as "free movies on weekends (post-theater but pre-DVD release)," "dances, fundraisers, activities, socials, concerts," LARPing, and robot competitions. "We definitely are a geeky campus," says a student. Now, "a geeky tech school is not the place someone would expect to find a flourishing Greek community," says a student. "But in fact the Panhellenic community on campus is excellent."

Student Body

"It's nice to know that no matter what you like, you're going to find a kindred spirit at WPI," says a student of the "rather smart," "open and friendly" crowd. The school is around 70 percent guys (and almost all of the student body is here for a STEM major) so fraternities and sports are popular (sororities and sports for girls, too), and all have a "nerdy side" that "brings us together." Still, don't get it wrong: WPI "is not a school full of Poindexters who never leave their rooms." "We have athletes, Greek life, theatre, and anything else you can find at any other school. However, we all have a common bond because of our love of math, science, and all things logical," says a student.

WORCESTER POLYTECHNIC INSTITUTE

FINANCIAL AID: 508-831-5469 • E-MAIL: ADMISSIONS@WPI.EDU • WEBSITE: WWW.WPI.EDU

THE PRINCETON REVIEW SAYS

Admissions

Very important factors considered include: rigor of secondary school record, academic GPA. *Important factors considered include:* class rank, standardized test scores, recommendation(s), extracurricular activities, character/personal qualities. *Other factors considered include:* application essay, interview, talent/ability, first generation, alumni/ae relation, geographical residence, volunteer work, work experience, level of applicant's interest. SAT or ACT considered if submitted; SAT Subject Tests considered if submitted. ACT with or without writing accepted. SAT with or without Essay component accepted. TOEFL required of all international applicants. High school diploma is required and GED is accepted. *Academic units required:* 4 English, 4 math, 2 science, 2 science labs. *Academic units recommended:* 4 science, 2 foreign language, 2 social studies, 1 history, 1 computer science.

Financial Aid

Students should submit: FAFSA, CSS/Financial Aid PROFILE, Noncustodial PROFILE. Regular filing deadline is 2/1. The Princeton Review suggests that all financial aid forms be submitted as soon as possible after October 1. *Need-based scholarships/grants offered:* Federal Pell, FSEOG, State scholarships/grants, Private scholarships, College/university scholarship or grant aid from institutional funds. *Loan aid offered:* Direct Subsidized Stafford Loans, Direct Unsubsidized Stafford Loans, Direct PLUS loans, Federal Perkins Loans, State Loans, College/university loans from institutional funds. Applicants will be notified of awards on or about 4/1. Federal Work-Study Program available. Institutional employment available.

The Inside Word

WPI's high admission rate is the result of a self-selecting applicant pool; those who don't have a decent chance of getting in here rarely bother to apply. The relatively low rate of conversion of accepted students to enrollees is due to the fact that WPI is a 'safety' school for many applicants. Those who get in here and at MIT, CalTech, Cornell, or Carnegie Mellon usually wind up elsewhere.

THE SCHOOL SAYS "..."

From the Admissions Office

"Projects and research enrich WPI's academic program. WPI believes that in these times simply passing courses and accumulating theoretical knowledge is not enough to truly educate tomorrow's leaders. Tomorrow's professionals ought to be involved in project work that prepares them today for future challenges. Projects at WPI come as close to professional experience as a college program can possibly achieve. In fact, WPI works with more than 200 companies, government agencies, and private organizations each year. These groups provide opportunities where students get a chance to work in real, professional settings. Students gain invaluable experience in planning, coordinating team efforts, meeting deadlines, writing proposals and reports, making oral presentations, doing cost analyses, and making decisions.

"Applicants are required to submit SAT or ACT scores, or in lieu of test scores may submit supplemental materials through WPI's Flex Path program. Students who choose the Flex Path are encouraged to submit examples of academic work or extracurricular projects that reflect a high level of organization, motivation, creativity and problem-solving ability."

SELECTIVITY

Admissions Rating	94
# of applicants	10,172
% of applicants accepted	49
% of acceptees attending	22
# offered a place on the wait list	2,472
% accepting a place on wait list	56
% admitted from wait list	3

FRESHMAN PROFILE

Range SAT Critical Reading	570–680
Range SAT Math	640–740
Range SAT Writing	560–670
Range ACT Composite	27–32
Minimum paper TOEFL	550
Minimum internet-based TOEFL	79
Average HS GPA	3.8
% graduated top 10% of class	65
% graduated top 25% of class	91
% graduated top 50% of class	98

DEADLINES

Early action	
Deadline	11/10
Notification	12/20
Regular	
Deadline	2/1
Notification	4/1
Nonfall registration?	Yes

APPLICANTS ALSO LOOK AT AND OFTEN PREFER

Massachusetts Institute of Technology; Cornell University; Carnegie Mellon University; Brown University

AND SOMETIMES PREFER

Tufts University; Rensselaer Polytechnic Institute; Boston University; University of Rochester

AND RARELY PREFER

University of Massachusetts Amherst

FINANCIAL FACTS

Financial Aid Rating	87
Annual tuition	$44,970
Room and board	$13,410
Required fees	$620
Books and supplies	$1,000
Average frosh need-based scholarship	$23,869
Average UG need-based scholarship	$22,103
% needy frosh rec. need-based scholarship or grant aid	100
% needy UG rec. need-based scholarship or grant aid	96
% needy frosh rec. non-need-based scholarship or grant aid	32
% needy UG rec. non-need-based scholarship or grant aid	34
% needy frosh rec. need-based self-help aid	53
% needy UG rec. need-based self-help aid	53
% frosh rec. any financial aid	98
% UG rec. any financial aid	95
% frosh need fully met	55
% ugrads need fully met	45
Average % of frosh need met	79
Average % of ugrad need met	77

XAVIER UNIVERSITY OF LOUISIANA

ONE DREXEL DRIVE, NEW ORLEANS, LA 70125 • ADMISSIONS: 504-520-7388 • FAX: 504-520-7941

STUDENTS SAY "..."

Academics

One of the top Historically Black Colleges/Universities (HBCU), Xavier University of Louisiana prides itself on educating students in a range of subjects, to provide a "thriving underlying foundation, upon which students can achieve the very best for themselves." Though perhaps best known for its science departments, the New Orleans-based school has both a College of Arts and Sciences and a College of Pharmacy and requires "high academic standards" for all of majors across the board. Between its academic reputation and the emphasis placed on community leadership, no matter the reason that you go to XU, you leave "fully educated." "I was challenged academically, but not broken. The workload was not overwhelming," says a student. Small class sizes means great interaction with professors, and the ensuing "close-knit relationships" are cited by many as a major part of their satisfaction with the school. Also on that list? "The education you receive at XU, considering the extremely low tuition cost and financial aid opportunities for a private university, is unparalleled." Professors at XU are dedicated to ensuring that all students "are proficient, if not masters, in the materials taught," and they provide "an excellent foundation for further academic and career success." XU produces a tremendous number of graduates who go on to medical school and other professional schools in "the pursuit of success." Most faculty members are "almost always available in some form or fashion to help you with any questions you may have," and the school itself provides "multiple resources for any problems that need reinforcement." One exception, however, is the financial aid and fiscal services departments, which "have very little time to discuss things with students."

Life

Despite its location, XU "is by no means a party school." Because the student body is mostly composed of science majors, people "are always studying," and "study groups are a common thing." Students "will take occasional breaks," but for the most part, grades are the important thing at XU. "We are not a school that places as much emphasis on 'fun' as we do making sure we are productive and contributing citizens by the time we graduate," says a student. Though the school offers "lots of opportunities to volunteer," many students complain that there aren't enough social activities to keep students occupied, and school spirit suffers as a result. "We have a strong academic standing, but our campus life is pretty limited," says one student. The dry campus also enforces a curfew ("Sometimes it feels like a boarding school"), so the typical college experience and hair-letting-loose happens off-campus: "Campus is a place to work." Not everyone is familiar with the city (there's no off-campus housing associated with XU), so going out to movies, clubs, and shopping on weekends usually happens in groups. There's also a fair amount of interaction with neighboring schools like Tulane, Loyola, and Dillard. "There are so many things to do right around the corner from Xavier; I can see musicals, watch the Saints, see the Pelicans play, salsa dance, get amazing Southern cuisine, listen to 'bounce' music, and learn how to dance, see parades and second lines," sums up a Big Easy lover.

Student Body

Studious, studious, studious. Most students are "very focused, driven, and destined for success," and unsurprisingly, you run into a lot of "aspiring" doctors and pharmacists. The majority of students are African American or Asian, and the female-to-male ratio is quite high. The student body as a whole has a "conservative mentality." It's "very easy" to make friends here, particularly through study groups, and the small campus means that "everyone recognizes everyone" and "gets along with each other."

XAVIER UNIVERSITY OF LOUISIANA

FINANCIAL AID: 504-520-7835 • E-MAIL: APPLY@XULA.EDU • WEBSITE: WWW.XULA.EDU

THE PRINCETON REVIEW SAYS

Admissions

Very important factors considered include: rigor of secondary school record, academic GPA, standardized test scores, recommendation(s). *Important factors considered include:* class rank, application essay. *Other factors considered include:* interview, extracurricular activities, talent/ability, character/personal qualities, alumni/ae relation, volunteer work, work experience. SAT or ACT required; SAT Subject Tests considered if submitted. ACT with Writing recommended. TOEFL required of all international applicants. High school diploma is required and GED is accepted. *Academic units required:* 4 English, 2 math, 2 science, 1 social studies, 7 academic electives. *Academic units recommended:* 4 math, 3 science, 1 foreign language, 1 history.

Financial Aid

Students should submit: FAFSA. Priority filing deadline is 1/1. The Princeton Review suggests that all financial aid forms be submitted as soon as possible after October 1. *Need-based scholarships/grants offered:* Federal Pell, FSEOG, State scholarships/grants, Private scholarships, College/university scholarship or grant aid from institutional funds, United Negro College Fund. *Loan aid offered:* Direct Subsidized Stafford Loans, Direct Unsubsidized Stafford Loans, Direct PLUS loans, Federal Perkins Loans. Applicants will be notified of awards on a rolling basis beginning 4/1. Federal Work-Study Program available. Institutional employment available.

Inside Word

This HBCU has a rolling admissions process, and applicants typically receive notification of the school's decision within one month of completed application submission. Campus visits are encouraged. If you want to be considered for scholarships, you'll need to include a strong personal statement that reflects evidence of leadership. Admission to the school's College of Pharmacy is separate from that of the College of Arts and Sciences and is subject to a different set of requirements.

THE SCHOOL SAYS "..."

From the Admissions Office

"You have made a great decision in planning to go to college. You will never regret it. It will help you reach your greatest potential as an individual and as a contributing member of our society. You will make another important decision when you select Xavier for your college education. For more than 80 years, Xavier has been expanding horizons, opening new worlds, enriching lives, developing leaders and sending graduates out to conquer their selected corner of the world. Xavier graduates have heeded the call of urban America, providing enlightened leadership in city government. They have served as mayors, headed municipal agencies, donned judicial robes. They have also served in state legislatures. In the health professions, Xavier is a national leader in providing graduates for schools of medicine and dentistry, including the country's top-ranked schools. College of Pharmacy graduates can be found in almost every state, serving in neighborhood pharmacies, in hospitals, and in the pharmaceutical industry. Xavier graduates are vital members of health care teams, while others conduct biomedical research.

"Xavier educators are found in classrooms of colleges and schools. They also serve as presidents, superintendents and principals. Business graduates rise quickly in the world of business and industry. Xavier alumni report the news on network television and in leading national publications. They perform on opera and concert stages in the music centers of the world. As lawyers and social scientists, they help right some of the wrongs of our society. They fulfill the Xavier tradition in leadership and service. Xavier seeks students to keep that tradition alive—students with great potential, who will not settle for less than high achievement, students who make a difference in the lives they touch. You can make your life count for something special by coming to Xavier."

SELECTIVITY

Admissions Rating	84
# of applicants	4,847
% of applicants accepted	66
% of acceptees attending	21
# offered a place on the wait list	0

FRESHMAN PROFILE

Range SAT Critical Reading	450–550
Range SAT Math	460–550
Range SAT Writing	440–520
Range ACT Composite	20–25
Minimum paper TOEFL	550
Average HS GPA	3.4
% graduated top 10% of class	36
% graduated top 25% of class	58
% graduated top 50% of class	83

DEADLINES

Regular	
Priority	3/1
Deadline	7/1
Nonfall registration?	Yes

FINANCIAL FACTS

Financial Aid Rating	73
Annual tuition	$19,800
Room and board	$8,200
Required fees	$2,549
Books and supplies	$1,220
Average frosh need-based scholarship	$5,701
Average UG need-based scholarship	$5,694
% needy frosh rec. need-based scholarship or grant aid	65
% needy UG rec. need-based scholarship or grant aid	65
% needy frosh rec. non-need-based scholarship or grant aid	91
% needy UG rec. non-need-based scholarship or grant aid	79
% needy frosh rec. need-based self-help aid	93
% needy UG rec. need-based self-help aid	95
% frosh rec. any financial aid	94
% UG rec. any financial aid	24
% frosh need fully met	0
% ugrads need fully met	1
Average % of frosh need met	14
Average % of ugrad need met	13

XAVIER UNIVERSITY (OH)

3800 VICTORY PARKWAY, CINCINNATI, OH 45207-5311 • ADMISSIONS: 513-745-3301 • FAX: 513-745-4319

STUDENTS SAY "..."

Academics

Xavier University is a Jesuit liberal arts university that encourages students to become well-rounded, reflective citizens through a comprehensive core curriculum and a focus on critical analysis and application. All students take part in the First-Year Experience, which includes a First-Year Seminar and the Goa program, a series of six small group meetings throughout the year in which students engage in discussion and activities. All of this togetherness and shared experience create a "great sense of community that allows students to feel welcomed and accepted." All in all, Xavier "helps students achieve what they set out for. We are provided the means to be successful, and it is our responsibility to take them."

The academics here "can be tough at times" but "really small" class sizes make it "very easy for you to know your professor and receive extra help." The "warm and caring" teachers can "maintain strong professional bonds with the students" while feeling like people the students can come easily talk to. They "take an actual interest in you as a student" and "do what they can to help you grow as an individual and to succeed in life."

Above everything, students speak of the inclusive environment as being the most enabling aspect of Xavier, and how important it is to attend a school with "an outstanding community, built on love, support, and understanding." The intimate university has a real "rising tide lifts all boats" feel, and the vast majority of students "put a lot of stock into getting an education and... will actually turn in quality work that they put thought and effort into."

Life

Weekdays are filled with "studying, classes, extra credit opportunities and club meetings," and weekends find students "attending athletic events or finding parties with peers." Other free hours are used for the standard issue college pastimes: "We watch movies, play games, and just enjoy each other's company." This "very peaceful campus" is also a very active one, with people frequently "playing sports on the mall or the student organization screening a movie." Many students participate in intramural sports, and everyone "has a lot of school pride," as well as moral pride. "Most people here have an awareness of the injustices in this world and want to do something about it," says a student. Downtown Cincinnati is a big hangout; the zoo is very popular, as well as Newport on the Levee (an entertainment center) and various restaurants. The "beautiful" campus is far enough from the city that students don't feel like they're right in the middle of Cincinnati, but also "close enough that [we] do not feel far away from the action." Men's basketball games are the highlighted sporting event, along with men's soccer, and events on campus such as Xavier Fest and Club Day on the yard have high attendance.

Student Body

This is a group of "independent and careful young adults who enjoy living life to the fullest" and hold doors open for one another. Xavier is the kind of school that does not discriminate by grade: "seniors talk to freshman and freshman talk to seniors." For the most part, everyone is "positive and outgoing" and "talks to everyone." "We are a small community—you see a familiar face everywhere you go," says a student. There's no question that "diversity could improve at Xavier," but regardless of the numbers "everyone is accepted and Xavier doesn't have a social order that could constrict individuals from becoming friends." There is an evident environment of respect among the school's students, staff and faculty, and "when students want to be heard, they can be and will be."

FINANCIAL AID: 513-745-3142 • E-MAIL: XUADMIT@XAVIER.EDU • WEBSITE: WWW.XAVIER.EDU

THE PRINCETON REVIEW SAYS

Admissions

Very important factors considered include: rigor of secondary school record, academic GPA, standardized test scores. *Important factors considered include:* application essay, recommendation(s), extracurricular activities, character/personal qualities, volunteer work. *Other factors considered include:* class rank, talent/ability, first generation, alumni/ae relation, work experience, level of applicant's interest. SAT or ACT required. ACT with or without writing accepted. SAT with or without Essay component accepted. TOEFL required of all international applicants. High school diploma is required and GED is accepted. *Academic units recommended:* 4 English, 3 math, 3 science, 2 foreign language, 3 social studies, 5 academic electives, and 1 unit from above areas or other academic areas.

Financial Aid

Students should submit: FAFSA. Priority filing deadline is 2/15. The Princeton Review suggests that all financial aid forms be submitted as soon as possible after October 1. *Need-based scholarships/grants offered:* Federal Pell, FSEOG, State scholarships/grants, Private scholarships, College/university scholarship or grant aid from institutional funds. *Loan aid offered:* Direct Subsidized Stafford Loans, Direct Unsubsidized Stafford Loans, Direct PLUS loans, Federal Perkins Loans. Applicants will be notified of awards on a rolling basis beginning 3/1. Federal Work-Study Program available. Institutional employment available.

The Inside Word

There will be no major hurdles for above-average students when it comes to winning admission to Xavier. For others, it will take a little more legwork. Look to provide credible demonstrations of commitment to academics and Jesuit ideals of service if you want to win over admissions officers.

THE SCHOOL SAYS "..."

From the Admissions Office

"Founded in 1831, Xavier University is the fourth oldest of the twenty-eight Jesuit colleges and universities in the United States. The Jesuit tradition is evident in the university's core curriculum, degree programs, and involvement opportunities. Xavier is home to approximately 7,000 total students; 4,300 degree-seeking undergraduates. The student population represents more than forty-five states and forty-three foreign countries. Xavier offers more than eighty undergraduate academic majors and more than fifty minors in the College of Arts and Sciences; the Williams College of Business; and the College of Social Sciences, Health, and Education. Most popular majors include business, natural sciences, nursing, communication arts, education, psychology, biology, sport management/marketing, and pre-professional study. Other programs of note include University Scholars; Honors AB; Philosophy, Politics, and the Public; Army ROTC, study abroad, academic service-learning, and community engagement fellowship. There are more than 100 academic clubs, social and service organizations, and recreational sports activities on campus. Students participate in groups such as student government, campus ministry, performing arts, and intramural sports as well as one of the largest service-oriented Alternative Break clubs in the country. Xavier is a member of the Division I Big East Conference and fields teams in men's and women's basketball, cross-country, track, golf, soccer, swimming, and tennis, as well as men's baseball and women's volleyball. Xavier is situated on more than 180 acres in a residential area of Cincinnati, Ohio. The face of Xavier continues to change with the addition of the technology-based Conaton Learning Commons and Smith Hall, a new building for the Williams College of Business, both which opened in fall 2010, Fenwick Place which includes a 535-bed residence hall, a dining hall and offices that opened in fall 2011 and a new classroom building that opened in fall 2015. Applicants must submit results from the SAT or ACT. The student's best score(s) from either test will be used. The writing portion of the SAT/ACT is not required and will not be used in admission and scholarship decisions."

SELECTIVITY

Admissions Rating	80
# of applicants	10,661
% of applicants accepted	72
% of acceptees attending	15
# offered a place on the wait list	98
% accepting a place on wait list	17
% admitted from wait list	47

FRESHMAN PROFILE

Range SAT Critical Reading	490–590
Range SAT Math	490–590
Range SAT Writing	480–590
Range ACT Composite	22–27
Minimum paper TOEFL	550
Minimum internet-based TOEFL	79
Average HS GPA	3.6
% graduated top 10% of class	23
% graduated top 25% of class	53
% graduated top 50% of class	84

DEADLINES

Priority	2/1
Nonfall registration?	Yes

APPLICANTS ALSO LOOK AT AND OFTEN PREFER

The Ohio State University–Columbus; Miami University; University of Cincinnati; University of Dayton

AND SOMETIMES PREFER

Indiana University Bloomington; Marquette University; Ohio University–Athens; University of Kentucky; Purdue University–West Lafayette

AND RARELY PREFER

Butler University; Saint Louis University

FINANCIAL FACTS

Financial Aid Rating	84
Annual tuition	$34,050
Room and board	$11,380
Required fees	$1,030
Books and supplies	$1,000
Average frosh need-based scholarship	$17,783
Average UG need-based scholarship	$16,829
% needy frosh rec. need-based scholarship or grant aid	97
% needy UG rec. need-based scholarship or grant aid	96
% needy frosh rec. non-need-based scholarship or grant aid	17
% needy UG rec. non-need-based scholarship or grant aid	15
% needy frosh rec. need-based self-help aid	74
% needy UG rec. need-based self-help aid	76
% frosh rec. any financial aid	99
% UG rec. any financial aid	92
% UG borrow to pay for school	67
Average cumulative indebtedness	$32,131
% frosh need fully met	21
% ugrads need fully met	19
Average % of frosh need met	75
Average % of ugrad need met	73

YALE UNIVERSITY

PO BOX 208234, NEW HAVEN, CT 06520-8234 • ADMISSIONS: 203-432-9300 • FAX: 203-432-9392

CAMPUS LIFE

Quality of Life Rating	94
Fire Safety Rating	62
Green Rating	95
Type of school	Private
Affiliation	No Affiliation
Environment	City

STUDENTS

Total undergrad enrollment	5,537
% male/female	51/49
% from out of state	93
% frosh from public high school	57
% frosh live on campus	100
% ugrads live on campus	84
% African American	7
% Asian	17
% Caucasian	47
% Hispanic	11
% Native American	1
% Pacific Islander	0
% Two or more races	6
% Race and/or ethnicity unknown	1
% international	11
# of countries represented	89

SURVEY SAYS...
Students are happy
Classroom facilities are great
Great library
Internships are widely available
School is well run
Great financial aid
Students are friendly
Diverse student types interact on campus
Students environmentally aware
Dorms are like palaces
Recreation facilities are great
Lots of beer drinking
Hard liquor is popular
Theater is popular
Campus newspaper is popular
Active minority support groups

ACADEMICS

Academic Rating	96
% students returning for sophomore year	99
students graduating within 4 years	87
students graduating within 6 years	96
Calendar	Semester
Student/faculty ratio	6:1
Profs interesting rating	90
Profs accessible rating	86

Most classes have 10–19 students.

MOST POPULAR MAJORS
Economics; Political Science; History

STUDENTS SAY "..."

Academics
Listening to Yale students wax rhapsodic about their school, one can be forgiven for wondering whether they aren't actually describing the platonic form of the university. By their own account, students here benefit not only from "amazing academics and extensive resources" that provide "phenomenal in- and out-of-class education," but also from participation in "a student body that is committed to learning and to each other." Unlike some other prestigious, prominent research universities, Yale "places unparalleled focus on undergraduate education," requiring all professors to teach at least one undergraduate course each year. "[You know] the professors actually love teaching, because if they just wanted to do their research, they could have easily gone elsewhere." A residential college system further personalizes the experience. Each residential college "has a Dean and a Master, each of which is only responsible for 300 to 500 students, so administrative attention is highly specialized and widely available." Students further enjoy access to "a seemingly never-ending supply of resources (they really just love throwing money at us)" that includes "the [13.8] million volumes in our libraries." In short, "the opportunities are truly endless." "The experiences you have here and the people that you meet will change your life and strengthen your dreams," says one student. Looking for the flip side to all this? "If the weather were a bit nicer, that would be excellent," one student offers. Guess that will have to do.

Life
Yale is, of course, extremely challenging academically, but students assure us that "aside from the stress of midterms and finals, life at Yale is relatively carefree." Work doesn't keep undergrads from participating in "a huge variety of activities for fun. There are more than 400 student groups, including singing, dancing, juggling fire, theater…the list goes on. Because of all of these groups, there are shows on-campus all the time, which are a lot of fun and usually free or less than five dollars. On top of that, there are parties and events on campus and off campus, as well as many subsidized trips to New York City and Boston." Many here "are politically active (or at least politically aware)" and "a very large number of students either volunteer or try to get involved in some sort of organization to make a difference in the world." When the weekend comes around, "there are always parties to go to, whether at the frats or in rooms, but there's definitely no pressure to drink if you don't want to. A good friend of mine pledged a frat without drinking and that's definitely not unheard of (but still not common)." The relationship between Yale and the city of New Haven "sometimes leaves a little to be desired, but overall it's a great place to be for four years."

Student Body
A typical Yalie is "tough to define because so much of what makes Yale special is the unique convergence of different students to form one cohesive entity. Nonetheless, the one common characteristic of Yale students is passion—each Yalie is driven and dedicated to what he or she loves most, and it creates a palpable atmosphere of enthusiasm on campus." True enough, the student body represents a wide variety of ethnic, religious, economic, and academic backgrounds, but they all "thrive on learning, whether in a class, from a book, or from a conversation with a new friend." Students here also "tend to do a lot." "Everyone has many activities that they are a part of, which in turn fosters the closely connected feel of the campus." Undergrads tend to lean to the left politically, but for "those whose political views aren't as liberal as the rest of the campus…there are several campus organizations that cater to them."

FINANCIAL AID: 203-432-2700 • E-MAIL: STUDENT.QUESTIONS@YALE.EDU • WEBSITE: WWW.YALE.EDU

THE PRINCETON REVIEW SAYS

Admissions

Very important factors considered include: rigor of secondary school record, class rank, academic GPA, standardized test scores, application essay, recommendation(s), extracurricular activities, talent/ability, character/personal qualities. *Other factors considered include:* interview, first generation, alumni/ae relation, geographical residence, state residency, racial/ethnic status, volunteer work, work experience. SAT or ACT with Writing required. TOEFL required of all international applicants. High school diploma or equivalent is not required.

Financial Aid

Students should submit: FAFSA, CSS/Financial Aid PROFILE, Noncustodial PROFILE. Regular filing deadline is 3/1. The Princeton Review suggests that all financial aid forms be submitted as soon as possible after October 1. *Need-based scholarships/grants offered:* Federal Pell, FSEOG, State scholarships/grants, Private scholarships, College/university scholarship or grant aid from institutional funds, United Negro College Fund. *Loan aid offered:* Direct Subsidized Stafford Loans, Direct Unsubsidized Stafford Loans, Direct PLUS loans, Federal Perkins Loans, State Loans. Applicants will be notified of awards on or about 4/1. Federal Work-Study Program available. Institutional employment available.

The Inside Word

Yale estimates that over three-quarters of all its applicants are qualified to attend the university, but less than 10 percent get in. That adds up to a lot of broken hearts among kids who, if admitted, could probably handle the academic program. With so many qualified applicants to choose from, Yale can winnow to build an incoming class that is balanced in terms of income level, racial/ethnic background, geographic origin, and academic interest. Legacies (descendents of Yale grads) gain some advantage—although they still need exceptionally strong credentials.

THE SCHOOL SAYS "..."

From the Admissions Office

"The most important questions the admissions committee must resolve are 'Who is likely to make the most of Yale's resources?' and 'Who will contribute significantly to the Yale community?' These questions suggest an approach to evaluating applicants that is more complex than whether Yale would rather admit well-rounded people or those with specialized talents. In selecting a class of 1,350 from roughly 30,000 applicants, the admissions committee looks for academic ability and achievement combined with such personal characteristics as motivation, curiosity, energy, and leadership ability. The nature of these qualities is such that there is no simple profile of grades, scores, interests, and activities that will assure admission. Diversity within the student population is important, and the admissions committee selects a class of able and contributing individuals from a variety of backgrounds and with a broad range of interests and skills.

"Applicants for the entering class are required to take the SAT or the ACT with Writing. For SATs taken in March 2016 or later, the Essayis required."

SELECTIVITY

Admissions Rating	99
# of applicants	30,236
% of applicants accepted	6
% of acceptees attending	69
# offered a place on the wait list	1,098
% accepting a place on wait list	65
% admitted from wait list	73

FRESHMAN PROFILE

Range SAT Critical Reading	720–800
Range SAT Math	710–800
Range SAT Writing	710–790
Range ACT Composite	31–35
Minimum paper TOEFL	600
Minimum internet-based TOEFL	100
% graduated top 10% of class	96
% graduated top 25% of class	99
% graduated top 50% of class	100

DEADLINES

Early action	
Deadline	11/1
Notification	12/15
Regular	
Deadline	1/1
Notification	4/1
Nonfall registration?	No

FINANCIAL FACTS

Financial Aid Rating	97
Annual tuition	$49,480
Room and board	$15,170
Books and supplies	$3,580
Average frosh need-based scholarship	$50,359
Average UG need-based scholarship	$47,960
% needy frosh rec. need-based scholarship or grant aid	100
% needy UG rec. need-based scholarship or grant aid	100
% needy frosh rec. non-need-based scholarship or grant aid	0
% needy UG rec. non-need-based scholarship or grant aid	0
% needy frosh rec. need-based self-help aid	73
% needy UG rec. need-based self-help aid	85
% frosh rec. any financial aid	51
% UG rec. any financial aid	50
% frosh need fully met	100
% ugrads need fully met	97
Average % of frosh need met	100
Average % of ugrad need met	100

In addition to the 381 schools in this book, we salute the following 274 schools that we consider academically outstanding and well worth consideration in your college search. For more information on these schools, check out the "Regional School Says" section on page 857 or visit PrincetonReview.com to find admissions information, costs, and more.

MIDWEST

Illinois
Augustana College
Elmhurst College
Lewis University
Millikin University
Monmouth College
North Central College
Rockford University
Southern Illinois University Carbondale
University of St. Francis
Western Illinois University

Indiana
Anderson University
Ball State University
Butler University
Grace College and Seminary
Huntington University
Indiana State University
Manchester University
Saint Joseph's College
Saint Mary's College
Taylor University
Trine University
University of Evansville
Valparaiso University

Iowa
Clarke University
Dordt College
Drake University
Graceland University
Luther College
Morningside College
Northwestern College
St. Ambrose University
University of Northern Iowa
Wartburg College

Kansas
Baker University
Emporia State University
Pittsburg State University
Sterling College
University of Saint Mary

Michigan
Alma College
Eastern Michigan University
Grand Valley State University
Hope College
Kettering University
Lawrence Technological University

Michigan State University
University of Michigan—Flint
Western Michigan University

Minnesota
Augsburg College
The College of Saint Scholastica
Gustavus Adolphus College
Hamline University
Saint Mary's University of Minnesota
St. Catherine University
University of Minnesota, Crookston
University of Saint Thomas
Winona State University

Missouri
Columbia College
Drury University
Southeast Missouri State University
University of Central Missouri
University of Missouri—Kansas City
Westminster College

Nebraska
Doane College
Hastings College
Nebraska Wesleyan University
University of Nebraska at Omaha

North Dakota
Mayville State University
University of Jamestown

Ohio
Ashland University
Baldwin Wallace University
Cedarville University
The Cleveland Institute of Art
Hiram College
John Carroll University
Lake Erie College
Lourdes University
Marietta College
The University of Akron
Wright State University

South Dakota
Augustana University

Wisconsin
Carthage College
Edgewood College
Milwaukee School of Engineering
Northland College
St. Norbert College

University of Wisconsin—Eau Claire
University of Wisconsin—Milwaukee
University of Wisconsin—River Falls

NORTHEAST

Connecticut
Central Connecticut State University
Eastern Connecticut State University

Maine
University of Maine—Fort Kent
University of Southern Maine

Maryland
Hood College
Maryland Institute College of Art
McDaniel College
Stevenson University
Towson University

Massachusetts
Hampshire College
Lesley University
Merrimack College
Nichols College
Regis College
University of Massachusetts Boston
Wentworth Institute of Technology
Worcester State University

New Hampshire
Keene State College

New Jersey
Ramapo College of New Jersey
Stockton University

New York
Adelphi University
Elmira College
Eugene Lang College of Liberal Arts
Hartwick College
Houghton College
Iona College
LIM College
Manhattanville College
Molloy College
Niagara University
Pace University
Polytechnic Institute of New York University—Brooklyn
Pratt Institute
Roberts Wesleyan College
State University of New York at Cortland
State University of New York at New Paltz
State University of New York—Fredonia
State University of New York—Maritime College
State University of New York—Oswego
State University of New York—The College at Brockport
State University of New York—University at Buffalo
Wells College

Pennsylvania
Albright College
Arcadia University

California University of Pennsylvania
Chatham University
Chestnut Hill College
Delaware Valley College
Elizabethtown College
King's College (PA)
Kutztown University of Pennsylvania
Lancaster Bible College
La Roche College
Lebanon Valley College
Lycoming College
Marywood University
Messiah College
Misericordia University
Moore College of Art and Design
Neumann University
Robert Morris University
Rosemont College
Saint Joseph's University (PA)
Seton Hill University
Slippery Rock University of Pennsylvania
University of the Arts
University of Pittsburgh at Bradford
University of Pittsburgh at Johnstown
Westminster College (PA)
Wilkes University
York College of Pennsylvania

Rhode Island
Roger Williams University
Salve Regina University

SOUTHEAST

Alabama
Auburn University at Montgomery
Birmingham-Southern College
Huntingdon College
Samford University
Troy University—Troy (formerly Troy State University)

Arkansas
Arkansas State University
Harding University
Hendrix College
Lyon College

Florida
Florida Agriculture and Mechanical University
Florida Atlantic University
Palm Beach Atlantic University
University of North Florida
University of West Florida
Webber International University

Georgia
Brenau University
Clark Atlanta University
Covenant College
Georgia College & State University
Oglethorpe University
Shorter University
Toccoa Falls College
University of West Georgia

Kentucky

Brescia University
Kentucky State University
Kentucky Wesleyan College

Mississippi

Mississippi College

North Carolina

Appalachian State University
Barton College
Belmont Abbey College
Campbell University
East Carolina University
High Point University
Meredith College
University of North Carolina—Pembroke
University of North Carolina—Wilmington

South Carolina

Anderson University
Coker College
Winthrop University

Tennessee

Belmont University
Christian Brothers University
East Tennessee State University
Fisk University
King University
Lee University
Maryville College
Middle Tennessee State University
Southern Adventist University
Tennessee Technological University
Union University
The University of Tennessee at Martin

Virginia

Averett University
Bridgewater College
Longwood University
Mary Baldwin College
Old Dominion University
Radford University
Sweet Briar College

West Virginia

Bethany College (WV)
Concord University
Shepherd University
University of Charleston
West Virginia Wesleyan College

WEST

Alaska

University of Alaska Fairbanks

California

American Jewish University
Azusa Pacific University
Biola University
California Institute of the Arts

California State Polytechnic University, Pomona
California State University—East Bay
California State University—Long Beach
California State University—San Bernardino
Hult International Business School
Humboldt State University
Menlo College
Otis College of Art and Design
University of California—Irvine
Westmont College

Colorado

Fort Lewis College

Hawaii

Hawaii Pacific University

Idaho

Northwest Nazarene University

New Mexico

New Mexico Institute of Mining and Technology
Santa Fe University of Art and Design

Oklahoma

Oklahoma Baptist University
Oklahoma Christian University
Oklahoma City University
Oklahoma State University
Oral Roberts University

Oregon

Corban University
George Fox University
Linfield College
Oregon State University
Pacific University
University of Portland

Texas

Abilene Christian University
Hardin-Simmons University
St. Edward's University
Texas Lutheran University
Texas State University
Texas Tech University
University of North Texas
University of St. Thomas
The University of Texas at Arlington

Utah

Southern Utah University
Utah State University
Weber State University

Washington

Pacific Lutheran University
Seattle Pacific University
University of Washington—Bothell
Walla Walla University
Whitworth University

PART 4

INDEXES

INDEX OF SCHOOLS

INDEX OF SCHOOLS BY LOCATION

INTERNATIONAL

Canada
McGill University	374
University of Toronto	742

Ireland
Maynooth University	372
Trinity College Dublin	570

INDEX OF SCHOOLS BY TUITION

Price categories are based on figures the schools reported to us in early spring 2015 for tuition (out-of-state tuition for public schools) and do not include fees, room, board, transportation, or other expenses.

University of Chicago	618	Williams College	810
University of Miami	666	Yale University	822
University of Notre Dame	698		
University of Richmond	716	**Over $50,000**	
University of Rochester	718	Brown University	120
University of Southern California	732	Carleton College	134
Ursinus College	758	Carnegie Mellon University	136
Villanova University	764	Cornell University	208
Wake Forest University	774	Franklin and Marshall College	256
Washington University in St. Louis	784	Haverford College	298
Webb Institute	786	Johns Hopkins University	324
Wellesley College	788	Macalester College	360
Wesleyan University	792	Vassar College	762
Wheaton College (MA)	800		
Whitman College	802		
Willamette University	806		

THE PRINCETON REVIEW NATIONAL COLLEGE COUNSELOR ADVISORY BOARD, 2016–2017

We thank the members of this board for their careful and considered input on our products and services.

Michael A. Acquilano, Director of College Guidance, Staten Island Academy, Staten Island, NY

Roland M. Allen, Director of College Counseling, St. Margaret's Episcopal School, San Juan Capistrano, CA

Carol I. Bernstein, Director of College Guidance, Chadwick School, Palos Verdes Peninsula, CA

Lee Bierer, Weekly *Countdown to College* Syndicated Columnist and Independent College Counselor, College Admissions Strategies, Charlotte, NC

Marianne M. Borgmann, Director of Guidance, Cincinnati Hills Christian Academy, Cincinnati, OH

Vicki Brunnick, MA, LPC, College Counselor, South Mecklenburg High School, Charlotte, NC

Judy S. Fairfull, Guidance Department Head, Doherty Memorial High School, Worcester, MA, Worcester Public School District, MA

Meghan Farley, Co-Director of College Counseling, Pingree School, South Hamilton, MA

Maureen Ferrell, Director of College Counseling, The Summit Country Day School, Cincinnati, OH

Nancy Griesemer, MPA, Columnist for Examiner.com and Independent College Consultant, College Explorations, Oakton, VA

Chuck Gutman, College Counselor, Waukegan High School, Waukegan, IL

Troy B. Hammond, Director of University Counseling, Bayview Glen School, Toronto, Ontario, Canada

Ann Herbener, College Counselor, Papillion-La Vista High School, Papillion, NE

William Hirt, College Counselor, Professional Children's School, New York, NY

Marilyn J. Kaufman, MEd, Independent College Counselor,
    President of College Admission Consultants, Dallas, TX

Geri Kellogg, LPC Counselor, J.J. Pearce High School, Richardson, TX

Joanne Levy-Prewitt, College Admissions Advisor, Moraga, CA

Susan S. Marrs, Director, College Counseling, Seven Hills School, Cincinnati OH

Erin M. McElligott, Director of College Counseling,
    Prospect Hill Academy Charter School, Cambridge, MA

Moira McKinnon, Director of College Counseling, Berwick Academy,
    South Berwick, ME

Bruce Richardson, Director of Guidance, Plano Senior High School, Plano, TX

Kimberly R. Simpson, Educational Consultant,
    Collegiate Admissions Consulting Services, LLC, Covington, LA

Theresa Urist, Director of College Counseling, Prospect Hill Academy Charter School,
    Cambridge, MA

Michael Wilner, Educational Consultant and Founder, Wilner Education, Putney, VT

SCHOOL SAYS . . .

In this section you'll find advertisements directly from colleges with information they'd like you to consider about their schools. The editorial in these pages is written by the schools, which pay a fee to offset the cost of printing their advertisements in this section.

The Princeton Review does not charge schools for inclusion in the School Profiles (pp 61-823) section in this book. The company has never required colleges, universities, or any institutions to pay a fee for their profiles or inclusions in our books.

For information about how we selected the 381 outstanding schools in this book, see page 21, "How and Why We Produce This Book."

Learn to thrive

A top research university
–National Science Foundation

A "Best College Value" for academic quality and affordability
–Kiplinger Personal Finance

Among the best-qualified graduates, according to employers
–The Wall Street Journal

asu.edu

BEST COLLEGES
U.S.News
MOST INNOVATIVE
2016

#1 in the U.S. for innovation
#1 ASU #2 Stanford #3 MIT

Students flourish at Assumption College. Strong academic programs in the liberal arts, sciences, business and professional studies, rooted in the rich Catholic intellectual tradition, will provide you with the skills you'll need to excel.

But there's more to education than coursework. At Assumption we'll help you cultivate the character and personal values you'll need to meet the demands of a changing world. The campus community will challenge and support you to achieve more than you thought possible, and put you on the path to leading a life of meaning.

Find your light at Assumption, and learn how to share it with the world.

500 Salisbury Street · Worcester, MA 01609
www.assumption.edu · 866.477.7776

GET THE FACTS

:: **43** majors and **48** minors in the liberal arts, sciences, business and professional studies

:: **2,000** undergraduates from 25 states and 36 countries

:: **90** percent of the students live on campus in guaranteed housing all four years

:: Founded in **1904,** Assumption is the fourth-oldest Catholic college in New England

:: Students can choose from more than **60** student clubs and organizations

:: **Recognized as a top tier school** by *U.S. News and World Report*

:: **24** top-performing NCAA Division II athletic teams

:: **12:1** student/faculty ratio

:: Merit scholarships up to **$20,000** annually

:: Located in the 2nd-largest city in New England, Worcester has more than **30,000** college students overall

:: **Our Rome campus** is ranked a **Top Ten study abroad program** in the nation

ARCHITECTURE. ART. ENGINEERING.

THE COOPER UNION NYC

photo: Mario Morgado

New York City has inspired generations of architects, artists and engineers with its energy, history, soaring architecture and people.

For students, The Cooper Union's East Village location acts as laboratory, provocation, case study and vision. As one of the most selective schools in the country, we provide a rigorous course of study taught by faculty who are both teachers and practitioners. Whether in the classroom, the studio or the lab, learning is a collaborative process of invention and critique. And with the resources of a global city, students have countless opportunities to find mentors, explore fields of study and test their ideas. Build your foundation at The Cooper Union.   cooper.edu

THE COOPER UNION

flsouthern.edu/*guarantees*

our GUARANTEES

Florida Southern goes beyond the conventional college experience, guaranteeing each student an internship, a travel-study experience, and graduation in four years. These signature opportunities, combined with our devoted faculty and stunning historic campus, create a college experience unlike any other.

"Junior Journey was an amazing opportunity that I wouldn't trade for anything in the world! All students should go on at least one international trip in their college career—there is no substitute for experiencing that adventure firsthand. It becomes part of you."

**– Kaci Kohlepp, Plowman Scholar
Australia/New Zealand/Fiji Option**

INTERNSHIPS | **JUNIOR JOURNEY** | **4-YEAR GRADUATION**

FLORIDA SOUTHERN COLLEGE

Prepared.
Not just for a job.
For your life's work.

Yomayra Guerrero '16
Interned at Steve Madden, New York City.

Learn more at naz.edu/internships

Learn more at **naz.edu**

Art and Design
Art Education
Art History
Art Studio
Visual Communication
    Design

Business and Management
Accounting
Business Management
Economics
Finance
International and Global
    Studies
Marketing
Music/Business
Visual Communication
    Design

Education
Art Education
Education, Adolescence
Education, Early
    Childhood and
    Elementary
Music Education
Special Education

Health and Human Services
Biomedical Sciences
Clinical Laboratory
    Sciences
Communication
    Sciences and
    Disorders (Speech
    Therapy)
Music Therapy
Nursing
Occupational Therapy
Physical Therapy
Public Health
Social Work

Humanities and Social Sciences
American Studies
Anthropology
Communication and
    Media
Community Youth
    Development
English
History
International and Global
    Studies
Law (3+3 degree with
    Syracuse University)
Legal Studies
Museums, Archives, and
    Public History
Peace and Justice
Philosophy
Political Science
Psychology
Religious Studies
Social Science
Sociology
Women and Gender
    Studies

Languages and International
Chinese
French
German
International and Global
    Studies
Italian
Modern Foreign
    Languages
Spanish

Music
Music
Music/Business
Music Education
Music Performance
Music Therapy
Musical Theatre

Sciences and Math
Biochemistry
Biology
Biomedical Sciences
Chemistry
Clinical Laboratory
    Sciences
Environmental Science
    and Sustainability
Mathematics
Public Health
Toxicology

Theatre and Performance
Acting
Dance Studies
Musical Theatre
Technical Production
Theatre Arts

NAZARETH COLLEGE   4245 East Avenue, Rochester, NY 14618 ▪ 585-389-2860 ▪ admissions@naz.edu

SAINT ANSELM COLLEGE

1889

Manchester, New Hampshire

A comprehensive liberal arts education where you'll gain true insight into how the world works— and how you can make it work better.

The facts

98
Percent of students are awarded financial aid

18
Our average class size

98%
of 2015 graduates are employed, in school or engaged in service

11:1
Our student/ faculty ratio

60
Minutes to skiing, beaches, and Boston

VISIT US!
www.anselm.edu/visit

CONNECT WITH US!
social.anselm.edu

University of New Haven

DISCOVER UNH!

QUICKFACTS

▶

- Enrollment: 4,600 full-time undergraduate students
- Majors and Programs: Over 100
- Student to Faculty Ratio: 16 to 1

- Athletics: NCAA Division II
- Location: West Haven, CT
- Average Class Size: 23 Students

BEST COLLEGES
U.S.News & WORLD REPORT
REGIONAL UNIVERSITIES
NORTH
2016

www.newhaven.edu/info

THE UNIVERSITY OF SCRANTON
A JESUIT UNIVERSITY

REVIEW THE NUMBERS
SEE HOW SCRANTON ADDS UP

FIND OUT MORE ABOUT SCRANTON

4000
UNDERGRADUATE
STUDENTS

AVERAGE CLASS SIZE: 21

AVERAGE
6-YEAR GRAD RATE
82%

FRESHMAN RETENTION RATE: 89%

EXPECT MORE
FROM SCRANTON

scranton.edu/**expect**more

A CATHOLIC AND JESUIT UNIVERSITY

The University of Tulsa's Collins College of Business is nationally ranked for both undergraduate (*Bloomberg*) and graduate programs (*U.S. News*). The college features small class sizes led by outstanding faculty, opportunities to gain hands-on experience through internships and study abroad partnerships and programs that foster innovation and creativity.

TU is a great investment. The Princeton Review profiled TU in the 2016 edition of *Colleges That Pay You Back,* and *Kiplinger's Personal Finance* named TU to its list of the Top 300 Best College Values of 2016.

Visit Us to Learn More
Apply online at **apply.utulsa.edu** or **commonapp.org**.

Students are encouraged to schedule an individual campus visit. **utulsa.edu/visit**

business.utulsa.edu • 800-331-3050
CollinsUndergradAdv@utulsa.edu

2017
BEST REGIONAL COLLEGES
SCHOOL SAYS . . .

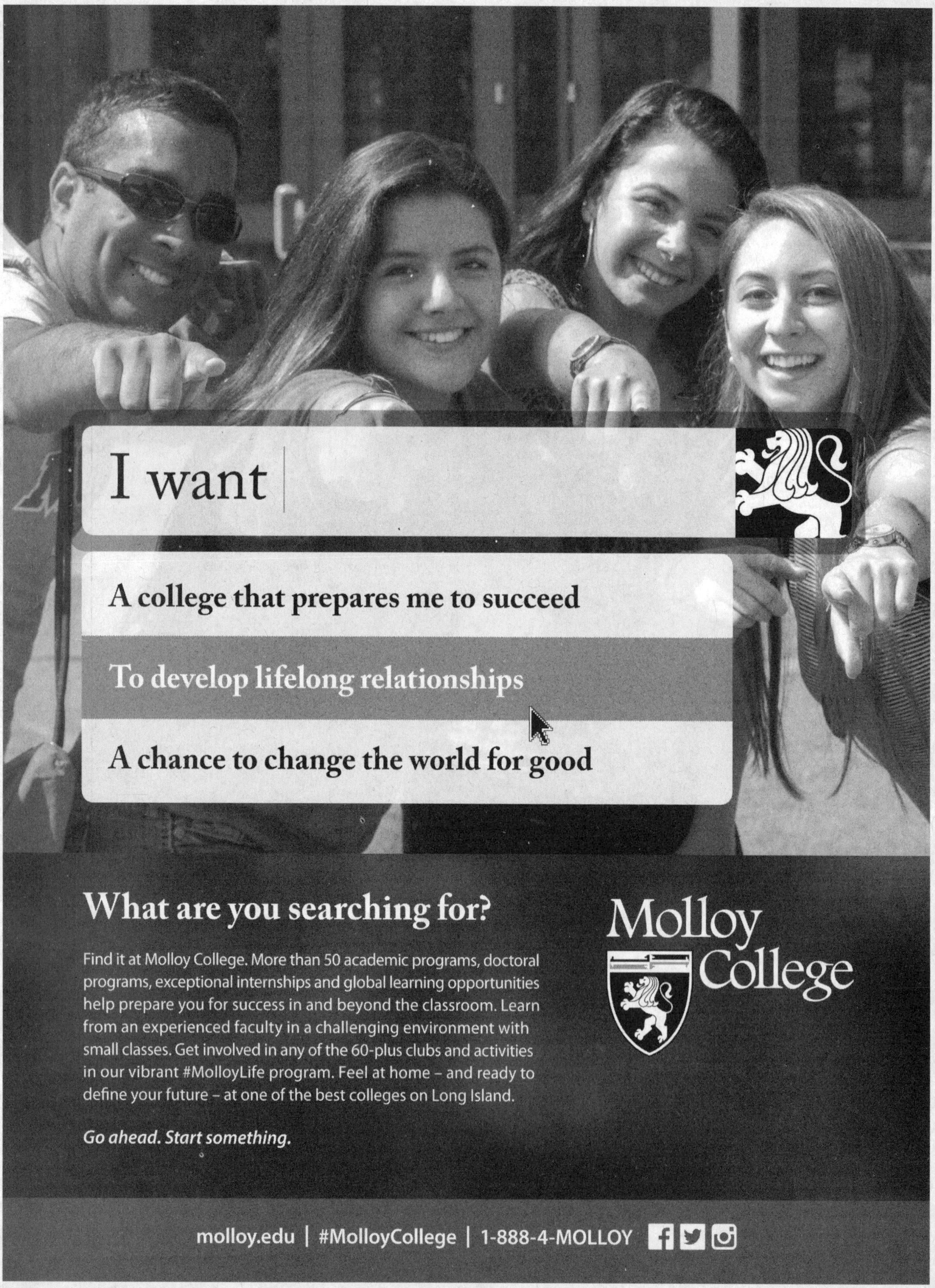
I want
A college that prepares me to succeed
To develop lifelong relationships
A chance to change the world for good
What are you searching for?
Find it at Molloy College. More than 50 academic programs, doctoral programs, exceptional internships and global learning opportunities help prepare you for success in and beyond the classroom. Learn from an experienced faculty in a challenging environment with small classes. Get involved in any of the 60-plus clubs and activities in our vibrant #MolloyLife program. Feel at home – and ready to define your future – at one of the best colleges on Long Island.
Go ahead. Start something.
Molloy College
molloy.edu | #MolloyCollege | 1-888-4-MOLLOY

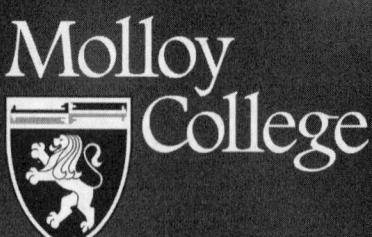

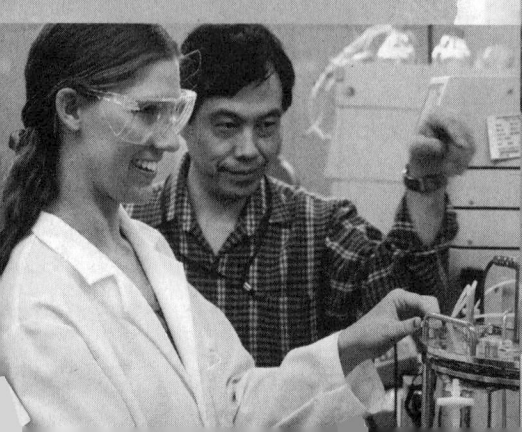

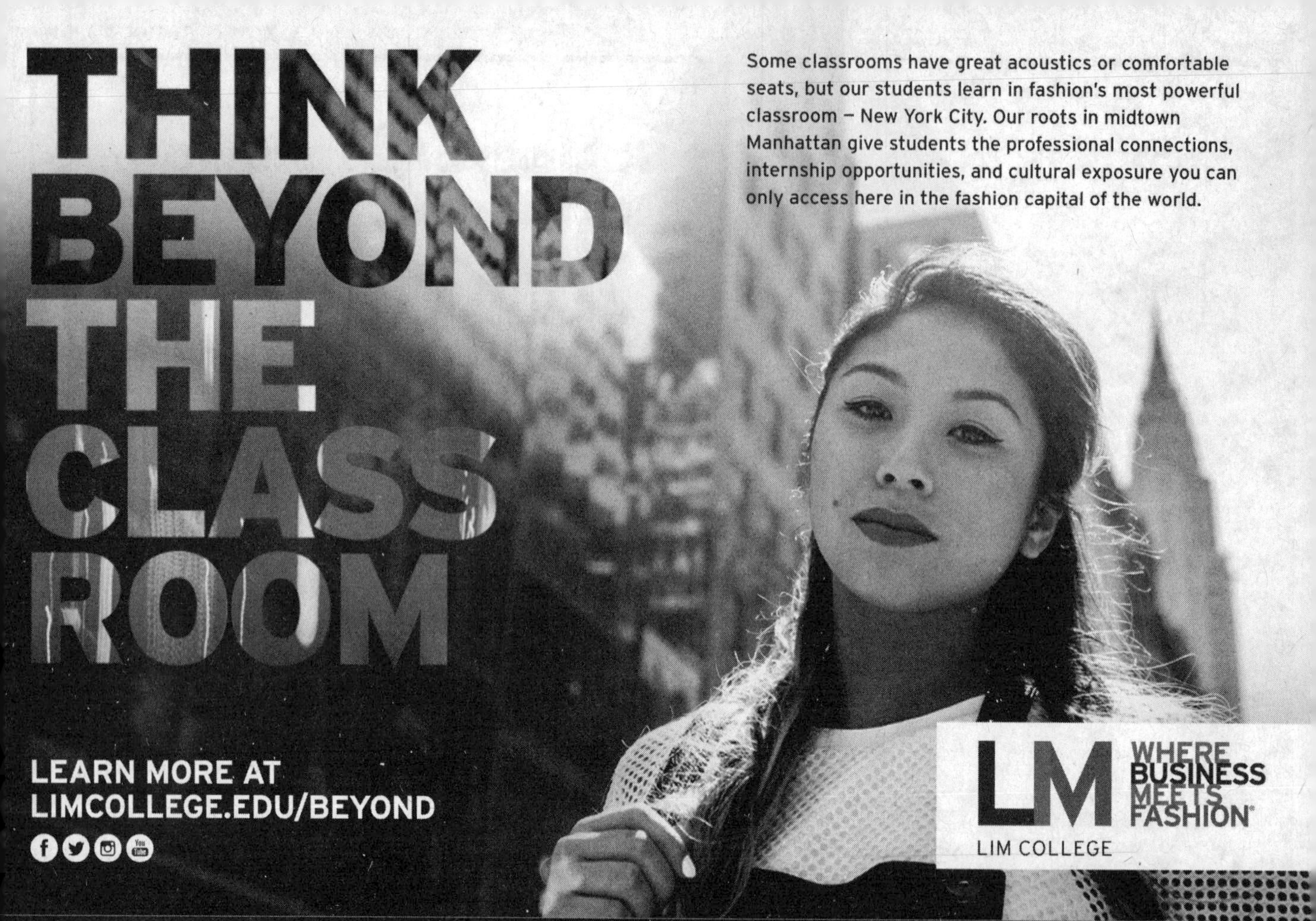
THINK BEYOND THE CLASS ROOM
Some classrooms have great acoustics or comfortable seats, but our students learn in fashion's most powerful classroom – New York City. Our roots in midtown Manhattan give students the professional connections, internship opportunities, and cultural exposure you can only access here in the fashion capital of the world.
LEARN MORE AT LIMCOLLEGE.EDU/BEYOND
LM WHERE BUSINESS MEETS FASHION®
LIM COLLEGE

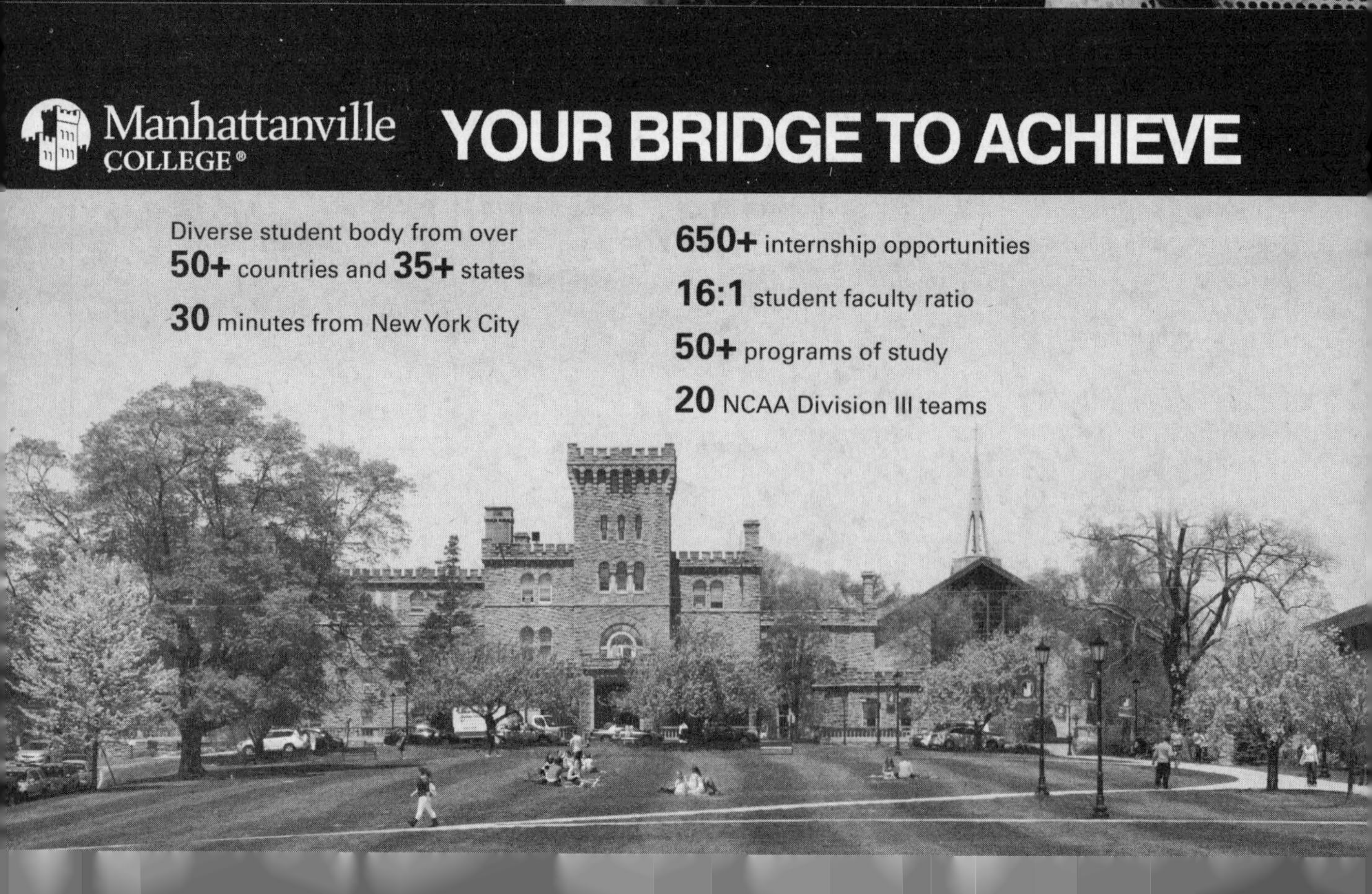
Manhattanville COLLEGE®
YOUR BRIDGE TO ACHIEVE
Diverse student body from over 50+ countries and 35+ states
30 minutes from New York City
650+ internship opportunities
16:1 student faculty ratio
50+ programs of study
20 NCAA Division III teams

Robert Franek, Senior Vice President-Publisher at The Princeton Review, is the company's chief expert on education and college issues. Over his 23-year career, he has served as a college admissions administrator, test prep teacher, author, and lecturer. Rob visits more than 50 colleges a year and oversees the company's line of 150 titles from best-selling test-prep guides to college- and graduate school-related books. Prior to joining The Princeton Review in 1999, Rob served as a college admissions administrator at Wagner College (New York City) for six years. He earned his BA at Drew University in Political Science and History. Follow him on Twitter: @RobFranek.

David Soto, Director of Content Development, is a graduate of the Walter Cronkite School of Journalism at Arizona State University and Director of Content Development for The Princeton Review. He helps create a line of guidebook titles on various aspects of the admissions process, including college, graduate school, and career-related topics, as well as the company website which serves more than half of all college-bound students. He lives in Brooklyn, NY.

Kristen O'Toole, Editorial Director, received a BA from Bates College and an MFA from Columbia University. She has written and edited information about college and graduate school admissions for The Princeton Review since 2008.

NOTES

NOTES

NOTES

WE KNOW APPLYING TO COLLEGES IS STRESSFUL.

Why Not Win $2,000 for It?

Participate in our 2017 "College Hopes & Worries Survey."

You might win our college scholarship prize!

The Princeton Review has conducted this survey of high school students applying to colleges and parents of applicants since 2005. Why? We're curious to know what concerns you the most about your application experiences and what your dream college would be.

Our survey has just 15 questions—way shorter than any college app. You can zip through it in less than three minutes. Plus, in addition to the $2,000 scholarship prize we'll give to one lucky participant chosen at random, we'll give another 25 participants (also chosen at random) a free copy of one of our college-related guidebooks. They can chose either *Paying for College Without Going Broke, Colleges That Create Futures,* or *Colleges That Pay You Back.* In March 2017, about the time you'll (hopefully) be receiving college acceptance and financial aid award letters, we'll post the survey findings on our site and inform the scholarship winner and book winners. For more information, see **Official Rules** below.

We know how exciting and how stressful college applications can be. We hope the information on our site and in our books helps you find, get in to, and get aid from the college best for you. We wish you great success in your applications and your college years ahead.

Official Rules:

Princeton Review 2017 "College Hopes & Worries Survey" Prize Sweepstakes

NO PURCHASE NECESSARY. OPEN TO RESIDENTS OF THE FIFTY UNITED STATES (AND WASHINTON, DC) THIRTEEN YEARS OF AGE AND OLDER ONLY.

1. HOW TO ENTER: To enter via the Internet, visit www.princetonreview.com/go/survey. LIMIT ONE ENTRY PER PERSON. All online entries must be received by 11:59 P.M. EDT on February 29, 2017. To enter without Internet access or answering the questionnaire, handwrite your name, complete address, and phone number on a postcard and mail to: The Princeton Review, 2017 College Hopes & Worries Survey, c/o Robert Franek, 555 W. 18th St. 4th Fl., New York, NY 10011. Mail-in entries must be received by February 29, 2017. Not responsible for lost, late, or misdirected mail.

2. ELIGIBILITY: Open to residents of the 50 United States and D.C., 13 years of age and older, except for employees of The Princeton Review ("Sponsor"), its affiliates, subsidiaries and agencies (collectively "Promotion Parties"), and members of their immediate family or persons living in the same household. Void where prohibited.

3. RANDOM DRAWINGS: A random drawing will be held on or about March 31, 2017. Odds of winning will depend upon the number of eligible entries received. Winner will be notified by e-mail/mail and/or telephone, at Sponsor's option and will be required to sign and return any required Affidavit of Eligibility, Release of Liability and Publicity Release within seven (7) days of attempted delivery or prize will be forfeited and an alternate winner may be selected. The return of any prize or prize notification as undeliverable may result in disqualification and an alternate winner may be selected.

4. PRIZES: One (1) Grand Prize: $2,000.00 Scholarship, awarded as a check. Twenty-Five (25) First Prizes: winner's choice of one of the following Princeton Review books: *Paying for College without Going Broke, Colleges That Create Futures,* or *Colleges That Pay You Back.* Approximate Retail Value: $19.00. Total prize value: $2,475.00. Limit one prize per family/household. All prizes will be awarded.

5. GENERAL RULES: All income taxes resulting from acceptance of prize are the responsibility of winner. By entering sweepstakes, entrant accepts and agrees to these Official Rules and the decisions of Sponsor, which shall be final in all matters. By accepting prize, winner agrees to hold Promotion Parties, their affiliates, directors, officers, employees and assigns harmless against any and all claims and liability arising out of use of prize. Acceptance also constitutes permission to the Promotion Parties to use winner's name and likeness for marketing purposes without further compensation or right of approval, unless prohibited by law. Promotion Parties are not responsible for lost or late mail, or for technical, hardware, or software malfunctions, lost or unavailable network connections, or failed, incorrect, inaccurate, incomplete, garbled, or delayed electronic communication whether caused by the sender or by any of the equipment or programming associated with or utilized in this sweepstakes, or by any human error which may occur in the processing of the entries in this sweepstakes. If, in the Sponsor's opinion, there is any suspected evidence of tampering with any portion of the promotion, or if technical difficulties compromise the integrity of the promotion, the Sponsor reserves the right to modify or terminate the sweepstakes in a manner deemed reasonable by the Sponsor, at the Sponsor's sole discretion. In the event a dispute arises as to the identity of a potentially winning online entrant, entries made by Internet will be declared made by the name on the online entry form. All federal and state laws apply.

6. WINNERS LIST: For the names of the winners, available after May 1, 2017, send a self-addressed, stamped (#10) envelope to: The Princeton Review, 2017 College Hopes & Worries Survey Contest Winners, c/o Robert Franek, 555 W. 18th St. 4th Fl., New York, NY 10011.

College Hopes & Worries Survey 2017

Mail to The Princeton Review, 2017 College Hopes & Worries Survey, c/o Robert Franek, 555 W. 18th St., 4th Fl., New York, NY 10011 (mailed entries must be received by February 20, 2017) or fill out online (online entries can be submitted between January 20 and February 29, 2017) at www.PrincetonReview.com/go/survey.

Name _____

Address (optional) _____

City / State / ZIP _____

Daytime phone _____

E-mail address_____

I am ____ a parent of a student ____ a student applying to attend college beginning in

____ Spring or Fall 2017 ____ Spring or Fall 2018 ____ Later (indicate year:_____).

1   What would be your "dream" college? What college would you most like to attend (or see your child attend) if chance of being accepted or cost were not an issue? (Please write complete name of school e.g. "Oklahoma University," not initials such as "OU" which could also be an abbreviation for Ohio University.)

_____

2   How many colleges will you (your child) apply to?

____ 1 to 4

____ 5 to 8

____ 9 to 12

____ 13 or more

3   What is (or will be) the toughest part of your (your child's) college application experience? (Choose one.)

____ Researching colleges

____ Taking the SAT, ACT, or AP exams

____ Completing applications for admission and financial aid

____ Waiting for the decision letters and deciding which college to attend

4   Which college admission exam do you wish you (your child) could take if all of the following options were available?

____ The ACT

____ The SAT

5   How would you rate the college application guidance and support you (your child) have (has) received from your (your child's) high school college advisor / guidance counselor?

____ Excellent

____ Good

____ Fair

____ Poor

6   What do you estimate your (or your child's) college degree will cost, including four years of tuition, room and board, fees, books and other expenses? (Choose one.)

   ____ More than $100,000

   ____ $75,000 to $100,000

   ____ $50,000 to 75,000

   ____ $25,000 to $50,000

   ____ Less than $25,000

7   How necessary will financial aid (education loans, scholarships, or grants) be to pay for your (your child's) college education? (Choose one.)

   ____ Extremely

   ____ Very

   ____ Somewhat

   ____ Not at all

8   What's your biggest concern about applying to or attending college? (Choose one.)

   ____ Won't get into first-choice college

   ____ Will get into first-choice college, but won't be able to afford to attend

   ____ Level of debt I (my child) will take on to pay for the degree

   ____ Will attend a college I (my child) may regret

9   How would you gauge your stress level about the college application process? (Choose one.)

   ____ Very High

   ____ High

   ____ Average

   ____ Low

   ____ Very Low

10 Ideally, how far from home would you like the college you (your child) attend(s) to be? (Choose one.)

   ____ Less than 250 miles

   ____ 250 to 500 miles

   ____ 500 to 1,000

   ____ More than 1,000 miles

11 When it comes to choosing the college you (your child) will attend, which of the following do you think it is most likely to be? (Choose one.)

   ____ College with best academic reputation

   ____ College with best program for my (my child's) career interests

   ____ College that will be the most affordable

   ____ College that will be the best overall fit